WORLDMARK
ENCYCLOPEDIA
OF THE STATES

ISSN 1531-1627

WORLDMARK ENCYCLOPEDIA
OF THE STATES,
SEVENTH EDITION

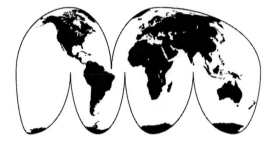

Volume 2
Nebraska to Wyoming
and District of Columbia, Puerto Rico,
U.S. Dependencies, and U.S. Overview

GALE
CENGAGE Learning

Detroit • New York • San Francisco • New Haven, Conn • Waterville, Maine • London

Worldmark Encyclopedia of the States, Seventh Edition
Timothy L. Gall, Editor in Chief

Project Editor
Mary Rose Bonk

Editorial
Jennifer Greve,
Kimberly Lewis,
Kate Potthoff

Imaging
Christine O'Bryan

Product Design
Jennifer Wahi

Manufacturing
Rita Wimberly

ISBN 1-4144-1058-1 (set)
ISBN 1-4144-1121-9 (v.1)
ISBN 1-4144-1122-7 (v.2)
ISSN 1531-1627 (set)

This title is also available as an e-book
ISBN 1-4144-1114-6
Contact your Gale sales representative for ordering information.

Printed in the United States of America
5 6 7 8   14 13

CONTENTS

PREFACE

In 1980, editor and publisher Moshe Y. Sachs set out to create the *Worldmark Encyclopedia of the Nations,* a new kind of reference work that would view every nation of the world as if through a "world mirror" and not from the perspective of any one country or group of countries. In 1981, a companion volume, the *Worldmark Encyclopedia of the States,* was introduced. It was selected as an "Outstanding Reference Source" by the Reference Sources Committee of the American Library Association, Reference and Adult Services Division. Gale now offers a revised and updated seventh edition of the *Worldmark Encyclopedia of the States.*

The fitness of the United States of America as a subject for encyclopedic study is plain. No discussion of world politics, economics, culture, technology, or military affairs would be complete without an intensive examination of the American achievement. What is not so obvious is why the editors chose to present this work as an encyclopedia of the *states* rather than of the United States. In so doing, they emphasize the fact that the United States is a federal union of separate states with divergent histories, traditions, resources, laws, and economic interests.

Every state, large or small, is treated in an individual chapter, within a framework of 50 standard subject headings; generally, the more populous the state, the longer the article. The District of Columbia and the Commonwealth of Puerto Rico each have their own chapters, and two additional articles describe in summary the other Caribbean and Pacific dependencies. The concluding chapter is an overview of the nation as a whole. Supplementing this textual material are tables of conversions and abbreviations, a glossary, and more than 50 black-and-white maps prepared especially for this encyclopedia.

Publication of this encyclopedia was a collective effort that enlisted the talents of scholars, government agencies, editor-writers, artists, cartographers, typesetters, proofreaders, and many others. Perhaps only those involved in the production of reference books fully appreciate how complex that endeavor can be. Readers customarily expect that a reference book will be correct in every particular; and yet, by the time it has been on the shelves for a few months, a conscientious editor may already have a long list of improvements and corrections to be made in a subsequent edition. We invite you, the reader, to add your suggestions to our list.

Send comments to:

Worldmark Encyclopedia of the States
Gale
27500 Drake Road
Farmington Hills, MI 48331

The Editors

GUIDE TO STATE ARTICLES

All information contained within a state article is uniformly keyed by means of small superior numerals to the left of the subject headings. A heading such as "Population," for example, carries the same key numeral (6) in every article. Thus, to find information about the population of Alabama, consult the table of contents for the page number where the Alabama article begins and look for section 6 thereunder.

Introductory matter for each state includes:

Origin of state name
Nickname
Capital
Date and order of statehood
Song
Motto
Flag
Official seal
Symbols (animal, tree, flower, etc.)
Legal holidays
Time zone

SUBJECT HEADINGS IN NUMERICAL ORDER

1	Location, size, and extent	27	Mining
2	Topography	28	Energy and power
3	Climate	29	Industry
4	Flora and fauna	30	Commerce
5	Environmental protection	31	Consumer protection
6	Population	32	Banking
7	Ethnic groups	33	Insurance
8	Languages	34	Securities
9	Religions	35	Public finance
10	Transportation	36	Taxation
11	History	37	Economic policy
12	State government	38	Health
13	Political parties	39	Social welfare
14	Local government	40	Housing
15	State services	41	Education
16	Judicial system	42	Arts
17	Armed forces	43	Libraries and museums
18	Migration	44	Communications
19	Intergovernmental cooperation	45	Press
20	Economy	46	Organizations
21	Income	47	Tourism, travel, and recreation
22	Labor		
23	Agriculture	48	Sports
24	Animal husbandry	49	Famous persons
25	Fishing	50	Bibliography
26	Forestry		

SUBJECT HEADINGS IN ALPHABETICAL ORDER

Agriculture	23	Intergovernmental cooperation	19
Animal husbandry	24	Judicial system	16
Armed forces	17	Labor	22
Arts	42	Languages	8
Banking	32	Libraries and museums	43
Bibliography	50	Local government	14
Climate	3	Location, size, and extent	1
Commerce	30	Migration	18
Communications	44	Mining	27
Consumer protection	31	Organizations	46
Economic policy	37	Political parties	13
Economy	20	Population	6
Education	41	Press	45
Energy and power	28	Public finance	35
Environmental protection	5	Religions	9
Ethnic groups	7	Securities	34
Famous persons	49	Social welfare	39
Fishing	25	Sports	48
Flora and fauna	4	State government	12
Forestry	26	State services	15
Health	38	Taxation	36
History	11	Topography	2
Housing	40	Tourism, travel, and recreation	47
Income	21	Transportation	10
Industry	29		
Insurance	33		

EXPLANATION OF SYMBOLS

A fiscal split year is indicated by a stroke (e.g. 1994/95).
A dollar sign ($) stands for US$ unless otherwise indicated.
Note that 1 billion = 1,000 million = 10^9.
The use of a small dash (e.g., 1990–94) normally signifies the full period of calendar years covered (including the end year indicated).

NOTES

GENERAL NOTE: In producing the seventh edition of *Worldmark Encyclopedia of the States*, the editors were aided by the wealth of information now available from state governments on the World Wide Web. The information included in this volume from postings by state agencies was supplemented by data from The Council of State Governments, the Census Bureau, the Bureau of Economic Analysis, the National Center for Education Statistics, the Bureau of Justice Statistics, the Department of Energy, the National Science Board, the National Center for Health Statistics, the Federal Highway Administration, the Department of Defense, the Department of Veterans Affairs, the Department of the Interior, the Federal Deposit Insurance Corporation, and a wide variety of additional federal agencies and offices. This state and federal information was indispensable to *Worldmark* editors in revising state articles. Space does not permit listing of the hundreds of additional documents from private sources which were consulted for each state's entry. Listed below are notable sources of data which were used in revising a majority of entries.

MAPS: The maps of the states were produced by the University of Akron Laboratory for Cartographic and Spatial Analysis under the direction of Joseph W. Stoll. The maps originated from the United States Geological Survey 1:2,000,000 Digital Line Graphs (DLG). Additional sources used to determine and verify the positioning of text and symbols include 1990 United States Census Data, USGS 1:500,000 Topographic State Maps, brochures and maps from the state visitor bureaus, and the *Rand McNally United States Road Atlas*. For definitions of abbreviations used on the maps please refer to the section entitled "Abbreviations and Acronyms" appearing on page xi.

WEIGHTS AND MEASURES: Recognizing the trend toward use of the metric system throughout the United States, the text provides metric equivalents for customary measures of length and area, and both Fahrenheit and Centigrade expressions for temperature. Production figures are expressed exclusively in the prevailing customary units.

LOCATION, SIZE, AND EXTENT: The lengths of interstate boundary segments and the total lengths of state boundaries appear in roman type when derived from official government sources; italic type indicates data derived from other sources. Discrepancies in the boundary lengths of neighboring states as specified by official sources arise from divergent methodologies of measurement.

FLORA AND FAUNA: Discussions of endangered species are based on the *List of Endangered and Threatened Wildlife and Plants* maintained by the Fish and Wildlife Service of the US Department of the Interior, and on data supplied by the states.

POPULATION: Population figures are from data released by the US Census Bureau's Population Estimates Program as of 2006. These data can be found at http://eire.census.gov/popest/estimates.php together with a wide variety of additional economic and demographic data collected by the US Department of Commerce and other related federal agencies. Tables of counties, county seats, county areas, and estimates of county populations as of 2006 accompany the articles on the 14 most populous states; the editors regret that space limitations prevented the publication of such a table for each state. Because of rounding of numbers, county areas in these tables may not equal the total.

LANGUAGES: Examples of lexical and pronunciation patterns cited in the text are meant to suggest the historic development of principal linguistic features and should not be taken as a comprehensive statement of current usage. Data on languages spoken in the home were obtained from "Languages Spoken at Home: 2000" issued online at http://factfinder.census.gov by the US Census Bureau.

TRANSPORTATION: Transportation statistics were compiled from the *Transportation Profile* for each of the states and the District of Columbia published by the Bureau of Transportation Statistics, US Department of Transportation.

JUDICIAL SYSTEM: *Uniform Crime Reports for the United States*, published annually by the Federal Bureau of Investigation and embodying the FBI Crime Index (tabulations of offenses known to the police), was the principal source for the crime statistics cited in the text.

ARMED FORCES: The number of veterans of US military service are as reported by Census Bureau as of 2006. Additional data came from the *State Summary* reports prepared by the Office of Public Affairs, Media Relations, Department of Veterans Affairs.

INCOME: Data on income was extracted in part from *State BEARFACTS 1994 – 2004* published online at http://www.bea.gov/bea/regional/bearfacts by the Bureau of Economic Analysis of the US Department of Commerce.

LABOR: Statistics on the labor force and union membership were obtained from Bureau of Labor Statistics, United States Department of Labor and are available online at http://www.bls.gov.

ENERGY AND POWER: Data for proved reserves and production of fossil fuels were derived from publications of the American Gas Association, American Petroleum Institute, National Coal Association, and US Department of Energy. Data on nuclear power facilities were obtained from the Nuclear Information and Resource Service and from state sources.

INSURANCE: The principal statistical sources for information on insurance were annual publications of the Insurance Information Institute and the American Council of Life Insurance.

PUBLIC FINANCE: Tables of state government revenues and expenditures were obtained from *2004 State Government Tax Collections* and *State Government Finances: 2004* issued by the US Census Bureau and available online at http://www.census.gov/govs/www/statetax02.html and http://www.census.gov/govs.state. Additional information came from the official web sites of the individual states.

HEALTH: The principal statistical sources for hospitals and medical personnel were annual publications of the American Dental Association, American Hospital Association, and American Medical Association.

LIBRARIES AND MUSEUMS: In most cases, library and museum names are listed in the *American Library Directory* by R. R. Bowker, and the *Official Museum Directory,* compiled by the National Register Publishing Co. in cooperation with the American Association of Museums.

PRESS: Circulation data follow the 2005 *Editor & Publisher International Yearbook.*

FAMOUS PERSONS: Entries are current through July 2006. Where a person described in one state is known to have been born in another, the state of birth follows the personal name, in parentheses.

BIBLIOGRAPHY: Bibliographies are intended as a guide to landmark works on each state for further research and not as a listing of sources in preparing the articles. Such listings would have far exceeded space limitations.

CONVERSION TABLES*

LENGTH

1 centimeter	0.3937 inch
1 centimeter	0.03280833 foot
1 meter (100 centimeters)	3.280833 feet
1 meter	1.093611 US yards
1 kilometer (1,000 meters)	0.62137 statute mile
1 kilometer	0.539957 nautical mile
1 inch	2.540005 centimeters
1 foot (12 inches)	30.4801 centimeters
1 US yard (3 feet)	0.914402 meter
1 statute mile (5,280 feet; 1,760 yards)	1.609347 kilometers
1 British mile	1.609344 kilometers
1 nautical mile (1.1508 statute miles or 6,076.10333 feet)	1.852 kilometers
1 British nautical mile (6,080 feet)	1.85319 kilometers

AREA

1 sq centimeter	0.154999 sq inch
1 sq meter (10,000 sq centimeters)	10.76387 sq feet
1 sq meter	1.1959585 sq yards
1 hectare (10,000 sq meters)	2.47104 acres
1 sq kilometer (100 hectares)	0.386101 sq mile
1 sq inch	6.451626 sq centimeters
1 sq foot (144 sq inches)	0.092903 sq meter
1 sq yard (9 sq feet)	0.836131 sq meter
1 acre (4,840 sq yards)	0.404687 hectare
1 sq mile (640 acres)	2.589998 sq kilometers

VOLUME

1 cubic centimeter	0.061023 cubic inch
1 cubic meter (1,000,000 cubic centimeters)	35.31445 cubic feet
1 cubic meter	1.307943 cubic yards
1 cubic inch	16.387162 cubic centimeters
1 cubic foot (1,728 cubic inches)	0.028317 cubic meter
1 cubic yard (27 cubic feet)	0.764559 cubic meter

LIQUID MEASURE

1 liter	0.8799 imperial quart
1 liter	1.05671 US quarts
1 hectoliter	21.9975 imperial gallons
1 hectoliter	26.4178 US gallons
1 imperial quart	1.136491 liters
1 US quart	0.946333 liter
1 imperial gallon	0.04546 hectoliter
1 US gallon	0.037853 hectoliter

WEIGHT

1 kilogram (1,000 grams)	35.27396 avoirdupois ounces
1 kilogram	32.15074 troy ounces
1 kilogram	2.204622 avoirdupois pounds
1 quintal (100 kg)	220.4622 avoirdupois pounds
1 quintal	1.9684125 hundredweights
1 metric ton (1,000 kg)	1.102311 short tons
1 metric ton	0.984206 long ton

1 avoirdupois ounce	0.0283495 kilogram
1 troy ounce	0.0311035 kilogram
1 avoirdupois pound	0.453592 kilogram
1 avoirdupois pound	0.00453592 quintal
1 hundred weight (cwt., 112 lb)	0.50802 quintal
1 short ton (2,000 lb)	0.907185 metric ton
1 long ton (2,240 lb)	1.016047 metric tons

ELECTRIC ENERGY

1 horsepower (hp)	0.7457 kilowatt
1 kilowatt (kw)	1.34102 horsepower

TEMPERATURE

Celsius (C)	Fahrenheit−32 x 5/9
Fahrenheit (F)	9/5 Celsius + 32

BUSHELS

	LB	METRIC TON	BUSHELS PER METRIC TON
Barley (US)	48	0.021772	45.931
(UK)	50	0.022680	44.092
Corn (UK, US)	56	0.025401	39.368
Linseed (UK)	52	0.023587	42.396
(Australia, US)	56	0.025401	39.368
Oats (US)	32	0.014515	68.894
(Canada)	34	0.015422	64.842
Potatoes (UK, US)	60	0.027216	36.743
Rice (Australia)	42	0.019051	52.491
(US)	45	0.020412	48.991
Rye (UK, US)	56	0.025401	39.368
(Australia)	60	0.027216	36.743
Soybeans (US)	60	0.027216	36.743
Wheat (UK, US)	60	0.027216	36.743

BAGS OF COFFEE

	LB	KG	BAGS PER METRIC TON
Brazil, Columbia Mexico, Venezuela	132.28	60	16.667
El Salvador	152.12	69	14.493
Haiti	185.63	84.2	11.876

BALES OF COTTON

	LB	METRIC TON	BALES PER METRIC TON
India	392	0.177808	5.624
Brazil	397	0.180000	5.555
US (net)	480	0.217724	4.593
US (gross)	500	0.226796	4.409

PETROLEUM

One barrel = 42 US gallons = 34.97 imperial gallons = 158.99 liters = 0.15899 cubic meter (or 1 cubic meter = 6.2898 barrels).

*Includes units of measure cited in the text, as well as certain other units employed in parts of the English-speaking world.

ABBREVIATIONS AND ACRONYMS

AD—Anno Domini
AFDC—Aid to Families with Dependent Children
AFL–CIO—American Federation of Labor–Congress of Industrial Organizations
AM—before noon
AM—amplitude modulation
American Ind.—American Independent Party
Amtrak—National Railroad Passenger Corp.
b.—born
BC—Before Christ
Btu—British thermal unit(s)
bu—bushel(s)
c.—circa (about)
C—Celsius (Centigrade)
CIA—Central Intelligence Agency
cm—centimeter(s)
Co.—company
comp.—compiler
Conrail—Consolidated Rail Corp.
Corp.—corporation
Cr.—creek
CST—Central Standard Time
cu—cubic
cwt—hundredweight(s)
d.—died
D—Democrat
e—evening
E—east
ed.—edition, editor
e.g.—exempli gratia (for example)
EPA—Environmental Protection Agency
est.—estimated
EST—Eastern Standard Time
et al.—et alii (and others)

etc.—et cetera (and so on)
F—Fahrenheit
FBI—Federal Bureau of Investigation
FCC—Federal Communications Commission
FM—frequency modulation
For.—forest
Ft.—fort
ft—foot, feet
GDP—gross domestic product
gm—gram
GMT—Greenwich Mean Time
GNP—gross national product
GRT—gross registered tons
Hist.—historic
I—interstate (highway)
i.e.—id est (that is)
in—inch(es)
Inc.—incorporated
Ind. Res.—Indian Reservation
Is.—isle, island
Jct.—junction
K—kindergarten
kg—kilogram(s)
km—kilometer(s)
km/hr—kilometers per hour
kw—kilowatt(s)
kwh—kilowatt-hour(s)
lb—pound(s)
m—meter(s); morning
m^3—cubic meter(s)
Mem.—memorial
mi—mile(s)
Mil. Res.—military reservation
Mon.—monument

mph—miles per hour
MST—Mountain Standard Time
Mt.—mount
Mtn.—mountain
mw—megawatt(s)
N—north
NA—not available
Natl.—National
Natl. Mon.—national monument
NATO—North Atlantic Treaty Organization
NCAA—National Collegiate Athletic Association
n.d.—no date
N.F.—national forest
N.P.—national park
N.W.R.—national wildlife refuge
oz—ounce(s)
PM—after noon
PST—Pacific Standard Time
r.—reigned
R—Republican
Ra.—range
Res.—reservoir, reservation
rev. ed.—revised edition
s—south
S—Sunday
Soc.—Socialist
S.P.—senic point
sq—square
St.—saint, state
UN—United Nations
US—United States
USIA—United States Information Agency
w—west
W.M.A.—wildlife management area

NAMES OF STATES AND OTHER SELECTED AREAS

	Standard Abbreviation(s)	Postal Abbreviation		Standard Abbreviation(s)	Postal Abbreviation
Alabama	Ala.	AL	Nebraska	Nebr. (Neb.)	NE
Alaska	*	AK	Nevada	Nev.	NV
Arizona	Ariz.	AZ	New Hampshire	N.H.	NH
Arkansas	Ark.	AR	New Jersey	N.J.	NJ
California	Calif.	CA	New Mexico	N.Mex. (N.M.)	NM
Colorado	Colo.	CO	New York	N.Y.	NY
Connecticut	Conn.	CT	North Carolina	N.C.	NC
Delaware	Del.	DE	North Dakota	N.Dak. (N.D.)	ND
District of Columbia	D.C.	DC	Ohio	*	OH
Florida	Fla.	FL	Oklahoma	Okla.	OK
Georgia	Ga.	GA	Oregon	Oreg. (Ore.)	OR
Hawaii	*	HI	Pennsylvania	Pa.	PA
Idaho	*	ID	Puerto Rico	P.R.	PR
Illinois	Ill.	IL	Rhode Island	R.I.	RI
Indiana	Ind.	IN	South Carolina	S.C.	SC
Iowa	*	IA	South Dakota	S.Dak. (S.D.)	SD
Kansas	Kans. (Kan.)	KS	Tennessee	Tenn.	TN
Kentucky	Ky.	KY	Texas	Tex.	TX
Louisiana	La.	LA	Utah	*	UT
Maine	Me.	ME	Vermont	Vt.	VT
Maryland	Md.	MD	Virginia	Va.	VA
Massachusetts	Mass.	MA	Virgin Islands	V.I.	VI
Michigan	Mich.	MI	Washington	Wash.	WA
Minnesota	Minn.	MN	West Virginia	W.Va.	WV
Mississippi	Miss.	MS	Wisconsin	Wis.	WI
Missouri	Mo.	MO	Wyoming	Wyo.	WY
Montana	Mont.	MT	*No standard abbreviation		

GLOSSARY

ANTEBELLUM: before the US Civil War.

BLUE LAWS: laws forbidding certain practices (e.g., conducting business, gaming, drinking liquor), especially on Sundays.

CAPITAL BUDGET: a financial plan for acquiring and improving buildings or land, paid for by the sale of bonds.

CAPITAL PUNISHMENT: punishment by death.

CIVILIAN LABOR FORCE: all persons 16 years of age or older who are not in the armed forces and who are now holding a job, have been temporarily laid off, are waiting to be reassigned to a new position, or are unemployed but actively looking for work.

CLASS I RAILROAD: a railroad having gross annual revenues of $83.5 million or more in 1983.

COMMERCIAL BANK: a bank that offers businesses and individuals a variety of banking services, including the right of withdrawal by check.

COMPACT: a formal agreement, covenant, or understanding between two or more parties.

CONSOLIDATED BUDGET: a financial plan that includes the general budget, federal funds, and all special funds.

CONSTANT DOLLARS: money values calculated so as to eliminate the effect of inflation on prices and income.

CONTINENTAL CLIMATE: the climate typical of the US interior, having distinct seasons, a wide range of daily and annual temperatures, and dry, sunny summers.

COUNCIL-MANAGER SYSTEM: a system of local government under which a professional administrator is hired by an elected council to carry out its laws and policies.

CREDIT UNION: a cooperative body that raises funds from its members by the sale of shares and makes loans to its members at relatively low interest rates.

CURRENT DOLLARS: money values that reflect prevailing prices, without excluding the effects of inflation.

DEMAND DEPOSIT: a bank deposit that can be withdrawn by the depositor with no advance notice to the bank.

ELECTORAL VOTES: the votes that a state may cast for president, equal to the combined total of its US senators and representatives and nearly always cast entirely on behalf of the candidate who won the most votes in that state on Election Day.

ENDANGERED SPECIES: a type of plant or animal threatened with extinction in all or part of its natural range.

FEDERAL POVERTY LEVEL: a level of money income below which a person or family qualifies for US government aid.

FISCAL YEAR: a 12-month period for accounting purposes.

FOOD STAMPS: coupons issued by the government to low-income persons for food purchases at local stores.

GENERAL BUDGET: a financial plan based on a government's normal revenues and operating expenses, excluding special funds.

GENERAL COASTLINE: a measurement of the general outline of the US seacoast. See also TIDAL SHORELINE.

GREAT AWAKENING: during the mid–18th century, a Protestant religious revival in North America, especially New England.

GROSS STATE PRODUCT: the total value of goods and services produced in the state.

GROWING SEASON: the period between the last 32°f (0°c) temperature in spring and the first 32°f (0°c) temperature in autumn.

HOME-RULE CHARTER: a document stating how and in what respects a city, town, or county may govern itself.

INSTALLED CAPACITY: the maximum possible output of electric power at any given time.

MAYOR-COUNCIL SYSTEM: a system of local government under which an elected council serves as a legislature and an elected mayor is the chief administrator.

MEDICAID: a federal-state program that helps defray the hospital and medical costs of needy persons.

MEDICARE: a program of hospital and medical insurance for the elderly, administered by the federal government.

METROPOLITAN AREA: in most cases, a city and its surrounding suburbs.

NO-FAULT INSURANCE: an automobile insurance plan that allows an accident victim to receive payment from an insurance company without having to prove who was responsible for the accident.

NORTHERN, NORTH MIDLAND: major US dialect regions.

OMBUDSMAN: a public official empowered to hear and investigate complaints by private citizens about government agencies.

PER CAPITA: per person.

POCKET VETO: a method by which a state governor (or the US president) may kill a bill by taking no action on it before the legislature adjourns.

PROVED RESERVES: the quantity of a recoverable mineral resource (such as oil or natural gas) that is still in the ground.

PUBLIC DEBT: the amount owed by a government.

RELIGIOUS ADHERENTS: the followers of a religious group, including (but not confined to) the full, confirmed, or communicant members of that group.

RETAIL TRADE: the sale of goods directly to the consumer.

REVENUE SHARING: the distribution of federal tax receipts to state and local governments.

RIGHT-TO-WORK LAW: a measure outlawing any attempt to require union membership as a condition of employment.

SAVINGS AND LOAN ASSOCIATION: a bank that invests the savings of depositors primarily in home mortgage loans.

SERVICE INDUSTRIES: industries that provide services (e.g., health, legal, automotive repair) for individuals, businesses, and others.

SOCIAL SECURITY: as commonly understood, the federal system of old age, survivors, and disability insurance.

SOUTHERN, SOUTH MIDLAND: major US dialect regions.

STOLPORT: an airfield for short-takeoff-and-landing (STOL) aircraft, which require runways shorter than those used by conventional aircraft.

SUNBELT: the southernmost states of the United States, extending from Florida to California.

SUPPLEMENTAL SECURITY INCOME: a federally administered program of aid to the aged, blind, and disabled.

TIDAL SHORELINE: a detailed measurement of the US seacoast that includes sounds, bays, other outlets, and offshore islands.

TIME DEPOSIT: a bank deposit that may be withdrawn only at the end of a specified time period or upon advance notice to the bank.

VALUE ADDED BY MANUFACTURE: the difference, measured in dollars, between the value of finished goods and the cost of the materials needed to produce them.

WHOLESALE TRADE: the sale of goods, usually in large quantities, for ultimate resale to consumers.

EDITORIAL STAFF

Editor in Chief: Timothy L. Gall
Senior Editors: Jeneen M. Hobby, Karen Ellicott, George Vukmanovich
Graphics Editor: Daniel Mehling
Associate Editors: Rachel Babura, Susan Bevan Gall, James Henry, Daniel M. Lucas, Maura E. Malone, Michael A. Parris, Seth E. Rosenberg, Gail Rosewater, Susan Stern, Jeanne-Marie Stumpf, Kimberly Tilly, Rosalie Wieder, Sarah Wang, Daiva Ziedonis
Proofreaders: Jane Hoehner, Deborah A. Ring
Cartography: University of Akron Laboratory for Cartographic and Spatial Analysis: Joseph W. Stoll, Supervisor; Scott Raypholtz; Mike Meyer

CONTRIBUTORS
TO THE FIRST EDITION

ALLEN, HAROLD B. Emeritus Professor of English and Linguistics, University of Minnesota (Minneapolis–St. Paul). LANGUAGES.

BASSETT, T. D. SEYMOUR. Former University Archivist, University of Vermont (Burlington). VERMONT.

BENSON, MAXINE. Curator of Document Resources, Colorado Historical Society. COLORADO.

BROWN, RICHARD D. Professor of History, University of Connecticut (Storrs). MASSACHUSETTS.

CASHIN, EDWARD J. Professor of History, Augusta College. GEORGIA.

CHANNING, STEVEN A. Professor of History, University of Kentucky (Lexington). KENTUCKY.

CLARK, CHARLES E. Professor of History, University of New Hampshire (Durham). MAINE.

COGSWELL, PHILIP, JR. Forum Editor, *The Oregonian.* OREGON.

CONLEY, PATRICK T. Professor of History and Law, Providence College. RHODE ISLAND.

CORLEW, ROBERT E. Dean, School of Liberal Arts, Middle Tennessee State University (Murfreesboro). TENNESSEE.

CREIGH, DOROTHY WEYER. Author and historian; member, Nebraska State Board of Education. NEBRASKA.

CUNNINGHAM, JOHN T. Author and historian. NEW JERSEY.

FISHER, PERRY. Director, Columbia Historical Society. DISTRICT OF COLUMBIA.

FRANTZ, JOE B. Professor of History, University of Texas (Austin). TEXAS.

GOODELL, LELE. Member, Editorial Board, *Hawaiian Journal of History.* HAWAII (in part).

GOODRICH, JAMES W. Associate Director, State Historical Society of Missouri. MISSOURI.

HAMILTON, VIRGINIA. Professor of History, University of Alabama (Birmingham). ALABAMA.

HAVIGHURST, WALTER. Research Professor of English Emeritus, Miami University (Oxford). OHIO.

HINTON, HARWOOD P. Editor, *Arizona and the West,* University of Arizona (Tucson). ARIZONA.

HOOGENBOOM, ARI. Professor of History, Brooklyn College of the City University of New York. PENNSYLVANIA.

HOOVER, HERBERT T. Professor of History, University of South Dakota (Vermillion). SOUTH DAKOTA.

HUNT, WILLIAM R. Historian; former Professor of History, University of Alaska. ALASKA.

JENSEN, DWIGHT. Author and historian. IDAHO.

JENSEN, RICHARD J. Professor of History, University of Illinois (Chicago). ILLINOIS.

LARSON, ROBERT W. Professor of History, University of Northern Colorado (Greeley). NEW MEXICO.

MAPP, ALF J., JR. Author, lecturer, and historian; Professor of English, Creative Writing, and Journalism, Old Dominion University (Norfolk). VIRGINIA.

MAY, GEORGE S. Professor of History, Eastern Michigan University (Ypsilanti). MICHIGAN.

MEYER, GLADYS. Professor emeritus, Columbia University. ETHNIC GROUPS.

MOODY, ERIC N. Historian, Nevada Historical Society. NEVADA.

MUNROE, JOHN A. H. Rodney Sharp Professor of History, University of Delaware. DELAWARE.

MURPHY, MARIAM. Associate Editor, *Utah Historical Quarterly.* UTAH.

O'BRIEN, KATHLEEN ANN. Project Director, Upper Midwest Women's History Center for Teachers. MINNESOTA.

PADOVER, SAUL K. Distinguished Service Professor Emeritus, Graduate Faculty, New School (New York City). UNITED STATES OF AMERICA.

PECKHAM, HOWARD H. Professor emeritus, University of Michigan. INDIANA.

PRYOR, NANCY. Research consultant and librarian, Washington State Library. WASHINGTON.

RAWLS, JAMES J. Instructor of History, Diablo Valley College (Pleasant Hill). CALIFORNIA.

RICE, OTIS K. Professor of History, West Virginia Institute of Technology (Montgomery). WEST VIRGINIA.

RICHMOND, ROBERT W. Assistant Executive Director, Kansas State Historical Society. KANSAS.

RIGHTER, ROBERT W. Assistant Professor of History, University of Wyoming (Laramie). WYOMING.

ROTH, DAVID M. Director, Center for Connecticut Studies, Eastern Connecticut State College (Willimantic). CONNECTICUT.

SCHEFFER, BARBARA MOORE. Feature Writer. OKLAHOMA (in part).

SCHEFFER, WALTER F. Regents' Professor of Political Science and Director, Graduate Program in Public Administration, University of Oklahoma (Norman). OKLAHOMA (in part).

SCHMITT, ROBERT C. Hawaii State Statistician. HAWAII (in part).

SCUDIERE, PAUL J. Senior Historian, New York State Education Department. NEW YORK.

SKATES, JOHN RAY. Professor of History, University of Southern Mississippi (Hattiesburg). MISSISSIPPI.

SMITH, DOUG. Writer, *Arkansas Gazette* (Little Rock). ARKANSAS.

STOUDEMIRE, ROBERT H. Professor of State and Local Government and Senior Research Associate, Bureau of Governmental Research, University of South Carolina (Columbia). SOUTH CAROLINA.

SULLIVAN, LARRY E. Librarian, New York Historical Society. MARYLAND.

TAYLOR, JOE GRAY. Professor of History, McNeese State University (Lake Charles). LOUISIANA.

TEBEAU, CHARLTON W. Emeritus Professor of History, University of Miami. FLORIDA.

THOMPSON, WILLIAM FLETCHER. Director of Research, State Historical Society of Wisconsin. WISCONSIN.

VIVO, PAQUITA. Author and consultant. PUERTO RICO.

WALL, JOSEPH FRAZIER. Professor of History, Grinnell College. IOWA.

WALLACE, R. STUART. Assistant Director/Editor, New Hampshire Historical Society. NEW HAMPSHIRE.

WATSON, HARRY L. Assistant Professor of History, University of North Carolina (Chapel Hill). NORTH CAROLINA.

WEAVER, KENNETH L. Associate Professor of Political Science, Montana State University (Bozeman). MONTANA.

WILKINS, ROBERT P. Professor of History, University of North Dakota (Grand Forks). NORTH DAKOTA.

WOODS, BOB. Editor, *Sierra Club Wildlife Involvement News.* FLORA AND FAUNA.

NEBRASKA

State of Nebraska

ORIGIN OF STATE NAME: Derived from the Oto Indian word *nebrathka*, meaning "flat water" (for the Platte River). **NICKNAME:** The Cornhusker State. **CAPITAL:** Lincoln. **ENTERED UNION:** 1 March 1867 (37th). **SONG:** "Beautiful Nebraska." **MOTTO:** Equality Before the Law. **FLAG:** The great seal appears in the center, in gold and silver, on a field of blue. **OFFICIAL SEAL:** Agriculture is represented by a farmer's cabin, sheaves of wheat, and growing corn; the mechanic arts, by a blacksmith. Above is the state motto; in the background, a steamboat plies the Missouri River and a train heads toward the Rockies. The scene is surrounded by the words "Great Seal of the State of Nebraska, March 1st 1867." **BIRD:** Western meadowlark. **FLOWER:** Goldenrod. **TREE:** Western cottonwood. **GEM:** Blue agate. **LEGAL HOLIDAYS:** New Year's Day, 1 January; Birthday of Martin Luther King Jr., 3rd Monday in January; Presidents' Day, 3rd Monday in February; Arbor Day, last Friday in April; Memorial Day, last Monday in May; Independence Day, 4 July; Labor Day, 1st Monday in September; Columbus Day, 2nd Monday in October; Veterans' Day, 11 November; Thanksgiving, 4th Thursday in November and following Friday; Christmas Day, 25 December. Other days for special observances include Pioneers' Memorial Day, 2nd Sunday in June; Nebraska Czech Day, 1st Sunday in August; and American Indian Day, 4th Monday in September. **TIME:** 6 AM CST = noon GMT; 5 AM MST = noon GMT.

¹LOCATION, SIZE, AND EXTENT

Located in the western north-central United States, Nebraska ranks 15th in size among the 50 states. The total area of the state is 77,355 sq mi (200,349 sq km), of which land takes up 76,644 sq mi (198,508 sq km) and inland water 711 sq mi (1,841 sq km). Nebraska extends about 415 mi (668 km) E–W and 205 mi (330 km) N–S.

Nebraska is bordered on the N by South Dakota (with the line formed in part by the Missouri River), on the E by Iowa and Missouri (the line being defined by the Missouri River), on the S by Kansas and Colorado, and on the W by Colorado and Wyoming. The boundary length of Nebraska totals 1,332 mi (2,143 km). The state's geographic center is in Custer County, 10 mi (16 km) NW of Broken Bow.

²TOPOGRAPHY

Most of Nebraska is prairie; more than two-thirds of the state lies within the Great Plains proper. The elevation slopes upward gradually from east to west, from a low of 840 ft (256 m) in the southeast along the Missouri River to 5,424 ft (1,654 m) in Johnson Twp. of Kimball County. The mean elevation of the state is approximately 2,600 ft (793 m). Rolling alluvial lowlands in the eastern portion of the state give way to the flat, treeless plain of central Nebraska, which in turn rises to a tableland in the west. The Sand Hills of the north-central plain is an unusual region of sand dunes anchored by grasses that cover about 18,000 sq mi (47,000 sq km).

The Sand Hills region is dotted with small natural lakes; in the rest of the state, the main lakes are artificial. The Missouri River—which, with its tributaries, drains the entire state—forms the eastern part of the northern boundary of Nebraska. Three rivers cross the state from west to east: the wide, shallow Platte River flows through the heart of the state for 310 mi (499 km), the Nio-brara River traverses the state's northern region, and the Republican River flows through southern Nebraska.

³CLIMATE

Nebraska has a continental climate, with highly variable temperatures from season to season and year to year. The central region has an annual normal temperature of 50°F (10°C), with a normal monthly maximum of 76°F (24°C) in July and a normal monthly minimum of 22°F (-6°C) in January. The record low for the state is -47°F (-44°C), registered in Morrill County on 12 February 1899; the record high of 118°F (48°C) was recorded at Minden on 24 July 1936.

Average yearly precipitation in Omaha is about 30 in (76 cm); in the semiarid panhandle in the west, 17 in (43 cm); and in the southeast, 30 in (76 cm). Snowfall in the state varies from about 21 in (53 cm) in the southeast to about 45 in (114 cm) in the northwest corner. Blizzards, droughts, and windstorms have plagued Nebraskans throughout their history.

⁴FLORA AND FAUNA

Nebraska's deciduous forests are generally oak and hickory; conifer forests are dominated by western yellow (ponderosa) pine. The tallgrass prairie may include various slough grasses and needle-grasses, along with big bluestem and prairie dropseed. Mixed prairie regions abound with western wheatgrass and buffalo grass. The prairie region of the Sand Hills supports a variety of blue-stems, gramas, and other grasses. Common Nebraska wildflowers are wild rose, phlox, petunia, columbine, goldenrod, and sunflower. Rare species of Nebraska's flora include the Hayden penstemon, yellow ladyslipper, pawpaw, and snow trillium. Three species were threatened as of 2006: Ute ladies' tresses, western prairie fringed orchid, and Colorado butterfly plant. The blowout penstemon was listed as endangered that year.

Common mammals native to the state are the pronghorn sheep, white-tailed and mule deer, badger, kit fox, coyote, striped ground squirrel, prairie vole, and several skunk species. There are more than 400 kinds of birds, the mourning dove, barn swallow, and western meadowlark (the state bird) among them. Three main wetland areas (Rainwater Basin wetlands, Big Bend reach of the Platte River, and the Sandhills wetlands) serve as important migrating and breeding grounds for waterfowl and nongame birds. Carp, catfish, trout, and perch are fished for sport. Rare animal species include the least shrew, least weasel, and bobcat. The US Fish and Wildlife Service listed nine animal species (vertebrates and invertebrates) as threatened or endangered in 2006, including the American burying beetle, bald eagle, whooping crane, black-footed ferret, Topeka shiner, pallid sturgeon, and Eskimo curlew.

5ENVIRONMENTAL PROTECTION

The Department of Environmental Quality was established in 1971 to protect and improve the quality of the state's water, air, and land resources. The Agricultural Pollution Control Division of the Department regulates disposal of feedlot wastes and other sources of water pollution by agriculture. The Water and Waste Management Division is responsible for administering the Federal Clean Water Act, the Federal Resources Conservation and Recovery Act, portions of the Federal Safe Drinking Water Act, and the Nebraska Environmental Protection Act as it relates to water, solid waste, and hazardous materials. In 2003, Nebraska had 255 hazardous waste sites listed in the US Environment Protection Agency (EPA) database, 12 of which were on the National Priorities List as of 2006. In 2005, the EPA spent over $15 million through the Superfund program for the cleanup of hazardous waste sites in the state. The same year, federal EPA grants awarded to the state included $8.2 million for its drinking water state revolving fund and $5.4 million for the clean water revolving fund.

A program to protect groundwater from such pollutants as nitrates, synthetic organic compounds, hydrocarbons, pesticides, and other sources was outlined in 1985. In 1996, the state spent $3.2 million on its Soil and Water Conservation Program. In 1994, the state imposed a tax on commercial fertilizers to create the Natural Resources Enhancement Fund, which distributes funds to local natural resource districts for water quality improvement programs. The Engineering Division regulates wastewater treatment standards and assists municipalities in securing federal construction grants for wastewater facilities. The Air Quality Division is responsible for monitoring and securing compliance with national ambient air quality standards. In 2003, 51.5 million lb of toxic chemicals were released in the state.

The state has three main wetland areas: Rainwater Basin wetlands, Big Bend reach of the Platte River, and the Sandhills wetlands. While these areas are protected, the state has lost about 1 million acres (405,000 hectares) of wetlands since pre-European settlement times.

6POPULATION

Nebraska ranked 38th in population in the United States with an estimated total of 1,758,787 in 2005, an increase of 2.8% since 2000. Between 1990 and 2000, Nebraska's population grew from 1,578,385 to 1,711,263, an increase of 8.4%. The population was projected to reach 1.78 million by 2015 and 1.81 million by 2025.

The population density in 2004 was 22.7 persons per sq mi. In 2004, the median age of all Nebraskans was 36. In the same year, 24.9% of the populace were under age 18 while 13.3% was age 65 or older. The largest cities in 2004 were Omaha, which ranked 43rd among the nation's cities with an estimated population of 409,416, and Lincoln, with 236,146 residents.

7ETHNIC GROUPS

Among Nebraskans reporting at least one specific ancestry in the 2000 census, 661,133 identified their ancestry as German, 163,651 as English, 229,805 as Irish, 93,286 as Czech, and 84,294 as Swedish. The 2000 population also included 68,541 black Americans 21,931 Asians, and 836 Pacific Islanders. There were 94,425 Hispanics and Latinos in 2000, representing 5.5% of the total population. In 2004, 4.3% of the population was black, 1.5% Asian, 0.1% Pacific Islander, 6.9% Hispanic or Latino, and 1.1% of the population claimed origin of two or more races. Foreign-born residents numbered 74,638, or 4.4% of the total population, in 2000.

There were 14,896 American Indians in Nebraska as of 2000, down from around 16,000 in 1990. The three Indian reservations maintained for the Omaha, Winnebago, and Santee Sioux tribes had the following populations as of 2000: Omaha, 5,194, and Winnebago, 2,588, and Santee Sioux, 603. In 2004, 0.9% of the population was American Indian.

8LANGUAGES

Many Plains Indians of the Macro-Siouan family once roamed widely over what is now Nebraska. Place names derived from the Siouan language include Omaha, Ogallala, Niobrara, and Keya Paha. In 1990, about 1,300 Nebraskans claimed Indian tongues as their first languages.

In 2000, 1, 469,046 Nebraskans—92.1% of the resident population five years old or older—spoke only English at home, down from 95.2% in 1990.

The following table gives selected statistics from the 2000 Census for language spoken at home by persons five years old and over. The category "Other Slavic languages" includes Czech, Slovak, and Ukrainian. The category "African languages" includes Amharic, Ibo, Twi, Yoruba, Bantu, Swahili, and Somali.

LANGUAGE	NUMBER	PERCENT
Population 5 years and over	1,594,700	100.0Speak only
English	1,469,046	92.1
Speak a language other than English	125,654	7.9
Speak a language other than English	**125,654**	**7.9**
Spanish or Spanish Creole	77,655	4.9
German	8,865	0.6
Vietnamese	5,958	0.4
Other Slavic languages	4,236	0.3
French (incl. Patois, Cajun)	3,631	0.2
Chinese	2,409	0.2
Arabic	1,628	0.1
Russian	1,559	0.1
African languages	1,472	0.1
Polish	1,420	0.1
Italian	1,419	0.1
Tagalog	1,311	0.1
Japanese	1,274	0.1

Nebraska English, except for a slight South Midland influence in the southwest and some Northern influence from Wisconsin and New York settlers in the Platte River Valley, is almost pure

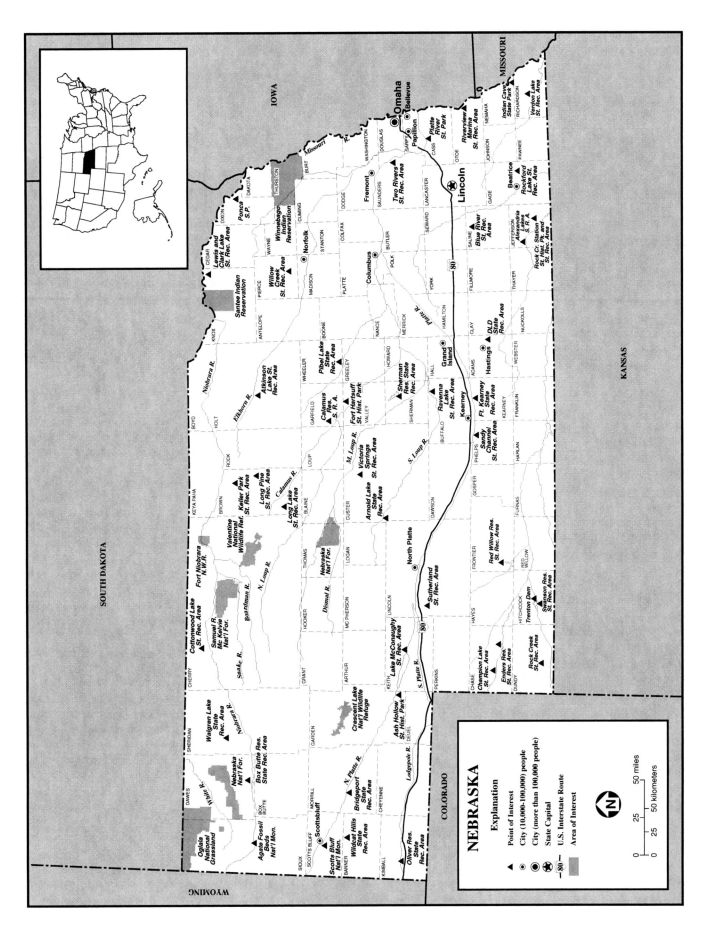

North Midland. A few words, mostly food terms like *kolaches* (fruit-filled pastries), are derived from the language of the large Czech population. Usual pronunciation features are *on* and *hog* with the /o/, *cow* and *now* as /kaow/ and /naow/, because with the /ah/ vowel, *cot* and *caught* as sound-alikes, and a strong final /r/. *Fire* sounds almost like *far,* and *our* like *are; greasy* is pronounced /greezy/.

9 RELIGIONS

Nebraska's religious history derives from its patterns of immigration. German and Scandinavian settlers tended to be Lutheran; Irish, Polish, and Czech immigrants were mainly Roman Catholic. Methodism and other Protestant religions were spread by settlers from other Midwestern states.

Though Protestants collectively outnumber Catholics, the Roman Catholic Church is the largest single Christian denomination within the state with about 376,843 adherents in 2004; of which 229,952 belong to the archdiocese of Omaha. As of a 2000 general survey, Lutherans constituted the largest Protestant group with 117,419 adherents of the Missouri Synod, 128,570 of the Evangelical Lutheran Church in America, and 5,829 of the Wisconsin Evangelical Lutheran Synod. In 2004, there were 84,337 members of the United Methodist Church. In 2000, there were 39,420 Presbyterians–USA. In 2006, there were 20,910 members of the Church of Jesus Christ of Latter-day Saints (Mormons); a Mormon temple was opened in Winter Quarters in 2001. As of 2005, there were 18,119 members of the United Church of Christ. The Jewish population was estimated at 7,100 in 2000 and Muslims numbered about 3,115. That year, there were 704,403 people (about 41% of the population) who were not counted as members of any religious organization.

10 TRANSPORTATION

Nebraska's development was profoundly influenced by two major railroads, the Union Pacific and the Chicago Burlington and Quincy (later merged along with the Great Northern and Northern Pacific railroads into the Burlington Northern in 1970), both of which were major landowners in the state in the late 1800s. As of 2003, the Union Pacific and the former railroads that make up the Burlington Northern (now the Burlington Northern Santa Fe) still operated in Nebraska, and constitute the state's two Class I railroads. Altogether, in that year, there were 11 railroads in the state with 3,548 rail mi (5,712 km) of track. As of 2006, Amtrak provided east–west service to five stations in Nebraska via its Chicago to Emreyville/San Francisco California Zephyr train

Nebraska's road system which totaled 93,245 mi (150,124 km) in 2004, is dominated by Interstate 80, the major east–west route and the largest public investment project in the state's history. Some 1.678 million motor vehicles were registered in 2004, of which around 829,000 were automobiles and about 820,000 were trucks of all types. There were 1,315,819 licensed drivers in the state that same year.

In 2005, Nebraska had a total of 303 public and private-use aviation-related facilities. This included 266 airports, 36 heliports, and one seaplane base. Eppley Airfield, Omaha's airport, is by far the busiest in the state. In 2004, Epply had 1,892,379 passengers enplaned.

Nebraska in 2004 had 318 mi (512 km) of navigable waterways. In 2003, waterborne shipments totaled only 50,000 tons.

11 HISTORY

Nebraska's first inhabitants, from about 10,000 BC, were nomadic Paleo-Indians. Successive groups were more sedentary, cultivating corn and beans. Archaeological excavations indicate that prolonged drought and dust storms before the 16th century caused these inhabitants to vacate the area. In the 16th and 17th centuries, other Indian tribes came from the East, some pushed by enemy tribes, others seeking new hunting grounds. By 1800, semisedentary Pawnee, Ponca, Omaha, and Oto, along with several nomadic groups, were in the region.

The Indians developed amiable relations with the first white explorers, French and Spanish fur trappers and traders who traveled through Nebraska in the 18th century using the Missouri River as a route to the West. The area was claimed by both Spain and France and was French territory at the time of the Louisiana Purchase, when it came under US jurisdiction. It was explored during the first half of the 19th century by Lewis and Clark, Zebulon Pike, Stephen H. Long, and John C. Frémont.

The Indian Intercourse Act of 1834 forbade white settlement west of the Mississippi River, reserving the Great Plains as Indian Territory. Nothing prevented whites from traversing Nebraska, however, and from 1840 to 1866, some 350,000 persons crossed the area on the Oregon, California, and Mormon trails, following the Platte River Valley, which was a natural highway to the West. Military forts were established in the 1840s to protect travelers from Indian attack.

The Kansas-Nebraska Act of 1854 established Nebraska Territory, which stretched from Kansas to Canada and from the Missouri River to the Rockies. The territory assumed its present shape in 1861. Still sparsely populated, Nebraska escaped the violence over the slavery issue that afflicted Kansas. The creation of Nebraska Territory heightened conflict between Indians and white settlers, however, as Indians were forced to cede more and more of their land. From mid-1860 to the late 1870s, western Nebraska was a battleground for Indians and US soldiers. By 1890, the Indians were defeated and moved onto reservations in Nebraska, South Dakota, and Oklahoma.

Settlement of Nebraska Territory was rapid, accelerated by the Homestead Act of 1862, under which the US government provided 160 acres (65 hectares) to a settler for a nominal fee, and the construction of the Union Pacific, the first transcontinental railroad. The Burlington Railroad, which came to Nebraska in the late 1860s, used its vast land grants from Congress to promote immigration, selling the land to potential settlers from the East and from Europe. The end of the Civil War brought an influx of Union veterans, bolstering the Republican administration, which began pushing for statehood. On 1 March 1867, Nebraska became the 37th state to join the Union. Farming and ranching developed as the state's two main enterprises. Facing for the first time the harsh elements of the Great Plains, homesteaders in central and western Nebraska evolved what came to be known as the sod-house culture, using grassy soil to construct sturdy insulated homes. They harnessed the wind with windmills to pump water, constructed fences of barbed wire, and developed dry-land farming techniques.

Ranching existed in Nebraska as early as 1859, and by the 1870s it was well established in the western part of the state. Some foreign investors controlled hundreds of thousands of acres of the free range. The cruel winter of 1886–87 killed thousands of cattle and bankrupted many of these large ranches.

By 1890, depressed farm prices, high railroad shipping charges, and rising interest rates were hurting the state's farmers, and a drought in the 1890s exacerbated their plight. These problems contributed to the rise of populism, a pro-agrarian movement. Many Nebraska legislators embraced populism, helping to bring about the first initiative and referendum laws in the United States, providing for the regulation of stockyards and telephone and telegraph companies, and instituting compulsory education.

World War I created a rift among Nebraskans as excessive patriotic zeal was directed against residents of German descent. German-language newspapers were censored, ministers were ordered to preach only in English (often to congregations that understood only German), and three university professors of German origin were fired. A Nebraska law (1919) that prohibited the teaching of any foreign language until high school was later declared unconstitutional by the US Supreme Court.

Tilling of marginal land to take advantage of farm prices that had been inflated during World War I caused economic distress during the 1920s. Nebraska's farm economy was already in peril when the dust storms of the 1930s began, and conditions worsened as drought, heat, and grasshopper invasions plagued the state. Thousands of people, particularly from the southwest counties in which dust-bowl conditions were most severe, fled Nebraska for the west coast. Some farmers joined protest movements—dumping milk, for example, rather than selling at depressed prices—while others marched on the state capital to demand a moratorium on farm debts, which they received. In the end, federal aid saved the farmers.

The onset of World War II brought prosperity to other sectors. Military airfields and war industries were placed in the state because of its safe inland location, bringing industrial growth that extended into the postwar years. Much of the new industry that developed during the postwar era was agriculture-related, including the manufacture of mechanized implements and irrigation equipment.

Farm output and income increased dramatically into the 1970s through wider use of hybrid seed, pesticides, fungicides, chemical fertilizers, close-row planting, and irrigation, but contaminated runoff adversely affected water quality and greater water use drastically lowered water-table levels. Many farmers took on large debt burdens to finance expanded output, their credit buoyed by strong farm-product prices and exports. When prices began to fall in the early 1980s, many found themselves overextended. By spring 1985, an estimated 10% of all farmers were reportedly close to bankruptcy. In the early 1990s farm prices rose; the average farm income in Nebraska rose more than 10% between 1989 and the mid-1990s. Increasingly, the state had fewer, larger, and more-mechanized farms. The growth of small industries and tourism also bolstered Nebraska's economy in the 1990s. By 1999 the state enjoyed one of the lowest unemployment rates in the nation—2.9%. But farmers were struggling again. A wildfire in the Sandhills of Nebraska's panhandle in 1999 scorched 74,840 acres and claimed 25,000 trees; it was the largest fire in the state's history. In the summer of 2000, areas of the state had had no substantial rain in a year. The previous autumn and winter were the driest on record. Drought conditions prevailed. Even with mitigation efforts, much of the state's corn crop was lost.

Challenges still facing the state have included a loss of population in rural areas, urban decay, and tension among various ethnic groups. In 1998 there were more Hispanics, accounting for 4.4% of the population, in the state than there were African Americans; Nebraska also has a small Native American population. Water conservation to avoid depletion of the state's aquifers for irrigation purposes remains a major priority. Nebraska was facing its worst recession since the 1980s in 2003. By 2004, the state was in its fifth straight year of severe drought conditions.

Lt. Governor Dave Heineman became Nebraska's governor in January 2005 when former Governor Mike Johanns resigned to serve as US Secretary of Agriculture. Heineman upon coming to office focused on four priorities: education, economic vitality, efficiency in government, and protecting families.

12 STATE GOVERNMENT

The first state constitution was adopted in 1866; a second, adopted in 1875, is still in effect. A 1919–20 constitutional convention proposed—and voters passed—41 amendments; by January 2005, the document had been revised an additional 222 times.

Nebraska's legislature is unique among the states; since 1934, it has been a unicameral body of 49 members elected on a nonpartisan basis. Members, who go by the title of senator, are chosen in even-numbered years for four-year terms. Legislative sessions begin in early January each year and are limited to 90 legislative days in odd-numbered years and to 60 legislative days in even-numbered years. Special sessions, not formally limited in duration, may be called by petition of two-thirds of the legislators. Legislators must be qualified voters, at least 21 years old, and should have lived in their district for a year prior to election. The legislative salary was $12,000 in 2004, unchanged from 1999.

Elected executives are the governor, lieutenant governor, secretary of state, auditor, treasurer, and attorney general, all of whom serve four-year terms. The governor and lieutenant governor are jointly elected; each must be a US citizen for at least five years, at least 30 years old, and have been a resident and citizen of Nebraska for at least five years. After serving two consecutive terms, the governor is ineligible for the office for four years. As of December 2004, the governor's salary was $85,000.

A bill becomes law when passed by a majority of the legislature and signed by the governor. If the governor does not approve, the bill is returned with objections, and a three-fifths vote of the members of the legislature is required to override the veto. A bill automatically becomes law if the governor does not take action within five days of receiving it.

A three-fifths majority of the legislature is required to propose an amendment to the state constitution. The people may propose an amendment by presenting a petition signed by 10% of total votes for governor at last election. The amendments are then submitted for approval at the next regular election or at a special election in which a majority of the votes tallied must be at least 30% of the total number of registered voters.

Nebraska Presidential Vote by Major Political Parties, 1948–2004

YEAR	ELECTORAL VOTE	NEBRASKA WINNER	DEMOCRAT	REPUBLICAN
1948	6	Dewey (R)	224,165	264,774
1952	6	*Eisenhower (R)	188,057	421,603
1956	6	*Eisenhower (R)	199,029	378,108
1960	6	Nixon (R)	232,542	380,553
1964	5	*Johnson (D)	307,307	276,847
1968	5	*Nixon (R)	170,784	321,163
1972	5	*Nixon (R)	169,991	406,298
1976	5	Ford (R)	233,692	359,705
1980	5	*Reagan (R)	166,424	419,214
1984	5	*Reagan (R)	187,866	460,054
1988	5	*Bush (R)	259,235	397,956
1992**	5	Bush (R)	217,344	344,346
1996**	5	Dole (R)	236,761	363,467
2000	5	*Bush, G. W. (R)	231,780	433,862
2004	5	*Bush, G. W. (R)	254,328	512,814

*Won US presidential election.
**IND. candidate Ross Perot received 174,687 votes in 1992 and 71,278 votes in 1996.

Voters in Nebraska must be US citizens, at least 18 years old, and state residents. Restrictions apply to convicted felons and those officially found mentally incompetent.

13 POLITICAL PARTIES

In the 2000 presidential elections, Republican candidate George W. Bush secured 63% of the vote; Democrat Al Gore, 33%; and Green Party candidate Ralph Nader, 3%. In 2004, Bush again dominated, with 66% of the vote to Democratic challenger John Kerry's 33%. In 2004 there were 1,160,000 registered voters. In 1998, 37% of registered voters were Democratic, 49% Republican, and 14% unaffiliated or members of other parties. The state had five electoral votes in the 2004 presidential election.

In the 2000 elections, Democrat Ben Nelson was elected to the Senate; Republican Chuck Hagel won election to the Senate in 1996 and was reelected in 2002. In 1998 Republican Mike Johanns was elected to succeed Nelson as governor; Johanns was reelected in 2002, but resigned before completing his term to become the US secretary of agriculture. Johanns was succeeded by Lieutenant Governor Dave Heineman in January 2005. Republicans won all three of the state's seats in the US House of Representatives in 1994, 1996, 1998, 2000, 2002, and 2004. Nebraska's unicameral state legislature is nonpartisan.

14 LOCAL GOVERNMENT

In 2005, Nebraska had 93 counties, 531 municipalities, and 576 public school districts. Some 1,146 special districts covered such services as fire protection, housing, irrigation, and sewage treatment. In 2002, there were 446 townships. Boards of supervisors or commissioners, elected by voters, administer at the county level. Municipalities are generally governed by a mayor (or city manager) and council. Villages elect trustees to governing boards.

In 2005, local government accounted for about 79,114 full-time (or equivalent) employment positions.

15 STATE SERVICES

To address the continuing threat of terrorism and to work with the federal Department of Homeland Security, homeland security in Nebraska operates under executive order; the lieutenant governor is designated as the state homeland security advisor.

As of 1 June 1971, the Office of Public Counsel (Ombudsman) was empowered to investigate complaints from citizens in relation to the state government. The Accountability and Disclosure Commission, established in 1977, regulates the organization and financing of political campaigns and investigates reports of conflicts of interest involving state officials.

The eight-member state Board of Education, elected on a nonpartisan basis, oversees elementary and secondary public schools and vocational education. The Board of Regents, which also consists of eight elected members, governs the University of Nebraska system. Special examining boards license architects, engineers, psychologists, and land surveyors. The Coordinating Commission for Postsecondary Education works to develop a statewide plan for an educationally and economically sound, progressive, and coordinated system of postsecondary education.

The Department of Roads maintains and builds highways, and the Department of Aeronautics regulates aviation, licenses airports, and registers aviators. The Department of Motor Vehicles provides vehicle and driver services. Natural resources are protected by the Forest Service, Energy Office, Game and Parks Commission, and the Natural Resources Department.

Public assistance, child welfare, medical care for the indigent, and a special program of services for children with disabilities are the responsibility of the Health and Human Service System, which also operates community health services, provides nutritional services, and is responsible for disease control.

The state's huge agricultural industry is aided and monitored by the Department of Agriculture, which is empowered to protect livestock, inspect food-processing areas, conduct research into crop development, and encourage product marketing. The Nebraska Corn Board works to enhance the profitability of the corn producer.

16 JUDICIAL SYSTEM

The Nebraska Supreme Court is the state's highest court, which consists of a chief justice and six other justices, all of whom are initially appointed by the governor. They must be elected after serving three years, and every six years thereafter, running unopposed on their own record. Below the Supreme Court are the district courts of which 53 judges serve 21 districts in the state. These are trial courts of general jurisdiction. County courts handle criminal misdemeanors and civil cases involving less than $5,000. In addition, there are a court of industrial relations, a worker's compensation court, two conciliation courts (family courts), two municipal courts (in Omaha and Lincoln), and juvenile courts in three counties.

As of 31 December 2004, a total of 4,130 prisoners were held in Nebraska's state and federal prisons, an increase from 4,040 of 2.2% from the previous year. As of year-end 2004, a total of 369 inmates were female, up from 323 or 14.2% from the year before. Among sentenced prisoners (one year or more), Nebraska had an incarceration rate of 230 per 100,000 population in 2004.

According to the Federal Bureau of Investigation, Nebraska in 2004 had a violent crime rate (murder/nonnegligent manslaughter, forcible rape, robbery, aggravated assault) of 308.7 reported incidents per 100,000 population, or a total of 5,393 reported incidents. Crimes against property (burglary, larceny/theft, and motor vehicle theft) in that same year totaled 61,512 reported incidents or 3,520.6 reported incidents per 100,000 people. Nebraska has a death penalty, of which electrocution is the sole method of execution. From 1976 through 5 May 2006, the state had executed only three people, the most recent of which was in December 1997. As of 1 January 2006, Nebraska had 10 inmates on death row.

In 2003, Nebraska spent $42,004,625 on homeland security, an average of $24 per state resident.

17 ARMED FORCES

The US military presence in the state is concentrated near Omaha, where Offutt Air Force Base serves as the headquarters of the US Strategic Air Command. In 2004, Nebraska firms were awarded $401.2 million in defense contracts, and defense payroll outlays were $925 million. In the same year, there were 7,332 active-duty military personnel and 3,769 civilian personnel stationed in Nebraska.

A total of 159,487 veterans of US military service resided in Nebraska as of 2003. Of these, 22,241 served in World War II, 20,282 in the Korean conflict, 48,499 in the Vietnam era, and 25,391 during the Persian Gulf War. For the fiscal year 2004, total Veterans Affairs expenditures in Nebraska amounted to $538 million.

As of 31 October 2004, the Nebraska State Patrol employed 498 full-time sworn officers.

18 MIGRATION

The pioneers who settled Nebraska in the 1860s consisted mainly of Civil War veterans from the North and foreign-born immigrants. Some of the settlers migrated from the East and easterly parts of the Midwest, but many came directly from Europe to farm the land. The Union Pacific and Burlington Northern railroads, which sold land to the settlers, actively recruited immigrants in Europe. Germans were the largest group to settle in Nebraska (in 1900, 65,506 residents were German-born), then Czechs from Bohemia, and Scandinavians from Sweden, Denmark, and Norway. The Irish came to work on the railroads in the 1860s and stayed to help build the cities. Another wave of Irish immigrants in the 1880s went to work in the packinghouses of Omaha. The city's stockyards also attracted Polish workers. The 1900 census showed that over one-half of all Nebraskans were either foreign-born or the children of foreign-born parents. For much of the 20th century, Nebraska was in a period of out-migration. From 1930 to 1960, the state suffered a net loss of nearly 500,000 people through migration, with more than one third of the total leaving during the dust-bowl decade, 1930–40. This trend continued, with Nebraska experiencing a net out-migration of 27,400 for the period 1985–90. Between 1990 and 1998, the state had net gains of 2,000 in domestic migration and 14,000 in international migration. In 1998, 1,267 foreign immigrants arrived in Nebraska. The state's overall population increased 5.3% between 1990 and 1998. In the period 2000–05, net international migration was 22,199 and net internal migration was -26,206, for a net loss of 4,007 people.

19 INTERGOVERNMENTAL COOPERATION

Nebraska's Commission on Intergovernmental Cooperation represents the state in the Council of State Governments. As an oil-producing state, Nebraska is a member of the Interstate Compact to Conserve Oil and Gas. In addition, the state belongs to several regional commissions. Of particular importance are the Republican River Compact with Colorado and Kansas, the Big Blue River Compact with Kansas, the South Platte River Compact with Colorado, the Ponca Creek Nebraska-South Dakota-Wyoming Water Compact, and the Upper Niobrara River Compact with Wyoming. The Nebraska Boundary Commission was authorized in 1982 to enter into negotiations to more precisely demarcate Nebraska's boundaries with Iowa, South Dakota, and Missouri. Nebraska is also a member of the Central Interstate Low-Level Radioactive Waste Compact, under which Nebraska, Kansas, Oklahoma, Louisiana, and Arkansas have located a suitable disposal site for such waste. Boundary pacts are in effect with Iowa, Missouri, and South Dakota. In fiscal year 2005, the state received $1.893 billion in federal grants, an estimated $1.927 billion in fiscal year 2006, and an estimated $1.994 billion in fiscal year 2007.

20 ECONOMY

Agriculture has historically been the backbone of Nebraska's economy, with cattle, corn, hogs, and soybeans leading the state's list of farm products. However, Nebraska is attempting to diversify its economy and has been successful in attracting new business, in large part because of its location near western coal and oil deposits.

The largest portion of the state's labor force is employed in agriculture, either directly or indirectly—as farm workers, as factory workers in the food-processing and farm-equipment industries, or as providers of related services. The service sector, which includes not only the servicing of equipment but also the high growth areas of health and business services and telemarketing, expanded at an annual rate of 4.4% during the 1980s. The trend intensified in the late 1990s, as general services grew at an average annual rate of 7.7% from 1998 to 2001, and financial services grew at an average rate of 5.7%. Nebraska was not deeply involved in the information technology (IT) boom of the 1990s, and therefore was not deeply affected by its bust in 2001. Coming into the 21st century, the state economy grew a moderate average rate of about 4.1% (1998 to 2000), which fell to 2.4% in 2001. In 2001, declines in manufacturing employment were off-set by increases in the services and government sectors. The job losses became more severe in 2002, by the fourth quarter, the unemployment rate had eased to 3.3%, down from 3.9% in April 2002.

With technological advances in farming and transportation, and consolidation in the agricultural sector, Nebraska's rural counties have been losing population since the 1970s. In 2002, sixty six of Nebraska's 93 counties had lower populations than in the 1970s, and population loss accelerated during the 1990s. Drought conditions in 2002 disrupted cattle production because of shortages of hay and pasture. Drought persisted into the winter of 2002-03, and the state is likely to face long-term water shortages.

Nebraska's gross state product (GSP) in 2004 was $68.183 billion, of which manufacturing (durable and nondurable goods) accounted for the largest share at $8.305 billion or 12.1% of GSP, followed by the real estate sector at $5.872 billion (8.6% of GSP), and health care and social assistance at $4.919 billion (7.2% of GSP). In that same year, there were an estimated 151,088 small businesses in Nebraska. Of the 46,161 businesses that had employees, an estimated total of 44,703 or 96.8% were small companies. An estimated 4,849 new businesses were established in the state in 2004, up 12.5% from the year before. Business terminations that same year came to 5,051, unchanged from 2003. There were 207 business bankruptcies in 2004, down 13% from the previous year. In 2005, the state's personal bankruptcy (Chapter 7 and Chapter 13) filing rate was 485 filings per 100,000 people, ranking Nebraska as the 28th highest in the nation.

21 INCOME

In 2005 Nebraska had a gross state product (GSP) of $70 billion which accounted for 0.6% of the nation's gross domestic product and placed the state at number 37 in highest GSP among the 50 states and the District of Columbia.

According to the Bureau of Economic Analysis, in 2004 Nebraska had a per capita personal income (PCPI) of $32,341. This ranked 21st in the United States and was 98% of the national average of $33,050. The 1994–2004 average annual growth rate of PCPI was 4.5%. Nebraska had a total personal income (TPI) of $56,523,179,000, which ranked 36th in the United States and reflected an increase of 5.8% from 2003. The 1994–2004 average annual growth rate of TPI was 5.2%. Earnings of persons employed in Nebraska increased from $41,452,474,000 in 2003 to $43,923,337,000 in 2004, an increase of 6.0%. The 2003–04 national change was 6.3%.

The US Census Bureau reports that the three-year average median household income for 2002 to 2004 in 2004 dollars was $44,623 compared to a national average of $44,473. During the same period an estimated 9.9% of the population was below the poverty line as compared to 12.4% nationwide.

22 LABOR

According to the US Department of Labor's Bureau of Labor Statistics (BLS), in April 2006 the seasonally adjusted civilian labor force in Nebraska numbered 988,200, with approximately 33,700 workers unemployed, yielding an unemployment rate of 3.4%, compared to the national average of 4.7% for the same period. Preliminary data for the same period placed nonfarm employment at 947,100. Since the beginning of the BLS data series in 1976, the highest unemployment rate recorded in Nebraska was 6.8% in February 1983. The historical low was 2.2% in February 1998. Preliminary nonfarm employment data by occupation for April 2006 showed that approximately 4.9% of the labor force was employed in construction; 10.9% in manufacturing; 21.2% in trade, transportation, and public utilities; 6.9% in financial activities; 10.4% in professional and business services; 13.7% in education and health services; 8.5% in leisure and hospitality services; and 17.1% in government.

The BLS reported that in 2005, a total of 69,000 of Nebraska's 830,000 employed wage and salary workers were formal members of a union. This represented 8.3% of those so employed, which was unchanged from 2004, and below the national average of 12%. Overall in 2005, a total of 79,000 workers (9.5%) in Nebraska were covered by a union or employee association contract, which includes those workers who reported no union affiliation. Nebraska is one of 22 states with a right-to-work law.

As of 1 March 2006, Nebraska had a state-mandated minimum wage rate of $5.15 per hour. In 2004, women in the state accounted for 47.1% of the employed civilian labor force.

23 AGRICULTURE

Territorial Nebraska was settled by homesteaders. Farmers easily adapted to the land and the relatively rainy eastern region, and corn soon became their major crop. In the drier central and western prairie regions, settlers were forced to learn new farming methods to conserve moisture in the ground. Droughts in the 1890s provided impetus for water conservation. Initially, oats and spring wheat were grown along with corn, but by the end of the 19th century, winter wheat became the main wheat crop. The drought and dust storms of the 1930s, which devastated the state's agricultural economy, once again drove home the need for water and soil conservation. In 2002, a total of 7.5 million acres (3 million hectares) were irrigated, a 21% increase from 1992. In 2004, there were 48,300 farms covering 45.9 million acres (18.6 million hectares).

With total cash receipts from farm marketings at over $11.2 billion in 2005, Nebraska ranked fourth among the 50 states. About $7.3 billion of all farm marketings came from livestock production, and $3.9 billion from cash crops (9.9% of US total). In 2004, corn accounted for 22% of farm receipts.

Crop production in 2004 (in bushels) included: corn, 1.3 billion; sorghum grain, 33.6 million; wheat, 61 million; oats, 3.7 million; and barley, 162,000. Hay production was 6.1 million tons and potato production, 9.3 million hundredweight (422 million kg). During 2000–04, Nebraska ranked third among the states in production of corn for grain and sorghum for grain, and fifth in sorghum for beans.

Farms in Nebraska are major businesses requiring large land holdings to justify investments. The average value of an acre of cropland in 2004 was $1,750. Nebraska farms still tend to be owned by individuals or families rather than by large corporations. The strength of state support for the family farm was reflected in the passage of a 1982 constitutional amendment, initiated by petition, prohibiting the purchase of Nebraska farm and ranch lands by other than a Nebraska family farm corporation.

24 ANIMAL HUSBANDRY

In 2005, Nebraska ranked third behind Texas and Kansas in the total number of cattle on farms (6.35 million), including 61,000 milk cows. Nebraska farmers had around 2.85 million hogs and pigs, valued at $313.5 million in 2004. During 2003, the state produced an estimated 10.3 million lb (4.7 million kg) of sheep and lambs, which grossed $10.8 million in income for Nebraska farmers. Dairy products included 1.13 billion lb (0.51 billion kg) of milk produced.

25 FISHING

Commercial fishing is negligible in Nebraska. The US Fish and Wildlife Service maintains 87 public fishing areas. In 2004, the state had 176,619 fishing license holders. There are five state hatcheries producing a variety of stock fish that includes largemouth bass, bluegill, black crappie, channel catfish, yellow perch, walleye, trout, and tiger musky.

26 FORESTRY

Arbor Day, now observed throughout the United States, originated in Nebraska in 1872 as a way of encouraging tree planting in the sparsely forested state. Forestland occupies 1,275,000 acres (516,000 hectares), or 2.6% of all Nebraska. Ash, boxelder, hackberry, cottonwood, honey locust, red and bur oaks, walnut, elm, and willow trees are common to eastern and central Nebraska, while ponderosa pine, cottonwood, eastern red cedar, and Rocky Mountain juniper prevail in the west. Lumber production amounted to only 15 million board ft in 2004. The state's two national forests—Nebraska and Samuel R. McKelvie—are primarily grassland and are managed for livestock grazing. In 2005, the National Forest Service maintained 257,628 acres (104,262 hectares) of forestland.

27 MINING

According to preliminary data from the US Geological Survey (USGS), the estimated value of nonfuel mineral production by Nebraska in 2003 was $94.2 million, a decrease from 2002 of about 4%.

According to the preliminary data for 2003, by value and in descending order, cement (portland and masonry), crushed stone, and construction sand and gravel were the state's top nonfuel minerals.

Preliminary data for 2003 showed crushed stone production totaling 6.9 million metric tons, with a value of $51.1 million, while construction sand and gravel output stood at 12.2 million metric tons, with a value of $42.1 million.

Most clay mining occurs in the southeast region, but sand and gravel mining takes place throughout the state. Industrial sand was used in the production of glass and had some applications outside of construction activities. Nebraska in 2003 was also a producer of common clays and lime.

28 ENERGY AND POWER

Nebraska is the only state with an electric power system owned by the public through regional, cooperative, and municipal systems. As of 2003, Nebraska had 162 electrical power service providers, of which 151 were publicly owned, 23 were cooperatives and one was federally operated. As of that same year there were 930,822 retail customers. Of that total, 909,089 received their power from publicly owned service providers. Cooperatives accounted for 21,721 customers and 12 were 48 federal customers.

Total net summer generating capability by the state's electrical generating plants in 2003 stood at 6.685 million kW, with total production that same year at 30.455 billion kWh. Of the total amount generated, 99.7% came from electric utilities, with the remainder coming from independent producers and combined heat and power service providers. The largest portion of all electric power generated, 20.954 billion kWh (68.8%), came from coal-fired plants, with nuclear plants in second place at 7.996 billion kWh (26.3%) and hydroelectric plants in third at 980.110 million kWh (3.2%). Other renewable power sources, natural gas fueled plants, and petroleum fired plants accounted for the remainder.

As of 2006, Nebraska had two operating nuclear power plants: the Cooper plant in Brownville and the Fort Calhoun Station near Omaha.

As of 2004, Nebraska had proven crude oil reserves of 15 million barrels, or less than 1% of all proven US reserves, while output that same year averaged 8,000 barrels per day. Including federal offshore domains, the state that year ranked 22nd (21st excluding federal offshore) in proven reserves and 23rd (22nd excluding federal offshore) in production among the 31 producing states. In 2004, Nebraska had 1,639 producing oil wells and accounted for under 1% of all US production. The state has no refineries.

In 2004, Nebraska had 111 producing natural gas and gas condensate wells. In that same year, marketed gas production (all gas produced excluding gas used for repressuring, vented and flared, and nonhydrocarbon gases removed) totaled 1.454 billion cu ft (0.041 billion cu m). There was no data available on the state's proven reserves of natural gas.

Nebraska has no commercial coal industry.

29 INDUSTRY

According to the US Census Bureau's Annual Survey of Manufactures (ASM) for 2004, Nebraska's manufacturing sector covered some 15 product subsectors. The shipment value of all products manufactured in the state that same year was $34.433 billion. Of that total, food manufacturing accounted for the largest share at $19.037 billion. It was followed by machinery manufacturing at $2.061 billion, transportation equipment manufacturing at $2.034 billion, chemical manufacturing at $1.904 billion, and miscellaneous manufacturing at $1.623 billion.

In 2004, a total of 99,706 people in Nebraska were employed in the state's manufacturing sector, according to the ASM. Of that total, 76,578 were actual production workers. In terms of total employment, the food manufacturing industry accounted for the largest portion of all manufacturing employees at 36,190, with 29,537 actual production workers. It was followed by machinery manufacturing at 8,590 employees (5,617 actual production workers), fabricated metal product manufacturing at 8,306 employees (6,112 actual production workers), transportation equipment manufacturing at 7,841 employees (6,508 actual production workers), plastics and rubber products manufacturing at 5,159 employees (4,078 actual production workers), and miscellaneous manufacturing with 5,025 employees (4,070 actual production workers).

ASM data for 2004 showed that Nebraska's manufacturing sector paid $3.532 billion in wages. Of that amount, the food manufacturing sector accounted for the largest share at $1.131 billion. It was followed by machinery manufacturing at $350.037 million, fabricated metal product manufacturing at $307.681 million, transport equipment manufacturing at $291.760 million, and plastics and rubber products manufacturing at $184.551 million.

Nebraska has a small but growing manufacturing sector, the largest portion of which is in the Omaha metropolitan area. Other manufacturing centers are located in Lincoln and the Sioux City, Iowa, metropolitan area that is located in Nebraska.

30 COMMERCE

According to the 2002 Census of Wholesale Trade, Nebraska's wholesale trade sector had sales that year totaling $26.1 billion from 2,907 establishments. Wholesalers of durable goods accounted for 1,542 establishments, followed by nondurable goods wholesalers at 1,193 and electronic markets, agents, and brokers accounting for 172 establishments. Sales by durable goods wholesalers in 2002 totaled $6.2 billion, while wholesalers of nondurable goods saw sales of $16.5 billion. Electronic markets, agents, and brokers in the wholesale trade industry had sales of $3.3 billion.

In the 2002 Census of Retail Trade, Nebraska was listed as having 8,157 retail establishments with sales of $20.2 billion. The leading types of retail businesses by number of establishments were: motor vehicle and motor vehicle parts dealers (1,126), gasoline stations (1,116), building material/garden equipment and supplies dealers (1,022), and food and beverage stores (892). In terms of sales, motor vehicle and motor vehicle parts dealers accounted for the largest share of retail sales at $5.07 billion, followed by general merchandise stores at $2.8 billion, food and beverage stores at $2.4 billion, and building material/garden equipment and supplies dealers at $2.1 billion. A total of 105,634 people were employed by the retail sector in Nebraska that year.

Nebraska's exports of goods produced within the state totaled $3 billion in 2005. Major export items included: food, electronic equipment, agricultural crops, transport equipment, and chemicals. The majority of exports went to Japan, Canada, and Mexico.

31CONSUMER PROTECTION

Nebraska's consumer protection activities are generally the responsibility of the Office of the Attorney General's Consumers Protection Division. The Division also operates a mediation service to help the state's consumers to resolve complaints against business. Consumer protection involving railroads, telephone companies motor transport and other common carriers within the state is the responsibility of the Nebraska Public Service Commission.

When dealing with consumer protection issues, the state's attorney general's office can initiate civil and criminal proceedings, represent the state before state and federal regulatory agencies, administer consumer protection and education programs, handle formal consumer complaints, and exercise broad subpoena powers. In antitrust actions, the attorney general's office can act on behalf of those consumers who are incapable of acting on their own; initiate damage actions on behalf of the state in state courts; initiate criminal proceedings; and represent counties, cities and other governmental entities in recovering civil damages under state or federal law. However, the state's attorney general's office cannot provide private legal advice.

The offices of the Consumer Protection Division are located in Lincoln, the state capital.

32BANKING

As of June 2005, Nebraska had 262 insured banks, savings and loans, and saving banks, plus 25 state-chartered and 53 federally chartered credit unions (CUs). Excluding the CUs, the Omaha-Council Bluffs market area accounted for the largest portion of the state's financial institutions and deposits in 2004, with 74 institutions and $14.442 billion in deposits. As of June 2005, CUs accounted for 5.3% of all assets held by all financial institutions in the state, or some $2.577 billion. Banks, savings and loans, and savings banks collectively accounted for the remaining 94.7% or $46.120 billion in assets held.

In 2004, the median net interest margin (NIM)—the difference between the lower rates offered to savers and the higher rates charged on loans—was 4.18%, down from 4.19% in 2003. In fourth quarter 2005, the median NIM was 4.15%. The median percentage of past-due/nonaccrual loans to total loans in 2004 was 1.68%, down from 1.85% in 2003and was 1.47% in fourth quarter 2005.

Regulation of Nebraska's state-chartered banks and other financial institutions is the responsibility of the Nebraska Department of Banking and Finance.

33INSURANCE

The insurance industry is important in Nebraska's economy. The major company in the state is Mutual of Omaha. In 2004, there were about 1.2 million individual life insurance policies in force with a total value of over $91.9 billion; total value for all categories of life insurance (individual, group, and credit) was over $145 billion. The average coverage amount is $76,500 per policy holder. Death benefits paid that year totaled at over $399 million.

In 2003, there were 29 life and health and 38 property and casualty insurance companies domiciled in the state. Direct premiums for property and casualty insurance totaled $3 billion in 2004. That year, there were 13,617 flood insurance policies in force in the state, with a total value of $1.49 billion.

In 2004, 57% of state residents held employment-based health insurance policies, 8% held individual policies, and 22% were covered under Medicare and Medicaid; 11% of residents were uninsured. In 2003, employee contributions for employment-based health coverage averaged at 29% for family coverage. The employee contribution for single coverage averaged at 25%, the highest rate in the nation. The state offers a six-month health benefits expansion program for small-firm employees in connection with the Consolidated Omnibus Budget Reconciliation Act (COBRA, 1986), a health insurance program for those who lose employment-based coverage due to termination or reduction of work hours.

In 2003, there were over 1.3 million auto insurance policies in effect for private passenger cars. Required minimum coverage includes bodily injury liability of up to $25,000 per individual and $50,000 for all persons injured in an accident, as well as property damage liability of $25,000. In 2003, the average expenditure per vehicle for insurance coverage was $624.26.

34SECURITIES

The Bureau of Securities within the Department of Banking and Finance regulates the sale of securities. There are no stock exchanges in the state. In 2005, there were 410 personal financial advisers employed in the state and 1,440 securities, commodities, and financial services sales agents. In 2004, there were over 29 publicly traded companies within the state, with over 11 NASDAQ companies, 9 NYSE listings, and 1 AMEX listing. In 2006, the state had five Fortune 500 companies; Berkshire Hathaway ranked first in the state and 13th in the nation with revenues of over $81.6 billion, followed by ConAgra Foods, Union Pacific, Peter Kiewit Sons', Inc, and Mutual of Omaha Insurance. Peter Kiewit Sons', Inc. is an employee-owned company that does not trade in public stock. The other four companies listed are on the NYSE.

³⁵PUBLIC FINANCE

Nebraska's constitution prohibits the state from incurring debt in excess of $100,000. However, there is a provision in the constitution that permits the issuance of revenue bonds for highway and water conservation and management structure construction. There are $10 million of bonds payable by a separate legal entity that has been blended into the financial activity of the state. These bonds do not represent a general obligation of the state and are secured by revenues from the equipment that the debt was incurred to purchase.

Nebraska—State Government Finances

(Dollar amounts in thousands. Per capita amounts in dollars.)

	AMOUNT	PER CAPITA
Total Revenue	8,316,470	4,757.71
General revenue	7,337,829	4,197.84
Intergovernmental revenue	2,383,391	1,363.50
Taxes	3,639,811	2,082.27
General sales	1,524,591	872.19
Selective sales	463,487	265.15
License taxes	201,921	115.52
Individual income tax	1,242,603	710.87
Corporate income tax	167,429	95.78
Other taxes	39,780	22.76
Current charges	652,712	373.41
Miscellaneous general revenue	661,915	378.67
Utility revenue	–	–
Liquor store revenue	–	–
Insurance trust revenue	978,641	559.86
Total expenditure	6,979,917	3,993.09
Intergovernmental expenditure	1,695,613	970.03
Direct expenditure	5,284,304	3,023.06
Current operation	4,072,878	2,330.02
Capital outlay	652,374	373.21
Insurance benefits and repayments	334,290	191.24
Assistance and subsidies	128,728	73.64
Interest on debt	96,034	54.94
Exhibit: Salaries and wages	1,827,865	1,045.69
Total expenditure	6,979,917	3,993.09
General expenditure	6,645,627	3,801.85
Intergovernmental expenditure	1,695,613	970.03
Direct expenditure	4,950,014	2,831.82
General expenditures, by function:		
Education	2,324,444	1,329.77
Public welfare	1,899,089	1,086.44
Hospitals	202,775	116.00
Health	308,713	176.61
Highways	595,128	340.46
Police protection	69,651	39.85
Correction	188,457	107.81
Natural resources	146,969	84.08
Parks and recreation	30,384	17.38
Government administration	178,182	101.93
Interest on general debt	96,034	54.94
Other and unallocable	605,801	346.57
Utility expenditure	–	–
Liquor store expenditure	–	–
Insurance trust expenditure	334,290	191.24
Debt at end of fiscal year	1,949,654	1,115.36
Cash and security holdings	10,272,986	5,876.99

Abbreviations and symbols: – zero or rounds to zero; (NA) not available; (X) not applicable.

SOURCE: *U.S. Census Bureau, Governments Division, 2004 Survey of State Government Finances,* January 2006.

The constitution also authorizes the Board of Regents of the University of Nebraska, the Board of Trustees of the Nebraska State Colleges, and the State Board of Education to issue revenue bonds to construct, purchase, or remodel educational buildings and facilities. The payment of these bonds is generally made from revenue collected from use of the buildings and facilities. The legislature has authorized the creation of two financing authorities that are not subject to state constitutional restrictions on the incurrence of debt. These financing authorities were organized to assist in providing funds for the construction of capital improvement projects at the colleges and the University. Although the state has no legal responsibility for the debt of these financing authorities, they are considered part of the reporting entity.

The Nebraska state budget is prepared by the Budget Division of the Department of Administrative Services and is submitted annually by the governor to the legislature. The fiscal year runs from 1 July to 30 June.

Fiscal year 2006 general funds were estimated at $3.3 billion for resources and $2.9 billion for expenditures. In fiscal year 2004, federal government grants to Nebraska were $2.5 billion.

In the fiscal year 2007 federal budget, Nebraska was slated to receive $5 million to co-locate the Terminal Radar Approach Control (TRACON) in Lincoln with the TRACON in Omaha.

³⁶TAXATION

In 2005, Nebraska collected $3,797 million in tax revenues or $2,158 per capita, which placed it 24th among the 50 states in per capita tax burden. The national average was $2,192 per capita. Property taxes accounted for 0.1% of the total, sales taxes 39.9%, selective sales taxes 12.0%, individual income taxes 36.7%, corporate income taxes 5.2%, and other taxes 6.0%.

As of 1 January 2006, Nebraska had four individual income tax brackets ranging from 2.56 to 6.84%. The state taxes corporations at rates ranging from 5.58 to 7.81% depending on tax bracket.

In 2004, state and local property taxes amounted to $2,007,118,000 or $1,148 per capita. The per capita amount ranks the state 16th highest nationally. Local governments collected $2,004,782,000 of the total and the state government $2,336,000.

Nebraska taxes retail sales at a rate of 5.5%. In addition to the state tax, local taxes on retail sales can reach as much as 1.5%, making for a potential total tax on retail sales of 7%. Food purchased for consumption off-premises is tax exempt. The tax on cigarettes is 64 cents per pack, which ranks 30th among the 50 states and the District of Columbia. Nebraska taxes gasoline at 27 cents per gallon. This is in addition to the 18.4 cents per gallon federal tax on gasoline.

According to the Tax Foundation, for every federal tax dollar sent to Washington in 2004, Nebraska citizens received $1.07 in federal spending.

³⁷ECONOMIC POLICY

The Department of Economic Development (DED) was created in 1967 to plan, promote, and develop the economy of the state. Nebraska offers loans for businesses which create or maintain employment for persons of low and moderate income. It provides tax credits to companies which increase investment and add jobs. The Bio Nebraska Life Sciences Association was formed in 2005 to coordinate and expand life sciences in the state. Grow Nebraska is a nonprofit marketing program whose mission is to expand the state's arts and craft industry. The Nebraska "Edge" programs are rural entrepreneurial training programs that are hosted by local communities, organizations and associations. The Nebraska Investment Finance Authority provides tax-exempt bond financing and technical assistance for agriculture, business, housing, and community development. In 2006, the US Chamber of Commerce ranked all 50 states on legal fairness towards business. The chamber found Nebraska to be one of five states with the best legal environment for business. The other four were Iowa, Virginia, Connecticut, and Delaware.

38HEALTH

The infant mortality rate in October 2005 was estimated at 5.7 per 1,000 live births. The birth rate in 2003 was 14.9 per 1,000 population. The abortion rate stood at 11.6 per 1,000 women in 2000. In 2003, about 83.4% of pregnant woman received prenatal care beginning in the first trimester. In 2004, approximately 82% of children received routine immunizations before the age of three.

The crude death rate in 2003 was 8.9 deaths per 1,000 population. As of 2002, the death rates for major causes of death (per 100,000 resident population) were: heart disease, 245.3; cancer, 189.5; cerebrovascular diseases, 63.8; chronic lower respiratory diseases, 54; and diabetes, 22.7. The mortality rate from HIV infection was 1.2 per 100,000 population. In 2004, the reported AIDS case rate was at about 3.9 per 100,000 population. In 2002, about 57% of the population was considered overweight or obese. As of 2004, about 20.2% of state residents were smokers.

University Hospital and University of Nebraska Medical Center are in Omaha. In 2003, Nebraska had 85 community hospitals with about 7,500 beds. There were about 212,000 patient admissions that year and 3.7 million outpatient visits. The average daily inpatient census was about 4,400 patients. The average cost per day for hospital care was $1,043. Also in 2003, there were about 228 certified nursing facilities in the state with 16,378 beds and an overall occupancy rate of about 83%. In 2004, it was estimated that about 75.3% of all state residents had received some type of dental care within the year. Nebraska had 243 physicians per 100,000 resident population in 2004 and 936 nurses per 100,000 in 2005. In 2004, there were a total of 1,114 dentists in the state.

About 15% of state residents were enrolled in Medicaid programs in 2003; 15% were enrolled in Medicare programs in 2004. Approximately 11% of the state population was uninsured in 2004. In 2003, state health care expenditures totaled $2.1 million.

39SOCIAL WELFARE

In 2004, about 43,000 people received unemployment benefits, with the average weekly unemployment benefit at $220. In fiscal year 2005, the estimated average monthly participation in the food stamp program included about 117,415 persons (46,948 households); the average monthly benefit was about $84.83 per person. That year, the total of benefits paid through the state for the food stamp program was about $119.5 million.

Temporary Assistance for Needy Families (TANF), the system of federal welfare assistance that officially replaced Aid to Families with Dependent Children (AFDC) in 1997, was reauthorized through the Deficit Reduction Act of 2005. TANF is funded through federal block grants that are divided among the states based on an equation involving the number of recipients in each state. Nebraska's TANF program is called Employment First. In 2004, the state program had 27,000 recipients; state and federal expenditures on this TANF program totaled $59 million in fiscal year 2003.

In December 2004, Social Security benefits were paid to 290,580 Nebraska residents. This number included 190,650 retired workers, 29,720 widows and widowers, 31,910 disabled workers, 18,070 spouses, and 20,230 children. Social Security beneficiaries represented 16.6% of the total state population and 94.3% of the state's population age 65 and older. Retired workers received an average monthly payment of $937; widows and widowers, $927; disabled workers, $847; and spouses, $475. Payments for children of retired workers averaged $510 per month; children of deceased workers, $648; and children of disabled workers, $240. Federal Supplemental Security Income payments in December 2004 went to 22,100 Nebraska residents, averaging $368 a month. An additional $519,000 of state-administered supplemental payments were distributed to 5,574 residents.

40HOUSING

In 2004, there were an estimated 757,743 housing units in Nebraska, 687,456 of which were occupied; 68.4% were owner-occupied. About 73.8% of all units were single-family, detached homes. Utility gas and electricity were the most common heating energy sources. It was estimated that 35,566 units lacked telephone service, 1,426 lacked complete plumbing facilities, and 3,513 lacked complete kitchen facilities. The average household had 2.47 members.

In 2004, 10,900 new privately owned units were authorized for construction. The median home value was $106,656. The median monthly cost for mortgage owners was $1,051. Renters paid a median of $547 per month. In 2006, the state received over $12.3 million in community development block grants from the US Department of Housing and Urban Development (HUD).

41EDUCATION

In 2004, 91.3% of Nebraskans age 25 and older were high school graduates, exceeding the national average of 84%. Some 24.8% had obtained a bachelor's degree or higher, lower than the national average of 26%.

The total enrollment for fall 2002 in Nebraska's public schools stood at 285,000. Of these, 195,000 attended schools from kindergarten through grade eight, and 90,000 attended high school. Approximately 79.5% of the students were white, 7.1% were black, 10.1% were Hispanic, 1.7% were Asian/Pacific Islander, and 1.6% were American Indian/Alaskan Native. Total enrollment was estimated at 282,000 in fall 2003 and expected to be 285,000 by fall 2014, a decline of 0.2% during the period 2002 to 2014. there were 39,454 students enrolled in 242 private schools in fall 2003. Expenditures for public education in 2003/04 were estimated at $2.6 billion. Since 1969, the National Assessment of Educational Progress (NAEP) has tested public school students nationwide. The resulting report, *The Nation's Report Card,* stated that in 2005 eighth graders in Nebraska scored 284 out of 500 in mathematics compared with the national average of 278.

As of fall 2002, there were 116,737 students enrolled in college or graduate school; minority students comprised 9.8% of total postsecondary enrollment. In 2005, Nebraska had 39 degree-granting institutions, including 7 public four-year schools, 8 public two-year schools, and 16 nonprofit, private four-year institutions. The University of Nebraska is the state's largest postsecondary institution, with campuses in Kearney, Lincoln, and Omaha.

42 ARTS

The 15-member Nebraska Arts Council (NAC), appointed by the governor, is empowered to receive federal and state funds and to plan and administer statewide and special programs in all the arts. Funds are available for arts education, organizational support, multicultural arts projects, special arts-related programs, touring, and fellowships. Affiliation with the Mid-America Arts Alliance allows the council to help sponsor national and regional events. In 2005, the NAC and other Nebraska arts organizations received nine grants totaling $747,800 from the National Endowment for the Arts.

The Nebraska Humanities Council, founded in 1972, sponsors two annual festivals: The Great Plains Chautauqua and the Nebraska Book Festival. The Nebraska Book Festival celebrates local writers and books, but also emphasizes the importance of reading and writing worldwide; the 2005 theme "Local Wonders" featured US Poet Laureate and 2005 Pulitzer Prize winner, Ted Kooser, and his title, *Local Wonders: Seasons in the Bohemian Alps*. In 2005, the National Endowment for the Humanities contributed $782,580 to seven programs in the state.

The Omaha Theater Company for Young People sponsors a number of theatrical performances as well as the Omaha Theater Ballet Company. The Omaha Symphony was founded in 1921, and Opera Omaha was founded in 1958. In their 2006/07 season, the Omaha Symphony hosted special guest performances by pop and Christian music artist, Amy Grant, and Tony-Award winning actress, Bernadette Peters.

The Lied Center for Performing Arts in Lincoln was created in 1990 and sponsors a wide variety of dance, theater, and musical programs. The facility brings major regional, national, and international events to the state and works with the University of Nebraska–Lincoln, providing opportunities in teaching and training in the performing arts departments. Offering a wide variety of events, in 2006, performances included Cuban-American recording artist, Maria Del Rey and the musical *Sweeney Todd* performed by local musical company, TADA.

43 LIBRARIES AND MUSEUMS

For the fiscal year ending in December 2001, Nebraska had 272 public library systems, with 289 libraries, of which 17 were branches. In that same year, there was a total of 6,004,000 volumes of books and serial publications in the public library system, while total circulation was 11,366,000. The system also had 209,000 audio and 175,000 video items, 15,000 electronic format items (CD-ROMs, magnetic tapes, and disks), and nine bookmobiles. In fiscal year 2001, operating income for the state's public library system came to $37,036,000 and included $289,000 in federal grants and $511,000 in state grants. The Omaha public library system had 916,560 books and 2,471 periodical subscriptions in nine branches.

The Joslyn Art Museum in Omaha is the state's leading museum. Other important museums include the Nebraska State Museum of History, the University of Nebraska State Museum (natural history), and the Sheldon Memorial Art Gallery, all in Lincoln; the Western Heritage Museum in Omaha; the Stuhr Museum of the Prairie Pioneer in Grand Island; and the Hastings Museum in Hastings. In all, the state had 107 museums in 2000. The Agate Fossil Beds National Monument in northwestern Nebraska features mammal fossils from the Miocene era and a library of paleontological and geologic material.

44 COMMUNICATIONS

Telephone service is regulated by the Public Service Commission. About 95.7% of the state's occupied housing units had telephones in 2004. Additionally, by June of that same year there were 984,355 mobile wireless telephone subscribers. In 2003, 66.1% of Nebraska households had a computer and 55.4% had Internet access. By June 2005, there were 253,974 high-speed lines in Nebraska, 228,965 residential and 25,009 for business. In 2005, 52 major FM stations and 19 major AM stations were operating. There were 8 major network TV stations. A total of 23,752 Internet domain names were registered in the state in 2000.

45 PRESS

In 2005, Nebraska had 6 morning dailies, 12 evening dailies, and 6 Sunday newspapers. The leading newspaper is the *Omaha World–Herald*, with a daily circulation in 2005 of 192,607 and a Sunday circulation of 242,964. The *Lincoln Journal–Star* had a daily circulation of 74,893 and a Sunday circulation of 84,149.

46 ORGANIZATIONS

In 2006, there were over 2,835 nonprofit organizations registered within the state, of which about 1,874 were registered as charitable, educational, or religious organizations. Among the national organizations based in Nebraska are the Great Plains Council at the University of Nebraska (Lincoln), the American Shorthorn Society (Omaha), the Morse Telegraph Club (Lincoln), Girls and Boys Town (Boys Town), Wellness Councils of America (Omaha), USA Roller Sports (Lincoln), and the National Arbor Day Foundation (Nebraska City). The state's arts, culture, and history are represented in part by the Nebraska Humanities Council and the Nebraska State Historical Society. Special interest and hobbyist associations include the Antique Barbed Wire Society based in Kearney and the Centennial Model T Club of Omaha.

47 TOURISM, TRAVEL, AND RECREATION

Tourism is Nebraska's third-largest source of outside revenue (after agriculture and manufacturing). In 2004, the state hosted some 19.6 million travelers. Out-of-state visitors were primarily from Kansas, Iowa, Colorado, Missouri, South Dakota, Illinois, and Minnesota. Total travel expenditures were at $2.9 billion. The industry supports nearly 43,000 jobs.

The 8 state parks, 9 state historical parks, 12 federal areas, and 55 recreational areas are main tourist attractions; fishing, swimming, picnicking, and sightseeing are the principal activities. The most attended Nebraska attractions in 2002 were: Omaha's Henry Doorly Zoo (1,420,556 visitors), Cabela's in Sidney (1,025,000), Eugene T. Mahoney State Park (1,100,000), Lake McConaughy State Recreation Area (859,624), Fort Robinson State Park (357,932), Joslyn Art Museum (186,646), Strategic Air and Space

Museum (173,889), the Great Platte River Road Archway Monument (163,000), University of Nebraska State Museum (133,343), and Scotts Bluff National Monument (111,293). There is a Lewis and Clark Discovery Center in Crofton. An unusual exhibit, called Carhenge is a re-creation of Stonehenge made with wrecked cars.

48 SPORTS

There are no major professional sports teams in Nebraska. Minor league baseball's Omaha Royals play in the Triple-A Pacific Coast League. The most popular spectator sport is college football. Equestrian activities, including racing and rodeos, are popular. Major annual sporting events are the National Collegiate Athletic Association (NCAA) College Baseball World Series at Rosenblatt Stadium and the River City Roundup and Rodeo, both held in Omaha. Pari-mutuel racing is licensed by the state.

The University of Nebraska Cornhuskers compete in the Big Twelve Conference. The football team often places high in national rankings and was named National Champion in 1970 (with Texas), 1971, 1994, 1995, and 1997. The Cornhuskers won the Orange Bowl in 1964, 1971, 1972, 1973, 1983, 1995, 1997, and 1998; the Cotton Bowl in 1974 (January); the Sugar Bowl in 1974 (December), 1985, and 1987; the Alamo Bowl in 2001; and the Fiesta Bowl in 1996 and 2000. The basketball team won the National Invitational Tournament in 1996.

49 FAMOUS NEBRASKANS

Nebraska was the birthplace of only one US president, Gerald R. Ford (Leslie King Jr., b.1913). When Spiro Agnew resigned the vice presidency in October 1973, President Richard M. Nixon appointed Ford, then a US representative from Michigan, to the post. Upon Nixon's resignation on 9 August 1974, Ford became the first nonelected president in US history.

Four native and adoptive Nebraskans have served in the presidential cabinet. J. Sterling Morton (b.New York, 1832–1902), who originated Arbor Day, was secretary of agriculture under Grover Cleveland. William Jennings Bryan (b.Illinois, 1860–1925), a US representative from Nebraska, served as secretary of state and was three times the unsuccessful Democratic candidate for president. Frederick A. Seaton (b.Washington, 1909–74) was Dwight Eisenhower's secretary of the interior, and Melvin Laird (b.1922) was Richard Nixon's secretary of defense.

George W. Norris (b.Ohio, 1861–1944), the "fighting liberal," served 10 years in the US House of Representatives and 30 years in the Senate. Norris's greatest contributions were in rural electrification (his efforts led to the creation of the Tennessee Valley Authority), farm relief, and labor reform; he also promoted the unicameral form of government in Nebraska. Theodore C. Sorensen (b.1928) was an adviser to President John F. Kennedy.

Indian leaders important in Nebraska history include Oglala Sioux chiefs Red Cloud (1822–1909) and Crazy Horse (1849?–77). Moses Kinkaid (b.West Virginia, 1854–1920) served in the US House and was the author of the Kinkaid Act, which encouraged homesteading in Nebraska. Educator and legal scholar Roscoe Pound (1870–1964) was also a Nebraskan. In agricultural science, Samuel Aughey (b.Pennsylvania, 1831–1912) and Hardy W. Campbell (b.Vermont, 1850–1937) developed dry-land farming techniques. Botanist Charles E. Bessey (b.Ohio, 1845–1915) encouraged forestation. Father Edward Joseph Flanagan (b.Ireland,

1886–1948) was the founder of Boys Town, a home for underprivileged youth. Two native Nebraskans became Nobel laureates in 1980: Lawrence R. Klein (b.1920) in economics and Val L. Fitch (b.1923) in physics.

Writers associated with Nebraska include Willa Cather (b.Virginia, 1873–1947), who used the Nebraska frontier setting of her childhood in many of her writings and won a Pulitzer Prize in 1922; author and poet John G. Neihardt (b.Illinois, 1881–1973), who incorporated Indian mythology and history in his work; Mari Sandoz (1901–66), who wrote of her native Great Plains; writer-photographer Wright Morris (1910–98); and author Tillie Olsen (b.1912). Rollin Kirby (1875–1952) won three Pulitzer Prizes for political cartooning. Composer-conductor Howard Hanson (1896–1982), born in Wahoo, won a Pulitzer Prize in 1944.

Nebraskans important in entertainment include actor-dancer Fred Astaire (Fred Austerlitz, 1899–1984); actors Harold Lloyd (1894–1971), Henry Fonda (1905–82), Robert Taylor (Spangler Arlington Brugh, (1911–69), Marlon Brando (1924–2004), and Sandy Dennis (1937–93); television stars Johnny Carson (b.Iowa, 1925–2005) and Dick Cavett (b.1936); and motion-picture producer Darryl F. Zanuck (1902–79).

50 BIBLIOGRAPHY

Calloway, Bertha W., and Alonzo N. Smith. *Visions of Freedom on the Great Plains: An Illustrated History of African Americans in Nebraska.* Virginia Beach, Va.: Donning Co., 1998.

Council of State Governments. *The Book of the States, 2006 Edition.* Lexington, Ky.: Council of State Governments, 2006.

Iowa Nebraska Travel-Smart. Santa Fe: John Muir Publications, 2000.

Luebke, Frederick C. *Nebraska: An Illustrated History.* Lincoln: University of Nebraska Press, 1995.

McArthur, Debra. *The Kansas-Nebraska Act and "Bleeding Kansas" in American History.* Berkeley Heights, N.J.: Enslow, 2003.

Mobil Travel Guide. Great Plains 2006: Iowa, Kansas, Missouri, Nebraska, Oklahoma. Lincolnwood, Ill.: ExxonMobil Travel Publications, 2006.

Olson, James C., and Ronald C. Naugle. *History of Nebraska.* 3rd ed. Lincoln: University of Nebraska Press, 1997.

Preston, Thomas. *Great Plains: North Dakota, South Dakota, Nebraska, Kansas, Oklahoma, and Texas.* Vol. 4 in *The Double Eagle Guide to 1,000 Great Western Recreation Destinations.* Billings, Mont.: Discovery Publications, 2003.

State of Nebraska. Department of Economic Development. *Nebraska Statistical Handbook, 1993–1994.* Lincoln, 1994.

US Department of Commerce, Economics and Statistics Administration, US Census Bureau. *Nebraska, 2000. Summary Social, Economic, and Housing Characteristics: 2000 Census of Population and Housing.* Washington, D.C.: US Government Printing Office, 2003.

Wishart, David J. *An Unspeakable Sadness: The Dispossession of the Nebraska Indians.* Lincoln: University of Nebraska Press, 1994.

NEVADA

State of Nevada

ORIGIN OF STATE NAME: Named for the Sierra Nevada mountain range, *nevada* meaning "snow-covered" in Spanish. **NICKNAME:** The Silver State; the Sagebrush State; the Battle-born State. **CAPITAL:** Carson City. **ENTERED UNION:** 31 October 1864 (36th). **SONG:** "Home Means Nevada." **MOTTO:** All for Our Country. **FLAG:** On a blue field, two sprays of sagebrush and a golden scroll in the upper lefthand corner frame a silver star with the word "Nevada," below the star and above the sprays; the scroll, reading "Battle Born," recalls that Nevada was admitted to the Union during the Civil War. **OFFICIAL SEAL:** A quartz mill, ore cart, and mine tunnel symbolize Nevada's mining industry. A plow, sickle, and sheaf of wheat represent its agricultural resources. In the background are a railroad, a telegraph line, and a sun rising over the snow-covered mountains. Encircling this scene are 36 stars and the state motto. The words "The Great Seal of the State of Nevada" surround the whole. **BIRD:** Mountain bluebird. **FISH:** Lahontan cutthroat trout. **FLOWER:** Sagebrush. **TREE:** Single-leaf piñon; Bristlecone pine. **LEGAL HOLIDAYS:** New Year's Day, 1 January; Birthday of Martin Luther King Jr., 3rd Monday in January; Washington's Birthday, 3rd Monday in February; Memorial Day, last Monday in May; Independence Day, 4 July; Labor Day, 1st Monday in September; Nevada Day, last Friday in October; Veterans' Day, 11 November; Thanksgiving Day, 4th Thursday in November; Family Day, Friday after Thanksgiving; Christmas Day, 25 December. **TIME:** 4 AM PST = noon GMT.

1 LOCATION, SIZE, AND EXTENT

Situated between the Rocky Mountains and the Sierra Nevada in the western United States, Nevada ranks seventh in size among the 50 states.

The total area of Nevada is 110,561 sq mi (286,352 sq km), with land comprising 109,894 sq mi (284,624 sq km) and inland water covering 667 sq mi (1,728 sq km). Nevada extends 320 mi (515 km) E–W; the maximum N–S extension is 483 mi (777 km).

Nevada is bordered on the N by Oregon and Idaho; on the E by Utah and Arizona (with the line in the SE formed by the Colorado River); and on the S and W by California (with part of the line passing through Lake Tahoe). The total boundary length of Nevada is 1,480 mi (2,382 km). The state's geographic center is in Lander County, 26 mi (42 km) SE of Austin.

2 TOPOGRAPHY

Almost all of Nevada belongs physiographically to the Great Basin, a plateau characterized by isolated mountain ranges separated by arid basins. These ranges generally trend north–south; most are short, up to 75 mi (121 km) long and 15 mi (24 km) wide, and rise to altitudes of 7,000–10,000 ft (2,100–3,000 m). Chief among them are the Schell Creek, Ruby, Toiyabe, and Carson (within the Sierra Nevada). Nevada's highest point is Boundary Peak, 13,140 ft (4,007 m), in the southwest. The mean elevation of the state is approximately 5,500 ft (1,678 m).

Nevada has a number of large lakes and several large saline marshes known as sinks. The largest lake is Pyramid, with an area of 188 sq mi (487 sq km), in the west. Nevada shares Lake Tahoe with California, and Lake Mead, created by Hoover Dam on the Colorado River, with Arizona. The streams of the Great Basin frequently disappear during dry spells; many of them flow into local lakes or sinks without reaching the sea. The state's longest river, the Humboldt, flows for 290 mi (467 km) through the northern half of the state into the Humboldt Sink. The Walker, Truckee, and Carson rivers drain the western part of Nevada. The canyon carved by the mighty Colorado, the river that forms the extreme southeastern boundary of the state, is the site of Nevada's lowest elevation, 479 ft (146 m).

3 CLIMATE

Nevada's climate is sunny and dry, with wide variation in daily temperatures. The normal daily temperature at Reno is 50°F (10°C), ranging from 32°F (0°C) in January to 70°F (21°C) in July. The all-time high, 125°F (52°C), was set at Laughlin on 29 June 1994; the record low, -50°F (-46°C), at San Jacinto on 8 January 1937.

Nevada is the driest state in the United States, with overall average annual precipitation of about 7.3 in (18 cm) at Reno. Snowfall is abundant in the mountains, however, reaching 60 in (152 cm) a year on the highest peaks.

4 FLORA AND FAUNA

Various species of pine—among them the single-leaf pinon, the state tree—dominate Nevada's woodlands. Creosote bush is common in southern Nevada, as are many kinds of sagebrush throughout the state. Wildflowers include shooting star and white and yellow violets. Eight plant species were listed as threatened or endangered in 2006. Endangered species that year were Amargosa niterwort and steamboat buckwheat.

Native mammals include the black bear, white-tailed and mule deer, pronghorn antelope, Rocky Mountain elk, cottontail rabbit, and river otter. Grouse, partridge, pheasant, and quail are the leading game birds, and a diversity of trout, char, salmon, and whitefish thrive in Nevada waters. Rare and protected reptiles are the Gila monster and desert tortoise.

Ash Meadows National Wildlife Refuge, an oasis ecosystem in the Mojave Desert, is home to at least 25 species of rare and endangered plants and animals. These include the Devil's Hole pupfish, which is found only in one single limestone cave, and the Ash Meadows naucorid, an insect found only by one spring. Six plant species are unique to the site.

The US Fish and Wildlife Service listed 25 Nevada animal species (vertebrates and invertebrates) as threatened or endangered in April 2006, including the desert tortoise, six species of dace, three species of pupfish, woundfin, and three species of chub.

5 ENVIRONMENTAL PROTECTION

Preservation of the state's clean air, scarce water resources, and no longer abundant wildlife are the major environmental challenges facing Nevada. The Department of Fish and Game sets quotas on the hunting of deer, antelope, bighorn sheep, and other game animals. The Department of Conservation and Natural Resources has broad responsibility for environmental protection, state lands, forests, and water and mineral resources. The Division of Environmental Protection within the department has primary responsibility for the control of air pollution, water pollution, waste management, and groundwater protection. In 2003, 409.1 million lb of toxic chemicals were released in the state; Nevada ranked second in the country (after Alaska) for the highest level of toxic chemicals released. In 2003, Nevada had 33 hazardous waste sites listed in the US Environment Protection Agency (EPA) database; only one, Carson River Mercury Site, was on the National Priorities List as of 2006. In 2005, the EPA spent over $400,000 through the Superfund program for the cleanup of hazardous waste sites in the state. The same year, federal EPA grants awarded to the state included $16.5 million for the safe drinking water state revolving fund and $6.4 million for the water pollution control revolving fund.

Although wetlands cover only about 1% of the mainly barren state, they are some of the most valuable lands in the state. Ash Meadows National Wildlife Refuge, an oasis ecosystem in the Mojave Desert, was established in 1984 and designated as a Ramsar Wetland of International Importance in 1986.

6 POPULATION

Nevada ranked 35th in the United States with an estimated total population of 2,414,807 in 2005, an increase of 20.8% since 2000. Between 1990 and 2000, Nevada's population grew from 1,201,833 to 1,998,257, an increase of 66.3%, the decade's largest increase by far among the 50 states (followed by 40% for Arizona). It was also the fourth consecutive decade in which Nevada was the country's fastest-growing state and had a population growth rate over 50%. The population was projected to reach 3 million by 2015 and 3.8 million by 2025. In 2004, the median age of Nevada residents was 35.1. In the same year, nearly 25.9% of the populace was under the age of 18 while 11.2% was age 65 or older.

With a population density of 21.3 persons per sq mi in 2004 (up from 15.9 in 1998), Nevada remains one of the most sparsely populated states. Approximately 90% of Nevada residents live in cities, the largest of which, Las Vegas, had an estimated 534,847 residents in 2004. Henderson had an estimated population of 224,829, and

Reno had 197,963. The Greater Las Vegas metropolitan area had an estimated 1,650,671 residents in 2004; the Reno metropolitan area had an estimated 384,491.

7 ETHNIC GROUPS

Some 135,477 black Americans made up about 6.8% of Nevada's population, up sharply from 79,000 in 1990, although the percentage at that time remained about the same. By 2004, however, the percentage of the state's population that was black was 7.5%. The American Indian population was 26,420 in 2000, down from 31,000 in 1990. In 1990, tribal landholdings totaled 1,138,462 acres (460,721 hectares). Major tribes are the Washo, Northern Paiute, Southern Paiute, and Shoshoni. In 2004, 1.4% of the population was American Indian.

Both the number and percentage of foreign-born residents rose sharply in the 1990s, from 104,828 persons (8.7%) in 1990 to 316,593 state residents (15.8%) in 2000—the sixth-highest percentage of foreign born in the 50 states. In 2000, Hispanics and Latinos numbered 393,970 (19.7% of the state total), and 285,764 reported Mexican ancestry, up sharply from 72,281 in 1990. In 2004, 22.8% of the population was of Hispanic or Latino origin, 5.5% of the population was Asian, and 0.5% Pacific Islander. That year, 2.5% of the population reported origin of two or more races.

8 LANGUAGES

Midland and Northern English dialects are so intermixed in Nevada that no clear regional division appears; an example of this is the scattered use of both Midland *dived* (instead of dove) as the past tense of *dive* and the Northern /krik/ for *creek*. In 2000, 1,425,748 Nevadans—76.9% of the resident population five years old or older—spoke only English at home, down from 86.8% in 1990.

The following table gives selected statistics from the 2000 Census for language spoken at home by persons five years old and over. The category "Other Pacific Island languages" includes Chamorro, Hawaiian, Ilocano, Indonesian, and Samoan.

LANGUAGE	NUMBER	PERCENT
Population 5 years and over	**1,853,720**	**100.0**
Speak only English	1,425,748	76.9
Speak a language other than English	427,972	23.1
Speak a language other than English	**427,972**	**23.1**
Spanish or Spanish Creole	299,947	16.2
Tagalog	29,476	1.6
Chinese	11,787	0.6
German	10,318	0.6
French (incl. Patois, Cajun)	7,912	0.4
Korean	6,634	0.4
Italian	6,169	0.3
Japanese	5,678	0.3
Other Pacific Island languages	4,552	0.2
Vietnamese	3,808	0.2
Thai	3,615	0.2

9 RELIGIONS

In 2004, Nevada had 607,926 Roman Catholics, a significant increase from 331,844 members in 2000. The second-largest single denomination is the Church of Jesus Christ of Latter-day Saints (Mormons), which reported a statewide membership of 165,498 members in 298 congregations in 2006. There are two Mormon temples in the state, at Las Vegas (opened in 1989) and Reno (2000). Other major Protestant groups (with 2000 membership

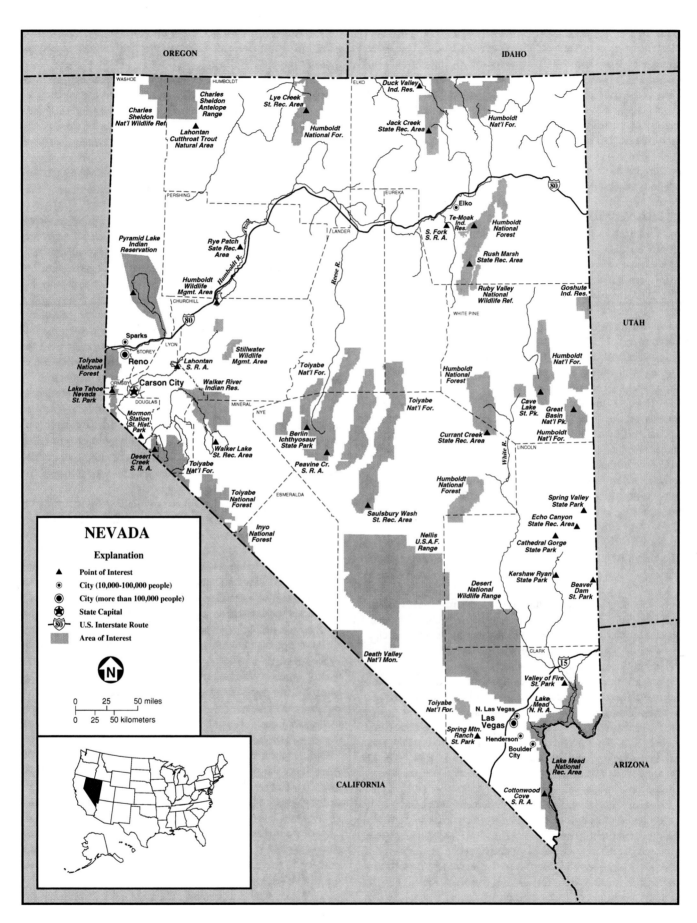

data) include Southern Baptists, 40,233 (with 1,373 newly baptized members reported in 2002); Assemblies of God, 22,699 (an increase of 220% from 1990); Evangelical Lutherans, 10,663; and United Methodists, 10,452. The Salvation Army, though still relatively small, experienced membership growth of 145% from 1990 to report a total of 1,239 adherents in 2000. Also in 2000, there were an estimated 77,100 Jews living in Nevada, representing an increase of 277% from 1990. Muslims numbered about 2,291 and there were about 1,124 adherents to the Baha'i faith. About 1.3 million people (about 65.7% of the population) did not claim any religious affiliation.

¹⁰TRANSPORTATION

As of 2003, Nevada had 2,009 mi (3,234 km) of railroad trackage, all of which is Class I right-of-way. As of 2006, Amtrak provided passenger service to four stations across northern Nevada en route from Chicago to Oakland via its California Zephyr train.

In 2003, there were 33,977 mi (54,702 km) of public roads and streets in Nevada. In 2004, there were some 1.301 million registered vehicles in the state, of which about 633,000 were automobiles, around 622,000 were trucks of all types, and some 2,000 were buses. Licensed drivers in that same year numbered 1,548,097. The major highways, I-80 and I-15, link Salt Lake City with Reno and Las Vegas, respectively.

In 2005, Nevada had a total of 132 public and private-use aviation-related facilities. This included 99 airports, 32 heliports, and 1 STOLport (Short Take-Off and Landing). The leading commercial air terminals are McCarran International Airport in Las Vegas and Reno-Tahoe International Airport. In 2004, McCarran International Airport had 19,943,025 enplanements, making it the sixth-busiest airport in the United States. Reno-Tahoe International in that same year had 2,478,179 enplanements.

¹¹HISTORY

The first inhabitants of what is now Nevada arrived about 12,000 years ago. They were fishermen, as well as hunters and food gatherers, for the glacial lakes of the ancient Great Basin were then only beginning to recede. Numerous sites of early human habitation have been found, the most famous being Pueblo Grande de Nevada (also known as Lost City). In modern times, four principal Indian groups have inhabited Nevada: Southern Paiute, Northern Paiute, Shoshoni, and Washo.

Probably the first white explorer to enter the state was the Spanish priest Francisco Garces, who apparently penetrated extreme southern Nevada in 1776. The year 1826 saw Peter Skene Ogden of the British Hudson's Bay Company enter the northeast in a prelude to his later exploration of the Humboldt River; the rival American trapper Jedediah Smith traversed the state in 1826–27. During 1843–44, John C. Frémont led the first of his several expeditions into Nevada.

Nevada's first permanent white settlement, Mormon Station (later Genoa), was founded in 1850 in what is now western Nevada, a region that became part of Utah Territory the same year. (The southeastern tip of Nevada was assigned to the Territory of New Mexico.) Soon other Mormon settlements were started there and in Las Vegas Valley. The Las Vegas mission failed, but the farming communities to the northwest succeeded, even though friction between Mormons and placer miners in that area caused

political unrest. Most of the Mormons in western Nevada departed in 1857, when Salt Lake City was threatened by an invasion of federal troops.

A separate Nevada Territory was established in 1861; only three years later, on 31 October 1864, Nevada achieved statehood, although the present boundaries were not established until 18 January 1867. Two factors accelerated the creation of Nevada: the secession of the southern states, whose congressmen had been blocking the creation of new free states, and the discovery, in 1859, of the Comstock Lode, an immense concentration of silver and gold which attracted thousands of fortune seekers and established the region as a thriving mining center.

Nevada's development during the rest of the century was determined by the economic fortunes of the Comstock, whose affairs were dominated, first, by the Bank of California (in alliance with the Central Pacific Railroad) and then by the "Bonanza Firm" of John W. Mackay and his partners. The lode's rich ores were exhausted in the late 1870s and Nevada slipped into a 20-year depression. A number of efforts were made to revive the economy, one being an attempt to encourage mining by increasing the value of silver. To this end, Nevadans wholeheartedly supported the movement for free silver coinage during the 1890s and the Silver Party reigned supreme in state politics for most of the decade.

Nevada's economy revived following new discoveries of silver at Tonopah and gold at Goldfield early in the 20th century. A second great mining boom ensued, bolstered and extended by major copper discoveries in eastern Nevada. Progressive political ferment in this pre-World War I period added recall, referendum, and initiative amendments to the state constitution and brought about the adoption of women's suffrage (1914).

The 1920s was a time of subdued economic activity; mining fell off, and not even the celebrated divorce trade, centered in Reno, was able to compensate for its decline. Politically, the decade was conservative and Republican, with millionaire George Wingfield dominating state politics through a so-called bipartisan machine. Nevada went Democratic during the 1930s, when the hard times of the Depression were alleviated by federal public-works projects, most notably the construction of the Hoover (Boulder) Dam, and by state laws aiding the divorce business and legalizing gambling.

Gaming grew rapidly after World War II, becoming by the mid-1950s not only the mainstay of Nevada tourism but also the state's leading industry. Revelations during the 1950s and 1960s that organized crime had infiltrated the casino industry and that casino income was being used to finance narcotics and other rackets in major East Coast cities led to a state and federal crackdown and the imposition of new state controls.

From 1960 to 1980, Nevada was the fastest-growing of the 50 states, increasing its population by 70% in the 1960s and 64% in the 1970s. In the mid-1980s the state's population growth continued to outpace that of the nation, reaching 14% in the first half of the 1980s in contrast to the national average of 4%. Much of this growth was associated with expansion of the gambling industry—centered in the casinos of Las Vegas and Reno—and of the military. In the 1980s, Nevada began to try to reduce its dependence on gambling by diversifying its economy. In an attempt to attract new businesses, particularly in the high-tech industry, the state promoted such features as its absence of state, corporate, or personal income taxes, inexpensive real estate, low wages, and its ready access by air or land to California.

In the first half of the 1990s, Nevada was once again the nation's fastest growing state, increasing its population by nearly 25%; by 2001 the state's population exceeded 2.1 million. Efforts to diversify the state's economy yielded results as its industrial base expanded. In the early 1990s, Nevada was the only state reporting an increase in manufacturing jobs. Meanwhile Las Vegas continued to prosper, expanding its offerings to attract new visitors. During the decade, several extravagant new hotel and casino complexes opened, many of them featuring amusement parks and other family-oriented entertainment. The booming Las Vegas economy helped push Nevada unemployment to an all-time low of 3.1% in December 1999, one-half a percentage point below the prior record of 3.6% set in 1962. Due in large measure to the 2001 US recession and its aftermath, however, Nevada faced a $704 million budget deficit in 2003, and the unemployment rate stood at 5.4% in July 2003, albeit below the national average of 6.2%. In September 2005, Nevada's unemployment rate had dropped to 4.2%, below the national average of 5.1%. In 2005, the state had a budget surplus, and decided to return a portion of it to taxpayers in the form of a one-time $300 million tax rebate. The 2005 state budget approved by Nevada's legislature was $5.9 billion. Nevada had the fastest growing state budget in the nation that year.

Nevadans' opposition to the Yucca Mountain nuclear waste disposal site, first proposed by Congress in 1987, has been a continuing issue. In 2002, US Energy Secretary Spencer Abraham recommended the Yucca Mountain site to President George W. Bush as a nuclear waste repository, which Bush approved. Nevada Governor Kenny Guinn vetoed the project, but the US Congress overrode his veto. President Bush signed Congress's joint resolution into law, and Yucca Mountain became the nation's nuclear waste repository site. Nevada filed major lawsuits against the US Department of Energy, the Nuclear Regulatory Commission, President Bush, and Secretary Abraham, which were consolidated into four major cases and heard before the District of Columbia Court of Appeals on 14 January 2004. The judges dismissed most of Nevada's claims, but they did rule in favor of the state's complaint against radiation standards for the nuclear waste repository.

12 STATE GOVERNMENT

Nevada's 1864 constitution, as amended (132 times by January 2005), continues to govern the state. In 2002 voters gave final approval to an amendment defining marriage as a union between a man and a woman. The state legislature consists of a Senate with 21 members, each elected to a four-year term, and a House of Representatives with 42 members, each serving two years. Legislative sessions are held in odd-numbered years only, beginning on the first Monday in February and lasting no more than 120 calendar days. Only the governor may call special sessions, which have no limit, but legislators are only paid for up to 20 calendar days during a special session. Legislators must be qualified voters, at least 21 years old, should have lived in the state for at least a year, and should have lived in the district for at least 30 days prior to the close of filing for declaration of candidacy. The legislative salary was $130 per diem during regular sessions in 2004, unchanged from 1999.

Executive officials elected statewide include the governor and lieutenant governor (who run separately), secretary of state, attorney general, treasurer, and comptroller, all of whom serve for four years. The governor is limited to a maximum of two consecutive terms. Candidates for governor must be at least 25 years old, a qualified voter, and must have been a citizen and resident of the state for at least two years prior to election. As of December 2004, the governor's salary was $117,000, unchanged from 1999.

Bills approved by the legislature are sent to the governor, who has five days when the legislature is in session (or 10 days if adjourned) to sign or veto it. If the governor does not act within the required time period, the bill automatically becomes law. A two-thirds vote of the elected members of each house is required to override a gubernatorial veto.

Constitutional amendments may be submitted to the voters for ratification if the proposed amendments have received majority votes in each house in two successive sessions or under an initiative procedure calling for petitions signed by 10% of those who voted in the last general election. Legislative amendments need a majority vote; initiative amendments require majorities in two consecutive elections. Voters must be US citizens, at least 18 years old, continuous state and county residents for at least 30 days and precinct residents for at least 10 days prior to election day. Restrictions apply to convicted felons and those declared mentally incompetent by the court.

13 POLITICAL PARTIES

Since World War II neither the Democrats nor the Republicans have dominated state politics, which are basically conservative. As of 2004, there were 1,094,000 registered voters. In the 2000 presidential election, Republican George W. Bush received 49% of the vote to Democrat Al Gore's 46%. In 2004, Bush garnered 50.5% to Democratic challenger John Kerry's 47.9%. Republican Kenny Guinn, first elected governor in 1998, was reelected in 2002. Democrat Harry Reid was elected US Senator in 1986; he was reelected in 1992, 1998, and 2004. Republican Senator John Ensign was elected in 2000. Following the 2004 elections, Nevada sent one Democrat and two Republicans to the US House of Representa-

Nevada Presidential Vote by Major Political Parties, 1948–2004				
YEAR	ELECTORAL VOTE	NEVADA WINNER	DEMOCRAT	REPUBLICAN
1948	3	*Truman (D)	31,290	29,357
1952	3	*Eisenhower (R)	31,688	50,502
1956	3	*Eisenhower (R)	40,640	56,049
1960	3	*Kennedy (D)	54,880	52,387
1964	3	*Johnson (D)	79,339	56,094
1968	3	*Nixon (R)	60,598	73,188
1972	3	*Nixon (R)	66,016	115,750
1976	3	Ford (R)	92,479	101,273
1980	3	*Reagan (R)	66,666	155,017
1984	4	*Reagan (R)	91,655	188,770
1988	4	*Bush (R)	132,738	206,040
1992**	4	*Clinton (D)	189,148	175,828
1996**	4	*Clinton (D)	203,974	199,244
2000	4	*Bush, G. W. (R)	279,978	301,575
2004	5	*Bush, G. W. (R)	397,190	418,690

*Won US presidential election.
**IND. candidate Ross Perot received 132,580 votes in 1992 and 43,986 votes in 1996.

tives. As of mid-2005, there were 12 Republicans and 9 Democrats in the state Senate, and 16 Republicans and 26 Democrats in the state House. The state had five electoral votes in the 2004 presidential election.

14 LOCAL GOVERNMENT

As of 2005, Nevada was subdivided into 17 counties and 19 municipal governments, most of them county seats. The state had 17 public school districts and 158 special districts that year. The county is the primary form of local government. Elected county officials include commissioners, public administrator, district attorney, and sheriff. Most municipalities use the mayor-council system of government.

In 2005, local government accounted for about 74,642 full-time (or equivalent) employment positions.

15 STATE SERVICES

To address the continuing threat of terrorism and to work with the federal Department of Homeland Security, homeland security in Nevada operates under the authority of the governor; the adjutant general is appointed to oversee the state's homeland security activities.

The Commission on Ethics oversees financial disclosure by state officials. The Department of Education and the Nevada System of Higher Education are the main state educational agencies. The Department of Health and Human Services has divisions covering public health, rehabilitation, mental health and developmental disabilities, welfare, youth services, and programs for the elderly. Regulatory functions are exercised by the Business and Industry Department (insurance, banking, consumer affairs, real estate), the Public Utilities Commission, the Gaming Control Board, and other state agencies. Other organizations include the Division of Minerals, the Commission on Tourism, the Division of Wildlife, and the Department of Information Technology.

16 JUDICIAL SYSTEM

Nevada's Supreme Court consists of a chief justice and six other justices. There are 51 district court judges organized into nine judicial districts. All judges are elected by nonpartisan ballot to six-year terms.

As of 31 December 2004, a total of 11,365 prisoners were held in Nevada's state and federal prisons, an increase from 10,543 of 7.8% from the previous year. As of year-end 2004, a total of 878 inmates were female, down from 880 or 0.2% from the year before. Among sentenced prisoners (one year or more), Nevada had an incarceration rate of 474 per 100,000 population in 2004.

According to the Federal Bureau of Investigation, Nevada in 2004 had a violent crime rate (murder/nonnegligent manslaughter; forcible rape; robbery; aggravated assault) of 615.9 reported incidents per 100,000 population, or a total of 14,379 reported incidents. Crimes against property (burglary; larceny/theft; and motor vehicle theft) in that same year totaled 98,215 reported incidents or 4,206.6 reported incidents per 100,000 people. Nevada has a death penalty, of which lethal injection is the sole method of execution. For the period 1976 through 5 May 2006, the state has executed 12 people, including one execution carried out in 2006, prior to 5 May. As of 1 January 2006, Nevada had 83 inmates on death row.

In 2003, Nevada spent $63,105,669 on homeland security, an average of $30 per state resident.

17 ARMED FORCES

In 2004, there were 9,251 active-duty military personnel and 2,089 civilian personnel stationed in Nevada. The largest installations are the Hawthorne Army Depot near Reno and the Nellis Air Force Base near Las Vegas. The state has been the site of both ballistic missile and atomic weapons testing. In 2004, Nevada firms received about $439 million in federal defense contracts and defense payroll outlays were more than $1.1 billion.

As of 2003, 243,716 military veterans were living in the state, including 27,496 of World War II; 26,015 of the Korean conflict; 75,775 from the Vietnam era; and 36,607 in the Gulf War. For the fiscal year 2004, total Veterans Affairs expenditures in Nevada amounted to more than $642 million.

As of 31 October 2004, the Nevada Highway Patrol employed 367 full-time sworn officers.

18 MIGRATION

In 1870, about half of Nevada's population consisted of foreign immigrants, among them Chinese, Italians, Swiss, British, Irish, Germans, and French Canadians. Though their origins were diverse, their numbers were few—no more than 21,000 in all. Not until the 1940s did migrants come in large volume. Between 1940 and 1980, Nevada gained a total of 507,000 residents through migration, equal to 63% of the 1980 population; there was an additional net gain from migration of 233,000 during the 1980s, accounting for 75% of the net population increase. Between 1990 and 1998, Nevada had net gains of 397,000 in domestic migration and 45,000 in international migration. In 1998, the state admitted 6,106 foreign immigrants, of whom 2,881 were from Mexico. Between 1990 and 1998, the state's overall population grew 45.4%, making it the fastest growing state in the nation. In the period 2000–05, net international migration was 66,098 and net internal migration was 270,945, for a net gain of 337,043 people.

19 INTERGOVERNMENTAL COOPERATION

Nevada takes part in the Colorado River Compact, the Tahoe Regional Planning Authority, and the California-Nevada Interstate Compact, under which the two states administer water rights involving Lake Tahoe and the Carson, Truckee, and Walker rivers. Other river compacts influence use of the Upper Niobrara river and the boundary between Arizona and Nevada on the Colorado River. The state also is a signatory to the Interstate Oil and Gas Compact, the Western Interstate Commission for Higher Education, and the Western Interstate Energy Compact. Federal grants in fiscal year 2005 totaled $1.652 billion, an estimated $1.714 billion in fiscal year 2006, and an estimated $1.759 billion in fiscal year 2007.

20 ECONOMY

Nevada is disadvantaged by a lack of water and a shortage of arable land, but blessed with a wealth of mineral resources—gold, silver, copper, and other metals. Mining remains important, though overshadowed since World War II by tourism and gambling, which generate more than 50% of the state's income. Legalized gaming alone produces nearly half of Nevada's tax revenues.

Throughout the 1990s, employment growth averaged 5.2% annually. The state economy roared into the 21st century, posting annual growth rates of 7.7% in 1998, 9% in 1999, and 8.6% in 2000. The national recession and slowdown in 2001 caused the pace of job growth to fall to 2.4% and the overall growth rate to fall to 4.9%, but these remain well above national averages. Job growth in Nevada has been centered on growth in services, the retail trade, government and the construction sector.

Nevada's gross state product (GSP) in 2004 was $100.317 billion, of which the lodging and food service industries accounted for the largest share at $14.196 billion or 14.1% of GSP, followed by the real estate sector at $12.722 billion (12.6% of GSP) and the construction industry at $10.313 billion (10.2% of GSP). In that same year, there were an estimated 177,282 small businesses in Nevada. Of the 51,424 businesses that had employees, an estimated total of 49,209 or 95.7% were small companies. An estimated 10,483 new businesses were established in the state in 2004, up 7.5% from the year before. Business terminations that same year came to 9,012, up 0.8% from 2003. There were 257 business bankruptcies in 2004, down 19.9% from the previous year. In 2005, the state's personal bankruptcy (Chapter 7 and Chapter 13) filing rate was 931 filings per 100,000 people, ranking Nevada as the third-highest in the nation.

21 INCOME

In 2005 Nevada had a gross state product (GSP) of $111 billion which accounted for 0.9% of the nation's gross domestic product and placed the state at number 31 in highest GSP among the 50 states and the District of Columbia.

According to the Bureau of Economic Analysis, in 2004 Nevada had a per capita personal income (PCPI) of $33,787. This ranked 18th in the United States and was 102% of the national average of $33,050. The 1994–2004 average annual growth rate of PCPI was 3.6%. Nevada had a total personal income (TPI) of $78,822,134,000, which ranked 32nd in the United States and reflected an increase of 10.1% from 2003. The 1994–2004 average annual growth rate of TPI was 8.3%. Earnings of persons employed in Nevada increased from $55,064,306,000 in 2003 to $61,541,717,000 in 2004, an increase of 11.8%. The 2003–04 national change was 6.3%.

The US Census Bureau reports that the three-year average median household income for 2002–04 in 2004 dollars was $46,984 compared to a national average of $44,473. During the same period an estimated 10.2% of the population was below the poverty line as compared to 12.4% nationwide.

22 LABOR

According to the Bureau of Labor Statistics (BLS), in April 2006 the seasonally adjusted civilian labor force in Nevada numbered 1,264,900, with approximately 52,300 workers unemployed, yielding an unemployment rate of 4.1%, compared to the national average of 4.7% for the same period. Preliminary data for the same period placed nonfarm employment at 1,279,200. Since the beginning of the BLS data series in 1976, the highest unemployment rate recorded in Nevada was 10.7% in December 1982. The historical low was 3.6% in January 2006. Preliminary nonfarm employment data by occupation for April 2006 showed that approximately 11.5% of the labor force was employed in construction;

3.8% in manufacturing; 17.6% in trade, transportation, and public utilities; 5.2% in financial activities; 12.2% in professional and business services; 6.8% in education and health services; 26.2% in leisure and hospitality services; and 11.5% in government.

The US Department of Labor's Bureau of Labor Statistics reported that in 2005, a total of 145,000 of Nevada's 1,051,000 employed wage and salary workers were formal members of a union. This represented 13.8% of those so employed, up from 12.5% in 2004 and above the national average of 12%. Overall in 2005, a total of 158,000 workers (15.1%) in Nevada were covered by a union or employee association contract, which includes those workers who reported no union affiliation. Nevada is one of 22 states with a right-to-work law.

As of 1 March 2006, Nevada had a state-mandated minimum wage rate of $5.15 per hour. In 2004, women in the state accounted for 44% of the employed civilian labor force.

23 AGRICULTURE

Agricultural income in 2005 totaled $478 million (45th in the United States), of which $172 million was from crops and $306 million from livestock and animal products. Chief crops in 2004 included 960,000 bushels of wheat, 1.48 million tons of hay, and 2,881,000 hundredweight of potatoes. Nevada's barley crop in 2004 was 210,000 bushels, down from 2,700,000 in 1983. Virtually all of the state's cropland requires irrigation.

24 ANIMAL HUSBANDRY

In 2005, Nevada ranches and farms had 500,000 cattle and calves, valued at $450 million. In 2003, the state produced 2.5 million lb (1.1 million kg) of sheep and lambs which brought in around $4 million in gross income. In 2004, the shorn wool production was an estimated 510,000 lb (231,800 kg) of wool. Nevada's total milk yield in 2003 was 485 million lb (220 million kg) from 26,000 milk cows.

25 FISHING

There is no commercial fishing industry in Nevada. The state has four fish culture facilities that produce about 430,000 lb of trout annually. The Lahontan National Fish Hatchery also distributes cutthroat trout within the state. In 2004, Nevada issued 124,408 sport fishing licenses.

26 FORESTRY

Nevada in 2004 had 9,767,000 acres (3,953,000 hectares) of forestland. In 2005, four national forests had 5,841,209 acres (2,363,937 hectares) in the National Forest System. Less than 2% of all forested land in Nevada was classified as commercial timberland.

27 MINING

According to preliminary data from the US Geological Survey (USGS), the estimated value of nonfuel mineral production by Nevada in 2003 was over $2.9 billion, an increase from 2002 of about 1%. The USGS data ranked Nevada as second among the 50 states by the total value of its nonfuel mineral production, accounting for over 7.5% of total US output.

According to the preliminary data for 2003, gold, construction sand and gravel, crushed stone and silver were the state's top nonfuel minerals. These commodities accounted for 83%, 6%, 1.5%, and 1.5%, respectively, of all nonfuel mineral production in the state. In that same year, Nevada provided 81% of the gold mined in the United States and 24% of the silver, making the state first in gold and second in silver production. Nevada in 2003 was also the only state to produce magnesite and lithium carbonate minerals. In addition, Nevada ranked first in the production of barite, brucite, and diatomite, third in gypsum, fifth in perlite, sixth in gemstones, and seventh in lime.

Preliminary data for 2003 showed gold production at 216,000 kg, with a value of $2.440 billion, with silver output at 292,000 kg and a value of $43.700 million. Construction sand and gravel output totaled 38 million metric tons for a value of $173 million, while crushed stone output stood at 8.7 million metric tons with a value of $46.1 million, according to the USGS data for 2003.

In 2003, Nevada was also a producer of fuller's earth and industrial sand and gravel.

28 ENERGY AND POWER

As of 2003, Nevada had 19 electrical power service providers, of which eight were publicly owned and eight were cooperatives. Of the remainder, two were investor owned and one was federally operated. As of that same year there were 1,019,075 retail customers. Of that total, 964,923 received their power from investor-owned service providers. Cooperatives accounted for 29,792 customers, while publicly owned providers had 24,358 customers. There were only two federal customers.

Total net summer generating capability by the state's electrical generating plants in 2003 stood at 7.508 million kW, with total production that same year at 33.194 billion kWh. Of the total amount generated, 74.2% came from electric utilities, with the remainder coming from independent producers and combined heat and power service providers. The largest portion of all electric power generated, 17.085 billion kWh (51.5%), came from coal-fired plants, with natural gas fueled plants in second place at 13.252 billion kWh (39.9%) and hydroelectric plants in third at 1.756 billion kWh (5.3%). Other renewable power sources accounted for 3.2% of all power generated, with plants using other types of gases and petroleum fired plants at 0.1% each.

Because Nevada produces more electricity than it consumes, the remainder is exported, principally to California. Hoover Dam, anchored in the bedrock of Black Canyon east of Las Vegas, is the state's largest hydroelectric installation, with an installed capacity of 1,039,000 kW in 2003. The first six of the dam's eight turbines came onstream during 1936–38, while the other two were added in 1944 and 1961.

As of 2004, Nevada had proven crude oil reserves of less than 1% of all proven US reserves, while output that same year averaged 1,000 barrels per day. Including federal offshore domains, the state that year ranked 27th (26th excluding federal offshore) in production among the 31 producing states. In 2004 Nevada had 57 producing oil wells and accounted for under 1% of all US production. In 2005, the state's single refinery had a combined crude oil distillation capacity of 1,707 barrels per day.

In 2004, Nevada had four producing natural gas and gas condensate wells. In 2003 (the latest year for which data was available), marketed gas production (all gas produced excluding gas used for repressuring, vented and flared, and nonhydrocarbon gases removed) totaled 6 million cu ft (170,400 cu m). There was no data available on the state's proven reserves of natural gas.

29 INDUSTRY

Industry in Nevada is limited but diversified, producing communications equipment, pet food, chemicals, and sprinkler systems, among other products.

According to the US Census Bureau's Annual Survey of Manufactures (ASM) for 2004, Nevada's manufacturing sector covered some 13 product subsectors. The shipment value of all products manufactured in the state that same year was $9.551 billion. Of that total, miscellaneous manufacturing accounted for the largest share at $1.680 billion. It was followed by food manufacturing at $1.172 billion, nonmetallic mineral product manufacturing at $1.045 billion, and fabricated metal product manufacturing at $846.723 million.

In 2004, a total of 43,967 people in Nevada were employed in the state's manufacturing sector, according to the ASM. Of that total, 28,876 were actual production workers. In terms of total employment, the miscellaneous manufacturing industry accounted for the largest portion of all manufacturing employees at 8,147, with 3,546 actual production workers. It was followed by fabricated metal product manufacturing at 5,368 employees (3,894 actual production workers); nonmetallic mineral product manufacturing at 3,820 employees (3,215 actual production workers); food manufacturing at 3,428 employees (2,272 actual production workers); and computer and electronic product manufacturing with 3,426 employees (1,477 actual production workers).

ASM data for 2004 showed that Nevada's manufacturing sector paid $1.849 billion in wages. Of that amount, the miscellaneous manufacturing sector accounted for the largest share at $466.410 million. It was followed by fabricated metal product manufacturing at $201.834 million; computer and electronic product manufacturing at $171.943 million; and nonmetallic mineral product manufacturing at $166.519 million.

30 COMMERCE

According to the 2002 Census of Wholesale Trade, Nevada's wholesale trade sector had sales that year totaling $16.5 billion from 2,612 establishments. Wholesalers of durable goods accounted for 1,658 establishments, followed by nondurable goods wholesalers at 850 and electronic markets, agents, and brokers accounting for 104 establishments. Sales by durable goods wholesalers in 2002 totaled $8.4 billion, while wholesalers of nondurable goods saw sales of $5.8 billion. Electronic markets, agents, and brokers in the wholesale trade industry had sales of $2.2 billion.

In the 2002 Census of Retail Trade, Nevada was listed as having 7,214 retail establishments with sales of $26.9 billion. The leading types of retail businesses by number of establishments were clothing and clothing accessories stores (1,195); miscellaneous store retailers (1,062); food and beverage stores (769), motor vehicle and motor vehicle parts dealers (681), and gasoline stations (671). In terms of sales, motor vehicle and motor vehicle parts dealers accounted for the largest share of retail sales, at $6.6 billion, followed by general merchandise stores, at $3.8 billion; food and beverage stores, at $3.6 billion; and nonstore retailers, at $3.4 billion. A total of 112,339 people were employed by the retail sector in Nevada that year.

Exporters located in Nevada exported $3.9 billion in merchandise during 2005.

31 CONSUMER PROTECTION

The state of Nevada has two entities dedicated to consumer protection: the Bureau of Consumer Protection (BCP) at the Office of the Attorney General, and the Nevada Consumer Affairs Division.

The BCP was created in 1997 by the Nevada Legislature to protect consumers from deceptive or fraudulent sales practices and represent consumers' interests in government. The BCP has the authority to file lawsuits on behalf of the public and the state of Nevada. It operates consumer education and awareness programs, reviews consumer complaints and can act as an advocate for consumers over utilities related issues before the Public Utilities Commission of Nevada, as well as federal utility regulatory agencies and courts. The BCP can also pursue civil and criminal enforcement of the state's antitrust law. It is also authorized to file civil actions under federal antitrust laws.

The Nevada Consumer Affairs Division regulates deceptive trade practices through its investigatory powers and through its authority to require the registration and bonding of buying clubs, charitable solicitors, credit repair organizations, dance and martial arts studios, health clubs, magazine sales, recovery rooms, sports betting information services, telemarketers, travel agents and tour operators/brokers, and weight loss clinics.

When dealing with consumer protection issues, the state's Attorney General's Office can initiate civil and criminal proceedings; represent the state before state and federal regulatory agencies; administer consumer protection and education programs; and exercise broad subpoena powers. However, the Attorney General's Office has only limited power to handle formal consumer complaints due to the state having a separate consumer affairs department (the Consumer Affairs Division). In antitrust actions, the Attorney General's Office can act on behalf of those consumers who are incapable of acting on their own; initiate damage actions on behalf of the state in state courts; initiate criminal proceedings; and represent counties, cities and other governmental entities in recovering civil damages under state or federal law.

Offices of the Bureau of Consumer Protection are located in Las Vegas. The state's Consumer Affairs Division has offices in Las Vegas and Reno.

32 BANKING

As of June 2005, Nevada had 38 insured banks, savings and loans, and saving banks, plus 12 state-chartered and 17 federally chartered credit unions (CUs). Excluding the CUs, the Las Vegas–Paradise market area accounted for the largest portion of the state's financial institutions and deposits in 2004, with 42 institutions and $33.605 billion in deposits. As of June 2005, CUs accounted for 7.2% of all assets held by all financial institutions in the state, or some $4.562 billion. Banks, savings and loans, and savings banks collectively accounted for the remaining 92.8% or $58.650 billion in assets held.

In 2004, the median net interest margin (the difference between the lower rates offered to savers and the higher rates charged on loans) stood at 4.85%, up from 4.77% in 2003. As of fourth quarter 2005, the rate stood at 5.40%. Regulation of Nevada's state-chartered banks and financial institutions is the responsibility of the Division of Financial Institutions.

33 INSURANCE

Nevadans held 639,000 individual life insurance policies in 2004 with a total value of over $83 billion; total value for all categories of life insurance (individual, group, and credit) was about $121 billion. The average coverage amount is $130,600 per policy holder. Death benefits paid that year totaled $422.5 million.

As of 2003, there were nine property and casualty and three life and health insurance companies domiciled in the state. Direct premiums for property and casualty insurance totaled $3.8 billion in 2004. That year, there were 15,525 flood insurance policies in force in the state, with a total value of $3 billion.

In 2004, 57% of state residents held employment-based health insurance policies, 4% held individual policies, and 18% were covered under Medicare and Medicaid; 19% of residents were uninsured. Nevada ties with four other states as having the fourth-highest percentage of uninsured residents in the nation. In 2003, employee contributions for employment-based health coverage averaged at 13% for single coverage and 24% for family coverage. The state offers an 18-month health benefits expansion program for small-firm employees in connection with the Consolidated Omnibus Budget Reconciliation Act (COBRA, 1986), a health insurance program for those who lose employment-based coverage due to termination or reduction of work hours.

In 2003, there were over 1.4 million auto insurance policies in effect for private passenger cars. Required minimum coverage includes bodily injury liability of up to $15,000 per individual and $30,000 for all persons injured in an accident, as well as property damage liability of $10,000. In 2003, the average expenditure per vehicle for insurance coverage was $913.05.

34 SECURITIES

There are no securities exchanges in Nevada. In 2005, there were 1,350 personal financial advisers employed in the state and 1,210 securities, commodities, and financial services sales agents. In 2004, there were over 116 publicly traded companies within the state, with over 22 NASDAQ companies, 11 NYSE listings, and 3 AMEX listings. In 2006, the state had two Fortune 500 companies; Harrah's Entertainment ranked first in the state and 309th in the nation with revenues of over $4.4 billion, followed by MGM Mirage at 334th in the nation and $6.4 billion in revenues.

35 PUBLIC FINANCE

The budget is prepared biennially by the Budget Division of the Department of Administration and submitted by the governor to the legislature, which has unlimited power to change it.

Fiscal year 2006 general funds were estimated at $3.0 billion for resources and $2.9 billion for expenditures. In fiscal year 2004, federal government grants to Nevada were $2.3 billion.

In the fiscal year 2007 federal budget, Nevada was slated to receive $51.7 million in State Children's Health Insurance Program (SCHIP) funds to help the state provide health coverage to low-income, uninsured children who do not qualify for Medicaid. This funding is a 23% increase over fiscal year 2006. Nevada was also to receive $12.9 million in federal funds for the HOME Investment Partnership Program to help Nevada fund a wide range of

Nevada—State Government Finances

(Dollar amounts in thousands. Per capita amounts in dollars.)

	AMOUNT	PER CAPITA
Total Revenue	10,136,127	4,344.68
General revenue	7,318,255	3,136.84
Intergovernmental revenue	1,625,188	696.61
Taxes	4,738,877	2,031.24
General sales	2,264,749	970.75
Selective sales	1,559,853	668.60
License taxes	623,400	267.21
Individual income tax	–	–
Corporate income tax	–	–
Other taxes	290,875	124.68
Current charges	605,144	259.38
Miscellaneous general revenue	349,046	149.61
Utility revenue	143,048	61.32
Liquor store revenue	–	–
Insurance trust revenue	2,674,824	1,146.52
Total expenditure	8,686,071	3,723.13
Intergovernmental expenditure	2,948,274	1,263.73
Direct expenditure	5,737,797	2,459.41
Current operation	3,756,367	1,610.10
Capital outlay	744,452	319.10
Insurance benefits and repayments	985,326	422.34
Assistance and subsidies	107,240	45.97
Interest on debt	144,412	61.90
Exhibit: Salaries and wages	1,230,195	527.30
Total expenditure	8,686,071	3,723.13
General expenditure	7,555,705	3,238.62
Intergovernmental expenditure	2,948,274	1,263.73
Direct expenditure	4,607,431	1,974.90
General expenditures, by function:		
Education	3,011,529	1,290.84
Public welfare	1,292,137	553.85
Hospitals	145,759	62.48
Health	210,948	90.42
Highways	893,516	382.99
Police protection	62,023	26.59
Correction	234,116	100.35
Natural resources	118,250	50.69
Parks and recreation	19,240	8.25
Government administration	201,243	86.26
Interest on general debt	140,358	60.16
Other and unallocable	1,226,586	525.75
Utility expenditure	145,040	62.17
Liquor store expenditure	–	–
Insurance trust expenditure	985,326	422.34
Debt at end of fiscal year	3,607,292	1,546.20
Cash and security holdings	21,351,168	9,151.81

Abbreviations and symbols: – zero or rounds to zero; (NA) not available; (X) not applicable.

SOURCE: *U.S. Census Bureau, Governments Division, 2004 Survey of State Government Finances*, January 2006.

activities that build, buy, or rehabilitate affordable housing for rent or homeownership, or provide direct rental assistance to low-income people. This funding is a 12% increase over fiscal year 2006. Another $55 million in federal funds was allocated to replace the air traffic control tower at McCarran International Airport in Las Vegas.

36 TAXATION

In 2005, Nevada collected $5,010 million in tax revenues or $2,075 per capita, which placed it 28th among the 50 states in per capita

tax burden. The national average was $2,192 per capita. Property taxes accounted for 3.0% of the total, sales taxes 45.0%, selective sales taxes 33.6%, and other taxes 18.4%.

As of 1 January 2006, Nevada had no state income tax, a distinction it shared with Wyoming, Washington, Alaska, Florida, Texas, and South Dakota.

In 2004, state and local property taxes amounted to $2,147,294,000 or $920 per capita. The per capita amount ranks the state 30th highest nationally. Local governments collected $2,014,826,000 of the total and the state government $132,468,000.

Nevada taxes retail sales at a rate of 6.5%. In addition to the state tax, local taxes on retail sales can reach as much as 1%, making for a potential total tax on retail sales of 7.5%. Food purchased for consumption off-premises is tax exempt. The tax on cigarettes is 80 cents per pack, which ranks 25th among the 50 states and the District of Columbia. Nevada taxes gasoline at 24.805 cents per gallon. This is in addition to the 18.4 cents per gallon federal tax on gasoline.

According to the Tax Foundation, for every federal tax dollar sent to Washington in 2004, Nevada citizens received $0.73 in federal spending.

37 ECONOMIC POLICY

Federal projects have played an especially large role in Nevada's development. During the depression of the 1930s, Hoover (Boulder) Dam was constructed to provide needed jobs, water, and hydroelectric power for the state. Other public works—Davis Dam (Lake Mohave) and the Southern Nevada Water Project—serve similar purposes. The fact that some 87% of Nevada land is owned by the US government further increases the federal impact on the economy. Gaming supplies a large proportion of state revenues.

The Nevada Commission on Economic Development (NCED) offers a number of incentives to encourage the growth of primary businesses in Nevada and to promote economic diversification. There is no corporate or personal income tax and other state taxes are low. The Department of Business and Industry issues tax-exempt industrial development bonds which provide low-interest financing of new construction or improvement of manufacturing facilities and other projects. The State Development Corporation, a private financial corporation certified by the US Small Business Administration, offers long-term loans for expanding or new businesses. Rural small businesses can obtain loans from the Rural Nevada Development Corporation and the Nevada Revolving Loan Fund Program. Almost 30% of foreign-based companies in Nevada are Japanese.

38 HEALTH

The infant mortality rate in October 2005 was estimated at 5.3 per 1,000 live births. The birth rate in 2003 was 15 per 1,000 population. The abortion rate stood at 32.2 per 1,000 women in 2000. In 2003, about 75.8% of pregnant woman received prenatal care beginning in the first trimester. In 2004, approximately 68% of children received routine immunizations before the age of three; this was the lowest immunization rate in the country.

The crude death rate in 2003 was 8 deaths per 1,000 population. As of 2002, the death rates for major causes of death (per 100,000 resident population) were: heart disease, 203.4; cancer, 181.1; cerebrovascular diseases, 44.9; chronic lower respiratory diseases,

54; and diabetes, 15.8. The mortality rate from HIV infection was 3.5 per 100,000 population. In 2004, the reported AIDS case rate was at about 13.1 per 100,000 population. In 2002, about 54.8% of the population was considered overweight or obese. As of 2004, about 23.2% of state residents were smokers.

In 2003, Nevada had 24 community hospitals with about 4,300 beds. There were about 213,000 patient admissions that year and 2.3 million outpatient visits. The average daily inpatient census was about 3,000 patients. The average cost per day for hospital care was $1,608. Also in 2003, there were about 44 certified nursing facilities in the state with 5,197 beds and an overall occupancy rate of about 82.9%. In 2004, it was estimated that about 64.5% of all state residents had received some type of dental care within the year. Nevada had 196 physicians per 100,000 resident population in 2004 and 579 nurses per 100,000 in 2005. In 2004, there was a total of 1,123 dentists in the state.

About 11% of state residents were enrolled in Medicaid programs in 2003; 12% were enrolled in Medicare programs in 2004. Approximately 19% of the state population was uninsured in 2004. In 2003, state health care expenditures totaled $1.6 million.

39 SOCIAL WELFARE

In 2004, about 66,000 people received unemployment benefits, with the average weekly unemployment benefit at $245. In fiscal year 2005, the estimated average monthly participation in the food stamp program included about 121,707 persons (54,877 households); the average monthly benefit was about $88.26 per person. That year, the total of benefits paid through the state for the food stamp program was about $128.9 million.

Temporary Assistance for Needy Families (TANF), the system of federal welfare assistance that officially replaced Aid to Families with Dependent Children (AFDC) in 1997, was reauthorized through the Deficit Reduction Act of 2005. TANF is funded through federal block grants that are divided among the states based on an equation involving the number of recipients in each state. In 2004, the state TANF program had 21,000 recipients; state and federal expenditures on this TANF program totaled $54 million in fiscal year 2003.

In December 2004, Social Security benefits were paid to 340,680 Nevada residents. This number included 230,990 retired workers, 26,440 widows and widowers, 43,030 disabled workers, 15,120 spouses, and 25,100 children. Social Security beneficiaries represented 14.5% of the total state population and 91% of the state's population age 65 and older. Retired workers received an average monthly payment of $962; widows and widowers, $939; disabled workers, $960; and spouses, $473. Payments for children of retired workers averaged $471 per month; children of deceased workers, $671; and children of disabled workers, $271. Federal Supplemental Security Income payments in December 2004 went to 32,129 Nevada residents, averaging $396 a month.

40 HOUSING

In 2004, there were an estimated 976,446 housing units, of which 871,915 were occupied; 61.2% were owner-occupied. About 54.6% of all units were single-family, detached dwellings; 18.6% were in buildings containing three to nine units. Over 1,700 units were listed in a category of boats, RVs, vans, etc. Utility gas and electricity were the most common heating energy sources. It was es-

timated that 41,658 units lacked telephone service, 3,041 lacked complete plumbing facilities, and 3,683 lacked complete kitchen facilities. The average household had 2.64 members.

In 2004, 44,600 new privately owned units were authorized for construction. The median home value was $202,937. The median monthly cost for mortgage owners was $1,274. Renters paid a median of $787 per month. In 2006, the state received over $2.7 million in community development block grants from the US Department of Housing and Urban Development (HUD).

41 EDUCATION

In 2004, 86.3% of Nevada residents age 25 and older were high school graduates; 24.5% had obtained a bachelor's degree or higher.

The total enrollment for fall 2002 in Nevada's public schools stood at 369,000. Of these, 271,000 attended schools from kindergarten through grade eight, and 99,000 attended high school. Approximately 50.8% of the students were white, 10.7% were black, 30.2% were Hispanic, 6.7% were Asian/Pacific Islander, and 1.7% were American Indian/Alaskan Native. Total enrollment was estimated at 385,000 in fall 2003 and expected to be 474,000 by fall 2014, an increase of 28.4% during the period 2002–14. In fall 2003 there were 18,219 students enrolled in 111 private schools. Expenditures for public education in 2003/04 were estimated at $3.2 billion or $6,399 per student, the sixth-lowest among the 50 states. Since 1969, the National Assessment of Educational Progress (NAEP) has tested public school students nationwide. The resulting report, *The Nation's Report Card*, stated that in 2005, eighth graders in Nevada scored 270 out of 500 in mathematics compared with the national average of 278.

As of fall 2002, there were 95,671 students enrolled in college or graduate school; minority students comprised 30.1% of total postsecondary enrollment. Nearly all students enroll in the University of Nevada system, which has campuses in Las Vegas and Reno. In 2005 Nevada had 15 degree-granting institutions, including Sierra Nevada College.

42 ARTS

The Nevada Arts Council (NAC), a division of the Department of Cultural Affairs, consists of a 10-memeber staff and a 9-member board appointed by the governor. In 2005, the NAC and other Nevada arts organizations received six grants totaling $673,300 from the National Endowment for the Arts (NEA). The state also provided significant funding to the Arts Council. The Nevada Humanities Council sponsors annual programs that include a Chautauqua in Reno, Boulder City and Lake Tahoe, and the Vegas Valley Book Festival. In 2005, the National Endowment for the Humanities contributed $532,792 to four state programs.

Major exhibits are mounted by the Las Vegas Art Museum, formally the Las Vegas Art League, and the Sierra Arts Foundation in Reno. Upon becoming the Las Vegas Art Museum in 1974, it became the first fine-arts museum in southern Nevada. The Nevada Opera, Reno Chamber Orchestra, and the Nevada Festival Ballet are all based in Reno. The Las Vegas Philharmonic was founded in 1998 and as of 2005 had become the third-largest arts organizations in the state. The Western Folklife Center in Elko, founded in 1980, promotes public awareness of the American West culture and traditions. Every year, the Western Folklife Center presents a National Cowboy Poetry Gathering in the last week of January.

43 LIBRARIES AND MUSEUMS

In 2001, Nevada had 23 public library systems, with a total of 87 libraries, of which 67 were branches. The system, that same year, had a combined book and serial publication stock of 4,382,000 volumes, and a total circulation of 10,206,000. The system also had 209,000 audio and 148,000 video items, 27,000 electronic format items (CD-ROMs, magnetic tapes, and disks), and four bookmobiles. The University of Nevada had 956,282 books in its Reno campus library system and 861,362 at Las Vegas. The Nevada State Library in Carson City had 76,445. In fiscal year 2001, operating income for the state's public library system amounted to $62,888,000 and included $782,000 in federal grants and $520,000 in state grants.

There are some 29 museums and historic sites. Notable are the Nevada State Museum in Carson City and Las Vegas; the museum of the Nevada Historical Society and the Fleischmann Planetarium, University of Nevada, in Reno; and the Museum of Natural History, University of Nevada, at Las Vegas.

44 COMMUNICATIONS

In 2004, 92.2% of Nevada's occupied housing units had telephones. In addition, by June of that same year there were 1,319,684 mobile wireless telephone subscribers. In 2003, 61.3% of Nevada households had a computer and 55.2% had Internet access. By June 2005, there were 402,030 high-speed lines in Nevada, 360,627 residential and 41,403 for business. In 2005, broadcast facilities comprised 27 major radio stations (7 AM, 20 FM) and 12 network television stations. In 2000, at least two large cable television systems served the Las Vegas and Reno areas. A total of 72,183 Internet domain names were registered in the state in that same year.

45 PRESS

In 2005, the state had four morning newspapers, four evening papers, and four Sunday papers. The leading newspaper was the *Las Vegas Review-Journal*, with a daily circulation of 159,507 and a Sunday circulation of 218,624. The *Reno Gazette-Journal*, with a daily circulation of 66,409 and Sunday circulation of 82,745, is the most influential newspaper in the northern half of the state. The regional interest *Nevada* magazine is published six times a year.

46 ORGANIZATIONS

In 2006, there were over 900 nonprofit organizations registered within the state, of which about 626 were registered as charitable, educational, or religious organizations. Notable national organizations with headquarters in Nevada include the Western History Association, the American Chess Association, the American Gem Society, the Gaming Standards Association, and the North American Boxing Federation.

Local arts and history are represented in part by the Central Nevada Historical Society, the Lake Tahoe Arts Council, the Sierra Contra Dance Society, the National Association for Outlaw and Lawman History, and the Nevada Opera Association.

47 TOURISM, TRAVEL, AND RECREATION

Tourism remained Nevada's most important industry, employing over 228,000 people. In 2005, approximately 51.1 million travelers visited the state. About 25 million people visited state and national parks. A majority of all tourists flock to "Vegas" for gambling and for the top-flight entertainers who perform there. In 2005, there were 180,000 hotel rooms of which 133,186 were in Las Vegas. The gaming industry had total revenues of $11.6 billion in 2005. Las Vegas is one the most used cities for conventions. The Nevada Commission on Tourism has branch offices in Japan, the United Kingdom, and Seoul, Korea.

Nevada attractions include Pyramid Lake, Lake Tahoe, Lake Mead, and Lehman Caves National Monument. In Las Vegas, there is the Atomic Testing Museum, the Fremont Street Experience (outdoor sound and light show), the Guggenheim Hermitage Museum at the Venetian Hotel, and Red Rock scenic adventure tours. The city of Laughlin has Colorado River tours. For motorsports enthusiasts, there are 14 raceways in Nevada. Hoover Dam, built on the Nevada-Arizona border, is a marvel of engineering; visitors can view films and take tours to view the construction. There are 21 state parks and recreation areas, and the Great Basin National Park. Lake Mead National Recreation Area attracts 43% of all park visitors (totaling over 24 million people in 1999). Grand Canyon National Park is the second most popular parks destination, with 18% of all parks visitors.

48 SPORTS

There are no major professional sports teams in Nevada. Las Vegas has a minor league baseball team, the 51s, in the Triple-A Pacific Coast League. The Las Vegas Wranglers are a minor league hockey team that play in the West Division of the ECHL. Las Vegas and Reno have hosted many professional boxing title bouts. Golfing and rodeo are also popular.

The basketball team at the University of Nevada–Las Vegas emerged as a national powerhouse in the late 1980s and early 1990s. The Runnin' Rebels won the national championship in 1990.

Other annual sporting events include the Greens.com Open at Reno-Tahoe in Reno in August, the Invensys Classic at Las Vegas in October, the Nationals Finals Rodeo staged in Las Vegas each December, and the UAW-DaimlerChrysler 400 at the Las Vegas Motor Speedway.

49 FAMOUS NEVADANS

Nevadans who have held important federal offices include Raymond T. Baker (1877–1935) and Eva B. Adams (1908–91), both directors of the US Mint, and Charles B. Henderson (b.California, 1873–1954), head of the Reconstruction Finance Corporation. Prominent US senators have been James W. Nye (b.New York, 1815–76), also the only governor of Nevada Territory; William M. Stewart (b.New York, 1827–1909), author of the final form of the 15th Amendment to the US Constitution, father of federal mining legislation, and a leader of the free-silver-coinage movement in the 1890s; and Francis G. Newlands (b.Mississippi, 1848–1917), author of the federal Reclamation Act of 1902.

Probably the most significant state historical figure is George Wingfield (b.Arkansas, 1876–1959), a mining millionaire who exerted great influence over Nevada's economic and political life in the early 20th century. Among the nationally recognized personalities associated with Nevada is Howard R. Hughes (b.Texas, 1905–76), an aviation entrepreneur who became a casino and hotel owner and wealthy recluse in his later years.

Leading creative and performing artists have included operatic singer Emma Nevada (Emma Wixon, 1862–1940); painter Robert Caples (1908–79); and, among writers, Dan DeQuille (William Wright, b.Ohio, 1829–98); Lucius Beebe (b.Massachusetts, 1902–66); and Walter Van Tilburg Clark (b.Maine, 1909–71).

50 BIBLIOGRAPHY

Busby, Mark (ed.). *The Southwest.* Vol. 8 in *The Greenwood Encyclopedia of American Regional Cultures.* Westport, Conn.: Greenwood Press, 2004.

Council of State Governments. *The Book of the States, 2006 Edition.* Lexington, Ky.: Council of State Governments, 2006.

Davies, Richard O. (ed.). *The Maverick Spirit: Building the New Nevada.* Reno: University of Nevada Press, 1999.

Driggs, Don W. *Nevada Politics and Government: Conservatism in an Open Society.* Lincoln: University of Nebraska Press, 1996.

Hulse, James W. *The Silver State: Nevada's Heritage Reinterpreted.* 3rd ed. Reno: University of Nevada Press, 2004.

Parzybok, Tye W. *Weather Extremes in the West.* Missoula, Mont.: Mountain Press, 2005.

Peck, Donna. *Nevada: Off the Beaten Path.* Old Saybrook, Conn.: Globe Pequot Press, 1999.

Preston, Thomas. *Intermountain West: Idaho, Nevada, Utah, and Arizona.* Vol. 2 of *The Double Eagle Guide to 1,000 Great Western Recreation Destinations.* 2nd ed. Billings, Mont.: Discovery Publications, 2003.

US Department of Commerce, Economics and Statistics Administration, US Census Bureau. *Nevada, 2000. Summary Social, Economic, and Housing Characteristics: 2000 Census of Population and Housing.* Washington, D.C.: US Government Printing Office, 2003.

Zanjani, Sally Springmeyer. *Devils Will Reign: How Nevada Began.* Reno: University of Nevada Press, 2006.

NEW HAMPSHIRE

State of Hampshire

ORIGIN OF STATE NAME: Named for the English county of Hampshire. **NICKNAME:** The Granite State. **CAPITAL:** Concord. **ENTERED UNION:** 21 June 1788 (9th). **SONG:** "Old New Hampshire." **MOTTO:** Live Free or Die. **FLAG:** The state seal, surrounded by laurel leaves with nine stars interspersed, is centered on a blue field. **OFFICIAL SEAL:** In the center is a broadside view of the frigate *Raleigh;* in the left foreground is a granite boulder; in the background is a rising sun. A laurel wreath and the words "Seal of the State of New Hampshire 1776" surround the whole. **BIRD:** Purple finch. **FLOWER:** Purple lilac. **TREE:** White birch. **GEM:** Smoky quartz. **LEGAL HOLIDAYS:** New Year's Day, 1 January; Civil Rights Day and Birthday of Martin Luther King Jr., 3rd Monday in January; Presidents' Day, 3rd Monday in February; Memorial Day, last Monday in May; Independence Day, 4 July; Labor Day, 1st Monday in September; Columbus Day, 2nd Monday in October; Election Day, Tuesday following 1st Monday in November in even-numbered years; Veterans' Day, 11 November; Thanksgiving Day, 4th Thursday in November plus the day after; Christmas Day, 25 December. **TIME:** 7 AM EST = noon GMT.

¹LOCATION, SIZE, AND EXTENT

Situated in New England in the northeastern United States, New Hampshire ranks 44th in size among the 50 states. The total area of New Hampshire is 9,279 sq mi (24,033 sq km), comprising 8,993 sq mi (23,292 sq km) of land and 286 sq mi (741 sq km) of inland water. The state has a maximum extension of 93 mi (150 km) E–W and 180 mi (290 km) N–S. New Hampshire is shaped roughly like a right triangle, with the line from the far N to the extreme SW forming the hypotenuse.

New Hampshire is bordered on the N by the Canadian province of Quebec; on the E by Maine (with part of the line formed by the Piscataqua and Salmon Falls rivers) and the Atlantic Ocean; on the S by Massachusetts; and on the W by Vermont (following the west bank of the Connecticut River) and Quebec (with the line formed by Halls Stream).

The three southernmost Isles of Shoals lying in the Atlantic belong to New Hampshire. The state's total boundary line is 555 mi (893 km). Its geographic center lies in Belknap County, 3 mi (5 km) E of Ashland.

²TOPOGRAPHY

The major regions of New Hampshire are the coastal lowland in the southeast; the New England Uplands, covering most of the south and west; and the White Mountains (part of the Appalachian chain) in the north, including Mt. Washington, at 6,288 ft (1,918 m), the highest peak in the northeastern United States. With a mean elevation of about 1,000 ft (305 m), New Hampshire is generally hilly, rocky, and in many areas densely wooded.

There are some 1,300 lakes and ponds, of which the largest is Lake Winnipesaukee, covering 70 sq mi (181 sq km). The principal rivers are the Connecticut (forming the border with Vermont), Merrimack, Salmon Falls, Piscataqua, Saco, and Androscoggin. Near the coast are the nine rocky Isles of Shoals, three of which belong to New Hampshire. About 10% of the state land area is

covered by wetlands. Sea level at the Atlantic Ocean is the lowest elevation of the state.

³CLIMATE

New Hampshire has a changeable climate, with wide variations in daily and seasonal temperatures. Summers are short and cool, winters long and cold. Concord has an average yearly temperature of 46°F (7°C), ranging from 20°F (-6°C) in January to 70°F (21°C) in July. The record low temperature, -47°F (-44°C), was set at Mt. Washington on 29 January 1934; the all-time high, 106°F (41°C) at Nashua, 4 July 1911. Annual precipitation at Concord averages 36.7 in (93 cm); the average snowfall in Concord is 63.2 in (160 cm) a year, with more than 100 in (254 cm) yearly in the mountains. The strongest wind ever recorded, other than during a tornado—231 mi/h (372 km/h)—occurred on Mt. Washington on 12 April 1934.

⁴FLORA AND FAUNA

Well forested, New Hampshire supports an abundance of elm, maple, beech, oak, pine, hemlock, and fir trees. Among wild flowers, several orchids are considered rare. Three New Hampshire plant species were listed as threatened or endangered in 2006; the small whorled pogonia was threatened and Jesup's milk-vetch and Northeastern bulrush were endangered.

Among native New Hampshire mammals are the white-tailed deer, muskrat, beaver, porcupine, and snowshoe hare. Nine animal species (vertebrates and invertebrates) were listed by the US Fish and Wildlife Service as threatened or endangered in 2006, including the Karner blue butterfly, bald eagle, dwarf wedgemussel, finback whale, and leatherback sea turtle.

⁵ENVIRONMENTAL PROTECTION

State agencies concerned with environmental protection include the Fish and Game Department, the Department of Resources and

Economic Development (DRED), and the Department of Environmental Services (DES). DRED oversees the state's forests, lands and parks and, in the late 1980s, DRED was the lead state agency in the acquisition and long-term protection of open space. DES was created in 1987, consolidating several preexisting commissions and boards into four divisions which protect the environmental quality of air, groundwater, the state's surface waters, and solid waste. In the 1990s, DES focused on such issues as ground-level ozone, landfill closures, groundwater remediation and protection of lakes, rivers, and other wetlands in New Hampshire. In 2003, 5.9 million lb of toxic chemicals were released in the state. Also in 2003, New Hampshire had 91 hazardous waste sites listed in the US Environment Protection Agency (EPA) database, 20 of which were on the National Priorities List as of 2006, including Pease Air Force Base and the Mottolo Pig Farm in Raymond. In 2005, the EPA spent over $10 million through the Superfund program for the cleanup of hazardous waste sites in the state. The same year, federal EPA grants awarded to the state included $13 million for the clean water state revolving fund and $8.2 million for the drinking water state revolving fund.

6 POPULATION

New Hampshire ranked 41st in population in the United States with an estimated total of 1,309,940 in 2005, an increase of 6% since 2000. Between 1990 and 2000, New Hampshire's population grew from 1,109,252 to 1,235,786, an increase of 11.4%. The population is projected to reach 1.45 million by 2015 and 1.58 million by 2025. The population density in 2004 was 144.9 persons per sq mi. In 2004, the median age was 39.1. Persons under 18 years old accounted for 23.5% of the population while 12.1% was age 65 or older.

In 2004, Manchester, the largest city, had an estimated population of 109,310. The Manchester-Nashua metropolitan area had an estimated population of 398,574. In 2003, the capital city of Concord had a population of 41,823

7 ETHNIC GROUPS

In 2000, a total of 223,026 New Hampshirites claimed English ancestry. Those claiming French ancestry numbered 180,947, and Irish 240,804. There are also about 127,153 French Canadians. In 2000, there were 9,035 black Americans, 15,931 Asians, 371 Pacific Islanders, and 2,964 Native Americans living in New Hampshire. In the same year, there were 20,489 residents of Hispanic origin, or 1.7% of the total population. The foreign-born population numbered 54,154, or 4.4% of the total population, in 2000.

In 2004, 2.1% of the population was Hispanic or Latino, 1.7% Asian, 0.9% black, and 0.2% American Indian or Alaskan Native; 0.9% of the population reported origin of two or more races.

8 LANGUAGES

Some place-names, such as Ossipee, Mascoma, and Chocorua, preserve the memory of the Pennacook and Abnaki Algonkian tribes living in the area before white settlement.

New Hampshire speech is essentially Northern, with the special features marking eastern New England, especially the loss of the final /r/, as in *park* and *father,* and /yu/ in *tube* and *new. Raspberries* sounds like /rawzberries/, a wishbone is a *luckybone,* gut-ters are *eavespouts,* and cows are summoned by "Loo!" Canadian French is heard in the northern region.

In 2000, 91.7% of all state residents aged five and above—a total of 935,825—spoke only English at home.

The following table gives selected statistics from the 2000 Census for language spoken at home by persons five years old and over. The category "Other Indo-European languages" includes Albanian, Gaelic, Lithuanian, and Rumanian. The category "Other Asian languages" includes Dravidian languages, Malayalam, Telugu, Tamil, and Turkish.

LANGUAGE	NUMBER	PERCENT
Population 5 years and over	**1,160,340**	**100.0**
Speak only English	1,064,252	91.7
Speak a language other than English	96,088	8.3
Speak a language other than English	**96,088**	**8.3**
French (incl. Patois, Cajun)	39,551	3.4
Spanish or Spanish Creole	18,647	1.6
German	4,788	0.4
Greek	3,411	0.3
Chinese	3,268	0.3
Italian	2,649	0.2
Portuguese or Portuguese Creole	2,394	0.2
Polish	2,094	0.2
Other Indo-European languages	1,468	0.1
Arabic	1,462	0.1
Vietnamese	1,449	0.1
Other Asian languages	1,240	0.1
Korean	1,228	0.1
Serbo-Croatian	1,182	0.1
Russian	1,009	0.1

9 RELIGIONS

The first settlers of New Hampshire were Separatists, precursors of the modern Congregationalists (United Church of Christ) and their first church was probably built around 1633. The first Episcopal church was built in 1638 and the first Quaker meetinghouse in 1701; Presbyterians, Baptists, and Methodists built churches later in the 18th century. The state remained almost entirely Protestant until the second half of the 19th century, when Roman Catholics (French Canadian, Irish, and Italian) began arriving in significant numbers, along with some Greek and Russian Orthodox Christians.

In 2004, Roman Catholics numbered at about 327,353 adherents. In 2005, there were 25,794 members of the United Church of Christ. Other leading Protestant denominations (with 2000 membership data) are the United Methodist Church, 18,927; the American Baptist Churches–USA, 16,359; and the Episcopal Church, 16,148. There were about 10,020 Jews and 3,782 Muslims throughout the state in 2000. A few small groups have reported considerable growth since 1990. These include the Salvation Army, which went from 763 members in 1990 to 2,651 members in 2000. The International Church of the Foursquare Gospel grew from 51 adherents in 1990 to 1,203 in 2000 and the Christian Churches and Churches of Christ reported a membership of 1,503 in 2000, up from 396 in 1990.

10 TRANSPORTATION

New Hampshire's first railroad, between Nashua and Lowell, Massachusetts, was chartered in 1835 and opened in 1838. Two years later, Exeter and Boston were linked by rail. The state had more than 1,200 mi (1,900 km) of track in 1920, but by 2003, the total route mileage in New Hampshire shrunk to 473 mi (761 km).

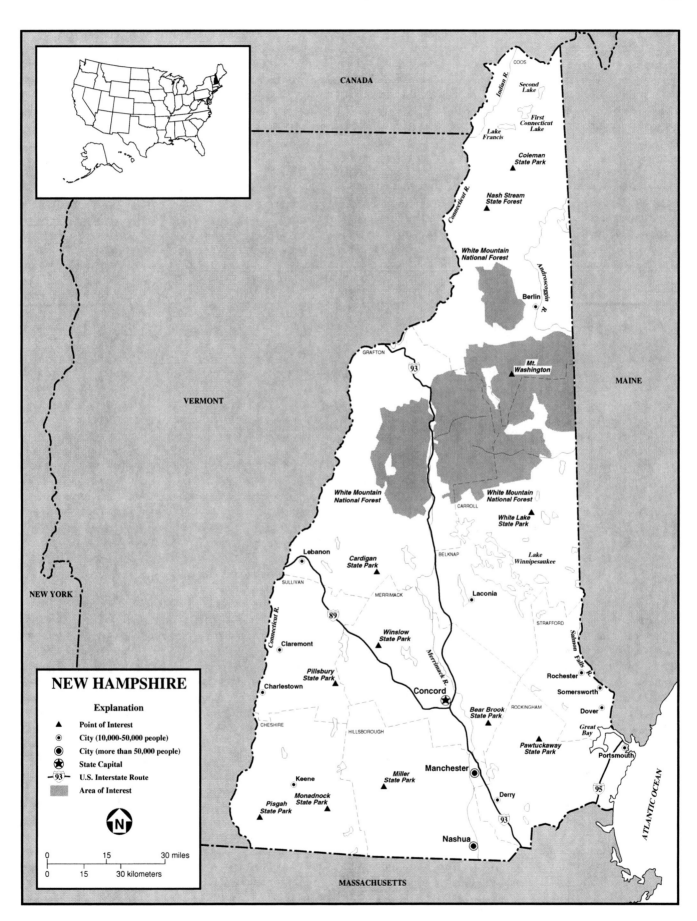

NEW HAMPSHIRE

Explanation

▲ Point of Interest
⊙ City (10,000-50,000 people)
◉ City (more than 50,000 people)
★ State Capital
—93— U.S. Interstate Route
░ Area of Interest

N

0   15   30 miles
0   15   30 kilometers

There were no Class I railroads operating in the state as of that year. As of 2006, Amtrak provided service to three stations in New Hampshire via its Boston to Portland Downeaster train

In 2003, the state had a total of 15,628 mi (25,161 km) of roads. The main north–south highway is I-93. As of 2004, there were some 668,000 automobiles, around 491,000 trucks of all types, about 66,000 motorcycles, and some 1,000 buses registered in the state, along with 985,775 licensed drivers. In 2005, New Hampshire had a total of 127 public and private-use aviation-related facilities. This included 51 airports, 67 heliports, and nine seaplane bases. The state's main airport is Manchester Municipal Airport. In 2004, the airport had 1,973,142 enplanements.

Portsmouth is the state's primary port. In 2004, the Portsmouth handled 4.794 million tons of cargo. For that same year, New Hampshire had only eight mi (12 km) of navigable inland waterways. In 2003, total waterborne shipments totaled 4.971 million tons.

11 HISTORY

The land called New Hampshire has supported a human population for at least 10,000 years. Prior to European settlement, Indian tribes of the Algonkian language group lived in the region. During the 17th century, most of New Hampshire's Indians, called Pennacook, were organized in a loose confederation centered along the Merrimack Valley.

The coast of New England was explored by Dutch, English, and French navigators throughout the 16th century. Samuel de Champlain prepared the first accurate map of the New England coast in 1604, and Captain John Smith explored the Isles of Shoals in 1614. By this time, numerous English fishermen were summering on New England's coastal banks, using the Isles of Shoals for temporary shelter and to dry their catch.

The first English settlement was established along the Piscataqua River in 1623. From 1643 to 1680, New Hampshire was a province of Massachusetts, and the boundary between them was not settled until 1740. During the 18th century, as settlers moved up the Merrimack and Connecticut river valleys, they came into conflict with the Indians. By 1760, however, the Pennacook had been expelled from the region.

Throughout the provincial period, people in New Hampshire made their living through fishing, farming, cutting and sawing timber, shipbuilding, and coastal and overseas trade. By the first quarter of the 18th century, Portsmouth, the provincial capital, had become a thriving commercial port. New Hampshire's terrain worked against Portsmouth's commercial interests, however, by dictating that roads (and later railroads) run in a north–south direction—making Boston, and not Portsmouth, New England's primary trading center. During the Revolutionary War, extensive preparations were made to protect the harbor from a British attack that never came. Although nearly 18,500 New Hampshire men enlisted in the war, no battle was fought within its boundaries. New Hampshire was the first of the original 13 colonies to establish an independent government—on 5 January 1776, six months before the Declaration of Independence.

During the 19th century, as overseas trade became less important to the New Hampshire economy, textile mills were built, principally along the Merrimack River. By midcentury, the Merrimack Valley had become the social, political, and economic center of the state. So great was the demand for workers in these mills that immigrant labor was imported during the 1850s; a decade later, French Canadian workers began pouring south from Quebec.

Although industry thrived, agriculture did not; New Hampshire hill farms could not compete against Midwestern farms. The population in farm towns dropped, leaving a maze of stone walls, cellar holes, and new forests on the hillsides. The people who remained began to cluster in small village centers.

World War I, however, marked a turning point for New Hampshire industry. As wartime demand fell off, the state's old textile mills were unable to compete with newer cotton mills in the South, and New Hampshire's mill towns became as depressed as its farm towns; only in the north, the center for logging and paper manufacturing, did state residents continue to enjoy moderate prosperity. Industrial towns in the southern counties responded to the decline in textile manufacture by making other items, particularly shoes, but the collapse of the state's railroad network spelled further trouble for the slumping economy. The growth of tourism aided the rural areas primarily, as old farms became spacious vacation homes for "summer people," who in some cases paid the bulk of local property taxes.

During the 1960s, New Hampshire's economic decline began to reverse, except in agriculture. In the 1970s and early 1980s, growth in the state's northern counties remained modest, but the combination of Boston's urban sprawl, interstate highway construction, and low state taxes encouraged people and industry—notably high-technology businesses—to move into southern New Hampshire. The state's population doubled between 1960 and 1988, from 606,921 to 1.1 million. Most of the arrivals were younger, more affluent, and better educated than the natives. The newcomers shared the fiscally conservative views of those born in New Hampshire but tended to be more liberal on social questions such as gun control and abortion. The rise in population strained government services, prompted an increase in local taxes, and provoked concern over the state's vanishing open spaces. The state's population has held fairly steady since 1988, with an estimated 1.3 million people in 2004.

Like other New England states, New Hampshire was hard hit by the recession of the early 1990s, with the unemployment rate rising to 10% by 1992. But by the mid-1990s a recovery was underway, and about 30,000 of the more than 60,000 jobs lost during the recession had been regained. By 1999 the state enjoyed the second-lowest unemployment rate in the nation—just 2.7%. Population growth in the state threatened to do away with the annual town meeting. A study released in 2000 showed that more towns had replaced the celebrated tradition with the official ballot form of governance.

In 2000, New Hampshire Chief Justice David Brock faced an unprecedented trial on charges he influenced a lower-court judge about a powerful state senator's case, allowed a Supreme Court colleague to have a say in the handling of his own divorce, permitted disqualified justices to participate in cases, and lied to a house committee investigating the court. Brock was the first New Hampshire official impeached in 210 years and his trial was to be the first in the state's history. The last impeachment of a New Hampshire official was in 1790; Supreme Court Justice Woodbury Langdon resigned before he was tried. Brock was acquitted by the New Hampshire Senate in October 2000.

Like other New England states in the early 2000s, New Hampshire faced record-breaking budget deficits. Republican Governor Craig Benson vetoed a 2003 two-year budget passed by the state legislature, saying it would increase the deficit and raise taxes. Democrat John Lynch, who was inaugurated as New Hampshire's governor in January 2005 after defeating Benson in the November 2004 election, put his attention to improving education, reducing health care costs, protecting the environment, and creating good jobs. In his first few months in office he worked with the legislature to pass legislation stabilizing health care costs for small businesses; eliminating a projected $300 million budget deficit; and making progress on education funding.

12 STATE GOVERNMENT

New Hampshire's constitution, adopted in 1784 and extensively revised in 1792, is the second-oldest state-governing document still in effect. Every 10 years, the people vote on the question of calling a convention to revise it; proposed revisions must then be approved by two-thirds of the voters at a referendum. Amendments may also be placed on the ballot by a three-fifths vote of both houses of the state legislature. If placed on the ballot, an amendment must be approved by two-thirds of the voters on the amendment in order to be ratified. The constitution was amended 143 times by January 2005.

The state legislature, called the General Court, consists of a 24-member Senate and a 400-seat House of Representatives, larger than that of any other state. Legislative sessions begin each January and are limited to 45 legislative days. Special sessions, indirectly limited to 15 legislative days, may be called by a two-thirds vote of the members of each house. Senators must be at least 30 years old, representatives 18. The state residency requirement for senators is a minimum of seven years and for representatives a minimum of two. Legislators, who must reside in their districts, serve two-year terms, for which they were paid $200 ($100 per year) as of 2004, unchanged from 1999.

The only executive elected statewide is the governor, who serves a two-year term and is assisted by a five-member executive council, elected for two years by district. As of 2006, New Hampshire and Vermont were the only two states whose governors served two-year terms. The council must approve all administrative and judicial appointments. The secretary of state and state treasurer are elected by the legislature. The governor must be at least 30 years old and must have been a state resident for seven years before election. As of December 2004, the governor's salary was $96,060.

A bill becomes law if signed by the governor, if passed by the legislature and left unsigned by the governor for five days whether or not the legislature is in or out of session, or if passed over a gubernatorial veto by two-thirds of the legislators present in each house. A voter must be at least 18 years old, a US citizen, and must have a permanent established domicile in the state of New Hampshire. Restrictions apply to convicted felons.

13 POLITICAL PARTIES

New Hampshire has almost always gone with the Republican presidential nominee in recent decades, but the Democratic and Republican parties were much more evenly balanced in local and state elections. New Hampshire's quadrennial presidential preference primary, the second state primary of the campaign season

New Hampshire Presidential Vote by Major Political Parties, 1948–2004

YEAR	ELECTORAL VOTE	NEW HAMPSHIRE WINNER	DEMOCRAT	REPUBLICAN
1948	4	Dewey (R)	107,995	121,299
1952	4	*Eisenhower (R)	106,663	166,287
1956	4	*Eisenhower (R)	90,364	176,519
1960	4	Nixon (R)	137,772	157,989
1964	4	*Johnson (D)	182,065	104,029
1968	4	*Nixon (R)	130,589	154,903
1972	4	*Nixon (R)	116,435	213,724
1976	4	Ford (R)	147,635	185,935
1980	4	*Reagan (R)	108,864	221,705
1984	4	*Reagan (R)	120,347	267,050
1988	4	*Bush (R)	163,696	281,537
1992**	4	*Clinton (D)	209,040	202,484
1996**	4	*Clinton (D)	246,214	196,532
2000	4	*Bush, G. W. (R)	266,348	273,559
2004	4	Kerry (D)	340,511	331,237

*Won US presidential election.
**IND. candidate Ross Perot received 121,337 votes in 1992 and 48,390 votes in 1996.

after Iowa, accords to New Hampshirites a degree of national political influence and a claim on media attention far out of proportion to their numbers. In the 1992 presidential election, New Hampshire voters defied their tradition and chose Democrat Bill Clinton over Republican incumbent George Bush by a scant 6,556 votes. Clinton won the state again in 1996. In the 2000 presidential election, Republican George W. Bush received 48% of the vote to Democrat Al Gore's 47%; Green Party candidate Ralph Nader garnered 4% of the vote. In 2004, Bush won 40.3% to Democratic challenger John Kerry's 49.0%. In 2004, there were 690,000 registered voters. In 1998, 27% of registered voters were Democratic, 36% Republican, and 36% unaffiliated or members of other parties. The state had four electoral votes in the 2004 presidential election.

As of 2005, both of New Hampshire's senators, John Sununu (elected in 2002) and Judd Gregg (reelected in 2004), were Republicans. Following the 2004 election, both House seats were held by Republicans. In 2002, Republican Craig Benson was elected governor; he was defeated by Democrat John Lynch in 2004. The New Hampshire state Senate in mid-2005 had 16 Republicans and 8 Democrats, and the state House had 253 Republicans and 147 Democrats.

14 LOCAL GOVERNMENT

As of 2005, New Hampshire has 10 counties, each governed by three commissioners. Other elected county officials include the sheriff, attorney, treasurer, registrar of deeds, and registrar of probate.

New Hampshire also had 13 municipal governments in 2005, as well as 178 public school districts, and 148 special districts. In 2002, there were 221 townships. Most municipalities have elected mayors and councils. Some municipal charters provide for the council-manager or commission system of government. The basic unit of town government is the traditional town meeting, held once a year, when selectmen and other local officials are chosen.

In 2005, local government accounted for about 49,709 full-time (or equivalent) employment positions.

15 STATE SERVICES

To address the continuing threat of terrorism and to work with the federal Department of Homeland Security, homeland security in New Hampshire operates under the authority of the governor; the emergency management director is designated as the state homeland security advisor.

The Department of Education, governed by the seven-member State Board of Education (which appoints an education commissioner), has primary responsibility for public instruction. The Department of Transportation and the Division of Ports and Harbors share transport responsibilities, while the Department of Health and Human Services oversees public health and mental health and welfare. Executive branch departments include the departments of agriculture, markets, and food; cultural resources; fish and game; justice; revenue administration; and parks and recreation. Authorities, boards, and commissions include the Liquor Commission and the Sweepstakes Commission.

16 JUDICIAL SYSTEM

All judges in New Hampshire are appointed by the governor, subject to confirmation by the executive council. Appointments are to age 70, with retirement compulsory at that time. The state's highest court, the Supreme Court, consists of a chief justice and four associate justices. The main trial court is the Superior Court for which there were 28 judges in 1999.

As of 31 December 2004, a total of 2,448 prisoners were held in New Hampshire's state and federal prisons, an increase from 2,434 of 0.6% from the previous year. As of year-end 2004, a total of 119 inmates were female, up from 117 or 1.7% from the year before. Among sentenced prisoners (one year or more), New Hampshire had an incarceration rate of 187 per 100,000 population in 2004.

According to the Federal Bureau of Investigation, New Hampshire in 2004, had a violent crime rate (murder/nonnegligent manslaughter; forcible rape; robbery; aggravated assault) of 167 reported incidents per 100,000 population, or a total of 2,170 reported incidents. Crimes against property (burglary; larceny/theft; and motor vehicle theft) in that same year totaled 26,511 reported incidents or 2,040.1 reported incidents per 100,000 people. New Hampshire has a death penalty, which consists of lethal injection or hanging, the latter of which is used only if lethal injection cannot be used. Since 1930, New Hampshire has executed only one person and as of 1 January 2006 no prisoners were under sentence of death in the state. For the period 1976 through 5 May 2006, there have been no executions carried out by the state.

In 2003, New Hampshire spent $45,536,983 on homeland security, an average of $36 per state resident.

17 ARMED FORCES

In 2004, there were 218 active-duty military personnel and 1,059 civilian personnel stationed in New Hampshire. The principal military installation is the Portsmouth Naval Shipyard. Firms in the state received nearly $715 million in defense contract awards in 2004, and defense payroll outlays were $384 million.

As of 2003, veterans living in New Hampshire numbered 131,074, of whom 16,623 were veterans of World War II; 14,381, the Korean conflict; 41,627, the Vietnam era; and 16,940 served during the Gulf War. For the fiscal year 2004, total Veterans Affairs expenditures in New Hampshire amounted to more than $325 million.

As of 31 October 2004, the New Hampshire State Police employed 267 full-time sworn officers.

18 MIGRATION

From the time of the first European settlement until the middle of the 19th century, the population of New Hampshire was primarily of British origin. Subsequently, immigrants from Quebec and from Ireland, Italy, and other countries began arriving in significant numbers. New Hampshire's population growth since 1960 has been fueled by migrants from other states. The net gain from migration was 74,000 from 1985 to 1990. Between 1990 and 1998, New Hampshire had net gains of 19,000 in domestic migration and 6,000 in international migration. In 1998, the state admitted 1,010 foreign immigrants. Between 1990 and 1998, the state's overall population increased 6.8%. In the period 2000–05, net international migration was 11,107 and net internal migration was 40,861, for a net gain of 51,968 people.

19 INTERGOVERNMENTAL COOPERATION

New Hampshire participates in the American and Canadian French Cultural Exchange Commission, Atlantic States Marine Fisheries Commission, Connecticut River Valley Flood Control Compact, Maine-New Hampshire Interstate School Compact, Northeastern Forest Fire Protection Compact, and various New England regional compacts (including compacts on radiological health protection, higher education, corrections, police, trucking fees and permits, water pollution control, sewage and garbage disposal, fire protection, and the lotto). Federal grants to New Hampshire totaled $1.243 billion in fiscal year 2005, an estimated $1.253 billion in fiscal year 2006, and an estimated $1.271 billion in fiscal year 2007.

20 ECONOMY

New Hampshire is one of the most industrialized states in the United States, ranking well above the national median in proportion of labor force employed in manufacturing and in value added by manufacture. Between 1977 and 1982, manufacturing employment rose 13%, to 107,500, as many high-technology firms moved into the southern portion of the state. Since World War II, tourism has been one of the state's fastest-growing sources of income. Coming into the 21st century, the state's economy was booming, posting annual growth rates of 8.2% in 1998, 7% in 1999, and 9.3% in 2000. It was clearly headed for a correction, and in the national recession and slowdown of 2001 it was one of the few states that experienced a contraction for the year, albeit a small 0.4% contraction. Due to the large growth of information technology (IT) related jobs in southern New Hampshire in the 1990s, this was the region of New England that saw the greatest fall in personal income between mid-2000 and mid-2002.

New Hampshire's gross state product (GSP) in 2004 was $51.871 billion of which the real estate sector accounted for the largest share at $7.232 billion or 13.9% of GSP, followed by manufacturing (durable and nondurable goods) at $6.47 billion (12.4% of GSP), and healthcare and social assistance at $4.195 billion (8% of GSP). In that same year, there were an estimated 133,052 small businesses in New Hampshire. Of the 40,151 businesses that had employees, an estimated total of 38,820 or 96.7% were small companies. An estimated 4,865 new businesses were established in the state in 2004, up 4.6% from the year before. Business terminations that same year came to 5,401, up 17.5% from 2003. There were 158 business bankruptcies in 2004, down 11.2% from the previous year. In 2005, the state's personal bankruptcy (Chapter 7 and Chapter 13) filing rate was 333 filings per 100,000 people, ranking New Hampshire as the 47th highest in the nation.

21 INCOME

In 2005, New Hampshire had a gross state product (GSP) of $56 billion which accounted for 0.4% of the nation's gross domestic product and placed the state at number 39 in highest GSP among the 50 states and the District of Columbia.

According to the Bureau of Economic Analysis, in 2004 New Hampshire had a per capita personal income (PCPI) of $36,616. This ranked seventh in the United States and was 111% of the national average of $33,050. The 1994–2004 average annual growth rate of PCPI was 4.5%. New Hampshire had a total personal income (TPI) of $47,569,847,000, which ranked 38th in the United States and reflected an increase of 7.1% from 2003. The 1994–2004 average annual growth rate of TPI was 5.8%. Earnings of persons employed in New Hampshire increased from $32,481,694,000 in 2003 to $34,921,009,000 in 2004, an increase of 7.5%. The 2003–04 national change was 6.3%.

The US Census Bureau reports that the three-year average median household income for 2002–04 in 2004 dollars was $57,352 compared to a national average of $44,473. During the same period an estimated 5.7% of the population was below the poverty line as compared to 12.4% nationwide.

22 LABOR

According to the Bureau of Labor Statistics (BLS), in April 2006 the seasonally adjusted civilian labor force in New Hampshire numbered 735,300 with approximately 24,700 workers unemployed, yielding an unemployment rate of 3.4%, compared to the national average of 4.7% for the same period. Preliminary data for the same period placed nonfarm employment at 642,500. Since the beginning of the BLS data series in 1976, the highest unemployment rate recorded in New Hampshire was 7.7% in June 1982. The historical low was 1.9% in April 1987. Preliminary nonfarm employment data by occupation for April 2006 showed that approximately 4.8% of the labor force was employed in construction; 12% in manufacturing; 22.1% in trade, transportation, and public utilities; 6.3% in financial activities; 9.5% in professional and business services; 15.7% in education and health services; 9.9% in leisure and hospitality services; and 13.9% in government.

The US Department of Labor's Bureau of Labor Statistics reported that in 2005, a total of 65,000 of New Hampshire's 627,000 employed wage and salary workers were formal members of a union. This represented 10.4% of those so employed, up from 9.9% in 2004, but still below the national average of 12%. Overall in 2005, a total of 72,000 workers (11.5%) in New Hampshire were covered by a union or employee association contract, which includes those workers who reported no union affiliation. New Hampshire is one of 28 states that does not have a right-to-work law.

As of 1 March 2006, New Hampshire had a state-mandated minimum wage rate of $5.15 per hour. In 2004, women in the state accounted for 46.7% of the employed civilian labor force.

23 AGRICULTURE

Only Rhode Island and Alaska generate less income from farming than New Hampshire. Farm income in 2005 was $168 million, 56% of which was in crops.

In 2004, there were about 3,400 farms occupying about 450,000 acres (182,000 hectares). Leading crops and their output in 2004 were hay, 105,000 tons, and commercial apples, 31 million lb (14 million kg).

24 ANIMAL HUSBANDRY

Dairy and poultry products are the mainstays of New Hampshire's agriculture. In 2003, the state had 16,000 milk cows, with a total milk yield of 305 million lb (139 million kg). Poultry items included 1,183,000 lb (538,000 kg) of chickens, sold for $28,000; 132,000 lb (60,000 kg) of turkey, valued at $224,000, and 43 million eggs, valued at $3.2 million.

25 FISHING

New Hampshire's commercial catch in 2004 consisted of 21.9 million lb (10 million kg), worth $8.8 million. Most of the catch includes cod and lobster. In 2003, the state had 3 processing and 20 wholesale plants with about 497 employees. The commercial fleet in 2001 had about 580 boats and vessels. The state sponsors six hatcheries. The Nashua National Fish Hatchery is also located in the state. In 2004, the state issued 143,835 sport fishing licenses.

26 FORESTRY

New Hampshire had 4,824,000 acres (1,952,000 hectares) of forestland in 2004, of which 4,503,000 acres (1,822,000 hectares) were considered suitable for commercial use. Of that total, 83% was privately owned. Forests cover about 84% of New Hampshire. Lumber production in 2004 was 232 million board feet, 72% softwood.

27 MINING

According to preliminary data from the US Geological Survey (USGS), the estimated value of nonfuel mineral production by New Hampshire in 2003 was $63.9 million, a decrease from 2002 of about 3%.

By value, according to the preliminary data for 2003, construction sand and gravel was the state's leading nonfuel mineral commodity, accounting for around 69% of all nonfuel mineral production. In second place was crushed stone.

Preliminary data for 2003 showed production of construction sand and gravel totaling 9.1 million metric tons, with a value of $44.1 million, while crushed stone output that year totaled 3.89 million metric tons, and a value of $19.8 million. New Hampshire in 2003 was also a producer of dimension granite, and gem stones which were collected by hobbyists. Sand and gravel are mined in every county, and dimension granite is quarried in Hillsborough, Merrimack, and Coos counties.

²⁸ENERGY AND POWER

As of 2003, new Hampshire had 20 electrical power service providers, of which five were publicly owned and one was a cooperative. Of the remainder, four were investor owned, four were owners of independent generators that sold directly to customers, four were generation-only suppliers and two were delivery-only providers. As of that same year there were 661,773 retail customers. Of that total, 576,788 received their power from investor-owned service providers. The state's lone cooperative accounted for 73,727 customers, while publicly owned providers had 11,147 customers. There were five independent generator or "facility" customers, while generation-only suppliers had 106 customers. There was no data on the number of delivery-only customers.

Total net summer generating capability by the state's electrical generating plants in 2003 stood at 4.244 million kW, with total production that same year at 21.597 billion kWh. Of the total amount generated, 28.9% came from electric utilities, with the remaining 71.1% coming from independent producers and combined heat and power service providers. The largest portion of all electric power generated, 9.276 billion kWh (43%), came from nuclear power, with natural gas fired plants in second place at 4.165 billion kWh (19.3%) and coal-fired plants in third at 3.923 billion kWh (18.2%). Other renewable power sources accounted for 4% of all power generated, with hydroelectric at 6.2% and petroleum fired plants at 9.5%.

In 1990, the controversial nuclear power plant at Seabrook, built by Public Service Co. of New Hampshire, began operating. Originally planned as a two-reactor, 2,300-Mw facility, Seabrook was scaled back to one 1,150 MW reactor whose cost was about five times the original $1 billion two-reactor estimate. As of 2003, the plant had a generating capability of 1,159 MW and was the largest reactor in New England.

New Hampshire has no refineries, nor any proven reserves or production of crude oil and natural gas.

²⁹INDUSTRY

During the provincial era, shipbuilding was New Hampshire's major industry. By 1870, cotton and woolen mills, concentrated in the southeast, employed about one-third of the labor force and accounted for roughly half the value of all manufactures.

According to the US Census Bureau's Annual Survey of Manufactures (ASM) for 2004, New Hampshire's manufacturing sector covered some 16 product subsectors. The shipment value of all products manufactured in the state that same year was $15.439 billion. Of that total, computer and electronic product manufacturing accounted for the largest share at $3.982 billion. It was followed by machinery manufacturing at $1.867 billion; fabricated metal product manufacturing at $1.627 billion; miscellaneous manufacturing at $1.017 billion; and electrical equipment, appliance and component manufacturing at $983.270 million.

In 2004, a total of 72,498 people in New Hampshire were employed in the state's manufacturing sector, according to the ASM. Of that total, 452,589 were actual production workers. In terms of total employment, the computer and electronic product manufacturing industry accounted for the largest portion of all manufacturing employees at 14,068, with 6,127 actual production workers. It was followed by fabricated metal product manufacturing

at 10,776 employees (8,023 actual production workers); machinery manufacturing at 8,534 employees (4,497 actual production workers); miscellaneous manufacturing at 5,307 employees (2,997 actual production workers); and plastics and rubber products manufacturing with 4,555 employees (3,543 actual production workers).

ASM data for 2004 showed that New Hampshire's manufacturing sector paid $3.332 billion in wages. Of that amount, the computer and electronic product manufacturing sector accounted for the largest share at $863.134 million. It was followed by fabricated metal product manufacturing at $436.288 million; machinery manufacturing at $430.462 million; miscellaneous manufacturing at $255.064 million; and electrical equipment, appliance and component manufacturing at $175.557 million.

³⁰COMMERCE

According to the 2002 Census of Wholesale Trade, New Hampshire's wholesale trade sector had sales that year totaling $13.7 billion from 2,004 establishments. Wholesalers of durable goods accounted for 1,326 establishments, followed by nondurable goods wholesalers at 508 and electronic markets, agents, and brokers accounting for 170 establishments. Sales by durable goods wholesalers in 2002 totaled $6.6 billion, while wholesalers of nondurable goods saw sales of $5.4 billion. Electronic markets, agents, and brokers in the wholesale trade industry had sales of $1.5 billion.

In the 2002 Census of Retail Trade, New Hampshire was listed as having 6,702 retail establishments with sales of $20.8 billion. The leading types of retail businesses by number of establishments were: miscellaneous store retailers (839); motor vehicle and motor vehicle parts dealers (822); clothing and clothing accessories stores (806); and food and beverage stores (752). In terms of sales, motor vehicle and motor vehicle parts dealers accounted for the largest share of retail sales at $5.3 billion, followed by food and beverage stores at $3.3 billion; general merchandise stores at $2.8 billion; nonstore retailers at $1.85 billion; and building material/garden equipment and supplies dealers $1.80 billion. A total of 93,804 people were employed by the retail sector in New Hampshire that year.

Foreign exports of goods originating in New Hampshire totaled $2.5 billion in 2005.

³¹CONSUMER PROTECTION

Consumer protection issues are handled by the Consumer Protection and Antitrust Bureau, which is under the jurisdiction of the state of New Hampshire's Department of Justice. Specific legal action however, is handled by the state's Attorney General's Office, which is also under the state's Department of Justice.

When dealing with consumer protection issues, the state's Attorney General's Office can initiate civil and criminal proceedings; represent the state before state and federal regulatory agencies; administer consumer protection and education programs; handle formal consumer complaints; and exercise broad subpoena powers. In antitrust actions, the Attorney General's Office can act on behalf of those consumers who are incapable of acting on their own; initiate damage actions on behalf of the state in state courts; and initiate criminal proceedings. However, the Attorney General's Office cannot represent counties, cities and other governmental entities in recovering civil damages under state or federal law.

The offices of the Consumer Protection and Antitrust Bureau are located in Concord.

32 BANKING

As of June 2005, New Hampshire had 30 insured banks, savings and loans, and saving banks, plus 21 state-chartered and six federally chartered credit unions (CUs). Excluding the CUs, the Manchester-Nashua market area accounted for the largest portion of the state's financial institutions and deposits in 2004, with 15 institutions and $6.435 billion in deposits. As of June 2005, CUs accounted for 9.6% of all assets held by all financial institutions in the state, or some $3.349 billion. Banks, savings and loans, and savings banks collectively accounted for the remaining 90.4% or $31.670 billion in assets held.

Twenty percent of New Hampshire's banks have long-term asset concentrations greater than 30% of earnings assets. This is due in large measure to the large percentage of thrifts and residential lenders in the state. Over one-half of all insured banks in New Hampshire are savings institutions.

Regulation of state-chartered banks and other financial institutions is the responsibility of the Banking Department.

33 INSURANCE

In 2004, there were 631,000 individual life insurance policies in force in New Hampshire, with a total value of about $59.5 billion; total value for all categories of life insurance (individual, group, and credit) was $90 billion. The average coverage amount is $94,400 per policy holder. Death benefits paid that year totaled $209.2 million.

As of 2003, there were 33 property and casualty and 3 life and health insurance companies domiciled in the state. Direct premiums for property and casualty insurance totaled $2.1 billion in 2004. That year, there were 5,211 flood insurance policies in force in the state, with a total value of $758 million.

In 2004, 67% of state residents held employment-based health insurance policies, 3% held individual policies, and 18% were covered under Medicare and Medicaid; 11% of residents were uninsured. New Hampshire has the highest percentage of employment-based insurance in the country. In 2003, employee contributions for employment-based health coverage averaged at 21% for single coverage and 25% for family coverage. The state offers an 18-month health benefits expansion program for small-firm employees in connection with the Consolidated Omnibus Budget Reconciliation Act (COBRA, 1986), a health insurance program for those who lose employment-based coverage due to termination or reduction of work hours.

In 2003, there were 862,145 auto insurance policies in effect for private passenger cars. Insurance coverage is not mandatory but motorists are expected to take financial responsibility and uninsured motorist coverage is available. In 2003, the average expenditure per vehicle for insurance coverage was $776.47.

34 SECURITIES

New Hampshire has no securities exchanges. In 2005, there were 490 personal financial advisers employed in the state and 1,950 securities, commodities, and financial services sales agents. In 2004, there were over 36 publicly traded companies within the state, with over 14 NASDAQ companies, 8 NYSE listings, and 4 AMEX listings. In 2006, the state had one Fortune 500 company; Fisher Scientific Intl, based in Hampton and listed on the NYSE, ranked 389th in the nation with revenues of over $5.5 billion. Timberland in Stratham (NYSE) and PC Connection in Merrimack (NASDAQ) made the Fortune 1,000 list.

35 PUBLIC FINANCE

The New Hampshire state budget is drawn up biennially by the Department of Administrative Services and then submitted by the governor to the legislature for amendment and approval. The fiscal year (FY) runs from 1 July to 30 June.

New Hampshire—State Government Finances

(Dollar amounts in thousands. Per capita amounts in dollars.)

	AMOUNT	PER CAPITA
Total Revenue	6,174,660	4,753.39
General revenue	5,024,122	3,867.68
Intergovernmental revenue	1,676,883	1,290.90
Taxes	2,005,389	1,543.79
General sales	–	–
Selective sales	674,354	519.13
License taxes	199,170	153.33
Individual income tax	54,769	42.16
Corporate income tax	407,603	313.78
Other taxes	669,493	515.39
Current charges	723,942	557.31
Miscellaneous general revenue	617,908	475.68
Utility revenue	110	.08
Liquor store revenue	371,766	286.19
Insurance trust revenue	778,662	599.43
Total expenditure	5,654,063	4,352.63
Intergovernmental expenditure	1,278,988	984.59
Direct expenditure	4,375,075	3,368.03
Current operation	3,288,655	2,531.68
Capital outlay	293,670	226.07
Insurance benefits and repayments	384,809	296.23
Assistance and subsidies	106,111	81.69
Interest on debt	301,830	232.36
Exhibit: Salaries and wages	780,172	600.59
Total expenditure	5,654,063	4,352.63
General expenditure	4,942,244	3,804.65
Intergovernmental expenditure	1,278,988	984.59
Direct expenditure	3,663,256	2,820.06
General expenditures, by function:		
Education	1,667,818	1,283.92
Public welfare	1,441,935	1,110.03
Hospitals	50,196	38.64
Health	137,669	105.98
Highways	374,149	288.03
Police protection	37,454	28.83
Correction	94,423	72.69
Natural resources	61,365	47.24
Parks and recreation	13,657	10.51
Government administration	200,118	154.06
Interest on general debt	301,830	232.36
Other and unallocable	561,630	432.36
Utility expenditure	9,294	7.15
Liquor store expenditure	317,716	244.59
Insurance trust expenditure	384,809	296.23
Debt at end of fiscal year	5,894,106	4,537.42
Cash and security holdings	10,175,057	7,832.99

Abbreviations and symbols: – zero or rounds to zero; (NA) not available; (X) not applicable.

SOURCE: U.S. Census Bureau, Governments Division, 2004 Survey of State Government Finances, January 2006.

Fiscal year 2006 general funds were estimated at $1.37 billion for resources and $1.34 billion for expenditures. In fiscal year 2004, federal government grants to New Hampshire were $1.8 billion

On 5 January 2006 the federal government released $100 million in emergency contingency funds targeted to the areas with the greatest need, including $900,000 for New Hampshire.

36 TAXATION

In 2005, New Hampshire collected $2,022 million in tax revenues or $1,544 per capita, which placed it 48th among the 50 states in per capita tax burden. The national average was $2,192 per capita. Property taxes accounted for 19.4% of the total, selective sales taxes 34.9%, individual income taxes 3.3%, corporate income taxes 23.6%, and other taxes 18.8%.

As of 1 January 2006, state income tax was limited to dividends and interest income only. The state taxes corporations at a flat rate of 8.5%.

In 2004, state and local property taxes amounted to $2.5 billion or $1,940 per capita. The per capita amount ranks the state third-highest nationally. Local governments collected $2,026,125,000 of the total and the state government $493,589,000.

New Hampshire taxes gasoline at 19.625 cents per gallon. This is in addition to the 18.4 cents per gallon federal tax on gasoline.

According to the Tax Foundation, for every federal tax dollar sent to Washington in 2004, New Hampshire citizens received $0.67 in federal spending, which ranks the state third-lowest among all states.

37 ECONOMIC POLICY

Business incentives in New Hampshire include a generally favorable tax climate (which includes the absence of sales, personal income, and capital gains taxes), specific tax incentives and exemptions, and relatively low wage rates. The state has offered loan programs through the New Hampshire Business Finance Authority since 1992, aimed at encouraging economic development and job creation and at assisting small businesses. The state also participates in a joint venture with Maine and Vermont which provides loans to export companies. Foreign Trade Zone No. 81 provides economic incentives to companies doing business in the international markets. New Hampshire's Division of Economic Development (DED), within the Department of Resources and Economic Development, has the main responsibility for state support of programs to increase jobs and revenues in the state. Major operational units within the DED have been focused on assistance for business relocations and expansions; New Economy Ventures; community development; Internet development; exports of states products, imports of state products and tourism. Under the program NH Works, employers were offered free assistance on all facets of hiring the right employees.

38 HEALTH

The infant mortality rate in October 2005 was estimated at 5.4 per 1,000 live births. The birth rate in 2003 was 11.2 per 1,000 population. The abortion rate stood at 11.2 per 1,000 women in 2000. In 2003, about 92.8% of pregnant woman received prenatal care beginning in the first trimester; this was the highest rate for pre-

natal care in the nation. In 2004, approximately 86% of children received routine immunizations before the age of three.

The crude death rate in 2003 was 7.5 deaths per 1,000 population. As of 2002, the death rates for major causes of death (per 100,000 resident population) were: heart disease, 217.7; cancer, 198.3; cerebrovascular diseases, 49.2; chronic lower respiratory diseases, 45.3; and diabetes, 24.4. The mortality rate from HIV infection was not available. In 2004, the reported AIDS case rate was at about 3.2 per 100,000 population. In 2002, about 53.5% of the population was considered overweight or obese. As of 2004, about 21.6% of state residents were smokers.

In 2003, New Hampshire had 28 community hospitals with about 2,800 beds. There were about 118,000 patient admissions that year and 3.1 million outpatient visits. The average daily inpatient census was about 1,700 patients. The average cost per day for hospital care was $1,389. Also in 2003, there were about 81 certified nursing facilities in the state with 7,811 beds and an overall occupancy rate of about 91.5%. New In 2004, it was estimated that about 77.5% of all state residents had received some type of dental care within the year. Hampshire had 267 physicians per 100,000 resident population in 2004 and 932 nurses per 100,000 in 2005. In 2004, there were a total of 795 dentists in the state.

About 10% of state residents were enrolled in Medicaid programs in 2003; 14% were enrolled in Medicare programs in 2004. Approximately 11% of the state population was uninsured in 2004. In 2003, state health care expenditures totaled $1.3 million.

39 SOCIAL WELFARE

In 2004, about 21,000 people received unemployment benefits, with the average weekly unemployment benefit at $251. In fiscal year 2005, the estimated average monthly participation in the food stamp program included about 52,310 persons (25,198 households); the average monthly benefit was about $80.56 per person. That year, the total of benefits paid through the state for the food stamp program was about $50.5 million, the lowest total in the nation.

Temporary Assistance for Needy Families (TANF), the system of federal welfare assistance that officially replaced Aid to Families with Dependent Children (AFDC) in 1997, was reauthorized through the Deficit Reduction Act of 2005. TANF is funded through federal block grants that are divided among the states based on an equation involving the number of recipients in each state. New Hampshire's TANF program for work-exempt families is called the Family Assistance Program (FAP), while aid to work-mandated families under TANF is called the New Hampshire Employment Program (NHEP). In 2004, the state program had 14,000 recipients; state and federal expenditures on this TANF program totaled $37 million in fiscal year 2003.

In December 2004, Social Security benefits were paid to 219,080 New Hampshire residents. This number included 143,580 retired workers, 18,050 widows and widowers, 30,090 disabled workers, 8,850 spouses, and 18,510 children. Social Security beneficiaries represented 16.6% of the total state population and 96.9% of the state's population age 65 and older. Retired workers received an average monthly payment of $978; widows and widowers, $948; disabled workers, $897; and spouses, $505. Payments for children of retired workers averaged $513 per month; children of deceased workers, $681; and children of disabled workers, $282. Federal

Supplemental Security Income payments in December 2004 went to 13,029 New Hampshire residents, averaging $377 a month. An additional $873,000 of state-administered supplemental payments were distributed to 16,784 residents.

40 HOUSING

In 2004, there were 575,671 housing units in New Hampshire, 491,589 of which were occupied; 72.6% were owner-occupied. About 62.8% of all units were single-family, detached homes. Fuel oil and kerosene were the most common heating energy sources. It was estimated that 8,724 units lacked telephone service, 2,770 lacked complete plumbing facilities, and 2,725 lacked complete kitchen facilities. The average household had 2.57 members.

In 2004, 8,700 new privately owned units were authorized for construction. The median home value was $216,639. The median monthly cost for mortgage owners was $1,472. Renters paid a median of $810. In 2006, the state received over $9.2 million in community development block grants from the US Department of Housing and Urban Development (HUD).

41 EDUCATION

In 2004, 90.8% of New Hampshire residents age 25 and older were high school graduates, significantly higher than the national average of 84%. Some 35.4% had obtained a bachelor's degree or higher, surpassing the national average of 26%.

The total enrollment for fall 2002 in New Hampshire's public schools stood at 208,000. Of these, 144,000 attended schools from kindergarten through grade eight, and 64,000 attended high school. Approximately 94.2% of the students were white, 1.4% were black, 2.4% were Hispanic, 1.7% were Asian/Pacific Islander, and 0.3% were American Indian/Alaskan Native. Total enrollment was estimated at 205,000 in fall 2003 but expected to be 193,000 by fall 2014, a decline of 7.1% during the period 2002–14. Expenditures for public education in 2003/04 were estimated at $2.1 billion. In fall 2003 there were 23,692 students enrolled in 165 private schools. Since 1969, the National Assessment of Educational Progress (NAEP) has tested public school students nationwide. The resulting report, *The Nation's Report Card,* stated that in 2005 eighth graders in New Hampshire scored 285 out of 500 in mathematics compared with the national average of 278.

As of fall 2002, there were 68,523 students enrolled in college or graduate school; minority students comprised 7.2% of total postsecondary enrollment. In 2005, New Hampshire had 25 degree-granting institutions. The best-known institution of higher education is Dartmouth College, which originated in Connecticut in 1754 as Moor's Indian Charity School and was established at Hanover in 1769. When the state of New Hampshire attempted to amend Dartmouth's charter to make the institution public in the early 19th century, the US Supreme Court handed down a precedent-setting ruling prohibiting state violation of contract rights. The University of New Hampshire, the leading public institution, was founded at Hanover in 1866 and relocated at Durham in 1891. The university also has a campus in Manchester. Other colleges include Franklin Pierce College, Keene State College, and Southern New Hampshire University.

42 ARTS

The New Hampshire State Council on the Arts was established in 1965 with the mission of making the arts more prevalent in the community and education. In 2005, the New Hampshire State Council on the Arts and other New Hampshire arts organizations received 7 grants totaling $682,100 from the National Endowment for the Arts. State and private sources also contributed substantial funding to the state's arts programs.

As of 2006, the New Hampshire Humanities Council sponsored a number of ongoing programs including What Is New Hampshire Reading?, a statewide reading and discussion program; a Literature and Medicine series that hosts discussions on what matters in health care and why, and an annual summer Chautauqua. In 2005, the National Endowment for the Humanities contributed $743,861 to eight state programs.

Hopkins Center at Dartmouth College features musical events throughout the year. Ballet groups include Ballet New England in Portsmouth, City Center Ballet in Lebanon, and Petit Papillon in Concord. Opera groups include the Granite State Opera in Temple, and Opera North in Hanover. Classical music groups include the Nashua Chamber Orchestra, the Nashua Symphony Orchestra, the Granite State Symphony in Concord, the New England Wind Ensemble in Franklin, and the New Hampshire Philharmonic Orchestra and New Hampshire Symphony Orchestra (both in Manchester). The Lakes Region Symphony Orchestra based in Meredith, celebrated its 30th anniversary during the 2005/06 season.

The New Hampshire Music Festival in Center Harbor serves as a year-round educational institute and performing arts center and sponsors an annual summer festival featuring the New Hampshire Music Festival Orchestra. The festival began in 1952 and as of 2006 it hosted more than 160 events per year, over 50 presented during the summer festival. Monadnock Music in Peterborough is an organization sponsoring a variety of musical programs, including "Lend an Ear!"—a program geared towards educating young people, primarily elementary school children, about chamber music. This program in particular served over 1600 students from 18 different schools during the 2004/05 school year.

Patricia Fargnoli, of Walpole, New Hampshire was named the state's poet laureate for the January 2006–March 2009 term. She has published works that include *Necessary Light* and *Duties of the Spirit* (2005) and has won several awards such as the May Swenson Poetry Prize and the Jane Kenyon Poetry Book Award. The artist laureate as of 2006 was James Aponovich, an internationally acclaimed still life painter and teacher at the New Hampshire Institute of Art.

Principal galleries include the Currier Gallery of Art in Manchester, the University Art Gallery at the University of New Hampshire in Durham, Hood Museum—the Dartmouth College Art Museum at Hanover, and the Lamont Gallery at Phillips Exeter Academy in Exeter.

43 LIBRARIES AND MUSEUMS

As of December 2001, New Hampshire had 229 public library systems, with a total of 238 libraries, of which there were nine branches. The system, that same year, had a total book and serial publication stock of 5,572,000 volumes and a total combined circulation of 8,647,000. The system also had 172,000 audio and 158,000 video items, 18,000 electronic format items (CD-ROMs, magnetic tapes, and disks), and two bookmobiles. Leading academic and historical collections include Dartmouth College's Baker Memorial Library in Hanover (2,309,626 volumes); the New Hampshire State Library (519,319) and New Hampshire Historical Society Library (50,000), both in Concord; and the University of New Hampshire's Ezekiel W. Diamond Library (1,151,203) in Durham. In fiscal year 2001, operating income for the state's public library system was $35,575,000 and included $$50,000 in federal grants and $35,000 in state grants.

Among the more than 76 museums and historic sites are the Museum of New Hampshire History in Concord and the Franklin Pierce Homestead in Hillsboro.

44 COMMUNICATIONS

In 2004, 96.4% of New Hampshire's occupied housing units had telephones. Additionally, by June of that same year there were 686,746 mobile wireless telephone subscribers. In 2003, 71.5% of New Hampshire households had a computer and 65.2% had Internet access. By June 2005, there were 238,502 high-speed lines in New Hampshire, 223,102 residential and 15,400 for business. In 2005, the state had 32 major radio stations (7 AM, 25 FM), and 5 television stations. State residents also receive broadcasts from neighboring Massachusetts, Vermont, and Maine. A total of 38,887 Internet domain names were registered in the state in 2000.

45 PRESS

In 2005, New Hampshire had eight morning newspapers, four evening newspapers, and eight Sunday papers. The best-known newspaper in the state is Manchester's *The Union Leader* (59,384 daily and 81,144 Sunday), published by conservative William Loeb until his death in 1981. In the capital, the *Concord Monitor* circulates 20,107 papers daily and 22,747 on Sundays. The Dover *Foster's Daily Democrat* has a circulation of 22,720 for its weekday evening edition and 27,728 for the Sunday edition. The Nashua *Telegraph* has a circulation of 25,566 daily and 32,672 Sundays.

46 ORGANIZATIONS

In 2006, there were over 2,015 nonprofit organizations registered within the state, of which about 1,469 were registered as charitable, educational, or religious organizations. National organizations with headquarters in New Hampshire include the Student Conservation Association (Charlestown), Interhostel (Durham), the International Association of Reiki Professionals (Nashua), and the Academy of Applied Science (Concord). The regional Atlantic Offshore Lobstermen's Association is based in Bedford. The New Hampshire Historical Society us based in Concord. There are a number of municipal and county historical societies.

47 TOURISM, TRAVEL, AND RECREATION

Tourism is a major part of the economy of New Hampshire. It has been estimated that the industry brings in revenues of $8.6 billion per year and sponsors over 65,000 jobs.

Skiing, camping, hiking, and boating are the main outdoor attractions. Other attractions include Strawberry Banke, a restored village in Portsmouth; Daniel Webster's birthplace near Franklin; and the Mt. Washington Cog Railway. Merrimack Valley is the most visited area, generating 36% of all tourism revenue. There are over 72 state parks and recreation areas. Many tourists come to New Hampshire for skiing. One of the most famous natural attractions, "The Old Man on the Mountain," collapsed in May 2003. Motorsports enthusiasts can visit the New Hampshire Speedway. In 2006, Squam Lake celebrated the 25th anniversary of the filming of the feature film, *On Golden Pond*.

48 SPORTS

There are no major professional sports teams in New Hampshire, although there are minor league baseball teams in Nashua and Manchester. Major national and international skiing events are frequently held in the state, as are such other winter competitions as snowmobile races and the Annual World Championship Sled Dog Derby in Laconia. Thoroughbred, harness, and greyhound racing are the warm-weather spectator sports. The annual Whaleback Yacht Race is held in early August.

Dartmouth College competes in the Ivy League, and the University of New Hampshire belongs to the America East Conference, both Division I-AA Conferences.

The New Hampshire International Speedway, which opened in Loudon in 1994, plays host to a NASCAR Busch Series and Nextel Cup races in July and September.

49 FAMOUS NEW HAMPSHIRITES

Born in Hillsboro, Franklin Pierce (1804–69), the nation's 14th president, serving from 1853 to 1857, was the only US chief executive to come from New Hampshire. Henry Wilson (Jeremiah Jones Colbath, 1812–75), US vice president from 1873 to 1875, was a native of Farmington.

US Supreme Court chief justices Salmon P. Chase (1808–73), Harlan Fiske Stone (1872–1946), and David Souter (b.1939) were New Hampshirites, and Levi Woodbury (1789–1851) was a distinguished associate justice. John Langdon (1741–1819) was the first president pro tempore of the US Senate; two other US senators from New Hampshire, George Higgins Moses (b.Maine, 1869–1944) and Henry Styles Bridges (b.Maine, 1898–1961), also held this position. US cabinet members from New Hampshire included Henry Dearborn (1751–1829), secretary of war; Daniel Webster (1782–1852), secretary of state; and William E. Chandler (1835–1917), secretary of the Navy. Other political leaders of note were Benning Wentworth (1696–1770), royal governor Meshech Weare (1713–86), the state's leader during the American Revolution; Josiah Bartlett (b.Massachusetts, 1729–95), a physician, governor, and signer of the Declaration of Independence; Isaac Hill (b.Massachusetts, 1789–1851), a publisher, governor, and US senator; and John Parker Hale (1806–73), senator, antislavery agitator, minister to Spain, and presidential candidate of the Free Soil Party. John Sununu, a former Governor of New Hampshire (b.1939, Cuba) was chief of staff during the Bush administration.

Military leaders associated with New Hampshire during the colonial and Revolutionary periods include John Stark (1728–1822), Robert Rogers (b.Massachusetts, 1731–95), and John Sullivan (1710–95). Among other figures of note are educator Eleazar Wheelock (b.Connecticut, 1711–79), the founder of Dartmouth College; physicians Lyman Spaulding (1775–1821), Reuben D. Mussey (1780–1866), and Amos Twitchell (1781–1850), as well as Samuel Thomson (1769–1843), a leading advocate of herbal medicine; religious leaders Hosea Ballou (1771–1852), his grand-nephew of the same name (1796–1861), and Mary Baker Eddy (1821–1910), founder of Christian Science; George Whipple (1878–1976), winner of the 1934 Nobel Prize for physiology or medicine; and labor organizer and US Communist Party leader Elizabeth Gurley Flynn (1890–1964).

Sarah Josepha Hale (1788–1879), Horace Greeley (1811–72), Charles Dana (1819–97), Thomas Bailey Aldrich (1836–1907), Bradford Torrey (b.Massachusetts, 1843–1912), Alice Brown (1857–1948), and J(erome) D(avid) Salinger (b.New York, 1919) are among the writers and editors who have lived in New Hampshire, along with poets Edna Dean Proctor (1829–1923), Celia Laighton Thaxter (1826–94), Edward Arlington Robinson (b.Maine, 1869–1935), and Robert Frost (b.California, 1874–1963), one of whose poetry volumes is entitled *New Hampshire* (1923). Painter Benjamin Champney (1817–1907) and sculptor Daniel Chester French (1850–1931) were born in New Hampshire, while Augustus Saint-Gaudens (b.Ireland, 1848–1907) created much of his sculpture in the state.

Vaudevillian Will Cressey (1863–1930) was a New Hampshire man. More recent celebrities include newspaper publisher William Loeb (b.New York, 1905–81) and astronaut Alan B. Shepard Jr. (1923–98).

50 BIBLIOGRAPHY

Casanave, Suki. *Natural Wonders of New Hampshire: Exploring Wild and Scenic Places.* Lincolnwood, Ill.: Country Roads Press, 1998.

Council of State Governments. *The Book of the States, 2006 Edition.* Lexington, Ky.: Council of State Governments, 2006.

Dubois, Muriel L. *New Hampshire Facts and Symbols.* Mankato, Minn.: Hilltop Books, 2000.

Lawson, Russell M. *New Hampshire.* New York: Interlink Books, 2006.

Mobil Travel Guide. *New England, 2004: Connecticut, Maine, Massachusetts, New Hampshire, Rhode Island, Vermont.* Guilford, Conn.: Globe Pequot, 2003.

Sletcher, Michael (ed.). *New England.* Vol. 4 in *The Greenwood Encyclopedia of American Regional Cultures.* Westport, Conn.: Greenwood Press, 2004.

US Department of Commerce, Economics and Statistics Administration, US Census Bureau. *New Hampshire, 2000. Summary Social, Economic, and Housing Characteristics: 2000 Census of Population and Housing.* Washington, D.C.: US Government Printing Office, 2003.

NEW JERSEY

State of New Jersey

ORIGIN OF STATE NAME: Named for the British Channel Island of Jersey. **NICKNAME:** The Garden State. **CAPITAL:** Trenton. **ENTERED UNION:** 18 December 1787 (3rd). **SONG:** "I'm from New Jersey" (unofficial). **MOTTO:** Liberty and Prosperity. **COAT OF ARMS:** In the center is a shield with three plows, symbolic of agriculture. A helmet above indicates sovereignty, and a horse's head atop the helmet signifies speed and prosperity. The state motto and the date "1776" are displayed on a banner below. **FLAG:** The coat of arms on a buff field. **OFFICIAL SEAL:** The coat of arms surrounded by the words "The Great Seal of the State of New Jersey." **BIRD:** Eastern goldfinch. **FLOWER:** Violet. **TREE:** Red oak; dogwood (memorial tree). **LEGAL HOLIDAYS:** New Year's Day, 1 January; Birthday of Martin Luther King Jr. 3rd Monday in January; Lincoln's Birthday, 12 February (sometimes observed on a Friday or Monday closest to this date); Washington's Birthday, 3rd Monday in February; Good Friday, Friday before Easter, March or April; Memorial Day, last Monday in May; Independence Day, 4 July; Labor Day, 1st Monday in September; Columbus Day, 2nd Monday in October; Election Day, 1st Tuesday after 1st Monday in November; Veterans' Day, 11 November; Thanksgiving Day, 4th Thursday in November; Christmas Day, 25 December. **TIME:** 7 AM EST = noon GMT.

[1] LOCATION, SIZE, AND EXTENT

Situated in the northeastern United States, New Jersey is the smallest of the Middle Atlantic states and ranks 46th among the 50 states.

The total area of New Jersey is 7,787 sq mi (20,168 sq km), of which 7,468 sq mi (19,342 sq km) constitute land and 319 sq mi (826 sq km) are inland water. New Jersey extends 166 mi (267 km) N–S; the extreme width E–W is 57 mi (92 km).

New Jersey is bordered on the N and NE by New York State (with the boundary formed partly by the Hudson River, New York Bay, and Arthur Kill, and passing through Raritan Bay); on the E by the Atlantic Ocean; on the S and SW by Delaware (with the line passing through Delaware Bay); and on the W by Pennsylvania (separated by the Delaware River). Numerous barrier islands lie off the Atlantic coast.

New Jersey's total boundary length is 480 mi (773 km), including a general coastline of 130 mi (209 km); the tidal shoreline is 1,792 mi (2,884 km). The state's geographic center is in Mercer County, near Trenton.

[2] TOPOGRAPHY

Although small, New Jersey has considerable topographic variety. In the extreme northwest corner of the state are the Appalachian Valley and the Kittatinny Ridge and Valley. This area contains High Point, the state's peak elevation, at 1,803 ft (550 m) above sea level. To the east and south is the highlands region, an area of many natural lakes and steep ridges, including the Ramapo Mountains, part of the Appalachian chain. East of the highlands is a flat area broken by the high ridges of the Watchungs and Sourlands and—most spectacularly—by the Palisades, a column of traprock rising some 500 ft (150 m) above the Hudson River. The mean elevation of the state is approximately 250 ft (76 m). T

he Atlantic Coastal Plain, a flat area with swamps and sandy beaches, claims the remaining two-thirds of the state. Its most notable feature is the Pine Barrens, 760 sq mi (1,968 sq km) of pitch pines and white oaks. Sandy Hook, a peninsula more than 5 mi (8 km) long, extending northward into the Atlantic from Monmouth County, is part of the Gateway National Recreation Area. Sea level at the Atlantic Ocean is the lowest elevation in the state.

Major rivers include the Delaware, forming the border with Pennsylvania, and the Passaic, Hackensack, and Raritan. The largest natural lake is Lake Hopatcong, about 8 mi (13 km) long. Some 550 to 600 million years ago, New Jersey's topography was the opposite of what it is now, with mountains to the east and a shallow sea to the west. Volcanic eruptions about 225 million years ago caused these eastern mountains to sink and new peaks to rise in the northwest; the lava flow formed the Watchung Mountains and the Palisades. The shoreline settled into its present shape at least 10,000 years ago.

[3] CLIMATE

Bounded by the Atlantic Ocean and the Delaware River, most of New Jersey has a moderate climate with cold winters and warm, humid summers. Winter temperatures are slightly colder and summer temperatures slightly milder in the northwestern hills than in the rest of the state.

In Atlantic City, the yearly average temperature is 54°F (12°C), ranging from 32°F (0°C) in January to 75°F (23°C) in July. Precipitation is plentiful, averaging 46 in (117 cm) annually; snowfall totals about 16 in (41 cm). At Atlantic City, annual precipitation is about 40.3 cm (102 cm). The annual average humidity is 81% at 7 AM, reaching a normal high of 87% in September.

Statewide, the record high temperature is 110°F (43°C), set in Runyon on 10 July 1936; the record low is -34°F (-37°C), set in River Vale on 5 January 1904. A 29.7-in. (75.4-cm) accumulation on Long Beach Island in 1947 was the greatest 24-hour snowfall in the state's recorded history. Occasional hurricanes and violent spring storms have damaged beachfront property over the years, and floods along northern New Jersey rivers especially in the Passaic River basin, are not uncommon. A serious drought occurs, on average, about once every 15 years.

4 FLORA AND FAUNA

Although highly urbanized, New Jersey still provides a diversity of natural regions, including a shady coastal zone, the hilly and wooded Allegheny zone, and the Pine Barrens in the south. Birch, beech, hickory, and elm all grow in the state, along with black locust, red maple, and 20 varieties of oak; common shrubs include the spicebush, staggerbush, and mountain laurel. Vast stretches beneath pine trees are covered with pyxie, a small creeping evergreen shrub. Common wild flowers include meadow rue, butterflyweed, black-eyed Susan, and the ubiquitous eastern (common) dandelion. Among rare plants are Candy's lobelia, floating heart, and pennywort. Six plant species were listed as threatened or endangered in 2006, including the American chaffseed and small whorled pogonia.

Among mammals indigenous to New Jersey are the white-tailed deer, black bear, gray and red foxes, raccoon, woodchuck, opossum, striped skunk, eastern gray squirrel, eastern chipmunk, and common cottontail. The herring gull, sandpiper, and little green and night herons are common shore birds, while the red-eyed vireo, hermit thrush, English sparrow, robin, cardinal, and Baltimore oriole are frequently sighted inland. The Edwin B. Forsythe National Wildlife Refuge, a Ramsar Wetland of International Importance, serves as an important breeding and wintering site for over 70,000 birds each year. The site also supports 38 mammal species, 8 amphibian species, and 11 types of reptiles.

Anglers in the state prize the northern pike, chain pickerel, and various species of bass, trout, and perch. Declining or rare animals include the whippoorwill, hooded warbler, eastern hognose snake, northern red salamander, and northern kingfish. Sixteen animal species (vertebrates and invertebrates) were listed by the US Fish and Wildlife Service as threatened or endangered in April 2006, including four species of turtle, the Indiana bat, bald eagle, shortnose sturgeon, roseate tern, and three species of whale.

5 ENVIRONMENTAL PROTECTION

Laws and policies regulating the management and protection of New Jersey's environment and natural resources are administered by the Department of Environmental Protection (DEP). The state devoted 1.4% of its total budget appropriations, or $225.1 million, to environmental protection in 1996–97.

The proximity of the populace to industrial plants and to the state's expansive highway system makes air pollution control a special concern in the state. New Jersey had one of the most comprehensive air pollution control programs in the United States, maintaining a network of 105 air pollution monitoring stations, as well as 60 stations that monitor just for particulates and 10 that monitor for radiation. New Jersey was the first state to begin a statewide search for sites contaminated by dioxin, a toxic by-product in the manufacture of herbicides.

The DEP reported that a 1984 review of water quality in the state showed that water quality degradation had been halted and that the quality of streams had been stabilized or improved. The

greatest improvements had been made in certain bays and estuaries along the Atlantic coast, where the elimination of discharges from older municipal sewage treatment plants resulted in the reopening of shellfish-harvesting grounds for the first time in 20 years. However, some rivers in highly urbanized areas were still severely polluted.

Approximately 1,500 treatment facilities discharge waste water into New Jersey's surface and groundwaters. Nearly 80% of these facilities comply with the requirements of federal and state clean water laws. Solid waste disposal in New Jersey became critical as major landfills reached capacity. In 1977, the state had more than 300 operating landfills; in 1991 there were about 50 landfills. The state's solid waste stream is 1,100 tons per capita. Some counties and municipalities were implementing recycling programs in 1985, and the state legislature was considering a bill to make recycling mandatory. By the mid-1990s the state of New Jersey had about 30 curbside recycling programs.

New Jersey's toxic waste cleanup program is among the most serious in the United States. In 2003, 23.1 million lb of toxic chemicals were released in the state. In 2003, New Jersey had 551 hazardous waste sites listed in the US Environment Protection Agency (EPA) database, 113 of which were on the National Priorities List as of 2006, including the Federal Aviation Administration Technical Center, the Middlesex Sampling Plant (of the US Department of Energy), and the US Radium Corp., as well as several farm sites. In 2004, New Jersey ranked first in the nation for the highest number of sites on the National Priorities List. In 2005, the EPA spent over $85 million through the Superfund program for the cleanup of hazardous waste sites in the state. The same year, federal EPA grants awarded to the state included $44 million for the clean water state revolving fund and $19 million for the drinking water revolving fund.

The New Jersey Spill Compensation Fund was established by the state legislature in 1977 and amended in 1980. A tax based on the transfer of hazardous substances and petroleum products is paid into the fund and used for the cleanup of spills.

New Jersey first acquired land for preservation purposes in 1907. Since 1961, the state has bought more than 240,000 acres (97,000 hectares) under a "Green Acres" program for conservation and recreation. In 1984, an $83-million Green Trust Fund was established to expand land acquisition. The Green Acres Program has assisted county and municipal governments in acquiring over 70,000 acres (28,000 hectares). Additionally, Green Acres is assisting nonprofit conservation groups in acquiring over 20,000 acres (8,000 hectares) in a 50% matching grant program established in 1989. The US Congress designated 1.1 million acres (445,000 hectares) in the southern part of the state as the Pinelands National Reserve in 1978. Since then, the state has purchased more than 60,000 acres (24,000 hectares) in the region, bringing the state open-space holding in the Pinelands to more than 270,000 acres (109,000 hectares). As of 1 July 1993, there were approximately 790,000 acres (319,000 hectares) of preserved public open space and recreation land in New Jersey.

There are about 916,000 acres (370,692 hectares) of wetlands in the state. The Edwin B. Forsythe National Wildlife Refuge on the Atlantic coast was established in 1984 through the merger of the Brigantine and Barnegat National Wildlife Refuges. The site was designated as a Ramsar Wetland of International Importance in

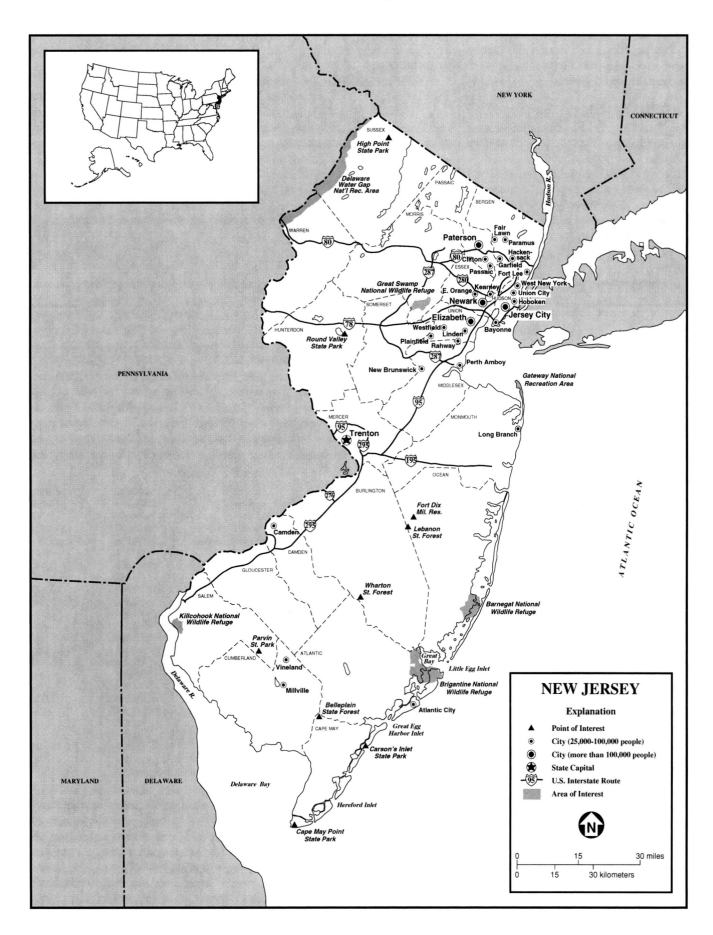

High Point State Park

Delaware Water Gap Nat'l Rec. Area

SUSSEX

PASSAIC

MORRIS

BERGEN

WARREN

NEW YORK

CONNECTICUT

Hudson R.

Fair Lawn

Paterson

Paramus

Hacken-sack

Clifton

Garfield

Passaic

Fort Lee

West New York

Great Swamp National Wildlife Refuge

E. Orange

Kearney

Union City

ESSEX

Hoboken

Newark

HUDSON

Jersey City

UNION

Elizabeth

Westfield

Bayonne

Plainfield

Linden

Rahway

SOMERSET

HUNTERDON

Round Valley State Park

New Brunswick

Perth Amboy

Gateway National Recreation Area

MIDDLESEX

PENNSYLVANIA

MERCER

MONMOUTH

Trenton

Long Branch

OCEAN

BURLINGTON

Fort Dix Mil. Res.

Lebanon St. Forest

Camden

CAMDEN

GLOUCESTER

Wharton St. Forest

Barnegat National Wildlife Refuge

SALEM

Killcohook National Wildlife Refuge

Parvin St. Park

CUMBERLAND

ATLANTIC

Vineland

Great Bay

Little Egg Inlet

Millville

Brigantine National Wildlife Refuge

Belleplain State Forest

Atlantic City

Delaware R.

CAPE MAY

Great Egg Harbor Inlet

Carson's Inlet State Park

MARYLAND

DELAWARE

Delaware Bay

Hereford Inlet

Cape May Point State Park

ATLANTIC OCEAN

NEW JERSEY

Explanation

▲ Point of Interest

◉ City (25,000–100,000 people)

◉ City (more than 100,000 people)

✪ State Capital

⬡95 U.S. Interstate Route

▨ Area of Interest

N

| 0 | 15 | 30 miles |
| 0 | 15 | 30 kilometers |

1986, primarily for its role as a habitat for breeding and wintering waterbirds. Part of the Delaware Bay Estuary wetlands lie within New Jersey, but jurisdiction of this Ramsar site (designated 1992) lies with the state of Delaware.

6 POPULATION

New Jersey ranked 10th in population in the United States with an estimated total of 8,717,925 in 2005, an increase of 3.6% since 2000. Between 1990 and 2000, New Jersey's population grew from 7,730,188 to 8,414,350, an increase of 8.9%. In 2004, New Jersey had the highest population density among the 50 states: 1,175.60 persons per sq mi. The population is projected to reach 9.2 million by 2015 and 9.6 million by 2025.

In 2004, the median age was 37.8. Persons under 18 years old accounted for 24.8% of the population while 12.9% was age 65 or older.

Sparsely populated at the time of the Revolutionary War, New Jersey did not pass the one million mark until the 1880 census. Most of the state's subsequent growth came through migration, especially from New York during the period after 1950 when the New Jersey population stood at 4,835,329. The most significant population growth came in older cities in northern New Jersey and in commuter towns near New York and Philadelphia. The average annual population growth declined from 2.3% in the 1950s to 1.7% in the 1960s, and the state actually experienced a net loss from migration of 275,000 during the 1970s. Total growth rose to 5% during the 1980s.

New Jersey's major population centers, with estimated 2004 population figures, are Newark, 280,451; Jersey City, 239,079; Paterson, 150,869; and Elizabeth, 124,724.

7 ETHNIC GROUPS

New Jersey is one of the most ethnically heterogeneous states. As of 2000, 1,476,327 New Jerseyites (17.5% of the state's population) were of foreign birth. The leading countries of origin were Italy, 7.3%; Cuba, 6.5%; India, 5.4%; and Germany, 4.4%. As of 2001, New Jersey had the third-highest percentage of foreign-born residents among the 50 states, surpassed only by California and New York.

Blacks first came to New Jersey as slaves in the 1600s; the state abolished slavery in 1804, one of the last of the northern states to do so. Today black people constitute the state's largest (13.6%) ethnic minority, 1,141,821 as of 2000. Newark elected its first black mayor, Kenneth Gibson, in 1970, three years after the city was torn by racial disorders that killed 26 people and injured some 1,500 others. In 2004, 14.5% of the state's population was black.

The estimated Hispanic and Latino population in 2000 was 1,117,191 (up from 868,000 in 1996), or 13.3% of the total. The Puerto Rican population, which increased from 55,361 in 1960 to 366,788 in 2000, lived mostly in Newark, Jersey City, Elizabeth, Paterson, and Passaic. There were 77,337 Cubans in 2000, many of them in Union City and Elizabeth; their numbers were augmented by the migration of Cuban refugees in 1980. Smaller Spanish-speaking groups included Colombians and Dominicans. In 2004, 14.9% of the state's population was Hispanic or Latino.

The estimated number of Asians living in New Jersey in 2000 was 480,276, the fifth-largest total among the 50 states. Pacific Islanders numbered 273,000. The largest group of Asians reported was from India (169,180 in 2000, up from 54,039 in 1990); there were 85,245 Filipinos, 100,355 Chinese (more than double the 1990 figure of 47,068), 65,349 Koreans, and 14,672 Japanese. In 2004, 7% of the state's population was Asian.

The state's total Native American population, including Eskimos and Aleuts, numbered 19,492 in 2000. Among the state's American Indians is a group claiming to be descended from Dutch settlers, black slaves, British and German soldiers, and Leni-Lenape and Tuscarora Indians; incorporated as the Ramapough Mountain Indians in 1978, they live in the Ramapo hills near Ringwood and Mahwah. In 2004, 0.3% of the state's population was American Indian.

In 2004, 1.2% of the state's population reported origin of two or more races.

8 LANGUAGES

European settlers found New Jersey inhabited largely by the Leni-Lenape Indians, whose legacy can still be found in such place-names as Passaic, Totowa, Hopatcong, Kittatinny, and Piscataway.

In 2000, 5,854,578 New Jerseyites—74.5% of the resident population five years old or older—spoke only English at home, down from 80.5% in 1990.

The following table gives selected statistics from the 2000 Census for language spoken at home by persons five years old and over. The category "Other Asian languages" includes Dravidian languages, Malayalam, Telugu, Tamil, and Turkish. The category "Other Indic languages" includes Bengali, Marathi, Punjabi, and Romany. The category "African languages" includes Amharic, Ibo, Twi, Yoruba, Bantu, Swahili, and Somali.

LANGUAGE	NUMBER	PERCENT
Population 5 years and over	**7,856,268**	**100.0**
Speak only English	5,854,578	74.5
Speak a language other than English	2,001,690	25.5
Speak a language other than English	**2,001,690**	**25.5**
Spanish or Spanish Creole	967,741	12.3
Italian	116,365	1.5
Chinese	84,345	1.1
Polish	74,663	1.0
Portuguese or Portuguese Creole	72,870	0.9
Tagalog	66,851	0.9
Korean	55,340	0.7
Gujarathi	47,324	0.6
French (incl. Patois, Cajun)	47,225	0.6
Arabic	47,052	0.6
German	41,025	0.5
Russian	38,566	0.5
Other Asian languages	36,573	0.5
Other Indic languages	35,718	0.5
Hindi	31,395	0.4
French Creole	28,783	0.4
Greek	26,566	0.3
African languages	21,514	0.3

English in New Jersey is rather evenly divided north and south between Northern and Midland dialects. Special characteristics of some New York metropolitan area speech occur in the northeast portion, such as the absence of /r/ after a vowel, a consonant like /d/ or /t/ instead of the /th/ sounds in *this* or *thin,* and pronunciations as *coop* rhyming with *stoop, food* with *good,* and *goal* and *fool; faucet* has the vowel of *father.* Dominant in the southern half are *run* (small stream), *baby coach* (baby carriage) in the Philadelphia trading area, *winnering owl* (screech owl), and *eel worm* (earthworm). Heard also are *out* as /aot/, *muskmelon* as /muskmillon/, and *keg* rhyming with *bag*, *scarce* with *fierce*, *spook* with *book*, and *haunted* with *panted*.

⁹RELIGIONS

With a history of religious tolerance, New Jersey has welcomed many denominations to its shores. Dutch immigrants founded a Reformed Church in 1662, the first in the state. After the English took control, Puritans came from New England and Long Island, Congregationalists from Connecticut, and Baptists from Rhode Island. Quaker settlements in Shrewsbury and western New Jersey during the early 1670s predated the better-known Quaker colony in Pennsylvania. Episcopalians, Presbyterians, German Lutherans, and Methodists arrived during the 18th century. The state's first synagogue was established in 1848, in Newark.

About the only religion not tolerated by New Jerseyites was Catholicism; the first Catholic parish was not organized until 1814 and laws excluding Catholics from holding office were on the books until 1844. The Catholic numbers swelled as a result of Irish immigration after 1845, and even more with the arrival of Italians after 1880. Today, Roman Catholics constitute the state's single largest religious group. Passaic is the headquarters of the Byzantine-Ruthenian Rite in the Byzantine Catholic Church.

In 2004, the number of Roman Catholics within the state was at about 3,479,158. The next largest group is Jewish, with about 468,000 members in 2000. The largest Protestant denomination (with 2000 data) is the United Methodist Church, with 140,133 adherents, followed by the Presbyterian Church USA, with 119,735; the Episcopal Church, 91,964; and the Evangelical Lutheran Church in America, 79,264. There were about 120,724 Muslims in the state. Nearly 3.5 million people (about 42.3% of the population) were not counted as members of any religious organization.

American Atheists, a national organization founded by Madalyn Murray O'Hair in 1958, is based in Parsippany.

¹⁰TRANSPORTATION

Ever since the first traders sought the fastest way to get from New York to Philadelphia, transportation has been of central importance to New Jersey and has greatly shaped its growth. In the mid-1820s, Hoboken engineer John Stevens built the first steam locomotive operated in the United States. Over the protests of the dominant stagecoach operators, his son Robert obtained a charter in 1830 for the Camden and Amboy Railroad. The line opened in 1834, and six years later it held a monopoly on the lucrative New York–Philadelphia run. Other lines, such as the Elizabeth and Somerville, the Morris and Essex, the Paterson and Hudson, and the Jersey Central, were limited to shorter runs, largely because the Camden and Amboy's influence with the legislature gave it a huge competitive advantage. Camden and Amboy stock was leased to the Pennsylvania Railroad in 1871, and the ensuing controversy over whether New Jersey transit should be entrusted to an "alien" company led to the passage of a law opening up the state to rail competition. Industry grew around the rail lines, and the railroads became a vital link in the shipment of products from New York and northern New Jersey.

As of 2003, the major freight operations were run by CSX and Northfolk Southern. In that same year, there were 2,798 route mi (4,504 km) of track in the state, of which 1,581 mi (2,545 km) was

Class I track. In addition, there were one regional, one Canadian, six local, and six switching and terminal railroads operating in the state. As of 2006, daily Amtrak service linked Newark, Trenton, and four other New Jersey cities along the main eastern rail corridor. But the bulk of interstate passenger traffic consists of commuters to New York and Philadelphia on trains operated by the Port Authority of New York and New Jersey (PA) and the Port Authority Transit Corp. (PATCO), a subsidiary of the Delaware River Port Authority.

The New Jersey Transit Corporation, called NJ TRANSIT, is a public corporation created under the Public Transportation Act of 1979. The corporation is charged with coordinating and improving bus and rail services throughout the state. It is the nation's third largest pubic transit agency, providing 223 million passenger trips annually. It operates 711 daily trains on 11 rail lines, and 2,027 buses on 236 routes throughout the state. It also owns and operates the Newark City Subway, a 4.3-mile light rail system providing service through downtown Newark.

Although associated more with the West, the first stagecoach service began in New Jersey, as part of a New York–Philadelphia trek that took some five days in 1723. For a time, colonial law required towns along the way to provide taverns for the passengers, and it was not uncommon for coach operators who were also tavern owners to find some way to prolong the journey an extra night. They traveled on roads that were barely more passable than the Leni-Lenape trails from which they originated. Improvement was slow, but by 1828, the legislature had granted 54 turnpike charters.

Road building has continued ever since. In 2004, there were 38,122 mi (61,376 km) of public roads in the state. The major highways are the New Jersey Turnpike, opened in 1952 and extending 133 mi (214 km) between Bergen and Salem counties, and the Garden State Parkway, completed in 1955 and stretching 173 mi (278 km) from the New York State line to Cape May. There were some 6.218 million registered vehicles in the state in 2004, including about 3.974 million automobiles, approximately 2.076 million trucks of all types, and around 19,000 buses. There were 5,799,532 licensed New Jersey drivers in that same year.

Many bridges and tunnels link New Jersey with New York State, Pennsylvania, and Delaware. Twenty-seven bridges cross the Delaware River, connecting New Jersey with Pennsylvania and Delaware.

At the gateway to New York Harbor, ports at Elizabeth and Newark have overtaken New York City ports in cargo volume, and contribute greatly to the local economy. Operated by the Port Authority of New York and New Jersey, Port Newark has almost 4 mi (6.4 km) of berthing space along Newark Bay, while nearby Port Elizabeth, with better than 3 mi (4.8 km) of berths, is a major handler of containerized cargo. In 2004, ports under the jurisdiction of the Port Authority of New York and New Jersey handled 152.377 million tons of cargo. Private piers in Jersey City and Bayonne handle both containerized and bulk cargoes. The tonnage handled by northern New Jersey port facilities, taken as a whole, make it the largest port on the east coast, and second largest overall in the United States. The Ports of Philadelphia and Camden, Inc., headquartered in Philadelphia, operate facilities along the Delaware River, including the Beckett Street and Broadway Terminals in Camden, that were formerly operated by the South Jersey Port Corporation. The port facility at Paulsboro is the most active in the state, with 30.485 million tons of cargo handled in 2004. The port of Camden-Gloucester handled 7.189 million tons that same year. New Jersey in 2004 had 360 mi (579 km) of navigable inland waterways. In 2003, waterborne shipments totaled 111.661 million tons.

In 2005, New Jersey had a total of 389 public and private-use aviation-related facilities. This included 119 airports, 256 heliports, and 13 seaplane bases. Newark Liberty International Airport is the state's busiest airport, with 15,827,675 passengers enplaned in 2004, making it the 12th-busiest airport in the United States.

11 HISTORY

The first known inhabitants of what is now New Jersey were the Leni-Lenape (meaning "Original People"), who arrived in the land between the Hudson and Delaware rivers about 6,000 years ago. Members of the Algonkian language group, the Leni-Lenape were an agricultural people supplementing their diet with freshwater fish and shellfish. The peace-loving Leni-Lenape believed in monogamy, educated their children in the simple skills needed for wilderness survival, and clung rigidly to a tradition that a pot of food must always be warm on the fire to welcome all strangers.

The first European explorer to reach New Jersey was Giovanni da Verrazano, who sailed into what is now Newark Bay in 1524. Henry Hudson, an English captain sailing under a Dutch flag, piloted the Half Moon along the New Jersey shore and into Sandy Hook Bay in the late summer of 1609, a voyage that established a Dutch claim to the New World. Hollanders came to trade in what is now Hudson County as early as 1618, and in 1660, they founded New Jersey's first town, called Bergen (now part of Jersey City). Meanwhile, across the state, Swedish settlers began moving east of the Delaware River in 1639. Their colony of New Sweden had only one brief spurt of glory, from 1643 to 1653, under Governor Johan Printz.

The Leni-Lenape lost out to the newcomers, whether Dutch, Swedish, or English, despite a series of treaties that the Europeans thought fair. State and local records describe these agreements: huge tracts of land exchanged for trinkets, guns, and alcohol. The guns and alcohol, combined with smallpox (another European import), doomed the "Original People." In 1758, when a treaty established an Indian reservation at Brotherton (now the town of Indian Mills), only a few hundred Indians remained.

England assumed control in March 1664, when King Charles II granted a region from the Connecticut River to the Delaware River to his brother James, the Duke of York. The duke, in turn, deeded the land between the Hudson and Delaware rivers, which he named New Jersey, to his court friends John Berkeley, 1st Baron Berkeley of Stratton, and Sir George Carteret, on 23 June 1664. Lord Berkeley and Sir George became proprietors, owning the land and having the right to govern its people. Subsequently, the land passed into the hands of two boards of proprietors in two provinces called East Jersey and West Jersey, with their capitals in Perth Amboy and Burlington, respectively. East Jersey was settled mainly by Puritans from Long Island and New England, West Jersey by Quakers from England. The split cost the colony dearly in 1702, when Queen Anne united East and West Jersey but placed them under New York rule. The colony did not get its own "home rule" until 1738, when Lewis Morris was named the first royal governor.

By this time, New Jersey's divided character was already established. Eastern New Jersey looked toward New York, western New Jersey toward Philadelphia. The level plain connecting those two major colonial towns made it certain that New Jersey would serve as a pathway. Along the makeshift roads that soon crossed the region—more roads than in any other colony—travelers brought conflicting news and ideas. During the American Revolution, the colony was about equally divided between Revolutionists and Loyalists. William Franklin (illegitimate son of Benjamin Franklin), royal governor from 1763 until 1776, strove valiantly to keep New Jersey sympathetic to England, but failed and was arrested. Throughout the Revolutionary period, he remained a leading Loyalist; after the war, he left for England.

Franklin's influence caused New Jersey to dally at first over independence, but in June 1776, the colony sent five new delegates to the Continental Congress—Abraham Clark, John Hart, Frances Hopkinson, Richard Stockton, and the Reverend John Witherspoon—all of whom voted for the Declaration of Independence. Two days before the Declaration was proclaimed, New Jersey adopted its first state constitution. William Livingston, a fiery anti-British propagandist, was the first elected governor of the state.

New Jersey played a pivotal role in the Revolutionary War, for the side that controlled both New York and Philadelphia would almost certainly win. George Washington and his battered troops made their winter headquarters in the state three times during the first four years of the war, twice in Morristown and once in Somerville. Five major battles were fought in New Jersey, the most important being the Battle of Trenton on 26 December 1776 and the Battle of Monmouth on 28 June 1778. At war's end, Princeton became the temporary capital of the United States from 26 June 1783 to 4 November 1783.

The state languished after the Revolution, with many of its pathway towns ravaged by the passing of competing armies, its trade dependent on New York City, and its ironworks (first established in 1676) shut down because of decreased demand. The state's leaders vigorously supported a federation of the 13 states, in which all states, regardless of size, would be represented equally in one national legislative body. This so-called New Jersey Plan led to the establishment of the US Senate.

Railroads and canals brought life to the state in the 1830s and set it on a course of urbanization and industrialization. The 90-mi (145-km) Morris Canal linked northern New Jersey with the coal fields of Pennsylvania. Considered one of the engineering marvels of the 19th century, the canal rose to 914 feet (279 meters) from sea level at Newark Bay to Lake Hopatcong, then fell 760 feet (232 meters) to a point on the Delaware River opposite Easton, Pa. Old iron mines beside the canal found markets, the dyeing and weaving mills of Paterson prospered, and Newark, most affected by the emerging industries, became the state's first incorporated city in 1836. Another canal, the Delaware and Raritan, crossed the relatively flat land from Bordentown, Trenton, and New Brunswick boomed. Princeton, whose leaders fought to keep the canal away from the town, settled into a long existence as a college community built around the College of New Jersey, founded in Elizabeth in 1746 and transferred to Princeton in 1756.

The canals were doomed by railroad competition almost from the start. The Morris Canal was insolvent long before World War I, and the Delaware Canal, although operative until 1934, went into a long, slow decline after the Civil War. The first railroad, from Bordentown to South Amboy, closely paralleled the Delaware and Raritan Canal and in 1871 became an important part of the Pennsylvania Railroad. The coal brought in on railroad cars freed industry from waterpower; factories sprang up wherever the rails went. The Hudson County waterfront, eastern terminus for most of the nation's railway systems, became the most important railroad area in the United States. Rail lines also carried vacationers to the Jersey shore, building an important source of income for the state.

The Civil War split New Jersey bitterly. Leaders in the Democratic Party opposed the war as a "Black Republican" affair. Prosperous industrialists in Newark and Trenton feared that their vigorous trade with the South would be impaired, Cape May innkeepers fretted about the loss of tourists from Virginia, and even Princeton students were divided. As late as the summer of 1863, after the Battle of Gettysburg, many state "peace Democrats" were urging the North to make peace with the Confederacy. Draft calls were vigorously opposed in 1863, yet the state sent its full quota of troops into service throughout the conflict. Most important, New Jersey factories poured forth streams of munitions and other equipment for the Union army. At war's end, political leaders stubbornly opposed the 13th, 14th, and 15th Amendments to the US Constitution, and blacks were not permitted to vote in the state until 1870.

During the last decades of the 19th century, New Jersey developed a reputation for factories capable of making the components necessary for thousands of other manufacturing enterprises. Few factories were large, although in 1873, Isaac M. Singer opened a huge sewing machine plant at Elizabeth that employed 3,000 persons. Oil refineries on the Hudson County waterfront had everexpanding payrolls, pottery firms in Trenton thrived, and Newark gained strength from many diversified manufacturers and also saw its insurance companies become nationally powerful.

Twentieth-century wars stimulated New Jersey's industries. During World War I, giant shipyards at Newark, Kearny, and Camden made New Jersey the nation's leading shipbuilding state. The Middlesex County area refined 75% of the nation's copper, and nearly 75% of US shells were loaded in the state. World War II revived the shipbuilding and munitions industries, while chemical and pharmaceutical manufacturing, spawned by the World War I cutoff of German chemicals, showed further growth during the second world conflict. Paterson, preeminent in locomotive building during the 19th century, became the nation's foremost airplane engine manufacturing center. Training and mobilization centers at Ft. Dix and Camp Kilmer moved millions of soldiers into the front lines.

The US Census Bureau termed New Jersey officially "urban" in 1880, when the state population rose above 1 million for the first time. Urbanization intensified throughout the 20th century and especially after World War II, as people left the old cities in New Jersey and other northeastern states to buy homes in developments on former farmlands. Places like Cherry Hill, Woodbridge, Clifton, and Middletown Township boomed after 1945, increasing their population as much as sixfold in the decades that followed.

New Jersey also experienced many of the problems of urbanization. Its cities have declined; traffic congestion is intense in the morning, when commuters stream into urban areas to work, and again in the evening, when they return home to what once was called "the country." That country now knows the problems of urban growth: increased needs for schools, sewers, police and fire protection, and road maintenance, along with rising taxes.

The state has not surrendered to its problems, however. In 1947, voters overwhelmingly approved a new state constitution, a terse, comprehensive document that streamlined state government, reformed the state's chaotic court system, and mandated equal rights for all. Governor Alfred E. Driscoll promptly integrated the New Jersey National Guard, despite strong federal objectives; integration of all US armed forces soon followed. After 1950 voters passed a wide variety of multi-million-dollar bond issues to establish or rebuild state colleges. Funds were allocated for the purchase and development of new park and forest lands. Large bond issues have financed the construction of highways, reservoirs, and rapid transit systems. In 2000, the state legislature approved the largest construction program in New Jersey history. Settling a long-running battle over how to rebuild the state's deteriorating and overcrowded schools, lawmakers agreed to spend $12 billion system-wide, with benefits to be seen in inner cities as well as in suburbs.

In the 1970s and early 1980s, New Jersey experienced a recession. The unemployment rate climbed to almost 10%. Over 270,000 people left the state. The state's cities were hit particularly hard, suffering both from the loss of manufacturing jobs and from a flight of retailing to suburban malls. The economy of New Jersey in these decades also underwent a dramatic restructuring. While the state lost over 200,000 manufacturing jobs it gained 670,000 jobs in service industries. The economy rebounded during the 1980s, but began to contract again at the end of the decade, declining further during the recession of early 1990s. In 1996 the state's unemployment rate fell below 6% for the first time in six years. By 1999 it had dropped to 4.6%. Observers credited the recovery of the 1990s in part to a skilled workforce that attracted pharmaceutical, biotechnology, electronics, and other high-tech firms to the state. Tax and economic incentives also helped bring business to the state. The state ranked second in the nation in both per capita personal income ($33,953) and low poverty rate (8.6%) in 1998. However, the state faced a severe budget crisis from 2002–05. Nevertheless, the state's per capita personal income in 2004 was $41,332, third in the nation behind Connecticut and Massachusetts.

In September 1999 New Jersey experienced one of the worst natural disasters in its history; Hurricane Floyd damaged more than 8,000 homes and destroyed several hundred more. A federal aid package approved in 2000 promised victims some relief.

During the second half of the 1900s New Jersey had no predictable political pattern. It gave huge presidential majorities to Republican Dwight D. Eisenhower and Democrat Lyndon B. Johnson, narrowly supported Democrat John F. Kennedy, favored Republican Gerald Ford over Democrat Jimmy Carter by a small margin, gave two big majorities to Republican Ronald Reagan, favored Democrat Bill Clinton in the 1990s, and favored Democrat Al Gore over George W. Bush in 2000. New Jersey gave its 15 electoral votes to Democrat John Kerry in 2004, in a 53% to 46% margin over George W. Bush. For more than 20 years, the state's two

US senators, Clifford B. Case (R) and Harrison A. Williams (D), were recognized as like-minded liberals. Democrat Bill Bradley, former Princeton University and New York Knickerbockers basketball star, was elected to Case's seat in 1978. (In 1999 Bradley made a run for the presidency. Though gaining considerable support from the electorate, he dropped his bid for the Democratic nomination in the face of competition from Vice President Al Gore.) In 2006, New Jersey was represented by US Senators Frank R. Lautenberg and Robert Menendez, both Democrats.

Republican Governor Thomas Kean, who served from 1983–89, helped improve the public image of New Jersey, long perceived as dominated by smoke-belching factories and troubled cities. Kean was succeeded by Democrat Jim Florio who sought to redistribute wealth throughout the state by doubling the income tax of those in the top bracket, raising the sales tax, lowering property taxes for middle- and low-income homeowners and renters, and shifting state aid from public schools in affluent areas to schools in poor and moderate income communities. In 1992, Florio lost his bid for reelection to Republican Christine Todd Whitman, who promised to lower income taxes by 30%. As soon as she took office, Whitman implemented a 5% cut and pushed through another 10% cut as part of her budget package in 1993. Whitman won a second term in the 1996 election. Whitman was named President George W. Bush's head of the Environmental Protection Agency; she took office in January 2001 and resigned in May 2003.

Democrat Richard J. Codey, former state Senate president, became acting governor in November 2004 after Governor James E. McGreevey resigned before his term expired. McGreevey announced his resignation in August 2004 after revealing that he is gay and that he had an adulterous affair with a man.

12 STATE GOVERNMENT

New Jersey's first state constitution took effect in 1776. A second constitution was written in 1844, and a third in 1947. This last document, as amended (36 times as of January 2005), continues to govern the state today.

The state legislature consists of a 40-member Senate and an 80-member General Assembly. Annual legislative sessions begin in early January and are not limited in length. Special sessions, also of unlimited duration, may be called by petition of a majority of the members in each house. Senators, elected to four-year terms, must be at least 30 years old, and have been New Jersey residents for four years and district residents for a year. Assembly members, elected to two-year terms, must be at least 21 years old, and have been New Jersey residents for two years and district residents for a year. All legislators must be qualified voters prior to election. Both houses of the legislature meet in unlimited annual sessions. The legislative salary was $49,000 as of 2004.

New Jersey is one of only four states—the others are Maine, New Hampshire, and Tennessee—in which the governor is the only statewide elected administrative official. Given broad powers by the state constitution, the governor appoints the heads or commissioners of the major state departments with the advice and consent of the Senate; not subject to Senate approval are more than 500 patronage positions. The governor is also commander-in-chief of the state's armed forces, submits the budget to the legislature each January, presents an annual message on the condition of the state, and may grant pardons and, with the aid of the Pa-

role Board, grant executive clemency. Elected to a four-year term in the odd-numbered year following the presidential election, the governor may run for a second term but not for a third until four years have passed. A candidate for governor must be at least 30 years old and must have been a US citizen for 20 years and a New Jersey resident for seven years in order to qualify for the ballot. As of December 2004, the governor's salary was $157,000.

A bill may be introduced in either house of the legislature. Once passed, it goes to the governor, who may sign it, return it to the legislature with recommendations for change, or veto it in its entirety. A two-thirds vote by the members in each house is needed to override a veto. If the governor neither signs nor vetoes a bill, it becomes law after 45 days as long as the legislature is in session.

Amendments to the state constitution may originate in either house. If, after public hearings, both houses pass the proposal by a three-fifths vote, the amendment is placed on the ballot at the next general election. If approved by a majority, but by less than a three-fifths vote in both houses, the amendment is referred to the next session of the legislature, at which time, if again approved by a majority, it is placed on the ballot. The amendment goes into effect 30 days after ratification by the electorate.

To vote in New Jersey, one must be at least 18 years old, a US citizen, and a New Jersey and county resident for at least 30 days prior to election day. Restrictions apply to those convicted of crimes in New Jersey or another state.

13 POLITICAL PARTIES

From the 1830s through the early 1850s, Democrats and Whigs dominated the political life of New Jersey. Exercising considerable, though subtle, influence in the decade before the Civil War was the Native American (Know-Nothing) Party, an anti-immigrant, anti-Catholic group that won several assembly and Senate seats. Wary of breaking ties with the South and ambivalent about the slavery issue, New Jerseyites, especially those in Essex and Bergen counties, did not lend much support to the abolitionist cause. Early Republicans thus found it advantageous to call themselves simply "Opposition;" the state's first Opposition governor was elected in 1856. Republicans controlled the state for most of the 1860s; but with heavy support from business leaders, the Democrats regained control in 1869 and held the governorship through 1896. They were succeeded by a series of Progressive Republican governors whose efforts were largely thwarted by a conservative legislature. Sweeping reforms- including a corrupt-practices act, a primary election law, and increased support for public education- were implemented during the two years that Woodrow Wilson, a Democrat, served as governor before being elected to the presidency. Between 1913 and 1985, Democrats held the statehouse almost two-thirds of the time.

New Jersey's unenviable reputation for corruption in government dates back at least to 1838, when ballot tampering resulted in the disputed election of five Whigs to the US House of Representatives. (After a House investigation, the Whigs were barred and their Democratic opponents given the seats.) Throughout the rest of the century, corruption was rampant in local elections: Philadelphians, for example, were regularly imported to vote in Atlantic City elections, and vote buying was a standard election-day procedure in Essex and Hudson counties. Wilson's 1911 reform bill eliminated some of these practices, but not the bossism that had come to dominate big-city politics. Frank Hague of Jersey City controlled patronage and political leaders on the local, state, and national level from 1919 to 1947; during the 1960s and 1970s, Hague's successor John V. Kenny, Jersey City mayor Thomas Whelan, and Newark mayor Hugh Addonizio, along with numerous other state and local officials, were convicted of corrupt political dealings. From 1969 to mid-1975, federal prosecutors indicted 148 public officials, securing 72 convictions. Brendan Byrne, who had never before held elective office, won the governorship in 1973, mainly on the strength of a campaign that portrayed him as the "judge who couldn't be bought." On the national level, New Jersey Representative Peter Rodino gained a reputation for honesty and fairness when he chaired the House Judiciary Committee's impeachment hearings against Richard Nixon. However, the state's image suffered a further blow in 1980, when, as a result of the FBI's "ABSCAM" investigation, charges of influence peddling were brought against several state officials, including members of the Casino Control Commission, whose function was to prevent corruption and crime in Atlantic City's gambling establishments.

Later in the year, New Jersey Democrat Harrison Williams became the nation's first US senator to be indicted, on charges of bribery and conspiracy, as a result of the ABSCAM probe. He was convicted in 1981 and sentenced to prison. As a result of the same investigation, US Representative Frank Thompson Jr., was convicted in 1980 on bribery and conspiracy charges. A New Jerseyite, Raymond Donovan, was named secretary of labor by President Ronald Reagan in 1981, but he resigned in 1985 after being indicted late in 1984 for allegedly seeking to defraud the New York City Transit Authority while serving as vice president of the Schiavone Construction Company in Secaucus.

In the 2000 presidential voting, Democrat Al Gore defeated Republican George W. Bush, picking up 56% of the vote to Bush's 41%. Independent Ralph Nader garnered 3%. In 2004, Democratic challenger John Kerry won 52.7% of the vote to incumbent George W. Bush's 46.5%. In 2004, there were 5,009,000 registered voters. In 1998, 25% of registered voters were Democratic, 19% Republican, and 56% unaffiliated or members of other parties. The state had 15 electoral votes in the 2004 presidential election.

In 1993, New Jersey elected its first woman as governor, Republican Christine Todd Whitman; she was reelected in 1997. In late 2000 she was named by President George W. Bush to head the Environmental Protection Agency, a post she resigned in June 2003. Democrat James McGreevey was elected New Jersey's governor in 2001; he resigned in August 2004 and was succeeded by state Senate president Richard Codey. In fall 2005 elections, Democratic US senator Jon Corzine was elected governor. Democrat Frank Lautenberg, first elected to the Senate in 1982, and reelected in 1988 and 1994, returned to the Senate in 2002 after having retired in 2000. Following 2004 national elections, the state's delegation to the US House consisted of seven Democrats and six Republicans. Following the 2005 statewide elections, the state Senate contained 22 Democrats and 18 Republicans, while the General Assembly consisted of 48 Democrats and 32 Republicans.

New Jersey Presidential Vote by Political Parties, 1948–2004

YEAR	ELECTORAL VOTES	NEW JERSEY WINNER	DEMOCRAT	REPUBLICAN	PROGRESSIVE	SOCIALIST	PROHIBITION	SOCIALIST LABOR	SOCIALIST WORKERS
1948	16	Dewey (R)	895,455	981,124	42,683	10,521	10,593	3,354	5,825
1952	16	*Eisenhower (R)	1,015,902	1,373,613	5,589	8,593	—	5,815	3,850
					CONSTITUTION				
1956	16	*Eisenhower (R)	850,337	1,606,942	5,317	—	9,147	6,736	4,004
					CONSERVATIVE				
1960	16	*Kennedy (D)	1,385,415	1,363,324	8,708	—	—	4,262	11,402
1964	17	*Johnson (D)	1,867,671	963,843	—	—	—	7,075	8,181
					AMERICAN IND.	PEACE AND FREEDOM			
1968	17	*Nixon (R)	1,264,206	1,325,467	262,187	8,084	—	6,784	8,667
					PEOPLE'S	AMERICAN			
1972	17	*Nixon (R)	1,102,211	1,845,502	—	5,355	34,378	4,544	2,233
					US LABOR	LIBERTARIAN			COMMUNIST
1976	17	Ford (R)	1,444,653	1,509,688	7,716	1,650	9,449	3,686	1,662
1980	17	*Reagan (R)	1,147,364	1,546,557	8,203	—	20,652	2,198	2,555
						WORKERS WORLD			
1984	16	*Reagan (R)	1,261,323	1,933,630	—	8,404	6,416	—	1,564
					NEW ALLIANCE	PEACE AND FREEDOM		CONSUMER	SOCIALIST
1988	16	* Bush (R)	1,320,352	1,743,192	5,139	9,953	8,421	3,454	2,587
						IND. (Perot)		IND. (Bradford)	TAXPAYERS
1992	15	* Clinton (D)	1,436,206	1,356,865	3,513	521,829	6,822	4,749	2,670
					GREEN (NADER)				
1996	15	*Clinton (D)	1,652,329	1,103,078	32,465	262,134	14,763	—	—
						IND. (Buchanan)			
2000	15	Gore (D)	1,788,850	1,284,173	94,554	6,989	6,312	—	—
					IND. (Nader)	GREEN (Cobb)		CONSTITUTION (Peroutka)	SOCIALIST (Brown)
2004	15	Kerry (D)	1,911,430	1,670,003	19,418	1,807	4,514	2,750	664

*Won US presidential election.

[14]LOCAL GOVERNMENT

As of 2005, New Jersey had 21 counties, 324 municipal governments, 604 public school districts, and 276 special districts. In 2002, there were 242 townships. Counties are classed by population and whether or not they border the Atlantic Ocean. Cities, boroughs, and towns may employ the mayor-council system, council-manager system, commission system, or other forms of their own devising. Most townships and villages are governed by committee or by a council and a mayor with limited powers. Cities, like counties, are classed by population and location: first-class cities are those over 150,000 in population; second-class, 12,000–150,000; third-class, all others except ocean resorts; and fourth-class, ocean resorts.

The budgets of all local units are supervised by the New Jersey Department of Community Affairs, which also offers municipal aid programs.

In 2005, local government accounted for about 347,538 full-time (or equivalent) employment positions.

[15]STATE SERVICES

To address the continuing threat of terrorism and to work with the federal Department of Homeland Security, homeland security in New Jersey operates under executive order and state statute; a counterterrorism office director is named to oversee the state's homeland security activities.

The constitution of 1947 limited the number of state government departments to 20. New Jersey in 1974 became the first state to establish a Public Advocate Department (as of 2006 the Office of the Public Defender), empowered to provide legal assistance for indigent criminal defendants, mental patients, and any citizen with a grievance against a government agency or regulated industry. A Code of Ethics, adopted by the legislature in 1976, seeks to prevent state employees from using their positions for personal gain. By executive order, more than 500 state executive officials must file financial disclosure statements.

The Education Department administers state and federal aid to all elementary and secondary schools, oversees pupil transportation, and has jurisdiction over the state library, museum, and historical commission. State-run colleges and universities and higher education policy are the province of the Commission on Higher Education. All state-maintained highways and bus and rail transportation are the responsibility of the Department of Transportation, which also operates New Jersey Transit, whose function is to acquire and operate public transportation services.

The Human Services Department administers welfare, Medicaid, mental health, and developmentally disabled programs, as well as veterans' institutions and programs and other state-supported social services. Alcohol, drug abuse, and many other health-related programs are monitored by the Health and Senior Services Department, which also oversees hospitals and compiles statewide health statistics.

The Office of the Attorney General, officially titled the Department of Law and Public Safety, is the statewide law enforcement agency. Its functions include criminal justice, consumer affairs, civil rights, alcoholic beverage control, and gaming enforcement; also within this department are the State Police, State Racing Commission, Violent Crimes Compensation Board, and a number of regulatory boards. The Department of Military and Veterans Affairs controls the Army and Air National Guard. Correctional institutions, training schools, treatment centers, and parole offices are administered by the Corrections Department.

The Division of Energy monitors the supply and use of fuel and administers the state master plan for energy use and conservation; it forms part of the Board of Public Utilities, which has broad regulatory jurisdiction, ranging from garbage collection to public broadcasting. Other agencies are the departments of agriculture, banking and insurance, commerce, community affairs, environmental protection, labor and workforce development, state, and treasury.

[16]JUDICIAL SYSTEM

All judges in New Jersey, except municipal court judges, are appointed by the governor with the consent of the Senate. Initial terms for supreme and superior court judges are seven years; after reappointment, judges may serve indefinitely.

The supreme court, the state's highest, consists of six associate justices and a chief justice, who is also the administrative head of the state court system. As the court of highest authority, the supreme court hears appeals on constitutional questions and on certain cases from the superior court, which comprises three divisions: chancery, law, and appellate. The chancery division has original jurisdiction over general equity cases, most probate cases, and divorce actions. All other original cases are tried within the law division. The appellate division hears appeals from the chancery and law divisions, from lower courts, and from most state administrative agencies. A state tax court, empowered to review local property tax assessments, equalization tables, and state tax determinations, has been in operation since 1979; by statute, it may have from 6 to 12 judges. Municipal court judges, appointed by local governing bodies for three-year terms, hear minor criminal matters, motor vehicle cases, and violations of municipal ordinances.

The legislature approved a sweeping reform of the state's criminal law code in 1978. Strict sentencing standards were established, and one result was an overcrowding of the state's prison system. Governor Brendan Byrne signed a law in 1981 imposing a minimum three-year sentence on anyone committing a crime with a gun.

As of 31 December 2004, a total of 26,757 prisoners were held in New Jersey's state and federal prisons, a decrease from 27,246 of 1.6% from the previous year. As of year-end 2004, a total of 1,470 inmates were female, down from 1,517 or 3.1% from the year before. Among sentenced prisoners (one year or more), New Jersey had an incarceration rate of 306 per 100,000 population in 2004.

According to the Federal Bureau of Investigation, New Jersey in 2004, had a violent crime rate (murder/nonnegligent manslaughter; forcible rape; robbery; aggravated assault) of 355.7 reported incidents per 100,000 population, or a total of 30,943 reported incidents. Crimes against property (burglary; larceny/theft; and motor vehicle theft) in that same year totaled 211,313 reported incidents or 2,429.2 reported incidents per 100,000 people. As of 1982, New Jersey has had a death penalty, of which lethal injection is the sole method of execution. However, as of that year through 5 May 2006, the state has yet to carry out an execution. As of 1 January 2006, New Jersey had 13 inmates on death row.

In 2003, New Jersey spent $272,195,275 on homeland security, an average of $32 per state resident.

[17] ARMED FORCES

In 2004, there were 6,392 active-duty military personnel and 13,628 civilian personnel stationed in New Jersey. The largest installation in the state is McGuire Air Force Base in Wrightstown. The US Coast Guard operates a training center in Cape May. New Jersey firms received over $4.1 billion in defense contracts awards in 2004, defense payroll outlays were $1.8 billion.

Of the 582,917 veterans living in New Jersey in 2003, World War II veterans numbered 110,844; Korean conflict, 80,677; Vietnam era, 167,895; and 58,244 served in the Persian Gulf War. For the fiscal year 2004, total Veterans Affairs expenditures in New Hampshire exceeded $1.0 billion.

As of 31 October 2004, the New Jersey State Police employed 2,684 full-time sworn officers.

[18] MIGRATION

New Jersey's first white settlers were inter-colonial migrants: Dutch from New Amsterdam, Swedes from west of the Delaware River, and Puritans from New England and Long Island. By 1776, New Jersey's population was about 138,000, of whom perhaps 7% were black slaves.

Population growth lagged during the early 19th century, as discouraged farmers left their worn-out plots for more fertile western soil; farmers in Salem County, for example, went off to found new Salems in Ohio, Indiana, Iowa, and Oregon. Not until the rapid industrial growth of the mid-1800s did New Jersey attract great waves of immigrants. Germans and Irish were the first to arrive, the latter comprising 37% of Jersey City's population by 1870. The late 1800s and early 1900s brought newcomers from Eastern Europe, including many Jews, and a much larger number of Italians to the cities. By 1900, 43% of all Hudson County residents were foreign-born. More recently, migration from Puerto Rico and Cuba has been substantial. In 1990, 143,974 New Jersey residents age 5 and older had lived in Puerto Rico in 1985. In 1996, 1,152,000 New Jersey residents, or 14%, were foreign born. In 1998, 35,091 foreign immigrants entered the state, the fifth-highest total for any state that year.

From World War I on, there has been a steady migration of blacks from southern states; Newark's black population grew by 130,000 between 1950 and 1970. Black as well as Hispanic newcomers settled in major cities just as whites were departing for the suburbs. New Jersey's suburbs were also attractive to residents of New York City, Philadelphia, and other adjacent areas, who began a massive move to the state just after World War II; nearly all of these suburbanites were white. From 1940 to 1970, New Jersey gained a net total of 1,360,000 residents. Between 1970 and 1990, however, the state lost about 250,000 residents through migration. Between 1990 and 1998, New Jersey had a net loss of 350,000 in domestic migration and a net gain of 360,000 in international migration. While the black, Hispanic, and Asian populations were still rising, whites were departing from New Jersey in increasing numbers. As of 1998, New Jersey's black population numbered 1,188,000; Hispanic, 866,000; and Asian, 453,000. Between 1990 and 1998, the state's overall population increased 4.7%. In the period 2000–05, net international migration was 290,194 and net internal migration was -194,901, for a net gain of 95,293 people.

[19] INTERGOVERNMENTAL COOPERATION

New Jersey participates in such regional bodies as the Interstate Sanitation Commission, Atlantic States Marine Fisheries Commission, and Mid-Atlantic Fishery Management Council. Of primary importance to the state are its relations with neighboring Pennsylvania and New York. With Pennsylvania, New Jersey takes part in the Delaware Valley Regional Planning Commission, Delaware River Joint Toll Bridge Commission, and Delaware River Port Authority; with New York, the Port Authority of New York and New Jersey, the Palisades Interstate Park Commission, and the Waterfront Commission, established to eliminate corruption and stabilize employment at the Hudson River ports. The Delaware River Basin Commission manages the water resources of the 12,750-sq mi (33,000-sq km) basin under the jurisdiction of Delaware, New Jersey, New York, and Pennsylvania. The Delaware River and Bay Authority operates a bridge and ferry between New Jersey and Delaware. In fiscal year 2005, the state received $8.694 billion in federal grants, an estimated $9.086 billion in fiscal year 2006, and an estimated $9.509 billion in fiscal year 2007.

[20] ECONOMY

New Jersey was predominantly agricultural until the mid-1800s, when the rise of the railroads stimulated manufacturing in northern New Jersey and opened the Jersey shore to resort development. The steady growth of population in the 1900s fostered the growth of service-related industries, construction, and trade, for which the state's proximity to New York and Philadelphia had long been advantageous.

During the 1970s, New Jersey's economy followed national trends, except that the mid-decade recession was especially severe. Conditions in most areas improved in the latter part of the decade, particularly in Atlantic City, with the construction of gambling casinos and other entertainment facilities. Manufacturing in the central cities declined, however, as industries moved to suburban locations.

Although petroleum refining, chemicals and pharmaceuticals, food processing, apparel, fabricated metals, electric and electronic equipment, and other machinery are all important, the state is more noteworthy for the diversity of its manufacturers than for any dominant company or product. The service sector of the economy, led by wholesale and retail trade, continued to grow rapidly during the 1990s. The heaviest concentrations of jobs are in and near metropolitan New York and Philadelphia, but employment opportunities in the central and north-central counties have been increasing. Fresh market vegetables are the leading source of farm income. Overall growth in the state economy was robust coming into the 21st century, with annual growth rates averaging over 6% 1998 to 2000. The national recession and slowdown of 2001 slowed annual growth to 2.2%, but in 2002 the state economy was showing resiliency. Employment losses for the state as a whole started later and were milder than for the nation as a whole.

New Jersey's gross state product (GSP) in 2004 was $416.053 billion of which the real estate sector accounted for the largest share at $65.656 billion or 15.7% of GSP, followed by manufacturing (durable and non durable goods) at $45.357 billion (10.9% of

GSP), and professional and technical services at $33.652 billion (8% of GSP). In that same year, there were an estimated 766,323 small businesses in New Jersey. Of the 256,863 businesses that had employees, an estimated total of 252,831 or 98.4% were small companies. An estimated 35,895 new businesses were established in the state in 2004, up 22.8% from the year before. Business terminations that same year came to 50,034, up 35.9% from 2003. There were 684 business bankruptcies in 2004, down 6.8% from the previous year. In 2005, the state's personal bankruptcy (Chapter 7 and Chapter 13) filing rate was 485 filings per 100,000 people, ranking New Jersey as the 29th highest in the nation.

²¹INCOME

In 2005, New Jersey had a gross state product (GSP) of $431 billion which accounted for 3.5% of the nation's gross domestic product and placed the state at number 8 in highest GSP among the 50 states and the District of Columbia.

According to the Bureau of Economic Analysis, in 2004 New Jersey had a per capita personal income (PCPI) of $41,626. This ranked fourth in the United States and was 126% of the national average of $33,050. The 1994–2004 average annual growth rate of PCPI was 4.2%. New Jersey had a total personal income (TPI) of $361,524,402,000, which ranked seventh in the United States and reflected an increase of 5.6% from 2003. The 1994–2004 average annual growth rate of TPI was 5.1%. Earnings of persons employed in New Jersey increased from $252,207,195,000 in 2003 to $265,438,128,000 in 2004, an increase of 5.2%. The 2003–04 national change was 6.3%.

The US Census Bureau reports that the three-year average median household income for 2002–04 in 2004 dollars was $56,772 compared to a national average of $44,473. During the same period an estimated 8.2% of the population was below the poverty line as compared to 12.4% nationwide.

²²LABOR

According to the Bureau of Labor Statistics (BLS), in April 2006 the seasonally adjusted civilian labor force in New Jersey numbered 4,501,800, with approximately 231,300 workers unemployed, yielding an unemployment rate of 5.1%, compared to the national average of 4.7% for the same period. Preliminary data for the same period placed nonfarm employment at 4,074,900. Since the beginning of the BLS data series in 1976, the highest unemployment rate recorded in New Jersey was 10.6% in February 1977. The historical low was 3.5% in June 2000. Preliminary nonfarm employment data by occupation for April 2006 showed that approximately 4.2% of the labor force was employed in construction; 7.8% in manufacturing; 21.5% in trade, transportation, and public utilities; 6.9% in financial activities; 14.6% in professional and business services; 13.9% in education and health services; 8.4% in leisure and hospitality services; and 15.8% in government.

Although migrant workers are still employed at south Jersey tomato farms and fruit orchards, the number of farm workers coming into the state is declining with the increased use of mechanical harvesters.

The state's first child labor law was passed in 1851, and in 1886, workers were given the right to organize. Labor's gains were slow and painful, however. In Paterson, no fewer than 137 strikes were called between 1881 and 1900, every one of them a failure. A 1913 strike of Paterson silkworkers drew nationwide headlines but, again, few results. Other notable strikes were a walkout at a Carteret fertilizer factory in 1915, during which six picketers were killed by guards; a yearlong work stoppage by Passaic textile workers in 1926; and another Paterson silkworkers' strike in 1933, this one finally leading to union recognition and significant wage increases. That year, the state enacted a law setting minimum wages and maximum hours for women. This measure was repealed in 1971, in line with the trend toward nonpreferential labor standards.

The BLS reported that in 2005, a total of 791,000 of New Jersey's 3,868,000 employed wage and salary workers were formal members of a union. This represented 20.5% of those so employed, up from 19.8% in 2004, well above the national average of 12%. New Jersey is one of only five states whose union membership rate exceeds 20%. Overall in 2005, a total of 838,000 workers (21.7%) in New Jersey were covered by a union or employee association contract, which includes those workers who reported no union affiliation. New Jersey is also one of 28 states that does not have a right-to-work law.

As of 1 March 2006, New Jersey had a state-mandated minimum wage rate of $6.15 per hour, which will increase on October 1, 2006 to $7.15 per hour. In 2004, women in the state accounted for 46.2% of the employed civilian labor force.

²³AGRICULTURE

New Jersey is a leading producer of fresh fruits and vegetables. Its total farm income was $862 million in 2005. In 2004, it ranked fourth in cranberries, spinach, and lettuce, and eighth in fresh market tomatoes.

Some 820,000 acres (about 332,000 hectares) were in 9,900 farms in 2004. The major farm counties are: Warren for grain and milk production, Gloucester and Cumberland for fruits and vegetables, Atlantic for blueberries, Burlington for nursery production and berries, Salem for processing vegetables, and Monmouth for nursery and equine.

In 2004, New Jersey produced 265,140 tons of fresh market vegetables. Leading crops (in hundredweight units) were: bell peppers, 962,000; cabbage, 928,000; sweet corn, 525,000; tomatoes, 690,000; and head lettuce, 164,000. New Jersey farmers also produced 56,440 tons of vegetables for processing. Fruit crops in 2004 (in pound units) included apples, 40,000,000, and peaches, 32,500,000. In 2004, cranberry production was 40 million lb. The expansion of housing and industry has increased the value of farm acreage and buildings in New Jersey to over $9,750 per acre, fourth highest in the nation after Connecticut, Rhode Island, and Massachusetts.

²⁴ANIMAL HUSBANDRY

In 2005, New Jersey had an estimated 44,000 cattle and calves, valued at $48.8 million. During 2004, New Jersey farmers had an estimated 11,000 hogs and pigs valued at $1.3 million. In 2003, poultry farmers produced 686,000 million lb (312 million kg) of turkey, 3 million lb (1.4 million kg) of chickens, and 556 million eggs. The state's total milk yield was 216 million lb (98.1 million kg) in 2003.

25FISHING

In 2004, New Jersey had a commercial fish catch of 185.6 million lb (84.3 million kg) worth $139.4 million, the eighth highest catch volume in the nation. Cape May–Wildwood had the 15th-highest value and 13th-largest volume of all US ports, bringing in 97.5 million lb (44.3 million kg) of fish, worth $68.1 million. Clams, scallops, swordfish, tuna, squid, lobster, and flounder are the most valuable species. The state ranked second in the nation for volume of Atlantic mackerel landings, at 35.5 million lb (16.1 million kg). The state also led the nation in landings of surf clams (43.5 million lb/19.8 million kg) and quahogs (17.6 million lb/8 million kg). In 2003, there were 15 processing and 83 wholesale plants in the state with about 2,050 employees. The commercial fleet in 2001 had 397 vessels.

The US Fish and Wildlife Service of the Department of the Interior maintains a total of 190,000 acres (76,900 hectares) on 12 different sites with boating access. The state stocks over 1.8 million fish per year to lakes, ponds, rivers, and streams. The Hackettstown State Fish Hatchery and the Pequest Trout Hatchery are major suppliers.

Recreational fishermen catch finfish and shellfish along the Atlantic coast and in the rivers and lakes of northern New Jersey. In 2004, the state issued 169,418 sport fishing licenses.

26FORESTRY

Over 42% of New Jersey's land area, or 1,876,000 acres (759,000 hectares), was forested in 2003. Of that total, 1,288,000 acres (521,000 hectares) were private commercial timberland. The forests of New Jersey are important for their function in conservation and recreation. Wood that is harvested contributes to specialty markets and quality veneer products. State forests cover 382,000 acres (155,000 hectares).

27MINING

According to preliminary data from the US Geological Survey (USGS), the estimated value of nonfuel mineral production by new Jersey in 2003 was $272 million, an increase from 2002 of about 5%.

According to the preliminary data for 2003, crushed stone, and construction sand and gravel were the state's top nonfuel minerals, by value. These were followed by industrial sand and gravel, and greens and marl.

According to preliminary figures for 2003, a total of 22.5 million metric tons of crushed stone were produced, for a total value of $142 million, while construction sand and gravel output totaled 15.2 million metric tons, with a value of $92 million. Industrial sand and gravel production in 2003 totaled 1.51 million metric tons, for a value of $33.8 million. New Jersey in 2003 continued to be the only state that produced greensand marl, also known as the mineral glauconite, which is processed and sold mainly as a water-softening filtration medium to remove soluble iron and manganese from well water. A secondary use is as an organic conditioner for soils.

28ENERGY AND POWER

As of 2003, New Jersey had 37 electrical power service providers, of which nine were publicly owned and one was a cooperative. Of the remainder, four were investor owned, six were owners of independent generators that sold directly to customers, 12 were generation-only suppliers and five were delivery-only providers. As of that same year there were 3,737,697 retail customers. Of that total, 3,624,915 received their power from investor-owned service providers. Cooperatives accounted for 11,267 customers, while publicly owned providers had 56,447 customers. There were seven independent generator or "facility" customers, 12 generation-only customers. There was no data on the number of delivery-only customers.

Total net summer generating capability by the state's electrical generating plants in 2003 stood at 18.647 million kW, with total production that same year at 57.399 billion kWh. Of the total amount generated, only 3.3% came from electric utilities, with the remaining 96.7% coming from independent producers and combined heat and power service providers. The largest portion of all electric power generated, 29.709 billion kWh (51.8%), came from nuclear generating plants, with natural gas fired plants in second place at 14.775 billion kWh (25.7%) and coal fueled plants in third at 9.789 billion kWh (17.1%). Other renewable power sources accounted for 2.4% of all power generated, with petroleum fired plants at 2.7%. Pumped storage and hydroelectric generation, and plants using other types of gases made up the remainder.

As of 2006, New Jersey had three operating nuclear power stations: the Hope Creek in Lower Alloways Township; the Oyster Creek plant at Forked River; and the Salem Creek plant near Salem.

New Jersey has no known proven reserves or production of crude oil and natural gas. However, the state has six crude oil refineries, some of which are the largest in the United States. As of 2005, the state's refineries had a distillation capacity of 615,000 barrels per day. New Jersey produces little of its own energy, importing much of its electric power and virtually all of its fossil fuels.

29INDUSTRY

New Jersey's earliest industries were glassmaking and iron working. In 1791, Alexander Hamilton proposed the development of a planned industrial town at the Passaic Falls. The Society for Establishing Useful Manufactures, an agency charged with developing the town, tried but failed to set up a cotton mill at the site, called Paterson, in 1797. By the early 1800s, however, Paterson had become the country's largest silk manufacturing center and by 1850, it was producing locomotives as well. On the eve of the Civil War, industry already had a strong foothold in the state. Newark had breweries, hat factories, and paper plants; Trenton, iron and paper; Jersey City, steel and soap; and Middlesex, clays and ceramics. The late 1800s saw the birth of the electrical industry, the growth of oil refineries on Bayonne's shores, and emerging chemical, drug, paint, and telephone manufacturing centers. All these products retain their places among the state's diverse manufactures.

According to the US Census Bureau's Annual Survey of Manufactures (ASM) for 2004, New Jersey's manufacturing sector covered some 20 product subsectors. The shipment value of all products manufactured in the state that same year was $94.125 billion. Of that total, chemical manufacturing accounted for the largest share at $26.911 billion. It was followed by petroleum and coal products manufacturing at $12.222 billion; food manufacturing at $9.481 billion; computer and electronic product manufacturing at $6.115 billion; and fabricated metal product manufacturing at $5.241 billion.

In 2004, a total of 308,566 people in New Jersey were employed in the state's manufacturing sector, according to the ASM. Of that total, 201,419 were actual production workers. In terms of total employment, the chemical manufacturing industry accounted for the largest portion of all manufacturing employees at 50,881 with 25,643 actual production workers. It was followed by fabricated metal product manufacturing at 30,235 employees (21,120 actual production workers); food manufacturing at 28,958 employees (18,783 actual production workers); computer and electronic product manufacturing at 28,710 employees (14,868 actual production workers); and plastics and rubber products manufacturing with 25,186 employees (18,778 actual production workers).

ASM data for 2004 showed that New Jersey's manufacturing sector paid $14.447 billion in wages. Of that amount, the chemical manufacturing sector accounted for the largest share at $3.084 billion. It was followed by computer and electronic product manufacturing at $1.603 billion; fabricated metal product manufacturing at $1.241 billion; printing and related support activities at $1.111 billion; and miscellaneous manufacturing at $1.078 billion.

³⁰COMMERCE

With one of the nation's busiest ports, one of the busiest airports (Newark), the largest length of highways and railroads per state area, and many regional distribution centers, New Jersey is an important commercial state.

According to the 2002 Census of Wholesale Trade, New Jersey's wholesale trade sector had sales that year totaling $256.9 billion from 16,803 establishments. Wholesalers of durable goods accounted for 9,293 establishments, followed by nondurable goods wholesalers at 6,281 and electronic markets, agents, and brokers accounting for 1,229 establishments. Sales by durable goods wholesalers in 2002 totaled $125.9 billion, while wholesalers of nondurable goods saw sales of $107.06 billion. Electronic markets, agents, and brokers in the wholesale trade industry had sales of $23.9 billion. The state's wholesale trade is largely concentrated near manufacturing centers and along the New Jersey Turnpike. Bergen, Union, and Essex counties accounted for most of the state's wholesale trade.

In the 2002 Census of Retail Trade, New Jersey was listed as having 34,741 retail establishments with sales of $102.1 billion. The leading types of retail businesses by number of establishments were: food and beverage stores (6,824); clothing and clothing accessories stores (5,782); miscellaneous store retailers (3,423); and health and personal care stores (2,866). In terms of sales, motor vehicle and motor vehicle parts stores accounted for the largest share of retail sales at $26.3 billion, followed by food and beverage stores at $19.1 billion; general merchandise stores at $10.3 billion; nonstore retailers at $8.01 billion; and building material/garden equipment and supplies dealers at $7.4 billion. A total of 434,574 people were employed by the retail sector in New Jersey that year.

Port Newark and the Elizabeth Marine Terminal, foreign-trade zones operated by the Port Authority of New York and New Jersey, have been modernized and enlarged in recent years, and together account for most of the cargo unloaded in New York Harbor. In 2005, New Jersey exported $21.08 billion to foreign countries. Leading exports were chemicals, electronics, and industrial machinery. Most exports went to Canada, Japan, the UK, and Mexico.

³¹CONSUMER PROTECTION

Consumer fraud cases are handled by the Division of Consumer Affairs and the Office of the Attorney General, both of which are under the Department of Law and Public Safety. The Division of Consumer Affairs also supervises the activities of 41 boards and committees, which are responsible for regulating over 80 occupations and professions.

When dealing with consumer protection issues, the state's Attorney General's Office can initiate civil and criminal proceedings; represent the state before state and federal regulatory agencies; administer consumer protection and education programs; handle formal consumer complaints; and exercise broad subpoena powers. In antitrust actions, the Attorney General's Office can act on behalf of those consumers who are incapable of acting on their own; initiate damage actions on behalf of the state in state courts; initiate criminal proceedings; and represent counties, cities and other governmental entities in recovering civil damages under state or federal law.

The offices of the Division of Consumer Affairs are located in Newark. County government consumer affairs offices are located in Atlantic City, Blackwood, Bridgeton, Cape May Court House, East Orange, Flemington, Freehold, Hackensack, Jersey City, Mount Holly, New Brunswick, Somerville, Toms River, Trenton, Wayne, Westfield and Woodbury. City government consumer affairs offices are located in Middlesex, Nutley, Perth Amboy, Plainfield, Secaucus, Union and Woodbridge.

³²BANKING

The colonies' first bank of issue opened in Gloucester in 1682. New Jersey's first chartered bank, the Newark Banking and Insurance Co., was the first of many banks to open in that city. By the mid-1800s, Newark was indisputably the financial center of the state. For the most part, commercial banking in New Jersey is overshadowed by the great financial centers of New York City and Philadelphia.

As of June 2005, New Jersey had 136 insured banks, savings and loans, and saving banks, plus 20 state-chartered and 226 federally chartered credit unions (CUs). Excluding the CUs, the New York-Northern New Jersey-Long Island market area accounted for the largest portion of the state's financial institutions and deposits in 2004, with 233 institutions and $770.488 billion in deposits, followed by the Trenton-Ewing market area with 25 institutions and $9.302 billion in deposits. As of June 2005, CUs accounted for 5.1% of all assets held by all financial institutions in the state, or some $9.559 billion. Banks, savings and loans, and savings banks collectively accounted for the remaining 94.9% or $178.820 billion in assets held.

Regulation of all state-chartered banks, savings banks, savings and loan associations and limited purpose trust companies is the responsibility of the Department of Banking and Insurance. National or federally chartered banks are regulated by the Office of Comptroller of the Currency. The principal regulator of federally chartered savings and loan associations is the Office of Thrift Supervision.

In 2004, the median net interest margin (the difference between the lower rates offered to savers and the higher rates charged on loans) was 3.54%, down slightly from 3.55% in 2003. A large number of New Jersey's banks are residential lenders, and the widespread use of long-term mortgages in results in higher concentrations of long-term assets in New Jersey, around twice that reported by other banks elsewhere in the nation.

In 2004, the median percentage of past-due/nonaccrual loans to total loans was 0.88%, up from 0.85% in 2003.

33 INSURANCE

In 2004, there were over 4.4 million individual life insurance policies in force in New Jersey, with a total value of over $540.6 billion; total value for all categories of life insurance (individual, group, and credit) was $902.4 billion. The average coverage amount is $120,600 per policy holder. Death benefits paid that year totaled $2.1 billion.

As of 2003, there were 81 property and casualty and 7 life and health insurers domiciled in the state. In 2004, direct premiums for property and casualty insurance totaled $16.9 billion. That year, there were 189,830 flood insurance policies in force in the state, with a total value of $33.1 billion. About $6 billion of coverage was held through FAIR plans, which are designed to offer coverage for some natural circumstances, such as wind and hail, in high risk areas.

In 2004, 62% of state residents held employment-based health insurance policies, 3% held individual policies, and 20% were covered under Medicare and Medicaid; 15% of residents were uninsured. New Jersey ranks as having the third-highest percentage of employment-based insureds among the fifty states. In 2003, employee contributions for employment-based health coverage averaged at 16% for single coverage and 20% for family coverage. The state offers a 12-month health benefits expansion program for small-firm employees in connection with the Consolidated Omnibus Budget Reconciliation Act (COBRA, 1986), a health insurance program for those who lose employment-based coverage due to termination or reduction of work hours.

In 2003, there were over 5.1 million auto insurance policies in effect for private passenger cars. Required minimum coverage includes bodily injury liability of up to $15,000 per individual and $30,000 for all persons injured in an accident, as well as property damage liability of $5,000. Personal injury protection is also required. In 2003, the average expenditure per vehicle for insurance coverage was $1,188.42, which ranked as the highest average in the nation.

All insurance agents, brokers, and companies in the state are licensed and regulated by the Department of Banking and Insurance.

34 SECURITIES

There are no stock or commodity exchanges in New Jersey. Regulation of securities trading in the state is under the control of the Bureau of Securities of the Division of Consumer Affairs, within the Department of Law and Public Safety.

In 2005, there were 5,310 personal financial advisers employed in the state and 12,690 securities, commodities, and financial services sales agents. In 2004, there were over 517 publicly traded companies within the state, with over 167 NASDAQ companies, 112 NYSE listings, and 45 AMEX listings. In 2006, the state had 22 Fortune 500 companies; Johnson and Johnson (based in New Brunswick) ranked first in the state and 32nd in the nation with revenues of over $50.5 billion, followed by Medco Health Solutions (Franklin Lakes), Prudential Financial (Newark), Honeywell Intl., (Morristown), and Merck (Whitehouse Station). All five of these companies are listed on the NYSE.

35 PUBLIC FINANCE

The annual budget, prepared by the Treasury Department's Division of Budget and Accounting, is submitted by the governor to the legislature for approval. The fiscal year (FY) runs from 1 July through 30 June.

Fiscal year 2006 general funds were estimated at $28.4 billion for resources and $27.5 billion for expenditures. In fiscal year 2004, federal government grants to New Jersey were $11.3 billion.

In the fiscal year 2007 federal budget, New Jersey was slated to receive: $110.5 million in State Children's Health Insurance Program (SCHIP) funds to help the state provide health coverage to low-income, uninsured children who do not qualify for Medicaid. This funding is a 23% increase over fiscal year 2006; and $52 million for the HOME Investment Partnership Program to help New Jersey fund a wide range of activities that build, buy, or rehabilitate affordable housing for rent or homeownership, or provide direct rental assistance to low-income people. This funding is a 12% increase over fiscal year 2006.

36 TAXATION

In 2005, New Jersey collected $22,934 million in tax revenues or $2,631 per capita, which placed it 10th among the 50 states in per capita tax burden. The national average was $2,192 per capita. Sales taxes accounted for 28.6% of the total, selective sales taxes 15.8%, individual income taxes 35.9%, corporate income taxes 9.7%, and other taxes 10.1%.

As of 1 January 2006, New Jersey had six individual income tax brackets ranging from 1.4 to 8.97%. The state taxes corporations at a flat rate of 9.0%.

In 2004, state and local property taxes amounted to $18,229,254,000 or $2,099 per capita. The per capita amount ranks the state as having the highest property taxes in the nation. Local governments collected $18,225,594,000 of the total and the state government $3,660,000.

New Jersey taxes retail sales at a rate of 6%. Food purchased for consumption off-premises is tax exempt. The tax on cigarettes is 240 cents per pack, which ranks second among the 50 states and the District of Columbia. New Jersey taxes gasoline at 14.50 cents per gallon. This is in addition to the 18.4 cents per gallon federal tax on gasoline.

Per dollar of federal tax paid in 2004, New Jersey citizens received only $0.55 in federal spending, the lowest amount in the nation and down from 1922 when it received $0.66 per dollar sent to Washington.

37 ECONOMIC POLICY

New Jersey's controlled budget and relatively low business tax burden have helped encourage new businesses to enter the state. The New Jersey Commerce, Economic Growth and Tourism Commission is the state's lead agency in coordinating efforts between gov-

New Jersey—State Government Finances

(Dollar amounts in thousands. Per capita amounts in dollars.)

	AMOUNT	PER CAPITA
Total Revenue	50,588,543	5,824.82
General revenue	37,904,075	4,364.31
Intergovernmental revenue	9,580,081	1,103.06
Taxes	20,981,428	2,415.82
General sales	6,261,700	720.98
Selective sales	3,478,584	400.53
License taxes	1,177,242	135.55
Individual income tax	7,400,733	852.13
Corporate income tax	1,896,998	218.42
Other taxes	766,171	88.22
Current charges	4,316,948	497.06
Miscellaneous general revenue	3,025,618	348.37
Utility revenue	591,310	68.08
Liquor store revenue	–	–
Insurance trust revenue	12,093,158	1,392.42
Total expenditure	46,455,897	5,348.98
Intergovernmental expenditure	9,813,688	1,129.96
Direct expenditure	36,642,209	4,219.02
Current operation	23,411,920	2,695.67
Capital outlay	3,465,474	399.02
Insurance benefits and repayments	8,131,855	936.31
Assistance and subsidies	471,762	54.32
Interest on debt	1,161,198	133.70
Exhibit: Salaries and wages	3,129,159	360.29
Total expenditure	46,455,897	5,348.98
General expenditure	36,064,484	4,152.50
Intergovernmental expenditure	9,813,688	1,129.96
Direct expenditure	26,250,796	3,022.54
General expenditures, by function:		
Education	12,122,842	1,395.84
Public welfare	8,593,086	989.42
Hospitals	1,616,323	186.11
Health	770,150	88.68
Highways	2,388,481	275.01
Police protection	431,279	49.66
Correction	1,375,329	158.36
Natural resources	330,844	38.09
Parks and recreation	399,223	45.97
Government administration	1,404,840	161.75
Interest on general debt	1,156,794	133.19
Other and unallocable	5,475,293	630.43
Utility expenditure	2,259,558	260.17
Liquor store expenditure	–	–
Insurance trust expenditure	8,131,855	936.31
Debt at end of fiscal year	35,770,241	4,118.62
Cash and security holdings	87,493,366	10,074.08

Abbreviations and symbols: – zero or rounds to zero; (NA) not available; (X) not applicable.

SOURCE: *U.S. Census Bureau, Governments Division, 2004 Survey of State Government Finances,* January 2006.

ernment and the private sector to provide access to a broad range of technical, financial and other assistance that helps businesses grow and contribute to economic development. The commission administers a number of development programs designed to retain and attract business and jobs. The state's Economic Development Authority (EDA) is an independent authority established to provide financing programs, including loans, loan guarantees, and tax-free and taxable bond packages.

The Urban Enterprise Zone Program seeks to revitalize urban areas by granting tax incentives and relaxing some government regulations. The Office of Business Services was established as a clearinghouse to help, support, and promote the development of small, women- and minority-owned enterprises. The Office of International Trade and Protocol seeks to boost the state's exports and bring more foreign companies into the state. Other offices within the department promote tourism and motion picture production. Besides financing, EDA offers a full range of real estate development services, training for entrepreneurs, and technical support. Specific categories targeted for assistance are small and mid-size businesses, high-tech businesses, nonprofits, and brownfields. There are also separate divisions for advocating Smart Growth principles and for trade adjustment assistance.

38HEALTH

The infant mortality rate in October 2005 was estimated at 4.9 per 1,000 live births. The birth rate in 2003 was 13.5 per 1,000 population. The abortion rate stood at 36.3 per 1,000 women in 2000, representing the third-highest rate in the country (after the District of Columbia and New York). In 2003, about 80.2% of pregnant woman received prenatal care beginning in the first trimester. In 2004, approximately 83% of children received routine immunizations before the age of three.

The crude death rate in 2003 was 8.5 deaths per 1,000 population. As of 2002, the death rates for major causes of death (per 100,000 resident population) were: heart disease, 262; cancer, 207.5; cerebrovascular diseases, 46.8; chronic lower respiratory diseases, 33.6; and diabetes, 29.5. The mortality rate from HIV infection was 8.9 per 100,000 population. In 2004, the reported AIDS case rate was at about 21.2 per 100,000 population. In 2002, about 52.9% of the population was considered overweight or obese. As of 2004, about 18.8% of state residents were smokers.

In 2003, New Jersey had 78 community hospitals with about 22,800 beds. There were about 1.1 million patient admissions that year and 14.7 million outpatient visits. The average daily inpatient census was about 16,900 patients. The average cost per day for hospital care was $1,411. Also in 2003, there were about 356 certified nursing facilities in the state with 50,551 beds and an overall occupancy rate of about 87.7%. In 2004, it was estimated that about 75.8% of all state residents had received some type of dental care within the year. New Jersey had 333 physicians per 100,000 resident population in 2004 and 928 nurses per 100,000 in 2005. In 2004, there were a total of 7,045 dentists in the state.

About 11% of state residents were enrolled in Medicaid programs in 2003; 14% were enrolled in Medicare programs in 2004. Approximately 15% of the state population was uninsured in 2004. In 2003, state health care expenditures totaled $12.7 million.

The state's only medical school, the University of Medicine and Dentistry of New Jersey, is a public institution that combines three medical schools, one dental school, a school of allied professions, and a graduate school of biomedical sciences.

39SOCIAL WELFARE

Through the Department of Human Services, New Jersey administers the major federal welfare programs, as well as several programs specifically designed to meet the needs of New Jersey minority groups. Among the latter in the 1990s was the Cuban-Haitian Entrant Program. Additional assistance went to refugees from such areas as Southeast Asia and Eastern Europe.

In 2004, about 332,000 people received unemployment benefits, with the average weekly unemployment benefit at $331. In fiscal year 2005, the estimated average monthly participation in the food stamp program included about 392,416 persons (186,661 households); the average monthly benefit was about $92.89 per person. That year, the total of benefits paid through the state for the food stamp program was about $437.4 million.

Temporary Assistance for Needy Families (TANF), the system of federal welfare assistance that officially replaced Aid to Families with Dependent Children (AFDC) in 1997, was reauthorized through the Deficit Reduction Act of 2005. TANF is funded through federal block grants that are divided among the states based on an equation involving the number of recipients in each state. New Jersey's TANF program is called Work First New Jersey (WFNJ). In 2004, the state program had 108,000 recipients; state and federal expenditures on this TANF program totaled $274 million in fiscal year 2003.

In December 2004, Social Security benefits were paid to 1,370,440 New Jersey residents. This number included 939,010 retired workers, 123,960 widows and widowers, 148,650 disabled workers, 57,990 spouses, and 100,810 children. Social Security beneficiaries represented 15.7% of the total state population and 91.3% of the state's population age 65 and older. Retired workers received an average monthly payment of $1.054; widows and widowers, $993; disabled workers, $976; and spouses, $509. Payments for children of retired workers averaged $516 per month; children of deceased workers, $705; and children of disabled workers, $310. Federal Supplemental Security Income payments in December 2004 went to 150,151 New Jersey residents, averaging $415 a month.

⁴⁰HOUSING

Before 1967, New Jersey took a laissez-faire attitude toward housing. With each locality free to fashion its own zoning ordinances, large tracts of rural land succumbed to "suburban sprawl"—single-family housing developments spread out in two huge arcs from New York City and Philadelphia. Meanwhile, the tenement housing of New Jersey's central cities was left to deteriorate. Because poor housing was at least one of the causes of the Newark riot in 1967, the state established the Department of Community Affairs to coordinate existing housing aid programs and establish new ones. The state legislature also created the Mortgage Finance Agency and Housing Finance Agency to stimulate home buying and residential construction. In an effort to halt suburban sprawl, local and county planning boards were encouraged during the 1970s to adopt master plans for controlled growth. Court decisions in the late 1970s and early 1980s challenged the constitutionality of zoning laws that precluded the development of low-income housing in suburban areas.

In 2004, the state had an estimated 3,414,739 housing units, of which 3,134,481 were occupied; 68.1% were owner-occupied. About 54.6% of all units were single-family, detached homes. Nearly 60% of the entire housing stock was built before 1969. Utility gas is the most common heating energy source, followed by fuel oil and kerosene. It was estimated that 98,620 units lacked telephone service, 10,054 lacked complete plumbing facilities, and 16,364 lacked complete kitchen facilities. The average household had 2.71 members.

In 2004, 36,900 new privately owned units were authorized for construction. The median home value was $291,294, the fifth highest in the country. The median monthly cost for mortgage owners was $1,847, the highest rate in the country. Renters paid a median of $877, the second-highest rate in the country, after California. In 2006, the state received over $8.3 million in community development block grants from the US Department of Housing and Urban Development (HUD).

⁴¹EDUCATION

Public education in New Jersey dates from 1828, when the legislature first allocated funds to support education; by 1871, a public school system was established statewide. In 2004, 87.6% of persons 25 years and older were high school graduates. Some 34.6% of persons obtained a bachelor's degree or higher.

The total enrollment for fall 2002 in New Jersey's public schools stood at 1,367,000. Of these, 979,000 attended schools from kindergarten through grade eight, and 389,000 attended high school. Approximately 57.9% of the students were white, 17.7% were black, 17.2% were Hispanic, 7% were Asian/Pacific Islander, and 0.2% were American Indian/Alaskan Native. Total enrollment was estimated at 1,386,000 in fall 2003 and was expected to be 1,415,000 by fall 2014, an increase of 3.5% during the period 2002–14. Expenditures for public education in 2003–04 were estimated at $20.8 billion or $12,981 per student, the highest among the 50 states. There were 204,732 students enrolled in 964 private schools. Since 1969, the National Assessment of Educational Progress (NAEP) has tested public school students nationwide. The resulting report, *The Nation's Report Card,* stated that in 2005 eighth graders in New Jersey scored 284 out of 500 in mathematics compared with the national average of 278.

As of fall 2002, there were 361,733 students enrolled in institutions of higher education; minority students comprised 34.3% of total postsecondary enrollment. In 2005, New Jersey had 58 degree-granting institutions including, 14 public four-year schools, 19 public two-year schools, and 21 nonprofit, private four-year schools. Rutgers, the state university, began operations as Queen's College in 1766 and was placed under state control in 1956, encompassing the separate colleges of Rutgers, Douglass, Livingston, and Cook, among others. As of 2005, the university had campuses at New Brunswick/Piscataway, Camden, and Newark. The major private university in the state and one of the nation's leading institutions is Princeton University, founded in 1746. Other major private universities are Seton Hall (1856); Stevens Institute of Technology (1870); and Fairleigh Dickinson (1942), with three main campuses.

The New Jersey Commission on Higher Education offers tuition aid grants and scholarships to state residents who attend colleges and universities in the state. Guaranteed loans for any qualified resident are available through the New Jersey Higher Education Assistance Authority.

⁴²ARTS

During the late 1800s and early 1900s, New Jersey towns, especially Atlantic City and Newark, were tryout centers for shows bound for Broadway. The New Jersey Theater Group, a service organization for nonprofit professional theaters, was established in 1978; several theaters—including the Tony Award–winning McCarter

Theater at Princeton and Paper Mill Playhouse in Millburn—are members of the Theater Group.

Around the turn of the century, Ft. Lee was the motion picture capital of the world. Most of the best-known "silents"—including the first, *The Great Train Robbery,* and episodes of *The Perils of Pauline*—were shot there, and in its heyday the state film industry supported 21 companies and 7 studios. New Jersey's early preeminence in cinema, an era that ended with the rise of Hollywood, stemmed partly from the fact that the first motion picture system was developed by Thomas Edison at Menlo Park in the late 1880s. The state created the New Jersey Motion Picture and Television Commission in 1977; in the next six years, production companies spent $57 million in the state. Notable productions during this period included two Woody Allen pictures, *Broadway Danny Rose* and *The Purple Rose of Cairo.*

The New Jersey State Council of the Arts consists of 17 members appointed by the governor. In 2005, the New Jersey State Council of the Arts and other New Jersey arts organizations received 29 grants totaling $1,186,200 from the National Endowment for the Arts. State and private sources also contributed funding to New Jersey's arts programs. The New Jersey Council for the Humanities (NJCH) was founded in 1973 and consists of a 25-member board of trustees. As of 2006 ongoing programs associated with the NJCH included the annual Humanities Festival Week, a week of programs adhering to a particular humanities theme chosen each year; Ideas at Work, promoting forums for thoughts on humanity topics in the work place; and the Horizons Speakers Bureau, providing lectures in humanities across the state. In 2005, the National Endowment for the Humanities contributed $2.6 million to 36 state programs.

The state's long history of support for classical music dates at least to 1796, when William Dunlap of Perth Amboy wrote the libretto for *The Archers,* the first American opera to be commercially produced. The state's leading orchestra is the New Jersey Symphony, which makes its home in the new New Jersey Performing Arts Center in Newark; there are other symphony orchestras in Plainfield and Trenton. As of 2006 the New Jersey Symphony of Newark was noted for providing educational and community programs that included the Newark Early Strings Program, which provides free string instruction to second, third and fourth grade students in the Newark Public School District, and REACH (Resources for Education and Community Harmony,) which presents a variety of musical programs that allow for personal interaction with the artists. The New Jersey State Opera performs in Newark's Symphony Hall, while the Opera Festival of New Jersey makes its home in Lawrenceville. Noteworthy dance companies include the American Repertory Ballet, New Jersey Ballet, and the Nai-Ni Chen Dance Company, described as a "cross-cultural contemporary dance company."

The jazz clubs of northern New Jersey and the seaside rock clubs in Asbury Park have helped launch the careers of many local performers. The city of Asbury Park was scheduled to host its 18th annual Jazz Festival in June 2006. Famous rock music star Bruce Springsteen grew up in southern New Jersey and titled his first album with Columbia Records, *Greetings From Asbury Park, NJ* (1973). Atlantic City's hotels and casinos host numerous star performances every year.

⁴³LIBRARIES AND MUSEUMS

For calendar year 2001, New Jersey had 309 public library systems, with a total of 458 libraries, 149 of which were branches. The state's public library systems that same year housed 31,035,000 volumes of books and serial publications, and had a total circulation of 49,171,000. The system also had 1,076,000 audio and 789,000 video items, 43,000 electronic format items (CD-ROMs, magnetic tapes, and disks), and 15 bookmobiles. The Newark Public Library was the largest municipal system with 1,452,336 volumes and 10 branches. Distinguished by special collections on African-American studies, art and archaeology, economics, and international affairs, among many others, Princeton University's library is the largest in the state, with 4,973,619 volumes and 34,182 periodical subscriptions in 1998; Rutgers University ranked second with 3,238,416. The New Jersey State Library in Trenton contained 470,000 volumes, mostly on the state's history and government. One of the largest business libraries, emphasizing scientific and technical data, is the AT&T Bell Laboratories' library system, based in Murray Hill. In 2001, operating income for the state's public library system was $315,890,000 and included $1,509,000 in federal grants and $9,730,000 in state grants.

New Jersey has more than 177 museums, historic sites, botanical gardens and arboretums. Among the most noteworthy museums are the New Jersey Historical Society in Newark and New Jersey State Museum in Trenton; the Newark Museum, containing both art and science exhibits; Princeton University's Art Museum and Museum of Natural History; and the Jersey City Museum. Also of interest are the early waterfront homes and vessels of Historic Gardner's Basin in Atlantic City, as well as Grover Cleveland's birthplace in Caldwell; the Campbell Museum in Camden (featuring the soup company's collection of bowls and utensils); Cape May County Historical Museum; Clinton Historical Museum Village; US Army Communications-Electronics Museum at Ft. Monmouth; Batsto Village, near Hammonton; Morristown National Historic Park (where George Washington headquartered during the Revolutionary War); Sandy Hook Museum; and one of the most popular attractions, the Edison National Historic Site, formerly the home and workshop of Thomas Edison, in West Orange. In 1984, the grounds at the Skylands section of Ringwood State Park were designated as the official state botanical garden.

⁴⁴COMMUNICATIONS

Many communications breakthroughs—including Telstar, the first communications satellite—have been achieved by researchers at Bell Labs in Holmdel, Whippany, and Murray Hill. Three Bell Labs researchers shared the Nobel Prize in physics (1956) for developing the transistor, a device that has revolutionized communications and many other fields. In 1876, at Menlo Park, Thomas Edison invented the carbon telephone transmitter, a device that made the telephone commercially feasible.

The first mail carriers to come to New Jersey were, typically enough, on their way between New York and Philadelphia. Express mail between the two cities began in 1737, and by 1764, carriers could speed through the state in 24 hours. In colonial times, tavern keepers generally served as the local mailmen. The nation's largest bulk-mail facility is in Jersey City. In 2004, 95.1% of the state's occupied housing units had telephones. Additionally, by

June of that same year there were 6,326,459 mobile wireless telephone subscribers. In 2003, 65.5% of New Jersey households had a computer and 60.5% had Internet access. By June 2005, there were 1,654,477 high-speed lines in New Jersey, 1,479,635 residential and 174,842 for business.

Because the state lacks a major television broadcasting outlet, New Jerseyites receive more news about events in New York City and Philadelphia than in their own towns and cities. In 2005, there were 60 major radio stations (8 AM, 52 FM) and 7 television stations, none of which commanded anything like the audiences and influence of the stations across the Hudson and Delaware rivers. In 1978, in cooperation with public television's WNET (licensed in Newark but operated in New York), New Jersey's public stations began producing New Jersey's first nightly newscast.

A total of 251,401 Internet domain names were registered in New Jersey in the year 2000.

⁴⁵PRESS

New Jersey has not been known for having a very powerful press. In 1702, Queen Anne banned printers from the colony. The state's first periodical, founded in 1758, died two years later. New Jersey's first daily paper, the *Newark Daily Advertiser,* did not arrive until 1832.

Many present-day newspapers, most notably the *Newark Star–Ledger,* have amassed considerable circulation. However, no newspaper has been able to muster statewide influence or match the quality and prestige of the nearby *New York Times* or *Philadelphia Inquirer,* both of which are read widely in the state, along with other New York City and Philadelphia papers. In 2005, there were 18 morning dailies, 1 evening, and 15 Sunday papers. Most of the largest papers are owned by either Gannett Co., Inc (of Virginia) or Advance Publications (of New York).

The following table shows leading New Jersey dailies with their approximate 2005 circulation:

AREA	NAME	DAILY	SUNDAY
Atlantic City	*Press* (m,S)	74,655	93,129
Camden-Cherry Hill	*Courier-Post** (m,S)	75,408	89,922
Hackensack (Bergen County)	*Record* (m,S)	176,177	212,333
Neptune-Asbury Park	*Asbury Park Press** (m,S)	160,399	212,471
Newark	*Star–Ledger*+ (m,S)	400,042	608,257
Trenton	*Times*+ (m,S)	67,600	73,006

*owned by Gannett Co., Inc. +owned by Advance Publications.

Numerous scholarly and historical works have been published by the university presses of Princeton and Rutgers. The offices of Pearson Education and its division, Prentice-Hall, are located in Upper Saddle River. Several New York City publishing houses maintain their production and warehousing facilities in the state. Periodicals published in New Jersey include *Home, Medical Economics, New Jersey Monthly,* and *Personal Computing.*

⁴⁶ORGANIZATIONS

In 2006, there were over 10,065 nonprofit organizations registered within the state, of which about 6,826 were registered as charitable, educational, or religious organizations.

Princeton is the headquarters of several education-related groups, including the Educational Testing Service, Graduate Record Examinations Board, the International Mathematical Union, Independent Educational Services, and Woodrow Wilson National Fellowship Foundation.

Seeing Eye of Morristown was one of the first organizations to provide seeing-eye dogs for the blind. Other medical and health-related organizations are National Industries for the Blind (Wayne), the American Council for Headache Education (Mount Royal), the Multiple Sclerosis Association of America (Cherry Hill), and the American Association of Veterinary State Boards (Teaneck). Birthright USA, an anti-abortion counseling service, has its headquarters in Woodbury; the National Council on Crime and Delinquency is in Ft. Lee. The Institute of Electrical and Electronics Engineers in Piscataway is a professional organization with national membership. There are statewide professional organizations representing most professions.

Hobby and sports groups include the US Golf Association, the International Golf Federation, and the World Amateur Golf Council in Far Hills; US Equestrian Team in Gladstone; Babe Ruth Baseball/Softball in Trenton; the International Boxing Federation in East Orange; the American Double Dutch League in Cherry Hill; and National Intercollegiate Women's Fencing Association in Upper Montclair. The Miss America Organization, established in 1921, sponsors the annual Miss America competition in Atlantic City. The American Vegan Society is based in Malaga.

Several religious organizations have base offices in New Jersey, including the American Coptic Association, the Blue Army of Our Lady of Fatima, USA, the National Interfaith Hospitality Network, and the Xaverian Missionaries of the United States. The American Atheists organization is also based in the state.

There are numerous arts and cultural organizations. Some of national interest include the Music Critics Association of North America, the Musical Heritage Society, the National Music Council, the Royal Academy of Dance, and the World Congress of Teachers of Dancing. The American Accordionist's Associations and an American Accordion Musicological Society are both based in New Jersey. There are a number of local historical societies. The Heritage Institute of Ellis Island is located in Jersey City.

⁴⁷TOURISM, TRAVEL, AND RECREATION

Tourism is a leading industry in New Jersey, accounting for a sizeable part of the state's revenues. One out of nine New Jersey workers has a job in tourism, which was the fastest growing economic sector in 2005, with $36.6 billion in revenue. In 2005, there were 72.2 million visitors to the state, 57% of which were day-trip travelers. About 34% of all trips are made by residents within the state. Nearly 25% of all visitors are from New York and 19% are from Pennsylvania. The Jersey shore has been a popular attraction since 1801, when Cape May began advertising itself as a summer resort. Dining, entertainment, and gambling are also popular.

Of all the shore resorts, the largest has long been Atlantic City, which by the 1890s was the nation's most popular resort city and by 1905 was the first major city with an economy almost totally dependent on tourism. That proved to be its downfall, as improvements in road and air transportation made more modern resorts in other states easily accessible to easterners. By the early 1970s, the city's only claims to fame were the Miss America pageant and the game of Monopoly, whose standard version uses its street names. In an effort to restore Atlantic City to its former luster and revive its economy, New Jersey voters approved a constitutional amendment in 1976 to allow casinos in the resort. Some 33 million people visit Atlantic City annually. New Jersey has 127 miles of beaches from Sandy Hook to Cape May and Ocean City. Casino taxes were earmarked to reduce property taxes of senior citizens. New Jersey's close proximity to New York also makes it attractive to visitors. New Jersey hosts the Liberty Science Center with ferry rides to the Statue of Liberty. Camden has a Six Flags amusement park and Columbia features the Lakota Wolf Preserve.

State attractions include 10 ski areas in northwestern New Jersey (on Hamburg Mountain alone, more than 50 slopes are available), canoeing and camping at the Delaware Water Gap National Recreation Area, 3 national wildlife refuges, 31 public golf courses, and 30 amusement parks, including Great Adventure in central Jersey. Dutch Neck Village, created in 1976, includes a living museum and the Old Hickory Arboretum. Jersey Greens, the largest outlet mall in New Jersey, opened in 1999, anticipating revenues of $5.6 million annually.

48 SPORTS

New Jersey did not have a major league professional team until 1976, when the New York Giants of the National Football League moved across the Hudson River into the newly completed Giants Stadium in the Meadowlands Sports Complex at East Rutherford. The NFL's New York Jets began playing their home games at the Meadowlands in 1984. The Continental Airlines Arena, located at the same site, is the home of the New Jersey Nets of the National Basketball Association and the New Jersey Devils of the National Hockey League. As New York teams that no longer play in their home state, the Giants and the Jets are scorned by some New York sports purists. When the Giants won the Super Bowl in 1987, New York's then mayor, Ed Koch, refused them the ticker-tape parade traditionally given to local sports champions on the grounds that since they play in New Jersey they are not a New York team.

The state did celebrate a championship it could call its own, however, when the Devils won the Stanley Cup in 1995. The Devils repeated their success with two more Stanley Cup victories in 2000 and 2003.

The New Jersey Nets have made a surge in the recent past, becoming one of the most successful teams in the NBA. They captured berths in consecutive NBA Finals in 2002 and 2003, falling short on both occasions, however.

The Meadowlands is also the home of a dual thoroughbred-harness-racing track. Other racetracks are Garden State Park (Cherry Hill), Monmouth Park (Oceanport), and Atlantic City Race Course for thoroughbreds, and Freehold Raceway for harness racing. Auto racing is featured at speedways in Bridgeport, East Windsor, and New Egypt. Trenton has a minor league baseball team, the Thunder, in the Eastern League. New Jersey has several world-class golf courses, including Baltusrol, the site of seven US Opens and the 2005 PGA Championship. Numerous championship boxing matches have been held in Atlantic City.

New Jersey is historically significant for the births of two major national sports. Princeton and Rutgers played what is claimed to be the first intercollegiate football game on 6 November 1869 at New Brunswick. (Princeton was named national champion several times around the turn of the century, for the last time in 1911). The first game of what is known today as baseball was played in New Jersey at the Elysion Field in Hoboken between the Knicker-bockers and the New York Nine on 19 June 1846. Several important college games are held at Giants Stadium each fall. In college basketball, Seton Hall placed high in the rankings repeatedly in the late 1980s and early 1990s, winning the National Invitational Tournament in 1953. In 1989 they made it to the finals, losing to Michigan by one point in overtime. Rutgers had a formidable men's basketball team in the 1970s, making it to the Final Four in 1976.

Other annual sporting events include the New Jersey Offshore Grand Prix Ocean Races held at Point Pleasant Beach in July and the National Marbles Tournament in Wildwood.

49 FAMOUS NEW JERSEYITES

While only one native New Jerseyite, (Stephen) Grover Cleveland (1837–1908), has been elected president of the United States, the state can also properly claim (Thomas) Woodrow Wilson (b.Virginia, 1856–1924), who spent most of his adult life there. Cleveland left his birthplace in Caldwell as a little boy, winning his fame and two terms in the White House (1885–89, 1893–97) as a resident of New York State. After serving as president, he retired to Princeton, where he died and is buried. Wilson, a member of Princeton's class of 1879, returned to the university in 1908 as a professor and became its president in 1902. Elected governor of New Jersey in 1910, Wilson pushed through a series of sweeping reforms before entering the White House in 1913. Wilson's two presidential terms were marked by his controversial decision to declare war on Germany and his unsuccessful crusade for US membership in the League of Nations after World War I.

Two vice presidents hail from New Jersey: Aaron Burr (1756–1836) and Garret A. Hobart (1844–99). Burr, born in Newark and educated at what is now Princeton University, is best remembered for killing Alexander Hamilton in a duel at Weehawken in 1804. Hobart was born in Long Branch, graduated from Rutgers College, and served as a lawyer in Paterson until elected vice president in 1896; he died in office.

Four New Jerseyites have become associate justices of the US Supreme Court: William Paterson (b.Ireland, 1745–1806), Joseph P. Bradley (1813–92), Mahlon Pitney (1858–1924), and William J. Brennan Jr. (1906-1997). Among the relatively few New Jerseyites to serve in the US cabinet was William E. Simon (1927), secretary of the treasury under Gerald Ford.

Few New Jerseyites won important political status in colonial years because the colony was so long under New York's political and social domination. Lewis Morris (b.New York, 1671–1746) was named the first royal governor of New Jersey when severance from New York came in 1738. Governors who made important contributions to the state included William Livingston (b.New York, 1723–90), first governor after New Jersey became a state in 1776; Marcus L. Ward (1812–84), a strong Union supporter; and Alfred E. Driscoll (1902–75), who persevered in getting New Jersey a new state constitution in 1947 despite intense opposition from the Democratic Party leadership. Other important historical figures are Molly Pitcher (Mary Ludwig Hays McCauley, 1754?–1832), a heroine of the American Revolution, and Zebulon Pike (1779–1813), the noted explorer.

Two New Jersey persons have won the Nobel Peace Prize: Woodrow Wilson in 1919, and Nicholas Murray Butler (1862–1947) in 1931. A three-man team at Bell Laboratories in Murray Hill won the 1956 physics award for their invention of the transistor: Walter Brattain (b.China, 1902–87), John Bardeen (b.Wisconsin, 1908–91), and William Shockley (b.England, 1910). Dr. Selman Waksman (b.Russia, 1888–1973), a Rutgers University professor, won the 1952 prize in medicine and physiology for the discovery of streptomycin. Dickinson Woodruff (1895–1973) won the medicine and physiology prize in 1956, and Joshua Lederberg (b.1925) was a co-winner in 1958. Theoretical physicist Albert Einstein (b.Germany, 1879–1955), winner of a Nobel Prize in 1921, spent his last decades in Princeton. One of the world's most prolific inventors, Thomas Alva Edison (b.Ohio, 1847–1931) patented over 1,000 devices from workshops at Menlo Park and West Orange. David Dinkins (b.1927), first African-American mayor of New York was born in Trenton, New Jersey. Norman Schwarzkopf (b.1934), commander of US forces in Desert Storm (Gulf War), was born August 22, 1934 in Trenton, New Jersey. Michael Chang (b.1972), 1989 French Open tennis champion, was born in Hoboken.

The state's traditions in the arts began in colonial times. Patience Lovell Wright (1725–86) of Bordentown was America's first recognized sculptor. Jonathan Odell (1737–1818) was an anti-Revolutionary satirist, while Francis Hopkinson (b.Pennsylvania, 1737–91), lawyer, artist, and musician, lampooned the British. Authors of note after the Revolution included William Dunlap (1766–1839), who compiled the first history of the stage in America; James Fenimore Cooper (1789–1851), one of the nation's first novelists; Mary Mapes Dodge (b.New York, 1838–1905), noted author of children's books; Stephen Crane (1871–1900), famed for *The Red Badge of Courage* (1895); and Albert Payson Terhune (1872–1942), beloved for his collie stories.

Quite a number of prominent 20th-century writers were born in or associated with New Jersey. They include poets William Carlos Williams (1883–1963) and Allen Ginsberg (1926-1997); satirist Dorothy Parker (1893–1967); journalist-critic Alexander Woollcott (1887–1943); Edmund Wilson (1895–1972), influential critic, editor, and literary historian; Norman Cousins (1912–90); Norman Mailer (b.1923); Thomas Fleming (b.1927); John McPhee (b.1931); Philip Roth (b.1933); Imamu Amiri Baraka (LeRoi Jones, b.1934); and Peter Benchley (b.New York, 1940–2006).

Notable 19th-century artists were Asher B. Durand (1796–1886) and George Inness (b.New York, 1825–94). The best-known 20th-century artist associated with New Jersey was Ben Shahn (1898–1969); cartoonist Charles Addams (1912–88) was born in Westfield. Noted photographers born in New Jersey include Alfred Stieglitz (1864–1946) and Dorothea Lange (1895–1965). Important New Jersey composers were Lowell Mason (b.Massachusetts, 1792–1872), called the "father of American church music," and Milton Babbitt (b.Pennsylvania, 1916), long active at Princeton. The state's many concert singers include Anna Case (1889–1984), Paul Robeson (1898–1976), and Richard Crooks (1900–72). Popular singers include Francis Albert "Frank" Sinatra (1915–98),

Sarah Vaughan (1924-1990), Dionne Warwick (b.1941), Paul Simon (b.1942), and Bruce Springsteen (b.1949). Jazz musician William "Count" Basie (1904–84) was born in Red Bank.

Other celebrities native to New Jersey are actors Jack Nicholson (b.1937), Michael Douglas (b.1944), Meryl Streep (b.1948), and John Travolta (b.1954). Comedians Lou Costello (1906–59), Ernie Kovacs (1919–62), Jerry Lewis (b.1926), and Clerow "Flip" Wilson (1933–98) were also born in the state. New Jersey-born athletes include figure skater Richard "Dick" Button (b.1929), winner of two Olympic gold medals.

50 BIBLIOGRAPHY

Cunningham, John T. *This is New Jersey.* 4th ed. New Brunswick, N.J.: Rutgers University Press, 1994.

Council of State Governments. *The Book of the States, 2006 Edition.* Lexington, Ky.: Council of State Governments, 2006.

DeGrove, John Melvin. *Planning Policy and Politics: Smart Growth and the States.* Cambridge, Mass.: Lincoln Institute of Land Policy, 2005.

Doak, Robin S. *Voices from Colonial America. New Jersey.* Washington, D.C.: National Geographic, 2005.

Gillette, William. *Jersey Blue: Civil War Politics in New Jersey, 1854-1865.* New Brunswick, N.J.: Rutgers University Press, 1995.

League of Women Voters of New Jersey. *New Jersey: Spotlight on New Jersey Government.* 6th ed. New Brunswick, N.J.: Rutgers University Press, 1992.

Lee, Francis Bazley (ed.). *Genealogical and Memorial History of the State of New Jersey: A Record of the Achievements of Her People in the Making of a Commonwealth and the Founding of a Nation.* Baltimore, Md.: reprinted for Clearfield Company, Inc. by Genealogical Pub. Co., 2000.

Marzec, Robert P. (ed.). *The Mid-Atlantic Region.* Vol. 2 in *The Greenwood Encyclopedia of American Regional Cultures.* Westport, Conn.: Greenwood Press, 2004.

A New Jersey Anthology. Newark: New Jersey Historical Society, 1994.

Roberts, Russell. *Discover the Hidden New Jersey.* New Brunswick, N.J.: Rutgers University Press, 1995.

Santelli, Robert. *Guide to the Jersey Shore: from Sandy Hook to Cape May.* Guilford, Conn.: Globe Pequot Press, 2000.

Simon, Bryant. *Boardwalk of Dreams: Atlantic City and the Fate of Urban America.* New York: Oxford University Press, 2004.

US Department of Commerce, Economics and Statistics Administration, US Census Bureau. *New Jersey, 2000. Summary Social, Economic, and Housing Characteristics: 2000 Census of Population and Housing.* Washington, D.C.: US Government Printing Office, 2003.

NEW MEXICO

State of New Mexico

ORIGIN OF STATE NAME: Spanish explorers in 1540 called the area "the new Mexico." **NICKNAME:** Land of Enchantment. **CAPITAL:** Santa Fe. **ENTERED UNION:** 6 January 1912 (47th). **SONG:** "O Fair New Mexico;" "Así es Nuevo México." **MOTTO:** *Crescit eundo* (It grows as it goes). **FLAG:** The sun symbol of the Zia Indians appears in red on a yellow field. **OFFICIAL SEAL:** An American bald eagle with extended wings grasps three arrows in its talons and shields a smaller eagle grasping a snake in its beak and a cactus in its talons (the emblem of Mexico, and thus symbolic of the change in sovereignty over the state). Below the scene is the state motto. The words "Great Seal of the State of New Mexico 1912" surround the whole. **BIRD:** Roadrunner (chaparral bird). **FISH:** Cutthroat trout. **FLOWER:** Yucca (Our Lords Candles). **TREE:** Piñon pine. **GEM:** Turquoise. **LEGAL HOLIDAYS:** New Year's Day, 1 January; Birthday of Martin Luther King Jr., 3rd Monday in January; Memorial Day, last Monday in May; Independence Day, 4 July; Labor Day, 1st Monday in September; Columbus Day, 2nd Monday in October; Veterans' Day, 11 November; Thanksgiving Day, 4th Thursday in November; President's Day, day after Thanksgiving; Christmas Day, 25 December. **TIME:** 5 AM MST = noon GMT.

¹LOCATION, SIZE, AND EXTENT

New Mexico is located in the southwestern United States. Smaller only than Montana of the eight Rocky Mountain states, it ranks fifth in size among the 50 states. The area of New Mexico is 121,593 sq mi (314,926 sq km), of which land comprises 121,335 sq mi (314,258 sq km) and inland water 258 sq mi (668 sq km). Almost square in shape except for its jagged southern border, New Mexico extends about 352 mi (566 km) E–W and 391 mi (629 km) N–S.

New Mexico is bordered on the N by Colorado; on the E by Oklahoma and Texas; on the s by Texas and the Mexican state of Chihuahua (with a small portion of the south-central border formed by the Rio Grande); and on the w by Arizona. The total boundary length of New Mexico is 1,434 mi (2,308 km).

The geographic center of the state is in Torrance County, 12 mi (19 km) ssw of Willard.

²TOPOGRAPHY

The Continental Divide extends from north to south through central New Mexico. The north-central part of the state lies within the Southern Rocky Mountains, and the northwest forms part of the Colorado Plateau. The eastern two-fifths of the state fall on the western fringes of the Great Plains.

Major mountain ranges include the Southern Rockies, the Chuska Mountains in the northwest, and the Caballo, San Andres, San Mateo, Sacramento, and Guadalupe ranges in the south and southwest. The highest point in the state is Wheeler Peak, at 13,161 ft (4,014 m); the lowest point, 2,842 ft (867 m), is at Red Bluff Reservoir. The mean elevation of the state is approximately 5,700 ft (1,739 m).

The Rio Grande traverses New Mexico from north to south and forms a small part of the state's southern border with Texas. Other major rivers include the Pecos, San Juan, Canadian, and Gila. The largest bodies of inland water are the Elephant Butte Reservoir and Conchas Reservoir, both created by dams.

The Carlsbad Caverns, the largest known subterranean labyrinth in the world, penetrate the foothills of the Guadalupes in the southeast. The caverns embrace more than 37 mi (60 km) of connecting chambers and corridors and are famed for their stalactite and stalagmite formations.

³CLIMATE

New Mexico's climate ranges from arid to semiarid, with a wide range of temperatures. Average January temperatures vary from about 35°F (2°C) in the north to about 55°F (13°C) in the southern and central regions. July temperatures range from about 78°F (26°C) at high elevations to around 92°F (33°C) at lower elevations. The record high temperature for the state is 122°F (50°C), set most recently on 27 July 1994 at Lakewood; the record low, -50°F (-46°C), was set on 1 February 1951 at Gavilan.

Average annual precipitation is about 8.5 in (21 cm) in Albuquerque in the desert; at high elevations, annual precipitation averaged over 20 in (50 cm). Nearly one-half the annual rainfall comes during July and August, and thunderstorms are common in the summer. Snow is much more frequent in the north than in the south; Albuquerque gets about 11 in (28 cm) of snow per year, and the northern mountains receive up to 100 in (254 cm).

⁴FLORA AND FAUNA

New Mexico is divided into the following six life zones: lower Sonoran, upper Sonoran, transition, Canadian, Hudsonian, and arctic-alpine.

Characteristic vegetation in each zone includes, respectively, desert shrubs and grasses; piñon/juniper woodland, sagebrush, and chaparral; ponderosa pine and oak woodlands; mixed conifer and aspen forests; spruce/fir forests and meadows; tundra wild flowers and riparian shrubs. The yucca has three varieties in New Mexico and is the state flower. Thirteen plant species were listed as threatened or endangered in 2006, including Sacramento prickly poppy, Moncos milk-vetch, and two species of cacti.

Indigenous animals include pronghorn antelope, javelina, and black-throated sparrow in the lower Sonoran zone; mule and white-tailed deer, ringtail, and brown towhee in the upper Sonoran zone; elk and wild turkey in the transition zone; black bear and hairy woodpecker in the Canadian zone; pine marten and blue grouse in the Hudsonian zone; and bighorn sheep, pika, ermine, and white-tailed ptarmigan in the arctic-alpine zone. Among notable desert insects are the tarantula, centipede, and vinegarroon. The coatimundi, Baird's sparrow, and brook stickleback are among rare animals. Twenty-eight New Mexican animal species (vertebrates and invertebrates) were classified as threatened or endangered by the US Fish and Wildlife Service in April 2006, including two species of bat, whooping crane, bald eagle, southwestern willow flycatcher, Mexican spotted owl, three species of shiner, and razorback sucker.

5 ENVIRONMENTAL PROTECTION

Agencies concerned with the environment include the New Mexico Environment Department (NMED), the Environmental Improvement Board, the Water Quality Control Commission, and the Energy, Minerals and Natural Resources Department. As the state's leading environmental agency, the NMED's mission is to preserve, protect, and perpetuate New Mexico's environment for present and future generations. The Department is comprised of four divisions, 14 bureaus, four districts, and 17 field offices. Each entity is responsible for different areas and functions of environmental protection (or administrative support) concerning air, water, and land resources. Under the authority of state/federal laws and regulations, the NMED fulfills its mission through the judicious application of statewide regulatory, technical assistance, planning, enforcement, educational, and related functions in the service of its citizens.

Wetlands cover about 482,000 acres (195,058 hectares) of the state and include such diverse areas as forested wetlands, marshes, alpine snow glades, and salt meadows. Conversion of land for agricultural and urban development are the primary threats to these lands, which lie primarily in the eastern and northern areas of the state.

In 2003, 17.9 million lb of toxic chemicals were released in the state. Also in 2003, New Mexico had 120 hazardous waste sites listed in the US Environment Protection Agency (EPA) database, 12 of which were on the National Priorities List as of 2006. In 2005, the EPA spent over $3.2 million through the Superfund program for the cleanup of hazardous waste sites in the state. The same year, federal EPA grants awarded to the state included $8.3 million for the drinking water state revolving fund and $6.8 million for improvements in municipal wastewater treatment programs.

6 POPULATION

New Mexico ranked 36th in population in the United States with an estimated total of 1,928,384 in 2005, an increase of 6% since 2000. Between 1990 and 2000, New Mexico's population grew from 1,515,069 to 1,819,046, an increase of 20.1%. The population is projected to reach 2 million by 2015 and 2.1 million by 2025. The population density in 2004 was 15.7 persons per sq mi. In 2004 the median age was 35.8. Persons under 18 years old accounted for 25.9% of the population while 12.1% was age 65 or older.

In 2004, an estimated 484,246 people lived in Albuquerque. An estimated 781,447 lived in the Albuquerque metropolitan area. The Santa Fe metropolitan area had 138,705 inhabitants.

7 ETHNIC GROUPS

New Mexico has two large minorities: Indians and Hispanics. In 2000, the estimated American Indian population was 173,483 (9.5% of the total population— the second-highest percentage of any state). In 2004, 10.1% of the population was American Indian. Part of Arizona's great Navaho reservation extends across the border into New Mexico. New Mexico's Navaho population was recorded as 67,397 in 2000. There are 2 Apache reservations, 19 Pueblo villages (including one for the Zia in Sandoval County), and lands allotted to other tribes. Altogether, Indian lands cover 8,152,895 acres (3,299,477 hectares), 10.5% of New Mexico's area (second only to Arizona in proportion of Indian lands). In 2000 the Zuni lands had a population of 7,758, and the Acoma reservation had 2,802 residents.

The Hispanic population is an old one, descending from Spanish-speaking peoples who lived there before the territory was annexed by the United States. In 2000, Hispanics and Latinos (including a small number of immigrants from modern Mexico) numbered 765,386 or 42.1% of the total state population. That percentage had increased to 43.3% of the state population in 2004.

As of 2000, an estimated 19,255 Asians, 1,503 Pacific Islanders, and 34,343 black Americans lived in the state. In 2004, 2.4% of the state's population was black, 1.3% Asian, and 0.1% Pacific Islander. That year, 1.5% of the population reported origin of two or more races.

8 LANGUAGES

New Mexico has large Indian and Spanish-speaking populations. But just a few place-names, like Tucumcari and Mescalero, echo in English the presence of the Apache, Zuni, Navaho, and other tribes living there. Numerous Spanish borrowings include *vigas* (rafters) in the northern half, and *canales* (gutters) and *acequia* (irrigation ditch) in the Rio Grande Valley. New Mexico English is a mixture of dominant Midland, with some Northern features (such as *sick to the stomach*) in the northeast, and Southern and South Midland features such as *spoonbread* and *carry* (escort) in the eastern agricultural fringe.

In 2000, 1,072,947 New Mexicans—63.5% of the resident population five years of age and older—spoke only English at home, down slightly from 64.5% in 1990.

The following table gives selected statistics from the 2000 Census for language spoken at home by persons five years old and over.

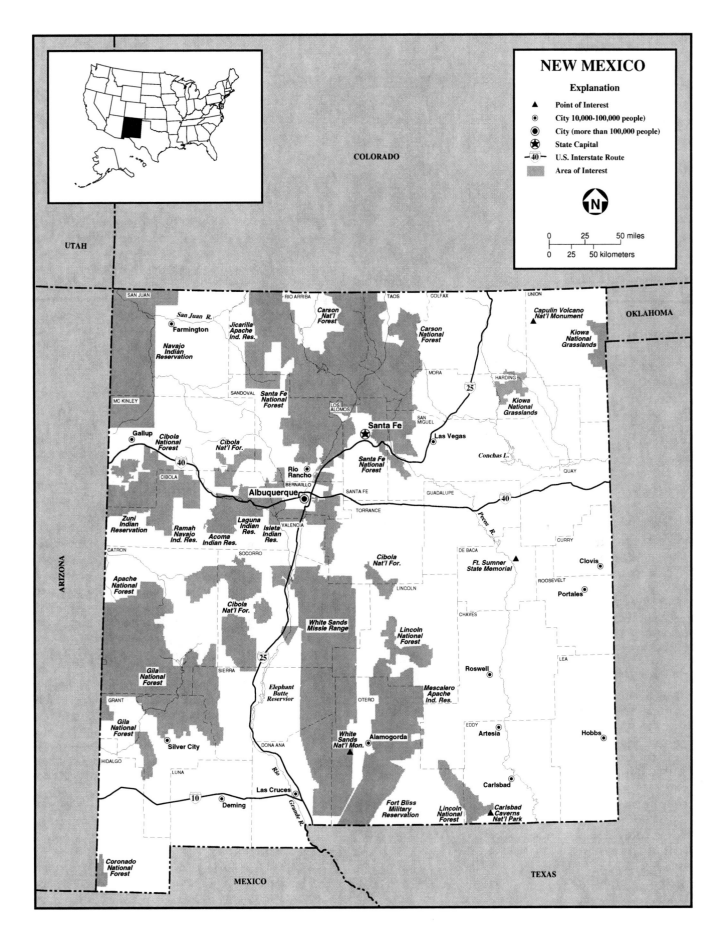

The category "Other Native North American languages" includes Apache, Cherokee, Choctaw, Dakota, Keres, Pima, and Yupik.

LANGUAGE	NUMBER	PERCENT
Population 5 years and over	**1,689,911**	**100.0**
Speak only English	1,072,947	63.5
Speak a language other than English	616,964	36.5
Speak a language other than English	**616,964**	**36.5**
Spanish or Spanish Creole	485,681	28.7
Navajo	68,788	4.1
Other Native North American languages	26,880	1.6
German	7,871	0.5
French (incl. Patois, Cajun)	4,332	0.3
Chinese	2,983	0.2
Vietnamese	2,523	0.1
Italian	1,931	0.1
Tagalog	1,603	0.1
Japanese	1,263	0.1
Korean	1,197	0.1
Arabic	980	0.1

9 RELIGIONS

The first religions in New Mexico were practiced by Pueblo and Navaho Indians. Franciscan missionaries arrived at the time of Coronado's conquest in 1540, and the first Roman Catholic church in the state was built in 1598. Roman Catholicism has long been the dominant religion, though from the mid-1800s there has also been a steady increase in the number of Protestants. The first Baptist missionaries arrived in 1849, the Methodists in 1850, and the Mormons in 1877.

The state's Roman Catholic churches had about 435,244 members in 2004. The next largest denomination is the Southern Baptist Convention, with 132,675 in 2000; 2,856 newly baptized members reported in 2002. In 2004, there were 39,865 United Methodists statewide. In 2000, there were 22,070 members of Assemblies of God, 18,985 members of Churches of Christ, and 13,224 Presbyterians (USA). The Church of Jesus Christ of Latter-day Saints reported about 61,862 members in 123 congregation in 2006; the state's first Mormon temple was dedicated in Albuquerque in 2000. The Jewish population was estimated at 10,500 in 2000 and the Muslim congregations had 2,604 adherents. The same year, about 761,218 people (about 41.8% of the population) were not counted as members of any religious organization.

10 TRANSPORTATION

Important early roads included El Camino Real, extending from Mexico City, Mexico, up to Santa Fe and the Santa Fe Trail, leading westward from Independence, Missouri. By 2004, New Mexico had 64,004 mi (103,046 km) of public roads and streets.

In 2004, some 1.539 million motor vehicles were registered in the state, of which around 681,000 were automobiles, approximately 820,000 were trucks of all types, some 36,000 were motorcycles, and about 2,000 were buses. In that same year, there were 1,271,365 licensed drivers in the state.

Rail service did not begin in New Mexico until 1879. New Mexico had 2,388 mi (3,844 km) of track in 2003, with Class I roads making up close to 94% of that total. The main rail lines serving the state are the Union Pacific and the Burlington Northern Santa Fe. As of 2006, Amtrak provided passenger service to five stations in New Mexico via its Chicago to Los Angeles Southwest Chief train and via its New Orleans to Los Angeles train the Sunset Limited.

In 2005, New Mexico had a total of 176 public and private-use aviation-related facilities. This included 150 airports, 25 heliports, and one seaplane base. Albuquerque International is the state's main airport. In 2004, the airport had 3,079,172 enplanements.

11 HISTORY

The earliest evidence of human occupation in what is now New Mexico, dating from about 20,000 years ago, has been found in Sandia Cave near Albuquerque. This so-called Sandia man was later joined by other nomadic hunters—the Clovis and Folsom people from the northern and eastern portions of the state, and the Cochise culture, which flourished in southwestern New Mexico from about 10,000 to 500 BC. The Mogollon people tilled small farms in the southwest from 300 BC to about 100 years before Columbus came to the New World. Also among the state's early inhabitants were the Basket Makers, a seminomadic people who eventually evolved into the Anasazi, or Cliff Dwellers. The Anasazi, who made their home in the Four Corners region (where present-day New Mexico meets Colorado, Arizona, and Utah), were the predecessors of the modern Pueblo Indians.

The Pueblo people lived along the upper Rio Grande, except for a desert group east of Albuquerque, who lived in the same kind of apartment-like villages as the river Pueblos. During the 13th century, the Navajo settled in the Four Corners area to become farmers, sheepherders, and occasional enemies of the Pueblos. The Apache, a more nomadic and warlike group who came at about the same time, later posed a threat to all the non-Indians who arrived in New Mexico during the Spanish, Mexican, and American periods.

Francisco Vásquez de Coronado led the earliest major expedition to New Mexico, beginning in 1540, 80 years before the Pilgrims landed at Plymouth Rock. In 1598, Don Juan de Onate led an expedition up the Rio Grande, where, one year later, he established the settlement of San Gabriel, near present-day Espanola; in 1610, the Spanish moved their center of activity to Santa Fe. For more than two centuries, the Spaniards, who concentrated their settlements, farms, and ranches in the upper Rio Grande Valley, dominated New Mexico, except for a period from 1680 to about 1693, when the Pueblo Indians temporarily regained control of the region.

In 1821, Mexico gained its independence from Spain, and New Mexico came under the Mexican flag for 25 years. The unpopularity of government officials sent from Mexico City and the inability of the new republic to control the Apache led to the revolt of 1837, which was put down by a force from Albuquerque led by General Manuel Armijo. In 1841, as governor of the Mexican territory, Armijo defeated an invading force from the Republic of Texas, but he later made a highly controversial decision not to defend Apache Pass east of Santa Fe during the Mexican-American War, instead retreating and allowing US forces under the command of General Stephen Watts Kearny to enter the capital city unopposed on 18 August 1846.

Kearny, without authorization from Congress, immediately attempted to make New Mexico a US territory. He appointed the respected Indian trader Charles Bent, a founder of Bent's Fort on the Santa Fe Trail, as civil governor, and then led his army on to

California. After Kearny's departure, a Mexican and Indian revolt in Taos resulted in Bent's death; the suppression of the Taos uprising by another US Army contingent secured American control over New Mexico, although the area did not officially become a part of the United States until the Treaty of Guadalupe-Hidalgo ended the Mexican-American War in 1848.

New Mexico became a US territory as part of the Compromise of 1850, which also brought California into the Union as a free state. Territorial status did not bring about rapid or dramatic changes in the lives of those who were already in New Mexico. However, an increasing number of people traveling on the Santa Fe Trail—which had been used since the early 1820s to carry goods between Independence, Mo., and Santa Fe—were Americans seeking a new home in the Southwest. One issue that divided many of these new settlers from the original Spanish-speaking inhabitants was land. Native New Mexicans resisted, sometimes violently, the efforts of new Anglo residents and outside capital to take over lands that had been allocated during the earlier Spanish and Mexican periods. Anglo lawyers such as Thomas Benton Catron acquired unprecedented amounts of land from native grantees as payment of legal fees in the prolonged litigation that often accompanied these disputes. Eventually, a court of private land claims, established by the federal government, legally processed 33 million acres (13 million hectares) of disputed land from 1891 to 1904.

Land disputes were not the only cause of violence during the territorial period. In 1862, Confederate General Henry Hopkins Sibley led an army of Texans up the Rio Grande and occupied Santa Fe; he was defeated at Glorieta Pass in northern New Mexico by a hastily assembled army that included volunteers from Colorado and New Mexico and Union regulars, in a battle that has been labeled the Gettysburg of the West. The so-called Lincoln County War of 1878–81, a range war pitting cattlemen against merchants and involving, among other partisans, William H. Bonney (Billy the Kid), helped give the territory the image of a lawless region unfit for statehood.

Despite the tumult, New Mexico began to make substantial economic progress. In 1879, the Atchison, Topeka and Santa Fe Railroad entered the territory. General Lew Wallace, who was appointed by President Rutherford B. Hayes to settle the Lincoln County War, was the last territorial governor to enter New Mexico by stagecoach and the first to leave it by train.

By the end of the 19th century, the Indian threat that had plagued the Anglos, like the Spanish-speaking New Mexicans before them, had finally been resolved. New Mexicans won the respect of Theodore Roosevelt by enlisting in his Rough Riders during the Spanish-American War, and when he became president, he returned the favor by working for statehood. New Mexico finally became a state on 6 January 1912, under President William H. Taft.

In March 1916, irregulars of the Mexican revolutionary Pancho Villa crossed the international boundary into New Mexico, killing, robbing, and burning homes in Columbus. US troops under the command of General John J. Pershing were sent into Mexico on a long and unsuccessful expedition to capture Villa, while National Guardsmen remained on the alert in the Columbus area for almost a year.

The decade of the 1920s was characterized by the discovery and development of new resources. Potash salts were found near Carlsbad, and important petroleum reserves in the south-east and northwest were discovered and exploited. Oil development made possible another important industry, tourism, which began to flourish as gasoline became increasingly available. This period of prosperity ended, however, with the onset of the Great Depression.

World War II revived the economy, but at a price. In 1942, hundreds of New Mexicans stationed in the Philippines were among the US troops forced to make the cruel "Bataan march" to Japanese prison camps. Scientists working at Los Alamos ushered in the Atomic Age with the explosion of the first atomic bomb at White Sands Proving Ground in June 1945.

The remarkable growth that characterized the Sunbelt during the postwar era has been noticeable in New Mexico. Newcomers from many parts of the country moved to the state, a demographic shift with profound social, cultural, and political consequences. Spanish-speaking New Mexicans, once an overwhelming majority, became a minority. As of the 2000 census, Hispanics accounted for 42% of the state's population, and Native Americans accounted for 9.5% of the population.

Defense-related industries have been a mainstay of New Mexico's economy in the postwar period. Income from this sector declined in the early 1990s due to reductions in military spending following the end of the Cold War. However, this decline was offset by New Mexico's diversification into nonmilitary production, including such high-tech projects as Intel's Rio Rancho plant, which, in the mid-1990s, was the world's largest computer-chip factory. Tourism also played a major role in New Mexico's economy through the 1990s, and the state remains a leading center of space and nuclear research.

Today New Mexico's leaders struggle with two persistent problems—poverty and crime. In 1998, with 20.4% of its residents living below the poverty level (the highest percentage in the nation), the state's children were found to be suffering. More than one in four children in New Mexico was poor, posing the immediate problems of hunger and malnutrition, lack of education, and a strain on the public health system as well as the long-term challenge to the juvenile justice system. Government figures in 1998 showed the state ranked as the most violent in the nation, with 961 crimes per 100,000 residents. New Mexico was one of four states (Louisiana, Mississippi, and Arkansas were the other three) with a poverty rate for 2002–04 (based on a three-year average) of over 17%. (New Mexico's rate was 17.5%.)

The state's public education system also posed a major issue in 2000, with the debate centering on proposed voucher legislation that would help parents pay for private schools. Opponents, including New Mexico's Democratic Party, argued in favor of legislation that would boost public schools instead—increasing teacher pay, reducing class sizes, and improving early childhood education.

Democratic Governor Bill Richardson, elected in 2002 by the largest margin of any candidate since 1964, came to the job with a long list of political credentials: former US Representative, UN ambassador, and Energy Secretary. He has been nominated several times for the Nobel Peace Prize. By 2005 he had made progress on such target issues as tax cuts, school reform, job creation, water projects, and efforts to combat drunk driving.

12 STATE GOVERNMENT

The constitution of New Mexico was drafted in 1910, approved by the voters in 1911, and came into effect when statehood was achieved in 1912. A new constitution drawn up by a convention of elected delegates was rejected by the voters in 1969. By January 2005, the 1912 document had been amended 151 times.

The legislature consists of a 42-member Senate and a 70-member House of Representatives. Senators must be at least 25 years old, qualified voters, and residents of their districts; they serve four-year terms. House members must be 21 years old, qualified voters, and residents of their districts; they serve two-year terms. The legislature meets every year, for 60 calendar days in odd-numbered years and 30 calendar days in even-numbered years. The legislature may call special sessions, limited to 30 calendar days, by petition of three-fifths of the members of each house. Legislators do not receive a salary from the state.

The executive branch consists of the governor and lieutenant governor (elected jointly), secretary of state, auditor, treasurer, attorney general, and commissioner of public lands. They are elected for four-year terms; none may serve more than two successive terms. Candidates for governor must be 30 years old, US citizens, qualified voters, and residents of New Mexico for at least five years prior to election. As of December 2004, the governor's salary was $110,000. Three elected members of the Corporation Commission, which has various regulatory and revenue-raising responsibilities, serve six-year terms.

A bill passed by the legislature becomes law if signed by the governor, if left unsigned by the governor for three days while the legislature is in session, or if passed over the governor's veto by two-thirds of the members present in each house. If the governor does not act on a bill after the legislature adjourns, the bill dies after 20 days.

In general, constitutional amendments must be approved by majority vote in each house and by a majority of the electorate. Amendments dealing with voting rights, school lands, and linguistic requirements for education can be proposed only by three-fourths of each house, and subsequently must be approved by three-fourths of the total electorate and two-thirds of the electorate in each county.

In order to vote in state elections, a person must be 18 years old, a US citizen, and a state resident. Restrictions apply to convicted felons and those declared mentally incompetent by the court.

13 POLITICAL PARTIES

Although Democrats hold a very substantial edge in voter registration—53% of registered voters to the Republicans' 33% as of 1998—New Mexico has been a "swing state" in US presidential elections since it entered the Union. Between 1948 and 1992, New Mexicans voted for Democratic presidential candidates four times and Republican presidential candidates eight times, choosing in every election except 1976 and 1992 the candidate who was also the presidential choice of voters nationwide. In the 2000 presidential election, Democrat Al Gore beat Republican candidate George W. Bush by a mere 366 votes, out of approximately 615,000 cast statewide. In 2004, Bush won the state, with 50% of votes cast to 49% for Democratic challenger John Kerry. In 2004 there were 1,105,000 registered voters. The state had five electoral votes in the 2004 presidential election.

New Mexico's US senators in 2003 were Democrat Jeff Bingaman, elected in 2000 to his fourth term, and Republican Peter V. Domenici, who was elected to his sixth term in 2002. Following the 2004 elections, New Mexico's US House delegation consisted of two Republicans and one Democrat. As of mid-2005 there were 23 Democrats and 19 Republicans in the state Senate and 42 Democrats and 28 Republicans in the state House. Governor Bill

New Mexico Presidential Vote by Political Parties, 1948–2004

YEAR	ELECTORAL VOTE	NEW MEXICO WINNER	DEMOCRAT	REPUBLICAN	PROGRESSIVE
1948	4	*Truman (D)	105,240	80,303	1,037
1952	4	*Eisenhower (R)	105,435	132,170	225
					CONSTITUTION
1956	4	*Eisenhower (R)	106,098	146,788	364
1960	4	*Kennedy (D)	156,027	153,733	570
1964	4	*Johnson (D)	194,015	132,838	1,217
					AMERICAN IND.
1968	4	*Nixon (R)	130,081	169,692	25,737
					AMERICAN
1972	4	*Nixon (R)	141,084	235,606	8,767
					SOC. WORKERS
1976	4	Ford (R)	201,148	211,419	2,462
					LIBERTARIAN
1980	4	*Reagan (R)	167,826	250,779	4,365
1984	4	*Reagan (R)	201,769	307,101	4,459
1988	4	*Bush (R)	244,497	270,341	3,268
1992**	5	*Clinton (D)	261,617	212,824	1,615
1996**	5	*Clinton (D)	273,495	232,751	2,996
2000	5	Gore (D)	286,783	286,417	2,058
2004***	5	*Bush, G. W. (R)	376,930	370,942	2,382

*Won US presidential election.
**IND. candidate Ross Perot received 91,895 votes in 1992 and 32,257 votes in 1996.
***IND. candidate Ralph Nader received 4,053 votes in 2004.

Richardson, Democrat, was first elected in 2002. He had previously served as a US Representative, UN ambassador, and Energy Secretary under President Bill Clinton.

¹⁴LOCAL GOVERNMENT

There were 33 counties in New Mexico as of 2005. Each is governed by commissioners elected for two-year terms. Other county officers include the clerk, assessor, treasurer, surveyor, sheriff, and probate judge. Municipalities are incorporated as cities, towns, or villages. As of 2005, there were 101 municipalities, 89 public school districts, and 628 special districts.

The Indian Reorganization Act of 1934 reaffirmed the right of Indians to govern themselves, adopt constitutions, and form corporations to do business under federal law. Indians also retain the right to vote in state and federal elections. Pueblo Indians elect governors from each pueblo to form a coalition called the All-Indian Pueblo Council. The Apache elect a tribal council headed by a president and vice-president. The Navajo—one-third of whom live in New Mexico—elect a chairman, vice-chairman, and council members from their reservation in New Mexico and Arizona.

In 2005, local government accounted for about 77,894 full-time (or equivalent) employment positions.

¹⁵STATE SERVICES

To address the continuing threat of terrorism and to work with the federal Department of Homeland Security, homeland security in New Mexico operates under executive order; a special assistant to the governor is designated as the state homeland security advisor.

The Department of Transportation (until 2003 the State Highway Commission) supervises the state transportation system; with it is included the Division of Aviation.

Welfare services are provided through the Human Services Department. A related service agency is the Department of Indian Affairs. Health services are provided by the Department of Health. The various public protection agencies include the divisions of consumer protection, criminal appeals, civil, litigation, prosecutions and investigations, violence against women, and Medicaid fraud—all within the purview of the Attorney General's Office; the Department of Public Safety; the Department of Corrections; and the New Mexico State Police. Education is regulated by the Department of Education.

The state's natural resources are protected by the Department of Game and Fish, the Environment Department, the Energy Minerals and Natural Resources Department, and the Tourism Department.

¹⁶JUDICIAL SYSTEM

New Mexico's judicial branch consists of a supreme court, an appeals court, district courts, probate courts, magistrate courts, and other lesser courts as created by law.

The New Mexico Supreme Court is composed of a chief justice and four associate justices. The Appeals Court, created to take over some of the Supreme Court's caseload, is composed of 10 judges. All are elected for eight-year terms.

The state's 33 counties are divided into 13 judicial districts, served by 72 district judges, each elected for a six-year term. District courts have unlimited general jurisdiction and are commonly referred to as trial courts. They also serve as courts of review for decisions of lower courts and administrative agencies. Each county has a probate court, served by a probate judge who is elected from within the county for a two-year term.

As of 31 December 2004, a total of 6,379 prisoners were held in New Mexico's state and federal prisons, an increase from 6,223 of 2.5% from the previous year. As of year-end 2004, a total of 581 inmates were female, up from 576 or 0.9% from the year before. Among sentenced prisoners (one year or more), New Mexico had an incarceration rate of 318 per 100,000 population in 2004.

According to the Federal Bureau of Investigation, New Mexico in 2004, had a violent crime rate (murder/nonnegligent manslaughter; forcible rape; robbery; aggravated assault) of 687.3 reported incidents per 100,000 population, or a total of 13,081 reported incidents. Crimes against property (burglary; larceny/theft; and motor vehicle theft) in that same year totaled 79,895 reported incidents or 4,197.7 reported incidents per 100,000 people. New Mexico has a death penalty, of which lethal injection is the sole method of execution. From 1976 through 5 May 2006, the state has carried out only one execution, on November 6, 2001. As of 1 January 2006, New Mexico had only two inmates on death row.

In 2003, New Mexico spent $71,574,810 on homeland security, an average of $36 per state resident.

¹⁷ARMED FORCES

In 2004, there were 11,994 active-duty military personnel and 6,805 civilian personnel stationed in New Mexico, 6,523 of whom were in the Air Force. The major installations are Kirtland Air Force Base in the Albuquerque area, Holloman Air Force Base at Alamogordo, and White Sands Missile Range north of Las Cruces. Defense contract awards totaled more than $1.07 billion in 2004, and payroll outlays were $1.4 billion.

There were 180,172 veterans living in New Mexico in 2003. Of these, 22,349 served in World War II; 18,976 in the Korean conflict; 56,308 during the Vietnam era; and 28,154 served in the Persian Gulf War. For the fiscal year 2004, total Veterans Affairs expenditures in New Mexico amounted to $686 million.

As of 31 October 2004, the New Mexico State Police employed 565 full-time sworn officers.

¹⁸MIGRATION

Prior to statehood, the major influx of migrants came from Texas and Mexico; many of these immigrants spoke Spanish as their primary language.

Wartime prosperity during the 1940s brought a wave of Anglos into the state. New Mexico experienced a net gain through migration of 78,000 people during 1940–60, a net loss of 130,000 during the economic slump of the 1960s, and another net gain of 154,000 between 1970 and 1983. In the 1980s, New Mexico had a net gain from migration of 63,000 residents, accounting for 28% of the state's population increase during those years. Between 1990 and 1998, the state had net gains of 55,000 in domestic migration and 36,000 in international migration. In 1998, 2,199 foreign immigrants entered New Mexico. The state's overall population increased 14.6% between 1990 and 1998. In the period 2000–05, net international migration was 27,974 and net internal migration was 9,527, for a net gain of 37,501 people.

[19] INTERGOVERNMENTAL COOPERATION

New Mexico participates in the Interstate Oil and Gas Compact; Interstate Compact for Juveniles; Western Interstate Commission for Higher Education; Western Interstate Corrections Compact; Western Interstate Nuclear Compact; compacts governing use of the Rio Grande and the Canadian, Costilla, Colorado, La Plata, and Pecos rivers; and other interstate agreements including the Cumbres and Toltec Scenic Railroad Compact. It is an associate member of the Interstate Mining Compact. In fiscal year 2005, New Mexico received $3.018 billion in federal grants, an estimated $3.070 billion in fiscal year 2006, and an estimated $3.142 billion in fiscal year 2007.

[20] ECONOMY

New Mexico was primarily an agricultural state until the 1940s, when military activities assumed major economic importance. Currently, major industries include manufacturing, petroleum, and food. Tourism also continues to flourish. Major employers range from Wal-Mart, Intel, Kirtland Air Force Base, to Los Alamos National Laboratory, and Honeywell Inc. New Mexico's economy had an unusually large public sector, accounting for over 18% of total state product in 2001, compared to the state average of 12%. The state was relatively unaffected by both the boom of the late 1990s and the bust of 2001. In 1998 and 1999, the state posted anemic growth rates of 1.4% and 1.5%, and although this picked up to a strong 6.8% in 2000, growth continued at 5.4% in the recession year of 2001. The basis for the improvement—growth in general services, the government, transportation and utilities sector, and financial services offsetting steady losses in mining, manufacturing and construction—continued into 2002. As was true with the previous national recession in the early 1990s, New Mexico has not experienced net job losses.

New Mexico's gross state product (GSP) in 2004 was $61.012 billion, of which the real estate sector accounted for the largest share at $7.105 billion or 11.6% of GSP, followed by manufacturing (durable and nondurable goods) at $5.446 billion (8.9% of GSP), and health care and social assistance services at $4.107 billion (6.7% of GSP). In that same year, there were an estimated 143,909 small businesses in New Mexico. Of the 42,241 businesses that had employees, an estimated total of 40,611 or 96.1% were small companies. An estimated 5,683 new businesses were established in the state in 2004, up 3.2% from the year before. Business terminations that same year came to 5,592, down 3.1% from 2003. There were 727 business bankruptcies in 2004, down by 6.1% from the previous year. In 2005, the state's personal bankruptcy (Chapter 7 and Chapter 13) filing rate was 485 filings per 100,000 people, ranking New Mexico as the 27th highest in the nation.

[21] INCOME

In 2005 New Mexico had a gross state product (GSP) of $69 billion which accounted for 0.6% of the nation's gross domestic product and placed the state at number 38 in highest GSP among the 50 states and the District of Columbia.

According to the Bureau of Economic Analysis, in 2004 New Mexico had a per capita personal income (PCPI) of $26,184. This ranked 48th in the United States and was 79% of the national average of $33,050. The 1994–2004 average annual growth rate of PCPI was 4.0%. New Mexico had a total personal income (TPI) of $49,827,505,000, which ranked 37th in the United States and reflected an increase of 6.5% from 2003. The 1994–2004 average annual growth rate of TPI was 5.3%. Earnings of persons employed in New Mexico increased from $34,637,098,000 in 2003 to $37,209,628,000 in 2004, an increase of 7.4%. The 2003–04 national change was 6.3%.

The US Census Bureau reports that the three-year average median household income for 2002–04 in 2004 dollars was $37,587 compared to a national average of $44,473. During the same period an estimated 17.5% of the population was below the poverty line as compared to 12.4% nationwide.

[22] LABOR

According to the Bureau of Labor Statistics (BLS), in April 2006 the seasonally adjusted civilian labor force in New Mexico numbered 958,000, with approximately 41,100 workers unemployed, yielding an unemployment rate of 4.3%, compared to the national average of 4.7% for the same period. Preliminary data for the same period placed nonfarm employment at 824,800. Since the beginning of the BLS data series in 1976, the highest unemployment rate recorded in New Mexico was 9.9% in April 1983. The historical low was 4% in March 2006. Preliminary nonfarm employment data by occupation for April 2006 showed that approximately 6.9% of the labor force was employed in construction; 4.5% in manufacturing; 17.1% in trade, transportation, and public utilities; 4.2% in financial activities; 11.4% in professional and business services; 13% in education and health services; 10.2% in leisure and hospitality services; and 24.7% in government.

The US Department of Labor's Bureau of Labor Statistics reported that in 2005, a total of 63,000 of New Mexico's 777,000 employed wage and salary workers were formal members of a union. This represented 8.1% of those so employed, up from 6.7% in 2004, but still below the national average of 12%. Overall in 2005, a total of 83,000 workers (10.7%) in New Mexico were covered by a union or employee association contract, which includes those workers who reported no union affiliation. New Mexico is one of 28 states that does not have a right-to-work law.

As of 1 March 2006, New Mexico had a state-mandated minimum wage rate of $5.15 per hour. In 2004, women in the state accounted for 46.8% of the employed civilian labor force.

[23] AGRICULTURE

The first farmers of New Mexico were the Pueblo Indians, who raised corn, beans, and squash. Wheat and barley were introduced from Europe, and indigo and chiles came from Mexico.

In 2005, New Mexico's total farm marketings were $2.67 billion. About 25% came from crops and 75% from livestock products. Leading crops included hay and wheat. In 2004, hay production was 1,365,000 tons, valued at $163,900,000, and wheat production was 7,800,000 bushels, valued at $24,570,000. The state also produced 10,440,000 bushels of corn for grain, and 594,000 hundredweight of potatoes in 2004.

[24] ANIMAL HUSBANDRY

Meat animals, especially cattle, represent the bulk of New Mexico's agricultural income. In 2005, there were nearly 1.5 million cattle and calves, valued at $1.64 billion. In 2004, there were an estimated 2,500 hogs and pigs, valued at $275,000 on New Mexico farms. During 2003, New Mexico farms and ranches produced around 7.6 million lb (3.4 million kg) of sheep and lambs which brought in a gross income of some $7.7 million. The main stock-raising regions are in the east, northeast, and northwest.

25 FISHING

There is no commercial fishing in New Mexico. In 2004, the state issued 205,291 sport fishing licenses. The native cutthroat trout is prized by sport fishermen, however, and numerous species have been introduced into state lakes and reservoirs. The federal government sponsors two fish hatcheries and technology centers in New Mexico: in Dexter and Mora. The Dexter center is the only facility in the nation dedicated to studying and distributing endangered fish for restocking in waters where they naturally occur. The center works with 14 imperiled fish species including the razorback sucker, Colorado squawfish, Guzman beautiful shiner, bonytail chub, and the Yaqui catfish.

26 FORESTRY

Lumber production was 111 million board feet in 2002. Although lumbering ranks low as a source of state income, the forests of New Mexico are of crucial importance because of the role they play in water conservation and recreation.

In 2004, 16,680,000 acres (670,000 hectares), or more than 20% of New Mexico's land area, was forestland. Of the state total, 9,522,000 acres (3,854,000 hectares) were federally owned or managed, and 825,000 acres (334,000 hectares) were owned by the state. Privately owned lands accounted for 6,331,000 acres (2,562,000 hectares). Seven national forests covered 9 million acres (3.7 million hectares) in 2005, the largest of which was Gila National Forest, at 2.7 million acres (1.1 million hectares).

27 MINING

According to preliminary data from the US Geological Survey (USGS), the estimated value of nonfuel mineral production by New Mexico in 2003 was $533 million, a decrease from 2002 of about 5%. The USGS data ranked New Mexico as 25th among the 50 states by the total value of its nonfuel mineral production, accounting for almost 1.5% of total US output.

According to the preliminary data for 2003, potash and copper, followed by construction sand and gravel, cement (portland and masonry), and crushed stone were the state's top nonfuel minerals by value. Collectively, these five commodities accounted for around 90% of all nonfuel mineral output, by value. By volume, New Mexico in 2003, was the nation's leading producer of perlite, potash, and zeolites. The state also ranked third in copper, mica, and pumice output and fifth in molybdenum.

In 2003, preliminary data showed that New Mexico produced 85,000 metric tons of copper ore, valued at $153 million, and 14 million metric tons of construction sand and gravel valued at $68.6 million. Crushed stone output that same year totaled 3.9 million metric tons, with a value of $25.2 million.

According to the state, the vast majority of the potash finds its way as a soil amendment in agriculture; the remainder is used in industry for such things as manufacturing television tubes, chinaware, soaps, and synthetic rubber.

28 ENERGY AND POWER

As of 2003, New Mexico had 34 electrical power service providers, of which eight were publicly owned and 21 were cooperatives. Of the remainder, four were investor owned, and one was federally operated. As of that same year there were 894,309 retail customers. Of that total, 624,777 received their power from investor-owned service providers. Cooperatives accounted for 189,781 customers, while publicly owned providers had 79,747 customers. There were four federal customers.

Total net summer generating capability by the state's electrical generating plants in 2003 stood at 6.289 million kW, with total production that same year at 32.735 billion kWh. Of the total amount generated, 97.1% came from electric utilities, with the remainder coming from independent producers and combined heat and power service providers. The largest portion of all electric power generated, 28.812 billion kWh (88%), came from coal-fired plants, with natural gas fueled plants in second place at 3.518 billion kWh (10.7%). Other renewable power sources accounted for 0.6% of all power generated, with hydroelectric generation and petroleum fired plants accounting for 0.5% and 0.2%, respectively.

New Mexico is a major producer of oil and natural gas, and has significant reserves of low-sulfur bituminous coal.

Most of New Mexico's natural gas and oil fields are located in the southeastern counties of Eddy, Lea, and Chaves, and in the northwestern counties of McKinley and San Juan. As of 2004, New Mexico had proven crude oil reserves of 669 million barrels, or 3% of all proven US reserves, while output that same year averaged 176,000 barrels per day. Including federal offshore domains, the state that year ranked fifth (fourth excluding federal offshore) in proven reserves and sixth (fifth excluding federal offshore) in production among the 31 producing states. In 2004 New Mexico had 27,389 producing oil wells and accounted for 3% of all US production. As of 2005, the state's Three refineries had a combined crude oil distillation capacity of 112,600 barrels per day.

In 2004, New Mexico had 38,574 producing natural gas and gas condensate wells. In that same year, marketed gas production (all gas produced excluding gas used for repressuring, vented and flared, and nonhydrocarbon gases removed) totaled 1,632.539 billion cu ft (46.36 billion cu m). As of 31 December 2004, proven reserves of dry or consumer-grade natural gas totaled 18,512 billion cu ft (525.7 billion cu m).

New Mexico in 2004, had four producing coal mines, three of which were surface operations. Coal production that year totaled 27,250,000 short tons, up from 26,389,000 short tons in 2003. Of the total produced in 2004, surface mines accounted for 19,565,000 short tons. Recoverable coal reserves in 2004 totaled 1.3 billion short tons. One short ton equals 2,000 lb (0.907 metric tons).

29 INDUSTRY

More than 50% of the manufacturing jobs in the state are located in and around Albuquerque, in Bernalillo County. Other counties with substantial manufacturing activity include Santa Fe, San Juan, Otero, McKinley, and Dona Ana.

According to the US Census Bureau's Annual Survey of Manufactures (ASM) for 2004, New Mexico's manufacturing sector covered some 12 product subsectors. The shipment value of all products manufactured in the state that same year was $17.392 billion.

Of that total, computer and electronic product manufacturing accounted for the largest share at $9.714 billion. It was followed by food manufacturing at $1.669 billion; miscellaneous manufacturing at $796.981 million; nonmetallic mineral product manufacturing at $437.260 million; and transportation equipment manufacturing at $416.578 million.

In 2004, a total of 32,927 people in New Mexico were employed in the state's manufacturing sector, according to the ASM. Of that total, 22,821 were actual production workers. In terms of total employment, the computer and electronic product manufacturing industry accounted for the largest portion of all manufacturing employees at 9,352 with 5,410 actual production workers. It was followed by food manufacturing at 3,875 employees (3,011 actual production workers); miscellaneous manufacturing at 3,248 employees (2,229 actual production workers); and fabricated metal product manufacturing with 2,519 employees (1,825 actual production workers).

ASM data for 2004 showed that New Mexico's manufacturing sector paid $1.343 billion in wages. Of that amount, the computer and electronic product manufacturing sector accounted for the largest share at $512.917 million. It was followed by food manufacturing at $128.635 million; miscellaneous manufacturing at $90.758 million; fabricated metal product manufacturing at $83.089 million; and transportation equipment manufacturing at $79.082 million.

30 COMMERCE

According to the 2002 Census of Wholesale Trade, New Mexico's wholesale trade sector had sales that year totaling $8.9 billion from 2,046 establishments. Wholesalers of durable goods accounted for 1,295 establishments, followed by nondurable goods wholesalers at 650 and electronic markets, agents, and brokers accounting for 101 establishments. Sales by durable goods wholesalers in 2002 totaled $3.7 billion, while wholesalers of nondurable goods saw sales of $4.3 billion. Electronic markets, agents, and brokers in the wholesale trade industry had sales of $903.6 million.

In the 2002 Census of Retail Trade, New Mexico was listed as having 7,227 retail establishments with sales of $18.3 billion. The leading types of retail businesses by number of establishments were: miscellaneous store retailers (1,085); gasoline stations tied with clothing and clothing accessories stores (958 each); motor vehicle and motor vehicle parts dealers (851); and food and beverage stores (639). In terms of sales, motor vehicle and motor vehicle parts dealers accounted for the largest share of retail sales at $4.7 billion, followed by general merchandise stores at $3.3 billion; gasoline stations at $2.09 billion; and food and beverage stores at $2.02 billion. A total of 89,413 people were employed by the retail sector in New Mexico that year.

New Mexico's foreign exports totaled $2.5 billion in 2005.

31 CONSUMER PROTECTION

Consumer protection in New Mexico is the responsibility of the Office of the Attorney General's Consumer Protection Division, which is authorized by the state's primary consumer law, the Unfair Practices Act, to provide a range of services designed to protect consumers and to resolve disputes between business and consumers. These services can involve the mediation of a dispute, educating the public on consumer issues, investigating suspicious business activities, the proposing of legislation, and through the Attorney General's Office, the initiation of litigation.

When dealing with consumer protection issues, the state's Attorney General's Office can initiate civil and criminal proceedings; represent the state before state and federal regulatory agencies; administer consumer protection and education programs; handle formal consumer complaints; and exercise broad subpoena powers. In antitrust actions, the Attorney General's Office can act on behalf of those consumers who are incapable of acting on their own; initiate damage actions on behalf of the state in state courts; initiate criminal proceedings; and representing other governmental entities in recovering civil damages under state or federal law. However, neither the Attorney General's office nor the Consumer Protection Division are authorized to act in a private capacity for an individual citizen.

The offices of the Consumer Protection Division are located in Santa Fe.

32 BANKING

New Mexico's first bank, the First National Bank of Santa Fe, was organized in 1870. After the turn of the century, banking establishments expanded rapidly in the state, mainly because of growth in the livestock industry.

As of June 2005, New Mexico had 57 insured banks, savings and loans, and saving banks, plus 25 state-chartered and 28 federally chartered credit unions (CUs). Excluding the CUs, the Albuquerque market area accounted for the largest portion of the state's financial institutions and deposits in 2004, with 24 institutions and $8.645 billion in deposits. As of June 2005, CUs accounted for 21.8% of all assets held by all financial institutions in the state, or some $4.516 billion. Banks, savings and loans, and savings banks collectively accounted for the remaining 78.2% or $16.230 billion in assets held.

In 2004, the median percentage of past-due/nonaccrual loans to total loans was 1.23%, down from 1,58% in 2003. The median net interest margin (the difference between the lower rates offered savers and the higher rates charged on loans) was 4.65% in 2004, up from 4.50% in 2003.

Regulation of state-chartered banks and other financial institutions is the responsibility of the Financial Institutions Division.

33 INSURANCE

In 2004, 679,000 individual life insurance policies were in force in the state, and their total value was about $52.7 billion; total value for all categories of life insurance (individual, group, and credit) was about $91.5 billion. The average coverage amount is $77,700 per policy holder. Death benefits paid that year totaled $297.2 million.

As of 2003, there were seven property and casualty and one life and health insurance company domiciled in the state. In 2004, direct premiums for property and casualty insurance totaled over $2.3 billion. That year, there were 12,655 flood insurance policies in force in the state, with a total value of $.4 billion. About $654 million of coverage was held through FAIR plans, which are designed to offer coverage for some natural circumstances, such as wind and hail, in high risk areas.

In 2004, 42% of state residents held employment-based health insurance policies, 4% held individual policies, and 30% were covered under Medicare and Medicaid; 22% of residents were uninsured. New Mexico has the lowest percentage of employment-based insureds among the 50 states and the second-highest percentage of uninsured residents (following Texas). In 2003, employee contributions for employment-based health coverage averaged at 18% for single coverage and 27% for family coverage. The state offers a six-month health benefits expansion program for small-firm employees in connection with the Consolidated Omnibus Budget Reconciliation Act (COBRA, 1986), a health insurance program for those who lose employment-based coverage due to termination or reduction of work hours.

In 2003, there were over 1.2 million auto insurance policies in effect for private passenger cars. Required minimum coverage includes bodily injury liability of up to $25,000 per individual and $50,000 for all persons injured in an accident, as well as property damage liability of $10,000. In 2003, the average expenditure per vehicle for insurance coverage was $730.46.

The insurance industry is regulated by the State Insurance Board.

³⁴SECURITIES

There are no securities exchanges in New Mexico. In 2005, there were 290 personal financial advisers employed in the state and 490 securities, commodities, and financial services sales agents. In 2004, there were over 23 publicly traded companies within the state, with over five NASDAQ companies and two NYSE listings. In 2006, the state had two Fortune 1,000 companies; PNM Resources (Albuquerque) ranked 785th in the nation with revenues of over $2 billion, followed by Thornburg Mortgage (Santa Fe) at 951st in the nations with $1.5 billion in revenues. Both companies are listed on the NYSE.

³⁵PUBLIC FINANCE

The governor of New Mexico submits a budget annually to the legislature for approval. The fiscal year (FY) runs 1 July–30 June.

Fiscal year 2006 general funds were estimated at $5.9 billion for resources and $5.3 billion for expenditures. In fiscal year 2004, federal government grants to New Mexico were $4.6 billion.

In the fiscal year 2007 federal budget, New Mexico was slated to receive: $52 million in State Children's Health Insurance Program (SCHIP) funds to help New Mexico provide health coverage to low-income, uninsured children who do not qualify for Medicaid. This funding is a 23% increase over fiscal year 2006; $11.7 million for the HOME Investment Partnership Program to help New Mexico fund a wide range of activities that build, buy, or rehabilitate affordable housing for rent or homeownership, or provide direct rental assistance to low-income people. This funding is an 11% increase over fiscal year 2006; and $2.6 million for the site acquisition and design of a new replacement border station in Columbus.

³⁶TAXATION

In 2005, New Mexico collected $4,471 million in tax revenues or $2,319 per capita, which placed it 20th among the 50 states in per capita tax burden. The national average was $2,192 per capita. Property taxes accounted for 0.9% of the total, sales taxes 34.8%, selective sales taxes 13.7%, individual income taxes 24.3%, corporate income taxes 5.4%, and other taxes 20.8%.

As of 1 January 2006, New Mexico had four individual income tax brackets ranging from 1.7% to 5.3%. The state taxes corporations at rates ranging from 4.8% to 7.6% depending on tax bracket.

In 2004, state and local property taxes amounted to $840,068,000 or $441 per capita. The per capita amount ranks the state third-lowest nationally. Local governments collected $786,994,000 of the total and the state government $52,779,000.

New Mexico taxes retail sales at a rate of 5%. In addition to the state tax, local taxes on retail sales can reach as much as 2.25%,

New Mexico—State Government Finances

(Dollar amounts in thousands. Per capita amounts in dollars.)

	AMOUNT	PER CAPITA
Total Revenue	11,809,742	6,205.85
General revenue	9,798,429	5,148.94
Intergovernmental revenue	3,546,494	1,863.63
Taxes	4,001,780	2,102.88
General sales	1,443,300	758.43
Selective sales	595,140	312.74
License taxes	169,805	89.23
Individual income tax	1,007,248	529.29
Corporate income tax	138,196	72.62
Other taxes	648,091	340.56
Current charges	758,043	398.34
Miscellaneous general revenue	1,492,112	784.08
Utility revenue	–	–
Liquor store revenue	–	–
Insurance trust revenue	2,011,313	1,056.92
Total expenditure	11,024,686	5,793.32
Intergovernmental expenditure	3,031,473	1,593.00
Direct expenditure	7,993,213	4,200.32
Current operation	6,029,536	3,168.44
Capital outlay	447,139	234.97
Insurance benefits and repayments	1,011,307	531.43
Assistance and subsidies	341,021	179.20
Interest on debt	164,210	86.29
Exhibit: Salaries and wages	1,787,554	939.33
Total expenditure	11,024,686	5,793.32
General expenditure	10,013,379	5,261.89
Intergovernmental expenditure	3,031,473	1,593.00
Direct expenditure	6,981,906	3,668.89
General expenditures, by function:		
Education	3,813,208	2,003.79
Public welfare	2,492,564	1,309.81
Hospitals	487,280	256.06
Health	240,706	126.49
Highways	633,467	332.88
Police protection	111,883	58.79
Correction	254,639	133.81
Natural resources	173,372	91.10
Parks and recreation	59,457	31.24
Government administration	391,194	205.57
Interest on general debt	164,210	86.29
Other and unallocable	1,191,399	626.06
Utility expenditure	–	–
Liquor store expenditure	–	–
Insurance trust expenditure	1,011,307	531.43
Debt at end of fiscal year	5,411,287	2,843.56
Cash and security holdings	33,923,425	17,826.29

Abbreviations and symbols: – zero or rounds to zero; (NA) not available; (X) not applicable.

SOURCE: *U.S. Census Bureau, Governments Division, 2004 Survey of State Government Finances,* January 2006.

making for a potential total tax on retail sales of 7.25%. Food purchased for consumption off-premises is taxable. The tax on cigarettes is 91 cents per pack, which ranks 22nd among the 50 states and the District of Columbia. New Mexico taxes gasoline at 18.9 cents per gallon. This is in addition to the 18.4 cents per gallon federal tax on gasoline.

According to the Tax Foundation, for every federal tax dollar sent to Washington in 2004, New Mexico citizens received $2.00 in federal spending, one of the highest rates in the nation.

37 ECONOMIC POLICY

The Economic Development Department (EDD) promotes industrial and community development through such measures as tax-free bonds for manufacturing facilities; tax credits for investment and for job training, venture capital funds; and community development block grants. The state also seeks export markets for New Mexico's products and encourages use of the state by the film industry. Total incentives to employ 100 workers in a rural area, exporting most of the product, and investing at least $15 million amounted to almost $4 billion in 2000. The Economic Development Partnership, the biggest part of the Economic Development Department, focuses on business and community development. Separate divisions include International Trade, the Film Office, the Office of Science and Technology, and the New Mexico Office for Space Commercialization (NMOSC). In 2006, New Mexico targeted the following areas for economic development: aerospace, biotechnology, film, food processing, manufacturing, maquila suppliers, renewable energy, and technology.

38 HEALTH

The infant mortality rate in October 2005 was estimated at 5.8 per 1,000 live births. The birth rate in 2003 was 14.9 per 1,000 population. The abortion rate stood at 14.7 per 1,000 women in 2000. In 2003, about 68.9% of pregnant woman received prenatal care beginning in the first trimester, this was the lowest rate for prenatal care in the nation. In 2004, approximately 84% of children received routine immunizations before the age of three.

The crude death rate in 2003 was 7.9 deaths per 1,000 population. As of 2002, the death rates for major causes of death (per 100,000 resident population) were: heart disease, 181.1; cancer, 165.3; cerebrovascular diseases, 38.5; chronic lower respiratory diseases, 46.2; and diabetes, 31.4. The mortality rate from HIV infection was 1.9 per 100,000 population. In 2004, the reported AIDS case rate was at about 9.6 per 100,000 population. In 2002, about 54.4% of the population was considered overweight or obese. As of 2004, about 20.3% of state residents were smokers.

In 2003, New Mexico had 37 community hospitals with about 3,700 beds. There were about 166,000 patient admissions that year and 4.5 million outpatient visits. The average daily inpatient census was about 2,100 patients. The average cost per day for hospital care was $1,563. Also in 2003, there were about 81 certified nursing facilities in the state with 7,443 beds and an overall occupancy rate of about 84.4%. In 2004, it was estimated that about 67.9% of all state residents had received some type of dental care within the year. New Mexico had 238 physicians per 100,000 resident population in 2004 and 579 nurses per 100,000 in 2005. In 2004, there were a total of 832 dentists in the state.

About 26% of state residents were enrolled in Medicaid programs in 2003; 13% were enrolled in Medicare programs in 2004. Approximately 22% of the state population was uninsured in 2004; this percentage ranked the state as second in the nation for uninsured residents, following Texas. In 2003, state health care expenditures totaled $2.4 million.

39 SOCIAL WELFARE

In 2004, about 32,000 people received unemployment benefits, with the average weekly unemployment benefit at $220. For 2005, the estimated average monthly participation in the food stamp program included about 240,637 persons (93,094 households); the average monthly benefit was about $87.07 per person. That year, the total of benefits paid through the state for the food stamp program was about $251.4 million.

Temporary Assistance for Needy Families (TANF), the system of federal welfare assistance that officially replaced Aid to Families with Dependent Children (AFDC) in 1997, was reauthorized through the Deficit Reduction Act of 2005. TANF is funded through federal block grants that are divided among the states based on an equation involving the number of recipients in each state. New Mexico's TANF program is called NM Works. In 2004, the state program had 46,000 recipients; state and federal expenditures on this TANF program totaled $79 million in fiscal year 2003.

In December 2004, Social Security benefits were paid to 303,610 New Mexico residents. This number included 180,860 retired workers, 29,700 widows and widowers, 42,150 disabled workers, 21,530 spouses, and 29,370 children. Social Security beneficiaries represented 15.9% of the total state population and 89.6% of the state's population age 65 and older. Retired workers received an average monthly payment of $892; widows and widowers, $825; disabled workers, $861; and spouses, $421. Payments for children of retired workers averaged $408 per month; children of deceased workers, $520; and children of disabled workers, $249. Federal Supplemental Security Income payments in December 2004 went to 51,656 New Mexico residents, averaging $377 a month. An additional $18,000 of state-administered supplemental payments were distributed to 177 residents.

The state maintains the Carrie Tingley Crippled Children's Hospital in Truth or Consequences, the Miners' Hospital of New Mexico in Raton, and the New Mexico School for the Visually Handicapped in Alamogordo.

40 HOUSING

In 2004, New Mexico had an estimated 825,540 housing units, 711,827 of which were occupied; 69.3% were owner-occupied. About 37.6% of all housing units in New Mexico were built from 1970 to 1989. About 62.5% of all units were single-family, detached homes; about 16% were mobile homes. Utility gas and electricity were the most common heating energy sources. It was estimated that 40,178 units lacked telephone service, 9,673 lacked complete plumbing facilities, and 10, 186 lacked complete kitchen facilities. The average household had 2.62 members.

In 2004, 12,600 new privately owned units were authorized for construction. The median home value was $110,788. The median monthly cost for mortgage owners was $935. Renters paid a median of $546 per month. In September 2005, the state received grants of over $1.5 million from the US Department of Housing and Urban Development (HUD) for rural housing and economic development programs. For 2006, HUD allocated to the state over $14.2 million in community development block grants.

41 EDUCATION

In 2004, 82.9% of New Mexicans age 25 and older were high school graduates. Some 25.1% had obtained a bachelor's degree or higher.

The total enrollment for fall 2002 in New Mexico's public schools stood at 320,000. Of these, 224,000 attended schools from kindergarten through grade eight, and 96,000 attended high school. Approximately 32.8% of the students were white, 2.4% were black, 52.5% were Hispanic, 1.2% were Asian/Pacific Islander, and 11.2% were American Indian/Alaskan Native. Total enrollment was estimated at 318,000 in fall 2003 and expected to be 338,000 by fall 2014, an increase of 5.7% during the period 2002–14. Expenditures for public education in 2003/04 were estimated at $2.8 billion. There were 22,416 students enrolled in 176 private schools in fall 2003. Since 1969, the National Assessment of Educational Progress (NAEP) has tested public school students nationwide. The resulting report, *The Nation's Report Card,* stated that in 2005 eighth graders in New Mexico scored 263 out of 500 in mathematics compared with the national average of 278.

As of fall 2002, there were 120,997 students enrolled in institutions of higher education; minority students comprised 53.4% of total postsecondary enrollment. In 2005 New Mexico had 42 degree-granting institutions including, 7 public four-year institutions, 20 public two-year institutions, and 6 nonprofit, private four-year institutions. The leading public schools are the University of New Mexico, with its main campus at Albuquerque, and New Mexico State University in Las Cruces.

42 ARTS

New Mexico Arts, the state arts commission, consists of 15 governor-appointed members and provides financial support for statewide art programs. In 2005, New Mexico Arts and other New Mexico arts organizations received 29 grants totaling $1,194,567 from the National Endowment for the Arts (NEA). State and private sources also contribute funding to the state's arts programs. New Mexico Arts has contributed funding to promote multicultural arts programs that reflect the Spanish and American Indian cultural influences of the area. The New Mexico Humanities Council was founded in 1972. In 2005, the National Endowment for the Humanities contributed $1,640,966 for 13 state programs.

New Mexico is a state rich in Indian, Spanish, Mexican, and contemporary art. Major exhibits can be seen at the University of New Mexico Art Museum in Albuquerque, which as of 2006, holding close to 30,000 pieces was considered the largest fine art collection in the state. The city of Taos is an artists' colony of renown and is home to the Hardwood Museum of Art, established in 1923. The Hardwood Museum of Art's permanent collection focuses both on the multicultural heritage of the state as well as the city's influence on the development of American art.

The Santa Fe Opera, established in 1957, has become one of the nation's most distinguished regional opera companies. In 2006, the Sante Fe Opera celebrated its 50th anniversary with a Golden Anniversary Gala Weekend. The New Mexico Symphony Orchestra (also called the Albuquerque Symphony Orchestra, established in 1932) and the Orchestra Chorus present a variety of musical programs from classical to pops.

The Santa Fe Chamber Music Festival began in 1972. After the 2005 season the Open Arts Foundation decided to end its annual Santa Fe Jazz and International Music Festival.

43 LIBRARIES AND MUSEUMS

In June 2001, New Mexico had 80 public library systems, with a total of 101 libraries, of which 21 were branches. The systems in that same year, had a combined total of 4,132,000 volumes of books and serial publications, and a circulation of 7,716,000. The system also had 91,000 audio and 64,000 video items, 4,000 electronic format items (CD-ROMs, magnetic tapes, and disks), and three bookmobiles. The largest municipal library is the Albuquerque Public Library, with over 1,235,211 volumes. The largest university library is that of the University of New Mexico, with 1,882,136 volumes. There is a scientific library at Los Alamos and a law library at Santa Fe. In fiscal year 2001, operating income for the state's public library system totaled $28,885,000 and included $219,000 in federal grants and $506,000 in state grants.

New Mexico has 109 museums. Especially noteworthy are the Maxwell Museum of Anthropology at Albuquerque; the Museum of New Mexico, Museum of International Folk Art, and Institute of American Indian Arts Museum, all in Santa Fe; and several art galleries and museums in Taos. Historic sites include the Palace of the Governors (1610), the oldest US capitol and probably the nation's oldest public building, in Santa Fe; Aztec Ruins National Monument, near Aztec; and Gila Cliff Dwellings National Monument, 44 mi (71 km) north of Silver City. A state natural history museum, in Albuquerque, opened in 1985.

44 COMMUNICATIONS

The first regular monthly mail service between New Mexico and the other US states began in 1849. In 2004, 91.4% of the state's occupied housing units had telephones. In addition, by June of that same year there were 939,091 mobile wireless telephone subscribers. In 2003, 53.9% of New Mexico households had a computer and 44.5% had Internet access. By June 2005, there were 175,303 high-speed lines in New Mexico, 155,493 residential and 19,810 for business. In 2005 there were 5 major AM radio stations and 37 major FM stations. There were 9 major network television stations in 2005. The Albuquerque-Santa Fe area had 568,650 television households, 57% of which had cable in 1999. A total of 29,730 Internet domain names were registered in the state in 2000.

45 PRESS

The first newspaper published in New Mexico was *El Crep£sculo de la Libertad* (Dawn of Liberty), a Spanish-language paper established at Santa Fe in 1834. The *Santa Fe Republican,* established in 1847, was the first English-language newspaper.

In 2005, there were 9 morning, 9 evening, and 13 Sunday newspapers in the state. The leading dailies include the *Albuquerque Journal,* with a morning circulation of 107,306 (151,146 on Sundays); and the *Santa Fe New Mexican,* with a morning circulation of 24,667 (26,812 on Sundays).

La Herencia, (est. 1994) and *Tradición Revista* are magazines devoted to regional Hispanic history, art, and culture.

⁴⁶ORGANIZATIONS

In 2006, there were over 1,570 nonprofit organizations registered within the state, of which about 1,121 were registered as charitable, educational, or religious organizations. National organizations with headquarters in New Mexico include the National Association of Consumer Credit Administrators (Santa Fe), the American Indian Law Students Association, the American Holistic Medical Association, and Futures for Children, all located in Albuquerque.

The state is home to several organizations focusing on the rights and welfare of Native Americans. These include the National Indian Youth Council, the All Indian Pueblo Council, Gathering of Nations, the Inter-Tribal Indian Ceremonial Association, and the National Tribal Environmental Council.

Art and cultural organizations include the El Paso Symphony Orchestra Association, the Indian Arts and Crafts Association, the Institute of American Indian Arts, the New Mexico Art League, the New Mexico Ballet Company, the Wordcraft Circle of Native Writers and Storytellers, and Spanish Colonial Arts Society. Special interest and hobbyist organizations based in New Mexico include the 3HO Foundation (yoga) and the American Amateur Baseball Congress.

⁴⁷TOURISM, TRAVEL, AND RECREATION

The development of New Mexico's natural recreational resources has made tourism a leading economic activity. In May 2006, the governor declared a national tourism week to celebrate the achievement of $5 billion in tourism revenue. An estimated 80,000 people employed in tourism. In 2002, the state hosted some 11.5 million travelers. About 28.6% of all trips were instate travel by residents, with 53% of visitors traveling from five states: Texas, Colorado, California, Arizona, and Oklahoma. The most popular vacation area was the Albuquerque-Sante Fe region (with 22.9% of all visitors), followed by Taos. Shopping, outdoor activities, and historical sites were the most popular attractions.

Hunting, fishing, camping, boating, and skiing are among the many outdoor attractions. Sandia Mountain is a popular ski destination. The state has a national park—Carlsbad Caverns—and 13 national monuments, among them Aztec Ruins, Bandelier, Capulin Mountain, Chaco Canyon, El Morro (Inscription Rock), Fort Union, Gila Cliff Dwellings, Gran Quivira, Pecos, and White Sands. In 1984, the US House of Representatives designated 27,840 acres (11,266 hectares) of new wilderness preserves in New Mexico's San Juan basin, including a 2,720-acre (1,100-hectare) "fossil forest." New Mexico has an annual hot air balloon festival, a summer opera season, and the famous Indian Corn Mart outdoor art festival. Santa Fe is known for its many art galleries. Taos has skiing and also Indian sacred sites.

⁴⁸SPORTS

New Mexico has no major professional sports teams, though Albuquerque does have a minor league baseball team, the Isotopes, in the Class-AAA Pacific Coast League. Thoroughbred and quarter-horse racing with pari-mutuel betting is an important spectator sport. Sunland Park, south of Las Cruces, has a winterlong schedule. From May to August there is racing and betting at Ruidoso Downs, Sun Ray Park, and the Downs at Albuquerque.

The Lobos of the University of New Mexico compete in the Mountain West Conference, while the Aggies of New Mexico State University belong to the Big West Conference. New Mexico State finished third in the 1970 National Collegiate Athletic Association (NCAA) basketball tournament.

Other annual sporting events include the Great Overland Windsail Race in Lordsburg in June, the Silver City RPCA Wild, Wild West Rodeo Week in Gila in June, and the International Balloon Fiesta in Albuquerque in October.

⁴⁹FAMOUS NEW MEXICANS

Among the earliest Europeans to explore New Mexico were Francisco Vasquez de Coronado (b.Spain, 1510–54) and Juan de Oñate (b.Mexico, 1549?–1624?), the founder of New Mexico. Diego de Vargas (b.Spain, 1643–1704) reconquered New Mexico for the Spanish after the Pueblo Revolt of 1680, which was led by Popé (d.1685?), a San Juan Pueblo medicine man. Later Indian leaders include Mangas Coloradas (1795?–1863) and Victorio (1809?–80), both of the Mimbreño Apache. Two prominent native New Mexicans during the brief period of Mexican rule were Manuel Armijo (1792?–1853), governor at the time of the American conquest, and the Taos priest José Antonio Martinez (1793–1867).

Army scout and trapper Christopher Houston "Kit" Carson (b.Kentucky, 1809–68) made his home in Taos, as did Charles Bent (b.Virginia, 1799–1847), one of the builders of Bent's Fort, a famous landmark on the Santa Fe Trail. A pioneer of a different kind was Jean Baptiste Lamy (b.France, 1814–88), the first Roman Catholic bishop in the Southwest; his life inspired Willa Cather's novel *Death Comes for the Archbishop*. Among the more notorious of the frontier figures in New Mexico was Billy the Kid (William H. Bonney, b.New York, 1859–81); his killer was New Mexico lawman Patrick Floyd "Pat" Garrett (b.Alabama, 1850–1908).

Notable US senators from New Mexico were Thomas Benton Catron (b.Missouri, 1840–1921), a Republican who dominated New Mexico politics during the territorial period; Albert Bacon Fall (b.Kentucky, 1861–1944), who later, as secretary of the interior, gained notoriety for his role in the Teapot Dome scandal; Dennis Chavez (1888–1962), the most prominent and influential native New Mexican to serve in Washington; Carl A. Hatch (b.Kansas, 1889–1963), best known for the Hatch Act of 1939, which limited partisan political activities by federal employees; and Clinton P. Anderson (b.South Dakota, 1895–1975) who was also secretary of agriculture.

New Mexico has attracted many artists and writers. Painters Bert G. Phillips (b.New York, 1868–1956) and Ernest Leonard Blumenschein (b.Ohio 1874–1960) started the famous Taos art colony in 1898. Mabel Dodge Luhan (b.New York, 1879–1962) did much to lure the creative community to Taos through her writings; the most famous person to take up residence there was English novelist D. H. Lawrence (1885–1930). Peter Hurd (1940–84) was a muralist, portraitist, and book illustrator. New Mexico's best-known artist is Georgia O'Keeffe (b.Wisconsin, 1887–1986). Maria Povera Martinez (1887?–1980) was known for her black-on-black pottery.

Other prominent persons who have made New Mexico their home include rocketry pioneer Robert H. Goddard (b.Massachusetts, 1882–1945), Pulitzer Prize-winning editorial cartoonist Bill Mauldin (1921–2003), novelist and popular historian Paul Horgan (b.New York, 1903–95), novelist N. Scott Momaday (b.Oklahoma, 1934), and golfer Nancy Lopez-Melton (b.California, 1957). Al Unser Sr., four-time winner of the Indianapolis 500, was born in Albuquerque, New Mexico, 29 May 1939.

50BIBLIOGRAPHY

Busby, Mark (ed.). *The Southwest.* Vol. 8 in *The Greenwood Encyclopedia of American Regional Cultures.* Westport, Conn.: Greenwood Press, 2004.

Council of State Governments. *The Book of the States, 2006 Edition.* Lexington, Ky.: Council of State Governments, 2006.

Enchanted Lifeways: The History, Museums, Arts & Festivals of New Mexico. Compiled by the New Mexico Office of Cultural Affairs. Santa Fe: New Mexico Magazine, 1995.

Parzybok, Tye W. *Weather Extremes in the West.* Missoula, Mont.: Mountain Press, 2005.

Preston, Christine, Douglas Preston, and José Antonio Esquibel. *The Royal Road: El Camino Real from Mexico City to Santa Fe.* Albuquerque: University of New Mexico Press, 1998.

Preston, Thomas. *Rocky Mountains: Montana, Wyoming, Colorado, New Mexico,* 2nd ed. Vol. 3 of *The Double Eagle Guide to 1,000 Great Western Recreation Destinations.* Billings, Mont.: Discovery Publications, 2003.

Rees, Amanda (ed.). *The Great Plains Region.* Vol. 1 in *The Greenwood Encyclopedia of American Regional Cultures.* Westport, Conn.: Greenwood Press, 2004.

Etulain, Richard W., and Ferenc M. Szasz (eds.). *Religion in Modern New Mexico.* Albuquerque: University of New Mexico Press, 1997.

Reséndez, Andrés. *Changing National Identities at the Frontier: Texas and New Mexico, 1800–1850.* New York: Cambridge University Press, 2005.

Roberts, David. *The Pueblo Revolt: The Secret Rebellion that Drove the Spaniards Out of the Southwest.* New York: Simon & Schuster, 2004.

Samora, Julian, and Patricia Vandel Simon. *A History of the Mexican-American People.* Rev. ed. Notre Dame, Ind.: University of Notre Dame Press, 1993.

Staats, Todd. *New Mexico: Off the Beaten Path.* Guilford, Conn.: Globe Pequot Press, 1999.

US Department of Commerce, Economics and Statistics Administration, US Census Bureau. *New Mexico, 2000. Summary Social, Economic, and Housing Characteristics: 2000 Census of Population and Housing.* Washington, D.C.: US Government Printing Office, 2003.

NEW YORK

State of New York

ORIGIN OF STATE NAME: Named for the Duke of York (later King James II) in 1664. **NICKNAME:** The Empire State. **CAPITAL:** Albany. **ENTERED UNION:** 26 July 1788 (11th). **SONG:** "I Love New York". **MOTTO:** *Excelsior* (Ever upward). **COAT OF ARMS:** Liberty and Justice stand on either side of a shield showing a mountain sunrise. Above the shield is an eagle on a globe. In the foreground are a three-masted ship and a Hudson River sloop, both representing commerce. Liberty's left foot has kicked aside a royal crown. Beneath the shield is the state motto. **FLAG:** Dark blue with the coat of arms in the center. **OFFICIAL SEAL:** The coat of arms surrounded by the words "The Great Seal of the State of New York." **BIRD:** Bluebird. **FISH:** Brook or speckled trout. **FLOWER:** Rose. **TREE:** Sugar maple. **GEM:** Garnet. **LEGAL HOLIDAYS:** New Year's Day, 1 January; Birthday of Martin Luther King Jr., 3rd Monday in January; Lincoln's Birthday, 12 February, sometimes observed on the Friday closest to this date; Washington's Birthday, 3rd Monday in February; Memorial Day, last Monday in May; Independence Day, 4 July; Labor Day, 1st Monday in September; Columbus Day, 2nd Monday in October; General Election Day, 1st Tuesday after the 1st Monday in November; Veterans' Day, 11 November; Thanksgiving Day, 4th Thursday in November; Christmas Day, 25 December. **TIME:** 7 AM EST = noon GMT.

¹LOCATION, SIZE, AND EXTENT

Located in the northeastern United States, New York State is the largest of the three Middle Atlantic states and ranks 30th in size among the 50 states.

The total area of New York is 49,108 sq mi (127,190 sq km), of which land takes up 47,377 sq mi (122,707 sq km) and the remaining 1,731 sq mi (4,483 sq km) consist of inland water. New York's width is about 320 mi (515 km) E–W, not including Long Island, which extends an additional 118 mi (190 km) SW–NE; the state's maximum N–S extension is about 310 mi (499 km). New York State is shaped roughly like a right triangle: the line from the extreme NE to the extreme SW forms the hypotenuse, with New York City as the right angle.

Mainland New York is bordered on the NW and N by the Canadian provinces of Ontario (with the boundary line passing through Lake Ontario and the St. Lawrence River) and Quebec; on the E by Vermont (with part of the line passing through Lake Champlain and the Poultney River), Massachusetts, and Connecticut; on the S by the Atlantic Ocean, New Jersey (part of the line passes through the Hudson River), and Pennsylvania (partly through the Delaware River); and on the W by Pennsylvania (with the line extending into Lake Erie) and Ontario (through Lake Erie and the Niagara River).

Two large islands lie off the state's SE corner. Long Island is bounded by Connecticut (through Long Island Sound) to the N, Rhode Island (through the Atlantic Ocean) to the NE, the Atlantic to the S, and the East River and the Narrows to the W. Staten Island (a borough of New York City) is separated from New Jersey by Newark Bay in the N, Raritan Bay in the S, and Arthur Kill channel in the W, and from Long Island by the Narrows to the E. Including these two islands, the total boundary length of New York State is 1,430 mi (2,301 km). Long Island, with an area of 1,396 sq mi (3,616 sq km), is the largest island belonging to one of the 48 coterminous states.

The state's geographic center is in Madison County, 12 mi (19 km) s of Oneida.

²TOPOGRAPHY

Two upland regions—the Adirondack Mountains and the Appalachian Highlands—dominate the topography of New York State.

The Adirondacks cover most of the northeast and occupy about one-fourth of the state's total area. The Appalachian Highlands, including the Catskill Mountains and Kittatinny Mountain Ridge (or Shawangunk Mountains), extend across the southern half of the state, from the Hudson River Valley to the basin of Lake Erie. Between these two upland regions, and also along the state's northern and eastern borders, lies a network of lowlands, including the Great Lakes Plain; the Hudson, Mohawk, Lake Champlain, and St. Lawrence valleys; and the coastal areas of New York City and Long Island.

The state's highest peaks are found in the Adirondacks: Mt. Marcy, 5,344 feet (1,629 meters), and Algonquin Peak, 5,114 feet (1,559 meters). The mean elevation of the state is approximately 1,000 ft (305 m). Nestled among the Adirondacks are many scenic lakes, including Lake Placid, Saranac Lake, and Lake George. The region is also the source of the Hudson and Ausable rivers. The Adirondack Forest Preserve covers much of this terrain, and both public and private lakes are mainly for recreational use.

The highest peak in the Catskills is Slide Mountain, at 4,204 feet (1,281 meters). Lesser upland regions of New York include the Hudson Highlands, projecting into the Hudson Valley; the Taconic Range, along the state's eastern border; and Tug Hill Plateau, set amid the lowlands just west of the Adirondacks.

Three lakes—Erie, Ontario, and Champlain—form part of the state's borders. The state has jurisdiction over 594 sq mi (1,538 sq km) of Lake Erie and 3,033 sq mi (7,855 sq km) of Lake Ontario. New York contains some 8,000 lakes; the largest lake wholly within the state is Oneida, about 22 mi (35 km) long, with a maximum width of 6 mi (10 km) and an area of 80 sq mi (207 sq km). Many smaller lakes are found in the Adirondacks and in the Finger Lakes region in west-central New York, renowned for its vineyards and great natural beauty. The 11 Finger Lakes themselves (including Owasco, Cayuga, Seneca, Keuka, Canadaigua, and Skaneateles) are long and narrow, fanning southward from a line that runs roughly from Syracuse westward to Geneseo. Sea level at the Atlantic Ocean is the lowest elevation of the state.

New York's longest river is the Hudson, extending from the Adirondacks to New York Bay for a distance of 306 mi (492 km). The Mohawk River flows into the Hudson north of Albany. The major rivers of central and western New York State—the Black, Genesee, and Oswego—all flow into Lake Ontario. Rivers defining the state's borders are the St. Lawrence in the north, the Poultney in the east, the Delaware in the southeast, and the Niagara in the west. Along the Niagara River, Niagara Falls forms New York's most spectacular natural feature. The falls, with an estimated mean flow rate of more than 1,585,000 gallons (60,000 hectoliters) per second, are both a leading tourist attraction and a major source of hydroelectric power.

About 2 billion years ago, New York State was entirely covered by a body of water that periodically rose and fell. The Adirondacks and Hudson River Palisades were produced by undersea volcanic action during this Grenville period. At about the same time, the schist and other crystalline rock that lie beneath Manhattan were formed. The Catskills were worn down by erosion from what was once a high, level plain. Glaciers from the last Ice Age carved out the inland lakes and valleys and determined the surface features of Staten Island and Long Island.

³CLIMATE

Although New York lies entirely within the humid continental zone, there is much variation from region to region. The three main climatic regions are the southeastern lowlands, which have the warmest temperatures and the longest season between frosts; the uplands of the Catskills and Adirondacks, where winters are cold and summers cool; and the snow belt along the Great Lakes Plain, one of the snowiest areas of the United States. The growing (frost-free) season ranges from 100 to 120 days in the Adirondacks, Catskills, and higher elevations of the hills of southwestern New York to 180–200 days on Long Island.

Among the major population centers, New York City has an annual average temperature of 55°F (12°C), with a normal maximum of 63°F (17°C) and a normal minimum of 47°F (8°C). Albany has an annual average of 48°F (8°C), with a normal maximum of 58°F (14°C) and a normal minimum of 37°F (2°C). The average in Buffalo is 48°F (8°C), the normal maximum 57°F (13°C), and the normal minimum 40°F (4°C). The record low temperature for the state is -52°F (-47°C), recorded at Stillwater Reservoir in the Adirondacks on 9 February 1934 and at Old Forge on 18 February 1979; the record high is 108°F (42°C), registered at Troy on 22 July 1926.

Annual precipitation ranges from over 50 in (127 cm) in the higher elevations to about 30 in (76 cm) in the areas near Lake Ontario and Lake Champlain, and in the lower half of the Genesee River Valley. New York City has an average annual precipitation of 46.7 in (118 cm), with an average annual snowfall of 28 in (71 cm); Albany receives an average annual precipitation of 35.7 in (90 cm); and Buffalo, 38.3 in (97 cm). In the snow belt, Buffalo receives 91 in (231 cm) of snow. Rochester averages 89 in (218 cm), and Syracuse 114 in (289 cm). New York City has fewer days of precipitation than other major populated areas (120 days annually, compared with 168 for Buffalo). Buffalo is the windiest city in the state, with a mean hourly wind speed of about 12 mph (19 km/hr). Tornadoes are rare, but hurricanes and tropical storms sometimes cause heavy damage to Long Island.

⁴FLORA AND FAUNA

New York has some 150 species of trees. Post and willow oak, laurel magnolia, sweet gum, and hop trees dominate the Atlantic shore areas, while oak, hickory, and chestnut thrive in the Hudson and Mohawk valleys and the Great Lakes Plain. Birch, beech, basswood, white oak, and commercially valuable maple are found on the Appalachian Plateau and in the foothills of the Adirondack Mountains. The bulk of the Adirondacks and Catskills is covered with red and black spruce, balsam fir, and mountain ash, as well as white pine and maple. Spruce, balsam fir, paper birch, and mountain ash rise to the timberline while only the hardiest plant species grow above it. Larch, mulberry, locust, and several kinds of willow are among the many varieties that have been introduced throughout the state. Apple trees and other fruit-bearing species are important in western New York and the Hudson Valley.

Common meadow flowers include several types of rose (the state flower), along with dandelion, Queen Anne's lace, goldenrod, and black-eyed Susan. Wild sarsaparilla, Solomon's seal, Indian pipe, bunchberry, and goldthread flourish amid the forests. Cattails grow in profusion along the Hudson, and rushes cover the Finger Lakes shallows. Among protected plants are all species of fern, bayberry, lotus, all native orchids, five species of rhododendron (including azalea), and trillium. Five plant species were listed as threatened or endangered in 2006, including the sandplain gerardia, American hart's tongue fern, and Leedy's roseroot.

Some 600 species of mammals, birds, amphibians, and reptiles are found in New York, of which more than 450 species are common. Mammals in abundance include many mouse species, the snowshoe hare, common and New England cottontails, woodchuck, squirrel, muskrat, and raccoon. The deer population has been estimated at as many as 500,000, making them a pest causing millions of dollars annually in crop damage. The wolverine, elk, and moose were all wiped out during the 19th century, and the otter, mink, marten, and fisher populations were drastically reduced; but the beaver, nearly eliminated by fur trappers, had come back strongly by 1940.

More than 260 bird species have been observed. The most common year-round residents are the crow, hawk, and several types of woodpecker. Summer visitors are many, and include the bluebird (the state bird). The wild turkey, which disappeared during the 19th century, was successfully reestablished in the 1970s. The house (or English) sparrow has been in New York since its introduction in the 1800s.

The common toad, newt, and several species of frog and salamander inhabit New York waters. Garter snakes, water snakes, grass snakes, and milk snakes are common; rattlesnakes formerly thrived in the Adirondacks. There are 210 known species of fish; 130 species are found in the Hudson, 120 in the Lake Ontario wa-

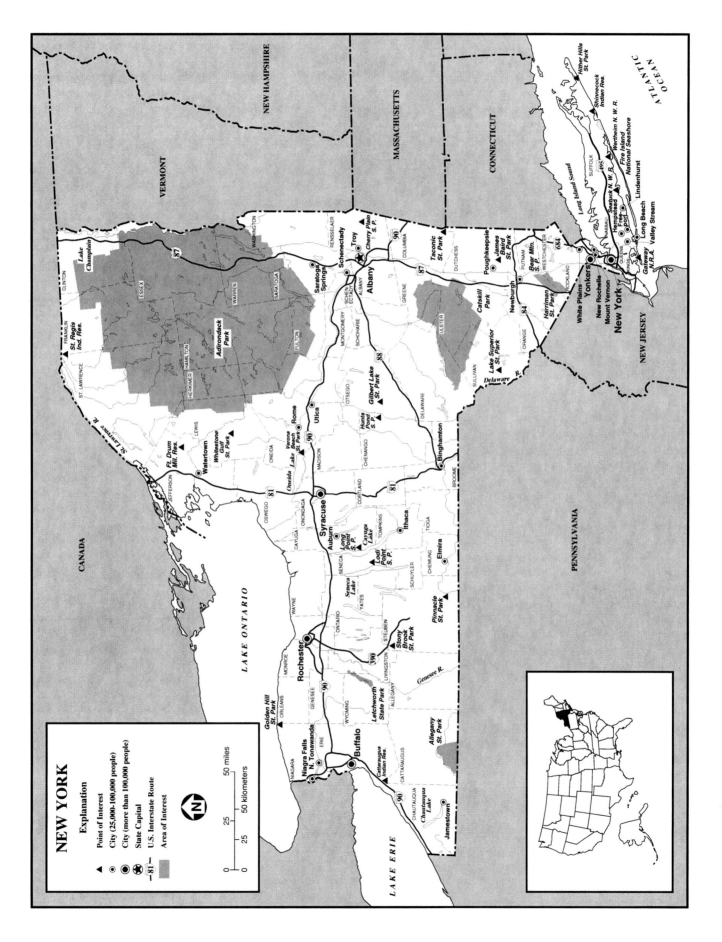

tershed. Freshwater fish include species of perch, bass, pike, and trout (the state fish). Oysters, clams, and several saltwater fish species are found in Long Island Sound. Of insect varieties, the praying mantis is looked upon as a friend (since it eats insects that prey on crops and trees) while the gypsy moth has been singled out as an enemy in periodic state-run pest-control programs.

In April 2006, twenty animal species (vertebrates and invertebrates) were classified by the US Fish and Wildlife Service as threatened or endangered, including the Indiana bat, Karner blue butterfly, piping plover, bald eagle, shortnose sturgeon, three species of whale, and five species of turtle.

[5]ENVIRONMENTAL PROTECTION

New York was one of the first states to mount a major conservation effort. In the 1970s, well over $1 billion was spent to reclaim the state from the ravages of pollution. State conservation efforts date back at least to 1885, when a forest preserve was legally established in the Adirondacks and Catskills. Adirondack Park was created in 1892, Catskill Park in 1904. Then, as now, the issue was how much if any state forestland would be put to commercial use. Timber cutting in the forest preserve was legalized in 1893, but the constitution of 1895 forbade the practice. By the late 1930s, the state had spent more than $16 million on land purchases and controlled 2,159,795 acres (874,041 hectares) in the Adirondacks and some 230,000 acres (more than 93,000 hectares) in the Catskills. The constitutional revision of 1894 expressly outlawed the sale, removal, or destruction of timber on forestlands. That requirement was modified by constitutional amendment in 1957 and 1973, however, and the state is now permitted to sell forest products from the preserves in limited amounts.

All state environmental programs are run by the Department of Environmental Conservation (DEC), established in 1970. The department oversees pollution control programs, monitors environmental quality, manages the forest preserves, and administers fish and wildlife laws (including the issuance of hunting and fishing licenses). The state's national parks totaled 35,914 acres (14,534 hectares). State parks and recreational areas totaled 258,000 acres (104,000 hectares). Wetlands covered 2.5 million acres of the state as of 2000. About one-half of the 160 species identified as endangered or threatened by the Department of Environmental Conservation are wetlands-dependent.

The chief air-quality problem areas are Buffalo, where levels of particles (especially from the use of coke in steelmaking) are high, and New York City, where little progress has been made in cutting carbon monoxide emissions from motor vehicles. Despite air-quality efforts, acid rain has been blamed for killing fish and trees in the Adirondacks, Catskills, and other areas. In 1984, the legislature passed the first measure in the nation designed to reduce acid rain, calling for a cut of 12% in sulfur dioxide emissions by 1988 and further reductions after that. In 2000, the state legislature passed the Air Pollution Mitigation Law, which penalized New York utilities for selling sulfur dioxide allowances other states; the law was overturned in April 2002, when a federal district court ruled that the law both restricted interstate commerce and was preempted by the federal Clean Air Act. In 2003, 44 million lb of toxic chemicals were released in the state.

Before the 1960s, the condition of New York's waters was a national scandal. Raw sewage, arsenic, cyanide, and heavy metals were regularly dumped into the state's lakes and rivers, and fish were rapidly dying off. Two Pure Waters Bond Acts during the 1960s, the Environmental Quality Bond Act of 1972, and a state fishery program have helped reverse the damage. The state has also taken action against corporate polluters, including a $7-million settlement with General Electric over that company's discharge of toxic polychlorinated biphenyls (PCBs) into the Hudson. In addition, the state and federal government spent perhaps $45 million between 1978 and 1982 on the cleanup of the Love Canal area of Niagara Falls, which was contaminated by the improper disposal of toxic wastes, and on the relocation of some 400 families that had lived there. Remaining problems include continued dumping of sewage and industrial wastes into New York Bay and Long Island Sound, sewage overflows into the Lower Hudson, industrial dumping in the Hudson Valley, nuclear wastes in West Valley in Cattaraugus County, and contamination of fish in Lake Erie. Toxic pollutants, such as organic chemicals and heavy metals, appear in surface and groundwater to an extent not yet fully assessed.

In 2003, New York had 485 hazardous waste sites listed in the US Environment Protection Agency (EPA) database, 86 of which were on the National Priorities List in 2006, including Brookhaven National Laboratory and General Motors Central Foundry Division in Massena. In 2006, New York ranked fourth in the nation for the highest number of sites on the National Priorities List, following New Jersey, Pennsylvania, and California. In 2005, the EPA spent over $32 million through the Superfund program for the cleanup of hazardous waste sites in the state. The same year, federal EPA grants awarded to the state included $64.2 million for the drinking water state revolving fund and over $4.8 million for projects to implement air pollution controls. Other EPA grants received that year included $2.4 million for projects involved with the Long Island Sound Restoration Act and $330,152 for the Lake Champlain Basin Program.

A 1982 law requires a deposit on beer and soft-drink containers sold in the state, to encourage return and recycling of bottles and cans.

[6]POPULATION

New York is no longer the most populous state, having lost that position to California in the 1970 census. However, New York City remains the most populous US city, as it has been since at least 1790. New York state ranked third in population in the United States with an estimated total of 19,254,630 in 2005, an increase of 1.5% since 2000. Between 1990 and 2000, New York's population grew from 17,990,455 to 18,976,457, an increase of 5.5%. The population is projected to reach 19.5 million by 2015. New York's population density in 2004 was 407.2 persons per sq mi, the seventh-highest in the nation. In 2004, the median age for New Yorkers was 37.3, with nearly 23.8% of the populace under age 18 and 13% over 65.

First in the state as well as the nation in population was New York City, with 8,104,079 residents in 2004 (up from 7,323,000 in 1990). The growth of New York City has been remarkable. In 1790, when the first national census was taken, the city had 49,401 residents. By 1850, its population had boomed to 696,115; by 1900, to 3,437,202, double that of Chicago, the city's closest rival. Manhattan alone housed more people in 1900 than any city outside New York. In 1990, if Brooklyn, Queens, Manhattan, and the Bronx had each been a separate city, they would still have ranked third, fourth, sixth, and seventh in the nation, respectively.

Other leading cities, with their estimated 2004 populations were Buffalo, 282,864; Rochester, 212,481; Yonkers, 197,126; and Syracuse, 143,101. All these cities have lost population since the 1970s. With 18,709,802 people in 2004 (down from 20,196,649 in 1999), the tri-state New York City metropolitan area remained the nation's largest; other major metropolitan areas included those of Buffalo-Niagara Falls, with an estimated 1,154,378 people, and Rochester, with 1,041,499. Albany, the state capital, had an estimated metropolitan population of 845,269 in 2004.

7 ETHNIC GROUPS

During the 19th and 20th centuries, New York was the principal gateway for European immigrants. In the great northern migration that began after World War I, large numbers of blacks also settled there; more recently there has been an influx of Hispanics and Latinos and, to a lesser extent, of Asians. As of 2000, New York had the largest black and second-largest Asian population among the 50 states, and the second-highest percentage of foreign-born residents.

According to the US Bureau of the Census, New York had 82,461 Indians in 2000. In 1996, there were an estimated 16,014 Indians living on or adjacent to the reservations of the following seven tribes: the Cayuga, Oneida, Onondaga, Seneca, and Tuscarora nations, the St. Regis Mohawk Tribe, and the Tonawanda Band of

Senecas. In 2004, 0.5% of the state's population was American Indian or Alaskan Native.

Blacks have been in New York since 1624. All black slaves were freed by a state law in 1827. Rochester was a major center of the antislavery movement; Frederick Douglass, a former slave, settled and published his newspaper North Star there, while helping to run the Underground Railroad. After World War I, blacks moving into New York City displaced the Jews, Italians, Germans, and Irish then living in Harlem, which went on to become the cultural capital of black America. The black population of New York State was 3,014,385 as of 2000—15.9% of the state's population. That percentage had increased to 17.5% by 2004. In 2000, the black population of New York City alone was 2,129,762, larger than the black populations of all but four of the 50 states, and representing 26.6% of all city residents.

The population of Hispanics and Latinos as of 2000 was 2,867,583, or 15% of the state population. Of this total, New York City accounted for roughly 75%. Puerto Ricans in New York state numbered 1,050,293. Cubans, Dominicans, Colombians, Central Americans, and Mexicans are also present in growing numbers, including a large but undetermined number of illegal immigrants. In 2004, 16% of the state's population was Hispanic or Latino.

New York's Asian population is surpassed only by that of California. In 2000 it was estimated at 1,044,976, up from 694,000 in 1990. Pacific Islanders numbered 8,818. In 2000, state residents included 424,774 Chinese, 251,724 Asian Indians (up from 80,430

New York—Counties, County Seats, and County Areas and Populations

COUNTY	COUNTY SEAT	LAND AREA (SQ MI)	POPULATION (2005 EST.)	COUNTY	COUNTY SEAT	LAND AREA (SQ MI)	POPULATION (2005 EST.)
Albany	Albany	584	297,414	Oneida	Utica	1,819	234,105
Allegany	Belmont	1,032	50,602	Onondaga	Syracuse	785	458,053
Bronx	Bronx	42	1,357,589	Ontario	Canandaigua	644	104,461
Broome	Binghamton	712	196,947	Orange	Goshen	826	372,893
Cattaraugus	Little Valley	1,306	82,502	Orleans	Albion	391	43,387
Cayuga	Auburn	695	81,454	Oswego	Oswego	954	123,373
Chautauqua	Mayville	1,064	136,409	Otsego	Cooperstown	1,004	62,746
Chemung	Elmira	411	89,512	Putnam	Carmel	231	100,507
Chenango	Norwich	897	51,755	Queens	Queens	109	2,241,600
Clinton	Plattsburgh	1,043	82,047	Rensselaer	Troy	655	155,251
Columbia	Hudson	628	63,622	Richmond	Staten Island	59	464,573
Cortland	Cortland	500	48,622	Rockland	New City	175	292,916
Delaware	Delhi	1,440	47,534	St. Lawrence	Canton	2,728	111,380
Dutchess	Poughkeepsie	804	294,849	Saratoga	Ballston Spa	810	214,859
Erie	Buffalo	1,046	930,703	Schenectady	Schenectady	206	149,078
Essex	Elizabethtown	1,806	38,676	Schoharie	Schoharie	624	32,277
Franklin	Malone	1,648	51,033	Schuyler	Watkins Glen	329	19,342
Fulton	Johnstown	497	55,625	Seneca	Waterloo	327	34,855
Genesee	Batavia	495	59,257	Steuben	Bath	1,396	98,632
Greene	Catskill	648	49,682	Suffolk	Riverhead	911	1,474,927
Hamilton	Lake Pleasant	1,721	5,228	Sullivan	Monticello	976	76,539
Herkimer	Herkimer	1,416	63,780	Tioga	Owego	519	51,475
Jefferson	Watertown	1,273	116,384	Tompkins	Ithaca	477	100,018
Kings	Brooklyn	70	2,486,235	Ulster	Kingston	1,131	182,693
Lewis	Lowville	1,283	26,571	Warren	Town of Queensbury*	882	65,548
Livingston	Geneseo	633	64,205	Washington	Hudson Falls**	836	63,024
Madison	Wampsville	656	70,337	Wayne	Lyons	605	93,609
Monroe	Rochester	663	733,366	Westchester	White Plains	438	940,807
Montgomery	Fonda	404	48,968	Wyoming	Warsaw	595	42,693
Nassau	Mineola	287	1,333,137	Yates	Penn Yan	339	24,756
New York	New York	22	1,593,200	**TOTALS**		48,033	19,254,630
Niagara	Lockport	526	217,008				

a decade earlier), 119,846 Koreans, 81,681 Filipinos, 37,279 Japanese, and 23,818 Vietnamese (up from 12,116 in 1990). New York City has the second-largest Chinatown in the United States. In 2004, 6.5% of the state's population was Asian.

In 2000 there were 3,868,133 foreign-born New Yorkers (20.4% of the total state population), a million more than there had been in 1990 (2,851,861, or 15.8%) and more than any other state except California. Among persons who reported at least one specific ancestry group, 2,122,620 named German; 2,737,146 Italian; 2,454,469 Irish; 1,140,036 English; 986,141 Polish; and 460,261 Russian. These figures do not distinguish the large numbers of European Jewish immigrants who would identify themselves as Jews rather than by their country of origin.

The ethnic diversity of the state is reflected in such Manhattan neighborhoods as Harlem, Chinatown, Little Italy, and "Spanish," or East, Harlem, with its large Puerto Rican concentration. Many of the more successful ethnics have moved to the suburbs; on the other hand, new immigrants still tend to form ethnic communities, often in the outer boroughs, such as Asians and South Americans in certain parts of Queens and Russian Jews in south Brooklyn. Outside New York City there are also important ethnic enclaves in the Buffalo metropolitan area, with its large populations of Polish and Italian origin.

8 LANGUAGES

Just as New York for three centuries has channeled immigrant speakers of other languages into the English-speaking population, so it has helped to channel some of their words into English, with much more rapid dissemination because of the concentration of publishing and communications industries in New York City.

Little word-borrowing followed contacts by European settlers with the unfriendly Iroquois, who between the 14th and 17th centuries had dispersed the several Algonkian tribes of Montauk, Delaware, and Mahican Indians. In New York State, the effect on English has been almost entirely the adoption of such place-names as Manhattan, Adirondack, Chautauqua, and Skaneateles.

Although the speech of metropolitan New York has its own characteristics, in the state as a whole the Northern dialect predominates. New York State residents generally say /hahg/ and /fahg/ for *hog* and *fog*, /krik/ for *creek*, *greasy* with an /s/ sound, and *half* and *path* with the vowel of *cat*. They keep the /r/ after a vowel, as in *far* and *cord;* sharply differentiate *horse* and *hoarse* by pronouncing the former with the vowel of *haw* and the latter with the vowel of *hoe;* and call a clump of hard maples a *sugarbush*.

There are many regional variations. In the Hudson Valley, *horse* and *hoarse* tend to be pronounced alike, and a sugarbush is called a *sap bush*. In the eastern sector, New England *piazza* for porch and *buttonball* for sycamore are found, as is the Hudson Valley term *nightwalker* for a large earthworm. In the Niagara peninsula, Midland *eavespout* (gutter) and *bawl* (how a calf sounds) have successfully moved north from Pennsylvania to invade Northern speech. In the North Country, some Canadian influence survives in *stook* (shock), *boodan* (liver sausage), and *shivaree* (wedding celebration). In the New York City area, many speakers pronounce *bird* almost as if it were /boyd/, do not sound the /h/ in *whip* or the /r/ after a vowel—although the trend now is toward the /r/ pronunciation—may pronounce initial /th/ almost like /t/ or /d/, *stand on line* (instead of in a line) while waiting to buy a huge sandwich

they call a *hero* and may even pronounce *Long Island* with an inserted /g/ as /long giland/. From the high proportion of New York Yiddish speakers (nearly 40% of all those in the United States in 1990) have come such terms as *schlock*, *schmaltz*, and *chutzpah*.

Serious communication problems have arisen in New York City, especially in the schools, because of the major influx since World War II of Spanish speakers from the Caribbean region, speakers of so-called black English from the South, and, more recently, Asians, in addition to the ever-present large numbers of speakers of other languages. As a result, schools in some areas have emphasized teaching English as a second language.

According to the 2000 census, 72% of all New Yorkers five years of age or older spoke only English at home, down from 76.7% in 1990.

The following table gives selected statistics from the 2000 Census for language spoken at home by persons five years old and over. The category "Other Indic languages" includes Bengali, Marathi, Punjabi, and Romany. The category "Other Indo-European languages" includes Albanian, Gaelic, Lithuanian, and Rumanian. The category "African languages" includes Amharic, Ibo, Twi, Yoruba, Bantu, Swahili, and Somali. The category "Other Asian languages" includes Dravidian languages, Malayalam, Telugu, Tamil, and Turkish. The category "Other Slavic languages" includes Czech, Slovak, and Ukrainian. The category "Other West Germanic languages" includes Dutch, Pennsylvania Dutch, and Afrikaans. The category "Scandinavian languages" includes Danish, Norwegian, and Swedish.

LANGUAGE	NUMBER	PERCENT
Population 5 years and over	**17,749,110**	**100.0**
Speak only English	12,786,189	72.0
Speak a language other than English	4,962,921	28.0
Speak a language other than English	**4,962,921**	**28.0**
Spanish or Spanish Creole	2,416,126	13.6
Chinese	374,627	2.1
Italian	294,271	1.7
Russian	218,765	1.2
French (incl. Patois, Cajun)	180,809	1.0
French Creole	114,747	0.6
Yiddish	113,514	0.6
Polish	111,730	0.6
Korean	102,105	0.6
Other Indic languages	97,212	0.5
German	92,709	0.5
Greek	86,659	0.5
Arabic	69,959	0.4
Hebrew	67,675	0.4
Tagalog	65,506	0.4
Other Indo-European languages	61,128	0.3
African languages	54,271	0.3
Other Asian languages	53,400	0.3
Urdu	52,448	0.3
Portuguese or Portuguese Creole	41,378	0.2
Hindi	41,151	0.2
Other Slavic languages	39,619	0.2
Japanese	34,569	0.2
Serbo-Croatian	31,553	0.2
Persian	25,975	0.1
Vietnamese	20,249	0.1
Hungarian	18,421	0.1
Guajarati	16,908	0.1
Other West Germanic languages	13,415	0.1
Scandinavian languages	11,974	0.1

9RELIGIONS

Before the 1800s, Protestant sects dominated the religious life of New York, although religion did not play as large a role in the public life of New Netherland as it did in New England, with its Puritan population. The first Jews were permitted by the Dutch to settle in New Amsterdam in 1654, but their numbers remained small for the next 200 years. Both the Dutch and later the English forbade the practice of Roman Catholicism. Full religious freedom was not permitted until the constitution of 1777, and there was no Roman Catholic church in upstate New York until 1797. During the early 19th century, Presbyterian, Methodist, Universalist, Baptist, and Quaker pioneers carried their faith westward across the state. Many Protestant churches took part enthusiastically in the abolitionist movement, and the blacks who fled northward out of slavery formed their own Protestant churches and church organizations.

For Roman Catholics and Jews, the history of the 19th century is the story of successive waves of immigration: Roman Catholics first from Ireland and Germany, later from Italy and Poland, Jews first from Germany, Austria, and England, later (in vast numbers) from Russia and other Eastern European nations. The Jews who settled in New York City tended to remain there, the Roman Catholic immigrants were more dispersed throughout the state, with a large German and Eastern European group settling in Buffalo. Irish Catholics were the first group to win great political influence, but since World War II, Jews and Italian Catholics have played a leading role, especially in New York City.

As of 2004, New York had 7,761,801 Roman Catholics, representing about 41% of the total population. About 2,521,087 Roman Catholics were members of the New York Archdiocese. In 2000, there were 1,653,870 adherents of Jewish congregations. Membership of leading Protestant denominations in 2000 included United Methodists, 403,362; Episcopalians, 201,797; Presbyterians (USA), 162,227; and Evangelical Lutherans, 169,329. About 39.6% of the population did not specify a religious affiliation.

The Church of Jesus Christ of Latter-day Saints has reported a fairly strong and steady growth in membership over the past decade. In 1990, membership was reported at 29,997; in 2000 membership grew to 44,987. In 2006, statewide membership was reported at 69,682 in 151 congregations. Three Mormon temples have been established in the state: Harrison (est. 1995), Palmyra (est. 2000), and Manhattan (est. 2004).

Because of diversified immigration, New York City has small percentages but significant numbers of Buddhists, Muslims, Hindus, and Orthodox Christians. There were about 223,968 members of Muslim congregations. Though exact membership numbers were not available, there were about 121 Buddhist congregations and 83 Hindu congregations statewide. There is also a wide variety of religious-nationalist sects and cults, including the World Community of Islam in the West, also called the Nation of Islam (Black Muslims), the Hare Krishna group, and the Unification Church of the Reverend Sun Myung Moon.

The National Council of Churches, founded in 1950 and based in New York City, is one of the leading Christian ecumenical organizations in the country, representing over 45 million people in over 100,000 local congregations. The World Council of Churches, the largest international Christian ecumenical organization, has its US offices in New York City. New York City also serves as the home base for a number of national Jewish organizations, including the American Board of Rabbis–Vaad Harabonim of America, the American Jewish Congress, the Rabbinical Council of America, and the American Sephardi Federation. Opus Dei, a conservative Catholic organization with about 87,000 members worldwide, has its US headquarters in New York City; the organization gained controversial attention in 2006 based on its mention in The Da-Vinci Code, a movie and best-selling novel by Dan Brown.

10TRANSPORTATION

New York City is a major transit point for both domestic and international passenger and freight traffic. The Port of New York and New Jersey is among the nation's busiest harbors; New York City hosts two major airports, Kennedy International and La Guardia, both in Queens. New York City is connected with the rest of the state by an extensive network of good roads, although road and rail transport within the metropolitan region is sagging with age.

The first railroad in New York State was the Mohawk and Hudson, which made its initial trip from Albany to Schenectady on 9 August 1831. A series of short inter-city rail lines, built during the 1830s and 1840s, were united into the New York Central in 1853. Cornelius Vanderbilt gained control of the New York Central in 1867 and by 1873 had connected New York with Chicago. Under Vanderbilt and his son William, rail links were also forged between New York and Boston, Buffalo, Montreal, and western Pennsylvania.

The height of the railroads' power and commercial importance came during the last decades of the 19th century. After World War I, road vehicles gradually replaced the railroads as freight carriers. In 2003, New York had 4,879 mi (7,855 km) of track. In the same year, there were two Class I lines, in addition to two Canadian lines, four regional, 20 local, and seven switching and terminal railroads operating within the state.

The decline in freight business, and the railroads' inability to make up the loss of passenger traffic, led to a series of reorganizations and failures, of which the best known is the merger of the New York Central with the Pennsylvania Railroad, and the subsequent bankruptcy of the Penn Central. Today, much of New York's rail network is operated by either CSX or the Norfolk Southern. The National Railroad Passenger Corporation (Amtrak) owns and operates lines along the eastern corridor from Boston through New York City to Washington, DC. Regularly scheduled daily trains are operated through New York State, stopping at 25 stations. New York City's Penn Station is the busiest station in the entire Amtrak system. The Long Island Railroad, an important commuter carrier, is run by the Metropolitan Transportation Authority (MTA), which also operates the New York City subways. Construction of the New York City subway system began in 1900, with service starting on 27 October 1904. The route network is about 230 mi (370 km) long, of which 137 mi (220 km) are underground.

The only other mass-transit rail line in the state is Buffalo's 6.4 mi (10.3 km) light rail system, of which 5.2 mi (8.4 km) is underground. In 1984, regular trolley service resumed in Buffalo for the first time since 1950 on the other 1.2 mi (1.9 km) of track, running through the downtown shopping district. Among cities served by municipal, county, or metropolitan-area bus systems are Albany, Binghamton, Buffalo, Elmira, and Syracuse.

In 2004, there were some 11.048 million motor vehicles registered in New York State, including around 8.468 million automobiles, some 25,000 buses, and about 2.386 million trucks of all types. In addition, around 169,000 motorcycles were also registered as of that same year. The state in 2004, had 113,341 mi (182,479 km) of public roads and highways. The major toll road, and the nation's longest toll superhighway, is the Thomas E. Dewey Thruway, operated by the New York State Thruway Authority, which extends 559 mi (900 km) from just outside New York City to Buffalo and the Pennsylvania border in southwestern New York. Toll-free expressways include the Adirondack Northway (I-87), from Albany to the Canadian border, and the North–South Expressway (I-81), from the Canadian to the Pennsylvania border.

A number of famous bridges and tunnels connect the five boroughs of New York City with each other and with New Jersey. The Verrazano–Narrows Bridge, opened to traffic in 1964, spans New York Harbor between Brooklyn and Staten Island. Equally famous, and especially renowned for their beauty, are the Brooklyn Bridge (1883), the city's first suspension bridge, and the George Washington Bridge (1931). The Holland (1927) and Lincoln (1937–57) tunnels under the Hudson River link Manhattan with New Jersey. Important links among the five boroughs include the Triborough Bridge, Manhattan Bridge, Williamsburg Bridge, Queensboro Bridge, Bronx-Whitestone Bridge, Throgs Neck Bridge, Brooklyn-Battery Tunnel, and Queens-Midtown Tunnel. The Staten Island Ferry conveys passengers and autos between the borough and lower Manhattan.

Until the early 1800s, almost all the state's trade moved on the Atlantic Ocean, Hudson River, and New York Bay. This waterway transportation system was expanded starting in the 1820s. Off the Hudson, one of the country's major arteries, branched the main elements of the New York Barge Canal System: the Erie Canal, linking the Atlantic with Lake Erie, and New York City with Buffalo; the Oswego Canal, connecting the Erie Canal with Lake Ontario; the Cayuga and Seneca Canal, connecting the Erie Canal with Cayuga and Seneca lakes; and the Champlain Canal, extending the state's navigable waterways from the Hudson to Lake Champlain, and so to Vermont and Quebec Province. By 1872, New York's canal system was carrying over 6 million tons of cargo per year; however, an absolute decline in freight tonnage began after 1890 (the relative decline had begun 40 years earlier, with the rise of the railroads). By the mid-1980s, the canals carried less than 10% of the tonnage for 1880.

Buffalo, on Lake Erie, is the most important inland port. In 2004, it handled 1.592 million tons of cargo. Albany, the major port on the Hudson, handled 7.450 million tons of cargo, and Port Jefferson, on Long Island Sound, handled 2.398 million tons in 2004. In that same year, New York had 394 mi (634 km) of navigable inland waterways. Waterborne shipments in 2003 totaled 99.406 million tons.

It would be difficult to exaggerate the historic and economic importance of New York Harbor—haven for explorers, point of entry for millions of refugees and immigrants, and the nation's greatest seaport until recent years, when it was surpassed by Greater New Orleans and Houston in terms of cargo tonnage. Harbor facilities, including those of Bayonne, Jersey City, and Newark, New Jersey, add up to 755 mi (1,215 km) of frontage, with some 700 piers and wharves. The entire port is under the jurisdiction of the Port Authority of New York and New Jersey. In 2004, it handled 152.377 million tons of cargo. In the mid-1990s, the port was served by 1,000 trucking companies, 80 steamship lines, and 12 intermodal rail terminals.

In 2005, the state of New York had a total of 582 public and private-use aviation-related facilities. This included 397 airports, 167 heliports, and 18 seaplane bases. By far the busiest airports in the state are John F. Kennedy International (18,586,863 passengers enplaned in 2004) and La Guardia (12,312,561 passengers enplaned in 2004), both in New York City, and making them the 8th- and 20th-busiest airports in the United States, respectively. Buffalo Niagara International Airport was the state's largest airport outside of New York City, with 2,206,385 passengers enplaned in 2004.

[11] HISTORY

The region now known as New York State has been inhabited for about 10,000 years. The first Indians probably came across the Bering Strait and most likely reached New York via the Niagara Peninsula. Remains have been found in southwestern New York of the Indians called Mound Builders (for their practice of burying their dead in large mounds), who cultivated food crops and tobacco. The Mound Builders were still living in the state well after AD 1000, although by that time most of New York was controlled by later migrants of the Algonkian linguistic group. These Algonkian tribes included the Mahican in the northeast, the Wappinger in the Hudson Valley and on Long Island, and the Leni-Lenape (or Delaware) of the Delaware Valley.

Indians of the Iroquoian language group invaded the state from the north and west during the early 14th century. In 1570, after European explorers had discovered New York but before the establishment of any permanent European settlements, the main Iroquois tribes—the Onondaga, Oneida, Seneca, Cayuga, and Mohawk—established the League of the Five Nations. For the next 200 years, members of the League generally kept peace among themselves but made war on other tribes, using not only traditional weapons but also the guns they were able to get from the French, Dutch, and English. In 1715, a sixth nation joined the League—the Tuscarora, who had fled the British in North Carolina. For much of the 18th century, the Iroquois played a skillful role in balancing competing French and British interests.

The first European known to have entered New York Harbor was the Florentine navigator Giovanni da Verrazano, on 17 April 1524. The Frenchman Samuel de Champlain began exploring the St. Lawrence River in 1603. While Champlain was aiding the Huron Indians in their fight against the League in 1609, the English mariner Henry Hudson, in the service of the Dutch East India Company, entered New York Bay and sailed up the river that would later bear his name, reaching about as far as Albany. To the Dutch the area did not look especially promising, and there was no permanent Dutch settlement until 1624, three years after the Dutch West India Company had been founded. The area near Albany was first to be settled. The Dutch were mainly interested in fur trading and agriculture in the colony—named New Netherland—was slow to develop. New Amsterdam was founded in 1626, when Director-General Peter Minuit bought Manhattan (from the Indian word manahatin, "hill island") from the Indians for goods worth—as tradition has it—about $24.

New Amsterdam grew slowly, and by 1650 had no more than 1,000 people. When the British took over New Netherland in 1664, only 8,000 residents lived in the colony. Already, however, the population was remarkably diverse: there were the Dutch and English, of course, but also French, Germans, Finns, Swedes, and Jews, as well as black slaves from Angola. The Swedes lived in what had been New Sweden, a territory along the Delaware River ceded to the Netherlands during the administration of Peter Stuyvesant. Equally famed for his wooden leg and his hot temper, Stuyvesant had become director general of the New Netherland colony in 1647. Three years later, after skirmishes with the English settlers of New England, the colony gave up all claims to the Connecticut Valley in the Treaty of Hartford.

Though small and weak, New Netherland was an annoyance to the English. The presence of Dutch traders in New York Bay made it difficult for England to enforce its monopolies under the Navigation Acts. Moreover, the Dutch colony was a political barrier between New England and two other English colonies, Maryland and Virginia. So, in 1664, King Charles II awarded "all the land from the west side of the Connecticutte River to the East Side of De La Ware Bay" to his brother, the Duke of York and Albany, the future King James II. The British fleet arrived in New York Bay on 18 August 1664. Stuyvesant wanted to fight, but his subjects refused, and the governor had no choice but to surrender. The English agreed to preserve the Dutch rights of property and inheritance, and to guarantee complete liberty of conscience. Thus New Netherland became New York. It remained an English colony for the next 112 years, except for a period in 1673 when Dutch rule was briefly restored.

The first decades under the English were stormy. After repeated demands from the colonists, a General Assembly was called in 1683. The assembly adopted a Charter of Liberties and Privileges, but the document, approved by James before his coronation, was revoked after he became king in 1685. The assembly itself was dissolved in 1686, and James II acted to place New York under the dominion of New England. The plan was aborted by the Glorious Revolution of 1688, when James was forced to abdicate. Power in New York fell to Jacob Leisler, a German merchant with local backing. Leisler ruled until 1691, when a new royal governor arrived and had Leisler hanged for treason.

The succeeding decades were marked by conflict between the English and French and by the rising power of the provincial assembly in relations with the British crown. As early as 1690, a band of 150 Frenchmen and 100 Indians attacked and burned Schenectady. New York contributed men and money to campaign against the French in Canada in 1709 and 1711 (during Queen Anne's War) and in 1746 (during King George's War). In 1756, the English determined to drive the French out of the region once and for all. After some early reverses, the English defeated the French in 1760. The Treaty of Paris (1763), ending the French and Indian War, ceded all territory east of the Mississippi to England, except for New Orleans and two islands in the mouth of the St. Lawrence River. The Iroquois, their power weakened during the course of the war, signed treaties giving large areas of their land to the New York colony.

The signing of the Treaty of Paris was followed by English attempts to tighten control over the colonies, in New York as elsewhere. New York merchants vehemently protested the Sugar Act and Stamp Act, and the radical Sons of Liberty made their first appearance in the colony in October 1765. Later, in 1774, after Paul Revere brought news of the Boston Tea Party to New York City, British tea was also dumped into that city's harbor. Nevertheless, New York hesitated before committing itself to independence. The colony's delegates to the Continental Congress in Philadelphia were not permitted by the Third Provincial Congress in New York to vote either for or against the Declaration of Independence on 4 July 1776. The Fourth Provincial Congress, meeting at White Plains, did ratify the Declaration five days later. On 6 February 1778, New York became the second state to ratify the Articles of Confederation.

Nearly one-third of all battles during the Revolutionary War took place on New York soil. The action there began when troops under Ethan Allen captured Fort Ticonderoga in May 1775, and Seth Warner and his New England forces took Crown Point. Reverses came in 1776, however, when George Washington's forces were driven from Long Island and Manhattan by the British; New York City was to remain in British hands for the rest of the war. Troops commanded by British General John Burgoyne recaptured Ticonderoga in July 1777, but were defeated in October at Saratoga, in a battle that is often considered the turning point of the war. In 1778, General Washington made his headquarters at West Point, which General Benedict Arnold tried unsuccessfully to betray to the British in 1780. Washington moved his forces to Newburgh in 1782, and marched into New York City on 25 November 1785, the day the British evacuated their forces. On 4 December, he said farewell to his officers at Fraunces Tavern in lower Manhattan, a landmark that still stands.

Even as war raged, New York State adopted its first constitution on 20 April 1777. The constitution provided for an elected governor and house of assembly, but the franchise was limited to property holders. The first state capital was Kingston, but the capital was moved to Albany in January 1797. After much debate, in which the Federalist Alexander Hamilton played a leading role, the state ratified the US Constitution (with amendments) on 26 July 1788. New York City served as the seat of the US government from 11 January 1785 to 12 August 1790, and the first US president, George Washington, was inaugurated in the city on 30 April 1789.

George Clinton was the state's first elected governor, serving from 1777 to 1795 and again from 1801 to 1804. The achievements under his governorship were considerable. Commerce and agriculture expanded, partly because of Clinton's protectionist policies and partly because of the state's extremely favorable geographical situation.

The end of the War of 1812 signaled the opening of an era of unprecedented economic expansion for the state. By this time, the Iroquois were no longer a threat (most had sided with the British during the Revolutionary War, and many later fled to Canada). Migrants from New England were flocking to the state, which the census of 1810 showed was the most populous in the country. Small wonder that New York was the site of the early 19th century's most ambitious engineering project: construction of the Erie Canal. Ground was broken for the canal in 1817, during the first term of Governor De Witt Clinton, the nephew of George Clinton; the first vessels passed through the completed canal in 1825.

Actually, New York had emerged as the nation's leading commercial center before the canal was even started. The textile industry had established itself by the mid-1820s, and the dairy industry was thriving. The effects of the canal were felt most strongly in foreign trade—by 1831, 50% of US imports and 27% of US exports passed through the state—and in the canal towns of Utica, Syracuse, Rochester, and Buffalo, where business boomed.

Commercial progress during this period was matched by social and cultural advancement. New York City became a center of literary activity during the 1820s, and by the 1840s was already the nation's theatrical capital. A new state constitution drafted in 1821 established universal white male suffrage, but retained the property qualifications for blacks. Slavery was abolished as of 4 July 1827 (few slaves actually remained in the state by this time), and New Yorkers soon took the lead in the growing antislavery movement. The first women's rights convention in the United States was held in Seneca Falls in 1848—though women would have to wait until 1917 before winning the right to vote in state elections. Also during the 1840s, the state saw the first of several great waves of European immigration. The Irish and Germans were the earliest major arrivals during the 19th century, but before World War I they would be joined—not always amicably—by Italians and European Jews.

New Yorkers voted for Abraham Lincoln in the presidential election of 1860 and were among the readiest recruits to the Union side. Enthusiasm for the conflict diminished during the next two years, however. When the military draft reached New York City on 11 July 1863, the result was three days of rioting in which blacks were lynched and the homes of prominent abolitionists were burned. But New York was not a wartime battleground, and overall the war and Reconstruction were very good for business.

The decades after the Civil War ushered in an era of extraordinary commercial growth and political corruption. This was the Gilded Age, during which entrepreneurs became multimillionaires and New York was transformed from an agricultural state to an industrial giant. In 1860, the leading manufactures in the state were flour and meal, men's clothing, refined sugar, leather goods, liquor, and lumber; 90 years later, apparel, printing and publishing, food, machinery, chemicals, fabricated metal products, electrical machinery, textiles, instruments, and transportation equipment had became the dominant industries.

The key to this transformation was the development of the railroads. The boom period for railroad construction started in the 1850s and reached its high point after 1867, when "Commodore" Cornelius Vanderbilt, who had been a steamboat captain in 1818, took over the New York Central. During the 1860s, native New Yorkers like Jay Gould and Russell Sage made their fortunes through investment and speculation. Especially during the century's last two decades, corporate names that became household words began to emerge: Westinghouse Electric in 1886, General Electric (as Edison Electric) in 1889, Eastman Kodak in 1892. In 1882, another native New Yorker, John D. Rockefeller, formed the Standard Oil Trust; although the trust would eventually be broken up, the Rockefeller family would help shape New York politics for many decades to come.

The period immediately following the Civil War also marked a new high in political influence for the Tammany Society (or "Tammany Hall"), founded in 1789 as an anti-Federalist organization. From 1857 until his exposure by the press in 1871, Democrat William March "Boss" Tweed ruled Tammany and effectively dominated New York City by dispersing patronage, buying votes, and bribing legislators and judges. Tammany went into temporary eclipse after the Tweed Ring was broken up, and Republicans swept the state in 1872. The first result was a series of constitutional changes, including one abolishing the requirement that blacks hold property in order to vote. A new constitution approved in 1894, and effective in 1895, remains the basic law of New York State today.

During the Union's first 100 years, New York's political life had projected into national prominence such men as Alexander Hamilton, John Jay, George and De Witt Clinton, Martin Van Buren, and Millard Fillmore. The state's vast population—New York held more electoral votes than any other state between 1812 and 1972—coupled with its growing industrial and financial power, enhanced the prestige of state leaders during the nation's second century. Grover Cleveland, though born in New Jersey, became mayor of Buffalo, then governor of New York, and finally the 22d US president in 1885. Theodore Roosevelt was governor of New York, then became vice president and finally president of the United States in 1901. In 1910, Charles Evans Hughes resigned the governorship to become an associate justice of the US Supreme Court; he also served as secretary of state, and in 1930 was appointed chief justice of the United States. By the 1920s, Tammany had rebounded from the Tweed Ring breakup and from another scandal during the 1890s to reach its peak of prestige: Alfred E. Smith, a longtime member of Tammany, as well as an able and popular official, was four times elected governor and in 1928 became the first Roman Catholic candidate to be nominated by a major party for the presidency of the United States. That year saw the election of Franklin D. Roosevelt as governor of New York.

The 1930s, a period of depression, ushered in a new wave of progressive government. From 1933 until 1945, FDR was in the White House. Roosevelt's successor in the statehouse was Herbert H. Lehman, whose Little New Deal established the basic pattern of present state social welfare policies that had begun on a much more modest scale during Smith's administration. The Fusion mayor of New York City at this time—propelled into office by yet another wave of exposure of Tammany corruption—was the colorful and popular Fiorello H. La Guardia.

The decades following World War II saw extraordinary expansion of New York social services, including construction of the state university system, but also an erosion of the state's industrial base. Fiscal crises were not new to the state—reformers in the 1920s railed against New York City's "spendthrift" policies—but the greatly increased scale of government in the 1970s made the fiscal crisis of 1975 unprecedented in its scope and implications. The city's short-term debt grew from virtually zero to about $6 billion between 1970 and 1975, although its government reported consistently balanced budgets. Eventually a package totaling $4.5 billion in aid was needed to avoid bankruptcy. The decreasing pace of population and industrial growth during the 1950s and 1960s, and the decline during the 1970s, also led to a dimming of New York's political fortunes. The single dominant political figure in New York after World War II, Nelson A. Rockefeller (governor, 1958–73), tried and failed three times to win the Republican presidential nomination before his appointment to the vice-presidency in 1974. Unable to overcome the hostility of his party's conservative wing, he was not renominated for the vice-presidency in 1976. In 1984, however, US Representative Geraldine Ferraro of Queens was the Democratic Party's vice-presidential standard-bearer, and Governor Mario M. Cuomo emerged as an influential Democratic spokesman. After serving for 12 years, Cuomo was replaced in 1995 by State Senator George Pataki, the first Republican elected New York governor since 1970.

From the late 1970s through the late 1980s, New York enjoyed an economic boom, particularly in finance, insurance, real estate and construction. The state budget increased in constant dollars by 20%. While much of that increase compensated for cuts in federal aid to states and was directed at education, municipalities, schools and prisons, some went to meet new needs such as homelessness and AIDS victims. Prosperity did not reach all sectors of the economy or the population, however. In 1984, 25% of the residents of New York City lived below the poverty line. The collapse of the stock market in October of 1987, in which the market plunged 36% in two months, not only forced a retrenchment on Wall Street but also signaled the end of the boom and the beginning of a recession that was quite severe in New York, exacerbated by the curtailment of federal funding by the Reagan and Bush administrations. Unemployment peaked in 1992, and by 1994 a recovery was under way.

The boom economy of the late 1990s boosted Wall Street, with the bulls dominating the stock market despite some historic losses, particularly in the technology sector, which analysts later categorized as "market corrections." In 1998 New York had the fourth-highest per capita income in the nation ($31,679) but it also had more people living below the poverty level than 45 other states, again indicating prosperity had not reached into all sectors.

The 1990s witnessed the settlement of the lawsuits surrounding Love Canal in Buffalo, where leaking chemical wastes in the 1970s and early 1980s had prompted the state and federal governments to pay to move families from the area. In the largest legal settlement in New York's history, in 1994 Occidental Petroleum Corp. agreed to pay $98 million in damages for the dumping of hazardous wastes at Love Canal, ending 16 years of litigation.

The state, which dropped from the nation's second to third most populous in 1994, retained the ranking in 2005. According to Census Bureau estimates, the state had over 19 million people in 2005—surpassed only by California and Texas. New York's Hispanic population in 2003 was estimated to be roughly the same in number as its African American population (African Americans 15.9%; Hispanics 15.1%).

In mid-1999, in the midst of a budget impasse in the state legislature, the government determined it would sell state facilities. A resulting deal, reached in 2000, saw the state selling two nuclear plants for a total asking price of $967 million. It was the largest privatization of state assets in New York history.

Transportation in and around New York City was the focus of the statehouse and legislature in 2000. Governor George Pataki and New Jersey Governor Christine Todd Whitman, a fellow Republican, had squared off over issues surrounding the Port Authority, which the states jointly control. The governors resolved their differences in June 2000. They cleared the way for the construction of a $200-million cargo hub for the world's largest ocean carrier (Maersk Sealand) and reopened the possibility that the World Trade Center, which the Port Authority still controlled, could be turned over to a private developer. Meanwhile, lawmakers heard arguments for and against a proposed $17-billion project to be undertaken by the Metropolitan Transit Authority (MTA). Advocates argued the public works plan, which would result in the largest sale of municipal bonds in US history, was necessary to build a new generation of subways, buses, and trains to serve the greater New York area. Opponents believed the project would pose disaster for the MTA, burying the agency under a mountain of debt and rendering it unable to maintain the existing transportation systems.

New York City was one site of the nation's terrorist attacks on 11 September 2001, when hijackers from the al-Qaeda terrorist organization flew two passenger airliners into the North and South Towers of the World Trade Center, destroying them. Another aircraft hit the Pentagon building in Washington, DC, and a fourth crashed into a field in Stony Creek Township, Pennsylvania. Approximately 3,000 people had died, were missing, or presumed dead as a result of the attacks. The city and the nation went into a long period of mourning. New York City Mayor Rudolph Giuliani was praised for his effective handling of the crisis.

Berlin-based architect Daniel Libeskind's design for rebuilding "Ground Zero" (the site of the demolished World Trade Center) was accepted in 2003; New Yorkers had expressed dissatisfaction with the original designs, which were thought to be uninspiring. Libeskind's design features a complex of angular towers and a spire that would be among the world's tallest structures.

New York was one of the states affected by the 14 August 2003 massive power blackout in Canada, the Northeast and Midwestern states. The largest electrical outage in US history affected 9,300 square miles and a population of over 50 million.

Following the decline of the stock market on Wall Street and the US recession in the early 2000s, New York in 2003 was plagued with economic woes. The state faced a budget deficit of $10 billion that year. Although the economy began to improve in 2004 and 2005, the state still faced a budget gap of $4.2 billion in 2005–06. In 2004, New York had the fifth-highest per capita personal income in the nation, at $38,228, behind Connecticut, Maryland, Massachusetts, and New Jersey. The poverty rate for New York in 2003–04 was 14.6%, above the national rate of 12.6% (measured as a two-year average).

12 STATE GOVERNMENT

New York has had four constitutions, adopted in 1777, 1822, 1846, and 1895. The 1895 constitution was extensively revised in 1938, and the basic structure of state government has not changed since then, although the document had been amended 216 times by January 2005. In 1993 the Temporary State Commission on Constitutional Revision was created in anticipation of a referendum on a constitutional convention in 1997.

The legislature consists of a 62-member Senate and 150-member assembly. Senators and assembly members serve two-year terms and are elected in even-numbered years. Each house holds regular annual sessions, which begin in January and are not formally limited in length; special sessions may be called by the governor or initiated by petition of two-thirds of the membership of each body. All legislators must be at least 18 years old, US citizens, and must have been residents of the state for at least five years and residents of their districts for at least one year prior to election. The legislative salary was $79,500 in 2004, unchanged from 1999.

Either senators or assembly members may introduce or amend a bill; the governor may introduce a budget bill. To pass, a bill requires a majority vote in both houses; a two-thirds majority (of the elected members in each house) is required to override the governor's veto. If the governor neither signs nor vetoes a bill, it becomes law after 10 days, as long as the legislature is in session.

The state's only elected executives are the governor, lieutenant governor, comptroller, and attorney general. Each serves a four-year term. The governor and lieutenant governor are jointly elected; there is no limit to the number of terms they may serve. The governor must be at least 25 years old, a US citizen, and a resident of the state for at least one year prior to the date of election. The lieutenant governor is next in line for the governorship (should the governor be unable to complete his term in office) and presides over the Senate. As of December 2004, the governor's salary was $179,000, unchanged from 1999.

The governor appoints the heads of most of the major executive departments, with some of the appointments requiring the advice and consent of the Senate. The exceptions are the comptroller and attorney general, who are elected by the voters; the commissioner of education, who is named by the Regents of the University of the State of New York; the commissioner of social services, elected by the Board of Social Services; and the chief of the Executive Department, which the governor heads ex officio.

A bill becomes law when passed by both houses of the legislature and signed by the governor. While the legislature is in session, a bill may also become law if the governor fails to act on it within 10 days of its receipt. The governor may veto a bill or, if the legislature has adjourned, may kill a bill simply by taking no action on it for 30 days.

A proposed amendment to the state constitution must receive majority votes in both houses of the legislature during two successive sessions. Amendments so approved are put on the ballot in November and adopted or rejected by majority vote. The constitution also provides that the voters must be permitted every 20 years to decide whether a convention should be called to amend the present constitution. Voters in New York must be US citizens, at least 18 years old, residents of the county (or New York City) for 30 days prior to election day, and unable to claim the right to vote elsewhere. Restrictions apply to convicted felons and those declared mentally incompetent by the court.

13 POLITICAL PARTIES

In addition to the Democratic and Republican parties, the major political groups, there has always been a profusion of minor parties in New York, some of which have significantly influenced the outcomes of national and state elections.

Party politics in the state crystallized into their present form around 1855. Up to that time, a welter of parties and factions—including such short-lived groups as the Anti-Masons, Bucktails, Clintonians, Hunkers, and Barnburners (split into Hardshell and Softshell Democrats), Know-Nothings (Native American Party),

New York Presidential Vote by Political Parties, 1948–2004

YEAR	ELECTORAL VOTE	NEW YORK WINNER	DEMOCRAT	LIBERAL[1]	REPUBLICAN	PROGRESSIVE[2]	SOCIALIST	SOCIALIST WORKERS	PEACE AND FREEDOM
1948	47	Dewey (R)	2,557,642	222,562	2,841,163	509,559	40,879	2,675	—
1952	45	*Eisenhower (R)	2,687,890	416,711	3,952,815	64,211	2,664	2,212	—
1956	45	*Eisenhower (R)	2,458,212	292,557	4,340,340	—	—	—	—
1960	45	*Kennedy (D)	3,423,909	406,176	3,446,419	—	—	14,319	—
							SOC. LABOR		
1964	43	*Johnson (D)	4,570,670	342,432	2,243,559		6,118	3,228	—
						AMERICAN IND.[3]			
1968	43	Humphrey (D)	3,066,848	311,622	3,007,932	358,864	8,432	11,851	24,517
						CONSERVATIVE[4]			COMMUNIST
1972	41	*Nixon (R)	2,767,956	183,128	3,824,642	368,136	4,530	7,797	5,641
							LIBERTARIAN		
1976	41	*Carter (D)	3,244,165	145,393	2,825,913	2,724,878	12,197	6,996	10,270
								RIGHT TO LIFE	CITIZENS
1980	41	*Reagan (R)	2,728,372	467,801	2,637,700	256,131	52,648	24,159	23,186
									COMMUNIST
1984	36	*Reagan (R)	3,001,285	118,324	3,376,519	288,244	11,949	—	4,226
								NEW ALLIANCE	
1988	36	Dukakis (D)	3,255,487	92,395	2,838,414	243,457	12,109	15,845	20,497
1992[5]	22	*Clinton (D)	3,346,894	97,556	2,041,690	177,000	13,451	15,472	11,318
								FREEDOM[4]	GREEN (Nader)
1996[5]	33	*Clinton (D)	3,649,630	106,547	1,738,707	183,392	12,220	11,393	75,956
2000	33	Gore (D)	3,942,215	77,087	2,258,877	144,797	7,649		244,030
			DEM./WORKING FAMILIES		WRITE-IN (Cobb)	REP. AND CONSERVATIVE	WRITE-IN (Peroutka)	SOCIALIST WORKERS	IND. (Nader)
2004	31	Kerry (D)	4,314,280	87	2,962,567	207	11,607	2,405	99,873

*Won US presidential election.
1 Supported Democratic candidate except in 1980, when John Anderson ran on the Liberal line.
2 Ran in the state as the American Labor Party.
3 Appeared on the state ballot as the Courage Party.
4 Supported Republican candidate.
5 IND. candidate Ross Perot received 1,090,721 votes in 1992 and 503,458 votes in 1996.

Wooly Heads and Silver-Grays (factions of the Whigs), and the Liberty Party—jockeyed for power in New York State.

Roughly speaking, the Democratic Party evolved out of the Democratic Republican factions of the old Republican Party and had become a unified party by the 1850s. The Democratic power base was—and has remained—the big cities, especially New York City. The most important big-city political machine from the 1860s through the 1950s, except for a few brief periods, was the Tammany Society ("Tammany Hall"). Tammany controlled the Democratic Party in New York City and, through that party, the city itself.

The Republican Party in New York State emerged in 1855 as the heir of the Whigs, the Liberty Party, and the Softshell Democratic faction. The Republican Party's power base includes the state's rural counties, the smaller cities and towns, and (though not so much in the 1970s and early 1980s as in earlier decades) the New York City suburbs. Although New York Republicans stand to the right of the Democrats on social issues, they have usually been well to the left of the national Republican party. The liberal "internationalist" strain of Republicanism was personified during the 1960s by Governor Nelson Rockefeller, US Senator Jacob Javits, and New York City Mayor John V. Lindsay (who later became a Democrat).

The disaffection of more conservative Republicans and Democrats within the state led to the formation of the Conservative Party in 1963. At first intended as a device to exert pressure on the state Republican establishment, the Conservative Party soon became a power in its own right, electing a US senator, James Buckley, in 1970. Its power decreased in the late 1970s as the Republican Party embraced some of its positions. The Conservative Party has its left-wing counterpart in the Liberal Party, which was formed in 1944 by dissidents in the American Labor Party who claimed the ALP was Communist-influenced. Tied strongly to labor interests, the Liberals have normally supported the national Democratic ticket. Their power, however, has waned considerably in recent years.

Minor parties have sometimes meant the difference between victory and defeat for major party candidates in state and national elections. The Liberal Party line provided the victory margin in the state, and therefore the nation, for Democratic presidential candidate John F. Kennedy in 1960. Other significant, though not victorious, minor-party presidential candidates have included the American Labor Party with Henry Wallace in 1948 (8% of the vote), the Courage Party with George Wallace in 1968 (5%), and the Liberal Party with John Anderson in 1980 (7%). Among radical parties, the Socialists qualified for the presidential ballot continuously between 1900 and 1952, reaching a peak of 203,201 votes (7% of the total) in 1920.

Democrat Mario M. Cuomo was defeated in his run for a fourth term as governor in November 1994 by Republican George Pataki; Pataki was elected to a third term in 2002. In 2003 New York's US senators were Democrat Charles Schumer, elected to his first term in 1998 to succeed three-term Republican Alphonse D'Amato was reelected in 2004, and Democrat Hillary Rodham Clinton, first elected in 2000. Following the 2004 elections, New York's US representatives included 20 Democrats and 9 Republicans. Republicans held 35 seats in the state Senate while Democrats held 27. In the State Assembly there were 105 Democrats and 45 Republicans.

In the November 1980 presidential elections, Republican nominee Ronald Reagan (with Conservative Party backing) won the state's then-41 electoral votes, apparently because John Anderson, running in New York State on the Liberal Party line, siphoned enough votes from the Democratic incumbent, Jimmy Carter, to give Reagan a plurality. Reagan carried the state again in 1984, despite the presence on the Democratic ticket of US Representative Geraldine Ferraro of Queens as the running mate of Walter Mondale; Ferraro was the first woman candidate for president or vice president on a major party ticket. New Yorkers chose Democratic nominees Michael Dukakis and Bill Clinton in 1988 and 1992, respectively, and Clinton again won the state in 1996. In the 2000 presidential election, Democrat Al Gore won 60% of the vote to Republican George W. Bush's 35%; Green Party candidate Ralph Nader garnered 4% of the vote. In 2004, Democratic challenger John Kerry won 57.8% to incumbent George W. Bush's 40.5%. In 2004 there were 11,837,000 registered voters. In 1998, 47% of registered voters were Democratic, 29% Republican, and 24% unaffiliated or members of other parties. The state had 31 electoral votes in the 2004 presidential election, a loss of 2 votes over the 2000 election.

In November 1993, New York City mayor David Dinkins, a Democrat and New York's first black mayor, who had served since 1990, was defeated by Republican Rudolph Giuliani. Giuliani was legally barred from seeking a third term, and billionaire media tycoon Michael Bloomberg won the mayoral contest in 2001; Bloomberg was reelected in 2005.

14 LOCAL GOVERNMENT

The state constitution, endorsing the principle of home rule, recognizes many different levels of local government. In 2005, New York had 62 counties, 616 municipal governments, 703 public school districts, and 1,135 special districts. In 2002, there were 929 townships.

Cities are contained within counties, with one outstanding exception: New York City is made up of five counties, one for each of its five boroughs. Traditionally, counties are run by an elected board of supervisors or county legislature; however, a growing number of counties have vested increased powers in a single elected county executive. With the exception of some counties within New York City, each county has a county attorney and district attorney, sheriff, fiscal officer (treasurer), county clerk, and commissioner of social services.

Towns are run by a town board; the town supervisor is the board's presiding officer and acts as town treasurer. A group of people within a town or towns may also incorporate themselves into a village, with their own elected mayor and elected board of trustees. Some villages have administrators or managers. Members of the village remain members of the town, and must pay taxes to both jurisdictions. The constitution grants the state legislature the power to decide which taxes the local governments may levy and how much debt they may incur.

New York City is governed by a mayor and city council, but much practical power resides in the Board of Estimate. On this board sit the city's three top elected officials—the mayor, comptroller, and city council president. The board also includes the five borough presidents, elected officials who represent (and, to a limited extent, govern) each of the five boroughs. New York City government is further complicated by the fact that certain essential services are provided not by the city itself but by independent "authorities." The special district of the Port Authority of New York and New Jersey, for example, operates New York Harbor, sets interstate bridge and tunnel tolls, and supervises the city's bus and air terminals; it is responsible not to the mayor but to the governors of New York and New Jersey. Similarly, the Metropolitan Transportation Authority, which controls the city's subways and some of its commuter rail lines, is an independent agency responsible to the state rather than the city.

In 2005, local government accounted for about 938,753 full-time (or equivalent) employment positions.

15 STATE SERVICES

To address the continuing threat of terrorism and to work with the federal Department of Homeland Security, homeland security in New York operates under state statute; the homeland security director is designated as the state homeland security advisor.

Educational services are provided through the Education Department. Under this department's jurisdiction are the State Library, the State Museum, the State Archives, the New York State School for the Blind at Batavia, and the New York State School for the Deaf at Rome. The Education Department also issues licenses for 38 professions, including architecture, engineering and land surveying, massage, pharmacy, public accountancy, social work, and various medical specialties. The state university system is administered by a separate agency headed by a chancellor.

Transportation services are under the direction of the Department of Transportation, which has responsibility for highways, aviation, mass transit, railroads, water transport, transportation safety, and intrastate rate regulation. The Department of Motor Vehicles licenses all road vehicles, motor vehicle dealers, motor vehicle operators, and driving schools.

Human services are provided through several state departments. Among the programs and facilities operated by the Department of Health are three research and treatment facilities; the New York State Veterans' Home at Oxford, Roswell Park Memorial Institute at Buffalo, and Helen Hayes Hospital at West Haverstraw. The state provides care for the mentally ill, retarded, and alcoholics and other substance-dependent persons through the Office of Mental Health, the Office of Mental Retardation and Development Disabilities, and the Office of Alcoholism and Substance Abuse Services. The Office of Mental Health maintains psychiatric centers and developmental centers for developmental disabilities. The Office of Temporary and Disability Assistance within the Department of Family Assistance supervises and sets standards for locally administered public and private welfare and health programs, including Food Stamps and TANF (Temporary Assistance to Needy Families). The Office of Children and Family Services, also within the Department of Family Assistance, has special responsibilities for the blind and visually handicapped and over Indian affairs. Other human services are provided through the Division of Veterans' Affairs, the Division of Human Rights, and the Office for the Aging, all within the Executive Department.

Public protection services include state armed forces, corrections, and consumer protection. Included within the Division of Military and Naval Affairs, in the Executive Department, are the Army National Guard, Air National Guard, Naval Militia, and New York Guard. The Division of State Police operates within the Executive Department, while prisons are administered by the separate Department of Correctional Services. The State Consumer Protection Board (Executive Department) coordinates the consumer protection activities of the various agencies and departments. The major legal role in consumer protection is played by the attorney general.

Housing services are provided through the Division of Housing and Community Renewal of the Executive Department, and through the quasi-independent New York State Housing Finance Agency/State of New York Mortgage Agency. The Department of State serves as a keeper of records and licensing agency, as well as serving the financial, corporate, and legal community. The Governor's office has a Women's Advisory.

Natural resources protection services are centralized in the Department of Environmental Conservation. The administration of the state park and recreation system is carried out by the Office of Parks, Recreation and Historic Preservation, in the Executive Department. The Department of Agriculture and Markets serves the interests of farmers and also administers the state's Pure Food Law. Energy is the province of the Department of Public Service. The quasi-independent Power Authority of the State of New York finances, builds, and operates electricity-generating and transmission facilities.

The Department of Labor provides most labor services for the state. Its responsibilities include occupational health and safety, human resource development and allocation, administration of unemployment insurance and other benefit programs, and maintenance of labor standards, including enforcement of minimum wage and other labor laws. The Employment Relations Board tries to settle labor disputes and prevent work stoppages.

16 JUDICIAL SYSTEM

New York's highest court is the Court of Appeals in Albany, with appellate jurisdiction only. The Court of Appeals consists of a chief judge and six associate judges, appointed by the governor and approved by the Senate for 14-year terms. Below the Court of Appeals is the state's Supreme Court, with nearly 570 justices in 12 judicial districts. The Supreme Court of New York State does not sit as one body, instead most supreme court justices are assigned original jurisdiction in civil and criminal matters, while 56 justices are assigned to the appellate division of supreme court and 15 to appellate terms of supreme court. Supreme Court justices are elected by district and serve 14-year terms.

The New York Court of Claims sits in Albany, with judges appointed by the governor to nine-year terms, along with judges sitting as acting Supreme Court justices in felony trials. This special trial court hears civil cases involving claims by or against the state.

Outside New York City, each county has its own county court to handle criminal cases, although some are delegated to be handled by lower courts. County court judges are elected to 10-year terms. Many counties have a surrogate's court to handle such matters as wills and estates; surrogates are elected to 10-year terms except in New York City counties, where they are elected to 14-year terms. Each county has its own family court. In New York City, judges are appointed by the mayor for 10-year terms; elsewhere they are elected for 10 years. A county's district attorney has authority in criminal matters. Most cities (including New York City) have their own court systems; in New York City, the mayor appoints judges of city criminal and family courts. Village police justices and town justices of the peace handle minor violations and other routine matters.

The Department of Correctional Services maintains correctional facilities throughout the state, as well as regional parole offices. As of 31 December 2004, a total of 63,751 prisoners were held in New York's state and federal prisons, a decrease from 65,198 of 2.2% from the previous year. As of year-end 2004, a total of 2,789 inmates were female, down from 2,914 or 4.3% from the year before. Among sentenced prisoners (one year or more), New York had an incarceration rate of 331 per 100,000 population in 2004.

According to the Federal Bureau of Investigation, New York in 2004, had a violent crime rate (murder/nonnegligent manslaughter; forcible rape; robbery; aggravated assault) of 441.6 reported incidents per 100,000 population, or a total of 84,914 reported incidents. Crimes against property (burglary; larceny/theft; and motor vehicle theft) in that same year totaled 422,734 reported incidents or 2,198.6 reported incidents per 100,000 people. In 1995, the state instituted a new death penalty statute, of which lethal injection was the sole method of execution. However, on 24 June, 2004 New York's death penalty statute was declared unconstitutional. The last execution in the state took place in 1963. As of 1 January 2006, only one inmate remained on the state's death row.

In 2003, New York spent $4,309,416,130 on homeland security, an average of $236 per state resident.

17ARMED FORCES

The US Military Academy at West Point was founded in 1802. In 2004, there were 22,714 active-duty military personnel and 11,409 civilian personnel stationed in New York, more than half of whom were at Fort Drum. In 2004, New York firms received more than $5.2 billion in defense contracts. In addition, defense spending outlays, including retires military pay, were $2.4 billion.

In 2003, there were 1,711,900 veterans of US military service in the state. The statistics for living veterans of wartime service were as follows: World War II, 212,726; Korea, 159,501; Vietnam era, 337,162; and 129,275 from the Persian Gulf War. For the fiscal year 2004, total Veterans Affairs expenditures in New York exceeded $3.1 billion.

As of 31 October 2004, the New York State Police employed 4,659 sworn officers.

18MIGRATION

Since the early 1800s, New York has been the primary port of entry for Europeans coming to the United States. The Statue of Liberty—dedicated in 1886 and beckoning "your tired, your poor, / Your huddled masses yearning to breathe free" to the shores of America—was often the immigrants' first glimpse of America. The first stop for some 20 million immigrants in the late 19th and early 20th centuries was Ellis Island, where they were processed, often given Americanized names, and sent onward to an uncertain future.

The first great wave of European immigrants arrived in the 1840s, impelled by the potato famine in Ireland. By 1850, New York City had 133,730 Irish-born inhabitants, and by 1890, 409,224. Although smaller in number, German immigration during this period was more widespread; during the 1850s, German-speaking people were the largest foreign-born group in Rochester and Buffalo, and by 1855 about 30,000 of Buffalo's 74,000 residents were German.

The next two great waves of European immigration—Eastern European Jews and Italians—overlapped. Vast numbers of Jews began arriving from Eastern Europe during the 1880s, by which time some 80,000 German-speaking Jews were already living in New York City. By 1910, the Jewish population of the city was about 1,250,000, growing to nearly 2,000,000 by the mid-1920s. The flood of Italians began during the 1800s, when the Italian population of New York City increased from 75,000 to more than 200,000; in 1950, nearly 500,000 Italian-born immigrants were living in the state. Migration from the 1840s onward followed a cyclical pattern: as one group dispersed from New York City throughout the state and the nation, it was replaced by a new wave of immigrants.

Yankees from New England made up the first great wave of domestic migration. Most of the migrants who came to New York between 1790 and 1840 were Yankees; it has been estimated that by 1850, 52,000 natives of Vermont (20% of that state's population) had become residents of New York. There was a slow, steady migration of African Americans from slave states to New York before the Civil War, but massive black migration to New York, and especially to New York City, began during World War I and continued well into the 1960s. The third great wave of domestic migration came after World War II, from Puerto Rico. Nearly 40,000 Puerto Ricans settled in New York City in 1946, and 58,500 in 1952–53. By 1960, the census showed well over 600,000 New Yorkers of Puerto Rican birth or parentage. As of 1990, Puerto Rican-born New Yorkers numbered 143,974. Nearly 41,800 state residents in 1990 had lived in Puerto Rico in 1985. Many other Caribbean natives—especially Dominicans, Jamaicans, and Haitians—followed. In 1996, there were a reported 3,232,000 state residents who were foreign-born (about 17% of the state's population). In 1998, 96,559 foreign immigrants entered New York, the second-highest total of any state (surpassed only by California) and over 15% of the total immigration for that year.

The fourth and most recent domestic migratory trend is unique in New York history—the net outward migration from New York to other states. During the 1960s, New York suffered a net loss of more than 100,000 residents through migration; between 1970 and 1980, the estimated net loss was probably in excess of 1,500,000, far greater than that in any other state: probably 80% of the migration was from New York City. From 1980 to 1990, net loss from migration exceeded 340,000. Between 1990 and 1998, New York had a net loss of 1,722,000 in domestic migration. These general estimates hide a racial movement of historic proportions: during the 1960s, while an estimated net total of 638,000 whites were moving out of the state, 396,000 blacks were moving in; during 1970–75, according to Census Bureau estimates, 701,000 whites left New York, while 60,000 blacks were arriving. According to a private study, a net total of 700,000 whites and 50,000 blacks left the state during 1975–80. It appears that many of the white emigrants went to suburban areas of New Jersey and Connecticut, but many also went to two Sunbelt states, Florida and California. Overwhelmingly, the black arrivals came from the South. During the 1980s, the black population of the New York City area increased by 16.4%. By 1997, blacks comprised 19.4% of the New York City area's total population.

Intrastate migration has followed the familiar pattern of rural to urban, urban to suburban. In 1790, the state was 88% rural; the rural population grew in absolute terms (though not as a percentage of the total state population) until the 1880s when the long period of decline began. New York's farm population decreased by 21% during the 1940s, 33% during the 1950s, 38% during the 1960s, and 49% during the 1970s. By 1990, 84% of all New Yorkers lived in urban areas; by 1996, 91.8%. Meanwhile, the suburban population has grown steadily. In 1950, 3,538,620 New Yorkers (24% of the state total) lived in suburbs; by 1980, this figure had grown to 7,461,161 (42% of all state residents). It should be remembered, of course, that this more than doubling of the suburban population reflects natural increase and direct migration from other states and regions, as well as the intrastate migratory movement from central cities to suburbs. Between 1990 and 1998, New York's overall population only increased by 1%.

In the period 2000–05, net international migration was 667,007 and net internal migration was -1,001,100, for a net loss of 334,093 people.

[19]INTERGOVERNMENTAL COOPERATION

New York State is a member of the Council of State Governments and its allied organizations. The state participates in many interstate regional commissions (and in commissions with the Canadian provinces of Ontario and Quebec). Among the more active interstate commissions are the Appalachian Regional Commission, Atlantic States Marine Fisheries Commission, Delaware River Basin Commission, Great Lakes Commission, Interstate Oil and Gas Compact Commission, Mid-Atlantic Fishery Management Council, New England Interstate Water Pollution Control Commission, Northeastern Forest Fire Protection Commission, and the Ohio River Valley Water Sanitation Commission. In 1985, New York joined seven other Great Lakes states and two Canadian provinces in the Great Lakes Charter, for the purpose of protecting the lakes' water reserves.

The three most important interstate bodies for the New York metropolitan area are the Palisades Interstate Park Commission, Interstate Sanitation Commission, and Port Authority of New York and New Jersey. The Palisades Interstate Park Commission was founded in 1900 (with New Jersey) in order to preserve the natural beauty of the Palisades region. The Interstate Sanitation Commission (with New Jersey and Connecticut; established in 1961) monitors and seeks to control pollution within the tri-state Interstate Sanitation District. The Port Authority of New York and New Jersey, created in 1921 and the most powerful of the three, is a public corporation with the power to issue its own bonds. Its vast holdings include 4 bridges, 2 tunnels, 5 airports and heliports, 2 motor vehicle terminals, 6 marine terminals, the trans-Hudson rapid transit system, an industrial park in the Bronx, and the 110-story twin-towered World Trade Center in lower Manhattan, until it was destroyed in 2001. Bridge compacts include those on the Buffalo and Fort Erie bridge, the Ogdensburg bridge and port, and the Canada and New York International bridge. Other compacts include the New York-Connecticut Railroad Service, and the Susquehanna River Basin Compact (with Maryland and Pennsylvania). Federal grants to New York state and local governments

totaled $38.313 billion in fiscal year 2005, higher than any other state except California. In fiscal year 2006, New York received an estimated $40.606 billion in federal grants, and an estimated $41.817 billion in fiscal year 2007.

[20]ECONOMY

From the Civil War through the 1950s, New York State led the nation in just about every category by which an economy can be measured. In the colonial and early national periods, New York was a leading wheat-growing state. When the wheat crop declined, dairying and lumbering became the state's mainstays. New York then emerged as the national leader in wholesaling, retailing, and manufacturing—and remained so well into the 1960s.

By 1973, however, the state was running neck and neck with California by most output measures, or had already been surpassed. The total labor force, the number of workers in manufacturing, and the number of factories all declined during the 1960s and 1970s. New York City's manufacturing base and its skilled laborers have been emigrating to the suburbs and to other states since World War II. Between 1969 and 1976, the city lost 600,000 jobs. With the departure of much of the middle class, the city's tax base shrank, a factor that contributed to the fiscal crisis of 1975, when a package of short-term aid from Congress, the state government, and the labor union pension funds saved the city from default.

The 1980s saw the state's fortunes on the rise. A shift in dependence from manufacturing to services, and particularly to finance, helped the state and New York City weather the 1981–82 recession. In 1983, the state's three largest industrial and commercial employers (excluding public utilities) were all banks based in New York City. From 1980 to 1990, the state's economy acquired approximately one million jobs, in contrast to 50,000 the previous decade. Financial services led the city's economic expansion, adding 100,000 jobs from 1980 to 1987. Long Island also experienced growth in the first half of the decade, benefiting from the defense build-up by the federal government in the early and mid-eighties.

New York's economy not only grew during the eighties but also underwent a restructuring. Manufacturing witnessed a decline in its share of total employment from 20% in 1980 to 14% in 1990. Apparel, industrial machinery and equipment, and primary metals accounted for 40% of the total loss of jobs. Industrial output, however, increased 10.1% between 1980 and 1987. Productivity gains produced both the rise in output and the decline in employment. Construction boomed from 1982–89, increasing its share of employment from 2.9% to 3.8%. The service sector, particularly business-related, health care, education and social services grew 52% in the decade, increasing services' share of employment from 24% in 1980 to 29% in 1990. Finance, insurance, and the real estate industry expanded 64%. The surge in financial services employment ended with the crash of the stock market in October of 1987, in which stock prices dropped 36% in two months. The crash prompted the layoff of 9,000 employees on Wall Street and a downsizing of the banking and securities industries. More than $1 trillion in financial transactions took place per day on the NYSE in 2000.

About one in 11 New York City residents received some form of public assistance (including Medicaid and Supplemental Security Income benefits) in 1994. The high number of people on welfare prompted the New York State government to turn the welfare program into a "workfare" program that put the able-bodied to work. By 1998, the welfare roles had been reduced by over 600,000 from 1995 numbers, a 35% decrease. Job growth rose steadily through the 1990s. Coming into the 21st century, the state economy was growing briskly, with annual growth rates of 8.3% in 1998, 3.5% in 1999, and 7.3% in 2000. Even in the national recession of 2001, and with the events of 9/11, the state economy posted 3.5% annual growth. Employment growth in the state lagged the nation as a whole during 2001 and 2002, but was close to the national average by the end of 2002. New York City's rate of job losses, however, continued to exceed the state and the nation. However, office vacancy rates in New York City in the fourth quarter 2002, at 8% for midtown, and 12% for downtown (where the twin World Trade Center towers had been located), were well below the national average of 16.5%. The state's manufacturing sector, which had been contracting for decades, fell from 10.8% of gross state product in 1997 to 9.4% of the total in 2001. In 2002, the highest percentages of manufacturing job losses were in the cities of Buffalo, Rochester and Syracuse.

New York's gross state product (GSP) in 2004 was $896.739 billion, of which the real estate sector accounted for the largest share at $114.056 billion or 12.7% of GSP, followed by professional and technical services at $75.337 billion (8.4% of GSP), and health care and social assistance services at 70.059 billion (7.8% of GSP). In that same year, there were an estimated 1,779,932 small businesses in New York. Of the 481,858 businesses that had employees, an estimated total of 477,260 or 99% were small companies. An estimated 62,854 new businesses were established in the state in 2004, up 3.8% from the year before. Business terminations that same year came to 64,013, up 4.6% from 2003. There were 4,070 business bankruptcies in 2004, up 104.8% from the previous year. In 2005, the state's personal bankruptcy (Chapter 7 and Chapter 13) filing rate was 385 filings per 100,000 people, ranking New York as the 42nd highest in the nation.

21INCOME

In 2005 New York had a gross state product (GSP) of $963 billion which accounted for 7.8% of the nation's gross domestic product and placed the state at number 3 in highest GSP among the 50 states and the District of Columbia.

According to the Bureau of Economic Analysis, in 2004 New York had a per capita personal income (PCPI) of $38,264. This ranked sixth in the United States and was 116% of the national average of $33,050. The 1994–2004 average annual growth rate of PCPI was 4.0%. New York had a total personal income (TPI) of $737,755,932,000, which ranked second in the United States and reflected an increase of 6.7% from 2003. The 1994–2004 average annual growth rate of TPI was 4.5%. Earnings of persons employed in New York increased from $558,688,257,000 in 2003 to $596,716,261,000 in 2004, an increase of 6.8%. The 2003–04 national change was 6.3%.

The US Census Bureau reports that the three-year average median household income for 2002–04 in 2004 dollars was $44,228 compared to a national average of $44,473. During the same period an estimated 14.4% of the population was below the poverty line as compared to 12.4% nationwide.

22LABOR

According to the Bureau of Labor Statistics (BLS), in April 2006 the seasonally adjusted civilian labor force in New York numbered 9,516,800, with approximately 467,000 workers unemployed, yielding an unemployment rate of 4.9%, compared to the national average of 4.7% for the same period. Preliminary data for the same period placed nonfarm employment at 8,583,500. Since the beginning of the BLS data series in 1976, the highest unemployment rate recorded in New York was 10.5% in July 1976. The historical low was 4% in April 1988. Preliminary nonfarm employment data by occupation for April 2006 showed that approximately 3.8% of the labor force was employed in construction; 6.5% in manufacturing; 17.5% in trade, transportation, and public utilities; 8.4% in financial activities; 12.7% in professional and business services; 18.2% in education and health services; 7.8% in leisure and hospitality services; and 17.3% in government.

The labor force participation rate of women increased from 42.0% in 1974 to 55.8% in 1998. Over the same period, participation rates for men declined from 75.9% to 71.4%. Among minority groups, the unemployment rate in 1998 was 11.4% for blacks and 8.9% for Hispanics.

At the turn of the century, working conditions in New York were among the worst in the country. The flood of immigrants into the labor market and the absence of labor laws to protect them led to the development in New York City of cramped, ill-lit, poorly ventilated, and unhealthy factories—the sweatshops for which the garment industry became notorious. Since that time working conditions in the garment factories have improved, primarily through the efforts of the International Ladies' Garment Workers Union and, later, its sister organization, the Amalgamated Clothing and Textiles Workers Union.

Under the state's Taylor Law, public employees do not have the right to strike. Penalties for striking may be exacted against both the unions and their leaders.

The BLS reported that in 2005, a total of 2,090,000 of New York's 8,008,000 employed wage and salary workers were formal members of a union. This represented 26.1% of those so employed, up from 25.3% in 2004, and well above the national average of 12%. Overall in 2005, a total of 2,201,000 workers (27.5%) in New York were covered by a union or employee association contract, which includes those workers who reported no union affiliation. New York is one of five states whose union membership rate is greater than 20%. The New York is also one of 28 states that does not have a right-to-work law.

As of 1 March 2006, New York had a state-mandated minimum wage rate of $6.75 per hour, which will increase to $7.15 per hour on 1 January 2007. In 2004, women in the state accounted for 47% of the employed civilian labor force.

23AGRICULTURE

New York ranked 28th in farm income in 2005, with cash receipts from farming at over $3.5 billion. About 62% came from livestock products, mostly dairy goods. In 2004, the state ranked second in apples, third in the production of corn for silage, third in cauliflower, fourth in tart cherries and snap beans, and ninth in oats.

Corn was the leading crop for the Indians and for the European settlers of the early colonial period. During the early 1800s, however, wheat was the major crop grown in eastern New York. With the opening of the Erie Canal, western New York (especially the Genesee Valley) became a major wheat-growing center as well. By the late 1850s, when the state's wheat crop began to decline, New York still led the nation in barley, flax, hops, and potato production and was a significant grower of corn and oats. The opening of the railroads took away the state's competitive advantage, but as grain production shifted to the Midwest, the state emerged as a leading supplier of meat and dairy products.

New York remains an important dairy state, but urbanization has reduced its overall agricultural potential. In 2004, 14% of the state's land area was devoted to crop growing; in 2004, there were only 36,000 farms, with 7.6 million acres (3.1 million hectares).

The west-central part of the state is the most intensively farmed. Chautauqua County, in the extreme southwest, leads the state in grape production, while Wayne County, along Lake Ontario, leads in apples and cherries. The dairy industry is concentrated in the St. Lawrence Valley; grain growing dominates the plains between Syracuse and Buffalo. Potatoes are grown mostly in Suffolk County, on eastern Long Island.

Leading filed crops in 2004 included hay, of which 2.9 million tons were produced, worth $327 million; corn, 61 million bushels worth $146.4 million; oats, 3.3 million bushels worth $5.5 million; and wheat, 5.3 million bushels, worth $13.8 million.

Farms in 2004 also produced 941,010 tons of commercial vegetables. Leading vegetable crops were cabbage, onions, sweet corn, and snap beans. State vineyards produced 145,000 tons of grapes for wine and juice in 2004, while the apple crop totaled 1.1 billion lb.

24 ANIMAL HUSBANDRY

The St. Lawrence Valley is the state's leading cattle-raising region, followed by the Mohawk Valley and Wyoming County, in western New York. The poultry industry is more widely dispersed. In 2005, an estimated 1.41 million cattle and calves were worth around $1.73 billion. There were an estimated 84,000 hogs and pigs, worth $8.4 million in 2004. During 2003, around 14.6 million lb (6.6 million kg) of broilers were produced, worth $5.1 million, and 13.3 million lb (6 million kg) of turkey, worth $4.8 million.

New York is a leading dairy state. In 2003, New York was third in the United States in milk production with 11.9 million lb (5.4 million kg) of milk from 671,000 milk cows.

Also during 2003, New York farmers produced around 3 million lb (1.4 million kg) of sheep and lambs, which brought in around $2.7 million in gross income. The state produced around 1.05 billion eggs, valued at $56.3 million in 2003. Duck raising is an industry of local importance on Long Island.

25 FISHING

Fishing, though an attraction for tourists and sportsmen, plays only a marginal role in the economic life of the state. In 2004, the Atlantic commercial catch by New York fishers was 33.7 million lb (15.3 million kg), valued at $46.4 million. The Great Lakes commercial catch the same year was 10,000 lb (4,500 kg) valued at $11,000. Important species for commercial use are clams and oysters. In 2004, the state ranked second in the nation (after New Jersey) in volume of surf clams (6.8 million lb/3.1 million kg) and third for soft clams (234,000 lb/106,000 kg). Virtually all of New

York's commercial fishing takes place in the Atlantic waters off Long Island. Montauk, on the eastern end of Long Island, is the state's leading fishing port. In 2003, there were 6 processing and 271 wholesale plants in the state with about 2,154 employees.

Pollution and poor wildlife management have seriously endangered the state's commercial and sport fishing in the ocean, rivers, and lakes. Commercial fishing for striped bass in the Hudson River was banned in 1976 because of contamination by polychlorinated biphenyls (PCBs). Commercial fishing in the river for five other species—black crappie, brown bullhead, carp, goldfish, and pumpkinseed—was banned in 1985. Also banned in 1985 was commercial fishing for striped bass in New York Harbor and along both shores of western Long Island.

In recent decades, however, the Department of Environmental Conservation has taken an active role in restocking New York's inland waters. The US Fish and Wildlife Service distributes large numbers of lake trout and Atlantic salmon fingerlings and rainbow and brook trout fry throughout the state. There are 12 state hatcheries producing over 1 million lb (over 453,000 kg) of fish per year, including brook trout, brown trout, rainbow trout, lake trout, steelhead, chinook salmon, coho salmon, landlocked salmon, walleye, muskellunge, and tiger muskellunge.

In 2004, the state issued 983,812 sport fishing licenses.

26 FORESTRY

About 61% of New York's surface area is forestland. The most densely forested counties are Hamilton, Essex, and Warren in the Adirondacks, and Delaware, Greene, and Ulster in the Catskills. The total forested area was about 18,432,000 acres (7,459,000 hectares) in 2004, of which 15,389,000 acres (6,228,000 hectares) were classified as commercial forest, meaning they were available for the harvest of wood products such as sawlogs, veneer, and pulpwood or firewood. In 2004, lumber production totaled 480 million board feet.

Finger Lakes National Forest, the only national forest within the state, covered 16,211 acres (6,560 hectares) in 2005. The state Department of Environmental Conservation manages about 3,000,000 acres (1,200,000 hectares) in the Catskills and Adirondacks as Forest Preserves, and an additional 800,000 acres in State Forests and Wildlife Management Areas (where timber harvesting is allowed as part of their management plans).

27 MINING

According to preliminary data from the US Geological Survey (USGS), the estimated value of nonfuel mineral production by New York in 2003 was $978 million, a decrease from $991 million in 2002. The USGS data ranked New York as 14th among the 50 states by the total value of its nonfuel mineral production, accounting for over 2.5% of total US output.

According to the preliminary data for 2003, crushed stone, followed by cement (portland and masonry), salt, construction sand and gravel, and wollastonite were the state's top nonfuel minerals by value. Collectively, these five commodities accounted for around 98% of all nonfuel mineral output, by value. About 75% of the state's nonfuel minerals, by value, were major construction material commodities: cement, common clays, construction sand and gravel, and crushed stone. New York in 2003 was the nation's only producer of wollastonite. The state also ranked third in salt, fourth in talc, and tenth in portland and masonry cement. New York was the leading state (out of two) in the production of industrial grade garnets and eighth in the production of dimension stone.

Preliminary data for 2003 showed that New York's production of crushed stone totaled 51.5 million metric tons, with a value of $358 million, while output of salt totaled 4.9 million metric tons, valued at $190 million. Construction sand and gravel production in that same year came to 32 million metric tons, and was valued at $171 million. Common clays output totaled 641,000 metric tons and was valued at $7.99 million.

Other commodities produced in New York included gypsum and peat. Major uses of wollastonite (a type of calcium silicate) are as a filler in ceramic tile, marine wallboard, paint, plastics, and refractory liners in steel mills.

28 ENERGY AND POWER

As of 2003, New York had 96 electrical power service providers, of which 48 were publicly owned and four were cooperatives. Of the remainder, nine were investor owned, three were owners of independent generators that sold directly to customers, 25 were generation-only suppliers and seven were delivery-only providers. As of that same year there were 7,876,995 retail customers. Of that total, 6,245,232 received their power from investor-owned service providers. Cooperatives accounted for 16,816 customers, while publicly owned providers had 1,243,176 customers. There were 1,867 independent generator or "facility" customers, and 369,904 generation-only customers. There was no data on the number of delivery-only customers.

Total net summer generating capability by the state's electrical generating plants in 2003 stood at 36.696 million kW, with total production that same year at 137.643 billion kWh. Of the total amount generated, 30.2% came from electric utilities, with the remaining 69.8% coming from independent producers and combined heat and power service providers. The largest portion of all electric power generated, 40.697 billion kWh (29.6%), came from nuclear power generation, with natural gas fueled plants in second place at 28.156 billion kWh (20.5%) and hydroelectric plants in third at 24.268 billion kWh (17.6%). Other renewable power sources, coal and petroleum fired plants (17.1% and 14%, respectively) and pumped storage facilities accounted for the remaining power generated.

Electric bills for New York City are the highest in the nation, and customers in Buffalo and Rochester also pay above the national median. Sales of public and private electric power totaled 144.045 billion kWh in 2003, of which 50.3% went to commercial users, 15.1% to industrial purchasers, 32.7% to residential users, and 1.9% for transportation.

As of 2006, New York had four operating nuclear power stations: the James A. Fitzpatrick and the Nile Mile Point plants, both near Oswego; the Indian Point plant in Westchester County; and the Robert E. Ginna plant near Rochester.

As of 2004, New York had proven crude oil reserves of less than 1% of all proven US reserves, while output that same year averaged 464 barrels per day. Including federal offshore domains, the state that year ranked 29th (28th excluding federal offshore) in production among the 31 producing states. In 2004 New York had 3,095 producing oil wells and accounted for under 1% of all US production. There are no refineries in the state of New York.

In 2004, New York had 5,781 producing natural gas and gas condensate wells. In that same year, marketed gas production (all gas produced excluding gas used for repressuring, vented and flared, and nonhydrocarbon gases removed) totaled 36.137 billion cu ft (1.02 billion cu m). As of 31 December 2004, proven reserves of dry or consumer-grade natural gas totaled 324 billion cu ft (9.2 billion cu m).

29 INDUSTRY

Until the 1970s, New York was the nation's foremost industrial state, ranking first in virtually every general category. However, US Commerce Department data show that by 1975 the state had slipped in manufacturing to second in number of employees, payroll, and value added, fourth in value of shipments of manufactured goods, and sixth in new capital spending. Important sectors are instruments and related products, industrial machinery and equipment, electronic and electric equipment, printing and publishing, and textiles.

The Buffalo region, with its excellent transport facilities and abundant power supply, is the main center for heavy industry in the state, while light industry is dispersed throughout the state. Rochester is especially well known for its photographic (Kodak) and optical equipment and office machines. The state's leadership in electronic equipment is in large part attributable to the International Business Machines Corp. (IBM), which was founded in 1911 at Endicott, near Binghamton. The presence of two large General Electric plants has long made Schenectady a leader in the manufacture of electric machinery.

New York City excels not only in the apparel and publishing trades but also in food processing, meat packing, chemicals, leather goods, metal products, and many other manufactures. In addition, the city serves as headquarters for many large industrial corporations whose manufacturing activities often take place entirely outside New York.

According to the US Census Bureau's Annual Survey of Manufactures (ASM) for 2004, New York's manufacturing sector covered some 21 product subsectors. The shipment value of all products manufactured in the state that same year was $146.691 billion. Of that total, chemical manufacturing accounted for the largest share at $35.291 billion. It was followed by computer and electronic product manufacturing at $14.565 billion; food manufacturing at $14.090 billion; transport equipment manufacturing at $11.717 billion; machinery manufacturing at $10.449 billion; and miscellaneous manufacturing at $9.031 billion.

In 2004, a total of 569,641 people in New York were employed in the state's manufacturing sector, according to the ASM. Of that total, 370,674 were actual production workers. In terms of total employment, the computer and electronic product manufacturing industry accounted for the largest portion of all manufacturing employees at 65,291, with 29,738 actual production workers. It was followed by chemical manufacturing at 57,004 employees (28,401 actual production workers); fabricated metal product manufacturing at 55,711 employees (39,809 actual production workers); miscellaneous manufacturing at 47,587 employees (31,212 actual production workers); and food manufacturing with 46,847 employees (31,160 actual production workers).

ASM data for 2004 showed that New York's manufacturing sector paid $24.145 billion in wages. Of that amount, the computer and electronic product manufacturing sector accounted for the largest share at $3.713 billion. It was followed by chemical manufacturing at $2.874 billion; fabricated metal product manufacturing at $2.193 billion; machinery manufacturing at $2030 billion; transport equipment manufacturing at $1.989 billion; and miscellaneous manufacturing at $1.708 billion.

³⁰COMMERCE

According to the 2002 Census of Wholesale Trade, New York's wholesale trade sector had sales that year totaling $343.6 billion from 35,845 establishments. Wholesalers of durable goods accounted for 18,400 establishments, followed by nondurable goods wholesalers at 15,236 and electronic markets, agents, and brokers accounting for 2,209 establishments. Sales by durable goods wholesalers in 2002 totaled $127.7 billion, while wholesalers of nondurable goods saw sales of $184.6 billion. Electronic markets, agents, and brokers in the wholesale trade industry had sales of $31.2 billion.

In the 2002 Census of Retail Trade, New York was listed as having 76,425 retail establishments with sales of $178.06 billion. The leading types of retail businesses by number of establishments were: food and beverage stores (15,210); clothing and clothing accessories stores (12,531); miscellaneous store retailers (8,346); and health and personal care stores (6,648). In terms of sales, motor vehicle and motor vehicle parts stores accounted for the largest share of retail sales at $37.3 billion, followed by food and beverage stores at $29.6 billion; general merchandise stores at $19.7 billion; clothing and clothing accessories stores at $17.2 billion; and health and personal care stores at $16.2 billion. A total of 837,806 people were employed by the retail sector in New York that year.

The state's long border with Canada, its important ports on Lakes Erie and Ontario, and its vast harbor on New York Bay ensure it a major role in US foreign trade. About one-quarter of US waterborne imports and exports pass through the New York Customs District (including New York City, Albany, and Newark and Perth Amboy, N.J.). Exports of goods from New York totaled $50.4 billion in 2005, third among the states.

³¹CONSUMER PROTECTION

The New York State Consumer Protection Board (CPB) was created in 1970, and is headed by an executive director appointed by the governor with the advice and consent of the Senate. The CPB is divided into three organizations: the Consumer Assistance Unit; the Law and Investigations Unit; and the Office of Strategic Programs (which in turn is composed of an Outreach and Education Unit, and a Utility Intervention Unit). The Board coordinates the activities of all state agencies performing consumer protection functions, represents consumer interests before federal, state, and local bodies (including the Public Service Commission), and encourages consumer education and research, but it has no enforcement powers. These are vested in the Bureau of Consumer Frauds and Protection within the Department of Law, under the direction of the Attorney General. The Department of Public Service has regulatory authority over several areas of key interest to consumers, including gas, electric, and telephone rates.

State law outlaws unfair or deceptive trade practices and provides for small-claims courts, where consumers can take action at little cost to themselves. New York licenses and regulates automobile repair services, permits advertising of prescription drug prices, and requires unit pricing. A "cooling-off" period for home purchase contracts is mandated, and standards have been established for mobile-home construction. New York also has no-fault automobile insurance. In 1974, the legislature outlawed sex discrimination in banking, credit, and insurance policy transactions. The state's fair-trade law, which allowed price fixing on certain items, was repealed in 1975. The Fair Credit Reporting Act passed in 1977, allows consumers access to their credit bureau files. A 1984 "Lemon Law" entitles purchasers of defective new cars to repairs, a refund, or a replacement under specified circumstances. A similar law for used cars requires a written warranty for most essential mechanical components.

When dealing with consumer protection issues, New York's Attorney General can initiate civil and criminal proceedings; represent the state before state and federal regulatory agencies; administer consumer protection and education programs; handle formal consumer complaints; and exercise broad subpoena powers. In antitrust actions, the Attorney General can act on behalf of those consumers who are incapable of acting on their own; initiate damage actions on behalf of the state in state courts; initiate criminal proceedings; and represent counties, cities and other governmental entities in recovering civil damages under state or federal law.

The offices of the New York State Consumer Protection Board are located in Albany. The offices of the Bureau of Consumer Frauds and Protection are located in Albany and in New York City. The Office of the Attorney General has regional offices in Binghamton, Brooklyn, Buffalo, Hauppauge, Mineola, Harlem (New York City), Plattsburgh, Rochester, Syracuse, Utica, Watertown and in White Plains. County government consumer affairs offices are located in Albany, Buffalo, Carmel, Goshen, Kingston, Mineola, Monticello, New York City, Poughkeepsie, Schenectady, and White Plains. City government consumer affairs offices are located in Mount Vernon, New York City, Newtonville, Schenectady, and in Yonkers.

³²BANKING

New York City is the major US banking center. Banking is one of the state's leading industries, ranking first in the United States. As of June 2005, the state of New York had 209 insured banks, savings and loans, and saving banks, plus 32 state-chartered and 519 federally chartered credit unions (CUs). Excluding the CUs, the New York–Northern New Jersey–Long Island market area accounted for the largest portion of the state's financial institutions and deposits in 2004, with 233 institutions and $770.488 billion in deposits. As of June 2005, CUs accounted for 2.9% of all assets held by all financial institutions in the state, or some $36.484 billion. Banks, savings and loans, and savings banks collectively accounted for the remaining 97.1% or $1,202.550 billion in assets held.

In 2004, the state's insured banks reported a median past-due/nonaccrual loan to total loans percentage of 1.20%, down from 1.46% in 2003. The median net interest margin (the difference between the lower rates offered to savers and the higher rates charged on loans) in 2004 was 3.77%, down slightly from 3.78% in 2003.

New York has a higher percentage of residential mortgage lenders than the rest of the nation, and its median ratio of long-term assets-to-average earning assets remains above that of the nation.

Regulation of state-chartered banks and other financial institutions is the responsibility of the New York State Banking Department. It was established in 1851 and is the oldest bank regulatory body in the United States.

33 INSURANCE

Like banking, insurance is big business in New York. Three of the ten top US life insurance companies—Metropolitan Life, New York Life, and Equitable Life Assurance—had their headquarters in New York.

As of 2003, there were 195 property and casualty and 186 life and health insurance companies domiciled in the state. Direct premiums for property and casualty insurance totaled over $33.3 billion in 2004. That year, there were 100,121 flood insurance policies in force in the state, with a total value of $17.5 billion. About $11 billion of coverage was held through FAIR plans, which are designed to offer coverage for some natural circumstances, such as wind and hail, in high risk areas.

In 2004, New Yorkers held over 9 million individual life insurance policies with a value of about $999 billion; total value for all categories of life insurance (individual, group, and credit) was $1.6 trillion. The average coverage amount is $110,100 per policy holder. Death benefits paid that year totaled $3.8 billion.

In 2004, 53% of state residents held employment-based health insurance policies, 3% held individual policies, and 28% were covered under Medicare and Medicaid; 15% of residents were uninsured. In 2003, employee contributions for employment-based health coverage averaged at 17% for single coverage and 19% for family coverage. The state offers an 18-month health benefits expansion program for small-firm employees in connection with the Consolidated Omnibus Budget Reconciliation Act (COBRA, 1986), a health insurance program for those who lose employment-based coverage due to termination or reduction of work hours.

In 2003, there were over 9 million auto insurance policies in effect for private passenger cars. Required minimum coverage includes bodily injury liability of up to $25,000 per individual and $50,000 for all persons injured in an accident, as well as property damage liability of $10,000. Personal injury protection is also required. In 2003, the average expenditure per vehicle for insurance coverage was $1,160.80, which ranked as the second-highest average in the nation (following New Jersey).

34 SECURITIES

The New York Stock Exchange (NYSE) is by far the largest organized securities market in the nation and the world. The exchange began as an agreement among 24 brokers, known as the Buttonwood Agreement, in 1792; the exchange adopted its first constitution in 1817 and took on its present name in 1863. A clear sign of the growth of the NYSE is the development of its communications system. Stock tickers were first introduced in 1867; a faster ticker, installed in 1930, was capable of printing 500 characters a minute. By 1964, this was no longer fast enough, and a 900-character-a-minute ticker was introduced. Annual registered share volume increased from 1.8 billion in 1965 to 7.6 billion in 1978 following the introduction in 1976 of a new data line capable of handling 36,000 characters a minute. In August 2000, the NYSE switched to a decimal system. The New York Futures Exchange was incorporated in 1979 as a wholly owned subsidiary of the NYSE and began trading in 1980. It also deals in options on futures. In 2006, The NYSE merged with Archipelago Holdings (ArcaEx and the Pacific Exchange) to form the for-profit NYSE Group, Inc. As of 2005, there were about 2,672 issuers listed on the NYSE, including about 453 foreign companies. NYSE listed companies represent a total global market value of $21 trillion.

The American Stock Exchange (AMEX) is the second-leading US securities floor-based market, but the AMEX ranks far below the NYSE in both volume and value of securities. The AMEX traces its origins to the outdoor trading in unlisted securities that began on Wall and Hanover streets in the 1840s, the exchange was organized as the New York Curb Agency in 1908; the exchange moved indoors, but continued to use the hand signals developed by outdoor traders. The AMEX adopted its current name in 1953. Constitutional changes in 1976 for the first time permitted qualified issues to be traded on both the AMEX and the NYSE as well as on other exchanges. This Intermarket Trading System (ITS) began in 1978. In 1996, the hand signals used in trading on the AMEX for over 100 years were replaced by a computerized communication system. AMEX has about 661 regular trading members, and 203 options members.

The National Association of Securities Dealers Automated Quotations (NASDAQ), created in 1971, is a highly active exchange for over-the-counter securities. New York City is also a major center for trading in commodity futures. Leading commodity exchanges are the New York Coffee and Sugar Exchange; the New York Cocoa Exchange; the New York Cotton Exchange; the Commodity Exchange, Inc. (COMEX), specializing in gold, silver, and copper futures; and the New York Mercantile Exchange, which trades in futures for potatoes, platinum, palladium, silver coins, beef, and gold, among other items. Bonds may be issued in New York by cities, counties, towns, villages, school districts, and fire districts, as well as by quasi-independent authorities.

In 2005, there were 16,530 personal financial advisers employed in the state and 34,860 securities, commodities, and financial services sales agents. In 2004, there were over 1,097 publicly traded companies within the state, with over 280 XX NASDAQ companies, 378 NYSE listings, and 114 AMEX listings. In 2006, the state had 55 Fortune 500 companies, including 20 companies in the Fortune 100; Citigroup ranked first in the state and eighth in the nation with revenues of over $131 billion, followed by American Intl. Group (ninth), Intl. Business Machines (10th), J.P. Morgan Chase and Co. (17th), and Verizon Communications (18th). All five if these companies are listed on the NYSE.

35 PUBLIC FINANCE

New York State has the second largest budget (behind California), of all states in the United States.

The New York State budget is prepared by the Division of the Budget and submitted annually by the governor to the legislature for amendment and approval. The fiscal year (FY) runs from 1 April to 31 March.

New York—State Government Finances

(Dollar amounts in thousands. Per capita amounts in dollars.)

	AMOUNT	PER CAPITA
Total Revenue	136,520,762	7,080.59
General revenue	106,300,211	5,513.21
Intergovernmental revenue	47,838,143	2,481.10
Taxes	45,826,429	2,376.77
General sales	10,050,291	521.25
Selective sales	6,428,674	333.42
License taxes	1,193,019	61.88
Individual income tax	24,647,225	1,278.32
Corporate income tax	2,044,504	106.04
Other taxes	1,462,716	75.86
Current charges	6,537,484	339.06
Miscellaneous general revenue	6,098,155	316.28
Utility revenue	6,091,450	315.93
Liquor store revenue	–	–
Insurance trust revenue	24,129,101	1,251.44
Total expenditure	132,883,277	6,891.93
Intergovernmental expenditure	44,112,115	2,287.85
Direct expenditure	88,771,162	4,604.07
Current operation	60,269,027	3,125.82
Capital outlay	8,786,756	455.72
Insurance benefits and repayments	14,365,484	745.06
Assistance and subsidies	1,392,954	72.24
Interest on debt	3,956,941	205.22
Exhibit: Salaries and wages	14,032,761	727.80
Total expenditure	132,883,277	6,891.93
General expenditure	108,248,168	5,614.24
Intergovernmental expenditure	44,112,115	2,287.85
Direct expenditure	64,136,053	3,326.39
General expenditures, by function:		
Education	31,359,362	1,626.44
Public welfare	41,154,459	2,134.46
Hospitals	3,860,409	200.22
Health	5,231,209	271.31
Highways	3,672,833	190.49
Police protection	818,700	42.46
Correction	2,586,817	134.16
Natural resources	356,697	18.50
Parks and recreation	475,625	24.67
Government administration	4,264,941	221.20
Interest on general debt	3,020,332	156.65
Other and unallocable	11,446,784	593.68
Utility expenditure	10,269,625	532.63
Liquor store expenditure	–	–
Insurance trust expenditure	14,365,484	745.06
Debt at end of fiscal year	95,709,813	4,963.94
Cash and security holdings	262,375,039	13,607.96

Abbreviations and symbols: – zero or rounds to zero; (NA) not available; (X) not applicable.

SOURCE: *U.S. Census Bureau, Governments Division, 2004 Survey of State Government Finances,* January 2006.

Fiscal year 2006 general funds were estimated at $50.2 billion for resources and $47.2 billion for expenditures. In fiscal year 2004, federal government grants to New York were $50.0 billion.

In the fiscal year 2007 federal budget, New York state was slated to receive: $2 billion in tax credits for transportation infrastructure to replace underutilized provisions of the Liberty Zone tax package; $628.5 million for major cities throughout the state to fund buses, railcars, and maintenance facilities essential to sustaining public transportation systems that serve their communities; $300 million to begin construction of the Long Island Rail Road East Side commuter rail extension on Manhattan's East Side.

This extension will carry an estimated 166,000 daily passengers when complete in 2012; $46 million for the modernization of the Thurgood Marshall US Courthouse in New York City, including safety and accessibility upgrades; $24 million to improve public transportation in New York for the elderly, persons with disabilities, and persons with lower-incomes, providing access to job and health care facilities; $15.3 million to provide transportation in rural areas statewide meeting the needs of individuals that may have no other means of transportation; and $7.6 million to expand a national cemetery in Saratoga.

On 5 January 2006 the federal government also released $100 million in emergency contingency funds targeted to the areas with the greatest need, including $15 million for New York.

36 TAXATION

In 2005, New York collected $50,190 million in tax revenues or $2,607 per capita, which placed it 11th among the 50 states in per capita tax burden. The national average was $2,192 per capita. Sales taxes accounted for 21.9% of the total; selective sales taxes, 10.3%; individual income taxes, 56.0%; corporate income taxes, 5.5%; and other taxes, 6.3%.

As of 1 January 2006, New York had five individual income tax brackets ranging from 4.0% to 6.85%. The state taxes corporations at a flat rate of 7.5%.

In 2004, local property taxes amounted to $32,333,564,000 or $1,677 per capita. The per capita amount ranks the state fourth-highest nationally. New York does not have property taxes at the state level.

New York taxes retail sales at a rate of 4.25%. In addition to the state tax, local taxes on retail sales can reach as much as 4.50%, making for a potential total tax on retail sales of 8.75%. Food purchased for consumption off-premises is tax exempt. The tax on cigarettes is 150 cents per pack, which ranks 10th among the 50 states and the District of Columbia. New York taxes gasoline at 23.9 cents per gallon. This is in addition to the 18.4 cents per gallon federal tax on gasoline.

According to the Tax Foundation, for every federal tax dollar sent to Washington in 2004, New York citizens received $0.79 in federal spending.

37 ECONOMIC POLICY

New York has created a number of incentives for business to foster new jobs and encourage economic prosperity. Among these are government-owned industrial park sites, state aid in the creation of county and city master plans, state recruitment and screening of industrial employees, programs for the promotion of research and development, and state help in bidding on federal procurement contracts. Through Empire State Development (ESD), New York State provides a full range of technical assistance. Representatives of the ESD call on firms in Canada, Asia, Latin America, and Europe; the division maintains offices in London, Tokyo, Montreal, Toronto, Jerusalem, and Mexico City. The ESD, through its ten regional offices, encourages the retention and expansion of existing facilities and the attraction of new job-creating investments. Other divisions aid small business and minority and women's business.

The state administers a number of financial programs to attract or retain businesses. Among these are low interest loans and grants for small businesses or for firms that create substantial numbers of jobs; grants and low cost loans for the development of industrial parks; and working capital loans to help companies at risk of downsizing. The state awards both grants and loans to manufacturing companies to encourage productivity improvements and modernization. It also seeks to encourage economic development in distressed rural communities with low interest loans for small businesses located in such areas. To promote technological innovation, the state provides debt and equity financing for technology based start-up companies.

In 2002, the ESD announced that to assist businesses affected by the World Trade Center (WTC) tragedy, it was implementing a $700 million Community Development Block Grant (CDBG) provided by the federal government. The funds were to be made available in the form of loans and grants to affected businesses that committed to job retention, job creation and investment in New York City, with priority on Lower Manhattan. Other WTC assistance programs of the ESD include a Disaster Assistance Program for Individuals, Disaster Recovery Resources for Small Businesses, Liberty Zone Tax Benefits, a New York Liberty Bond Program, and the World Trade Center Relief Fund. The Lower Manhattan Development Corporation (LMDC), created after the terrorist attacks of 11 September 2001, was charged with planning and coordinating the rebuilding and revitalization of lower Manhattan.

38 HEALTH

Health presents a mixed picture in New York State. The state has some of the finest hospital and medical education facilities in the United States, but it also has large numbers of the needy with serious health problems.

The infant mortality rate in October 2005 was estimated at 5.8 per 1,000 live births. The birth rate in 2003 was 13.2 per 1,000 population. The abortion rate stood at 39.1 per 1,000 women in 2000, representing the second-highest rate in the country (following the District of Columbia). In 2003, about 82.4% of pregnant woman received prenatal care beginning in the first trimester. In 2004, approximately 82% of children received routine immunizations before the age of three.

The crude death rate in 2003 was 8.1 deaths per 1,000 population. As of 2002, the death rates for major causes of death (per 100,000 resident population) were: heart disease, 295.8; cancer, 191.4; cerebrovascular diseases, 39.8; chronic lower respiratory diseases, 36.4; and diabetes, 20.5. The mortality rate from HIV infection was 10.3 per 100,000 population, representing the third-highest rate in the country (following the District of Columbia and Maryland). In 2004, the reported AIDS case rate was at about 39.7 per 100,000 population, the second-highest rate in the country (following the District of Columbia). In 2002, about 54.4% of the population was considered overweight or obese. As of 2004, about 19.9% of state residents were smokers.

In 2003, New York had 207 community hospitals with about 64,700 beds. There were about 2.49 million patient admissions that year and 48 million outpatient visits. The average daily inpatient census was about 50,600 patients. The average cost per day for hospital care was $1,402. Also in 2003, there were about 671 certified nursing facilities in the state with 122,633 beds and an overall occupancy rate of about 92.5%. In 2004, it was estimated that about 71.7% of all state residents had received some type of dental care within the year. New York had 401 physicians per 100,000 resident population in 2004 and 854 nurses per 100,000 in 2005. In 2004, there were a total of 14,498 dentists in the state.

In 2005, the New York–Presbyterian University Hospital of Columbia and Cornell ranked seventh on the Honor Roll of Best Hospitals 2005 by *U.S. News & World Report.* In the same report, it also ranked fifth for best pediatric care and seventh for best care in heart disease and heart surgery. The Memorial Sloan-Kettering Cancer Center ranked first in the nation for cancer care.

About 24% of state residents were enrolled in Medicaid programs in 2003; 14% were enrolled in Medicare programs in 2004. Approximately 15% of the state population was uninsured in 2004. In 2003, state health care expenditures totaled $44.5 million.

39 SOCIAL WELFARE

A 1938 New York constitutional provision mandated that the care and support of the needy shall be a state concern. Social welfare is a major public enterprise in the state; the growth of poverty relief programs has been enormous. In 2004, about 513,000 people received unemployment benefits, with the average weekly unemployment benefit at $271. For 2005, the estimated average monthly participation in the food stamp program included about 1,754,861 persons (915,703 households); the average monthly benefit was about $101.43 per person. That year, the total of benefits paid through the state for the food stamp program was over $2.1 billion.

Temporary Assistance for Needy Families (TANF), the system of federal welfare assistance that officially replaced Aid to Families with Dependent Children (AFDC) in 1997, was reauthorized through the Deficit Reduction Act of 2005. TANF is funded through federal block grants that are divided among the states based on an equation involving the number of recipients in each state. New York's TANF program is called the Family Assistance Program (FA). In 2004, the state program had 336,000 recipients; state and federal expenditures on this TANF program totaled $2 billion in fiscal year 2003.

In December 2004, Social Security benefits were paid to 3,045,290 New York residents. This number included 1,985,530 retired workers, 277,600 widows and widowers, 383,800 disabled workers, 149,780 spouses, and 248,580 children. Social Security beneficiaries represented 15.8% of the total state population and 87.7% of the state's population age 65 and older. Retired workers received an average monthly payment of $1,011; widows and widowers, $947; disabled workers, $943; and spouses, $480. Payments for children of retired workers averaged $490 per month; children of deceased workers, $666; and children of disabled workers, $273. Federal Supplemental Security Income payments in December 2004 went to 626,593 New York residents, averaging $461 a month.

40 HOUSING

In 2004, the state had an estimated 7,819,359 housing units, of which 7,087,566 were occupied. That year, the state ranked fourth in the nation for the highest number of housing units (following California, Texas, and Florida). An estimated 3,259,092 units, or 41.6%, are located in New York City (NYC). The housing stock in New York is relatively old. About 33.7% of all units in the state were built before or during 1939; 49.7% were built between 1940 and 1979. In NYC, 83% of all housing units were built before 1960; in Buffalo, 73% of all units were built before 1939.

Statewide in 2004, 42.3% of all units were single-family, detached homes. In NYC, however, only 9% were single, detached units; 46.9% of the city's housing units are located in buildings of 20 units or more. The average household had 2.63 members. Housing differences in New York City offer far greater contrasts than units per structure: the posh apartment houses of Manhattan and the hovels of the South Bronx both count as multi-unit dwellings. In 2004, New York State had the second-lowest percentage of owner-occupied housing in the nation, at 55.6% (only the District of Columbia was lower). In 2004, it was estimated that 140,133 units in NYC lacked telephone service, 19,137 lacked complete plumbing facilities, and 20,630 lacked complete kitchen facilities. Statewide, about 247,421 units lacked telephone service, 32,130 lacked complete plumbing facilities, and 211,862 lacked complete kitchen facilities. Characteristic of housing in New York is a system of rent controls that began in 1943.

The tight housing market—which may have contributed to the exodus of New Yorkers from the state—was not helped by the slump in housing construction from the mid-1970s to the mid-1980s. In New York City, more units were demolished than built every year from 1974 to 1981. The drop in construction of multi-unit dwellings was even more noticeable: from 64,959 units in 1972 to 11,740 units in 1982. In 1993, only 7,723 multi-unit dwellings were authorized. The overall decline in construction was coupled with a drastic drop in new public housing. In 1972, permits were issued for 111,282 units valued at $2.1 billion. By 1975, however, only 32,623 units worth $756 million were authorized; in 1982 there were only 25,280 units worth $1.1 billion, and in 1996, 34,895 units valued at $3.1 billion were authorized. In 1998, numbers were on the rebound with 38,400 new privately owned housing units.

In 2004, 53,500 new privately owned housing units were authorized for construction. The median home value for the state was $220,981. The median home value in NYC was $373,176. The median monthly cost for mortgage owners statewide was $1,525; renters paid a median of $796 per month. In NYC, the median monthly cost for mortgage owners was $1,920; renters paid a median of $856 per month.

Direct state aid for housing is limited. Governmental and quasi-independent agencies dealing with housing include the following: the Division of Housing and Community Renewal of the Executive Department, which makes loans and grants to municipalities for slum clearance and construction of low-income housing, supervises the operation of more than 400 housing developments, and administers rent-control and rent-stabilization laws; the New York State Housing Finance Agency, which is empowered to issue notes and bonds for various construction projects, not limited to housing; the State of New York Mortgage Agency, which may purchase existing mortgage loans from banks in order to make funds available for the banks to make new mortgage loans, and which also offers mortgage insurance; and the New York State Urban Development Corporation (UDC), a multibillion dollar agency designed to raise capital for all types of construction, including low-income housing. In 2006, the state received over $48.5 million in community development block grants (CDBG) from the US Department of Housing and Urban Development (HUD). New York City received $185.5 million in CDBGs and Buffalo received $16.5 million.

41 EDUCATION

The Board of Regents and the State Education Department govern education from pre-kindergarten to graduate school. They are constitutionally responsible for setting educational policy, standards, and rules and legally required to ensure that the entities they oversee carry them out. The board and department also provide vocational and educational services to people with disabilities.

In 2004, 85.4% of New Yorkers age 25 and older were high school graduates. Some 30.6% had obtained a bachelor's degree or higher.

The total enrollment for fall 2002 in New York's public schools stood at 2,888,000. Of these, 2,017,000 attended schools from kindergarten through grade eight, and 871,000 attended high school. Approximately 53.9% of the students were white, 19.7% were black, 19.4% were Hispanic, 6.6% were Asian/Pacific Islander, and 0.5% were American Indian/Alaskan Native. Total enrollment was estimated at 2,872,000 in fall 2003 and expected to be 2,715,000 by fall 2014, a decline of 6% during the period 2002–14. Expenditures for public education in 2003/04 were estimated at $42.5 billion or $12,930 per student, the second-highest among the 50 states. In fall 2003 there were 458,079 students enrolled in 1,959 private schools. Since 1969, the National Assessment of Educational Progress (NAEP) has tested public school students nationwide. The resulting report, *The Nation's Report Card,* stated that in 2005 eighth graders in New York scored 280 out of 500 in mathematics compared with the national average of 278.

As of fall 2002, there were 1,107,270 students enrolled in institutions of higher education; minority students comprised 32.4% of total postsecondary enrollment. In 2005 New York had 309 degree-granting institutions including, 45 public four-year schools, 35 public two-year schools, and 163 nonprofit, private four-year schools.

There are two massive public university systems: the State University of New York (SUNY) and the City University of New York (CUNY). Established in 1948, SUNY is one of the largest university systems in the country and encompasses university colleges of arts and sciences, specialized colleges, agricultural and technical colleges, statutory colleges (allied with private universities), health sciences centers, and locally sponsored community colleges. University centers include Buffalo, Albany, and Binghamton. The City University of New York was created in 1961, although many of its component institutions (including 12 four-year institutions) were founded much earlier. Under an open-enrollment policy adopted in 1970, every New York City resident with a high school diploma is guaranteed the chance to earn a college degree within the CUNY system (which CUNY campus the student attends is determined by grade point average).

The oldest private university in the state is Columbia University, founded in New York City as Kings College in 1754. Also part of Columbia are Barnard College (all women) and Columbia University Teachers College. Other major private institutions are Cornell University in Ithaca (1865); Fordham University in Manhattan and the Bronx (1841); New York University in Manhattan (1831); Rensselaer Polytechnic Institute in Troy (1824); St. John's University in Queens (1870); Syracuse University (1870); and the

University of Rochester (1850). Among the state's many smaller but highly distinguished institutions are Hamilton College, the Juilliard School, the New School for Social Research, Rockefeller University, Sarah Lawrence College, Vassar College, and Yeshiva University.

Unique features of education in New York are the "Regents exams," uniform subject examinations administered to all high school students, and the Regents Scholarships Tuition Assistance Program (TAP), a higher-education aid program. The state passed a "truth in testing" law in 1979, giving students the right to see their graded college and graduate school entrance examinations, as well as information on how the test results were validated.

42 ARTS

New York City is the cultural capital of the state, and leads the nation in both the creative and the performing arts. The state's foremost arts center is Lincoln Center for the Performing Arts, in Manhattan. Facilities at Lincoln Center include Avery Fisher Hall (which opened as Philharmonic Hall in 1962), the home of the New York Philharmonic; the Metropolitan Opera House (1966), where the Metropolitan Opera Company performs; and the New York State Theater, which presents both the New York City Opera and the New York City Ballet. Also at Lincoln Center are the Julliard School and the Library and Museum of the Performing Arts. The best-known arts center outside New York City is the Saratoga Performing Arts Center at Saratoga Springs. During the summer, the Saratoga Center presents performances by the New York City Ballet and the Philadelphia Orchestra. Artpark, a state park at Lewiston, has a 2,324-seat theater for operas and musicals, and offers art exhibits during the summer.

The New York State Council on the Arts (NYSCA) consists of 20 governor-appointed members. In 2005, the NYSCA and other New York arts organizations received 440 grants totaling over $16,204,450 from the National Endowment for the Arts. The Council on the Arts also receives funding from the state as well as contributions from private sources. The New York State Council on the Arts contributed to the Arts Connection of New York City—a program dedicated to providing the New York City public schools with interactive programming associated with the various arts—and to the National Book Foundation—centered in New York city and created to promote literacy as well as the appreciation of great American writing.

The New York Council for the Humanities was established in 1975; as of 2006 the state's Council for the Humanities had provided programs to over 4,000 institutions reaching over 250,000 New Yorkers annually. In 2005, the National Endowment for the Humanities contributed $13,421,970 to 124 state programs.

The city's most famous artists' district is Greenwich Village, which still holds an annual outdoor art fair. In 2005, the 57th Greenwich Village Art Fair featured over 100 artists, working in numerous different mediums. After the 1950s many artists moved to SoHo (Manhattan on the West Side between Canal and Houston Streets), NoHo (immediately north of Houston Street), the East Village, and Tribeca (between Canal Street and the World Trade Center). By the early 1980s, artists seeking space at reasonable prices were moving to Long Island City in Queens, to areas of Brooklyn, or out of the city entirely, to places such as Hoboken and Paterson in New Jersey. During the late 1940s and early 1950s,

abstract painters—including Jackson Pollock, Mark Rothko, and Willem de Kooning—helped make the city a center of the avant garde.

At the same time, poets such as Frank O'Hara and John Ashbery sought verbal analogues to developments in the visual arts, and an urbane, improvisatory literature was created. New York has enjoyed a vigorous poetic tradition throughout its history, most notably with the works of Walt Whitman (who served as editor of the Brooklyn Eagle from 1846 to 1848) and through Hart Crane's mythic vision of the city in his long poem, *The Bridge*. The emergence of New York as the center of the US publishing and communications industries fostered the growth of a literary marketplace, attracting writers from across the country and the world. Early New York novelists included Washington Irving, Edgar Allan Poe, and Herman Melville; among the many who made their home in the city in the 20th century were Thomas Wolfe and Norman Mailer. The simultaneous growth of the Broadway stage made New York City a vital forum for playwriting, songwriting, and theatrical production. New York City is also a major link in the US songwriting, music publishing, and recording industries.

There are more than 35 Broadway theaters—large theaters in midtown Manhattan presenting full-scale, sometimes lavish productions with top-rank performers. "Off Broadway" productions are often of high professional quality, though typically in smaller theaters, outside the midtown district, often with smaller casts and less costly settings. "Off-Off Broadway" productions range from small experimental theaters on the fringes of the city to performances in nightclubs and cabarets. The New York metropolitan area has hundreds of motion picture theaters—more than 65 in Manhattan alone, not counting special series at the Museum of Modern Art and other cultural institutions. In the 1970s, New York City made a determined and successful effort to attract motion picture production companies.

New York's leading symphony orchestra, the New York Philharmonic, is the oldest symphony orchestra in the United States with a history that dates back to the founding of the Philharmonic Society of New York in 1842. Among the principal conductors of the orchestra have been Gustav Mahler, Josef Willem Mengelberg, Wilhelm Furtwangler, Arturo Toscanini, Leonard Bernstein, Pierre Boulez, and Zubin Mehta. As of its 2004/05 season the orchestra had performed in over 416 cities and 57 countries. Leading US and foreign orchestras and soloists appear at both Avery Fisher Hall and Carnegie Hall, built in 1892 and famed for its acoustics. Important orchestras outside New York City include the Buffalo Philharmonic, which performs at Kleinhans Music Hall, the Rochester Philharmonic, and the Eastman Philharmonic, the orchestra of the Eastman School of Music (University of Rochester).

New York City is one of the world centers of ballet. Of special renown is the New York City Ballet; the company consisted of approximately 90 dancers—the largest in America. The New York City Ballet's principal choreographer until his death in 1983 was George Balanchine. Many other ballet companies, including the American Ballet Theatre and the Alvin Ailey American Dance Theater, make regular appearances in New York. Rochester, Syracuse, Cooperstown, Chautauqua, and Binghamton have opera companies, and Lake George has an opera festival. The Lake George Opera marked its 45th summer season in 2006. The North

Fork Theatre at Westbury presents wide-ranging musical and comedic programs.

⁴³LIBRARIES AND MUSEUMS

In 2001, the state of New York had 750 public library systems, with a total of 1,089 libraries, of which 340 were branches. In that same year, the state's public library system had 78,546,000 volumes of books and serial publications on its shelves, and a total circulation of 126,796,000. The system also had 4,371,000 audio and 2,115,000 video items, 665,000 electronic format items (CD-ROMs, magnetic tapes, and disks), and 10 bookmobiles. The state also had three of the world's largest libraries, and New York City has several of the world's most famous museums. In fiscal year 2001, operating income for the public library system totaled $902,746,000 and included $3,981,000 from the federal government, $51,055,000 from the state government, and the rest from local sources.

The leading public library systems and their operating statistics as of 1999 were the New York Public Library, 17,762,034 volumes in 127 branches; Brooklyn Public Library, 6,800,000 volumes and 10,077,559 circulation; Queens Borough Public Library, 8,668,948 volumes and 14,829,837 circulation; and Buffalo and Erie County system, 5,240,965 volumes and 8,734,854 circulation.

Chartered in 1895, the New York Public Library (NYPL) is the most complete municipal library system in the world. The library's main building, at 5th Avenue and 42d St., is one of the city's best-known landmarks; serving the needs of Manhattan, the Bronx, and Staten Island. The NYPL is a repository for every book published in the United States. The NYPL also operates the Library and Museum of the Performing Arts at Lincoln Center; the Schomburg Center for Research in Black Culture; and the Science, Industry, and Business Library that opened in May 1996.

Two private university libraries—at Columbia University (7,018,408 volumes in 1999) and Cornell University (6,617,242)–rank among the world's major libraries. Other major university libraries in the state, with their 1999 book holdings, are Syracuse University, 2,650,995; New York University, 2,987,062; the State University of New York at Buffalo, 2,534,500; and the University of Rochester, 2,446,729.

There are about 671 museums in New York State; about 150 are major museums, of which perhaps 80% are in New York City. In addition, some 579 sites of historic importance are maintained by local historical societies. Major art museums in New York City include the Metropolitan Museum of Art, with more than one million art objects and paintings from virtually every period and culture; the Cloisters, a branch of the Metropolitan Museum devoted entirely to medieval art and architecture; the Frick collection; the Whitney Museum of American Art; the Brooklyn Museum; and two large modern collections, the Museum of Modern Art and the Solomon R. Guggenheim Museum (the latter designed by Frank Lloyd Wright in a distinctive spiral pattern). The Jewish Museum, the Museum of the American Indian, and the museum and reference library of the Hispanic Society of America specialize in cultural history.

The sciences are represented by the American Museum of Natural History, famed for its dioramas of humans and animals in natural settings and for its massive dinosaur skeletons; the Hayden Planetarium; the New York Botanical Garden and New York Zoological Society Park (Bronx Zoo), both in the Bronx. Also of interest are the Museum of the City of New York, the Museum of the New-York Historical Society, the South Street Seaport Museum, and the New York Aquarium.

The New York State Museum in Albany contains natural history collections and historical artifacts. Buffalo has several museums of note, including the Albright-Knox Art Gallery (for contemporary art), the Buffalo Museum of Science, and the Buffalo and Erie County Historical Society museum.

Among the state's many other fine museums, the Everson Museum of Art (Syracuse), the Rochester Museum and Science Center, the National Baseball Hall of Fame and Museum (Cooperstown), and the Corning Museum of Glass deserve special mention. Buffalo, New Rochelle, Rochester, Syracuse, and Utica have zoos.

⁴⁴COMMUNICATIONS

New York City is the hub of the entire US communications network. Postal service was established in New York State in 1692; at the same time, the first General Letter Office was begun in New York City. By the mid-19th century, postal receipts in the state accounted for more than 20% of the US total. "Fast mail" service by train started in the 1870s, with the main routes leading from New York City to either Chicago or St. Louis via Indianapolis and Cincinnati. Mail was carried by air experimentally from Garden City to Mineola, Long Island, in 1911; the first regular airmail service in the United States started in 1917, between New York City and Washington, DC, via Philadelphia.

Telephone service in New York is provided primarily by the New York Telephone Co., but also by more than 40 smaller companies throughout the state. As of 2004, 94.5% of New York's occupied housing units had telephones. Additionally, by June of that same year there were 9,939,759 mobile wireless telephone subscribers. In 2003, 60.0% of New York households had a computer and 53.3% had Internet access. By June 2005, there were 3,188,033 high-speed lines in New York, 2,833,478 residential and 354,555 for business.

Until 31 December 1983, New York Telephone was part of the Bell System, whose parent organization was the American Telephone and Telegraph Co. (AT&T). Effective 1 January 1984, as the result of a US Justice Department antitrust suit, AT&T divested itself of 22 Bell operating companies, which regrouped into seven independent regional telephone companies to provide local telephone service in the United States. One of these companies, NYNEX, is the parent company of New York Telephone. AT&T, which continued to supply long-distance telephone services to New Yorkers (along with competitive carriers such as MCI, ITT, and GTE), is headquartered in New York City.

Domestic telegraph service is provided by the Western Union Telegraph Co., ITT World Communications, RCA Global Communications, and Western Union International. All four companies have their headquarters in New York City. New York State had 58 major AM stations and 181 major FM stations operating in 2005. New York City operates its own radio stations, WNYC-AM and FM, devoted largely to classical music and educational programming. There were 46 major television stations in the state in 2005. The city is the headquarters for most of the major US television networks, including the American Broadcasting Co. (now part of Walt Disney Corp.), Columbia Broadcasting System (owned by the Westinghouse Corp.), National Broadcasting Co.

(owned by General Electric), Westinghouse Broadcasting (Group W), Metromedia, and the Public Broadcasting Service (PBS). The metropolitan area's PBS affiliate, WNET (licensed in Newark, N.J.), is a leading producer of programs for the PBS network. As of 1999, the New York metropolitan area had 6,874,990 television households, 74% of which received cable. The Buffalo region had 621,460 television homes, with a 77% penetration rate.

A total of 589,963 Internet domain names were registered in the state in the year 2000; the second highest number of all states.

45 PRESS

A pioneer in the establishment of freedom of the press, New York is the leader of the US newspaper, magazine, and book-publishing industries. The first major test of press freedom in the colonies came in 1734, when a German-American printer, John Peter Zenger, was arrested on charges of sedition and libel. In his newspaper, the *New-York Weekly Journal*, Zenger had published articles criticizing the colonial governor of New York. Zenger's lawyer, Andrew Hamilton, argued that because the charges in the article were true, they could not be libelous. The jury's acceptance of this argument freed Zenger and established the right of the press to criticize those in power. Two late decisions involving a New York newspaper also struck blows for press freedom. In *New York Times v. Sullivan* (1964), the US Supreme Court ruled that a public official could not win a libel suit against a newspaper unless he could show that its statements about him were not only false but also malicious or in reckless disregard of the truth. In 1971, the *New York Times* was again involved in a landmark case when the federal government tried—and failed—to prevent the newspaper from publishing the Pentagon Papers, a collection of secret documents concerning the war in Vietnam.

In 2005, New York had 37 morning newspapers, 23 evening papers, and 38 Sunday editions.

The following table shows leading papers in New York, with their average daily and Sunday circulations in 2005:

AREA	NAME	DAILY	SUNDAY
Albany	*Times–Union* (m,S)	100,628	146,464
Buffalo	*News* (all day,S)	196,429	282,618
Long Island	*Newsday* (m,S)	481,816	574,081
New York City	*Daily News* (m,S)	715,052	786,952
	Post (m,S)	481,860	455,511
	Times (m,S)	1,121,057	1,680,583
	Wall Street Journal (m)	1,780,605	
Rochester	*Democrat and Chronicle* (m,S)	166,727	224,408
Syracuse	*Post-Standard* (m,S)	118,926	175,020

All of New York City's major newspapers have claims to fame. The *Times* is the nation's "newspaper of record," excelling in the publication of speeches, press conferences, and government reports. It is widely circulated to US libraries and is often cited in research. In 2005, the *Times* Sunday edition was the number one Sunday newspaper in the nation, based on circulation figures. The *New York Post*, founded in 1801, is the oldest US newspaper published continuously without change of name. The *Wall Street Journal*, published Monday through Friday, is a truly national paper, presenting mostly business news in four regional editions. In 2005, the *Wall Street Journal*, the *Times*, the New York *Daily News*, the Long Island *Newsday*, and the *Post* were among the top thirteen largest daily newspapers in the nation. Many historic New

York papers first merged and then—bearing compound names like the *Herald-Tribune, Journal-American,* and *World-Telegram & Sun Newspaper*—died in the 1950s and 1960s. In 2001, the Syracuse *Herald-American* and *Herald-Journal* merged to form the *Post-Standard*

There are two Spanish dailies published in New York City: *El Diario La Prensa,* with a circulation of 50,019 daily and 34,636 Sundays; and *Hoy,* with a circulation of 49,681 daily and 25,465 Sundays.

The leading newspaper chain is the Gannett Co., Inc. (headquarters in Virginia). Other groups include Ogden Newspapers, Inc.(West Virginia), Hearst Newspapers (New York), and Johnson Newspaper Corp. (New York). All the major news agencies have offices in New York City, and the Associated Press has its headquarters there.

In 2005, there were 354 weekly publications in New York. Of these there are 208 paid weeklies, 53 free weeklies, and 93 combined weeklies. The total circulation of paid weeklies (1,635,143) and free weeklies (2,420,539) is 4,055,682. Two of New York City's paid weeklies, *People's Weekly World* and *Observer* ranked first and sixth, respectively, in the United States based on circulations of 67,700 and 52,000. Based on circulation in the United States in 2005, among free weeklies the Suffolk County *Life Newspapers* ranked second in the United States with a circulation of 548,657. The Nassau County *This Week/Pennysaver* (circulation 993,913) ranked seventh in the United States among shopping publications.

Many leading US magazines are published in New York City, including the newsmagazines *Time* and *Newsweek,* business journals like *Fortune, Forbes,* and *Business Week,* and hundreds of consumer and trade publications. *Reader's Digest* is published in Pleasantville. Two weeklies closely identified with New York are of more than local interest. While the *New Yorker* carries up-to-date listings of cultural events and exhibitions in New York City, the excellence of its journalism, criticism, fiction, and cartoons has long made it a literary standard-bearer for the entire nation. *New York* magazine influenced the writing style and graphic design of the 1960s and set the pattern for a new wave of state and local magazines that avoided boosterism in favor of independent reporting and commentary. Another weekly, the *Village Voice* (actually a tabloid newspaper), became the prototype for a host of alternative or "underground" journals during the 1960s.

New York City is also the center of the nation's book-publishing industry. New York publishers include McGraw–Hill, Macmillan, Simon & Schuster, and Random House; many book publishers are subsidiaries of other companies.

46 ORGANIZATIONS

In 2006, there were over 25,673 nonprofit organizations registered within the state, of which about 19,427 were registered as charitable, educational, or religious organizations.

The United Nations is the best-known organization to have its headquarters in New York. The UN Secretariat, completed in 1951, remains one of the most familiar landmarks of New York City. Hundreds of US nonprofit organizations also have their national headquarters in New York City. General and service organizations operating out of New York City include the American Field Service, Boys Clubs of America, Girls Clubs of America, Girl

Scouts of the USA, Young Women's Christian Associations of the USA (YWCA), and Associated YM-YWHAs of Greater New York (the Jewish equivalent of the YMCA and YWCA).

Among the cultural and educational groups of national interest are the American Academy of Arts and Letters, Authors League of America, Children's Book Council, Modern Language Association of America, and PEN American Center. State organizations include the Folk Music Society of New York, the New York Center for Books and Reading, the New York Academy of Sciences, the New York Drama Critics Circle, and the New York State Historical. The Statue of Liberty–Ellis Island Foundation sponsors educational programs as well as maintaining the monument and museum. There are numerous local musical and theater groups. There are also several regional historical societies.

Among the national environmental and animal welfare organizations with headquarters in the city are the American Society for the Prevention of Cruelty to Animals (ASPCA), Friends of Animals, Fund for Animals, National Audubon Society, Bide-A-Wee Home Association, Environmental Defense Fund, and American Kennel Club. State groups include the New York City Community Garden Coalition, the New York Conservation Foundation, and the New York State Conservation Council.

Many medical, health, and charitable organizations have their national offices in New York City, including Alcoholics Anonymous, American Foundation for the Blind, National Society to Prevent Blindness, CARE, American Cancer Society, United Cerebral Palsy Associations, Child Welfare League of America, American Diabetes Association, National Multiple Sclerosis Society, Muscular Dystrophy Association, and Planned Parenthood Federation of America.

Leading ethnic and religious organizations based in the city include the American Bible Society, National Conference of Christians and Jews, Hadassah, United Jewish Appeal, American Jewish Committee, American Jewish Congress, United Negro College Fund, Congress of Racial Equality, and National Urban League.

There are many commercial, trade, and professional organizations headquartered in New York City. Among the better known are the Actors' Equity Association, American Arbitration Association, American Booksellers Association, American Federation of Musicians, American Institute of Chemical Engineers, American Society of Civil Engineers, American Society of Composers, Authors, and Publishers (ASCAP), American Society of Journalists and Authors, American Insurance Association, Magazine Publishers Association, American Management Associations, American Society of Mechanical Engineers, and American Institute of Physics.

Sports organizations centered in New York City include the National Football League, the American and the National Leagues of Professional Baseball Clubs, the National Thoroughbred Racing Association, National Basketball Association, the Polar Bear Club–USA, and the US Tennis Association.

Influential political and international affairs groups include the American Civil Liberties Union, Council on Foreign Relations, Trilateral Commission, United Nations Association of the USA, and US Committee for UNICEF.

Virtually every other major US organization has one or more chapters within the state.

47 TOURISM, TRAVEL, AND RECREATION

New York City is the primary travel destination in the state. In 2001, there were 35.2 million visitors to New York City, including 5.7 million international visitors. The projection for 2006 was 43.3 millions visitors to New York City. New York City alone brings in $39 billion in revenue. New York City also supported 291,977 jobs in tourism in 2004. A typical visit to New York City might include a boat ride to the Statue of Liberty; a three-hour boat ride around Manhattan; the Empire State Building, the United Nations, Rockefeller Center, and the New York Stock Exchange; walking tours of the Bronx Zoo, Chinatown, and the theater district; and a sampling of the city's many museums, restaurants, shops, and shows.

Second to New York City as a magnet for tourists comes Long Island, with its beaches, racetracks, and other recreational facilities. Attractions of the Hudson Valley include the US Military Academy (West Point), the Franklin D. Roosevelt home at Hyde Park, Bear Mountain State Park, and several wineries. North of Hudson Valley is Albany, with its massive government center, Governor Nelson A. Rockefeller Plaza, often called the Albany Mall; Saratoga Springs, home of an arts center, racetrack, and spa; and the Adirondack region, with its forest preserve, summer and winter resorts, and abundant hunting and fishing. Northwest of the Adirondacks, in the St. Lawrence River, are the Thousand Islands—actually some 1,800 small islands extending over some 50 mi (80 km) and popular among freshwater fishermen and summer vacationers.

Scenic sites in central New York include the summer resorts and ski areas of the Catskills and the scenic marvels and wineries of the Finger Lakes region, including Taughannock Falls in Trumansburg, the highest waterfall east of the Rockies. Further west lie Buffalo and Niagara Falls. Niagara Falls alone attracts over 12 million visitors annually. Charter boat fishing is available on Lake Ontario. Chautauqua Lake and Allegany State Park, the state's largest, lie south of Buffalo and Niagara Falls. Elmont is the home of the Belmont race track, the third leg in the Triple Crown of thoroughbred horse racing. Motorsports fans can visit the Adirondacks International Speedway.

48 SPORTS

New York has eleven major league professional sports teams: the New York Yankees and the New York Mets of Major League Baseball; the New York Giants, the New York Jets (although the Giants' and Jets' stadiums are located in New Jersey), and the Buffalo Bills of the National Football League; the New York Knickerbockers (usually called the Knicks) of the National Basketball Association; the New York Islanders, the New York Rangers, and the Buffalo Sabres of the National Hockey League; the New York Liberty of the Women's National Basketball Association, and Red Bull New York of Major League Soccer.

The Yankees have a record of excellence spanning most of the twentieth century. They won the American League Pennant 39 times and the World Series 26 times, most recently in 2000, when they defeated the New York Mets in five games. The series was coined the "Subway Series" because both teams were from New York City. Other championship streaks include the American League Pennant in 1927 and 1928; 1936–39; 1941–43; 1949–53; 1955–58; 1960–64; 1998–2001. In the 28 years between 1936 and

1964, the Yankees competed in 23 World Series, winning 16. The Mets have played in four World Series, winning in 1969 and 1986. The Giants won Super Bowls in 1987 and 1991, and the Jets did so in 1969 in a memorable upset victory over the Baltimore Colts. The Buffalo Bills won the American Football Conference Championship in 1991, 1992, 1993, and 1994, losing the Super Bowl each time. The Knicks won the NBA championship in 1970 and 1973, and lost in the NBA finals in 1951, 1952, 1953, 1972, 1994, and 1999. The Islanders won the Stanley Cup in 1980, 1981, 1982, and 1983. The Rangers won it in 1928, 1933, 1940, and 1994.

Three New York teams, the Nets, Giants, and Jets, moved to New Jersey during the 1970s and 1980s. The Giants and Jets remained, in name, New York teams (unlike the Nets, who are now the New Jersey Nets), although the move remains controversial. In 1987, when the Giants won the Super Bowl, then mayor of New York Ed Koch refused them the ticker-tape parade through the city traditionally given in honor of championship teams on the grounds that, their name notwithstanding, they are a New Jersey team.

The state also has 13 minor league baseball teams and six minor league hockey teams.

Horse racing is important to New York State, both as a sports attraction and because of the tax revenues that betting generates. The main thoroughbred racetracks are Aqueduct in Queens, Belmont in Nassau County, and the Saratoga Race Course in Saratoga Springs. Belmont is the home of the Belmont Stakes, one of the three jewels in the Triple Crown of US racing. Saratoga Springs also has a longer harness-racing season at its Saratoga Equine Sports Center facility. Thoroughbred racing is also offered at the Finger Lakes track in Canandaigua. The top track for harness racing is Monticello Raceway (in the Catskills).

The New York City Off-Track Betting Corporation (OTB), which began operations in April 1971, takes bets on races at the state's major tracks, as well as on some out-of-state races. Off-track betting services operate on a smaller scale on Long Island and in upstate New York.

New York City hosts several major professional tennis tournaments every year, including the US Open in Flushing Meadows; the Last Minute Travel.com Masters (men) in Central Park, and the Chase Championships of the WTA Tour (women) at Madison Square Garden.

Among other professional sports facilities, the Watkins Glen International automobile racetrack was, until 1980, the site of a Grand Prix race every October. It now hosts a NASCAR Nextel Cup race in August. Lake Placid, an important winter-sports region, hosted the 1932 and 1980 Winter Olympics, and continues to host amateur winter sports competitions, such as bobsled racing and ski jumping. New York City's Madison Square Garden is a leading venue for professional boxing and hosts many other sporting events.

In collegiate sports, basketball is perhaps most popular. Historically, the City College of New York produced many nationally ranked teams including the National Collegiate Athletic Association (NCAA) champions of 1950; in that year, they also won the National Invitational Basketball Tournament (NIT). St. John's and Syracuse have produced nationally prominent teams, including the 1989 St. John's team that won the NIT. The Syracuse Orangemen won the 2003 National Championship.

The US Military Academy at West Point (Army) won college football national championships in 1944 and 1945, and, as of 1997, ranked 12th all-time among Division I-A teams with more than 600 victories.

Hockey and lacrosse are popular sports at the collegiate level and have been well represented by New York colleges and universities. Both the Syracuse Orangemen and Cornell Big Red have captured multiple national championships on the Division-I level. Cornell has been equally successful on the ice, advancing to the Frozen Four on a number of occasions (most recently in 2003). The Big Red captured the national championship in both 1967 and 1970.

In 1978, New York became the first state to sponsor a statewide amateur athletic event, the Empire State Games. More than 50,000 athletes now compete for a place in the finals, held each summer; the Winter Games, held each February in Lake Placid, host more than 1,000.

The New York City marathon, which is held in late October or early November, has become one of the largest, most prestigious marathons in the world.

Other annual sporting events include the Adirondack Hot Air Balloon Festival in Glens Falls in September and the Westminster Kennel Club Dog Show in New York City in February. The Baseball Hall of Fame is located in Cooperstown.

⁴⁹ FAMOUS NEW YORKERS

New York State has been the home of five US presidents, eight US vice presidents (three of whom also became president), many statesmen of national and international repute, and a large corps of writers and entertainers.

Martin Van Buren (1782–1862), the eighth US president, became governor of New York in 1828. He was elected to the vice presidency as a Democrat under Andrew Jackson in 1832, and succeeded Jackson in the election of 1836. An unpopular president, Van Buren ran for reelection in 1840 but was defeated, losing even his home state. The 13th US president, Millard Fillmore (1800–74), was elected vice president under Zachary Taylor in 1848. He became president in 1850 when Taylor died. Fillmore's party, the Whigs, did not renominate him in 1852; four years later, he unsuccessfully ran for president as the candidate of the Native American (or Know-Nothing) Party.

Chester Alan Arthur (1829–86), a transplanted New Yorker born in Vermont, became the 21st US president when James Garfield was assassinated. New York's other US presidents had more distinguished careers. Although he was born in New Jersey, Grover Cleveland (1837–1908) served as mayor of Buffalo and as governor of New York before his election to his first presidential term in 1884; he was again elected president in 1892. Theodore Roosevelt (1858–1919), a Republican, was elected governor in 1898. He won election as vice president under William McKinley in 1900, and became the nation's 26th president after McKinley was murdered in 1901. Roosevelt pursued an aggressive foreign policy, but also won renown as a conservationist and trustbuster. Reelected in 1904, he was awarded the Nobel Peace Prize in 1906 for helping to settle a war between Russia and Japan. Roosevelt declined to run again in 1908. However, he sought the Republican nomination in 1912 and, when defeated, became the candidate of the

Progressive (or Bull Moose) Party, losing the general election to Woodrow Wilson.

Franklin Delano Roosevelt (1882–1945), a fifth cousin of Theodore Roosevelt, first ran for national office in 1920, when he was the Democratic vice-presidential choice. A year after losing that election, FDR was crippled by poliomyelitis. He then made an amazing political comeback: he was elected governor of New York in 1928 and served until 1932, when US voters chose him as their 32d president. Reelected in 1936, 1940, and 1944, FDR is the only president ever to have served more than two full terms in office. Roosevelt guided the United States through the Great Depression and World War II, and his New Deal programs greatly enlarged the federal role in promoting social welfare.

In addition to Van Buren, Fillmore, and Theodore Roosevelt, five US vice presidents were born in New York: George Clinton (1739–1812), who was also New York State's first elected governor; Daniel D. Tompkins (1774–1825); William A. Wheeler (1819–87); Schuyler Colfax (1823–85); and James S. Sherman 1855–1912). Two other US vice presidents, though not born in New York, were New Yorkers by the time they became vice president. The first was Aaron Burr (1756–1836), perhaps best known for killing Alexander Hamilton in a duel in 1804; Hamilton (b.Nevis, West Indies, 1757–1804) was a leading Federalist, George Washington's treasury secretary, and the only New York delegate to sign the US Constitution in 1787. The second transplanted New Yorker to become vice president was Nelson Aldrich Rockefeller (1908–79). Born in Maine, Rockefeller served as governor of New York State from 1959 to 1973, was for two decades a major force in national Republican politics, and was appointed vice president by Gerald Ford in 1974, serving in that office through January 1977. Alan Greenspan (b.1926), a chairman of the Federal Reserve, was born in New York City.

Two native New Yorkers have become chief justices of the United States: John Jay (1745–1829) and Charles Evans Hughes (1862–1948). A third chief justice, Harlan Fiske Stone (1872–1946), born in New Hampshire, spent most of his legal career in New York City and served as dean of Columbia University's School of Law. Among New Yorkers who became associate justices of the US Supreme Court, Benjamin Nathan Cardozo (1870–1938) is noteworthy. Ruth Bader Ginsberg (b.1933) was President Bill Clinton's first appointment to the Supreme Court.

Other federal officeholders born in New York include US secretaries of state William Henry Seward (1801–72), Hamilton Fish (1808–93), Elihu Root (1845–1937), Frank B. Kellogg (1856–1937), and Henry L. Stimson (1867–1950). Prominent US senators have included Robert F. Wagner (1877–1953), who sponsored many New Deal laws; Robert F. Kennedy (1925–68), who though born in Massachusetts was elected to represent New York in 1964; Jacob K. Javits (1904–86), who served continuously in the Senate from 1957 through 1980; and Daniel Patrick Moynihan (1927–2003), a scholar, author, and former federal bureaucrat who has represented New York since 1977. Colin Powell (b.1937), first African American to lead the Armed Forces, attended the City University of New York.

The most important—and most colorful—figure in colonial New York was Peter Stuyvesant (b.Netherlands, 1592–1672); as director general of New Netherland, he won the hearty dislike of the Dutch settlers. Signers of the Declaration of Independence in 1776 from New York were Francis Lewis (1713–1803); Philip Livingston (1716–78); Lewis Morris (1726–98), the half-brother of the colonial patriot Gouverneur Morris (1752–1816); and William Floyd (1734–1821).

Other governors who made important contributions to the history of the state include DeWitt Clinton (1769–1828); Alfred E. Smith (1873–1944); Herbert H. Lehman (1878–1963); W. Averell Harriman (1891–1986), who has also held many US diplomatic posts; and Thomas E. Dewey (1902–71). Mario M. Cuomo (b.1932) served three terms as governor from 1982–94. Robert Moses (b.Connecticut, 1888–1981) led in the development of New York's parks and highway transportation system. One of the best-known and best-loved mayors in New York City history was Fiorello H. La Guardia (1882–1947), a reformer who held the office from 1934 to 1945. Edward I. Koch (b.1924) was first elected to the mayoralty in 1977.

Native New Yorkers have won Nobel prizes in every category. Winners of the Nobel Peace Prize besides Theodore Roosevelt were Elihu Root in 1912 and Frank B. Kellogg in 1929. The lone winner of the Nobel Prize for literature was Eugene O'Neill (1888–1953) in 1936. The chemistry prize was awarded to Irving Langmuir (1881–1957) in 1932, John H. Northrop (1891–1987) in 1946, and William Howard Stein (1911–80) in 1972. Winners in physics include Carl D. Anderson (b.1905-1991) in 1936, Robert Hofstadter (1915–90) in 1961, Richard Phillips Feynman (1918–88) and Julian Seymour Schwinger (1918–94) in 1965, Murray Gell-Mann (b.1929) in 1969, Leon N. Cooper (b.1930) in 1972, Burton Richter (b.1931) in 1976, and Steven Weinberg (b.1933) and Sheldon L. Glashow (b.1923) in 1979.

The following New Yorkers have been awarded the Nobel Prize for physiology or medicine: Hermann Joseph Muller (1890–1967) in 1946, Arthur Kornberg (b.1918) in 1959, George Wald (1906–97) in 1967, Marshall Warren Nirenberg (b.1927) in 1968, Julius Axelrod (1912–2004) in 1970, Gerald Maurice Edelman (b.1929) in 1972, David Baltimore (b.1938) in 1975, Baruch Samuel Blumberg (b.1925) and Daniel Carlton Gajdusek (b.1923) in 1976, Rosalyn Sussman Yalow (b.1921) in 1977, and Hamilton O. Smith (b.1931) in 1978.

The Nobel Prize for economic science was won by Kenneth J. Arrow (b.1921) in 1972, Milton Friedman (b.1912) in 1976, Richard Stone (1928–91) in 1984, and Robert Fogel (b.1926) in 1993. New York is also the birthplace of national labor leader George Meany (1894–1980) and economist Walter Heller (1915–87). Other distinguished state residents were physicist Joseph Henry (1797–1878), Mormon leader Brigham Young (b.Vermont, 1801–77), botanist Asa Gray (1810–88), inventor-businessman George Westinghouse (1846–1914), and Jonas E. Salk (1914–95), developer of a poliomyelitis vaccine. Melvin Schwartz (b.New York City, 1932) was a co-recipient of the 1988 Nobel prize in physics. Gertrude Belle Elion (1918–99), Nobel Prize winner in medicine 1988, was born in New York City. Leon Max Lederman (b.1922) was a co-recipient of the 1988 Nobel Prize in physics.

Writers born in New York include the storyteller and satirist Washington Irving (1783–1859); poets Walt Whitman (1819–92) and Ogden Nash (1902–71); and playwrights Eugene O'Neill (1888–1953), Arthur Miller (1915–2005), Paddy Chayefsky (1923–81), and Neil Simon (b.1927). Two of America's greatest novelists were New Yorkers: Herman Melville (1819–91), who was also an important poet, and Henry James (1843–1916), whose short stories are equally well known. Other novelists include James Fenimore Cooper (b.New Jersey, 1789–1851), Henry Miller (1891–1980), James Michener (1907–97), J(erome) D(avid) Salinger (b.1919), Joseph Heller (1923–99), James Baldwin (1924–87), and Gore Vidal (b.1925). Lionel Trilling (1905–75) was a well-known literary critic; Barbara Tuchman (1912–89), a historian, has won both scholarly praise and popular favor. New York City has produced two famous journalist-commentators, Walter Lippmann (1889–1974) and William F. Buckley Jr. (b.1925), and a famous journalist-broadcaster Walter Winchell (1897–1972).

Broadway is the showcase of American drama and the birthplace of the American musical theater. New Yorkers linked with the growth of the musical include Jerome Kern (1885–1945), Lorenz Hart (1895–1943), Oscar Hammerstein II (1895–1960), Richard Rodgers (1902–79), Alan Jay Lerner (1918–86), and Stephen Sondheim (b.1930). George Gershwin (1898–1937), whose *Porgy and Bess* raised the musical to its highest artistic form, also composed piano and orchestral works. Other important US composers from New York include Irving Berlin (b.Russia, 1888–1989), Aaron Copland (1900–90), Elliott Carter (b.1908), and William Schuman (1910–92). New York was the adopted home of ballet director and choreographer George Balanchine (b.Russia, 1904–83); his associate Jerome Robbins (1918–98) was born in New York City, as was choreographer Agnes De Mille (1905–93). Leaders in the visual arts include Frederic Remington (1861–1909), the popular illustrator Norman Rockwell (1894–1978), Willem de Kooning (b.Netherlands, 1904–97), and the photographer Margaret Bourke-White (1906–71).

Many of America's best-loved entertainers come from the state. A small sampling would include comedians Groucho Marx (Julius Marx, 1890–1977), Mae West (1892–1980), Eddie Cantor (Edward Israel Iskowitz, 1892–1964), James "Jimmy" Durante (1893–1980), Bert Lahr (Irving Lahrheim, 1895–1967), George Burns (1896–1996), Milton Berle (Berlinger, b.1908), Lucille Ball (1911–1989), Danny Kaye (David Daniel Kominsky, 1913–87), and Sid Caesar (b.1922); comedian-film directors Mel Brooks (Melvin Kaminsky, b.1926) and Woody Allen (Allen Konigsberg, b.1935); stage and screen stars Humphrey Bogart (1899–1957), James Cagney (1904–86), Zero Mostel (Samuel Joel Mostel, 1915–77), and Lauren Bacall (Betty Joan Perske, b.1924); pop, jazz, and folk singers Cab Calloway (1907–90), Lena Horne (b.1917), Pete Seeger (b.1919), Sammy Davis Jr. (1925–90), Harry Belafonte (b.1927), Joan Baez (b.1941), Barbra Streisand (b.1942), Carly Simon (b.1945), Arlo Guthrie (b.1947), Billy Joel (b.1951), and Mariah Carey, Grammy Award-winning pop singer, (b.1969); and opera stars Robert Merrill (1919–2004), Maria Callas (Kalogeropoulos, 1923–77), and Beverly Sills (Belle Silverman, b.1929). Also noteworthy are producers Irving Thalberg (1899–1936), David Susskind (1920–87), Joseph Papp (1921–91), and Harold Prince (b.1928) and directors George Cukor (1899–1983), Stanley Kubrick (1928–99), John

Frankenheimer (1930–2002), Peter Bogdanovich (b.1939), and actor Tom Cruise (b.1962 in Syracuse, New York).

Among many prominent sports figures born in New York are first-baseman Lou Gehrig (1903–41), football coach Vince Lombardi (1913–70), pitcher Sanford "Sandy" Koufax (b.1935), and basketball stars Kareem Abdul-Jabbar (Lew Alcindor, b.1947) and Julius Erving (b.1950). Orel Leonard Hershiser IV (b.1958), who set the record for most consecutive scoreless innings pitched, was born in Buffalo, New York.

50 BIBLIOGRAPHY

Berrol, Selma Cantor. *The Empire City: New York and Its People, 1624-1996.* Westport, Conn.: Praeger, 1997.

Burgan, Michael. *New York, 1609-1776.* Washington, D.C.: National Geographic Society, 2006.

Council of State Governments. *The Book of the States, 2006 Edition.* Lexington, Ky.: Council of State Governments, 2006.

Cuomo, Mario M. *Diaries of Mario M. Cuomo: The Campaign for Governor.* New York: Random House, 1984.

Fabend, Firth Haring. *Zion on the Hudson: Dutch New York and New Jersey in the Age of Revivals.* New Brunswick, N.J.: Rutgers University Press, 2000.

Galie, Peter J. *The New York State Constitution: A Reference Guide.* New York, Greenwood Press, 1991.

———. *Ordered Liberty: A Constitutional History of New York.* New York: Fordham University Press, 1996.

Gellman, David Nathaniel. *Emancipating New York: The Politics of Slavery and Freedom, 1777-1827.* Baton Rouge: Louisiana State University Press, 2006.

Hansen, Joyce, and Gary McGowan. *Breaking Ground, Breaking Silence: The Story of New York's African Burial Ground.* New York: Henry Holt, 1998.

Homberger, Eric. *The Historical Atlas of New York City: A Visual Celebration of Nearly 400 Years of New York City's History.* New York: Henry Holt, 1996.

Silbey, Joel H. *Martin Van Buren and the Emergence of American Popular Politics.* Lanham, Md.: Rowman & Littlefield, 2002.

Stout, Glenn. *Nine Months at Ground Zero: The Story of the Brotherhood of Workers Who Took on a Job Like No Other.* New York: Scribner, 2006.

Torres, Andrés. *Between Melting Pot and Mosaic: African Americans and Puerto Ricans in the New York Political Economy.* Philadelphia: Temple University Press, 1995.

US Department of Commerce, Economics and Statistics Administration, US Census Bureau. *New York, 2000. Summary Social, Economic, and Housing Characteristics: 2000 Census of Population and Housing.* Washington, D.C.: US Government Printing Office, 2003.

NORTH CAROLINA

State of North Carolina

ORIGIN OF STATE NAME: Named in honor of King Charles I of England. **NICKNAME:** The Tarheel State; Old North State. **CAPITAL:** Raleigh. **ENTERED UNION:** 21 November 1789 (12th). **SONG:** "The Old North State." **MOTTO:** *Esse quam videri* (To be rather than to seem). **FLAG:** Adjacent to the fly of two equally sized bars, red above and white below, is a blue union containing a white star in the center, flanked by the letters N and C in gold. Above and below the star are two gold scrolls, the upper one reading "May 20th 1775," the lower one "April 12th 1776." **OFFICIAL SEAL:** Liberty, clasping a constitution and holding aloft on a pole a liberty cap, stands on the left, while Plenty sits besides a cornucopia on the right; behind them, mountains run to the sea, on which a three-masted ship appears. "May 20, 1775" appears above the figures; the words "The Great Seal of the State of North Carolina" and the state motto surround the whole. **BIRD:** Cardinal. **FISH:** Channel bass. **FLOWER:** Dogwood. **TREE:** Long leaf pine. **GEM:** Emerald. **LEGAL HOLIDAYS:** New Year's Day, 1 January; Birthday of Martin Luther King Jr., 3rd Monday in January; Good Friday, Friday before Easter, March or April; Memorial Day, last Monday in May; Independence Day, 4 July; Labor Day, 1st Monday in September; Veterans' Day, 11 November; Thanksgiving Day, 4th Thursday in November and the day following; Christmas Day, 25 December and the day following. **TIME:** 7 AM EST = noon GMT.

¹LOCATION, SIZE, AND EXTENT

Located in the southeastern United States, North Carolina ranks 28th in size among the 50 states.

The total area of North Carolina is 52,669 sq mi (136,413 sq km), of which land accounts for 48,843 sq mi (126,504 sq km) and inland water 3,826 sq mi (9,909 sq km). North Carolina extends 503 mi (810 km) E–W; the state's maximum N–S extension is 187 mi (301 km).

North Carolina is bordered on the N by Virginia; on the E by the Atlantic Ocean; on the S by South Carolina and Georgia; and on the W by Tennessee. A long chain of islands or sand banks, called the Outer Banks, lies off the state's Atlantic coast. The total boundary line of North Carolina is 1,270 mi (2,044 km), including a general coastline of 301 mi (484 km); the tidal shoreline extends 3,375 mi (5,432 km). The state's geographic center is in Chatham County, 10 mi (16 km) NW of Sanford.

²TOPOGRAPHY

North Carolina's three major topographic regions belong to the Atlantic Coastal Plain, the Piedmont Plateau, and the Appalachian Mountains.

The Outer Banks, narrow islands of shifting sandbars, screen most of the coastal plain from the ocean. Treacherous navigation conditions and numerous shipwrecks have earned the name of "Graveyard of the Atlantic" for the shoal waters off Cape Hatteras, which, like Cape Lookout and Cape Fear, juts out from the banks into the Atlantic. Cape Hatteras Lighthouse is the tallest in the United States, rising 208 ft (63 m). The shallow Pamlico and Albemarle sounds and broad salt marshes lying behind the Outer Banks serve not only as valuable habitats for marine life but as further hindrances to water transportation. Sea level at the Atlantic Ocean is the lowest elevation of the state.

On the mainland, the coastal plain extends westward from the sounds for 100 to 140 mi (160–225 km) and upward from sea level to nearly 500 ft (150 m). Near the ocean, the outer coastal plain is very flat and often swampy; this region contains all the natural lakes in North Carolina, the largest being Lake Mattamuskeet (67 sq mi/174 sq km), followed by lakes Phelps and Waccamaw. The inner coastal plain is more elevated and better drained. Infertile sand hills mark its southwestern section, but the rest of the region constitutes the state's principal farming country.

The Piedmont is a rolling plateau of red clay soil roughly 150 mi (240 km) wide, rising from 30 to 600 ft (90–180 m) in the east to 1,500 ft (460 m) in the west. The fall line, a sudden change in elevation, separates the piedmont from the coastal plain and produces numerous rapids in the rivers that flow between the regions.

The Blue Ridge, a steep escarpment that parallels the Tennessee border, divides the piedmont from North Carolina's westernmost region, containing the highest and most rugged portion of the Appalachian chain. The two major ranges are the Blue Ridge itself, which averages 3,000–4,000 ft high (900–1,200 m), and the Great Smoky Mountains, which have 43 peaks higher than 6,000 ft (1,800 m). Several smaller chains intersect these two ranges; one of them, the Black Mountains, contains Mt. Mitchell, at 6,684 ft (2,039 m) the tallest peak east of the Mississippi River. The mean elevation of the state is approximately 700 ft (214 m).

No single river basin dominates North Carolina. The Hiwassee, Little Tennessee, French Broad, Watauga, and New rivers flow from the mountains westward to the Mississippi River system. East of the Blue Ridge, the Chowan, Roanoke, Tar, Neuse, Cape Fear, Yadkin, and Catawba drain the piedmont and coastal plain. The largest artificial lakes are Lake Norman on the Catawba, Lake Gaston on the Roanoke, and High Rock Lake on the Yadkin.

3CLIMATE

North Carolina has a humid, subtropical climate. Winters are short and mild, while summers are usually very sultry; spring and fall are distinct and refreshing periods of transition. In most of North Carolina, temperatures rarely go above 100°F (38°C) or fall below 10°F (-12°C), but differences in altitude and proximity to the ocean create significant local variations. Average January temperatures range from 36°F (2°C) to 48°F (9°C), with an average daily maximum January temperature of 51°F (11°C) and minimum of 29°F (-2°C). Average July temperatures range from 68°F (20°C) to 80°F (27°C), with an average daily high of 87°F (31°C) and a low of 66°F (19°C). The coldest temperature ever recorded in North Carolina was -34°F (-37°C), registered on 21 January 1985 on Mt. Mitchell; the hottest, 110°F (43°C), occurred on 21 August 1983 at Fayetteville.

In the southwestern section of the Blue Ridge, moist southerly winds rising over the mountains drop more than 80 in (203 cm) of precipitation per year, making this region the wettest in the eastern states; the other side of the mountains receives less than half that amount. Average annual precipitation at Charlotte is about 43 in (109 cm). The piedmont gets between 44 and 48 in (112 to 122 cm) of precipitation per year, while 44 to 56 in (112 to 142 cm) annually fall on the coastal plain. Average winter snowfalls vary from 50 in (127 cm) on Mt. Mitchell to only a trace amount at Cape Hatteras. In the summer, North Carolina weather responds to the Bermuda High, a pressure system centered in the mid-Atlantic. Winds from the southwest bring masses of hot humid air over the state; anticyclones connected with this system frequently lead to upper-level thermal inversions, producing a stagnant air mass that cannot disperse pollutants until cooler, drier air from Canada moves in. During late summer and early autumn, the eastern region is vulnerable to high winds and flooding from hurricanes. Hurricane Diana struck the Carolina coast in September 1984, causing $36 million in damage. A series of tornadoes in March of that year killed 61 people, injured over 1,000, and caused damage exceeding $120 million. Hurricanes Hugo (1989) and Fran (1996) caused major damage.

4FLORA AND FAUNA

North Carolina has approximately 300 species and subspecies of trees and almost 3,000 varieties of flowering plants. Coastal plant life begins with sea oats predominating on the dunes and salt meadow and cordgrass in the marshes, then gives way to wax myrtle, yaupon, red cedar, and live oak further inland. Blackwater swamps support dense stands of cypress and gum trees. Pond pine favors the peat soils of the Carolina bays, while longleaf pine and turkey oak cover the sand hills and other well-drained areas. Weeds take root when a field is abandoned in the piedmont, followed soon by loblolly, shortleaf, and Virginia pine; sweet gum and tulip poplars spring up beneath the pines, later giving way to an oak-hickory climax forest. Dogwood decorates the understory, but kudzu—a rank, weedy vine introduced from Japan as an antierosion measure in the 1930s—is a less attractive feature of the landscape. The profusion of plants reaches extraordinary proportions in the mountains. The deciduous forests on the lower slopes contain Carolina hemlock, silver bell, yellow buckeye, white basswood, sugar maple, yellow birch, tulip poplar, and beech, in addition to the common trees of the piedmont. Spruce and fir dominate the high mountain peaks. There is no true treeline in the North Carolina mountains, but unexplained treeless areas called "balds" appear on certain summits. Twenty-seven plant species were listed as threatened or endangered in 2006, including Blue Ridge goldenrod, bunched arrowhead, Heller's blazingstar, Virginia spiraea, seabeach amaranth, and rough-leaved loosestrife.

The white-tailed deer is the principal big-game animal of North Carolina, and the black bear is a tourist attraction in the Great Smoky Mountains National Park. The wild boar was introduced to the mountains during the 19th century; beavers have been reintroduced and are now the state's principal furbearers. The largest native carnivore is the bobcat.

North Carolina game birds include the bobwhite quail, mourning dove, wild turkey, and many varieties of duck and goose. Trout and smallmouth bass flourish in North Carolina's clear mountain streams, while catfish, pickerel, perch, crappie, and largemouth bass thrive in fresh water elsewhere. The sounds and surf of the coast yield channel bass, striped bass, flounder, and bluefish to anglers. Among insect pests, the pine bark beetle is a threat to the state's forests and forest industries.

The gray wolf, elk, eastern cougar, and bison are extinct in North Carolina; the American alligator, protected by the state, has returned in large numbers to eastern swamps and lakeshores. Thirty animal species (vertebrates and invertebrates) were listed by the US Fish and Wildlife Service as threatened or endangered in April 2006, including Indiana and Virginia big-eared bats, bald eagle, red-cockaded woodpecker, four species of whale, and five species of sea turtle.

5ENVIRONMENTAL PROTECTION

State actions to safeguard the environment began in 1915 with the purchase of the summit of Mt. Mitchell as North Carolina's first state park. North Carolina's citizens and officials worked actively (along with those in Tennessee) to establish the Great Smoky Mountains National Park during the 1920s, the same decade that saw the establishment of the first state agency for wildlife conservation. In 1937, a state and local program of soil and water conservation districts began to halt erosion and waste of natural resources.

Interest in environmental protection intensified during the 1970s. In 1971, the state required its own agencies to submit environmental impact statements in connection with all major project proposals; it also empowered local governments to require such statements from major private developers. Voters approved a $150 million bond issue in 1972 to assist in the construction of wastewater treatment facilities by local governments. The Coastal Management Act of 1974 mandated comprehensive land-use planning for estuaries, wetlands, beaches, and adjacent areas of environmental concern. The most controversial environmental action occurred mid-decade, when a coalition of state officials, local residents, and national environmental groups fought the proposed construction of a dam that would have flooded the New River Valley in northwestern North Carolina. Congress quashed the project when it designated the stream as a national scenic river in 1976.

Air quality in most of North Carolina's eight air-quality-control regions is good, although the industrialized areas of the piedmont and mountains experience pollution from vehicle exhausts and

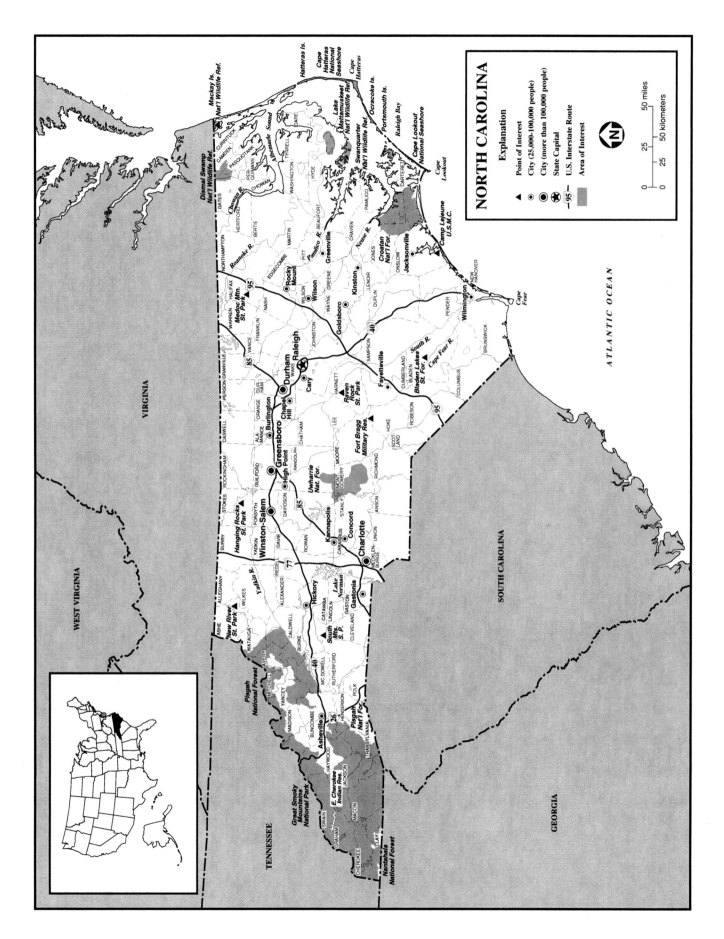

NORTH CAROLINA

Explanation

▲ Point of Interest
◉ City (25,000–100,000 people)
◉ City (more than 100,000 people)
✪ State Capital
—95— U.S. Interstate Route
▨ Area of Interest

50 miles
50 kilometers
0 25 50

North Carolina—Counties, County Seats, and County Areas and Populations

COUNTY	COUNTY SEAT	LAND AREA (SQ MI)	POPULATION (2005 EST.)	COUNTY	COUNTY SEAT	LAND AREA (SQ MI)	POPULATION (2005 EST.)
Alamance	Graham	433	140,533	Jones	Trenton	470	10,311
Alexander	Taylorsville	259	35,492	Lee	Sanford	259	55,704
Alleghany	Sparta	234	10,900	Lenoir	Kinston	402	57,961
Anson	Wadesboro	533	25,499	Lincoln	Lincolnton	298	69,851
Ashe	Jefferson	426	25,347	Macon	Franklin	517	32,148
Avery	Newland	247	17,641	Madison	Marshall	451	20,256
Beaufort	Washington	826	46,018	Martin	Williamston	461	24,643
Bertie	Windsor	701	19,480	McDowell	Marion	437	43,201
Bladen	Elizabethtown	879	32,938	Mecklenburg	Charlotte	528	796,372
Brunswick	Bolivia	861	89,162	Mitchell	Bakersville	222	15,784
Buncombe	Asheville	659	218,876	Montgomery	Troy	490	27,322
Burke	Morganton	505	89,399	Moore	Carthage	701	81,685
Cabarrus	Concord	364	150,244	Nash	Nashville	540	91,378
Caldwell	Lenoir	471	79,122	New Hanover	Wilmington	185	179,553
Camden	Camden	241	8,967	Northampton	Jackson	538	21,483
Carteret	Beaufort	525	62,525	Onslow	Jacksonville	763	152,440
Caswell	Yanceyville	427	23,608	Orange	Hillsborough	400	118,386
Catawba	Newton	396	151,641	Pamlico	Bayboro	341	12,735
Chatham	Pittsboro	708	58,002	Pasquotank	Elizabeth City	228	38,270
Cherokee	Murphy	452	25,796	Pender	Burgaw	875	46,429
Chowan	Edenton	181	14,528	Perquimans	Hertford	246	12,080
Clay	Hayesville	214	9,765	Person	Roxboro	398	37,217
Cleveland	Shelby	468	98,288	Pitt	Greenville	656	142,570
Columbus	Whiteville	939	54,746	Polk	Columbus	238	19,134
Craven	New Bern	702	90,795	Randolph	Asheboro	789	138,367
Cumberland	Fayetteville	657	304,520	Richmond	Rockingham	477	46,781
Currituck	Currituck	256	23,112	Robeson	Lumberton	949	127,586
Dare	Manteo	391	33,903	Rockingham	Wentworth	569	92,614
Davidson	Lexington	548	154,623	Rowan	Salisbury	519	135,099
Davie	Mocksville	267	39,136	Rutherford	Rutherfordton	568	63,771
Duplin	Kenansville	819	51,985	Sampson	Clinton	947	63,063
Durham	Durham	298	242,582	Scotland	Laurinburg	319	37,180
Edgecombe	Tarboro	506	54,129	Stanly	Albemarle	396	58,964
Forsyth	Winston-Salem	412	325,967	Stokes	Danbury	452	45,858
Franklin	Louisburg	494	54,429	Surry	Dobson	539	72,601
Gaston	Gastonia	357	196,137	Swain	Bryson City	526	13,167
Gates	Gatesville	338	11,224	Transylvania	Brevard	378	29,626
Graham	Robbinsville	289	8,085	Tyrrell	Columbia	407	4,157
Granville	Oxford	534	53,674	Union	Monroe	639	162,929
Greene	Snow Hill	266	20,026	Vance	Henderson	249	43,771
Guilford	Greensboro	651	443,519	Wake	Raleigh	854	748,815
Halifax	Halifax	724	56,023	Warren	Warrenton	427	19,729
Harnett	Lillington	601	103,692	Washington	Plymouth	332	13,282
Haywood	Waynesville	555	56,482	Watauga	Boone	314	42,472
Henderson	Hendersonville	375	97,217	Wayne	Goldsboro	554	114,448
Hertford	Winton	356	23,574	Wilkes	Wilkesboro	752	67,390
Hoke	Racford	391	41,016	Wilson	Wilson	374	76,281
Hyde	Swanquarter	624	5,413	Yadkin	Yadkinville	336	37,668
Iredell	Statesville	574	140,924	Yancey	Burnsville	314	18,201
Jackson	Sylva	490	35,368	**TOTALS**		**48,843**	**8,683,242**
Johnston	Smithfield	795	146,437				

coal-fired electric generating plants. Water quality ranges from extraordinary purity in numerous mountain trout streams to serious pollution in major rivers and coastal waters. Soil erosion and municipal and industrial waste discharges have drastically increased the level of dissolved solids in some piedmont streams, while runoffs from livestock pastures and nitrates leached from fertilized farmland have over stimulated the growth of algae in slow-moving eastern rivers. Pollution also has made certain areas of the coast unsafe for commercial shellfishing.

About 5.7 million acres (2.3 million hectares) of the state are wetlands; since 1997 the North Carolina Wetlands Partnership has overseen wetlands conservation. About 70% of North Car-

olina's rare and endangered plants and animals are considered wetland-dependent.

The Department of Environment, Health and Natural Resources, the state's main environmental agency, issues licenses to industries and municipalities and seeks to enforce clean air and water regulations. In 2003, 129.1 million lb of toxic chemicals were released in the state. In 2003, North Carolina had 311 hazardous waste sites listed in the US Environment Protection Agency (EPA) database, 31 of which were on the National Priorities List as of 2006, including the Barber Orchard in Waynesville and ABC One Hour Cleaners in Jacksonville. In 2005, the EPA spent over $461,000 through the Superfund program for the cleanup of hazardous waste sites in the state. The same year, federal EPA grants awarded to the state included $19.4 million for the water pollution control revolving fund and $14.5 million for the drinking water revolving fund.

6 POPULATION

North Carolina ranked 11th in population in the United States with an estimated total of 8,683,342 in 2005, an increase of 7.9% since 2000. Between 1990 and 2000, North Carolina's population grew from 6,628,637 to 8,049,313, an increase of 21.4%, making North Carolina the sixth-fastest-growing state of the decade. The population is projected to reach 10 million by 2015 and 11.4 million by 2025. The population density in 2004 was 175.4 persons per sq mi (67.7 persons per sq km). As of 2004, the state's population had a median age of 36. In the same year, 24.8% of the populace were under the age of 18 while 12.1% was age 65 or older.

At the time of the first census in 1790, North Carolina ranked third among the 13 states, with a population of 393,751, but it slipped to tenth by 1850. In the decades that followed, North Carolina grew slowly by natural increase and suffered from net out-migration, while the rest of the nation expanded rapidly. Out-migration abated after 1890, however, and North Carolina's overall growth rate in the 20th century was slightly greater than that of the nation as a whole.

Most North Carolinians live in and around a relatively large number of small and medium-sized cities and towns, many of which are concentrated in the Piedmont Crescent, between Charlotte, Greensboro, and Raleigh. Leading cities in 2004 were Charlotte, 594,359; Raleigh, 326,653; Greensboro, 231,543; Durham, 201,726; and Winston-Salem, 191,523. The Charlotte metropolitan area had an estimated 1,474,734 people in 2004.

7 ETHNIC GROUPS

North Carolina's white population is descended mostly from English settlers who arrived in the east in the 17th and early 18th centuries and from Scottish, Scots-Irish, and German immigrants who poured into the piedmont in the middle of the 18th century. Originally very distinct, these groups assimilated with one another in the first half of the 19th century to form a relatively homogeneous body of native-born white Protestants. By 1860, North Carolina had the lowest proportion of foreign-born whites of any state; more than a century later, in 1990, only 1.7% (115,077) of North Carolina residents were foreign born, mostly from Germany, the United Kingdom, and Mexico. Within the following decade, however, the foreign-born population increased dramatically, to 430,000 (5.3%) in 2000. In the same year, the estimated Hispanic and Latino population was 378,963 (4.7% of the state total), up from 161,000 (2.1%) in 1990. In 2004, 6.1% of the population was of Hispanic or Latino origin.

According to the 2000 federal census there were some 99,551 Native Americans (including Eskimos and Aleuts) living in North Carolina, the sixth-largest number in any state, and the largest number in any state east of the Mississippi. In 2004, 1.3% of the state's population was American Indian or Alaskan Native. The Lumbee of Robeson County and the surrounding area are the major Indian group. The total population of their lands in 2000, including non-Indians, was 474,100. Their origins are mysterious, but they are probably descended from many small tribes, deci-

mated by war and disease, that banded together in the Lumber River swamps in the 18th century. The Lumbee have no language other than English, have no traditional tribal culture, and are not recognized by the Bureau of Indian Affairs.

The Haliwa, Waccamaw Siouan, Coharie, and Person County Indians are smaller groups in eastern North Carolina who share the Lumbee's predicament. The only North Carolina Indians with a reservation, a tribal language and culture, and federal recognition are the Cherokee, whose ancestors hid in the Smokies when the majority of their tribe was removed to Indian Territory (now Oklahoma) in 1838. The North Carolina Cherokee have remained in the mountains ever since, living in a community that now centers on the Qualla Boundary Reservation near Great Smoky Mountains National Park.

The 1,737,545 blacks in North Carolina made up 21.6% of its total population in 2000. In 2004, 21.8% of the state's population was black. Black slaves came to North Carolina from the 17th century through the early 19th; like most white immigrants, they usually arrived in North Carolina after previous residence in other colonies. Although black slaves performed a wide variety of tasks and lived in every county of the state, they were most often field laborers on the large farms in the eastern region. The distribution of black population today still reflects the patterns of plantation agriculture: the coastal plain contains a much higher than average concentration of black inhabitants. The overall proportion of blacks in North Carolina rose throughout the 19th century but fell steadily in the 20th, until about 1970, as hundreds of thousands migrated to northern and western states. Some of the earliest demonstrations of the civil rights movement, most notably a 1960 lunch counter sit-in at Greensboro, took place in the state.

In 2000 North Carolina's Asian population numbered 113,689, including 26,197 Asian Indians, 18,984 Chinese, 15,596 Vietnamese, 12,600 Koreans, 9,592 Filipinos, and 7,093 Hmong. Pacific Islanders numbered 3,983. In 2004, 1.7% of the state's population was Asian, and 0.1% Pacific Islander. That year, 1% of the population reported origin of two or more races.

8 LANGUAGES

Although most of the original Cherokee Indians were removed to Indian Territory around 1838, descendants of those who resisted and remained have formed a strong Indian community in the Appalachian foothills. Among Indian place-names are Pamlico, Nantahala, and Cullasaja.

Many regional language features are widespread, but others sharply distinguish two subregions: the western half, including the piedmont and the Appalachian Highlands, and the eastern coastal plain. Terms common to South Midland and Southern speech occur throughout the state: both *dog irons* and *firedogs* (andirons), *bucket* (pail), *spicket* (spigot), *seesaw*, *comfort* (tied and filled bedcover), *pullybone* (wishbone), *ground squirrel* (chipmunk), *branch* (small stream), *light bread* (white bread), *polecat* (skunk), and *carry* (escort). Also common are *greasy* with the /z/ sound, *new* as /nyoo/ and *due* as /dyoo/, *swallow it* as /swaller it/, *can't* rhyming with *paint*, *poor* with the vowel sound /aw/, and *horse* and *hoarse* with different vowels.

Distinct to the western region are *snake feeder* (dragonfly), *blinds* (roller shades), *poke* (paper bag), *redworm* (earthworm), a *little piece* (a short distance), *plum peach* (clingstone peach), *sick on the stomach* (also found in the Pee Dee River Valley), *boiled* as /bawrld/, *fog* as /fawg/, *Mary* sounding like *merry* and *bulge* with the vowel of *good*. Setting off eastern North Carolina are *lightwood* (kindling), *mosquito hawk* (dragonfly), *earthworm, press peach* (instead of plum peach), *you-all* as second-person plural, and *sick in the stomach*. Distinctive eastern pronunciations include the loss of /r/ after a vowel, *fog* as /fagh/, *scarce* and *Mary* with the vowel of *gate, bulge* with the vowel sound /ah/. Along the coast, peanuts are *goobers* and a screech owl is a *shivering owl*.

In 2000, 6,909,648 North Carolinians—92% of the population five years of age and older—spoke only English at home, down from 96.1% in 1990.

The following table gives selected statistics from the 2000 Census for language spoken at home by persons five years old and over. The category "African languages" includes Amharic, Ibo, Twi, Yoruba, Bantu, Swahili, and Somali.

LANGUAGE	NUMBER	PERCENT
Population 5 years and over	**7,513,165**	**100.0**
Speak only English	6,909,648	92.0
Speak a language other than English	603,517	8.0
Speak a language other than English	**603,517**	**8.0**
Spanish or Spanish Creole	378,942	5.0
French (incl. Patois, Cajun)	33,201	0.4
German	28,520	0.4
Chinese	15,698	0.2
Vietnamese	13,594	0.2
Korean	11,386	0.2
Arabic	10,834	0.1
African languages	9,181	0.1
Miao, Hmong	7,493	0.1
Tagalog	6,521	0.1
Greek	6,404	0.1
Japanese	6,317	0.1
Italian	6,233	0.1

9RELIGIONS

The Church of England was the established church of colonial North Carolina but was never a dominant force among the early immigrants. Scottish Presbyterians settled in the upper Cape Fear Valley, and Scots-Irish Presbyterians occupied the piedmont after 1757. Lutheran Evangelical Reformed Germans later moved into the Yadkin and Catawba valleys of the same region. The Moravians, a German sect, founded the town of Salem (later merging with Winston to become Winston-Salem) in 1766 as the center of their utopian community at Wachovia. Methodist circuit riders and Separate Baptists missionaries won thousands of converts among blacks and whites, strengthening their appeal in the Great Revival of 1801. In the subsequent generation, a powerful evangelical consensus dominated popular culture. After the Civil War, blacks left the white congregations to found their own churches, but the overall strength of Protestantism persisted. When many North Carolinians left their farms at the end of the 19th century, they moved to mill villages that were well supplied with churches, often at the mill owners' expense.

The majority of North Carolinians are Protestant. The largest denomination in 2000 was the Southern Baptist Convention which reported 1,512,058 adherents; there were 28,169 newly baptized members reported in 2002. The United Methodist Church claimed 529,272 members in 2004 and the Presbyterian Church USA had 203,647 in 2000. The next largest Protestant denominations in 2000 were the Evangelical Lutheran Church in Ameri-

ca, 88,830 adherents; the Church of God (Cleveland, Tennessee), 81,037; the Episcopal Church, 80,068; the United Church of Christ, 50,088; the International Pentecostal Holiness Church, 50,265; the Original Free Will Baptists, 46,020; Independent Charismatic Churches, 42,559. In 2006, the Church of Jesus Christ of Latter-day Saints (Mormons) reported a statewide membership of 66,497 in 135 congregations; a Mormon temple was built in Raleigh-Durham in 1999. In 2000, the state had an estimated 25,545 Jews, and about 20,137 Muslims. There are still about 18,180 Moravians in the state. Over 4.3 million people (about 54.6% of the population) were not counted as members of any religious organization. In 2004, there were 319,492 Roman Catholics in the state.

The Advent Christian Church General Conference of America, representing 306 local Advent Christian churches in the United States and Canada, is based in Charlotte. The Billy Graham Evangelistic Association has its headquarters in Charlotte as well.

10TRANSPORTATION

The history of North Carolina's growth and prosperity has been inextricably linked to the history of transportation in the state, especially the history of highway development. North Carolina has the largest state-maintained highway system in the nation. To provide and maintain this system, North Carolina relies strictly on user-related sources of funds, such as motor fuel taxes and state license and registration fees.

The early settlers widened and improved the Indian trails into bridle trails and then dirt roads. In colonial times, waterways were the avenues of commerce. Almost all products moved on rivers and streams within the state, and most manufactured goods arrived by sea. When it became necessary to transport goods farther inland, local laws were passed which directed that a road be built to the nearest landing. By this piecemeal process, the state slowly acquired a system of dirt roads.

As the population of the state grew, so did the demand for roads. From 1830 onward, a new element was introduced into the picture—railroads, representing the newest and most efficient means of travel. In the 1850s, transportation took yet another turn when the state invested in plank roads, which did not prove financially practical.

With the coming of the Civil War, transportation improvements in North Carolina ground to a halt. During the war, the existing railroads were used heavily for military purposes. Renovations and improvements were delayed during the early years of the Reconstruction period because of poor economic conditions in the state. By 1870, the state gave up on assistance to railroads and left their further development to private companies. In 1895, the Southern Railway acquired a 99-year lease on the piedmont section of the North Carolina Railroad while eastern routes fell to the Atlantic Coast Line and the Seaboard Air Line Railway.

In the early years of the 20th century, the principal emphasis was on the further development of the investor-owned railroads. In 1911, there was 4,608 mi (7,414 km) of railroad right-of-way in the state, and by 1937 this figure had increased, if only slightly, to a total of 4,763 (7,663 km). By 2003, railroad track in North Carolina had fallen to 3,344 route mi (5,383 km). Two Class I railroads operate in the state, along with 13 local and eight switching and terminal lines. As of 2006, Amtrak provided service to 12 stations in the state via its New York to Charlotte Carolinian and its daily Charlotte to Raleigh Piedmont trains.

By the second decade of the century, the building of roads received new emphasis. It was during this period that North Carolina earned the label "the Good Roads State." In 1915, the Highway Commission was created, and in 1921 the General Assembly approved a $40 million state highway bond to construct a system of hard-surface roads connecting each of the 100 county seats with all of the others. The new hard-surface roads soon proved ideal for automobiles and trucks. More highway bonds were approved to pay for a statewide system of paved highways, giving the state more roads by the end of the decade than any other southern state except Texas. The state government took over the county roads in 1931.

In 2004, North Carolina had 102,666 mi (165,529 km) of public roads. There were some 6.195 million motor vehicles registered in the state that same year, including around 3.627 million automobiles, approximately 2,458 million trucks, and some 10,000 buses. Licensed drivers numbered 6,122,137 in 2004. The major interstate highways are I-95, which stretches north–south across the coastal plain, and I-85, which parallels it across the piedmont. I-40 leads from the mountains to the coast at Wilmington, and I-26 and I-77 handle north–south traffic in the western section. I-73 and I-74 add 325 mi (523 km) of interstate highway and will handle north–south traffic in the eastern section of the state.

Transportation 2001, a plan to speed up highway construction and complete key corridors, eliminate the road maintenance backlog, and develop a master plan for public transportation, was unveiled in 1994. A $950 million highway bond was approved by North Carolina voters in 1996 to accelerate construction of urban loops and intrastates and to pave secondary roads. Transit 2001, the master plan to improve public transportation was unveiled in February 1997. A major incentive has been placed on high-speed rail service from Raleigh to Charlotte, reducing travel time to two hours by 2000.

There are nine types of public transportation currently operating in North Carolina: human service transportation, rural general public transportation, urban transit, regional transit, vanpool and carpool programs, inter-city buses, inter-city rail passenger service, pupil transportation, and passenger ferry service. There are 17 publicly owned urban transit systems operating in North Carolina. More than three million North Carolinians have access to rural public transportation services operating in approximately 45 counties and towns.

The Atlantic Intracoastal Waterway follows sounds, rivers, and canals down the entire length of eastern North Carolina. The North Carolina ferry system, the second largest in the nation, transports more than 23 million passengers and 820,000 vehicles each year. Twenty-four ferry vessels move passengers and vehicles between the state's coastal communities. Seventeen of the vessels feature the colors and seals of North Carolina's public and private colleges and universities to promote the ferry system. There are major ports at Morehead City and Wilmington. In 2004, Morehead City handled 3.407 million tons of cargo, while Wilmington handled 7.888 million tons. In 2003, waterborne shipments totaled 10.231 million tons. In 2004, North Carolina had 1,152 mi (1,854 km) of navigable inland waterways.

In 2005, North Carolina had a total of 382 public and private-use aviation-related facilities. This included 305 airports, 74 heliports, and 3 STOLports (Short Take-Off and Landing). The state's two busiest airports are Charlotte-Douglas International and Raleigh-Durham International. In 2004, Charlotte–Douglas had 12,499,476 passengers enplaned, making it the 19th-busiest airport in the United States, while Raleigh-Durham had 4,371,883 enplanements that same year, making it the 43rd-busiest airport in the United States. Other major airports were at Asheville, Fayetteville, Greensboro, Kinston, Wilmington, and Winston-Salem.

11 HISTORY

Paleo-Indian peoples came to North Carolina about 10,000 years ago. These early inhabitants hunted game with spears and gathered nuts, roots, berries, and freshwater mollusks. Around 500 BC, with the invention of pottery and the development of agriculture, the Woodland Culture began to emerge. The Woodland way of life—growing corn, beans, and squash, and hunting game with bows and arrows—prevailed on the North Carolina coast until the Europeans arrived.

Living in North Carolina by this time were Indians of the Algonkian-, Siouan-, and Iroquoian-language families. The Roanoke, Chowanoc, Hatteras, Meherrin, and other Algonkian-speaking tribes of the coast had probably lived in the area the longest; some of them belonged to the Powhatan Confederacy of Virginia. The Siouan groups were related to larger tribes of the Great Plains. Of the Iroquoian-speakers, the Cherokee probably had lived in the mountains since before the beginning of the Christian era, while the Tuscarora had entered the upper coastal plain somewhat later. After their defeat by the colonists in the Tuscarora War of 1711–13, the tribe fled to what is now upper New York State to become the sixth member of the Iroquois Confederacy.

Contact with whites brought war, disease, and enslavement of the Algonkian and Siouan tribes. Banding together, the survivors probably gave rise to the present-day Lumbee and to the other Indian groups of eastern North Carolina. The Cherokee tried to avoid the fate of the coastal tribes by selectively adopting aspects of white culture. In 1838, however, the federal government responded to the demands of land-hungry whites by expelling most of the Cherokee to Indian Territory along the so-called Trail of Tears.

European penetration began when Giovanni da Verrazano, a Florentine navigator in French service, discovered the North Carolina coast in 1524. Don Lucas Vásquez de Ayllón led an unsuccessful Spanish attempt to settle near the mouth of the Cape Fear River two years later. Hernando de Soto tramped over the North Carolina mountains in 1540 in an unsuccessful search for gold, but the Spanish made no permanent contribution to the colonization of North Carolina.

Sixty years after Verrazano's voyage, North Carolina became the scene of England's first experiment in American empire. Sir Walter Raleigh, a courtier of Queen Elizabeth I, gained the queen's permission to send out explorers to the New World. They landed on the Outer Banks in 1584 and returned with reports so enthusiastic that Raleigh decided to sponsor a colony on Roanoke Island between Albemarle and Pamlico sounds. After a second expedition returned without founding a permanent settlement, Raleigh sent out a third group in 1587 under John White as governor. The passengers included White's daughter Eleanor and her husband, Ananias Dare. Shortly after landfall, Eleanor gave birth to Virginia Dare, the first child born of English parents in the New World. Several weeks later, White returned to England for supplies, but the threat of the Spanish Armada prevented his prompt return. By the time White got back to Roanoke in 1590, he found no trace of the settlers—only the word "Croatoan" carved on a tree. The fate of this "Lost Colony" has never been satisfactorily explained.

The next English venture focused on the more accessible Jamestown colony in the Chesapeake Bay area of Virginia. England tended to ignore the southern region until 1629, when Charles I laid out the territory between 30° and 36°N, named it Carolana for himself, and granted it to his attorney general, Sir Robert Heath. Heath made no attempt to people his domain, however, and Carolana remained empty of whites until stragglers drifted in from the mid-17th century onward. Events in England transformed Virginia's outpost into a separate colony. After the execution of Charles I in 1649, England had no ruling monarch until a party of noblemen invited Charles II back to England in 1660. Charles thanked eight of his benefactors three years later by making them lord proprietors of the province, now called Carolina. The vast new region eventually stretched from northern Florida to the modern boundary between North Carolina and Virginia, and from the Atlantic to the Pacific Ocean.

The proprietors divided Carolina into three counties and appointed a governor for each one. Albemarle County embraced the existing settlements in northeastern North Carolina near the waters of Albemarle Sound; it was the only one that developed a government within the present state boundaries. From the beginning, relations between the older pioneers and their newly imposed government were stormy. The English philosopher John Locke drew up the Fundamental Constitutions of Carolina, but his political blueprints proved unworkable. The proprietors' arbitrary efforts to collect royal customs touched off factional violence, culminating in Culpepper's Rebellion of 1677, one of the first American uprisings against a corrupt regime.

For a few years afterward, local residents had a more representative government, until the proprietors attempted to strengthen the establishment of the Anglican Church in the colony. In 1711, Cary's Rebellion was touched off by laws passed against the colony's Quakers. During the confusion, Tuscarora Indians launched a war against the white intruders on their lands. The whites won the Tuscarora War in 1713 with assistance from South Carolina, but political weakness in the north persisted. Proprietary officials openly consorted with pirates—including the notorious Edward Teach, alias Blackbeard—and royal inspectors questioned the fitness of proprietary government. South Carolina officially split off in 1719 and received a royal governor in 1721. Ten years later, all but one of the proprietors relinquished their rights for £2,500 each, and North Carolina became a royal colony. The remaining proprietor, Lord Granville, gave up his governing rights but retained ownership of one-eighth of the original grant; the Granville District thus included more than half of the unsettled territory in the North Carolina colony.

In the decades that followed, thousands of new settlers poured into North Carolina; by 1775 the population had swollen to 345,000, making North Carolina the fourth—most populous colony. Germans and Scots-Irish trekked down the Great Wagon Road from Pennsylvania to the Piedmont. Scottish Highlanders spread over the upper Cape Fear Valley as more Englishmen filled up the coastal plain. Backcountry settlers practiced self-sufficient farming, but eastern North Carolinians used slave labor to carve out rice and tobacco plantations. The westerners were often exploited by an eastern-dominated colonial assembly that sent corrupt and overbearing officials to govern them. Organizing in 1768 and calling themselves Regulators, unhappy westerners first petitioned for redress and then took up arms. Royal Governor William Tryon used eastern militia to crush the Regulators in a two-hour pitched battle at Alamance Creek in 1771.

The eastern leaders who dominated the assembly opposed all challenges to their authority, whether from the Regulators or from the British ministry. When England tightened its colonial administration, North Carolinians joined their fellow colonists in protests against the Stamp Act and similar impositions by Parliament. Meeting at Halifax in April 1776, the North Carolina provincial congress resolved in favor of American independence, the first colonial representative body to do so. Years later, citizens of Mecklenburg County recalled a gathering in 1775 during which their region declared independence, but subsequent historians have not verified their claim. The two dates on the North Carolina state flag nevertheless commemorate the Halifax Resolves and the "Mecklenburg Declaration of Independence."

Support for Britain appeared among recent Scottish immigrants, who answered the call to aid the royal governor but were ambushed by patriot militia at Moore's Creek Bridge on 27 February 1776. The incident effectively prevented a planned British invasion of the South. There was little further military action in North Carolina until late in the War for Independence, when Gen. Charles Cornwallis invaded the state from South Carolina in the fall of 1780. Guerrilla bands harassed his troops, and North Carolina militia wiped out a Loyalist detachment at King's Mountain. Pursuing the elusive American army under Gen. Nathanael Greene, Cornwallis won a costly victory at Guilford Courthouse in March 1781 but could neither eliminate his rival nor pacify the countryside. For the rest of 1781, Cornwallis wearied his men in marches and countermarches across North Carolina and Virginia before he finally succumbed to a trap set at Yorktown, Va., by an American army and a French fleet.

Numerous problems beset the new state. The government had a dire need of money, but when the victors sought to pay debts by selling land confiscated from the Loyalists, conservative lawyers objected strenuously, and a bitter political controversy ensued. Suspicious of outside control, North Carolina leaders hesitated before joining the Union. The state waited until November 1789 to ratify the US Constitution—a delay that helped stimulate the movement for adoption of a Bill of Rights. North Carolina relinquished its lands beyond the Great Smokies in 1789 (after an unsuccessful attempt by settlers to create a new state called Franklin), and thousands of North Carolinians migrated to the new western territories. The state did not share in the general prosperity of the early federal period. Poor transportation facilities hampered all efforts to expand commercial agriculture, and illiteracy remained widespread. North Carolina society came to appear so backward that some observers nicknamed it the "Rip Van Winkle state."

In 1815, state senator Archibald D. Murphey of Orange County began to press for public schools and for improved transportation to open up the Piedmont. Most eastern planters resisted Murphey's suggestions, partly because they refused to be taxed for the benefit of the westerners and partly because they feared the destabilizing social effects of reform. As long as the east controlled the General Assembly, the ideas of Murphey and his sympathizers had little practical impact, but in 1835, as a result of reforms in the state constitution, the west obtained reapportionment and the political climate changed. North Carolina initiated a program of state aid to railroads and other public works, and established the first state—supported system of common schools in the South.

Like other southern whites, North Carolina's white majority feared for the security of slavery under a national Republican administration, but North Carolinians reacted to the election of Abraham Lincoln with caution. When South Carolina and six other states seceded and formed the Confederate States of America in 1861, North Carolina refused to join, instead making a futile attempt to work for a peaceful settlement of the issue. However, after the outbreak of hostilities at Ft. Sumter, S.C., and Lincoln's call for troops in April 1861, neutrality disappeared and public opinion swung to the Confederate side. North Carolina became the last state to withdraw from the Union, joining the Confederacy on 20 May 1861.

North Carolina provided more troops to the Confederacy than any other state, and its losses added up to more than one-fourth of the total for the entire South, but support for the war was mixed. State leaders resisted the centralizing tendencies of the Richmond government, and even Governor Zebulon B. Vance opposed the Confederacy's conscription policies. North Carolina became a haven for deserters from the front lines in Virginia. William W. Holden, a popular Raleigh editor, organized a peace movement when defeat appeared inevitable, and Unionist sentiment flourished in the mountain counties; nevertheless, most white North Carolinians stood by Vance and the dying Confederate cause. At the war's end, Gen. Joseph E. Johnston surrendered the last major Confederate army to Gen. William T. Sherman at Bennett House near Hillsborough on 26 April 1865.

Reconstruction was marked by a bitter political and social struggle in North Carolina. United in the Conservative Party, most of the prewar slaveholding elite fought to preserve as much as possible of the former system, but a Republican coalition of blacks and nonslaveholding white Unionists defended freedmen's rights and instituted democratic reforms for the benefit of both races. After writing a new constitution in 1868, Republicans elected Holden as governor, but native whites fought back with violence and intimidation under the robes of the Ku Klux Klan. Holden's efforts to restore order were ineffectual, and when the Conservatives recaptured the General Assembly in 1870, they impeached him and removed him from office. Election of a Conservative governor in 1876 signaled the end of the Reconstruction era.

Once in power, the Conservatives—or Democrats, as they renamed themselves—slashed public services and enacted legislation to guarantee the power of landlords over tenants and sharecroppers. They cooperated with the consolidation of railroads under northern ownership, and they supported a massive drive to build cotton mills on the swiftly flowing streams of the Piedmont. By 1880, industry had surpassed its prewar level. But it was not until 1900 that blacks and their white allies were entirely eliminated as contenders for political power.

As the Industrial Revolution gained ground in North Carolina, small farmers protested their steadily worsening condition. The Populist Party expressed their demands for reform, and for a brief period in the 1890s shared power with the Republican Party in the Fusion movement. Under the leadership of Charles Brantley Aycock, conservative Democrats fought back with virulent denunciations of "Negro rule" and a call for white supremacy. In 1900, voters elected Aycock governor and approved a constitutional amendment that barred all illiterates from voting, except for those whose ancestors had voted before 1867. This literacy test and "grandfather clause" effectively disenfranchised blacks, while providing a temporary loophole for uneducated whites. To safeguard white rights after 1908 (the constitutional limit for registration under the grandfather clause), Aycock promised substantial improvements in the school system to put an end to white illiteracy.

In the decades after Aycock's election, an alliance of business interests and moderate-to-conservative Democrats dominated North Carolina politics. The industrial triumvirate of textile, tobacco, and furniture manufacturers, joined by banks and insurance companies, controlled the state's economy. The Republican Party shrank to a small remnant among mountain whites as blacks were forced out of the electorate.

In the years after World War II, North Carolina took its place in the booming Sunbelt economy. The development of Research Triangle Park—equidistant from the educational facilities of Duke University, North Carolina State University, and the University of North Carolina at Chapel Hill—provided a home for dozens of scientific and technology laboratories for government and business. New industries, some of them financed by foreign capital, appeared in formerly rural areas, and a prolonged population drain was effectively reversed.

The process of development has not been smooth or uniform, however. The late 1980s and early 1990s saw a shift in employment patterns as financial and high-technology industries boomed while jobs in the state's traditional industries, notably textiles and tobacco, declined. North Carolina possessed both the largest percentage of manufacturing jobs in the country and the lowest manufacturing wages. In 1990, 30% of all jobs paid annual wages below the poverty line for a family of four, resulting in 13% of North Carolinians living below the nationally established poverty line. Despite widespread prosperity in the 1990s, North Carolina was one of only 15 states where poverty—and child poverty—were on the rise. The rate had climbed to 14% by 1998, and to 15.1% by 2003–04 (measured as a two-year average). The national poverty rate in 2003–04 was 12.6%.

The excellence of many of North Carolina's universities contrasted with the inferior education provided by its primary and secondary public schools. North Carolina students' SAT scores placed them last nationally in 1989. In the ongoing effort to improve the public school system, in 2000 Democratic Governor Jim Hunt's top two priorities were raising teacher pay by 6.5% and funding the Smart Start (early childhood education) program. But Hunt's stance was not popular with the state's workers, who were lobbying the governor and the General Assembly for pay raises.

Racial tensions have created divisions within the state, which has one of the highest levels of Ku Klux Klan activity in the country. While Charlotte integrated its schools peacefully in 1971 through court-ordered busing, the militancy of black activists in the late 1960s and early 1970s provoked a white backlash. That backlash, along with the identification of the Democratic party in the early 1970s with liberal causes and with opposition to the Vietnam War, helped the conservative wing of the Republican party gain popularity in a state whose six military bases had given it a hawkish tradition. In 1972, North Carolina elected its first Republican US senator (Jesse A. Helms) and governor (James E. Holshouser Jr.) since Fusion days, and Republican strength continued to build into the mid-1990s. But after 1998 elections, the state was leaning toward a more bipartisan representation: Democratic candidate John Edwards took the state's second Senate seat while conservative Republican Helms retained the other; and voters sent seven Republicans and five Democrats to represent them in the US House. In 2004, John Edwards was the Democratic Party's vice-presidential nominee; he and Democratic presidential candidate John Kerry were defeated by President George W. Bush and Vice-President Richard B. Cheney by a margin of 3 million popular votes. As of 2005, North Carolina was represented by two Republican senators, Elizabeth Dole and Richard Burr, but Democrat Michael Easley remained governor.

Rising crime rates were among the leading public policy issues in the 1990s. The state legislature enacted laws imposing tough penalties on adults who supply guns to minors, and mandating life imprisonment without parole for three-time violent offenders.

Mother Nature has posed serious problems for North Carolinians in recent times. In September 1999, successive hurricanes moved onshore, water logging the low-lying eastern part of the state. The worst flooding in North Carolina history was intensified by more rainfall in the weeks that followed. The death toll climbed to 40 while property damages and agricultural losses rose. Cleanup of the state's waterways, which were polluted by waste from pigs and other livestock as well as from flooded sewage plants, remained a major health concern. In January 2000 the same region was blanketed in record snowfalls, adding further hardships to those who were struggling to recover. A month earlier, in an emergency legislative session, the General Assembly approved Governor Jim Hunt's plan to send $836 million to flood victims. By July 2000 the federal government had approved more than $1 billion in aid to the state. But it was estimated that the conditions had put thousands of farmers permanently out of business. North Carolina experienced a harsh winter in 2002–03, with some of the heaviest snowfalls since 1989.

The state's agricultural producers were also facing the declining demand for tobacco. The documented health hazards of smoking, state and federal excise taxes, ongoing lawsuits, and declining exports combined to cut cigarette production (also hurting the state's manufacturing sector in the process). With Kentucky, North Carolina farmers produced more than 65% of the total US crop. The state's historical dependency on the cash crop caused lawmakers to allocate half the funds from the national tobacco settlement to tobacco communities—to support educational and job training programs, provide employment assistance for farmers and displaced laborers, fund rural health care and social service programs, and invest in local public works and economic development projects to attract new businesses to areas that had been dependent on tobacco. The other half of the settlement was evenly divided between statewide health care and a trust fund for (former) tobacco growers and farm laborers.

Governor Mike Easley set his 2003 executive agenda on education, proposing a state lottery to fund education. In August 2005, Easley signed into law the North Carolina State Lottery Act, which enacted the North Carolina Education Lottery. One hundred percent of the net lottery proceeds will go to educational expenses, including reduced class sizes in early grades, academic pre-kindergarten programs, school construction, and scholarships for needy college and university students.

In 2005, Easley also focused on bringing more highly-skilled and high-tech jobs to the state, providing a quality transportation system for all of North Carolina, enacting strong Patients Bill of Rights legislation, helping seniors cope with the high costs of prescription drugs, promoting land and water conservation, and providing a strong environmental enforcement program.

12 STATE GOVERNMENT

North Carolina has operated under three constitutions, adopted in 1776, 1868, and 1971, respectively. The first was drafted hurriedly under wartime pressures and contained several inconsistencies and undemocratic features. The second, a product of Reconstruction, was written by native white Republicans and a sprinkling of blacks and northern-born Republicans. When conservative whites regained power, they left the basic framework of this constitution intact, though they added the literacy test, poll tax, and grandfather clause to it.

A century after the Civil War, the document had become unwieldy and partially obsolete. A constitutional study commission submitted to the General Assembly in 1969 a rewritten constitution, which the electorate ratified, as amended, in 1971. As of January 2005, the document had been amended a total of 34 times. One amendment permits the governor and lieutenant governor to serve a maximum of two successive four-year terms.

Under the 1971 constitution, the General Assembly consists of a 50-member Senate and a 120-member House of Representatives. Regular sessions are held in odd-numbered years, with the provision that the legislature may (and in practice, does) divide to meet in even-numbered years. Sessions begin in January and are not formally limited in length. Special sessions may be called by three-fifths petition of each house. Senators must be at least 25 years old and must have been residents of the state for at least two years and residents of their districts for at least one year prior to election. Representatives must have lived in their district for at least a year; the constitution establishes 21 as the minimum age for elective office. All members of the General Assembly serve two-year terms. The legislative salary was $13,951 in 2004, unchanged from 1999.

The governor and lieutenant governor (who run separately) must be 30 years old and a qualified voter; each must have been a US citizen for five years and a state resident for two. As of December 2004, the governor's salary was $121,391. North Carolina's chief executive has powers of appointment, supervision, veto, and budgetary recommendation. The voters also elect a secretary of state, treasurer, auditor, superintendent of public instruction, attorney general, and commissioners of agriculture, insurance, and labor; all serve four-year terms. These officials preside over their respective departments and sit with the governor and lieutenant governor as the council of state. The governor appoints the heads of the other executive departments.

Bills become law when they have passed three readings in each house of the General Assembly, and take effect 60 days after adjournment. Bills that are not signed or vetoed by the governor become law after 10 days when the legislature is in session and after 30 days if the legislature adjourns. A three-fifths vote of the elected members in each house is required to override a gubernatorial veto. Constitutional amendments may be proposed by a convention called by a two-thirds vote of both houses and a majority of the voters, or may be submitted directly to the voters by a three-fifths consent of each house. In either case, the proposed amendments must be ratified by a popular majority before becoming part of the constitution.

To vote in North Carolina a person must be a US citizen, at least 18 years old, a resident of the state and county for at least 30 days prior to election day, and not registered to vote in another state. Restrictions apply to convicted felons.

13 POLITICAL PARTIES

Prior to the Civil War, Whigs and Democrats were the two major political groups in North Carolina. The Republican Party emerged during Reconstruction as a coalition of newly enfranchised blacks, northern immigrants, and disaffected native whites, especially from non-slaveholding areas in the mountains. The opposing Conservative Party, representing a coalition of antebellum Democrats and former Whigs, became the Democratic Party after winning the governorship in 1876; from that time and for most of the 20th century, North Carolina was practically a one-party state.

Beginning in the 1930s, however, as blacks reentered the electorate as supporters of the New Deal and the liberal measures associated with Democratic presidents, the Republican Party attracted new white members who objected to national Democratic policies. Republican presidential candidates picked up strength in the 1950s and 1960s, and Richard Nixon carried North Carolina in 1968 and 1972, when Republicans also succeeded in electing Governor James E. Holshouser Jr., and US Senator Jesse A. Helms. The Watergate scandal cut short this movement toward a revitalized two-party system, and in 1976, Jimmy Carter became the first Democratic presidential candidate to carry the state since 1964.

Republican presidential candidate Ronald Reagan narrowly carried North Carolina in 1980, and a second Republican senator, John P. East, was elected that year. In 1984, the Republican Party had its best election year in North Carolina. Reagan won the state by a landslide, Helms won a third term—defeating two-term Governor James B. Hunt in the most expensive race to date in Senate history (more than $26 million was spent)—and Republican James G. Martin, a US representative, was elected governor, succeeding Hunt. In 1990, Helms was reelected to the Senate, defeating black mayor Harvey Gantt in a bitterly contested race. In 1996 Gantt challenged Helms again, and once again Helms was the victor. Helms subsequently announced he would not run for reelection in 2002, and Republican Elizabeth H. Dole won his seat. In 2000 and 2004, Republican George W. Bush won 56% of the presidential vote, to Democrat Al Gore's 43% (2000) and Democrat John Kerry's 44% (2004).

But by the mid-1990s the states' Democrats were influential again. In 1993 Democrat James B. Hunt returned to the governor's office after a hiatus of eight years. He was elected to his third term (having served the first two between 1977 and 1985) in the 1992 election, and went on to a fourth term following the 1996 elections. Having served the limit, Hunt was leaving the gubernatorial race open for 2000, and Democrat Mike Easley won the governorship in 2000. In 1998 elections the second US Senate seat, which had been won by Republican Lauch Faircloth in 1992, was won by

North Carolina Presidential Vote by Political Parties, 1948–2004

YEAR	ELECTORAL VOTE	NORTH CAROLINA WINNER	DEMOCRAT	REPUBLICAN	STATES' RIGHTS DEMOCRAT	PROGRESSIVE
1948	14	*Truman (D)	459,070	258,572	69,652	3,915
1952	14	Stevenson (D)	652,803	558,107	—	—
1956	14	Stevenson (D)	590,530	575,069	—	—
1960	14	*Kennedy (D)	713,136	655,420	—	—
1964	13	*Johnson (D)	800,139	624,841	—	—
						AMERICAN IND.
1968	13	*Nixon (R)	464,113	627,192	—	496,188
						AMERICAN
1972	13	*Nixon (R)	438,705	1,054,889	—	25,018
					LIBERTARIAN	
1976	13	Carter (D)	927,365	741,960	2,219	5,607
1980	13	*Reagan (R)	875,635	915,018	9,677	—
1984	13	*Reagan (R)	824,287	1,346,481	3,794	—
						NEW ALLIANCE
1988	13	*Bush (R)	890,167	1,237,258	1,263	5,682
						IND. (Perot)
1992	14	Bush (R)	1,114,042	1,134,661	5,171	357,864
1996	14	Dole (R)	1,107,849	1,225,938	8,740	168,059
						REFORM
2000	14	*Bush, G. W. (R)	1,257,692	1,631,163	12,307	8,874
						WRITE-IN (Nader)
2004	15	*Bush, G. W. (R)	1,525,849	1,961,166	11,731	1,805

*Won US presidential election.

Democrat John Edwards. In 2003 Edwards was running for president and had announced he would not seek reelection in 2004; the seat he vacated was won by Republican Richard Burr.

In 2004 there were 5,537,000 registered voters. In 1998, 53% of registered voters were Democratic, 34% Republican, and 14% unaffiliated or members of other parties. The state had 15 electoral votes in the 2005 presidential election, an increase of 1 vote over 2000.

Following the 2004 elections, 6 of North Carolina's 13 US Representatives were Democrats and 7 were Republicans. In mid-2005 the State Assembly had 63 Democrats and 57 Republicans, and there were 21 Republicans and 29 Democrats in the state Senate.

Minor parties have had a marked influence on the state. George Wallace's American Independent Party won 496,188 votes in 1968, placing second with more than 31% of the total vote. In 1992, Independent Ross Perot captured 14% of the vote.

¹⁴LOCAL GOVERNMENT

As of 2005, North Carolina had 100 counties, 541 municipalities, and 319 special districts. That year the state has 120 public school systems.

Counties have been the basis of local government in North Carolina for more than 300 years, and are still the primary governmental units for most citizens. All counties are led by boards of commissioners; commissioners serve either two- or four-year terms, and most are elected at large rather than by district. Most boards elect their own chairman from among their members, but voters in some counties choose a chairman separately. More than half the counties employ a county manager to supervise day-to-day operations of county government. Other elected officials are the sheriff, register of deeds, and the school board. Counties are subdivided into townships, but these are for administrative convenience only; they do not exercise any independent government functions.

County and municipal governments share many functions, but the precise allocation of authority varies in each case. Although the city of Charlotte and Mecklenburg County share a common school system, most often schools, streets, sewers, garbage collection, police and fire protection, and other services are handled separately. Most cities use the council-manager form of government, with council members elected from the city at large. Proliferation of suburban governments was hampered by a 1972 constitutional amendment that forbids the incorporation of a new town or city within 1 mi (1.6 km) of a city of 5,000–9,999 people, within 3 mi (4.8 km) of a city of 10,000–24,999, within 4 mi (6.4 km) of a city of 25,000–49,999, and within 5 mi (8 km) of a city of 50,000 or more unless the General Assembly acts to do so by a three-fifths vote of all members of each house.

In 2005, local government accounted for about 348,179 full-time (or equivalent) employment positions.

¹⁵STATE SERVICES

To address the continuing threat of terrorism and to work with the federal Department of Homeland Security, homeland security in North Carolina operates under executive order; the public safety director/secretary is designated as the state homeland security advisor.

The Department of Public Instruction administers state aid to local public school systems, a board of governors directs the 16 state-supported institutions of higher education, and the Department of Community Colleges administers the 58 community colleges. The Department of Cultural Resources offers a variety of educational and enrichment services to the public, maintaining historical sites, operating two major state museums, funding the North Carolina Symphony, and providing for the State Library. The Department of Transportation plans, builds, and maintains state highways; registers motor vehicles; develops airport facilities; administers public transportation activities; and operates 24 ferries.

Within the Department of Health and Human Resources, the Division of Mental Health, Developmental Disabilities, and Substance Abuse Services operates psychiatric hospitals, mental retardation centers, and alcoholic rehabilitation centers; it also coordinates mental health programs that include community mental health centers, group homes for the developmentally disabled and emotionally disturbed, shelter workshops, halfway houses, a special-care facility, and reeducation programs for emotionally disturbed children and adolescents. The Division of Social Services administers public assistance programs, and other divisions license medical facilities, promote public health, administer programs for juvenile delinquents and the vocationally handicapped, and operate a school for the blind and visually impaired and schools for the deaf. The Department of Agriculture and Consumer Services protects the consumer.

The Department of Crime Control and Public Safety includes the Highway Patrol and the National Guard, while the Department of Correction manages the prison system. Local law enforcement agencies receive assistance from the Department of Justice's State Bureau of Investigation. The Department of Environment and Natural Resources addresses the issues of air and water quality, coastal management, environmental health, forest and land resources, marine fisheries, wildlife resources, waste management, and the Museum of Natural Sciences. The Department of Labor administers the state Occupational Safety and Health Act; inspects boilers, elevators, amusement rides, mines, and quarries; offers conciliation, mediation, and arbitration services to settle labor disputes; and enforces state laws governing child labor, minimum wages, maximum working hours, and uniform wage payment.

¹⁶JUDICIAL SYSTEM

North Carolina's general court of justice is a unified judicial system that includes appellate courts (Court of Appeals) and trial courts (Superior Court). District court judges are elected to four-year terms. Judges above that level are elected for eight years.

The state's highest court is the North Carolina Supreme Court, which consists of a chief justice and six associate justices. It hears cases from the Court of Appeals as well as certain cases from lower courts. The Court of Appeals comprises 12 judges who hear cases in 3-judge panels. Superior courts, in 44 districts, have original jurisdiction in most major civil and criminal cases. There are 99 superior court judges appointed by the governor to eight-year terms. All Superior Court justices rotate between the districts within their divisions. District courts try misdemeanors, civil cases involving less than $5,000, and all domestic cases. They have no juries in criminal cases, but these cases may be appealed to Superior Court and be given a jury trial de novo; in civil cases, jury trial is provided on demand.

As of 31 December 2004, a total of 35,434 prisoners were held in North Carolina's state and federal prisons, an increase from 33,560 of 5.6% from the previous year. As of year-end 2004, a total of 2,430 inmates were female, up from 2,256 or 7.7% from the year before. Among sentenced prisoners (one year or more), North Carolina had an incarceration rate of 357 per 100,000 population in 2004.

According to the Federal Bureau of Investigation, North Carolina in 2004, had a violent crime rate (murder/nonnegligent manslaughter; forcible rape; robbery; aggravated assault) of 447.8 reported incidents per 100,000 population, or a total of 38,244 reported incidents. Crimes against property (burglary; larceny/theft; and motor vehicle theft) in that same year totaled 355,328 reported incidents or 4,160.2 reported incidents per 100,000 people. North Carolina has a death penalty, of which lethal injection is the sole method of execution. From 1976 through 5 May 2006, the state has carried out 42 executions, of which five were carried out in 2005 and three in 2006 (as of 5 May 2006). As of 1 January 2006, North Carolina had 190 inmates on death row.

In 1976, the US Supreme Court invalidated North Carolina's death penalty statute and the sentences of all inmates then on death row reverted to life imprisonment. However, the state passed a new capital punishment statute in 1977 which apparently assuaged the Court's objections. Two persons were executed in 1984—the state's first executions since 1961. One of the prisoners executed that year, Velma Barfield, was the first woman executed in the United States since 1962 and the first in North Carolina since 1944.

In 2003, North Carolina spent $354,328,968 on homeland security, an average of $43 per state resident.

17 ARMED FORCES

North Carolina holds the headquarters of the 3rd Army at Ft. Bragg in Fayetteville. By population, Fort Bragg is the largest Army installation in the world, providing a home to almost 10% of the Army's active component forces. Approximately 43,000 military and 8,000 civilian personnel work at Fort Bragg. Fort Bragg hosts America's only airborne corps and airborne division, the "Green Berets" of the Special Operations Command, and the Army's largest support command. The 82nd Airborne Division soldiers and others make 100,000 parachute jumps each year at Fort Bragg. The Marine Corps Camp Lejeune in Jacksonville is home base for the II Marine Expeditionary Force, 2nd Marine Division, 2nd Force Service Support Group and other combat units and support commands with a population of more than 41,000 Marine and Sailors. The Marine Corps air stations at Cherry Point and New River and Seymour Johnson Air Force Base in Goldsboro are the state's other important military installations. North Carolina firms received more than $2.2 billion in defense contract awards in 2004. Additionally, defense payroll outlays, including retired military pay, were $6.5 billion. In 2002, there were 94,296 active duty military personnel and 16,444 civilian personnel stationed in North Carolina, most of whom were at Ft. Bragg.

There were 767,051 veterans living in North Carolina in 2003. Of these, 90,599 saw service in World War II; 77,617 in the Korean conflict; 225,498 during the Vietnam era; and 140,170 in the

Persian Gulf War. For the fiscal year 2004, total Veterans Affairs expenditures in New Carolina exceeded $2.0 billion.

As of 31 October 2004, the North Carolina State Highway Patrol employed 1,686 full-time sworn officers.

18 MIGRATION

For most of the state's history, more people have moved away every decade than have moved into the state, and population growth has come only from net natural increase. In 1850, one-third of all free, native-born North Carolinians lived outside the state, chiefly in Tennessee, Georgia, Indiana, and Alabama. The state suffered a net loss of population from migration in every decade from 1870 to 1970.

Before 1890, the emigration rate was higher among whites than among blacks; since then, the reverse has been true, but the number of whites moving into North Carolina did not exceed the number of white emigrants until the 1960s. Between 1940 and 1970, 539,000 more blacks left North Carolina than moved into the state; most of these emigrants sought homes in the North and West. After 1970, however, black out-migration abruptly slackened as economic conditions in eastern North Carolina improved. Net migration to North Carolina was estimated at 278,000 (sixth among the states) from 1970 to 1980, at 83,000 (ninth among the states) from 1980 to 1983; and 347,000 (fifth among the states) from 1985 to 1990. Between 1990 and 1998, the state had net gains of 501,000 in domestic migration and 49,000 in international migration. In 1998, 6,415 foreign immigrants arrived in North Carolina. The state's overall population increased 13.8% between 1990 and 1998. In the period 2000–05, net international migration was 158,224 and net internal migration was 232,448, for a net gain of 390,672 people.

19 INTERGOVERNMENTAL COOPERATION

North Carolina adheres to at least 23 interstate compacts, including 4 that promote regional planning and development. The oldest of the 4, establishing the Board of Control for Southern Regional Education, pools the resources of southern states for the support of graduate and professional schools. The Southeastern Forest Fire Protection Compact promotes regional forest conservation, while the Southern States Energy Board fosters cooperation in nuclear power development. The Southern Growth Policies Board, formed in 1971 at the suggestion of former North Carolina Governor Terry Sanford, collects and publishes data for planning purposes from its headquarters in Research Triangle Park. The Tennessee Valley Authority operates four dams in western North Carolina to aid in flood control, generate hydroelectric power, and assist navigation downstream on the Tennessee River; most of the electricity generated is exported to Tennessee. North Caroline also belongs to the Mid-Atlantic Fishery Management Council, the Atlantic States Marine Fisheries Commission, the Ohio River Basin Commission, and the Appalachian Regional Commission. Total federal grants in fiscal year 2005 were $9.657 billion, an estimated $10.285 billion in fiscal year 2006, and an estimated $10.8 billion in fiscal year 2007.

20 ECONOMY

North Carolina's economy was dominated by agriculture until the closing decades of the 19th century, with tobacco the major cash crop. Today, tobacco is still the central factor in the economy of the coastal plain. In the piedmont, industrialization accelerated after 1880 when falling crop prices made farming less attractive. During the "cotton mill crusade" of the late 19th and early 20th centuries, local capitalists put spinning or weaving mills on swift streams throughout the region, until nearly every hamlet had its own factory. Under the leadership of James B. Duke, the American Tobacco Co. (now American Brands, with headquarters in New York City) expanded from its Durham headquarters during this same period to control, for a time, virtually the entire US market for smoking products. After native businessmen had established a successful textile boom, New England firms moved south in an effort to cut costs, and the piedmont became a center of southern industrial development.

As more and more Tar Heels left agriculture for the factory, their per capita income rose from 47% of the national average in 1930 to slightly less than 100% of the national average in 2000. The biggest employers are the textile and furniture industries. State government has made a vigorous effort to recruit outside investment and to improve the state's industrial mix. Major new firms now produce electrical equipment, processed foods, technical instruments, fabricated metals, plastics, and chemicals. The greatest industrial growth, however, has come not from wholly new industries, but from fields related to industries that were firmly established. Apparel manufacture spread across eastern North Carolina as an obvious extension of the textile industry, while other new firms produced chemicals and machinery for the textile and furniture business. Manufacturing remains the dominant sector in the state's economy, peaking at an output of nearly $62 billion (23.8% of total output) in 1999, as the overall state economy grew at a rate of 8.8% in 1998 and 8% in 1999. A decline in manufacturing output of 4.9% by 2001 was accompanied by declining overall growth rates, of 4.7% in 2000, and 0.98% in the national recession of 2001. While the nation's unemployment rose 1.4 percentage points between the third quarter 1999 and third quarter 2002, the rise in North Carolina over this period was 6.4%, reflecting mainly layoffs in its manufacturing sector.

North Carolina's gross state product (GSP) in 2004 totaled $336.398 billion, of which manufacturing (durable and nondurable goods) accounted for $72.295 billion or 21.4% of GSP, followed by the real estate sector, at $32.848 billion (9.7% of GSP), and healthcare and social assistance services, at $19.862 billion (5.9% of GSP). In that same year, there were an estimated 671,810 small businesses in North Carolina. Of the 182,598 businesses that had employees, an estimated total of 179,008 or 98% were small companies. An estimated 23,387 new businesses were established in the state in 2004, up 4.1% from the year before. Business terminations that same year came to 22,055, down 5.1% from 2003. There were 486 business bankruptcies in 2004, down 8% from the previous year. In 2005, the state's personal bankruptcy (Chapter 7 and Chapter 13) filing rate was 464 filings per 100,000 people, ranking North Carolina 33rd in the nation.

21INCOME

In 2005 North Carolina had a gross state product (GSP) of $345 billion which accounted for 2.8% of the nation's gross domestic product and placed the state at number 12 in highest GSP among the 50 states and the District of Columbia.

According to the Bureau of Economic Analysis, in 2004 North Carolina had a per capita personal income (PCPI) of $29,322. This ranked 38th in the United States and was 89% of the national average of $33,050. The 1994–2004 average annual growth rate of PCPI was 3.7%. North Carolina had a total personal income (TPI) of $250,426,537,000, which ranked 13th in the United States and reflected an increase of 6.7% from 2003. The 1994–2004 average annual growth rate of TPI was 5.5%. Earnings of persons employed in North Carolina increased from $181,840,239,000 in 2003 to $193,812,229,000 in 2004, an increase of 6.6%. The 2003–04 national change was 6.3%.

The US Census Bureau reports that the three-year average median household income for 2002–04 in 2004 dollars was $39,000 compared to a national average of $44,473. During the same period an estimated 14.8% of the population was below the poverty line as compared to 12.4% nationwide.

22LABOR

According to the Bureau of Labor Statistics (BLS), in April 2006 the seasonally adjusted civilian labor force in North Carolina numbered 4,396,000, with approximately 189,800 workers unemployed, yielding an unemployment rate of 4.3%, compared to the national average of 4.7% for the same period. Preliminary data for the same period placed nonfarm employment at 3,962,200. Since the beginning of the BLS data series in 1976, the highest unemployment rate recorded in North Carolina was 10.2% in February 1983. The historical low was 3.1% in April 1999. Preliminary nonfarm employment data by occupation for April 2006 showed that approximately 6% of the labor force was employed in construction; 14.1% in manufacturing; 18.4% in trade, transportation, and public utilities; 5.1% in financial activities; 11.3% in professional and business services; 11.9% in education and health services; 9.1% in leisure and hospitality services; and 17% in government.

North Carolina working conditions have brought the state considerable notoriety over the years. North Carolina is one of 22 states with a right-to-work law, and public officials are legally barred from negotiating a collective bargaining agreement.

The US Department of Labor's Bureau of Labor Statistics reported that in 2005, a total of 107,000 of North Carolina's 3,631,000 employed wage and salary workers were formal members of a union. This represented 2.9% of those so employed, up from 2.7% in 2004, well below the national average of 12% and the second-lowest in the United States. Overall in 2005, a total of 143,000 workers (3.9%) in North Carolina were covered by a union or employee association contract, which includes those workers who reported no union affiliation. North Carolina is one of 22 states with a right-to-work law.

As of 1 March 2006, North Carolina had a state-mandated minimum wage rate of $5.15 per hour. In 2004, women in the state accounted for 46.3% of the employed civilian labor force.

23AGRICULTURE

Farm marketings in North Carolina totaled $7.7 billion in 2005, eighth among the 50 states, with 34% from crop marketings. North Carolina led the nation in the production of tobacco and sweet potatoes, ranked fifth in peanuts, and was also a leading producer of corn, grapes, pecans, apples, tomatoes, and soybeans. Farm life plays an important role in the culture of the state.

The number of farms fell from 301,000 in 1950 to 52,000 in 2004, while the number of acres in farms declined from 17,800,000 to 9,000,000 (7,203,000 to 3,642,000 hectares). At 173 acres (70 hectares), the average North Carolina farm was only 39% the size of the average US farm— a statistic that in part reflects the smaller acreage requirements of tobacco, the state's principal crop. The relatively large number of family farm owner-operators who depend on a modest tobacco allotment to make their small acreages profitable is the basis for North Carolina's opposition to the US government's antismoking campaign and its fight to preserve tobacco price supports.

Although farm employment continues to decline, a significant share of North Carolina jobs—perhaps more than one-third—are still linked to agriculture either directly or indirectly. North Carolina's most heavily agricultural counties are massed in the coastal plain, the center of tobacco, corn, and soybean production, along with a bank of northern piedmont counties on the Virginia border. Virtually all peanut production is in the eastern part of the state, while tobacco, corn, and soybean production spills over into the piedmont. Cotton is grown in scattered counties along the South Carolina border and in a band leading northward across the coastal plain. Beans, tomatoes, cucumbers, strawberries, and blueberries are commercial crops in selected mountain and coastal plain locations. Apples are important to the economy of the mountains, and the sand hills are a center of peach cultivation.

In 2004, tobacco production was 351,630,000 lb (159,496,685 kg), 40% of US production. Production and value data for North Carolina's other principal crops were as follows: corn, 86,580,000 bushels, $203,463,000; soybeans, 51,000,000 bushels, $257,550,000; peanuts, 357,000,000 lb, $77,112,000; and sweet potatoes, 6,880,000 hundredweight, $92,880,000.

24 ANIMAL HUSBANDRY

North Carolina farms and ranches had an estimated 870,000 cattle and calves in 2005, valued at $661.2 million. In 2004, the state had around 9.8 million hogs and pigs, valued at $823.2 million. During 2003, North Carolina led the nation in turkey production with 1.1 billion lb (0.5 billion kg) of turkey, worth $397.8 million; the state was fourth in broiler production with 4.3 billion lb (2 billion kg), worth $1.51 billion; egg production totaled 2.52 billion eggs, worth $241.8 million. Milk cows numbered 61,000 in 2003 and they produced 1.04 million lb (0.48 million kg) of milk.

25 FISHING

In 2004, the commercial catch in North Carolina totaled over 136.4 million lb (62 million kg) valued at $77.1 million. The record landing for the state was in 1981, with a total of 432 million lb. Flounder, menhaden, and sea trout are the most valuable finfish; shrimp, crabs, and clams are the most sought-after shellfish. In 2004, the state catch for hard blue crab accounted for 20% of the total national supply, the second-highest percentage in the nation (after Louisiana). The port at Beaufort-Morehead City ranked 19th in the nation for volume, with a catch of 63.5 million lb (28.9 million kg).

In 2003, there were 31 processing and 78 wholesale plants in the state with about 1,471 employees. In 2001, the commercial fleet had 773 vessels.

North Carolina lakes and streams are stocked in part by three state fish hatcheries and two national hatcheries within the state (Edenton and KcKinney Lake). In 2004, the state issued 692,497 sport fishing licenses.

26 FORESTRY

As of 2004, forests covered 18,269,000 acres (6,179,000 hectares) in North Carolina, or about 59% of the state's land area. North Carolina's forests constitute 2.5% of all US forestland, and 97% of the state's wooded areas have commercial value. The largest tracts are found along the coast and in the Western Mountains, where most counties are more than 70% tree-covered. Hardwoods make up 53% of the state's forests. Mixed stands of oak and pine account for an additional 14%. The remaining 33% is pine and other conifers. More than 90% of the acreage harvested for timber is reforested.

National forests cover 6% of North Carolina's timberlands, and state and local governments own another 2%. The remainder is privately owned. In the days of wooden sailing vessels, North Carolina pine trees supplied large quantities of "naval stores"—tar, pitch, and turpentine for waterproofing and other nautical purposes. Today, the state produces mainly saw logs, pulpwood, veneer logs, and Christmas trees.

In 2004, lumber production totaled 2.62 billion board feet, eighth in the United States and 5.3% of national production.

27 MINING

According to data from the US Geological Survey (USGS), the value of nonfuel mineral production by North Carolina in 2004 was $805 million, an increase from 2003 of about 9.7%. The USGS data ranked North Carolina as 21st among the 50 states by the total value of its nonfuel mineral production, accounting for about 2% of total US output.

According to the data for 2004, crushed stone was the state's top nonfuel mineral produced, accounting for 68% by value of all nonfuel mineral output that year. It was followed by phosphate rock, construction sand and gravel, industrial sand and gravel, feldspar, dimension stone, common clays and mica. By volume, North Carolina was the leading state in the production of feldspar, common clays, mica, olivine, and pyrophyllite, of which the state was the sole producer. The state also ranked third in phosphate rock output, seventh in the production of industrial sand and gravel, and eighth in crushed stone.

Crushed stone production in 2004 totaled 72.3 million metric tons and was valued at $548 million, while construction sand and gravel output that year totaled 11.5 million metric tons, with a value of $59.7 million. Industrial sand and gravel production in 2004 totaled 1.630 million metric tons and was valued at $29 million. Feldspar output totaled 351,000 metric tons and was valued at $20.5 million. Dimension stone production in 2004 came to 43,000 metric tons and was valued at $18.2 million.

North Carolina in 2004 was ranked 11th in the production (by value) of gemstones.

28 ENERGY AND POWER

As of 2003, North Carolina had 111 electrical power service providers, of which 72 were publicly owned and 32 were cooperatives. Of the remainder, three were investor owned, one was federally operated and three were owners of independent generators that sold directly to customers. As of that same year there were 4,365,692 retail customers. Of that total, 2,934,296 received their power from investor-owned service providers. Cooperatives accounted for 892,553 customers, while publicly owned providers had 538,836 customers. There were four federal customers and three were independent generator or "facility" customers.

Total net summer generating capability by the state's electrical generating plants in 2003 stood at 27.263 million kW, with total production that same year at 127.582 billion kWh. Of the total amount generated, 92.8% came from electric utilities, with the remainder coming from independent producers and combined heat and power service providers. The largest portion of all electric power generated, 74.776 billion kWh (58.6%), came from natural gas fired plants, with nuclear power generation in second place at 40.906 billion kWh (32.1%) and hydroelectric plants in third at 7.200 billion kWh (5.6%). Other renewable power sources, pumped storage facilities, petroleum and natural gas fired plants, and other types of generation accounted for the remainder.

As of 2006, North Carolina had three operating nuclear power stations: the Brunswick plant in Brunswick County; the McGuire plant near Charlotte; and the Shearon-Harris plant near Raleigh.

No petroleum or natural gas has been found in North Carolina, but major companies have expressed interest in offshore drilling. The state has no refineries. There is also no coal mining, and proven coal reserves are minor, at only 10.7 million short tons. One short ton equals 2,000 lb (0.907 metric tons).

29 INDUSTRY

North Carolina has had a predominantly industrial economy for most of the 20th century. Today, the state is a major manufacturer of textiles, cigarettes, and furniture, as well as of chemicals and allied products, industrial machinery, food products, electronics/electrical equipment, and rubber and plastics products.

The industrial regions of North Carolina spread out from the piedmont cities. Roughly speaking, each movement outward represents a step down in the predominant level of skills and wages and a step closer to the primary processing of raw materials.

According to the US Census Bureau's Annual Survey of Manufactures (ASM) for 2004, North Carolina's manufacturing sector covered some 20 product subsectors. The shipment value of all products manufactured in the state that same year was $163.838 billion. Of that total, chemical manufacturing accounted for the largest share at $26.387 billion. It was followed by beverage and tobacco product manufacturing at $24.029 billion; food manufacturing at $15.294 billion; transportation equipment manufacturing at $14.360 billion; and machinery manufacturing at $9.664 billion.

In 2004, a total of 550,217 people in North Carolina were employed in the state's manufacturing sector, according to the ASM. Of that total, 411,087 were actual production workers. In terms of total employment, the furniture and related product manufacturing industry accounted for the largest portion of all manufacturing employees at 59,457, with 48,753 actual production workers. It was followed by food manufacturing at 54,848 employees (41,503 actual production workers); textile mills at 52,459 employees (44,442 actual production workers); plastics and rubber products manufacturing at 39,711 employees (30,816 actual produc-

tion workers); and fabricated metal product manufacturing with 38,355 employees (29,699 actual production workers).

ASM data for 2004 showed that North Carolina's manufacturing sector paid $19.861 billion in wages. Of that amount, the chemical manufacturing sector accounted for the largest share at $1.882 billion. It was followed by furniture and related product manufacturing at $1.632 billion; food manufacturing at $1.558 billion; textile mills at $1.509 billion; and computer and electronic product manufacturing at $1.488 billion.

30 COMMERCE

According to the 2002 Census of Wholesale Trade, North Carolina's wholesale trade sector had sales that year totaling $104.3 billion from 11,913 establishments. Wholesalers of durable goods accounted for 7,300 establishments, followed by nondurable goods wholesalers at 3,535 and electronic markets, agents, and brokers accounting for 1,078 establishments. Sales by durable goods wholesalers in 2002 totaled $45.1 billion, while wholesalers of nondurable goods saw sales of $43.3 billion. Electronic markets, agents, and brokers in the wholesale trade industry had sales of $15.8 billion.

In the 2002 Census of Retail Trade, North Carolina was listed as having 35,851 retail establishments with sales of $88.8 billion. The leading types of retail businesses by number of establishments were: gasoline stations (4,818); motor vehicle and motor vehicle parts dealers (4,589); clothing and clothing accessories stores (4,508); miscellaneous store retailers (4,044); and food and beverage stores (3,814). In terms of sales, motor vehicle and motor vehicle parts dealers accounted for the largest share of retail sales at $24.1 billion, followed by food and beverage stores at $12.7 billion; general merchandise stores at $12.2 billion; and gasoline stations at $8.3 billion. A total of 435,421 people were employed by the retail sector in North Carolina that year.

The state ports at Wilmington and Morehead City handle a growing volume of international trade. In 2005, North Carolina exported $19.4 billion worth of its goods to foreign markets (14th in the United States).

31 CONSUMER PROTECTION

Consumer protection issues in North Carolina are the responsibility of the Consumer Protection Division, which is a function of the state's Attorney General, both of which are part of the North Carolina Department of Justice. The Division has as its function the protection of North Carolina consumers from unfair and deceptive trade practices and from dishonest and unethical business competition. Although it assists in the resolution of disputes, investigates cases of consumer fraud, and initiates action to halt proscribed trade practices, it does not represent individual consumers in court. It also represents the public before the North Carolina Utilities Commission.

When dealing with consumer protection issues, the state's Attorney General can initiate civil and to a limited extent, criminal proceedings; represent the state before state and federal regulatory agencies; administer consumer protection and education programs; handle formal consumer complaints; and exercise broad subpoena powers. In antitrust actions, the Attorney General's Office can act on behalf of those consumers who are incapable of acting on their own; initiate damage actions on behalf of the state in state courts; initiate criminal proceedings; and represent counties, cities and other governmental entities in recovering civil damages under state or federal law.

The offices of the Consumer Protection Division are located in Raleigh.

³²BANKING

As of June 2005, North Carolina had 108 insured banks, savings and loans, and saving banks, plus 84 state-chartered and 48 federally chartered credit unions (CUs). Excluding the CUs, the Charlotte-Gastonia-Concord market area accounted for the largest portion of the state's financial institutions and deposits in 2004, with 43 institutions and $90.216 billion in deposits. As of June 2005, CUs accounted for 3.5% of all assets held by all financial institutions in the state, or some $21.984 billion. Banks, savings and loans, and savings banks collectively accounted for the remaining 96.5% or $607.160 billion in assets held.

In 2004, the median net interest margin (the difference between the lower rates offered to savers and the higher rates charged on loans) was 3.67%, up from 3.65% in 2003. The median percentage of past-due/nonaccrual loans to total loans in 2004 was 1.23%, down from 1.58% in 2003.

Regulation of state-chartered banks and other state-chartered financial institutions is the responsibility of the Office of the Commissioner of Banks and the North Carolina Banking Commission.

³³INSURANCE

In 2004, there were over 6.5 million individual life insurance policies in force, with a total value of over $390 billion; total value for all categories of life insurance (individual, group, and credit) was over $604 billion. The average coverage amount is $59,300 per policy holder. Death benefits paid that year totaled $1.66 billion.

As of 2003, there were 70 property and casualty and 6 life and health insurance companies domiciled in the state. In 2004, direct premiums for property and casualty insurance totaled over $10.6 billion. That year, there were 109,097 flood insurance policies in force in the state, with a total value of $19.4 billion.

In 2004, 52% of state residents held employment-based health insurance policies, 5% held individual policies, and 24% were covered under Medicare and Medicaid; 17% of residents were uninsured. In 2003, employee contributions for employment-based health coverage averaged at 16% for single coverage and 28% for family coverage. The state offers an 18-month health benefits expansion program for small-firm employees in connection with the Consolidated Omnibus Budget Reconciliation Act (COBRA, 1986), a health insurance program for those who lose employment-based coverage due to termination or reduction of work hours.

In 2003, there were over 6.2 million auto insurance policies in effect for private passenger cars. Of those, 23% (over 1.4 million) were issued through the shared market, a system of insurance companies assigned by the state to offer coverage to high risk drivers. Of the 50 states and the District of Columbia, North Carolina has the highest percentage of insureds in the shared market. Required minimum coverage includes bodily injury liability of up to $30,000 per individual and $60,000 for all persons injured in an accident, as well as property damage liability of $25,000. In 2003,

the average expenditure per vehicle for insurance coverage was $604.75.

³⁴SECURITIES

There are no securities exchanges in North Carolina. The Securities Division of the Office of Secretary of State is authorized to protect the public against fraudulent issues and sellers of securities. In 2005, there were 3,240 personal financial advisers employed in the state and 4,720 securities, commodities, and financial services sales agents. In 2004, there were over 167 publicly traded companies within the state, with over 65 NASDAQ companies, 39 NYSE listings, and 6 AMEX listings. In 2006, the state had 14 Fortune 500 companies; Bank of America Corp. (based in Charlotte) ranked first in the state and 12th in the nation with revenues of over $83.9 billion, followed by Lowe's, based in Mooresville, and Wachovia Corp., Duke Energy, and Nucor, all based in Charlotte. All five of these companies are listed on the NYSE.

³⁵PUBLIC FINANCE

The North Carolina budget is prepared biennially by the governor and reviewed annually by the Office of State Budget and Management, in consultation with the Advisory Budget Commission, an independent agency composed of five gubernatorial appointees, five members from the Senate, and five from the House of Representatives. It is then submitted to the General Assembly for amendment and approval. The fiscal year (FY) runs from 1 July to 30 June.

Fiscal year 2006 general funds were estimated at $17.4 billion for resources and $17.3 billion for expenditures. In fiscal year 2004, federal government grants to North Carolina were $12.6 billion.

³⁶TAXATION

In 2005, North Carolina collected $18,640 million in tax revenues or $2,147 per capita, which placed it 25th among the 50 states in per capita tax burden. The national average was $2,192 per capita. Sales taxes accounted for 24.7% of the total; selective sales taxes, 16.2%; individual income taxes, 45.2%; corporate income taxes, 6.8%; and other taxes, 7.1%.

As of 1 January 2006, North Carolina had four individual income tax brackets ranging from 6.0 to 8.25%. The state taxes corporations at a flat rate of 6.9%.

In 2004, local property taxes amounted to $6,093,170,000 or $713 per capita. The per capita amount ranks the state 38th highest nationally. North Carolina does not collect property taxes at the state level.

North Carolina taxes retail sales at a rate of 4.50%. In addition to the state tax, local taxes on retail sales can reach as much as 3%, making for a potential total tax on retail sales of 7.50%. Food purchased for consumption off-premises is exempt from state tax, but subject to local taxes. The tax on cigarettes is 30 cents per pack, which ranks 45th among the 50 states and the District of Columbia. North Carolina taxes gasoline at 30.15 cents per gallon. This is in addition to the 18.4 cents per gallon federal tax on gasoline.

According to the Tax Foundation, for every federal tax dollar sent to Washington in 2004, North Carolina citizens received $1.10 in federal spending.

North Carolina—State Government Finances

(Dollar amounts in thousands. Per capita amounts in dollars.)

	AMOUNT	PER CAPITA
Total Revenue	44,371,161	5,195.69
General revenue	32,951,167	3,858.45
Intergovernmental revenue	11,608,798	1,359.34
Taxes	16,836,454	1,971.48
General sales	4,351,822	509.58
Selective sales	2,917,379	341.61
License taxes	1,017,247	119.12
Individual income tax	7,510,978	879.51
Corporate income tax	837,085	98.02
Other taxes	201,943	23.65
Current charges	2,794,075	327.18
Miscellaneous general revenue	1,711,840	200.45
Utility revenue	–	–
Liquor store revenue	–	–
Insurance trust revenue	11,419,994	1,337.24
Total expenditure	37,050,568	4,338.47
Intergovernmental expenditure	10,326,743	1,209.22
Direct expenditure	26,723,825	3,129.25
Current operation	18,871,108	2,209.73
Capital outlay	2,961,676	346.80
Insurance benefits and repayments	3,939,093	461.25
Assistance and subsidies	511,322	59.87
Interest on debt	440,626	51.60
Exhibit: Salaries and wages	6,142,326	719.24
Total expenditure	37,050,568	4,338.47
General expenditure	33,009,076	3,865.23
Intergovernmental expenditure	10,326,743	1,209.22
Direct expenditure	22,682,333	2,656.01
General expenditures, by function:		
Education	13,290,923	1,556.31
Public welfare	8,755,747	1,025.26
Hospitals	1,107,043	129.63
Health	1,274,446	149.23
Highways	3,198,090	374.48
Police protection	378,278	44.29
Correction	1,041,109	121.91
Natural resources	516,959	60.53
Parks and recreation	151,009	17.68
Government administration	764,436	89.51
Interest on general debt	440,626	51.60
Other and unallocable	2,090,410	244.78
Utility expenditure	102,399	11.99
Liquor store expenditure	–	–
Insurance trust expenditure	3,939,093	461.25
Debt at end of fiscal year	14,102,900	1,651.39
Cash and security holdings	73,703,368	8,630.37

Abbreviations and symbols: – zero or rounds to zero; (NA) not available; (X) not applicable.

SOURCE: *U.S. Census Bureau, Governments Division, 2004 Survey of State Government Finances,* January 2006.

37 ECONOMIC POLICY

North Carolina's government has actively stimulated economic growth ever since the beginning of the 19th century. During the administration of Governor Luther H. Hodges (1954–61), the state began to recruit outside investment directly, developing such forward-looking facilities as Research Triangle Park. Since the 1970s, other policies and legislation have been aimed at the fostering of development in rural areas, where per capita income is lower and unemployment is higher than elsewhere in the state. In 1996, under the administration of Governor James B. Hunt, the General Assembly adopted the William S. Lee Quality Jobs and Business Expansion Act. The act groups North Carolina's counties into Enterprise Tiers, and provides for graduated tax credit amounts, depending upon Enterprise Tier location, for specific company activities including job creation, machinery and equipment investment, worker training, and research and development. The North Carolina Economic Development Board's goal has been to help the transformation of the economy from manufacturing to more high-technology enterprises.

The state also actively participates in programs involving industrial revenue bonds, state and federally assisted loan and grant programs, business energy loans, and assistance to local communities with shell buildings that can be customized to meet the needs of a company in a shorter period of time. The Business and Industry ServiCenter is a one-stop information and resource center for businesses.

38 HEALTH

Health conditions and health care facilities in North Carolina vary widely from region to region. In the larger cities-and especially in proximity to the excellent medical schools at Duke University and the University of North Carolina at Chapel Hill, quality health care is as readily available as anywhere in the United States.

The infant mortality rate in October 2005 was estimated at 8.4 per 1,000 live births. The birth rate in 2003 was 14.1 per 1,000 population. The abortion rate stood at 21 per 1,000 women in 2000. In 2003, about 84.5% of pregnant woman received prenatal care beginning in the first trimester. In 2004, approximately 82% of children received routine immunizations before the age of three.

The crude death rate in 2003 was 8.7 deaths per 1,000 population. As of 2002, the death rates for major causes of death (per 100,000 resident population) were: heart disease, 222.6; cancer, 194.8; cerebrovascular diseases, 63.2; chronic lower respiratory diseases, 44.2; and diabetes, 26.5. The mortality rate from HIV infection was 5.8 per 100,000 population. In 2004, the reported AIDS case rate was at about 13.3 per 100,000 population. In 2002, about 54.5% of the population was considered overweight or obese. As of 2004, about 23.1% of state residents were smokers.

In 2003, North Carolina had 113 community hospitals with about 23,300 beds. There were about 987,000 patient admissions that year and 14.5 million outpatient visits. The average daily inpatient census was about 16,600 patients. The average cost per day for hospital care was $1,020. Also in 2003, there were about 423 certified nursing facilities in the state with 43,022 beds and an overall occupancy rate of about 88.2%. In 2004, it was estimated that about 69.4% of all state residents had received some type of dental care within the year. North Carolina had 252 physicians per 100,000 resident population in 2004 and 831 nurses per 100,000 in 2005. In 2004, there was a total of 3,903 dentists in the state.

The state acted to increase the supply of doctors in eastern North Carolina in the 1970s by the establishment of a new medical school at East Carolina University in Greenville. Medical schools and superior medical research facilities are also located at Duke University Medical Center in Durham, UNC Hospitals at the University of North Carolina in Chapel Hill, and the Bowman

Gray School of Medicine at Wake Forest University in Winston-Salem. In 2005, Duke University Medical Center ranked eighth on the Honor Roll of Best Hospitals 2005 by *U.S. News & World Report*. In the same report, the hospital ranked fourth in the nation for best care in heart disease and heart surgery, sixth for best care in cancer, and in the top 20 for pediatric care.

About 17% of state residents were enrolled in Medicaid programs in 2003; 14% were enrolled in Medicare programs in 2004. Approximately 17% of the state population was uninsured in 2004. In 2003, state health care expenditures totaled $10.5 million.

39 SOCIAL WELFARE

In 2004, about 273,000 people received unemployment benefits, with the average weekly unemployment benefit at $256. For 2005, the estimated average monthly participation in the food stamp program included about 799,747 persons (343,397 households); the average monthly benefit was about $89.21 per person. That year, the total of benefits paid through the state for the food stamp program was about $856 million.

Temporary Assistance for Needy Families (TANF), the system of federal welfare assistance that officially replaced Aid to Families with Dependent Children (AFDC) in 1997, was reauthorized through the Deficit Reduction Act of 2005. TANF is funded through federal block grants that are divided among the states based on an equation involving the number of recipients in each state. North Carolina's TANF program is called Work First. In 2004, the state program had 77,000 recipients; state and federal expenditures on this TANF program totaled $136 million in fiscal year 2003.

In December 2004, Social Security benefits were paid to 1,467,400 North Carolina residents. This number included 910,400 retired workers, 131,150 widows and widowers, 236,680 disabled workers, 59,010 spouses, and 130,160 children. Social Security beneficiaries represented 17.2% of the total state population and 94.7% of the state's population age 65 and older. Retired workers received an average monthly payment of $934; widows and widowers, $828; disabled workers, $877; and spouses, $464. Payments for children of retired workers averaged $480 per month; children of deceased workers, $606; and children of disabled workers, $263. Federal Supplemental Security Income payments in December 2004 went to 195,654 North Carolinians, averaging $359 a month. An additional $10.8 of state-administered supplemental payments were distributed to 24,056 residents.

40 HOUSING

In 2004, there were an estimated 3,860,078 units of housing in North Carolina, of which 3,340,330 were occupied; 69% were owner-occupied. About 64.7% of all housing units were single-family, detached homes. The state had one of the highest percentages of mobile home units in the nation at 16.8%. Nearly 36% of the entire housing stock was built between 1970 and 1989. The most common energy source for heating was electricity. It was estimated that 183,095 units lacked telephone service, 11,661 lacked complete plumbing facilities, and 11,745 lacked complete kitchen facilities. The average household had 2.48 members.

Also in 2004, 93,100 new privately owned units were authorized for construction. The median home value was $117,771. The median monthly cost for mortgage owners was $1,028. renters paid a median of $610 per month. In September 2005, the state received grants of $679,942 from the US Department of Housing and Urban Development (HUD) for rural housing and economic development programs. For 2006, HUD allocated to the state over $45 million in community development block grants.

41 EDUCATION

North Carolina's commitment to education was strengthened with legislative and financial support for improving student achievement through high standards; teacher accountability; an emphasis on teaching the basics of reading, writing and mathematics; and moving state control of schools to the local, community level. Legislation passed in 1996 allowed for the state's first public charter schools, up to 100 of them, and the first ones approved began operating in 1997. In 2004, 80.9% of North Carolinians age 25 and older were high school graduates, lower than the national average of 84%. Some 23.4% had obtained a bachelor's degree or higher; the national average was 26%.

North Carolina has a rich educational history, having started the first state university in the United States, in 1795, and the first free system of common schools in the South in 1839. North Carolina led the nation in the construction of rural schools in the 1920s. In 1957, Charlotte, Greensboro, and Winston-Salem were the first cities in the South to admit black students voluntarily to formerly all-white schools. But, as was the case throughout the South, widespread desegregation took much longer. In 1971, the US Supreme Court, in the landmark decision Swann v. Charlotte-Mecklenburg Board of Education, upheld the use of busing to desegregate that school system. The remainder of the state soon followed suit.

North Carolina established a statewide testing program in 1977 and increased high school graduation requirements in 1983, becoming the first state to require that students pass Algebra I in order to earn a diploma. North Carolina has been active in providing special programs for gifted students. Governor's School, a summer residential program for the gifted, was founded in 1963. Other talented students are served by the highly regarded North Carolina School of the Arts in Winston-Salem, which began operating in 1965, and the North Carolina School of Science and Mathematics, located in Durham, which opened in 1980.

The total enrollment for fall 2002 in North Carolina's public schools stood at 1,336,000. Of these, 964,000 attended schools from kindergarten through grade eight, and 372,000 attended high school. Approximately 58.3% of the students were white, 31.6% were black, 6.7% were Hispanic, 2% were Asian/Pacific Islander, and 1.5% were American Indian/Alaskan Native. Total enrollment was estimated at 1,355,000 in fall 2003 and was expected to be 1,381,000 by fall 2014, an increase of 3.3% during the period 2002–14. Expenditures for public education in 2003/04 were estimated at $10.2 billion. In fall 2003, there were 102,642 students enrolled in 661 private schools. Since 1969, the National Assessment of Educational Progress (NAEP) has tested public school students nationwide. The resulting report, *The Nation's Report Card*, stated that in 2005, eighth graders in North Carolina scored 282 out of 500 in mathematics compared with the national average of 278.

As of fall 2002, there were 447,335 students enrolled in college or graduate school; minority students comprised 28.5% of total postsecondary enrollment. In 2005 North Carolina had 130 degree-granting institutions. The University of North Carolina (UNC) was chartered in 1789 and opened at Chapel Hill in 1795. The state university system now embraces 16 campuses under a common board of governors. The three oldest and largest campuses, all of which offer research and graduate as well as undergraduate programs, are UNC-Chapel Hill, North Carolina State University in Raleigh (the first land-grant college for the study of agriculture and engineering), and UNC-Greensboro. North Carolina had 58 community colleges and 1 specialized technology center as of 2005.

Duke University in Durham is North Carolina's premier private institution and takes its place with the Chapel Hill and Raleigh public campuses as the third key facility in the Research Triangle. In addition to the public institutions and community colleges, there are also 49 private, four-year schools, of which Wake Forest University in Winston-Salem and Davidson College in Davidson are most noteworthy.

42 ARTS

North Carolina has been a pioneer in exploring new channels for state support of the arts. It was the first state to fund its own symphony, to endow its own art museum, to found a state school of the arts, to create a statewide arts council, and to establish a cabinet-level Department of Cultural Resources. The North Carolina Arts Council was established in 1964 and as of 2006 it was providing 1,000 grants annually to nonprofit organizations and artists. The council was instrumental in funding two of the first arts-based curriculum experiments in the state. The Arts Council's Grassroots Arts Program, established in 1977, was the nation's first per capita funding program for the local arts initiatives in which decision-making remained at the local level.

In 2005, North Carolina arts organizations received 41 grants totaling $1,535,926 from the National Endowment for the Arts. The North Carolina Humanities Council (NCHC), founded in 1972, is active in a number of programs. In 2005, the National Endowment for the Humanities contributed $2,475,754 to 29 state programs.

The North Carolina Symphony, based in Raleigh, is noted for having one of the most extensive educational programs of any orchestra nationwide. As of the 2006/07 season, its 75th anniversary, the North Carolina Symphony performed approximately 55 free concerts for more than 100,000 children annually. The North Carolina Museum of Art features one of the finest collections of early European master paintings in the country. The museum's collection spans 5,000 years and includes work by Dutch masters, Renaissance masterpieces, Egyptian artifacts, classical statues, and tribal and contemporary art. In 2005, the museum received a gift of 23 works by French sculptor Auguste Rodin, including 22 bronze sculptures. The gift made the museum one of the top Rodin repositories worldwide; the works of art were to be on display in new galleries that were part of a $75 million expansion project, scheduled to be completed in 2008.

Summer dance and music festivals, as well as professional theaters and historical outdoor dramas, galleries and museums, and the crafts community all serve as anchors for the state's tourism industry. North Carolina's Pulitzer Prize–winning playwright Paul Green created the genre of historical drama with the 1937 production of The Lost Colony.

Based for 20 years in Durham, the American Dance Festival (ADF) has commissioned new dance works, preserved dance history, trained dancers, and presented the best in contemporary dance. The African American Dance Ensemble, established in 1984 and based in North Carolina, performs for people across the United States promoting the preservation of African and African American dance. In 1961 Flat Rock Playhouse was officially designated the state theater of North Carolina.

Folk and traditional arts thrive across North Carolina in all disciplines. The North Carolina Folk Heritage Awards are given to recognize the state's leading folk artists. Penland School of Crafts, the John C. Campbell Folk School, the Southern Highland Craft Guild, Qualla Arts and Crafts Mutual, Inc., the Core Sound Waterfowl Museum, and the North Carolina Pottery Center are but a few of the organizations in North Carolina that help to keep the craft traditions alive.

43 LIBRARIES AND MUSEUMS

For the fiscal year ending in June 2001, North Carolina had 76 public library systems, with 379 libraries, of which 314 were branches. Libraries, in nearly every North Carolina community, are linked together through the State Library, ensuring that users in all parts of the state can have access to printed, filmed, and recorded materials. In that same year, the state's 76 public library systems had 15,916,000 volumes of books and serial publications on their shelves, and a total circulation of 43,313,000. The system also had 521,000 audio and 438,000 video items, 68,000 electronic format items (CD-ROMs, magnetic tapes, and disks), and 47 bookmobiles. Major university research libraries are located at the Chapel Hill, Raleigh, and Greensboro campuses of the University of North Carolina and at Duke University in Durham. The North Carolina Collection and Southern Historical Collection at the Chapel Hill campus are especially noteworthy. In fiscal year 2001, operating income for the public system totaled $156,375,000 and included $1,334,000 in federal grants and $17,910,000 in state grants.

North Carolina had 188 museums and historical sites in 2000. Established in 1956, the North Carolina Museum of Art, in Raleigh, is one of only two state-supported art museums in the United States (the other is in Virginia); the museum had an attendance of 233,893 in 1999. The North Carolina Museum of History is in Raleigh, with an annual attendance of 239,642. The Department of Cultural Resources administers 20 state historical sites and Tryon Place Restoration in New Bern. The Museum of Natural History in Raleigh is maintained by the state Department of Agriculture; smaller science museums exist in Charlotte, Greensboro, and Durham.

44 COMMUNICATIONS

Government postal service in North Carolina began in 1755 but did not become regular until 1771, with the establishment of a central post office for the southern colonies. Mails were slow and erratic, and many North Carolinians continued to entrust their letters to private travelers until well into the 19th century. Rural free delivery in the state began on 23 October 1896 in Rowan County.

Telephone service began in Wilmington and Raleigh in October 1879, and long distance connections between Wilmington and Petersburg, Va., began later that same year. In 2004, 93.3% of the state's occupied housing units had telephones. In addition, by June of that same year there were 4,875,916 mobile wireless telephone subscribers. In 2003, 57.7% of North Carolina households had a computer and 51.1% had Internet access. By June 2005, there were 1,237,877 high-speed lines in North Carolina, 1,124,284 residential and 113,593 for business.

There were 50 major AM radio stations in North Carolina in 2005, and 106 major FM stations. Major television stations numbered 33. In 1999, the Greenville-Spartanburg-Asheville-Anderson area had 732,490 television households, 61% of which received cable. The Raleigh-Durham area had 858,490 television-viewing households, 62% of which had cable. Finally, the Greensboro-High Point-Winston Salem viewing area boasted 64% of all television households with cable.

A total of 120,858 Internet domain names were registered in the state in the year 2000.

⁴⁵PRESS

As of 2005, North Carolina had 34 morning newspapers, 13 evening dailies, and 39 Sunday papers.

The following table shows the circulation of the largest dailies as of 2005:

AREA	NAME	DAILY	SUNDAY
Charlotte	*Observer* (m,S)	226,082	278,573
Greensboro	*News & Record* (m,S)	90,436	111,257
Raleigh	*News & Observer* (m,S)	176,550	211,735
Winston–Salem	*Journal* (m,S)	84,459	95,179

The *Charlotte Observer* won a 1981 Pulitzer Prize for its series on brown lung disease. The (Raleigh) *News &Observer* won a 1996 Pulitzer Prize for its series on the hog industry in North Carolina.

North Carolina has been the home of several nationally recognized "little reviews" of literature, poetry, and criticism, including *The Rebel, Crucible, Southern Poetry Review, The Carolina Quarterly, St. Andrews Review, The Sun, Pembroke Magazine,* and *Miscellany.* The *North Carolina Historical Review* is a quarterly scholarly publication of the Division of Archives and History.

⁴⁶ORGANIZATIONS

In 2006, there were 8,500 nonprofit organizations registered within the state, of which about 6,404 were registered as charitable, educational, or religious organizations.

The North Carolina Citizens Association serves as the voice of the state's business community. A teachers' organization, the North Carolina Association of Educators, is widely acknowledged as one of the most effective political pressure groups in the state, as is the North Carolina State Employees Association. Every major branch of industry has its own trade association; most are highly effective lobbying bodies. Carolina Action, the North Carolina Public Interest Research Group, the Kudzu Alliance, and the Brown Lung Association represent related consumer, environmental, antinuclear power, and public health concerns.

National organizations headquartered in the state include the American Board of Pediatrics, Association of Professors of Medicine, the American Senior Citizens Association, the Institute for Southern Studies, the Tobacco Association of the United States, the US Power Squadrons, the Improved Benevolent Protective Order of Elks of the World, the Independent Order of Odd Fellows, the World Methodist Council, and the Center for Creative Leadership. The Billy Graham Evangelistic Association is based in Charlotte.

Cultural and educational organizations at the local and national levels include the American Dance Festival, the Appalachian Consortium, the Moravian Music Foundation, Art in the Public Interest, the Center for Urban and Regional Studies, the National Humanities Center, the National Institute of Statistical Sciences, the North Carolina Humanities Council, and Preservation North Carolina. There are several clan associations for those of Scottish heritage.

⁴⁷TOURISM, TRAVEL, AND RECREATION

North Carolina promotes itself as "the heart of motorsports." Raleigh and Charlotte are right in the heart of NASCAR racing. In 2002, there were 44.4 million visitors to North Carolina, with total travel expenditures reaching $11.9 billion. About 30% of all trips are made by residents traveling within the state. About 53% of visitors travel from the following states: Virginia, South Carolina, Georgia, Florida, Pennsylvania, Tennessee, New York, Maryland, and Ohio.

Tourists are attracted by North Carolina's coastal beaches (301 miles of coastline); by golf and tennis opportunities; and by parks and scenery in the North Carolina mountains. Sites of special interest are the Revolutionary War battlegrounds at Guilford Courthouse and Moore's Creek Bridge; Bennett Place, near Hillsborough, where the last major Confederate army surrendered; Ft. Raleigh, the site of the Lost Colony's misadventures; and the Wright Brothers National Memorial at Kitty Hawk. With more than 600 golf courses across the state, North Carolina is often nicknamed the "Golf Capital of the World." North Carolina is the home of three United States presidents; Andrew Jackson, James K. Polk, and Andrew Johnson.

Cape Hatteras and Cape Lookout national seashores, which protect the beauty of the Outer Banks, together cover 58,563 acres (23,700 hectares). The Blue Ridge Parkway, a scenic motor route operated by the National Park Service that winds over the crest of the Blue Ridge in Virginia, North Carolina, and Georgia, attracts millions of visitors to North Carolina yearly. There are 300 mi (500 km) of the Appalachian Trail in North Carolina. Another popular attraction, Great Smoky Mountains National Park, straddles the North Carolina-Tennessee border. There are more than 1.2 million acres of national forest land located in North Carolina, 1,500 lakes of 10 acres or more, and 37,000 miles of freshwater streams. North Carolina was first settled by residents of Scotland and still maintains its Scottish heritage with festivals and crafts.

⁴⁸SPORTS

There are four major professional sports teams in North Carolina: the Charlotte Bobcats of the National Basketball Association, the Charlotte Sting of the Women's National Basketball Association, the Carolina Panthers of the National Football League, and the Carolina Hurricanes of the National Hockey League, who relocated to Raleigh from Hartford, Connecticut, in 1997. The Charlotte

Hornets, now located in New Orleans, left North Carolina in 2002. Minor league baseball's Carolina League is based in North Carolina, and 14 minor league teams call the state home. Additionally, there is minor league hockey in Charlotte, Fayetteville, and Winston-Salem. Two other professional sports that figure prominently in the state are golf and stock-car racing. The Greater Greensboro Chrysler Classic in April is a major tournament on the Professional Golfers' Association tour. The Lowe's Motor Speedway in Charlotte is the home of the Nextel All-Star Challenge, the Coca-Cola 600, and the Bank of America 500 on the NASCAR Nextel Cup circuit.

College basketball is the ruling passion of amateur sports fans in North Carolina. Organized in the Atlantic Coast Conference, the University of North Carolina at Chapel Hill, North Carolina State University, Wake Forest University, and Duke University consistently field nationally ranked basketball teams. North Carolina won the National Collegiate Athletic Association (NCAA) Championship in 1957, 1982, 1993, and 2005, North Carolina State captured the title in 1974 and 1983, and Duke won back-to-back championships in 1991 and 1992, and in 2001.

Other annual sporting events include the Stoneybrook Steeplechase in Southern Pines in April and the National Hollerin' Contest in Spivey's Corner, which tests farmers' ability to call livestock.

Track and field star Marion Jones and boxing great Sugar Ray Leonard were born in North Carolina.

⁴⁹ FAMOUS NORTH CAROLINIANS

Three US presidents had North Carolina roots, but all three reached the White House from Tennessee. Andrew Jackson (1767–1845), the seventh president, was born in an unsurveyed border region, probably in South Carolina, but studied law and was admitted to the bar in North Carolina before moving to frontier Tennessee in 1788. James K. Polk (1795–1849), the 11th president, was born in Mecklenburg County but grew up in Tennessee. Another native North Carolinian, Andrew Johnson (1808–75), was a tailor's apprentice in Raleigh before moving to Tennessee at the age of 18. Johnson served as Abraham Lincoln's vice president for six weeks in 1865 before becoming the nation's 17th president when Lincoln was assassinated. William Rufus King (1786–1853), the other US vice president from North Carolina, also served for only six weeks, dying before he could exercise his duties.

Three native North Carolinians have served as speaker of the US House of Representatives. The first, Nathaniel Macon (1758–1837), occupied the speaker's chair from 1801 to 1807 and served as president pro tem of the US Senate in 1826-27. The other two were James K. Polk and Joseph G. "Uncle Joe" Cannon (1836–1926), who served as speaker of the House from 1903 to 1911, but as a representative from Illinois.

Sir Walter Raleigh (or Ralegh, b.England, 1552?–1618) never came to North Carolina, but his efforts to found a colony there led state lawmakers to give his name to the new state capital in 1792. Raleigh's "Lost Colony" on Roanoke Island was the home of Virginia Dare (1587–?), the first child of English parents to be born in America. More than a century later, the infamous Edward Teach (or Thatch, b.England, ?–1716) made his headquarters at Bath and terrorized coastal waters as the pirate known as Blackbeard.

Principal leaders of the early national period included Richard Caswell (b.Maryland, 1729–89), Revolutionary War governor;

William Richardson Davie (b.England, 1756–1820), governor of the state and founder of the University of North Carolina; and Archibald De Bow Murphey (1777–1832), reform advocate, legislator, and judge. Prominent black Americans of the 19th century who were born or who lived in North Carolina were John Chavis (1763–1838), teacher and minister; David Walker (1785–1830), abolitionist; and Hiram Revels (1827–1901), first black member of the US Senate.

North Carolinians prominent in the era of the Civil War and Reconstruction included antislavery author Hinton Rowan Helper (1829–1909), Civil War governor Zebulon B. Vance (1830–94), Reconstruction governor William W. Holden (1818–92), and "carpetbagger" judge Albion Winegar Tourgee (b.Ohio, 1838–1905). Among major politicians of the 20th century are Furnifold McLendell Simmons (1854–1940), US senator from 1901 to 1931; Charles Brantley Aycock (1859–1912), governor from 1901 to 1905; Frank Porter Graham (1886–1972), University of North Carolina president, New Deal adviser, and US senator, 1949–50; Luther H. Hodges (b.Virginia, 1898–1974), governor from 1954 to 1960, US secretary of commerce from 1961 to 1965, and founder of Research Triangle Park; Samuel J. Ervin Jr. (1896–1985), US senator from 1954 to 1974 and chairman of the Senate Watergate investigation; Terry Sanford (1917–98), governor from 1961 to 1965, US presidential aspirant, and president of Duke University; and Jesse Helms (b.1921), senator from 1973 to 2003. Civil rights leader Jesse Jackson (b.1941) began his career as a student activist in Greensboro. The most famous North Carolinian living today is probably evangelist Billy Graham (b.1918).

James Buchanan Duke (1856–1925) founded the American Tobacco Co. and provided the endowment that transformed Trinity College into Duke University. The most outstanding North Carolina-born inventor was Richard J. Gatling (1818–1903), creator of the "Gatling gun," the first machine gun. The Wright brothers, Wilbur (b.Indiana, 1867–1912) and Orville (b.Ohio, 1871–1948), achieved the first successful powered airplane flight at Kitty Hawk, on the Outer Banks, on 17 December 1903. Psychologist Joseph Banks Rhine (b.Pennsylvania, 1895–1980) was known for his research on extrasensory perception. Kary Mullis, 1993 winner of the Nobel Prize for chemistry, was born in Lenoir, North Carolina.

A number of North Carolinians have won fame as literary figures. They include Walter Hines Page (1855–1918), editor and diplomat; William Sydney Porter (1862–1910), a short-story writer who used the pseudonym O. Henry; playwright Paul Green (1894–1984); and novelists Thomas Wolfe (1900–38) and Reynolds Price (b.1933). Major scholars associated with the state have included sociologist Howard W. Odum (b.Georgia, 1884–1954) and historians W. J. Cash (1901–41) and John Hope Franklin (b.Oklahoma, 1915). Journalists Edward R. Murrow (1908–65), Tom Wicker (b.1926), and Charles Kuralt (1934–97) were all North Carolina natives. Harry Golden (Harry L. Goldhurst, b.New York, 1903–81), a Jewish humorist, founded the Carolina Israelite.

Jazz artists Thelonious Monk (1918–82), John Coltrane (1926–67), and Nina Simone (1933–2003) were born in the state, as were pop singer Roberta Flack (b.1939), folksinger Arthel "Doc" Watson (b.1923), bluegrass banjo artist Earl Scruggs (b.1924), and actor Andy Griffith (b.1926). North Carolina athletes include former heavyweight champion Floyd Patterson (1935–2006), NASCAR driver Richard Petty (1937–2000), football quarterbacks Sonny Jurgenson (b.1934) and Roman Gabriel (b.1940), baseball pitchers Gaylord Perry (b.1938) and Jim "Catfish" Hunter (1946–99), and basketball player Meadowlark Lemon (b.1932), long a star with the Harlem Globetrotters. Michael Jordan (b.New York, 1963) played college basketball at the University of North Carolina, and went on to fame as a National Basketball Association star.

50 BIBLIOGRAPHY

Byrd, William L. *In Full Force and Virtue: North Carolina Emancipation Records, 1713–1860.* Bowie, Md.: Heritage Books, 1999.

Coastal Southeast 2005: Georgia, North Carolina, South Carolina. Park Ridge, Ill.: ExxonMobil Travel Publications, 2005.

Council of State Governments. *The Book of the States, 2006 Edition.* Lexington, Ky.: Council of State Governments, 2006.

Doherty, Craig A. *North Carolina.* New York: Facts On File, 2005.

Fleer, Jack D. *North Carolina Government & Politics.* Lincoln: University of Nebraska, 1994.

Hossfeld, Leslie H. *Narrative, Political Unconscious, and Racial Violence in Wilmington, North Carolina.* New York: Routledge, 2004.

Jones, H.G. *North Carolina History: An Annotated Bibliography.* Westport, Conn.: Greenwood Press, 1995.

McKinney, Gordon B. *Zeb Vance: North Carolina's Civil War Governor and Gilded Age Political Leader.* Chapel Hill: University of North Carolina Press, 2004.

North Carolina Handbook. Chico, Calif.: Moon Publications, 1999.

Ready, Milton. *The Tar Heel State: A History of North Carolina.* Columbia: University of South Carolina Press, 2005.

Rodenbough, Charles D. *Governor Alexander Martin: Biography of a North Carolina Revolutionary War Statesman.* Jefferson, N.C.: McFarland, 2004.

US Department of Commerce, Economics and Statistics Administration, US Census Bureau. *North Carolina, 2000. Summary Social, Economic, and Housing Characteristics: 2000 Census of Population and Housing.* Washington, D.C.: US Government Printing Office, 2003.

NORTH DAKOTA

State of North Dakota

ORIGIN OF STATE NAME: The state was formerly the northern section of Dakota Territory; *dakota* is a Siouan word meaning "allies." **NICKNAME:** Peace Garden State; Flickertail State. **CAPITAL:** Bismarck. **ENTERED UNION:** 2 November 1889 (39th). **SONG:** "North Dakota Hymn;" "Flickertail March." (march). **MOTTO:** Liberty and Union, Now and Forever, One and Inseparable. **FLAG:** The flag consists of a blue field with yellow fringes; on each side is depicted an eagle with outstretched wings, holding in one talon a sheaf of arrows, in the other an olive branch, and in his beak a banner inscribed with the words "*E Pluribus Unum.*" Below the eagle are the words "North Dakota"; above it are 13 stars surmounted by a sunburst. **OFFICIAL SEAL:** In the center is an elm tree; beneath it are a sheaf of wheat, a plow, an anvil, and a bow and three arrows, and in the background a Native American chases a buffalo toward a setting sun. The depiction is surrounded by the state motto, and the words "Great Seal State of North Dakota October 1st 1889" encircle the whole. **BIRD:** Western meadowlark. **FISH:** Northern pike. **FLOWER:** Wild prairie rose. **TREE:** American elm. **LEGAL HOLIDAYS:** New Year's Day, 1 January; Birthday of Martin Luther King Jr., 3rd Monday in January; Presidents' Day, 3rd Monday in February; Good Friday, Friday before Easter, March or April; Memorial Day, last Monday in May; Independence Day, 4 July; Labor Day, 1st Monday in September; Veterans' Day, 11 November; Thanksgiving Day, 4th Thursday in November; Christmas Day, 25 December. **TIME:** 6 AM CST = noon GMT; 5 AM MST = noon GMT.

¹LOCATION, SIZE, AND EXTENT

Located in the western north-central United States, North Dakota ranks 17th in size among the 50 states.

The total area of North Dakota is 70,703 sq mi (183,121 sq km), comprising 69,300 sq mi (179,487 sq km) of land and 1,403 sq mi (3,634 sq km) of inland water. Shaped roughly like a rectangle, North Dakota has three straight sides and one irregular border on the E. Its maximum length E–W is about 360 mi (580 km), its extreme width N–S about 210 mi (340 km).

North Dakota is bordered on the N by the Canadian provinces of Saskatchewan and Manitoba; on the E by Minnesota (with the line formed by the Red River of the North); on the S by South Dakota; and on the W by Montana. The total boundary length is 1,312 mi (2,111 km). The state's geographic center is in Sheridan County, 5 mi (8 km) SW of McClusky.

²TOPOGRAPHY

North Dakota straddles two major US physiographic regions: the Central Plains in the east and the Great Plains in the west. Along the eastern border is the generally flat Red River Valley, with the state's lowest point, 750 ft (229 m); this valley was once covered by the waters of a glacial lake. Most of the eastern half of North Dakota consists of the Drift Prairie, at 1,300–1,600 ft (400–500 m) above sea level. The Missouri Plateau occupies the western half of the state and has the highest point in North Dakota—White Butte, 3,506 ft (1,069 m)—in Slope County in the southwest. Separating the Missouri Plateau from the Drift Prairie is the Missouri Escarpment, which rises 400 ft (122 m) above the prairie and extends diagonally from northwest to southeast. The mean elevation of the state is approximately 1,900 ft (580 m).

North Dakota has two major rivers: the Red River of the North, flowing northward into Canada; and the Missouri River, which enters in the northwest and then flows east and, joined by the Yellowstone River, southeast into South Dakota.

³CLIMATE

North Dakota lies in the northwestern continental interior of the United States. Characteristically, summers are hot, winters very cold, and rainfall sparse to moderate, with periods of drought. The average annual temperature is 40°F (4°C), ranging from 7°F (-14°C) in January to 69°F (21°C) in July. The record low temperature, -60°F (-51°C), was set at Parshall on 15 February 1936; the record high, 121°F (49°C), at Steele on 6 July 1936.

The average yearly precipitation was about 15.8 in (40 cm) at Bismarck. The total annual snowfall averages 41.9 in (106 cm) at Bismarck.

⁴FLORA AND FAUNA

North Dakota is predominantly a region of prairie and plains, although the American elm, green ash, box elder, and cottonwood grow there. Cranberries, juneberries, and wild grapes are also common. Indian, blue, grama, and buffalo grasses grow on the plains; the wild prairie rose is the state flower. The western prairie fringed orchid was the only plant species classified by the US Fish and Wildlife Service as threatened in 2006; no plant species were listed as endangered that year.

Once on the verge of extinction, the white-tailed and mule deer and pronghorn antelope have been restored. The elk and grizzly bear, both common until about 1880, had disappeared by 1900; bighorn sheep, reintroduced in 1956, are beginning to flourish.

North Dakota claims more wild ducks than any other state except Alaska, and it has the largest sharptailed grouse population in the United States. Six animal species (vertebrates and invertebrates) were listed as threatened or endangered in North Dakota in April 2006, including the bald eagle, Eskimo curlew, pallid sturgeon, least tern, and whooping crane.

5 ENVIRONMENTAL PROTECTION

North Dakota has little urban or industrial pollution. An environmental issue confronting the state in the mid-1980s and early 1990s was how to use its coal resources without damaging the land through strip mining or polluting the air with coal-fired industrial plants. Major environmental issues confronting the state are importation of non-hazardous and hazardous solid wastes for treatment or disposal, non-point surface water pollution from agricultural and native land, groundwater contamination by fuel storage tanks and by irrigation, and air pollution by energy conversion plants.

The Environmental Health Section of the North Dakota Department of Health oversees programs to ensure water and air quality. North Dakota has little urban air pollution with one exception: motor vehicle traffic is causing excess ambient carbon monoxide in an area within the city of Fargo. The major industrial sources of air contaminants within the state are seven coal-fired electrical generating plants, a coal gasification plant, a refinery, and agricultural commodity processing facilities. The ambient air quality has been in compliance with federal standards, although an epidemiological study has associated certain air contaminants with a higher incidence of respiratory illness among persons living in the vicinity of coal-burning plants. In 2003, 23.6 million lb of toxic chemicals were released in the state.

To conserve water and provide irrigation, nearly 700 dams have been built, including Garrison Dam, completed in 1960. The Garrison Diversion Project, authorized by the US Congress in 1965, was intended to draw water from Lake Sakakawea, the impoundment behind Garrison Dam. As of the 1980s, there were about 2.7 million acres of wetlands in the state. This total has been diminishing, however, by agricultural development.

Diversion of household waste to recycling grew to about nearly 15% of the waste stream. Yard wastes, household appliances, and scrap tires are also diverted for compost, recycling, or fuel, respectively. In 2003, North Dakota had 17 hazardous waste sites listed in the US Environment Protection Agency (EPA) database, but none were on the National Priorities List as of 2006. In 2005, the EPA spent over $2.6 million through the Superfund program for the cleanup of hazardous waste sites in the state. The same year, federal EPA grants awarded to the state included $11.7 million for the water pollution control state revolving fund and $8.2 for the safe drinking water revolving fund.

6 POPULATION

North Dakota ranked 48th in population in the United States with an estimated total of 636,677 in 2005 a decrease of 0.9% from 2000. Between 1990 and 2000, North Dakota's population grew from 638,800 to 642,200, an increase of 0.5%. The population is projected to decrease to 620,777 by 2025. The population density in 2004 was 9.2 persons per sq mi, the fourth-lowest in the nation (after Alaska, Wyoming, and Montana). In 2004, the median age

in North Dakota was 38.8; 21.9% of the populace were under age 18 while 14.7% was age 65 or older.

North Dakota is one of the most rural states in the United States, with over half of its population living outside metropolitan areas. The Fargo metropolitan area had an estimated population of 181,520 in 2004. The Bismarck metropolitan area had a population of about 97,924 and the Grand Forks area had a population of about 96,046.

7 ETHNIC GROUPS

As of 2000, about 92.4% of the state's population was white. The American Indian population was 31,329, or about 4.9% of the total; that percentage had increased to 5.2% by 2004. In 2000, there were some 3,916 blacks, representing 0.6% of the population. That percentage had increased to 0.7% by 2004. Among Americans of European origin, the leading groups were Germans, who made up 44% of the total population, and Norwegians, who made up 30%. Only about 1.9% of the state's population (12,114) was foreign born as of 2000, predominantly from neighboring Canada. In the same year, the Asian population totaled 3,606, with 230 Pacific Islanders. In 2000, 7,786 North Dakotans were Hispanic or Latino, representing 1.2% of the state's total population. In 2004, 1.5% of the population was Hispanic or Latino, 0.7% Asian, 0.9% of the population reported origin of two or more races.

8 LANGUAGES

Although a few Indian words are used in the English spoken near the reservations where Ojibwa and Sioux live in North Dakota, the only general impact of Indian speech on English is in such place-names as Pembina, Mandan, Wabek, and Anamoose.

A few Norwegian food terms like *lefse* and *lutefisk* have entered the Northern dialect that is characteristic of North Dakota, and some Midland terms have intruded from the south.

In 2000, 93.7% of the population five years old or older spoke only English at home, down slightly from 92.1% in 1990.

The following table gives selected statistics from the 2000 Census for language spoken at home by persons five years old and over. The category "Scandinavian languages" includes Danish, Norwegian, and Swedish. The category "Other Native North American languages" includes Apache, Cherokee, Choctaw, Dakota, Keres, Pima, and Yupik. The category "African languages" includes Amharic, Ibo, Twi, Yoruba, Bantu, Swahili, and Somali.

LANGUAGE	NUMBER	PERCENT
Population 5 years and over	**603,106**	**100.0**
Speak only English	565,130	93.7
Speak a language other than English	37,976	6.3
Speak a language other than English	**37,976**	**6.3**
German	14,931	2.5
Spanish or Spanish Creole	8,263	1.4
Scandinavian languages	3,193	0.5
Other Native North American languages	2,536	0.4
French (incl. Patois, Cajun)	1,597	0.3
Other Slavic languages	1,350	0.2
Serbo-Croatian	825	0.1
African languages	459	0.1
Polish	452	0.1
Chinese	437	0.1
Russian	331	0.1
Tagalog	330	0.1

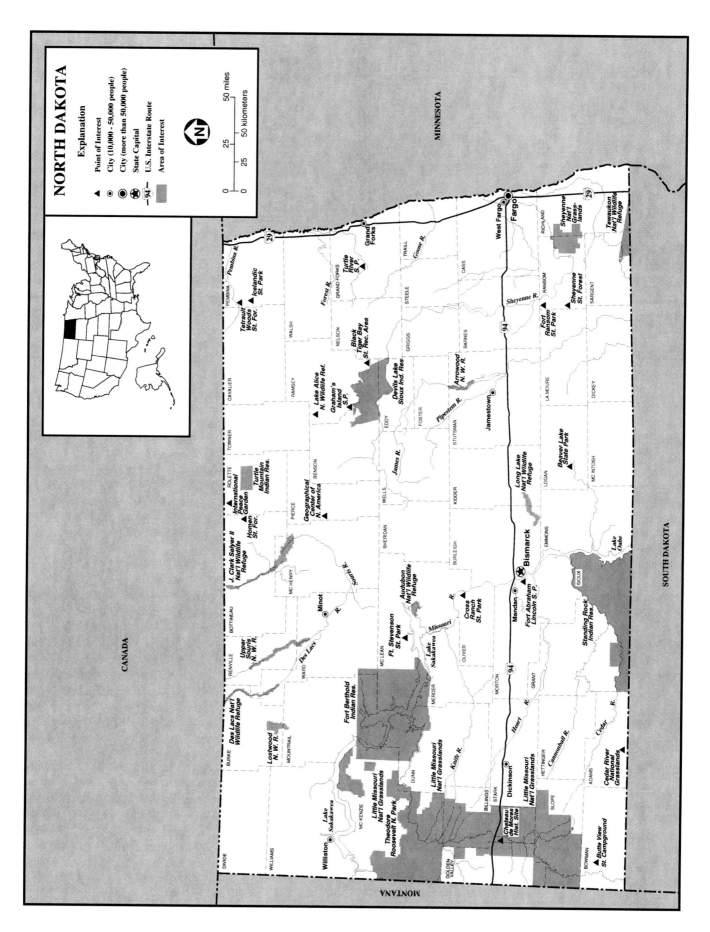

9 RELIGIONS

Most of the state population is mainline Protestant, with the leading denominations being the Evangelical Lutheran Church in America with 174,554 adherents (in 2000) and the Untied Methodist Church with 20,159 adherents. The Lutheran Church—Missouri Synod had about 23,720 members. The Roman Catholic Church had about 148,435 members in 2004. There were an estimate 920 Muslims and 730 Jews in the state in 2000. About 26.8% of the population did not specify a religious affiliation.

10 TRANSPORTATION

In 2003, there was 3,727 mi (6,000 km) of rail trackage in North Dakota. The largest railroad lines are the Burlington Northern Santa Fe (BNSF) and the Soo Line. Farm products and coal accounted for most of the state originated tonnage carried by the railroads. As of 2006, Amtrak passenger service was provided to seven stations in the state via its Chicago–Seattle/Portland Empire Builder train.

There were 86,782 mi (139,719 km) of public roads, streets, and highways in North Dakota in 2004. There were also some 707,000 registered motor vehicles of all types and 461,780 licensed drivers in the state for that same year.

In 2005, North Dakota had a total of 308 public and private-use aviation-related facilities. This included 292 airports, 15 heliports, and 1 seaplane base. Hector International Airport at Fargo is the state's main airport, with 261,872 passengers enplaned in 2004.

11 HISTORY

Human occupation of what is now North Dakota began about 13,000 BC in the southwestern corner of the state, which at that time was covered with lush vegetation. Drought drove away the aboriginal hunter-gatherers, and it was not until about 2,000 years ago that Indians from the more humid regions to the east moved into the easternmost third of the Dakotas. About AD 1300 the Mandan Indians brought an advanced agricultural economy up the Missouri River. They were joined by the Hidatsa and Arikara about three or four centuries later. Moving from the Minnesota forests during the 17th century, the Yanktonai Sioux occupied the southeastern quarter of the state. Their cousins west of the Missouri River, the Teton Sioux, led a nomadic life as hunters and mounted warriors. The Ojibwa, who had driven the Sioux out of Minnesota, settled in the northeast.

European penetration of the Dakotas began in 1738, when Pierre Gaultier de Varennes, Sieur de la Vérendrye, of Trois Riviéres in New France, traded for furs in the Red River region. Later the fur trade spread farther into the Red and Missouri river valleys, especially around Pembina, where the North West Company and the Hudson's Bay Company had their posts. After the Lewis and Clark expedition (1804–06) explored the Missouri, the American Fur Company traded there, with buffalo hides the leading commodity.

In 1812, Scottish settlers from Canada moved up the Red River to Pembina. This first white farming settlement in North Dakota also attracted numerous métis, half-breeds of mixed Indian and European ancestry. An extensive trade in furs and buffalo hides, which were transported first by heavy carts and later by steamboats, sprang up between Pembina, Ft. Garry (Winnipeg, Canada), and St. Paul, Minn.

Army movements against the Sioux during and after the Civil War brought white men into central North Dakota, which in 1861 was organized as part of the Dakota Territory, including the present-day Dakotas, Montana, and Wyoming. The signing of treaties confining the agricultural Indians to reservations, the arrival of the Northern Pacific Railroad at Fargo in 1872, and its extension to the Missouri the following year led to the rise of homesteading on giant "bonanza farms." Settlers poured in, especially from Canada. This short-lived "Great Dakota boom" ended in the mid-1880s with drought and depressed farm prices. As many of the original American and Canadian settlers left in disgust, they were replaced by Norwegians, Germans, and other Europeans. By 1910, North Dakota, which had entered the Union in 1889, was among the leading states in percentage of foreign-born residents.

From the time of statehood onward, Republicans dominated politics in North Dakota. Their leader was Alexander McKenzie, a Canadian immigrant who built a reputation as an agent of the railroads, protecting them from regulation. Between 1898 and 1915, the "Second Boom" brought an upsurge in population and railroad construction. In politics, Republican Progressives enacted reforms, but left unsolved the basic problem of how North Dakota farmers could stand up to the powerful grain traders of Minneapolis-St. Paul. Agrarian revolt flared in 1915, when Arthur C. Townley organized the Farmers' Nonpartisan Political League. Operating through Republican Party machinery, Townley succeeded in having his gubernatorial candidate, Lynn J. Frazier, elected in 1916. State-owned enterprises were established, including the Bank of North Dakota, the Home Building Association, the Hail Insurance Department, and a mill and grain elevator. However, the league was hurt by charges of "socialism" and, after 1917, by allegations of pro-German sympathies in World War I, as well as of mismanagement. In 1921, Frazier and Attorney General William Lemke were removed from office in the nation's first recall election.

The 1920s, a period of bank failures, low farm prices, drought, and political disunity, saw the beginnings of an exodus from the state. Matters grew worse during the Great Depression. Elected governor by hard-pressed farmers in 1932, William Langer took spectacular steps to save farms from foreclosure and to raise grain prices, until a conflict with the Roosevelt administration led to his removal from office on charges that he had illegally solicited political contributions.

World War II brought a quiet prosperity to North Dakota that lasted into the following decades. The Arab oil embargo of 1973 and the rise of oil prices throughout the decade spurred drilling for oil, encouraged the mining of lignite for electrical generation, and led to the construction of the nation's first coal gasification plant, at a cost of $2 billion, in a lignite mining area near Beulah. In the 1980s, however, North Dakota's economy suffered a setback when oil prices dropped. In addition, a drought that began in 1987 damaged over 5.3 million acres of land by 1988 and persisted into the 1990s and early 2000s. Agricultural production was strong in early 1990s. However, severe storms and flooding in 1994 damaged about $600 million in crops. The state continues to experience extreme weather conditions.

The state's economy was boosted by the 1991 repeal of the "blue laws" enforcing the closing of all retail businesses on Sundays. Republican Governor Ed Schafer, elected in 1992 and reelected in 1996, set an aggressive plan for the state's economic development, resulting in an estimated 10% increase in the number of jobs and record-low unemployment. By 2000 Fargo boasted one of the lowest unemployment rates in the nation. Nevertheless, poverty was on the rise in the 1990s. With 15.1% of its residents living below the nationally established poverty line, North Dakota ranked as the ninth-poorest in the United States in 1998. The state had begun the decade ranked nineteenth, with a 13.7% rate. It was also one of just 15 states where child poverty was on the rise—one in five children lived in poverty in 1998. However, by 2003–04, North Dakota had turned its poverty statistics around: the poverty rate during that two-year average was 9.7%, well below the national average of 12.6%. Per capita personal income in 2004 was $31,398, just below the US average of $32,937. In 2003, North Dakota led the nation in personal income and wage growth.

Census Bureau figures in 2000 showed the state (population 642,200) continued to be one of the least populated in the nation—only Alaska, Vermont, and Wyoming had fewer residents. Stemming the tide of North Dakotans moving out of state was a top priority. The state enjoyed the rank of safest in the nation in 1999, with only 89 crimes per 100,000 people.

As of 2005, it was illegal for unmarried couples to cohabitate in North Dakota, one of seven states to have such laws. Republican governor John Hoeven, during his second term in office, was committed to enhancing the state's business climate. In 2005, the state had a budget surplus and the budget called for tax relief through higher state funding for K–12 education, additional revenue sharing with cities and counties, tax credits for farms and businesses, and a property tax break for seniors and people with disabilities.

12 STATE GOVERNMENT

North Dakota is governed by the constitution of 1889, as amended (145 times by January 2005). The constitution may be amended by a majority vote in the legislature; a majority vote of the state electorate is required for ratification. Amendments may also be proposed by initiative (by petition of 4% of the state's population).

State elected officials are the governor and lieutenant governor (elected jointly), secretary of state, auditor, treasurer, attorney general, superintendent of public instruction, three public service commissioners, and the commissioners of insurance, taxation, and agriculture. With the exception of the public service commissioners, who serve six-year terms, all terms are four years. Candidates for governor must be 30 years old, US citizens, qualified voters, and state residents for at least five years prior to election. As of December 2004, the governor's salary was $85,506.

The legislature, which convenes every two years (in odd-numbered years) beginning in early January, is bicameral, with a 47-member Senate and a 94-member House of Representatives. Regular sessions are limited to 80 legislative days. The governor or a legislative council may call for a special session. All legislators must be at least 18 years old, state residents for at least one year, and qualified voters in their districts prior to election; they serve four-year terms. In 2004 legislators received a per diem salary during regular sessions of $125 per calendar day. A two-thirds vote of the elected members of each house is required to override a gubernatorial veto. Bills that are not vetoed or signed by the governor become law after three days (or after 15 days if the legislature adjourns).

Voters in North Dakota must be US citizens, at least 18 years old, and a precinct resident for at least 30 days prior to election. The state does not require voters to register. Restrictions apply to convicted felons and those declared mentally incompetent by the court.

13 POLITICAL PARTIES

Between 1889 and 1960, Republicans held the governorship for 58 years. North Dakota politics were not monolithic, however, for aside from the Populist and Democratic opposition, the Republican Party was itself torn by factionalism, with Progressive and Nonpartisan League challenges to the conservative, probusiness party establishment. Between 1960 and 1980, the statehouse was in Democratic hands. In the early and mid-nineties, the Republican party increased its influence at the state level, gaining dominance in both houses of the state legislature, having wrestled control of the Senate away from the Democrats in the November 1994 election. The state had 481,351 registered voters in 2002, 49% of whom turned out to vote. Following the 2004 election, the state Senate had 32 Republicans and 15 Democrats. The state House was dominated by the Republicans, who held 67 seats, while the Democrats had 27.

In the 2000 presidential election, Republican George W. Bush won 61% of the vote to Democrat Al Gore's 33%. Independent candidate Ralph Nader and Reform Party candidate Pat Buchanan each received 3% of the vote. In 2004, Bush won 66% of the vote to Democratic challenger John Kerry's 33%. North Dakota had three electoral votes in the 2004 presidential election.

Republican John Hoeven was elected governor in 2000. North Dakota's US senators in 2003 were Kent Conrad, a Democrat elected in 1992 to fill a seat vacated by the death of Quentin D. Burdick and reelected to full terms in 1994 and 2000, and Democrat Byron Dorgan, who was also reelected for second and third terms in 1998 and 2004. Following the 2004 elections, North Dakota's sole representative to the US House was a Democrat.

North Dakota Presidential Vote by Major Political Parties, 1948–2004

YEAR	ELECTORAL VOTE	N. DAKOTA WINNER	DEMOCRAT	REPUBLICAN
1948	4	Dewey (R)	95,812	115,139
1952	4	*Eisenhower (R)	76,694	191,712
1956	4	*Eisenhower (R)	96,742	156,766
1960	4	Nixon (R)	123,963	154,310
1964	4	*Johnson (D)	149,784	108,207
1968	4	*Nixon (R)	94,769	138,669
1972	3	*Nixon (R)	100,384	174,109
1976	3	Ford (R)	136,078	153,470
1980	3	*Reagan (R)	79,189	193,695
1984	3	*Reagan (R)	104,429	200,336
1988	3	*Bush (R)	127,739	166,559
1992**	3	Bush (R)	99,168	136,244
1996**	3	Dole (R)	106,905	125,050
2000	3	*Bush, G. W. (R)	95,284	174.852
2004	3	*Bush, G. W. (R)	111,052	196,651

*Won US presidential election.
**IND. candidate Ross Perot received 71,084 votes in 1992 and 32,515 votes in 1996.

¹⁴LOCAL GOVERNMENT

In 2005, North Dakota had 53 counties, 360 municipalities (all designated as cities regardless of size), 230 public school districts, and 764 special districts. In 2002, there were 1,332 special districts. Typical elected county officials are commissioners, a sheriff, a court clerk, a county judge, a county justice, and a state's attorney. Counties are divided into townships, each with its own elected administrative officers. Most municipalities operate by the mayor-council system of government.

In 2005, local government accounted for about 23,093 full-time (or equivalent) employment positions.

¹⁵STATE SERVICES

To address the continuing threat of terrorism and to work with the federal Department of Homeland Security, homeland security in North Dakota operates under the authority of the governor; the emergency management director was designated as the state homeland security advisor.

Educational services are under the jurisdiction of the Department of Public Instruction and the Board of Higher Education; there are state schools for the deaf, blind, handicapped, and developmentally disabled. Health and welfare agencies include the State Health Department, Department of Agriculture, Department of Economic Development and Finance, Council on the Arts, Veterans Affairs Department, Department of Human Services, and Indian Affairs Commission. Agricultural services include an extensive program of experiment and extension stations.

¹⁶JUDICIAL SYSTEM

North Dakota has a supreme court of five justices, seven district courts with 43 justices, and a system of local (county) courts. Supreme court justices are elected for 10-year terms, district court judges for 6-year terms.

As of 31 December 2004, a total of 1,327 prisoners were held in North Dakota's state and federal prisons, an increase from 1,239 of 7.1% from the previous year. As of year-end 2004, a total of 129 inmates were female, up from 113 or 14.2% from the year before. Among sentenced prisoners (one year or more), North Dakota had an incarceration rate of 195 per 100,000 population in 2004.

According to the Federal Bureau of Investigation, North Dakota in 2004, had a violent crime rate (murder/nonnegligent manslaughter; forcible rape; robbery; aggravated assault) of 79.4 reported incidents per 100,000 population (the lowest in the United States), or a total of 504 reported incidents. Crimes against property (burglary; larceny/theft; and motor vehicle theft) in that same year totaled 12,158 reported incidents or 1,916.6 reported incidents per 100,000 people. North Dakota does not have a death penalty. It was abolished in 1973, with the last execution in that state taking place in 1930. North Dakota does provide for life without parole.

In 2003, North Dakota spent $26,679,568 on homeland security, an average of $39 per state resident.

¹⁷ARMED FORCES

In 2004, there were 7,840 active-duty military personnel and 1,706 civilian personnel stationed in North Dakota, the majority of whom were stationed at the Strategic Air Command bases at Minot and Grand Forks. North Dakota firms received more than $309 million in defense contract awards in 2004. Defense Department payroll outlays in that same year were $498 million.

In 2003, 55,374 veterans were living in North Dakota, including 7,558 from World War II; 6,787 from the Korean conflict; 17,850 from the Vietnam era; and 8,680 in the Persian Gulf War. A total of more than $156 million was spent on major veterans' benefit programs in the state in 2004.

As of 31 October 2004, the North Dakota Highway Patrol employed 134 full-time sworn officers.

¹⁸MIGRATION

During the late 19th century, North Dakota was largely settled by immigrants of German and Scandinavian stock. The state reached a peak population in 1930, but then suffered steady losses until well into the 1970s because of out-migration. This trend has shown some signs of abating, however. From 1980 to 1983, the state's population grew 4.3%, in part because of a net gain in migration of about 5,000 people. Also during the 1980s, the urban population grew to outnumber the rural population, rising from 48.8% to 53.3% of the total populace. From 1985 to 1990, North Dakota had a net loss of 44,142 from migration. Between 1990 and 1998, the state had a net loss of 30,000 in domestic migration but a net gain of 4,000 in international migration. In 1998, the state admitted 472 foreign immigrants. North Dakota's overall population decreased by 0.1% between 1990 and 1998. In the period 2000–05, net international migration was 3,687 and net internal migration was -18,568, for a net loss of 14,881 people.

¹⁹INTERGOVERNMENTAL COOPERATION

North Dakota participates in such interstate agreements as the Yellowstone River Compact, Western Interstate Commission for Higher Education, Interstate Compact for Juveniles, and Interstate Oil and Gas Compact. A Minnesota–North Dakota Boundary Compact was ratified in 1961. Federal grants in fiscal year 2001 totaled almost $1.3 billion. Mirroring a national trend, that figure declined significantly by fiscal year 2005, to $935 million. Federal grants were estimated at $908 million in fiscal year 2006, and an estimated $921 million in fiscal year 2007.

²⁰ECONOMY

North Dakota has been and still is an important agricultural state, especially as a producer of wheat, much of which finds its way onto the world market. Many segments of the economy are affected by agriculture; for example, a substantial wholesale trade is involved in moving grain and livestock to market. Like other Midwestern farmers, North Dakotans suffered from high interest rates and a federal embargo on grain shipments to the Soviet Union in the early 1980s. Farm numbers have continued to decline, posing a threat to the vitality of the state's rural lifestyle. From 1970, 43 of North Dakota's 53 counties have lost population, and for 23 of these the population decline accelerated in the 1990s. The exodus has been aggravated by prolonged drought conditions, which in 2002 helped reduce wheat production (representing a quarter of the state's total agricultural revenues) by 24% and disrupted cattle production. Not being deeply involved in the dot.com frenzy of the 1990s, North Dakota was only slightly affected by the national recession and slowdown of 2001 and 2002. By December 2002, state unemployment which had risen to 3.6% in October, had fallen back to 3%.

Growth industries for the state include petroleum and the mining of coal, chiefly lignite. North Dakota has more coal resources than any other state. Manufacturing is concentrated to a great extent on farm products and machinery.

North Dakota's gross state product (GSP) in 2004 was $22.687 billion, of which manufacturing accounted for the largest share at $2.366 billion or 10.4% of GSP, followed by health care and social assistance services at $2.069 billion (9.1% of GSP), and the real estate sector at $1.840 billion (8.1% of GSP). In that same year, there were an estimated 59,158 small businesses in North Dakota. Of the 19,177 businesses that had employees, an estimated total of 18,522 or 96.6% were small companies. An estimated 1,747 new businesses were established in the state in 2004, up 20% from the year before. Business terminations that same year came to 2,621, up 27.9% from 2003. There were 85 business bankruptcies in 2004, down 19% from the previous year. In 2005, the state's personal bankruptcy (Chapter 7 and Chapter 13) filing rate was 345 filings per 100,000 people, ranking North Dakota as the 46th highest in the nation.

21 INCOME

In 2005 North Dakota had a gross state product (GSP) of $24 billion which accounted for 0.2% of the nation's gross domestic product and placed the state at number 50 in highest GSP among the 50 states and the District of Columbia.

According to the Bureau of Economic Analysis, in 2004 North Dakota had a per capita personal income (PCPI) of $29,494. This ranked 37th in the United States and was 89% of the national average of $33,050. The 1994–2004 average annual growth rate of PCPI was 4.5%. North Dakota had a total personal income (TPI) of $18,767,503,000, which ranked 50th in the United States and reflected an increase of 2.8% from 2003. The 1994–2004 average annual growth rate of TPI was 4.4%. Earnings of persons employed in North Dakota increased from $14,513,974,000 in 2003 to $14,966,009,000 in 2004, an increase of 3.1%. The 2003–04 national change was 6.3%.

The US Census Bureau reports that the three-year average median household income for 2002 to 2004 in 2004 dollars was $39,594 compared to a national average of $44,473. During the same period an estimated 10.3% of the population was below the poverty line as compared to 12.4% nationwide.

22 LABOR

According to the Bureau of Labor Statistics (BLS), in April 2006 the seasonally adjusted civilian labor force in North Dakota numbered 363,900, with approximately 12,000 workers unemployed, yielding an unemployment rate of 3.3%, compared to the national average of 4.7% for the same period. Preliminary data for the same period placed nonfarm employment at 349,800. Since the beginning of the BLS data series in 1976, the highest unemployment rate recorded in North Dakota was 6.9% in March 1983. The historical low was 2.5% in January 1998. Preliminary nonfarm employment data by occupation for April 2006 showed that approximately 5.6% of the labor force was employed in construction; 10.4% in manufacturing; 21.5% in trade, transportation, and public utilities; 5.4% in financial activities; 7.7% in professional and business services; 14% in education and health services; 9.2% in leisure and hospitality services; and 21.5% in government.

The US Department of Labor's Bureau of Labor Statistics reported that in 2005, a total of 21,000 of North Dakota's 289,000 employed wage and salary workers were formal members of a union. This represented 7.3% of those so employed, down from 7.7% in 2004, and below the national average of 12%. Overall in 2005, a total of 26,000 workers (9.2%) in North Dakota were covered by a union or employee association contract, which includes those workers who reported no union affiliation. North Dakota is one of 22 states with a right-to-work law.

As of 1 March 2006, North Dakota had a state-mandated minimum wage rate of $5.15 per hour. In 2004, women in the state accounted for 47.8% of the employed civilian labor force.

23 AGRICULTURE

North Dakota's farm marketings totaled $3.96 billion in 2005. Typically, North Dakota is the number one producer of hard spring wheat, durum wheat, sunflowers, barley, oats, flax, all dry edible beans, and pinto beans. In 2004, North Dakota led the nation in spring wheat, drum wheat, barley, dry edible beans, sunflowers, and was second in the nation in overall wheat production. production.

The total number of farms has declined over the years as the average size of farming operations has increased. In 2004, the state had approximately 30,300 farms and ranches occupying 39.4 million acres (16 million hectares) and producing 306.5 million bushels of wheat (second after Kansas), 91.7 million bushels of barley (1st), 791.7 million lb of sunflowers, 14.1 million bushels of oats, 4.75 hundredweight of dry edible beans (1st), 120.8 million bushels of corn, 4.8 million tons of sugar beets (third), and 26.7 million hundredweight of potatoes. The average farm is 1,300 acres (526 hectares).

24 ANIMAL HUSBANDRY

North Dakota farms and ranches had an estimated 1.7 million cattle and calves, valued at $1.83 billion in 2005. During 2004, there were around 169,000 hogs and pigs, worth $18.6 million. North Dakota farmers produced nearly 7 million lb (3.2 million kg) of sheep and lambs, which brought in $7.5 million in gross income in 2003, and nearly 29.4 million lb (13.4 million kg) of turkey were produced in that same year. North Dakota was the leading producer of honey in 2004, with 9.1 million lb (4.1 million kg), worth $31.9 million.

25 FISHING

There is little commercial fishing in North Dakota. The Garrison Dam National Fish Hatchery produces up to 3 million northern pike and nearly 10 million walleye each year. Other species produced there and at the Valley City National Fish Hatchery include smallmouth bass, crappie, rainbow trout, lake trout, brown trout, cutthroat trout, chinook salmon, paddlefish, and pallid sturgeon. In 2004, the state issued 168,497 sport fishing licenses.

26 FORESTRY

The dispersed forests on the rolling prairie are not a dominant feature of the landscape; North Dakota's climate is more favorable to grassland ecosystems. At the time of settlement, native forests covered about 700,000 acres (283,000 hectares). In 2004, there were 673,000 acres (272,000 hectares) of forestland, with 441,000 acres (178,000 hectares) classified as viable timberland. Agricultural clearing, inundation by reservoirs, and other land use changes have resulted in a 9% reduction in total forestland since 1954.

27 MINING

According to preliminary data from the US Geological Survey (USGS), the estimated value of nonfuel mineral production by North Dakota in 2003 was $37.7 million, an increase from 2002 of about 3%.

According to the preliminary data for 2003, construction sand and gravel was the state's leading nonfuel mineral by value and accounted for around 75% of all nonfuel minerals produced, by value. In second place was lime, which was followed by crushed stone.

The preliminary data for 2003 showed that a total of 10.6 million metric tons of construction sand and gravel were produced, having a value of $8.1 million. Lapidary and collectible materials such as petrified wood, agates, jasper, and flint are also found in North Dakota. The state is also a producer of leonardite, an oxidized lignite that is used for viscosity control in oil well drilling muds, as a dispersant, a soil conditioner, and as a stabilizer for ion-exchange resins.

28 ENERGY AND POWER

As of 2003, North Dakota had 39 electrical power service providers, of which 12 were publicly owned and 23 were cooperatives. Of the remainder, three were investor owned and one was federally operated. As of that same year there were 354,323 retail customers. Of that total, 213,027 received their power from investor-owned service providers. Cooperatives accounted for 130,081 customers, while publicly owned providers had 11,197 customers. There were 18 federal customers.

Total net summer generating capability by the state's electrical generating plants in 2003 stood at 4.644 million kW, with total production that same year at 31.322 billion kWh. Of the total amount generated, 99.2% came from electric utilities, with the remainder coming from independent producers and combined heat and power service providers. The largest portion of all electric power generated, 29.427 billion kWh (94%), came from coal-fired plants, with hydroelectric plants in second place at 1.723 billion kWh (5.5%). Other renewable power sources, petroleum fired plants, and plants using other types of gases each accounted for 0.2%.

North Dakota in 2004, had four producing coal mines, all of which were surface operations. Coal production that year totaled 29,943,000 short tons, down from 30,775,000 short tons in 2003. Recoverable coal reserves in 2004 totaled 1.19 billion short tons. One short ton equals 2,000 lb (0.907 metric tons).

As of 2004, North Dakota had proven crude oil reserves of 389 million barrels, or over 2% of all proven US reserves, while output that same year averaged 85,000 barrels per day. Including federal offshore domains, the state that year ranked ninth (eighth excluding federal offshore) in proven reserves and tenth (ninth excluding federal offshore) in production among the 31 producing states. In 2004 North Dakota had 3,072 producing oil wells and account-

ed for 2% of all US production. As of 2005, the state's sole refinery had a crude oil distillation capacity of 58,000 barrels per day.

In 2004, North Dakota had 117 producing natural gas and gas condensate wells. In that same year, marketed gas production (all gas produced excluding gas used for repressuring, vented and flared, and nonhydrocarbon gases removed) totaled 55.009 billion cu ft (1.56 billion cu m). As of 31 December 2004, proven reserves of dry or consumer-grade natural gas totaled 417 billion cu ft (11.8 billion cu m).

29 INDUSTRY

According to the US Census Bureau's Annual Survey of Manufactures (ASM) for 2004, North Dakota's manufacturing sector covered some seven product subsectors. The shipment value of all products manufactured in the state that same year was $7.371 billion. Of that total, food manufacturing accounted for the largest share at $2.370 billion. It was followed by machinery manufacturing at $1.874 billion; computer and electronic product manufacturing at $454.510 million; wood product manufacturing at $305.188 million; and fabricated metal product manufacturing at $261.463 million.

In 2004, a total of 22,027 people in North Dakota were employed in the state's manufacturing sector, according to the ASM. Of that total, 16,485 were actual production workers. In terms of total employment, the food manufacturing industry accounted for the largest portion of all manufacturing employees at 4,902 with 3,808 actual production workers. It was followed by machinery manufacturing at 4,707 employees (3,331 actual production workers); wood product manufacturing at 1,908 employees (1,745 actual production workers); computer and electronic product manufacturing at 1,785 employees (1,192 actual production workers); transportation equipment manufacturing at 1,573 employees (1,208 actual production workers); and fabricated metal product manufacturing with 1,417 employees (1,132 actual production workers).

ASM data for 2004 showed that North Dakota's manufacturing sector paid $764.390 million in wages. Of that amount, the machinery manufacturing sector accounted for the largest share at $182.480 million. It was followed by food manufacturing at $159.059 million; wood product manufacturing at $68.594 million; computer and electronic product manufacturing at $66.649 million; and fabricated metal product manufacturing at $55.437 million.

30 COMMERCE

According to the 2002 Census of Wholesale Trade, North Dakota's wholesale trade sector had sales that year totaling $8.8 billion from 1,485 establishments. Wholesalers of durable goods accounted for 751 establishments, followed by nondurable goods wholesalers at 691 and electronic markets, agents, and brokers accounting for 43 establishments. Sales by durable goods wholesalers in 2002 totaled $2.7 billion, while wholesalers of nondurable goods saw sales of $5.4 billion. Electronic markets, agents, and brokers in the wholesale trade industry had sales of $627.3 million.

In the 2002 Census of Retail Trade, North Dakota was listed as having 3,433 retail establishments with sales of $7.7 billion. The leading types of retail businesses by number of establishments were: gasoline stations (496); motor vehicle and motor vehicle parts dealers (471); building material/garden equipment and supplies dealers (432); food and beverage stores (368); and miscellaneous store retailers (353). In terms of sales, motor vehicle and motor vehicle parts dealers accounted for the largest share of retail sales at $2.08 billion, followed by general merchandise stores at $1.1 billion; gasoline stations at $1.01 billion; and food and beverage stores at $902.4 million. A total of 41,342 people were employed by the retail sector in North Dakota that year.

Exports of North Dakota origin totaled nearly $1.2 billion in 2005, ranking the state 46th in the nation.

³¹CONSUMER PROTECTION

Allegations of consumer fraud and other illegal business practices are handled by the Consumer Protection and Antitrust Division (CPAT) of the state's Attorney General's Office. The CPAT can investigate and prosecute instances of consumer fraud, as well as mediate consumer-business disputes and educates the public on how to avoid consumer fraud.

When dealing with consumer protection issues, the state's Attorney General's Office can initiate civil (but not criminal) proceedings; represent the state before state and federal regulatory agencies; administer consumer protection and education programs; handle formal consumer complaints; and exercise broad subpoena powers. In antitrust actions, the Attorney General's Office can act on behalf of those consumers who are incapable of acting on their own; initiate damage actions on behalf of the state in state courts; and represent counties, cities and other governmental entities in recovering civil damages under state or federal law. However the Office cannot initiate criminal proceedings in antitrust cases.

The offices of the Consumer Protection and Antitrust Division are located in Bismarck.

³²BANKING

As of June 2005, North Dakota had 100 insured banks, savings and loans, and saving banks, plus 38 state-chartered and 20 federally chartered credit unions (CUs). Excluding the CUs, the Fargo market area accounted for the largest portion of the state's financial institutions and deposits in 2004, with 25 institutions and $3.412 billion in deposits. As of June 2005, CUs accounted for 8.3% of all assets held by all financial institutions in the state, or some $1.458 billion. Banks, savings and loans, and savings banks collectively accounted for the remaining 91.7% or $16.180 billion in assets held.

Regulation of state-chartered banks and other state-chartered financial institutions is the responsibility of the North Dakota Department of Financial Institutions and its three divisions: the Banking Division; the Credit Union Division; and the Consumer Division.

In 2004, the median net interest margin (the difference between the lower rates offered to savers and the higher rates charged on loans) stood at 4.15%, down from 4.17% in 2003.

³³INSURANCE

In 2004, North Dakota had 416,000 life insurance policies in force, worth over $38.8 billion; total value for all categories of life insurance (individual, group, and credit) was about $56 billion. The average coverage amount is $93,500 per policy holder. Death benefits paid that year totaled over $138.3 million.

As of 2003, there were 19 property and casualty and 4 life and health insurance companies domiciled in the state. In 2004, direct premiums for property and casualty insurance totaled over $1.2 billion. That year, there were 5,136 flood insurance policies in force in the state, with a total value of $685 million.

In 2004, 55% of state residents held employment-based health insurance policies, 10% held individual policies, and 21% were covered under Medicare and Medicaid; 11% of residents were uninsured. North Dakota has the highest percentage of individual (non employment-based) policy holders among the fifty states. In 2003, employee contributions for employment-based health coverage averaged at 19% for single coverage and 27% for family coverage. The state offers a 39-week health benefits expansion program for small-firm employees in connection with the Consolidated Omnibus Budget Reconciliation Act (COBRA, 1986), a health insurance program for those who lose employment-based coverage due to termination or reduction of work hours.

In 2003, there were 554,234 auto insurance policies in effect for private passenger cars. Required minimum coverage includes bodily injury liability of up to $25,000 per individual and $50,000 for all persons injured in an accident, as well as property damage liability of $25,000. In 2003, the average expenditure per vehicle for insurance coverage was $565.30, which is the lowest average of the 50 states and the District of Columbia.

³⁴SECURITIES

North Dakota has no securities exchanges. In 2005, there were 170 personal financial advisers employed in the state and 480 securities, commodities, and financial services sales agents. In 2004, there were over six publicly traded companies within the state, with over four NASDAQ companies and two NYSE listings. In 2006, the state had one Fortune 1,000 company; MDU Resources Group, listed on the NYSE and based in Bismarck, ranked 546th in the nation with revenues of over $3.4 billion.

³⁵PUBLIC FINANCE

Total expenditures for fiscal years 1995–97 (including federal and special funds) totaled approximately $3.6 billion, including $500 million for transportation, a total of $1.1 billion for health and human services, and a total of $1.3 billion for education. North Dakota has the only state-owned bank and state-owned mill, contributing $50 million and $3 million, respectively, to the general fund during the fiscal year 1999–01 biennium.

Fiscal year 2006 general funds were estimated at $1.1 billion for resources and $975 million for expenditures. In fiscal year 2004, federal government grants to North Dakota were $1.5 billion.

In the fiscal year 2007 federal budget, North Dakota was slated to receive: $7.8 million in State Children's Health Insurance Program (SCHIP) funds to help the state provide health coverage to low-income, uninsured children who do not qualify for Medicaid. This funding is a 23% increase over fiscal year 2006; $4 million for the HOME Investment Partnership Program to help North Dakota fund a wide range of activities that build, buy, or rehabilitate affordable housing for rent or homeownership, or provide direct rental assistance to low-income people. This funding is a 13% increase over fiscal year 2006; and $12 million to complete the

North Dakota—State Government Finances

(Dollar amounts in thousands. Per capita amounts in dollars.)

	AMOUNT	PER CAPITA
Total Revenue	5,228,053	8,220.21
General revenue	3,172,034	4,987.47
Intergovernmental revenue	1,220,547	1,919.10
Taxes	1,228,890	1,932.22
General sales	367,304	577.52
Selective sales	299,434	470.81
License taxes	118,377	186.13
Individual income tax	213,982	336.45
Corporate income tax	49,807	78.31
Other taxes	179,986	283.00
Current charges	516,265	811.74
Miscellaneous general revenue	206,332	324.42
Utility revenue	–	–
Liquor store revenue	–	–
Insurance trust revenue	2,056,019	3,232.73
Total expenditure	3,197,884	5,028.12
Intergovernmental expenditure	613,513	964.64
Direct expenditure	2,584,371	4,063.48
Current operation	1,960,581	3,082.67
Capital outlay	281,143	442.05
Insurance benefits and repayments	223,187	350.92
Assistance and subsidies	42,952	67.53
Interest on debt	76,508	120.30
Exhibit: Salaries and wages	560,791	881.75
Total expenditure	3,197,884	5,028.12
General expenditure	2,974,697	4,677.20
Intergovernmental expenditure	613,513	964.64
Direct expenditure	2,361,184	3,712.55
General expenditures, by function:		
Education	1,057,056	1,662.04
Public welfare	683,035	1,073.95
Hospitals	44,002	69.19
Health	57,081	89.75
Highways	385,158	605.59
Police protection	13,866	21.80
Correction	45,458	71.47
Natural resources	133,888	210.52
Parks and recreation	13,934	21.91
Government administration	123,047	193.47
Interest on general debt	76,508	120.30
Other and unallocable	341,664	537.21
Utility expenditure	–	–
Liquor store expenditure	–	–
Insurance trust expenditure	223,187	350.92
Debt at end of fiscal year	1,662,390	2,613.82
Cash and security holdings	7,301,736	11,480.72

Abbreviations and symbols: – zero or rounds to zero; (NA) not available; (X) not applicable.

SOURCE: *U.S. Census Bureau, Governments Division, 2004 Survey of State Government Finances*, January 2006.

Army Corps of Engineers' urban flood damage reduction project in Grand Forks-East Grand Forks.

³⁶TAXATION

In 2005, North Dakota collected $1,403 million in tax revenues or $2,203 per capita, which placed it 21st among the 50 states in per capita tax burden. The national average was $2,192 per capita. Property taxes accounted for 0.1% of the total; sales taxes, 29.2%; selective sales taxes, 21.3%; individual income taxes, 17.2%; corporate income taxes, 5.4%; and other taxes, 26.7%.

As of 1 January 2006, North Dakota had five individual income tax brackets ranging from 2.1 to 5.54%. The state taxes corporations at rates ranging from 2.6 to 7.0% depending on tax bracket.

In 2004, state and local property taxes amounted to $584,622,000 or $919 per capita. The per capita amount ranks the state 31st nationally. Local governments collected $583,144,000 of the total and the state government $1,478,000.

North Dakota taxes retail sales at a rate of 5%. In addition to the state tax, local taxes on retail sales can reach as much as 2.50%, making for a potential total tax on retail sales of 7.50%. Food purchased for consumption off-premises is tax exempt. The tax on cigarettes is 44 cents per pack, which ranks 38th among the 50 states and the District of Columbia. North Dakota taxes gasoline at 23 cents per gallon. This is in addition to the 18.4 cents per gallon federal tax on gasoline.

According to the Tax Foundation, for every federal tax dollar sent to Washington in 2004, North Dakota citizens received $1.73 in federal spending, which ranks the state fifth-highest nationally.

³⁷ECONOMIC POLICY

The North Dakota Economic Development and Finance Division of the Department of Commerce seeks to attract new industry, retain and expand existing industry, promote start-up businesses, and develop markets for state products. The state uses a local approach to provide business incentives, including job training, financing, and tax-abatement programs. The main operating units within the division include the Rural Development Council, Research, Marketing, and Business Development. Other divisions within the Department of Commerce focus on Community Services, Tourism and Workforce Development.

³⁸HEALTH

The infant mortality rate in October 2005 was estimated at 5.8 per 1,000 live births. The birth rate in 2003 was 12.6 per 1,000 population. The abortion rate stood at 9.9 per 1,000 women in 2000. In 2003, about 87.3% of pregnant woman received prenatal care beginning in the first trimester. In 2004, approximately 82% of children received routine immunizations before the age of three.

The crude death rate in 2003 was 9.6 deaths per 1,000 population. As of 2002, the death rates for major causes of death (per 100,000 resident population) were: heart disease, 255.9; cancer, 203.9; cerebrovascular diseases, 74; chronic lower respiratory diseases, 50.8; and diabetes, 33.7. North Dakota and Ohio share the distinction of having the third-highest diabetes mortality rate in the nation (following West Virginia and Louisiana). The mortality rate from HIV infection was not available in 2002. In 2004, the reported AIDS case rate was at about 2.7 per 100,000 population, on of the lowest in the nation. In 2002, about 59.3% of the population was considered overweight or obese. As of 2004, about 19.8% of state residents were smokers.

In 2003, North Dakota had 40 community hospitals with about 3,600 beds. There were about 88,000 patient admissions that year and 1.8 million outpatient visits. The average daily inpatient census was about 2,100 patients. The average cost per day for hospital care was $859. Also in 2003, there were about 84 certified nursing facilities in the state with 6,582 beds and an overall occupancy rate of about 93.2%. In 2004, it was estimated that about 69.6% of all state residents had received some type of dental care within the year. North Dakota had 244 physicians per 100,000 resident population in 2004 and 1,059 nurses per 100,000 in 2005. In 2004, there were a total of 319 dentists in the state.

About 12% of state residents were enrolled in Medicaid programs in 2003; 16% were enrolled in Medicare programs in 2004. Approximately 11% of the state population was uninsured in 2004. In 2003, state health care expenditures totaled $767,000.

39 SOCIAL WELFARE

In 2004, about 13,000 people received unemployment benefits, with the average weekly unemployment benefit at $226. For 2005, the estimated average monthly participation in the food stamp program included about 42,204 persons (18,927 households); the average monthly benefit was about $88.21 per person. That year, the total of benefits paid through the state for the food stamp program was about $44.6 million.

Temporary Assistance for Needy Families (TANF), the system of federal welfare assistance that officially replaced Aid to Families with Dependent Children (AFDC) in 1997, was reauthorized through the Deficit Reduction Act of 2005. TANF is funded through federal block grants that are divided among the states based on an equation involving the number of recipients in each state. North Dakota's TANF program is called Training, Employment, Education Management (TEEM). In 2004, the state program had 8,000 recipients; state and federal expenditures on this TANF program totaled $29 million in fiscal year 2003.

In December 2004, Social Security benefits were paid to 114,720 North Dakota residents. This number included 71,820 retired workers, 15,650 widows and widowers, 10,820 disabled workers, 9.330 spouses, and 7,100 children. Social Security beneficiaries represented 18% of the total state population and 94.9% of the state's population age 65 and older. Retired workers received an average monthly payment of $891; widows and widowers, $869; disabled workers, $840; and spouses, $447. Payments for children of retired workers averaged $489 per month; children of deceased workers, $582; and children of disabled workers, $274. Federal Supplemental Security Income payments in December 2004 went to 7,966 North Dakota residents, averaging $337 a month. An additional $160,000 of state-administered supplemental payments were distributed to 355 residents.

40 HOUSING

In 2004, North Dakota had 300,815 housing units, 262,585 of which were occupied; 68.1% were owner-occupied. About 63.2% of all housing units were single-family, detached homes. Utility gas and electricity were the most common energy sources for heating. It was estimated that 10,860 units lacked telephone services, 1,161 lacked complete plumbing facilities, and 1,825 lacked complete kitchen facilities. The average household had 2.32 members.

In 2004, 4,000 new privately owned units were authorized for construction. The median home value was $84,354, one of the lowest in the nation. The median monthly cost for mortgage owners was $902. Renters paid a median of $466 per month, representing the second-lowest rate in the nation (above West Virginia). In 2006, the state received over $4.9 million in community development block grants from the US Department of Housing and Urban Development (HUD).

41 EDUCATION

In 2004, 89.5% of North Dakota residents age 25 and older were high school graduates; 25.2% had obtained a bachelor's degree or higher.

The total enrollment for fall 2002 in North Dakota's public schools stood at 104,000. Of these, 69,000 attended schools from kindergarten through grade eight, and 35,000 attended high school. Approximately 88% of the students were white, 1.2% were black, 1.4% were Hispanic, 0.8% were Asian/Pacific Islander, and 8.5% were American Indian/Alaskan Native. Total enrollment was estimated at 102,000 in fall 2003 and expected to be 94,000 by 2014, a decline of 10.2% during the period 2002–14. Expenditures for public education in 2003/04 were estimated at $901 million. There were 6,209 students enrolled in 52 private schools. Since 1969, the National Assessment of Educational Progress (NAEP) has tested public school students nationwide. The resulting report, *The Nation's Report Card,* stated that in 2005, eighth graders in North Dakota scored 287 out of 500 in mathematics compared with the national average of 278.

As of fall 2002, there were 45,800 students enrolled in college or graduate school; minority students comprised 9.4% of total postsecondary enrollment. In 2005 North Dakota had 21 degree-granting institutions. The chief universities are the University of North Dakota in Grand Forks and North Dakota State University in Fargo. The North Dakota Student Financial Assistance Program offers scholarships for North Dakota college students, and the state Indian Scholarship Board provides aid to Native Americans attending college in the state.

42 ARTS

The North Dakota Council on the Arts (NDCA) was established in 1967 and is a branch of the North Dakota state government. NDCA provides grants to local artists and groups such as the Trollwood Performing Arts School and the Annual United Tribes Indian Art Expo; encourages visits by out-of-state artists and exhibitions; and provides information and other services to the general public.

In 2005, the North Dakota Council of the Arts and other North Dakota arts organizations received 9 grants totaling $647,800 from the National Endowment for the Arts. The state also provided the council with funding. In 2006, the North Dakota Humanities Council, established in 1973, provided programs that included Read North Dakota, to promote literature from and about the state, and the Great Plains Chautauqua Society. In 2005, the National Endowment for the Humanities contributed $778,772 to six state programs.

The historic Fargo Theater presents live theatrical performances as well as films and sponsors the annual Fargo Film Festival. Fargo is also the center for the Fargo-Moorhead Opera and the Fargo-Moorhead Symphony. The Northern Plains Ballet is based in Bismarck but tours to Sioux Falls, Fargo, Billings, and Grand Forks.

Two popular musical events are the Old Time Fiddlers Contest (at Dunseith in June) and the Medora Musical (Medora, June through Labor Day); the latter features Western songs and dance.

The North Dakota Museum of Art is the official state art museum. Founded in the mid-1970s, its permanent collection focuses on, but is not exclusive to, contemporary Native American Art.

[43]LIBRARIES AND MUSEUMS

In 2001, North Dakota had 82 public library systems, with a total of 89 libraries, of which eight were branches. In that same year, North Dakota public libraries had 2,158,000 volumes of books and serial publications on their shelves, and a total circulation of 3,937,000. The system also had 61,000 audio and 51,000 video items, 7,000 electronic format items (CD-ROMs, magnetic tapes, and disks), and 14 bookmobiles. The leading academic library was that of the University of North Dakota (Grand Forks), with 1,221,953 items. In 2001, operating income for the state's public library system totaled $8,837,000 and included $75,000 in federal funding and $565,000 in state funding. Operating expenditures that year totaled $8,185,000, of which 60.5% was spent on staff, and 19.6% on the collection.

Among the most notable of the state's 50 museums are the Art Galleries and Zoology Museum of the University of North Dakota and the North Dakota Heritage Center at Bismarck, which has an outstanding collection of Indian artifacts. Theodore Roosevelt National Park contains relics from the Elkhorn ranch where Roosevelt lived in the 1880s.

[44]COMMUNICATIONS

In 2004, 95.0% of North Dakota's occupied housing units had telephones. Additionally, by June 2002 there were 245,578 mobile wireless telephone subscribers. In 2003, 61.2% of North Dakota households had a computer and 53.2% had Internet access. By June 2005, there were 56,057 high-speed lines in North Dakota, 47,278 residential and 8,799 for business. There were 28 major radio stations (10 AM, 18 FM) in 2005. As of 2005, 9 major network television stations were in operation. A total of 15,091 Internet domain names were registered in North Dakota in 2000.

[45]PRESS

As of 2005, there were six morning dailies and four evening dailies. There were also seven Sunday papers in the state. The leading dailies were the *Fargo Forum,* with a daily circulation of 51,106, Sunday, 62,097; the *Grand Forks Herald,* 31,524 morning, 34,763 Sunday; the *Minot Daily News,* 20,974 morning, 21,848 Sunday; and the *Bismarck Tribune,* 27,620 morning, 31,081 Sunday. In addition, there were about 15 periodicals. The leading historical journal is *North Dakota Horizons,* a quarterly founded in 1971.

[46]ORGANIZATIONS

In 2006, there were over 1,276 nonprofit organizations registered within the state, of which about 770 were registered as charitable, educational, or religious organizations. Two of the state's largest organizations are the Friends (Service Club) and the Northwest Farm Managers Association, both headquartered in Fargo.

State organizations focusing on arts, culture, history, and the environment include Arts on the Prairie, ArtWise, the Bluegrass and Old Time Music Association of North Dakota, the Crazy Horse Memorial Foundation, Fargo Garden Society, the North Dakota Council on Arts, the Badlands Conservation Alliance. and the North Dakota Wildlife Federation. The North Dakota Academy of Science is located in Grand Forks. There are at least three chapters of the Sons of Norway active in the state.

The National Sunflower Association is in Bismarck.

[47]TOURISM, TRAVEL, AND RECREATION

North Dakota's 17 state parks received 922,434 visitors in 2003, a 5% decline over 2002. Visitors to Theodore Roosevelt National Park and other national historic sites in the state in 2003 numbered 517,356, representing a 15% increase over 2002. Some 40% of all park users come from other states and countries.

A $1.8-million tourism campaign in 2005 brought $88 million in tourism revenue to the state. Tourism is North Dakota's second-largest industry, accounting for $3 billion of economic impact.

Among the leading tourist attractions is the International Peace Garden, covering 2,200 acres (890 hectares) in North Dakota and Manitoba; it commemorates friendly relations between the United States and Canada. Ft. Abraham Lincoln State Park, south of Mandan, has been restored to evoke the 1870s, when General Custer left the area for his "last stand" against the Sioux. The most spectacular scenery in North Dakota is found in the Theodore Roosevelt National Park. The so-called "badlands," an integral part of the park, consist of strangely colored and intricately eroded buttes and other rock formations. Hunting and fishing are major recreational activities in North Dakota.

[48]SPORTS

There are no major professional sports teams in North Dakota. In collegiate football, the University of North Dakota Fighting Sioux and the North Dakota State University Bison compete in the North Central Conference. The University of North Dakota competes in collegiate ice hockey, winning National Collegiate Athletic Association (NCAA) championships in 1959, 1963, 1980, 1982, 1987, 1997, and 2000.

Other annual sporting events include the PWT Championship (a walleye fishing tournament) in Bismarck in September, and several rodeos throughout the state. Former New York Yankee slugger Roger Maris grew up in Fargo, North Dakota.

[49]FAMOUS NORTH DAKOTANS

Preeminent among North Dakota politicians known to the nation was Gerald P. Nye (b.Wisconsin, 1892–1971), a US senator and a leading isolationist opponent of President Franklin D. Roosevelt's foreign policy, as was Senator William Langer (1886–1959). Another prominent senator, Porter J. McCumber (1858–1933), supported President Woodrow Wilson in the League of Nations battle. US Representative William Lemke (1878–1950) sponsored farm-relief legislation and in 1936 ran for US president on the Union Party ticket. Usher L. Burdick (1879–1960), a maverick isolationist and champion of the American Indian, served 18 years in the US House of Representatives.

Vilhjalmur Stefansson (b.Canada, 1879–1962) recorded in numerous books his explorations and experiments in the high Arctic. Orin G. Libby (1864–1952) made a significant contribution to the study of American history. Other North Dakota–nurtured writers and commentators include Maxwell Anderson (b.Pennsylvania, 1888–1959), a Pulitzer Prize–winning playwright; Edward K. Thompson (Minnesota, 1907–96), editor of *Life* magazine and founder-editor of *Smithsonian;* radio and television commentator Eric Severeid (1912–1992); and novelist Larry Woiwode (b.1941).

To the entertainment world North Dakota has contributed band leaders Harold Bachman (1892–1972), Lawrence Welk (1903–92), and Tommy Tucker (Gerald Duppler, 1908–89); jazz vocalist Peggy Lee (Norma Delores Egstrom, b.1920) and country singer Lynn Anderson (b.1947); and actresses Dorothy Stickney (1900–98) and Angie Dickinson (Angeline Brown, b.1931).

Sports personalities associated with the state include outfielder Roger Maris (1934–85), who in 1961 broke Babe Ruth's record for home runs in one season.

⁵⁰BIBLIOGRAPHY

Barbour, Barton H. *Fort Union and the Upper Missouri Fur Trade.* Norman: University of Oklahoma Press, 2001.

Council of State Governments. *The Book of the States, 2006 Edition.* Lexington, Ky.: Council of State Governments, 2006.

DeLorme Mapping Company. *North Dakota Atlas & Gazetteer: Topo Maps of the Entire State: Back Roads, Outdoor Recreation.* Yarmouth, Me.: DeLorme, 1999.

Hintz, Martin. *North Dakota.* New York: Children's Press, 2000.

Hoover, Herbert T. *The Sioux and Other Native American Cultures of the Dakotas: An Annotated Bibliography.* Westport, Conn.: Greenwood Press, 1993.

McMacken, Robin. *The Dakotas: Off the Beaten Path.* Old Saybrook, Conn.: Globe Pequot Press, 1998.

Ostler, Jeffrey. *The Plains Sioux and U.S. Colonialism from Lewis and Clark to Wounded Knee.* New York: Cambridge University Press, 2004.

Parzybok, Tye W. *Weather Extremes in the West.* Missoula, Mont.: Mountain Press, 2005.

Preston, Thomas. *Great Plains: North Dakota, South Dakota, Nebraska, Kansas, Oklahoma, and Texas.* Vol. 4 in *The Double Eagle Guide to 1,000 Great Western Recreation Destinations.* Billings, Mont.: Discovery Publications, 2003.

Raaen, Aagot. *Grass of the Earth: Immigrant Life in Dakota Country.* St. Paul: Minnesota Historical Society Press, 1994.

Rees, Amanda (ed.). *The Great Plains Region.* Vol. 1 in *The Greenwood Encyclopedia of American Regional Cultures.* Westport, Conn.: Greenwood Press, 2004.

US Department of Commerce, Economics and Statistics Administration, US Census Bureau. *North Dakota, 2000. Summary Social, Economic, and Housing Characteristics: 2000 Census of Population and Housing.* Washington, D.C.: US Government Printing Office, 2003.

OHIO

State of Ohio

ORIGIN OF STATE NAME: From the Iroquois Indian word *oheo,* meaning "beautiful." **NICKNAME:** The Buckeye State. **CAPITAL:** Columbus. **ENTERED UNION:** 1 March 1803 (17th). **SONG:** "Beautiful Ohio." **MOTTO:** With God All Things Are Possible. **FLAG:** The flag is a burgee, with three red and two white lateral stripes. At the staff is a blue triangular field covered with 17 stars (signifying Ohio's order of entry into the Union), which is grouped around a red disk superimposed on a white circular "O." **OFFICIAL SEAL:** In the foreground are a sheaf of wheat and a sheaf of 17 arrows; behind, a sun rises over a mountain range, indicating that Ohio is the first state west of the Alleghenies. Surrounding the scene are the words "The Great Seal of the State of Ohio." **BIRD:** Cardinal. **FLOWER:** Scarlet carnation. **TREE:** Buckeye. **LEGAL HOLIDAYS:** New Year's Day, 1 January; Birthday of Martin Luther King Jr., 3rd Monday in January; Presidents' Day, 3rd Monday in February; Memorial Day, last Monday in May; Independence Day, 4 July; Labor Day, 1st Monday in September; Columbus Day, 2nd Monday in October; Veterans' Day, 11 November; Thanksgiving Day, 4th Thursday in November; Christmas Day, 25 December. **TIME:** 7 AM EST = noon GMT.

¹LOCATION, SIZE, AND EXTENT

Located in the eastern north-central United States, Ohio is the 11th largest of the 12 Midwestern states and ranks 35th in size among the 50 states.

The state's total area is 41,330 sq mi (107,044 sq km), of which land comprises 41,004 sq mi (106,201 sq km) and inland water 326 sq mi (823 sq km). Ohio extends about 210 mi (338 km) E–W; its maximum N–S extension is 230 mi (370 km).

Ohio is bordered on the N by Michigan and the Canadian province of Ontario (with the line passing through Lake Erie); on the E by Pennsylvania and West Virginia (with the Ohio River forming part of the boundary); on the S by West Virginia and Kentucky (with the entire line defined by the Ohio River); and on the W by Indiana.

Five important islands lie off the state's northern shore, in Lake Erie: the three Bass Islands, Kelleys Island, and Catawba Island. Ohio's total boundary length is 997 mi (1,605 km).

The state's geographic center is in Delaware County, 25 mi (40 km) NNE of Columbus.

²TOPOGRAPHY

Ohio has three distinct topographical regions: the foothills of the Allegheny Mountains in the eastern half of the state; the Erie lakeshore, extending for nearly three-fourths of the northern boundary; and the central plains in the western half of the state.

The Allegheny Plateau in eastern Ohio consists of rugged hills and steep valleys that recede gradually as the terrain sweeps westward toward the central plains. The highest point in the state is Campbell Hill (1,549 ft/472 m), located in Logan County about 50 mi (80 km) northwest of Columbus. The mean elevation of the state is approximately 850 ft (259 m).

The Erie lakeshore, a band of level lowland that runs across the state to the northwestern corner on the Michigan boundary, is distinguished by sandy beaches. The central plains extend to the western boundary with Indiana. In the south, undulating hills decline in altitude as they reach the serpentine Ohio River, which forms the state's southern boundary with Kentucky and West Virginia. The state's lowest point is on the bands of the Ohio River in the southwest, where the altitude drops to 455 ft (139 m) above sea level.

Most of Ohio's 2,500 lakes are situated in the east, and nearly all are reservoirs backed up by river dams. The largest, Pymatuning Reservoir, on the Pennsylvania border, has an area of 14,650 acres (5,929 hectares). Grand Lake (St. Mary's), located near the western border, covering 12,500 acres (5,059 hectares), is the largest lake wholly within Ohio.

Ohio has two drainage basins separated by a low ridge extending from the northeast corner to about the middle of the western border with Indiana. North of the ridge, more than one-third of Ohio's area is drained by the Maumee, Portage, Sandusky, Cuyahoga, and Grand rivers into Lake Erie. South of the ridge, the remaining two-thirds of the state is drained mainly by the Muskingum, Hocking, Raccoon, Scioto, Little Miami, and Miami rivers into the Ohio River, which winds for about 450 mi (725 km) along the eastern and southern borders.

Ohio's bedrock of sandstone, shale, and limestone was formed during the Paleozoic era some 300–600 million years ago. The oldest limestone rocks are found in the Cincinnati anticline, a ridge of sedimentary rock layers about 3,000 ft (900 m) thick that extends from north to south in west-central Ohio. Inland seas filled and receded periodically to form salt and gypsum, also creating peat bogs that later were pressurized into the coal beds of southeastern Ohio. At the end of the Paleozoic era, the land in the eastern region uplifted to form a plateau that was later eroded by wind and water into hills and gorges.

About two million years ago, glaciers covering two-thirds of the state leveled the western region into plains and deposited fertile limestone topsoil. As the glaciers retreated, the melting ice formed a vast lake, which overflowed southward into the channels that became the Ohio River. Perhaps 15,000 years ago, during the last Ice Age, the glacial waters ran off and reduced Lake Erie to its present size. Limestone rocks in Glacier Grooves State Park on Kelley's Island bear the marks of the glaciers' movements.

³CLIMATE

Lying in the humid continental zone, Ohio has a generally temperate climate. Winters are cold and summers mild in the eastern highlands. The southern region has the warmest temperatures and longest growing season—198 days on the average, compared with 150 to 178 days in the remainder of the state. More than half of the annual rainfall occurs during the growing season, from May to October.

Among the major cities, Columbus, in the central region, has an annual average temperature of 52°F (11°C), with a normal maximum of 62°F (16°C) and a normal minimum of 42°F (5°C). Cleveland, in the north, has an annual average of 51°F (10°C), with a normal maximum of 59°F (15°C) and minimum of 41°F (5°C). The average temperature in Cincinnati, in the south, is 54.5°F (12°C), the normal maximum 64.6°F (18°C), and the normal minimum 44.3°F (6°C). Cleveland has an average of 122 days per year in which the temperature drops to 32° (0°C) or lower, Columbus 117 days, and Cincinnati 90 days. The record low temperature for the state is -39°F (-39°C), set at Milligan on 10 February 1899. The record high is 113°F (45°C), registered near Gallipolis on 21 July 1934.

Cleveland has an average annual snowfall of 55.4 in (140 cm), while Columbus receives 27.6 in (70 cm), and Cincinnati 14.2 in (36 cm). The average annual precipitation in Cincinnati is about with 40.7 in (103 cm), compared with 37.8 in (96 cm) for Columbus and 37.2 in (94 cm) for Cleveland. Because of its proximity to Lake Erie, Cleveland is the windiest city, with winds that average 11 mph (18 km/hr).

⁴FLORA AND FAUNA

More than 2,500 plant species have been found in Ohio. The southeastern hill and valley region supports pitch pine, bigleaf magnolia, and sourwood, with undergrowths of sassafras, witchhazel, pawpaw, hornbeam, and various dogwoods. At least 14 species of oak, 10 of maple, 9 of poplar, 9 of pine, 7 of ash, 7 of elm, 6 of hickory, 5 of birch, and 2 of beech grow in the state, along with butternut, eastern black walnut, wild black cherry, black locust, and sycamore. A relative of the horse chestnut (introduced to Ohio from Asia), the distinctive buckeye—first called the Ohio buckeye and now the official state tree—is characterized by its clusters of cream-colored flowers that bloom in spring and later form large, brown, thick-hulled nuts. Five Ohio plant species were listed as threatened in 2006, including eastern prairie fringed orchid, northern wild monkshood, and lakeside daisy; the running buffalo clover was listed as endangered that year by the US Fish and Wildlife Service.

The Buckeye State is rich in mammals. White-tailed deer, badger, mink, raccoon, red and gray foxes, coyote, beaver, eastern cottontail, woodchuck, least shrew, and opossum are found throughout the state's five wildlife districts; the bobcat, woodland jumping mouse, and red-backed mole are among many species with more restricted habitats. Common birds include the eastern great blue heron, green-winged teal, mourning dove, eastern belted kingfisher, eastern horned lark, blue-gray gnatcatcher, eastern cowbird, and a great variety of ducks, woodpeckers, and warblers; the cardinal is the state bird, and the ruffed grouse, mostly confined to the Allegheny Plateau, is a favorite game species. Bass, pickerel, perch, carp, pike, trout, catfish, sucker, and darter thrive in Ohio's lakes and streams. The snapping, midland painted, and spiny softshelled turtles, five-lined skink, northern water snake, midland brown snake, eastern hognose, and eastern milk snake appear throughout Ohio. The northern copperhead, eastern massasauga (swamp rattler), and timber rattlesnake are Ohio's only poisonous reptiles. Fowler's toad, bullfrog, green pickerel frog, and marbled and red-backed salamanders are common native amphibians.

Acting on the premise that the largest problem facing wildlife is the destruction of their habitat, the Division of Wildlife of the Department of Natural Resources has instituted an ambitious endangered species program. The US Fish and Wildlife Service listed 17 Ohio animal species (vertebrates and invertebrates) as threatened or endangered in April 2006, including the bald eagle, Indiana bat, Scioto madtom, and piping plover.

⁵ENVIRONMENTAL PROTECTION

Early conservation efforts in Ohio were aimed at controlling the ravages of spring floods and preventing soil erosion. After the Miami River floods of March 1913, which took 361 lives and resulted in property losses of more than $100 million in Dayton alone, the Miami Conservancy District was formed; five earth dams and 60 mi (97 km) of river levees were completed by 1922, at a cost of $40 million, to hold back cresting water. In the Muskingum Conservancy District in eastern Ohio, construction of flood-control dams has prevented spring flooding and the washing away of valuable topsoil into the Ohio River.

In recent years, the state's major environmental concerns have been to reverse the pollution of Lake Erie, control the air pollution attributable to industries and automobiles, clean up dumps for solid and hazardous wastes, improve water quality, and prevent pollution. Of recent concern is the problem with so-called "brownfields"—polluted industrial sites whose cleanup costs present barriers to development. In November 2000, voters approved the Clean Ohio Fund; it will provide $200 million to help revitalize abandoned commercial and industrial sites, promoting reuse of existing infrastructure, and helping to reduce sprawl. The Clean Ohio Revitalization Fund awarded nearly $40 million to 17 projects in its first round of funding.

The state's regulatory agency for environmental matters is the Ohio Environmental Protection Agency (EPA), established in 1972. The agency has long-range programs to deal with pollution of air, water, and land resources. Ohio EPA also coordinates state, local, and federal funding of environmental programs.

Since 1972, antipollution efforts in Lake Erie have focused on reducing the discharge of phosphorus into the lake from sewage and agricultural wastes; sewage treatment facilities have been upgraded with the aid of more than $750 million in federal grants, and efforts have been made to promote reduced-tillage farming to control runoff. By the early 1980s, numerous beaches had been reopened, and sport fishing was once again on the increase. Since 1972, Ohio industries spent billions of dollars on efforts to control

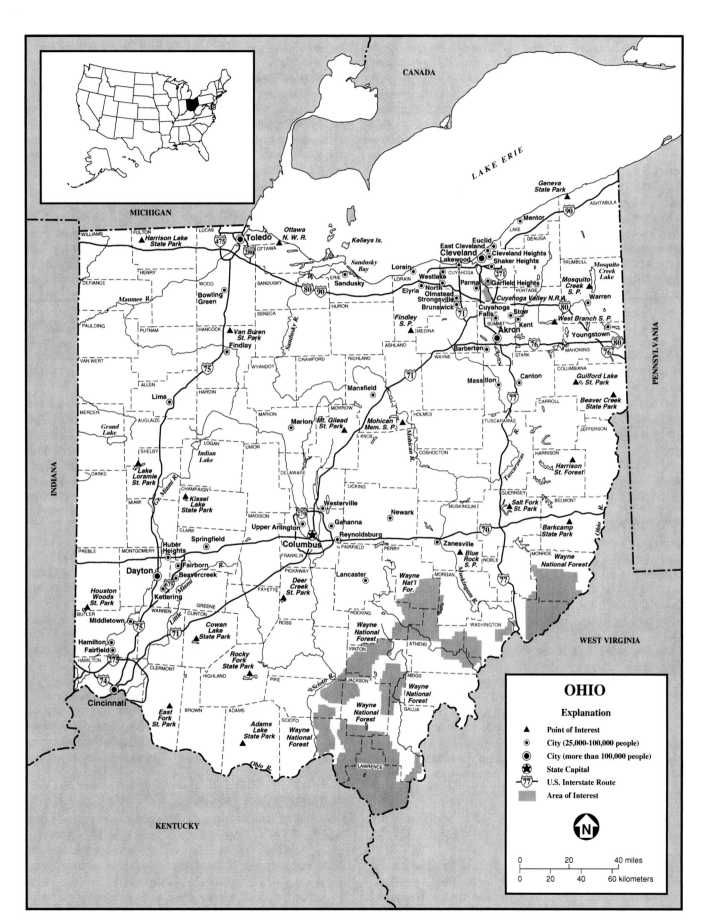

OHIO

Explanation

▲ Point of Interest

⊙ City (25,000-100,000 people)

◉ City (more than 100,000 people)

★ State Capital

〰77〰 U.S. Interstate Route

▨ Area of Interest

0   20   40 miles

0   20   40   60 kilometers

air pollution. Peak ozone levels have dropped by 25% overall and by up to 50% in some urban areas. Lead levels in the outdoor air have dropped 98% since 1978 and particulate levels have dropped 80%. From 1967 to 1983, through the efforts of local health departments and with the eventual help of the EPA, over 1,300 open garbage dumps were closed down and more than 200 sanitary landfills constructed to replace them. In 2003, 251.6 million lb of toxic chemicals were released in the state; Ohio ranks fourth in the nation for highest levels of toxic chemicals released (following Alaska, Nevada, and Texas).

In 1980, Ohio passed its first legislation aimed at controlling hazardous wastes, and by the mid-1980s, with the aid of more than $11 million in federal Superfund grants, cleanup had been completed or begun at 16 major sites. In 2003, Ohio had 318 hazardous waste sites listed in the US Environment Protection Agency (EPA) database. In 2006, 30 of these sites were on the National Priorities List, including Wright-Patterson Air Force Base. Rickenbacker Air National Guard base has been proposed as a National Priority List Site. In 2005, the EPA spent over $5.1 million through the Superfund program for the cleanup of hazardous waste sites in the state. The same year, federal EPA grants awarded to the state included $25.2 million for its safe drinking water revolving fund. An addition grant of $60.6 million was awarded to provide assistance for water resource protection and improvement projects in small and hardship communities.

Another agency, the Ohio Department of Natural Resources, is responsible for the development and use of the state's natural resources. The state's parks and recreational areas totaled 208,000 acres (84,000 hectares). The department also assists in soil conservation, issues permits for dams, promotes conservation of oil and gas, and allocates strip-mining licenses.

6 POPULATION

Ohio ranked seventh in population in the United States with an estimated total of 11,464,042 in 2005, an increase of 1% since 2000. Between 1990 and 2000, Ohio's population grew from 10,847,115 to 11,353,140, an increase of 4.7%. The population is projected to reach 11.63 million by 2015, but a decline to 11.6 is projected by 2025. The population density in 2004 was 280.1 persons per sq mi.

Ohio's population grew slowly during the colonial period and totaled 45,365 persons in 1800. Once the territory became a state in 1803, settlers flocked to Ohio and the population quintupled to 230,760 by 1810, The state's population doubled again by 1820, approached 2,000,000 in 1850, and totaled 3,198,062 by 1880. Ohio's annual rate of population increase slowed considerably after 1900, when its population was 4,157,545; nevertheless, in the period between 1900 and 1960, the total population more than doubled to 9,706,397. A slow rate of population increase during the 1970s, and a population decline during 1980–85, resulted from a net migration loss and a declining birthrate.

In 2004, the median age in Ohio was 37.5. In the same year, more than 24.3% of the populace were under age 18 while 13.3% was age 65 or older.

As of the 1990 census, Columbus became Ohio's largest city, with a population of 632,910, trading second place with Cleveland, which had 505,616 residents. Whereas Columbus increased its population by 12% during the 1980s, Cleveland's population de-

creased by 11.9%. The 2004 estimated populations of the two cities were Columbus, 730,008, and Cleveland, 458,684. The Columbus metropolitan area had an estimated population of 1,693,906. The Cleveland metropolitan area (including Elyria and Mentor) had a population of about 2,137,073. Cincinnati and other large cities also lost population during this period, largely because of the shift of the middle class from the inner cities to the suburbs or to other states. In 2004, Cincinnati's estimated population was 314,154, followed by Toledo, 304,973; Akron, 212,179; and Dayton, 160,293. The Cincinnati metropolitan area had an estimated population of 2,058,221.

7 ETHNIC GROUPS

Ohio was first settled by migrants from the eastern states and from the British Isles and northern Europe, especially Germany. Cincinnati had such a large German population that its public schools were bilingual until World War I. With the coming of the railroads and the development of industry, Slavic and other south Europeans were recruited in large numbers.

By 2000, however, only about 3% of Ohioans were foreign born, the major places of origin being Germany, Italy, and the United Kingdom. Ethnic clusters persist in the large cities, and some small communities retain a specific ethnic flavor, such as Fairport Harbor on Lake Erie, with its large Finnish population.

As of 2000 there were 1,301,307 blacks, representing 11.5% of the population. That percentage increased to 11.9% by 2004. Most live in the larger cities, especially Cleveland, which in 2000 had a black population of 243,939, or 51.0% of the city total. Historically, Ohio was very active in the antislavery movement. Oberlin College, established in 1833 by dissident theological students, admitted blacks from its founding and maintained a "station" on the Underground Railroad. Cleveland elected its first black mayor, Carl B. Stokes, in 1967.

Some 217,123 people in Ohio (1.9% of the total population) were Hispanic or Latino in 2000, up from 140,000 in 1990. The largest number (90,663) were of Mexican descent, but there were also many Puerto Ricans. In 2004, 2.2% of the population was Hispanic or Latino. In 2000, American Indians numbered about 24,486. In 2004, 0.2% of the population was American Indian. In 2000, Asians were estimated to number 132,633, including 30,425 Chinese (up from 16,829 in 1990), 12,393 Filipinos, 10,732 Japanese, and 13,376 Koreans. Pacific Islanders numbered 2,749. In 2004, Asians accounted for 1.4% of the population. In 2004, 1.2% of the population reported origin of two or more races.

Except for small Iroquoian groups like the Erie and Seneca, most of the Indian population before white settlement comprised four Algonkian tribes: Delaware, Miami, Wyandot, and Shawnee. Indian place-names include Ohio, Coshocton, Cuyahoga, and Wapakoneta.

8 LANGUAGES

Ohio English reflects three post-Revolutionary migration paths. Into the Western Reserve south of Lake Erie came Northern speech from New York and Connecticut. Still common there are the Northern pronunciation of the *ow* diphthong, as in *cow,* with a beginning like the /ah/ vowel in *father,* and the use of the /ah/ in *fog* and *college;* /krik/ is more common than /kreek/ for *creek.* A dragonfly is a *devil's darning needle;* doughnuts may be *fried cakes;*

a boy throws himself face down on a sled in a *bellyflop (per);* and a tied and filled bedcover is a *comforter.*

Most of nonurban Ohio has North Midland speech from Pennsylvania. Generally, except in the northern strip, *cot* and *caught* are sound-alikes, and *now* is /naow/, south of Columbus, because of the influence of South Midland patterns from Kentucky and extreme southern Pennsylvania, corn bread may be *corn pone,* lima beans are *butter beans,* and a tied quilt is a *comforter. Spouting,* yielding to *gutters,* barely reaches across to Indiana; and *sick at the stomach, dived,* and *wait on me* are competing with expanding Northern *to the stomach, dove,* and *wait for me.* A new Midland term, *bellybuster,* originated around Wheeling and has spread north to compete with *bellyflop.* Northern and Midland merge in the mixed dialect west of Toledo.

From Kentucky, South Midland speakers took *you-all* into Ohio River towns, and in the southwestern tip of the state can be heard their *evening* for *afternoon, terrapin* for *tortoise,* and *frogstool* for *toadstool.* Recent northward migration has introduced South Midland speech and black English, a southern dialect, into such industrial centers as Cleveland, Toledo, and Akron.

Localisms have developed. For the grass strip between sidewalk and street, Akron has *devil-strip* and Cleveland has *treelawn.* Foreign-language influence appears in such Pennsylvania Germanisms as *clook* (hatching hen), *snits* (dried apples), *smearcase* (cottage cheese), and *got awake.*

Of Ohioans aged five years or older 93.9% spoke only English at home in 2000, down from 94.6% in 1990.

The following table gives selected statistics from the 2000 Census for language spoken at home by persons five years old and over. The category "Other West Germanic languages" includes Dutch, Pennsylvania Dutch, and Afrikaans. The category "Other Slavic languages" includes Czech, Slovak, and Ukrainian. The category "African languages" includes Amharic, Ibo, Twi, Yoruba, Bantu,

Ohio—Counties, County Seats, and County Areas and Populations

COUNTY	COUNTY SEAT	LAND AREA (SQ MI)	POPULATION (2005 EST.)	COUNTY	COUNTY SEAT	LAND AREA (SQ MI)	POPULATION (2005 EST.)
Adams	West Union	586	28,454	Logan	Bellefontaine	458	46,580
Allen	Lima	405	106,234	Lorain	Elyria	495	296,307
Ashland	Ashland	424	54,123	Lucas	Toledo	341	448,229
Ashtabula	Jefferson	703	103,221	Madison	London	467	41,295
Athens	Athens	508	62,062	Mahoning	Youngstown	417	254,274
Auglaize	Wapakoneta	398	47,242	Marion	Marion	403	65,932
Belmont	St. Clairsville	537	69,228	Medina	Medina	422	167,010
Brown	Georgetown	493	44,398	Meigs	Pomeroy	432	23,232
Butler	Hamilton	469	350,412	Mercer	Celina	457	41,202
Carroll	Carrollton	393	29,388	Miami	Troy	410	101,619
Champaign	Urbana	429	39,698	Monroe	Woodsfield	458	14,698
Clark	Springfield	398	142,376	Montgomery	Dayton	458	547,435
Clermont	Batavia	456	190,589	Morgan	McConnelsville	420	14,958
Clinton	Wilmington	410	42,570	Morrow	Mt. Gilead	406	34,322
Columbiana	Lisbon	534	110,928	Muskingum	Zanesville	654	85,579
Coshocton	Coshocton	566	36,945	Noble	Caldwell	399	14,156
Crawford	Bucyrus	403	45,774	Ottawa	Port Clinton	253	41,583
Cuyahoga	Cleveland	459	1,335,317	Paulding	Paulding	419	19,537
Darke	Greenville	600	52,983	Perry	New Lexington	412	35,246
Defiance	Defiance	414	39,112	Pickaway	Circleville	503	52,989
Delaware	Delaware	443	150,268	Pike	Waverly	443	28,146
Erie	Sandusky	264	78,665	Portage	Ravenna	493	155,631
Fairfield	Lancaster	506	138,423	Preble	Eaton	426	42,527
Fayette	Washington Ct. House	405	28,199	Putnam	Ottawa	484	34,928
Franklin	Columbus	542	1,090,771	Richland	Mansfield	497	127,949
Fulton	Wauseon	407	42,955	Ross	Chillicothe	692	75,197
Gallia	Gallipolis	471	31,362	Sandusky	Fremont	409	61,676
Geauga	Chardon	408	95,218	Scioto	Portsmouth	614	76,561
Greene	Xenia	415	151,996	Seneca	Tiffin	553	57,483
Guernsey	Cambridge	522	41,123	Shelby	Sidney	409	48,736
Hamilton	Cincinnati	412	806,652	Stark	Canton	574	380,608
Hancock	Findlay	532	73,503	Summit	Akron	412	546,604
Hardin	Kenton	471	32,032	Trumbull	Warren	612	219,296
Harrison	Cadiz	400	15,920	Tuscarawas	New Philadelphia	569	91,944
Henry	Napoleon	415	29,453	Union	Marysville	437	45,751
Highland	Hillsboro	553	42,818	Van Wert	Van Wert	410	29,154
Hocking	Logan	423	29,009	Vinton	McArthur	414	13,429
Holmes	Millersburg	424	41,567	Warren	Lebanon	403	196,622
Huron	Norwalk	495	60,385	Washington	Marietta	640	62,210
Jackson	Jackson	420	33,526	Wayne	Wooster	557	113,697
Jefferson	Steubenville	410	70,599	Williams	Bryan	422	38,688
Knox	Mt. Vernon	529	58,398	Wood	Bowling Green	619	123,929
Lake	Painesville	231	232,466	Wyandot	Upper Sandusky	406	22,813
Lawrence	Ironton	457	63,112	**TOTALS**		41,005	11,464,042
Licking	Newark	686	154,806				

Swahili, and Somali. The category "Other Indo-European languages" includes Albanian, Gaelic, Lithuanian, and Rumanian.

LANGUAGE	NUMBER	PERCENT
Population 5 years and over	**10,599,968**	**100.0**
Speak only English	9,951,475	93.9
Speak a language other than English	648,493	6.1
Speak a language other than English	**648,493**	**6.1**
Spanish or Spanish Creole	213,147	2.0
German	72,647	0.7
French (incl. Patois, Cajun)	44,594	0.4
Italian	27,697	0.3
Other West Germanic languages	26,372	0.2
Chinese	25,704	0.2
Arabic	22,647	0.2
Other Slavic languages	21,230	0.2
Polish	16,462	0.2
Russian	16,030	0.2
Greek	13,656	0.1
African languages	13,261	0.1
Serbo-Croatian	12,577	0.1
Hungarian	11,859	0.1
Other Indo-European languages	11,070	0.1
Korean	11,028	0.1

[9] RELIGIONS

The first religious settlement in Ohio territory was founded among Huron Indians in 1751 by a Roman Catholic priest near what is now Sandusky. Shortly afterward, Moravian missionaries converted some Delaware Indians to Christianity; the first Protestant church was founded by Congregationalist ministers at Marietta in 1788. Dissident religious sects such as the Shakers, Amish, and Quakers moved into Ohio from the early 18th century onward, but the majority of settlers in the early 19th century were Presbyterians, Methodists, Baptists, Disciples of Christ, and Episcopalians.

The first Roman Catholic priest to be stationed permanently in Ohio was Father Edward Fenwick, who settled in Cincinnati in 1817. When the Protestant settlers there did not allow him to build a Catholic church in the town, he founded Christ Church (now St. Francis Church) just outside Cincinnati. In 1821, Father Fenwick became the first Catholic bishop in Ohio. The large influx of Irish and German immigrants after 1830 greatly increased the Catholic constituency in Cleveland, Cincinnati, Columbus, and Toledo. Among the German immigrants were many Lutherans and large number of Jews, who made Cincinnati a center of Reform Judaism. In the mid-19th century, Cincinnati had the nation's third-largest Jewish community; the Union of American Hebrew Congregations, the most important Reform body, was founded there in 1873, and Hebrew Union College, a rabbinical training school and center of Jewish learning, was founded two years later.

The Church of Jesus Christ of Latter-day Saints (Mormons), founded in 1930 by Joseph Smith Jr. of New York, built its first permanent place of worship in Kirtland, Ohio, in 1933. The Kirtland Temple, as it has been called, is still open today as a museum and educational center. A functioning temple was opened in Columbus in 1999. In 2006, the Latter-day Saints reported a statewide membership of 54,297 in 124 congregations.

In 2004, Ohio had a Roman Catholic population of about 2,139,524, with about 512,146 members belonging to the archdiocese of Cincinnati and 812,675 members within the Cleveland diocese. In 2000, the state's Jewish population was estimated at 142,255. Leading Jewish communities were in Cleveland, Cincinnati, and Columbus. The Muslim population was at about 41,281

people. Ohio communities of Amish and Mennonites are among the largest in the nation with over 24,000 Amish and over 20,000 Mennonites in the state (primarily central Ohio).

In the United Methodist Church is one of the largest Protestant denominations, with a membership of about 420,142 statewide in 2004. In 2000, the Evangelical Lutheran Church in America reported 301,749 members; the Southern Baptist Convention had 187,227 (with 5,251 newly baptized members in 2002); the Presbyterian Church USA, 160,800, Christian Churches and Churches of Christ, 142,571; and the American Baptist Churches USA, 117,757. In 2000, about 6.2 million people (55.1% of the population) were not counted as members of any religious organization. The national Office of General Ministries of the United Church of Christ is located in Cleveland. The Ohio conference of the United Church of Christ had about 118,449 members in 2005.

[10] TRANSPORTATION

Sandwiched between two of the country's largest inland water systems, Lake Erie and the Ohio River, Ohio has long been a leader in water transport. With its numerous terminals on the Ohio River and deepwater ports on Lake Erie, Ohio ranks as one of the major US states for shipping.

The building of railroads in the mid-19th century greatly improved transportation within the state by connecting inland counties with Lake Erie and the Ohio River. The Mad River and Lake Erie Railroad, between Dayton and Sandusky, was completed in 1844, and two years later, it was joined with the Little Miami Railroad, to provide through service to Cincinnati. By 1856, Cleveland was connected by rail with Columbus and Pittsburgh. Railroad building in the state reached a peak in the 1850s. At the outbreak of the Civil War, Ohio had more miles of track than any other state. By 1900, railroads were by far the most important system of transport.

In 2003, Class I railroads operated 4,510 rail mi (7,261 km) of track in the state, out of a total of 6,519 mi (10,495 km) of track in service. In that same year, Ohio had 19 railroads within its borders, including three Class I railroads. Freight service on branch lines to counties has been maintained through a state subsidy program.

Mass transit in Ohio's cities began in 1859 with horse-drawn carriages carrying paying passengers in Cleveland and Cincinnati, which added a cable car on rails about 1880. The electric trolley car, introduced to Cleveland in 1884, soon became the most popular mass transit system for the large cities. Inter-urban electric railways carried passengers to and from rural towns that had been bypassed by the railroads. There were 2,809 mi (4,521 km) of interurban track in the state by 1907. The use of electric railways declined with the development of the motor car in the 1920s, and by 1939, for example, the seven interurban lines serving Columbus had been abandoned. Today, suburbanites mostly commute to their workplaces in Columbus and other cities by automobile and bus lines. However, Cleveland continues to operate a light rail system, that as of 2004, had around 40 mi (64 km) of track, which stretched from the city's east side and eastern suburbs to the downtown lakefront and out to Cleveland Hopkins Airport on the city's southwestern side. In 2006, Amtrak operated three regularly scheduled trains through Ohio, connecting six cities.

Rough roads were used by settlers in the early 19th century. The National Road was built from Wheeling, West Virginia, to Zanesville in 1826, and was extended to Columbus by 1833. The increasing use of the automobile in the 1930s led to massive state and federal road-building programs in Ohio as elsewhere. The major interstate highways across Ohio connect Cleveland and the Toledo area in the north (I-80, I-90); link Columbus with Dayton, Zanesville, and Wheeling (I-70) and with Cincinnati and Cleveland (I-71); and extend north–south from Cleveland and Akron to Marietta in the east (I-77), and from Toledo to Dayton and Cincinnati in the west (I-75).

In 2004, Ohio had 124,752 mi (200,850 km) of roads. In that same year, there were some 6.395 million automobiles, about 4.061 million trucks of all types, some 298,000 motorcycles, and around 18,000 buses registered in the state, along with 7,675,007 licensed drivers.

Inland waterways have long been important for transport and commerce in Ohio. The first settlers traveled into Ohio by flatboat down the Ohio River to establish such towns as Marietta and Cincinnati. Lake Erie schooners brought the founders of Cleveland and Sandusky. Steamboat service began on the Ohio River in 1811, and at Lake Erie ports in 1818. The public demand for water transportation in the interior of the state, where few rivers were navigable, led to construction of the Ohio and Erie Canal from Portsmouth on the Ohio River to Cleveland, and the Miami and Erie Canal from Cincinnati to Toledo. Both canals were opened to traffic in 1827 but not completed for another 14 years. The canals gave Ohio's farmers better access to eastern and southern markets. Water transportation is still a principal means of shipping Ohio's products through the St. Lawrence Seaway to foreign countries, and the method by which millions of tons of cargo, particularly coal, are moved via the Ohio River to domestic markets.

Ohio's ports rank among the busiest of the 50 states in volume. In 2004, the state's most active ports were: Cleveland, with 15.774 million tons of cargo handled; Cincinnati with 13.898 million tons; Ashtabula with 10.938 million tons; and Toledo with 9.861 million tons. In 2003, waterborne shipments totaled 113.743 million tons. In 2004, Ohio had 444 mi (714 km) of navigable inland waterways.

Ohioans consider Dayton to be the birthplace of aviation because it was there that Wilbur and Orville Wright built the first motor-powered airplane in 1903. In 2005, Ohio had a total of 734 public and private-use aviation-related facilities. This included 519 airports, 209 heliports, 4 STOLports (Short Take-Off and Landing), and 2 seaplane bases. The state's major air terminals are the Greater Cincinnati airport (actually located across the Ohio River in Kentucky) and Hopkins International in Cleveland. In 2004, Cincinnati/Northern Kentucky International Airport had 10,864,547 passenger enplanements, while Cleveland Hopkins had 5,389,196 enplanements in that same year, making them the 22nd- and 35th-busiest airports in the United States, respectively.

11 HISTORY

The first people in Ohio, some 11,000 years ago, were hunters. Their stone tools have been found with skeletal remains of long-extinct mammoths and mastodons. Centuries later, Ohio was inhabited by the Adena people, the earliest mound builders. Their descendants, the Hopewell Indians, built burial mounds, fortifications, and ceremonial earthworks, some of which are now preserved in state parks.

The first European travelers in Ohio, during the 17th century, found four Indian tribes: Wyandot and Delaware in northern Ohio, Miami and Shawnee in the south. All were hunters who followed game trails that threaded the dense Ohio forest. All together, these four tribes numbered about 15,000 people. European exploration was begun by a French nobleman, Robert Cavelier, Sieur de la Salle, who, with Indian guides and paddlers, voyaged from the St. Lawrence River to the Ohio, which he explored in 1669–70. In the early 1700s, French and English traders brought knives, hatchets, guns, blankets, tobacco, rum, and brandy to exchange for the Indians' deer and beaver skins.

Both the French and the English claimed possession of Ohio, the French claim resting on La Salle's exploration, while the British claimed all territory extending westward from their coastal colonies. To reinforce the French claim, Celeron de Bienville led an expedition from Canada to Ohio in 1749 to warn off English traders, win over the Indians, and assert French possession of the land. Traveling by canoe, with marches overland, he found the Indians better disposed at that time to the English than to the French. The following year, a company of Virginia merchants sent Christopher Gist to map Ohio trade routes and to make friendship and trade agreements with the tribes. The clash of ambitions brought on the French and Indian War—during which the Indians fought on both sides—ending in 1763 with French defeat and the ceding of the vast western territory to the British. During the Revolutionary War, the American militiaman George Rogers Clark, with a small company of woodsmen-soldiers, seized British posts and trading stations in Ohio, and, in the Battle of Piqua, defeated Indian warriors allied with the British. It was largely Clark's campaigns that won the Northwest Territory for the United States.

The new nation had a huge public domain, extending from the Allegheny Mountains to the Mississippi River. To provide future government and development of the territory northwest of the Ohio River, the US Congress enacted the Land Ordinance of 1785 and the Northwest Ordinance of 1787. The Land Ordinance created a survey system of rectangular sections and townships, a system begun in Ohio and extended to all new areas in the expanding nation. The farsighted Northwest Ordinance provided a system of government under which territories could achieve statehood on a basis equal with that of the original colonies. When a specified area had a population of 60,000 free adult males, it could seek admission to the Union as a state.

The first permanent settlement in Ohio was made in 1788 by an organization of Revolutionary War veterans who had received land warrants as a reward for their military service. They trekked by ox-drawn wagons over the mountains and by flatboat down the Ohio River to the mouth of the Muskingum, where they built the historic town of Marietta. John Cleves Symes, a New Jersey official, brought pioneer settlers to his Miami Purchase in southwestern Ohio; their first settlement, in 1789, eventually became the city of Cincinnati. Access to the fertile Ohio Valley was provided by the westward-flowing Ohio River, which carried pioneer settlers and frontier commerce. Flatboats made a one-way journey, as families floated toward what they hoped would be new settlements. Keelboats traveled both downstream and upstream—an easy journey followed by a hard one. The keelboat trade, carrying military supplies and frontier produce, created an enduring river lore. Its legendary hero is burly, blustering Mike Fink, "half horse and half alligator," always ready for a fight or a frolic, for riot or rampage.

Increasing settlement of the Ohio Valley aroused Indian resistance. War parties raided outlying villages, burned houses, and drove families away. Two military expeditions against the Indians were shattered by Chief Little Turtle and his Miami warriors. Then, in 1793, Maj. Gen. "Mad Anthony" Wayne took command in the west. He built roads and forts in the Miami Valley, and trained a force of riflemen. On a summer morning in 1794, Wayne routed allied tribesmen, mostly Miami and Shawnee, in the decisive Battle of Fallen Timbers. In the ensuing Treaty of Greenville, Indian leaders surrendered claim to the southern half of Ohio, opening that large domain to uncontested American occupation.

When, in 1800, Connecticut ceded to the United States a strip of land along Lake Erie claimed by its colonial charter and called the Western Reserve, that region became a part of the Northwest Territory. Now the future seemed unclouded, and from the older colonies came a great migration to the promised land. By 1802, Ohio had enough population to seek statehood, and in November, a constitutional convention assembled at Chillicothe. In 25 days and at a total cost of $5,000, the 35 delegates framed a constitution that vested most authority in the state legislature and gave the vote to all white male taxpayers. On 1 March 1803, Ohio joined the Union as the 17th state.

Beyond Ohio's western border, Indians still roamed free. In 1811, the powerful Shawnee chief Tecumseh led a tribal resistance movement (supported by the British) seeking to halt the white man's advance into the new territory and to regain lands already lost to the Americans. Ohio militia regiments led by Gen. William Henry Harrison repulsed an Indian invasion near Toledo in the battle of Tippecanoe on 7 November 1811. Control of Lake Erie and of Great Lakes commerce was at stake when Commodore Oliver Hazard Perry won a decisive naval victory over a British fleet in western Lake Erie during the War of 1812. Tecumseh was slain in the Battle of Thames in Canada on 5 October 1813.

With peace restored in 1815, "Ohio fever" spread through New England. In a great migration, people streamed over the mountains and the lakes to a land of rich soil, mild climate, and beckoning opportunities. Across the Atlantic, especially in England, Ireland, and Germany, thousands of immigrants boarded ship for America. At newly opened land offices, public land was sold at $1.25 an acre. Forest became fields, fields became villages and towns, towns became cities. By 1850, Ohio was the third-most populous state in the Union.

Having cleared millions of acres of forest, Ohioans turned to economic development. Producing more than its people consumed, the state needed transportation routes to eastern markets. The National Road extended across the central counties in the 1830s, carrying stagecoach passengers and wagon commerce from Pennsylvania and Maryland. The Ohio canal system, created between 1825 and 1841, linked the Ohio River and Lake Erie, providing a waterway to the Atlantic via New York's Erie Canal. In 1826, state lands were valued at $16 million; 15 years later, their value exceeded $100 million. The chief products were wheat, corn, pork, beef, salt, wool, and leather. By 1850, when farm and factory production outstripped the capacity of mule teams and canal barges, railroad building had begun. In the next decade, railroads crisscrossed the state.

In 1861, Ohio, like the rest of the nation, was divided. The northern counties, teeming with former New Englanders, were imbued with abolitionist zeal. But Ohio's southern counties had close ties with Virginia and Kentucky across the river. From southeastern Ohio came Clement L. Vallandigham, leader of the Peace Democrats—called Copperheads by their opponents—who defended states' rights, opposed all of President Lincoln's policies, and urged compromise with the Confederacy. While Ohio surpassed its quota by providing a total of 320,000 Union Army volunteers, the Copperhead movement grew strong enough to nominate Vallandigham for state governor in 1863. Responding to the news of Vallandigham's defeat by the rugged Unionist John Brough, Lincoln telegraphed: "Ohio has saved the nation." Ohio became directly involved in the war for two weeks in 1863, when Confederate Gen. John Hunt Morgan led a Kentucky cavalry force on a daring but ineffectual raid through the southern counties.

Ohio gave the Union its greatest generals—Ulysses S. Grant, William Tecumseh Sherman, and Philip H. Sheridan—each of whom won decisive victories at crucial times. Also essential to the Union cause was the service of Ohio men in Lincoln's cabinet, including Treasury Secretary Salmon P. Chase and War Secretary Edwin M. Stanton.

Mid-19th-century Ohio was primarily an agricultural state, but war demands stimulated Ohio manufacturing, and in the decade following the war, the state's industrial products surpassed the value of its rich farm production. The greatest commercial development came in northern Ohio, where heavy industry grew dramatically. To Toledo, Cleveland, and Youngstown via Lake Superior came iron ore that was converted into iron and steel with coal from the Ohio Valley. In the 1870s, John D. Rockefeller of Cleveland organized the Standard Oil Co., which soon controlled oil refining and distribution throughout the nation. At the same time, B. F. Goodrich of Akron began making fire hose, the first rubber product in an industry whose prodigious growth would make Akron the "rubber capital of the world." In the middle of the state, the capital city, Columbus, became a center of the brewing, railroad equipment, and farm implement industries. Cincinnati factories made steamboat boilers, machine tools, meat products, railroad cars, and soap. Dayton became known for its paper products, refrigerators, and cash registers. With industrial growth came political power. In the next half century, Ohio virtually took possession of the White House. Presidents Grant, Rutherford B. Hayes, James A. Garfield, Benjamin Harrison, William McKinley, William Howard Taft, and Warren G. Harding were all Ohioans.

The four great business pursuits—agriculture, commerce, mining, and manufacturing—were remarkably balanced in Ohio. Its ethnic strains were various. Following the earlier English, Irish, and German influx came Italian, Czech, Dutch, Finnish, Greek, Hungarian, Polish, Russian, Serbian, and Ukrainian immigrants, along with a growing number of blacks from the rural South. Thus Ohio provided an advantageous background for a president; to any segment of the nation, an Ohio candidate did not seem alien. In the 1920 campaign, both the Republican and Democratic nominees—Harding and James M. Cox—were Ohio men. Norman Thomas, a perennial Socialist candidate, was likewise an Ohioan.

During World War I, Ohio's heavy industry expanded and its cities grew. Progressivism developed in Toledo and Cleveland, under their respective mayors, Samuel M. "Golden Rule" Jones and

Tom L. Johnson, whose reforms resulted in the city-manager form of government that spread to other Ohio cities. In the postwar 1920s, Ohio's oil, rubber, and glass industries kept pace with accelerating automobile production. Yet none of these industries was immune to the prolonged depression of the 1930s. Widespread unemployment and a stagnant economy were not relieved until the outbreak of World War II. The war swept 641,000 Ohioans into military service and gave Ohio industry military contracts totaling $18 billion.

The state's economy prospered after World War II, with highway building, truck and tractor production, aircraft manufacture, and airport construction leading the field. The completion of the St. Lawrence Seaway in 1959 made active international ports of Toledo and Cleveland. Major problems during this period involved pollution created by the dumping of industrial wastes (especially in Lake Erie) and urban decay resulting from the departure of middle-class families to the suburbs, an exodus that left the central cities to growing numbers of the poor and underprivileged. Related to these problems were troubles in the Ohio school system. Deteriorating neighborhoods produced inadequate revenues for schools and public services, and attempts at racial integration brought controversy and disturbance. When political offices were won by minority leaders—in 1967, for example, Carl Stokes of Cleveland became the first black mayor of any major US city—friction and tension continued. A further shock to Ohioans was the May 1970 shooting of 13 Kent State University students, four of whom died, by national guardsmen who had been sent to the campus to preserve order during a series of demonstrations against US involvement in Vietnam.

During the early 1980s, Ohio was still beset by serious social and economic problems. While the state's population remained static, the unemployment rate in 1982 and 1983 reached 14%. A decline in manufacturing jobs was only partly offset by the employment brought by a growing service sector. In 1983, the state established the Thomas Edison Program to provide start-up companies with venture capital funds. The legislation helped jumpstart the state's economy. But by the end of the 1980s, economic progress slowed again. Unemployment rose in the recession of the early 1990s, reaching 6.9% in 1992. Within two years, as part of a national recovery, it had rebounded to 4.9%. In March 1995, Ohio was the site of the largest work stoppage in the auto industry in a quarter century, when almost 178,000 employees were laid off in response to a 17-day strike by auto workers at two General Motors plants in Dayton. In 1999 the economy was holding steady with an unemployment rate of 4.3%, in line with the national average. In July 2003, the unemployment rate stood at 6.2%, again on par with the national average. Ohio's unemployment rate stood at 5.8% in September 2005, above the national average of 5.1%. Ohio continued to experience job losses in a national economy that had just begun to recover from the 2001 recession.

Hunger and homelessness were on the rise in the late 1990s and early 2000s. A 1999 report by the Ohio Hunger Task Force found that nearly one million children in low-income family faced hunger, while the Coalition on Homelessness and Housing reported that need for emergency shelters for families had grown, stretching resources in the state's 10 largest counties.

In January 1999, newly elected Governor Robert Taft, the great grandson of President William Howard Taft, took office. His ad-ministration moved quickly to address the problem highlighted in a 1996 federal study that revealed the state had the worst school facilities in the nation. His plan to spend $23 billion on school repairs over 12 years was boosted in November 1999 by voters who approved Issue 1, a ballot initiative allowing Ohio to borrow money less expensively for school construction. The governor was also pushing for tougher gun control.

Conservancy programs at the state level encompassed the watersheds of the Muskingum and Miami rivers, which became models for such undertakings in other states in the 1980s. Pollution in Lake Erie, where poor water conditions had made national headlines, was successfully reversed through a coalition of government efforts. By the end of the 1990s, the state was viewed as a national leader in improving waterways. But, as the Environmental Protection Agency lined up partners to clean up the Cuyahoga River, Ohio still faced serious environmental threats. A study released in 2000 indicated air pollution in the Ohio River Valley was worse than that on the nation's East Coast. It was reported earlier that rain contaminated with mercury from coal-fired electric plants was polluting Midwest lakes and rivers. In 2000 the EPA released a study citing the state for failing to meet tighter federal ozone limits. Illegal dumping also posed a persistent problem, with an estimated 30 to 40 million tires having been unlawfully deposited at nearly 100 sites around the state.

In 2000 the state remained among the most populous in the nation, with its more than 11.3 million people giving it a rank of seventh among the states.

Ohio was one of the states affected by the 14 August 2003 massive power blackout in Canada, the Northeast and Midwestern states. The largest electrical outage in US history affected 9,300 square miles and a population of over 50 million. An initial power failure in Ohio was later found to be the trigger for the outage. Many areas of Cleveland were without safe drinking water for a number of days.

Ohio remained at the center of the nation's presidential politics in 2004: President George W. Bush narrowly defeated John Kerry in Ohio by less than 120,000 votes, which swung the election for him. Ohio politics in 2005 were also the subject of controversy. Beginning in April 2005, the Toledo Blade newspaper began publishing a series of stories revealing that Toledo coin dealer Tom Noe, chair of the Bush-Cheney campaign for Lucas County, was investing $50 million for the state through coin speculation: buying and selling rare coins to turn a profit. Noe could not account for $10–13 million in the fund. Noe had also been placed under federal investigation for money laundering—perhaps state money—to the Bush campaign. The "coingate" scandal was complicated further by the fact that a Blade reporter with close ties to the Republican Party reportedly knew about Noe's campaign violations in early 2004, but suppressed the information. The publisher and editor-in-chief of the Blade held that if the "coingate" scandal had become public knowledge before the November election, Kerry would have won Ohio and won the presidency. Republican governor Bob Taft was the subject of a scandal in 2005 in which he pleaded no contest to accepting certain gifts—including from Noe—without reporting them, as required by law.

In the November 2004 election, Ohio voters approved by initiative petition an amendment to the Ohio constitution that adopted a section declaring a valid and recognized marriage to be between one man and one woman only.

[12] STATE GOVERNMENT

The Ohio constitution of 1803 was replaced by a second constitution in 1851. Amendments proposed by a constitutional convention in 1912 and subsequently approved by the voters so heavily revised the 1851 constitution as to make it virtually a new document. This modified constitution, with subsequent amendments (a total of 161 by January 2005), provides for county and municipal home rule, direct primary elections, recall of elected officials, and constitutional amendments by initiative and referendum.

Ohio's General Assembly consists of a 99-member House of Representatives, elected for two years, and a Senate of 33 members serving four-year terms (half the members are chosen every two years). Regular sessions of the legislature convene the first Monday in January of each year and are not formally limited in length. The presiding officers of both houses may issue a joint call to convene a special session. Legislators must be at least 18 years old, have lived in their districts for at least one year, and be qualified voters. The legislative salary was $54,942 in 2004. Each house may introduce legislation, and both houses must approve a bill before it can be signed into law by the governor. The governor's veto of a bill can be overridden by three-fifths majority votes of the elected members of each houses. Bills not signed or vetoed by the governor become law after 10 days.

Officials elected statewide are the governor and lieutenant governor (elected jointly), secretary of state, attorney general, auditor, and treasurer, all of whom serve four-year terms. (Eleven members of the state Board of Education are elected; six are appointed: all serve four-year terms.) Effective in 1959, a constitutional amendment changed the governor's term from two to four years and forbade a governor from serving more than two successive terms. The governor appoints the heads of executive departments, as well as the adjutant general and members of most statutory boards. Candidates for governor must be 18 years old, US citizens, qualified voters, and state residents. As of December 2004, the governor's salary was $126,485.

The constitution may be amended legislatively by a three-fifths vote of each house; the proposed amendment must then receive majority approval by the voters at the next general election. Amendments may also be proposed by petition of 10% of the electors who voted for governor in the last general election; a majority vote in a subsequent referendum is required for passage.

The constitution provides that every 20 years (from 1932 onward), the voters must be given the chance to choose whether a constitutional convention should be held. Voters rejected this option in 1932, 1952, 1972, and again in 1992.

To vote in Ohio, one must be a US citizen, at least 18 years old, and have been a state resident for at least 30 days prior to election day. Restrictions apply to convicted felons and those declared mentally incompetent by the court.

[13] POLITICAL PARTIES

Ohio has sent seven native sons and one other state resident to the White House—equaling Virginia as the "mother of presidents." The state's two major political parties, Democratic and Republican, have dominated the political scene since 1856.

Ohioans scattered their votes among various political factions until 1836, when they rallied behind state resident William Henry Harrison and the Whig Party; they again supported Harrison in 1840, helping him win his second bid for the presidency. Whigs

Ohio Presidential Vote by Political Parties, 1948–2004

YEAR	ELECTORAL VOTE	OHIO WINNER	DEMOCRAT	REPUBLICAN	PROGRESSIVE	SOCIALIST LABOR	COMMUNIST	LIBERTARIAN
1948	25	*Truman (D)	1,452,791	1,445,684	37,487	—	—	—
1952	25	*Eisenhower (R)	1,600,367	2,100,391	—	—	—	—
1956	25	*Eisenhower (R)	1,439,655	2,262,610	—	—	—	—
1960	25	Nixon (R)	1,944,248	2,217,611	—	—	—	—
1964	26f	*Johnson (D)	2,498,331	1,470,865				
1968	26	*Nixon (R)	1,700,586	1,791,014	AMERICAN IND. 467,495	—	—	—
1972	25	*Nixon (R)	1,558,889	2,441,827	AMERICAN 80,067	7,107	6,437	—
1976	25	*Carter (D)	2,011,621	2,000,505	SOC. WORKERS 15,529	4,717	7,817	8,961
1980	25	*Reagan (R)	1,745,103	2,203,139	CITIZENS 8,979	4,436	5,030	49,604
1984	25	*Reagan (R)	1,825,440	2,678,560	—		—	5,886
1988	25	*Bush (R)	1,939,629	2,416,549	—	WORKERS LEAGUE 5,432	NEW ALLIANCE 12,017	11,989
1992	21	*Clinton (D)	1,984,942	1,894,310	IND. (Perot) 1,036,426	POPULIST/AM. FIRST 4,698	6,411	7,252
1996	21	*Clinton (D)	2,148,222	1,859,883	483,207	—	—	12,851
2000	21	*Bush, G. W. (R)	2,186,190	2,351,209	IND. (Nader) 117,857	IND. (Buchanan) 26,724	—	13,475
2004	20	*Bush, G. W. (R)	2,741,167	2,859,768	WRITE-IN (Cobb) 192	NONPARTISAN (Peroutka) 11,939	WRITE-IN (Schriner) 114	NONPARTISAN (Badnarik) 14,676

*Won US presidential election.

and Democrats divided the votes in 1844, 1848, and 1852; in 1856, however, Ohio supported the newly formed Republican Party, and after the Civil War, seven of the country's next 12 presidents were Ohio-born Republicans, beginning with Grant and ending with Harding. From 1856 to 1996, Ohioans voted for the Republican candidate in all presidential elections except those in which the following six Democrats were elected: Woodrow Wilson (twice), Franklin D. Roosevelt (three times), Harry S. Truman, Lyndon B. Johnson, Jimmy Carter, and Bill Clinton (twice). In 1920, when the presidential candidates of both major parties were Ohioans, the Republican, Warren G. Harding, carried Ohio as well as the nation.

Political bossism flourished in Ohio during the last quarter of the 19th century, when the state government was controlled by Republicans Mark Hanna in Cleveland and George B. Cox in Cincinnati. Hanna played an influential role in Republican national politics; in 1896, his handpicked candidate, William McKinley, was elected to the presidency. But the despotism of the bosses and the widespread corruption in city governments led to public demands for reform. In Toledo, a reform mayor, Samuel "Golden Rule" Jones, began to clean house in 1897. Four years later, another group of reformers, led by Mayor Tom L. Johnson, ousted the Hanna machine and instituted honest government in Cleveland. At the time, journalist Lincoln Steffens called Cleveland "the best-governed city in the United States" and Cincinnati "the worst." The era of bossism ended for Cincinnati in 1905, when the voters overthrew the Cox machine, elected a reform mayor on a fusion ticket, and instituted reforms that in 1925 made Cincinnati the first major US city with a nonpartisan city-manager form of government.

With the decline of big-city political machines, ticket splitting has become a regular practice among Ohio voters in state and local contests. Governor Frank J. Lausche, a Democrat, was elected to an unprecedented five two-year terms (1945–47, 1949–57), and Republican James A. Rhodes served four four-year terms (1963–71, 1975–83). In 1982, Ohioans elected a Democratic governor, Richard F. Celeste, and Democrats swept all state offices and won control of both houses of the state legislature. Republican George Voinovich won the governorship in 1990 and again in 1994. In 1998 elections, Republican candidate Bob Taft won the governor's office; he was reelected in 2002. In 2005 the Republicans also dominated the state Senate (22 seats as opposed to the Democrats' 11), and the state House, which had 61 Republicans and 38 Democrats.

Following November 2004 elections, there were 6 Democrats and 12 Republicans serving as US Representatives. In 1992 both Ohio senators—John Glenn, elected to a fourth term in 1992, and Howard Metzenbaum, elected to a third term in 1988—were Democrats. However, in 1994 Metzenbaum retired and a Republican, Mike DeWine, took the seat (he was reelected in 2000). In 1998, the seat held by retiring Senator John Glenn was won by former Ohio governor, Republican George Voinovich.

In general, third parties have fared poorly in Ohio since 1856. Exceptions were the 1968 presidential election, in which American Independent Party candidate George Wallace garnered nearly 12% of Ohio's popular vote, and the 1992 presidential election, when Independent Ross Perot captured 21% of the vote. A more typical voting pattern was displayed in the 1976 presidential election when the two major parties together received 97.7% of the

total votes cast, and only 2.3% of the votes were split among minor parties and independents. In 2000, independent candidate Ralph Nader took 3% of the vote, and independent candidate Pat Buchanan won 1%.

The result was not nearly so close in 1980, when Ronald Reagan, the Republican presidential nominee, won 51% of the popular vote to 41% for Jimmy Carter (with 6% going to John Anderson and 2% to minor party candidates), or in 1984, when Reagan won 59% of the popular vote to defeat Walter Mondale in the state. Republican George Bush won 55% of the vote in 1988. In 1992, however, Bush lost the state to Democratic nominee Bill Clinton, who captured 40% of the vote to Bush's 38%. In 1996, Clinton won 47% of the vote, Republican Bob Dole won 41%, and Independent Ross Perot received 11%. In 2000, Republican George W. Bush won 50% of the vote to Democrat Al Gore's 46%. In 2004, Bush increased his support slightly, to take 51% of the vote to John Kerry's 48.5%. In 2002 there were 7,973,000 registered voters. In 1998, 17% of registered voters were Democratic, 18% Republican, and 65% unaffiliated or members of other parties. The state had 20 electoral votes in the 2004 presidential election, a loss of 1 vote over 2000.

14 LOCAL GOVERNMENT

As of 2005, local government in Ohio is exercised by 88 counties, 942 municipal governments, 662 public school districts, and 631 special districts. In 2002, there were 1,308 townships.

Each county is administered by a board of commissioners, elected to four-year terms, whose authority is limited by state law. The county government is run by officials elected to four-year terms: auditor or financial officer, clerk of courts, coroner, engineer, prosecuting attorney, recorder, sheriff, and treasurer.

Within each county are incorporated areas with limited authority to govern their own affairs. Thirty voters in an area may request incorporation of the community as a village. A village reaching the population of 5,000 automatically becomes a city, which by law must establish executive and legislative bodies. There are three types of city government: the mayor-council plan, which is the form adopted by a majority of the state's cities; the city-manager form, under which the city council appoints a professional manager to conduct nonpartisan government operations; and the commission type, in which a board of elected commissioners administers the city government. In practice, most large cities have adopted a home-rule charter that permits them to select the form of government best suited to their requirements.

Cleveland experimented with the city-manager form of government from 1924 to 1932, at which time public disclosures of municipal corruption led the city's voters to return to the mayor-council plan. In 1967, Cleveland became the first major US city to elect a black mayor; Carl Stokes served two two-year terms but retired from politics in 1971. Cleveland again attracted national attention in 1978 when its 31-year-old mayor, Dennis J. Kucinich, publicly disputed the city's financial policies with members of the city council, and the city defaulted on $15 million in bank loans. Mayor Kucinich narrowly survived a recall election; in 1979, he was defeated for reelection.

Cincinnati has retained the city-manager form of government since 1925. The mayor, elected by the city council from among its members, has no administrative duties. Instead, the council appoints a city manager to a term as chief executive. Columbus, the state capital since 1816, has a mayor-council form of government.

Townships are governed by three trustees and a clerk, all elected to staggered four-year terms. These elected officials oversee zoning ordinances, parks, road maintenance, fire protection, and other matters within their jurisdiction.

In 2005, local government accounted for about 484,096 full-time (or equivalent) employment positions.

15 STATE SERVICES

To address the continuing threat of terrorism and to work with the federal Department of Homeland Security, homeland security in Ohio operates under the authority of the governor; the state police superintendent is designated as the state homeland security advisor.

The State Department of Education administers every phase of public school operations, including counseling and testing services, the federal school lunch program, and teacher education and certification. The department also oversees special schools for the blind and deaf. The department's chief administrator is the superintendent of public instruction.

Health and welfare services are provided by several departments. The Department of Health issues and enforces health and sanitary regulations. Violations of health rules are reviewed by a Public Health Council of seven members, including three physicians and a pharmacist. The Department of Mental Health administers mental health institutions; develops diagnostic, prevention, and rehabilitation programs; and trains mental health professionals. The Department of Job and Family Services helps the poor through TANF (temporary assistance to needy families), food stamps, and Medicaid. The Bureau of Workers' Compensation and the Division of Labor and Worker Safety administer labor benefit programs.

Public protection services include those of the State Highway Patrol and the Bureau of Motor Vehicles, both within the Department of Public Safety; the Department of Rehabilitation and Correction, which operates penal institutions; the Department of Youth Services, which administers juvenile correction centers; and the Environmental Protection Agency.

16 JUDICIAL SYSTEM

The Supreme Court of Ohio, the highest court in the state, reviews proceedings of the lower courts and of state agencies. The high court has a chief justice and six associate justices elected to six-year terms. Below the Supreme Court are 12 courts of appeals, which exercise jurisdiction over their respective judicial districts. Each court has at least three judges elected to six-year terms. The district that includes Cleveland has nine appeals court judges, while the Cincinnati district has six.

Trial courts include 88 courts of common pleas, one in each county. Judges are elected to six-year terms. Probate courts, domestic relations courts, and juvenile courts often function as divisions of the common pleas courts. In 1957, a system of county courts was established by the legislature to replace justices of the peace and mayor's courts at the local level. Large cities have their own municipal, juvenile, and police courts.

As of 31 December 2004, a total of 44,806 prisoners were held in Ohio's state and federal prisons, an increase from 44,778 of 0.1%

from the previous year. As of year-end 2004, a total of 3,185 inmates were female, up from 2,897 or 9.9% from the year before. Among sentenced prisoners (one year or more), Ohio had an incarceration rate of 391 per 100,000 population in 2004.

According to the Federal Bureau of Investigation, Ohio in 2004, had a violent crime rate (murder/nonnegligent manslaughter; forcible rape; robbery; aggravated assault) of 341.8 reported incidents per 100,000 population, or a total of 39,163 reported incidents. Crimes against property (burglary; larceny/theft; and motor vehicle theft) in that same year totaled 420,910 reported incidents or 3,673.2 reported incidents per 100,000 people. Ohio has a death penalty, of which lethal injection is the sole method of execution. From 1976 through 5 May 2006, the state has carried out 21 executions, including four in 2005 and two in 2006 (as of 5 May). As of 1 January 2006, Ohio had 196 inmates on death row.

In 2003, Ohio spent $278,109,346 on homeland security, an average of $24 per state resident.

17 ARMED FORCES

In 2004, there were 7,211 active-duty military personnel and 21,704 civilian personnel stationed in Ohio, the vast majority of whom were at Wright-Patterson Air Force Base near Dayton. Wright-Patterson AFB is one of the largest and most important bases in the United States Air Force and houses the National Museum of the United States Air Force. In 2004, it had a workforce numbering approximately 17,000 people including nearly 10,000 civilians, making it the one of the largest employers in the state of Ohio and the largest employer at a single location. In 2004, the Defense Department awarded over $4.6 billion in defense contracts to Ohio companies. Additionally, defense payroll outlays were $2.89 billion.

In 2003, Ohio had 1,051,007 living veterans, of whom 158,697 had served in World War II; 121,342 during the Korean conflict; 320,046 during the Vietnam era; and 145,893 during the Persian Gulf War. In 2004, the Veterans Administration expended more than $2.1 billion in pensions, medical assistance, and other major veterans' benefits.

As of 31 October 2004, the Ohio State Highway Patrol employed 1,481 full-time sworn officers.

18 MIGRATION

After the Ohio country became a US territory in 1785, Virginians, Connecticut Yankees, and New Jerseyites began arriving in significant numbers; tens of thousands of settlers from New England, Pennsylvania, and some southern states thronged into Ohio in subsequent decades. The great migration from the eastern states continued throughout most of the 19th century, and was bolstered by new arrivals from Europe. The Irish came in the 1830s, and many Germans began arriving in the 1840s. Another wave of European immigration brought about 500,000 people a year to Ohio during the 1880s, many of them from southern and eastern Europe. Former slaves left the South for Ohio following the Civil War, and a larger migratory wave brought blacks to Ohio after World War II to work in the industrial cities. In the 1910s, many emigrants from Greece, Albania, and Latvia settled in Akron to work in the rubber industry.

The industrialization of Ohio in the late 19th and the 20th centuries encouraged the migration of Ohioans from the farms to the cities. The large number of Ohioans who lived in rural areas and worked on farms declined steadily after 1900, with the farm population decreasing to under 1,000,000 during World War II and then to fewer than 400,000 by 1979. A more recent development has been the exodus of urbanites from Ohio's largest cities. From 1970 to 1990, Cleveland lost 245,000 residents, Cincinnati 90,000, Dayton 61,000, Akron 52,000, and Toledo 50,000. Columbus was the only major city to gain residents—93,000—during this period. Ohio lost more than one million people through migration during the period 1970–83. Net migration loss for the state from 1985 to 1990 came to 72,000. Between 1990 and 1998, Ohio had a net loss of 144,000 in domestic migration and a net gain of 48,000 in international migration. In 1998, 7,697 foreign immigrants arrived in Ohio; of these, the greatest number, 900, came from India. The state's overall population increased 3.3% between 1990 and 1998. In the period 2000–05, net international migration was 75,142 and net internal migration was -177,150, for a net loss of 102,008 people.

¹⁹INTERGOVERNMENTAL COOPERATION

The Ohio Commission on Interstate Cooperation represents the state in dealings with the Council of State Governments and its allied organizations. Ohio is a signatory to interstate compacts covering the Ohio River Valley, Pymatuning Reservoir, and the Great Lakes Basin, including the Great Lakes Charter signed in February 1985. The state also participates in the Interstate Mining Compact Commission, the Appalachian Regional Commission, the Midwest Interstate Low-Level Radioactive Waste Compact Commission, the Interstate Oil and Gas Compact, and other compacts. Federal grants to Ohio exceeded $13.734 billion in fiscal year 2005, an estimated $14.011 billion in fiscal year 2006, and an estimated $14.301 billion in fiscal year 2007.

²⁰ECONOMY

Ohio's economy has shown remarkable balance over the years. In the mid-19th century, Ohio became a leader in agriculture, ranking first among the states in wheat production in 1840, and first in corn and wool by 1850. With industrialization, Ohio ranked fourth in value added by manufacturing in 1900.

Coal mining in the southeastern part of the state and easy access to Minnesota's iron ore via the Great Lakes contributed to the growth of the iron and steel industry in the Cleveland-Youngstown area. Ohio led the nation in the manufacture of machine tools and placed second among the states in steel production in the early 1900s. Automobile manufacturing and other new industries developed after World War I. Hit hard by the depression of the 1930s, the state diversified its industrial foundation and enjoyed prosperity during and after World War II, as its population increased and its income grew.

In the 1970s, however, growth began to lag. By 1980, per capita income in Ohio had fallen well behind the national average. While the gross national product in constant dollars grew 99% from 1960 to 1980, the gross state product expanded only 66%. Manufacturing, which traditionally accounted for more than one-third of the gross state product, was shrinking, as demand for durable goods declined. Manufacturing employment peaked at 1.4 million in 1969; by 1982, the total was down to 1.1 million, and it was believed that many of these jobs would be permanently lost because of a reorientation of Ohio's economy from manufacturing toward services. With unemployment reaching peak levels, the state was forced to borrow from the federal government to fund the soaring cost of unemployment benefits.

Steel was produced primarily in Youngstown, automotive and aircraft parts in Cleveland, automobile tires and other rubber products in Akron, and office equipment in Dayton. Recessionary trends in 1980 led to the closing of a US Steel plant in Youngstown and of two Firestone tire and rubber factories in the Akron area, and to widespread layoffs in the auto parts industry. This bad economic news was partially offset when in 1983 the Honda Motor Co. opened Japan's first US automobile assembly plant at Marysville near Columbus, where Honda had already been manufacturing motorcycles. Honda suppliers also began establishing plants in the state.

Despite its shrinking size, manufacturing remains dominant in Ohio's economy. The sector centers on durable goods. Among manufacturers, transportation equipment and industrial machinery are the largest employers. Both durable and nondurable goods (instruments, chemicals, printing and lumber) enjoyed the greatest gains in employment between 1987 and 1993. However, durable goods' share of the gross state product, particularly primary metals, motor vehicles, and industrial machinery, fell 4.5% between 1977 and 1990 while nondurable goods industries' share of the gross state product remained constant and services, particularly business services, increased their share by 2.5%. In 2002, durable goods made up two-thirds of Ohio's manufacturing output. Output from Ohio's manufacturing sector peaked in 1998 at approximately $90.4 billion (about 26.1% of gross state product), and had fallen 11.9% by 2001, including a 7.1% dip in the national recession of 2001. Output from manufacturing in 2001 constituted only 21.3% of gross state product. The fall in manufacturing output helped bring down the state's annual growth rates down from 6.5% in 1998 to an average of 3.3% 1999-2000, and then to 0.83% in 2001. In 2002, Ohio lagged the rest of the nation in employment performance because of significant losses in manufacturing, employing 18% of the state's labor force. Employment losses were sharpest among manufacturers of durable goods (which make up two-thirds of Ohio's manufactures), falling 8.4% between the fourth quarter of 2000 and the fourth quarter of 2002. Ohio's recovery hinges on recovery in its durable manufacturing sector.

In 2004, Ohio's gross state product (GSP) was $419.866 billion, of which manufacturing (durable and nondurable goods) contributed $84.597 billion or 20.1% of GSP, followed by the real estate sector at $44.588 billion (10.6% of GSP), and health care and social assistance services at $33.201 billion (7.9% of GSP). In that same year, there were an estimated 850,961 small businesses in Ohio. Of the 231,374 businesses that had employees, an estimated total of 227,339 or 98.3% were small companies. An estimated 22,725 new businesses were established in the state in 2004, up 2.2% from the year before. Business terminations that same year came to 21,328, down 9.4% from 2003. There were 1,432 business bankruptcies in 2004, up 0.4% from the previous year. In 2005, the state's personal bankruptcy (Chapter 7 and Chapter 13) filing rate was 774 filings per 100,000 people, ranking Ohio as the eighth-highest in the nation.

21 INCOME

In 2005 Ohio had a gross state product (GSP) of $442 billion which accounted for 3.6% of the nation's gross domestic product and placed the state at number 7 in highest GSP among the 50 states and the District of Columbia.

According to the Bureau of Economic Analysis, in 2004 Ohio had a per capita personal income (PCPI) of $31,161. This ranked 26th in the United States and was 94% of the national average of $33,050. The 1994–2004 average annual growth rate of PCPI was 3.7%. Ohio had a total personal income (TPI) of $356,795,912,000, which ranked eighth in the United States and reflected an increase of 4.2% from 2003. The 1994–2004 average annual growth rate of TPI was 4.0%. Earnings of persons employed in Ohio increased from $263,241,162,000 in 2003 to $274,175,471,000 in 2004, an increase of 4.2%. The 2003–04 national change was 6.3%.

The US Census Bureau reports that the three-year average median household income for 2002–04 in 2004 dollars was $44,160 compared to a national average of $44,473. During the same period an estimated 10.8% of the population was below the poverty line as compared to 12.4% nationwide.

22 LABOR

According to the Bureau of Labor Statistics (BLS), in April 2006 the seasonally adjusted civilian labor force in Ohio numbered 5,927,300, with approximately 326,900 workers unemployed, yielding an unemployment rate of 5.5%, compared to the national average of 4.7% for the same period. Preliminary data for the same period placed nonfarm employment at 5,460,800. Since the beginning of the BLS data series in 1976, the highest unemployment rate recorded in Ohio was 13.8% in January 1983. The historical low was 3.9% in March 2001. Preliminary nonfarm employment data by occupation for April 2006 showed that approximately 4.3% of the labor force was employed in construction; 14.8 in manufacturing; 19.1% in trade, transportation, and public utilities; 5.7% in financial activities; 11.9% in professional and business services; 14.1% in education and health services; 9.3% in leisure and hospitality services; and 14.5% in government.

The first workers' organization in Ohio was formed by Dayton mechanics in 1811. The Ohio Federation of Labor was founded in 1884; the American Federation of Labor (AFL) was founded in Columbus in 1886, and Ohio native William Green became president of the AFL in 1924. But it was not until the 1930s that labor unions in Ohio were formed on a large scale. In 1934, the United Rubber Workers began to organize workers in Akron; through a successful series of sit-down strikes at the city's rubber plants, the union grew to about 70,000 members by 1937. In that year, the United Steelworkers struck seven steel plants in the Youngstown area and won the right to bargain collectively for 50,000 steelworkers. The number of union members increased from about 25% of the state's non-farm employees in 1939 to 32% in 1980 when about 1.4 million workers belonged to labor organizations.

Progressive labor legislation in the state began in 1852 with laws regulating working hours for women and children and limiting men to a 10-hour workday. In 1890, Ohio became the first state to establish a public employment service. Subsequent labor legislation included a workers' compensation act in 1911 and child labor and minimum wage measures in the 1930s. In 1983, a law was passed giving public employees, other than police officers and fire fighters, a limited right to strike.

The US Department of Labor's Bureau of Labor Statistics reported that in 2005, a total of 804,000 of Ohio's 5,039,000 employed wage and salary workers were formal members of a union. This represented 16% of those so employed, up from 15.2% in 2004, and above the national average of 12%. Overall in 2005, a total of 866,000 workers (17.2%) in Ohio were covered by a union or employee association contract, which includes those workers who reported no union affiliation. Ohio is one of 28 states that do not have a right-to-work law.

As of 1 March 2006, Ohio had a state-mandated minimum wage rate of $5.15 per hour. In 2004, women in the state accounted for 40.1% of the employed civilian labor force.

23 AGRICULTURE

Despite increasing urbanization and industrialization, agriculture retains its economic importance. Ohio ranked 17th in net farm income among the 50 states in 2005. In that year, the state's production of crops, dairy products, and livestock was valued at nearly $5.1 billion.

The number of farms in 2004 was 77,300, down from 234,000 in 1940. The average size of farms increased from 94 acres (38 hectares) in 1940 to 189 acres (76 hectares) in 2004.

Grain is grown and cattle and hogs are raised on large farms in the north-central and western parts of the state, while smaller farms predominate in the hilly southeastern region. Truck farming has continued to expand near the large cities.

Ohio was the third-leading producer of tomatoes for processing in 2004 with 177,320 tons. Field crops in 2004 (in bushels) included corn for grain, 491,380,000; soybeans, 207,740,000; wheat, 55,180,000; and oats, 3,150,000. The most valuable crops included soybeans, with sales of $1.2 billion, and corn, $1.0 billion. These two crops accounted for 41% of Ohio's farm receipts in 2004. Ohio farmers also produced 3,232,000 tons of hay and 34,000 tons of sugar beets in 2004.

24 ANIMAL HUSBANDRY

Cattle and hogs are raised in the central and western regions. In 2005, Ohio had 1.3 million cattle and calves, worth over $1.2 billion. In 2004, Ohio farmers had 1.5 million hogs and pigs, valued at $159.5 million. During 2003, Ohio farmers produced nearly 12.9 million lb (5.8 million kg) of sheep and lambs.

Dairying is common in most regions of the state, but especially in the east and southeast. In 2003, Ohio's 260,000 milk cows produced 4.5 billion lb (2 billion kg) of milk. The poultry industry is dispersed throughout the state. Ohio ranked second among the states in production of eggs with 7.6 billion eggs in 2003. Poultry farmers in Ohio also produced 212.3 million lb (96.5 million kg) of turkey and sold 225.5 million lb (102.3 million kg) of broilers worth $78.9 million in 2003.

25 FISHING

Commercial fishing, which once flourished in Lake Erie, has declined during the 20th century. In 2004, commercial fish landings brought about 3.9 million lb (1.8 million kg) valued at $2.9 million. The primary Lake Erie fish species are walleye, perch, lake trout, and small mouth bass. In 2001, the commercial fleet had 31 vessels and 19 boats.

A statewide fish hatchery system (of six locations) annually produces and stocks up to 30 million fry and yearling size fish—mostly walleye, saugeye, trout, catfish, bass, sunfish, muskellunge, and pike. In 2004, the state issued 917,902 sport fishing licenses.

26 FORESTRY

In 2003, Ohio had 7,855,000 acres (3,179,000 hectares) of forestland, representing 30% of the state's total land area, but only 1% of all US forests. Although scattered throughout the state, hardwood forests are concentrated in the hilly region of the southeast. Lawrence and Vinton counties are more than 70% forested. Commercial timberlands in 2002 totaled 7,568,000 acres (3,063,000 hectares), of which over 90% was privately owned.

The state's lumber and wood products industry supplies building materials, household furniture, and paper products. In 2004, total lumber production was 379 million board feet. In 2002 there were about 690,000 acres (279,000 hectares) of federal, state, county, and municipal forestland in Ohio.

27 MINING

According to preliminary data from the US Geological Survey (USGS), the estimated value of nonfuel mineral production by Ohio in 2003 was $968 million, down slightly from 2002. The USGS data ranked Ohio as 15th among the 50 states by the total value of its nonfuel mineral production, accounting for around 2.5% of total US output.

According to the preliminary data for 2003, crushed stone, followed by construction sand and gravel, salt, lime, cement (portland and masonry), and industrial sand and gravel were the state's top nonfuel minerals by value. Crushed stone and construction sand and gravel accounted for around 57% of all nonfuel mineral output, by value. Ohio in 2003 was the nation's third leading producer by volume of fire clay, fourth in the production of salt and lime, fifth in construction sand and gravel and common clays, and tenth in industrial sand and gravel.

Preliminary data for 2003 showed that a total of 68.8 million metric tons of crushed stone were produced, with a value of $310 million, while construction sand and gravel output totaled 47 million metric tons, and was valued at $242 million. Lime production that same year was 1.7 million metric tons, and was worth $110 million.

Ohio's mines produced only coal and industrial minerals. Metals production came from materials received from other states or foreign sources. Ohio ranked second in 2003 in the production of raw steel, for which output that year totaled 11.9 million metric tons.

28 ENERGY AND POWER

Ohio has abundant energy resources. The state government estimates that Ohio's coal reserves are sufficient to meet demand for 500 years and that oil and natural gas reserves are also ample.

As of 2003, Ohio had 136 electrical power service providers, of which 85 were publicly owned and 25 were cooperatives. Of the remainder, nine were investor owned, one was the owner of an in-

dependent generator that sold directly to customers, 10 were generation-only suppliers and six were delivery-only providers. As of that same year there were 5,397,308 retail customers. Of that total, 3,751,772 received their power from investor-owned service providers. Cooperatives accounted for 358,050 customers, while publicly owned providers had 370,524 customers. There was one independent generator or "facility" customer, and 916,961 generation-only customers. There was no data on the number of delivery-only customers.

Total net summer generating capability by the state's electrical generating plants in 2003 stood at 34.060 million kW, with total production that same year at 146.638 billion kWh. Of the total amount generated, 94.8% came from electric utilities, with the remainder coming from independent producers and combined heat and power service providers. The largest portion of all electric power generated, 134.769 billion kWh (91.9%), came from coal-fired plants, with nuclear power generation plants in second place at 8.475 billion kWh (5.8%) and natural gas fueled plants in third at 1.793 billion kWh (1.2%). Other renewable power sources accounted for 0.3% of all power generated. Petroleum fired plants, hydroelectric generation and plants using other types of gases accounted for the remainder.

As of 2006, Ohio had two operating nuclear power plants: the Davis-Besse plant in Oak Harbor; and the Perry plant in Lake County, near Cleveland.

In the 1880s, petroleum was discovered near Lima and natural gas near Toledo, both in the northwest. These fossil fuels have since been found and exploited in the central and eastern regions. As of 2004, Ohio had proven crude oil reserves of 49 million barrels, or less than 1% of all proven US reserves, while output that same year averaged 16,000 barrels per day. Including federal offshore domains, the state that year ranked 20th (19th excluding federal offshore) in proven reserves and 19th (20th excluding federal offshore) in production among the 31 producing states. In 2004 Ohio had 28,941 producing oil wells and accounted for under 1% of all US production. As of 2005, the state's four refineries had a combined crude oil distillation capacity of 551,400 barrels per day.

In 2004, Ohio had 33,828 producing natural gas and gas condensate wells. In that same year, marketed gas production (all gas produced excluding gas used for repressuring, vented and flared, and nonhydrocarbon gases removed) totaled 93.641 billion cu ft (2.65 billion cu m). As of 31 December 2004, proven reserves of dry or consumer-grade natural gas totaled 974 billion cu ft (27.66 billion cu m). A potential energy source is the rich bed of shale rock, underlying more than half of Ohio, which was estimated to contain more than 200 trillion cu ft (5.7 trillion cu m) of natural gas. But much research is needed before the gas can be extracted economically.

Coalfields lie beneath southeastern Ohio, particularly in Hocking, Athens, and Perry counties. In 2004, Ohio had 52 producing coal mines, 44 of which were surface operations and eight were underground. Coal production that year totaled 23,222,000 short tons, up from 22,009,000 short tons in 2003. Of the total produced in 2004, underground mines accounted for 14,270,000 short tons. Recoverable coal reserves in 2004 totaled 318 million short tons. One short ton equals 2,000 lb (0.907 metric tons).

29 INDUSTRY

Ohio has been a leading manufacturing state since the mid-1800s. During the last two decades of the 20th century, Ohio became the nation's leader in machine-tool manufacturing, the second-leading steel producer, and a pioneer in oil refining and in the production of automobiles and automotive parts, such as rubber tires.

In recent decades, Ohio has also become important as a manufacturer of glassware, soap, matches, paint, business machines, refrigerators—and even comic books and Chinese food products.

According to the US Census Bureau's Annual Survey of Manufactures (ASM) for 2004, Ohio's manufacturing sector covered some 21 product subsectors. The shipment value of all products manufactured in the state that same year was $258.799 billion. Of that total, transportation equipment manufacturing accounted for the largest share at $77.937 billion. It was followed by fabricated metal product manufacturing at $24.634 billion; chemical manufacturing at $22.736 billion; food manufacturing at $21.156 billion; and primary metal manufacturing at $20.363 billion.

In 2004, a total of 782,617 people in Ohio were employed in the state's manufacturing sector, according to the ASM. Of that total, 570,149 were actual production workers. In terms of total employment, the transportation equipment manufacturing industry accounted for the largest portion of all manufacturing employees at 138,306, with 108,070 actual production workers. It was followed by fabricated metal product manufacturing at 120,011 employees (90,874 actual production workers); plastics and rubber products manufacturing at 80,830 employees (62,397 actual production workers); machinery manufacturing at 75,954 employees (46,117 actual production workers); and food manufacturing with 51,607 employees (37,247 actual production workers).

ASM data for 2004 showed that Ohio's manufacturing sector paid $34.503 billion in wages. Of that amount, the transportation equipment manufacturing sector accounted for the largest share at $8.042 billion. It was followed by fabricated metal product manufacturing at $4.868 billion; machinery manufacturing at $3.392 billion; plastics and rubber products manufacturing at $2.924 billion; and primary metal manufacturing at $2.580 billion.

30 COMMERCE

Ohio is a major commercial state. According to the 2002 Census of Wholesale Trade, Ohio's wholesale trade sector had sales that year totaling $166.4 billion from 16,000 establishments. Wholesalers of durable goods accounted for 10,149 establishments, followed by nondurable goods wholesalers at 4,316 and electronic markets, agents, and brokers accounting for 1,535 establishments. Sales by durable goods wholesalers in 2002 totaled $78.5 billion, while wholesalers of nondurable goods saw sales of $70.04 billion. Electronic markets, agents, and brokers in the wholesale trade industry had sales of $17.8 billion.

In the 2002 Census of Retail Trade, Ohio was listed as having 42,280 retail establishments with sales of $119.7 billion. The leading types of retail businesses by number of establishments were: food and beverage stores (5,757); clothing and clothing accessories stores (5,139); motor vehicle and motor vehicle parts dealers (4,909); miscellaneous store retailers (4,863); and gasoline stations (4,460). In terms of sales, motor vehicle and motor vehicle parts stores accounted for the largest share of retail sales at $30.7 billion, followed by general merchandise stores at $17.9 billion; food and beverage stores at $17.4 billion; gasoline stations at $10.4 billion; and building material/garden equipment and supplies dealers at $9.1 billion. A total of 611,814 people were employed by the retail sector in Ohio that year.

In 2005, Ohio ranked seventh in the United States as an exporter of goods, with exports worth $34 billion. Transportation equipment, nonelectric machinery, chemicals, electric and electronic equipment, primary metals, fabricated metal products, stone, clay, and glass products, and rubber and plastic products account for most of the export value.

31 CONSUMER PROTECTION

Although Ohio has some of the toughest consumer protection laws in the United States, the state does not have a single, dedicated agency or department responsible for consumer protection. Instead, the state relies upon a range of state offices to provide consumer protection activities that are specific to that agency or department. Agencies involved in consumer protection include the Agriculture Department's Division of Food Safety, which operates inspection programs to protect consumers, and the Commerce Department's Office of Consumer Affairs (created in 2002), which protects consumers from abusive lending practices through education, fielding complaints, referring borrowers to organizations that can assist them, and initiating enforcement action if lending laws are violated. The Ohio Consumers' Counsel acts to protect the interests of residential consumers of public utilities and works to educate consumers about utility issues and resolve consumer complaints. The Attorney General's Office via its Consumer Protection Section, resolves consumer complaints and enforces consumer protection laws.

When dealing with consumer protection issues, the state's Attorney General's Office can initiate civil and criminal proceedings; represent the state before state and federal regulatory agencies; administer consumer protection and education programs; handle formal consumer complaints; and exercise broad subpoena powers. In antitrust actions, the Attorney General's Office can act on behalf of those consumers who are incapable of acting on their own; initiate damage actions on behalf of the state in state courts; initiate criminal proceedings; and represent counties, cities and other governmental entities in recovering civil damages under state or federal law.

The offices of the Ohio Consumer's Council and the Consumer Protection Section of the Attorney General's Office are located in Columbus. There is also a county government consumer affairs office in Akron.

32 BANKING

Ohio's first banks, in Marietta and Chillicothe, were incorporated in 1808, and a state bank was authorized in 1845. As of June 2005, Ohio had 281 insured banks, savings and loans, and saving banks, plus 223 state-chartered and 272 federally chartered credit unions (CUs). Excluding the CUs, the Cleveland-Elyria-Mentor market area accounted for the largest portion of the state's deposits in 2004, at $64.472 billion, but ranked third in the number of institutions at 44. The Cincinnati-Middletown market area (which includes a portion of Kentucky) ranks second in deposits with $37.080 billion, and first in the number of institutions at 87. The Columbus market area ranks second in the number of institutions at 57, and third in deposits at $28.762 billion. As of June 2005, CUs accounted for 1% of all assets held by all financial institutions in the state, or some $16.575 billion. Banks, savings and loans, and savings banks collectively accounted for the remaining 99% or $1,580.100 billion in assets held.

The median percentage of past-due/nonaccrual loans to total loans as of fourth quarter 2005 stood at 1.74%, down from 1.79% in 2004 and 1.89% in 2003. The median net interest margin (the difference between the lower rates offered savers and the higher rates charged on loans) for the state's insured institutions was 3.82% as of fourth quarter 2005, down from 3.83% in 2004 but up from 2003's rate of 3.80%.

State chartered banks and other state-chartered financial institutions are the responsibility of the Ohio Department of Commerce's Division of Financial Institutions. Federally charted institutions are regulated by the US government.

³³INSURANCE

In 2004, there were over 7.1 million individual life insurance policies in force, with a total value of over $480 billion; total value for all categories of life insurance (individual, group, and credit) was over $780.8 billion. The average coverage amount is $66,700 per policy holder. Death benefits paid that year totaled $2.4 billion. In 2000, 46 life and health insurance companies had headquarters in Ohio.

At the end of 2003, 134 property and casualty and 41 life and health insurance companies were domiciled in Ohio. In 2004, direct premiums for property and casualty insurance totaled over $13.8 billion. That year, there were 36,166 flood insurance policies in force in the state, with a total value of $3.9 billion. About $14.7 billion of coverage was held through FAIR plans, which are designed to offer coverage for some natural circumstances, such as wind and hail, in high risk areas.

In 2004, 61% of state residents held employment-based health insurance policies, 3% held individual policies, and 23% were covered under Medicare and Medicaid; 12% of residents were uninsured. In 2003, employee contributions for employment-based health coverage averaged at 17% for single coverage and 21% for family coverage. The state offers a six-month health benefits expansion program for small-firm employees in connection with the Consolidated Omnibus Budget Reconciliation Act (COBRA, 1986), a health insurance program for those who lose employment-based coverage due to termination or reduction of work hours.

In 2003, there were over 7.9 million auto insurance policies in effect for private passenger cars. Required minimum coverage includes bodily injury liability of up to $12,500 per individual and $25,000 for all persons injured in an accident, as well as property damage liability of $7,500. In 2003, the average expenditure per vehicle for insurance coverage was $671.23.

³⁴SECURITIES

The Cincinnati Stock Exchange (CSE) was organized on 11 March 1885 by 12 stockbrokers who agreed to meet regularly to buy and sell securities. In the mid-1990s, the Cincinnati Stock Exchange moved to Chicago and ceased operations in Ohio.

The Ohio securities marketplace is overseen by the Ohio Division of Securities of the Ohio Department of Commerce. The division provides investor protection, enhances capital formation, and protects the integrity of the securities marketplace by administering and enforcing the Ohio Securities Act, which was enacted in 1913. It requires that all securities sold in Ohio be registered with the division or properly exempted from registration and requires that each person transacting business in securities in Ohio be licensed by the division. It also imposes anti-fraud standards in connection with the sale of securities.

In 2005, there were 2,710 personal financial advisers employed in the state and 10,940 securities, commodities, and financial services sales agents. In 2004, there were over 279 publicly traded companies within the state, with over 93 NASDAQ companies, 93 NYSE listings, and 13 AMEX listings. In 2006, the state had 28 Fortune 500 companies; Cardinal Health (based in Dublin) ranked first in the state and ninth in the nation with revenues of over $74.9 billion, followed by Kroger, Procter and Gamble, and Federated Department Stores, all based in Cincinnati, and Nationwide Financial Services, based in Columbus. These five NYSE-listed companies are also part of the Fortune 100.

³⁵PUBLIC FINANCE

The state budget is prepared on a biennial basis by the Office of Budget and Management. It is submitted by the governor to the state legislature, which must act on it by the close of the current fiscal year (FY). The state's fiscal year runs from 1 July through 30 June.

The General Assembly has nearly total discretion in allocating general revenues, which are used primarily to support education, welfare, mental health facilities, law enforcement, property tax relief, and government operations. The assembly also allocates money from special revenue funds by means of specific legislative acts. More than one-half of all state expenditures come from the general fund.

Fiscal year 2006 general funds were estimated at $25.7 billion for resources and $25.3 billion for expenditures. In fiscal year 2004, federal government grants to Ohio totaled $16.5 billion.

³⁶TAXATION

In 2005, Ohio collected $24,007 million in tax revenues or $2,094 per capita, which placed it 27th among the 50 states in per capita tax burden. The national average was $2,192 per capita. Property taxes accounted for 0.2% of the total; sales taxes, 34.1%; selective sales taxes, 12.3%; individual income taxes, 39.3%; corporate income taxes, 5.5%; and other taxes, 8.6%.

As of 1 January 2006, Ohio had nine individual income tax brackets ranging from 0.712% to 7.185%. The state taxes corporations at rates ranging from 5.1% to 8.5% depending on tax bracket.

Ohio—State Government Finances

(Dollar amounts in thousands. Per capita amounts in dollars.)

	AMOUNT	PER CAPITA
Total Revenue	76,443,362	6,676.28
General revenue	45,732,357	3,994.09
Intergovernmental revenue	14,870,405	1,298.73
Taxes	22,475,528	1,962.93
General sales	7,881,510	688.34
Selective sales	2,901,794	253.43
License taxes	1,813,479	158.38
Individual income tax	8,705,161	760.28
Corporate income tax	1,060,594	92.63
Other taxes	112,990	9.87
Current charges	5,103,632	445.73
Miscellaneous general revenue	3,282,792	286.71
Utility revenue	–	–
Liquor store revenue	581,412	50.78
Insurance trust revenue	30,129,593	2,631.41
Total expenditure	58,874,466	5,141.87
Intergovernmental expenditure	15,730,201	1,373.82
Direct expenditure	43,144,265	3,768.06
Current operation	25,303,008	2,209.87
Capital outlay	3,097,504	270.52
Insurance benefits and repayments	11,984,509	1,046.68
Assistance and subsidies	1,566,629	136.82
Interest on debt	1,192,615	104.16
Exhibit: Salaries and wages	6,775,542	591.75
Total expenditure	58,874,466	5,141.87
General expenditure	46,524,145	4,063.24
Intergovernmental expenditure	15,730,201	1,373.82
Direct expenditure	30,793,944	2,689.43
General expenditures, by function:		
Education	17,006,672	1,485.30
Public welfare	13,558,685	1,184.16
Hospitals	1,579,696	137.96
Health	1,936,533	169.13
Highways	3,032,342	264.83
Police protection	254,436	22.22
Correction	1,558,121	136.08
Natural resources	416,181	36.35
Parks and recreation	113,070	9.88
Government administration	1,942,370	169.64
Interest on general debt	1,192,615	104.16
Other and unallocable	3,933,424	343.53
Utility expenditure	–	–
Liquor store expenditure	365,812	31.95
Insurance trust expenditure	11,984,509	1,046.68
Debt at end of fiscal year	22,183,360	1,937.41
Cash and security holdings	166,738,540	14,562.32

Abbreviations and symbols: – zero or rounds to zero; (NA) not available; (X) not applicable.

SOURCE: U.S. Census Bureau, Governments Division, 2004 Survey of State Government Finances, January 2006.

In 2004, state and local property taxes amounted to $11,232,828,000 or $981 per capita. The per capita amount ranks the state 25th nationally. Local governments collected $11,192,192,000 of the total and the state government $40,636,000.

Ohio taxes retail sales at a rate of 6%. In addition to the state tax, local taxes on retail sales can reach as much as 2%, making for a potential total tax on retail sales of 8%. Food purchased for consumption off-premises is tax exempt. The tax on cigarettes is 125 cents per pack, which ranks 13th among the 50 states and the District of Columbia. Ohio taxes gasoline at 28 cents per gallon. This is in addition to the 18.4 cents per gallon federal tax on gasoline.

According to the Tax Foundation, for every federal tax dollar sent to Washington in 2004, Ohio citizens received $1.01 in federal spending.

³⁷ECONOMIC POLICY

Although Ohio seeks to attract new industries, a substantial portion of the state's annual economic growth stems from the expansion of existing businesses.

Ohio offers numerous business incentives to spur industrial development. The state encourages capital investment by offering private developers property tax abatements for commercial redevelopment. A 1976 state law permits municipal corporations to exempt certain property improvements from real property taxes for periods of up to 30 years. The state's guaranteed-loan program for industrial developers provides repayment guarantees on 90% of loans up to $1 million. The state also offers revenue bonds to finance a developer's land, buildings, and equipment at interest rates below the going mortgage interest rates.

The Ohio Department of Development (ODOD) consists of several divisions, including the: Economic Development Division, Office of Business Development, Office of Tax Incentives, Office of Financial Incentives, Office of Industrial Training, and Office of Small and Developing Business. These organizations administer plans for economic growth in cooperation with city and county governments. They inform companies about opportunities and advantages in the state and promote the sale of Ohio's exports abroad. In the 1990s, the departments instituted research and development programs at state universities in such fields as biotechnology, clean coal technologies, welding and joining technologies, robotics, polymers, and artificial intelligence. Special attention has been paid to the development of Ohio's growing life science industry. The Third Frontier Internship Program is designed to keep Ohio's college graduates in the state by connecting them with Ohio businesses through student internships.

³⁸HEALTH

The infant mortality rate in October 2005 was estimated at 8.2 per 1,000 live births. The birth rate in 2003 was 13.3 per 1,000 population. The abortion rate stood at 16.5 per 1,000 women in 2000. In 2003, about 87.7% of pregnant woman received prenatal care beginning in the first trimester. In 2004, approximately 80% of children received routine immunizations before the age of three.

The crude death rate in 2003 was 9.5 deaths per 1,000 population. As of 2002, the death rates for major causes of death (per 100,000 resident population) were: heart disease, 274.8; cancer, 220.4; cerebrovascular diseases, 63.5; chronic lower respiratory diseases, 53.1; and diabetes, 33.7. Ohio and North Dakota share the distinction of having the third-highest diabetes mortality rate in the nation (following West Virginia and Louisiana). The mortality rate from HIV infection was 2.1 per 100,000 population. In 2004, the reported AIDS case rate was at about 5.8 per 100,000 population. In 2002, about 55.6% of the population was considered overweight or obese. As of 2004, about 25.8% of state residents were smokers, representing the fifth-highest rate in the country.

In 2003, Ohio had 163 community hospitals with about 33,000 beds. There were about 1.4 million patient admissions that year and 30 million outpatient visits. The average daily inpatient census was about 20,600 patients. The average cost per day for hospital care was $1,504. Also in 2003, there were about 989 certified nursing facilities in the state with 106,426 beds and an overall occupancy rate of about 75%. In 2004, it was estimated that about 72.2% of all state residents had received some type of dental care within the year. Ohio had 289 physicians per 100,000 resident population in 2004 and 930 nurses per 100,000 in 2005. In 2004, there was a total of 5,981 dentists in the state.

In 2005, the Cleveland Clinic ranked fourth on the Honor Roll of Best Hospitals 2005 by *U.S. News & World Report.* In the same report, it ranked first in the nation for care of heart disease and heart surgery. Rainbow Babies and Children's Hospital in Cleveland ranked sixth in the nation for best pediatric care. University Hospitals of Cleveland, Akron General Medical Center, Christ Hospital in Cincinnati, and Ohio State University Hospital in Columbus all ranked within the top 40 best hospitals in care for heart disease and heart surgery.

About 17% of state residents were enrolled in Medicaid programs in 2003; 15% were enrolled in Medicare programs in 2004. Approximately 12% of the state population was uninsured in 2004. In 2003, state health care expenditures totaled $13.3 million.

39 SOCIAL WELFARE

The growth of welfare programs in the state was remarkably rapid during the 1970s and early 1980s. From 1970 to 1978, for example, Aid to Families with Dependent Children (AFDC) nearly tripled, to $446 million; by 1996, there were 552,000 AFDC recipients; the average payment per family was $421.

In 2004, about 306,000 people received unemployment benefits, with the average weekly unemployment benefit at $252. For 2005, the estimated average monthly participation in the food stamp program included about 1,007,172 persons (448,524 households); the average monthly benefit was about $95.72 per person. That year, the total of benefits paid through the state for the food stamp program was about $1.15 billion.

Temporary Assistance for Needy Families (TANF), the system of federal welfare assistance that officially replaced Aid to Families with Dependent Children (AFDC) in 1997, was reauthorized through the Deficit Reduction Act of 2005. TANF is funded through federal block grants that are divided among the states based on an equation involving the number of recipients in each state. Ohio's TANF program is called Ohio Works First (OWF). In 2004, the state program had 186,000 recipients; state and federal expenditures on this TANF program totaled $310 million in fiscal year 2003.

In December 2004, Social Security benefits were paid to 1,950,740 Ohio residents. This number included 1,199,320 retired workers, 236,870 widows and widowers, 230,860 disabled workers, 134,780 spouses, and 148,910 children. Social Security beneficiaries represented 17% of the total state population and 92.6% of the state's population age 65 and older. Retired workers received an average monthly payment of $970; widows and widowers, $933; disabled workers, $876; and spouses, $489. Payments for children of retired workers averaged $501 per month; children of deceased workers, $636; and children of disabled workers, $263. Federal Supplemental Security Income payments in December 2004 went to 245,401 Ohio residents, averaging $418 a month.

40 HOUSING

In 2004, Ohio had an estimated 4,966,746 housing units, 4,514,723 of which were occupied; 69.8% were owner-occupied. About 68% of all units were single-family, detached homes. About 22.4% of the housing units were built in 1939 or earlier; 43.7% were built between 1950 and 1979. It was estimated that 173,724 units lacked telephone service, 16,483 lacked complete plumbing facilities, and 19,901 lacked complete kitchen facilities. Utility gas was the most common energy source for heating. The average household had 2.47 members.

In 2004, 51,700 new privately owned units were authorized for construction. The median home value was $122,384. The median monthly cost for mortgage owners was $1,090. Renters paid a median of $587 per month. In September 2005, the state received grants of $255,000 from the US Department of Housing and Urban Development (HUD) for rural housing and economic development programs. For 2006, HUD allocated to the state over $48.9 million in community development block grants (CDBG). The city of Cleveland received over $24.5 million in CDBGs.

41 EDUCATION

In 2004, 88.1% of Ohio residents age 25 and older were high school graduates, surpassing the national average of 84%. Some 24.6% had obtained a bachelor's degree or higher.

Ohio claims a number of "firsts" in US education: the first kindergarten, established by German settlers in Columbus in 1838; the first junior high school, also at Columbus, in 1909; the first municipal university, the University of Cincinnati, founded in 1870; and the first college to grant degrees to women, Oberlin, in 1837. The state's earliest school system was organized in Akron in 1847.

The total enrollment in Ohio's public schools for fall 2002 stood at 1,838,000. Of these, 1,284,000 attended schools from kindergarten through grade eight, and 554,000 attended high school. Approximately 79.4% of the students were white, 17% were black, 2.1% were Hispanic, 1.3% were Asian/Pacific Islander, and 0.1% were American Indian/Alaskan Native. Total enrollment was estimated at 1,825,000 in fall 2003 and expected to be 1,752,000 by fall 2014, a decline of 4.7% during the period 2002–14. Expenditures for public education in 2003/04 were estimated at $19.2 billion or $8,963 per student. In fall 2003, there were 239,323 students enrolled in 987 private schools. Since 1969, the National Assessment of Educational Progress (NAEP) has tested public school students nationwide. The resulting report, *The Nation's Report Card,* stated that in 2005, eighth graders in Ohio scored 283 out of 500 in mathematics compared with the national average of 278.

As of fall 2002, there were 587,996 students enrolled in college or graduate school; minority students comprised 15.1% of total postsecondary enrollment. In 2005 Ohio had 187 degree-granting institutions. State universities include Ohio State University (Columbus), Ohio University (Athens), Miami University (Oxford), and other state universities at Akron, Bowling Green, Cincinnati, Cleveland, Dayton, Kent, Toledo, Wilberforce, and Youngstown. The largest, Ohio State, was chartered in 1870 and also has campuses at Lima, Mansfield, Marion, Newark, and Wooster. Ohio has 36 public two-year colleges. Well-known private colleges and universities include Antioch (Yellow Springs), Case Western Reserve (Cleveland), Kenyon (Gambier), Muskingum (New Concord),

Oberlin, Wittenberg (Springfield), and Wooster. The conservatories at both Oberlin and the Cleveland Institute of Music have national reputations.

Ohio residents enrolled as full-time students at an eligible institution within the state may apply for instructional grants from the Student Assistance Office of the Ohio Board of Regents. Guaranteed loans are provided through the Ohio Student Loan Commission.

42 ARTS

The Ohio Arts Council was founded in 1965 with the mission of developing and preserving the state's cultural heritage. The council consists of a Board with 15 governor-appointed, voting members and 4 non-voting members 2 from the Ohio Senate and 2 from the House of Representatives. In 2005, the Ohio Arts Council and other Ohio arts organizations received 52 grants totaling $1,740,300 from the National Endowment for the Arts. State and private sources contributed funds to arts programming as well. As of 2006, the Ohio Humanities Council presented a number of historical and literary programs, including "Booked for the Day: Literary Retreats for Working Professionals" and the Ohio Chautauqua. In 2005, the National Endowment for the Humanities contributed $2,270,470 to 27 state programs.

The earliest center of artistic activities in Ohio was Cincinnati, where a group of young painters did landscapes and portraits as early as 1840. The state's first art gallery was established there in 1854; the Cincinnati Art Academy was founded in 1869, and the Art Museum in 1886. Famous American artists who worked in Cincinnati during part of their careers include Thomas Cole, a founder of the "Hudson River School" of landscape painting, and Columbus-born George Bellows, whose realistic *Stag at Sharkey's* is displayed at the Cleveland Museum of Art (founded in 1913). Other notable centers for the visual arts include the Akron Art Institute, Columbus Museum of Art, Dayton Art Institute, Toledo Museum of Art, and museums or galleries in Marion, Oberlin, Springfield, Youngstown, and Zanesville.

Cincinnati also was an early center for the theater; the Eagle Theater opened there in 1839, and shortly afterward, the first showboat on the Ohio River began making regular stops at the city. The first US minstrel show appeared in Ohio in 1842. Ohio has three professional theatrical companies: the Cincinnati Playhouse, the Cleveland Play House, and the Great Lakes Theatre Festival. Celebrating its 90th anniversary during the 2005/06 season, The Cleveland Play House is the nation's oldest permanent repertory theater. As of 2006, The Ohio Community Theater Association included groups in Akron, Canton, Columbus, Mansfield, Toledo, and Youngstown, among many other locations.

The Cincinnati Symphony was founded in 1895 and reorganized in 1909 with Leopold Stokowski as conductor. The Cincinnati Pops Orchestra acquired a new summer home in 1984 at the newly opened Riverbend Music Center. The Cincinnati Opera Association, founded in 1920, is the second-oldest opera company in the United States. Cincinnati is also the host of the annual Cincinnati May Festival, a classical music event that is considered to be the oldest continuous choral festival in the Western Hemisphere.

The Cleveland Orchestra, founded in 1918, has risen to world-class stature since 1946, when George Szell began his 24-year tenure as conductor and music director. Blossom Music Center, the Cleveland Orchestra's summer home located between Cleveland and Akron, has been a center for both classical and popular music in Northeast Ohio since opening in 1968. In 2002/2003 Blossom underwent major improvements to its structures and landscaping. A $36.7 million renovation and expansion of the orchestra's main home, Severance Hall, had been completed three years earlier.

Smaller professional musical groups in Cleveland include Apollo's Fire (the Cleveland Baroque Orchestra), the Cleveland Chamber Orchestra, and the Cleveland Pops Orchestra. The Cleveland Opera finds its home at the State Theatre and the Lyric Opera Cleveland is a resident of Playhouse Square.

There are civic symphony orchestras in Columbus, Dayton, Toledo, and Youngstown. Ballet companies are based in Cincinnati, Dayton, and Toledo. E. J. Thomas Hall in Akron is the home of the Ohio Ballet and the Akron Symphony. Operas are performed by resident companies in Cleveland, Columbus, Cincinnati, Toledo, and Dayton. There are numerous local arts festivals and craft shows. In 2005, Cleveland introduced the first ever Ingenuity Festival, a four-day event celebrating and promoting the awareness of the relationship between art and technology.

The nation's first college music department was established at Oberlin College in 1865; the Cincinnati Conservatory of Music was established in 1867, the Baldwin-Wallace College Conservatory in 1899, and the Cleveland Institute of Music in 1920. The Baldwin-Wallace Bach Festival, begun in 1932, is the oldest collegiate Bach festival in the country, celebrating its 75th Anniversary in 2007. Bach's four major choral works are performed at the festival in four-year cycles (one per year). Baldwin-Wallace is also home to the Riemenschneider Bach Institute, guardian of priceless Bach-related first editions and manuscripts.

The Cleveland International Piano Competition, held biennially at the Cleveland Institute of Music since 1975, has become one of the foremost events of its type, drawing contestants from 19 countries throughout the world. In 2005, the competition awarded a record cash prize of $50,000 to the winner.

43 LIBRARIES AND MUSEUMS

Ever since early settlers traded coonskins for books and established, in 1804, the Coonskin Library (now on display at the Ohio Historical Center in Columbus), Ohioans have stressed the importance of the public library system. In calendar year 2001, Ohio had 250 public library systems, with a total of 716 libraries, of which 482 were branches. For that same year, the state's public library system had 47,088,000 volumes of books and serial publications on its shelves, and a total circulation of 156,527,000. The system also had 3,418,000 audio and 2,716,000 video items, 127,000 electronic format items (CD-ROMs, magnetic tapes, and disks), and 66 bookmobiles.

Major public library systems include those of Cincinnati, with 4,721,766 volumes in 1998; Cleveland, 3,782,419; Cuyahoga County, 3,085,123; Dayton, 1,782,419; and Columbus, 2,433,636. Leading academic libraries include those of Ohio State University, over seven million books; Case Western Reserve University, 1,304,852 books; and the University of Cincinnati, over three million books. The State Library of Ohio in Columbus, founded in 1817, provides research and information services for Ohio's state government and agencies with more than two million books and periodicals. In 2001, operating income for the state's public library system came to $682,412,000 and included $1,085,000 in federal grants and $499,124,000 in state grants.

Among the state's more than 284 museums are the Museum of Art, Natural History Museum, and Western Reserve Historical Society Museum in Cleveland; the Museum of Natural History, Art Museum, and Taft Museum in Cincinnati; the Dayton Art Institute; and the Center of Science and Industry and Ohio Historical Center in Columbus. The Zanesville Art Center has collections of ceramics and glass made in the Zanesville area. Also noteworthy are the US Air Force Museum near Dayton, the Neil Armstrong Air and Space Museum at Wapakoneta, and the Ohio River Museum in Marietta. Cincinnati has a conservatory of rare plants, while Cleveland has botanical gardens and an aquarium; both cities have zoos. The National First Ladies' Library in Canton features the artwork and artifacts of First Lady Caroline Harrison.

Historical sites in Ohio include the Schoenbrunn Village State Memorial, a reconstruction of the state's first settlement by Moravian missionaries, near New Philadelphia; the early-19th-century Piqua Historical Area, with exhibits of Indian culture; and the Fort Meigs reconstruction at Perrysburg. Archaeological sites include the "great circle" mounds, built by the Hopewell Indians at present-day Newark, and Inscription Rock, marked by prehistoric Indians, on Kelley's Island.

44 COMMUNICATIONS

In 2004, 94.9% of Ohio's occupied housing units had telephones. In addition, by June of that same year there were 6,188,081 mobile wireless telephone subscribers. In 2003, 58.8% of Ohio households had a computer and 52.5% had Internet access. By June 2005, there were 1,505,272 high-speed lines in Ohio, 1,395,062 residential and 110,210 for business.

Many of the state's radio stations were established in the early 1920s, when the growth of radio broadcasting was fostered by the availability of low-priced sets manufactured by Crosley Radio of Cincinnati. In 2005, there were 46 major AM stations, 159 major FM stations, and 31 commercial and 11 noncommercial television stations. In 1999, the Cleveland area had 1,479,020 television households, 72% of which received cable. In that same year the Cincinnati area had 820,000 television households, 64% receiving cable. Finally, of the Columbus area's 757,860 television-viewing families, 66% watched cable. A total of 168,083 Internet domain names were registered in Ohio in 2000.

45 PRESS

The first newspaper published in the region north and west of the Ohio River was the *Centinel of the North–Western Territory,* which was written, typeset, and printed in Cincinnati by William Maxwell in 1793. The oldest newspaper in the state still published under its original name is the *Scioto Gazette,* which appeared in 1800. The oldest extant weekly, the *Lebanon Western Star,* began publication in 1807, and the first daily, the *Cincinnati Commercial Register,* appeared in 1826. By 1840 there were 145 newspapers in Ohio.

Two of the state's most influential newspapers, the *Cleveland Plain Dealer* and the *Cincinnati Enquirer,* were founded in 1841.

In 2005, the *Cleveland Plain Dealer* was the twentieth-largest daily newspaper in the country. In 1878, Edward W. Scripps established the Cleveland *Penny Press* (later called the *Press*), the first newspaper in what would become the extensive Scripps-Howard chain (though the *Press* folded in 1982). He later added to his newspaper empire the *Cincinnati Post* (1881) and the *Columbus Citizen* (1899), as well as papers in Akron, Toledo, and Youngstown.

In 2005, the state had 30 mornings dailies, 54 evening editions, and 41 Sunday editions. With a total of 84 daily newspapers, Ohio has the third-largest number of daily papers in the country (following California and Texas).

The following table lists leading Ohio newspapers with their approximate daily circulation in 2005:

AREA	NAME	DAILY	SUNDAY
Akron	*Beacon Journal* (m,S)	173,975	185,963
Cincinnati	*Enquirer* (m,S)	183,051	192,240
	Post (e)	43,398	68,910 (Sat.)
Cleveland	*Plain Dealer* (m,S)	354,309	479,131
Columbus	*Dispatch* (m,S)	251,045	361,304
Dayton	*Daily News* (m,S)	178,099	185,122
Toledo	*Blade* (m,S)	139,398	183,632
Youngstown	*Vindicator* (e,S)	66,487	94,710

*Sun Newspapers,*a weekly newspaper, founded in 1969, produces 25 regional editions to serve 82 communities in the greater Cleveland and Akron areas, with a weekly circulation of 270,000. It is the largest chain of fully paid weekly newspapers in the United States. *Crain's Cleveland Business* has reported a readership of about 90,000 per week. Regional interest periodicals include *Cleveland Magazine, Cincinnati Magazine, Ohio Magazine,* and *Northern Ohio Live.*

46 ORGANIZATIONS

In 2006, there were over 15,895 nonprofit organizations registered within the state, of which about 10,308 were registered as charitable, educational, or religious organizations. Service organizations with headquarters in Ohio include Disabled American Veterans and the National Exchange Club.

Commercial and professional organizations include the American Ceramic Society, the Order of United Commercial Travelers of America, Music Teachers National Association, ASM International, the United States Police Canine Association, the Association for Systems Management, and the Brotherhood of Locomotive Engineers.

Sports associations operating out of Ohio are the Lighter-Than-Air Society and Professional Bowlers Association, American Motorcyclist Association, the Amateur Trapshooting Association, the International Soap Box Derby, the Freethrowers Boomerang Association, US Flag and Touch Football League, US Speedskating, and Indoor Sports Club. Special interest and hobbyist groups include the Etch-A-Sketch Club, the National Quilting Association, and the American Bonsai Society.

Arts, culture, and history are promoted in the state through such organizations as the Botanical Society of America, the American Guild of English Handbell Ringers, the American-Slovenian Polka Foundation, the Ohio and Erie Canal Association, the Ohio Art League, the Ohio Arts Council, and the Ohio Valley

Art League. There are also numerous local arts groups and historical societies.

47TOURISM, TRAVEL, AND RECREATION

Ohio visitors spend more than $30.7 billion annually on travel and tourism and the industry supports nearly 529,100 travel-related positions. Ohio has a $162 million dollar travel market. Visitors spend more than one billion annually in Ashtabula County alone. It is known as the Covered Bridge Capital (16) and the Wine Capital (11) of Ohio, and offers more campsites than any other county in Ohio (18).

Cleveland, Columbus, and Cincinnati all offer major attractions of museums, restaurants, shopping, parks, and concerts. The Rock and Roll Hall of Fame and Museum and the Great Lakes Science Center, both in Cleveland, are major attractions. Major league sports (Indians baseball, Cavaliers basketball, Browns football) also draw visitors to Cleveland. The semiannual Cleveland International Piano Competition, with its $50,000 first prize, draws crowds to see performances with the Cleveland Orchestra. The NFL Hall of Fame is located in Canton. Popular amusement parks include Cedar Point in Sandusky, King's Island in Cincinnati, and Six Flags Worlds of Adventure in Aurora. Sandusky is also the launching point for visiting the Lake Erie Islands of Put-in-Bay and Middle Bass Island. There visitors can see the monument to William Hazard Perry (naval hero of the War of 1812) and visit wineries.

Beaches and parks in the Lake Erie region are especially popular with tourists during the summer, including the Mentor Headlands State Park. The Cuyahoga Valley National Park is also a popular attraction, linking the urban centers of Cleveland and Akron. The Cleveland Metroparks system creates an "Emerald Necklace" around the greater Cleveland area.

Ohio state parks comprise 204,274 acres (84,000 hectares). Among the most visited state parks are Alum Creek, East Harbor and Kelleys Island (both on Lake Erie), Grand Lake, St. Mary's, Hocking Hills, Hueston Woods, Mohican, Pymatuning (on the Pennsylvania border), Rocky Fork, Salt Fork, Scioto Trail, and West Branch. Ohio is the home of many Indian communities and archaeological sites such as the Great Circle Earthworks and the Miamisburg Mound and the Serpent Mound are popular visitor sites.

The most popular sport fish are bass, catfish, bullhead, carp, perch, and rainbow trout. The deer-hunting season varies for shotgun, primitive arms, and bows.

The eastern Allegheny region has several ski resorts for winter sports enthusiasts. Popular tourist attractions here include the Amish settlement around Millersburg, the National Road-Zane Grey Museum near Zanesville, and the restored Roscoe Village on the Ohio-Erie Canal. The southern region offers scenic hill country and the showboat *Majestic*, the last of the original floating theaters, in Cincinnati.

In the western region, tourist sites include the Wright brothers' early flying machines in Dayton's Carillon Park, the Ohio Caverns at West Liberty, and the Zane Caverns near Bellefontaine. The central region is "Johnny Appleseed" country; the folk hero (a frontiersman whose real name was John Chapman) is commemorated in Mansfield by the blockhouse to which he directed settlers in order to save them from an Indian raid. In Columbus are the reconstructed Ohio Village and the Exposition Center, site of the annual Ohio State Fair, held for 13 days in mid-August.

Other leading tourist attractions include Ohio's presidential memorials and homes: the William Henry Harrison Memorial at North Bend, Ulysses S. Grant's birthplace at Point Pleasant, the James A. Garfield home at Mentor, the Rutherford B. Hayes home at Fremont, the William McKinley Memorial at Canton, the Taft National Historic Site in Cincinnati, and the Warren G. Harding home in Marion. Also of interest are the Thomas A. Edison birthplace at Milan, and Malabar Farm, in Richland County, home of author and conservationist Louis Bromfield.

48SPORTS

There are seven major professional sports teams in Ohio: the Cleveland Indians and the Cincinnati Reds of Major League Baseball, the Columbus Crew of Major League Soccer, the Cincinnati Bengals and the Cleveland Browns of the National Football League, the Columbus Blue Jackets of the National Hockey League, and the Cleveland Cavaliers of the National Basketball Association.

The state is also home to Triple-A minor league baseball teams in Columbus and Toledo, a Double-A team in Akron, and Single-A teams in Eastlake, Niles, and Dayton. In addition, there are minor league hockey teams in Cleveland, Columbus, Dayton, and Toledo.

The Cincinnati Reds (traditionally short for Redstockings) were the first professionally organized baseball team, playing their first season in 1869. Their record was 64–0. The Reds won the World Series in 1919, 1940, 1975, 1976, and 1990. The Indians won the World Series in 1920 and 1948. In 1995, the Indians won their first American League pennant since 1954, but lost to the Atlanta Braves in the World Series. They returned to the Series in 1997, this time losing to the Florida Marlins. The original Cleveland Browns, who moved to Baltimore in 1995, won four NFL titles, football's championship prior to the Super Bowl, the last in 1964. An expansion or relocation NFL team began play as the Browns in a new stadium in Cleveland beginning in 1999. The Bengals won the American Football Conference Championship in both 1981 and 1988, but lost each year's Super Bowl.

Akron has been headquarters for the Professional Bowlers Association (PBA) since its founding in 1958. The PBA's top tournament is played there each year, and the PBA Hall of Fame is also located in Akron. The NEC Invitational is played annually in Akron, and the Memorial Golf Tournament in Dublin.

Major horse-racing tracks include Cleveland's Thistledown, Cincinnati's River Downs, Columbus's Scioto Downs, and other tracks at Toledo, Lebanon, Grove City, and Northfield. The Cleveland Gold Cup race is held annually at Thistledown, as is the Ohio Derby. The Little Brown Jug classic for three-year-old pacers takes place every year at the Delaware Fairgrounds, and the Ohio State race for two-year-old trotters is held during the state fair at Columbus.

Several new facilities have been constructed, including the new Cleveland Browns Stadium in 1999, Jacobs Field in 1994 (home of the Indians), Columbus Crew Stadium, and most recently, the Great American Ballpark in Cincinnati (2003). The Cincinnati Reds make it their home park.

In collegiate sports, Ohio State University has long been a football powerhouse, winning over 25 Big Ten titles. Ohio State won the Rose Bowl in 1950, 1955, 1958, 1969, 1974, and 1997. The Buckeyes were named national champions in 1942, 1954 (with UCLA), 1957 (with Auburn), 1968, and in 2003 after upsetting Miami (Fl) in the Fiesta Bowl. Ohio State also has won National Collegiate Athletic Association (NCAA) championships in baseball, basketball, fencing, golf, gymnastics, and swimming, while Cincinnati and Dayton universities have had highly successful basketball teams. The Pro Football Hall of Fame is located in Canton, where the sport was first organized professionally in 1920.

Other annual sporting events include the grand tournament of the American Trapshooting Association in Vandalia, the Grand Prix or Cleveland Indy car race, and the All-American Soap Box Derby in Akron, a nationally covered event in which 9- to 15-year-olds compete.

49 FAMOUS OHIOANS

Ohio has been the native state of seven US presidents and the residence of another. Inventions by Ohioans include the incandescent light, the arc light, and the airplane.

William Henry Harrison (b.Virginia, 1773–1841), the ninth US president, came to Ohio as a US Army ensign in territorial times. After serving in the Indian wars under Gen. Anthony Wayne, he became secretary of the Northwest Territory. As the territorial delegate to Congress, he fostered the Harrison Land Act, which stimulated settlement of the public domain. Named territorial governor in 1800, Harrison conducted both warfare and peace negotiations with the Indians. After the defeat of British and Indian forces in 1813, he became known as the "Washington of the West." After settling at North Bend on the Ohio River, he began a political career that carried him to the White House in 1841. Harrison caught a chill from a cold March wind and died of pneumonia exactly one month after his inauguration.

From 1869 to 1881, the White House was occupied by three Ohioans. All were Republicans who had served with distinction as Union Army generals. The first, Ulysses Simpson Grant (Hiram Ulysses Grant, 1822–85), the 18th US president, was an Ohio farm boy educated at West Point. After service in the Mexican War, he left the US Army, having been charged with intemperance. He emerged from obscurity in 1861, when he was assigned to an Illinois regiment. Grant rose quickly in command; after victories at Shiloh and Vicksburg, he was commissioned major general. In 1864, he directed the Virginia campaign that ended with Confederate surrender, and this rumpled, slouching, laconic man became the nation's hero. In 1868, he was elected president, and he was reelected in 1872. His second term was rocked with financial scandals, though none were directly connected to Grant. After leaving the presidency in 1877, he went bankrupt, and to discharge his debts, he wrote his memoirs. That extraordinary book was completed four days before his death from throat cancer in 1885. Grant is buried in a monumental tomb in New York City.

Rutherford B. Hayes (1822–93), the 19th US president, was born in Delaware, Ohio, and educated at Kenyon College and Harvard Law School. Following Army service, he was elected to Congress, and in 1876 became the Republican presidential nominee. In a close and disputed election, he defeated New York's Governor Samuel J. Tilden. Hayes chose not to run for re-election, returning instead to Ohio to work on behalf of humanitarian causes.

In 1893, Hayes died in Fremont, where the Hayes Memorial was created—the first presidential museum and library in the nation.

James A. Garfield (1831–81), 20th US president, was born in a log cabin in northern Ohio. Between school terms, he worked as a farmhand and a mule driver on the Ohio Canal. After holding several Civil War commands, he served in Congress for 18 years. Elected president in 1880, he held office but a few months; he was shot by a disappointed office seeker in the Washington, DC, railroad station on 2 July and died 11 weeks later.

Benjamin Harrison (1833–1901), 23rd US president and grandson of William Henry Harrison, was born in North Bend. After graduation from Miami University, he studied law and began to practice in Indianapolis. Military command in the Civil War was followed by service in the US Senate and the Republican presidential nomination in 1888. As president, Harrison gave impetus to westward expansion, moved toward annexation of Hawaii, and enlarged the civil-service system.

US presidents in the 20th century include three more native Ohioans. William McKinley (1843–1901) was born in Niles. Elected in 1896 as the 25th president, he established the gold standard and maintained tariff protection for US manufactures. Early in his second term, while greeting a throng of people, he was shot to death by a young anarchist. William Howard Taft (1857–1930), of Cincinnati, was the 27th US president. He gained a national reputation in 1904 as President Theodore Roosevelt's secretary of war; five years later, he succeeded Roosevelt in the White House. Defeated in 1912, Taft then left Washington for a law professorship at Yale. In 1921, under President Warren G. Harding (1865–1923), he became US chief justice, serving in that office until a month before his death. Harding, the last Ohioan to win the White House, was born in Blooming Grove. He went into politics from journalism, after serving as editor of the *Marion Star*. After eight years in the US Senate, he was a dark-horse candidate for the Republican presidential nomination in 1920. He won the election from James M. Cox (1870–1957), another Ohio journalist-politician, and became the 29th US president. Harding, who died in office, was surrounded by graft and corruption in his own cabinet.

Three US vice presidents were natives of Ohio. Thomas A. Hendricks (1819–85) was elected on the Democratic ticket with Grover Cleveland in 1884. Charles W. Fairbanks (1852–1918) served from 1905 to 1909 under Theodore Roosevelt. Charles Gates Dawes (1865–1951) became vice president under Calvin Coolidge in 1925, the same year the Dawes Plan for reorganizing German finances brought him the Nobel Peace Prize; from 1929 to 1932, he served as US ambassador to Great Britain.

Three Ohioans served as chief justice on the Supreme Court: Salmon P. Chase (b.New Hampshire, 1808–73), Morrison R. Waite (b.Connecticut, 1816–88), and Taft. Most notable among nearly 40 cabinet officers from Ohio were Secretary of State Lewis Cass (b.New Hampshire, 1783–1866), Treasury Secretaries Chase and John Sherman (1823–1900), and Secretary of War Edwin M. Stanton (1814–69). William Tecumseh Sherman (1820–91) was a Union general in the Civil War whose Georgia campaign in 1864 helped effect the surrender of the Confederacy. Although disappointed in his quest for the presidency, US Senator Robert A. Taft (1889–1953) was an enduring figure, best remembered for his authorship of the Taft-Hartley Labor Management Relations Act of 1947.

Nobel Prize winners from Ohio include Dawes and physicists Arthur Compton (1892–1962) and Donald Glaser (b.1926). Notable Pulitzer Prize winners include novelist Louis Bromfield (1896–1956), dramatist Russell Crouse (1893–1966), historian Paul Herman Buck (1899–1979), and historian and biographer Arthur Schlesinger Jr. (b.1917). Ohio writers of enduring fame are novelists William Dean Howells (1837–1920), Zane Grey (1875–1939), and Sherwood Anderson (1876–1941), whose short story collection *Winesburg, Ohio* was set in his hometown of Clyde; poets Paul Laurence Dunbar (1872–1906) and Hart Crane (1899–1932); and humorist James Thurber (1894–1961). Toni Morrison (b.1931), winner of the 1988 Pulitzer Prize for literature and the 1993 Nobel Prize for literature, was born in Lorain, Ohio. Among Ohio's eminent journalists are Whitelaw Reid (1837–1912), satirists David R. Locke (1833–88) and Ambrose Bierce (1842–1914), columnist O. O. McIntyre (1884–1938), newsletter publisher W. M. Kiplinger (1891–1967), and James Reston (b.Scotland, 1909–95), an editor and columnist for the *New York Times* along with author-commentator Lowell Thomas (1892–1981). Important in the art world were painters Thomas Cole (b.England, 1801–48), Frank Duveneck (b.Kentucky, 1848–1919), and George Bellows (1882–1925), as well as architects Cass Gilbert (1859–1934) and Philip Johnson (1906–2005). Defense lawyer Clarence Darrow (1857–1938) was also an Ohioan.

Ohio educators whose books taught reading, writing, and arithmetic to the nation's schoolchildren were William Holmes McGuffey (b.Pennsylvania, 1800–73), Platt R. Spencer (1800–64), and Joseph Ray (1807–65). In higher education, Horace Mann (b.Massachusetts, 1796–1859) was the first president of innovative Antioch College, and William Rainey Harper (1856–1906) founded the University of Chicago.

Several Ohio-born inventor-scientists have furthered the nation's industrial progress. Thomas A. Edison (1847–1931) produced the incandescent lamp, the phonograph, and the movie camera. Charles Brush (1849–1929) invented the arc light. John H. Patterson (1844–1922) helped develop the cash register. The Wright brothers, Orville (1871–1948) and Wilbur (b.Indiana, 1867–1912), made the first flight in a powered aircraft. Charles F. Kettering (1876–1958) invented the automobile self-starter. Ohio's leading industrialist was John D. Rockefeller (b.New York, 1839–1937), founder of Standard Oil of Ohio. Harvey S. Firestone (1868–1938) started the tire company that bears his name. Edward "Eddie" Rickenbacker (1890–1973), an ace pilot in World War I, was president of Eastern Airlines.

The most notable Ohioans in the entertainment field are markswoman Annie Oakley (Phoebe Anne Oakley Mozee, 1860–1926);

movie actors Clark Gable (1901–60) and Roy Rogers (Leonard Slye, 1912–98); movie director Stephen Spielberg (b.1947); comedian Bob Hope (Leslie Townes Hope, b.England, 1903); actors Paul Newman (b.1925), Hal Holbrook (b.1925), and Joel Grey (b.1932); jazz pianist Art Tatum (1910–56); and composer Henry Mancini (1924–94).

Leading sports figures from Ohio are boxing champion Jim Jeffries (1875–1953), racing driver Barney Oldfield (1878–1946), baseball pitcher Cy Young (1867–1955), baseball executive Branch Rickey (1881–1965), baseball star Peter "Pete" Rose (b.1941), who broke Ty Cobb's record for the most hits, track star Jesse Owens (b.Alabama, 1912–80), jockey George Edward "Eddie" Arcaro (1916–97), and golfer Jack Nicklaus (b.1940).

Astronauts from Ohio include John Glenn (b.1921), the first American to orbit Earth, who was elected US senator from Ohio in 1974; and Neil Armstrong (b.1930), the first man to walk on the moon.

50 BIBLIOGRAPHY

Council of State Governments. *The Book of the States, 2006 Edition.* Lexington, Ky.: Council of State Governments, 2006.

Curtin, Michael F. *Ohio Politics Almanac.* 2nd ed. Kent: Kent State University Press, 2006.

Feagler, Dick. *Feagler's Cleveland.* Cleveland: Gray & Co., 1996.

Middleton, Stephen. *The Black Laws: Race and the Legal Process in Early Ohio.* Athens: Ohio University Press, 2005.

Ohio Politics. Edited by Alexander P. Lamis. Kent: Kent State University Press, 1994.

Owen, Lorrie K. (ed.). *Dictionary of Ohio Historic Places.* St. Clair Shores, Mich.: Somerset Publishers, 1999.

Peacefull, Leonard (ed.). *A Geography of Ohio.* Kent: Kent State University Press, 1996.

Platt, Carolyn V. *Cuyahoga Valley National Park Handbook.* Kent: The Kent State University Press, 2006.

Shriver, Phillip R., and Clarence E. Wunderlin Jr. (eds.). *The Documentary Heritage of Ohio.* Athens: Ohio University Press, 2000.

Thurber, James. *My Life and Hard Times.* New York: Harper, 1933.

US Department of Commerce, Economics and Statistics Administration, US Census Bureau. *Ohio, 2000. Summary Social, Economic, and Housing Characteristics: 2000 Census of Population and Housing.* Washington, D.C.: US Government Printing Office, 2003.

OKLAHOMA

State of Oklahoma

ORIGIN OF STATE NAME: Derived from the Choctaw Indian words *okla humma,* meaning "land of the red people." **NICKNAME:** The Sooner State. **CAPITAL:** Oklahoma City. **ENTERED UNION:** 16 November 1907 (46th). **SONG:** "Oklahoma!" **MOTTO:** *Labor omnia vincit* (Labor conquers all things). **FLAG:** On a blue field, a peace pipe and an olive branch cross an Osage warrior's shield, which is decorated with small crosses and from which seven eagle feathers descend. The word "Oklahoma" appears below. **OFFICIAL SEAL:** Each point of a five-pointed star incorporates the emblem of a Native American nation: (clockwise from top) Chickasaw, Choctaw, Seminole, Creek, and Cherokee. In the center, a frontiersman and Native American shake hands before the goddess of justice; behind them are symbols of progress, including a farm, train, and mill. Surrounding the large star are 45 small ones and the words "Great Seal of the State of Oklahoma 1907." **BIRD:** Scissor-tailed flycatcher. **FISH:** White bass (sand bass). **FLOWER:** Mistletoe. **TREE:** Redbud. **LEGAL HOLIDAYS:** New Year's Day, 1 January; Birthday of Martin Luther King Jr., 3rd Monday in January; Presidents' Day, 3rd Monday in February; Confederate Memorial Day, May 10; National Memorial Day, last Monday in May; Independence Day, 4 July; Labor Day, 1st Monday in September; Veterans' Day, 11 November; Thanksgiving Day, 4th Thursday in November and the following day; Christmas Day, 25 December and the day following. **TIME:** 6 AM CST = noon GMT.

¹LOCATION, SIZE, AND EXTENT

Situated in the western south-central United States, Oklahoma ranks 18th in size among the 50 states.

The total area of Oklahoma is 69,956 sq mi (181,186 sq km), of which land takes up 68,655 sq mi (177,817 sq km) and inland water 1,301 sq mi (3,369 sq km). Oklahoma extends 464 mi (747 km) E–W including the panhandle in the NW, which is about 165 mi (266 km) long. The maximum N–S extension is 230 mi (370 km).

Oklahoma is bordered on the N by Colorado and Kansas; on the E by Missouri and Arkansas; on the S and SW by Texas (with part of the line formed by the Red River); and on the extreme W by New Mexico. The total estimated boundary length of Oklahoma is 1,581 mi (2,544 km). The state's geographic center is in Oklahoma County, 8 mi (13 km) N of Oklahoma City.

²TOPOGRAPHY

The land of Oklahoma rises gently to the west from an altitude of 289 ft (88 m) at Little River in the southeastern corner (the lowest point in the state) to a height of 4,973 ft (1,517 m) at Black Mesa, the highest elevation, on the tip of the panhandle. The mean elevation of the state is approximately 1,300 ft (397 m). Four mountain ranges cross this Great Plains state: the Boston Mountains (part of the Ozark Plateau) in the northeast, the Quachitas in the southeast, the Arbuckles in the south-central region, and the Wichitas in the southwest. Much of the northwest belongs to the High Plains, while northeastern Oklahoma is mainly a region of buttes and valleys.

Not quite two-thirds of the state is drained by the Arkansas River, and the remainder by the Red River. Within Oklahoma, the Arkansas is joined by the Verdigris, Grand (Neosho), and Illinois rivers from the north and northeast, and by the Cimarron and Canadian rivers from the northwest and west. The Red River, which marks most of the state's southern boundary, is joined by the Washita, Salt Fork, Blue, Kiamichi, and many smaller rivers. There are few natural lakes but many artificial ones, of which the largest is Lake Eufaula, covering 102,500 acres (41,500 hectares).

³CLIMATE

Oklahoma has a continental climate with cold winters and hot summers. Normal daily average temperatures in Oklahoma City range from 37°F (2°C) in January to 82°F (27°C) in July. The record low temperature of -27°F (-33°C) was set at Watts on 18 January 1930; the record high, 120°F (49°C), occurred at Tipton on 27 June 1994.

Dry, sunny weather generally prevails throughout the state. Precipitation varies from an average of 15 in (38 cm) annually in the panhandle to over 50 in (127 cm) in the southeast. Average annual precipitation in Oklahoma City is about 33.3 in (84 cm). Snowfall averages 9 in (23 cm) a year in Oklahoma City, which is also one of the windiest cities in the United States, with an average annual wind speed of 13 mph (20 km/hr).

Oklahoma is tornado-prone. One of the most destructive windstorms was the tornado that tore through Ellis, Woods, and Woodward counties on 9 April 1947, killing 101 people and injuring 782 others.

⁴FLORA AND FAUNA

Grasses grow in abundance in Oklahoma. Bluestem, buffalo, sand lovegrass, and grama grasses are native, with the bluestem found mostly in the eastern and central regions, and buffalo grass most common in the western counties, known as the "short grass country." Deciduous hardwoods stand in eastern Oklahoma, and red and yellow cactus blossoms brighten the Black Mesa area in the northwest. The eastern prairie fringed orchid was listed as threatened in 2006; there were no plant species listed as endangered that year in Oklahoma.

The white-tailed deer is found in all counties, and Rio Grande wild turkeys are hunted across much of the state. Pronghorn antelope inhabit the panhandle area, and elk survive in the Wichita Mountains Wildlife Refuge, where a few herds of American buffalo (bison) are also preserved. The bobwhite quail, ring-necked pheasant, and prairie chicken are common game birds. Native sport fish include largemouth, smallmouth, white, and spotted bass; catfish; crappie; and sunfish.

In April 2006, the US Fish and Wildlife Service listed 18 species of animals (vertebrates and invertebrates) as threatened or endangered. These included three species of bat (Ozark big-eared, Indiana, and gray), bald eagle, whooping crane, black-capped vireo, red-cockaded woodpecker, Eskimo curlew, and Neosho madtom.

5ENVIRONMENTAL PROTECTION

The Oklahoma Department of Environment Quality has overall responsibility for coordinating all pollution control activities by other state agencies and for developing a comprehensive water quality management program for Oklahoma. The Oklahoma Conservation Commission is responsible for conservation of renewable natural resources through land use planning, small watershed upstream flood control, reclamation of abandoned mine land, water quality monitoring and soil and water conservation, as well as environmental education and wetlands conservation. The Department of Wildlife Conservation manages wildlife resources and habitat specifically for hunters, anglers, and others who appreciate wildlife.

The Department of Health is responsible for the monitoring of air quality standards; the enforcement of regulations covering control of industrial and solid waste; the enforcement of regulations covering radioactive materials at the Kerr-McGee processing facility at Gore and elsewhere; and the maintenance of standards at all public waterworks and sewer systems. The Water Resources Board has broad statutory authority to protect the state's waters.

Toxic industrial wastes remain an environmental concern, and old mines in the Tar Creek area of northeastern Oklahoma still exude groundwater contaminated by zinc, iron, and cadmium. In 2003, 30 million lb of toxic chemicals were released in the state. Also in 2003, Oklahoma had 165 hazardous waste sites listed in the US Environment Protection Agency (EPA) database, 10 of which were on the National Priorities List as of 2006; among these were Tar Creek in Ottawa County and Tinker Air Force Base. In 2005, the EPA spent over $8.8 million through the Superfund program for the cleanup of hazardous waste sites in the state. The same year, federal EPA grants awarded to the state included $10.7 million for wastewater system improvements. A special grant of $4.96 million was awarded for the Oklahoma Plan Demonstration Project in Tar Creek, Ottawa County, which is designed to offer demonstration programs for land restoration and environmental management.

Lands devastated by erosion during the droughts of the 1930s were purchased by the federal government and turned over to the Soil Conservation Service for restoration. When grasses were firmly established in the mid-1950s, the land was turned over to the US Forest Service and is now leased for grazing. In 2003, the state had about 890,000 acres of wetlands—about 2% of the land.

6POPULATION

Oklahoma ranked 28th in population in the United States with an estimated total of 3,547,884 in 2005, an increase of 2.8% since 2000. Between 1990 and 2000, Oklahoma's population grew from 3,145,585 to 3,450,654, an increase of 9.7%. The population is projected to reach 3.6 million by 2015 and 3.8 million by 2025. The population density in 2004 was 51.3 persons per sq mi. In 2004 the median age in Oklahoma was 36.5; 24.4% of the on under age 18 while 13.2% was age 65 or older.

The largest city is Oklahoma City, which in 2004 had an estimated 528,042 inhabitants in the city proper and an estimated population of 1,144,327 in the metropolitan statistical area. Tulsa, the second-largest city, had an estimated population of 383,764 in the city proper and a 881,815 in the metropolitan area. Norman ranked third with a population of 100,923 in 2004. The Lawton metropolitan area had a population of about 110,514.

7ETHNIC GROUPS

According to the 1990 Census, Oklahoma had more American Indians—252,420—than any other state, but by 1998 its estimated American Indian population of 281,000 had been surpassed by California's (292,000), and it remained in second place in 2000, with an Indian population of 273,230, or 7.9% of the state's total population—the fourth-highest percentage ranking in the United States. Oklahoma was also home to some of the nation's largest Indian reservations, including those of the Creek, Cherokee, Chickasaw, and Choctaw Indians. By 2004, the state's American Indian population had increased to 8.1% of the total population.

Black slaves came to Oklahoma (then known as Indian Territory) with their Indian masters after Congress forced the resettlement of Indians from the southeast to lands west of the Mississippi River in 1830. By the time of the Civil War, there were 7,000 free Negroes in Oklahoma. After the depression of the 1930s, blacks left the farms and small towns and concentrated in Oklahoma City and Tulsa. In 2000, the black population of 260,968 was smaller than the American Indian population. It remained thus in 2004, when the black population accounted for 7.7% of the state's total population.

Mexicans came to Oklahoma during the 19th century as laborers on railroads and ranches, and in coal mines. Later they worked in the cotton fields until the depression of the 1930s and subsequent mechanization reduced the need for seasonal labor. Today, most first- and second-generation Mexicans live in Oklahoma City, Tulsa, and Lawton. In 2000, Oklahomans who were classified as Hispanics or Latinos numbered 179,304 and represented 5.2% of the state's total population. Of this total, 132,813 were Mexican. In 2004, 6.3% of the state's population was Hispanic or Latino.

Italians, Czechs, Germans, Poles, Britons, Irish, and others of European stock also came to Oklahoma during the 19th century. Foreign immigration has been small since that time, however, and in 2000, less than 4% of the population consisted of the foreign born (who numbered 131,747). Persons claiming at least one specific ancestry group in 2000 included English, 291,553; German, 435,245; and Irish, 354,802. In 2000, the Asian population numbered 46,767 and there were 2,372 Pacific Islanders. In 2004, 1.5% of the population was Asian, and 0.1% of the population was Pa-

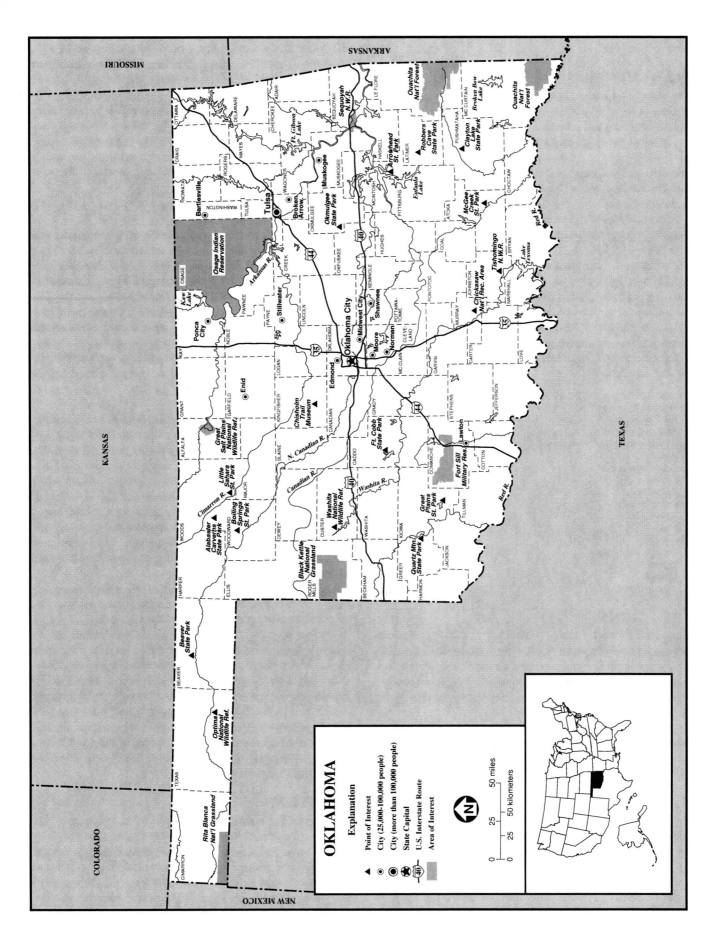

cific Islander. A full 4% of the population reported origin of two or more races that year.

8 LANGUAGES

Once the open hunting ground of the Osage, Comanche, and Apache Indians, what is now Oklahoma later welcomed the deported Cherokee and other transferred eastern tribes. The diversity of tribal and linguistic backgrounds is reflected in numerous place-names such as Oklahoma itself, Kiamichi, and Muskogee. Almost equally diverse is Oklahoma English, with its uneven blending of features of North Midland, South Midland, and Southern dialects.

In 2000, 2,977,187 Oklahomans—92.6% of the resident population five years or older—spoke only English at home, down from 95% in 1990.

The following table gives selected statistics from the 2000 Census for language spoken at home by persons five years old and over. The category "Other Native North American languages" includes Apache, Cherokee, Choctaw, Dakota, Keres, Pima, and Yupik. The category "Other Asian languages" includes Dravidian languages, Malayalam, Telugu, Tamil, and Turkish. The category "African languages" includes Amharic, Ibo, Twi, Yoruba, Bantu, Swahili, and Somali.

LANGUAGE	NUMBER	PERCENT
Population 5 years and over	**3,215,719**	**100.0**
Speak only English	2,977,187	92.6
Speak a language other than English	238,532	7.4
Speak a language other than English	**238,532**	**7.4**
Spanish or Spanish Creole	141,060	4.4
Other Native North American languages	18,871	0.6
German	13,445	0.4
Vietnamese	11,330	0.4
French (incl. Patois, Cajun)	8,258	0.3
Chinese	6,413	0.2
Korean	3,948	0.1
Arabic	3,265	0.1
Other Asian languages	3,134	0.1
Tagalog	2,888	0.1
Japanese	2,546	0.1
African languages	2,546	0.1

9 RELIGIONS

Evangelical Protestant groups predominate in Oklahoma with adherents representing about 41.4% of the total population in 2000. This group was influential in keeping the state "dry"—that is, banning the sale of all alcoholic beverages—until 1959 and resisting legalization of public drinking until 29 counties voted to permit the sale of liquor by the drink in 1985.

The leading Protestant group in 2000 was the Southern Baptist Convention with 967,223 adherents; in 2002 there were 16,563 new baptized members. Other leading Evangelical Protestant denominations in 2000 included the Assemblies of God, 88,301 adherents; the Churches of Christ, 83,047; the Christian Church (Disciples of Christ), 53,729; and the Christian Churches, 42,708. Free Will Baptists, Nazarenes, Missouri Synod Lutherans, and those of various other Pentecostal traditions are also fairly well represented. The largest Mainline Protestant denominations are the United Methodist Church, with 253,375 adherents (in 2004), and the Presbyterian Church USA, with 35,211 adherents (in 2000) In 2006 there were 38,011 members of the Church of Jesus Christ of Latter-day Saints (Mormons) in 75 congregations.

In 2004, there were about 169,045 Roman Catholics in the state, of which 112,951 reside in the archdiocese of Oklahoma City. In 2000, there were 6,145 Muslims and about 5,050 Jews throughout the state. About 39.2% of the population did not claim any religious affiliation.

Oral Roberts, a popular minister, has established a college and faith-healing hospital in Tulsa, and his "Tower of Faith" broadcasts by radio and television have made him a well-known preacher throughout the United States. A Mormon temple was built in Oklahoma City in 2000. The offices of the Unitarian Universalist Christian Fellowship are in Turley.

10 TRANSPORTATION

In 1930, the high point for railroad transportation in Oklahoma, there were 6,678 mi (10,747 km) of railroad track in the state. In 2003, there were 3,853 rail mi (6,201 km) of track. As of that same year, there were three Class I railroads operating in Oklahoma: the Burlington Northern Santa Fe; the Union Pacific; and the Kansas City Southern. Together, they operated 2,536 mi (4,82 km) of right-of-way in the state as of 2003. As of 2006, Amtrak provided passenger service to five stations in Oklahoma via its Oklahoma City to Fort Worth Heartland Flyer train. Inter-urban transit needs, formerly served by streetcars (one of the most popular routes operated between Oklahoma City and Norman), are now supplied by buses.

The Department of Transportation is responsible for construction and maintenance of the state road system, which in 2004 included state roads and highways, and interstate highways. The main east–west highways are I-44, connecting Tulsa and Oklahoma City, and I-40; the major north–south route is I-35, which links Oklahoma City with Topeka, Kansas and Dallas–Ft. Worth, Texas. Overall in 2004, Oklahoma had 112,713 mi (181,467 km) of roadway. A total of some 3.156 million motor vehicles were registered in the state that same year, including 1.622 million automobiles and 1.448 million trucks of all types. There were 2,369,621 licensed drivers in 2004.

The opening of the McClellan–Kerr Arkansas River Navigation System in 1971 linked Oklahoma with the Mississippi River and thus to Gulf coast ports. Tulsa, Port of Catoosa, is the chief port on the system, handling 2.159 million tons of cargo in 2004. In 2003, waterborne shipments totaled 4.895 million tons. In 2004, Oklahoma had 150 mi (241 km) of navigable inland waterways.

In 2005, Oklahoma had a total of 439 public and private-use aviation-related facilities. This included 346 airports, 91 heliports, 1 STOLport (Short Take-Off and Landing), and 1 seaplane base. Will Rogers World Airport in Oklahoma City and Tulsa International Airport are the state's largest airports. In 2004, Will Rogers had 1,695,096 passengers enplaned, while Tulsa International had 1,462,799 enplanements.

11 HISTORY

There is evidence—chiefly from the Spiro Mound in eastern Oklahoma, excavated in 1930—that an advanced Indian civilization inhabited the region around AD 900–1100. By the time the Spanish conquistadores, led by Hernando de Soto and Francisco Vasquez de Coronado, arrived there in the 16th century, however, only a few scattered tribes remained. Two centuries later, French trappers moved up the rivers of Oklahoma.

Except for the panhandle, which remained a no-man's-land until 1890, all of present-day Oklahoma became part of US territory with the Louisiana Purchase in 1803. Under the Indian Removal Act of 1830, Indian tribes from the southeastern United States were resettled in what was then known as Indian Country. Although 4,000 Indians died along the "Trail of Tears" (from Georgia to Oklahoma) between the time of removal and the Civil War, the Five Civilized Tribes—Cherokees, Chickasaw, Choctaw, Creek, and Seminole—prospered in the new land. The eastern region that they settled, comprising not quite half of modern Oklahoma and known as Indian Territory since the early 19th century (although not formally organized under that name until 1890), offered rich soil and luxurious vegetation. White settlers also came to farm the land, but their methods depleted the soil, preparing the way for the dust bowl of the 1930s. Meanwhile, the increasing movement of people and goods between Santa Fe and New Orleans spurred further growth in the region. Military posts such as Ft. Gibson, Ft. Supply, and Ft. Towson were established between 1824 and the 1880s, with settlements growing up around them.

During the early Civil War period, the Five Civilized Tribes—some of whose members were slaveholders—allied with the Confederacy. After Union troops captured Ft. Gibson in 1863, the Union Army controlled one-half of Indian Territory. From the end of the Civil War to the 1880s, the federal government removed the eastern tribes from certain lands that were especially attractive to the railroads and to interested white settlers. Skirmishes between the Indians and the federal troops occurred, culminating in a massacre of Cheyenne Indians on 27 November 1868 by Colonel George Custer and his 7th Cavalry at the Battle of the Washita.

Amid a clamor for Indian lands, Congress opened western Oklahoma—formerly reserved for the Cherokee, Cheyenne, Fox, and other tribes—to homesteaders in 1889. Present-day Oklahoma City, Norman, Guthrie, Edmond, and Stillwater represent the eastern boundary for the 1889 "run" on Oklahoma lands; eight more runs were to follow. The greatest was in 1893, when about 100,000 people stormed onto the newly opened Cherokee outlet. The drive to get a land claim was fierce, and thousands of "Sooners" staked their claims before the land was officially opened. The western region became Oklahoma Territory, governed by a territorial legislature and a federally appointed governor in 1890; Guthrie was named the capital. Most of eastern Oklahoma continued to be governed by the Five Civilized Tribes.

Although an Oklahoma statehood bill was introduced in Congress as early as 1892, the Five Civilized Tribes resisted all efforts to unite Indian Territory until their attempt to form their own state was defeated in 1905. Congress passed an enabling act in June 1906, and Oklahoma became the 46th state on 16 November 1907 after a vote of the residents of both territories. Oklahoma City was named the state capital in 1910.

When President Theodore Roosevelt signed the statehood proclamation, Oklahoma's population was about 1,500,000—75% rural, 25% urban—most of them drawn by the state's agricultural and mineral resources. The McAlester coal mines had opened in 1871, and lead and zinc were being mined in Ottawa County. But it was oil that made the state prosperous. Prospecting began in 1882, and the first commercial well was drilled at Bartlesville in 1897. The famous Glenn Pool gusher, near Tulsa, was struck in 1905. Oil wells were producing more than 40 million barrels annually when Oklahoma entered the Union, and the state led all others in oil production until 1928.

Generally, the decade of the 1920s was a tumultuous period for Oklahoma. A race riot in Tulsa in 1921 was put down by the National Guard. (In February 2001, a state commission recommended that the surviving victims be compensated for what has been called the nation's most violent instance of racial oppression. The recommendation launched an intense debate over whether today's taxpayers should have to pay restitution for yesterday's crimes.) Also in 1921, the Ku Klux Klan claimed close to 100,000 Oklahomans. The Klan was outlawed when Governor John C. Walton declared martial law in 1923, during a period of turmoil and violence that culminated in Walton's impeachment and conviction on charges of incompetence, corruption, and abuse of power. The 1930s brought a destructive drought, dust storms, and an exodus of "Okies," many of them to California. Colorful Governor William "Alfalfa Bill" Murray led the call for federal relief for the distressed dust bowl region—though he insisted on his right to administer the funds. When Oklahoma oil fields were glutting the market at 15 cents a barrel, Murray placed 3,106 producing wells under martial law from August 1931 to April 1933. Kansas, New Mexico, and Texas also agreed to control their oil production and under the leadership of Governor E. W. Marland, the Interstate Oil Compact was created in 1936 to conserve petroleum and stabilize prices.

Oklahoma's first native-born governor, Robert Kerr (later a senator for 14 years) held the statehouse during World War II and brought the state national recognition by promoting Oklahoma as a site for military, industrial, and conservation projects. Under early postwar governors Roy Turner, Johnston Murray, and Raymond Gary, tax reductions attracted industry, major highways were built, a loyalty oath for state employees was declared unconstitutional, and Oklahoma's higher educational facilities were integrated. The term of Governor Howard Edmondson saw the repeal of prohibition in 1959, the establishment of merit and central purchasing systems, and the introduction of a state income tax withholding plan.

Oil and gas again brought increased wealth to the state in the 1960s, 1970s, and early 1980s, as state revenues from oil and gas increased from $72 million in 1972 to $745 million in 1982. Nearly $1 billion was spent for new highways, schools, and state offices; new police were hired; and teacher salaries were raised to nationally competitive levels. Unemployment fell to 3.6% in 1981 while an influx of job seekers from other states made Oklahoma one of the fastest-growing states in the nation in the early 1980s.

In 1983, as oil prices fell in the face of a growing worldwide oil glut, the oil boom suddenly ended. Between 1982 and 1986, jobs in the extraction of oil and gas dropped by 50%. The failure of 24 banks, home mortgage foreclosures, and mounting distress among the state's farmers added to Oklahoma's financial woes. Falling state revenues and a balanced budget requirement in the state constitution compelled Governor George Nigh in 1983 to cut appropriations and to preside over a series of tax increases that lost for Oklahoma its claim to one of the lowest tax burdens in the nation.

The oil bust did not entirely devastate the Oklahoma economy. Those industries with a national rather than a regional base, such as distribution, transportation, food processing, and light manufacturing, continued to prosper, and the state's leaders made a concerted effort to diversify Oklahoma's industries even further by attracting both private enterprise and defense contracts. By the end of the decade, the economy had begun to recover, and recovery continued into the 1990s. By 1999 the unemployment rate had dropped to 3.4%, below the national average. Poverty was on the decline in the state: 15.6% of Oklahomans lived below the federal poverty level in 1990; in 1998 the rate dipped to 14.1%. But with the tenth-lowest median income in the nation, the state's income levels lagged behind, causing some analysts to predict that Oklahoma might have problems competing in a strong economy.

On 19 April 1995, the Alfred P. Murrah Federal Building in Oklahoma City was destroyed in a bomb blast that claimed 168 lives and constituted the most serious act of terrorism in the history of the United States until the events of 11 September 2001. Governor Frank Keating was commended for his strong leadership during the crisis. A memorial to the victims was unveiled in April 2000, the five-year anniversary of the tragedy. Timothy McVeigh was executed in 2001 for his part in the Oklahoma bombing.

In 2003 Oklahoma faced its largest budget deficit in state history ($600 million). Democratic Governor Brad Henry pledged to eliminate taxes on retirement income for senior citizens, provide access to affordable prescription drugs, retain jobs in the state, improve Oklahoma schools, and increase teachers' salaries. Henry proposed a state lottery to fund education; voters overwhelmingly passed the lottery in November 2004. He secured a state vote to fund healthcare initiatives through an increase in the tobacco tax. Henry promoted tort reform, Medicaid screening for breast and cervical cancer, voluntary relocation assistance for the troubled Tar Creek region, and expansion of pre-school programs. He secured a workers' compensation reform package that business groups applauded, worked on funding for road and bridge repair, created a successful anti-methamphetamine program, and ensured that assistance went to Oklahoma National Guard members and their families. The projected 2005 fiscal year budget gap in Oklahoma was $5.3 billion.

12 STATE GOVERNMENT

Oklahoma's first and only constitution became effective on 16 November 1907. By January 2005, that document had been amended 171 times (including five amendments that were subsequently nullified by the courts).

The Oklahoma legislature consists of two chambers, a 48-member Senate and a 101-member House of Representatives. To serve in the legislature one must be a qualified voter, US citizen, and district resident; also, senators must be at least 25 years old and representatives at least 21. Senators hold office for four years, representatives for two. The legislature meets annually, beginning on the first Monday in February; the regular session ends on the last Friday in May. Special sessions may be called by a vote of two-thirds of the members of each house. The legislative salary in 2004 was $38,400, unchanged from 1999.

State elected officials are the governor, lieutenant governor, attorney general, auditor, state treasurer, superintendent of public instruction, commissioner of labor, and commissioner of insurance, all of whom serve four-year terms, and three corporation commissioners, who serve staggered six-year terms. The governor is limited to serving two consecutive terms. A candidate for gov-

ernor must be at least 31 years old and a qualified voter in Oklahoma. As of December 2004, the governor's salary was $110,298.

Any member of either house may introduce legislation. A bill passed by the legislature becomes law if signed by the governor, if left unsigned by the governor for five days while the legislature is in session, or if passed over the governor's veto by two-thirds of the elected members of each house (three-fourths in the case of emergency bills). A bill dies after 15 days if the governor takes no action and the legislature has adjourned. Constitutional amendments may be placed on the ballot by majority vote in both houses, by initiative petition of 15% of the electorate, or by constitutional convention. To be ratified, proposed amendments must receive a majority vote of the electorate.

To vote in Oklahoma, one must be a US citizen, at least 18 years old, and a state resident. Restrictions apply to convicted felons and those declared mentally incapacitated by the court.

13 POLITICAL PARTIES

The history of the two major political groups in Oklahoma, the Democratic and Republican parties, dates back to 1890, when Indian Territory and Oklahoma Territory were separately organized. Indian Territory was dominated by Democrats, reflecting the influence of southern immigrants, while Oklahoma Territory was primarily Republican because of immigration from the northern states. When the two territories joined for admission to the Union in 1907, Democrats outnumbered Republicans, as they have ever since. Democrats have continued to dominate the lesser state offices, but the Republicans won the governorship three times between 1962 and 1990, and the Republican presidential nominee out-polled his Democratic counterpart in ten of twelve presidential elections between 1948 and 1992. The best showing by a minor party in a recent presidential race was 25% garnered by Independent Ross Perot in 1992.

Oklahomans cast 60% of their popular vote for Republican George W. Bush in the 2000 presidential election, and 38% for Al Gore. In 2004, 65.6% of the vote went for the incumbent President Bush, with 32.4% to the challenger, Democrat John Kerry. In 2004 there were 2,143,000 registered voters. In 1998, 57% of registered

Oklahoma Presidential Vote by Political Parties, 1948–2004

YEAR	ELECTORAL VOTE	OKLAHOMA WINNER	DEMOCRAT	REPUBLICAN
1948	10	*Truman (D)	452,782	2687,817
1952	8	*Eisenhower (R)	430,939	518,045
1956	8	*Eisenhower (R)	385,581	473,769
1960	8	Nixon (R)	370,111	533,039
1964	8	*Johnson (D)	519,834	412,665
1968	8	*Nixon (R)	301,658	449,697
1972	8	*Nixon (R)	247,147	759,025
1976	8	Ford (R)	532,442	545,708
1980	8	*Reagan (R)	402,026	695,570
1984	8	*Reagan (R)	385,080	861,530
1988	8	*Bush (R)	483,423	678,367
1992**	8	Bush (R)	473,066	592,929
1996**	8	Dole (R)	488,105	582,315
2000***	8	*Bush, G. W. (R)	474,276	744,337
2004	7	*Bush, G. W. (R)	503,966	959,792

*Won US presidential election.
**IND. candidate Ross Perot received 319,878 votes in 1992 and 130,788 votes in 1996.

voters were Democratic, 35% Republican, and 8% unaffiliated or members of other parties. The state had seven electoral votes in the 2000 presidential election, a loss of one vote over 2000.

Democrat Brad Henry was elected governor in 2002. Republican senator James Inhofe, first elected in a special election in 1994, was reelected to full terms in 1996 and 2002. Republican senator Don Nickles, first elected in 1980, was reelected in 1998 to a fourth term; in 2004, Republican Tom Coburn won a seat in the US Senate. In 2004, Oklahoma sent four Republicans and one Democrat to the US House of Representatives. In 2005, there were 26 Democrats and 20 Republicans in the state House, and 44 Democrats and 57 Republicans in the state Senate.

[14] LOCAL GOVERNMENT

As of 2005, local governmental units in Oklahoma included 77 counties, 590 municipal governments, 544 public school districts and 560 special districts.

County government consists of three commissioners elected by districts, a county clerk, assessor, treasurer, sheriff, surveyor, and (in most counties) superintendent of schools. Towns of 1,000 residents or more may incorporate as cities. Any city of 2,000 or more people may vote to become a home-rule city, determining its own form of government, by adopting a home-rule charter. Cities electing not to adopt a home-rule charter operate under aldermanic, mayor-council, or council-manager systems. A large majority of home-rule cities have council-manager systems.

In 2005, local government accounted for about 140,324 full-time (or equivalent) employment positions.

[15] STATE SERVICES

To address the continuing threat of terrorism and to work with the federal Department of Homeland Security, homeland security in Oklahoma operates under state statute and executive order; the homeland security director is designated as the state homeland security advisor.

The Oklahoma Department of Education, functioning under a six-member appointed Board of Education and an elected superintendent of public instruction, has responsibility for all phases of education through the first 12 grades. Postsecondary study is under the general authority of the Oklahoma State Regents for Higher Education and other separate boards of regents associated with one or more institutions. Vocational and technical education, a federal-state cooperative program, is administered in Oklahoma under the Department of Career and Technology Education. The Department of Transportation has authority over the planning, construction, and maintenance of the state highway system. The Oklahoma Corporation Commission regulates transportation and transmission companies, public utilities, motor carriers, and the oil and gas industry, while the Oklahoma Aeronautics Commission participates in financing airports.

The Department of Health has as a major function the control and prevention of communicable diseases; it administers community health program funds and licenses most health-related facilities. The Department of Human Services oversees the care of neglected children, delinquent youths, and the developmentally disabled and operates various facilities and programs for the handicapped, the elderly, and the infirm.

Protective services are supplied through the Oklahoma Military Department, which administers the Army and Air National Guard; the Department of Corrections, overseeing the state penitentiary and reformatory, adult correctional centers, and community treatment centers; and the Department of Public Safety, with general safety and law enforcement responsibilities, among which are licensing drivers and patrolling the highways. Natural resource protection services are centered principally in the Oklahoma Conservation Commission. The Department of Wildlife Conservation administers the game and fish laws.

[16] JUDICIAL SYSTEM

In 1967, following some of the worst judicial scandals in the history of the state, in which one supreme court justice was imprisoned for income tax evasion and another impeached on charges of bribery and corruption, Oklahoma approved a constitutional amendment to reform the state's judicial system. Under the new provisions, the Supreme Court, the state's highest court, consists of nine justices initially elected to six-year terms, but with additional terms pursuant to nonpartisan, noncompetitive elections. If a justice is rejected by the voters, the vacancy is filled by gubernatorial appointment, subject to confirmation by the electorate. The court's appellate jurisdiction includes all civil cases (except those which it assigns to the courts of appeals), while its original jurisdiction extends to general supervisory control over all lesser courts and agencies created by law.

The highest appellate court for criminal cases is the Court of Criminal Appeals, a five-member body filled in the same manner as the Supreme Court. Courts of Civil Appeals, created by the legislature in 1968, are located in Tulsa and Oklahoma City. Each has six elective judges with powers to hear civil cases assigned to them by the Supreme Court. When final, their decisions are not appealable to any other state court, a system unique to Oklahoma.

District courts have original jurisdiction over all judicial matters and some review powers over administrative actions. There are 26 districts with 131 district judges who are elected to four-year terms. Municipal courts hear cases arising from local ordinances.

As of 31 December 2004, a total of 23,319 prisoners were held in Oklahoma's state and federal prisons, an increase from 22,821 of 2.2% from the previous year. As of year-end 2004, a total of 2,361 inmates were female, up from 2,320 or 1.8% from the year before. Among sentenced prisoners (one year or more), Oklahoma had an incarceration rate of 649 per 100,000 population in 2004.

According to the Federal Bureau of Investigation, Oklahoma in 2004, had a violent crime rate (murder/nonnegligent manslaughter; forcible rape; robbery; aggravated assault) of 500.5 reported incidents per 100,000 population, or a total of 17,635 reported incidents. Crimes against property (burglary; larceny/theft; and motor vehicle theft) in that same year totaled 149,472 reported incidents or 4,242.1 reported incidents per 100,000 people. Oklahoma has a death penalty, of which lethal injection is the sole method of execution. However, should lethal injection be declared unconstitutional, electrocution would be authorized, and if electrocution was found to be unconstitutional, the law authorizes the use of a firing squad. From 1976 through 5 May 2006, the state has carried out 80 executions, of which four were carried out in 2005 and one in 2006 (as of 5 May). As of 1 January 2006, Oklahoma had 91 inmates on death row.

In 2003, Oklahoma spent $75,847,874 on homeland security, an average of $22 per state resident.

17 ARMED FORCES

In 2004, there were 23,476 active-duty military personnel and 21,860 civilian personnel stationed in Oklahoma, the majority of whom were at Ft. Sill, near Lawton, the training facility for the Artillery Branch. A total of nearly $1.5 billion in prime military contracts was received by local businesses in 2004. Defense Department payroll outlays were $2.97 billion.

In 2003, 355,312 veterans were living in Oklahoma, of whom 45,491 saw service in World War II; 36,837 in the Korean conflict; 113,616 during the Vietnam era; and 59,264 during the Gulf War. In 2004, the Veterans Administration expended more than $1.2 billion in pensions, medical assistance, and other major veterans' benefits.

As of 31 October 2004, the Oklahoma Department of Public Safety employed 808 full-time sworn officers.

18 MIGRATION

Early immigrants to what is now Oklahoma included explorers, adventurers, and traders who made the country conscious of the new territory, and Indian tribes forcibly removed from the East and Midwest. The interior plains of Oklahoma remained basically unchanged until white settlers came in the late 1880s.

Coal mining brought miners from Italy to the McAlester and Krebs area in the 1870s, and Poles migrated to Bartlesville to work in the lead and zinc smelters. British and Irish coal miners came to Indian Territory because they could earn higher wages there than in their native countries, and Czechs and Slovaks arrived from Nebraska, Kansas, Iowa, and Texas when railroad construction began. Mexicans also worked as railroad laborers, ranch hands, and coal miners before statehood. The oil boom of the early 20th century brought an influx of workers from the eastern and Midwestern industrial regions. In 1907, the population of Oklahoma was 75% rural and 25% urban; by 1990, however, 67.7% of all inhabitants resided in urban areas. Oklahoma lost population during the 1930s because of dust bowl and drought conditions, and the trend toward out-migration continued after World War II; from 1940 through 1960, the net loss from migration was 653,000. Migration patterns were reversed, however, after 1960. From 1960 to 1970 nearly 21,000 more people moved into the state than out of it. In the period 1970–80, a total of 293,500 more people came than left, the migration accounting for nearly two-thirds of Oklahoma's total increase of 466,000 persons in that decade. From 1980 to 1983, Oklahoma ranked fourth among the states with a total net gain from migration of 186,000 people. From 1985 to 1990, a net migration loss of about 95,500 was reported. Between 1990 and 1998, the state had net gains of 48,000 in domestic migration and 26,000 in international migration. In 1998, 2,273 foreign immigrants arrived in Oklahoma. The state's overall population increased 6.4% between 1990 and 1998. In the period 2000–05, net international migration was 36,546 and net internal migration was -15,418, for a net gain of 21,128 people.

19 INTERGOVERNMENTAL COOPERATION

Oklahoma participates in a number of regional intergovernmental agreements, among them the Arkansas River Compact, Arkansas River Basin Compact, Canadian River Compact, Interstate Oil and Gas Compact, Red River Compact, South Central Interstate Forest Fire Protection Compact, Southern Growth Policies Board, Southern States Energy Board, Southern Regional Education Board, Interstate Mining Compact Commission, and the Central Interstate Low-Level Radioactive Waste Compact. Federal grants in fiscal year 2005 totaled $4.047 billion, an estimated $4.197 billion in fiscal year 2006, and an estimated $4.424 billion in fiscal year 2007.

20 ECONOMY

Primarily an agricultural state through the first half of the 20th century, Oklahoma has assumed a broader economic structure since the 1950s. Manufacturing heads the list of growth sectors, followed by wholesale and retail trade, services, finance, insurance, and real estate. Oil and gas extraction continues to play a major role. The oil industry boomed from the mid-1970s through the mid-1980s. In 1985, however, the boom ended. Prices dropped from $27 a barrel to $13 a barrel within a month in 1985. In 1998, gas and oil production was valued at only $3.4 billion; one-third of what it was worth in the mid-1980s. Oklahoma's unemployment rate, which averaged about 3% in the early 1980s, jumped to 9% in 1983, and then fell to 7% in 1985, and rose again, to 8%, in 1986. Since then, the economy has undergone a slow but steady recovery. Unemployment was at 3.4% in 1999. Gains in manufacturing made up for the losses in mining. Manufacturing output, however, peaked in 1999, and by 2001 had fallen 9.2%. The state's overall growth rate, which accelerated from 3.5% in 1998 to 3.9% in 1999 to 6.5% in 2000, fell back to 3.2% in the national recession and slowdown of 2001. The main growth sectors in terms of output coming into the 21st century (1997 to 2001) were general services (up 26.8%), government (up 24.2%), financial services (up 2.5%) and trade (up 21.3%). Oklahoma's military installations, Fort Sill and Tinder Air Force Base, are two of the state's top five employers and with rising defense spending, and oil and gas prices, the state's economy is seen as heading upward.

In 2004, Oklahoma's gross state product (GSP) was $107.600 billion, of which manufacturing (durable and nondurable goods) accounted for the largest share at $11.981 billion or 11.1% of GSP, followed by the real estate sector at $10.494 billion (9.7% of GSP), and healthcare and social assistance services at $7.518 billion (6.9% of GSP). In that same year, there were an estimated 303,135 small businesses in Oklahoma. Of the 77,027 businesses that had employees, an estimated total of 75,058 or 97.4% were small companies. An estimated 9,263 new businesses were established in the state in 2004, up 5.2% from the year before. Business terminations that same year came to 8,018, down 4.9% from 2003. There were 659 business bankruptcies in 2004, up 7.7% from the previous year. In 2005, the state's personal bankruptcy (Chapter 7 and Chapter 13) filing rate was 761 filings per 100,000 people, ranking Oklahoma as the 10th highest in the nation.

21 INCOME

In 2005 Oklahoma had a gross state product (GSP) of $121 billion which accounted for 1.0% of the nation's gross domestic product and placed the state at number 29 in highest GSP among the 50 states and the District of Columbia.

According to the Bureau of Economic Analysis, in 2004 Oklahoma had a per capita personal income (PCPI) of $27,840. This ranked 40th in the United States and was 84% of the national average of $33,050. The 1994–2004 average annual growth rate of PCPI was 4.2%. Oklahoma had a total personal income (TPI) of $98,095,384,000, which ranked 29th in the United States and reflected an increase of 5.4% from 2003. The 1994–2004 average annual growth rate of TPI was 5.0%. Earnings of persons employed in Oklahoma increased from $68,758,304,000 in 2003 to $73,134,429,000 in 2004, an increase of 6.4%. The 2003–04 national change was 6.3%.

The US Census Bureau reports that the three-year average median household income for 2002 to 2004 in 2004 dollars was $38,281 compared to a national average of $44,473. During the same period an estimated 12.6% of the population was below the poverty line as compared to 12.4% nationwide.

22LABOR

According to the Bureau of Labor Statistics (BLS), in April 2006 the seasonally adjusted civilian labor force in Oklahoma numbered 1,757,900, with approximately 69,000 workers unemployed, yielding an unemployment rate of 3.9%, compared to the national average of 4.7% for the same period. Preliminary data for the same period placed nonfarm employment at 1,537,100. Since the beginning of the BLS data series in 1976, the highest unemployment rate recorded in Oklahoma was 9.4% in August 1986. The historical low was 2.7% in January 2001. Preliminary nonfarm employment data by occupation for April 2006 showed that approximately 4.4% of the labor force was employed in construction; 18.3% in trade, transportation, and public utilities; 5.5% in financial activities; 11.3% in professional and business services; 12.1% in education and health services; 8.7% in leisure and hospitality services; and 20.5% in government. Data was unavailable for manufacturing.

The US Department of Labor's Bureau of Labor Statistics reported that in 2005, a total of 77,000 of Oklahoma's 1,432,000 employed wage and salary workers were formal members of a union. This represented 5.4% of those so employed, down from 6.1% in 2004, well below the national average of 12%. Overall in 2005, a total of 91,000 workers (6.4%) in Oklahoma were covered by a union or employee association contract, which includes those workers who reported no union affiliation. Oklahoma is one of 22 states with a right-to-work law.

As of 1 March 2006, Oklahoma had a two-tiered state-mandated minimum wage rate. Employers with annual sales of more than $100,000 came under the $5.15 per hour rate, while all others came under a $2.00 per hour rate. In 2004, women in the state accounted for 46.3% of the employed civilian labor force.

23AGRICULTURE

Agriculture remains an important economic activity in Oklahoma, even though its relative share of personal income and employment has declined since 1950. Total farm income, estimated at $5.04 billion, ranked 18th in the United States in 2005. Crop marketings contributed $1.03 billion; livestock, $4.01 billion.

As of 2004, Oklahoma had 83,500 farms and ranches covering 33,700,000 acres (13,640,000 hectares). The state ranked fifth in the United States for wheat production in 2004, with 164,500,000 bushels worth $542.8 million. Peanut production ranked seventh in 2004, with 102,300,000 lb, valued at $19,232,000. Other 2004 crop figures include sorghum for grain, 14,400,000 bushels, $25,402,000; soybeans, 8,700,000 bushels, $43,500,000; corn for grain, 30,000,000 bushels, $75,000,000; and oats, 555,000 bushels, $944,000.

Virtually all of Oklahoma's wheat production is located in the western half of the state; cotton (310,000 bales in 2004) is grown in the southwest corner. Sorghum-producing regions include the panhandle, central to southwestern Oklahoma, and the northeast corner of the state.

24ANIMAL HUSBANDRY

In 2005, there were 5.4 million cattle and calves, worth $4.4 billion. During 2004, Oklahoma farmers had 2.4 million hogs and pigs, valued at $194.4 million. In 2003, the state produced around 4 million lb (1.8 million kg) of sheep and lambs which brought in nearly $3.8 million in gross income. Also during 2003, poultry farmers produced 1.11 billion lb (0.5 billion kg) of broilers valued at $379.1 million, and 933 million eggs valued at $72 million. Oklahoma's 82,000 dairy cows produced an estimated 1.31 billion lb (0.59 billion kg) of milk in 2003.

25FISHING

Commercial fishing is of minor importance in Oklahoma. The prolific white bass (sand bass), Oklahoma's state fish, is abundant in most large reservoirs. Smallmouth and spotted bass, bluegill, and channel catfish have won favor with fishermen. Rainbow trout are stocked year round in the Illinois River, and walleye and sauger are stocked in most reservoirs. The Tishomingo National Fish Hatchery produces primarily smallmouth bass for distribution to federal wildlife areas in Oklahoma and Texas. In 2004, the state issued 668,924 sport fishing licenses.

26FORESTRY

While Oklahoma is not generally known as a forested state, a significant amount of forest is found there. Oklahoma's forests cover approximately 7,665,000 acres (3,102,000 hectares) or nearly 17% of the state's land area. Approximately 65% of this is commercially productive forestland. These forests are about 95% privately owned. They are intensively utilized for lumber, plywood, paper, fuelwood, and other products. They also provide high quality drinking water for the state's two largest cities, excellent wildlife habitat, substantial protection against soil erosion, and numerous recreational opportunities.

Oklahoma's forests play a vital role in the economy in the eastern half of the state. Much of the timber harvested in Oklahoma is shipped to processing plants in western Arkansas. Nearly two million acres of the loblolly-shortleaf pine and shortleaf pine-oak forests support several major wood processing plants in the southeastern corner of the state. Hardwood processing is scattered over the entire forested area in smaller sawmills. In the late 1980s and early 1990s, Oklahoma's eastern red cedar forests and woodlands supported a surge in processing plants.

In 2004 lumber output from Oklahoma's forests totaled 355 million board ft, 97% softwood.

27MINING

According to preliminary data from the US Geological Survey (USGS), the estimated value of nonfuel mineral production by Oklahoma in 2003 was $479 million, an increase from 2002 of about 1%. The USGS data ranked Oklahoma as 28th among the 50 states by the total value of its nonfuel mineral production, accounting for over 1% of total US output.

According to the preliminary data for 2003, crushed stone was the leading nonfuel mineral produced by Oklahoma, accounting for over 40% of all nonfuel mineral output, by value. It was followed by cement (portland and masonry), construction sand and gravel, industrial sand and gravel, iodine, and gypsum, by value. By volume, Oklahoma in 2003, was the nation's leading producer of gypsum and ranked second in tripoli output. It ranked fifth in feldspar, seventh in common clays, and eighth in industrial sand and gravel. Oklahoma was the only state to produce iodine.

Preliminary data for 2003 showed that a total of 45.8 million metric tons of crushed stone were produced, with a value of $202 million, while construction sand and gravel output came to 9.8 million metric tons, with a value of $39.7 million. Industrial sand and gravel production that same year totaled 1.32 million metric tons, and had a value of $28.4 million. Crude iodine output totaled 1,750 metric tons and was valued at $19.7 million. Crude gypsum production in 2003 stood at 2.41 million metric tons, with a value of $18.7 million.

According to the Oklahoma Department of Mines in 2003, the state had 233 mine operators and 307 operating mines. A total of 26,702 people were directly employed by the state's mining industry, excluding those employed by helium and iodine mine operators.

28ENERGY AND POWER

As of 2003, Oklahoma had 98 electrical power service providers, of which 62 were publicly owned and 30 were cooperatives. Of the remainder, four were investor owned, one was federally operated and one was the owner of an independent generator that sold directly to customers. As of that same year there were 1,805,442 retail customers. Of that total, 1,179,570 received their power from investor-owned service providers. Cooperatives accounted for 436,446 customers, while publicly owned providers had 189,346 customers. There was one federal customers and 79 were independent generator or "facility" customers.

Total net summer generating capability by the state's electrical generating plants in 2003 stood at 18.239 million kW, with total production that same year at 60.626 billion kWh. Of the total amount generated, 82.1% came from electric utilities, with the remainder coming from independent producers and combined heat and power service providers. The largest portion of all electric power generated, 36.676 billion kWh (60.5%), came from coal-fired plants, with natural gas fueled plants in second place at 21.822 billion kWh (36%) and hydroelectric facilities in third at 1.798 billion kWh (3%). Other renewable power sources, pumped storage facilities, petroleum fired plants and plants using other types of gases accounted for the remainder.

Oklahoma is rich in fossil fuel resources, producing oil, natural gas, and coal. Crude oil production declined from 223.6 million barrels in 1968, to 150.5 million barrels in 1978, to 70.6 mil-

lion barrels in 1999. As of 2004, Oklahoma had proven crude oil reserves of 570 million barrels, or 3% of all proven US reserves, while output that same year averaged 171,000 barrels per day. Including federal offshore domains, the state that year ranked seventh (sixth excluding federal offshore) in both proven reserves and production among the 31 producing states. In 2004 Oklahoma had 83,750 producing oil wells and accounted for 3% of all US production. As of 2005, the state's five refineries had a combined crude oil distillation capacity of 484,961 barrels per day.

In 2004, Oklahoma had 35,612 producing natural gas and gas condensate wells. In that same year, marketed gas production (all gas produced excluding gas used for repressuring, vented and flared, and nonhydrocarbon gases removed) totaled 1,663.148 billion cu ft (47.23 billion cu m). As of 31 December 2004, proven reserves of dry or consumer-grade natural gas totaled 16,238 billion cu ft (461.15 billion cu m).

Oklahoma in 2004, had eight producing coal mines, seven of which were surface operations. Coal production that year totaled 1,792,000 short tons, up from 1,565,000 short tons in 2003. Of the total produced in 2004, the surface mines accounted for 1,383,000 short tons. Recoverable coal reserves in 2004 totaled 17 million short tons. One short ton equals 2,000 lb (0.907 metric tons).

29INDUSTRY

Oklahoma's earliest manufactures were based on agricultural and petroleum production. As late as 1939, the food-processing and petroleum-refining industries together accounted for one-third of the total value added by manufacture. Although resource-related industries continue to predominate, manufacturing has become much more diversified.

According to the US Census Bureau's Annual Survey of Manufactures (ASM) for 2004, Oklahoma's manufacturing sector covered some 17 product subsectors. The shipment value of all products manufactured in the state that same year was $45.710 billion. Of that total, petroleum and coal products manufacturing accounted for the largest share at $8.904 billion. It was followed by transportation equipment manufacturing at $7.902 billion; machinery manufacturing at $5.378 billion; food manufacturing at $5.035 billion; and fabricated metal product manufacturing at $3.891 billion.

In 2004, a total of 132,540 people in Oklahoma were employed in the state's manufacturing sector, according to the ASM. Of that total, 98,281 were actual production workers. In terms of total employment, the fabricated metal product manufacturing industry accounted for the largest portion of all manufacturing employees at 22,319, with 16,497 actual production workers. It was followed by machinery manufacturing at 20,438 employees (12,935 actual production workers); transportation equipment manufacturing at 17,071 employees (13,166 actual production workers); food manufacturing at 14,277 employees (10,905 actual production workers); and plastics and rubber products manufacturing with 12,104 employees (9,765 actual production workers).

ASM data for 2004 showed that Oklahoma's manufacturing sector paid $5.241 billion in wages. Of that amount, the machinery manufacturing sector accounted for the largest share at $900.746 million. It was followed by fabricated metal product manufacturing at $799.199 million; transport equipment manufacturing at

$714.183 million; plastics and rubber products manufacturing at $528.999 million; and food manufacturing at $480.609 million.

³⁰COMMERCE

According to the 2002 Census of Wholesale Trade, Oklahoma's wholesale trade sector had sales that year totaling $30.7 billion from 4,770 establishments. Wholesalers of durable goods accounted for 2,993 establishments, followed by nondurable goods wholesalers at 1,489 and electronic markets, agents, and brokers accounting for 288 establishments. Sales by durable goods wholesalers in 2002 totaled $11.1 billion, while wholesalers of nondurable goods saw sales of $15.9 billion. Electronic markets, agents, and brokers in the wholesale trade industry had sales of $3.6 billion.

In the 2002 Census of Retail Trade, Oklahoma was listed as having 13,922 retail establishments with sales of $32.1 billion. The leading types of retail businesses by number of establishments were: gasoline stations (2,020); motor vehicle and motor vehicle parts dealers (1,830); miscellaneous store retailers (1,652); and food and beverage stores (1,558). In terms of sales, motor vehicle and motor vehicle parts dealers accounted for the largest share of retail sales at $9.4 billion, followed by general merchandise stores at $6.2 billion; gasoline stations at $3.7 billion; and food and beverage stores at $3.3 billion. A total of 167,949 people were employed by the retail sector in Oklahoma that year.

Exporters located in Oklahoma exported $4.3 billion in merchandise during 2005. Major exports included industrial machinery and transportation equipment.

³¹CONSUMER PROTECTION

Consumer protection issues in Oklahoma are generally the responsibility of the Consumer Protection Division of the Attorney General's Office. Among the Division's duties are the resolution of complaints against businesses, the provision of information on those complaints and of publications to consumers to help educate the public and the enforcement of the state's laws regarding unfair and deceptive practices. However, consumer protection issues involving "Supervised Lenders," such as finance companies, and non-lender extenders of credit is the responsibility of the Commission on Consumer Credit, which also maintains a program of consumer education and has the power to require lawful and businesslike procedures by lending agencies under the state's Uniform Credit Code.

When dealing with consumer protection issues, the state's Attorney General's Office can initiate civil and criminal proceedings; represent the state before state and federal regulatory agencies; administer consumer protection and education programs; handle formal consumer complaints; and exercise broad subpoena powers. In antitrust actions, the Attorney General's Office can act on behalf of those consumers who are incapable of acting on their own; initiate damage actions on behalf of the state in state courts; initiate criminal proceedings; and represent counties, cities and other governmental entities in recovering civil damages under state or federal law.

The offices of the Commission on Consumer Credit and of the Consumer Protection Division are located in Oklahoma City.

³²BANKING

As of June 2005, Oklahoma had 274 insured banks, savings and loans, and saving banks, plus 26 state-chartered and 60 federally chartered credit unions (CUs). Excluding the CUs, the Oklahoma City market area accounted for the largest portion of the state's financial institutions and deposits in 2004, with 70 institutions and $15.734 billion in deposits, followed by the Tulsa market area with 68 institutions and $13.276 billion. As of June 2005, CUs accounted for 9.7% of all assets held by all financial institutions in the state, or some $6.412 billion. Banks, savings and loans, and savings banks collectively accounted for the remaining 90.3% or $59.840 billion in assets held.

The State Banking Department has the responsibility for supervising all state-chartered banks, savings and loan associations, credit unions, and trust companies.

The median percentage of past-due/non accrual loans to total loans stood at 1.98% as of fourth quarter 2005, down from 2004's rate of 2.17% and 2003's level of 2.37%, mark an ongoing improvement in the state's lending environment. In 2004, the median net internal margin (the difference between the lower rates offered savers and the higher rates charged on loans) for the state's insured institutions stood at 4.49%, up from 4.45% in 2003, but down from the 4.54% rate as of fourth quarter 2005.

³³INSURANCE

As of 2003, there were 54 property and casualty and 29 life and health insurance companies domiciled in the state. In 2004, direct premiums for property and casualty insurance totaled over $4.8 billion. That year, there were 13,843 flood insurance policies in force in the state, with a total value of $1.5 billion.

In 2004, there were over 1.6 million individual life insurance policies in force, with a total value of about $111 billion; total value for all categories of life insurance (individual, group, and credit) was over $174 billion. The average coverage amount is $67,700 per policy holder. Death benefits paid that year totaled $604 million.

In 2004, 48% of state residents held employment-based health insurance policies, 4% held individual policies, and 25% were covered under Medicare and Medicaid; 20% of residents were uninsured. Oklahoma has the third-highest percentage of uninsured residents among the fifty states (following Texas and New Mexico). In 2003, employee contributions for employment-based health coverage averaged at 19% for single coverage and 28% for family coverage. The state offers a 30-day health benefits expansion program for small-firm employees (in some cases) in connection with the Consolidated Omnibus Budget Reconciliation Act (COBRA, 1986), a health insurance program for those who lose employment-based coverage due to termination or reduction of work hours.

In 2003, there were over 2.4 million auto insurance policies in effect for private passenger cars. Required minimum coverage includes bodily injury liability of up to $25,000 per individual and $50,000 for all persons injured in an accident, as well as property damage liability of $25,000. In 2003, the average expenditure per vehicle for insurance coverage was $688.64.

³⁴SECURITIES

There are no stock or commodity exchanges in Oklahoma. In 2005, there were 560 personal financial advisers employed in the state and 1,320 securities, commodities, and financial services sales agents. In 2004, there were over 75 publicly traded companies within the state, with over 20 NASDAQ companies, 15 NYSE listings, and 5 AMEX listings. In 2006, the state had six Fortune 500 companies; ONEOK ranked first in the state and 176th in the nation with revenues of over $12.8 billion, followed by Williams (energy), Devon Energy, Kerr-McGee, OGE Energy, and Chesa-peake Energy. Devon Energy is listed on AMEX; the other listed companies are on the NYSE.

³⁵PUBLIC FINANCE

The Oklahoma budget is prepared by the director of state finance and submitted by the governor to the legislature each February. Article 10, section 23 of the Oklahoma Constitution requires a balanced budget. The constitution establishes a "Rainy Day" Fund into which general revenue fund revenues in excess of the certified estimate are deposited for emergency appropriation at a later date. All funds are "appropriated" pursuant to the constitution. In addition, state law authorizes a cash-flow reserve fund that can be up to 10% of the approved budget. The fiscal year (FY) is 1 July through 30 June.

2006 general funds were estimated at $5.6 billion for resources and $5.5 billion for expenditures. In fiscal year 2004, federal government grants to Oklahoma were $5.2 billion.

In the fiscal year 2007 federal budget, Oklahoma was slated to receive:$70.8 million in State Children's Health Insurance Program (SCHIP) funds to help the state provide health coverage to low-income, uninsured children who do not qualify for Medicaid. This funding is a 23% increase over fiscal year 2006; and $21.7 million for the HOME Investment Partnership Program to help Oklahoma fund a wide range of activities that build, buy, or rehabilitate affordable housing for rent or homeownership, or provide direct rental assistance to low-income people. This funding is a 12% increase over fiscal year 2006.

³⁶TAXATION

In 2005, Oklahoma collected $6,859 million in tax revenues or $1,933 per capita, which placed it 34th among the 50 states in per capita tax burden. The national average was $2,192 per capita. Sales taxes accounted for 24.2% of the total; selective sales taxes, 12.2%; individual income taxes, 36.0%; corporate income taxes, 2.5%; and other taxes, 25.1%.

As of 1 January 2006, Oklahoma had eight individual income tax brackets ranging from 0.5% to 6.25%. The state taxes corporations at a flat rate of 6.0%.

In 2004, local property taxes amounted to $1,637,457,000 or $465 per capita. The per capita amount ranks the state 47th highest nationally. Oklahoma does not collect property taxes at the state level.

Oklahoma taxes retail sales at a rate of 4.50%. In addition to the state tax, local taxes on retail sales can reach as much as 6%, making for a potential total tax on retail sales of 10.50%. Food purchased for consumption off-premises is taxable. The tax on cigarettes is 103 cents per pack, which ranks 18th among the 50 states and the District of Columbia. Oklahoma taxes gasoline at 17 cents per gallon. This is in addition to the 18.4 cents per gallon federal tax on gasoline.

According to the Tax Foundation, for every federal tax dollar sent to Washington in 2004, Oklahoma citizens received $1.48 in federal spending.

³⁷ECONOMIC POLICY

Pro-business measures in Oklahoma include comparatively low property tax rates, limits on annual increases in property tax rates,

Oklahoma—State Government Finances

(Dollar amounts in thousands. Per capita amounts in dollars.)

	AMOUNT	PER CAPITA
Total Revenue	17,520,326	4,971.72
General revenue	13,700,103	3,887.66
Intergovernmental revenue	4,565,639	1,295.58
Taxes	6,426,713	1,823.70
General sales	1,594,246	452.40
Selective sales	744,782	211.35
License taxes	840,421	238.48
Individual income tax	2,319,123	658.09
Corporate income tax	133,309	37.83
Other taxes	794,832	225.55
Current charges	1,686,097	478.46
Miscellaneous general revenue	1,021,654	289.91
Utility revenue	353,290	100.25
Liquor store revenue	–	–
Insurance trust revenue	3,466,933	983.81
Total expenditure	14,914,919	4,232.38
Intergovernmental expenditure	3,715,417	1,054.32
Direct expenditure	11,199,502	3,178.07
Current operation	8,241,628	2,338.71
Capital outlay	864,752	245.39
Insurance benefits and repayments	1,531,825	434.68
Assistance and subsidies	204,201	57.95
Interest on debt	357,096	101.33
Exhibit: Salaries and wages	2,183,778	619.69
Total expenditure	14,914,919	4,232.38
General expenditure	13,078,274	3,711.20
Intergovernmental expenditure	3,715,417	1,054.32
Direct expenditure	9,362,857	2,656.88
General expenditures, by function:		
Education	5,594,067	1,587.42
Public welfare	3,535,155	1,003.17
Hospitals	154,342	43.80
Health	495,409	140.58
Highways	1,050,621	298.13
Police protection	102,790	29.17
Correction	501,001	142.17
Natural resources	205,152	58.22
Parks and recreation	77,230	21.92
Government administration	571,760	162.25
Interest on general debt	286,610	81.33
Other and unallocable	504,137	143.06
Utility expenditure	304,820	86.50
Liquor store expenditure	–	–
Insurance trust expenditure	1,531,825	434.68
Debt at end of fiscal year	6,930,071	1,966.54
Cash and security holdings	28,273,456	8,023.11

Abbreviations and symbols: – zero or rounds to zero; (NA) not available; (X) not applicable.

SOURCE: *U.S. Census Bureau, Governments Division, 2004 Survey of State Government Finances,* January 2006.

and requirements that tax increases be submitted to a vote of the people or pass the legislature with a 75% vote.

Business incentives include wage rebates of up to 5% for 10 years for qualifying basic firms that add at least $2.5 million of new payroll in the state over a three-year period. This incentive, known as the Oklahoma Quality Jobs Program, was adopted in 1993. Since that time, more than 130 firms have received in excess of $35 million in incentive payments while adding more than 26,000 jobs to the Oklahoma economy. More than 55,000 jobs were planned to be added as of 2005.

Other incentives include a job tax credit of $1,000 per year for five years for new manufacturing jobs in state enterprise zones; a 30% investment tax credit for investment in qualifying agricultural processing ventures or cooperatives; and free customized training for qualifying firms from the Oklahoma Department of Vocational and Technical Education through its Training in Industry Program (TIP). The state has placed emphasis on the Oklahoma Main Street Program, a statewide downtown revitalization program providing training, resources, and technical assistance to 36 targeted Main Street communities. The Oklahoma Main Street Program was first created in late 1985. By 2006, there were 44 communities in the Main Street program.

38 HEALTH

The infant mortality rate in October 2005 was estimated at 8.2 per 1,000 live births. The birth rate in 2003 was 14.4 per 1,000 population. The abortion rate stood at 10.1 per 1,000 women in 2000. In 2003, about 77.8% of pregnant woman received prenatal care beginning in the first trimester. In 2004, approximately 72% of children received routine immunizations before the age of three.

The crude death rate in 2003 was 10.2 deaths per 1,000 population. As of 2002, the death rates for major causes of death (per 100,000 resident population) were: heart disease, 321.4; cancer, 213.9; cerebrovascular diseases, 69.5; chronic lower respiratory diseases, 56.9; and diabetes, 30.5. Oklahoma had the second-highest heart disease death rate in the country (following West Virginia). The mortality rate from HIV infection was 2.6 per 100,000 population. In 2004, the reported AIDS case rate was at about 5.5 per 100,000 population. In 2002, about 56.2% of the population was considered overweight or obese. As of 2004, about 26% of state residents were smokers, representing the fourth-highest percentage in the country.

In 2003, Oklahoma had 108 community hospitals with about 11,000 beds. There were about 450,000 patient admissions that year and 5.5 million outpatient visits. The average daily inpatient census was about 6,500 patients. The average cost per day for hospital care was $1,777. Also in 2003, there were about 370 certified nursing facilities in the state with 32,733 beds and an overall occupancy rate of about 66.2%. In 2004, it was estimated that about 61.3% of all state residents had received some type of dental care within the year. Oklahoma had 205 physicians per 100,000 resident population in 2004 and 695 nurses per 100,000 in 2005. In 2004, there were a total of 1,728 dentists in the state.

About 19% of state residents were enrolled in Medicaid programs in 2003; 15% were enrolled in Medicare programs in 2004. Approximately 20% of the state population was uninsured in 2004, ranking the state as third in the nation for highest percentage of uninsured residents (following Texas and New Mexico). In 2003, state health care expenditures totaled $3.4 million.

39 SOCIAL WELFARE

In 2004, about 60,000 people received unemployment benefits, with the average weekly unemployment benefit at $219. For 2005, the estimated average monthly participation in the food stamp program included about 424,402 persons (172,837 households); the average monthly benefit was about $86.32 per person. That year, the total of benefits paid through the state for the food stamp program was about $439.5 million.

Temporary Assistance for Needy Families (TANF), the system of federal welfare assistance that officially replaced Aid to Families with Dependent Children (AFDC) in 1997, was reauthorized through the Deficit Reduction Act of 2005. TANF is funded through federal block grants that are divided among the states based on an equation involving the number of recipients in each state. In 2004, the state TANF program had 34,000 recipients; state and federal expenditures on this TANF program totaled $174 million in fiscal year 2003.

In December 2004, Social Security benefits were paid to 623,160 Oklahoma residents. This number included 381,090 retired workers, 68,000 widows and widowers, 84,630 disabled workers, 36,180 spouses, and 53,260 children. Social Security beneficiaries represented 17.7% of the total state population and 93.1% of the state's population age 65 and older. Retired workers received an average monthly payment of $916; widows and widowers, $869; disabled workers, $880; and spouses, $449. Payments for children of retired workers averaged $477 per month; children of deceased workers, $589; and children of disabled workers, $257. Federal Supplemental Security Income payments in December 2004 went to 77,100 Oklahoma residents, averaging $382 a month. An additional $3.2 million of state-administered supplemental payments were distributed to 76,939 residents.

40 HOUSING

Indian tepees and settlers' sod houses dotted the Oklahoma plains when the "eighty-niners" swarmed into the territory; old neighborhoods in cities and towns of Oklahoma still retain some of the modest frame houses they built. Oklahomans continue to prefer single-family dwellings, despite a recent trend toward condominiums. Modern underground homes and solar-heated dwellings can be seen in the university towns of Norman and Stillwater.

In 2004, there were an estimated 1,572,756 housing units, of which 1,360,032 were occupied; 68.2% were owner-occupied. About 72.5% of all units were single-family, detached homes. Utility gas and electricity were the most common energy sources for heating. It was estimated that 85,609 units lacked telephone service, 2,351 lacked complete plumbing facilities, and 7,496 lacked complete kitchen facilities. The average household had 2.51 members.

In 2004, 17,100 new privately owned units were authorized for construction. The median home value was $85,060. The median monthly cost for mortgage owners was $871. Renters paid a median of $525 per month. In September 2005, the state received grants of $300,000 from the US Department of Housing and Urban Development (HUD) for rural housing and economic development programs. For 2006, HUD allocated to the state over $17.2 million in community development block grants.

41 EDUCATION

In 2004, 85.2% of Oklahomans 25 years of age or older were high school graduates; during the same year, 22.9% had obtained a bachelor's degree or higher.

The total enrollment for fall 2002 in Oklahoma's public schools stood at 625,000. Of these, 449,000 attended schools from kindergarten through grade eight, and 176,000 attended high school. Approximately 61.5% of the students were white, 10.9% were black, 7.6% were Hispanic, 1.5% were Asian/Pacific Islander, and 18.5% were American Indian/Alaskan Native. Total enrollment was estimated at 615,000 in fall 2003 and expected to be 626,000 by fall 2014, an increase of 0.3% during the period 2002–14. Expenditures for public education in 2003/04 were estimated at $4.4 billion or $6,176 per student the fourth-lowest among the 50 states. There were 27,603 students enrolled in 168 private schools in fall 2003. Since 1969, the National Assessment of Educational Progress (NAEP) has tested public school students nationwide. The resulting report, *The Nation's Report Card*, stated that in 2005, eighth graders in Oklahoma scored 271 out of 500 in mathematics, compared with the national average of 278.

As of fall 2002, there were 198,423 students enrolled in college or graduate school; minority students comprised 23.8% of total postsecondary enrollment. In 2005 year Oklahoma had 53 degree-granting institutions including 15 public four-year schools, 14 public two-year schools, and 17 nonprofit, private four-year schools. The comprehensive institutions, the University of Oklahoma (Norman) and Oklahoma State University (Stillwater), also offer major graduate-level programs. Well-known institutions include Oral Roberts University and the University of Tulsa.

42 ARTS

The Oklahoma Arts Council was founded in 1965. In 2005, the State Arts Council of Oklahoma and other Oklahoma arts organizations received 12 grants totaling $828,700 from the National Endowment for the Arts. The State Arts Council of Oklahoma also received funding from the state and private sources. Among the organizations that typically benefit from federal funding are the Metropolitan Library Commission of Oklahoma Country, the Red Earth Native American Cultural Festival, and the Theater of North Tulsa. The Oklahoma Humanities Council (OHC) was founded in 1971. In 2005, the National Endowment for the Humanities contributed $760,924 for 12 state programs.

Major arts centers are located in Tulsa and Oklahoma City, but there are many arts and crafts museums throughout the state. Oklahoma City's leading cultural institution is the Oklahoma City Philharmonic, formed in 1924. The Tulsa Philharmonic, Tulsa Ballet Theater, and Tulsa Opera all appear at the Tulsa Performing Arts Center, a municipally owned and operated facility. As of 2005, this six-level center consisted of the 2,365-seat Chapman Music Hall, the 437-seat John H. Williams Theater, and two multilevel experimental theaters (the Liddy Doenges Theater and Charles E. Norman Theater).

There are five other ballet companies located in Oklahoma City, Bartlesville, Clinton, Lawton, and Norman. The intermingling of Native American, American West, and Euro-American art traditions infuses all aspects of Oklahoma culture. Native American contributions to the arts include achievements in art and sculpture, as well as the international acclaim accorded to ballerinas Maria and Marjorie Tallchief, Rosella Hightower, and Moscelyne Larkin.

The Oklahoma City Museum of Art was noted for serving over 130,000 visitors annually as of 2005. The museum's permanent collection covers five centuries, emphasizing the 19th and 20th centuries.

Bartlesville is home to a symphony orchestra, a show choir, a civic ballet, and a theater guild. It is also the host of the annual OK Mozart International Festival, established in 1985, which features the Solisti New York Orchestra and attracts world-class guest artists. In 2006, the festival celebrated its 22nd season and Mozart's 250th birthday.

43 LIBRARIES AND MUSEUMS

In June 2001, Oklahoma had 115 public library systems, with a total of 210 libraries, of which 95 were branches. In that same year, the public library system had 6,316,000 volumes of books and serial publications on its shelves, and a total circulation of 15,354,000. The system also had 174,000 audio and 151,000 video items, 6,000 electronic format items (CD-ROMs, magnetic tapes, and disks), and five bookmobiles. The Five Civilized Tribes Museum Library in Muskogee has a large collection of Indian documents and art, while the Cherokee archives are held at the Cherokee National Historical Society in Tahlequah. The Morris Swett Library at Ft. Sill has a special collection on military history, particularly field artillery. The Oklahoma Department of Libraries in Oklahoma City has holdings covering law, library science, Oklahoma history, and other fields. Large academic libraries include those of the University of Oklahoma (Norman), with 3,642,653 volumes and 10,496 periodical subscriptions in 1998, and Oklahoma State University Library (Stillwater), with 2,025,168. In fiscal year 2001, operating income for the state's public library system totaled $63,440,000 and included $313,000 in federal grants and $1,792,000 in state grants.

Oklahoma has 113 museums and historic sites. The Philbrook Art Center in Tulsa houses important collections of Indian, Renaissance, and Oriental art. Also in Tulsa are the Thomas Gilcrease Institute of American History and Art. Major museums in Norman are the University of Oklahoma's Museum of Art and the Stovall Museum of Science and Industry. The Oklahoma Art Center, National Cowboy Hall of Fame and Western Heritage Center, Oklahoma Heritage Association, Oklahoma Historical Society Museum, Oklahoma Museum of Art, State Museum of Oklahoma, and the Omniplex Science Museum are major attractions in Oklahoma City. Other museums of special interest include the Museum of the Great Plains in Lawton, the Will Rogers Memorial in Claremore, Cherokee National Museum in Tahlequah, and the Woolaroc Museum in Bartlesville.

44 COMMUNICATIONS

The Butterfield Stage and Overland Mail delivered the mail to Millerton on 18 September 1858 as part of the first US transcontinental postal route. After the Civil War, the early railroads delivered mail and parcels to the Oklahoma and Indian territories.

In 2004, 91.0% of Oklahoma's occupied housing units had telephones. Additionally, by June of that same year there were 1,724,505 mobile wireless telephone subscribers. In 2003, 55.4% of Oklahoma households had a computer and 48.4% had Internet access. By June 2005, there were 449,631 high-speed lines in Oklahoma, 409,046 residential and 40,585 for business. In 2005, Oklahoma had 25 major AM and 64 major FM radio stations, and 19 major television channels. Oklahoma City had 600,240 television households, 63% of which received cable in 1999. A total of 44,743 Internet domain names were registered in the state in 2000.

45 PRESS

In 2005, Oklahoma had 13 morning dailies, 29 evening dailies, and 34 Sunday newspapers. In 2004, the *Oklahoman* ranked 50th in the United States according to circulation among the top 100 daily newspapers, and the *Tulsa World* ranking 82nd.

Leading dailies and their approximate circulation in 2005 were as follows:

AREA	NAME	DAILY	SUNDAY
Oklahoma City	*Oklahoman* (m,S)	250,496	288,948
Tulsa	*Tulsa World* (m,S)	158,965	198,477

As of 2005 there were 143 newspapers that appeared weekly or up to three times a week; most had circulations of less than 10,000 copies.

Tulsa and Oklahoma City each have monthly city-interest publications and the University of Oklahoma has a highly active university press.

46 ORGANIZATIONS

In 2006, there were over 2,810 nonprofit organizations registered within the state, of which about 2,000 were registered as charitable, educational, or religious organizations. Among the organizations headquartered in Oklahoma are the Football Writers Association of America, the International Professional Rodeo Association, the National Judges Association, the National Pigeon Association and the American Racing Pigeon Union, the Amateur Softball Association of America, the International Softball Federation, the American Association of Petroleum Geologists, the Gas Processors Association, and the US Jaycees.

Organizations focusing on the arts include the American Choral Directors Association and Sweet Adelines International. Historical and cultural organizations include the Cherokee National Historical Society, the Institute of the Great Plains, and the National Cowboy and Western Heritage Museum. Organizations dedicated to the rights and welfare of Native Americans include the American Indian Institute, American Indian Research and Development, and the Institute for the Development of Indian Law.

47 TOURISM, TRAVEL, AND RECREATION

Tourism has become a growing sector of Oklahoma's economy. Domestic travelers spent $3.9 billion on overnight and day trips in 2002, a 5.2% increase over 1999. The travel industry employed over 69,200 people in the same year. Oklahoma and Tulsa received the most visitors.

Oklahoma's 50 state parks and recreational areas draw some 16 million visitors annually. The national park service maintains one facility in Oklahoma-Chickasaw National Recreation Area, centering on artificial Lake Arbuckle.

The state also maintains and operates the American Indian Hall of Fame, in Anadarko; Black Kettle Museum, in Cheyenne; the T. B. Ferguson Home in Watonga; the Murrell Home, south of Tahlequah; the Pawnee Bill Museum, in Pawnee; the Pioneer Woman Statue and Museum, in Ponca City; the Chisholm Trail Museum, in Kingfisher; and the Western Trails Museum, in Clinton.

National wildlife refuges include Optima, Salt Plains, Sequoyah, Tishomingo, Washita, and Wichita Mountains; they have a combined area of 140,696 acres (56,938 hectares). The Great Salt Plains National Park extends over 14 counties. Fort Sill, in Lawton, is the army's principal artillery school. Oklahoma is also the winter quarters for many traveling circuses. Many Indian tribes were forcibly relocated to Oklahoma on a march which became known as the Trail of Tears. There are 39 tribes still located in Oklahoma.

48 SPORTS

Oklahoma has no major professional sports teams. The Triple-A baseball Red Hawks play in Oklahoma City, and the Tulsa Drillers play in the Double-A Texas League. Collegiate sports, however, is the primary source of pride for Oklahomans. As of 2003, the University of Oklahoma Sooners had won seven national football titles. They won the Orange Bowl in 1954, 1956, 1958, 1959, 1968, 1976, 1979, 1980, 1981, 1986, 1987, and 2001. They have also produced championships in wrestling, baseball, softball, and gymnastics. Recently, the Sooners have had a resurgence in basketball. The Oklahoma State University Cowboys have captured National Collegiate Athletic Association (NCAA) and Big Eight titles in basketball, baseball, and golf, and are a perennial national contender in wrestling.

Oklahoma City hosts the rodeo at the Oklahoma state fair every September and October. In golf, Tulsa has been the site of several US Open tournaments. The Softball Hall of Fame is in Oklahoma City.

Jim Thorpe, possibly the greatest athlete of all time, was born in Oklahoma, as were baseball greats Mickey Mantle and Johnny Bench.

49 FAMOUS OKLAHOMANS

Carl Albert (1908–2000), a McAlester native, has held the highest public position of any Oklahoman. Elected to the US House of Representatives in 1947, he became majority leader in 1962 and served as speaker of the House from 1971 until his retirement in 1976. Patrick Jay Hurley (1883–1963), the first Oklahoman appointed to a cabinet post, was secretary of war under Herbert Hoover and later ambassador to China.

William "Alfalfa Bill" Murray (b.Texas, 1869–1956) was president of the state constitutional convention and served as governor from 1931 to 1935. Robert S. Kerr (1896–1963), founder of Kerr-McGee Oil, was the state's first native-born governor, serving from 1943 to 1947; elected to the US Senate in 1948, he became an influential Democratic leader. A(lmer) S(tillwell) Mike Monroney (1902–80) served as US representative from 1939 to 1951 and senator from 1951 to 1969.

Oklahomans have been prominent in literature and the arts. Journalist and historian Marquis James (b.Missouri, 1891–1955) won a Pulitzer Prize in 1930 for his biography of Sam Houston and another in 1938 for Andrew Jackson; John Berryman (1914–72) won the 1965 Pulitzer Prize in poetry for *77 Dream Songs, 1964*; and Ralph Ellison (1914–94) won the 1953 National Book Award for his novel *Invisible Man.* The popular musical *Oklahoma!* by Richard Rodgers and Oscar Hammerstein II is based on *Green Grow the Lilacs* by Oklahoman Lynn Riggs (1899–1954). N(avarre) Scott Momaday (b.1934), born in Lawton, received a Pulitzer Prize in 1969 for *House Made of Dawn.* Woodrow Crumbo (1912–89) and Allen Houser (1914–94) are prominent Indian artists born in the state.

Just about the best-known Oklahoman was William Penn Adair "Will" Rogers (1879–1935), the beloved humorist and writer who spread cheer in the dreary days of the Depression. Part Cherokee, Rogers was a horse rider, trick roper, and stage and movie star until he was killed in a plane crash in Alaska. Among his gifts to the American language are the oft-quoted expressions "I never met a man I didn't like" and "All I know is what I read in the newspapers." Other prominent performing artists include singer-songwriter Woody Guthrie (1912–67), composer of "This Land Is Your Land," among other classics; ballerina Maria Tallchief (b.1925); popular singer Patti Page (b.1927); and operatic soprano Roberta Knie (b.1938). Famous Oklahoma actors include (Francis) Van Heflin (1910–71), Ben Johnson (1918–96), Jennifer Jones (b.1919), Tony Randall (1920–2004), James Garner (James Baumgardner, b.1928), and Cleavon Little (1939–92). Paul Harvey (b.1918) is a widely syndicated radio commentator. James Francis "Jim" Thorpe (1888–1953) became known as the "world's greatest athlete" after his pentathlon and decathlon performances at the 1912 Olympic Games; of Indian ancestry, Thorpe also starred in baseball, football, and other sports. Bud Wilkinson (b.Minnesota, 1916–94) coached the University of Oklahoma football team to a record 47-game unbeaten streak in the 1950s. Baseball stars Paul Warner (1903–65) and his brother Lloyd (1906–82), Mickey Mantle (1931–95), Wilver Dornel "Willie" Stargell (1941–2001), and Johnny Bench (b.1947) are native Oklahomans.

50 BIBLIOGRAPHY

Brophy, Alfred L. *Reconstructing the Dreamland: The Tulsa Riot of 1921: Race, Reparations, and Reconciliation.* New York: Oxford University Press, 2002.

Council of State Governments. *The Book of the States, 2006 Edition.* Lexington, Ky.: Council of State Governments, 2006.

Hamill, James F. *Going Indian.* Urbana: University of Illinois Press, 2006.

Harris, LaDonna. *LaDonna Harris: A Comanche Life.* Lincoln: University of Nebraska Press, 2000.

Mobil Travel Guide. Great Plains 2006: Iowa, Kansas, Missouri, Nebraska, Oklahoma. Lincolnwood, Ill.: ExxonMobil Travel Publications, 2006.

Preston, Thomas. *Great Plains: North Dakota, South Dakota, Nebraska, Kansas, Oklahoma, and Texas.* Vol. 4 in *The Double Eagle Guide to 1,000 Great Western Recreation Destinations.* Billings, Mont.: Discovery Publications, 2003.

Rees, Amanda (ed.). *The Great Plains Region.* Vol. 1 in *The Greenwood Encyclopedia of American Regional Cultures.* Westport, Conn.: Greenwood Press, 2004.

Stein, Howard F., and Robert F. Hill (eds.). *The Culture of Oklahoma.* Norman: University of Oklahoma Press, 1993.

Sullivan, Lynn M. *Adventure Guide to Oklahoma.* Edison, N.J.: Hunter Publishing, 1999.

US Department of Commerce, Economics and Statistics Administration, US Census Bureau. *Oklahoma, 2000. Summary Social, Economic, and Housing Characteristics: 2000 Census of Population and Housing.* Washington, D.C.: US Government Printing Office, 2003.

OREGON

State of Oregon

ORIGIN OF STATE NAME: Unknown; name first applied to the river now known as the Columbia, possibly from the Algonquian for "beautiful water." **NICKNAME:** The Beaver State. **CAPITAL:** Salem. **ENTERED UNION:** 14 February 1859 (33rd). **SONG:** "Oregon, My Oregon." **MOTTO:** She Flies With Her Own Wings. **FLAG:** The flag consists of a navy-blue field with gold lettering and illustrations. Obverse: the shield from the state seal, supported by 33 stars, with the words "State of Oregon" above and the year of admission below. Reverse: a beaver. **OFFICIAL SEAL:** A shield, supported by 33 stars and crested by an American eagle, depicts mountains and forests, an elk, a covered wagon and ox team, wheat, a plow, a pickax, and the state motto. In the background, as the sun sets over the Pacific, an American merchant ship arrives as a British man-o'-war departs. The words "State of Oregon 1859" surround the whole. **BIRD:** Western meadowlark. **FISH:** Chinook salmon. **FLOWER:** Oregon grape. **TREE:** Douglas fir. **GEM:** Sunstone. **LEGAL HOLIDAYS:** New Year's Day, 1 January; Birthday of Martin Luther King Jr., 3rd Monday in January; Presidents', Day, 3rd Monday in February; Memorial Day, last Monday in May; Independence Day, 4 July; Labor Day, 1st Monday in September; Veterans' Day, 11 November; Thanksgiving Day, 4th Thursday in November; Christmas Day, 25 December. **TIME:** 5 AM MST = noon GMT; 4 AM PST = noon GMT.

¹LOCATION, SIZE, AND EXTENT

Located on the Pacific coast of the northwestern United States. Oregon ranks 10th in size among the 50 states.

The total area of Oregon is 97,073 sq mi (251,419 sq km), with land comprising 96,184 sq mi (249,117 sq km) and inland water 889 sq mi (2,302 sq km). Oregon extends 395 mi (636 km) E–W; the state's maximum N–S extension is 295 mi (475 km).

Oregon is bordered on the N by Washington (with most of the line formed by the Columbia River); on the E by Idaho (with part of the line defined by the Snake River); on the S by Nevada and California; and on the W by the Pacific Ocean. The total boundary length of Oregon is 1,444 mi (2,324 km), including a general coastline of 296 mi (476 km); the tidal shoreline extends 1,410 mi (2,269 km). The state's geographic center is in Crook County, 25 mi (40 km) SSE of Prineville.

²TOPOGRAPHY

The Cascade Range, extending north–south, divides Oregon into distinct eastern and western regions, each of which contains a great variety of landforms.

At the state's western edge, the Coast Range, a relatively low mountain system, rises from the beaches, bays, and rugged headlands of the Pacific coast. Between the Coast and Cascade ranges lie fertile valleys, the largest being the Willamette Valley, Oregon's heartland. The two-thirds of the state lying east of the Cascade Range consists generally of arid plateaus cut by river canyons, with rolling hills in the north-central portion giving way to the Blue Mountains in the northeast. The Great Basin in the southeast is characterized by fault-block ridges, weathered buttes, and remnants of large prehistoric lakes.

The Cascades, Oregon's highest mountains, contain nine snow-capped volcanic peaks more than 9,000 ft (2,700 m) high, of which the highest is Mt. Hood, at 11,239 ft (3,428 m). A dormant volcano,

Mt. Hood last erupted in 1865. (Mt. St. Helen's, which erupted in 1980, is only 60 mi/97 km to the northwest, in Washington.) The Blue Mountains include several rugged subranges interspersed with plateaus, alluvial basins, and deep river canyons. The Klamath Mountains in the southwest form a jumble of ridges where the Coast and Cascade ranges join. The mean elevation of the state is approximately 3,300 ft (1,007 m).

Oregon is drained by many rivers, but the Columbia, demarcating most of the northern border with Washington, is by far the biggest and most important. Originating in Canada, it flows more than 1,200 mi (1,900 km) to the Pacific Ocean. With a mean flow rate of 250,134 cu ft per second, the Columbia is the third-largest river in the United States. It drains some 58% of Oregon's surface by way of a series of northward-flowing rivers, including the Deschutes, John Day, and Umatilla. The largest of the Columbia's tributaries in Oregon, and longest river entirely within the state, is the Willamette, which drains a fertile valley more than 100 mi (160 km) long. Better than half of Oregon's eastern boundary with Idaho is formed by the Snake River, which flows through Hell's Canyon, one of the deepest canyons in North America.

Oregon has 19 natural lakes with a surface area of more than 3,000 acres (1,200 hectares), and many smaller ones. The largest is Upper Klamath Lake, which covers 58,922 acres (23,845 hectares) and is quite shallow. The most famous, however, is Crater Lake, which formed in the crater created by the violent eruption of Mt. Mazama several thousand years ago and is now a national park. Its depth of 1,932 ft (589 m)—greater than any other lake in the United States—and its nearly circular expanse of bright-blue water, edged by the crater's rim, make it a natural wonder. Sea level at the Pacific Ocean is the lowest elevation in the state.

³CLIMATE

Oregon has a generally temperate climate, but there are marked regional variations. The Cascade Range separates the state into two broad climatic zones: the western third, with relatively heavy precipitation and moderate temperatures, and the eastern two-thirds, with relatively little precipitation and more extreme temperatures. Within these general regions, climate depends largely on elevation and land configuration.

In January, normal daily mean temperatures range from more than 45°F (7°C) in the coastal sections to between 25°F (-4°C) and 28°F (-2°C) in the southeast. In July, the normal daily means range between 65°F (18°C) and 70°F (21°C) in the plateau regions and central valleys and between 70°F (21°C) and 78°F (26°C) along the eastern border. Oregon's record low temperature, -54°F (-48°C), was registered at Seneca on 10 February 1933; the all-time high, 119°F (48°C), at Pendleton on 10 August 1898.

The Cascades serve as a barrier to the warm, moist winds blowing in from the Pacific, confining most precipitation to western Oregon. The average annual rainfall in Portland is about 37 in (94 cm); rainfall elsewhere varied from less than 8 in (20 cm) in the drier plateau regions to as much as 200 in (508 cm) at locations on the upper west slopes of the Coast Range. In the Blue Mountains and the Columbia River Basin, totals are about 15 in (38 cm) to 20 in (51 cm). In Portland, fog is common, with about 123 days of fog per year, and the sun shines, on average, during only 48% of the daylight hours. From 300 in (760 cm) to 550 in (1,400 cm) of snow falls each year in the highest reaches of the Cascades.

4 FLORA AND FAUNA

With its variety of climatic conditions and surface features, Oregon has a diverse assortment of vegetation and wildlife, including 78 native tree species. The coastal region is covered by a rain forest of spruce, hemlock, and cedar rising above dense underbrush. A short distance inland, the stands of Douglas fir—Oregon's state tree and dominant timber resource—begin, extending across the western slopes to the summit of the Cascade Range. Where the Douglas fir has been destroyed by fire or logging, alder and various types of berries grow. In the high elevations of the Cascades, Douglas fir gives way to pines and true firs. Ponderosa pine predominates on the eastern slopes, while in areas too dry for pine the forests give way to open range, which, in its natural state, is characterized by sagebrush, occasional juniper trees, and sparse grasses. The state's many species of smaller indigenous plants include Oregon grape—the state flower—as well as salmonberry, huckleberry, blackberry, and many other berries. Fifteen Oregon plant species were listed as threatened or endangered in 2006, including the Willamette daisy, Western lily, Malheur wire-lettuce, rough popcornflower, and MacFarlane's four-o'clock.

More than 130 species of mammal are native to Oregon, of which 28 are found throughout the state. Many species, such as the cougar and bear, are protected, either entirely or through hunting restrictions. The bighorn sheep, once extirpated—deliberately exterminated—in Oregon, has been reintroduced in limited numbers; the Columbian white-tailed deer, with an extremely limited habitat along the Columbia River, is still classified as endangered. Deer and elk are popular game mammals, with herds managed by the state: mule deer predominate in eastern Oregon, black-tailed deer in the west. Among introduced mammals, the nutria and opossum are now present in large numbers. At least 60 species of fish are found in Oregon, including five different salmon species, of which the Chinook is the largest and the coho most common.

Salmon form the basis of Oregon's sport and commercial fishing, although dams and development have blocked many spawning areas, causing a decline in numbers and heavy reliance on hatcheries to continue the runs. Hundreds of species of birds inhabit Oregon, either year-round or during particular seasons. The state lies in the path of the Pacific Flyway, a major route for migratory waterfowl, and large numbers of geese and ducks may be found in western Oregon and marshy areas east of the Cascades. Extensive bird refuges have been established in various parts of the state. Thirty-three Oregon animal species (vertebrates and invertebrates) were classified as threatened or endangered by the US Fish and Wildlife Service in April 2006, including the short-tailed albatross, bald eagle, Fender's blue butterfly, three species of chub, brown pelican, northern spotted owl, and three species of sea turtle.

5 ENVIRONMENTAL PROTECTION

Oregon has been among the most active states in environmental protection. In 1938, the polluted condition of the Willamette River led to the enactment, by initiative, of one of the nation's first comprehensive water pollution control laws, which helped restore the river's quality for swimming and fishing. An air pollution control law was enacted in 1951, and air and water quality programs were placed under the Department of Environmental Quality (DEQ), established in 1969. This department is Oregon's major environmental protection agency, enforcing standards for air and water quality and solid and hazardous waste disposal. A vehicle inspection program has been instituted to reduce exhaust emissions in the Portland area and in Rogue Valley. The DEQ also operates an asbestos program to protect the public from asbestos in buildings that are being demolished or remodeled. The DEQ monitors 18 river basins for water quality and issues permits to businesses, industries, and government bodies that discharge waste water into public waters. A Wetland Conservation Strategy has been developed to protect the nearly 1.4 million acres (566,559 hectares) of wetlands in the state.

In 2003, 42.1 million pounds of toxic chemicals were released in the state. In 2003, Oregon had 112 hazardous waste sites listed in the US Environment Protection Agency (EPA) database, 11 of which were on the National Priorities List as of 2006, including Portland Harbor and the Union Pacific Railroad Tie Treating Plant. In 2005, the EPA spent over $8.7 million through the Superfund program for the cleanup of hazardous waste sites in the state. The same year, federal EPA grants awarded to the state included $14.5 million for the drinking water state revolving fund and $12.1 million for the water pollution control/clean water revolving fund.

In 1973, the legislature enacted what has become known as the Oregon Bottle Bill, the first state law prohibiting the sale of non-returnable beer or soft-drink containers. The DEQ estimates that more than 95% of beverage containers are returned for recycling. The success of the Bottle Bill was partly responsible for the passage in 1983 of the Recycling Opportunity Act, which reduces the amount of solid waste generated. Furthermore, all cities with 5,000 or more residents are required to provide curbside recycling services.

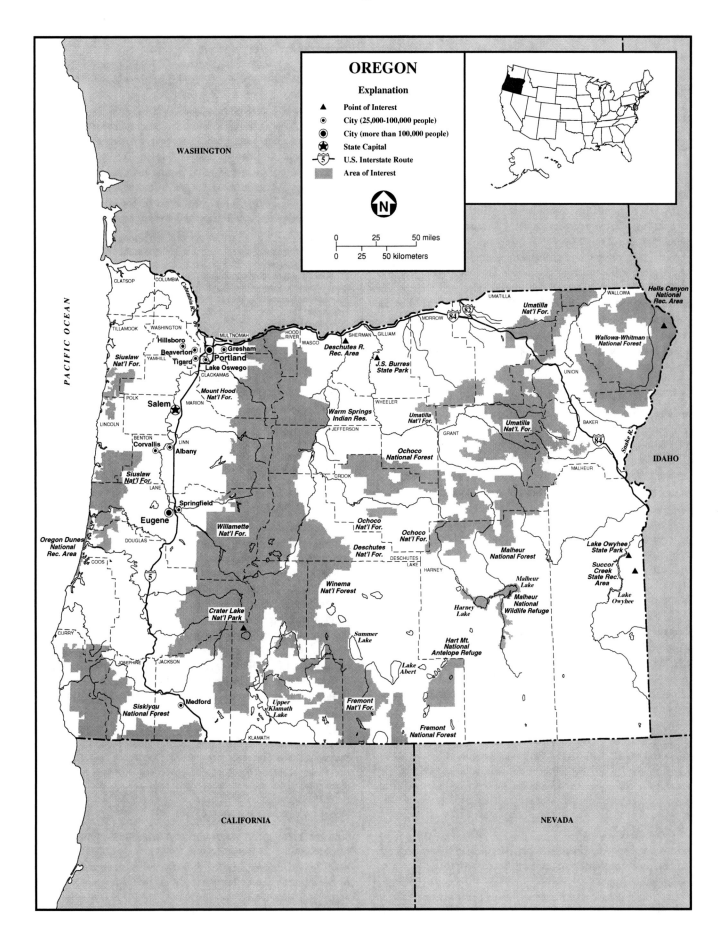

⁶POPULATION

Oregon ranked 27th in population in the United States with an estimated total of 3,641,056 in 2005, an increase of 6.4% since 2000. Between 1990 and 2000, Oregon's population grew from 2,842,321 to 3,421,399, an increase of 20.4%, making it one of the fastest-growing states in the nation. The population is projected to reach 4 million by 2015 and 4.5 million by 2025. In 2004 the median age was 37. Persons under 18 years old accounted for 23.7% of the population while 12.8% was age 65 or older.

Like other western states, Oregon experienced more rapid population growth than that of the United States as a whole in the 1970s, when population expanded 26%. The 1990 census figure represented a 7.9% increase over the 1980 census population. The population density in 2004 was 37.5 persons per sq mi.

As of 2000, more than half of all Oregonians lived in the Portland region, while much of the remainder also lived in the Willamette Valley, particularly in and around Salem and Eugene. The city of Portland had an estimated 533,492 residents in 2004; the Portland metropolitan area (which includes Vancouver and Beaverton) had an estimated 2004 population of 2,064,336. The estimated population of Salem was 146,120 and Eugene had a population of about 142,681.

⁷ETHNIC GROUPS

In 2000, the estimated number of American Indians was 45,211, with most of the population living in urban areas. The state's four reservations (with estimated 1995 population) are the Umatilla (2,154), Siletz (1,778), Spokane (1,416), and Kalispel (170). Important salmon fishing rights in the north are reserved under treaty. In 2004, 1.4% of the state's population was American Indian or Alaskan Native.

About 55,662 blacks were estimated to live in Oregon in 2000, up from 46,000 in 1990; most blacks reside in the Portland area. In 2004, 1.8% of the state's population was black. In 2000, Hispanics and Latinos numbered about 275,314, or 8% of the state total population, up from 113,000 in 1990. In 2004, 9.5% of the state's population was of Hispanic or Latino origin. In 2000, Asians numbered 101,350. There were 20,930 Chinese, 12,131 Japanese, 12,387 Koreans, 10,627 Filipinos, 18,890 Vietnamese (up from 8,130 in 1990), 9,575 Asian Indians (more than triple the 1990 population of 2,726), and 4,392 Laotians. Pacific Islanders numbered 7,976. In 2004, 3.4% of the population was Asian, and 0.3% Pacific Islander. In 2004, 2.3% of the total population reported origin of two or more races.

French Canadians have lived in Oregon since the opening of the territory, and they have continued to come in a small but steady migration. As of 2000, 31,354 Oregonians reported French Canadian ancestry. In all, the 2000 census counted some 289,702 Oregonians of foreign birth, accounting for 8.5% of the population (up from 139,307, or 4.9%, in 1990).

⁸LANGUAGES

Place-names such as Umatilla, Coos Bay, Klamath Falls, and Tillamook reflect the variety of Indian tribes that white settlers found in Oregon territory.

The midland dialect dominates Oregon English, except for an apparent Northern dialect influence in the Willamette Valley.

Throughout the state, *foreign* and *orange* have the /aw/ vowel, and *tomorrow* has the /ah/ of *father*.

In 2000, 2,810,654 Oregonians—87.9 of the population five years old or older—spoke only English at home, down from 92.7% in 1990.

The following table gives selected statistics from the 2000 Census for language spoken at home by persons five years old and over. The category "Other Indo-European languages" includes Albanian, Gaelic, Lithuanian, and Rumanian. The category "Other Slavic languages" includes Czech, Slovak, and Ukrainian. Samoan. The category "Other Asian languages" includes Dravidian languages, Malayalam, Telugu, Tamil, and Turkish. The category "Scandinavian languages" includes Danish, Norwegian, and Swedish.

LANGUAGE	NUMBER	PERCENT
Population 5 years and over	**3,199,323**	**100.0**
Speak only English	2,810,654	87.9
Speak a language other than English	388,669	12.1
Speak a language other than English	**388,669**	**12.1**
Spanish or Spanish Creole	217,614	6.8
German	18,400	0.6
Vietnamese	17,805	0.6
Russian	16,344	0.5
Chinese	15,504	0.5
French (incl. Patois, Cajun)	11,837	0.4
Japanese	9,377	0.3
Korean	9,185	0.3
Tagalog	6,181	0.2
Other Indo-European languages	5,945	0.2
Other Slavic languages	5,630	0.2
Other Pacific Island languages	4,331	0.1
Other Asian languages	4,109	0.1
Arabic	3,723	0.1
Scandinavian languages	3,276	0.1
Italian	3,104	0.1

⁹RELIGIONS

Just over one-third of Oregon's population is affiliated with an organized religion. About 2.3 million people, 68% of the population, were not counted as members of any religious organization in a 2000 survey. The leading Christian denomination is the Roman Catholic Church, with 425,765 members in 2004. The next largest denomination is the Church of Jesus Christ of Latter-day Saints, which reported a 2006 membership of 141,482 people in 294 congregations. There are two Mormon temples in the state: Portland (est. in 1989) and Medford (est. 2000). Other major Protestant groups (with 2000 membership data), are the Assemblies of God, 49,357; the Evangelical Lutheran Church in America, 46,807; Christian Churches and Churches of Christ, 39,011; United Methodists, 34,101; Presbyterians (USA), 33,909; and Southern Baptists, 32,433. The International Church of the Foursquare Gospel (established in California in 1923) had 44,826 members in Oregon in 2000. The same year, Jewish Oregonians were estimated to number 31,625, a figure which represents a 195% increase from 1990; there were about 5,225 Muslims throughout the state.

¹⁰TRANSPORTATION

With the state's major deepwater port and international airport, Portland is the transportation hub of Oregon. As of 2003, the state had 2,863 rail mi (4,609 km) of track and is served by two major rail systems: the Union Pacific; and the Burlington Northern Santa Fe. Lumber and wood products are the major commodities originating in Oregon. Farm products and chemicals are the major commodities terminating in Oregon, primarily at the Port of Portland. As of 2006, Amtrak provided north–south passenger service to seven stations in the state via its Amtrak Cascade and Coast Starlight trains, and east–west service from Portland to Chicago via its Empire Builder train.

Starting with pioneer trails and toll roads, Oregon's roads and highways had become a network extending 65,861 mi (106,036 km) by 2004. The main interstate highways are I-5, running the length of the state north–south connecting the major cities, and I-84, running northwest from Ontario in eastern Oregon and then along the northern border. In 2004, there were some 3.006 million registered vehicles in the state, including about 1.447 million passenger cars registered in Oregon, and 2,625,856 licensed drivers.

The Columbia River forms the major inland waterway for the Pacific Northwest, with barge navigation possible for 464 mi (747 km) upstream to Lewiston, Idaho, via the Snake River. Wheat from eastern Oregon and Washington is shipped downstream to Portland for reloading onto oceangoing vessels. The Port of Portland owns five major cargo terminals and handled more than 29.995 million tons of cargo in 2004. Oregon also has several important coastal harbors, including Astoria, Newport, and Coos Bay. In 2003, waterborne shipments totaled 31.811 million tons. In 2004, Oregon had 681 mi (1,096 km) of navigable inland waterways.

In 2005, Oregon had a total of 455 public and private-use aviation-related facilities. This included 346 airports, 104 heliports, two STOLports (Short Take-Off and Landing), and three seaplane bases. The state's largest and busiest airport is Portland International, with 6,379,884 passengers enplaned in 2004, making it the 33rd-busiest airport in the United States.

[11]HISTORY

The land now known as Oregon has been inhabited for at least 10,000 years, the age assigned to woven brush sandals found in caves along what was once the shore of a large inland lake. Later, a variety of Indian cultures evolved. Along the coast and lower Columbia River lived peoples of the Northern Coast Culture, who ate salmon and other marine life, built large dugout canoes and cedar plank houses, and possessed a complex social structure, including slavery, that emphasized status and wealth. East of the Cascade Range were hunter-gatherers who migrated from place to place as the food supply dictated.

The first European to see Oregon was probably Sir Francis Drake. In 1578, while on a raiding expedition against the Spanish, Drake reported sighting what is believed to be the Oregon coast before being forced to return southward by "vile, thicke and stinking fogges." For most of the next 200 years, European contact was limited to occasional sightings by mariners, who considered the coast too dangerous for landing. In 1778, however, British Captain James Cook, on his third voyage of discovery, visited the Northwest and named several Oregon capes. Soon afterward, American ships arrived in search of sea otter and other furs. A Yankee merchant captain, Robert Gray, discovered the Columbia River (which he named for his ship) in 1792, contributing to the US claim to the Northwest.

The first overland trek to Oregon was the Lewis and Clark Expedition, which traveled from St. Louis to the mouth of the Columbia, where it spent the winter of 1805–06. In 1811, a party of fur traders employed by New York merchant John Jacob Astor arrived by ship at the mouth of the Columbia and built a trading post named Astoria. The venture was not a success and was sold three years later to British interests, but some of the Astor party stayed, becoming Oregon's first permanent white residents. For the next 20 years, European and US interest in Oregon focused on the quest for beaver pelts. Agents of the British North West Company (which merged in 1821 with the Hudson's Bay Company) and some rival American parties explored the region, mapped trails, and established trading posts. Although Britain and the United States had agreed to a treaty of joint occupation in 1818, the de facto governor from 1824 to the early 1840s was Dr. John McLoughlin, the Hudson's Bay Company chief factor at Ft. Vancouver in Washington.

Another major influence on the region was Protestant missionary activity, which began with the arrival of Jason Lee, a Methodist missionary, in 1834. Lee started his mission in the Willamette Valley, near present-day Salem. After a lecture tour of the East, he returned to Oregon in 1840 with 50 settlers and assistants. While Lee's mission was of little help to the local Indians, most of whom had been killed off by white men's diseases, it served as a base for subsequent American settlement and as a counterbalance to the Hudson's Bay Company.

The first major wagon trains arrived by way of the Oregon Trail in the early 1840s. On 2 May 1843, as a "great migration" of 875 men, women, and children was crossing the plains, about 100 settlers met at the Willamette Valley community of Champoeg and voted to form a provisional government. That government remained in power until 1849, when Oregon became a territory, three years after the Oregon Treaty between Great Britain and the United States established the present US-Canadian boundary. As originally constituted, Oregon Territory included present-day Washington and much of Montana, Idaho, and Wyoming. A constitution prepared by an elected convention was approved in November 1857, and after a delay caused by North-South rivalries, on 14 February 1859, Congress voted to make Oregon, reduced to its present borders, the 33rd state.

Oregon remained relatively isolated until the completion of the first transcontinental railroad link in 1883. State politics, which had followed a pattern of venality and influence buying, underwent an upheaval in the early 1900s. Reformers led by William S. U'Ren instituted what became known as the "Oregon System" of initiative, referendum, and recall, by which voters could legislate directly and removed corrupt elected officials.

Oregon's population grew steadily in the 20th century as migration into the state continued. (By 2004, its population was almost 3.6 million.) Improved transportation helped make the state the nation's leading lumber producer and a major exporter of agricultural products. Development was also aided by hydroelectric projects, many undertaken by the federal government. The principal economic changes after World War II were the growth of the aluminum industry, a rapid expansion of the tourist trade, and the creation of a growing electronics industry. The dominant industries in the Oregon economy, however, remained those centered on its abundant natural resources—agriculture, timber, and coal. These industries suffered in the late 1970s and 1980s when interest rates skyrocketed, reducing demand for houses and therefore for wood. Employment in the lumber and wood industry dropped from 81,000 jobs in 1979 to 64,000 in 1985. High interest rates, by boosting the value of the dollar, also lowered foreign demand for lumber and produce.

It was hoped that the construction of high-technology plants in the mid-1980s would help immunize Oregon from the fluctuating fortunes of the extractive (mining and timber) and agricultural industries. However, a slump in the computer industry delayed the building of planned facilities in the state. By the early 1990s, Oregon did boast a burgeoning electronics industry, but the greatest job growth had occurred in the service sector. Agricultural industries also helped boost the state's economy. By 1994, unemployment stood at a 25-year low of 5%. Nevertheless, by 1999 it had increased to 5.7%, well above the national average (it was the third-highest jobless rate in the nation). Other statistics pointed out problems in Oregon. Poverty was on the rise during the decade—climbing from 9.2% in 1990 to 15% in 1998. The dramatic increase came as levels in most other states were on the decline, so that Oregon began the decade as the 43rd-poorest (one of the best-off states) in the nation and was set to close the decade as the 10th-poorest state. Children were a large part of these statistics: Oregon's child poverty rate shot up 25% between 1993 and 1998 alone, so that in 1998 one in five children in the state was living in poverty.

By 1990, the struggle between environmentalists and the timber industry over logging in Oregon's forests had become a major public policy debate. Federal legislation passed in 1993 set limits on commercial exploitation of older forests that were home to the spotted owl. With the shift in focus from timber production to protecting habitat, timber harvests in national forests declined 70% during the 1990s. The decline of logging resulted in severe economic downturns in rural areas and a loss of school funding, which the National Education Association called a "crisis for many forest county education systems" in western states, including Oregon. To assist communities affected by the downturn, Congress considered disparate proposals—from requiring the US Forest Service to generate more income (a portion of which, by a 1908 law, funds schools) from logging on public lands to issuing US Treasury payments to afflicted counties as they transition from logging-based economies. Conservationists were being backed by analysts who forecasted the state's greatest job growth would come from the environmentally friendly high-tech sector and the environmentally dependent tourism industry.

In 2003, Oregon faced a $2.5 billion budget deficit. Upon being elected in 2002, Democratic Governor Ted Kulongoski supported a temporary income tax increase, which voters rejected in a January 2003 referendum. The state then had to face cuts of over $300 million in education, health care, and other programs in order to balance the $11.6 billion budget for 2003–05. By 2005, Kulongoski had made inroads in creating jobs and expanding business opportunities in both rural and urban areas, while protecting the environment. He also promoted investment in post-secondary education, so that more Oregonians would be able to attend college, with the intent that graduates would remain in the state and put their skills back into the economy.

Despite Oregon's fiscal woes, its poverty rate improved slightly in the early 2000s: the 2003–04 two-year average poverty rate in the state was 12.1%, compared with a national average of 12.6%. However, the state unemployment rate in 2004 was 7.4%, well above the national average of 5.5%. Per capita personal income

in Oregon for 2004 was $29,971, below the national average of $32,937.

12 STATE GOVERNMENT

The Oregon constitution—drafted and approved in 1857, effective in 1859, and amended 238 times by January 2005—governs the state today. The first decade of the 20th century saw the passage of numerous progressive amendments, including provisions for the direct election of senators, the rights of initiative, referendum, recall, and a direct primary system.

The constitution establishes a 60-member House of Representatives, elected for two years, and a Senate of 30 members, serving four-year terms. Legislative sessions, which are not formally limited in length, begin in January of odd-numbered years. Special sessions may be called by the majority petition of each house. Legislators must be US citizens, at least 21 years old, and must have lived in their districts for at least one year. In 2004 the legislative salary was $15,396 for the biennial session.

State elected officials are the governor, secretary of state, attorney general, state treasurer, superintendent of public instruction, and a commissioner of labor and industries, all elected for four-year terms. The governor, who may serve no more than eight years in any 12-year period, must be a US citizen, a qualified voter, must be at least 30 years old, and must have been a resident of the state for three years before assuming office. As of December 2004, the governor's salary was $93,600. Much policy in Oregon is set by boards and commissions whose members are appointed by the governor, subject to confirmation by the Senate.

Bills become law when approved by a majority of the House and Senate and either signed by the governor or left unsigned for five days when the legislature is in session or for 30 days after it has adjourned. Measures presented to the voters by the legislature or by petition become law when approved by a majority of the electorate. The governor may veto a legislative bill, but the legislature may override a veto by a two-thirds vote of those present in each house. Proposed constitutional amendments require voter approval to take effect, and they may be placed on the ballot either by the legislature or by initiative petition (8% of total votes for all candidates for governor at last election).

To vote in Oregon a person must be a US citizen, age 18 or older, and a state resident. Restrictions apply to convicted felons.

13 POLITICAL PARTIES

Oregon has two major political parties, Democratic and Republican. Partly because of the role the direct primary system plays in choosing nominees, party organization is relatively weak. There is a strong tradition of political independence, evidenced in 1976 when Oregon gave independent presidential candidate Eugene McCarthy 3.9% of the vote—his highest percentage in any state—a total that probably cost Jimmy Carter Oregon's then six electoral votes. Another independent, John Anderson, won 112,389 votes (9.5%) in the 1980 presidential election.

Democrat Barbara Roberts was elected governor in 1990. She did not run for reelection in 1994, and John Kitzhaber, a Democrat and physician who designed Oregon's health care rationing system, defeated Republican congressman Denny Smith to become governor. Kitzhaber won a second term in 1998. In 2002, Democrat Ted Kulongoski won the governorship.

Oregonians elected two US senators in 1996. In a special election in January, Democrat Ron Wyden was chosen to serve the remainder of Robert Packwood's term after Packwood resigned from the Senate due to allegations of sexual misconduct; Wyden was elected to his first full term in 1998 and was reelected in 2004. In the November 1996 election, Republican Gordon Smith won the seat vacated by five-term senator Mark Hatfield; he was reelected in 2002. Following 2004 elections, all but one of the state's five US representatives were Democrats.

In mid-2005 there were 18 Democrats and 12 Republicans in the state Senate and 33 Republicans and 27 Democrats in the state House. In 2000, Oregon voters gave Democratic presidential candidate Al Gore a very slight victory over Republican George W. Bush. (Gore won by a margin of 6,765 votes out of over 1.5 million cast statewide.) In 2004, Democratic challenger John Kerry won 51.5% of the vote to incumbent President Bush's 47.6%. In 2004 there were 2,120,000 registered voters. In 1998, 40% of registered voters were Democratic, 36% Republican, and 24% unaffiliated or members of other parties. The state had seven electoral votes in the 2004 presidential election.

14 LOCAL GOVERNMENT

As of 2005, Oregon had 36 counties, 240 municipal governments, 197 public school districts, and 927 special districts. Towns and cities enjoy home rule, the right to choose their own form of government and enact legislation on matters of local concern. In 1958, home rule was extended to counties. Most of Oregon's larger cities have council-manager forms of government while smaller communities are governed by a city council and mayor. At the county level, typical elected officials are commissioners, judge, assessor, district attorney, sheriff, and treasurer.

The state constitution gives voters strong control over local government revenue by requiring voter approval of property tax levies.

In 2005, local government accounted for about 124,458 full-time (or equivalent) employment positions.

15 STATE SERVICES

To address the continuing threat of terrorism and to work with the federal Department of Homeland Security, homeland security in Oregon operates under executive order; the homeland security director is designated as the state homeland security advisor.

Special offices within the governor's office include the Economic Revitalization Team, the state Affirmative Action Office, and the Advocate for Minority, Women, and Emerging Small Business. The Office of the Long-Term Care Ombudsman is now a separate agency. The Oregon Government Standards and Practices Commission investigates conflicts of interest involving public officials and to levy civil penalties for infractions. Responsibility for educational matters is divided among the Board of Education, which oversees primary and secondary schools and community colleges; the Board of Higher Education, which controls the state college and university system; and the Childhood Care and Education Coordinating Council. The economy is guided by the departments of agriculture, consumer and business services, revenue, and economic and community development.

State highways, airfields, and public transit systems are under the jurisdiction of the Department of Transportation, which is headed by an appointed commission. The largest state agency is the Department of Human Services, encompassing children's services, adult and family services, health, mental health, seniors, and people with disabilities. State agencies involved in environmental matters include the Department of Environmental Qual-

Oregon Presidential Vote by Political Parties, 1948–2004

YEAR	ELECTORAL VOTE	OREGON WINNER	DEMOCRAT	REPUBLICAN	PROGRESSIVE	SOCIALIST	LIBERTARIAN
1948	6	Dewey (R)	243,147	260,904	14,978	5,051	—
1952	6	*Eisenhower (R)	270,579	420,815	3,665	—	—
1956	6	Eisenhower (R)	329,204	406,393	—	—	—
1960	6	Nixon (R)	367,402	408,065	—	—	—
1964	6	*Johnson (D)	501,017	282,779	—	—	—
						AMERICAN IND.	
1968	6	*Nixon (R)	358,866	408,433	—	49,683	—
						AMERICAN	
1972	6	*Nixon (R)	392,760	486,686	—	46,211	—
1976	6	Ford (R)	490,407	492,120	—	—	—
						CITIZENS	
1980	6	*Reagan (R)	456,890	571,044	—	13,642	25,838
1984	7	*Reagan (R)	536,479	685,700	—	—	—
					NEW ALLIANCE		
1988	7	Dukakis (D)	678,367	483,423	2,985	—	6,261
						IND. (Perot)	
1992	7	*Clinton (D)	621,314	475,757	3,030	354,091	4,277
					GREEN		
1996	7	*Clinton (D)	649,641	538,152	49,415	121,221	8,903
						IND. (Buchanan)	
2000	7	Gore (D)	720,342	713,577	77,357	7,063	7,447
					PACIFIC GREEN (Cobb)	CONSTITUTION	
2004	7	Kerry (D)	943,163	866,831	5,315	5,257	7,260

*Won US presidential election.

ity, the Department of Land Conservation and Development, and the departments of Energy, Forestry, Fish and Wildlife, and Water Resources. State-owned lands are administered through the Land Board.

16 JUDICIAL SYSTEM

Oregon's highest court is the Supreme Court, consisting of seven justices who elect one of their number to serve as chief justice. It accepts cases on review from the 10-judge Court of Appeals, which has exclusive jurisdiction over all criminal and civil appeals from lower courts and over certain actions of state agencies. Circuit courts and tax courts are the trial courts of original jurisdiction for civil and criminal matters. The 30 more-populous counties also have district courts, which hear minor civil, criminal, and traffic matters. In 1998, the circuit courts and district courts were merged. The circuit courts are thus the only state-level trial courts. Thirty localities retain justices of the peace, also with jurisdiction over minor cases. State judges and local justices of the peace are elected by nonpartisan ballot for six-year terms.

Oregon's penal system is operated by the Oregon Department of Corrections. As of 31 December 2004, a total of 13,183 prisoners were held in Oregon's state and federal prisons, an increase from 12,715 of 3.7% from the previous year. As of year-end 2004, a total of 985 inmates were female, up from 883 or 11.6% from the year before. Among sentenced prisoners (one year or more), Oregon had an incarceration rate of 365 per 100,000 population in 2004.

According to the Federal Bureau of Investigation, Oregon in 2004, had a violent crime rate (murder/nonnegligent manslaughter; forcible rape; robbery; aggravated assault) of 298.3 reported incidents per 100,000 population, or a total of 10,724 reported incidents. Crimes against property (burglary; larceny/theft; and motor vehicle theft) in that same year totaled 166,475 reported incidents or 4,631.3 reported incidents per 100,000 people. Oregon has a death penalty, of which lethal injection is the sole method of execution. From 1976 through 5 May 2006, the state has carried out only two executions, one in September 1996 and the other in May 1997. As of 1 January 2006, Oregon had 33 inmates on death row.

In 2003, Oregon spent $144,873,368 on homeland security, an average of $40 per state resident.

17 ARMED FORCES

In 2004, there were 667 active duty military personnel and 3,276 civilian personnel stationed in Oregon. The US Coast Guard does maintain search-and-rescue facilities, and the Army Corps of Engineers operates a number of hydroelectric projects in the state. Military contract awards in 2004 totaled nearly $530 million, and defense payroll outlays were $804 million.

In 2003, 366,780 military veterans were living in Oregon, of whom 51,587 served in World War II; 37,648 during the Korean conflict; 121,365 during the Vietnam era; and 49,235 during in the Persian Gulf War. Federal veterans' benefits in Oregon totaled more than $1.0 billion in 2004.

As of 31 October 2004, the Oregon State Police employed 610 full-time sworn officers.

18 MIGRATION

The Oregon Trail was the route along which thousands of settlers traveled to Oregon by covered wagon in the 1840s and 1850s. This early immigration was predominantly from Midwestern states. After the completion of the transcontinental railroad, northeastern states supplied an increasing proportion of the newcomers.

Foreign immigration began in the 1860s with the importation of Chinese contract laborers, and reached its peak about 1900. Germans and Scandinavians (particularly after 1900) were the most numerous foreign immigrants; Japanese, who began arriving in the 1890s, met a hostile reception in some areas. Canadians have also come to Oregon in significant numbers. Nevertheless, immigration from other states has predominated. Between 1970 and 1980, the state's net gain from migration was about 341,000; from 1980 to 1983, however, the state suffered a net loss of about 37,000, and from 1985 to 1990, the net migration gain was 123,500. Between 1990 and 1998, Oregon had net gains of 260,000 in domestic migration and 58,000 in international migration. In 1998, 5,909 foreign immigrants arrived in Oregon; of these, the greatest number, 1,879, came from Mexico. The state's overall population increased 15.5% between 1990 and 1998, making it one of the fastest growing states in the nation. In the period 2000–05, net international migration was 72,263 and net internal migration was 77,821 for a net gain of 150,084 people.

19 INTERGOVERNMENTAL COOPERATION

Oregon participates in such regional accords as the Columbia River Compact (between Oregon and Washington on fishing), Columbia River Gorge Compact, Columbia River Boundary Compact, Klamath River Compact (with California), Pacific States Marine Fisheries Commission, Pacific Ocean Resources Compact, Northwest Power and Conservation Council (with Idaho, Montana, and Washington), and several western groups concerned with corrections, education, and energy matters.

While Oregon receives federal assistance for a variety of programs, federal involvement is particularly heavy in the areas of energy and natural resources, through federal development, operation, and marketing of hydroelectric power and federal ownership of forest and grazing lands. Approximately 49% of Oregon's land area is owned by the federal government. Federal grants to Oregon totaled more than $4.3 billion in fiscal year 2001. Following a national trend, that figure decreased significantly to $3.682 billion in fiscal year 2005, an estimated $3.745 billion in fiscal year 2006, and an estimated $3.767 billion in fiscal year 2007.

20 ECONOMY

Since early settlement, Oregon's natural resources have formed the basis of its economy. Vast forests have made lumber and wood products the leading industry in the state. Since World War II, however, the state has striven to diversify its job base. The aluminum industry has been attracted to Oregon, along with computer and electronics firms, which now constitute the fastest-growing manufacturing sector. Development, principally in the "Silicon Forest" west of Portland, was expected to bring as many as 3,000 jobs a year during the mid- and late 1980s. Meanwhile, the trend in employment has been toward white-collar and service jobs, with agriculture and manufacturing holding a declining share of the civilian labor force. Tourism and research-related businesses growing out of partnerships between government and higher education are on the rise.

A large portion of manufacturing jobs outside the Portland area are in the lumber and wood products field, making them dependent on the health of the US construction industry. Jobs are plentiful when US housing starts rise, but unemployment increases when nationwide construction drops off. The cyclical changes in demand for forest products are a chronic problem, with rural areas and small towns particularly hard hit by the periodic closing of local lumber and plywood mills. State efforts at diversification in the 1990s were very effective, however, resulting in an astounding 79.8% growth in output from the electronics field of manufactures 1997 to 2000, the main component in an overall increase in output from manufactures of 43% across this period. Oregon was almost unique among the states in that growth in manufacturing, instead of services, led overall growth coming into the 21st century, with the state economy's annual growth rate accelerating from 5.6% in 1998, to 7.2% in 1999 to 10% in 2000. Oregon's economy was clearly headed for a correction, which came abruptly in the national recession of 2001, in which manufacturing output fell 7.7% and the state economy contracted overall -1.1% (one of the few states to register negative growth for the year). As a result, the personal bankruptcy rate soared, and foreclosures were running at rates not seen since the mid-1980s. By the end of 2002, employment in the electronic products and industrial machinery manufacturing sectors (which produce semiconductors and computers) had fallen 3%, and Oregon was posting the second highest unemployment rate in the country (7%).

In 2004, Oregon's gross state product (GSP) was $128.103 billion, of which manufacturing (durable and nondurable goods) contributed the largest share at $19.581 billion or 15.2% of GSP, followed by the real estate sector at $17.937 billion (14% of GSP) and healthcare and social assistance services at $9.770 billion (7.6% of GSP). In that same year, there were an estimated 320,019 small businesses in Oregon. Of the 104,114 businesses that had employees, an estimated total of 101,693 or 97.7% were small companies. An estimated 13,481 new businesses were established in the state in 2004, down 2.6% from the year before. Business terminations that same year came to 14,407, up 1.5% from 2003. There were 852 business bankruptcies in 2004, down 46.4% from the previous year. In 2005, the state's personal bankruptcy (Chapter 7 and Chapter 13) filing rate was 675 filings per 100,000 people, ranking Oregon as the 13th highest in the nation.

21INCOME

In 2005 Oregon had a gross state product (GSP) of $145 billion which accounted for 1.2% of the nation's gross domestic product and placed the state at number 26 in highest GSP among the 50 states and the District of Columbia.

According to the Bureau of Economic Analysis, in 2004 Oregon had a per capita personal income (PCPI) of $30,561. This ranked 30th in the United States and was 92% of the national average of $33,050. The 1994–2004 average annual growth rate of PCPI was 3.8%. Oregon had a total personal income (TPI) of $109,756,586,000, which ranked 28th in the United States and reflected an increase of 5.6% from 2003. The 1994–2004 average annual growth rate of TPI was 5.3%. Earnings of persons

employed in Oregon increased from $80,090,192,000 in 2003 to $85,554,132,000 in 2004, an increase of 6.8%. The 2003–04 national change was 6.3%.

The US Census Bureau reports that the three-year average median household income for 2002–04 in 2004 dollars was $42,617 compared to a national average of $44,473. During the same period an estimated 11.7% of the population was below the poverty line as compared to 12.4% nationwide.

22LABOR

According to the Bureau of Labor Statistics (BLS), in April 2006 the seasonally adjusted civilian labor force in Oregon numbered 1,877,400, with approximately 103,700 workers unemployed, yielding an unemployment rate of 5.5%, compared to the national average of 4.7% for the same period. Preliminary data for the same period placed nonfarm employment at 1,704,100. Since the beginning of the BLS data series in 1976, the highest unemployment rate recorded in Oregon was 12.1% in November 1982. The historical low was 4.7% in April 1995. Preliminary nonfarm employment data by occupation for April 2006 showed that approximately 5.8% of the labor force was employed in construction; 12.4% in manufacturing; 19.6% in trade, transportation, and public utilities; 6.2% in financial activities; 11.2% in professional and business services; 12.1% in education and health services; 9.6% in leisure and hospitality services; and 16.7% in government.

The US Department of Labor's Bureau of Labor Statistics reported that in 2005, a total of 213,000 of Oregon's 1,470,000 employed wage and salary workers were formal members of a union. This represented 14.5% of those so employed, down from 15.2% in 2004, but still above the national average of 12%. Overall in 2005, a total of 231,000 workers (15.7%) in Oregon were covered by a union or employee association contract, which includes those workers who reported no union affiliation. Oregon is one of 28 states that do not have a right-to-work law.

As of 1 March 2006, Oregon had a state-mandated minimum wage rate of $7.50 per hour. As of 1 January 2004, Oregon is required to annually adjust its minimum wage rate for inflation. In 2004, women in the state accounted for 45.6% of the employed civilian labor force.

23AGRICULTURE

Oregon ranked 27th in the United States in agricultural output in 2005, with cash receipts of $3.7 billion. Crops accounted for 72% of the total. While wheat has been Oregon's leading crop since the state was first settled, in recent years nursery and greenhouse products, valued at more than $951 million in 2004, have taken over the number-one spot, followed by hay and ryegrass production which bring in $262 million and $204 million respectively. Additionally, more than 170 farm and ranch commodities are commercially produced in the state. Oregon leads the nation in the production of hazelnuts, peppermint oil, blackberries, black raspberries, boysenberries, loganberries, several grass and seed crops, and Christmas trees.

Farmland covers about 17.2 million acres (7 million hectares), or 28% of Oregon's total area. Oregon's average farm is 427 acres (173 hectares), around the same size as the national average. In 2004, the state had some 40,000 farms. Quantity and value of selected crops in 2004 were as follows: hay, 3.6 million tons (valued at $381 million); wheat, 55.9 million bushels (valued at $201.7 million); potatoes, 19,775,000 hundred weight; pears, 208,000 tons (valued at $72.8 million).

Oregon produces about 98% of the nation's supply of ryegrass seed, with sales of nearly $198 million in 2005. In recent years, the growth of Oregon's wine industry has become noteworthy.

24 ANIMAL HUSBANDRY

Most beef cattle are raised on the rangeland of eastern Oregon, while dairy operations are concentrated in the western portion of the state. Sheep and poultry are also raised largely in the west.

After greenhouse/nursery products, cattle and calf production is Oregon's leading agricultural activity in terms of value, although income varies greatly with market conditions. Ranchers lease large tracts of federally owned grazing land under a permit system.

In 2005, Oregon ranches and farms had around 1.4 million cattle and calves, worth an estimated $1.37 billion. During 2003, the state produced nearly 10.1 million lb (4.6 million kg) of sheep and lambs, which brought in $11.7 million in gross income; in 2004 shorn wool production was an estimated 1.1 million lb (0.5 million kg) of wool. The 2003 milk output was estimated at 2.2 billion lb (1 billion kg). Oregon's poultry farmers produced nearly 2.8 million lb (1.3 million kg) of chickens in 2003, and 783 million eggs.

25 FISHING

Oregon's fish resources have long been of great importance to its inhabitants. For centuries, salmon provided much of the food for Indians, who gathered at traditional fishing grounds when the salmon were returning upstream from the ocean to spawn.

In 2004, Oregon ranked seventh among the states in the total amount of its commercial catch, at over 294.7 million lb (134 million kg) valued at $101 million. The port at Astoria ranked ninth in the nation in catch volume with 135.8 million lb (61.7 million kg). Newport ranked 11th the same year with 111.2 million lb (50.5 million kg). The catch included salmon, especially chinook and silver; groundfish such as flounder, rockfish, and lingcod; shellfish such as shrimp and oysters; and albacore tuna. Salmon landings in 2004 totaled 5.9 million lb (2.7 million kg), the third largest salmon catch in the nation, and were valued at $13 million. Oregon led the nation in dungeness crab landings, with 27.3 million lb (12.4 million kg), which accounted for 38% of the total for the nation.

In 2003, there were 26 processing plants in the state with about 1,012 employees. In 2002, the commercial fishing fleet consisted of 998 boats and vessels.

Sport fishing, primarily for salmon and trout, is a major recreational attraction. In 2004, the state issued 666,454 sport fishing licenses. Hatchery production of salmon and steelhead has taken on increased importance, as development has destroyed natural fishspawning areas. There are 34 public fish hatcheries in the state, including two national fish hatcheries (Eagle Creek and Warm Springs).

26 FORESTRY

About 48% (29.7 million acres/12 million hectares) of Oregon is forested. Oregon's forests are divided into two major geographic regions. Douglas-fir is a primary conifer species in western Oregon, with western hemlock and sitka spruce found along the coast.

In eastern Oregon, ponderosa pine is the main species. Several species of true fir, larch, and lodgepole pine also grow east of the Cascades. Noncommercial forests are found along the crest of the Cascade Range and in the high-desert country of eastern Oregon. These species include alpine fir, mountain hemlock and western juniper.

Over 60% of Oregon's forests are publicly owned. National Forest Service lands cover 17.5 million acres (7.1 million hectares). Most of these are federal lands. Federal timber harvest levels have steadily declined over the last several years as timber sales have been appealed and forest set-asides for habitat protection have increased. Reduced revenues have affected local services and infrastructure—where a percentage of harvest tax dollars are reinvested—and the overall structure and funding of federal agencies. The Oregon Department of Forestry manages about 786,000 acres (318,000 hectares) of forestland. About 654,000 acres (265,000 hectares) are managed by the department for the counties, and a further 132,000 acres (53,000 hectares) are Common School Fund forestlands, managed for the State Land Board. State forestlands are not managed with the same "multiple-use" strategy as lands managed by the US Forest Service. According to statute, state lands are managed to produce sustainable revenue for counties, schools, and local taxing districts. About 80% of the state's forestland, or 23.8 million acres (9.6 million hectares), is land capable of producing timber for commercial harvest. However, less than 60% of this commercial land is available for full-yield timber production. The remaining forestland base contains commercial forest, but at reduced levels, and provides vital environmental and recreational functions.

Forestland available for commercial timber management has decreased since the 1970s. Estimates show that Oregon's commercial land base has decreased by more than 24% since 1945. Private forestland has been lost due to urban expansion and other non-timber uses. Private forestlands, however, have assumed a much more important role as Oregon's timber supplier due to harvest limitations placed on federal forestland. Timber harvest levels on non-industrial forestlands—parcels typically smaller than 5,000 acres (2,000 hectares) and owned by individuals, not corporations—have more than doubled since 1981, and harvest levels on industry-owned forestlands have also increased during the same period. The relative percentage of overall harvest, however, emphasizes the importance of Oregon's private forestlands.

In 2004, Oregon led the nation in total lumber production, with 7.08 billion board feet, and contributed 14.3% to the national total. Nearly all of the timber harvested from private forestlands is second-growth—trees originating from 1920 to 1940. Private forestlands are being reforested and play a major role in sustaining Oregon's long-term timber supply. Oregon law has required reforestation following timber harvesting since 1941. Oregon was the first state to pass a Forest Practices Act, in 1971. About 100 million seedlings are planted in Oregon each year.

27 MINING

According to preliminary data from the US Geological Survey (USGS), the estimated value of nonfuel mineral production by Oregon in 2003 was $311 million, a decrease from 2002 of about 3%. The USGS data ranked Oregon as 35th among the 50 states by the total value of its nonfuel mineral production, accounting for about 1% of total US output.

According to the preliminary data for 2003, construction sand and gravel and crushed stone were the state's top nonfuel minerals by value. They were followed in descending order of value by portland cement, diatomite, and lime. Collectively, these five commodities accounted for approximately 96% of all nonfuel mineral production, by value. Oregon in 2003 was the nation's only producer of emery; it ranked second in the output of perlite and pumice, third in diatomite and (by value) gemstones, and fifth in talc.

Preliminary figures for 2003 showed Oregon produced 19 million metric tons of construction sand and gravel, valued at $113 million, and 18.8 million metric tons of crushed stone, worth $96.8 million.

In 2003, Oregon was also a producer of zeolites and common clays. Zeolites are used as an ammonia absorbent in aquarium systems, as animal feed supplements, anticaking agents, fungicide carriers, in odor control, and in wastewater treatment.

28 ENERGY AND POWER

As of 2003, Oregon had 41 electrical power service providers, of which 18 were publicly owned and 19 were cooperatives. Of the remainder, three were investor owned, and one was federally operated. As of that same year there were 1,739,659 retail customers. Of that total, 1,282,670 received their power from investor-owned service providers. Cooperatives accounted for 183,752 customers, while publicly owned providers had 273,235 customers. There were two federal customers.

Total net summer generating capability by the state's electrical generating plants in 2003 stood at 12.882 million kW, with total production that same year at 48.966 billion kWh. Of the total amount generated, 78.8% came from electric utilities, with the remainder coming from independent producers and combined heat and power service providers. The largest portion of all electric power generated, 33.250 billion kWh (67.9%), came from hydroelectric plants, with natural gas fired plants in second place at 10.243 billion kWh (20.9%) and coal-fired plants in third at 4.304 billion kWh (8.8%). Other renewable power sources accounted for 2.3% of all power generated, with petroleum fired plants at 0.1.

Oregon ranks high in the development of hydroelectric power, which supplies more than half of the state's energy needs. Multipurpose federal projects, including four dams on the Columbia River and eight in the Willamette Basin, and projects owned by private or public utilities give Oregon a hydroelectric capacity of over 8,100,000 kW. In recent decades, low-cost power from dams has proved inadequate to meet the state's energy needs, with coal and natural gas fired steam plants being built to supply additional electric power. As of 2003, however, there were no nuclear power plants in operation.

Oregon has no proven reserves or production of crude oil. Although the state has one refinery, it is used to produce asphalt.

In 2004, Oregon had 15 producing natural gas and gas condensate wells. In that same year, marketed gas production (all gas produced excluding gas used for repressuring, vented and flared, and nonhydrocarbon gases removed) totaled 467 million cu ft (13.26 million cu m). There is no data available on the state's proven reserves of natural gas.

29 INDUSTRY

According to the US Census Bureau's Annual Survey of Manufactures (ASM) for 2004, Oregon's manufacturing sector covered some 17 product subsectors. The shipment value of all products manufactured in the state that same year was $54.836 billion. Of that total, computer and electronic product manufacturing accounted for the largest share at $17.849 billion. It was followed by wood product manufacturing at $8.782 billion; food manufacturing at $5.876 billion; transportation equipment manufacturing at $3.211 billion; and paper manufacturing at $2.849 billion.

In 2004, a total of 174,214 people in Oregon were employed in the state's manufacturing sector, according to the ASM. Of that total, 124,218 were actual production workers. In terms of total employment, the wood product manufacturing industry accounted for the largest portion of all manufacturing employees at 31,497 with 26,622 actual production workers. It was followed by computer and electronic product manufacturing at 25,481 employees (12,966 actual production workers); food manufacturing at 18,625 employees (14,659 actual production workers); fabricated metal product manufacturing at 15,335 employees (10,930 actual production workers); and transportation equipment manufacturing with 14,784 employees (11,931 actual production workers).

ASM data for 2004 showed that Oregon's manufacturing sector paid $7.276 billion in wages. Of that amount, the computer and electronic product manufacturing sector accounted for the largest share at $1.459 billion. It was followed by wood product manufacturing at $1.148 billion; food manufacturing at $628.849 million; fabricated metal product manufacturing at $599.949 million; and transportation equipment manufacturing at $564.379 million.

More than half of Oregon's industrial workers are employed in the Portland area. The Willamette Valley is the site of one of the nation's largest canning and freezing industries.

30 COMMERCE

According to the 2002 Census of Wholesale Trade, Oregon's wholesale trade sector had sales that year totaling $56.8 billion from 5,770 establishments. Wholesalers of durable goods accounted for 3,620 establishments, followed by nondurable goods wholesalers at 1,707 and electronic markets, agents, and brokers accounting for 443 establishments. Sales by durable goods wholesalers in 2002 totaled $27.7 billion, while wholesalers of nondurable goods saw sales of $22.7 billion. Electronic markets, agents, and brokers in the wholesale trade industry had sales of $6.4 billion.

In the 2002 Census of Retail Trade, Oregon was listed as having 14,277 retail establishments with sales of $37.8 billion. The leading types of retail businesses by number of establishments were: miscellaneous store retailers (1,964); food and beverage stores (1,938); motor vehicle and motor vehicle parts dealers (1,805); and clothing and clothing accessories stores (1,514). In terms of sales, motor vehicle and motor vehicle parts dealers accounted for the largest share of retail sales at $10 billion, followed by general merchandise stores at $7.02 billion; food and beverage stores at $6.07 billion; and gasoline stations at $2.4 billion. A total of 183,706 people were employed by the retail sector in Oregon that year.

Exports moving through Oregon were valued at $12.3 billion in 2005. Exports went primarily to Canada, Japan, Korea, and the Philippines.

31 CONSUMER PROTECTION

The Department of Consumer and Business Services (DCBS) is Oregon's largest regulatory and consumer protection agency. It is a part of the state's Department of Justice, along with the Office of the Attorney General, the latter of which litigates consumer protection issues. The DCBS administers laws and rules regarding workmen's compensation, occupational safety and health, building codes, financial institutions and insurance companies, and securities offerings. The Financial Fraud/Consumer Protection Section of the state's Department of Justice coordinates consumer services carried on by other government agencies, conducts studies and research in consumer services, and advises executive and legislative branches in matters affecting consumer interests. In addition, it is responsible for the enforcement of Oregon's Unlawful Trade Practices Act. Also responsible for consumer protection are the Department of Agriculture (measurement standards division); and the state's public utilities commission.

When dealing with consumer protection issues, the state's Attorney General's Office can initiate civil and to a limited extent, criminal proceedings; represent the state before state and federal regulatory agencies; administer consumer protection and education programs; handle formal consumer complaints; and exercise broad subpoena powers. In antitrust actions, the Attorney General's Office can act on behalf of those consumers who are incapable of acting on their own; initiate damage actions on behalf of the state in state courts; and initiate criminal proceedings. However, the Attorney General's Office cannot represent counties, cities and other governmental entities in recovering civil damages under state or federal law.

The offices of the Financial Fraud/Consumer Protection Section are located in Salem.

32 BANKING

Consolidations and acquisitions transformed Oregon's banking system from one characterized by a large number of local banks into one dominated by two large chains—the US National Bank of Oregon and Wells Fargo.

As of June 2005, Oregon had 39 insured banks, savings and loans, and saving banks, plus 23 state-chartered and 70 federally chartered credit unions (CUs). Excluding the CUs, the Portland-Vancouver-Beaverton market area accounted for the largest portion of the state's financial institutions and deposits in 2004, with 40 institutions and $25.150 billion in deposits. As of June 2005, CUs accounted for 34.4% of all assets held by all financial institutions in the state, or some $11.810 billion. Banks, savings and loans, and savings banks collectively accounted for the remaining 65.6% or $22.560 billion in assets held.

The median percentage of past-due/nonaccrual loans to total loans as of fourth quarter 2005 stood at 0.32%, down from 0.44% in 2004 and 0.84 in 2003, reflecting solid economic growth in the state. The median net interest margin (the difference between the lower rates offered to savers and the higher rates charged on loans) has increased as the Federal Reserve has continued a policy of interest rate hikes. As of fourth quarter 2005, the NIM rate stood at 5.45%, up from 4.95% in 2004 and 5.04% in 2003.

Regulation of Oregon's state charted banks and other state-chartered financial institutions is the responsibility of the Oregon Division of Finance and Corporate Securities.

33 INSURANCE

In 2004, there were over 1.18 million individual life insurance policies in force, with a total value of over $128 billion; total value for all categories of life insurance (individual, group, and credit) was over $195 billion. The average coverage amount is $108,800 per policy holder. Death benefits paid that year totaled $512.9 million.

As of the end of 2003, there were 14 property and casualty and 3 life and health insurance companies domiciled in the state. In 2003, direct premiums for property and casualty insurance totaled over $5 billion. That year, there were 26,351 flood insurance policies in force in the state, with a total value of $4.4 million. About $424 million of coverage was held through FAIR plans, which are designed to offer coverage for some natural circumstances, such as wind and hail, in high risk areas.

In 2004, 53% of state residents held employment-based health insurance policies, 6% held individual policies, and 23% were covered under Medicare and Medicaid; 17% of residents were uninsured. In 2003, employee contributions for employment-based health coverage averaged at 13% for single coverage and 24% for family coverage. The state offers a six-month health benefits expansion program for small-firm employees in connection with the Consolidated Omnibus Budget Reconciliation Act (COBRA, 1986), a health insurance program for those who lose employment-based coverage due to termination or reduction of work hours.

In 2003, there were over 2.4 million auto insurance policies in effect for private passenger cars. Required minimum coverage includes bodily injury liability of up to $25,000 per individual and $50,000 for all persons injured in an accident, as well as property damage liability of $10,000. Personal injury protection and uninsured motorist coverage are also required. In 2003, the average expenditure per vehicle for insurance coverage was $734.99.

34 SECURITIES

There are no securities or commodities exchanges in Oregon. In 2005, there were about 2,350 securities, commodities, and financial services sales agents employed in the state. In 2004, there were over 100 publicly traded companies within the state, with over 51 NASDAQ companies, 13 NYSE listings, and 1 AMEX listings. In 2006, the state had one Fortune 500 companies; Nike, based in Beaverton and listed on the NYSE, ranked 163rd in the nation with revenues of over $13.7 billion. The NYSE-listed companies Precision Catparts, Lithia Motors, and StanCorp Financials were included on the Fortune 1,000.

35 PUBLIC FINANCE

Oregon's biennial budget, covering a period from 1 July of each odd-numbered year to 30 June of the next odd-numbered year, is prepared by the Executive Department and submitted by the governor to the legislature for amendment and approval. Unlike some state budgets, Oregon's is not contained in a single omnibus appropriations bill. Instead, each agency appropriation is considered as a separate measure. When the legislature is not in session, an emergency board of 17 legislators considers fiscal problems; this board may adjust budgets, allocate money from a special emergency fund, and establish new expenditure limitations, but it cannot enact new general fund appropriations. The Oregon constitution prohibits a state budget deficit and requires that all general obligation bond issues be submitted to the voters.

Fiscal year 2005 general funds were estimated at $4.8 billion for resources and $4.6 billion for expenditures. In fiscal year 2004, federal government grants to Oregon were nearly $5.2 billion.

Oregon—State Government Finances

(Dollar amounts in thousands. Per capita amounts in dollars.)

	AMOUNT	PER CAPITA
Total Revenue	24,488,705	6,819.47
General revenue	13,766,126	3,833.51
Intergovernmental revenue	4,160,915	1,158.71
Taxes	6,103,071	1,699.55
General sales	–	–
Selective sales	748,882	208.54
License taxes	651,016	181.29
Individual income tax	4,270,740	1,189.29
Corporate income tax	320,065	89.13
Other taxes	112,368	31.29
Current charges	2,143,679	596.96
Miscellaneous general revenue	1,358,461	378.30
Utility revenue	2,016	.56
Liquor store revenue	289,365	80.58
Insurance trust revenue	10,431,198	2,904.82
Total expenditure	18,788,196	5,232.02
Intergovernmental expenditure	4,637,052	1,291.30
Direct expenditure	14,151,144	3,940.73
Current operation	8,562,329	2,384.39
Capital outlay	787,202	219.22
Insurance benefits and repayments	4,074,456	1,134.63
Assistance and subsidies	351,104	97.77
Interest on debt	376,053	104.72
Exhibit: Salaries and wages	3,105,615	864.83
Total expenditure	18,788,196	5,232.02
General expenditure	14,560,257	4,054.65
Intergovernmental expenditure	4,637,052	1,291.30
Direct expenditure	9,923,205	2,763.35
General expenditures, by function:		
Education	5,465,246	1,521.93
Public welfare	3,517,473	979.52
Hospitals	677,811	188.75
Health	285,489	79.50
Highways	1,232,642	343.26
Police protection	196,166	54.63
Correction	494,152	137.61
Natural resources	380,247	105.89
Parks and recreation	73,727	20.53
Government administration	946,791	263.66
Interest on general debt	376,053	104.72
Other and unallocable	914,460	254.65
Utility expenditure	9,083	2.53
Liquor store expenditure	144,400	40.21
Insurance trust expenditure	4,074,456	1,134.63
Debt at end of fiscal year	10,495,671	2,922.77
Cash and security holdings	59,094,738	16,456.35

Abbreviations and symbols: – zero or rounds to zero; (NA) not available; (X) not applicable.

SOURCE: *U.S. Census Bureau, Governments Division, 2004 Survey of State Government Finances,* January 2006.

In the fiscal year 2007 federal budget, Oregon was slated to receive: $107.6 million to begin construction on two Portland-area fixed guideway transit systems. The first, an eight-mile MAX system extension parallel to Interstate 205, was forecast to have a 2009 ridership of over 25,000 additional weekday boardings. The second, a 15-mile project, would serve rapidly growing suburban communities west of Portland in Washington County. The state also was to receive $40 million in incremental funding for a $160 million project for I-5 bridge repair and for other improvements in the I-5 corridor; $39.8 million for major cities throughout the state to fund buses, railcars, and maintenance facilities essential to sustaining public transportation systems that serve their communities; $13 million (a $12 million increase over fiscal year 2006) to continue actions to remove the Savage Rapids Dam on Oregon's Rogue River; $8.5 million to provide transportation in rural areas statewide; and $3.8 million to improve public transportation in Oregon for the elderly, persons with disabilities, and persons with lower-incomes, providing access to job and health care facilities.

[36]TAXATION

In 2005, Oregon collected $6,523 million in tax revenues or $1,791 per capita, which placed it 41st among the 50 states in per capita tax burden. The national average was $2,192 per capita. Property taxes accounted for 0.4% of the total; selective sales taxes, 10.7%; individual income taxes, 72.0%; corporate income taxes, 5.6%; and other taxes, 11.3%.

As of 1 January 2006, Oregon had three individual income tax brackets ranging from 5.0% to 9.0%. The state taxes corporations at a flat rate of 6.6%.

In 2004, state and local property taxes amounted to $3,459,371,000 or $963 per capita. The per capita amount ranks the state 28th nationally. Local governments collected $3,443,506,000 of the total and the state government $15,865,000.

Oregon taxes gasoline at 24 cents per gallon. This is in addition to the 18.4 cents per gallon federal tax on gasoline.

According to the Tax Foundation, for every federal tax dollar sent to Washington in 2004, Oregon citizens received $0.97 in federal spending.

[37]ECONOMIC POLICY

Oregon actively seeks balanced economic growth in order to diversify its industrial base, reduce its dependence on the wood products industry, and provide jobs for a steadily growing labor force. The Oregon Economic and Community Development Department (OECDD) offers a variety of financial assistance and incentives to companies which create jobs, particularly for low-income residents. It extends loans and issues industrial development bonds for manufacturing, processing and tourism-related facilities in Oregon. The bonds are exempt from federal taxes. The Department enables banks to make loans to projects that carry higher than conventional risk by creating reserve accounts which function as insurance for the banks. To promote new technologies, the Oregon Resource and Technology Development Corporation invests in applied research. Enterprise zones offer incentives for new businesses. The state offers tax credits to encourage businesses to use pollution control facilities, to invest in energy conservation and to employ renewable energy resources. The Department provides a Guidebook and Readiness Assessment Tool to help communities assess their economic development potentials. Oregon also launched a Brand Oregon campaign in 2003, which was a statewide effort to stimulate the economy through the promotion of Oregon's local characteristics and products. The program began with the promotion of seafood. Since then, wines and cheeses have been promoted, as have organic foods.

38HEALTH

The infant mortality rate in October 2005 was estimated at 5.5 per 1,000 live births. The birth rate in 2003 was 12.9 per 1,000 population. The abortion rate stood at 23.5 per 1,000 women in 2000. In 2003, about 81.2% of pregnant woman received prenatal care beginning in the first trimester. In 2004, approximately 79% of children received routine immunizations before the age of three.

The crude death rate in 2003 was 8.7 deaths per 1,000 population. As of 2002, the death rates for major causes of death (per 100,000 resident population) were: heart disease, 206.2; cancer, 205.8; cerebrovascular diseases, 75.1; chronic lower respiratory diseases, 52.4; and diabetes, 29.6. Oregon had the third-highest death rate for cerebrovascular diseases in the nation, following Arizona and Iowa. The mortality rate from HIV infection was 2.6 per 100,000 population. In 2004, the reported AIDS case rate was at about 7.8 per 100,000 population. In 2002, about 54.4% of the population was considered overweight or obese. As of 2004, about 19.9% of state residents were smokers.

In 2003, Oregon had 58 community hospitals with about 6,800 beds. There were about 342,000 patient admissions that year and 8.2 million outpatient visits. The average daily inpatient census was about 4,000 patients. The average cost per day for hospital care was $1,842. Also in 2003, there were about 141 certified nursing facilities in the state with 12,789 beds and an overall occupancy rate of about 67.6%. In 2004, it was estimated that about 68.5% of all state residents had received some type of dental care within the year. Oregon had 269 physicians per 100,000 resident population in 2004 and 768 nurses per 100,000 in 2005. In 2004, there were a total of 1,768 dentists in the state.

About 18% of state residents were enrolled in Medicaid programs in 2003; 15% were enrolled in Medicare programs in 2004. Approximately 17% of the state population was uninsured in 2004. In 2003, state health care expenditures totaled $3.8 million.

The only medical and dental schools in the state are at the University of Oregon Health Sciences University in Portland.

39SOCIAL WELFARE

The Department of Human Resources was created in 1971 to coordinate social service activities. In 2004, about 148,000 people received unemployment benefits, with the average weekly unemployment benefit at $252. For 2005, the estimated average monthly participation in the food stamp program included about 429,358 persons (218,297 households); the average monthly benefit was about $88.49 per person. That year, the total of benefits paid through the state for the food stamp program was about $455.9 million.

Temporary Assistance for Needy Families (TANF), the system of federal welfare assistance that officially replaced Aid to Families with Dependent Children (AFDC) in 1997, was reautho-

rized through the Deficit Reduction Act of 2005. TANF is funded through federal block grants that are divided among the states based on an equation involving the number of recipients in each state. Oregon's TANF program is called JOBS (Job Opportunities and Basic Skills). In 2004, the state program had 42,000 recipients; state and federal expenditures on this TANF program totaled $120 million in fiscal year 2003.

In December 2004, Social Security benefits were paid to 611,490 Oregon residents. This number included 406,330 retired workers, 57,330 widows and widowers, 73,750 disabled workers, 34,460 spouses, and 39,620 children. Social Security beneficiaries represented 16.8% of the total state population and 95.5% of the state's population age 65 and older. Retired workers received an average monthly payment of $964; widows and widowers, $944; disabled workers, $894; and spouses, $482. Payments for children of retired workers averaged $501 per month; children of deceased workers, $653; and children of disabled workers, $283. Federal Supplemental Security Income payments in December 2004 went to 58,842 Oregon residents, averaging $395 a month. An additional $1.7 million of state-administered supplemental payments were distributed to 16,972 residents.

40HOUSING

During the 1970s and early 1980s, a growing percentage of new construction went for rental units. Between 1970 and 1980, the proportion of the housing stock in single-family units fell from 77% to 68%. In 2004, there were an estimated 1,535,381 housing units in Oregon, of which 1,427,711 were occupied; 63% owner-occupied. About 62.5% of all units were single-family, detached homes. Electricity and utility gas were the most common energy sources for heat. It was estimated that 56,590 units lacked telephone service, 4,834 lacked complete plumbing facilities, and 10,081 lacked complete kitchen facilities. The average household had 2.46 members.

In 2004, 27,300 new privately owned units were authorized for construction. The median home value was $181,544. The median monthly cost for mortgage owners was $1,217. Renters paid a median of $681 per month. In September 2005, the state received grants of $649,984 from the US Department of Housing and Urban Development (HUD) for rural housing and economic development programs. For 2006, HUD allocated to the state over $14.2 million in community development block grants. The city of Portland received $10.4 million in community development block grants.

41EDUCATION

Passed by Oregon's legislature in 1991, the Educational Act for the 21st Century set into motion an extensive restructuring of the state's kindergarten through 12th grade public school system. Key components of the Act include raising academic standards for all students, increasing student skills and abilities needed in the workplace, involving parents in decision-making, assessing student performance, requiring accountability for results, emphasizing early childhood education, providing learning opportunities in partnership with communities, and giving local schools more freedom and autonomy.

In 2004, 87.4% of Oregon residents age 25 and older were high school graduates. Some 25.9% had obtained a bachelor's degree or higher. The total enrollment for fall 2002 in Oregon's public schools stood at 554,000. Of these, 382,000 attended schools from kindergarten through grade eight, and 172,000 attended high school. Approximately 76.6% of the students were white, 3.1% were black, 13.6% were Hispanic, 4.4% were Asian/Pacific Islander, and 2.3% were American Indian/Alaskan Native. Total enrollment was estimated at 555,000 in fall 2003 and was expected to be 591,000 by fall 2014, an increase of 6.7% during the period 2002–14. Expenditures for public education in 2003/04 were estimated at $5.7 billion. In fall 2003 there were 46,968 students enrolled in 362 private schools. Since 1969, the National Assessment of Educational Progress (NAEP) has tested public school students nationwide. The resulting report, *The Nation's Report Card,* stated that in 2005, eighth graders in Oregon scored 282 out of 500 in mathematics compared with the national average of 278.

As of fall 2002, there were 204,565 students enrolled in college or graduate school; minority students comprised 14.6% of total postsecondary enrollment. In 2005 Oregon had 59 degree-granting institutions including 9 public four-year schools, 17 public two-year schools, and 25 nonprofit, private four-year schools. The University of Oregon in Eugene has the highest regular enrollment, followed by Portland State University in Portland, and Oregon State University in Corvallis. The Oregon State Scholarship Commission (OSSC) administers an extensive financial aid program for state college students.

Major private higher education institutions include Willamette University, Salem; George Fox College, Newberg; Linfield College, McMinnville; and University of Portland, Reed College, Lewis and Clark College, and Oregon Graduate Institute of Science and Technology, all in Portland.

42 ARTS

The Oregon Arts Commission was established in 1967 and became a division of the Oregon Economic and Community Development Department in 1993. In 2005, the Oregon Arts Commission and other Oregon arts organizations received 31 grants totaling $1,187,500 from the National Endowment for the Arts. The state and private sources contribute funding for the arts as well.

The Oregon Council for the Humanities (OCH) has a number of annual historical and literary programs. In 2005, the National Endowment for the Humanities contributed $1,221,549 for 15 state programs.

The Portland Art Museum, with an associated art school, is the city's center for the visual arts. A $125 million preservation and renovation project was completed in October 2005 on the Portland Art Museum's Mark Building, featuring a new Center for Modern and Contemporary Art. The University of Oregon's Jordan Schnitzer Museum of Art, specializes in Oriental art. The Jordan Schnitzer Museum of Art reopened in January 2005, after a $14.2 million expansion project almost doubled the size of the building.

The state's most noted theatrical enterprise is the Tony Award-winning Oregon Shakespeare Festival (OSF) in Ashland, with a complex of theaters drawing actors and audiences from around the nation. Founded in 1935, the OSF is one of the oldest and largest professional nonprofit theaters in the United States. As of 2005, OSF had presented over 780 performances annually serving approximately 360,000 visitors. The Portland Center for the Performing Arts is home to the Oregon Symphony Orchestra, the Portland Opera, Oregon Ballet Theatre, Oregon Children's Theatre, Portland Center Stage, Portland Youth Philharmonic, Tears of Joy Puppet Theatre, and Broadway in Portland. Salem and Eugene have small symphony orchestras of their own; in 2005 the Oregon Symphony Association in Salem celebrated its 50th anniversary.

43 LIBRARIES AND MUSEUMS

For the fiscal year ending in June 2001, Oregon had 125 public library systems, with a total of 210 libraries, of which 89 were branches. In that same year, the total book/serial publication stock of all public libraries was 8,476,000 volumes and their combined circulation was 38,047,000. The system also had 473,000 audio and 359,000 video items, 12,000 electronic format items (CD-ROMs, magnetic tapes, and disks), and nine bookmobiles. Most cities and counties in Oregon have public library systems, the largest being the Multnomah County library system in Portland, with 14 branches and 1,288,634 volumes in 1999. The State Library in Salem serves as a reference agency for state government. In fiscal year 2001, operating income for the state's public library system was $112,473,000 and included $1,151,000 in federal grants and $729,000 in state grants.

Oregon has 105 museums, historic sites, botanical gardens and arboretums. Historical museums emphasizing Oregon's pioneer heritage appear throughout the state, with Ft. Clatsop National Memorial—featuring a replica of Lewis and Clark's winter headquarters—among the notable attractions. The Oregon Historical Society operates a major historical museum in Portland, publishes books of historical interest, and issues the Oregon Historical Quarterly. In Portland's Washington Park area are the Oregon Museum of Science and Industry, Washington Park Zoo, Western Forestry Center, and an arboretum and other gardens.

44 COMMUNICATIONS

As of 2004, 95.5% of Oregon's households had telephones. In addition, by June of that same year there were 1,894,285 mobile wireless telephone subscribers. In 2003, 67.0% of Oregon households had a computer and 61.0% had Internet access. By June 2005, there were 561,867 high-speed lines in Oregon, 505,260 residential and 56,607 for business. Oregon had 37 major AM and 86 major FM commercial radio stations in 2005; and 24 major television stations. A state-owned broadcasting system provides educational radio and television programming. The Portland area had over one million television households, 62% of which ordered cable in 1999. A total of 97,453 Internet domain names were registered in the state as of 2000.

45 PRESS

Oregon's first newspaper was the weekly *Oregon Spectator,* which began publication in 1846. Early newspapers engaged in what became known as the "Oregon style" of journalism, characterized by intemperate, vituperative, and fiercely partisan comments. As of 2005, 7 morning, 13 evening, and 12 Sunday newspapers were published in Oregon. The state's largest newspaper, the *Oregonian,* published in Portland, is owned by Advance Publications.

The following table lists leading Oregon newspapers with their approximate 2005 circulations:

AREA	NAME	DAILY	SUNDAY
Eugene	*Register–Guard* (m,S)	79,266	75,460
Portland	*Oregonian* (all day,S)	324,863	405,295
Salem	*Statesman-Journal* (m,S)	53,366	61,652

46 ORGANIZATIONS

In 2006, there were over 3,390 nonprofit organizations registered within the state, of which about 2,459 were registered as charitable, educational, or religious organizations. Among the many forestry-related organizations in Oregon are the International Woodworkers of America (AFL-CIO), Association of Western Pulp and Paper Workers, Pacific Lumber Exporters Association, Western Forest Industries Association, and Western Wood Products Association, all with their headquarters in Portland. State and national conservation issues are represented in part by the Native Fish Society, the Native Forest Council, and the Natural Areas Association. The National Indian Child Welfare Association is based in Portland.

Other national organizations based in the state are the Hop Growers of America and the North American Bungee Association. Local history is represented in part through the Big Butte Historical Society and the Oregon Trail Travelers, as well as several other regional historical societies. The United States Judo Federation is based in Ontario.

47 TOURISM, TRAVEL, AND RECREATION

Oregon's abundance and variety of natural features and recreational opportunities make the state a major tourist attraction. Travel and tourism is the state's third-largest employer, generating over 94,500 jobs. In 2002, travel revenues reached $6.3 billion. The Oregon Tourism Commission maintains an active tourist advertising program, and Portland hotels busily seek major conventions.

Among the leading attractions are the rugged Oregon coast, with its offshore salmon fishing; Crater Lake National Park; the Rogue River, for river running and fishing; the Columbia Gorge, east of Portland; the Cascades wilderness; and Portland's annual Rose Festival. Oregon has one national park, Crater Lake, and three other areas—John Day Fossil Beds National Monument, Oregon Caves National Monument, and Ft. Clatsop National Memorial—managed by the National Park Service. The US Forest Service administers the Oregon Dunes National Recreation Area, on the Oregon coast; the Lava Lands Visitor Complex near Bend; and the Hells Canyon National Recreation Area, east of Enterprise. Oregon has one of the nation's most extensive state park systems: 225 parks and recreation areas cover 90,000 acres (36,400 hectares). Portland and the Mt. Hood area attracts many mountain climbers and outdoor recreation seekers. There are places one can travel the original Oregon Trail of Westward expansion. In 2006 Oregon was celebrating the bicentennial of the Lewis and Clark expedition.

48 SPORTS

Oregon has one major league team, based in Portland. The Portland Trail Blazers, winners of the National Basketball Association championship in 1977, play in the NBA. The Portland Beavers are a Triple-A affiliate of the San Diego Padres. The state fields three teams that compete in baseball's class-A Northwest League, in Eugene and Salem.

Horse racing takes place at Portland Meadows in Portland and, in late August and early September, at the Oregon State Fair in Salem. There is greyhound racing at the Multnomah Greyhound Park near Portland. Pari-mutuel betting is permitted at the tracks, but off-track betting is prohibited.

The University of Oregon and Oregon State University belong to the Pacific 10 Conference. The Oregon State Ducks won the Rose Bowl in 1942 and appeared in, but lost, in 1965. Oregon was a surprise winner at the Pac-10 in 1994, and made its first Rose Bowl appearance in 37 years. The Ducks lost to Penn State in the 1995 Rose Bowl. Since 1996, the Ducks have won several bowl contests, highlighted by a victory over the Colorado Buffaloes in the 2002 Fiesta Bowl.

Other annual sporting events include sled dog races in Bend and Union Creek, the All-Indian Rodeo in Tygh Valley in May (one of many rodeos), and the Cycle Oregon Bike Ride.

49 FAMOUS OREGONIANS

Prominent federal officeholders from Oregon include Senator Charles McNary (1874–1944), a leading advocate of federal reclamation and development projects and the Republican vice-presidential nominee in 1940; Senator Wayne Morse (b.Wisconsin, 1900–1974), who was an early opponent of US involvement in Viet-Nam; Representative Edith Green (1910–1984), a leader in federal education assistance; and Representative Al Ullman (b.Montana, 1914–1986), chairman of the House Ways and Means Committee until his defeat in 1980. Recent cabinet members from Oregon have been Douglas McKay (1893–1959), secretary of the interior; and Neil Goldschmidt (b.1940) secretary of transportation.

A major figure in early Oregon history was sea captain Robert Gray (b.Rhode Island. 1755–1806), discoverer of the Columbia River. Although never holding a government position, fur trader Dr. John McLoughlin (b.Canada, 1784–1857) in effect ruled Oregon from 1824 to 1845; he was officially designated the "father of Oregon" by the 1957 state legislature. Also of importance in the early settlement was Methodist missionary Jason Lee (b.Canada, 1803–45). Oregon's most famous Indian was Chief Joseph (1840?–1904), leader of the Nez Percé in northeastern Oregon; when tension between the Nez Percé and white settlers erupted into open hostilities in 1877, Chief Joseph led his band of about 650 men, women, and children from the Oregon-Idaho border across the Bitterroot Range evading three army detachments before being captured in northern Montana.

Other important figures in the early days of statehood were Harvey W. Scott (b.Illinois 1838–1910), longtime editor of the Portland *Oregonian,* and his sister, Abigail Scott Duniway (b.Illinois, 1823–1915), the Northwest's foremost advocate of women's suffrage, a cause her brother strongly opposed. William Simon U'Ren (b.Wisconsin, 1859–1949) was a lawyer and reformer whose influence on Oregon politics and government endures to this day. Journalist and Communist John Reed (1887–1920), author of *Ten Days That Shook the World,* an eyewitness account of the Bolshevik Revolution, was born in Portland, and award-winning science-fiction writer Ursula K. LeGuin (b.California, 1929) is a Portland resident. Linus Pauling (1901–94), two-time winner of the Nobel Prize (for chemistry in 1954, for peace in 1962) was another Portland native. Other scientists prominent in the state's history include botanist David Douglas (b.Scotland, 1798–1834), who made two trips to Oregon and after whom the Douglas fir is named; and geologist and paleontologist Thomas Condon (b.Ireland, 1822–1907), discoverer of major fossil beds in eastern Oregon.

⁵⁰BIBLIOGRAPHY

Allerfeldt, Kristofer. *Race, Radicalism, Religion, and Restriction: Immigration in the Pacific Northwest, 1890–1924.* Westport, Conn.: Praeger, 2003.

Blair, Karen J. *Northwest Women: An Annotated Bibliography of Sources on the History of Oregon and Washington Women, 1787–1970.* Pullman: Washington State University Press, 1997.

Council of State Governments. *The Book of the States, 2006 Edition.* Lexington, Ky.: Council of State Governments, 2006.

Cressman, Luther Sheeleigh. *The Sandal & the Cave: The Indians of Oregon.* Corvallis: Oregon State University Press, 2005.

Dary, David. *The Oregon Trail: An American Saga.* New York: Alfred A. Knopf, 2004.

DeGrove, John Melvin. *Planning Policy and Politics: Smart Growth and the States.* Cambridge, Mass.: Lincoln Institute of Land Policy, 2005.

Goggans, Jan (ed.). *The Pacific Region.* Vol. 5 in *The Greenwood Encyclopedia of American Regional Cultures.* Westport, Conn.: Greenwood Press, 2004.

Lansing, Jewel Beck. *Portland: People, Politics, and Power, 1851–2001.* Corvallis: Oregon State University Press, 2003.

McArthur, Lewis A. *Oregon Geographic Names.* 7th ed. Portland: Oregon Historical Society Press, 2003.

Parzybok, Tye W. *Weather Extremes in the West.* Missoula, Mont.: Mountain Press, 2005.

Peterson del Mar, David. *Oregon's Promise: An Interpretive History.* Corvallis: Oregon State University Press, 2003.

Preston, Thomas. *Pacific Coast: Washington, Oregon, California.* 2nd ed. Vol. 1 in *The Double Eagle Guide to 1,000 Great Western Recreation Destinations.* Billings, Mont.: Discovery Publications, 2003.

US Department of Commerce, Economics and Statistics Administration, US Census Bureau. *Oregon, 2000. Summary Social, Economic, and Housing Characteristics: 2000 Census of Population and Housing.* Washington, D.C.: US Government Printing Office, 2003.

Webber, Bert, and Margie Webber. *Awesome Caverns of Marble in the Oregon Caves National Monuement.* Medford, Ore.: Webb Research Group Publishers, 1998.

Yuskavitch, Jim, and Leslie D. Cole. *The Insider's Guide to Bend & Central Oregon.* Helena, Mont.: Falcon Pub., Inc., 1999.

PENNSYLVANIA

Commonwealth of Pennsylvania

ORIGIN OF STATE NAME: Named for Admiral William Penn, father of the founder of Pennsylvania. **NICKNAME:** The Keystone State. **CAPITAL:** Harrisburg. **ENTERED UNION:** 12 December 1787 (2nd). **SONG:** "Pennsylvania." **MOTTO:** Virtue, Liberty and Independence. **COAT OF ARMS:** A shield supported by two horses displays a sailing ship, a plow, and three sheaves of wheat; an eagle forms the crest. Beneath the shield an olive branch and a cornstalk are crossed, and below them is the state motto. **FLAG:** The coat of arms appears in the center of a blue field. **OFFICIAL SEAL:** OBVERSE: a shield displays a sailing ship, a plow, and three sheaves of wheat, with a cornstalk to the left, an olive branch to the right, and an eagle above, surrounded by the inscription "Seal of the State of Pennsylvania." REVERSE: a woman representing Liberty holds a wand topped by a liberty cap in her left hand and a drawn sword in her right, as she tramples a lion representing Tyranny. The legend "Both Can't Survive" encircles the design. **BIRD:** Ruffed grouse. **FISH:** Brook trout. **FLOWER:** Mountain laurel. **TREE:** Hemlock. **LEGAL HOLIDAYS:** New Year's Day, 1 January; Birthday of Martin Luther King Jr., 3rd Monday in January; Presidents' Day, 3rd Monday in February; Memorial Day, last Monday in May; Independence Day, 4 July; Labor Day, 1st Monday in September; Columbus Day, 2nd Monday in October; Veterans' Day, 11 November; Thanksgiving Day, 4th Thursday in November and the following day; Christmas Day, 25 December. **TIME:** 7 AM EST = noon GMT.

¹LOCATION, SIZE, AND EXTENT

Located in the northeastern United States, the Commonwealth of Pennsylvania is the second-largest of the three Middle Atlantic states and ranks 33rd in size among the 50 states.

The total area of Pennsylvania is 45,308 sq mi (117,348 sq km), of which land occupies 44,888 sq mi (116,260 sq km) and inland water 420 sq mi (1,088 sq km). The state extends 307 mi (494 km) E–W and 169 mi (272 km) N–S. Pennsylvania is rectangular in shape, except for an irregular side on the E and a break in the even boundary in the NW where the line extends N-E for about 50 mi (80 km) along the shore of Lake Erie.

Pennsylvania is bordered on the N by New York; on the E by New York and New Jersey (with the Delaware River forming the entire boundary); on the SE by Delaware; on the S by Maryland and West Virginia (demarcated by the Mason-Dixon line); on the w by West Virginia and Ohio; and on the NW by Lake Erie. The total boundary length of Pennsylvania is 880 mi (1,416 km). The state's geographical center lies in Centre County, 2.5 mi (4 km) SW of Bellefonte.

²TOPOGRAPHY

Pennsylvania may be divided into more than a dozen distinct physiographic regions, most of which extend in curved bands from east to south. Beginning in the southeast, the first region (including Philadelphia) is a narrow belt of coastal plain along the lower Delaware River; this area, at sea level, is the state's lowest region. The next belt, dominating the southeastern corner, is the Piedmont Plateau, a wide area of rolling hills and lowlands. The Great Valley, approximately 10–15 mi (16–24 km) in width, runs from the middle of the state's eastern border to the middle of its southern border. The eastern, central, and western parts of the Great Valley are known as the Lehigh, Lebanon, and Cumberland

valleys, respectively. West and north of the Great Valley, the Pocono Plateau rises to about 2,200 ft (700 m). Next, in a band 50–60 mi (80–100 km) wide, most of the way from the north-central part of the eastern border to the west-central part of the southern border are the Appalachian Mountains, a distinctive region of parallel ridges and valleys.

The Allegheny High Plateau, part of the Appalachian Plateaus, makes up the western and northern parts of the state. The Allegheny Front, the escarpment along the eastern edge of the plateau, is the most striking topographical feature in Pennsylvania, dissected by many winding streams to form narrow, steep-sided valleys; the southwestern extension of the Allegheny High Plateau contains the state's highest peak, Mt. Davis, at 3,213 ft (980 m). A narrow lowland region, the Erie Plain, borders Lake Erie in the extreme northwestern part of the state. The mean elevation of the state is approximately 1,100 ft (336 m).

According to federal sources, Pennsylvania has jurisdiction over 735 sq mi (1,904 sq km) of Lake Erie; the state government gives a figure of 891 sq mi (2,308 sq km). Pennsylvania contains about 250 natural lakes larger than 20 acres (8 hectares), most of them in the glaciated regions of the northeast and northwest. The largest natural lake within the state's borders is Conneaut Lake, about 30 mi (48 km) south of the city of Erie, with an area of less than 1.5 sq mi (39 sq km); the largest manmade lake is Lake Wallenpaupack, in the Poconos, occupying about 9 sq mi (23 sq km). Pennsylvania claims more than 21 sq mi (54 sq km) of the Pymatuning Reservoir on the Ohio border.

The Susquehanna River and its tributaries drain more than 46% of the area of Pennsylvania, much of it in the Appalachian Mountains. The Delaware River forms Pennsylvania's eastern border and, like the Susquehanna, flows southeastward to the Atlantic Ocean. Most of the western part of the state is drained by the Allegheny and Monongahela rivers, which join at Pittsburgh to form the Ohio. The Beaver, Clarion, and Youghiogheny rivers are also important parts of this system.

During early geological history, the topography of Pennsylvania had the reverse of its present configurations, with mountains in the southeast and a large inland sea covering the rest of the state. This sea, which alternately expanded and contracted, interwove layers of vegetation (which later became coal) with layers of sandstone and shale.

³CLIMATE

Although Pennsylvania lies entirely within the humid continental zone, its climate varies according to region and elevation. The regions with the warmest temperatures and the longest growing seasons are the low-lying southwest Ohio valley and the Monongahela valley in the southeast. The region bordering Lake Erie also has a long growing season, as the moderating effect of the lake prevents early spring and late autumn frosts. The first two areas have hot summers, while the Erie area is more moderate. The rest of the state, at higher elevations, has cold winters and cool summers.

Among the major population centers, Philadelphia has an annual average temperature of 55°F (12°C), with a normal minimum of 46°F (7°C) and a normal maximum of 64°F (17°C). Pittsburgh has an annual average of 51°F (10°C), with a minimum of 41°F (5°C) and a maximum of 60°F (15°C). In the cooler northern areas, Scranton has a normal annual average ranging from 40°F (4°C) to 59°F (15°C); Erie, from 41°F (5°C) to 57°F (13°C). The record low temperature for the state is -42°F (-41°C), set at Smethport on 5 January 1904; the record high, 111°F (44°C), was reached at Phoenixville on 10 July 1936.

Philadelphia has about 40.9 in (103 cm) of precipitation annually, and Pittsburgh has 37 in (93 cm). Pittsburgh, however, has much more snow—43.1 in (109 cm), compared with 21 in (52 cm) for Philadelphia. The snowfall in Erie, in the snow belt, averages 85.5 in (217 cm) per year, with heavy snows sometimes experienced late in April. In Philadelphia, the sun shines an average of 56% of the time; in Pittsburgh, 45%.

The state has experienced several destructive floods. On 31 May 1889, the South Fork Dam near Johnstown broke after a heavy rainfall, and its rampaging waters killed 2,200 people and devastated the entire city in less than 10 minutes. On 19–20 July 1977, Johnstown experienced another flood, resulting in 68 deaths. Three tornadoes raked the southwestern part of the commonwealth on 23 June 1944, killing 45 persons and injuring another 362. Rains from Hurricane Agnes in June 1972 resulted in floods that caused 48 deaths and more than $1.2 billion worth of property damage in the Susquehanna Valley.

⁴FLORA AND FAUNA

Maple, walnut, poplar, oak, pine, ash, beech, and linden trees fill Pennsylvania's extensive forests, along with sassafras, sycamore, weeping willow, and balsam fir (Abies fraseri). Red pine and paper birch are found in the north while the sweet gum is dominant in the extreme southwest. Mountain laurel (the state flower), Juneberry, dotted hawthorn, New Jersey tea, and various dogwoods are among the shrubs and small trees found in most parts of the state, and dewberry, wintergreen, wild columbine, and wild ginger are also common. In April 2006, the small whorled pogonia and Virginia spirea were classified as threatened, with the northeastern bulrush as endangered.

Numerous mammals persist in Pennsylvania, among them the white-tailed deer (the state animal), black bear, red and gray foxes, opossum, raccoon, muskrat, mink, snowshoe hare, common cottontail, and red, gray, fox, and flying squirrels. Native amphibians include the hellbender, Fowler's toad, and the tree, cricket, and true frogs; among reptilian species are the five-lined and black skinks and five varieties of lizard. The ruffed grouse, a common game species, is the official state bird; other game birds are the wood dove, ring-necked pheasant, bobwhite quail, and mallard and black ducks. The robin, cardinal, English sparrow, red-eyed vireo, cedar waxwing, tufted titmouse, yellow-shafted flicker, barn swallow, blue jay, and killdeer are common non-game birds. More than 170 types of fish have been identified in Pennsylvania, with brown and brook trout, grass pickerel, bigeye chub, pirate perch, and white bass among the common native varieties.

In 1978, the Pennsylvania Game Commission and the US Fish and Wildlife Service signed a cooperative agreement under which the federal government provides two dollars for each dollar spent by the state to determine the status of and improve conditions for threatened or endangered species. On the threatened or endangered list in April 2006 were 12 animal species (vertebrates and invertebrates), including the Indiana bat, bald eagle, orangefoot pimpleback pearly mussel, dwarf wedgemussel, and pink mucket pearly mussel.

⁵ENVIRONMENTAL PROTECTION

Pennsylvania's environment was ravaged by uncontrolled timber cutting in the 19th century, and by extensive coal mining and industrial development until recent times. Pittsburgh's most famous landmarks were its smokestacks, and it was said that silverware on ships entering the port of Philadelphia would tarnish immediately from the fumes of the Delaware River. The anthracite-mining regions were filled with huge, hideous culm piles, and the bituminous and anthracite fields were torn up by strip-mining.

In 1895, Pennsylvania appointed its first commissioner of forestry, in an attempt to repair some of the earlier damage. Gifford Pinchot, who twice served as governor of Pennsylvania, was the first professionally trained forester in the United States (he studied at the École National Forestiere in Paris), developed the US Forest Service, and served as Pennsylvania forest commissioner from 1920 to 1922. In 1955, the state forests were put under scientific management.

In 1972, Pennsylvania voters ratified a state constitutional amendment adopted 18 May 1971, acknowledging the people's "right to clean air, pure water, and to the preservation of the natural, scenic, historic, and esthetic values of the environment" and naming the state as trustee of these resources. Passage of the amendment came only two years after establishment of the Pennsylvania Department of Environmental Resources, which in the 1990s was reorganized into two separate entities. The Department of Conservation and Natural Resources (DCNR) was established on 1 July 1995 to maintain and preserve the state's 116 state parks, manage the 2.1 million acres of state forest land, and provide information on the state's ecological and geologic resources. The DCNR also oversees environmental education and provides assistance and grants for preserving rivers, community trails, parks,

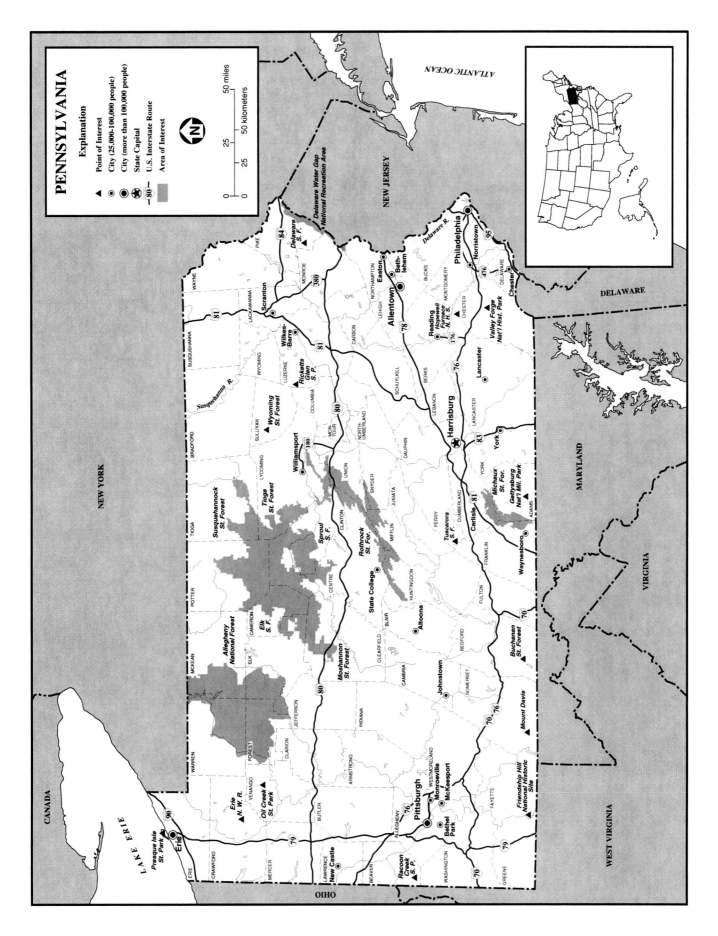

and recreation. The Pennsylvania Department of Environmental Protection (DEP) was established to protect the state's air, land, and water from pollution and to provide a cleaner environment for the health and safety of Pennsylvania's citizens.

In March 1979, Pennsylvania suffered the worst nuclear-power accident in US history when a nuclear reactor on Three Mile Island malfunctioned and radioactive gases escaped. A second reactor was shut down immediately even though it was not damaged. The cleanup of radioactive waste cost about $1 billion, and it was not until late 1985 that the undamaged unit was placed back in operation.

An oil spill at Marcus Hook, near the Delaware Border, released 435,000 gallons of crude oil into the Delaware River in September 1985; damage to birds and wetlands was more extensive in Delaware than in Pennsylvania. In 1996, there were 404,000 acres (163,492 hectares) of wetlands in the state. There are about 50 private conservancy groups that work with the state to protect these lands.

As of the early 1990s, sewage and industrial wastes were the major pollutants in areas with high industrial and population concentrations. In western and parts of central Pennsylvania, drainage from abandoned bituminous coal mines created serious water quality problems; active mines in this region were also potentially polluting. A similar situation prevailed in the anthracite areas of northeastern Pennsylvania. Oil and gas well operations, located primarily in the northwestern portion of the commonwealth, were additional pollution sources. In 2003, 166.9 million lb of toxic chemicals were released in the state.

After miners were trapped (and subsequently successfully rescued) in an accident at Quecreek Mine in July 2002, the DEP launched a program to build a database of abandoned mine locations to minimize the risk of another such accident occurring.

In 2003, Pennsylvania had 572 hazardous waste sites listed in the US Environment Protection Agency (EPA) database. In 2006, Pennsylvania ranked second in the nation (following New Jersey) for the highest number of hazardous waste sites on the National Priorities List, with 94 sites; these included the Rodale Manufacturing Co. Westinghouse Electric Corp. (Sharon), and Saegertown Industrial Area. At least 26 sites have been deleted from the list in past years. In 2005, the EPA spent over $14 million through the Superfund program for the cleanup of hazardous waste sites in the state. In 2004, the state received a federal EPA grant of $52.5 million for the clean water state revolving fund.

[6] POPULATION

Pennsylvania ranked sixth in population in the United States with an estimated total of 12,429,616 in 2005, an increase of 1.2% since 2000. Between 1990 and 2000, Pennsylvania's population grew from 11,881,643 to 12,281,054, an increase of 3.4%. The population is projected to reach 12.7 million by 2015 and 12.8 million by

Pennsylvania—Counties, County Seats, and County Areas and Populations

COUNTY	COUNTY SEAT	LAND AREA (SQ MI)	POPULATION (2005 EST.)	COUNTY	COUNTY SEAT	LAND AREA (SQ MI)	POPULATION (2005 EST.)
Adams	Gettysburg	521	99,749	Lackawanna	Scranton	461	209,525
Allegheny	Pittsburgh	727	1,235,841	Lancaster	Lancaster	952	490,562
Armstrong	Kittanning	646	70,586	Lawrence	New Castle	363	92,809
Beaver	Beaver	436	177,377	Lebanon	Lebanon	363	125,578
Bedford	Bedford	1,017	50,091	Lehigh	Allentown	348	330,433
Berks	Reading	861	396,314	Luzerne	Wilkes-Barre	891	312,861
Blair	Hollidaysburg	527	126,795	Lycoming	Williamsport	1,237	118,395
Bradford	Towanda	1,152	62,537	McKean	Smethport	1,237	44,370
Bucks	Doylestown	610	621,342	Mercer	Mercer	672	119,598
Butler	Butler	789	182,087	Mifflin	Lewistown	413	46,235
Cambria	Ebensburg	691	148,073	Monroe	Stroudsburg	609	163,234
Cameron	Emporium	398	5,639	Montgomery	Norristown	486	775,883
Carbon	Jim Thorpe	384	61,959	Montour	Danville	131	18,032
Centre	Bellefonte	1,106	140,561	Northampton	Easton	376	287,767
Chester	West Chester	758	474,027	Northumberland	Sunbury	461	92,610
Clarion	Clarion	607	40,589	Perry	New Bloomfield	557	44,728
Clearfield	Clearfield	1,149	82,783	Philadelphia	Philadelphia	136	1,463,281
Clinton	Lock Haven	891	37,439	Pike	Milford	550	56,337
Columbia	Bloomsburg	486	64,939	Potter	Coudersport	1,081	17,834
Crawford	Meadville	1,011	89,442	Schuylkill	Pottsville	782	147,447
Cumberland	Carlisle	547	223,089	Snyder	Middleburg	329	38,207
Dauphin	Harrisburg	528	253,995	Somerset	Somerset	1,073	78,907
Delaware	Media	184	555,648	Sullivan	Laporte	451	6,391
Elk	Ridgeway	830	33,577	Susquehanna	Montrose	826	42,124
Erie	Erie	804	280,446	Tioga	Wellsboro	1,131	41,649
Fayette	Uniontown	794	146,142	Union	Lewisburg	317	43,131
Forest	Tionesta	428	5,739	Venango	Franklin	679	55,928
Franklin	Chambersburg	774	137,409	Warren	Warren	885	42,033
Fulton	McConnellsburg	438	14,673	Washington	Washington	858	206,406
Greene	Waynesburg	577	39,808	Wayne	Honesdale	731	50,113
Huntingdon	Huntingdon	877	45,947	Westmoreland	Greensburg	1,033	367,635
Indiana	Indiana	829	88,703	Wyoming	Tunkhannock	399	28,160
Jefferson	Brookville	657	45,759	York	York	906	408,801
Juniata	Mifflintown	392	23,507	**TOTALS**		45,150	12,429,616

2025. In 2004, the median age for Pennsylvanians was 39.3. In the same year, 22.9% of the populace was under age 18 while 15.3% was age 65 or older. The population density in 2004 was 276.9 persons per sq mi.

As recently as 1940, Pennsylvania was the second most populous state in the United States. By the 1980 census, however, the state had slipped to fourth place, with a population of 11,863,895; it dropped to fifth place in 1990 with a population of 11,881,643.

The largest city in the state, Philadelphia, was the fifth-largest US city as of 2004, with a population of 1,470,151. Philadelphia's population has declined since 1970, when 1,949,996 people lived there. The population of the Philadelphia-Camden-Wilmington metropolitan area was estimated 5,800,614 in 2004. Pittsburgh's population declined from 616,806 in 1950 to an estimated 322,450 in 2004 in the city proper. In 2004, the Pittsburgh metropolitan area had an estimated population of 2,401,575. The 2004 estimated populations of Pennsylvania's other major cities were Allentown, 106,732, and Erie, 103,925. Other cities with large populations include Reading, Scranton, Bethlehem, Lancaster, Harrisburg, Altoona, and Wilkes-Barre.

7ETHNIC GROUPS

During the colonial period, under the religious tolerance of a Quaker government, Pennsylvania was a haven for dissident sectarians from continental Europe and the British Isles. Some German sectarians, including the Amish, have kept up their traditions to this day. An initially friendly policy toward the Indians waned in the late 18th century under the pressures of population growth and the anxieties of the French and Indian War. The famous Carlisle Indian School (1879–1918) educated many leaders from various tribes throughout the United States. In Pennsylvania itself, however, there were only 18,348 American Indians in 2000, up from 15,000 in 1990. In 2004, American Indians accounted for 0.2% of the population.

Modest numbers of black slaves were utilized as domestics, field workers, and iron miners in colonial Pennsylvania. Antislavery sentiment was stirred in the 18th century through the efforts of a Quaker, John Woolman, and other Pennsylvanians. The Gradual Abolition of Slavery Act was passed in 1780, and the important antislavery newspaper *The Liberator* appeared in Philadelphia in 1831. As of 2000, black Americans numbered 1,224,612 (10% of the total state population), and were concentrated in the large cities. Philadelphia was 43.2% black in 2000, with 655,824 African American residents. In 2004, 10.5% of the state's population was black.

The late 19th and early 20th centuries brought waves of immigrants from Ireland, Wales, various Slavic nations, and the eastern Mediterranean and the Balkans. Many of the new immigrants settled in the east-central anthracite coal-mining region. In 2000, 508,291 Pennsylvania residents, or 4.1% of the total population, were foreign born, up from 3.1% in 1990. Italy, Germany, the United Kingdom, India, the former Soviet Union, Korea, and Poland were the leading countries of origin. In the valleys surrounding Pittsburgh there are still self-contained ethnic enclaves, and there has been increased interest in preserving distinctive ethnic traditions.

Hispanics and Latinos in Pennsylvania numbered 394,088 in 2000 (3.2%), up from 232,000 in 1990. Most were Puerto Ricans, with smaller numbers of Cubans and Central Americans. In 2004, 3.8% of the population was of Hispanic or Latino origin. In 2000, Asians numbered 219,813; the Asian population included 50,650 Chinese (almost double the 1990 total of 25,908), 31,612 Koreans, 57,241 Asian Indians (almost triple the 1990 figure of 19,769), 14,506 Filipinos, and 30,037 Vietnamese, up sharply from 14,126 in 1990. Pacific Islanders numbered 3,417. In 2004, Asians accounted for 2.2% of the population. That year, 0.9% of the population reported origin of two or more races.

8LANGUAGES

Once home to several Algonkian tribes, Pennsylvania still has such Algonkian place-names as Punxsutawney, Aliquippa, Pocono, Towanda, Susquehanna, and Shamokin. An Iroquoian tribe gave its name to the Conestoga region. The word came to identify first the pioneers' covered wagons manufactured in the area and then, in shortened form, a cheap cigar called a *stogie.*

Although not quite homogeneous, Pennsylvania's North Midland dialect is significant as the source of much Midwestern and western speech. The only non-Midland sector is the northern tier of counties, settled from southern New York State, where features of the northern dialect predominate.

On the whole, Pennsylvania North Midland is distinguished by the presence of *want off* a tram or bus, *snake feeder* (dragonfly), *run* (small stream), *waterspouts* and *spouts* (gutters), and *creek* as /krik/. With these features are found others that commonly occur in Southern Pennsylvania, such as *corn pone, roasting ears,* and *spiket* (spigot). Western Pennsylvania, however, contrasts with the eastern half by the dominance of /nawthing/ for *nothing,* /greezy/ for *greasy,* /kao/ for *cow, sugar tree* (sugar maple), *hap* (quilt), and *clothes press* (closet), as well as by the influential merging of the /ah/ vowel and the /aw/ vowel so that *cot* and *caught* sound alike. Southern Pennsylvania has *flannel cakes* for pancakes and *ground hackie* for chipmunk. Within this region, Philadelphia and its suburbs have distinctive *baby coach* for baby carriage, *pavement* for sidewalk, *hoagie* for a large sandwich, the vowel of *put* in *broom* and *Cooper,* and the vowel of *father* in *on* and *fog.* In the east and northeast, a doughnut is a *cruller,* one is *sick in the stomach,* and *syrup* has the vowel of *sit.*

In much of central Pennsylvania, descendants of the colonial Palatinate German population retain their speech as Deutsch, often misnamed Pennsylvania Dutch, which has influenced English in the state through such loanwords as *toot* (bag), *rainworm* (earthworm), *snits* (dried apples), and *smearcase* (cottage cheese).

In 2000, 10,583,054 Pennsylvanians—91.6% of the population five years old or older—spoke only English at home, down slightly from 92.7% in 1990.

The following table gives selected statistics from the 2000 Census for language spoken at home by persons five years old and over. The category "Other West Germanic languages" includes Dutch, Pennsylvania Dutch, and Afrikaans. The category "Other Slavic languages" includes Czech, Slovak, and Ukrainian. The category "Other Asian languages" includes Dravidian languages, Malayalam, Telugu, Tamil, and Turkish. The category "Other Indic languages" includes Bengali, Marathi, Punjabi, and Romany. The category "Other Indo-European languages" includes Albanian, Gaelic, Lithuanian, and Rumanian.

LANGUAGE	NUMBER	PERCENT
Population 5 years and over	**11,555,538**	**100.0**
Speak only English	10,583,054	91.6
Speak a language other than English	972,484	8.4
Speak a language other than English	**972,484**	**8.4**
Spanish or Spanish Creole	356,754	3.1
Italian	70,434	0.6
German	68,672	0.6
Other West Germanic languages	51,073	0.4
French (incl. Patois, Cajun)	47,735	0.4
Chinese	42,790	0.4
Russian	32,189	0.3
Polish	31,717	0.3
Korean	25,978	0.2
Vietnamese	25,880	0.2
Other Slavic languages	24,423	0.2
Arabic	19,557	0.2
Greek	17,348	0.2
Other Asian languages	16,196	0.1
Other Indic languages	12,297	0.1
Other Indo-European languages	11,656	0.1
Hindi	10,045	0.1

9 RELIGIONS

With a long history of toleration, Pennsylvania has been a haven for numerous religious groups. The first European settlers were Swedish Lutherans; German Lutherans began arriving 1703. William Penn brought the Quakers to Pennsylvania during the 1680s and the climate of religious liberty soon attracted other dissident groups, including German Mennonites, Dunkars, Moravians, and Schwenkfelders; French Huguenots; Scots-Irish Presbyterians; and English Baptists. Descendants of the 16th-century Anabaptists, the Mennonites for the most part settled as farmers; they and the Quakers were the first religious groups openly to advocate abolition of slavery and to help runaway slaves to freedom via the Underground Railroad. The Amish-Mennonite followers of Jacob Amman continue to dress in black clothing, shun the use of mechanized tools, automobiles and electrical appliance, and observe Sundays by singing 16th-century hymns.

The Presbyterians, who built their first church in the state in 1704, played a major role both in the establishment of schools in the colony and in the later development of Pittsburgh and other cities in the western part of the state. Methodists held their first services in Philadelphia in 1768; for many years thereafter, Methodist circuit riders proselytized throughout the state.

Immigration during the 19th century brought a major change in patterns of worship. The Quakers gradually diminished in number and influence, while Roman Catholic and Greek Orthodox churches and Jewish synagogues opened in many of the mining and manufacturing centers. The bulk of the Jewish migration came, after 1848, from Germany and, after 1882, from East Europe and Russia. The Gilded Age saw the founding of a new group in Pittsburgh by clergyman Charles Taze Russell; first called the Russellites, members of this group (established in 1872) are known today as Jehovah's Witnesses.

Roman Catholics constitute the largest religious group in the state, with a total membership of about 3,686,088 in 2004, with about 1,486,058 belonging to the archdiocese of Philadelphia. The largest Protestant denomination in 2000 was the United Methodist Church, with 659,350 adherents; however, member-

ship in 2004 was reported at about 471,311. Other major Protestant groups (with 2000 membership data) were the Evangelical Lutheran Church in America, 611,913; the Presbyterian Church USA, 324,714; the American Baptist Church USA, 132,858; and the Episcopal Church, 116,511. The historically important Mennonites, of various traditions, had over 68,000 adherents in 2000. Amish communities had over 25,000 members and Moravians numbered over 10,000. Friends USA (Quakers) reported a membership of about 11,844. Jewish congregations included an estimated 283,000 members and the Muslim congregations had about 71,190 adherents. About 5.1 million people (42.1% of the population) were not counted as members of any religious organization. In 2005, the United Church of Christ reported about 182,779 members statewide.

The American Council of Christian Churches maintains executive offices in Bethlehem. The Mennonite Central Committee, a relief organization, is based in Akron. The Moravian Historical Society can be found in Nazareth,

10 TRANSPORTATION

Like so many of its industrial assets, Pennsylvania's well-developed road and rail networks are showing signs of old age. Nevertheless, the state remains an important center of transportation, and its ports are among the busiest in the United States.

The early years of railroad building left Pennsylvania with more miles of track than any other state. The first railroad charter, issued in 1819, provided for a horse-drawn railroad from the Delaware Valley to the headwaters of the Lehigh River. The state authorized construction of a line between Columbia and Philadelphia in 1828, and partial service began four years later as part of the State Works. The roadbed was state-owned, and private rail car companies paid a toll to use the rails. During this time, Pennsylvanians John Jervis and Joseph Harrison were developing steam-powered locomotives. Taking advantage of the new technology were separate rail lines connecting Philadelphia with Germantown (1834), Trenton, New Jersey (1838), and Reading (1839), with the Lehigh Valley (1846), and with New York City (1855). In December 1852, the Pennsylvania Central completed lines connecting Philadelphia and Pittsburgh. Five years later, the Pennsylvania Railroad purchased the State Works, eliminating state competition and tolls. By 1880, the company (which had added many smaller coal hauling lines to its holdings) was the world's largest corporation, with more than 30,000 employees and $400 million in capital. Although railroad revenues declined with the rise of the automobile, the Pennsylvania Railroad remained profitable until the 1960s, when the line merged with the New York Central to form the Penn Central. In 1970, the Penn Central separated its real estate holdings from its transportation operation, on which it declared bankruptcy.

As of 2003, the state had 6,942 rail mi (11,176 km) of track, of which 3,566 mi (5,741 km) were operated by the two Class I railroads serving the state: CSX Transportation and the Norfolk Southern. Overall that same year, Pennsylvania was served by 60 railroads, more than any other state. Coal was the top commodity by tonnage, carried by rail originating and terminating within the state. As of 2006, Amtrak operated passenger service through Pennsylvania to Philadelphia, Pittsburgh, and other cities along the east–west route, and from Philadelphia to New York and Washington, DC, along the northeast corridor.

Mass transit systems exist in metropolitan Philadelphia and Pittsburgh, in Bucks, Chester, Delaware, Montgomery, and Philadelphia counties, and in Altoona, Allentown, Erie, Harrisburg. Johnstown, Lancaster, Reading, Scranton, State College, and Wilkes-Barre. The Philadelphia Rapid Transit System, the state's first subway, was established in 1902 and is operated by the Southeastern Pennsylvania Transportation Authority, (SEPTA), which also runs buses, trolleys, trackless trolleys, and commuter trains in Bucks, Chester, Delaware, Montgomery, and Philadelphia counties. In 1985, a 1.1-mile (1.8-km) subway was opened in Pittsburgh as part of a 10.5-mile (16.9-km) light-rail (trolley) transit system linking downtown Pittsburgh with the South Hills section of the city.

Throughout its history, Pennsylvania has been a pioneer in road transportation. One of the earliest roads in the colonies was a "king's highway," connecting Philadelphia to Delaware in 1677; a "queen's road" from Philadelphia to Chester opened in 1706. A flurry of road building connected Philadelphia with other eastern Pennsylvania communities between 1705 and 1735. The first interior artery, the Great Conestoga Road, was opened in 1741 and linked Philadelphia with Lancaster. Indian trails in western Pennsylvania were developed into roadways, and a thoroughfare to Pittsburgh was completed in 1758. During the mid-1700s, a Lancaster County artisan developed an improved wagon for transporting goods across the Alleghenies. Called a Conestoga wagon after the region from which it came, this vehicle later became the prime means of transport for westward pioneers. Another major improvement in land transportation came with the opening in 1792 of the Philadelphia and Lancaster Turnpike, one of the first stone-surfaced roads in the United States. The steel-cable suspension bridge built by John Roebling over the Monongahela River at Pittsburgh in 1846 revolutionized bridge building, leading to the construction of spans longer and wider than had previously been thought possible. During the 1920s, Pennsylvania farmers were aided by the building of inexpensive rural roads connecting them with their markets.

A major development in automotive transport, the limited-access highway came to fruition with the Pennsylvania Turnpike, which opened in 1940 and was the first high-speed, multilane highway in the United States. In 2004, Pennsylvania had 120,623 mi (194,203 km) of public roads. Besides the Turnpike, the major highways are I-80 (Keystone Shortway), crossing the state from East Stroudsburg to the Ohio Turnpike; I-81, from the New York to the Maryland border via Scranton, Wilkes–Barre, and Harrisburg; and I-79, from Erie to the West Virginia border via Pittsburgh. As of 2004, there were some 9.989 million motor vehicles registered, including around 5.593 million automobiles, about 3.716 million trucks of all types, and some 29,000 buses. In that same year, there were a total of 8,430,142 licensed drivers in the state.

Blessed with access to the Atlantic Ocean and the Great Lakes and with such navigable waterways as the Delaware, Monongahela, Allegheny, and Ohio rivers, Pennsylvania was an early leader in water transportation, and Philadelphia, Pittsburgh, and Erie all developed as major ports. The peak period of canal building came during the 1820s and 1830s, which saw the completion of the Main Line of Public Works, used to transport goods between Philadelphia and Pittsburgh from 1834 to 1854. This system used waterways and a spectacular portage railroad that climbed over and cut through, via a tunnel, the Allegheny Mountains. Monumental as it was, the undertaking was largely a failure. Built too late to challenge the Erie Canal's domination of east–west trade, the Main Line was soon made obsolete by the railroads, as was the rest of the state's 800-mi (1,300-km) canal system.

Philadelphia, Pittsburgh, and Erie are the state's major shipping ports. The Philadelphia Harbor (including ports in the Philadelphia metropolitan area) handled 35.219 million tons of cargo in 2004. Although no longer the dominant gateway to the Mississippi, Pittsburgh is still a major inland port, and handled 41.034 million tons of cargo that year, while Erie, the state's port on the Great Lakes, handled 1.099 million tons of cargo. In 2003, waterborne shipments totaled 104.404 million tons. In 2004, Pennsylvania had 259 mi (416 km) of navigable inland waterways.

In 2005, Pennsylvania had a total of 810 public and private-use aviation-related facilities. This included 468 airports, 329 heliports, three STOLports (Short Take-Off and Landing), and 10 seaplane bases. The busiest air terminal in the state is Philadelphia International Airport, with 13,824,332 passenger enplanements in 2004, followed by Pittsburgh International Airport with 6,606,117 enplanements in that same year, making them the 17th- and 32nd-busiest airports in the United States, respectively.

11 HISTORY

Soon after the glacier receded from what is now Pennsylvania, about 20,000 years ago, nomadic hunters from the west moved up the Ohio River, penetrated the passes through the Allegheny Mountains, and moved down the Susquehanna and Delaware rivers. By about AD 500, the earliest Indians, already accustomed to fishing and gathering nuts, seeds, fruit, and roots, were beginning to cultivate the soil, make pottery, and build burial mounds. Over the next thousand years, the Indians became semisedentary, or only seasonal, nomads.

Woodland Indians living in Pennsylvania, mostly of the Algonkian language family, were less inclined toward agriculture than other Indian tribes. The first Europeans to sail up the Delaware River found the Leni-Lenape ("original people"), who, as their name signified, had long occupied that valley, and whom the English later called the Delaware. Other Algonkian tribes related to the Leni-Lenape were the Nanticoke, who ranged along the Susquehanna River, and the Shawnee, who were scattered throughout central Pennsylvania. The other major Indian language group in Pennsylvania was Iroquoian. This group included the Susquehanna (Conestoga), living east of the Susquehanna River and south to the shores of Chesapeake Bay; the Wyandot, along the Allegheny River; and the Erie, south of Lake Erie. Proving that tribes related by language could be deadly enemies, the Iroquoian Confederacy of the Five Nations, located in what is now New York, destroyed the Iroquoian-speaking Erie in the 1640s and the Susquehanna by 1680. The confederacy conquered the Leni-Lenape by 1720 but failed to destroy them.

The first European to reach Pennsylvania was probably Cornelis Jacobssen, who in 1614 entered Delaware Bay for Dutch merchants interested in the fur trade. In 1638, the Swedes began planting farms along the Delaware River; they lived in peace with the Leni-Lenape and Susquehanna, with whom they traded for furs.

Under Governor Johan Printz, the Swedes expanded into present-day Pennsylvania with a post at Tinicum Island (1643) and several forts along the Schuylkill River. The Dutch conquered New Sweden in 1655, but surrendered the land in 1664 to the English, led by James, Duke of York, the brother of King Charles II and the future King James II.

The English conquest was financed partly by Admiral William Penn, whose son, also named William, subsequently joined the Society of Friends (Quakers), a radical Protestant sect persecuted for espousing equality and pacifism. Dreaming of an ideal commonwealth that would be a refuge for all persecuted peoples, Penn asked Charles II, who had not paid the debt owed to Penn's father, to grant him land west of the Delaware. The Duke of York willingly gave up his claim to that land, and Charles II granted it in 1681 as a proprietary colony to the younger Penn and named it Pennsylvania in honor of Penn's father.

As proprietor of Pennsylvania, Penn was given enormous power to make laws and wars (subject to approval by the king and the freeman of Pennsylvania), levy taxes, coin money, regulate commerce, sell land, appoint officials, administer justice, and construct a government. From the beginning, Penn virtually gave up his lawmaking power and granted suffrage to property holders of 50 acres or £50. Even before coming to Pennsylvania, he forged his first Frame of Government, a document that went into effect on 25 April 1682 but lasted less than a year. Under it, a 72-member council, presided over by a governor, monopolized executive, legislative, and judicial power, although a 200-member assembly could veto or amend the council's legislation. Arriving in the colony in October 1682, Penn approved the location and layout of Philadelphia, met with the Leni-Lenape to acquire land and exchange vows of peace, called for elections to select an assembly, and proposed a Great Law that ranged from prescribing weights and measures to guaranteeing fundamental liberties.

When the First Frame proved unwieldy, Penn on 2 April 1683 approved a Second Frame, which created an 18-member council and a 36-member assembly. A conspicuous friend of the deposed James II, Penn lost control of Pennsylvania from 1692 to 1694, and it was during this period that the legislature began to assert its rights. Penn returned to the colony in 1699, and on 28 October 1701 approved yet another constitution, called the Charter of Privileges. This document lodged legislative power in an annually elected unicameral assembly, executive power in a governor and council, which he now appointed, and judicial power in appointed provincial judges and an elected county judiciary. The Charter of Privileges remained in force until 1776.

As Pennsylvania's government evolved, its population grew steadily. Most of the first immigrants were from the British Isles and Germany. From 1681 to 1710, numerous English and Welsh Quaker migrants populated a 25-mi (40-km) zone surrounding Philadelphia. By 1750, most German immigrants were settled in a semicircular zone some 25–75 mi (40–120 km) from Philadelphia. A third and outermost ring, extending roughly 75 mi (120 km) west and north of the Germans, was populated beginning in 1717 by the Scots-Irish, who were indifferent farmers, but known as aggressive pioneers. By 1776, each of the major groups—which remained quite distinct—constituted roughly a third of the 300,000 Pennsylvanians. Minorities included about 10,000 Scots, 10,000

Irish Catholics, 8,000 French Huguenots, 8,000 black slaves (despite Quaker hostility to slavery), and 1,000 Jews.

A key issue during the pre-Revolutionary period was the size and extent of the colony. Conflicting colonial charters, reflecting vague English ideas of American geography, brought all of Pennsylvania's boundaries except the Delaware River into dispute. After a protracted struggle, Pennsylvania and Maryland agreed upon a basis for Charles Mason and Jeremiah Dixon to run the famous line (1763–67) that divided North and South. Although Virginia and Pennsylvania both claimed the area around Pittsburgh, a joint commission agreed in 1779 to extend the Mason-Dixon line west the full five degrees prescribed in Penn's original charter. Five years earlier, the Penn family had abandoned to New York land north of the 42d parallel. This was confirmed as Pennsylvania's northern border in 1782, when the US Congress rejected Connecticut's claim to the Wyoming Valley area, where skirmishes (called the Yankee-Pennamite wars) had been going on since the 1760s.

Pennsylvania moved rapidly toward independence after the British victory in the French and Indian War. The Proclamation of 1763, preventing settlement west of the Alleghenies, outraged western Pennsylvania, while the Stamp Act (1765), Townshend Acts (1767), and Tea Act (1773) incensed Philadelphians. Although the Continental Congress began meeting in Philadelphia in September 1774, Pennsylvania revolted reluctantly. In July 1776, only three Pennsylvania delegates to the Second Continental Congress voted for independence, while two were opposed and two absented themselves from the vote. Nevertheless, the Declaration of Independence was proclaimed from Independence Hall, Pennsylvania's State House, on 4 July 1776. As the headquarters of the Congress, Philadelphia was an important British target. The American defeat at the Battle of Brandywine Creek on 11 September 1777 led to the British occupation of the city. The provisional capital was moved first to Lancaster and then to York, where the Articles of Confederation were drafted. Following battles at Germantown and Whitemarsh, General George Washington set up winter headquarters at Valley Forge, remaining there from December 1777 to June 1778. Faced with the threat of French naval power intervening on behalf of the Americans, the British evacuated Philadelphia during the spring of 1778, and Congress reconvened there on 2 July. Philadelphia would serve as the US capital until 1783, and again from 1790 to 1800.

With independence, Pennsylvania adopted the state constitution of 1776, which established a powerful unicameral assembly elected annually by all freemen supporting the Revolution, a weak administrative supreme executive council (with a figurehead president), an appointed judiciary, and a council of censors meeting every seven years in order to take a census, reapportion the assembly, and review the constitutionality of state actions. In 1780, Pennsylvania passed the first state law abolishing slavery. Seven years later, Pennsylvania became the second state to ratify the US Constitution and join the Union. In 1790, Pennsylvania adopted a new constitution, modeled on the federal one, allowing all taxpaying males to vote. This document provided for a powerful governor, elected for a three-year term and eligible to succeed himself twice, a bicameral legislature (with senators elected every four years and a house elected annually), and an appointed judiciary.

Opposition to national taxes was evidenced by two disturbances in the 1790s. In 1794, western Pennsylvania settlers, opposed to a federal excise tax on distilled spirits, waged the Whiskey Rebellion. The insurrection was soon quashed by state troops under federal command. The levying of a federal property tax inspired the unsuccessful Fries Rebellion (1799) among Pennsylvania Germans.

By 1800, the first stages of industrialization were at hand. Pittsburgh's first iron furnace was built in 1792, and the increasing use of coal as fuel made its mining commercially feasible. The completion of the Main Line of Public Works, a canal and rail system connecting Philadelphia with Pittsburgh, was a major development of the early 19th century, which was otherwise a period of political turmoil and shifting party alliances.

By 1838, Pennsylvania adopted a new constitution curtailing the governor's power (he could serve only two three-year terms in a nine-year period), making many judgeships elective for specific terms, restricting the charter of banks, and disenfranchising black people. The 1840s saw not only an influx of Irish immigrants but also the rise of the Native American (Know-Nothing) Party, an anti-Catholic movement. The antislavery crusade, which gave birth to the Republican Party, influenced state politics during the following decade.

Although a Pennsylvania Democrat, James Buchanan, carried the state and won the presidency in 1856, the Republicans captured Pennsylvania for Abraham Lincoln in 1860, partly by their strong support for a protective tariff. Protectionism attracted Pennsylvania because, in addition to its enormously productive farms, it was heavily industrialized, leading the nation in the production of iron, lumber, textiles, and leather.

Pennsylvania rallied to the Union cause, supplying some 338,000 men, a figure exceeded only by New York. The state was the scene of the Battle of Gettysburg (1–3 July 1863), a turning point in the war for the Union cause. Under General George Gordon Meade, the Union troops (one-third of whom were Pennsylvanians) defeated Confederate forces under General Robert E. Lee, who was then forced to lead a retreat to Virginia.

The Civil War left the Republican Party dominant in Pennsylvania, but, in the postwar years, the Republicans were themselves dominated by industry, particularly the Pennsylvania Railroad. Between 1890 and 1900, the state was the nation's chief producer of coal, iron, and steel, and for much of that period the main source of petroleum and lumber. Farmers' sons and daughters joined immigrants from abroad in flocking to the anthracite and bituminous coal regions and to Philadelphia, Pittsburgh, and other urban centers to work in mines, mills, and factories. As the state's industrial wealth increased, education, journalism, literature, art, and architecture flourished in Philadelphia and Pittsburgh. The 1876 Centennial Exhibition at Philadelphia illustrated America's advancement in the arts and industry.

Pennsylvania adopted a reform constitution in 1873, increasing the size of the Senate and house to reduce the threat of bribery, prescribing rules to prevent treachery in legislation and fraud at the polls, equalizing taxation, limiting state indebtedness, restricting the governor to one four-year term in eight years, and creating the office of lieutenant governor. None of this, however, seriously hampered the Republican political machine, led by Simon Cameron, Matthew Quay, and Boies Penrose, which dominated the state from the 1860s to the 1920s. Though Progressive reforms were enacted in subsequent years, the Penrose machine grew ever more efficient, while industrial leaders—supported both by the Pennsylvania state government and by society at large—smashed labor's efforts to unite, particularly in the great steel strike of 1919.

During the nationwide boom years of the 1920s, Pennsylvania did little more than hold its own economically, and its industrial growth rate was low. The state's share of the nation's iron and steel output no longer exceeded that of the rest of the country combined. Coal, textiles, and agriculture—all basic to the state's economy—were depressed. When Penrose died in 1921, at least five factions sought to control the powerful Pennsylvania Republican Party. In this confusion, Gifford Pinchot, a Progressive disciple of Theodore Roosevelt, won the governorship for 1923–27 and reorganized the state's administration, but failed in his attempt to enforce prohibition and to regulate power utilities.

The disastrous depression of the 1930s brought major changes to Pennsylvania. Serving again as governor (1931–35), Pinchot fought for state and federal relief for the unemployed. The Republican organization's lack of enthusiasm for Pinchot and Progressivism helped revive the state Democratic Party long enough to secure the election in 1934—for the first time since 1890—of its gubernatorial nominee, George H. Earle. As governor, Earle successfully introduced a Little New Deal, supporting labor, regulating utilities, aiding farmers, and building public works. With government support, coal miners, steelworkers, and other organized labor groups emerged from the Depression strong enough to challenge industry. Full employment and prosperity returned to Pennsylvania with the unprecedented demands on it for steel, ships, munitions, and uniforms during World War II.

Despite their professed opposition to government control, the Republican administrations (1939–55) that succeeded the Earle regime espoused and even enlarged Earle's program. They regulated industry, improved education, and augmented social services, at the same time increasing state bureaucracy, budgets, and taxes. Markets, transportation, banks, factories, machinery, and skilled labor remained abundant. Two Democratic governors were able to attract new industries to the state during the 1950s and early 1960s. However, the economy was still not healthy in 1963, when Republican William W. Scranton entered the statehouse (1963–67). Scranton continued both to enlarge state responsibilities (through increased taxes) and to secure federal aid for economic and social programs. He was rewarded with four years of steady economic growth. Pennsylvania's unemployment level, second-highest in the nation from 1950 to 1962, had dropped below the national average by 1966. The 1873 constitution was extensively revised at a constitutional convention held in 1967–68, during the administration of Raymond P. Shafer (1967–71), Scranton's Republican successor.

Pennsylvania faced an unresolved financial crisis in 1971 when Democrat Milton J. Shapp became governor. During his first term (1971–75), Shapp weathered the storm by securing passage of a state income tax. He virtually eliminated state patronage by signing union contracts covering state employees. Not only did he continue to attract business to Pennsylvania, but he also championed the consumer with no-fault auto insurance, adopted in 1974. Shapp's second term, however, was wrecked by his pursuit of the 1976 presidential nomination and by rampant corruption among Pennsylvania Democrats. Shapp's successor, Republican Richard L. Thornburgh, had scarcely been seated in the governor's chair before the release of radioactive gases resulting from the malfunction of one of the two nuclear reactors at Three Mile Island in March 1979 confronted him—and others—with vexing questions concerning the safety and wisdom of nuclear power. Nevertheless, in September 1985, during Thornburgh's second term, and following six years of cleanup of radioactive waste, the undamaged reactor at Three Mile Island was restarted.

In the mid-1980s, Pennsylvania found itself confronted with the problem of completing the transition from a manufacturing to a service economy. While some parts of the state, namely southeastern Pennsylvania and Philadelphia, had successfully negotiated the transition, the economies of Pittsburgh, Lehigh Valley, Scranton, and Wilkes-Barre remained centered on the depressed steel and coal industries. Under Governor Robert Casey, who took office in 1987, Pennsylvania created an organization called the Governor's Response Team to assist ailing industries in the state. The team helped companies obtain low-interest loans and subsidized companies that sought to retrain their workers. In the first year of its existence, the team reached out to assist 214 companies, saved 10,000 existing jobs, and created 10,000 new ones.

In the mid-1990s, steel was no longer the mainstay of industry in Pennsylvania, although the state still led the nation in production of specialty steel. Important manufacturing sectors included food processing and chemicals, especially pharmaceuticals. Philadelphia had become a center for high-technology industries, while Pittsburgh was a mecca for corporate headquarters. By 2000 the state's economy was described as "relentlessly strong" by one newspaper, and legislators considered $643.5 million in tax cuts to residents and businesses along with increased spending in education and health care. As in many other regions of the nation, one of the by-products of Pennsylvania's robust economy was urban sprawl. A landmark in the anti-sprawl movement, in June 2000 Republican Governor Tom Ridge signed into law a plan that encouraged local governments to work together, allowed them to determine growth areas, and required state agencies to comply with community development guidelines.

In 1996 Governor Ridge approved the deregulation of the state's electrical utilities. Four years later, a report indicated the move had helped the economy (by lower consumer bills) but would result in lower tax revenues (due to restructuring and lower prices). While computer models forecasted that by 2004 reductions in electric rates under deregulation would lead to $1.9 billion in additional economic output, a $1.4-billion increase in personal income, and 36,000 new jobs, legislators had not yet addressed the projected shortfall in tax revenues, which would affect public transportation and municipalities.

The state remained one of the nation's most populous, ranking fifth both in the 1990 census and 1995 estimates, before slipping to sixth (with over 12.2 million people) in 2000. The July 2004 population was 12.4 million, still ranking sixth in the nation.

Following the 11 September 2001 terrorist attacks on the United States, President George Bush proposed the creation of a cabinet-level Department of Homeland Security. Former Governor Tom Ridge was named first secretary of the department.

Democratic Governor Ed Rendell, elected in 2002, was the first former Philadelphia mayor to become Pennsylvania governor in 90 years. Rendell pledged to lower property taxes by one-third during his first year in office, raise income taxes, and to provide prescription drug coverage for senior citizens. He favored the introduction of slot machines at the state's racetracks and increasing school spending. In 2003, Pennsylvania faced a $2.4 billion budget deficit for fiscal year 2003/04.

Pennsylvania's 2005 budget was $22 billion; and the state's budget had been balanced. Governor Rendell was implementing his "Plan for a New Pennsylvania," by increasing education funding; passing an economic stimulus package to revitalize towns and communities; passing legislation to reduce property taxes; and expanding Pennsylvania's PACE and PACENET program to provide seniors with prescription drug coverage.

12 STATE GOVERNMENT

The 1873 constitution, substantially reshaped by a constitutional convention in 1967–68, is the foundation of state government in Pennsylvania. Between 1968 and January 2005, 30 amendments had been adopted.

The General Assembly consists of a 50-member Senate, elected to staggered four-year terms, and a 203-member House of Representatives, elected every two years. Regular sessions are two-years and begin on the first Tuesday in January of the odd-numbered year. The session ends on November 30 of the even-numbered year. Each calendar receives its own legislative number. Special sessions may be called by the majority petition of each house. To qualify for the General Assembly, a person must have been a state resident for four years and a district resident for at least one year; senators must be at least 25 years old, representatives at least 21. The legislative salary was $66,203.55 in 2004.

As head of the executive branch and chief executive officer of the state, the governor of Pennsylvania has the power to appoint heads of administrative departments, boards, and commissions, to approve or veto legislation, to grant pardons, and to command the state's military forces. The governor, who may serve no more than two four-year terms in succession, must be a US citizen, a qualified voter, be at least 30 years old, and have been a Pennsylvania resident for at least seven years before election. Elected with the governor is the lieutenant governor, who serves as president of the Senate and chairman of the board of pardons, and assumes the powers of the governor if the governor becomes unable to continue in that office. As of December 2004, the governor's salary was $155,753.

Other state elected officials are the auditor general, who oversees all state financial transactions; the state treasurer, who receives and keeps records of all state funds; and the attorney general, who heads the Department of Justice. All other department heads, or secretaries, are appointed by the governor and confirmed by a majority of the Senate.

A bill may be introduced in either house of the General Assembly. After the measure is passed by majority vote in each house, the governor has 10 days including Sundays (or 30 days, including Sundays, if the legislature has adjourned) in which to sign it, refuse to sign it (in which case it automatically becomes law), or veto it. Vetoes may be overridden by a two-thirds vote of the elected members of each house. A bill becomes effective 60 days after enactment.

A proposed constitutional amendment must be approved by a majority of both house and Senate members in two successive legislatures before it can be placed on the ballot. If approved by a majority of the voters in a general election, the amendment then becomes part of the constitution.

To vote in state elections a person must be a US citizen for at least one month before the next election, at least 18 years old, and a resident of Pennsylvania and of the precinct for at least 30 days preceding the election. Restrictions apply to convicted felons.

13 POLITICAL PARTIES

The Republican Party totally dominated Pennsylvania politics from 1860, when the first Republican governor was elected, to the early 1930s. During this period, there were 16 Republican and only two Democratic administrations. Most of the Republicans were staunchly probusiness, though one Republican Progressive, Gifford Pinchot, was elected governor in 1922 and again in 1930. A Democrat, George Earle, won the governorship in 1934, in the depths of the Depression, but from 1939 through 1955, Republicans again held the office without interruption. Only since the mid-1950s has Pennsylvania emerged as a two-party state, with Democrats electing governors in 1954, 1958, 1970, 1974, 1986 and 1990, and Republicans winning the governorships in 1962, 1966, 1978, 1982, and 1994. In 1998, Tom Ridge, the Republican first elected to the office in 1994, won a second term as governor. He was named the first secretary of the newly created Department of Homeland Security in November 2002, after having served as the first administrator of the Office of Homeland Security from September 2001. In 2002, Democrat Ed Rendell was elected governor.

Both US Senate seats were held by Republicans from 1968 to 1991. In November of 1991, a little-known Democrat and former college president named Harris Wofford defeated former governor Richard Thornburgh for the seat of Senator John Heinz, who died in 1991. In 1994, Republican Rick Santorum, a congressman from the Pittsburgh area, defeated Wofford; Santorum was reelected in 2000. Pennsylvania's other senator, Republican Arlen Specter, was elected to his fifth term in 2004. In 2005, Pennsylvania's 19 US House seats were held by 7 Democrats and 12 Republicans. In mid-2005, there were 30 Republicans and 20 Democrats in the state Senate, and 110 Republicans and 93 Democrats in the state House.

Democratic voters were heavily concentrated in metropolitan Philadelphia and Pittsburgh. Pennsylvania, a pivotal state for Jimmy Carter in 1976, was swept by the Republican tide in the 1980 presidential election; Ronald Reagan, the Republican nominee, won nearly 50% of the popular vote. In 1984, President Reagan received 53% of the popular vote, while Democrat Walter Mondale received 46%. In 1988, Republican and former vice president George Bush won 51% of the popular vote. Democratic nominee Bill Clinton garnered 45% of the vote in 1992, and in 1996, Clinton won 49% of the vote. In 2000, Democrat Al Gore won 51% of the vote to Republican George W. Bush's 47%; Green Party candidate Ralph Nader won 2% of the vote. In 2004, Democrat John Kerry won 50.8% of vote to incumbent President Bush's 48.6%. In 2004 there were 8,367,000 registered voters. In 1998, 48% of registered voters were Democratic, 42% Republican, and 9% unaffili-

Pennsylvania Presidential Vote by Political Parties, 1948–2004

YEAR	ELECTORAL VOTE	PENN. WINNER	DEMOCRAT	REPUBLICAN	PROGRESSIVE	SOCIALIST	PROHIBITION	SOC. LABOR
1948	35	Dewey (R)	1,752,426	1,902,197	55,161	11,325	10,538	1,461
						SOC. WORKERS		
1952	32	*Eisenhower (R)	2,146,269	2,415,789	4,222	1,508	8,951	1,377
1956	32	*Eisenhower (R)	1,981,769	2,585,252	—	2,035	—	7,447
1960	32	*Kennedy (D)	2,556,282	2,439,956	—	2,678	—	7,158
1964	29	*Johnson (D)	3,130,954	1,673,657	—	10,456	—	5,092
					PEACE/FREEDOM		AMERICAN IND.	
1968	29	Humphrey (D)	2,259,403	2,090,017	7,821	4,862	378,582	4,977
								AMERICAN
1972	27	*Nixon (R)	1,796,951	2,714,521	—	4,639	—	70,593
					COMMUNIST			US LABOR
1976	27	*Carter (D)	2,328,677	2,205,604	1,891	3,009	25,344	2,744
						LIBERTARIAN	SOC. WORKERS	
1980	27	*Reagan (R)	1,937,540	2,261,872	5,184	33,263	20,291	—
1984	25	*Reagan (R)	2,228,131	2,584,323	21,628	6,982	—	—
					CONSUMER		NEW ALLIANCE	POPULIST
1988	25	*Bush (R)	2,194,944	2,300,087	19,158	12,051	4,379	3,444
								IND. (Perot)
1992	23	*Clinton (D)	2,239,164	1,791,164	—	21,477	4,661	902,667
1996	23	*Clinton (D)	2,215,819	1,801,169	—	28,000	—	430,984
					GREEN		REFORM	
2000	23	Gore (D)	2,485,967	2,281,127	103,392	11,248	16,023	—
							WRITE-IN (Nader)	CONSTITUTION (Peroutka)
2004	21	Kerry (D)	2,938,095	2,793,847	6,319	21,185	2,656	6,318

*Won US presidential election.

ated or members of other parties. The state had 21 electoral votes in the 2004 presidential election, a loss of 2 votes over 2000.

14 LOCAL GOVERNMENT

As of 2005, Pennsylvania had 67 counties, 1,018 municipal governments, 501 public school districts, and 1,885 special districts. In 2002, there were 1,546 townships.

Under home-rule laws, municipalities may choose to draft and amend their own charter. Pennsylvania counties are responsible for state law enforcement, judicial administration, and the conduct of state elections: counties also are involved in public health, regional planning, and solid waste disposal. Counties can also maintain hospitals, homes for the aged, community colleges, libraries, and other community facilities. The chief governing body in each county is a three-member board of commissioners, each elected to a four-year term. Other elected officials generally include the sheriff, district attorney, notary, clerk of courts, register of wills, recorder of deeds, jury commissioners, auditor or controller, and treasurer. Among the appointed officials is a public defender. Counties are divided by law into nine classes, depending on population. Philadelphia's county offices were merged with the city government in 1952, pursuant to the home-rule charter of 1951.

There are four classes of cities. The only first-class city, Philadelphia, is governed by a mayor and city council. Other elected officials are the controller, district attorney, sheriff, register of wills, and three city commissioners. Major appointed officials include managing director, director of finance, city representative, and city solicitor. Both Pittsburgh and Scranton (classified as second-class cities) are governed under mayor-council systems that give the mayors strong discretionary powers.

Boroughs are governed under mayor-council systems giving the council strong powers. Other elected officials are the tax assessor, tax collector, and auditor or controller. The state's first-class townships, located mostly in metropolitan areas, are governed by elected commissioners who serve four-year overlapping terms. Second-class townships, most of them located in rural areas, have three supervisors who are elected at large to six-year terms.

In 2005, local government accounted for about 416,829 full-time (or equivalent) employment positions.

15 STATE SERVICES

To address the continuing threat of terrorism and to work with the federal Department of Homeland Security, homeland security in Pennsylvania operates under executive order; a homeland security director was appointed to oversee the state's homeland security activities.

Executive agencies under the governor's jurisdiction are the Advisory Commission on African American Affairs, the Advisory Commission on Asian American Affairs, Advisory Commission on Latino Affairs, Commission for Children and Families, Green Government Council, Sportsmen's Advisory Council, Office of Inspector General, Office of Public Liaison, Pennsylvania Rural Development Council, and the Council on the Arts. The State Ethics Commission enforces the Pennsylvania Public Official and Employee Ethics Act. The Liquor Control Board operates state liquor stores and claims to be the world's largest single purchaser of liquors and wines.

The Department of Education administers the school laws of Pennsylvania, oversees community colleges, licenses and regulates private schools, and administers the state public library program. Educational policy is the province of the State Board of Education, a panel with 17 members appointed by the governor to six-year terms. Also within the department are various boards that make policies for and review developments within the state's higher educational system.

The Department of Transportation maintains state-operated highways, mass transit, rail service, and aviation facilities. The Pennsylvania Turnpike Commission also has transport-related responsibilities. Agencies and departments providing health and welfare services include the Department of Aging, Department of Community and Economic Development, and Department of Health. All public assistance, social service, mental health, and developmental disability programs are administered by the Department of Public Welfare.

The Office of Attorney General has divisions on criminal law, legal services, and public protection. The National Guard, Bureau for Veterans' Affairs, and state veterans' homes are under the Department of Military and Veterans Affairs; the Pennsylvania State Police is a separate state agency. The Pennsylvania Commission on Crime and Delinquency allocates federal funds for crime control, juvenile justice, and delinquency prevention. The Pennsylvania Emergency Management Agency (formerly the State Council of Civil Defense) provides assistance in emergency situations resulting from natural or manmade disasters.

All state park and forest preservation programs, ecological and geological resource information programs, and community conservation partnerships are under the supervision of the Department of Conservation and Natural Resources and the Department of Environmental Protection. Land and water environmental protection programs are under the supervision of the Department of Environmental Protection. The Department of Labor and Industry administers safety, employment, and industrial standards; operates vocational rehabilitation and workers' compensation programs; and mediates labor disputes.

16 JUDICIAL SYSTEM

Since 1968, all Pennsylvania courts have been organized under the Unified Judicial System. The highest court in the state is the Supreme Court, which, having been established in 1722, is the oldest appellate court in the United States. The Court consists of 7 justices, elected to 10-year terms. The justice with the longest continuous service on the court automatically becomes chief justice. In general, the Supreme Court hears appeals from the commonwealth court. A separate appellate court, called the Superior Court, hears appeals from the courts of common pleas. There are 15 superior court judges, also elected to 10-year terms, as are the commonwealth and common pleas, which have original jurisdiction over all civil and criminal cases not otherwise specified.

In counties other than Philadelphia, misdemeanors and other minor offenses are tried by district justices, formerly known as justices of the peace. The Philadelphia municipal court consists of 22 judges, all of whom must be lawyers; the six judges who constitute the Philadelphia traffic court need not be lawyers. Pittsburgh's magistrates' court, appointed by the mayor, comprises 5 to 8 judges who need not be lawyers. All of Pennsylvania's judges, except traffic court judges and Pittsburgh's magistrates, are initially elected on a partisan ballot and thereafter on a nonpartisan retention ballot.

As of 31 December 2004, a total of 40,963 prisoners were held in Pennsylvania's state and federal prisons, an increase from 40,890 of 0.2% from the previous year. As of year-end 2004, a total of 1,827 inmates were female, up from 1,823 or 0.2% from the year before. Among sentenced prisoners (one year or more), Pennsylvania had an incarceration rate of 329 per 100,000 population in 2004.

According to the Federal Bureau of Investigation, Pennsylvania in 2004, had a violent crime rate (murder/nonnegligent manslaughter; forcible rape; robbery; aggravated assault) of 411.1 reported incidents per 100,000 population, or a total of 50,998 reported incidents. Crimes against property (burglary; larceny/theft; and motor vehicle theft) in that same year totaled 299,611 reported incidents or 2,415 reported incidents per 100,000 people. Pennsylvania has a death penalty, of which lethal injection is the sole method of execution. From 1976 through 5 May 2006, the state has carried out three executions, the last of which took place in July 1999. As of 1 January 2006, Pennsylvania had 231 inmates on death row.

In 2003, Pennsylvania spent $218,059,061 on homeland security, an average of $18 per state resident.

[17] ARMED FORCES

In 2004, there were 2,837 active-duty military personnel and 25,076 civilian personnel stationed in Pennsylvania. The US Army War College is in Carlisle, and there are army depots in Chambersburg, New Cumberland, and Scranton. Defense contracts worth more than $6.2 billion were awarded to Pennsylvania firms in 2004, tenth-highest in the United States for that year. In addition, there was another $2.9 billion in payroll outlays by the Department of Defense.

In 2003, there were 1,145,919 veterans living in the state, of whom 221,316 served in World War II; 149,673 in the Korean conflict; 335,124 during the Vietnam era; and 124,852 in the Gulf War. In 2004, the Veterans Administration expended more than $2.4 billion in pensions, medical assistance, and other major veterans' benefits.

As of 31 October 2004, the Pennsylvania State Police employed 4,227 full-time sworn officers.

[18] MIGRATION

When William Penn's followers arrived in Pennsylvania, they joined small groups of Dutch, Swedish, and Finnish immigrants who were already settled along the Delaware River. By 1685, 50% of Pennsylvania's European population was British. In 1683, the Frankfort Land Co. founded the Mennonite community of Germantown on 6,000 acres (2,400 hectares) east of the Schuylkill River. One hundred years later there were 120,000 Germans, about one-fourth of the state's census population; the Moravians, from Saxony, settled primarily in Bethlehem and Nazareth, and the Amish in Lancaster and Reading.

During the 19th century, more immigrants settled in Pennsylvania than in any other state except New York. Between 1840 and 1890, the anthracite mines in east-central Pennsylvania attracted the Irish, Welsh, and Slavs; Scots-Irish, Italian, Austrian, Hungar-ian, and Polish (and, after 1880, Russian) immigrants worked the western coal fields. The cities attracted Italian, French, and Slavic workers. East European and Russian Jews settled in Philadelphia and Pittsburgh between 1882 and 1900. By the turn of the century, the urban population surpassed the rural population.

During the 20th century, these patterns have been reversed. The trend among whites, particularly since World War II, has been to move out—from the cities to the suburbs, and from Pennsylvania to other states. Blacks, who began entering the state first as slaves and then as freemen, continued to migrate to the larger cities until the early 1970s, when a small out-migration began. Overall, between 1940 and 1980, Pennsylvania lost a net total of 1,759,000 residents through migration; it lost an additional 98,000 residents between 1980 and 1983. From 1985 to 1990, Pennsylvania had a net migration gain of nearly 21,000. Between 1990 and 1998, the state had a net loss of 219,000 in domestic migration but a net gain of 104,000 in international migration. In 1996, about 3% of Pennsylvania's population (421,000) was foreign-born. In 1998, 11,942 foreign immigrants arrived in the state; of these, the greatest number, 1,127, came from India. Pennsylvania's overall population increased only 1% between 1990 and 1998. In the period 2000–05, net international migration was 102,470 and net internal migration was -28,012, for a net gain of 74,458 people.

[19] INTERGOVERNMENTAL COOPERATION

Pennsylvania participates in such regional bodies as the Atlantic States Marine Fisheries Commission, Susquehanna River Basin Commission, Ohio River Valley Water Sanitation Commission, Wheeling Creek Watershed Protection and Flood Prevention Commission, and Great Lakes Commission. In 1985, Pennsylvania, seven other Great Lakes states, and the Canadian provinces of Quebec and Ontario signed the Great Lakes Compact to protect the lakes' water reserves. Other agreements include the Mid-Atlantic Fishery Management Council, Interstate Mining Compact Commission, Ohio River Basin Commission, Appalachian Regional Commission, Brandywine River Valley Compact, New Jersey-Pennsylvania Turnpike Bridge Compact, Potomac Valley Conservancy District, Pymatuning Lake Compact, and the Tri-State Agreement on the Chesapeake Bay.

Some of the most important interstate agreements concern commerce and development along the Delaware River. The Delaware River Basin Commission involves the governors of Delaware, New Jersey, New York, and Pennsylvania in the utilization and conservation of the Delaware and its surrounding areas. Through the Delaware River Port Authority, New Jersey and Pennsylvania control an interstate mass transit system. The two states also are signatories to the Delaware River Joint Toll Bridge Compact and Delaware Valley Regional Planning Commission. During fiscal year 2005, Pennsylvania received $15.561 billion in federal grants (fifth among the 50 states). Federal grants were estimated at $16.324 billion in fiscal year 2006, and an estimated $16.846 billion in fiscal year 2007.

[20] ECONOMY

Dominated by coal and steel, Pennsylvania is an important contributor to the national economy, but its role has diminished considerably since the early 20th Century. The state reached the height of its economic development by 1920, when its western oil wells and coal fields made it the nation's leading energy producer. By that time, however, Pennsylvania's oil production was already on the decline, and demand for coal had slackened. No longer did the state dominate US steel production. Pennsylvania produced 60% of the United States total in 1900, but only 30% in 1940 and 24% in 1960. Philadelphia, a diversified manufacturing center, began to lose many of its textile and apparel factories. The Great Depression of the 1930s hastened the decline. Industrial production in 1932 was less than half the 1929 level, and mineral production, already in a slump throughout the 1920s, dropped more than 50% in value between 1929 and 1933. By 1933, some 37% of the state's workforce was unemployed.

Massive federal aid programs and the production of munitions stimulated employment during the 1940s, but some sections of the state have never fully recovered from the damage of the Depression years. Declines in coal and steel production and the loss of other industries to the Sunbelt have not yet been entirely countered by gains in other sectors, despite a steady expansion of machinery production, increased tourism, and the growth of service-related industries and trade. Manufacturing, the second-largest employer in Pennsylvania—providing one million jobs in the 1990s—lost about 350,000 jobs during the 1980s. The outlook for the steel industry remains uncertain, as Pennsylvania's aging factories face severe competition from foreign producers. Services, in contrast, recorded about as much growth as manufacturing lost. The fastest growing service industries were concentrated in the medical and health fields. Coming into the 21st century, the annual growth rate for Pennsylvania's economy averaged 4.75% (1998 to 2000), which was then more than halved to 2.2% in the national recession of 2001. Manufacturing output, which grew 5.2% from 1997 to 2000 (although decreasing as a share of total output from 20.1% to 18.4%), fell 7.2% in 2001 (decreasing its share to 16.7%). The strongest growth in output was in various service sectors, with output from general services up 28% from 1997 to 2001; from financial services, up 22.1%, and from trade, up 19.5%.

In 2004, Pennsylvania's gross state product (GSP) was $468.089 billion, of which manufacturing (durable and nondurable goods) accounted for the largest share at $75.281 billion or 16% of GSP, followed by the real estate sector at $55.986 billion (11.9% of GSP), and healthcare and social assistance services at $42.035 billion (8.9% of GSP). In that same year, there were an estimated 927,369 small businesses in Pennsylvania. Of the 275,853 businesses that had employees, an estimated total of 271,410 or 98.4% were small companies. An estimated 33,188 new businesses were established in the state in 2004, up 6.3% from the year before. Business terminations that same year came to 34,507, up 4.8% from 2003. There were 1,138 business bankruptcies in 2004, down 4.6% from the previous year. In 2005, the state's personal bankruptcy (Chapter 7 and Chapter 13) filing rate was 472 filings per 100,000 people, ranking Pennsylvania as the 31st highest in the nation.

21INCOME

In 2005 Pennsylvania had a gross state product (GSP) of $487 billion which accounted for 3.9% of the nation's gross domestic product and placed the state at number 6 in highest GSP among the 50 states and the District of Columbia.

According to the Bureau of Economic Analysis, in 2004 Pennsylvania had a per capita personal income (PCPI) of $33,312. This ranked 19th in the United States and was 101% of the national average of $33,050. The 1994–2004 average annual growth rate of PCPI was 4.0%. Pennsylvania had a total personal income (TPI) of $412,890,270,000, which ranked sixth in the United States and reflected an increase of 5.1% from 2003. The 1994–2004 average annual growth rate of TPI was 4.2%. Earnings of persons employed in Pennsylvania increased from $291,978,764,000 in 2003 to $308,068,372,000 in 2004, an increase of 5.5%. The 2003–04 national change was 6.3%.

The US Census Bureau reports that the three-year average median household income for 2002 to 2004 in 2004 dollars was $44,286 compared to a national average of $44,473. During the same period an estimated 10.4% of the population was below the poverty line as compared to 12.4% nationwide.

22LABOR

According to the Bureau of Labor Statistics (BLS), in April 2006 the seasonally adjusted civilian labor force in Pennsylvania 6,318,700, with approximately 299,400 workers unemployed, yielding an unemployment rate of 4.7%, compared to the national average of 4.7% for the same period. Preliminary data for the same period placed nonfarm employment at 5,747,200. Since the beginning of the BLS data series in 1976, the highest unemployment rate recorded in Pennsylvania was 12.9% in March 1983. The historical low was 4% in March 2000. Preliminary nonfarm employment data by occupation for April 2006 showed that approximately 4.4% of the labor force was employed in construction; 11.6% in manufacturing; 19.7% in trade, transportation, and public utilities; 5.8% in financial activities; 11.6% in professional and business services; 18.3% in education and health services; 8.5% in leisure and hospitality services; and 13% in government.

The history of unionism in Pennsylvania dates back to 1724 when Philadelphia workers organized the Carpenters' Company, the first crafts association in the colonies. Its Carpenters' Hall gained fame as the site of the First Continental Congress in 1774; the carpenters were also responsible for the first strike in the United States in 1791. The nation's first labor union was organized by Philadelphia shoemakers in 1794. By 1827, the Mechanics' Union of Trade Associations, the country's first central labor body, was striking for a 10-hour workday and was the impetus behind the formation of the Organized Workingman's Party. Nine years later there were no fewer than 58 labor organizations in Philadelphia and 13 in Pittsburgh, but the Panic of 1837 resulted in a sharp decline of union strength and membership for many years. Union ranks were further depleted by the Civil War, despite the efforts of Pennsylvania labor leader William Sylvis, who later became an important figure in the national labor reform movement. After the Civil War ended, the Noble Order of the Knights of Labor was established in Philadelphia in 1869.

The coal fields were sites of violent organizing struggles. In 1835, low wages and long hours sparked the first general mine strikes, which, like a walkout by anthracite miners in 1849, proved unsuccessful. During the 1850s and 1870s, a secret society known as the Molly Maguires led uprisings in the anthracite fields, but its influence ended after the conviction of its leaders for terrorist activities. The demise of the Molly Maguires did not stop the violence, however. Eleven persons were killed during a mine strike at Connellsville in 1891, and a strike by Luzerne County miners in

1897 resulted in 20 deaths. Finally, a five-month walkout by anthracite miners in 1902 led to increased pay, reduced hours, and an agreement to employ arbitration to settle disputes.

Steelworkers, burdened for many years by 12-hour workdays and 7-day workweeks, called several major strikes during this period. An 1892 lockout at Andrew Carnegie's Homestead steel mill led to a clash between workers and Pinkerton guards hired by the company. After several months, the strikers went back to work, their resources exhausted. A major strike in 1919, involving half of the nation's steelworkers, shut down the industry for more than three months, but it too produced no immediate gains. The Steel Workers Organizing Committee, later the United Steelworkers, finally won a contract and improved benefits from US Steel in 1937, although other steel companies held out until the early 1940s, when the Supreme Court forced recognition of the union.

The US Department of Labor's Bureau of Labor Statistics reported that in 2005, a total of 753,000 of Pennsylvania's 5,456,000 employed wage and salary workers were formal members of a union. This represented 13.8% of those so employed, down from 15% in 2004, but still above the national average of 12%. Overall in 2005, a total of 818,000 workers (15%) in Pennsylvania were covered by a union or employee association contract, which includes those workers who reported no union affiliation. Pennsylvania is one of 28 states that do not have a right-to-work law.

As of 1 March 2006, Pennsylvania had a state-mandated minimum wage rate of $5.15 per hour. In 2004, women in the state accounted for 47.5% of the employed civilian labor force.

23 AGRICULTURE

Pennsylvania ranked 20th among the 50 states in agricultural income in 2005, with receipts of $4.7 billion.

During the colonial period, German immigrants farmed the fertile land in southeastern Pennsylvania, making the state a leader in agricultural production. Unlike farmers in other states, who worked the soil until it was depleted and then moved on, these farmers carefully cultivated the same plots year after year, using crop rotation techniques that kept the land productive. As late as 1840, the state led the nation in wheat production, thanks in part to planting techniques developed and largely confined to southeastern Pennsylvania. However, westward expansion and the subsequent fall in agricultural prices hurt farming in the state, and many left the land for industrial jobs in the cities. Today, most farms in the state produce crops and dairy items for Philadelphia and other major eastern markets.

As of 2004 there were about 58,200 farms averaging 132 acres (54 hectares) in size. The leading farm areas were all in southeastern Pennsylvania. Lancaster County is by far the most productive, followed by the counties of Chester, Berks, Franklin, and Lebanon. These five counties account for over 40% of state agricultural sales.

Field crops in 2004 included: hay, 4,296,000 tons (valued at $380 million); corn for grain, 137.2 million bushels (valued at $274.4 million); soybeans, 10.5 million bushels (valued at $97.5 million); wheat, 6.6 million bushels (valued at $21.8 million); oats, 6.1 million bushels (valued at $10.3 million); and barley, 3.4 million (valued at $7.7 million).

Pennsylvania is a major producer of mushrooms and greenhouse and nursery crops. Other crops are fresh vegetables, potatoes, strawberries, apples, pears, peaches, grapes, and cherries (sweet and tart). The value of fresh market vegetables exceeded $70.4 million in 2004; the value of vegetables for processing, $10.9 million.

24 ANIMAL HUSBANDRY

Most of Pennsylvania's farm income stems from livestock production, primarily in Lancaster County.

In 2005, there were an estimated 1.63 million cattle and calves, valued at $1.8 billion. During 2004, there were around 1.1 million hogs and pigs, worth $106.9 million. In 2003 the state produced 7 million lb (3.2 million kg) of sheep and lambs, which brought in $7.5 million in gross income.

Pennsylvania is a leading producer of chickens in the United States, selling 44.2 million lb (20 million kg) in 2003. An estimated 10.4 billion lb (4.7 billion kg) of milk (fourth among the 50 states) was produced from 575,000 milk cows in the same year.

25 FISHING

There is very little commercial fishing in Pennsylvania. In 2004, the commercial catch was only 14,000 lb (640 kg), worth $38,000. In 2003, there were 5 processing and 34 wholesale plants in the state with about 976 employees.

The state's many lakes and streams make it a popular area for sport fishing. All recreational fishing in the state is supervised by the Fish Commission, established in 1866 and one of the oldest conservation agencies in the United States. Walleye, trout, and salmon were the leading species. There are two national fish hatcheries in the state. In 2004, Pennsylvania issued 1,018,756 sport fishing licenses.

26 FORESTRY

Pennsylvania's richly diverse forests dominate the landscape, covering 58% (16,585,000 acres/6,712,000 hectares) of the total land area. For the northeastern United States, public ownership is high at 26% (4,403,000 acres/1,782,000 hectares), mostly owned by the commonwealth. The 1989 Forest Inventory identified 90 different tree species; most of the 2,076 species of native vascular plants are forest related. Eagles and ospreys are making a comeback, there is a resident elk herd (the largest east of the Mississippi), coyotes have moved in, and river otters and fishers have been reintroduced. Some species of forest birds which are experiencing declines regionally have increasing populations in Pennsylvania's forests.

The forest products industry and forest-based recreation are very important to Pennsylvania's economy. Ten commercial tree species dominate the average annual net growth, producing 74% of the wood grown each year. In 2004, the total lumber production was 1,143 million board feet, or 2.3% of the US total.

Camping, fishing, hiking, and hunting are traditional Pennsylvania pastimes and the clean streams, vistas, and flora and fauna of the forest provide a focal point for these activities.

27 MINING

According to preliminary data from the US Geological Survey (USGS), the estimated value of nonfuel mineral production by Pennsylvania in 2003 was $1.26 billion, a decrease from 2002 of about 2%. The USGS data ranked Pennsylvania as 10th among the

50 states by the total value of its nonfuel mineral production, accounting for over 3% of total US output.

According to the preliminary data for 2003, by descending order of value, crushed stone, cement (portland and masonry), and construction sand and gravel were the state's top nonfuel minerals by value. Collectively, these commodities accounted for almost 92% of all nonfuel mineral output, by value. By volume, Pennsylvania in 2003 was third in portland cement, fourth (out of four states) in the production of tripoli, and sixth in the production of masonry cement and lime.

Preliminary figures for 2003 showed that crushed stone production totaled 96 million metric tons, which had a value of $547 million, while portland cement output that year totaled 6.13 million metric tons and was valued at an estimated $457 million. Construction sand and gravel production in 2003 totaled 18 million metric tons and was worth $115 million. Lime output that same year stood at 1.25 million metric tons and was worth $91.3 million.

Although no metals were mined in Pennsylvania, the state was the nation's fifth leading producer of raw steel, processing 5.53 million metric tons of raw steel in 2003.

28 ENERGY AND POWER

As of 2003, Pennsylvania had 85 electrical power service providers, of which 35 were publicly owned and 13 were cooperatives. Of the remainder, 11 were investor owned, 17 were generation-only suppliers and nine were delivery-only providers. As of that same year there were 5,747,853 retail customers. Of that total, 5,161,605 received their power from investor-owned service providers. Cooperatives accounted for 207,495 customers, while publicly owned providers had 83,030 customers. Generation-only suppliers had 295,723 customers. There was no customer data on the number of delivery-only customers.

Total net summer generating capability by the state's electrical generating plants in 2003 stood at 42.368 million kW, with total production that same year at 206.349 billion kWh. Of the total amount generated, 14.6% came from electric utilities, with the remaining 85.4% coming from independent producers and combined heat and power service providers. The largest portion of all electric power generated, 116.009 billion kWh (56.2%), came from coal-fired plants, with nuclear power generation in second place at 74.360 billion kWh (36%). Other renewable power sources, pumped storage facilities, hydroelectric, petroleum, natural gas, and other types of gas fueled plants accounted for the remaining production.

Operating nuclear plants in Pennsylvania as of 2006 were: Peach Bottom in York County; Beaver Valley at Shippingsport, Susquehanna in Luzerne County; Limerick, near Philadelphia; and Unit 1 of the Three Mile Island plant near Harrisburg.

The nation's first oil well was struck in Titusville in 1859, and for the next five decades Pennsylvania led the nation in oil production. As of 2004, Pennsylvania had proven crude oil reserves of 12 million barrels, less than 1% of all proven US reserves, while output that same year averaged 7,000 barrels per day. Including federal offshore domains, the state that year ranked 24th (23rd excluding federal offshore) in proven reserves and 22nd (21st excluding federal offshore) in production among the 31 producing states. In 2004 Pennsylvania had 16,242 producing oil wells, accounting for

under 1% of all US production. As of 2005, the state's five refineries had a combined crude oil distillation capacity of 770,000 barrels per day.

In 2004, Pennsylvania had 44,227 producing natural gas and gas condensate wells. In that same year, marketed gas production (all gas produced excluding gas used for repressuring, vented and flared, and nonhydrocarbon gases removed) totaled 159.827 billion cu ft (4.5 billion cu m). As of 31 December 2004, proven reserves of dry or consumer-grade natural gas totaled 2,386 billion cu ft (67.76 billion cu m).

Virtually all the state's commercial oil and gas reserves lie beneath the Allegheny High Plateau, in western Pennsylvania.

Coal is the state's most valuable mineral commodity, accounting for more than two-thirds of all mine income. In 2004, Pennsylvania had 260 producing coal mines, 202 of which were surface operations and 58 were underground. Coal production that year totaled 65,996,000 short tons, up from 63,708,000 short tons in 2003. Of the total produced in 2004, underground mines accounted for most of the production at 53,224,000 short tons.

Pennsylvania is the only state to produce both anthracite (hard) and bituminous (soft or brown) coal. The state has a total of 66 anthracite mines (46 surface and 20 underground) and 194 bituminous (156 surface and 38 underground) mines. In 2004, anthracite production totaled 1,679,000 short tons, with bituminous output at 64,317,000 short tons.

Total recoverable coal reserves in 2004 totaled 614 million short tons. Of that total, recoverable anthracite reserves that year totaled 22 million short tons, while recoverable bituminous reserves were placed at 592 million short tons. Bituminous coal is mined in Washington, Clearfield, Greene, Cambria, Armstrong, Somerset, Clarion, Allegheny, and 19 other counties in the western part of the state. A anthracite mining is concentrated in Schuylkill, Luzerne, Lackawanna, Northumberland, Carbon, Columbia, Sullivan, and Dauphin counties in the east. One short ton equals 2,000 lb (0.907 metric tons).

29 INDUSTRY

At different times throughout its history, Pennsylvania has been the nation's principal producer of ships, iron, chemicals, lumber, oil, textiles, glass, coal, and steel. Although it is still a major manufacturing center, Pennsylvania's industrial leadership has diminished steadily during the 20th century.

The first major industry in colonial Pennsylvania was shipbuilding, centered in Philadelphia. Iron works, brick kilns, candle factories, and other small crafts industries also grew up around the city. By 1850, Philadelphia alone accounted for nearly half of Pennsylvania's manufacturing output, with an array of products including flour, preserved meats, sugar, textiles, shoes, furniture, iron, locomotives, pharmaceuticals, and books. The exploitation of the state's coal and oil resources and the discovery of new steel-making processes helped build Pittsburgh into a major industrial center.

According to the US Census Bureau's Annual Survey of Manufactures (ASM) for 2004, Pennsylvania's manufacturing sector covered some 21 product subsectors. The shipment value of all products manufactured in the state that same year was $190.370 billion. Of that total, chemical manufacturing accounted for the largest share at $29.876 billion. It was followed by food manufacturing at $23.707 billion; primary metal manufacturing at $17.760 billion; petroleum and coal product manufacturing at $17.471 billion; and fabricated metal product manufacturing at $15.090 billion.

In 2004, a total of 645,796 people in Pennsylvania were employed in the state's manufacturing sector, according to the ASM. Of that total, 457,003 were actual production workers. In terms of total employment, the fabricated metal product manufacturing industry accounted for the largest portion of all manufacturing employees with 85,795 (62,587 actual production workers). It was followed by food manufacturing, with 71,228 (51,734 actual production workers); machinery manufacturing, with 51,643 (32,815 actual production workers); plastics and rubber products manufacturing, with 44,095 (34,117 actual production workers); printing and related support activities, with 42,733 (31,705 actual production workers); and transportation equipment manufacturing, with 37,763 (27,124 actual production workers).

ASM data for 2004 showed that Pennsylvania's manufacturing sector paid $26.816 billion in wages. Of that amount, the fabricated metal product manufacturing sector accounted for the largest share at $3.402 billion. It was followed by food manufacturing at $2.468 billion; machinery manufacturing at $2.372 billion; primary metal manufacturing at $2.140 billion; and chemical manufacturing at $2.063 billion.

30 COMMERCE

A major component in Philadelphia's early economy, trade remains important to the state.

According to the 2002 Census of Wholesale Trade, Pennsylvania's wholesale trade sector had sales that year totaling $183.7 billion from 15,991 establishments. Wholesalers of durable goods accounted for 9,887 establishments, followed by nondurable goods wholesalers at 4,777 and electronic markets, agents, and brokers accounting for 1,327 establishments. Sales by durable goods wholesalers in 2002 totaled $77.5 billion, while wholesalers of nondurable goods saw sales of $83.2 billion. Electronic markets, agents, and brokers in the wholesale trade industry had sales of $22.9 billion.

In the 2002 Census of Retail Trade, Pennsylvania was listed as having 48,041 retail establishments with sales of $130.7 billion. The leading types of retail businesses by number of establishments were: food and beverage stores (6,949); clothing and clothing accessories stores (6,276); motor vehicle and motor vehicle parts dealers (5,465); miscellaneous store retailers (5,449); and gasoline stations (4,476). In terms of sales, motor vehicle and motor vehicle parts stores accounted for the largest share of retail sales at $33.1 billion, followed by food and beverage stores at $21.3 billion; general merchandise stores at $16.8 billion; nonstore retailers at $11.6 billion; gasoline stations at $9.6 billion; and building material/garden equipment and supplies dealers at $9.2 billion. A total of 661,993 people were employed by the retail sector in Pennsylvania that year.

During the colonial era, Philadelphia was one of the busiest Atlantic ports and the leading port for the lucrative Caribbean trade. Philadelphia remains one of the country's leading foreign trade centers. In 2005, total exports of Pennsylvania goods had a value of $22.2 billion (ninth in the United States).

31 CONSUMER PROTECTION

Consumer protection affairs in Pennsylvania are the responsibility of the Bureau of Consumer Protection, which is under the Office of Attorney General. The bureau investigates and mediates complaints, acts in an advisory position to the legislature on issues that would affect consumers, investigates claims of fraud and deception, and acts to promote consumer education. Also within the Office of Attorney General is the Charitable Trusts and Organizations section and the Office of Consumer Advocate, which is responsible for representing the state's consumers in matters that involve utility services. Pennsylvanians are encouraged to report instances of fraud, waste, or mismanagement of state funds through a toll-free telephone service run by the Auditor General. Additionally, the Department of Insurance and the Department of Banking protect state residents against insurance fraud and banking fraud, respectively.

When dealing with consumer protection issues, the state's Attorney General's Office can initiate civil and criminal proceedings; administer consumer protection and education programs; handle formal consumer complaints; and exercise broad subpoena powers. However, the Attorney General cannot represent the state before regulatory agencies. In antitrust actions, the Attorney General's Office can act on behalf of those consumers who are incapable of acting on their own; initiate damage actions on behalf of the state in state courts; initiate criminal proceedings; and represent counties, cities and other governmental entities in recovering civil damages under state or federal law.

The offices of the Bureau of Consumer Protection and of the Office of Consumer Advocate are located in Harrisburg. The Office of the Attorney General has regional offices in Allentown, Ebensburg, Erie, Harrisburg, Philadelphia, Pittsburgh and Scranton. County government consumer protection offices are located in Doylestown, Media, Norristown and West Chester.

32 BANKING

Philadelphia is the nation's oldest banking center, and Third Street, between Chestnut and Walnut, has been called the cradle of American finance. The first chartered commercial bank in the United States was the Bank of North America, granted its charter in Philadelphia by the federal government in December 1781 and by Pennsylvania in April 1782. The First Bank of the United States was headquartered in Philadelphia from its inception in 1791 to 1811, when its charter was allowed to expire. Its building was bought by Stephen Girard, a private banker whose new institution quickly became one of the nation's largest banks. Girard's bank was closed after he died in 1831, but a new Girard Bank was opened in 1832; it merged with Philadelphia National Bank in 1926.

By the early 1800s, Philadelphia had reached its zenith as the nation's financial center. It was the home of the Bank of Pennsylvania, founded in 1793; the Bank of Philadelphia (1804); the Farmers and Mechanics Bank (1809); the Philadelphia Savings Fund Society (1816), the first mutual savings bank; and, most powerful of all, the Second Bank of the United States (1816). After 1823, under the directorship of Nicholas Biddle, this bank became an international leader and the only rival to New York City's growing banking industry. When President Jackson vetoed the bank's recharter in 1831, Philadelphia lost its preeminence as a banking center.

Pittsburgh's rise to prominence during the late 1800s, was due in great part to the efforts of its most successful financier, Andrew Mellon. In March 1982, the state legalized multibank holding companies; subsequently, the Mellon Bank acquired Centre County Bank of State College, Girard Bank, and Northwest Bank. Other major institutions are: Pittsburgh National Bank, part of PNC Financial, and Philadelphia National Bank. First Pennsylvania, in financial difficulty for several years, was saved from possible failure early in 1980 through a loan package engineered by the Federal Deposit Insurance Corporation.

As of June 2005, Pennsylvania had 254 insured banks, savings and loans, and saving banks, plus 73 state-chartered and 579 federally chartered credit unions (CUs). Excluding the CUs, the Philadelphia-Camden-Wilmington market area accounted for the largest portion of the state's financial institutions and deposits in 2004, with 156 institutions and $221.259 billion in deposits. As of June 2005, CUs accounted for 6.2% of all assets held by all financial institutions in the state, or some $23.100 billion. Banks, savings and loans, and savings banks collectively accounted for the remaining 93.8% or $348.550 billion in assets held.

The median net interest margin (the difference between the lower rates offered to savers and the higher rates charged on loans) for the state's banks stood at 3.31% as of fourth quarter 2005, down from 3.37% in 2004 and 3.38% in 2003. Pennsylvania's banks' media past-due/nonaccrual loan to total loan ratios in fourth quarter 2005 stood at 1.26%, down from 1.36% in 2004 and 1.51% in 2003.

Regulation of Pennsylvania's state-charter banks and other state-chartered financial institutions is the responsibility of the state's Department of Banking.

[33]INSURANCE

In 2004, there were over 8.5 million individual life insurance policies in force, with a total value of about $551 billion; total value for all categories of life insurance (individual, group, and credit) was over $909.5 billion. The average coverage amount is $64,100 per policy holder. Death benefits paid that year totaled $2.67 billion.

There were 37 life and health and 200 property and casualty insurance companies domiciled in Pennsylvania in 2003. In 2004, direct premiums for property and casualty insurance totaled over $19.2 billion. That year, there were 60,779 flood insurance policies in force in the state, with a total value of $8 billion. About $2.2 billion of coverage was held through FAIR plans, which are designed to offer coverage for some natural circumstances, such as wind and hail, in high risk areas.

In 2004, 58% of state residents held employment-based health insurance policies, 5% held individual policies, and 25% were covered under Medicare and Medicaid; 12% of residents were uninsured. In 2003, employee contributions for employment-based health coverage averaged at 15% for single coverage and 23% for family coverage. The state does not offer a health benefits expansion program in connection with the Consolidated Omnibus Budget Reconciliation Act (COBRA, 1986), a health insurance program for those who lose employment-based coverage due to termination or reduction of work hours.

In 2003, there were over 8.3 million auto insurance policies in effect for private passenger cars. Required minimum coverage includes bodily injury liability of up to $15,000 per individual and $30,000 for all persons injured in an accident, as well as property damage liability of $5,000. Coverage for first party medical expenses is also required. In 2003, the average expenditure per vehicle for insurance coverage was $810.25.

[34]SECURITIES

Formally established in 1790, the Philadelphia Stock Exchange (PHLX) is the oldest stock exchange in the United States. It was also the nation's most important exchange until the 1820s, when the New York Stock Exchange (NYSE) eclipsed it. Since World War II, the Philadelphia exchange has merged with stock exchanges in Baltimore (1949), Washington, DC (1953), and Pittsburgh (1969). As the primary odd-lot market for Government National Mortgage Association securities and as a leading market for odd-lot government securities and stock options, PHLX ranks after only the NYSE and American exchanges (AMEX) in trading volume. PHLX was the first exchange in the United States to trade foreign currency options (1982) and the National Over-the-Counter Index (1985). Over 2,600 stocks and over 800 options are traded on the exchange.

Sales of securities are regulated by the Pennsylvania Securities Commission, which also licenses all securities dealers, agents, and investment advisers in the state.

In 2005, there were 5,490 personal financial advisers employed in the state and 7,680 securities, commodities, and financial services sales agents. In 2004, there were over 415 publicly traded companies within the state, with over 168 NASDAQ companies, 97 NYSE listings, and 26 AMEX listings. In 2006, the state had 26 Fortune 500 companies; AmerisouceBergen ranked first in the state and 27th in the nation with revenues of over $54.5 billion, followed by Sunoco, Comcast, Rite Aid, and Cigna. Comcast is listed on NASDAQ; the other top four are listed on the NYSE.

[35]PUBLIC FINANCE

Pennsylvania's budget is prepared annually by the Office of Budget and submitted by the governor to the General Assembly for amendment and approval. By law, annual operating expenditures may not exceed available revenues and surpluses from prior years. The fiscal year (FY) runs from 1 July to 30 June.

Fiscal year 2006 general funds were estimated at $24.7 billion for resources and $24.5 billion for expenditures. In fiscal year 2004, federal government grants to Pennsylvania were $19.9 billion.

On 5 January 2006 the federal government released $100 million in emergency contingency funds targeted to the areas with the greatest need, including $7.7 million for Pennsylvania.

[36]TAXATION

In 2005, Pennsylvania collected $27,263 million in tax revenues or $2,193 per capita, which placed it 22nd among the 50 states in per capita tax burden. The national average was $2,192 per capita. Property taxes accounted for 0.2% of the total; sales taxes, 29.6%; selective sales taxes, 18.9%; individual income taxes, 30.4%; corporate income taxes, 6.2%; and other taxes, 14.7%.

As of 1 January 2006, Pennsylvania had one individual income tax bracket of 3.07%. The state taxes corporations at a flat rate of 9.99%.

In 2004, state and local property taxes amounted to $12,518,226,000 or $1,010 per capita. The per capita amount

Pennsylvania—State Government Finances

(Dollar amounts in thousands. Per capita amounts in dollars.)

	AMOUNT	PER CAPITA
Total Revenue	69,212,674	5,584.37
General revenue	50,028,732	4,036.53
Intergovernmental revenue	15,298,110	1,234.32
Taxes	25,346,879	2,045.09
General sales	7,773,133	627.17
Selective sales	4,756,518	383.78
License taxes	2,547,850	205.57
Individual income tax	7,323,364	590.88
Corporate income tax	1,677,998	135.39
Other taxes	1,268,016	102.31
Current charges	5,706,808	460.45
Miscellaneous general revenue	3,676,935	296.67
Utility revenue	–	–
Liquor store revenue	1,109,204	89.50
Insurance trust revenue	18,074,738	1,458.35
Total expenditure	57,353,773	4,627.54
Intergovernmental expenditure	12,156,969	980.88
Direct expenditure	45,196,804	3,646.67
Current operation	31,408,588	2,534.18
Capital outlay	3,361,917	271.25
Insurance benefits and repayments	8,044,411	649.06
Assistance and subsidies	1,258,487	101.54
Interest on debt	1,123,401	90.64
Exhibit: Salaries and wages	7,457,562	601.71
Total expenditure	57,353,773	4,627.54
General expenditure	48,242,901	3,892.44
Intergovernmental expenditure	12,156,969	980.88
Direct expenditure	36,085,932	2,911.56
General expenditures, by function:		
Education	15,391,363	1,241.84
Public welfare	16,772,449	1,353.27
Hospitals	2,201,565	177.63
Health	1,471,027	118.69
Highways	4,026,416	324.87
Police protection	604,141	48.74
Correction	1,488,414	120.09
Natural resources	631,347	50.94
Parks and recreation	168,300	13.58
Government administration	2,068,165	166.87
Interest on general debt	1,123,401	90.64
Other and unallocable	2,296,313	185.28
Utility expenditure	48,285	3.90
Liquor store expenditure	1,018,176	82.15
Insurance trust expenditure	8,044,411	649.06
Debt at end of fiscal year	25,995,752	2,097.45
Cash and security holdings	104,532,372	8,434.11

Abbreviations and symbols: – zero or rounds to zero; (NA) not available; (X) not applicable.

SOURCE: *U.S. Census Bureau, Governments Division, 2004 Survey of State Government Finances,* January 2006.

According to the Tax Foundation, for every federal tax dollar sent to Washington in 2004, Pennsylvania citizens received $1.06 in federal spending.

37 ECONOMIC POLICY

The Center for Entrepreneurial Assistance directs and controls the Department of Community and Economic Development's economic assistance activities. Other agencies include the Pennsylvania Industrial Development Authority and the Pennsylvania Capital Loan Fund. Pennsylvania also encourages industrial development, domestic and foreign investment to the state, and export assistance to Pennsylvania companies.

The Pennsylvania Industrial Development Authority Board and the Pennsylvania Minority Business Development Authority provide loans to businesses that want to build new facilities or renovate and expand older ones. The Office of Minority Business Enterprise seeks to strengthen minority businesses by helping them obtain contracts with the state. The Small Business Development Center aids small businesses by providing a network of informational sources. Additional services are provided by the Appalachian Regional Commission, the Office of Corporate and Financial Regulation, the Ben Franklin Technology Development Authority, the Community Economic Development Loan Program, the Customized Job Training Program, the Enterprise Zone Program, the Export Finance Program, the First Industries Fund, the Industrial Sites Reuse Program, the Infrastructure Development Program, the Keystone Innovation Starter Kit, Keystone Opportunity Zones, the Pennsylvania Capital Access Program (PennCap), the Pennsylvania Economic Development Financing Authority, Small Business Development Centers, and the Tax Increment Financing Guarantee Program.

38 HEALTH

The infant mortality rate in October 2005 was estimated at 6.9 per 1,000 live births. The birth rate in 2003 was 11.4 per 1,000 population. The abortion rate stood at 14.3 per 1,000 women in 2000. In 2003, about 76% of pregnant woman received prenatal care beginning in the first trimester. In 2004, approximately 86% of children received routine immunizations before the age of three.

The crude death rate in 2003 was 10.5 deaths per 1,000 population, which was the second-highest rate in the country that year (following West Virginia). As of 2002, the death rates for major causes of death (per 100,000 resident population) were: heart disease, 315; cancer, 242 (the third-highest rate in the country); cerebrovascular diseases, 69.5; chronic lower respiratory diseases, 48.8; and diabetes, 30.1. The mortality rate from HIV infection was 4 per 100,000 population. In 2004, the reported AIDS case rate was at about 13.1 per 100,000 population. In 2002, about 57% of the population was considered overweight or obese. As of 2004, about 22.6% of state residents were smokers.

In 2003, Pennsylvania had 201 community hospitals with about 40,900 beds. There were about 1.8 million patient admissions that year and 33 million outpatient visits. The average daily inpatient census was about 28,200 patients. The average cost per day for hospital care was $1,326. Also in 2003, there were about 740 certified nursing facilities in the state with 90,857 beds and an overall occupancy rate of about 89.7%. In 2004, it was estimated that about 69.9% of all state residents had received some type of dental care within the year. Pennsylvania had 332 physicians per 100,000

ranks the state 24th nationally. Local governments collected $12,449,837,000 of the total and the state government $68,389,000.

Pennsylvania taxes retail sales at a rate of 6%. In addition to the state tax, local taxes on retail sales can reach as much as 1%, making for a potential total tax on retail sales of 7%. Food purchased for consumption off-premises is tax exempt. The tax on cigarettes is 135 cents per pack, which ranks 12th among the 50 states and the District of Columbia. Pennsylvania taxes gasoline at 31.2 cents per gallon. This is in addition to the 18.4 cents per gallon federal tax on gasoline.

resident population in 2004 and 995 nurses per 100,000 in 2005. In 2004, there were a total of 7,789 dentists in the state.

About 14% of state residents were enrolled in Medicaid programs in 2003. In 2004, Pennsylvania tied with Arkansas and Florida at third in the nation for the highest percentage of residents on Medicare (following West Virginia and Maine). Approximately 12% of the state population was uninsured in 2004. In 2003, state health care expenditures totaled $18.8 million.

The University of Pennsylvania School of Medicine, which originated as the medical school of the College of Philadelphia in 1765, is the nation's oldest medical school. One of the nation's newest is the Hershey Medical Center of Pennsylvania State University. Other medical schools in Pennsylvania are the University of Pittsburgh School of Medicine, Temple University's School of Medicine, the Medical College of Pennsylvania, and Allegheny University, the last three in Philadelphia. The state also aids colleges of osteopathic medicine, podiatric medicine, and optometry—all in Philadelphia. In 2005, the University of Pittsburgh Medical Center and the Hospital of the University of Pennsylvania, Philadelphia, ranked 13th and 15th respectively on the Honor Roll of Best Hospitals 2005 by *U.S. News & World Report.* The Children's Hospital of Philadelphia ranked first in the nation in reputation for pediatric care

39 SOCIAL WELFARE

In 2004, about 487,000 people received unemployment benefits, with the average weekly unemployment benefit at $294. For 2005, the estimated average monthly participation in the food stamp program included about 1,042,809 persons (471,960 households); the average monthly benefit was about $88.28 per person. That year, the total of benefits paid through the state for the food stamp program was about $1.1 billion.

Temporary Assistance for Needy Families (TANF), the system of federal welfare assistance that officially replaced Aid to Families with Dependent Children (AFDC) in 1997, was reauthorized through the Deficit Reduction Act of 2005. TANF is funded through federal block grants that are divided among the states based on an equation involving the number of recipients in each state. In 2004, the Pennsylvania TANF program had 231,000 recipients; state and federal expenditures on this TANF program totaled $346 million in fiscal year 2003.

In December 2004, Social Security benefits were paid to 2,405,080 Pennsylvania residents. This number included 1,556,970 retired workers, 266,100 widows and widowers, 275,950 disabled workers, 133,490 spouses, and 172,570 children. Social Security beneficiaries represented 19.3% of the total state population and 93.3% of the state's population age 65 and older. Retired workers received an average monthly payment of $982; widows and widowers, $945; disabled workers, $910; and spouses, $496. Payments for children of retired workers averaged $509 per month; children of deceased workers, $658; and children of disabled workers, $266. Federal Supplemental Security Income payments in December 2004 went to 316,917 Pennsylvania residents, averaging $437 a month.

40 HOUSING

Faced with a decaying housing stock, Philadelphia during the 1970s and 1980s encouraged renovation of existing units along

with the construction of new ones, effectively revitalizing several neighborhoods. About 22.4% of all units in the state were built in the period from 1970 to 1989.

In 2004, there were 5,385,729 housing units in Pennsylvania, 4,817,757 of which were occupied; 72.8% were owner-occupied. About 57.6% of all units were single-family, detached homes. About 30.7% of all units were built in 1939 or earlier. In 2004, utility gas and fuel oil were the most common sources of energy for heating. It was estimated that 135,756 units lacked telephone services, 23,755 lacked complete plumbing facilities, and 28,415 lacked complete kitchen facilities. The average household had 2.48 members.

In 2004, 49,700 new privately owned housing units were authorized for construction. The median home value was $116,520. The median monthly cost for mortgage owners was $1,114. Renters paid a median of $611 per month. In September 2005, the state received grants of $450,000 from the US Department of Housing and Urban Development (HUD) for rural housing and economic development programs. For 2006, HUD allocated to the state over $50 million in community development block grants. The city of Philadelphia was awarded over $53 million in community development block grants.

41 EDUCATION

Pennsylvania fell behind many of its neighbors in establishing a free public school system. From colonial times until the 1830s, almost all instruction in reading and writing took place in private schools. Called "dame schools" in the cities and "neighborhood schools" in rural areas, they offered primary courses, usually taught by women in their own homes. In addition, the Quakers, Moravians, and Scots-Irish Presbyterians all formed their own private schools, emphasizing religious study. Many communities also set up secondary schools, called academies, on land granted by the state; by 1850, there were 524 academies, some of which later developed into colleges. A public school law passed in 1834 was not mandatory in the school districts but was still unpopular. Thaddeus Stevens, then a state legislator, is credited with saving the law from repeal in 1835. Two years later, more than 40% of the state's children were in public schools.

As of 2004, 86.5% of the population 25 years old and older had completed four years of high school, and 25.3% had obtained a bachelor's degree or higher.

The total enrollment for fall 2002 in Pennsylvania's public schools stood at 1,817,000. Of these, 1,242,000 attended schools from kindergarten through grade eight, and 575,000 attended high school. Approximately 76.3% of the students were white, 15.8% were black, 5.5% were Hispanic, 2.3% were Asian/Pacific Islander, and 0.1% were American Indian/Alaskan Native. Total enrollment was estimated at 1,812,000 in fall 2003 and expected to be 1,676,000 by 2014, a decline of 7.7% during the period 2002 to 2014. Expenditures for public education in 2003/04 were estimated at $20.7 billion or $9,979 per student, the ninth-highest among the 50 states. In fall 2003 there were 316,337 students enrolled in 2,009 private schools. Since 1969, the National Assessment of Educational Progress (NAEP) has tested public school students nationwide. The resulting report, *The Nation's Report Card,* stated that in 2005 eighth graders in Pennsylvania scored 281 out of 500 in mathematics compared with the national average of 278.

As of fall 2002, there were 654,826 students enrolled in college or graduate school; minority students comprised 16.4% of total postsecondary enrollment. In 2005 Pennsylvania had 262 degree-granting institutions including 44 public four-year schools, 21 public two-year schools, and 98 nonprofit, private four-year schools. Indiana University of Pennsylvania, established in 1872, accounted for about 15% of enrollment. Four universities have nonprofit corporate charters but are classified as state-related: Pennsylvania State University, Temple University, the University of Pittsburgh, and Lincoln University. Of these, Penn State is by far the largest. Founded in 1855 as the Farmers' High School of Pennsylvania, Penn State now has its main campus at University Park and 23 smaller campus locations statewide as well as a Penn State World Campus that allows online access to a Penn State education.

State-aided private institutions receiving designated grants from the legislature include the University of Pennsylvania, the largest of these schools, founded in 1740 by Benjamin Franklin as the Philadelphia Academy and Charitable School; among its noteworthy professional schools is the Wharton School of Business. Other private colleges and universities, also eligible to receive state aid through a per-pupil funding formula, include Bryn Mawr College (founded in 1880), Bucknell University (1846) in Lewisburg, Carnegie-Mellon University (1900) in Pittsburgh, Dickinson College (1733) in Carlisle, Duquesne University (1878) in Pittsburgh, Haverford College (1833), Lafayette College (1826), Lehigh University (1865), Swarthmore College (1864), and Villanova University (1842). The Pennsylvania Higher Education Assistance Agency (PHEAA) offers higher education grants, guarantees private loans, and administers work-study programs for Pennsylvania students.

42 ARTS

The Pennsylvania Council on the Arts (PCA) was established in 1966 and consists of a Council comprised of 19 members—15 private citizens appointed by the governor and 4 members of the General Assembly. In 2005, the PCA and other Pennsylvania arts organizations received 103 grants totaling $3,135,800 from the National Endowment for the Arts. The Pennsylvania Humanities Council (PHC) was established in 1973. In 2005, the National Endowment for the Humanities contributed $6,181,059 for 59 state programs. The state and various private sources also provided funding for arts programs.

Philadelphia was the cultural capital of the colonies and rivaled New York as a theatrical center during the 1800s. In 1984, Philadelphia had five fully developed resident theaters, ranking third in the nation after New York and California. As of 2005 a number of regional and summer stock theaters were scattered throughout the state, the most noteworthy being in Bucks County, Lancaster, and Pittsburgh. The Bucks County Playhouse is recognized as the State Theater and carries a rich history of featuring well-known stars such as Grace Kelly, Robert Redford, and Walter Matthau. The Bucks County Playhouse is also noted for premiering the famous dramas, *Harvey, Nobody Loves Me (Barefoot In The Park)* and *Give 'Em Hell Harry*.

Pennsylvania's most significant contribution to the performing arts has come through music. One of America's first important songwriters, Stephen Foster, was born in 1826 in Lawrenceville and grew up in Pittsburgh. Some of Foster's songs include, "Oh!

Susanna" (1848), "Jeanie With the Light Brown Hair" (1854), and "Old Folks at Home (Swanee River)" (1851).The Pittsburgh Symphony, which began performing in 1896, first achieved prominence under Victor Herbert. Temporarily disbanded in 1910, the symphony was revived under Fritz Reiner in 1927; subsequent music directors have included William Steinberg and Andre Previn. Even more illustrious has been the career of the Philadelphia Orchestra, founded in 1900. Among this orchestra's best-known permanent conductors have been Leopold Stokowski and Eugene Ormandy, both of whom recorded extensively.

An important dance company, the Pennsylvania Ballet, is based in Philadelphia, which is also home to the Curtis Institute of Music, founded in 1924. Pittsburgh hosts the Pittsburgh Ballet Theater (PBT). In 1989 PBT began conducting educational programs; as of 2005 the outreach programs had reached over 65,000 students from more than 200 school districts. The National Choreographic Center was established in the mid-1980s in Carlisle in conjunction with the Central Pennsylvania Youth Ballet School. Opera companies include the Fulton Opera House in Lancaster, Pittsburgh Opera, and Opera Company of Philadelphia.

In 1997 the Philadelphia Fringe Festival was founded. Under a changed title, the Philadelphia Live Arts Festival and Philly Fringe evolved into a 16-day festival. The festival, which includes theater, dance, music, poetry and puppetry performances, has been recorded as drawing over 47,000 attendants. The *American Poetry Review,* published in Philadelphia, has become one of the nation's premier poetry journals. Favorite tourist sites featuring the arts include the Andy Warhol Museum in Pittsburgh and the Edgar J. Kaufmann House, more commonly known as, Fallingwater, a home designed by renowned architect Frank Lloyd Wright in Bear Run.

43 LIBRARIES AND MUSEUMS

As of December 2001, Pennsylvania had 459 public library systems, with a total of 636 libraries, of which there were 181 were branches. In that same year, the libraries had a combined 28,061,000 volumes of books and serial publications on their shelves, and a total circulation of 56,929,000. The system also had 1,957,000 audio and 831,000 video items, 29,000 electronic format items (CD-ROMs, magnetic tapes, and disks), and 35 bookmobiles. The largest public library in the state, and one of the oldest in the United States, is the Free Library of Philadelphia, with 6,700,000 volumes in 73 branches. The Carnegie Library in Pittsburgh has 3,439,666 volumes and 18 branches. Harrisburg offers the State Library of Pennsylvania, which had 1,000,494 volumes in 1998. The Alverthorpe Gallery Library in Jenkintown contains the Rosenwald collection of illustrated books dating from the 15th century. In fiscal year 2001, operating income for the state's public library system came to $277,782,000 and included $2,705,000 in federal grants and $73,274,000 in state grants.

Philadelphia is the site of the state's largest academic collection, the University of Pennsylvania Libraries, with 4,791,342 volumes. Other major academic libraries are at the University of Pittsburgh, 3,968,106 volumes; Penn State, over 2.5 million; Temple, 2,445,164; Carnegie-Mellon, 906,069; and Bryn Mawr, 1,062,594.

Pennsylvania has 362 museums and public gardens, with many of the museums located in Philadelphia. The Franklin Institute, established in 1824 as an exhibition hall and training center for inventors and mechanics, is a leading showcase for science and technology. Other important museums are the Philadelphia Museum of Art, Academy of Natural Sciences, Pennsylvania Academy of the Fine Arts, Afro-American Historical and Cultural Museum, American Catholic Historical Society, American Swedish Historical Foundation Museum, and Museum of American Jewish History.

The Carnegie Institute in Pittsburgh is home to several major museums, including the Carnegie Museum of Natural History and the Museum of Art. Also in Pittsburgh are the Buhl Planetarium and Institute of Popular Science and the Frick Art Museum. Other institutions scattered throughout the state include the Moravian Museum, Bethlehem; US Army Military History Institute, Carlisle; Erie Art Center, Museum, and Old Custom House; Pennsylvania Lumber Museum, Galeton; Pennsylvania Historical and Museum Commission and William Penn Memorial Museum, Harrisburg; Pennsylvania Dutch Folk Culture Society, Lenhartsville; Schwenkfelder Museum, Pennsburg; and Railroad Museum of Pennsylvania, Strasburg. A new exhibit at the Pittsburgh Zoo and Aquarium opened in June of 2000, featuring a $16.8 million aquarium that was twice as big as the old Aqua Zoo, and included 500 species of sea creatures.

Several old forts commemorate the French and Indian War, and George Washington's Revolutionary headquarters at Valley Forge is now a national historical park. Brandywine Battlefield (Chadds Ford) is another Revolutionary War site. Gettysburg National Military Park commemorates the Civil War. Other historic sites are Independence National Historical Park, Philadelphia; the Daniel Boone Homestead, Birdsboro; John Brown's House, Chambersburg; James Buchanan's home, Lancaster; and Ft. Augusta, Sunbury, a frontier outpost.

44 COMMUNICATIONS

Philadelphia already had mail links to surrounding towns and to Maryland and Virginia by 1737, when Benjamin Franklin was named deputy postmaster of the city, but service was slow and not always reliable. During the remainder of the century, significant improvements in delivery were made, but some townspeople devised ingenious ways of transmitting information even faster than the mails. Philadelphia stock exchange brokers, for instance, communicated with agents in New York by flashing coded signals with mirrors and lights from a series of high points across New Jersey, thereby receiving stock prices on the same day they were transacted. By 1846, the first telegraph service in the state linked Harrisburg and Lancaster.

In 2004, 95.6% of Pennsylvania's households had telephones. Additionally, by June of that same year there were 6,420,037 mobile wireless telephone subscribers. In 2003, 60.2% of Pennsylvania households had a computer and 54.7% had Internet access. By June 2005, there were 1,602,716 high-speed lines in Pennsylvania, 1,455,509 residential and 157,207 for business.

Pittsburgh's KDKA became the world's first commercial radio station in 1920. By 2005, it was one of 55 major AM and 144 major FM radio stations. In addition, there were 34 major television stations. WQED in Pittsburgh pioneered community-sponsored educational television when it began broadcasting in 1954. In 1999, the Philadelphia area had 2,670,710 households, 79% with cable; the Pittsburgh area had a 79% penetration rate in 1,135,290

households; and the Harrisburg-Lancaster-Lebanon-York area had 599,930 households, 78% with cable.

A total of 217,724 Internet domain names were registered in the state as of 2000.

45 PRESS

Benjamin Franklin may have been colonial Pennsylvania's most renowned publisher, but its first was Andrew Bradford, whose *American Weekly Mercury,* established in 1719, was the third newspaper to appear in the colonies. Founded nine years later, the *Pennsylvania Gazette* was purchased by Franklin in 1730 and served as the springboard for *Poor Richard's Almanack.*

During the 1800s, newspapers sprang up in all the major cities and many small communities. By 1880, Pittsburgh had 10 daily newspapers—more than any other city its size. After a series of mergers and closings, however, it is left with only one paper today—the *Post-Gazette.* Philadelphia has two newspapers, the *Inquirer* and the *Daily News.* The *Inquirer,* founded in 1829, has won numerous awards for its investigative reporting.

In 2005, Pennsylvania had 50 morning newspapers, 31 evening newspapers, and 41 Sunday papers.

The following table shows the approximate circulation of some of the leading dailies in 2005:

AREA	NAME	DAILY	SUNDAY
Allentown	*Morning Call* (m,S)	126,470	159,733
Erie	*Times-News* (m,S)	59,454	86,185
Harrisburg	*Patriot-News* (m,S)	100,129	150,061
Philadelphia	*Inquirer* (m,S)	368,833	750,780
	Daily News (m)	135,956	68,333 (Sat.)
Pittsburgh	*Post-Gazette* (m,S)	238,860	402,981
Wilkes-Barre	*Citizens' Voice* (m,S)	31,606	30,664
	Times Leader (m,S)	42,585	59,730

In 2005, there were 198 weekly publications in Pennsylvania. Of these there are 107 paid weeklies, 38 free weeklies, and 53 combined weeklies. The total circulation of paid weeklies (506,614) and free weeklies (1,556,969) is 1,679,404. The *Moon Record* of Crescent, Pennsylvania ranked eighth among paid weeklies in the United States based on a circulation of 49,000. Based on circulation in the United States in 2005, among free weeklies the Bucks County *Trend Midweek* ranked first with a circulation of 625,000, followed by two northeast Philadelphia publications, the *News Gleaner* and *Northeast Times*, ranking fourteenth and fifteenth, respectively, with circulations of 136, 070 and 119,673. The Pittsburgh *Pennysaver* (circulation 772,546) ranked ninth in the United States among shopping publications in 2005.

Farm Journal and *Current History,* both monthlies, are published in Philadelphia, and there are monthlies named for both Philadelphia and Pittsburgh. Of more specialized interest are the gardening, nutrition, and health magazines and books from Rodale Press in Emmaus which publishes *Prevention, Men's Health and Runner's World, Women's Health, Organic Gardening, Backpacker, Best Life, Bicycling* and *Mountain Bike.* The Chilton Co., publisher of automotive guides, was acquired by The Thompson Corporation in 2003.

46 ORGANIZATIONS

In 2006, there were over 17,340 nonprofit organizations registered within the state, of which about 11,572 were registered as charitable, educational, or religious organizations.

Philadelphia is the home for two major service organizations: Big Brothers/Big Sisters of America and the Grand United Order of Odd Fellows. Educational organizations in that city include the American Academy of Political and Social Science, the Academy of Natural Sciences, the American Philosophical Society, and Middle States Association of Colleges and Schools. The Association for Children with Learning Disabilities is located in Pittsburgh, the College Placement Council in Bethlehem, and the American Philatelic Society in State College.

State organizations for arts and culture include ArtsQuest, Dance Theatre of Pennsylvania, the Pittsburgh Center for the Arts, the Folk Heritage Institute, and the Pennsylvania Historical Association. There are also several municipal and regional historical societies and art councils. State environmental organizations include Preservation Pennsylvania and the Rodale Institute.

Professional and trade groups in the state include the American Board of Surgery, the American College of Physicians–American Society of Internal Medicine, the National Board of Medical Examiners, the United Steel Workers of America, and the Society of Automotive Engineers. Valley Forge is the home of the Patriotic Order of the Sons of America.

Among the many sports organizations headquartered in Pennsylvania are the US Squash Racquets Association, Pop Warner Football, US Rowing Association, and the Little League Foundation. The Major League Umpires Association is also based in the state.

The Jewish Publication Society is based in Philadelphia. The Mennonite Central Committee, a major international relief and service organization, is based in Akron. The Moravian Historical Society is based in Nazareth.

47 TOURISM, TRAVEL, AND RECREATION

Tourism is the second-largest industry in the state of Pennsylvania, which hosted a record 126 million travelers in 2003. Of these, some 1.3 million were international visitors with the majority from Canada, the United Kingdom, and Germany. Two-thirds of out-of-state visitors traveled to the state from New York, New Jersey, and Maryland; Virginians and Ohioans completed the list of top-five states providing tourists to Pennsylvania. The total economic impact from travel expenditures was $21.9 billion in 2003. The industry supported over 563,440 jobs.

Philadelphia—whose Independence National Historical Park has been called the most historic square mile in America—offers the Liberty Bell, Independence Hall, Carpenter's Hall, and many other sites. North of Philadelphia, in Bucks County, is the town of New Hope, with its numerous crafts and antique shops.

The Lancaster area is "Pennsylvania Dutch" country, featuring tours and exhibits of Amish farm life. Gettysburg contains not only the famous Civil War battlefield but also the home of Dwight D. Eisenhower, opened to the public in 1980. Among the most popular sites are Chocolate World and Hershey Park in the town of Hershey and Valley Forge National Historic Park. Annual parades and festivals include the Mummers Parade on 1 January in Philadelphia and the Kutztown Folk Festival, commemorating Pennsylvania Dutch life, held the first week of July. Fallingwater is a Frank Lloyd Wright-designed house and visitor center.

No less an attraction are the state's outdoor recreation areas. The Laurel Highlands have many ski areas. The Laurel Caverns feature guided tours of the caves. By far the most popular for both skiing and camping are the Delaware Water Gap and the Poconos, also a favorite resort region. The state park system includes 116 state parks, 20 state forests, 1 national forest, and 3 environmental education centers.

48 SPORTS

Pennsylvania has seven major professional sports teams: the Philadelphia Phillies and the Pittsburgh Pirates of Major League Baseball, the Philadelphia Eagles and the Pittsburgh Steelers of the National Football League, the Philadelphia 76ers of the National Basketball Association, and the Pittsburgh Penguins and Philadelphia Flyers of the National Hockey League.

The Phillies won the World Series in 1980; they won the National League Championship in 1993, but lost the World Series to the Toronto Blue Jays. The Pirates won the World Series in 1909, 1925, 1960, 1971, and 1979. The Steelers established a legendary football dynasty in the 1970s, winning Super Bowls in 1975, 1976, 1979, 1980, and 2006. They also played in the 1996 Super Bowl, losing to the Dallas Cowboys. The Eagles won the National Football Conference championship in 1981, but lost to Oakland in that year's Super Bowl. The 76ers won the NBA championship in 1947, 1956, 1967, and 1983, and lost the championship series in 1977, 1980, and 1982. The Flyers won the Stanley Cup in 1974 and 1975 and lost in the finals in 1976, 1980, 1985, 1987, and 1997. The Penguins won the Stanley Cup in 1991 and 1992.

There are also minor league baseball teams in Harrisburg, Scranton, Altoona, Reading, Williamsport, Allentown, and Erie, and minor league hockey teams in Hershey, Johnstown, Wilkes-Barre, and Philadelphia.

Horse racing is conducted at Keystone Race Track in Bucks County, Penn National Race Course in Dauphin County, and Commodore Downs in Erie County. Harness-racing tracks include Liberty Bell Park in northeast Philadelphia, the Meadows in Washington County, and Pocono Downs in Luzerne County. Each June, Pennsylvania hosts a major auto race, the Pocono 500. Each July, the state hosts a second NASCAR Nextel Cup event, the Pennsylvania 500. The Penn Relays, an important amateur track meet, are held in Philadelphia every April.

In collegiate sports, football is most prominent. The University of Pittsburgh Panthers were named national champions in 1918, 1937, and 1976. Pennsylvania State University was named champion in 1982 and 1986 and joined the Big Ten in 1990. The Nittany Lions of Penn State won the Rose Bowl in 1995; the Sugar Bowl in 1983; the Orange Bowl in 1969, 1970, and 2006; the Fiesta Bowl in 1997; the Outback Bowl in 1996 and 1999; and the Cotton Bowl in 1972, to name just a few of their bowl victories. The University of Pennsylvania, members of the Ivy League, traditionally field strong teams in football and basketball. Villanova University, located in Philadelphia, won the National Collegiate Athletic Association (NCAA) basketball championship in 1985.

Each summer, Williamsport hosts baseball's Little League World Series.

49 FAMOUS PENNSYLVANIANS

Johan Printz (b.Sweden, 1592-1663), the 400-lb, hard-drinking, hard-swearing, and hard-ruling governor of New Sweden, was Pennsylvania's first European resident of note. The founder of Pennsylvania was William Penn (b.England, 1644-1718), a Quaker of sober habits and deep religious beliefs. Most extraordinary of all Pennsylvanians, Benjamin Franklin (b.Massachusetts, 1706-90), a printer, author, inventor, scientist, legislator, diplomat, and statesman, served the Philadelphia, Pennsylvania, and US governments in a variety of posts.

Only one native Pennsylvanian, James Buchanan (1791-1868), has ever become US president. Buchanan was a state assemblyman, five-term US representative, two-term US senator, secretary of state, and minister to Russia and then to Great Britain before entering the White House as a 65-year-old bachelor in 1857. As president, he tried to maintain the Union by avoiding extremes and preaching compromise, but his toleration of slavery was abhorrent to abolitionists and his desire to preserve the Union was obnoxious to secessionists. Dwight D. Eisenhower (b.Texas, 1890-1969) retired to a farm in Gettysburg after his presidency was over. George M. Dallas (1792-1864), Pennsylvania's only US vice president, was James K. Polk's running mate.

The six Pennsylvanians who have served on the US Supreme Court have all been associate justices: James Wilson (1742-98), Henry Baldwin (1780-1844), Robert C. Grier (1794-1870), William Strong (1808-95), George Shiras Jr. (1832-1924), and Owen J. Roberts (1875-1955). Controversial supreme court nominee Robert Heron Bock (b.Pennsylvania 1927) served as a federal judge for many years.

Many other Pennsylvanians have held prominent federal positions. Albert Gallatin (b.Switzerland, 1761-1849), brilliant secretary of the treasury under Thomas Jefferson and James Madison, later served as minister to France and then to Great Britain. Richard Rush (1780-1859) was Madison's attorney general and John Quincy Adams's secretary of the treasury. A distinguished jurist, Jeremiah Sullivan Black (1810-83) was Buchanan's attorney general and later his secretary of state. John Wanamaker (1838-1922), an innovative department store merchandiser, served as postmaster general under Benjamin Harrison. Philander C. Knox (1853-1921) was Theodore Roosevelt's attorney general and William Howard Taft's secretary of state. Financier Andrew C. Mellon (1855-1937) was secretary of the treasury under Warren G. Harding, Calvin Coolidge, and Herbert Hoover. Recent Pennsylvanians in high office include Richard Helms (1913-2002), director of the US Central Intelligence Agency from 1966 to 1973, and Alexander Haig (b.1924), former commander of NATO forces in Europe, chief of staff under Richard Nixon, and Ronald Reagan's first choice for secretary of state.

Three US senators, Simon Cameron (1799-1889), Matthew Quay (1833-1904), and Boies Penrose (1860-1921), are best known as leaders of the powerful Pennsylvania Republican machine. Senator Joseph F. Guffey (1870-1959) sponsored legislation to stabilize the bituminous coal industry. After serving as reform mayor of Philadelphia, Joseph S. Clark (1901-1990) also distinguished himself in the Senate, and Hugh Scott (1900-94) was Republican minority leader from 1969 to 1977. Outstanding representatives from Pennsylvania include Thaddeus Stevens (1792-1868), leader of radical Republicans during the Civil War era; David Wilmot (1814-68), author of the proviso attempting to prohibit slavery in territory acquired from Mexico; and Samuel J. Randall (1828-90), speaker of the House of Representatives from 1876 to 1881.

Other notable historical figures were Joseph Galloway (b.Maryland, 1729?-1803), a loyalist; Robert Morris (England, 1734-1806), a Revolutionary financier; and Betsy Ross (Elizabeth Griscom, 1752-1836), the seamstress who allegedly stitched the first American flag. Pamphleteer Thomas Paine (England, 1737-1809), pioneer Daniel Boone (1734-1820), and General Anthony Wayne (1745-96) also distinguished themselves during this period. In the Civil War, General George B. McClellan (1826-85) led the Union army on the Peninsula and at the Battle of Antietam, while at the Battle of Gettysburg, Generals George Gordon Meade (b.Spain, 1815-72) and Winfield Scott Hancock (1824-86) both showed their military prowess.

Important state governors include John W. Geary (1819-73), Samuel W. Pennypacker (1843-1916), Robert E. Pattison (b.Maryland, 1850-1904), Gifford Pinchot (b.Connecticut 1865-1946), James H. Duff (1883-1969), George H. Earle (1890-1974), Milton J. Shapp (Ohio, 1912-88), William W. Scranton (b.Connecticut, 1917), George M. Leader (b.1918), and Richard L. Thornburgh (b.1932).

Pennsylvanians have won Nobel Prizes in every category except literature. General George C. Marshall (1880-1959), chief of staff of the US Army in World War II and secretary of state when the European Recovery Program (Marshall Plan) was adopted, won the 1953 Nobel Peace Prize. Simon Kuznets (b.Russia, 1901-85) received the 1971 Nobel Prize in economic science for work on economic growth, and Herbert A. Simon (b.Wisconsin, 1916-2001) received the 1978 award for work on decision making in economic organizations; in 1980, Lawrence R. Klein (b.Nebraska, 1920) was honored for his design and application of econometric models. In physics, Otto Stern (b.Germany, 1888-1969) won the 1943 prize for work on the magnetic momentum of protons. In chemistry, Theodore W. Richards (1868-1928) won the 1914 Nobel Prize for determining the atomic weight of many elements, and Christian Boehmer Anfinsen (1916-95) won the 1972 award for pioneering studies in enzymes. In physiology or medicine, Philip S. Hench (1896-1965) won in 1950 for his discoveries about hormones of the adrenal cortex, Haldane K. Hartline (1903-83) won in 1967 for work on the human eye, and Howard M. Temin (1934-94) was honored in 1975 for the study of tumor viruses.

Many other Pennsylvanians were distinguished scientists. Ebenezer Kinnersly (1711-78) studied electricity, and Benjamin Franklin's grandson Alexander Dallas Bache (1806-67) was an expert on magnetism. Caspar Wistar (b.Germany, 1761-1818) and Thomas Woodhouse (1770-1809) pioneered the study of chemistry, while William Maclure (b.Scotland, 1763-1840) and James Mease (1771-1846) were early geologists. David Rittenhouse (1732-96) was a distinguished astronomer. John Bartram (1699-1777) and his son William (1739-1823) won international repute as botanists. Benjamin Rush (1745-1813) was Pennsylvania's most distinguished physician. Philip Syng Physick (1768-1837) was a leading surgeon, and Nathaniel Chapman (b.Virginia, 1780-1853) was the first president of the American Medical Association. Rachel Carson (1907-64), a marine biologist and writer, became widely known for her crusade against the use of chemical pesticides. Noted inventors born in Pennsylvania include steamboat builder Robert Fulton (1765–1815) and David Thomas (1794–1882), the father of the American anthracite iron industry.

Pennsylvania played a large role in the economic development of the United States. In addition to Mellon, outstanding bankers include Stephen Girard (b.France, 1750–1831), Nicholas Biddle (1786–1844), Anthony J. Drexel (1826–93), and John J. McCloy (1895–1985). Andrew Carnegie (b.Scotland, 1835–1919) and his lieutenants, including Henry Clay Frick (1849–1919) and Charles M. Schwab (1862–1939), created the most efficient steel-manufacturing company in the 19th century. Wanamaker, Frank W. Woolworth (b.New York, 1852–1919), and Sebastian S. Kresge (1867–1966) were pioneer merchandisers.

Other prominent businessmen born in Pennsylvania are automobile pioneer Clement Studebaker (1831–1901), chocolate manufacturer Milton S. Hershey (1857–1945), and retired Chrysler chairman Lee A. Iacocca (b.1924).

Pennsylvania labor leaders include Uriah S. Stephens (1821–82) and Terence V. Powderly (1849–1924), leaders of the Knights of Labor; Philip Murray (b.Scotland, 1886–1952), president of the CIO; and David J. MacDonald (1902–79), leader of the steelworkers. Among economic theorists, Henry George (1839–97) was the unorthodox advocate of the single tax. Florence Kelley (1859–1932) was an important social reformer, as is Bayard Rustin (1910–1987).

Important early religious leaders, all born in Germany, include Henry Melchior Muhlenberg (1711–87), organizer of Pennsylvania's Lutherans; Count Nikolaus Ludwig von Zinzendorf (1700–1760), a Morovian leader; and Johann Conrad Beissel (1690–1768), founder of the Ephrata Cloister. Charles Taze Russell (1852–1916), born a Congregationalist, founded the group that later became Jehovah's Witnesses. Among the state's outstanding scholars are historians Henry C. Lee (1825–1909), John Bach McMaster (1852–1932), Ellis Paxson Oberholtzer (1868–1936), and Henry Steele Commager (1902–98); anthropologist Margaret Mead (1901–78); behavioral psychologist B(urrhus) F(rederic) Skinner (1904–1990); urbanologist Jane Jacobs (1916–2006); and language theorist Noam Chomsky (b.1928). Thomas Gallaudet (b.1787–1851) was a pioneer in education of the deaf.

Pennsylvania has produced a large number of distinguished journalists and writers. In addition to Franklin, newspapermen include John Dunlap (b.Ireland, 1747–1812), Benjamin Franklin Bache (1769–98), William L. McLean (1852–1931), and Moses L. Annenberg (1878–1942). Magazine editors were Sarah Josepha Buell Hale (b.New Hampshire, 1788–1879), Cyrus H. K. Curtis (b.Maine, 1850–1933), Edward W. Bok (b.Netherlands, 1863–1930), and I(sidor) F(einstein) Stone (1907–1989). Ida M. Tarbell (1857–1944) was perhaps Pennsylvania's most famous muckraker. Among the many noteworthy Pennsylvania-born writers are Charles Brockden Brown (1771–1810), Bayard Taylor (1825–78), novelist and physician Silas Weir Mitchell (1829–1914), Charles Godfrey Leland (1824–1903), Owen Wister (1860–1938), Richard Harding Davis (1864–1916), Gertrude Stein (1874–1946), Mary Roberts Rinehart (1876–1958), Hervey Allen (1889–1949), Christopher Morley (1890–1957), Conrad Richter (1890–1968), John O'Hara (1905–70), Donald Barthelme (1931–89), and John Updike (b.1932). James Michener (b.New York, 1907–97) was raised in the state. Pennsylvania playwrights include James Nel-

son Barker (1784–1858), Maxwell Anderson (1888–1959), George S. Kaufman (1889–1961), Marc Connelly (1890–1980), Clifford Odets (1906–63), and Ed Bullins (b.1935). Among Pennsylvania poets are Francis Hopkinson (1737–91), Philip Freneau (b.New York, 1753–1832), Thomas Dunn English (1819–1902), Thomas Buchanan Read (1822–72), and Wallace Stevens (1879–1955).

Composers include Stephen Collins Foster (1826–64), Ethelbert Woodbridge Nevin (1862–1901), Charles Wakefield Cadman (1881–1946), and Samuel Barber (1910–81). Among Pennsylvania painters prominent in the history of American art are Benjamin West (1738–1820), renowned as the father of American painting; Charles Willson Peale (1741–1827), who was also a naturalist; Thomas Sully (b.England, 1783–1872); George Catlin (1796–1872); Thomas Eakins (1844–1916); Mary Cassatt (1845–1926); Man Ray (1890–1976); Andrew Wyeth (b.1917); and Andy Warhol (1927–87). Outstanding sculptors include William Rush (1756–1833), George Grey Barnard (1863–1938), and Alexander Calder (1898–1976).

Pennsylvania produced and patronized a host of actors, including Edwin Forrest (1806–72) Lionel (1878–1954), Ethel (1879–1959), and John (1882–1942) Barrymore; W. C. Fields (William Claude Dukenfield, 1880–1946); Ed Wynn (Isaiah Edwin Leopold, 1886–1966); William Powell (1892–1987); Ethel Waters (1896–1977); Janet Gaynor (1906–84); James Stewart (1908–97); Broderick Crawford (1911–1986); Gene Kelly (1912–96); Charles Bronson (Charles Buchinsky, b.1922); Mario Lanza (1925–59); Shirley Jones (b.1934); and comedian Bill Cosby (b.1937). Film directors Joseph L. Mankiewicz (1909–1993), Arthur Penn (b.1922), and Sidney Lumet (b.1924) and film producer David O. Selznick (1902–65) also came from Pennsylvania.

Pennsylvania has produced outstanding musicians. Four important Pennsylvania-born vocalists are Marian Anderson (b.1897–1993), Blanche Thebom (b.1919), Marilyn Horne (b.1934), and Anna Moffo (1934–2006). Pianists include the versatile Oscar Levant (1906–72) and jazz interpreters Earl "Fatha" Hines (1905–83) and Erroll Garner (1921–77). Popular band leaders include Fred Waring (1900–84), Jimmy Dorsey (1904–57) and his brother Tommy (1905–56), and Les Brown (1912–2001). Perry Como (1913–2001), Daryl Hall (b.1949), and John Oates (b.New York, 1948) have achieved renown as popular singers. Dancers and choreographers from Pennsylvania include Martha Graham (1893–1991), Paul Taylor (b.1930), and Gelsey Kirkland (b.1952).

Of the many outstanding athletes associated with Pennsylvania, Jim Thorpe (b.Oklahoma, 1888–1953) was most versatile, having starred in Olympic pentathlon and decathlon events and football. Baseball Hall of Famers include Honus Wagner (1874–1955), Stan Musial (b.1920), and Roy Campanella (1921–1993). Outstanding Pennsylvania football players include Harold "Red" Grange (1903–91), George Blanda (b.1927), John Unitas (1933–2002), Joe Namath (b.1943), and Tony Dorsett (b.1954). Other stars include basketball's Wilt Chamberlain (1936–99); golf's Arnold Palmer (b.1929), tennis's Bill Tilden (1893–1953); horse racing's Bill Hartack (b.1932); billiards' Willie Mosconi (1913–93); swimming's Johnny Weissmuller (1904–84); and track and field's Bill Toomey (b.1939).

Pennsylvania has also been the birthplace of a duchess—Bessie Wallis Warfield, the Duchess of Windsor (1896–1986)—and of a princess—Grace Kelly, Princess Grace of Monaco (1929–82).

50 BIBLIOGRAPHY

Blockson, Charles L. *African Americans in Pennsylvania: A History and Guide.* Baltimore: Black Classic, 1994.

Bremer, Francis J., and Dennis B. Downey (eds.). *A Guide to the History of Pennsylvania.* Westport, Conn.: Greenwood, 1994.

Council of State Governments. *The Book of the States, 2006 Edition.* Lexington, Ky.: Council of State Governments, 2006.

Doherty, Craig A. *Pennsylvania.* New York: Facts On File, 2005.

Harper, Steven Craig. *Promised Land: Penn's Holy Experiment, the Walking Purchase, and the Dispossession of Delawares, 1600–1763.* Bethlehem, Pa.: Lehigh University Press, 2006.

Marzec, Robert P. (ed.). *The Mid-Atlantic Region.* Vol. 2 in *The Greenwood Encyclopedia of American Regional Cultures.* Westport, Conn.: Greenwood Press, 2004.

Miller, Arthur P. Jr., and Marjorie L. Miller. *Pennsylvania Battlefields and Military Landmarks.* Mechanicsburg, Pa.: Stackpole Books, 2000.

Miller, E. Willard (ed.). *A Geography of Pennsylvania.* University Park: Pennsylvania State University Press, 1995.

Root, Douglas. *Pennsylvania.* Oakland, Calif.: Compass American Guides, 2000.

Trumbauer, Lisa. *Voices from Colonial America. Pennsylvania, 1643–1776.* Washington, D.C.: National Geographic Society, 2005.

US Department of Commerce, Economics and Statistics Administration, US Census Bureau. *Pennsylvania, 2000. Summary Social, Economic, and Housing Characteristics: 2000 Census of Population and Housing.* Washington, D.C.: US Government Printing Office, 2003.

Wright, Robert E. *The First Wall Street: Chestnut Street, Philadelphia, and the Birth of American Finance.* Chicago: University of Chicago Press, 2005.

RHODE ISLAND

State of Rhode Island and Providence Plantations

ORIGIN OF STATE NAME: Named for Rhode Island in Narragansett Bay, which was likened to the isle of Rhodes in the Mediterranean Sea. **NICKNAME:** The Ocean State; Little Rhody. **CAPITAL:** Providence. **ENTERED UNION:** 29 May 1790 (13th). **SONG:** "Rhode Island." **MOTTO:** Hope. **COAT OF ARMS:** A golden anchor on a blue field. **FLAG:** In the center of a white field is a golden anchor with a blue ribbon containing the state motto in gold letters beneath it, all surrounded by a circle of 13 gold stars. **OFFICIAL SEAL:** The anchor of the arms is surrounded by four scrolls, the topmost bearing the state motto: the words "Seal of the State of Rhode Island and Providence Plantations 1636" encircle the whole. **BIRD:** Rhode Island Red. **FLOWER:** Violet. **TREE:** Red maple. **LEGAL HOLIDAYS:** New Year's Day, 1 January; Memorial Day, last Monday in May; Independence Day, 4 July; Victory Day, 2nd Monday in August; Labor Day, 1st Monday in September; Columbus Day, 2nd Monday in October; Veterans' Day and Armistice Day, 11 November; Thanksgiving Day, 4th Thursday in November; Christmas Day, 25 December. **TIME:** 7 AM EST = noon GMT.

[1] LOCATION, SIZE, AND EXTENT

One of the six New England states in the northeastern United States, Rhode Island is the smallest of all the 50 states. Rhode Island occupies only 0.03% of the total US area, and could fit inside Alaska, the largest state, nearly 486 times.

The total area of Rhode Island is 1,212 sq mi (3,139 sq km), of which land comprises 1,055 sq mi (2,732 sq km), and inland water 157 sq mi (407 sq km). The state extends 37 mi (60 km) E–W and 48 mi (77 km) N–S.

Rhode Island is bordered on the N and E by Massachusetts; on the S by the Atlantic Ocean (enclosing the ocean inlet, Narragansett Bay); and on the W by Connecticut (with part of the line formed by the Pawcatuck River). Three large islands—Prudence, Aquidneck (officially known as Rhode Island), and Conanicut—are situated within Narragansett Bay. Block Island, with an area of about 11 sq mi (28 sq km), lies some 9 mi (14 km) SW of Pt. Judith, on the mainland. There are 38 islands in all.

The total boundary length of Rhode Island is 160 mi (257 km). The state's geographic center is in Kent County, 1 mi (1.6 km) SSW of Cranston.

[2] TOPOGRAPHY

Rhode Island comprises two main regions. The New England Upland Region, which is rough and hilly and marked by forests and lakes, occupies the western two-thirds of the state, while the Seaboard Lowland, with its sandy beaches and salt marshes, occupies the eastern third. The highest point in the state is Jerimoth Hill, at 812 ft (248 m), in the northwest. The lowest elevation is sea level at the Atlantic Ocean. The mean elevation of the state is approximately 200 ft (61 m).

Rhode Island's principal river, the Blackstone, flows from Woonsocket past Pawtucket and thence into the Providence River, which, like the Sakonnet, is an estuary of Narragansett Bay; the

Pawcatuck River flows into Block Island Sound. There are about 65,000 acres (26,304 hectares) of wetlands in the state. The state has 38 islands, the largest being Aquidneck (Rhode Island), with an area of about 45 sq mi (117 sq km).

[3] CLIMATE

Rhode Island has a humid climate, with cold winters and short summers. The average annual temperature is 50°F (10°C). At Providence the temperature ranges from an average of 29°F (-1°C) in January to 73°F (22°C) in July. The record high temperature, 104°F (40°C), was registered in Providence on 2 August 1975; the record low, -23°F (-31°C), at Kingston on 11 January 1942. In Providence, the average annual precipitation is about 45.1 in (114 cm); snowfall averages 35.6 in (90 cm) a year. Rhode Island's weather is highly changeable, with storms and hurricanes an occasional threat. On 21 September 1938, a hurricane and tidal wave took a toll of 262 lives; Hurricane Carol, on 31 August 1954, left 19 dead, and property damage was estimated at $90 million. A blizzard on 6–7 February 1978 dropped a record 28.6 in (73 cm) of snow on the state, as measured at Warwick, and caused 21 storm-attributed deaths.

[4] FLORA AND FAUNA

Though small, Rhode Island has three distinct life zones: sandplain lowlands, rising hills, and highlands. Common trees are the tuliptree, pin and post oaks, and red cedar. Cattails are abundant in marsh areas, and 40 types of fern and 30 species of orchid are indigenous to the state. In April 2006, the small whorled pogonia was listed by the US Fish and Wildlife Service as threatened and the sandplain gerardia endangered.

Urbanization and industrialization have taken their toll of native mammals. Swordfish, bluefish, lobsters, and clams populate coastal waters; brook trout and pickerel are among the common freshwater fish. Fourteen Rhode Island animal species (vertebrates and invertebrates) were listed as threatened or endangered in April 2006, including the American burying beetle, bald eagle, finback and humpback whale, and four species of sea turtle.

5 ENVIRONMENTAL PROTECTION

The Department of Environmental Management (DEM) coordinates all of the state's environmental protection and management programs. The Air, Solid Waste, and Hazardous Materials Section enforces controls on solid waste disposal, hazardous waste management facilities, industrial air pollution, and site remediation; the Water Quality Management Section regulates waste-treatment facilities, the discharge of industrial and oil wastes into state waters and public sewer facilities, groundwater protection, freshwater wetlands, dam maintenance, and home sewage disposal systems; the Natural Resources Management Section oversees fish, wildlife and estuarine resources, forest management, parks and recreation, and the enforcement of conservation laws; Planning and Administrative Services assists industry in pollution prevention, administers recycling programs, administers land preservation programs, and coordinates land acquisitions. The department also oversees water supply management. In 2003, the DEM, working the Department of Health, operated a Mosquito Abatement Coordination Office to help citizens minimize the risk of contracting West Nile virus from the mosquito population.

In 2003, 0.9 million pounds of toxic chemicals were released in the state, the second lowest amount of all the states in the nation. Also in 2003, Rhode Island had 187 hazardous waste sites listed in the US Environment Protection Agency (EPA) database, 12 of which were on the National Priorities List as of 2006, including the Newport Naval Education & Training Center. In 1996, 10% of the state's area was wetland. In 2005, the EPA spent over $2.4 million through the Superfund program for the cleanup of hazardous waste sites in the state. The same year, federal EPA grants awarded to the state included $8.3 million for the drinking water state revolving fund and $7.2 million for the clean water revolving fund.

6 POPULATION

Rhode Island ranked 43rd in population in the United States with an estimated total of 1,076,189 in 2005, an increase of 2.7% since 2000. Between 1990 and 2000, Rhode Island's population grew from 1,003,464 to 1,048,319, an increase of 4.5%. The population is projected to reach 1.13 million by 2015 and over 1.15 million by 2025. The population density in 2004 was 1,041.3 persons per sq mi (402 persons per sq km), making Rhode Island the nation's second most densely populated state, after New Jersey. In 2004 the median age was 38.1. Persons under 18 years old accounted for 22.6% of the population while 13.9% was age 65 or older.

Providence, the capital, is the leading city, with an estimated population in 2004 of 178,126 (compared to the 1940 peak of 253,504). Other cities with large populations include Pawtucket and Woonsocket.

7 ETHNIC GROUPS

Rhode Island's black population numbered 46,908 in 2000, up from 39,000 in 1990 (and 4.5% of the state total). In 2004, 6.1% of the state's population was black. In 2000 there were 90,820 Hispanics and Latinos (8.7% of the total population), nearly twice the

1990 census count of 46,000. In 2004, 10.3% of the state's population was of Hispanic or Latino origin. In 2000, there were 5,121 American Indians, up from 4,000 in 1990. In 2004, 0.6% of the population was American Indian or Alaskan Native. The Asian population was 23,665; the 2000 census reported 4,974 Chinese, 4,522 Cambodians, 2,942 Asian Indians, and 2,062 Filipinos. Pacific Islanders numbered 567. In 2004, 2.7% of the population was Asian and 0.1% Pacific Islander. The foreign born made up 11.4% of the population in 2000, or 119,277 persons, up from 9.5% of the population in 1990. In 2004, 1.5% of the population reported origin of two or more races.

8 LANGUAGES

Many place-names in Rhode Island attest to the early presence of Mahican Indians: for instance, Sakonnet Point, Pawtucket, Matunuck, Narragansett.

English in Rhode Island is of the Northern dialect, with the distinctive features of eastern New England: absence of final /r/, and a vowel in *part* and *bath* intermediate between that in *father* and that in *bat*.

Rhode Island's immigrant tradition is reflected in the fact that in 2000, 20% of the state's residents reported speaking a language other than English in the home, up from 18% in 1990.

The following table gives selected statistics from the 2000 Census for language spoken at home by persons five years old and over. The category "African languages" includes Amharic, Ibo, Twi, Yoruba, Bantu, Swahili, and Somali.

LANGUAGE	NUMBER	PERCENT
Population 5 years and over	**985,184**	**100.0**
Speak only English	788,560	80.0
Speak a language other than English	196,624	20.0
Speak a language other than English	**196,624**	**20.0**
Spanish or Spanish Creole	79,443	8.1
Portuguese or Portuguese Creole	37,437	3.8
French (incl. Patois, Cajun)	19,385	2.0
Italian	13,759	1.4
Mon-Khmer, Cambodian	5,586	0.6
French Creole	4,337	0.4
Chinese	3,882	0.4
Laotian	3,195	0.3
Polish	2,966	0.3
German	2,841	0.3
African languages	2,581	0.3
Arabic	2,086	0.2

9 RELIGIONS

The first European settlement in Rhode Island was founded by an English clergyman, Roger Williams, who left Massachusetts to find freedom of worship. The Rhode Island Charter of 1663 proclaimed that a "flourishing civil state may stand and best be maintained with full liberty in religious concernments." Rhode Island has maintained this viewpoint throughout its history, and has long been a model of religious pluralism. The first Baptist congregation in the United States was established in 1638 in Providence. In Newport stands the oldest synagogue (1763) and the oldest Quaker meetinghouse (1699) in the United States.

A majority of the population of Rhode Island is Catholic, reflecting heavy immigration from Italy, Ireland, Portugal, and French Canada. In 2004, there were 679,275 Roman Catholics, accounting for about 64% of the total state population. According to 2000 data, the largest Protestant denominations were Episco-

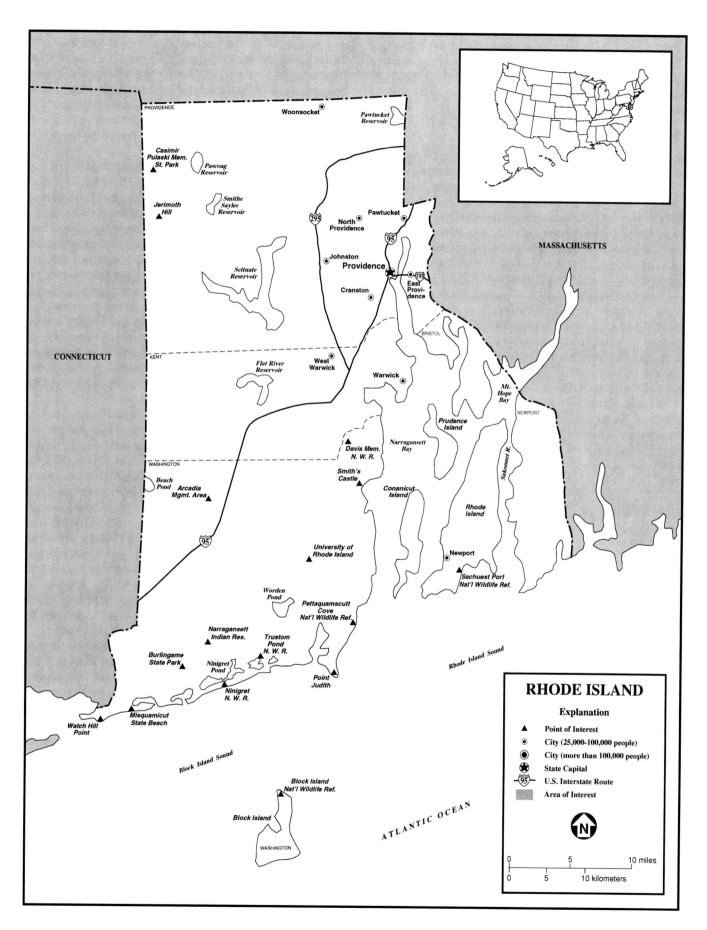

CONNECTICUT

MASSACHUSETTS

PROVIDENCE

Woonsocket

Pawtucket Reservoir

Casimir Pulaski Mem. St. Park

Pascoag Reservoir

Smithe Sayles Reservoir

Jerimoth Hill

North Providence

Pawtucket

Johnston

Providence

Cranston

East Providence

Scituate Reservoir

BRISTOL

KENT

Flat River Reservoir

West Warwick

Warwick

Mt. Hope Bay

NEWPORT

Prudence Island

Narragansett Bay

Davis Mem. N. W. R.

WASHINGTON

Smith's Castle

Conanicut Island

Rhode Island

Beach Pond

Arcadia Mgmt. Area

Sakonnet R.

University of Rhode Island

Newport

Sachuest Port Nat'l Wildlife Ref.

Worden Pond

Pettaquamscutt Cove Nat'l Wildlife Ref.

Narragansett Indian Res.

Trustom Pond N. W. R.

Burlingame State Park

Ninigret Pond

Point Judith

Ninigret N. W. R.

Rhode Island Sound

Misquamicut State Beach

Watch Hill Point

Block Island Sound

Block Island Nat'l Wildlife Ref.

Block Island

ATLANTIC OCEAN

WASHINGTON

RHODE ISLAND

Explanation

▲ Point of Interest
◉ City (25,000-100,000 people)
◉ City (more than 100,000 people)
★ State Capital
〰95〰 U.S. Interstate Route
▓ Area of Interest

0   5   10 miles
0   5   10 kilometers

palians, with 26,756 adherents, and American Baptists USA, with 20,997. There were about 7,686 members of the United Church of Christ in 2005. An estimated 16,10 Jews resided in the state the same year, as did about 1,827 Muslims. Friends–USA (Quakers) had only 599 members. About 36.5% of the population did not specify a religious affiliation.

[10]TRANSPORTATION

As of 2003, Rhode Island had only one operating railroad within its borders, the regional Providence & Worcester, which utilized the state's 102 rail mi (164 km) of track. In the same year, chemicals were the top commodity hauled from the state. As of 2006, Amtrak operated daily trains through Rhode Island, via its Acela Express train and its Regional northeast corridor trains.

In 2004, there were 6,419 mi (10,334 km) of public highways and roads. In that same year, some 824,000 motor vehicles were registered with the state, while there were 741,841 licensed drivers. The major route through New England, I-95, crosses Rhode Island. The Rhode Island Public Transit Authority provides commuter bus service connecting urbanized areas.

Some of the best deepwater ocean ports on the east coast are in Narragansett Bay. The port at Providence handled 9.558 million tons of cargo in 2004. In 2003, waterborne shipments totaled 9.417 million tons. In 2004, Rhode Island had only 39 mi (62 km) of navigable inland waterways.

In 2005, Rhode Island had a total of 28 public and private-use aviation-related facilities. This included 10 airports, 17 heliports and one seaplane base. Theodore Francis Green Airport is the state's major air terminal, with 2,732,524 passengers enplaned in 2004.

[11]HISTORY

Before the arrival of the first white settlers, the Narragansett Indians inhabited the area from what is now Providence south along Narragansett Bay. Their principal rivals, the Wampanoag, dominated the eastern shore region.

In 1524, Florentine navigator Giovanni da Verrazano, sailing in the employ of France, became the first European to explore Rhode Island. The earliest permanent settlement was established at Providence in 1636 by English clergyman Roger Williams and a small band of followers who left the repressive atmosphere of the Massachusetts Bay Colony to seek freedom of worship. Other nonconformists followed, settling Portsmouth (1638), Newport (1639), and Warwick (1642). In 1644, Williams journeyed to England, where he secured a parliamentary patent uniting the four original towns into a single colony, the Providence Plantations. This legislative grant remained in effect until the Stuart Restoration made it prudent to seek a royal charter. The charter, secured for Rhode Island and the Providence Plantations from Charles II in 1663, guaranteed religious liberty, permitting significant local autonomy, and strengthened the colony's territorial claims. Encroachments by white settlers on Indian lands led to the Indian uprising known as King Philip's War (1675–76), during which the Indians were soundly defeated.

The early 18th century was marked by significant growth in agriculture and commerce, including the rise of the slave trade. Having the greatest degree of self-rule, Rhode Island had the most to

lose from British efforts after 1763 to increase the mother country's supervision and control over the colonies. On 4 May 1776, Rhode Island became the first colony formally to renounce all allegiance to King George III. Favoring the weak central government established by the Articles of Confederation, the state quickly ratified them in 1778, but subsequently resisted the centralizing tendencies of the federal constitution. Rhode Island withheld ratification until 29 May 1790, making it the last of the original 13 states to join the Union.

The principal trends in 19th-century Rhode Island were industrialization, immigration, and urbanization. The state's royal charter (then still in effect) contained no procedure for its amendment, gave disproportionate influence to the declining rural towns, and conferred almost unlimited power on the legislature. In addition, suffrage was restricted by the General Assembly to owners of real estate and their eldest sons. Because earlier, moderate efforts at change had been virtually ignored by the assembly, political reformers decided to bypass the legislature and convene a People's Convention. Thomas Wilson Dorr, who led this movement, became the principal draftsman of a progressive "People's Constitution," ratified in a popular referendum in December 1841. A coalition of Whigs and rural Democrats used force to suppress the movement now known as Dorr's Rebellion, but they bowed to popular pressure and made limited changes via a new constitution, effective May 1843.

The latter half of the 19th century was marked by continued industrialization and urbanization. Immigration increased and became more diverse. Politically the state was dominated by the Republican Party until the 1930s. The Democrats, having seized the opportunity during the New Deal, consolidated their power during the 1940s, and from that time onward have captured most state and congressional elections. Present-day Rhode Island, though predominantly Catholic and Democratic, retains an ethnic and cultural diversity surprising in view of its size but consistent with its pluralist traditions. Rhode Island's residents have been moving from the cities to the suburbs, and in 1980 the state lost its ranking as the most urban state in the country to New Jersey. In the mid-1990s Rhode Island was still the nation's second most densely populated state, with more than three-quarters of its residents living within 15 mi (25 km) of the capital city of Providence.

From the 1950s to the 1980s, 30% of the workforce was in manufacturing jobs; in the 1990s many of these were still low-paid jobs in the jewelry and textile industries. Rhode Island experienced a real estate boom in the 1980s thanks to federal savings and loan deregulation and the state's proximity to the thriving Boston metropolitan area. However, real estate values declined at the end of the decade, and Rhode Island entered the 1990s with a banking crisis that forced its government to spend taxpayer dollars propping up uninsured financial institutions. The state was also hard hit by the recession of the early 1990s. By 1994 a slow recovery was under way, with unemployment fluctuating between 6% and 8%. Though the state's economy grew less quickly than that of its New England neighbors, it experienced a full recovery by the end of the 1990s and successfully made the transition from a manufacturing-based system to one reliant on the service sector. Further, it had done so without widening the gap between rich and poor, an achievement that had eluded other states. As of 1999,

Rhode Island's unemployment rate was 4.1%, in line with the national average. Between January 1999 and January 2000 alone, the state added 10,300 jobs. By 2001, however, the nation was in the grip of recession, and Rhode Island's unemployment rate by July 2003 was 5.6%, albeit below the national average of 6.2%. The state faced a $200 million budget deficit that year. In 2005, the state had a budget deficit of $164 million. The unemployment rate in 2004 was 5.2%, below the national average of 5.5%.

Rhode Island was the setting for a landmark lawsuit settlement in 1999. Three years earlier, the worst oil spill in the state's history contaminated waters and destroyed lobsters in Block Island Sound. Under the federal Oil Spill Act of 1990, those responsible for the spill settled separately with local lobstermen and the state, which was to direct $18 million in ongoing cleanup and recovery efforts. The cases were expected to set the standard for future negotiations in the wake of oil spills.

Republican Governor Donald Carcieri, elected in 2002, allowed a minimum wage increase of 60 cents to become law without his signature in 2003. Rhode Island's minimum wage law effective 1 January 2004 was $6.75 per hour. Carcieri pledged to revamp state government, create jobs, and balance the budget without raising taxes. In 2004, he proposed new state bonds to provide the funding necessary to preserve Narragansett Bay and to safeguard drinking water resources. Those measures were approved by voters in November 2004. He also formed the Narragansett Bay and Watershed Commission, which drafted a long-term plan for saving coastal resources.

12 STATE GOVERNMENT

Rhode Island has had two constitutions: the first based on the colonial charter (1842) and a revision (1986). In 1986, 8 amendments and a revision of the constitution were approved; subsequently, the constitution has been known as the 1986 Constitution. From 1986 through January 2005 there have been 8 amendments; total amendments since 1842 number 60.

Legislative authority is vested in the General Assembly, a bicameral body composed of 38 senators and 75 representatives. All legislators are elected for two-year terms from districts that are apportioned equally according to population after every federal decennial census. Annual sessions begin in January and are unlimited. The legislature may call for a special session by a joint call of the presiding officers of both houses. Legislators must be US citizens, qualified voters, at least 18 years of age, and residents of both state and district for at least 30 days. Among the more important checks enjoyed by the assembly is the power to override the governor's veto by a three-fifths vote of its members present and the power to establish all courts below the supreme court. The legislative salary in 2004 was $12,285.53.

State elected officials are the governor and lieutenant governor (elected separately), attorney general, secretary of state, and general treasurer. All are elected, in the odd-numbered year following presidential elections, for four-year terms. The governor is limited to serving two consecutive terms. The governor and lieutenant governor must be US citizens, qualified voters, at least 18 years of age, and 30 days a citizen and resident of Rhode Island. As of December 2004, the governor's salary was $105,194.

A bill passed by the legislature becomes law if signed by the governor, if left unsigned by the governor for six days while the legislature is in session (10 days if the legislature adjourns), or if passed over the governor's veto by three-fifths of the members present in each house. Legislation becomes effective upon enactment. Constitutional amendments are made by majority vote of the whole membership of each house of the legislature, and by a simple majority at the next general election.

Voters must be US citizens, 18 years old or over, and must have been residents of the state at least 30 days prior to an election. Restrictions apply to convicted felons and those declared mentally incompetent by the court.

13 POLITICAL PARTIES

For nearly five decades, Rhode Island has been one of the nation's most solidly Democratic states. It has voted for the Republican presidential candidate only four times since 1928, elected only one Republican (former Governor John H. Chafee) to the US Senate since 1934, and sent no Republicans to the US House from 1940 until 1980, when one Republican and one Democrat were elected. (They were reelected in 1982 and 1984.) Also in 1980, Rhode Island was one of only six states to favor Jimmy Carter. However, in 1984, Republican Edward DiPrete was elected governor, and Ronald Reagan narrowly carried the state in the presidential election. In the 2000 presidential election, Democrat Al Gore won 61% of the vote to Republican George W. Bush's 32%; independent candidate Ralph Nader took 6% of the popular vote. In 2004, Democrat John Kerry won 59.5% of the vote to incumbent President Bush's 38.9%.

In 1994, Republican John H. Chafee won a fourth term in the US Senate. Republican Lincoln D. Chafee was named senator in November 1999 upon the death of his father; he was elected to his first full term in 2000. In 1996, Democrat Jack Reed won the Senate seat vacated by Claiborne Pell after 36 years in office; Reed was reelected in 2002. Both US Representatives were Democrats in 2005. In mid-2005 there were 33 Democrats and 5 Republicans in the state Senate, and 59 Democrats and 16 Republicans in the

Rhode Island Presidential Vote, 1948–2004

YEAR	ELECTORAL VOTE	RHODE ISL. WINNER	DEMOCRAT	REPUBLICAN
1948	4	*Truman (D)	188,736	135,787
1952	4	*Eisenhower (R)	203,293	210,935
1956	4	*Eisenhower (R)	161,790	225,819
1960	4	*Kennedy (D)	258,032	147,502
1964	4	*Johnson (D)	315,463	74,615
1968	4	Humphrey (D)	246,518	122,359
1972	4	*Nixon (R)	194,645	220,383
1976	4	*Carter (D)	227,636	181,249
1980	4	Carter (D)	198,342	154,793
1984	4	*Reagan (R)	197,106	212,080
1988	4	Dukakis (D)	225,123	177,761
1992**	4	*Clinton (D)	213,299	131,601
1996**	4	*Clinton (D)	233,050	104,683
2000	4	Gore (D)	249,508	130,555
2004	4	Kerry (D)	259,760	169,046

*Won US presidential election.
**IND. candidate Ross Perot received 105,045 votes in 1992 and 43,723 votes in 1996.

state House; the governor's office was held by Republican Donald L. Carcieri, who was elected in 2002.

14 LOCAL GOVERNMENT

As of 2005, Rhode Island was subdivided into 5 counties, 8 municipal governments, 36 school districts, and 75 special districts. In 2002, there were 31 townships.

Many smaller communities retain the New England town meeting form of government, under which the town's eligible voters assemble to enact the local budget, set the tax levy, and approve other local measures. Larger cities and towns are governed by a mayor and/or city manager and a council.

In 2005, local government accounted for about 30,118 full-time (or equivalent) employment positions.

15 STATE SERVICES

To address the continuing threat of terrorism and to work with the federal Department of Homeland Security, homeland security in Rhode Island operates under the authority of the governor; the public safety director/secretary is designated as the state homeland security advisor.

The Department of Elementary and Secondary Education and the Board of Governors for Higher Education oversee all state educational services. Railroads, motor vehicle administration, and highway and bridge management come under the jurisdiction of the Department of Transportation. Health and welfare services are provided through the Department of Corrections; Department of the Attorney General; Department of Children, Youth, and Families; Department of Elderly Affairs; Department of Health; Department of Mental Health, Retardation, and Hospitals; and the Department of Human Services.

16 JUDICIAL SYSTEM

The five-member Supreme Court is the state's highest appellate tribunal. It may also issue, upon request, advisory opinions on the constitutionality of a questioned act to the governor or either house of the legislature. Supreme court justices are chosen by the legislature and, like other state judges, hold office for life ("during good behavior"), but in actuality they can be removed by a mere resolution of the General Assembly. In 1935, all five justices were ousted in this manner when a Democratic legislature replaced a court previously appointed by Republicans. In 1994, Chief Justice Thomas Fay resigned under impeachment pressure.

The General Trial Court is the superior court, with 1,012 justices in 1999. The state's trial court hears all jury trials in criminal cases and in civil matters involving more than $5,000, but can also hear non-jury cases. Superior and district court judges are appointed by the governor with the consent of the Senate.

District courts do not hold jury trials. Civil matters that involve $5,000 or less, small claims procedures, and non-jury criminal cases, including felony arraignments and misdemeanors, are handled at the district level. All cities and towns appoint judges to operate probate courts for wills and estates. Providence and a few other communities each have a municipal or police court.

As of 31 December 2004, a total of 3,430 prisoners were held in Rhode Island's state and federal prisons, a decrease from 3,527 of 2.8% from the previous year. As of year-end 2004, a total of 208 inmates were female, down from 222 or 6.3% from the year before.

Among sentenced prisoners (one year or more), New Mexico had an incarceration rate of 175 per 100,000 population in 2004.

According to the Federal Bureau of Investigation, Rhode Island in 2004, had a violent crime rate (murder/nonnegligent manslaughter; forcible rape; robbery; aggravated assault) of 247.4 reported incidents per 100,000 population, or a total of 2,673 reported incidents. Crimes against property (burglary; larceny/theft; and motor vehicle theft) in that same year totaled 31,166 reported incidents or 2,884.1 reported incidents per 100,000 people. Rhode Island has no death penalty.

17 ARMED FORCES

In 2004, there were 2,336 active duty military personnel and 4,370 civilian personnel stationed in Rhode Island, most of whom were at the US Naval Education and Training Center and Naval War College in Newport. Rhode Island firms received more than $417 million in defense contracts during 2004. Defense Department payroll outlays totaled $621 million.

In 2003, there were 91,161 US veterans living in the state, of whom 16,658 saw military service during World War II; 11,442 in the Korean conflict; 26,598 during the Vietnam era; and 10,008 in the Gulf War. In 2004, the Veterans Administration expended more than $254 million in pensions, medical assistance, and other major veterans' benefits.

As of 31 October 2004, the Rhode Island State Police employed 190 full-time sworn officers.

18 MIGRATION

During the 19th and early 20th centuries, the major immigrant groups who came to work in the state's growing industries were Irish, Italian, and French-Canadian. Significant numbers of British, Portuguese, Swedish, Polish, and German immigrants also moved to Rhode Island. Between 1940 and 1970, however, 2,000 more people left the state than moved to it, and between 1970 and 1983 there was a net loss of about 42,000. From 1985 to 1990, there was a net gain from migration of nearly 34,000. Between 1990 and 1998, Rhode Island had a net loss of 64,000 in domestic migration and a net gain of 16,000 in international migration. In 1998, 1,976 foreign immigrants arrived in the state. Rhode Island's overall population decreased 1.5% between 1990 and 1998.

During the 1980s, the urban proportion of the population remained virtually unchanged, dropping from 87% to 86%. By 1996, the metropolitan population had reached 93.8%. In the period 2000–05, net international migration was 18,965 and net internal migration was -4,964, for a net gain of 14,001 people.

19 INTERGOVERNMENTAL COOPERATION

Rhode Island participates in many interstate regional bodies, including the Atlantic States Marine Fisheries Commission, Interstate Compact for Juveniles, New England Interstate Water Pollution Control Commission, and Northeastern Forest Fire Protection Commission. New England regional agreements include those on tuberculosis control, radiological health protection, higher education, police, and dairy products. Federal grants to Rhode Island state and local governments totaled $1.697 billion in fiscal year 2005, an estimated $1.752 billion in fiscal year 2006, and an estimated $1.790 billion in fiscal year 2007.

²⁰ECONOMY

Rhode Island's economy was historically based overwhelmingly on industry, with agriculture, mining, forestry, and fishing making only small contributions. The state's leading manufactured products were jewelry, silverware, machinery, primary metals, textiles, and rubber products. In the late 1990s, manufacturing declined steadily as a contributor to state economic output, falling from 14.7% in 1997 to 11.1% in 2001. The recession of 2001 only accelerated the contraction in Rhode Island's manufacturing output to 3.3% from its previous rates of about 2% a year. The strongest growth sectors in terms of output coming into the 21st century were: financial services (up 44.3%); trade (up 28.5%); general services (up 25.6%); and government (up 20.6%). Unemployment rates in Rhode Island exceeded those of the United States throughout the 1970s, and the state's economic growth lagged behind that of the nation as a whole. Unemployment fell dramatically in 1983 and 1984, rose again to 8.7% in 1992, but had fallen to around 5% by 1996. Manufacturing employment declined 23% between 1983 and 1992 while service jobs increased 36%. In all, only about 1,000 jobs were lost between 1988 and 1998, mostly in the manufacturing sector, while service-related jobs rose, accounting for about half of all personal income in 1998. The impact of the 2001 national recession and slowdown on Rhode Island's employment and income was the mildest among the New England states. By mid-2002, job growth had surpassed the peak reached in 2000.

In 2004, Rhode Island's gross state product (GSP) was $41.679 billion, of which the real estate sector accounted for $5.421 billion or 13% of GSP, with health and social assistance at $3.798 billion (9.1% of GSP) and construction at $2.459 billion (5.8% of GSP). In that same year, there were an estimated 95,390 small businesses in Rhode Island. Of the 33,253 businesses that had employees, an estimated total of 32,098 or 96.5% were small companies. An estimated 3,932 new businesses were established in the state in 2004, up 13.5% from the year before. Business terminations that same year came to 4,250, up 3.6% from 2003. There were 74 business bankruptcies in 2004, up 54.2% from the previous year. In 2005, the state's personal bankruptcy (Chapter 7 and Chapter 13) filing rate was 422 filings per 100,000 people, ranking Rhode Island 35th in the nation.

²¹INCOME

In 2005 Rhode Island had a gross state product (GSP) of $44 billion which accounted for 0.4% of the nation's gross domestic product and placed the state at number 45 in highest GSP among the 50 states and the District of Columbia.

According to the Bureau of Economic Analysis, in 2004 Rhode Island had a per capita personal income (PCPI) of $34,207. This ranked 16th in the United States and was 104% of the national average of $33,050. The 1994–2004 average annual growth rate of PCPI was 4.5%. Rhode Island had a total personal income (TPI) of $36,940,300,000, which ranked 43rd in the United States and reflected an increase of 5.8% from 2003. The 1994–2004 average annual growth rate of TPI was 5.1%. Earnings of persons employed in Rhode Island increased from $24,586,561,000 in 2003 to $25,887,459,000 in 2004, an increase of 5.3%. The 2003–04 national change was 6.3%.

The US Census Bureau reports that the three-year average median household income for 2002–04 in 2004 dollars was $46,199 compared to a national average of $44,473. During the same period an estimated 11.3% of the population was below the poverty line as compared to 12.4% nationwide.

²²LABOR

According to the Bureau of Labor Statistics (BLS), in April 2006 the seasonally adjusted civilian labor force in Rhode Island 578,400, with approximately 31,100 workers unemployed, yielding an unemployment rate of 5.4%, compared to the national average of 4.7% for the same period. Preliminary data for the same period placed nonfarm employment at 495,000. Since the beginning of the BLS data series in 1976, the highest unemployment rate recorded in Rhode Island was 9.7% in November 1982. The historical low was 2.9% in July 1988. Preliminary nonfarm employment data by occupation for April 2006 showed that approximately 4.6% of the labor force was employed in construction; 10.7% in manufacturing; 16.3% in trade, transportation, and public utilities; 7.2% in financial activities; 11.4% in professional and business services; 19.4% in education and health services; 10.1% in leisure and hospitality services; and 13.1% in government.

The BLS reported that in 2005, a total of 79,000 of Rhode Island's 494,000 employed wage and salary workers were formal members of a union. This represented 15.9% of those so employed, down from 16.3% in 2004, but still above the national average of 12%. Overall in 2005, a total of 83,000 workers (16.8%) in Rhode Island were covered by a union or employee association contract, which includes those workers who reported no union affiliation. Rhode Island is one of 28 states with a right-to-work law.

As of 1 March 2006, Rhode Island had a state-mandated minimum wage rate of $7.10 per hour. In 2004, women in the state accounted for 49% of the employed civilian labor force.

²³AGRICULTURE

The state's total receipts from farm marketings were $63 million in 2005, 50th in the United States. Rhode Island had only about 850 farms in 2004 with an average size of just 71 acres (29 hectares), with the smallest area devoted to crops (21,000 acres, or 8,500 hectares) of any state. Nursery and greenhouse products were the main agricultural commodity. Total crop marketings amounted to $53 million in 2005.

²⁴ANIMAL HUSBANDRY

In 2005, Rhode Island had around 5,500 cattle and calves, valued at $5.5 million. During 2004, there were some 2,000 hogs and pigs, valued at $220,000. In 2003, the state produced 22 million lb (10 million kg) of milk, from 1,300 milk cows.

²⁵FISHING

The commercial catch in 2004 was 97.4 million lb (44.3 million kg), valued at $71.1 million. Point Judith is the main fishing port, ranking 24th in the United States, with catch value at $31.5 million. The state ranked second in the nation for squid catch with 38.1 million lb (17.3 million kg). Other valuable fish and shellfish include whiting, fluke and yellowtail flounders, cod, scup lobster, and clams. In 2001, the commercial fishing fleet consisted of 2,920 boats and 344 vessels. In 2003, there were 16 processing plants employing about 453 people.

In 2004, Rhode Island issued 26,629 sport-fishing licenses. Three hatcheries distribute nearly 326,000 lb (148,000 kg) of trout throughout the state each year.

26 FORESTRY

In 2004, forests covered 393,000 acres (159,000 hectares), about 60% of the state's land area. Some 340,000 acres (138,000 hectares) were usable as commercial timberland.

27 MINING

According to preliminary data from the US Geological Survey (USGS), the estimated value of nonfuel mineral production by Rhode Island in 2003 was $25.8 million, an increase from 2002 of about 1%.

According to the preliminary data for 2003, construction sand and gravel, and crushed stone were the state's top nonfuel minerals, accounting for around 52% and almost 48% of output by value, respectively. Industrial sand and gravel, and gemstones (by hobbyists) were also produced in Rhode Island, that same year.

Preliminary data for 2003 showed that a total of 1.9 million metric tons of construction sand and gravel was produced, with a value of $13.5 million, while crushed stone output that year totaled 1.9 million metric tons, valued at $12.3 million.

28 ENERGY AND POWER

Rhode Island is part of the New England regional power grid and imports most of its electric power. As of 2003, Rhode Island had eight electrical power service providers, of which one was publicly owned, three were investor owned, three were generation-only suppliers and two were delivery-only providers. As of that same year there were 476,316 retail customers. Of that total, 466,805 received their power from investor-owned service providers. Publicly owned providers had 4,525 customers, while generation-only suppliers had 4,986 customers. There was no data on the number of delivery-only customers.

Total net summer generating capability by the state's electrical generating plants in 2003 stood at 1.733 million kW, with total production that same year at 5.621 billion kWh. Of the total amount generated, only 0.2% came from electric utilities, with the remaining 99.8% coming from independent producers and combined heat and power service providers. The largest portion of all electric power generated, 5.454 billion kWh (97%), came from natural gas fired plants, with other renewable sources in second place at 101.768 billion kWh (1.8%) and petroleum fueled plants in third at 58.359 billion kWh (1%). Hydroelectric sources at 0.1% accounted for the remainder.

Rhode island has no refineries, nor any proven reserves or production of crude oil or natural gas.

29 INDUSTRY

The Industrial Revolution began early in Rhode Island. The first spinning jenny in the United States was built at Providence in 1787. Three years later, in Pawtucket, Samuel Slater opened a cotton mill, one of the first modern factories in America. By the end of the 18th century, textile, jewelry, and metal products were being manufactured in the state.

Over 1,000 manufacturers in the state produce finished jewelry and jewelry parts. Electronic and related products manufactured in the state include online lottery machines, circuit boards, and meteorological, navigational, and medical equipment. Chemicals and allied products made in the state include pigments and dyes, drugs and biomedical products, and liquid and aerosol consumer products.

According to the US Census Bureau's Annual Survey of Manufactures (ASM) for 2004, Rhode Island's manufacturing sector covered some 14 product subsectors. The shipment value of all products manufactured in the state that same year was $11.173 billion. Of that total, miscellaneous manufacturing accounted for the largest share at $1.949 billion. It was followed by electrical equipment, appliance and component manufacturing at $1.824 billion; fabricated metal product manufacturing at $1.561 billion; computer and electronic product manufacturing at $813.739 million; and plastics and rubber products manufacturing at $736.243 million.

In 2004, a total of 55,367 people in Rhode Island were employed in the state's manufacturing sector, according to the ASM. Of that total, 35,544 were actual production workers. In terms of total employment, the miscellaneous manufacturing industry accounted for the largest portion of all manufacturing employees at 11,614, with 7,618 actual production workers. It was followed by fabricated metal product manufacturing at 9,001 employees (6,706 actual production workers); computer and electronic product manufacturing at 4,825 employees (799 actual production workers); plastics and rubber products manufacturing with 4,083 employees (3,096 actual production workers); and electrical equipment, appliance and component manufacturing at 3,469 employees (2,052 actual production employees).

ASM data for 2004 showed that Rhode Island's manufacturing sector paid $2.235 billion in wages. Of that amount, the miscellaneous manufacturing sector accounted for the largest share at $384.278 million. It was followed by fabricated metal product manufacturing at $356.366 million; computer and electronic product manufacturing at $282.567 million; electrical equipment, appliance and component manufacturing at $169.127 million; and machinery manufacturing at $154.401 million.

30 COMMERCE

According to the 2002 Census of Wholesale Trade, Rhode Island's wholesale trade sector had sales that year totaling $8.5 billion from 1,479 establishments. Wholesalers of durable goods accounted for 936 establishments, followed by nondurable goods wholesalers at 442 and electronic markets, agents, and brokers accounting for 101 establishments. Sales by durable goods wholesalers in 2002 totaled $3.74 billion, while wholesalers of nondurable goods saw sales of $3.71 billion. Electronic markets, agents, and brokers in the wholesale trade industry had sales of $1.1 billion.

In the 2002 Census of Retail Trade, Rhode Island was listed as having 4,134 retail establishments with sales of $10.3 billion. The leading types of retail businesses by number of establishments were: food and beverage stores (695); clothing and clothing accessories stores (565); miscellaneous store retailers (504); and motor vehicle and motor vehicle parts dealers (429). In terms of sales, motor vehicle and motor vehicle parts dealers accounted for the largest share of retail sales at $2.6 billion, followed by food and beverage stores at $1.9 billion; health and personal care stores at $1.07 billion; general merchandise stores at $973.3 million; and gasoline stations at $655.7 million. A total of 50,665 people were employed by the retail sector in Rhode Island that year.

Rhode Island's foreign exports of manufactured goods totaled $1.2 billion in 2005.

31 CONSUMER PROTECTION

The Consumer Protection Unit of the Department of the Attorney General bears the primary responsibility for investigating and mediating consumer complaints of unlawful and unfair business practices and misleading advertising that arise from violations of the state's Deceptive Trade Practices Act. The unit also enforces the state's Telephone Sales Solicitation Act, the registration of health clubs under the state's Health Club Law, and provides information and referral services to the general public. In addition to the Consumer Protection Unit, the state's Attorney General's Office has other office units dedicated to other specific consumer protection related issues such as: charitable trusts (Charitable Trust Unit); antitrust violations (Antitrust Unit); environmental issues (Environmental Unit); insurance advocacy (Insurance Advocacy Unit (covers insurance rate hearings, healthcare and insurance fraud); public utilities (Public Utilities Regulation Unit); open government (complaints over access to public records and violations of the Open Meetings Act); and healthcare advocacy (Office of Health Care Advocate; helps patients with healthcare issues and can act on behalf of those consumers who are not able to act on their own).

When dealing with consumer protection issues, the state's Attorney General's office can initiate civil and criminal proceedings; administer consumer protection and education programs; handle formal consumer complaints; and exercise limited subpoena powers. However, the Attorney General's Office cannot represent the state before regulatory agencies. In antitrust actions, the Attorney General's office cannot act on behalf of those consumers who are incapable of acting on their own, but can initiate damage actions on behalf of the state in state courts and initiate criminal proceedings. The Attorney General's office, cannot represent counties, cities and other governmental entities in recovering civil damages under state or federal law.

The offices of the Consumer Protection Unit and the Department of the Attorney General are located in Providence.

32 BANKING

As of June 2005, Rhode Island had 14 insured banks, savings and loans, and saving banks, plus 11 state-chartered and 19 federally chartered credit unions (CUs). Excluding the CUs, the Providence-New Bedford-Fall River market area accounted for the largest portion of the state's financial institutions and deposits in 2004, with 40 institutions and $29.179 billion in deposits. As of June 2005, CUs accounted for 14.6% of all assets held by all financial institutions in the state, or some $3.518 billion. Banks, sav-

ings and loans, and savings banks collectively accounted for the remaining 85.4% or $20.500 billion in assets held.

As of 2002, about 50% of the state's banks had long-term asset concentrations of greater than 40%. Savings banks represented 50% of insured banks in Rhode Island and residential real estate loans made up 56% of the average loan portfolio in that year.

The median percentage of past-due/nonaccrual loans to total loans in the fourth quarter of 2005 stood at 0.56%, down from 0.56% in 2004 and 0.62% in 2003. regulation of state-chartered banks and other state-chartered financial institutions in Rhode Island is the responsibility of the state's Department of Business Regulation's Division of Banking.

33 INSURANCE

In 2004, 509,000 individual life insurance policies worth $51.6.0 billion were in force in Rhode Island; total value for all categories of life insurance (individual, group, and credit) was about $83.9 billion. The average coverage amount is $101,000 per policy holder. Death benefits paid that year totaled $233.6 million.

As of 2003, there were 23 property and casualty and 4 life and health insurance companies domiciled in the state. In 2004, direct premiums for property and casualty insurance totaled over $1.9 billion. That year, there were 11,774 flood insurance policies in force in the state, with a total value of $2 million. About $802 million of coverage was held through FAIR plans, which are designed to offer coverage for some natural circumstances, such as wind and hail, in high risk areas.

In 2004, 56% of state residents held employment-based health insurance policies, 4% held individual policies, and 28% were covered under Medicare and Medicaid; 11% of residents were uninsured. In 2003, employee contributions for employment-based health coverage averaged at 22% for single coverage and 27% for family coverage. The state offers an 18-month health benefits expansion program for small-firm employees in connection with the Consolidated Omnibus Budget Reconciliation Act (COBRA, 1986), a health insurance program for those who lose employment-based coverage due to termination or reduction of work hours.

In 2003, there were 672,295 auto insurance policies in effect for private passenger cars. Required minimum coverage includes bodily injury liability of up to $25,000 per individual and $50,000 for all persons injured in an accident, as well as property damage liability of $25,000. Uninsured motorist coverage is also required. In 2003, the average expenditure per vehicle for insurance coverage was $992.22, which ranked as the seventh-highest average in the nation.

34 SECURITIES

Rhode Island has no securities exchanges. In 2005, there were 500 personal financial advisers employed in the state. In 2004, there were over 21 publicly traded companies within the state, with over seven NASDAQ companies, five NYSE listings, and two AMEX listings. In 2006, the state had two Fortune 500 companies; CVS, based in Woonsocket and listed on the NYSE, ranked 1st in the state and 53rd in the nation, with revenues of over $37 billion, followed by Textron, based in Providence and also on the NYSE, ranked 190th in the nation with revenues of $11.9 billion. FM

Global, Hasbro, American Power Conversion, Nortek, and Amica Mutual Insurance were listed in the Fortune 1,000.

35 PUBLIC FINANCE

The annual budget is prepared by the State Budget Office in conjunction with the governor, and submitted to the legislature for approval. The fiscal year (FY) runs from 1 July through 30 June.

Fiscal year 2006 general funds were estimated at $3.13 billion for resources and $3.14 billion for expenditures. In fiscal year 2004, federal government grants to Rhode Island were $2.3 billion.

On 5 January 2006 the federal government released $100 million in emergency contingency funds targeted to the areas with the greatest need, including $844,000 for Rhode Island.

36 TAXATION

In 2005, Rhode Island collected $2,629 million in tax revenues or $2,443 per capita, which placed it 12th among the 50 states in per capita tax burden. The national average was $2,192 per capita. Property taxes accounted for 0.1% of the total; sales taxes, 32.1%; selective sales taxes, 20.3%; individual income taxes, 38.0%; corporate income taxes, 4.3%; and other taxes, 5.2%.

Rhode Island, as of 1 January 2006, taxed corporations at a flat rate of 9.0%.

In 2004, state and local property taxes amounted to $1.8 billion or $1,629 per capita. The per capita amount ranks the state fifth nationally. Local governments collected $1,757,602,000 of the total and the state government $1,532,000.

Rhode Island taxes retail sales at a rate of 7%. Food purchased for consumption off-premises is tax exempt. The tax on cigarettes is 246 cents per pack, which ranks first among the 50 states and the District of Columbia. Rhode Island taxes gasoline at 31 cents per gallon. This is in addition to the 18.4 cents per gallon federal tax on gasoline.

According to the Tax Foundation, for every federal tax dollar sent to Washington in 2004, Rhode Island citizens received $1.02 in federal spending.

37 ECONOMIC POLICY

The Rhode Island Economic Development Corporation (RIEDC) exists to preserve and expand Rhode Island businesses, and to attract new businesses to the state. Some of the services available to businesses through RIEDC are: job training assistance; financial assistance; government contracting assistance; site selection; and exporting assistance. The RIEDC includes a Job Creation Grant Fund, an Excellence Through Training Grant Program, an Employee Investment Grant Program, and an Export Management Training Grant Program.

The Innovation [T] Scale strategy is Rhode Island's effort to make its small size a competitive advantage. Innovators can take advantage of the state's manageable size, close knit networks, and densely concentrated resources to quickly and cost effectively test new ways of doing business.

38 HEALTH

The infant mortality rate in October 2005 was estimated at 5.9 per 1,000 live births. The birth rate in 2003 was 12.3 per 1,000 population. The abortion rate stood at 24.1 per 1,000 women in 2000. In 2003, about 90.9% of pregnant woman received prenatal care be-

Rhode Island—State Government Finances

(Dollar amounts in thousands. Per capita amounts in dollars.)

	AMOUNT	PER CAPITA
Total Revenue	7,266,196	6,727.96
General revenue	5,619,076	5,202.85
Intergovernmental revenue	2,095,870	1,940.62
Taxes	2,408,861	2,230.43
General sales	804,647	745.04
Selective sales	500,727	463.64
License taxes	94,481	87.48
Individual income tax	899,939	833.28
Corporate income tax	69,479	64.33
Other taxes	39,588	36.66
Current charges	447,628	414.47
Miscellaneous general revenue	666,717	617.33
Utility revenue	21,952	20.33
Liquor store revenue	–	–
Insurance trust revenue	1,625,168	1,504.79
Total expenditure	6,386,602	5,913.52
Intergovernmental expenditure	868,929	804.56
Direct expenditure	5,517,673	5,108.96
Current operation	3,817,330	3,534.56
Capital outlay	332,836	308.18
Insurance benefits and repayments	921,469	853.21
Assistance and subsidies	211,841	196.15
Interest on debt	234,197	216.85
Exhibit: Salaries and wages	1,274,120	1,179.74
Total expenditure	6,386,602	5,913.52
General expenditure	5,371,080	4,973.22
Intergovernmental expenditure	868,929	804.56
Direct expenditure	4,502,151	4,168.66
General expenditures, by function:		
Education	1,468,437	1,359.66
Public welfare	1,961,808	1,816.49
Hospitals	108,043	100.04
Health	205,720	190.48
Highways	256,348	237.36
Police protection	49,715	46.03
Correction	162,234	150.22
Natural resources	37,389	34.62
Parks and recreation	8,931	8.27
Government administration	297,829	275.77
Interest on general debt	234,197	216.85
Other and unallocable	580,429	537.43
Utility expenditure	94,053	87.09
Liquor store expenditure	–	–
Insurance trust expenditure	921,469	853.21
Debt at end of fiscal year	6,490,701	6,009.91
Cash and security holdings	12,755,483	11,810.63

Abbreviations and symbols: – zero or rounds to zero; (NA) not available; (X) not applicable.

SOURCE: *U.S. Census Bureau, Governments Division, 2004 Survey of State Government Finances,* January 2006.

ginning in the first trimester, this was the second-highest rate in the nation for prenatal care (after New Hampshire). In 2004, approximately 87% of children received routine immunizations before the age of three.

The crude death rate in 2003 was 9.3 deaths per 1,000 population. As of 2002, the death rates for major causes of death (per 100,000 resident population) were: heart disease, 290.6; cancer, 224.7; cerebrovascular diseases, 56.6; chronic lower respiratory diseases, 48.7; and diabetes, 24.6. The mortality rate from HIV infection was 2.2 per 100,000 population. In 2004, the reported AIDS case rate was at about 12.2 per 100,000 population. In 2002, about

52.9% of the population was considered overweight or obese. As of 2004, about 21.3% of state residents were smokers.

In 2003, Rhode Island had 11 community hospitals with about 2,400 beds. There were about 122,000 patient admissions that year and 2 million outpatient visits. The average daily inpatient census was about 1.8 patients. The average cost per day for hospital care was $1,591. Also in 2003, there were about 94 certified nursing facilities in the state with 9,376 beds and an overall occupancy rate of about 91%. In 2004, it was estimated that about 78.5% of all state residents had received some type of dental care within the year. Rhode Island had 361 physicians per 100,000 resident population in 2004 and 987 nurses per 100,000 in 2005. In 2004, there were a total of 557 dentists in the state.

About 20% of state residents were enrolled in Medicaid programs in 2003; 16% were enrolled in Medicare programs in 2004. Approximately 11% of the state population was uninsured in 2004. In 2003, state health care expenditures totaled $1.8 million.

39 SOCIAL WELFARE

In 2004, about 41,000 people received unemployment benefits, with the average weekly unemployment benefit at $324. For 2005, the estimated average monthly participation in the food stamp program included about 76,085 persons (34,751 households); the average monthly benefit was about $86 per person. That year, the total of benefits paid through the state for the food stamp program was about $78.5 million.

Temporary Assistance for Needy Families (TANF), the system of federal welfare assistance that officially replaced Aid to Families with Dependent Children (AFDC) in 1997, was reauthorized through the Deficit Reduction Act of 2005. TANF is funded through federal block grants that are divided among the states based on an equation involving the number of recipients in each state. Rhode Island's TANF program is called the Family Independence Program (FIP). In 2004, the state program had 32,000 recipients; state and federal expenditures on this TANF program totaled $91 million in fiscal year 2003.

In December 2004, Social Security benefits were paid to 191,710 Rhode Island residents. This number included 127,350 retired workers, 15,260 widows and widowers, 27,730 disabled workers, 6,480 spouses, and 14,890 children. Social Security beneficiaries represented 17.8% of the total state population and 92.7% of the state's population age 65 and older. Retired workers received an average monthly payment of $955; widows and widowers, $931; disabled workers, $877; and spouses, $471. Payments for children of retired workers averaged $461 per month; children of deceased workers, $664; and children of disabled workers, $256. Federal Supplemental Security Income payments in December 2004 went to 29,703 Rhode Island residents, averaging $430 a month.

40 HOUSING

In 2004, there were an estimated 446,305 housing units, 409,767 of which were occupied; 61.8% were owner-occupied. About 55.8% of all units were single-family, detached homes; 33.3% of all units were built in 1939 or earlier. Utility gas and fuel oil were the most common energy sources for heating. It was estimated that 13,132 units lacked telephone service, 1,435 lacked complete plumbing facilities, and 2,161 lacked complete kitchen facilities. The average household had 2.53 members.

In 2004, 2,500 new privately owned housing units were authorized for construction. Much of the new residential construction has taken place in the suburbs south and west of Providence. The median home value was $240,150. The median monthly cost for mortgage owners was $1,469. Renters paid a median of $740. In 2006, the state received over $5.2 million in community development block grants from the US Department of Housing and Urban Development (HUD). The city of Providence received $5.7 million in similar grant awards.

41 EDUCATION

In 2004, 81.1% of Rhode Islanders age 25 and older were high school graduates. Approximately 27.2% had obtained a bachelor's degree or higher.

The total enrollment for fall 2002 in Rhode Island's public schools stood at 159,000. Of these, 113,000 attended schools from kindergarten through grade eight, and 47,000 attended high school. Approximately 71.2% of the students were white, 8.5% were black, 16.4% were Hispanic, 3.2% were Asian/Pacific Islander, and 0.6% were American Indian/Alaskan Native. Total enrollment was estimated at 160,000 in fall 2003 and expected to be 154,000 by fall 2014, a decline of 3.6% during the period 2002 to 2014. Expenditures for public education in 2003/04 were estimated at $1.7 billion, or $9,903 per student, the 10th-highest among the 50 states. In fall 2003 there were 28,119 students enrolled in 139 private schools. Since 1969, the National Assessment of Educational Progress (NAEP) has tested public school students nationwide. The resulting report, *The Nation's Report Card,* stated that in 2005, eighth graders in Rhode Island scored 272 out of 500 in mathematics compared with the national average of 278.

As of fall 2002, there were 77,417 students enrolled in college or graduate school; minority students comprised 16.4% of total postsecondary enrollment. In 2005 Rhode Island had 13 degree-granting institutions. Leading institutions include Brown University (1764) in Providence; the University of Rhode Island (1892) in Kingston; and Providence College (1917). The Rhode Island School of Design (1877) is located in Providence.

42 ARTS

The Rhode Island State Council on the Arts (RISCA) was established in 1967. In 2005, RISCA and other Rhode Island arts organizations received 13 grants totaling $806,300 from the National Endowment for the Arts (NEA). The Rhode Island Council for the Humanities, founded in 1973, had awarded over $2.5 million to community and academic organizations as of 2005. In 2005, the National Endowment for the Humanities contributed $1,235,058 for eight state programs. The state, the New England Foundation for the Arts, and various private sources also provide funding for arts activities.

Newport and Providence have notable art galleries and museums, including the museum at the Rhode Island School of Design (RISD) in Providence. As of 2005, the RISD Museum housed over 80,000 pieces of art. Theatrical groups include the Trinity Repertory Company in Providence founded in 1964. As of 2005, hosting both an annual production of *A Christmas Carol* and Trinity Summer Shakespeare, the theater drew an annual audience of more than 185,000. The Rhode Island Philharmonic, with approximately 72 professional musicians, performs throughout the state. Newport is the site of the internationally famous Newport Jazz Festival, founded in 1954, and the Newport Music Festival. In 2006, the Newport Music Festival's 38th season hosted 67 concerts with 46 artists representing 17 countries. The Festival Ballet Providence and the State Ballet of Rhode Island are prominent dance groups. The Providence Performing Arts Center, restored to its original 1920s splendor in the late 1990s (and now listed on the National Register of Historic Places), hosts touring Broadway shows as well as concerts by a variety of performers.

The WaterFire public art installation on the riverfront in downtown Providence has played a key role in the revitalization of the city. The lighting of bonfires in 97 braziers placed in three rivers that flow through Providence has drawn thousands to the downtown area to enjoy music and other entertainment. As of 2006 there were 17 lightings scheduled from May until October.

43 LIBRARIES AND MUSEUMS

For the fiscal year ending in June 2001, Rhode Island had 48 public library systems, with a total of 72 libraries, of which 24 were branches. In that same year, the state's public libraries had a book and serial publication stock of 3,997,000 volumes, and a total combined circulation of 6,627,000. The system also had 109,000 audio and 117,000 video items, 6,000 electronic format items (CD-ROMs, magnetic tapes, and disks), and two bookmobiles. The Providence Public Library maintains several special historical collections. The Brown University Libraries, containing more than 2.6 million books and periodicals, include the Annmary Brown Memorial Library, with its collection of rare manuscripts, and the John Carter Brown Library, with an excellent collection of early Americana. In fiscal year 2001, operating income for the state's public library system totaled $36,378,000 and included $172,000 from federal sources and $6,031,000 in state funding.

Among the state's more than 53 museums and historic sites are the Haffenreffer Museum of Anthropology in Bristol, the Museum of Art of the Rhode Island School of Design in Providence, the Roger Williams Park Museum, also in Providence, the Nathanael Greene Homestead in Coventry, and the Slater Mill Historic Site in Pawtucket. Providence has the Roger Williams Park Zoo.

44 COMMUNICATIONS

The first automated post office in the US postal system was opened in Providence in 1960. As of 2004, 95.3% of the state's occupied housing units had telephones. In addition, by June of that same year there were 615,398 mobile wireless telephone subscribers. In 2003, 62.3% of Rhode Island households had a computer and 55.7% had Internet access. By June 2005, there were 186,743 high-speed lines in Rhode Island, 177,393 residential and 9,350 for business. In 2005, the state had 7 major AM and 9 major FM radio stations. Rhode Island had five television stations, including one public broadcasting affiliate operated by the state's Public Telecommunications Authority. The Providence-New Bedford area had 565,230 television-viewing homes, 79% with cable in 1999. A total of 23,508 Internet domain names were registered in Rhode Island as of 2000.

45 PRESS

The *Rhode Island Gazette*, the state's first newspaper, appeared in 1732. In 1850, Paulina Wright Davis established *Una*, one of the first women's rights newspapers in the country.

In 2005, Rhode Island had six daily newspapers with three Sunday editions.

The following table shows the approximate circulation for the state's leading dailies in 2005:

AREA	NAME	DAILY	SUNDAY
Newport	*Daily News* (e)	12,352	12,352 (Sat.)
Pawtucket	*Times* (m)	11,407	11,407 (Sat.)
Providence	*Journal* (m,S)	168,021	236,476
Woonsocket	*The Call* (m,S)	11,984	17,638

Regional interest periodicals include *Providence Monthly* and *Rhode Island Monthly*.

46 ORGANIZATIONS

In 2006, there were over 2,095 nonprofit organizations registered within the state, of which about 1,578 were registered as charitable, educational, or religious organizations. Among the professional and educational organizations with headquarters in Rhode Island are the Foundation for Gifted and Creative Children, Foster Parents Plan USA, The American Boat Builders and Repairers Association, the American Mathematical Society, the Manufacturing Jewelers and Silversmiths of America.

The US Sailing Association is based in Portsmouth and the International Tennis Hall of Fame is in Newport.

State art organizations include the Alliance of Artists' Communities, the Art League of Rhode Island, and the Summer Arts and Festival Organization.

47 TOURISM, TRAVEL, AND RECREATION

Tourism is the second-largest and fastest-growing industry in Rhode Island. In 2005, the state hosted over 15 million visitors, generating total revenues of $4.69 billion (a figure that represents an increase of 16.4% from 1999). The industry supports over 57,837 jobs.

Historic sites—especially the mansions of Newport and Providence—and water sports (particularly the America's Cup yacht races) are the main tourist attractions of Narragansett Bay. Rhode Island has over 400 miles of coastline. Block Island is a popular resort reachable by a ferry from Point Judith. Visitors can relax or participate in kayaking, sailing, sport fishing, or horseback riding. The Providence Place Mall, a 13-acre mega shopping complex with 150 specialty shops, restaurants, and cinemas opened in 1999. An architectural marvel, the shopping complex spans a highway, a river, and a train track bed. Rhode Island's state parks and recreational areas total 8,063 acres (3,263 hectares).

48 SPORTS

Rhode Island has no major league professional sports teams. Pawtucket has a Triple-A minor league baseball team and Providence has a minor league team in the American Hockey League. Providence College has competed successfully in collegiate basketball, winning National Invitational Tournament titles in 1961 and 1963, and advancing to the National Collegiate Athletic Association (NCAA) Final Four in 1973 and 1987.

Historically, Rhode Island has played an important part in the development of both yachting and tennis. The Newport Yacht Club hosted the America's Cup, international sailing's most prestigious event, from 1930 until 1983, when an Australian yacht won the race. It was the first time since 1851 that the cup had been won by a non-American. The cup was returned to America in 1987, but by a yacht from San Diego. Lawn tennis was first played in America at the Newport Casino, which was also the site of the United States Tennis championship from 1881 until 1915. Today it is home to the International Tennis Hall of Fame. The Museum of Yachting is located in Newport as well. Dog racing at Lincoln and jai alai at Newport are popular spectator sports with pari-mutuel betting.

Other annual sporting events include the Tennis Hall of Fame Championships in Newport in July, the Annual Tuna Tournament near Galilee and Narragansett in September, the Rhode Island Marathon in Newport in November, and summer college baseball league on Martha's Vineyard.

⁴⁹FAMOUS RHODE ISLANDERS

Important federal officeholders from Rhode Island have included US Senators Nelson W. Aldrich (1841–1915), Henry Bowen Anthony (1815–84), Theodore Francis Green (1867–1966), and John O. Pastore (1907–2000), and US Representative John E. Fogarty (1913–67). J. Howard McGrath (1903–66) held the posts of US senator, solicitor general, and attorney general.

Foremost among Rhode Island's historical figures is Roger Williams (b.England, 1603?–83), apostle of religious liberty and founder of Providence. Other significant pioneers, also born in England, include Anne Hutchinson (1591–1643), religious leader and cofounder of Portsmouth, and William Coddington (1601–78), founder of Newport. Other 17th-century Rhode Islanders of note were Dr. John Clarke (b.England, 1609–76), who secured the colony's royal charter, and Indian leader King Philip, known also as Metacomet (1639?–76). Important participants in the War for Independence were Commodore Esek Hopkins (1718–1802) and General Nathanael Greene (1742–86). The 19th century brought to prominence Thomas Wilson Dorr (1805–54), courageous leader of Dorr's Rebellion; social reformer Elizabeth Buffum Chace (1806–99); and naval officers Oliver Hazard Perry (1785–1819), who secured important US victories in the War of 1812, and his brother, Matthew C. Perry (1794–1858), who led the expedition that opened Japan to foreign trade in 1854. Among the state's many prominent industrialists and inventors are Samuel Slater (b.England, 1768–1835), pioneer in textile manufacturing, and

silversmith Jabez Gorham (1792–1869). Other significant public figures include Unitarian theologian William Ellery Channing (1780–1842); political boss Charles R. Brayton (1840–1910); Roman Catholic bishop and social reformer Matthew Harkins (b.Massachusetts, 1845–1921); and Dr. Charles V. Chapin (1856–1941), pioneer in public health.

Rhode Island's best-known creative writers are Gothic novelists H. P. Lovecraft (1890–1937) and Oliver La Farge (1901–63), and its most famous artist is portrait painter Gilbert Stuart (1755–1828). Popular performing artists include George M. Cohan (1878–1942), Nelson Eddy (1901–67), Bobby Hackett (1915–76), Van Johnson (b.1916), and Spalding Gray (1941–2004).

Important sports personalities include Baseball Hall of Famers Hugh Duffy (1866–1954), Napoleon Lajoie (1875–1959), and Charles "Gabby" Hartnett (1900–1972).

⁵⁰BIBLIOGRAPHY

Bilder, Mary Sarah. *The Transatlantic Constitution: Colonial Legal Culture and the Empire.* Cambridge, Mass.: Harvard University Press, 2004.

Council of State Governments. *The Book of the States, 2006 Edition.* Lexington, Ky.: Council of State Governments, 2006.

Gaustad, Edwin S. *Roger Williams.* New York: Oxford University Press, 2005.

Leazes, Francis J. *Providence, the Renaissance City.* Boston: Northeastern University Press, 2004.

Méras, Phyllis, and Tom Gannon. *Rhode Island, An Explorer's Guide.* Woodstock, Vt.: Countryman Press; New York: Distributed by W.W. Norton, 2000.

Sherman, Steve. *Country Roads of Connecticut and Rhode Island: Day Trips and Weekend Excursions.* Lincolnwood, Ill.: Country Roads Press, 1999.

Sletcher, Michael (ed.). *New England.* Vol. 4 in *The Greenwood Encyclopedia of American Regional Cultures.* Westport, Conn.: Greenwood Press, 2004.

Sterne, Evelyn Savidge. *Ballots & Bibles: Ethnic Politics and the Catholic Church in Providence.* Ithaca, N.Y.: Cornell University Press, 2004.

US Department of Commerce, Economics and Statistics Administration, US Census Bureau. *Rhode Island, 2000. Summary Social, Economic, and Housing Characteristics: 2000 Census of Population and Housing.* Washington, D.C.: US Government Printing Office, 2003.

SOUTH CAROLINA

State of South Carolina

ORIGIN OF STATE NAME: Named in honor of King Charles I of England. **NICKNAME:** The Palmetto State. **CAPITAL:** Columbia. **ENTERED UNION:** 23 May 1788 (8th). **SONG:** "Carolina;" "South Carolina on My Mind." **MOTTO:** *Animis opibusque parati* (Prepared in mind and resources); *Dum spiro spero* (While I breathe, I hope). **COAT OF ARMS:** A palmetto stands erect, with a ravaged oak (representing the British fleet) at its base; 12 spears, symbolizing the first 12 states, are bound crosswise to the palmetto's trunk by a band bearing the inscription "Quis separabit" (Who shall separate?). Two shields bearing the inscriptions "March 26" (the date in 1776 when South Carolina established its first independent government) and "July 4," respectively, hang from the tree. Under the oak are the words "Meliorem lapsa locavit" (Having fallen, it has set up a better one) and the year "1776." The words "South Carolina" and the motto *Animis opibusque parati* surround the whole. **FLAG:** Blue field with a white palmetto in the center and a white crescent at the union. **OFFICIAL SEAL:** The official seal consists of two ovals showing the original designs for the obverse and the reverse of South Carolina's great seal of 1777. LEFT (OBVERSE): same as the coat of arms. RIGHT (REVERSE): as the sun rises over the seashore, Hope, holding a laurel branch, walks over swords and daggers. The motto *Dum spiro spero* is above her, the word "Spes" (Hope) below. **BIRD:** Carolina wren; wild turkey (wild game bird). **FISH:** Striped bass. **FLOWER:** Yellow jessamine. **TREE:** Palmetto. **GEM:** Amethyst. **LEGAL HOLIDAYS:** New Year's Day, 1 January; Birthday of Martin Luther King Jr., 3rd Monday in January; Washington's Birthday/Presidents' Day, 3rd Monday in February; Confederate Memorial Day, 10 May; National Memorial Day, last Monday in May; Independence Day, 4 July; Labor Day, 1st Monday in September; Veterans' Day, 11 November; Thanksgiving Day, 4th Thursday in November; Christmas Eve, 24 December, when declared by the governor; Christmas Day, 25 December and the day following. **TIME:** 7 AM EST = noon GMT.

¹LOCATION, SIZE, AND EXTENT

Situated in the southeastern United States, South Carolina ranks 40th in size among the 50 states.

The state's total area is 31,113 sq mi (80,583 sq km), of which land takes up 30,203 sq mi (78,226 sq km) and inland water 910 sq mi (2,357 sq km). South Carolina extends 273 mi (439 km) E–W; its maximum N–S extension is 210 mi (338 km).

South Carolina is bounded on the N and NE by North Carolina; on the SE by the Atlantic Ocean; and on the SW and W by Georgia (with the line passing through the Savannah and Chattooga rivers).

Among the 13 major Sea Islands in the Atlantic off South Carolina are Bull, Sullivans, Kiawah, Edisto, Hunting, and Hilton Head, the largest island (42 sq mi—109 sq km) on the Atlantic seaboard between New Jersey and Florida. The total boundary length of South Carolina is 824 mi (1,326 km), including a general coastline of 187 mi (301 km); the tidal shoreline extends 2,876 mi (4,628 km). The state's geographic center is located in Richland County, 13 mi (21 km) SE of Columbia.

²TOPOGRAPHY

South Carolina is divided into two major regions by the fall line that runs through the center of the state from Augusta, Georgia, to Columbia and thence to Cheraw, near the North Carolina border. The area northwest of the line, known as the upcountry, lies within the Piedmont Plateau; the region to the southeast, called the low country, forms part of the Atlantic Coastal Plain. The rise

of the land from ocean to the fall line is very gradual: Columbia, 120 mi (193 km) inland, is only 135 ft (41 m) above sea level. In the extreme northwest, the Blue Ridge Mountains cover about 500 sq mi (1,300 sq km); the highest elevation, at 3,560 ft (1,086 m), is Sassafras Mountain. The mean elevation of the state is approximately 350 ft (107 m).

Among the many artificial lakes, mostly associated with electric power plants, is Lake Marion, the state's largest, covering 173 sq mi (48 sq km). Three river systems—the Pee Dee, Santee, and Savannah—drain most of the state. No rivers are navigable above the fall line.

³CLIMATE

South Carolina has a humid, subtropical climate. Average temperatures range from 68°F (20°C) on the coast to 58°F (14°C) in the northwest, with colder temperatures in the mountains. Summers are hot: in the central part of the state, temperatures often exceed 90°F (32°C), with a record of 111°F (44°C) set at Camden on 28 June 1954. In the northwest, temperatures of 32°F (0°C) or less occur from 50 to 70 days a year; the record low for the state is -20°F (-29°C), set at Caesars Head Mountain on 18 January 1977. The daily average temperature at Columbia is 45°F (7°C) in January and 82°F (27°C) in July.

Rainfall is ample throughout the state, averaging 48.7 in (123 cm) annually at Columbia and ranging from 38 in (97 cm) in the central region to 52 in (132 cm) in the upper piedmont. Snow and sleet (averaging 2 in/5 cm a year at Columbia) occur about three times annually, but more frequently and heavily in the mountains.

⁴FLORA AND FAUNA

Principal trees of South Carolina include palmetto (the state tree), balsam fir, beech, yellow birch, pitch pine, cypress, and several types of maple, ash, hickory, and oak; longleaf pine grows mainly south of the fall line. Rocky areas of the piedmont contain a wide mixture of moss and lichens. The coastal plain has a diversity of land formations—swamp, prairie, savannah, marsh, dunes—and, accordingly, a great number of different grasses, shrubs, and vines. Azaleas and camellias, not native to the state, have been planted profusely in private and pubic gardens. Nineteen plant species were listed as threatened or endangered in April 2006, including smooth coneflower, Schweinitz's sunflower, black spored quillwort, pondberry, and persistent trillium.

South Carolina mammals include white-tailed deer (the state animal), black bear, opossum, gray and red foxes, cottontail and marsh rabbits, mink, and woodchuck. Three varieties of raccoon are indigenous, one of them unique to Hilton Head Island. The state is also home to Bachman's shrew, originally identified in South Carolina by John Bachman, one of John J. Audubon's collaborators. Common birds include the mockingbird and Carolina wren (the state bird). Nineteen animal species (vertebrates and invertebrates) were listed as threatened or endangered in South Carolina in April 2006, including the Indiana bat, Carolina heelsplitter, bald eagle, five species of sea turtle, wood stork, and shortnose sturgeon.

⁵ENVIRONMENTAL PROTECTION

The Department of Health and Environmental Control (DHEC), established in 1973, is South Carolina's primary environmental protection agency. The agency's responsibilities were broadened in 1993 by government restructuring, which brought all natural resources permitting under the DHEC umbrella. The former Land Resources Commission and Water Resources Commission were dissolved by restructuring. The DHEC's areas of responsibility include all programs dealing with surface and groundwater protection; air quality; solid, hazardous, infectious and nuclear waste; mining; dam safety; public drinking water protection; shellfish; public swimming pool inspection; and environmental laboratory certification, among other things. In 2002, more than 99% of the state's 1,520 federally defined public water systems had complied with drinking water regulatory requirements.

The state has implemented an innovative river basin planning program for the modeling, permitting and protection of its surface water resources. South Carolina's five major river basins are to be studied, modeled, and subsequent permits renewed on a five-year rotating basis. The state's goal is to use the environmental permitting process to assess and control the overall health of the basin systems. About 25% of the state is covered with wetlands, most of which are forested and of freshwater.

In 2002 DHEC implemented programs to help citizens minimize risk of contracting West Nile virus, transmitted by mosquitoes.

South Carolina, as the rest of the nation, is preparing to implement an aggressive air quality permitting program. The state has in place an industrial fee system to support the air program which will include both stationary and mobile source activities.

In 1992, South Carolina passed the Solid Waste Management and Policy Act requiring county and regional solid waste planning to be in conformance with the State Solid Waste Management Plan. The state has in place innovative programs for source reduction, waste minimization, and recycling. Regulations have been approved for municipal and industrial waste land disposal systems, incineration, construction, and land clearing debris and other solid waste activities.

South Carolina has implemented aggressive regulatory reform. Coupled with "streamlined permitting," customer-friendly programs promote economic development without sacrificing environmental protection.

In 2003, 83.7 million lb of toxic chemicals were released in the state. In 2003, South Carolina had 194 hazardous waste sites listed in the US Environment Protection Agency (EPA) database, 26 of which were on the National Priorities List as of 2006, including the Parris Island Marine Corps Recruit Depot. In 2005, the EPA spent over $4.8 million through the Superfund program for the cleanup of hazardous waste sites in the state. The same year, federal EPA grants awarded to the state included $11 million for the clean water state revolving fund and $8 million for the drinking water revolving fund.

⁶POPULATION

South Carolina ranked 25th in population in the United States with an estimated total of 4,255,083 in 2005, an increase of 6.1% since 2000. Between 1990 and 2000, South Carolina's population grew from 3,486,703 to 4,012,012, an increase of 15.1%. The population is projected to reach 4.6 million by 2015 and 4.98 million by 2025. In 2004, the median age for South Carolinians was 36.9. In the same year, 24.4% of the populace was under age 18 while 12.4% was age 65 or older. The population density in 2004 was 139.4 persons per sq mi.

In 2004, Columbia was the largest city proper, with 116,331 residents. Other cities with large population concentrations include Charleston (104,883), Greenville, and Spartanburg. In 2004, the Columbia metropolitan area had an estimated 679,456 residents and the Charleston metropolitan area had 583,434.

⁷ETHNIC GROUPS

The white population of South Carolina is mainly of Northern European stock; the great migratory wave from Southern and Eastern Europe during the late 19th century left South Carolina virtually untouched. As of 2000, 115,978, or 2.9%, of South Carolinians were foreign born (up from 1.4% in 1990).

In 2000, the black population was 1,185,216, or 29.5% of the state's population (the third-highest percentage in the nation). In 2004, that percentage had dropped only slightly, to 29.4%. In the coastal regions and offshore islands there still can be found some vestiges of African heritage, notably the Gullah dialect. South Carolina has always had an urban black elite, much of it of mixed racial heritage. After 1954, racial integration proceeded relatively peacefully, with careful planning by both black and white leaders.

The 2000 census counted 13,718 American Indians, up from 8,000 in 1990. In 2004, 0.4% of the population was American Indian. In 1983, a federal appeals court upheld the Indians' claim that 144,000 acres (58,275 hectares) of disputed land still belonged to the Catawba tribe, who numbered an estimated 1,597 in 1995.

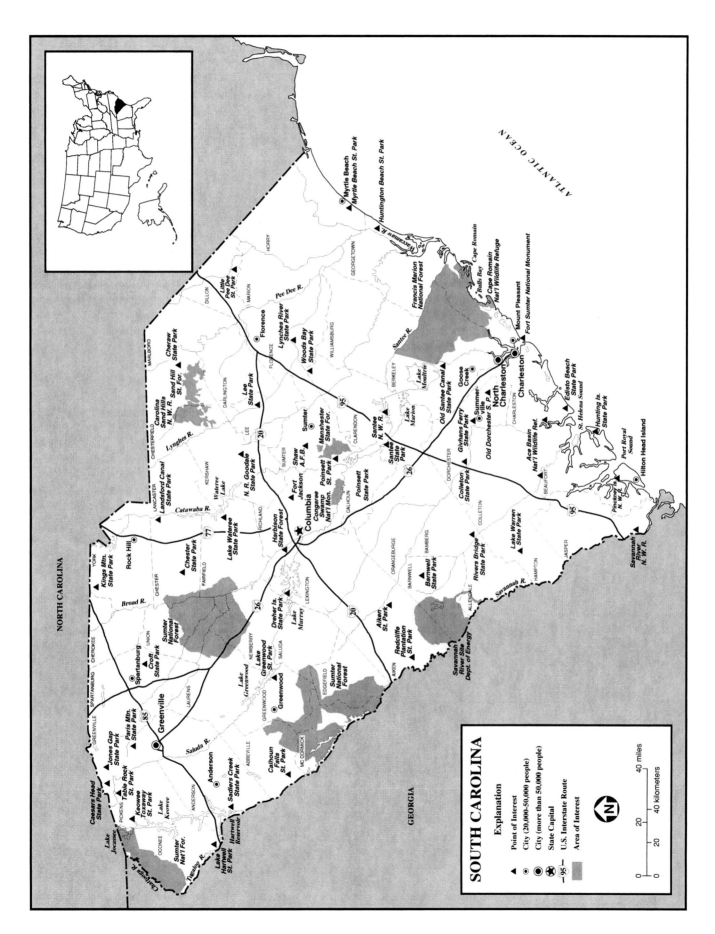

SOUTH CAROLINA

Explanation

▲ Point of Interest
◉ City (20,000-50,000 people)
◎ City (more than 50,000 people)
★ State Capital
─95─ U.S. Interstate Route
░ Area of Interest

In 2000, there were 95,076 Hispanics and Latinos (2.4% of the total population), nearly double the 1990 figure of 50,000 (1.3%). In 2004, 3.1% of the population was of Hispanic or Latino origin. In 2000, the census reported 52,871 Mexicans and 12.211 Puerto Ricans (up from 4,282 in 1990) in South Carolina. In the same year, South Carolina had 36,014 Asians, including 6,423 Filipinos, 2,448 Japanese, and 3,665 Koreans. Pacific Islanders numbered 1,628. In 2004, 1.1% of the population was Asian and 0.1% Pacific Islander. That year, 0.8% of the population reported origin of two or more races.

8LANGUAGES

English settlers in the 17th century encountered first the Yamasee Indians and then the Catawba, both having languages of the Hokan-Siouan family. Few Indians remain today, and a bare handful of their place-names persist: Cherokee Falls, Santee, Saluda.

South Carolina English is marked by a division between the South Midland of the upcountry and the plantation Southern of the coastal plain, where dominant Charleston speech has extensive cultural influence even in rural areas. Many upcountry speakers of Scotch-Irish background retain /r/ after a vowel, as in *hard,* a feature now gaining acceptance among younger speakers in Charleston. At the same time, a longtime distinctive Charleston feature, a centering glide after a long vowel, so that *date* and *eight* sound like /day-uht/ and /ay-uht/, is losing ground among younger speakers. Along the coast and on the Sea Islands, some blacks still use the Gullah dialect, based on a Creole mixture of pre-Revolutionary English and African speech. The dialect is rapidly dying in South Carolina, though its influence on local pronunciations persists.

In 2000, 94.8% of all state residents five years of age and older reported speaking English at home, up from 96.5% in 1990.

The following table gives selected statistics from the 2000 Census for language spoken at home by persons five years old and over.

LANGUAGE	NUMBER	PERCENT
Population 5 years and over	**3,748,669**	**100.0**
Speak only English	3,552,240	94.8
Speak a language other than English	196,429	5.2
Speak a language other than English	**196,429**	**5.2**
Spanish or Spanish Creole	110,030	2.9
French (incl. Patois, Cajun)	19,110	0.5
German	15,195	0.4
Chinese	5,648	0.2
Tagalog	4,496	0.1
Vietnamese	3,772	0.1
Korean	3,294	0.1
Italian	3,091	0.1
Japanese	2,807	0.1
Greek	2,566	0.1
Arabic	2,440	0.1
Gujarathi	2,101	0.1
Russian	1,618	0.0

9RELIGIONS

Evangelical Protestants account for a majority of the religiously active residents in the state. The largest single Christian denomination in 2000 was the Southern Baptist Convention with 928,341 adherents; there were 16,802 newly baptized members in 2002. The next largest of the Evangelical denominations were the Church of God (Cleveland, Tennessee) with 56,612 adherents and the Pentecostal Holiness Church with 33,820 adherents. The largest Mainline Protestant denomination is the United Methodist Church, which had 241,680 members in 2004. Other denominations (with 2000 figures) include the Presbyterian Church USA, 103,883; and the Evangelical Lutheran Church in America, 61,380. The Episcopal Church had great influence during colonial times, but in 2000 it had only 52,486 members. In 2004, there were 152,413 Roman Catholics in the state. In 2000, there were an estimated 11,000 Jews, 17,586 adherents to the Baha'i faith, and 5,761 Muslims. About 2.1 million people (52.4% of the population) were not counted as members of any religious organization.

10TRANSPORTATION

Since the Revolutionary War, South Carolina has been concerned with expanding the transport of goods between the upcountry and the port of Charleston and the Midwestern United States. Several canals were constructed north of the fall line, and the 136-mi (219-km) railroad completed from Charleston to Hamburg (across the Savannah River from Augusta, Georgia) in 1833 was the longest in the world at that time. Three years earlier, the *Best Friend of Charleston* had become the first American steam locomotive built for public railway passenger service; by the time the Charleston–Hamburg railway was completed, however, the *Best Friend* had blown up, and a new engine, the *Phoenix,* had replaced it. Many other efforts were made to connect Charleston to the interior by railway, but tunnels through the mountains were never completed. As of 2003, there were 2,423 rail mi (3,901 km) of track, utilized by two Class I, seven local, and four switching and terminal railroads. Lumber and wood products were the top commodities originating within the state that were carried by the railroads. Coal was the top commodity terminating in the state that was carried by the railroads. As of 2006, Amtrak provided north–south passenger train service to 11 cities in the state via its Crescent, Silver Services and Palmetto trains.

The public road network in 2004 was made up of 66,250 mi (106,662 km) of roads. Highway I-26, running northwest–southeast from the upcountry to the Atlantic, intersects I-85 at Spartanburg, I-20 at Columbia, and I-95 on its way toward Charleston. In 2004, there were some 1.912 million automobiles, approximately 1.290 million trucks of all types, and around 5,000 buses registered in the state, while the number of licensed drivers totaled 2,972,369 for that same year. City bus service is most heavily used in the Charleston and Columbia systems.

The state has three deepwater seaports. Charleston is one of the major ports on the Atlantic, handling 24.739 million tons of cargo in 2004, and the harbors of Georgetown and Port Royal also handle significant waterborne trade. The Atlantic Intracoastal Waterway, crossing the state slightly inward form the Atlantic Ocean, is a major thoroughfare. In 2003, waterborne shipments totaled 27.811 million tons. In 2004, South Carolina had 482 mi (776 km) of navigable inland waterways.

In 2005, South Carolina had a total of 193 public and private-use aviation-related facilities. This included 162 airports, 29 heliports, and two seaplane bases. Charleston International is the state's main airport. In 2004, Charleston had 909,084 passenger enplanements. Other major state airports were Greenville–Spartanburg International, Myrtle Beach International, and Columbia Metropolitan.

11 HISTORY

Prior to European settlement, the region now called South Carolina was populated by several Indian groups. Indians of Iroquoian stock, including the Cherokee, inhabited the northwestern section, while those of the Siouan stock—of whom the Catawba were the most numerous—occupied the northern and eastern regions. Indians of Muskogean stock lived in the south.

In the early 1500s, long before the English claimed the Carolinas, Spanish sea captains explored the coast. The Spaniards made an unsuccessful attempt to establish a settlement in 1526 at Winyah Bay, near the present city of Georgetown. Thirty-six years later, a group of French Huguenots under Jean Ribault landed at a site near Parris Island, but the colony failed after Ribault returned to France. The English established the first permanent settlement in 1670 under the supervision of the eight lords proprietors who had been granted "Carolana" by King Charles II. At first the colonists settled at Albemarle Point on the Ashley River: 10 years later, they moved across the river to the present site of Charleston.

Rice cultivation began in the coastal swamps, and black slaves were imported as field hands. The colony flourished, and by the mid-1700s, new areas were developing inland. Germans, Scots-Irish, and Welsh, who differed markedly from the original aristocratic settlers of the Charleston area, migrated to the southern part of the new province. Although the upcountry was developing and was taxed, it was not until 1770 that the settlers there were represented in the government. For the most part, the colonists had friendly relations with the Indians. In 1715, however, the Yamasee were incited by Spanish colonists at St. Augustine, Fla., to attack the South Carolina settlements. The settlers successfully resisted, with no help from the proprietors.

The original royal grant had made South Carolina a very large colony, but eventually the separate provinces of North Carolina and Georgia were established, two moves that destined South Carolina to be a small state. The colonists were successful in having the proprietors overthrown in 1719 and the government transferred to royal rule by 1721.

Skirmishes with the French, Spanish, Indians, and pirates, as well as a slave uprising in 1739, marked the pre-Revolutionary period. South Carolina opposed the Stamp Act of 1765 and took an active part in the American Revolution. The first British property seized by American Revolutionary forces was Ft. Charlotte in McCormick County in 1775. Among the many battles fought in South Carolina were major Patriot victories at Ft. Moultrie in Charleston (1776), Kings Mountain (1780), and Cowpens (1781), the last two among the war's most important engagements. Delegates from South Carolina, notably Charles Cotesworth Pinckney, were leaders at the federal constitutional convention of 1787. On 23 May 1788, South Carolina became the eighth state to ratify the Constitution.

Between the Revolutionary War and the Civil War, two issues dominated South Carolinians' political thinking: tariffs and slavery. Senator John C. Calhoun took an active part in developing the nullification theory by which a state claimed the right to abrogate unpopular federal laws. Open conflict over tariffs during the early 1830s was narrowly averted by a compromise on the rates, but in 1860, on the issue of slavery, no compromise was possible. At the time of secession, on 20 December 1860, more than half the state's population consisted of black slaves. The first battle of the Civil War took place at Ft. Sumter in Charleston Harbor on 12 April 1861. Federal forces soon captured the Sea Islands, but Charleston withstood a long siege until February 1865. In the closing months of the war, Union troops under General William Tecumseh Sherman burned Columbia and caused widespread destruction elsewhere. South Carolina contributed about 63,000 soldiers to the Confederacy out of a white population of some 291,000. Casualties were high: nearly 14,00 men were killed in battle or died after capture.

Federal troops occupied South Carolina after the war. During Reconstruction, as white South Carolinians saw it, illiterates, carpetbaggers, and scalawags raided the treasury, plunging the state into debt. The constitution was revised in 1868 by a convention in which blacks outnumbered whites by 76 to 48; given the franchise, blacks attained the offices of lieutenant governor and US representative. In 1876, bands of white militants called Red Shirts, supporting the gubernatorial candidacy of former Confederate General Wade Hampton, rode through the countryside urging whites to vote and intimidating potential black voters. Hampton, a Democrat, won the election, but was not permitted by the Republican incumbent to take office until President Rutherford B. Hayes declared an end to Reconstruction and withdrew federal troops from the state in April 1877.

For the next 100 years, South Carolina suffered through political turmoil, crop failures, and recessions. A major political change came in the 1880s with a large population increase upcountry and the migration of poor whites to cities. These trends gave farmers and industrial workers a majority of votes, and they found their leader in Benjamin Ryan "Pitchfork Ben" Tillman, a populist who stirred up class and racial hatreds by attacking the "Charleston ring." Tillman was influential in wresting control of the state Democratic Party from the coastal aristocrats; he served as governor from 1890 to 1894 and then as US senator until his death in 1918. However, his success inaugurated a period of political and racial demagoguery that saw the gradual (though not total) disfranchisement of black voters.

The main economic transformation after 1890 was the replacement of rice and cotton growing by tobacco and soybean cultivation and truck farming, along with the movement of tenant farmers, or sharecroppers, from the land to the cities. There they found jobs in textile mills, and textiles became the state's leading industry after 1900. With the devastation of the cotton crop by the boll weevil in the 1920s, farmers were compelled to diversify their crops, and some turned to raising cattle. Labor shortages in the North during and after World War II drew many thousands of African Americans from South Carolina to Philadelphia, Washington, DC, New York, and other cities.

In the postwar period, industry took over the dominant role formerly held by agriculture in South Carolina's economy, and the focus of textile production shifted from cotton to synthetic fabrics. In the 1990s the major industries were textiles and chemicals, and foreign investment played a major role in the state's economy. BMW, the German automobile company, established their North American plant in Greenville. Tourism also played a role, with the coastal areas drawing visitors from around the nation. In the early 2000s, South Carolina, along with other tobacco-producing states, was in the midst of a transition away from tobacco production.

Public school desegregation after the *Brown vs. Board of Education* ruling of 1954 proceeded peaceably, but very slowly, and blacks were gradually accepted alongside whites in the textile mills and other industries. In 1983, for the first time in 95 years, a black state senator was elected; the following year, four blacks were elected to the reapportioned Senate. Despite these changes, most white South Carolinians remained staunchly conservative in political and social matters, as witnessed by the 1999–2000 firestorm over the display of the Confederate flag on the dome of the State House. The controversy prompted the NAACP (National Association for the Advancement of Colored People) to call for a tourism boycott of the state. A January 2000 protest drew nearly 50,000 demonstrators, black and white, against the flag. Legislators brokered a compromise that moved the flag, viewed as a symbol of oppression by African Americans, to a spot in front of the capitol, where it flies from a 30-ft pole. The "solution," though favored by most South Carolinians who were polled, did not satisfy most of the black community. Tourism officials called for the NAACP to lift its boycott, but the organization refused to do so, maintaining the flag's only place is in a museum of history. The issue was raised by presidential candidate Al Sharpton in the 2004 presidential campaign.

In the postwar period, the Democrats' traditional control of the state weakened, and, beginning with Barry Goldwater, Republican presidential candidates have carried the state in every election except that of 1976, in which Southerner Jimmy Carter prevailed. Well-known conservative Republican J. Strom Thurmond represented South Carolina in the US Senate from 1954 to 2003, when he died at age 100. But his Democratic counterpart, Ernest Hollings (also a former governor) served in the Senate from 1966 to 2005.

In 1989, Hurricane Hugo struck South Carolina, packing 135-mph (217-kph) winds. Ripping roofs off buildings and sweeping boats onto city streets, the storm killed 37 people and produced over $700 million worth of property damage. Seven South Carolina counties were declared disaster areas. In 1993, flooding, followed by a record-breaking drought, caused an estimated $226 million in crop damage.

In response to a Supreme Court ruling, The Citadel (in Charleston), one of only two state-supported military schools in the country, admitted its first female cadet, Shannon Faulkner, in 1995. Faulkner left the institution after only six days. In 1997 two of four women attending the institution quit, alleging hazing and sexual harassment by their male peers. In May 1999 the institution graduated its first female cadet. By the following August, there were 75 female cadets enrolled at the Citadel, as the school fought a sexual harassment lawsuit of a former cadet.

In 1999 a settlement was reached in the worst oil spill in the state's history. A record $7-million fine was to be paid by a national pipeline company that admitted its negligence caused nearly one million gallons of diesel fuel to pollute the Upstate River.

South Carolina finished fiscal year 2003 with a $68.8 million budget deficit, down from the $248.8 million deficit at the end of fiscal year 2002. In 2003, Republican Governor Mark Sanford, elected in 2002, urged state legislators to reform the way the government conducts its business, from allowing state officials to hire and fire employees more easily, to funding schools with block grants rather than line items. The 2005–06 budget was $5.3 billion, and the state was struggling with a deficit of some $300–$500 million. South Carolina was among the 10 states in the nation with the lowest per capita personal incomes and the highest poverty rates.

[12] STATE GOVERNMENT

South Carolina has had seven constitutions, dating from 1776, 1778, 1790, 1861, 1865, 1868, and 1895, respectively. Beginning in 1970, most articles of the 1895 constitution were rewritten. The present document had been amended 485 times as of January 2005.

The General Assembly consists of a Senate of 46 members, elected for four-year terms, and a House of Representatives of 124 members, elected for two-year terms. Senators must be 25 years old, representatives 21; all legislators must be residents of the districts they represent. The legislative salary was $10,400 in 2004, unchanged from 1999.

Officials elected statewide are the governor and lieutenant governor (elected separately), attorney general, secretary of state, comptroller general, treasurer, adjutant general, secretary of agriculture, secretary of banking, and superintendent of education, all elected to four-year terms in odd-numbered years following presidential elections. The governor is limited to serving two consecutive terms. Eligibility requirements for the governor include a minimum age of 30, US and state citizenship for at least five years, and a five-year state residency. As of December 2004, the governor's salary was $106,078, unchanged from 1999.

Legislative sessions are held biennially, beginning in January; there is no limit to regular sessions. Special sessions can be called by a vote of two-thirds of the members of each house; there is no limit to special sessions. Bills may be introduced in either house, except for revenue measures, which are reserved to the House of Representatives. The governor has a regular veto, which may be overridden by a two-thirds vote of the elected members in each house of the legislature. Bills automatically become law after five days if the governor takes no action. The constitution may be amended by a two-thirds vote of each house of the General Assembly and by a majority of those casting ballots at the next general election. To take effect, however, the amendment must then be ratified by a majority vote of the next General Assembly.

US citizens 18 years old and older who are residents of the state are eligible to vote. Restrictions apply to convicted felons and those declared mentally incompetent by the court.

[13] POLITICAL PARTIES

South Carolina's major political organizations are the Democratic and Republican parties. From the end of Reconstruction, the Democratic Party dominated state politics. Dissatisfaction with the national party's position on civil rights in 1948 led to the formation of the States' Rights Democrat faction, whose candidate, South Carolina Governor J. Strom Thurmond, carried the state in 1948. Thurmond's subsequent switch to the Republicans while in the US Senate was a big boost for the state's Republican Party, which since 1964 has captured South Carolina's eight electoral votes in ten of the eleven presidential elections. In 2000, Republican George W. Bush received 57% of the vote to Democrat Al Gore's 41%. In 2004, Bush won 58% to 41% for Democrat John Kerry.

South Carolina's US senators are Republican James DeMint, who won the seat vacated by Democrat Ernest F. Hollings, who announced in August 2003 that he would retire at the end of his term, and Republican Lindsey Graham, elected in 2002. Republican Strom Thurmond, who was reelected in 1996 at the age of 93—was the oldest senator in the country's history. Thurmond died in June 2003 at the age of 100. As of 2005, there were two Democrats and four Republicans serving as US representatives. As on 2005, the state Senate had 19 Democrats and 27 Republicans; while in the state House there were 74 Republicans and 50 Democrats. In 2002 voters elected a Republican, Mark Sanford, to the governor's office.

Voters do not register according to political party in South Carolina. Instead, at primary elections, they simply take an oath that they have not participated in another primary. In 2004 there were 2,315,000 registered voters and the state held eight electoral votes for the 2004 presidential election.

14 LOCAL GOVERNMENT

As of 2005, South Carolina had 46 counties, 269 municipal governments, 90 public school districts, and 301 special districts of various types. Ten regional councils provide a broad range of technical and advisory services to county and municipal governments.

Under legislation enacted in 1975, all counties and municipalities have the same powers, regardless of size. Most municipalities operate under the mayor-council or city manager system; more than half the counties have a county administrator or manager. Customarily, each county has a council or commission, attorney, auditor, clerk of court, coroner, tax collector, treasurer, and sheriff. Many of these county officials are elected, but the only municipal officers elected are the mayor and the members of the council.

While the state shares revenues from many different sources with the counties and, municipalities, these local units derive virtually all their direct revenue from the property tax. The state's school districts have rapidly increased their own property tax levies, squeezing the counties' and municipalities' revenue base.

In 2005, local government accounted for about 167,783 full-time (or equivalent) employment positions.

15 STATE SERVICES

To address the continuing threat of terrorism and to work with the federal Department of Homeland Security, homeland security in South Carolina operates under state statute; a state police superintendent is appointed to oversee the state's homeland security activities.

The State Ethics Commission establishes rules covering possible conflicts of interest, oversees election campaign practices, and provides for officeholders' financial disclosure.

The Department of Education administers state and federal aid to the public schools, while the State Commission on Higher Education oversees the public colleges and universities, and the State Board for Technical and Comprehensive Education is responsible for postsecondary technical training schools. The state also runs special schools for the deaf and blind. Complementing both public and higher education is a state educational television network, under the jurisdiction of the South Carolina Educational Television Commission. Transportation services are provided by the Department of Transportation, which maintains most major roads, issues drivers' licenses, and has jurisdiction over the Highway Patrol. The Department of Public Safety regulates traffic, motor vehicles, and commercial vehicles. The Department of Commerce Division of Aeronautics oversees airport development.

South Carolina Presidential Vote by Political Parties, 1948–2004

YEAR	ELECTORAL VOTE	SOUTH CAROLINA WINNER	DEMOCRAT	REPUBLICAN	STATES' RIGHTS DEMOCRAT	LIBERTARIAN
1948	8	Thurmond (SRD)	34,423	5,386	102,607	—
1952	8	Stevenson (D)	172,957	168,043	—	—
					UNPLEDGED	—
1956	8	Stevenson (D)	136,278	75,634	88,509	
1960	8	*Kennedy (D)	198,121	188,558	—	—
1964	8	Goldwater (R)	215,723	309,048	—	
					AMERICAN IND.	
1968	8	*Nixon (R)	197,486	254,062	215,430	—
					AMERICAN	
1972	8	*Nixon (R)	1,868,824	477,044	10,075	—
1976	8	*Carter (D)	450,807	346,149	2,996	—
						LIBERTARIAN
1980	8	*Reagan (R)	430,385	441,841	—	4,975
1984	8	*Reagan (R)	344,459	615,539	—	4,359
1988	8	*Bush (R)	370,554	606,443	—	4,935
					IND. (Perot)	
1992	8	Bush (R)	479.514	577,507	138,872	2,719
1996	8	Dole (R)	506,283	573,458	64,386	4,271
					UNITED CITIZENS	
2000	8	*Bush, G., W. (R)	565,561	785,937	20,200	4,876
					IND. (Nader)	
2004**	8	*Bush, G. W. (R)	661,699	937,974	5,520	3,608

*Won US presidential election.
**CONSTITUTION Party candidate Michael Peroutka received 5,317 votes.

Through a variety of agencies, South Carolina offers a broad array of human services in the fields of mental health, developmental disabilities, vocational rehabilitation, veterans' affairs, care of the blind, and adoptions. An ombudsman for the aging handles complaints about nursing homes, which are licensed by the state. The South Carolina Law Enforcement Division provides technical aid to county sheriffs and municipal police departments. Emergency situations are handled by the Emergency Management Division and the National Guard.

The State Housing Finance and Development Authority is authorized to subsidize interest rates on mortgages for middle- and low-income families. The Employment Security Commission oversees unemployment compensation and job placement, while the Department of Labor, Licensing and Regulation offers arbitration and mediation services and enforces health and safety standards. The Human Affairs Commission looks into unfair labor practices based on sex, race, or age.

16JUDICIAL SYSTEM

South Carolina's unified judicial system is headed by the Chief Justice of the Supreme Court, who, along with four associate justices, is elected by the General Assembly to a 10-year term. The state's Supreme Court is the final court of appeal. A five-member intermediate court of appeals for criminal cases was established in 1979, but legal questions (specifically, about the election of General Assembly members to four of the five seats) prevented the court from convening until 1981. The court became a permanent constitutional court in 1984.

Sixteen circuit courts hear major criminal and civil cases. As of 1999 there were 154 circuit court judges, all of them elected by the General Assembly to six-year terms. The state also has a system of family courts for domestic and juvenile cases. In addition, there are magistrates' courts (justices of the peace) in all counties, municipal courts, and county probate judges.

The state penal system is rapidly becoming centralized under the state Department of Corrections. There is also a separate state system for juvenile offenders.

As of 31 December 2004, a total of 23,428 prisoners were held in South Carolina's state and federal prisons, a decrease from 23,719 of 1.2% from the previous year. As of year-end 2004, a total of 1,562 inmates were female, down from 1,576 or 0.9% from the year before. Among sentenced prisoners (one year or more), South Carolina had an incarceration rate of 539 per 100,000 population in 2004.

According to the Federal Bureau of Investigation, South Carolina in 2004, had a violent crime rate (murder/nonnegligent manslaughter; forcible rape; robbery; aggravated assault) of 784.2 reported incidents per 100,000 population (the highest of any state) or a total of 32,922 reported incidents. Crimes against property (burglary; larceny/theft; and motor vehicle theft) in that same year totaled 189,113 reported incidents or 4,504.8 reported incidents per 100,000 people. South Carolina has a death penalty, of which prisoners are allowed to choose between lethal injection or electrocution. From 1976 through 5 May 2006, the state has carried out 35 executions, of which three in 2005 were the most recent (as of 5 May 2006). As of 1 January 2006, South Carolina had 74 inmates on death row.

In 2003, South Carolina spent $101,287,819 on homeland security, an average of $25 per state resident.

17ARMED FORCES

In 2004, there were 38,213 active duty military personnel and 9,382 civilian personnel stationed in South Carolina. Ft. Jackson, in Columbia, is the largest and most active Initial Entry Training Center in the US Army, training 34% of all Soldiers and 69% of the women entering the Army each year. Air Force bases at Charleston and Sumter are major installations. Parris Island has long been one of the country's chief Marine Corps training bases. South Carolina firms received more than $1.59 billion in defense contract awards during 2004. In addition, there was another $3.3 billion in payroll outlays, including retired military pay, by the Department of Defense.

Veterans in South Carolina in 2003 totaled 413,551, including 45,135 from World War II; 39,518 from the Korean conflict; 122,974 who served during the Vietnam era; and 76,461 who served during in the Gulf War. In 2004, the Veterans Administration expended more than $1.2 billion in pensions, medical assistance, and other major veterans' benefits.

As of 31 October 2004, the South Carolina Highway Patrol employed 829 full-time sworn officers.

18MIGRATION

The original European migration into South Carolina consisted mostly of German, Welsh, and Scotch-Irish settlers. During the 19th century, many of the original settlers emigrated westward to Alabama, Mississippi, and Texas. In the 20th century, many blacks left the state for cities in the North. Between 1940 and 1970, South Carolina's net loss from migration was 601,000. During 1970–80, however, the state enjoyed a net gain of 210,000; in the 1980s, the net gain from migration was nearly 200,000. Between 1990 and 1998, the state had net gains of 119,000 in domestic migration and 16,000 in international migration. In 1998, 2,125 foreign immigrants arrived in South Carolina. The state's overall population increased 10% between 1990 and 1998. In the period 2000–05, international migration was 36,401 and net internal migration was 115,084, for a net gain of 151,485 people.

19INTERGOVERNMENTAL COOPERATION

The South Carolina Interstate Cooperation Commission represents the state before the Council of State Governments. South Carolina also participates in the Atlantic States Marine Fisheries Commission, Southeastern Forest Fire Protection Compact, Southern Growth Policies Board, Southern States Energy Board, Appalachian Regional Commission, Interstate Mining Compact Commission, and Southern Regional Education Board. In fiscal year 2005, the state received $4.918 billion in federal grants, an estimated $4.843 billion in fiscal year 2006, and an estimated $4.972 billion in fiscal year 2007.

20ECONOMY

During its early days, South Carolina was one of the country's richest areas. Its economy depended on foreign commerce and agriculture, especially indigo, rice, and later cotton. After the Civil War, the state suffered severe economic depression. Not until the

1880s did the textile industry—today the state's major employer—begin to develop.

Textiles and farming completely dominated the economy until after World War II, when efforts toward economic diversification attracted paper, chemical, and other industries to the state. During the postwar period, the state spent sizable amounts to improve its three ports, especially the harbor facilities of Charleston.

By 1999, manufacturing had become the most important sector in the South Carolina economy. Almost 25% of the labor force worked in manufacturing, well above the national average of 17%. The top ten manufacturers in the state employed over 40,000 workers. The Westinghouse Savannah River Site military base accounts for a significant portion of the state's manufacturing base. Employment at those facilities grew significantly during the 1980s when the Reagan administration increased military expenditures. In the 1990s, however, the federal government began cutting staff at the bases and considered phasing them out. Rising foreign and domestic investment, coupled with an abundance of first-class tourist facilities along the coast, contributed to the continuing growth of South Carolina's economy in the 1980s and were only temporarily hurt by the national recession of the early nineties. The state economy's annual growth rate, averaging 5.5% 1998 to 2000, dropped to 2.6% in the national recession of 2001. Manufacturing output, nearly flat from 1997 to 2001, dropped as a share of total state output from 24.5% to 20%. The strongest output growth was in the transportation and public utilities sector (up 41.9% 1997 to 2001). General services, including health, business, tourist, personal and educational services were up 30.3%, while financial services, including insurance and real estate were up 28%, and government services were up 25.7%.

In 2004, South Carolina's gross state product (GSP) was $136.125 billion, of which manufacturing (durable and nondurable goods) contributed $26.265 billion or 19.3% of GSP, followed by the real estate sector at $15.185 billion (11.1% of GSP), and construction at $7.670 billion (5.6% of GSP). In that same year, there were an estimated 312,108 small businesses in South Carolina. Of the 92,940 businesses that had employees, an estimated total of 90,416 or 97.3% were small companies. An estimated 11,745 new businesses were established in the state in 2004, up 9.2% from the year before. Business terminations that same year came to 10,975, up 2.5% from 2003. There were 175 business bankruptcies in 2004, up 23.2% from the previous year. In 2005, the state's personal bankruptcy (Chapter 7 and Chapter 13) filing rate was 391 filings per 100,000 people, ranking South Carolina as the 39th highest in the nation.

²¹INCOME

In 2005 South Carolina had a gross state product (GSP) of $140 billion which accounted for 1.1% of the nation's gross domestic product and placed the state at number 28 in highest GSP among the 50 states and the District of Columbia.

According to the Bureau of Economic Analysis, in 2004 South Carolina had a per capita personal income (PCPI) of $27,185. This ranked 45th in the United States and was 82% of the national average of $33,050. The 1994–2004 average annual growth rate of PCPI was 4.0%. South Carolina had a total personal income (TPI) of $114,121,015,000, which ranked 26th in the United States and reflected an increase of 6.0% from 2003. The 1994–2004 average

annual growth rate of TPI was 5.3%. Earnings of persons employed in South Carolina increased from $79,528,714,000 in 2003 to $84,052,494,000 in 2004, an increase of 5.7%. The 2003–04 national change was 6.3%.

The US Census Bureau reports that the three-year average median household income for 2002–04 in 2004 dollars was $39,326 compared to a national average of $44,473. During the same period an estimated 14.0% of the population was below the poverty line as compared to 12.4% nationwide.

²²LABOR

According to the Bureau of Labor Statistics (BLS), in April 2006 the seasonally adjusted civilian labor force in South Carolina 2,123,800, with approximately 139,900 workers unemployed, yielding an unemployment rate of 6.6%, compared to the national average of 4.7% for the same period. Preliminary data for the same period placed nonfarm employment at 1,907,100. Since the beginning of the BLS data series in 1976, the highest unemployment rate recorded in South Carolina was 11.4% in January 1983. The historical low was 3.1% in March 1998. Preliminary nonfarm employment data by occupation for April 2006 showed that approximately 6.4% of the labor force was employed in construction; 13.7% in manufacturing; 19.3% in trade, transportation, and public utilities; 5.3% in financial activities; 10% in education and health services; 10.7% in leisure and hospitality services; and 17.5% in government. Data was unavailable for professional and business services.

South Carolina has one of the lowest work stoppage rates in the nation and only a small percentage of the total labor force is organized. Textile, clothing, and ladies' garment workers' unions make up the bulk of the membership, followed by transportation and electrical workers. Several large textile companies have made major efforts to prevent their workers from organizing unions. Conflicts between management and workers have continued for years, but without serious violence.

The BLS reported that in 2005, a total of 40,000 of South Carolina's 1,739,000 employed wage and salary workers were formal members of a union. This represented 2.3% of those so employed, down from 3% in 2004, well below the national average of 12% and the lowest rate of all states. Overall in 2005, a total of 58,000 workers (3.3%) in South Carolina were covered by a union or employee association contract, which includes those workers who reported no union affiliation. South Carolina is one of 22 states with a right-to-work law.

As of 1 March 2006, South Carolina did not have a state-mandated minimum wage law. Employees in that state however, were covered under federal minimum wage statutes. In 2004, women in the state accounted for 48.1% of the employed civilian labor force.

²³AGRICULTURE

Agriculture is an integral part of the state's economy. The total cash receipts for agriculture were about $1.75 billion in 2004, but that figure represents only a fraction of the impact of agriculture and agribusiness in the state. Agriculture (food and fiber) along with forestry and forestry products contribute about 25% to the gross state product (GSP). Some 18% of all jobs in South Carolina are from agriculture and agribusiness. As of 2004 there were about

24,400 farms in the state, occupying 4.8 million acres (1.9 million hectares) with an average size of 199 acres (80 hectares). Agriculture in South Carolina supplies not only food for consumption, but also cotton for clothing and soybean oil for newsprint ink.

The main farming area is a 50-mi (80-km) band across the upper coastal plain. The Pee Dee region in the east is the center for tobacco production. Cotton is grown mostly south of the fall line, and feed crops thrive in the coastal and sand hill counties. Tobacco is the leading crop by value; in 2004, farmers in the state produced 60.75 million lb (27.61 million kg) of tobacco on 27,000 acres (10,900 hectares). Soybean and cotton production in that year were 14.8 million bushels and 390,000 bales, respectively. Peach production in 2004 was 70 million lb (31.8 million kg). Greenhouse and nursery products contributed 15.6% to total farm receipts in 2004.

South Carolina farmers and agribusinesses also produce apples, barley, beans, berries, canola, corn, cucumbers, hay, kiwifruit, mushrooms, oats, peanuts, pecans, popcorn, rye, sorghum, sweet potatoes, tea, turf grasses, tomatoes, ornamental trees, and wheat. As more people relocate and retire to the state, demand for agricultural products is increasing in order to supply restaurant, hotel, and landscaping businesses. The South Carolina Department of Agriculture operates three state farmers' markets in Columbia, Florence, and Greenville.

24 ANIMAL HUSBANDRY

In 2005, there were an estimated 435,000 cattle and calves, worth $339.3 million. During 2004, there were around 300,000 hogs and pigs, valued at $27 million. Dairy farmers produced around 318 million lb (144.5 million kg) of milk from 19,000 milk cows in 2003. Poultry farmers produced 1.4 billion eggs, worth some $87.9 million in the same year, and 14.8 million lb (6.7 million kg) of chicken, 1.14 billion lb (518 million kg) of broilers, and 494 million lb (224.5 million kg) of turkey.

25 FISHING

The state's oceanfront saltwater inlets and freshwater rivers and lakes provide ample fishing opportunities. Major commercial fishing is restricted to saltwater species of fish and shellfish, mainly shrimp, crabs, clams, and oysters. In 2004, the commercial catch totaled 12.4 million lb (5.6 million kg), valued at $18.5 million. In 2003, there were two processing plants in the state. In 2002, the commercial fleet had 556 vessels.

In 2004, the state issued 498,088 sport fishing licenses. There are two national fish hatcheries in the state (Orangeberg and Bears Bluff), stocking more than 5 million fish annually. In 2004, there were nine catfish farms covering 90 acres (36 hectares).

26 FORESTRY

South Carolina had 12,415,000 acres (5,024,000 hectares) of forestland in 2004—about two-thirds of the state's area and 1.7% of all US forests. The state's two national forests, Francis Marion and Sumter, comprised 5% of the forested area. Nearly all of South Carolina's forests are classified as commercial timberland, about 90% of it privately owned. Several varieties of pine, loblolly, longleaf, and shortleaf, are the major source of timber and of pulp for the paper industry. Total lumber production in 2004 was 1.57 billion board ft, 90% softwood.

27 MINING

According to preliminary data from the US Geological Survey (USGS), the estimated value of nonfuel mineral production by South Carolina in 2003 was $474 million, an increase from 2002 of 3%. The USGS data ranked South Carolina as 27th among the 50 states by the total value of its nonfuel mineral production, accounting for over 1% of total US output.

According to the preliminary data for 2003, portland cement was the state's leading nonfuel mineral commodity by value, and was followed by crushed stone, construction sand and gravel, kaolin, industrial sand and gravel, and vermiculite. Collectively, the initial three commodities accounted for 91% of all nonfuel mineral output, by value. By volume, South Carolina in 2003 ranked first in the production of vermiculite (out of two states), and was the nation's second leading producer of fire clay. It was third in masonry cement and kaolin, and ninth in common clays.

Preliminary data showed that production of portland cement in 2003 totaled 2.5 million metric tons, and was worth an estimated $183 million. It was followed by crushed stone, of which 26.3 million metric tons were produced, with a value of $171 million. Masonry cement output in 2003 totaled 425,000 metric tons and was worth an estimated $40.4 million, Construction sand and gravel production for that same year totaled 10.3 million metric tons and was valued at $36.1 million.

28 ENERGY AND POWER

As of 2003, South Carolina had 47 electrical power service providers, of which 22 were publicly owned and 21 were cooperatives. Of the remainder, four were investor owned. As of that same year there were 2,177,474 retail customers. Of that total, 1,235,618 received their power from investor-owned service providers. Cooperatives accounted for 645,551 customers, while publicly owned providers had 296,305 customers.

Total net summer generating capability by the state's electrical generating plants in 2003 stood at 20.658 million kW, with total production that same year at 93.772 billion kWh. Of the total amount generated, 97.6% came from electric utilities, with the remainder coming from independent producers and combined heat and power service providers. The largest portion of all electric power generated, 50.417 billion kWh (53.8%), came from nuclear power generation, with coal-fired plants in second place at 37.432 billion kWh (39.9%). Other renewable power sources, petroleum and natural gas fueled plants, hydroelectric and pumped storage facilities accounted for the remaining power generated.

Although it lacks fossil fuel resources, South Carolina produces more electricity than it consumes. South Carolina is heavily engaged in nuclear energy and is one of the nation's largest generators of nuclear power. As of 2006, the state had seven nuclear reactors in operation, two at the Catawba plant (the state's largest), three at the Oconee facility near Greenville, one at the H. B. Robinson plant near Hartsville, and one at the Virgil C. Summer plant near Jenkinsville. The vast Savannah River plant in Aiken County produces most of the plutonium for the nation's nuclear weapons; Chem-Nuclear Systems in Barnwell County stores about half of the country's low-level nuclear wastes; and a Westinghouse plant in Richland County makes fuel assemblies for nuclear reactors.

South Carolina has no proven reserves or production of crude oil or natural gas. There are no refineries in the state.

29 INDUSTRY

South Carolina's principal industry beginning in the 1880s was textiles, but many textile mills were closed during the 1970s and early 1980s because of the importation of cheaper textiles from abroad. The economic slack was made up, however, by the establishment of new industries, especially paper and chemical manufactures, and by increasing foreign investment in the state. Principal overseas investment came from Switzerland, Germany, the United Kingdom, and Japan. South Carolina's major manufacturing centers are concentrated north of the fall line and in the piedmont.

According to the US Census Bureau's Annual Survey of Manufactures (ASM) for 2004, South Carolina's manufacturing sector covered some 18 product subsectors. The shipment value of all products manufactured in the state that same year was $81.630 billion. Of that total, transportation equipment manufacturing accounted for the largest share at $15.251 billion. It was followed by chemical manufacturing at $12.722 billion; machinery manufacturing at $6.735 billion; textile mills at $6.445 billion; and plastics and rubber products manufacturing at $6.296 billion.

In 2004, a total of 258,222 people in South Carolina were employed in the state's manufacturing sector, according to the ASM. Of that total, 194,712 were actual production workers. In terms of total employment, the textile mill industry accounted for the largest portion of all manufacturing employees at 32,183, with 27,591 actual production workers. It was followed by chemical manufacturing at 29,896 employees (16,550 actual production workers); transportation equipment manufacturing at 29,655 employees (22,290 actual production workers); fabricated metal product manufacturing at 25,664 employees (19,819 actual production workers); and plastics and rubber products manufacturing with 20,292 employees (16,001 actual production workers).

ASM data for 2004 showed that South Carolina's manufacturing sector paid $10.293 billion in wages. Of that amount, the chemical manufacturing sector accounted for the largest share at $1.696 billion. It was followed by transport equipment manufacturing at $1.356 billion; textile mills at $958.880 million; fabricated metal product manufacturing at $929.957 million; and plastics and rubber products manufacturing at $877.816 million.

30 COMMERCE

According to the 2002 Census of Wholesale Trade, South Carolina's wholesale trade sector had sales that year totaling $32.9 billion from 4,917 establishments. Wholesalers of durable goods accounted for 3,031 establishments, followed by nondurable goods wholesalers at 1,559 and electronic markets, agents, and brokers accounting for 327 establishments. Sales by durable goods wholesalers in 2002 totaled $16.3 billion, while wholesalers of nondurable goods saw sales of $12.8 billion. Electronic markets, agents, and brokers in the wholesale trade industry had sales of $3.8 billion. Tobacco wholesale markets and warehouses are centered in the Pee Dee region, while soybean sales and storage facilities cluster around the port of Charleston. Truck crops, fruits, and melons are sold in large quantities at the state farmers' market in Columbia.

In the 2002 Census of Retail Trade, South Carolina was listed as having 18,416 retail establishments with sales of $40.6 billion. The leading types of retail businesses by number of establishments were: clothing and clothing accessories stores (2,647); gasoline stations (2,476); motor vehicle and motor vehicle parts dealers (2,237); and miscellaneous store retailers (2,131). In terms of sales, motor vehicle and motor vehicle parts dealers accounted for the largest share of retail sales at $10.4 billion, followed by general merchandise stores at $6.2 billion; food and beverage stores at $6.03 billion; and gasoline stations at $4.6 billion. A total of 212,926 people were employed by the retail sector in South Carolina that year.

In 2005, foreign exports were valued at $13.9 billion. Exports, mostly machinery, transportation equipment, and electronics; went primarily to Canada, Mexico, and Germany.

31 CONSUMER PROTECTION

The South Carolina Department of Consumer Affairs, established in 1974, has the authority to take, process, and investigate consumer complaints for probable basis and merit, represent the public at regulatory proceedings, and enforce consumer credit laws and consumer-related licensing laws. The Department is organized into five divisions: Administration; Consumer Services; Consumer Advocacy; Public Information and Education; and the Legal Division.

The Department is also responsible for the licensing and registration of pawnbrokers, motor clubs, physical fitness service organizations, mortgage loan brokers, athletic agents, prescription drug cards, continuing care retirement communities and prepaid legal representatives.

The state's Office of the Ombudsman, which is under the Governor's Office, also provides consumer services to the state's citizens on questions involving complaints, concerns and questions over the activities of the state government.

When dealing with consumer protection issues, the state's Attorney General's Office can initiate only limited civil, and only when permitted, criminal proceedings. It can represent the state before state and federal regulatory agencies, but cannot administer consumer protection and education programs. Formal consumer complaints can only be handled on a limited basis because of the authority granted to the Department of Consumer Affairs. The Attorney General's Office in consumer issues has limited subpoena powers. In antitrust actions, the Attorney General's Office can act on behalf of those consumers who are incapable of acting on their own; initiate damage actions on behalf of the state in state courts; initiate criminal proceedings; and represent counties, cities and other governmental entities in recovering civil damages under state or federal law.

The offices of the South Carolina Department of Consumer Affairs, the Office of the Attorney General and the State Ombudsman are located in Columbia.

32 BANKING

As of June 2005, South Carolina had 96 insured banks, savings and loans, and saving banks, plus 18 state-chartered and 69 federally chartered credit unions (CUs). Excluding the CUs, the Charleston-Gastonia-Concord market area accounted for the largest portion of the state's financial institutions and deposits in 2004, with

43 institutions and $90.216 billion in deposits. As of June 2005, CUs accounted for 11.9% of all assets held by all financial institutions in the state, or some $6.399 billion. Banks, savings and loans, and savings banks collectively accounted for the remaining 88.1% or $47.240 billion in assets held.

The median net interest margin (the difference between the lower rates offered to savers and the higher rates charged on loans) for the state's insured institutions as of fourth quarter 2005 stood at 4.21%, up from 4.02% in 2004 and 4.06% in 2003. The median percentage of past-due/nonaccrual loans to total loans in fourth quarter 2005 was 1.42%, up from 1.35% in 2004, but down from 1.67% in 2003.

Regulation of South Carolina's state-chartered banks and other financial institutions is the responsibility of the state's Board of Financial Institutions.

33 INSURANCE

The South Carolina Department of Insurance licenses and supervises the insurance companies doing business in the state. Most of these represent national insurance organizations. In 2004, over 3.5 million individual life insurance policies worth $163.9 billion were in force in South Carolina; total value for all categories of life insurance (individual, group, and credit) was $256.3 billion. The average coverage amount is $46,400 per policy holder. Death benefits paid that year totaled $874 million.

As of 2003, there were 32 property and casualty and 12 life and health insurance companies domiciled in the state. In 2004, direct premiums for property and casualty insurance totaled over $5.7 billion. That year, there were 148,301 flood insurance policies in force in the state, with a total value of $28.7 billion. There were also 21,440 beach and windstorm insurance policies against hurricane and other windstorm damage in force, with a total value of $6 billion.

In 2003, there were over 3.3 million auto insurance policies in effect for private passenger cars. Required minimum coverage includes bodily injury liability of up to $15,000 per individual and $30,000 for all persons injured in an accident, as well as property damage liability of $10,000. Uninsured motorist coverage is also required. In 2003, the average expenditure per vehicle for insurance coverage was $744.79.

In 2004, 51% of state residents held employment-based health insurance policies, 4% held individual policies, and 28% were covered under Medicare and Medicaid; 15% of residents were uninsured. In 2003, employee contributions for employment-based health coverage averaged at 20% for single coverage and 29% for family coverage. The state offers a six-month health benefits expansion program for small-firm employees in connection with the Consolidated Omnibus Budget Reconciliation Act (COBRA, 1986), a health insurance program for those who lose employment-based coverage due to termination or reduction of work hours.

34 SECURITIES

There are no securities exchanges in South Carolina. In 2005, there were 1,060 personal financial advisers employed in the state and 1,700 securities, commodities, and financial services sales agents. In 2004, there were over 64 publicly traded companies within the state, with over 18 NASDAQ companies, 8 NYSE listings, and 4 AMEX listings. In 2006, the state had one Fortune 500 company; SCANA, based in Columbia and listed on the NYSE, ranked 447th in the nation with revenues of over $4.7 billion. Sonoco Products (NYSE), Bowater (NYSE), and ScanSource (NASDAQ) were all listed in the Fortune 1,000.

Enforcement of the state Securities Act is vested in the securities commissioner within the Office of the Attorney General.

35 PUBLIC FINANCE

South Carolina's governor submits the annual budget to the General Assembly in January as the basis for enactment of an appropriation bill, effective for the fiscal year beginning July 1.

The state constitution requires that budget appropriations not exceed expected revenues. A General Reserve Fund (equaling 3% of General Fund revenues) is maintained to cover operating deficits. In addition, approximately 25% of projected revenue growth is set-aside and may be used as a surplus at the end of the fiscal year. Many tax revenues are earmarked for specific purposes and are deposited in accounts other than the general fund: all gasoline taxes and related charges are designated for highways, and a portion of the sales tax goes directly to public education. In addition, public education accounts for more than half of all general fund expenditures. The state shares tax collections with its subdivisions (counties and municipalities), which determine how their share of the money will be spent.

Fiscal year 2006 general funds were estimated at $6.4 billion for resources and $5.7 billion for expenditures. In fiscal year 2004, federal government grants to South Carolina were $6.1 billion.

36 TAXATION

In 2005, South Carolina collected $7,318 million in tax revenues or $1,720 per capita, which placed it 43rd among the 50 states in per capita tax burden. The national average was $2,192 per capita. Property taxes accounted for 0.1% of the total; sales taxes, 39.7%; selective sales taxes, 13.4%; individual income taxes, 36.8%; corporate income taxes, 3.4%; and other taxes 6.7%.

As of 1 January 2006, South Carolina had six individual income tax brackets ranging from 2.5% to 7.0%. The state taxes corporations at a flat rate of 5.0%.

In 2004, state and local property taxes amounted to $3,704,419,000 or $882 per capita. The per capita amount ranks the state 33rd highest nationally. Local governments collected $3,692,822,000 of the total and the state government $11,597,000.

South Carolina taxes retail sales at a rate of 5%. In addition to the state tax, local taxes on retail sales can reach as much as 2%, making for a potential total tax on retail sales of 7%. Food purchased for consumption off-premises is taxable. The tax on cigarettes is 7 cents per pack, which ranks 51st among the 50 states and the District of Columbia. South Carolina taxes gasoline at 16 cents per gallon. This is in addition to the 18.4 cents per gallon federal tax on gasoline.

According to the Tax Foundation, for every federal tax dollar sent to Washington in 2004, South Carolina citizens received $1.38 in federal spending.

37 ECONOMIC POLICY

The Department of Commerce seeks to encourage economic growth and to attract new industries; it has been successful in at-

South Carolina—State Government Finances

(Dollar amounts in thousands. Per capita amounts in dollars.)

	AMOUNT	PER CAPITA
Total Revenue	21,241,956	5,060.02
General revenue	16,836,232	4,010.54
Intergovernmental revenue	6,229,053	1,483.81
Taxes	6,803,568	1,620.67
General sales	2,726,657	649.51
Selective sales	963,329	229.47
License taxes	383,505	91.35
Individual income tax	2,438,712	580.92
Corporate income tax	196,510	46.81
Other taxes	94,855	22.60
Current charges	2,593,732	617.85
Miscellaneous general revenue	1,209,879	288.20
Utility revenue	1,047,934	249.63
Liquor store revenue	–	–
Insurance trust revenue	3,357,790	799.85
Total expenditure	21,427,748	5,104.28
Intergovernmental expenditure	4,159,942	990.93
Direct expenditure	17,267,806	4,113.34
Current operation	11,898,782	2,834.39
Capital outlay	1,771,527	421.99
Insurance benefits and repayments	2,293,201	546.26
Assistance and subsidies	695,601	165.70
Interest on debt	608,695	145.00
Exhibit: Salaries and wages	2,736,968	651.97
Total expenditure	21,427,748	5,104.28
General expenditure	17,960,507	4,278.35
Intergovernmental expenditure	4,159,942	990.93
Direct expenditure	13,800,565	3,287.41
General expenditures, by function:		
Education	6,091,352	1,451.01
Public welfare	4,936,352	1,175.88
Hospitals	978,551	233.10
Health	677,607	161.41
Highways	1,412,728	336.52
Police protection	182,727	43.53
Correction	419,758	99.99
Natural resources	201,047	47.89
Parks and recreation	68,284	16.27
Government administration	759,380	180.89
Interest on general debt	453,179	107.95
Other and unallocable	1,779,542	423.90
Utility expenditure	1,174,040	279.67
Liquor store expenditure	–	–
Insurance trust expenditure	2,293,201	546.26
Debt at end of fiscal year	11,162,865	2,659.09
Cash and security holdings	30,436,285	7,250.19

Abbreviations and symbols: – zero or rounds to zero; (NA) not available; (X) not applicable.

SOURCE: *U.S. Census Bureau, Governments Division, 2004 Survey of State Government Finances*, January 2006.

tracting foreign companies, especially to the Piedmont. The Community and Rural Development Division strengthens and improves the leadership capacity and education of local community leaders. The division offers technical assistance to all South Carolina communities.

The state exempts all new industrial construction from local property taxes (except the school tax) for five years. Moreover, industrial properties are assessed very leniently for tax purposes. State and local governments have cooperated in building necessary roads to industrial sites, providing water and sewer services, and helping industries to meet environmental standards. Counties are authorized to issue industrial bonds at low interest rates. Generally conservative state fiscal policies, relatively low wage rates, and an anti-union climate also serve as magnets for industry.

38 HEALTH

The infant mortality rate in October 2005 was estimated at 8.4 per 1,000 live births. The birth rate in 2003 was 13.4 per 1,000 population. The abortion rate stood at 9.3 per 1,000 women in 2000. In 2003, about 77.5% of pregnant woman received prenatal care beginning in the first trimester. In 2004, approximately 80% of children received routine immunizations before the age of three.

The crude death rate in 2003 was 9.2 deaths per 1,000 population. As of 2002, the death rates for major causes of death (per 100,000 resident population) were: heart disease, 235.2; cancer, 202.9; cerebrovascular diseases, 68.7; chronic lower respiratory diseases, 46; and diabetes, 27.1. The mortality rate from HIV infection was 7.3 per 100,000 population. In 2004, the reported AIDS case rate was at about 18.1 per 100,000 population. In 2002, about 59.3% of the population was considered overweight or obese. As of 2004, about 24.3% of state residents were smokers.

In 2003, South Carolina had 61 community hospitals with about 11,100 beds. There were about 506,000 patient admissions that year and 7.4 million outpatient visits. The average daily inpatient census was about 8,100 patients. The average cost per day for hospital care was $1,355. Also in 2003, there were about 178 certified nursing facilities in the state with 18,306 beds and an overall occupancy rate of about 88.6%. In 2004, it was estimated that about 68.7% of all state residents had received some type of dental care within the year. South Carolina had 231 physicians per 100,000 resident population in 2004 and 732 nurses per 100,000 in 2005. In 2004, there was a total of 1,949 dentists in the state.

About 24% of state residents were enrolled in Medicaid programs in 2003; 15% were enrolled in Medicare programs in 2004. Approximately 15% of the state population was uninsured in 2004. In 2003, state health care expenditures totaled $5.5 million.

39 SOCIAL WELFARE

In 2004, about 123,000 people received unemployment benefits, with the average weekly unemployment benefit at $211. In fiscal year 2005, the estimated average monthly participation in the food stamp program included about 521,125 persons (219,503 households); the average monthly benefit was about $90.48 per person. That year, the total of benefits paid through the state for the food stamp program was about $565.8 million.

Temporary Assistance for Needy Families (TANF), the system of federal welfare assistance that officially replaced Aid to Families with Dependent Children (AFDC) in 1997, was reauthorized through the Deficit Reduction Act of 2005. TANF is funded through federal block grants that are divided among the states based on an equation involving the number of recipients in each state. South Carolina's TANF program is called Family Independence. In 2004, the state program had 39,000 recipients; state and federal expenditures on this TANF program totaled $51 million in fiscal year 2003.

In December 2004, Social Security benefits were paid to 750,970 South Carolina residents. This number included 453,910 retired workers, 69,510 widows and widowers, 123,460 disabled workers,

30,770 spouses, and 73,320 children. Social Security beneficiaries represented 18% of the total state population and 93.8% of the state's population age 65 and older. Retired workers received an average monthly payment of $931; widows and widowers, $820; disabled workers, $884; and spouses, $468. Payments for children of retired workers averaged $490 per month; children of deceased workers, $597; and children of disabled workers, $270. Federal Supplemental Security Income payments in December 2004 went to 105,223 Pennsylvania residents, averaging $369 a month. An additional $937,000 of state-administered supplemental payments were distributed to 2,981 residents.

⁴⁰HOUSING

In 2004, there were an estimated 1,890,682 housing units, 1,611,401 of which were occupied; 69.7% were owner-occupied. About 60.6% of all housing units were single-family, detached homes. The state had one of the largest percentages of mobile home units with nearly 18.8% in 2004. Electricity and utility gas were the most common energy sources for heating. It was estimated 102,653 units lacked telephone service, 5,428 lacked complete plumbing facilities, and 8,284 lacked complete kitchen facilities. The average household had 2.52 members.

In 2004, 43,200 new privately owned housing units were authorized for construction. The median home value was $113,910. The median monthly cost for mortgage owners was $987. Renters paid a median of $610 per month. In 2006, the state received over $23.9 million in community development block grants from the US Department of Housing and Urban Development (HUD).

South Carolina has made a determined effort to upgrade housing. The State Housing Authority, created in 1971, is empowered to issue bonds to provide mortgage subsidies for low- and middle-income families.

⁴¹EDUCATION

For decades, South Carolina ranked below the national averages in most phases of education, including expenditures per pupil, median years of school completed, teachers' salaries, and literacy levels. During the 1970s, however, significant improvements were made through the adoption of five-year achievement goals, enactment of a statewide educational funding plan, provision of special programs for exceptional children and of kindergartens for all children, measurement of students' achievements at various stages, and expansion of adult education programs. As of 2004, 83.6% of residents 25 years or older had completed high school, almost meeting the national average of 84%. Some 24.9% had attended four or more years of college.

The total enrollment for fall 2002 in South Carolina's public schools stood at 695,000. Of these, 501,000 attended schools from kindergarten through grade eight, and 194,000 attended high school. Approximately 54.2% of the students were white, 41.3% were black, 3.2% were Hispanic, 1.1% were Asian/Pacific Islander, and 0.3% were American Indian/Alaskan Native. Total enrollment was estimated at 689,000 in fall 2003 and expected to be 675,000 by fall 2014, a decline of 2.7% during the period 2002–14. Expenditures for public education in 2003/04 were estimated at $6.1 billion. In fall 2003 there were 58,005 students enrolled in 345 private schools. Since 1969, the National Assessment of Educational Progress (NAEP) has tested public school students nationwide. The resulting report, *The Nation's Report Card,* stated that in 2005,

eighth graders in South Carolina scored 281 out of 500 in mathematics compared with the national average of 278.

As of fall 2002, there were 202,007 students enrolled in college or graduate school; minority students comprised 30.6% of total postsecondary enrollment. In 2005 South Carolina had 63 degree-granting institutions. The state has three major universities: the University of South Carolina, with its main campus in Columbia; Clemson University, at Clemson; and the Medical University of South Carolina in Charleston. In addition, there are four-year state colleges, as well as four-year and two-year branches of the University of South Carolina. The state also has 23 four-year nonprofit private colleges and universities; most are church-affiliated. The Lutheran Theological Southern Seminary in Columbia is the only major private graduate institution. South Carolina has an extensive technical education system, supported by both state and local funds. Tuition grants are offered for South Carolina students in need that are enrolled in private colleges in the state.

⁴²ARTS

The South Carolina Arts Commission, created in 1967, has developed apprenticeship programs, under the Folklife and Traditional Arts Apprenticeship Initiative, in which students learn from master artists. In 2005, the South Carolina Arts Commission and other South Carolina arts organizations received 15 grants totaling $933,200 from the National Endowment for the Arts (NEA). In 2005, the National Endowment for the Humanities contributed $769,885 for 10 state programs. The state and various private sources also provided funding for the council's activities.

South Carolina's three major centers for the visual arts are the Gibbes Museum of Art in Charleston, the Columbia Museum of Art, and the Greenville County Museum of Art. The Town Theater in Columbia was built in 1924 and is the nation's oldest community playhouse in continuous use. The theater building is also listed in the National Register of Historic Places. As of 2005, the Town Theater offered Summer Camps for youths between 2nd and 12th grade.

The Charleston Symphony Orchestra, founded in 1936, celebrated its 70th anniversary during the 2005/06 season. The Charlotte Symphony Orchestra celebrated its 75th anniversary during its 2006/07. Perhaps South Carolina's best-known musical event is the Spoleto Festival—held annually in Charleston during May and June and modeled on the Spoleto Festival in Italy—at which artists of international repute perform in original productions in opera, theater, dance, music, and circus.

⁴³LIBRARIES AND MUSEUMS

For the fiscal year ending in June 2001, South Carolina had 41 public library systems, with a total of 183 libraries, of which 143 were branches. In that same year, the South Carolina public library systems had a combined book/serial publication stock of 8,260,000 volumes and a total circulation of 18,166,000. The system also had 280,000 audio and 234,000 video items, 30,000 electronic format items (CD-ROMs, magnetic tapes, and disks), and 35 bookmobiles. The State Library in Columbia works to improve library services throughout the state and also provides reference and research services for the state government. The University of South Carolina and Clemson University libraries, with more than 3,067,457 and 1,024,289 volumes, respectively, have the most outstanding academic collections. Special libraries are maintained by the South Carolina Historical Society in Charleston and the Department of Archives and History in Columbia; the South Caroliniana Society at the University of South Carolina is a friends' group devoted to the USC library. In fiscal year 2001, operating income for the state's public library system totaled $75,829,000 and included $648,000 in federal funds and $6,990,000 in state funding.

There are 131 museums and historic sites, notably the State Museum in Columbia, with collections reflecting all areas of the state; Charleston Museum (specializing in history, natural history, and anthropology); and the University of South Carolina McKissick Museums (with silver, lapidary, and military collections) also in Columbia. Charleston is also famous for its many old homes, streets, churches, and public facilities; at the entrance to Charleston Harbor stands Ft. Sumter, where the Civil War began. Throughout the state, numerous battle sites of the American Revolution have been preserved; many antebellum plantation homes have been restored, especially in the low country. Restoration projects have proceeded in Columbia and Charleston, where the restored Exchange Building, dating to the Revolutionary War, was opened to the public in 1981.

Among the state's best-known botanical gardens are the Cypress, Magnolia, and Middleton gardens in the Charleston area. Edisto Garden in Orangeburg is renowned for its azaleas and roses, and Brookgreen Gardens near Georgetown displays a wide variety of plants, animals, and sculpture.

44 COMMUNICATIONS

In 2004, 93.4% of South Carolina's occupied housing units had telephones. Additionally, by June of that same year there were 2,337,367 mobile wireless telephone subscribers. In 2003, 54.9% of South Carolina households had a computer and 45.6% had Internet access. By June 2005, there were 464,917 high-speed lines in South Carolina, 414,608 residential and 50,309 for business. The state had 62 major radio stations (14 AM, 48 FM) and 20 major television stations in 2005. South Carolina has one of the most highly regarded educational television systems in the nation, with ten stations serving the public schools, higher education institutions, state agencies, and the general public through a multichannel closed-circuit network and seven open channels. The Charlotte area alone had 880,570 television households, 67% receiving cable in 1999. Some 45,839 Internet domain names were registered in the state as of 2000.

45 PRESS

Charleston *Courier*, founded in 1803, and the *Post*. founded in 1894 merged to form the Charleston *Post and Courier* in 1991. The Spartanburg *Herald-Journal* was founded in 1844 and the Greenville *News* began publication in 1874. Overall, as of 2005, South Carolina had 14 morning newspapers, 2 evening dailies, and 14 Sunday newspapers.

Leading dailies and their approximate 2005 circulation rates are as follows:

AREA	NAME	DAILY	SUNDAY
Charleston	*Post and Courier* (m,S)	95,588	106,061
Columbia	*The State* (m,S)	115,464	148,865
Greenville	*News* (m,S)	86,573	115,758
Spartanburg	*Herald-Journal* (m,S)	48,798	56,981

46 ORGANIZATIONS

In 2006, there were over 3,110 nonprofit organizations registered within the state, of which about 2,238 were registered as charitable, educational, or religious organizations. National professional and business organizations with headquarters in the state include the Association for Education in Journalism and Mass Communication, the National Peach Council, and the United States Sweet Potato Council. National offices for US Club Soccer and the Southern Conference of collegiate sports are located within the state. State educational and cultural organizations include the South Carolina Historical Society and the South Carolina Humanities Council. There are several local arts councils. The Congressional Medal of Honor Society in Mount Pleasant hosts a museum to honor recipients of this award.

47 TOURISM, TRAVEL, AND RECREATION

In 2004, the tourism and travel industry ranked first in the state as the largest employer and the largest "export." That year, the state hosted some 32 million visitors with total visitor spending at $7.8 billion. Approximately 132,400 South Carolinians are directly employed by the tourism industry. About 75% of travelers are from out-of-state. Nearly one-third of all trips are day trips. About 75% of out-of-state tourist revenue is spent by vacationers in Charleston, where visitors may tour in a horse-drawn buggy, and at the Myrtle Beach and Hilton Head Island resorts. The Marketplace at the center of Charleston marks the place where over 70% of all slaves were processed into the country. Outside of Charleston, several historic plantations offer tours.

The Cowpens National Battlefield and the Ft. Sumter and Ft. Moultrie and Kings Mountain national military sites are popular tourist attractions. Golf is a major attraction, generating more income than any other single entertainment or recreational activity. During the last week in May, Charleston hosts the Spoleto Festival, which features exhibits, plays, and musical presentations.

There are 46 state parks and 9 welcome centers in the state.

48 SPORTS

There are no major professional sports teams in South Carolina. Minor league baseball teams are located in Myrtle Beach and Charleston. There are also minor league hockey teams in North Charleston, Greenville, and Florence. Several steeplechase horse races are held annually in Camden, and important professional golf and tennis tournaments are held at Hilton Head Island.

In collegiate football, the Clemson Tigers of the Atlantic Coast Conference won the AP and UPI National Championship in 1981. The University of South Carolina of the Southeastern Conference and South Carolina State of the Mid-Eastern Athletic Conference also have football programs. Under the tutelage of former Notre Dame coach Lou Holtz, the South Carolina Gamecocks saw a turnaround in their football program, highlighted by consecutive Outback Bowl victories over Ohio State in 2001 and 2002.

Fishing, water-skiing, and sailing are popular sports. There are two major stock car races held at Darlington each year: the Mall.com 400 in March and the Southern 500 on Labor Day weekend.

Other annual sporting events include Polo Games held from February through Easter in Aiken, and the Governor's Annual Frog Jumping Contest held in Springfield on the Saturday before Easter.

⁴⁹ FAMOUS SOUTH CAROLINIANS

Many distinguished South Carolinians made their reputations outside the state. Andrew Jackson (1767–1845), the seventh US president, was born in a border settlement probably inside present-day South Carolina, but studied law in North Carolina before establishing a legal practice in Tennessee. Identified more closely with South Carolina is John C. Calhoun (1782–1850), vice president from 1825 to 1832; Calhoun also served as US senator and was a leader of the South before the Civil War.

John Rutledge (1739–1800), the first governor of the state and a leader during the America Revolution, served a term as US chief justice but was never confirmed by the Senate. Another Revolutionary leader, Charles Cotesworth Pinckney (1746–1825), was also a delegate to the US constitutional convention. A strong Unionist, Joel R. Poinsett (1779–1851) served as secretary of war and as the first US ambassador to Mexico; he developed the poinsettia, named after him, from a Mexican plant. Benjamin R. Tillman (1847–1918) was governor, US senator, and leader of the populist movement in South Carolina. Bernard M. Baruch (1870–1965), an outstanding financier, statesman, and adviser to presidents, was born in South Carolina. Another presidential adviser, James F. Byrnes (1879–1972), also served as US senator, associate justice of the Supreme Court, and secretary of state. The state's best-known recent political leader was J(ames) Strom Thurmond (1902–2003), who ran for the presidency as a States' Rights Democrat ("Dixiecrat") in 1948, winning 1,169,134 popular votes and 39 electoral votes, and served in the Senate from 1954 until his death.

Famous military leaders native to the state are the Revolutionary War General Francis Marion (1732?–95), known as the Swamp Fox, and James Longstreet (1821–1904), a Confederate lieutenant general during the Civil War, Mark W. Clark (b.New York, 1896–1984), US Army general and former president of the Citadel, lived in South Carolina after 1954. General William C. Westmoreland (1914–2005) was commander of US forces in Viet-Nam.

Notable in the academic world are Francis Lieber (b.Germany, 1800–1872), a political scientist who taught at the University of South Carolina and, later, Columbia University in New York City, and wrote for the United States the world's first comprehensive code of military laws and procedures; Mary McLeod Bethune (1875–1955), founder of Bethune-Cookman College in Florida and of the National Council of Negro Women; John B. Watson (1878–1958), a pioneer in behavioral psychology; and Charles H. Townes (b.1915), awarded the Nobel Prize in physics in 1964. South Carolinians prominent in business and the professions include architect Robert Mills (1781–1855), who designed the Washington Monument and many other buildings; William Gregg (b.Virginia, 1800–1867), a leader in establishing the textile industry in the South; David R. Coker (1870–1938), who developed many varieties of pedigreed seed; and industrial builder Charles E. Daniel (1895–1964), who helped bring many new industries to the state.

South Carolinians who made significant contributions to literature include William Gilmore Simms (1806–70), author of nearly 100 books; Julia Peterkin (1880–1961), who won the Pulit-

zer Prize for *Scarlet Sister Mary;* DuBose Heyward (1885–1940), whose novel *Porgy* was the basis of the folk opera *Porgy and Bess;* and James M. Dabbs (1896–1970), a writer who was also a leader in the racial integration movement.

Entertainers born in the state include singer Eartha Kitt (b.1928) and jazz trumpeter John Birks "Dizzy" Gillespie (1917–1993). Tennis champion Althea Gibson (1927–2003) was another South Carolina native.

⁵⁰ BIBLIOGRAPHY

Barefoot, Daniel W. *Touring South Carolina's Revolutionary War Sites.* Winston-Salem, N.C.: John F. Blair, 1999.

Cauthen, Charles E. *South Carolina Goes to War, 1860–65.* Chapel Hill: University of North Carolina Press, 2005.

Cities of the United States. 5th ed. Farmington Hills, Mich.: Thomson Gale, 2005.

Coastal Southeast 2005: Georgia, North Carolina, South Carolina. Park Ridge, Ill.: ExxonMobil Travel Publications, 2005.

Council of State Governments. *The Book of the States, 2006 Edition.* Lexington, Ky.: Council of State Governments, 2006.

Ferris, William (ed.). *The South.* Vol. 7 in *The Greenwood Encyclopedia of American Regional Cultures.* Westport, Conn.: Greenwood Press, 2004.

Graham, Cole Brease. *South Carolina Politics & Government.* Lincoln: University of Nebraska Press, 1994.

McAuliffe, Bill. *South Carolina Facts and Symbols.* New York: Hilltop Books, 1999.

McCaslin, Richard B. *Photographic History of South Carolina in the Civil War.* Fayetteville: University of Arkansas Press, 1994.

Poole, W. Scott. *South Carolina's Civil War: A Narrative History.* Macon, Ga.: Mercer University Press, 2005.

Rhyne, Nancy (ed.). *Voices of Carolina Slave Children.* Orangeburg, S.C.: Sandlapper Publishing Company, 1999.

Rogers, George C. *A South Carolina Chronology, 1497–1992.* Columbia: University of South Carolina Press, 1994.

US Department of Commerce, Economics and Statistics Administration, US Census Bureau. *South Carolina, 2000. Summary Social, Economic, and Housing Characteristics: 2000 Census of Population and Housing.* Washington, D.C.: US Government Printing Office, 2003.

US Department of Education, National Center for Education Statistics. Office of Educational Research and Improvement. *Digest of Education Statistics, 1993.* Washington, D.C.: US Government Printing Office, 1993.

US Department of the Interior, US Fish and Wildlife Service. *Endangered and Threatened Species Recovery Program.* Washington, D.C.: US Government Printing Office, 1990.

Yuhl, Stephanie E. *A Golden Haze of Memory: The Making of Historic Charleston.* Chapel Hill: University of North Carolina Press, 2005.

Zuczek, Richard. *State of Rebellion: Reconstruction in South Carolina.* Columbia: University of South Carolina Press, 1996.

SOUTH DAKOTA

State of South Dakota

ORIGIN OF STATE NAME: The state was formerly the southern part of Dakota Territory; *dakota* is a Sioux word meaning "friend" or "ally." **NICKNAME:** Mount Rushmore State; the Coyote State. **CAPITAL:** Pierre. **ENTERED UNION:** November 2, 1889 (40th). **SONG:** "Hail, South Dakota." **MOTTO:** Under God the People Rule. **COAT OF ARMS:** Beneath the state motto, the Missouri River winds between hills and plains; symbols representing mining (a smelting furnace and hills), commerce (a steamboat), and agriculture (a man plowing, cattle, and a field of corn) complete the scene. **FLAG:** The state seal, centered on a light-blue field and encircled by a serrated sun, is surrounded by the words "South Dakota" above and "The Mount Rushmore State" below. **OFFICIAL SEAL:** The words "State of South Dakota. Great Seal. 1889" encircle the arms. **BIRD:** Chinese ring-necked pheasant. **FISH:** Walleye. **FLOWER:** American Pasque (also called the May Day flower). **TREE:** Black Hills spruce. **GEM:** Fairburn agate. **LEGAL HOLIDAYS:** New Year's Day, 1 January; Birthday of Martin Luther King Jr., 3rd Monday in January; Presidents' Day, 3rd Monday in February; Memorial Day, last Monday in May; Independence Day, 4 July; Labor Day, 1st Monday in September; Native Americans' Day, 2nd Monday in October; Veterans' Day, 11 November; Thanksgiving Day, 4th Thursday in November; Christmas Day, 25 December. **TIME:** 6 AM CST = noon GM; 5 AM MST = noon GMT.

¹LOCATION, SIZE, AND EXTENT

Situated in the western north-central United States, South Dakota ranks 16th in size among the 50 states.

The state has a total area of 77,121 sq mi (199,730 sq km), comprising 75,896 sq mi (196,715 sq km) of land and 1,164 sq mi (3,015 sq km) of inland water. Shaped roughly like a rectangle with irregular borders on the E and SE, South Dakota extends about 380 mi (610 km) E–W and has a maximum N–S extension of 245 mi (394 km).

South Dakota is bordered on the N by North Dakota; on the E by Minnesota and Iowa (with the line in the NE passing through the Bois de Sioux River, Lake Traverse, and Big Stone Lake, and in the SE through the Big Sioux River); on the S by Nebraska (with part of the line formed by the Missouri River and Lewis and Clark Lake); and on the W by Wyoming and Montana.

The total boundary length of South Dakota is 1,316 mi (2,118 km). The state's geographic center is in Hughes County, 8 mi (13 km) NE of Pierre. The geographic center of the United States, including Alaska and Hawaii, is at 44°58′N, 103°46′W, in Butte County, 17 mi (27 km) W of Castle Rock.

²TOPOGRAPHY

The eastern two-fifths of South Dakota is prairie, belonging to the Central Lowlands. The western three-fifths falls within the Missouri Plateau, part of the Great Plains region; the High Plains extend into the southern fringes of the state. The Black Hills, an extension of the Rocky Mountains, occupy the southern half of the state's western border; the mountains, which tower about 4,000 ft (1,200 m) over the neighboring plains, include Harney Peak, at 7,242 ft (2,209 m) the highest point in the state. East of the southern Black Hills are the Badlands, a barren, eroded region with extensive fossil deposits. The mean elevation of the state is approximately 2,200 ft (671 m).

South Dakota's lowest elevation, 966 ft (295 m), is at Big Stone Lake, in the northeastern corner. Flowing south and southeast, the Missouri River cuts a huge swath through the heart of South Dakota before forming part of the southeastern boundary. Tributaries of the Missouri include the Grand, Cheyenne, Bad, Moreau, and White rivers in the west and the James, Vermillion, and Big Sioux in the east. The Missouri River itself is controlled by four massive dams, Gavins Point, Ft. Randall, Big Bend, and Oahe, which provide water for irrigation, flood control, and hydroelectric power. Major lakes in the state include Traverse, Big Stone, Lewis and Clark, Francis Case, and Oahe.

³CLIMATE

South Dakota has an interior continental climate, with hot summers, extremely cold winters, high winds, and periodic droughts. The normal January temperature is 12°F (-11°C); the normal July temperature, 74°F (23°C). The record low temperature is -58°F (-50°C), set at McIntosh on 17 February 1936; the record high, 120°F (49°C), at Gannvalley on 5 July 1936.

Normal annual precipitation averages about 25 in (63 cm) in Sioux Falls in the southeast, decreasing to less than 13 in (33 cm) in the northwest. Sioux Falls receives an average of 39.6 in (100 cm) of snow per year.

⁴FLORA AND FAUNA

Oak, maple, beech, birch, hickory, and willow are all represented in South Dakota's forests while thickets of chokecherry, wild plum, gooseberry, and currant are found in the eastern part of the state. Pasqueflower (Anemone ludoviciana) is the state flower; other wild flowers are beardtongue, bluebell, and monkshood. No South Dakota plant species were listed as threatened or endangered as of April 2006.

Familiar native mammals are the coyote (the state animal), porcupine, raccoon, bobcat, buffalo, white-tailed and mule deer, white-tailed jackrabbit, and black-tailed prairie dog. Nearly 300 species of birds have been identified; the sage grouse, bobwhite quail, and ring-necked pheasant are leading game birds. Trout, catfish, pike, bass, and perch are fished for sport.

Nearly 50% of the North American population of Franklin's gull have stopped at the site of the Sand Lake National Wildlife Refugee, which is also considered to be the world's largest nesting site for this bird. The site also serves as a nesting area for nearly 50% of the continental duck population.

In April 2006, the US Fish and Wildlife Service listed nine South Dakota animal species (vertebrates and invertebrates) as threatened or endangered, including the American burying beetle, whooping crane, Eskimo curlew, black-footed ferret, Topeka shiner, pallid sturgeon, least tern, and bald eagle.

5 ENVIRONMENTAL PROTECTION

The mission of the Department of the Environment and Natural Resources (DENR), the primary environmental agency in South Dakota, is to provide environmental services in a customer-oriented manner that promotes economic development; conserves natural resources; helps municipalities, industry, and citizens comply with regulations; and protects public health and the environment.

There are about 1.8 million acres (728,434 hectares) of wetlands in the state, accounting for about 3.6% of the land area. The Sand Lake National Wildlife Refuge, a freshwater cattail marsh, was designated as a Ramsar Wetland of International Importance in 1998.

In 2003, 10.3 million pounds of toxic chemicals were released in the state. In 2003, South Dakota had 39 hazardous waste sites listed in the US Environment Protection Agency (EPA) database, two of which, Ellsworth Air Force Base and Gilt Edge Mine, were on the National Priorities List as of 2006. In 2005, the EPA spent over $3 million through the Superfund program for the cleanup of hazardous waste sites in the state. The same year, federal EPA grants awarded to the state included $8.2 million for the drinking water state revolving fund and $5 million for the clean water revolving fund.

6 POPULATION

South Dakota ranked 46th in population in the United States with an estimated total of 775,933 in 2005, an increase of 2.8% since 2000. Between 1990 and 2000, South Dakota's population grew from 696,004 to 754,844, an increase of 8.5%. The population is projected to reach 796,954 by 2015 and 801,845 by 2025.

In 2004, the median age for South Dakotans was 37. In the same year, more than 24.8% of the populace was under the age of 18 while 14.2% was age 65 or older. The population density in 2004 was 10.2 persons per sq mi, making it the fifth most sparsely populated state in the nation.

Sioux Falls proper had an estimated 2004 population of 136,695. The Sioux Falls metropolitan area had an estimated population of 203,324. The Rapid City metropolitan area had an estimated 117,487 residents.

7 ETHNIC GROUPS

According to the 2000 census, South Dakota's population included some 62,283 American Indians, or 8.3% of the total state population—the third-highest percentage among the 50 states.. Many lived on the 5,099,000 acres (2,063,500 hectares) of Indian lands in 1982, but Rapid City also had a large Indian population. Among the state's largest reservations, with their populations as of 2000, are the Pine Ridge (15,521), Rosebud (10,469), and Cheyenne River (8,470) reservations. In 2004, 8.6% of the state's population was American Indian.

As of 2000, the black population was 4,685, up from 3,000 recorded in the 1990 census. The black population accounted for 0.8% of the state's total population in 2004. The estimated number of Asian residents was 4,378. In 2004, 0.7% of the population was Asian. Pacific Islanders numbered 261 in 2000. Of the South Dakotans who reported at least one specific ancestry in the 2000 census, 307,309 listed German, 115,292 Norwegian, 78,481 Irish, 53,2141 English, and 35,655 Dutch. In the same year, 13,495 South Dakotans—1.8% of the population—were foreign born, up from 7,731 in 1990. In 2000, the number of Hispanics and Latinos was 10,903, or 1.4% of the population. In 2004, 2% of the state's population was of Hispanic or Latino origin, and 1.2% reported origin of two or more races.

8 LANGUAGES

Despite hints given by such place-names as Dakota, Oahe, and Akaska, English has borrowed little from the language of the Sioux still living in South Dakota. *Tepee* is such a loanword, and *tado* (jerky) is heard near Pine Ridge. South Dakota English is transitional between the Northern and Midland dialects. Diffusion throughout the state is apparent, but many terms contrast along a curving line from the southeast to the northwest corner.

In 2000, 658,245 South Dakotans—93.5% of the resident population five years of age or older—spoke only English at home.

The following table gives selected statistics from the 2000 Census for language spoken at home by persons five years old and over. The category "Other Native North American languages" includes Apache, Cherokee, Choctaw, Dakota, Keres, Pima, and Yupik. The category "Other Slavic languages" includes Czech, Slovak, and Ukrainian. The category "African languages" includes Amharic, Ibo, Twi, Yoruba, Bantu, Swahili, and Somali. The category "Scandinavian languages" includes Danish, Norwegian, and Swedish.

LANGUAGE	NUMBER	PERCENT
Population 5 years and over	**703,820**	**100.0**
Speak only English	658,245	93.5
Speak a language other than English	45,575	6.5
Speak a language other than English	**45,575**	**6.5**
German	13,422	1.9
Other Native North American languages	11,246	1.6
Spanish or Spanish Creole	10,052	1.4
French (incl. Patois, Cajun)	1,256	0.2
Other Slavic languages	1,055	0.1
African languages	1,042	0.1
Scandinavian languages	1,024	0.1
Serbo-Croatian	573	0.1
Chinese	569	0.1
Vietnamese	553	0.1
Tagalog	457	0.1
Russian	411	0.1
Arabic	384	0.1

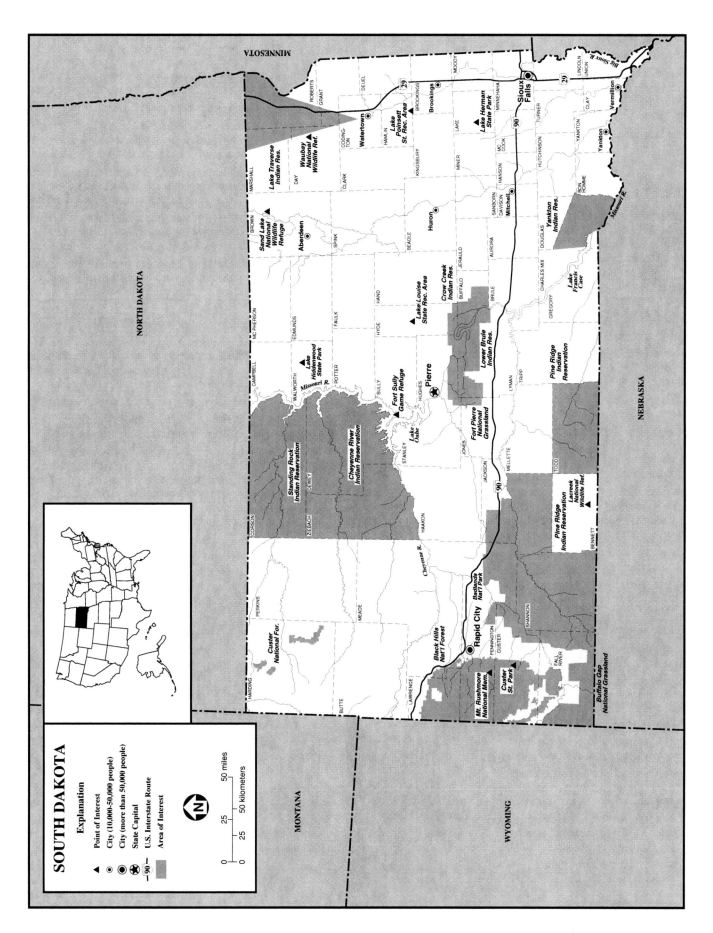

[9] RELIGIONS

The largest single denomination in the state is the Roman Catholic Church, which had 154,772 adherents, in 2004. According to 2000 data, leading Protestant denominations were the Evangelical Lutheran Church in America, with 121,871 adherents; the United Methodist Church, 37,280; and the Lutheran Church—Missouri Synod, 31,524. The Jewish population was estimated at 350 adherents. A few religious groups, though still relatively small in numbers, reported significant growth in membership since 1990. The Salvation Army grew from 732 members in 1990 to 2,804 in 2000, a difference of 283%. Likewise, the International Church of the Foursquare Gospel grew from 466 adherents in 1990 to 1,518 in 2000, a difference of 225%. In the 2000 survey, about 242,950 people (32.3% of the population) were not counted as members of any religious organization. The Church of Jesus Christ of Latter-day Saints reported a membership of about 8,957 adherents in 32 congregations in 2006.

[10] TRANSPORTATION

In 2003, a total of 1,940 mi (3,123 km) of railroad track was operated in South Dakota by nine railroads. The Burlington Northern Santa Fe (BNSF) and Soo Line were the state's two Class I railroads, operating a combined total of 937 mi (1,508 km) of track that same year. The remaining track was operated by nine other regional, local, or switching and terminal railroads. Freight was primarily coal and petroleum gas (terminating), and agricultural products (originating). As of 2006, there was no Amtrak passenger service in the state.

Public highways, streets, and roads covered 83,574 mi (134,554 km) in 2004 when the state had some 863,000 registered motor vehicles and 563,298 licensed drivers. In 2005, South Dakota had a total of 193 public and private-use aviation-related facilities. This included 159 airports, 33 heliports and one seaplane base. Joe Foss Field at Sioux Falls is the state's most active airport, with 333,338 passenger enplanements in 2004. South Dakota had 75 mi (120 km) of navigable inland waterways.

[11] HISTORY

People have lived in what is now South Dakota for at least 25,000 years. The original inhabitants, who hunted in the northern Great Plains until about 5000 BC, were the first of a succession of nomadic groups, followed by a society of semisedentary mound builders. After them came the prehistoric forebears of the modern riverine groups—Mandan, Hidatsa, and Arikara—who were found gathering, hunting, farming, and fishing along the upper Missouri River by the first European immigrants. These groups faced no challenge until the Sioux, driven from the Minnesota woodlands, began to move westward during the second quarter of the 18th century, expelling all other Native American groups form South Dakota by the mid-1830s.

Significant European penetration of South Dakota followed the Lewis and Clark expedition of 1804–06. White men came to assert US sovereignty, to negotiate Indian treaties, to "save Indian souls," and to traffic in hides and furs. Among the most important early merchants were Manuel Lisa, who pressed up the Missouri from St. Louis, and Pierre Chouteau Jr., whose offices in St. Louis dominated trade on both the upper Mississippi and upper Missouri

rivers from 1825 until his death in 1865, by which time all major sources of hides and furs were exhausted, negotiations for Indian land titles were in progress, and surveyors were preparing ceded territories for non-Indian settlers.

The Dakota Territory, which included much of present-day Wyoming and Montana as well as North and south Dakota, was established in 1861, with headquarters first at Yankton (1861–83) and later at Bismarck (1883–89). The territory was reduced to just the Dakotas in 1868; six years later, a gold rush brought thousands of prospectors and settlers to the Black Hills. South Dakota emerged as a state in 1889, with the capital in Pierre. Included within the state were nine Indian reservations, established, after protracted negotiations and three wars with the Sioux, by Indian Office personnel. Five reservations were established west of the Missouri for the Teton and Yanktonai Sioux, and four reserves east of the Missouri for the Yankton and several Isanti Sioux tribes. Sovereignty was thus divided among Indian agents, state officials, and tribal leaders, a division that did not always make for efficient government. Through the late 19th and early 20th centuries, South Dakotans had limited economic opportunities, for they depended mainly on agriculture. Some 30,000 Sioux barely survived on farming and livestock production, supplemented by irregular government jobs and off-reservation employment. The 500,000 non-Indians lived mainly off cattle-feeding enterprises and small grain sales east of the Missouri, mineral production (especially gold) in the Black Hills, and various service industries at urban centers throughout South Dakota.

The period after World War I saw extensive road building, the establishment of a tourist industry, and efforts to subdue and harness the waters of the Missouri. Like other Americans, South Dakotans were helped through the drought and depression of the 1930s by federal aid. Non-Indians were assisted by food relief, various work-relief programs, and crop-marketing plans, while Indians enjoyed an array of federal programs often called the "Indian New Deal." The economic revival brought about by World War II persisted into the postwar era. Rural whites benefited from the mechanization of agriculture, dam construction along the Missouri, rural electrification, and arid-land reclamation. Federal programs were organized for reservation Indians, relocating them in urban centers where industrial jobs were available, establishing light industries in areas already heavily populated by Indians, and improving education and occupational opportunities on reservations.

Meanwhile, the Sioux continued to bring their historic grievances to public attention. For 70 days in 1973, some 200 armed Indians occupied Wounded Knee, on the Pine Ridge Reservation, where hundreds of Sioux had been killed by US cavalry 83 years earlier. In 1980, reviewing one of several land claims brought by the Sioux, the US Supreme Court upheld compensation of $105 million for land in the Black Hills taken from the Indians by the federal government in 1877. But members of the American Indian Movement (AIM) opposed this settlement and demanded the return of the Black Hills to the Sioux. The economic plight of South Dakota's Indians worsened during the 1980s after the federal government reduced job training programs, and conditions on reservations remained bad in the 1990s, with unemployment in some cases as high as 70%. By 2005, unemployment on the Pine Ridge Reservation, the nation's second-largest, hovered at 80%; life expectancy for men was 48, and 52 for women. The alcoholism rate is the highest in the nation.

In sharp contrast, the state economy as a whole showed strength under the direction of Republican Governor William Janklow, elected in 1978 and reelected in 1982 and, after an eight-year hiatus, in 1994. Janklow, noted for his strong opposition to Indian claims, developed the state's water resources, revived railroad transportation, and attracted new industry to South Dakota, including Citicorp, the largest bank-holding company in the United States, which set up a credit-card operation in Sioux Falls and bought controlling interest in the American State Bank of Rapid City. In the 1990s, farm income had risen; record corn and soybean yields were reported in 1994, in spite of major flooding the year before that resulted in parts of the state being declared disaster areas. Manufacturing also prospered, expanding by up to 10% each year in the early 1990s. Legalized casino gambling has become an important source of government revenue since it was authorized in 1989.

Although the state had budget problems in the early 2000s, they were not as severe as other states. Republican Governor Mike Rounds, elected in 2002, asked legislators in 2003 to increase state aid to schools by $15 million and to create a prescription drug program. He planned a full-scale review of the state department of education. By 2004, Rounds had passed a balanced state budget; reduced the structural deficit from $28 to $20 million; increased state aid for local public schools and public universities; created the Homestake Underground Laboratory project; and created a program to give sales tax on food relief to individuals within 150% of the poverty level.

In the early 2000s South Dakota was experiencing severe drought conditions; damaging drought conditions have ruined crops, kept grass from growing, and led ranchers to sell off their cattle. The Great Plains states by 2005 were projected to face widespread drought in the coming decades.

12 STATE GOVERNMENT

South Dakota is governed by the constitution of 1889, which had been amended 212 times by January 2005. The legislature consists of a 35-seat Senate and 70-seat House of Representatives; all members serve two-year terms. Convening every January, regular sessions are limited to 40 legislative days in odd-numbered years and 35 legislative days in even-numbered years. To run for the legislature, a person must be at least 21 years old, a US citizen, a qualified voter in their district, and must have resided in the state for at least two years prior to election. As of 2004 the legislative salary was $12,000 for two years.

Executives elected statewide are the governor and lieutenant governor (elected jointly), secretary of state, attorney general, treasurer, the commissioner for school and public lands, who are all elected for four-year terms. (Voters also elect three public utility commissioners who serve six-year terms.) A candidate for governor must be a US citizen, at least 18 years old, and have been a resident of the state for at least two years. The governor is limited to serving two consecutive terms. As of December 2004, the governor's salary was $103,222.

A bill passed by the legislature becomes law if signed by the governor, if left unsigned by the governor for five days (including Sundays) while the legislature is in session (15 days, including Sundays, if has adjourned), or if passed over the governor's veto by two-thirds of the elected members of each house. Constitutional amendments may be proposed by the legislature with a majority vote in both houses. If the amendment is approved by a majority of voters during general elections, it becomes part of the constitution. Amendments may also be proposed by initiative (by petition of 10% of total votes for governor at last election).

Voters must be US citizens, at least 18 years old, and state residents. Restrictions apply to convicted felons and those declared mentally incompetent by the court.

13 POLITICAL PARTIES

For the most part, South Dakota has voted Republican in presidential elections, even when native-son George McGovern was the Democratic candidate in 1972. Conservatism runs strong at the local level, although between the two world wars, populist groups gained a broad agrarian following. South Dakotans chose George Bush in 1988 and again in 1992, and in 1996 they gave Republican Bob Dole 46% of the vote. In 2000 and 2004, Republican George W. Bush received 60% of the vote to Democrat Al Gore's 38% (2000) and Democrat John Kerry's 38% (2004). In 2004 there were 502,000 registered voters. In 1998, 40% were Democratic, 48% Republican, and 12% unaffiliated or members of other parties. The state had three electoral votes in the 2004 presidential election.

In 1994 voters elected Republican William Janklow to the governor's office; Janklow had earlier served in that capacity for two terms, 1979–83 and 1983–87. He was reelected in 1998. Republican Mike Rounds was elected governor in 2002 (Janklow had reached his term limit). Janklow was elected South Dakota's US Representative in 2002, but was convicted of second-degree manslaughter for his involvement in a fatal accident with a motorcyclist. In 2004, Democrat Stephanie Herseth won election to represent the state in the US House of Representatives.

Democrat Thomas Daschle won a third term in the Senate in 1998, but was narrowly defeated in his bid for a fourth term by Republican John Thune in 2004. In 1996, South Dakota's US rep-

South Dakota Presidential Vote by Major Political Parties, 1948–2004

YEAR	ELECTORAL VOTE	S. DAKOTA WINNER	DEMOCRAT	REPUBLICAN
1948	4	Dewey (R)	117,653	129,651
1952	4	*Eisenhower (R)	90,426	203,857
1956	4	*Eisenhower (R)	122,288	171,569
1960	4	Nixon (R)	128,070	178,417
1964	4	*Johnson (D)	163,010	130,108
1968	4	*Nixon (R)	118,023	149,841
1972	4	*Nixon (R)	139,945	166,476
1976	4	Ford (R)	147,068	151,505
1980	4	*Reagan (R)	103,855	198,343
1984	3	*Reagan (R)	116,113	200,267
1988	3	*Bush (R)	145,560	165,415
1992**	3	Bush (R)	124,888	136,718
1996**	3	Dole (R)	139,333	150,543
2000	3	*Bush, G. W. (R)	118,804	190,700
2004	3	*Bush, G. W. (R)	149,244	232,584

*Won US presidential election.
**IND. candidate Ross Perot received 73,295 votes in 1992 and 31,250 votes in 1996.

resentative, Democrat Tim Johnson, won the US Senate seat of Larry Pressler, who was seeking a fourth term; Johnson won re-election in 2002. There were 25 Republicans and 10 Democrats in the state Senate, and 46 Republicans and 19 Democrats in the state House in mid-2005.

14 LOCAL GOVERNMENT

As of 2005, South Dakota had 66 counties, 308 municipal governments, 176 public school districts, and 376 special districts, most of them concerned with agricultural issues such as soil conservation. Typical county officials include a treasurer, auditor, state's attorney, sheriff, register of deeds, and clerk of courts. In 2002, there were 940 townships.

In 2005, local government accounted for about 30,149 full-time (or equivalent) employment positions.

15 STATE SERVICES

To address the continuing threat of terrorism and to work with the federal Department of Homeland Security, homeland security in South Dakota operates under the authority of the governor; a homeland security director is appointed to oversee the state's homeland security activities.

The Department of Education oversees all elementary, secondary, and vocational education programs. The Board of Regents oversees the higher education system.

The Department of Social Services administers a variety of welfare programs, the Department of Labor aids the unemployed and underemployed, and the Department of Human Services serves disabled South Dakotans. Special agencies within the executive branch include the Office of Tribal Government Relations, the Office of Economic Development, and the State Energy Office.

16 JUDICIAL SYSTEM

South Dakota has a supreme court with five justices, and eight circuit courts with 167 judges. All are elected on a nonpartisan ballot with staggered eight-year terms.

As of 31 December 2004, a total of 3,095 prisoners were held in South Dakota's state and federal prisons, an increase from 3,026 of 2.3% from the previous year. As of year-end 2004, a total of 292 inmates were female, up from 269 or 8.6% from the year before. Among sentenced prisoners (one year or more), South Dakota had an incarceration rate of 399 per 100,000 population in 2004.

According to the Federal Bureau of Investigation, South Dakota in 2004, had a violent crime rate (murder/nonnegligent manslaughter; forcible rape; robbery; aggravated assault) of 171.5 reported incidents per 100,000 population, or a total of 1,322 reported incidents. Crimes against property (burglary; larceny/theft; and motor vehicle theft) in that same year totaled 14,905 reported incidents or 1,933.5 reported incidents per 100,000 people. Although South Dakota has a death penalty, in which lethal injection is the sole method of execution, the state has not carried out an execution since 1930, when only one inmate was executed. As of 1 January 2006, South Dakota had four inmates on death row.

In 2003, South Dakota spent $19,976,389 on homeland security, an average of $25 per state resident.

17 ARMED FORCES

In 2004, there were 3,698 active duty military personnel and 1,161 civilian personnel stationed in South Dakota, almost all of whom were at Ellsworth Air Force Base, near Rapid City, the state's only defense installation. South Dakota firms received more than $236 million in federal defense contracts in 2004. Defense Department payroll outlays totaled $396 million.

In 2003, 73,400 veterans were living in the state, including 9,765 from World War II; 9,865 from the Korean conflict; 21,938 from the Vietnam era; and 11,678 from the Persian Gulf War. In 2004, the Veterans Administration expended more than $299 million in pensions, medical assistance, and other major veterans' benefits.

As of 31 October 2004, the South Dakota Highway Patrol employed 150 full-time sworn officers.

18 MIGRATION

Since the 1930s, more people have left South Dakota than have settled in the state. Between 1940 and 1990, the net loss from migration amounted to almost 340,000. In 1980, the urban population stood at 46.4%, but had grown to equal the rural population (at 50%) by 1990. Between 1990 and 1998, South Dakota had net gains of 6,000 in domestic migration and 4,000 in international migration. In 1998, the state admitted 356 foreign immigrants. Between 1990 and 1998, the state's overall population increased 6.1%. In the period 2000–05, net international migration was 3,957 and net internal migration was -735, for a net gain of 3,222 people.

19 INTERGOVERNMENTAL COOPERATION

South Dakota participates in the Belle Fourche River Compact (with Wyoming), the Interstate Oil and Gas Compact, and the Western Interstate Commission for Higher Education, among other organizations; there are, in addition, boundary compacts with Minnesota and Nebraska. In fiscal year 2005, South Dakota received $1.010 billion in federal grants, an estimated $1.101 billion in fiscal year 2006, and an estimated $1.097 billion in fiscal year 2007.

20 ECONOMY

Agriculture has traditionally dominated South Dakota's economy. Grains and livestock have been the main farm products, and processed foods and farm equipment the leading manufactured items. However, since 1970, forty four of South Dakota's 67 counties have lost population, and for five these counties, the rate of depopulation accelerated during the 1990s. The prolonged drought affecting many western states helped to reduce the state's corn production by 10% and soybean production 6% in 2002, disrupted cattle production, and worsened the winter of 2002-2003. The historically important mining sector was contributing less than 1% of total state product in 2001. South Dakota's tax free environment was designed in part to attract high-technology, financial, and manufacturing investments during the 1990s. Manufacturing output grew at a substantial 16.9% from 1997 to 2000, but then plummeted 10% in the recession year of 2001, reducing manufacturing's share of gross state product from about 13% to 11.3%. The strongest growth in output has been in various services sectors. Coming into the 21st century (1997 to 2001), output from financial services increased 42.6%, while government services rose 29.4%, general services by 28.7% and wholesale and retail trade by 21.4%.

In 2004, South Dakota's gross state product (GSP) was $29.386 billion, of which manufacturing (durable and nondurable goods) accounted for the largest share at $3.181 billion or 10.8% of GSP, followed by health care and social assistance at $2.501 billion (8.5% of GSP), and the real estate sector at $2.237 billion (7.6% of GSP). In that same year, there were an estimated 72,949 small businesses in South Dakota. Of the 23,713 businesses that had employees, an estimated total of 22,958 or 96.8% were small companies. An estimated 1,691 new businesses were established in the state in 2004, up 26.4% from the year before. Business terminations that same year came to 2,251, up 18.5% from 2003. There were 108 business bankruptcies in 2004, down 1.8% from the previous year. In 2005, the state's personal bankruptcy (Chapter 7 and Chapter 13) filing rate was 360 filings per 100,000 people, ranking South Dakota 43rd in the nation.

21INCOME

In 2005 South Dakota had a gross state product (GSP) of $31 billion which accounted for 0.3% of the nation's gross domestic product and placed the state at number 47 in highest GSP among the 50 states and the District of Columbia.

According to the Bureau of Economic Analysis, in 2004 South Dakota had a per capita personal income (PCPI) of $30,209. This ranked 32nd in the United States and was 91% of the national average of $33,050. The 1994–2004 average annual growth rate of PCPI was 4.5%. South Dakota had a total personal income (TPI) of $23,279,500,000, which ranked 47th in the United States and reflected an increase of 4.6% from 2003. The 1994–2004 average annual growth rate of TPI was 5.1%. Earnings of persons employed in South Dakota increased from $16,303,502,000 in 2003 to $17,156,459,000 in 2004, an increase of 5.2%. The 2003–04 national change was 6.3%.

The US Census Bureau reports that the three-year average median household income for 2002–04 in 2004 dollars was $40,518 compared to a national average of $44,473. During the same period an estimated 12.5% of the population was below the poverty line as compared to 12.4% nationwide.

22LABOR

According to the Bureau of Labor Statistics (BLS), in April 2006 the seasonally adjusted civilian labor force in South Dakota 432,500, with approximately 13,000 workers unemployed, yielding an unemployment rate of 3%, compared to the national average of 4.7% for the same period. Preliminary data for the same period placed nonfarm employment at 398,700. Since the beginning of the BLS data series in 1976, the highest unemployment rate recorded in South Dakota was 5.9% in October 1982. The historical low was 2.4% in March 2000. Preliminary nonfarm employment data by occupation for April 2006 showed that approximately 5.7% of the labor force was employed in construction; 10.4% in manufacturing; 19.9% in trade, transportation, and public utilities; 7.3% in financial activities; 14.7% in education and health services; 10.7% in leisure and hospitality services; and 18.9% in government. Data were unavailable for professional and business services.

The US Department of Labor's Bureau of Labor Statistics reported that in 2005, a total of 21,000 of South Dakota's 350,000 employed wage and salary workers were formal members of a union. This represented 5.9% of those so employed, down slightly from 6% in 2004, and below the national average of 12%. Overall in 2005, a total of 29,000 workers (8.2%) in South Dakota were covered by a union or employee association contract, which includes those workers who reported no union affiliation. South Dakota is one of 22 states with a right-to-work law.

As of 1 March 2006, South Dakota had a state-mandated minimum wage rate of $5.15 per hour. In 2004, women in the state accounted for 48% of the employed civilian labor force.

23AGRICULTURE

South Dakota ranked 19th among the 50 states in 2005 in agricultural income, with receipts of $4.8 billion. In 2004 there were an estimated 31,600 farms and ranches in the state, covering about 43.8 million acres (17.7 million hectares).

Leading crops and their values during 2004 were hay, 6.87 million tons, $421.2 million; wheat, 128.6 million bushels, $416.9 million; corn for grain, 539.5 million bushels, $890.2 million; soybeans, 140.1 million bushels, $693.4 million; oats, 13.9 million bushels, $18.8 million; and barley, 3.1 million bushels, $6.3 million. In 2004, South Dakota ranked fifth among states in hay production, sixth in corn for grain as well as wheat, and seventh in grain sorghum.

24ANIMAL HUSBANDRY

The livestock industry is of great importance in South Dakota, particularly in the High Plains. In 2005 the state had an estimated 3.7 million cattle and calves, valued at around $3.8 billion. During 2004, there were 1.3 million hogs and pigs, valued at $146.3 million. In 2003 the state produced 30.1 million lb (13.7 million kg) of sheep and lambs, 152.7 million lb (69.4 million kg) of turkeys, 761 million eggs, and 1.7 million lb (0.8 million kg) of chickens. Dairy farmers produced nearly 1.33 billion lb (0.6 billion kg) of milk from around 82,000 milk cows in the same year.

25FISHING

Virtually all fishing is recreational. The state manages the maintenance of 5 million angler days of recreation per year. In 2004, South Dakota issued 206,349 sport fishing licenses. The D.C. Booth Historic National Fish Hatchery, established in 1896 (formerly Spearfish National Fish Hatchery), is one of the oldest operating hatcheries in the country. The facility primarily produces trout to stock the Black Hills region of the state. The Gavins Point National Fish Hatchery raises endangered pallid sturgeon and paddlefish. There are four state hatcheries.

26FORESTRY

In terms of geography and forests, east meets west in South Dakota in a rather dramatic way. The Prairie Plains in the east gradually give way to the grasslands of the Great Plains in the west as elevation increases by some 1,500 ft (450 m) between the Minnesota border and Rapid City.

The forests in the Plains regions are primarily associated with water-reservoirs, lakes, and the dominating Missouri River and its major tributaries such as the Cheyenne, Big White, Moreau,

Grand, and Bad rivers. Collectively these forests make up only 10% of the total forestland in the state and consist primarily of tree species associated with the eastern hardwood forests—elm, ash, basswood, and so forth. In the far western portion of the state and spilling over into northeastern Wyoming are the Black Hills. The forests in the Black Hills and at higher elevations west of the 103rd meridian to the southeast and north of the "Hills" are typically "western," consisting principally of ponderosa pine. About 90% of the forestland in South Dakota occurs west of the 103rd meridian, and most of it is in the Black Hills. Three counties, Pennington, Lawrence, and Custer, account for most of the State's forest area, which totals roughly 1,620,000 acres (656,000 million hectares).

The public sector owns 66% of South Dakota's forestland. The Black Hills and Custer National Forests administer about 90% of the public forestland. The rest is under the jurisdiction of the State and the US Department of the Interior, Bureau of Land Management (BLM). Most of the state-owned land is in the Custer State Park. East of Rapid City the 226,300 acres (91,500 hectares) of forestland is primarily privately owned.

Nonreserved timberland is the primary component of the state's forestland and occupies 1,511,000 acres (612,000 hectares). Woodland covers an additional 23,000 acres (9,300 hectares). Of the forestland, 1% contained primarily in national parks is reserved from harvesting wood products. Ponderosa pine is the state's predominant species. The second most predominant species is the bottomland hardwood group (elm/ash).

Sawtimber stands occupy 964,700 acres (390,400 hectares), which is more than half the total forested area; 675,000 acres (273,000 hectares) of this area is found in national forests. Poletimber stands account for a fifth of the timberland base, and sapling and seedling stands account for an additional 118,700 acres (48,000 hectares) of timberland.

South Dakota's timberland is not very productive when compared to other western states. Less than one-fifth of the state's timberland has the potential to produce greater than 50 cu ft (1.42 cu m) per acre per year. However, this is not to say that the state's timberland, and in particular the Black Hills area, has not been a good timber producer. The Black Hills have, for nearly a century, been successfully producing and supplying sawlogs, fuelwood, pulpwood, posts, and poles.

27MINING

According to preliminary data from the US Geological Survey (USGS), the estimated value of nonfuel mineral production by South Dakota in 2003 was $206 million, a decrease from 2002 of about 4.5%.

According to the preliminary data for 2003, by descending order of value, portland cement, construction sand and gravel, crushed stone, granite dimension stone, gypsum and common clays were the state's top nonfuel minerals. Collectively, these six commodity sectors accounted for around 81% of all nonfuel mineral output, by value. By volume, South Dakota in 2003, was the nation's second leading producer of granite dimension stone. The state also ranked fourth in mica, seventh in gold and feldspar, and 10th in dimension stone.

Preliminary data for 2003 showed that construction sand and gravel production totaled 13 million metric tons, with a value of $52.6 million, while crushed stone output that year, came to 6.7 million metric tons, with a value of $33.5 million.

Milbank Granite, a dark- to medium-red granite found in the northeastern part of the state, has been quarried continuously since 1907 and is the major source of dimension stone in the state.

28ENERGY AND POWER

As of 2003, South Dakota had 72 electrical power service providers, of which 35 were publicly owned and 30 were cooperatives. Of the remainder, six were investor owned, and one was federally operated. As of that same year there were 400,234 retail customers. Of that total, 212,384 received their power from investor-owned service providers. Cooperatives accounted for 132,379 customers, while publicly owned providers had 55,453 customers. There were 18 federal customers.

Total net summer generating capability by the state's electrical generating plants in 2003 stood at 2.690 million kW, with total production that same year at 7.943 billion kWh. Of the total amount generated, 99.5% came from electric utilities, with the remainder coming from independent producers and combined heat and power service providers. The largest portion of all electric power generated, 4.276 billion kWh (53.8%), came from hydroelectric plants, with coal-fired plants in second place at 3.431 billion kWh (43.2%) and natural gas fueled plants in third at 176.024 billion kWh (2.2%). Other renewable power sources and petroleum fired plants accounted for the remaining generation.

South Dakota has very modest fossil-fuel resources. As of 2004, the state had proven crude oil reserves of under 1% of all proven US reserves, while output that same year averaged 4,000 barrels per day. Including federal offshore domains, the state that year ranked 25th (24th excluding federal offshore) in production among the 31 producing states. In 2004 South Dakota had 148 producing oil wells and accounted for less than 1% of all US production. The state has no oil refineries.

In 2004, South Dakota had 61 producing natural gas and gas condensate wells. In 2003 (the latest year for which data was available), marketed gas production (all gas produced excluding gas used for repressuring, vented and flared, and nonhydrocarbon gases removed) totaled 1.103 billion cu ft (.031 billion cu m). There was no data on the state's proven reserves of natural gas.

South Dakota also has lignite reserves of 366,100,000 tons.

29INDUSTRY

According to the US Census Bureau's Annual Survey of Manufactures (ASM) for 2004, South Dakota's manufacturing sector covered some 11 product subsectors. The shipment value of all products manufactured in the state that same year was $12.083 billion. Of that total, computer and electronic equipment product manufacturing accounted for the largest share at $3.556 billion. It was followed by food manufacturing at $2.708 billion; miscellaneous manufacturing at $1.239 billion; machinery manufacturing at $1.104 billion; and transportation equipment manufacturing at $607.207 million.

In 2004, a total of 37,469 people in South Dakota were employed in the state's manufacturing sector, according to the ASM. Of that total, 28,628 were actual production workers. In terms of total employment, the food manufacturing industry accounted for the largest portion of all manufacturing employees at 7,257, with 6,136 actual production workers. It was followed by miscellaneous manufacturing at 4,778 employees (3,158 actual production workers); machinery manufacturing at 4,698 employees (3,369 actual production workers); fabricated metal product manufacturing at 3,537 employees (2,676 actual production workers); and computer and electronic product manufacturing with 3,262 employees (2,594 actual production workers).

ASM data for 2004 showed that South Dakota's manufacturing sector paid $1.222 billion in wages. Of that amount, the food manufacturing sector accounted for the largest share at $211.705 million. It was followed by machinery manufacturing at $176.672 million; miscellaneous manufacturing at $146.375 million; fabricated metal product manufacturing at $127.931 million; and computer and electronic product manufacturing at $107.559 million.

30 COMMERCE

According to the 2002 Census of Wholesale Trade, South Dakota's wholesale trade sector had sales that year totaling $7.8 billion from 1,329 establishments. Wholesalers of durable goods accounted for 690 establishments, followed by nondurable goods wholesalers at 565 and electronic markets, agents, and brokers accounting for 74 establishments. Sales by durable goods wholesalers in 2002 totaled $2.5 billion, while wholesalers of nondurable goods saw sales of $3.5 billion. Electronic markets, agents, and brokers in the wholesale trade industry had sales of $1.7 billion.

In the 2002 Census of Retail Trade, South Dakota was listed as having 4,249 retail establishments with sales of $9.6 billion. The leading types of retail businesses by number of establishments were: gasoline stations (678); motor vehicle and motor vehicle parts dealers tied with building material/garden equipment and supplies dealers (523 each); miscellaneous store retailers (522); and food and beverage stores (484). In terms of sales, motor vehicle and motor vehicle parts dealers accounted for the largest share of retail sales at $2.3 billion, followed by nonstore retailers at $1.29 billion; general merchandise stores at $1.26 billion; and gasoline stations at $1.1 billion. A total of 49,152 people were employed by the retail sector in South Dakota that year.

South Dakota's foreign exports in 2005 totaled $941.4 million, ranking the state 48th in the nation.

31 CONSUMER PROTECTION

The Division of Consumer Protection of the Office of the Attorney General enforces South Dakota's Deceptive Trade Practices Act, prosecutes cases of fraud and other illegal activities, and registers Charitable Solicitation organizations and Buying Clubs. Disputes are mediated between consumers and businesses. The Division also distributes consumer education materials, aids in the preparation of consumer related legislation, takes part in multi-jurisdictional actions with other state or federal law enforcement agencies, and advises consumers of complaints that are on file against specific companies.

When dealing with consumer protection issues, the state's Attorney General's Office can initiate civil and criminal proceedings; represent the state before state and federal regulatory agencies; administer consumer protection and education programs; handle formal consumer complaints; and exercise broad subpoena powers. In antitrust actions, the Attorney General's Office can act on behalf of those consumers who are incapable of acting on their own; initiate damage actions on behalf of the state in state courts; and initiate criminal proceedings. However, the state's Attorney General's Office cannot represent counties, cities and other governmental entities in recovering civil damages under state or federal law.

The offices of Division of Consumer Affairs are located in Pierre.

32 BANKING

As of June 2005, South Dakota had 91 insured banks, savings and loans, and saving banks, and 55 federally chartered credit unions (CUs). Excluding the CUs, the Sioux Falls market area accounted for the largest portion of the state's financial institution deposits in 2004, at $32.171 billion and ranked second in the number of financial institutions, at 32. The Sioux City market area, which includes portions of Nebraska and Iowa, ranked first in the number of financial institutions with 34, and second in deposits, at $2.051 billion. As of June 2005, CUs accounted for only 0.4% of all assets held by all financial institutions in the state, or some $1.525 billion. Banks, savings and loans, and savings banks collectively accounted for the remaining 99.6% or $433.470 billion in assets held.

Regulation of South Dakota's state-chartered banks and other state-chartered financial institutions is the responsibility of the state's Division of Banking.

33 INSURANCE

In 2004 there were 514,000 individual life insurance policies worth over $43.8 billion were in force in South Dakota; total value for all categories of life insurance (individual, group, and credit) was over $59.3 billion. The average coverage amount is $85,300 per policy holder. Death benefits paid that year totaled $160.8 million.

As of 2003, there were 20 property and casualty and one life and health insurance company domiciled in the state. In 2004, direct premiums for property and casualty insurance totaled over $1.4 billion. That year, there were 2,997 flood insurance policies in force in the state, with a total value of $364 million.

In 2004, 52% of state residents held employment-based health insurance policies, 9% held individual policies, and 25% were covered under Medicare and Medicaid; 12% of residents were uninsured. In 2003, employee contributions for employment-based health coverage averaged at 23% for single coverage and 27% for family coverage. The state offers an 18-month health benefits expansion program for small-firm employees in connection with the Consolidated Omnibus Budget Reconciliation Act (COBRA, 1986), a health insurance program for those who lose employment-based coverage due to termination or reduction of work hours.

In 2003, there were 627,527 auto insurance policies in effect for private passenger cars. Required minimum coverage includes bodily injury liability of up to $25,000 per individual and $20,000 for all persons injured in an accident, as well as property damage liability of $25,000. Uninsured motorist coverage is also required. In 2003, the average expenditure per vehicle for insurance coverage was $563.18, which ranked as the second-lowest average in the nation (before North Dakota).

34 SECURITIES

There are no securities exchanges in South Dakota. In 2005, there were 110 personal financial advisers employed in the state and 360 securities, commodities, and financial services sales agents. In 2004, there were over 12 publicly traded companies within the state, with over four NASDAQ companies (including Daktronics and HF Financial Corp), two NYSE listings (Black Hills Corp. and North Western Corp.), and one AMEX listing (The Credit Store).

35 PUBLIC FINANCE

The governor must submit the annual budget to the state legislature by 1 December. The fiscal year begins the following 1 July. The legislature may amend the budget at will, but the governor has a line item veto.

Fiscal year 2006 general funds were estimated at $1.0 billion for resources and $1.0 billion for expenditures. In 2004, federal government grants to South Dakota were $1.6 billion.

In the fiscal year 2007 federal budget, South Dakota was slated to receive $9.7 million in State Children's Health Insurance Program (SCHIP) funds (a 23% increase over 2006) to help provide health coverage to low-income, uninsured children who do not qualify for Medicaid. The state was also to receive $4.6 million for the HOME Investment Partnership Program to help South Dakota fund a wide range of activities that build, buy, or rehabilitate affordable housing for rent or homeownership, or provide direct rental assistance to low-income people; this was a 12% increase over fiscal year 2006. An addition $32 million was earmarked toward completion of the Mni Wiconi Rural Water Project, designed to provide a clean, reliable water supply to rural areas of South Dakota, including some of the poorest Native American communities in the country; and another $21 million (a $4 million increase over fiscal year 2006) for ongoing construction of the Lewis and Clark Regional Water System, which will bring high quality water to rural areas of South Dakota, as well as to the city of Sioux Falls.

36 TAXATION

In 2005, South Dakota collected $1,110 million in tax revenues or $1,430 per capita, which placed it 50th among the 50 states in per capita tax burden. The national average was $2,192 per capita. Sales taxes accounted for 56.0% of the total; selective sales taxes, 25.4%; corporate income taxes, 4.4%; and other taxes, 14.1%.

As of 1 January 2006, South Dakota had no state income tax, a distinction it shared with Wyoming, Washington, Nevada, Florida, Texas and Alaska.

In 2004, local property taxes amounted to $705,183,000, or $915 per capita. South Dakota has no state level property taxes. The per capita amount ranks the state 32nd nationally.

South Dakota taxes retail sales at a rate of 4%. In addition to the state tax, local taxes on retail sales can reach as much as 2%, making for a potential total tax on retail sales of 6%. Food purchased for consumption off-premises is taxable, although an income tax credit is allowed to offset sales tax on food. The tax on cigarettes is 53 cents per pack, which ranks 37th among the 50 states and the District of Columbia. South Dakota taxes gasoline at 22 cents per gallon. This is in addition to the 18.4 cents per gallon federal tax on gasoline.

According to the Tax Foundation, for every federal tax dollar sent to Washington in 2004, South Dakota citizens received $1.49 in federal spending, which ranks the state 10th nationally.

37 ECONOMIC POLICY

Efforts to attract industry to South Dakota and to broaden the state's economic base are under the jurisdiction of the Governor's

South Dakota—State Government Finances

(Dollar amounts in thousands. Per capita amounts in dollars.)

	AMOUNT	PER CAPITA
Total Revenue	3,863,621	5,011.18
General revenue	2,906,921	3,770.33
Intergovernmental revenue	1,239,324	1,607.42
Taxes	1,062,722	1,378.37
General sales	586,389	760.56
Selective sales	278,873	361.70
License taxes	138,877	180.13
Individual income tax	–	–
Corporate income tax	47,108	61.10
Other taxes	11,475	14.88
Current charges	209,524	271.76
Miscellaneous general revenue	395,351	512.78
Utility revenue	–	–
Liquor store revenue	–	–
Insurance trust revenue	956,700	1,240.86
Total expenditure	2,989,366	3,877.26
Intergovernmental expenditure	576,215	747.36
Direct expenditure	2,413,151	3,129.90
Current operation	1,602,276	2,078.18
Capital outlay	410,762	532.77
Insurance benefits and repayments	257,703	334.25
Assistance and subsidies	43,768	56.77
Interest on debt	98,642	127.94
Exhibit: Salaries and wages	488,804	633.99
Total expenditure	2,989,366	3,877.26
General expenditure	2,731,663	3,543.01
Intergovernmental expenditure	576,215	747.36
Direct expenditure	2,155,448	2,795.65
General expenditures, by function:		
Education	875,238	1,135.20
Public welfare	694,152	900.33
Hospitals	42,655	55.32
Health	93,611	121.42
Highways	417,467	541.46
Police protection	24,407	31.66
Correction	61,675	79.99
Natural resources	98,706	128.02
Parks and recreation	27,075	35.12
Government administration	110,392	143.18
Interest on general debt	98,642	127.94
Other and unallocable	187,643	243.38
Utility expenditure	–	–
Liquor store expenditure	–	–
Insurance trust expenditure	257,703	334.25
Debt at end of fiscal year	2,613,067	3,389.19
Cash and security holdings	9,467,630	12,279.68

Abbreviations and symbols: – zero or rounds to zero; (NA) not available; (X) not applicable.

SOURCE: U.S. Census Bureau, Governments Division, 2004 Survey of State Government Finances, January 2006.

Office of Economic Development. Among the advantages noted by the agency are the absence of corporate or personal income taxes, the low level of property taxes, the availability of community development corporations to finance construction of new facilities, various property tax relief measures, inventory tax exemptions, personal property tax exemptions, and a favorable labor climate in which work stoppages are few and union activity is limited by a right-to-work law. South Dakota is one of the few states to have enacted a statute of limitations on product liability—in this case, six years—a measure cited as further proof of the state's attempt to create an atmosphere conducive to manufacturing.

38 HEALTH

The infant mortality rate in October 2005 was estimated at 7.3 per 1,000 live births. The birth rate in 2003 was 14.4 per 1,000 population. The abortion rate stood at 5.5 per 1,000 women in 2000. In 2003, about 78.4% of pregnant woman received prenatal care beginning in the first trimester. In 2004, approximately 86% of children received routine immunizations before the age of three.

The crude death rate in 2003 was 9.3 deaths per 1,000 population. As of 2002, the death rates for major causes of death (per 100,000 resident population) were: heart disease, 254.5; cancer, 205.2; cerebrovascular diseases, 68.1; chronic lower respiratory diseases, 50.3; and diabetes, 25.6. The mortality rate from HIV infection was unavailable that year. In 2004, the reported AIDS case rate was at about 1.6 per 100,000 population, which was one of the lowest in the country. In 2002, about 58.2% of the population was considered overweight or obese. As of 2004, about 20.3% of state residents were smokers.

In 2003, South Dakota had 50 community hospitals with about 4,400 beds. There were about 103,000 patient admissions that year and 1,5 million outpatient visits. The average daily inpatient census was about 2,700 patients. The average cost per day for hospital care was $747. Also in 2003, there were about 113 certified nursing facilities in the state with 7,364 beds and an overall occupancy rate of about 92.4%. In 2004, it was estimated that about 72.1% of all state residents had received some type of dental care within the year. South Dakota had 217 physicians per 100,000 resident population in 2004 and 1,165 nurses per 100,000 in 2005. In 2004, there were a total of 345 dentists in the state.

About 16% of state residents were enrolled in Medicaid programs in 2003; 16% were enrolled in Medicare programs in 2004. Approximately 12% of the state population was uninsured in 2004. In 2003, state health care expenditures totaled $772,000.

39 SOCIAL WELFARE

In 2004, about 10,000 people received unemployment benefits, with the average weekly unemployment benefit at $205. In fiscal year 2005, the estimated average monthly participation in the food stamp program included about 56,095 persons (22,483 households); the average monthly benefit was about $91.33 per person. That year, the total of benefits paid through the state for the food stamp program was about $61.4 million.

Temporary Assistance for Needy Families (TANF), the system of federal welfare assistance that officially replaced Aid to Families with Dependent Children (AFDC) in 1997, was reautho-

rized through the Deficit Reduction Act of 2005. TANF is funded through federal block grants that are divided among the states based on an equation involving the number of recipients in each state. In 2004, the state TANF program had 6,000 recipients; state and federal expenditures on this TANF program totaled $19 million in fiscal year 2003.

In December 2004, Social Security benefits were paid to 139,770 South Dakota residents. This number included 90,220 retired workers, 15,560 widows and widowers, 13,960 disabled workers, 9,820 spouses, and 10,210 children. Social Security beneficiaries represented 18% of the total state population and 96.5% of the state's population age 65 and older. Retired workers received an average monthly payment of $878; widows and widowers, $859; disabled workers, $835; and spouses, $441. Payments for children of retired workers averaged $421 per month; children of deceased workers, $567; and children of disabled workers, $254. Federal Supplemental Security Income payments in December 2004 went to 12,469 South Dakota residents, averaging $353 a month. An additional $190,000 of state-administered supplemental payments were distributed to 3,641 residents.

40 HOUSING

In 2004, there were an estimated 342,620 housing units, of which 300,629 were occupied; 69.1% were owner-occupied. About 65.7% of all units were single-family, detached homes. Utility gas was the most common energy source for heating. It was estimated that 12,506 units lacked telephone service, 1,386 lacked complete plumbing facilities, and 1,550 lacked complete kitchen facilities. The average household had 2.47 members.

In 2004, 5,800 new privately owned housing units were authorized for construction. The median home value was $95,523. The median monthly cost for mortgage owners was $952. Renters paid a median of $493 per month. In September 2005, the state received grants of 680,000 from the US Department of Housing and Urban Development (HUD) for rural housing and economic development programs. For 2006, HUD allocated to the state over $6.6 million in community development block grants.

41 EDUCATION

As of 2004, 87.5% of South Dakotans 25 years of age or older were high school graduates, and 25.5% had four or more years of college.

The total enrollment for fall 2002 in South Dakota's public schools stood at 128,000. Of these, 87,000 attended schools from kindergarten through grade eight, and 41,000 attended high school. Approximately 84.9% of the students were white, 1.5% were black, 1.8% were Hispanic, 1% were Asian/Pacific Islander, and 10.7% were American Indian/Alaskan Native. Total enrollment was estimated at 126,000 in fall 2003 but expected to be 123,000 by fall 2014, a decline of 3.6% during the period 2002–14. Expenditures for public education in 2003/04 were estimated at $1 billion. There were 10,817 students enrolled in 95 private schools in fall 2003. Since 1969, the National Assessment of Educational Progress (NAEP) has tested public school students nationwide. The resulting report, *The Nation's Report Card*, stated that in 2005, eighth graders in South Dakota scored 287 out of 500 in mathematics compared with the national average of 278.

As of fall 2002, there were 47,751 students enrolled in college or graduate school; minority students comprised 10.2% of total postsecondary enrollment. In 2005 South Dakota had 26 degree-granting institutions. There are eight state-supported colleges and universities, of which the largest are the University of South Dakota and South Dakota State University. The South Dakota School of the Deaf as well as the South Dakota School for the Blind and Visually Impaired are also state-supported. In addition, the state has 12 private institutions of higher education.

⁴²ARTS

The South Dakota Arts Council, located at Pierre, and the South Dakota Humanities Council, at Brookings, aid and coordinate arts and humanities activities throughout the state. In 2005, the South Dakota Arts Council and other South Dakota arts organizations received six grants totaling $665,800 from the National Endowment for the Arts (NEA). In 2005, the National Endowment for the Humanities contributed $507,560 for four state projects. The state and various private sources also provided funding for the council's activities.

Artworks and handicrafts are displayed at the Dacotah Prairie Museum (Aberdeen), South Dakota Art Museum (Brookings), Sioux Indian Museum (Rapid City), Cultural Heritage Center (Pierre), and W. H. Over Museum (Vermillion). The state has nine tribal governments that present annual cultural arts events or powwows.

Symphony orchestras include the South Dakota Symphony in Sioux Falls and the Black Hills Symphony Orchestra in Rapid City. The Sioux Falls Jazz and Blues Society sponsors an annual festival, JazzFest. The annual Laura Ingalls Wilder Pageant in DeSmet includes outdoor performances as well as activities to recreate pioneer history.

⁴³LIBRARIES AND MUSEUMS

In 2001, South Dakota had 126 public library systems, with a total of 145 libraries, of which there were 19 branches. For that same year, the systems had a combined total of 2,835,000 volumes of book and serial publications, and a total circulation of 4,773,000. The system also had 77,000 audio and 71,000 video items, 5,000 electronic format items (CD-ROMs, magnetic tapes, and disks), and seven bookmobiles. Leading collections, each with more than 100,000 volumes, were those of South Dakota State University (Brookings), Northern State College and Alexander Mitchell Library (Aberdeen), Augustana College (Sioux Falls), the University of South Dakota (Vermillion), the South Dakota State Library (Pierre), and the Sioux Falls and Rapid City public libraries. In 2001, operating income for the state's public library system totaled $14,988,000 and included $167,000 from federal sources, and $13,825,000 from local sources.

South Dakota has 81 museums and historic sites, including the Cultural Heritage Museum (Pierre), Siouxland Heritage Museums and Delbridge Museum of Natural History (Sioux Falls), and the Shrine to Music Museum (Vermillion). Badlands National Park and Wind Cave National Park also display interesting exhibits.

⁴⁴COMMUNICATIONS

In 2004, 93.6% of South Dakota's occupied housing units had telephones. In addition, by June of that same year there were 382,906 mobile wireless telephone subscribers. In 2003, 62.1% of South Dakota households had a computer and 53.6% had Internet access. By June 2005, there were 61,856 high-speed lines in South Dakota, 51,283 residential and 10,573 for business. There were 65 major radio stations (21 AM, 44 FM) and 16 major television stations in 2005. Some 8,919 Internet domain names were registered in the state as of 2000.

⁴⁵PRESS

In 2002, South Dakota had six morning newspapers, five evening papers, and four Sunday papers. Leading newspapers included the *Rapid City Journal,* mornings 29,696, Sundays 34,222; and the Sioux Falls *Argus Leader,* mornings 53,395, Sundays 75,014.

⁴⁶ORGANIZATIONS

In 2006, there were over 1,345 nonprofit organizations registered within the state, of which about 828 were registered as charitable, educational, or religious organizations. There are several organizations focusing on the local and national interests of Native Americans. These include the Association of Community Tribal Schools, the Association on American Indian Affairs, and the Lakota Student Alliance. The South Dakota State Historical Society and the South Dakota Arts Council are located in Pierre. There are a number of municipal and county historical societies and art councils as well. The USA Deaf Sports Federation is based in Sioux Falls. Environmental groups include the Keep South Dakota Green Association and the South Dakota Wildlife Federation. The Evangelical Lutheran Good Samaritan Society, a nationwide service organization, is based in Sioux Falls.

⁴⁷TOURISM, TRAVEL, AND RECREATION

Tourism is the state's largest industry. Travelers spent an estimated $809 million in South Dakota in 2005, a 7.6% increase over 2004. The travel industry accounted for an estimated 33,100 jobs across the state that year.

Most of the state's tourist attractions lie west of the Missouri River, especially in the Black Hills region. Mt. Rushmore National Memorial consists of the heads of four US presidents—George Washington, Thomas Jefferson, Abraham Lincoln, and Theodore Roosevelt—carved in granite in the mountainside. Wind Cave National Park and Jewel Cave National Monument are also in the Black Hills region. Just to the east is Badlands National Monument, consisting of fossil beds and eroded cliffs almost bare of vegetation. Visitors can also tour the childhood home of Laura Ingalls Wilder, author of the popular *Little House on the Prairie* series, dig for dinosaurs in the Oligocene fossil beds, follow the Lewis and Clark trail, and visit more than 100 museums and cultural centers.

⁴⁸SPORTS

There are no major professional sports teams in South Dakota. However, the Sioux Falls Canaries are a minor league baseball club that plays in the American Association. Sioux Falls also is home to a minor league hockey team. The University of South Dakota

Coyotes and the Jackrabbits of South Dakota State both compete in the North Central Conference. Skiing and hiking are popular in the Black Hills. Other annual sporting events include the Black Hills Motorcycle Classic in Sturgis and many rodeos, including the Days of '76 in Deadwood. Former Olympic gold medalist Billy Mills and Football Hall of Famer Norm van Brocklin are among those athletes born in South Dakota.

⁴⁹FAMOUS SOUTH DAKOTANS

The only South Dakotan to win high elective office was Hubert H. Humphrey (1911–78), a native of Wallace who, after rising to power in Minnesota Democratic politics, served as US senator for 16 years before becoming vice president under Lyndon Johnson (1965–69).

Other outstanding federal officeholders from South Dakota were Newton Edmunds (1819–1908), second governor of the Dakota Territory; Charles Henry Burke (b.New York, 1861–1944), who as commissioner of Indian affairs improved education and health care for Native Americans; and Vermillion-born Peter Norbeck (1870–1936), a Progressive Republican leader, first while governor (1917–21) and then as US senator until his death. The son of a German-American father and a Brulé Indian mother, Benjamin Reifel (1906-1990) was the first American Indian elected to Congress from South Dakota; he later served as the last US commissioner of Indian affairs. George McGovern (b.1922) served in the US Senate from 1963 through 1980; an early opponent of the war in Viet Nam, he ran unsuccessfully as the Democratic presidential nominee in 1972.

Associated with South Dakota are several distinguished Indian leaders. Among them were Red Cloud (b.Nebraska 1822–1909), an Oglala warrior; Spotted Tail (b.Wyoming, 1833?–1881), the Brulé chief who was a commanding figure on the Rosebud Reservation; Sitting Bull (1834–90), a Hunkpapa Sioux most famous as the main leader of the Indian army that crushed George Custer's Seventh US Cavalry at the Battle of the Little Big Horn (1876) in Montana; and Crazy Horse (1849?–1877), an Oglala chief who also fought at Little Big Horn.

Ernest Orlando Lawrence (1901–58), the state's only Nobel Prize winner, received the physics award in 1939 for the invention of the cyclotron. The business leader with the greatest personal influence on South Dakota's history was Pierre Chouteau Jr. (b.Missouri, 1789–1865), a fur trader after whom the state capital is named.

South Dakota artists include George Catlin (b.Pennsylvania, 1796–1872), Karl Bodmer (1809–93), Harvey Dunn (1884–1952),
and Oscar Howe (1915–83). Gutzon Borglum (b.Idaho, 1871–1941) carved the faces on Mt. Rushmore. The state's two leading writers are Ole Edvart Rölvaag (b.Norway, 1876–1931), author of *Giants in the Earth* and other novels, and Frederick Manfred (b.Iowa, 1912–94), a Minnesota resident who served as writer-in-residence at the University of South Dakota and has used the state as a setting for many of his novels.

⁵⁰BIBLIOGRAPHY

Amerson, Robert. *From the Hidewood: Memories of a Dakota Neighborhood.* St. Paul: Minnesota Historical Society Press, 1996.

Council of State Governments. *The Book of the States, 2006 Edition.* Lexington, Ky.: Council of State Governments, 2006.

Fiffer, Steve. *Tyrannosaurus Sue: The Extraordinary Saga of the Largest, Most Fought Over T. Rex Ever Found.* New York: W. H. Freeman, 2000.

Hasselstrom, Linda M. *Feels Like Far: A Rancher's Life on the Great Plains.* New York: Lyons Press, 1999.

Nelson, Paula. *The Prairie Winnows Out Its Own: The West River Country of South Dakota in the Years of Depression and Dust.* Iowa City: University of Iowa Press, 1996.

Preston, Thomas. *Great Plains: North Dakota, South Dakota, Nebraska, Kansas, Oklahoma, and Texas.* Vol. 4 in *The Double Eagle Guide to 1,000 Great Western Recreation Destinations.* Billings, Mont.: Discovery Publications, 2003.

Rees, Amanda (ed.). *The Great Plains Region.* Vol. 1 in *The Greenwood Encyclopedia of American Regional Cultures.* Westport, Conn.: Greenwood Press, 2004.

Robertson, Paul. *The Power of the Land: Identity, Ethnicity, and Class among the Oglala Lakota.* New York: Routledge, 2002.

Schell, Herbert Samuel. *History of South Dakota.* 4th ed. Pierre: South Dakota State Historical Society Press, 2004.

Thompson, Harry F. (gen. ed.). *A New South Dakota History.* Sioux Falls, S.Dak.: Center for Western Studies/Augustana College, 2005.

US Department of Commerce, Economics and Statistics Administration, US Census Bureau. *South Dakota, 2000. Summary Social, Economic, and Housing Characteristics: 2000 Census of Population and Housing.* Washington, D.C.: US Government Printing Office, 2003.

TENNESSEE

State of Tennessee

ORIGIN OF STATE NAME: Probably derived from Indian name *Tenase,* which was the principal village of the Cherokee. **NICKNAME:** The Volunteer State. **CAPITAL:** Nashville. **ENTERED UNION:** 1 June 1796 (16th). **SONG:** "When It's Iris Time in Tennessee;" "The Tennessee Waltz;" "My Homeland, Tennessee;" "Rocky Top;" "My Tennessee;" "Tennessee;" The Pride of Tennessee." **MOTTO:** Agriculture and Commerce. **FLAG:** On a crimson field separated by a white border from a blue bar at the fly, three white stars on a blue circle edged in white represent the state's three main general divisions—East, Middle, and West Tennessee. **OFFICIAL SEAL:** The upper half consists of the word "Agriculture," a plow, a sheaf of wheat, a cotton plant, and the roman numeral XVI, signifying the order of entry into the Union. The lower half comprises the word "Commerce" and a boat. The words "The Great Seal of the State of Tennessee 1796" surround the whole. The date commemorates the passage of the state constitution. **BIRD:** Mockingbird. **FLOWER:** Iris (cultivated); Passion flower (wild flower). **TREE:** Tulip poplar. **GEM:** Freshwater pearl. **LEGAL HOLIDAYS:** New Year's Day, 1 January; Birthday of Martin Luther King Jr., 3rd Monday in January; Presidents' Day, 3rd Monday in February; Good Friday, Friday before Easter, March or April; Memorial Day, last Monday in May; Independence Day, 4 July; Labor Day, 1st Monday in September; Columbus Day, 2nd Monday in October (sometimes observed the day after Thanksgiving at the governor's discretion); Veterans' Day, 11 November; Thanksgiving Day, 4th Thursday in November; Christmas Day, 25 December. **TIME:** 7 AM EST = noon GMT; 6 AM CST = noon GMT.

¹LOCATION, SIZE, AND EXTENT

Situated in the eastern south-central United States, Tennessee ranks 34th in size among the 50 states.

The total area of the state is 42,144 sq mi (109,152 sq km), of which land occupies 41,155 sq mi (106,591 sq km) and inland water 989 sq mi (2,561 sq km). Tennessee extends about 430 mi (690 km) E–W and 110 mi (180 km) N–S.

Tennessee is bordered on the N by Kentucky and Virginia; on the E by North Carolina; on the S by Georgia, Alabama, and Mississippi; and on the W by Arkansas and Missouri (with the line formed by the Mississippi River). The boundary length of Tennessee totals 1,306 mi (2,102 km). The state's geographic center lies in Rutherford County, 5 mi (8 km) NE of Murfreesboro.

²TOPOGRAPHY

Long, narrow, and rhomboidal, Tennessee is divided topographically into six major physical regions: the Unaka Mountains, the Great Valley of East Tennessee, the Cumberland Plateau, the Highland Rim, the Central Basin, and the Gulf Coastal Plain. In addition, there are two minor physical regions: the Western Valley of the Tennessee River and the Mississippi Flood Plains.

The easternmost region is the Unaka Mountains, part of the Appalachian chain. The Unakas actually include several ranges, the most notable of which is the Great Smoky Mountains. The region constitutes the highest and most rugged surface in the state and covers an area of about 2,600 sq mi (6,700 sq km). Several peaks reach a height of 6,000 ft (1,800 m) or more: the tallest is Clingmans Dome in the Great Smokies, which rises to 6,643 ft (2,026 m) and is the highest point in the state. The mean elevation of the state is approximately 900 ft (275 m).

Lying due west of the Unakas is the Great Valley of East Tennessee. Extending from southwestern Virginia into northern Georgia, the Great Valley is a segment of the Ridge and Valley province of the Appalachian Highlands, which reach from New York into Alabama. This region, consisting of long, narrow ridges with broad valleys between them, covers more than 9,000 sq mi (23,000 sq km) of Tennessee. Since the coming of the Tennessee Valley Authority (TVA) in 1933, the area has been dotted with artificial lakes and dams, which supply electric power and aid in flood control.

The Cumberland Plateau, which extends in its entirety from southern Kentucky into central Alabama, has an area of about 5,400 sq mi (14,000 sq km) in Middle Tennessee. The plateau is a region of contrasts, including both the Cumberland Mountains, which rise to a height of 3,500 ft (1,100 m), and the Sequatchie Valley, the floor of which lies about 1,000 ft (300 m) below the surface of the adjoining plateau.

The Highland Rim, also in Middle Tennessee, is the state's largest natural region, consisting of more than 12,500 sq mi (32,400 sq km) and encircling the Central Basin. The eastern section is a gently rolling plain some 1,000 ft (300 m) lower than the Cumberland Plateau. The western part has an even lower elevation and sinks gently toward the Tennessee River.

The Central Basin, an oval depression with a gently rolling surface, has been compared to the bottom of an oval dish, of which the Highland Rim forms the broad, flat brim. With its rich soil, the region has attracted people from the earliest days of European settlement and is more densely populated than any other area in the state.

The westernmost of the major regions is the Gulf Coastal Plain. It embraces practically all of West Tennessee and covers an area of 9,000 sq mi (23,000 sq km). It is a broad plain, sloping gradually westward until it ends abruptly at the bluffs overlooking the Mississippi Flood Plains. In the northwest corner is Reelfoot Lake, the only natural lake of significance in the state, formed by a series of earthquakes in 1811 and 1812. The state's lowest point, 178 ft (54 m) above sea level, is on the banks of the Mississippi in the southwest.

Most of the state is drained by the Mississippi River system. Waters from the two longest rivers—the Tennessee, with a total length of 652 mi (1,049 km), and the Cumberland, which is 687 mi (1,106 km) long—flow into the Ohio River in Kentucky and join the Mississippi at Cairo, Illinois. Formed a few miles north of Knoxville by the confluence of the Holston and French Broad rivers, the Tennessee flows southwestward through the Great Valley into northern Alabama, then curves back into the state and flows northward into Kentucky. Other tributaries of the Tennessee are the Clinch, Duck, Elk, Hiwassee, and Sequatchie rivers. The Cumberland River rises in southeastern Kentucky, flows across central Tennessee, and then turns northward back into Kentucky; its principal tributaries are the Harpeth, Red, Obey, Caney Fork, and Stones rivers and Yellow Creek. In the western part of the state, the Forked Deer and Wolf rivers are among those flowing into the Mississippi, which forms the western border with Missouri and Arkansas.

3 CLIMATE

Generally, Tennessee has a temperate climate, with warm summers and mild winters. However, the state's varied topography leads to a wide range of climatic conditions.

The warmest parts of the state, with the longest growing season, are the Gulf Coastal Plain, the Central Basin, and the Sequatchie Valley. In the Memphis area in the southwest, the average date of the last killing frost is 20 March, and the growing season is about 235 days. Memphis has an annual average temperature of 62°F (17°C), 40°F (4°C) in January, and 83°F (28°C) in July. In the Nashville area, the growing season lasts about 225 days. Nashville has an annual average of 60°F (15°C), ranging from 38°F (3°C) in January to 80°F (26°C) in July. The Knoxville area has a growing season of 220 days. The city's annual average temperature is 59°F (15°C), with averages of 38°F (3°C) in January and 78°F (25°C) in July. In some parts of the mountainous east, where the temperatures are considerably lower, the growing season is as short as 130 days. The record high temperature for the state is 113°F (45°C), set at Perryville on 9 August 1930; the record low, -32°F (-36°C), was registered at Mountain City on 30 December 1917.

Severe storms occur infrequently. The greatest rainfall occurs in the winter and early spring, especially March; the early fall months, particularly September and October, are the driest. Average annual precipitation is about 52.4 in (133 cm) in Memphis and 48 in (122 cm) in Nashville. Snowfall varies and is more prevalent in East Tennessee than in the western section; Nashville gets about 10 in (25.4 cm) a year, Memphis only 5 in (12.7 cm).

4 FLORA AND FAUNA

With its varied terrain and soils, Tennessee has an abundance of flora, including at least 150 kinds of native trees. Tulip poplar (the state tree), shortleaf pine, and chestnut, black, and red oaks are commonly found in the eastern part of the state while the Highland Rim abounds in several varieties of oak, hickory, ash, and pine. Gum maple, black walnut, sycamore, and cottonwood grow in the west, and cypress is plentiful in the Reelfoot Lake area. In East Tennessee, rhododendron, mountain laurel, and wild azalea blossoms create a blaze of color in the mountains. More than 300 native Tennessee plants, including digitalis and ginseng have been utilized for medicinal purposes. In 2006, the US Fish and Wildlife Service listed 19 plant species as threatened or endangered in Tennessee, including the Blue Ridge goldenrod, Cumberland rosemary, Cumberland sandwort, Roan Mountain bluet, and Tennessee purple coneflower.

Tennessee mammals include the raccoon (the state animal), white-tailed deer, black bear, bobcat, muskrat, woodchuck, opossum, and red and gray foxes; the European wild boar was introduced by sportsmen in 1912. More than 250 bird species reside in Tennessee. Bobwhite quail, ruffed grouse, mourning dove, and mallard duck are the most common game birds. The state's 56 amphibian species include numerous frogs, salamanders, and newts; 58 reptile species include three types of rattlesnake. Of the 186 fish species in Tennessee's lakes and streams, catfish, bream, bass, crappie, pike, and trout are the leading game fish.

Tennessee's Wildlife Resources Agency conducts an endangered and threatened species protection program. Sixty-one animal species (vertebrates and invertebrates) were listed as endangered or threatened as of April 2006, including the seven species of darter, gray and Indiana bats, pallid sturgeon, bald eagle, Carolina northern flying squirrel, least tern, and white wartyback pearly mussel. The snail darter, cited by opponents of the Tellico Dam following the passage of the Endangered Species Act in 1973, is probably Tennessee's most famous threatened species.

5 ENVIRONMENTAL PROTECTION

Tennessee is historically an agricultural state but is geologically varied with mountains in the east, rolling hills in the central part of the state, and the wide floodplain of the Mississippi in the west.

The Great Smoky Mountains in east Tennessee are sensitive to changes in air quality. In 1997 the state forged an agreement with the US National Park Service and the US Forest Service to ensure that the process for issuing permits for new industries in the area take into account both business and environmental concerns. In 2003, 142.5 million lb of toxic chemicals were released in the state.

The first conservationists were agricultural reformers who, even before the Civil War, recommended terracing to conserve the soil and curtail erosion. Such conservation techniques as crop rotation and contour plowing were discussed at county fairs and other places where farmers gathered. In 1854, the legislature established the State Agricultural Bureau, which sought primarily to protect farmlands from floods. The streams of west Tennessee were extensively channelized for flood control beginning in the late 1800s, with a negative impact on both habitat and cropland. As of 2003, the state was working with local citizens and the US Army Corps of Engineers to reverse this process by restoring the natural meandering flow to the tributaries of the Mississippi.

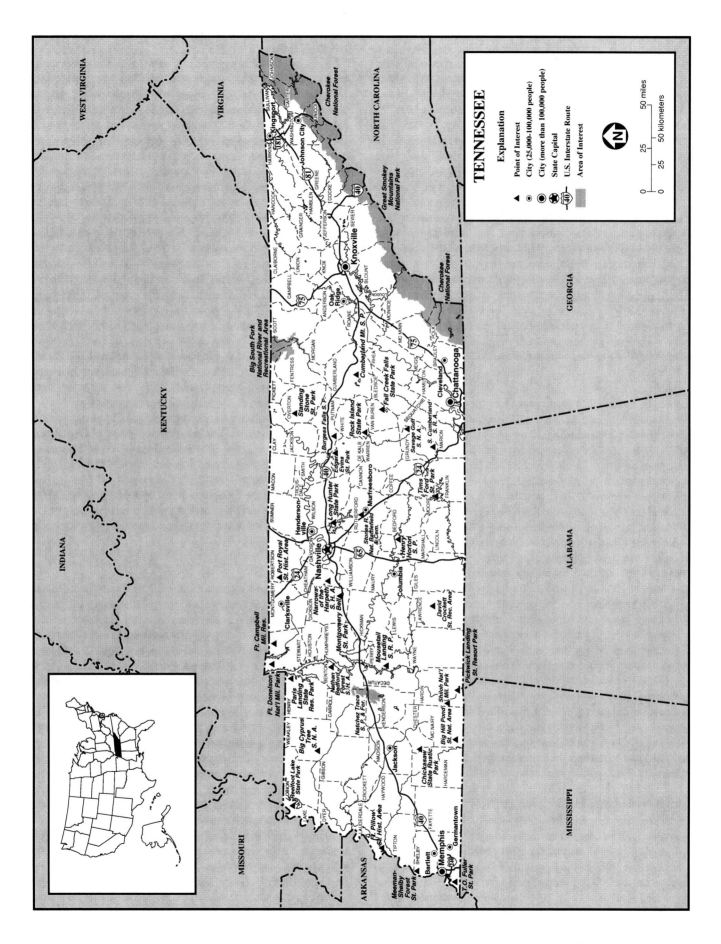

The Department of Environment and Conservation is responsible for air, land, and water protection in Tennessee. The department also manages the state park system and state natural areas. In 1996, Tennessee had approximately one million acres of wetlands. The Tennessee Wetland Act of 1986 authorized the acquisition of wetlands through the use of real estate taxes. In 1997, the state created four new natural areas.

When many of the first environmental laws were written in the 1970s, pollution of the air and water was widespread and severe. The early laws focused on tough enforcement tools and strict compliance measures to address this problem. In 1993, the Division of Pollution Prevention Assistance was established to provide information and support to industries attempting to reduce their pollution and waste. In 2003, Tennessee had 245 hazardous waste sites listed in the US Environment Protection Agency (EPA) database, 13 of which were on the National Priorities List as of 2006, including the Milan Army Ammunition Plant. In 2005, the EPA spent over $2.1 million through the Superfund program for the cleanup of hazardous waste sites in the state. The same year, federal EPA grants awarded to the state included $8.3 million for the drinking water state revolving fund and $15.7 million for loans on projects involving the waste water infrastructure.

6 POPULATION

Tennessee ranked 16th in population in the United States with an estimated total of 5,962,959 in 2005, an increase of 4.8% since 2000. Between 1990 and 2000, Tennessee's population grew from 4,877,185 to 5,689,283, an increase of 16.7%. The population is projected to reach 6.5 million by 2015 and 7 million by 2025. The population density in 2004 was 143.2 persons per sq mi. In 2004 the median age was 37. Persons under 18 years old accounted for 23.6% of the population while 12.5% was age 65 or older.

The first permanent white settlements in the state were established in the 1760s, when people from North Carolina and Virginia crossed the Unaka Mountains and settled in the fertile valleys. Between 1790 and 1800, the population increased threefold, from 35,690 to 105,600, and it doubled during each of the next two decades. After the Civil War, the population continued to increase, though at a slower rate, tripling between 1870 and 1970.

A pronounced urban trend became apparent after World War II. In 1960, for the first time in the state's history, census figures showed slightly more people living in urban than in rural areas. In the 1990s, approximately 70% of all Tennesseans lived in metropolitan areas. Memphis is the state's largest city; in 2004, it had an estimated population of 671,929. Nashville-Davidson had a population of 546,719, followed by Knoxville, 178,118, and Chattanooga, 154,853. The Memphis metropolitan area, including parts of Arkansas and Mississippi, had an estimated 1,250,293 residents in 2004, while metropolitan Nashville had 1,395,879.

7 ETHNIC GROUPS

For nearly a century after the earliest white settlements, Tennessee was inhabited by three ethno-racial populations: whites of English and Scotch-Irish descent, Cherokee Indians, and black Americans. Settlers crossing the Appalachians met Indian resistance as early as the late 1700s. Eventually, however, nearly all the Cherokee were forced to leave; in 2000 there were an estimated 15,152 American Indians in Tennessee, up from 10,000, the number re-

corded by the 1990 census. In 2004, 0.3% of the population was American Indian.

Blacks, originally brought into the state as slaves to work in the cotton fields of West Tennessee, made up about 10% of the population in 1790. White Tennesseans were divided on the issue of slavery. The small farmers of the eastern region were against it, and in the late 1820s and 1830s there were more antislavery societies in Tennessee than in any other southern state except North Carolina. The planters and merchants of southwest Tennessee, however, linked their sentiments and interests with those of the proslavery planters of the Mississippi Valley. The introduction of the cotton gin gave impetus to the acquisition of more slaves; by 1840, blacks accounted for 26% of the population, and Memphis had become a major market for the shipment of black slaves to large plantations farther south.

Immediately after the Civil War, many blacks, now free, migrated from Virginia and North Carolina to East Tennessee to become farmers, artisans, and owners of small businesses. After 1880, however, the black proportion of the population declined steadily. In 2000, the estimated black population was 932,809 (16% of the state total), up from 778,000 in 1990. In 2004, 16.8% of the population was black. In 2000, there were an estimated 56,662 Asians residing in the state; 12,835 Asian Indians constituted the largest group. Pacific Islanders numbered 2,205. In 2004, the Asian population in the state was 1.2% of the state's total population.

Descendants of European immigrants make up about half the population of Tennessee, the largest groups being of English and German descent. In 2000, 159,004 residents—2.8% of the population—were foreign-born, more than twice the 1990 total of 59,114 (1.2%). In 2000, there were 123,838 Hispanics and Latinos, representing 2.2% of the total population, up from 62,000 (1.1%) in 1990. In 2004, 2.8% of the state's population was Hispanic or Latino. That year, 0.9% of the population reported origin of two or more races.

8 LANGUAGES

White settlers found Tennessee inhabited by Cherokee Indians in the eastern mountains, Shawnee in most of the eastern and central region, and Chickasaw in the west—all of them speakers of Hokan-Siouan languages. Subsequently removed to Indian Territory, they left behind such place-names as Chickamauga, Chattanooga, and Chilhowee, as well as Tennessee itself.

Tennessee English represents a mixture of North Midland and South Midland features brought into the northeastern and north-central areas, of South Midland and Southern features introduced by settlers from Virginia and the Carolinas, and of a few additional Southern terms in the extreme western fringe, to which they were carried from Mississippi and Louisiana. Certain pronunciations exhibit a declining frequency from the Appalachians to the Mississippi River, such as /r/ after a vowel in the same syllable, as in *form* and *short,* and a rounded /aw/ before /r/ in *arm* and *barbed.* Others occur statewide, such as the /ah/ vowel in *forest* and *foreign, coop* and *Cooper* with the vowel of *book,* and simplification of the long /i/ vowel, so that *lice* sounds like *lass.* Common are such non-Northern terms as *wait on* (wait for), *pullybone* (along with Northern wishbone), *nicker* (neigh), *light bread* (white bread), and *snake feeder* (dragonfly), as well as *Jew's harp, juice harp,* and *French harp* (all for harmonica). In eastern Tennessee are found *goobers* (peanuts), *tote* (carry), *plum peach* (cling-stone peach), *ash cake* (a kind of cornbread), *fireboard* (mantel), *redworm* (earthworm), *branch* (stream), and *peckerwood* (woodpecker). Appearing in western Tennessee are *loaf bread, cold drink* (soft drink), and *burlap bag.* In Memphis, a large, long sandwich is a *poorboy.*

In 2000, 5,059,404 Tennesseans five years old and over—95.2% of the population in that age group—spoke only English at home, down from 97% in 1990.

The following table gives selected statistics from the 2000 Census for language spoken at home by persons five years old and over. The category "African languages" includes Amharic, Ibo, Twi, Yoruba, Bantu, Swahili, and Somali. The category "Other Indo-European languages" includes Albanian, Gaelic, Lithuanian, and Rumanian.

LANGUAGE	NUMBER	PERCENT
Population 5 years and over	**5,315,920**	**100.0**
Speak only English	5,059,404	95.2
Speak a language other than English	256,516	4.8
Speak a language other than English	**256,516**	**4.8**
Spanish or Spanish Creole	133,931	2.5
German	20,267	0.4
French (incl. Patois, Cajun)	17,557	0.3
Chinese	7,492	0.1
Vietnamese	6,625	0.1
Korean	6,550	0.1
Arabic	6,482	0.1
Laotian	4,496	0.1
African languages	4,480	0.1
Japanese	4,423	0.1
Other Indo-European languages	4,250	0.1
Tagalog	3,386	0.1
Italian	3,134	0.1

⁹RELIGIONS

Baptist and Presbyterian churches were organized on the frontier soon after permanent settlements were made. Many divisions have occurred in both groups. The Cumberland Presbyterian Church, which spread into other states, was organized near Nashville in 1810 because of differences within the parent church. Both the Baptists and the Presbyterians divided over slavery. Methodist circuit riders arrived with the early settlers, and they quickly succeeded in attracting many followers. Controversies over slavery and other sectional issues also developed within the Methodist Church and, as with the Baptists and Presbyterians, divisions emerged during the 1840s. The Methodists, however, were able to resolve their differences and regroup. The United Presbyterian Church and the Presbyterian Church in the United States finally ended their 122-year separation in 1983, reuniting to form the Presbyterian Church (USA).

Two other Protestant groups with large followings in the state had their origin on the Tennessee frontier in the first half of the 19th century: the Disciples of Christ and the Church of Christ. Both groups began with the followers of Thomas and Alexander Campbell and Barton W. Stone, among others, who deplored formal creeds and denominations and sought to return to the purity of early Christianity. As their numbers grew, these followers divided into Progressives, who supported missionary societies and instrumental music in church, and Conservatives, who did not. In 1906, a federal census of religions listed the Conservatives for the first time as the Church of Christ and the Progressives as the Dis-

ciples of Christ. The latter, now the Christian Church (Disciples of Christ) had 28,108 known adherents in 2000. The Church of God (Cleveland, Tennessee) was established in the state in 1886 as a result of the greater Pentecostal movement.

Tennessee has long been considered part of the Bible Belt because of the influence of fundamentalist Protestant groups that believe in the literal accuracy of the Bible. Evangelical Protestants still account for a majority of the religiously active population.

In 2000, the largest single religious group in the state was the Southern Baptist Convention with 1,414,199 adherents; there were 27,055 new baptized members reported in 2002. Other Evangelical groups in 2000 were the Churches of Christ, 216,648; the Church of God (Cleveland, Tennessee), 66,136; Independent, Non-Charismatic Churches, 50,003; and Assemblies of God, 40,430. The major Mainline Protestant denominations (with 2000 figures) were the United Methodist Church, 393,994; the Presbyterian Church USA, 67,800; and the Episcopal Church, 35,037. In 2004, there were about 185,486 Roman Catholics in the state. In 2000, there were 18,464 Muslims and an estimated 18,250 Jews in the state. About 2.7 million people (48.9% of the population) were not counted as members of any religious organization that year.

The Gideons International, an organization known for its free distribution of Bibles, is based in Nashville. The World Convention of Churches of Christ is also based in Nashville.

¹⁰TRANSPORTATION

Memphis, Nashville, Knoxville, and Chattanooga are the focal points for rail, highway, water, and air transportation. All are located on important rivers and interstate highways, and all have airports served by the major airlines.

Railroad building began in Tennessee as early as the 1820s. During the 1850s, the basis for 20th-century rail transportation was laid: the Louisville and Nashville Railroad linked Tennessee to the northern states, and the Memphis and Charleston line established ties with the East Coast. In 2003, Tennessee had 2,821 rail mi (4,541 km) of track, of which 2,097 mi (3,376 km) were Class I track. As of 2006, Amtrak provided north–south passenger train service to Memphis and Newbern, Tennessee via its Chicago to New Orleans City of New Orleans train.

The first roads, such as the Natchez Trace, which connected Nashville with the southwestern part of the state, often followed Indian trails. Many roads in the early 1800s were constructed by private individuals or chartered turnpike companies. The introduction of the automobile shortly after the beginning of the 20th century brought the development of modern roads and highways. After 1916, the federal government began to share the high cost of highway construction, and the 1920s were a decade of extensive road building.

In 2004, Tennessee had 88,988 mi (143,270 km) of roads. The major interstate highway is I-40, crossing east–west from Knoxville to Nashville and Memphis. In that same year, some 5.049 million motor vehicles were registered in the state, while 4,247,884 Tennesseans held drivers' licenses.

The principal means of transportation during Tennessee's early history was water, and all the early settlements were built on or near streams. The introduction of steamboats on the Cumberland River in the early 19th century helped make Nashville the state's largest city and its foremost trading center. By mid-century, however, Memphis, on the Mississippi River, had surpassed Nashville in population and trade, largely because of cotton. Tennessee in 2004 had 946 mi (1,523 km) of navigable inland waterways. The completion in 1985 of the 234-mi (377-km) Tennessee-Tombigbee Waterway gave Tennessee shippers a direct north–south route for all vessels between the Tennessee River and the Gulf of Mexico via the Black Warrior River in Alabama. Although none of the waterway runs through Tennessee, the northern terminus is on the Tennessee River near the common borders of Tennessee, Alabama, and Mississippi. In 2004, the ports of Memphis and Nashville handled 17.520 million tons and 3.941 million tons of freight, respectively. In 2003, waterborne shipments totaled 27.811 million tons.

In 2005, Tennessee had a total of 305 public and private-use aviation-related facilities. This included 195 airports, 100 heliports, 8 STOLports (Short Take-Off and Landing), and 2 seaplane bases. As of 2004, Memphis International Airport was among the world's busiest cargo-handling facilities and was also the state's major air terminal in terms of passenger traffic, with 5,295,062 passengers enplaned, making it the 36th busiest airport in the United States. Nashville International in that same year was the state's second busiest, with 4,298,703 passengers enplaned, making it the 44th busiest airport in the United States.

11 HISTORY

The lower Tennessee Valley was heavily populated with hunter-gatherers some 10,000 years ago. Their descendants, called Paleo-Indians, were succeeded by other native cultures, including the Archaic Indians, Woodland Indians, and Early Mississippians. When the first Spanish arrived in the early 16th century, Creek Indians were living in what is now East Tennessee, along with the Yuchi. About 200 years later, the powerful Cherokee—the largest single tribe south of the Ohio River, occupying parts of North Carolina, South Carolina, Georgia, and East Tennessee—drove the Creek and Yuchi out of the area and established themselves as the dominant tribe. Their settlements, varying in size from a dozen families to more than 200, were known as the Upper or Overhill Towns. The Cherokee retained their tribal dominance until they were forced out by the federal government in the 1830s. In West Tennessee, the Chickasaw were the major group. They lived principally in northern Mississippi but used Tennessee lands as a hunting ground. Shawnee occupied the Cumberland Valley in Middle Tennessee until driven north of the Ohio River by the Cherokee and Chickasaw.

Explorers and traders from continental Europe and the British Isles were in Tennessee for well over 200 years before permanent settlements were established in the 1760s. Hernando de Soto, a Spaniard, came from Florida to explore the area as early as 1540. He was followed during the 17th century by the French explorers Jacques Marquette, Louis Jolliet, and Robert Cavelier, Sieur de la Salle. Englishmen were not far behind: by the mid-1700s, hundreds—perhaps thousands—had crossed the Appalachian barrier and explored the transmontane country beyond, which was claimed first by the colony of Virginia and later assigned to North Carolina. They came in search of pelts, furs, and whatever else of value they might find. A fiercely independent breed, they were accustomed to hardship and unwilling to settle in a civilized community. Perhaps the best known was Daniel Boone, who by 1760 had found his way into present-day Washington County.

With the conclusion of the French and Indian War in 1763, many people from North Carolina and Virginia began to cross the Alleghenies. Elisha Walden was among those who first led groups of "long hunters" into the wilderness. By 1770, small pockets of white settlement were developing in the valley between the Unaka and Cumberland mountains. In the two decades that followed, more than 35,000 people settled on soil soon to become the State of Tennessee.

Two major areas of settlement developed. The larger one-in the northeast along the Holston, Nolichucky, and Watauga rivers-was organized as the Watauga Association in 1791. The second major area was in the Cumberland Basin, where James Robertson, under the sponsorship of the Transylvania Company (formed by eastern land speculators), established a settlement he called Nashborough (now Nashville) in 1779. There more than 250 adult males signed the Cumberland Compact, which established a government. They pledged to abide by the will of the majority and expressed their allegiance to North Carolina.

The Revolutionary War did not reach as far west as Tennessee, but many of the frontiersmen fought in the Carolinas and Virginia. The most famous battle involving these early Tennesseans was that of Kings Mountain, in South Carolina, where Colonel John Sevier and others defeated a superior force of British soldiers and captured more than 1,000 prisoners. Hardly was the Revolution over when Tennesseans began to think about statehood for themselves. As early as 1784, leaders in three mountain counties—Greene, Sullivan, and Washington—established the Free State of Franklin. John Sevier was chosen as governor, and an assembly was formed. Only after border warfare developed and factionalism weakened their cause did Franklin's leaders abandon their plans and return their allegiance to North Carolina. But the spirit of independence—indeed, defiance—persisted.

In 1790, less than two years after Franklin collapsed, North Carolina ceded its western lands to the United States. Tennessee became known as the Southwest Territory, with William Blount, a prominent North Carolina speculator and politician, as its governor. During his six-year tenure, a government was organized and a capital established at Knoxville. The population doubled to more than 70,000 in 1795, and steps were taken to convert the territory into a state. When the territorial legislature presented Congress with a petition for statehood, a lively debate ensued in the US Senate between Jeffersonian Democratic-Republicans, who urged immediate admission, and Federalists, who opposed it. The Jeffersonians triumphed, and on 1 June 1796, President George Washington signed a bill admitting Tennessee as the 16th state. Sevier became governor of the new state, Blount was elected to the US Senate, and Andrew Jackson became the state's first US representative.

Sevier dominated state politics for the first two decades of statehood, and he had little difficulty in thwarting the ambitions of Andrew Jackson and others who sought to challenge his leadership. Tennessee's population, about 85,000 when Sevier became governor, was more than 250,000 when he left the statehouse in 1809. Under Sevier's governorship, Nashville, Knoxville, and other early settlements became thriving frontier towns. Churches and schools were established, industry and agriculture developed, and Tennessee became a leading iron producer.

Andrew Jackson's rise to prominence came as a result of the Battle of New Orleans, fought at the conclusion of the War of 1812. Jackson, who had little difficulty raising troops in a state where volunteers for military service have always been abundant, lost only about a half dozen of his men, while British casualties exceeded 2,000. He returned to Nashville a hero, built a fine house that he named The Hermitage, received thousands of congratulatory messages, and conferred with friends about his political and military future. In 1823, Jackson was elected to the US Senate. Defeated the following year in a four-man race for the presidency, he ran again, this time successfully, in 1828, serving in that office for eight years.

Jackson alienated himself from many people in the state after 1835, when he announced his support of Martin Van Buren for president instead of Knoxvillian Hugh Lawson White, an avowed candidate. A majority of Tennesseans joined the new Whig Party, which arose in opposition to Jackson's Democratic Party, and voted in the 1836 presidential election for White instead of for Van Buren. The Whigs won every presidential election in Tennessee from 1836 to 1852, including the election of 1844, which sent Tennessean James Knox Polk, a Democrat, to the White House. Polk's term (1845–49) brought another war, this one with Mexico. Although Tennessee's quota was only 2,800, more than 25,000 men volunteered for service. Among the heroes of that war were William Trousdale and William B. Campbell, both of whom later were elected governor.

Social reform and cultural growth characterized the first half of the 19th century. A penitentiary was built, and the penal code made somewhat more humane. Temperance newspapers were published, temperance societies formed, and laws passed to curtail the consumption of alcoholic beverages. In 1834, a few women, embracing the feminist cause, were influential in giving the courts, rather than the legislature, the right to grant divorces. Many important schools were established, including the Nashville Female Academy, the University of Nashville, and more than two dozen colleges.

More than most other southern states, antebellum Tennessee was divided over the issue of slavery. Slaves had accompanied their owners into Tennessee in the 18th century, and by 1850, they constituted about one-fourth of the state's population. Although slaveholders lived in all sections of the state, they predominated in the west, where cotton was grown profitably, as well as in Middle Tennessee. In East Tennessee, where blacks made up less than 10% of the population, antislavery sentiment thrived. Most of those who supported emancipation urged that it be accomplished peacefully, gradually, and with compensation to the slave owners. Frances Wright, the Scottish reformer, founded the colony of Nashoba near Memphis in the 1820s as a place where freed blacks could learn self-reliance. After a few years the colony failed, however, and Wright took her colonists to Haiti. At the constitutional convention of 1834, hundreds of petitions were presented asking that the legislature be empowered to free the slaves. But while the convention endorsed several measures to democratize the constitution of 1796—abolishing property qualifications as a condition for holding office, for example—it decided against emancipation.

Considerable economic growth took place during this period. West Tennessee became a major cotton-growing area immediately after it was purchased form the Chickasaw in 1818, and Memphis, established in 1821, became the principal cotton-marketing center. The Volunteer State's annual cotton crop grew from less than 3,000 bales in 1810 to nearly 200,000 bales by midcentury. The counties of the Highland Rim produced tobacco in such abundance that, by 1840, Tennessee ranked just behind Kentucky and Virginia in total production. East Tennessee farmers practiced greater crop diversification, growing a variety of fruits and vegetables for market. Silk cultivation flourished briefly in the 1830s and 1840s.

Tennessee became a major battleground during the Civil War, as armies from both North and South crossed the state several times. Most Tennesseans favored secession. But the eastern counties remained staunchly Unionist, and many East Tennesseans crossed over into Kentucky to enlist in the Union Army. General Albert Sidney Johnston, the Confederate commander of the western theater, set up lines of defense across the northern border of the state and built forts on both the Cumberland and Tennessee rivers. In February 1862, Ft. Donelson and Ft. Henry were taken by General Ulysses S. Grant and naval Captain Andrew H. Foote, thereby opening the state to Union armies. Within two weeks Nashville was in the hands of the enemy. Northern troops pushed farther south and west, taking key positions on the Mississippi River. Less than two months later, on 6 April, Union forces near the Mississippi state line engaged Johnston's army in the Battle of Shiloh. Both sides suffered tremendous losses, including Johnston himself, who bled to death after sustaining a thigh wound. In the meantime President Abraham Lincoln had established a military government for the conquered state and appointed Andrew Johnson to head it. Johnson, who had served two terms as governor a decade earlier, had been elected to the US Senate in 1858; he remained there in 1861, the only southern senator to do so, refusing to follow his state into the Confederacy. In 1864, he was elected vice president under Lincoln.

Johnson's governorship did not mean the end of Confederate activities in Tennessee. Late in December 1862, Confederate forces made the first of two vigorous attempts to rid the state of the invader. General Braxton Bragg, who replaced Johnston as Confederate commander, established himself at Murfreesboro, 30 mi (48 km) southwest of Nashville, and threatened to retake the capital city. But at the Battle of Stones River, Union troops under General William S. Rosecrans forced Bragg to retreat to the southeast. Fighting did not resume until 19–20 September 1863, when the Confederates drove Union troops back to Chattanooga in the Battle of Chickamauga, one of the bloodiest engagements of the war. The second major Confederate drive occurred in November and December 1864, when General John B. Hood, commanding the Confederate Army of Tennessee, came out of Georgia and attacked the Union forces at Franklin and Nashville. Hood's army was destroyed, and these battles were the last major engagements in the state.

Returning to the Union in 1866, Tennessee was the only former Confederate state not to have a military government during Reconstruction. Economic readjustment was not as difficult as elsewhere in the South, and within a few years agricultural production exceeded antebellum levels. Extensive coal and iron deposits in

East Tennessee attracted northern capital, and by the early 1880s, flour, woolen, and paper mills were established in all the urban areas. By the late 1890s, Memphis was a leading cotton market and the nation's foremost producer of cottonseed oil. Politically, the Democratic Party became firmly entrenched, and would remain so until the 1950s.

As the 20th century dawned, the major issue in Tennessee was the crusade against alcohol, a movement with deep roots in the 19th century. Though the major cities still were "wet," earlier legislation had dried up the rural areas and small towns, and the Tennessee Anti-Saloon League and Women's Christian Temperance Union (WCTU) kept the matter in the public eye. In 1908, with "wet" forces controlling the state government, Edward Ward Carmack—a rabid prohibitionist, powerful politician, newspaper editor, and former US senator—was shot and killed in the street of Nashville. His assailants were convicted but pardoned immediately by the governor. In the following year, with Carmack as a martyr to their cause, "dry" forces enacted legislation that, in effect, imposed prohibition on the entire state. The dominant Democratic Party was divided and demoralized to such an extent that a Republican governor was elected—only the second since Reconstruction. The prohibition movement helped promote the cause of women's suffrage. A proposed state constitutional amendment giving women the right to vote failed in 1915, but in 1919, they were granted the franchise in municipal elections. One year later, Tennessee became the 36th state to ratify the 19th Amendment to the US Constitution, thereby granting women the right to vote nationwide.

The 1920s brought a resurgence of religious fundamentalism. When, in 1925, the legislature enacted a measure that prohibited the teaching of the theory of evolution in the public schools, a high school teacher named John T. Scopes decided to challenge the law. Three-time presidential candidate and fundamentalist spokesman William Jennings Bryan arrived in the tiny town of Dayton to aid in Scopes's prosecution, while the great civil liberties lawyer Clarence Darrow came from Chicago to lead the defense. The Scopes trial gave the Volunteer State unwanted notoriety throughout the civilized world. Scopes was convicted, and it was not until 1967 that the law was repealed.

The 1930s brought depression, but they also brought the Tennessee Valley Authority. Before TVA, residents of the Tennessee River Valley could boast of the beauty of the landscape, but of little else. The soil was so thin that little other than subsistence agriculture was possible, and many people lived on cash incomes of less than $100 a year. There were some senators, such as George Norris of Nebraska and Tennessee's own Kenneth D. McKellar, who saw great possibilities in valley development. Harnessing the Tennessee River with dams could not only generate electricity inexpensively but also greatly improve navigation; aid flood control, soil conservation, and reforestation; and produce nitrate fertilizer. Efforts to establish such a program failed, however, until Franklin D. Roosevelt included it in his New Deal. The law establishing the TVA was passed a few weeks after Roosevelt's inauguration in 1933, and dam construction began almost immediately. Before TVA, people in the valley consumed only 1.5 billion kWh of electricity annually; but consumption increased to 11.5 billion kWh by 1945 and to 57.5 billion kWh by 1960. Fewer than 2% of rural families in Tennessee had electricity in 1933; but by the late

1930s, power lines were being strung into remote areas, bringing to practically everyone the advantages that hitherto only urban residents had enjoyed. Inexpensive power became a magnet for industry, and industrial employment in the region nearly doubled in two decades. The building of a plant for the production of nuclear weapons at Oak Ridge in 1942 was due in large measure to the availability of TVA power.

The TVA notwithstanding, the depression caused many manufacturers to close or curtail operations, and farm prices declined drastically. Cotton, which had earlier brought farmers more than 30 cents a pound, declined to 5.7 cents, and the prices of corn, tobacco, and other crops fell proportionately. The state still was in the grip of financial depression when World War II began. Thousands of men volunteered for service before conscription was introduced; when the United States entered the war in 1941, several training posts were established in Tennessee. Tennessee firms manufacturing war materiel received contracts amounting to $1.25 billion and employed more than 200,000 people during the war. Industrial growth continued during the postwar period, while agriculture recovered and diversified. The chemical industry, spurred by high demand during and after World War II, became a leading sector, along with textiles, apparel, and food processing. Cotton and tobacco continued to be major crops, but by the early 1970s, soybeans had taken the lead, accounting for 22% of estimated farm income in 1980. Beef and dairy production also flourished.

Democratic boss Edward H. Crump, who ran an efficient political machine in Memphis, dominated state politics for most of the period between 1910 and the early 1950s, an era that saw the elevation of many Tennessee Democrats to national prominence. Considerable progress was made toward ending racial discrimination during the postwar years, although the desegregation of public schools was accomplished only after outbursts of violence at Clinton, Nashville, and Memphis. The killing of civil rights leader Martin Luther King Jr., in Memphis in 1968 resulted in rioting by blacks in that city, and in urban centers nationwide. The most notable political development during the 1970s was the resurgence of the Republican Party, making Tennessee one of the few true two-party states in the South.

The early 1980s saw the exposure of corruption in high places: former governor Ray Blanton and several aides were convicted for conspiracy to sell liquor licenses, and banker and former gubernatorial candidate Jacob F. "Jake" Butcher was convicted for fraud in the aftermath of the collapse of his banking empire. On the brighter side, there was a successful World's Fair in 1982, the Knoxville International Energy Exposition, and a fairly resilient state economy, bolstered by the much-heralded openings of the Nissan truck-assembly plant in Smyrna in 1983 and the General Motors Saturn plant in Spring Hill in 1990.

Manufacturing in Tennessee continued to grow throughout the 1980s, aided by the completion of the Tennessee-Tombigbee Waterway in 1985. The state gained nearly 45,000 manufacturing jobs between 1982 and 1992, many of them in the automotive and other transport-related industries. Tennessee's unemployment rate fell to a 16-year low of 4.7% in 1994.

The state legislature passed school reform laws in 1992 and, in 1993, a health-care package mandating the creation of TennCare, an insurance program designed to replace Medicaid coverage for 1.5 million uninsured residents of the state.

Democratic governor Phil Bredesen, elected in 2002, served two terms as Nashville mayor and hoped in 2003, despite the state's budget problems, to repeat statewide the significant economic growth he spearheaded in Nashville. The state was a leader in the nation in attempting to collect Internet and mail-order sales taxes. Tennessee officials estimated the state could lose up to $300 million in uncollected Internet and mail-order sales taxes in 2003.

Bredesen by 2005 had issued executive orders establishing tough ethics rules in the executive branch; managed the state through its fiscal crisis without raising taxes or cutting funds for education; raised teachers' pay to levels above the Southeastern average; expanded Tennessee's pre-kindergarten program; reformed the state's workers' compensation program and invested in retraining programs to help out-of-work employees develop new skills in the growing, competitive economy; launched a war on methamphetamine; and reformed TennCare, the state health-insurance program.

12 STATE GOVERNMENT

Tennessee's first constitution was adopted in 1796, just before the state was admitted to the Union. It vested executive authority in a governor, elected for two years, who had to be at least 25 years old and own at least 500 acres (202 hectares) of land. The governor could approve or veto bills adopted by the legislature, as commander-in-chief of the militia, and could grant pardons and reprieves, among other powers. Legislative power was placed in a General Assembly, consisting of a house and Senate, whose members served terms of two years. Candidates for the legislature were required to fulfill residence and age requirements and to own at least 200 acres (81 hectares). Property qualifications were not required for voting, and all freemen—including free blacks—could vote.

The basic governmental structure established in 1796 remains the fundamental law today. The constitution has been amended 36 times as of January 2005, however. The spirit of Jacksonian democracy prompted delegates at the constitutional convention of 1834 to remove property qualifications as a requirement for public office, reapportion representation, transfer the right to select county officials from justices of the peace to the voters, and reorganize the court system. At the same time, though, free blacks were disfranchised. In 1870, another constitutional convention confirmed the abolition of slavery and the enfranchisement of black men but imposed a poll tax as a requirement for voting. Membership of the House was fixed at 99 and the Senate at 33-numbers, these numbers are retained today. Assembling each January, regular sessions are limited to 90 legislative days. Special sessions, limited to 30 legislative days, may be called by petition of two-thirds of each house. All legislators must be US citizens, qualified voters in their districts, citizens of the state, and must have lived in the state for at least 3 years and in the district for one year. Further, senators are required to be at least 30 years old and representatives 21. The legislative salary in 2004 was $16,500, unchanged from 1999.

In the constitutional convention held in 1953, delegates increased the gubernatorial term from two to four years, gave the governor item-veto, eliminated the poll tax, authorized home rule for cities, and provided for the consolidation of county and city

functions. Later conventions extended the term of state senators from two to four years, sought to improve and streamline county government, and placed a constitutional limit on state spending. A limited convention in 1965 required the apportionment of the legislature according to population. This change greatly increased the weight of urban, and particularly black, votes.

The governor, the only executive elected statewide, appoints a cabinet of 21 members. The speaker of the state Senate automatically becomes lieutenant governor; the secretary of state, treasurer, and comptroller of the treasury are chosen by the legislature. The governor is limited to serving two consecutive terms. A candidate for governor must be at least 30 years old, a US citizen, and must have been a state citizen for at least seven years prior to election. As of December 2004, the governor's salary was $85,000, unchanged from 1999.

Legislation is enacted after bills are read and approved three times in each house and signed by the governor. If the governor vetoes a measure, the legislature may override the veto by majority vote of the elected members of each house. If the governor does not act on a bill, it becomes law after 10 days. Not more often than once every six years the legislature may submit to the voters the question of calling a convention to amend the constitution. If the vote is favorable, delegates are chosen. Changes proposed by the convention must be approved by a majority vote in a subsequent election. To amend the constitution, a majority of the members elected to both houses must first approve the proposed change. A second (two-thirds) vote by the legislature is required before the measure is put before the state's voters for majority approval.

Voters must be US citizens, at least 18 years old, and state residents. Restrictions apply to convicted felons and those declared mentally incompetent by the court.

13 POLITICAL PARTIES

The major political groups are the Democratic and Republican parties. Minor parties have seldom affected the outcome of an election in Tennessee.

When Tennessee entered the Union in 1796, it was strongly loyal to the Democratic-Republican Party. The Jacksonian era brought a change in political affiliations, and for more than 20 years, Tennessee had a vibrant two-party system. Jackson's followers formed the Democratic Party, which prevailed for a decade over the National Republican Party led by John Quincy Adams and Henry Clay. But by 1835, Tennesseans had become disillusioned with Jackson, and they joined the new Whig Party in large numbers. A Whig governor was elected in that year, and Whig presidential nominees consistently garnered Tennessee's electoral votes until the party foundered over the slavery issue in the 1850s.

After the Civil War and Reconstruction, Tennessee was part of the solid Democratic South for nearly a century. Only three Republican governors were elected during that period, and only then because bitter factionalism had divided the dominant party. East Tennessee remained a Republican stronghold. However, the 2nd Congressional district, which includes Knoxville, was the only district in the country to elect a Republican continuously from 1860 on. Republicans Warren G. Harding and Herbert Hoover carried the state in the presidential elections of 1920 and 1928. But whereas the 1920s saw a tendency away from one-party domination, Franklin D. Roosevelt and the New Deal brought the Volunteer State decisively back into the Democratic fold. Tennesseans voted overwhelmingly Democratic in the four elections that Roosevelt won (1932–44).

After World War II, the one-party system in Tennessee was shaken anew. Dwight D. Eisenhower narrowly won the state in 1952 and 1956, although Tennessee Senator Estes Kefauver was the Democratic vice-presidential nominee in the latter year. Tennesseans chose Richard Nixon all three times he ran for president. In fact, between 1948 and 1976, the only Democratic nominees to carry the state came from the South (Lyndon Johnson and Jimmy Carter) or from a border state (Harry Truman).

In state elections, the Republicans made deep inroads into Democratic power during the 1960s and 1970s. In 1966, Howard Baker became the first popularly elected Republican US senator in the state history. In 1970, voters elected Winfield Dunn as the first Republican governor in more than 50 years, and in the same year, they sent Republican Bill Brock to join Baker in the Senate. The Democrats regained the governorship in 1974 and Brock's seat in 1976, but Republicans again won the governorship in 1978 when Lamar Alexander defeated Jacob F. "Jake" Butcher. In 1982, Alexander became the first Tennessee governor to be elected to two successive four-year terms. Ned McWherter, a Democrat, was elected governor in 1990. Republican Don Sundquist became governor in 1994 and was reelected in 1998. Democrat Phil Bredesen was elected governor in 2002.

In 1994, Bill Frist, a heart surgeon, was elected to the US Senate on the Republican ticket, defeating Democrat James Sasser. He was reelected in 2000, and elected Senate Majority Leader in December 2002 after former Majority Leader Trent Lott aroused controversy by praising the 1948 presidential candidacy of segregationist Strom Thurmond. Democrat Harlan Matthews was appointed to fill the seat vacated by Al Gore in 1992 when Gore became vice president. In 1994, Republican Fred Thompson defeated Jim Cooper for the remaining two years of Gore's term. Thompson was elected to his first full term in 1996, but retired in 2002. That November, former Governor Lamar Alexander was elected US Senator from Tennessee. US representatives included four Republicans and five Democrats after the November 2004 elections. There were 16 Democrats and 17 Republicans in the state Senate and 53 Democrats and 46 Republicans in the state House in mid-2005.

Tennessee voters, who gave Republican George Bush 57.4% of the vote in 1988, chose Bill Clinton in 1992 and 1996. In 2000, Republican George W. Bush received 51% of the vote to Democrat Al Gore's 48%. In 2004, support for incumbent President Bush had increased to 56.8% to Democratic challenger John Kerry's 42.5%. In 2004 there were 3,532,000 registered voters; there is no party registration in the state. The state had 11 electoral votes in the 2004 presidential election.

¹⁴LOCAL GOVERNMENT

In 2005, local government in Tennessee was exercised by 95 counties and 349 municipalities. The county, a direct descendant of the Anglo-Saxon shire, has remained remarkably unaltered in Tennessee since it was brought from Virginia and North Carolina in frontier days. The constitution specifies that county officials must include at least a register, trustee (the custodian of county funds), sheriff, and county clerk, all of whom hold office for four years. Other officials have been added by legislative enactment: county commissioners, county executives (known for many years as county judges or county chairmen), tax assessors, county court clerks, and superintendents of public schools.

Tennessee Presidential Vote by Political Parties, 1948–2004

YEAR	ELECTORAL VOTE	TENNESSEE WINNER	DEMOCRAT	REPUBLICAN	STATES' RIGHTS DEMOCRAT	SOCIALIST	PROGRESSIVE	PROHIBITION
1948	11	*Truman (D)	270,402	202,914	73,815	1,288	1,864	—
					CONSTITUTION	—	—	—
1952	11	*Eisenhower (R)	443,710	446,147	379	—	887	1,432
1956	11	*Eisenhower (R)	456,507	462,288	19,820	—	—	789
					NAT'L STATES' RIGHTS			
1960	11	Nixon (R)	481,453	556,577	11,298	—	—	2,450
1964	11	*Johnson (D)	635,047	508,965	—	—	—	—
					AMERICAN IND.			
1968	11	*Nixon (R)	351,233	472,592	424,792	—	—	—
							AMERICAN	
1972	10	*Nixon (R)	357,293	813,147	—	—	30,373	—
								LIBERTARIAN
1976	10	*Carter (D)	825,897	633,969	2,303	—	5,769	1,375
					NAT'L STATESMAN		CITIZENS	
1980	10	*Reagan (R)	783,051	787,761	5,0211	—	1,112	7,116
1984	11	*Reagan (R)	711,714	990,212	—	—	978	3,072
1988	11	*Bush (R)	679,794	947,233	—	—	1,334	2,041
					IND. (Perot)			
1992	11	*Clinton (D)	933,521	841,300	199,968	1,356	727	1,847
1996	11	*Clinton (D)	909,146	863,530	105,918	—	—	5,020
					IND. (nader)		IND. (Buchanan)	
2000	11	*Bush, G. W. (R)	981,720	1,061,949	19,781	—	4,250	4,284
					WRITE-IN (Cobb)	IND. (Peroutka)	IND. (Badnarik)
2004	11	*Bush, G. W. (R)	1,036,477	1,384,375	8,992	33	2,570	4,866

*Won US presidential election.

City government is of more recent origin than county government. There are three forms of municipal government: mayor-council (or mayor-alderman), council-manager, and commission. The mayor-council system is the oldest and by far the most widely employed. There were 138 school districts and 475 special districts in 2005.

In 2005, local government accounted for about 239,168 full-time (or equivalent) employment positions.

15 STATE SERVICES

To address the continuing threat of terrorism and to work with the federal Department of Homeland Security, homeland security in Tennessee operates under executive order; a homeland security director oversees the state's homeland security activities.

The commissioner of education oversees the public schools as well as special and vocational-technical education; the higher education commission oversees higher education. Highways, aeronautics, mass transit, and waterways are the responsibility of the Department of Transportation. The Department of Safety and the State Highway Patrol are charged with enforcing the safety laws on all state roads and interstate highways. Public protection services are provided by the Military Department, which includes the Army and Air National Guard. The Department of Correction maintains prisons for adult offenders, a work-release program, and correctional and rehabilitation centers for juveniles. The Department of Environment and Conservation concerns itself with the environment.

The Department of Health licenses medical facilities, provides medical care for the indigent, operates tuberculosis treatment centers, and administers pollution control programs. The Department of Mental Health and Developmental Disabilities supervises mental hospitals, mental health clinics, and homes for the developmentally disabled. The Department of Human Services administers aid to the blind, aged, disabled, and families with dependent children, and determines eligibility for families receiving food stamps. The Department of Employment Security administers unemployment insurance and provides job training and placement services. State laws governing workers' compensation, occupational and mine safety, child labor, and wage standards are enforced by the Department of Labor and Workforce Development.

16 JUDICIAL SYSTEM

The Tennessee Supreme Court is the highest court in the state. It consists of five justices, not more than two of whom may reside in any one grand division of the state—East, Middle, or West Tennessee. The justices are elected by popular vote for terms of eight years and must be at least 35 years of age. The court has appellate jurisdiction only, holding sessions in Nashville, Knoxville, and Jackson. The position of chief justice rotates every 19 months.

Immediately below the Supreme Court are two appellate courts (each sitting in three divisions), established by the legislature to relieve the crowded high court docket. The Court of Appeals has appellate jurisdiction in most civil cases. The Court of Criminal Appeals hears cases from the lower courts involving criminal matters. Judges on both appellate courts are elected for eight-year terms.

Circuit courts have original jurisdiction in both civil and criminal cases. Tennessee still has chancery courts, vestiges of the Eng-lish courts designed to hear cases where there was no adequate remedy at law. They administer cases involving receiverships of corporations, settle disputes regarding property ownership, hear divorce cases, and adjudicate on a variety of other matters. In some districts, judges of the circuit and chancery courts, all of whom are elected for eight-year terms, have concurrent jurisdiction.

At the bottom of the judicial structure are general sessions courts. A comprehensive juvenile court system was set up in 1911. Other courts created for specific services include domestic relations courts and probate courts.

As of 31 December 2004, a total of 25,884 prisoners were held in Tennessee's state and federal prisons, an increase from 25,403 of 1.9% from the previous year. As of year-end 2004, a total of 1,905 inmates were female, up from 1,826 or 4.3% from the year before. Among sentenced prisoners (one year or more), Tennessee had an incarceration rate of 437 per 100,000 population in 2004.

According to the Federal Bureau of Investigation, Tennessee in 2004, had a violent crime rate (murder/nonnegligent manslaughter; forcible rape; robbery; aggravated assault) of 695.2 reported incidents per 100,000 population, or a total of 41,024 reported incidents. Crimes against property (burglary; larceny/theft; and motor vehicle theft) in that same year totaled 254,123 reported incidents or 4,306.5 reported incidents per 100,000 people. Tennessee has a death penalty, of which lethal injection is the sole method of execution for those sentenced after 1 January 1999. Those sentenced prior to that date can select electrocution over lethal injection. From 1976 through 5 May 2006, the state has carried out only one execution, in April 2000. As of 1 January 2006, Tennessee had 108 inmates on death row.

In 2003, Tennessee spent $186,916,752 on homeland security, an average of $31 per state resident.

17 ARMED FORCES

Tennessee supplied so many soldiers for the War of 1812 and the Mexican War that it became known as the Volunteer State. During the Civil War, more than 100,000 Tennesseans fought for the Confederacy and about half that number for the Union. In World War I, some 91,000 men served in the armed forces, and in World War II, 316,000 Tennesseans saw active duty.

In 2004, there were 2,430 active-duty military personnel and 5,390 civilian personnel stationed in Tennessee, most of whom were at Millington Naval Air Station near Memphis. Tennessee firms were awarded defense contracts totaling more than $2.1 billion in 2004. In addition, there was another $1.6 billion in payroll outlays by the Department of Defense.

On 2003, 540,778 veterans were living in Tennessee, of whom 62,502 served in World War II; 55,605 in the Korean conflict; 169,911 during the Vietnam era; and 87,253 during the Persian Gulf War. In 2004, the Veterans Administration expended more than $1.4 billion in pensions, medical assistance, and other major veterans' benefits.

As of 31 October 2004, the Tennessee Department of Public Safety employed 935 full-time sworn officers.

18 MIGRATION

The first white settlers in Tennessee, who came across the mountains from North Carolina and Virginia, were almost entirely of English extraction. They were followed by an influx of Scotch-

Irish, mainly from Pennsylvania. About 3,800 German and Irish migrants arrived during the 1830s and 1840s. In the next century, Tennessee's population remained relatively stable, except for an influx of blacks immediately following the Civil War. There was a steady out-migration of blacks to industrial centers in the North during the 20th century. The state suffered a net loss through migration of 462,000 between 1940 and 1970 but gained over 465,000 between 1970 and 1990. Between 1990 and 1998, Tennessee had net gains of 338,000 in domestic migration and 27,000 in international migration. In 1998, 2,806 foreign immigrants arrived in the state, the greatest concentrations coming from Mexico (300) and India (291). Tennessee's overall population increased 11.3% between 1990 and 1998.

The major in-state migration has been away from rural areas and into towns and cities. Blacks, especially, have tended to cluster in large urban centers. The population of metropolitan Memphis, for example, was more than 42% black in 1997. In the period 2000–05, net international migration was 49,973 and net internal migration was 109,707, for a net gain of 159,680 people.

[19] INTERGOVERNMENTAL COOPERATION

Tennessee participates in such interstate agreements as the Appalachian Regional Commission, Interstate Mining Compact Commission, Southeastern Forest Fire Protection Compact, Southern Regional Education Board, Southern Growth Policies Board, and the Southern States Energy Board. There are boundary accords with Arkansas, Kentucky, and Virginia, and an agreement with Alabama, Kentucky, and Mississippi governing development of the Tennessee-Tombigbee waterway. Federal grants to Tennessee amounted to $8.086 billion in fiscal year 2005, an estimated $7.890 billion in fiscal year 2006, and an estimated $8.114 billion in fiscal year 2007.

[20] ECONOMY

Tennessee's economy is based primarily on industry. Since the 1930s, the number of people employed in industry has grown at a rapid rate, while the number of farmers has declined proportionately. The principal manufacturing areas are Memphis, Nashville, Chattanooga, Knoxville, and Kingsport-Bristol. With the construction in the 1980s of a Nissan automobile and truck plant and a General Motors automobile facility, both in the area southeast of Nashville, Tennessee has become an important producer of transportation equipment. Since 1995, however, employment in Tennessee's manufacturing sector has fallen, and since 1999, total output from the sector has fallen 3.2% between 1999 and 2001. The pace of job loss in manufacturing accelerated in the 2001 national recession and slowdown, with 36,000 jobs lost during the year, 42% higher than any previous year. Manufacturing as a share of the state gross product fell from 21.5% in 1997 to 18.7% in 2001. The influx of new residents, from which Tennessee's economy benefited throughout the 1990s, fell to an eleven-year low with the fall in job growth in 2001. As of 2002, manufacturing jobs made up 17% of total employment in Tennessee, still above the national average of 13%. Income from agricultural products currently comes more from dairy and beef cattle, and soybeans than from traditional crops, tobacco, cotton, and corn. Coming into the 21st century (1997 to 2001) the strongest growth in terms of contributions to state gross product has been in the various services sectors. Output from general services increased 27.4%, with financial services rising 29.5%, transportation and utilities sector up by 27.4%, government up by 22.8%, and trade up by 17.8%.

In 2004, Tennessee's gross state product (GSP) was $217.626 billion, of which manufacturing accounted for the largest share at $38.142 or 17.5% of GSP, followed by the real estate sector at $23.219 (10.6% of GSP), and health care and social assistance at $17.985 billion (8.2% of GSP). In that same year, there were an estimated 471,316 small businesses in Tennessee. Of the 109,853 businesses that had employees, an estimated total of 106,729 or 97.2% were small companies. An estimated 17,415 new businesses were established in the state in 2004, down 1.6% from the year before. Business terminations that same year came to 16,520, up 1.3% from 2003. There were 548 business bankruptcies in 2004, down 8.2% from the previous year. In 2005, the state's personal bankruptcy (Chapter 7 and Chapter 13) filing rate was 1,117 filings per 100,000 people, ranking Tennessee as first in the nation.

[21] INCOME

In 2005 Tennessee had a gross state product (GSP) of $227 billion which accounted for 1.8% of the nation's gross domestic product and placed the state at number 18 in highest GSP among the 50 states and the District of Columbia.

According to the Bureau of Economic Analysis, in 2004 Tennessee had a per capita personal income (PCPI) of $29,844. This ranked 35th in the United States and was 90% of the national average of $33,050. The 1994–2004 average annual growth rate of PCPI was 4.0%. Tennessee had a total personal income (TPI) of $175,880,336,000, which ranked 19th in the United States and reflected an increase of 5.9% from 2003. The 1994–2004 average annual growth rate of TPI was 5.2%. Earnings of persons employed in Tennessee increased from $133,081,409,000 in 2003 to $141,576,558,000 in 2004, an increase of 6.4%. The 2003–04 national change was 6.3%.

The US Census Bureau reports that the three-year average median household income for 2002–04 in 2004 dollars was $38,550 compared to a national average of $44,473. During the same period an estimated 14.9% of the population was below the poverty line as compared to 12.4% nationwide.

[22] LABOR

According to the Bureau of Labor Statistics (BLS), in April 2006 the seasonally adjusted civilian labor force in Tennessee 2,960,500, with approximately 161,200 workers unemployed, yielding an unemployment rate of 5.4%, compared to the national average of 4.7% for the same period. Preliminary data for the same period placed nonfarm employment at 2,780,300. Since the beginning of the BLS data series in 1976, the highest unemployment rate recorded in Tennessee was 12.4% in December 1982. The historical low was 3.8% in March 2000. Preliminary nonfarm employment data by occupation for April 2006 showed that approximately 4.5% of the labor force was employed in construction; 14.6% in manufacturing; 21.9% in trade, transportation, and public utilities; 5.2% in financial activities; 11.3% in professional and business services; 12% in education and health services; 9.7% in leisure and hospitality services; and 15% in government.

The BLS reported that in 2005, a total of 128,000 of Tennessee's 2,368,000 employed wage and salary workers were formal members of a union. This represented 5.4% of those so employed, down from 6.7% in 2004, and well below the national average of 12%. Overall in 2005, a total of 156,000 workers (6.6%) in Tennessee were covered by a union or employee association contract, which includes those workers who reported no union affiliation. Tennessee is one of 22 states with a right-to-work law.

As of 1 March 2006, Tennessee did not have a state-mandated minimum wage law. Employees in that state however, were covered under federal minimum wage statutes. In 2004, women in the state accounted for 47.1% of the employed civilian labor force.

23 AGRICULTURE

Tennessee ranked 32d among the 50 states in 2005 with farm receipts of over $2.5 billion. There were 85,000 farms in 2004.

From the antebellum period to the 1950s, cotton was the leading crop, followed by corn and tobacco. But during the early 1960s, soybeans surpassed cotton as the principal source of income. In 2004, 48.4 million bushels of soybeans, valued at $251.6 million, were harvested. Tobacco production in 2004 was 67.9 million lb. The main types of tobacco are burley, a fine leaf used primarily for cigarettes, and eastern and western dark-fired, which are used primarily for cigars, pipe tobacco, and snuff. The corn harvest in 2004 was about 86.1 million bushels, valued at $180.8 million. In 2004, cotton production was 990,000 bales, valued at $225.1.9 million. In 2004, soybeans, greenhouse/nursery products, and cotton together accounted for 30% of state farm receipts.

24 ANIMAL HUSBANDRY

Cattle are raised throughout the state, but principally in middle and east Tennessee. In 1930, fewer than a million cattle and calves were raised on Tennessee farms; by 2005, there were an estimated 2.17 million cattle and calves, valued at $1.67 billion. During 2004, hogs and pigs numbered around 215,000 and were valued at $18.9 million. In 2003, Tennessee poultry farmers produced 948 million lb (431 million kg) of broilers, worth $322.3 million, and 290 million eggs, valued at $31.9 million. Tennessee dairy farmers produced 1.2 billion lb (0.5 billion kg) of milk from some 79,000 milk cows.

25 FISHING

Fishing is a major attraction for sport but plays a relatively small role in the economic life of Tennessee. There are 17 TVA lakes and 7 other lakes, all maintained by the Army Corps of Engineers; 10 of these lakes span an area of 10,000 acres (4,000 hectares) or more, and there are thousands of miles of creeks and mountain streams, all of which attract anglers. Tennessee has no closed season, except on trout.

In the 1970s, pollution from industrial waste dumping killed millions of fish and seriously endangered sport fishing. By the 1980s, however, industrial establishments in the state were complying more fully with the 1974 Water Pollution Act. In 2004, the state issued 1,028,386 sport fishing licenses. In 2004, Tennessee had 14 trout farms, selling 54,000 lb (24,500 kg). There are two national fish hatcheries in the state (Dale Hollow and Erwin), which together stock more than 1.9 million fish and produce more than 12 million trout eggs annually to support fishery mitigation efforts.

26 FORESTRY

Forests covered 14,404,000 acres (5,827,000 hectares) in 2004, or more than 50% of the state's total land area. Commercial timberlands in 2004 totaled 12,396,000 acres (5,017,000 hectares). In 2004, 86% of the forested area was privately owned, 10% federally owned, 3% state-owned, and 1% municipally owned. The counties of the Cumberland Plateau and Highland Rim are the major sources of timber products, and in Lewis, Perry, Polk, Scott, Sequatchie, Unicoi, and Wayne counties, more than 75% of the total area is commercial forest.

About 96% of Tennessee's timber is in hardwoods, and nearly one-half of that is in white and red oak. Of the softwoods, pine—shortleaf, loblolly, Virginia, pitch, and white—accounts for 80%. Red cedar accounts for about 5% of the softwood supply. Total lumber production in 2004 was 891 million board ft.

Wood products manufacturing is among the state's largest basic industries. The wood products industry in Tennessee falls into three main categories: paper and similar products, lumber and similar products, and furniture. Manufacturing uses only about a third of the wood grown by forests in Tennessee each year. The remaining two-thirds continues to accumulate on aging trees or is lost through decomposition of diseased and dead trees. The most common method of cutting timber in Tennessee has long been "high-grading," that is, cutting only the most valuable trees and leaving those of inferior quality and value. Clearcutting, patch cutting, and group selection are silviculturally preferable, but, with the exception of clearcutting on industry lands, are rarely practiced.

27 MINING

According to preliminary data from the US Geological Survey (USGS), the estimated value of nonfuel mineral production by Tennessee in 2003 was $606 million, a decrease from 2002 of about 6.5%. The USGS data ranked Tennessee as 23rd among the 50 states by the total value of its nonfuel mineral production, accounting for over 1.5% of total US output.

According to the preliminary data for 2003 crushed stone was the state's top nonfuel mineral commodity, accounting for over 50% of all nonfuel minerals produced, by value. In second place was cement (portland and masonry), followed by construction sand and gravel, zinc and ball clay. By volume, Tennessee in 2003, was the nation's leading producer of ball clay and gemstones. The state also ranked third in zinc and was ninth in the production of industrial stone and gravel.

Preliminary data for 2003 showed production of crushed stone to total 53.5 million metric tons, with a value of $321 million, while construction sand and gravel output that year totaled 9.7 million metric tons, valued at $54.8 million. Ball clay production in 2003 totaled 660,000 metric tons, with a valued of $28.1 million, with industrial sand and gravel output at 1.04 million metric tons, valued at $22.5 million.. In 2003, gemstone production consisted largely of cultured freshwater pearls and mother-of-pearl derived from freshwater mussel shells. The state was home to the nation's only freshwater pearl farm.

28 ENERGY AND POWER

The Tennessee Valley Authority (TVA) is the principal supplier of power in the state, providing electricity to more than 100 cities and 50 rural cooperatives. As of 2003, Tennessee had 94 electrical power service providers, of which 62 were publicly owned and 25 were cooperatives. Of the remainder, three were investor owned, one was federally operated and three were owners of independent generators that sold directly to customers. As of that same year there were 2,923,615 retail customers. Of that total, 45,628 received their power from investor-owned service providers. Cooperatives accounted for 848,844 customers, while publicly owned providers had 2,029,100 customers. There were 40 federal customers and three were independent generator or "facility" customers.

Total net summer generating capability by the state's electrical generating plants in 2003 stood at 20.893 million kW, with total production that same year at 92.221 billion kWh. Of the total amount generated, 96.2% came from electric utilities, with the remainder coming from independent producers and combined heat and power service providers. The largest portion of all electric power generated, 54.921 billion kWh (59.6%), came from coal-fired plants, with nuclear plants in second place at 24.152 billion kWh (26.2%) and hydroelectric plants in third at 12.003 billion kWh (13%). Other renewable power sources, natural gas, pumped storage and petroleum fired plants accounted for the remaining output.

As of 2006, Tennessee had two operating nuclear power plants: the Sequoyah plant near Chattanooga and the Watts Bar plant between Chattanooga and Knoxville. Both plants are operated by the Tennessee Valley Authority.

Tennessee in 2004, had 32 producing coal mines, 20 of which were surface operations and 12 were underground. Coal production that year totaled 2,887,000 short tons, up from 2,564,000 short tons in 2003. Of the total produced in 2004, surface mines accounted for 2,061,000 short tons. Recoverable coal reserves in 2004 totaled 26 million short tons. One short ton equals 2,000 lb (0.907 metric tons). Surface mine operators are now required to reclaim mined land. Most of the coal mined in the state is used for producing electricity, although some is used for home heating.

As of 2004, Tennessee had proven crude oil reserves of under 1% of all proven US reserves, while output that same year averaged 1,000 barrels per day. Including federal offshore domains, the state that year ranked 28th (27th excluding federal offshore) in production among the 31 producing states. In 2004 Tennessee had 400 producing oil wells and accounted for less than 1% of all US production. As of 2005, the state had one refinery with a crude oil distillation capacity of 180,000 barrels per day.

In 2004, Tennessee had 280 producing natural gas and gas condensate wells. In 2003 (the latest year for which data was available), marketed gas production (all gas produced excluding gas used for repressuring, vented and flared, and nonhydrocarbon gases removed) totaled 1.803 billion cu ft (.051 billion cu m). There was no data available on the state's proven reserves of natural gas.

29 INDUSTRY

On the eve of the Civil War, only 1% of Tennessee's population was employed in manufacturing, mostly in the iron, cotton, lumber, and flour-milling industries. Rapid industrial growth took place during the 20th century, however, and by 1981, Tennessee ranked third among the southeastern states and 15th in the United States in value of shipments. Tennessee's four major metropolitan areas, Memphis, Nashville, Knoxville, and Chattanooga, and collectively employ the largest share of all the state's industrial workers.

According to the US Census Bureau's Annual Survey of Manufactures (ASM) for 2004, Tennessee's manufacturing sector covered some 21 product subsectors. The shipment value of all products manufactured in the state that same year was $125.530 billion. Of that total, transportation equipment manufacturing accounted for the largest share at $26.256 billion. It was followed by computer and electronic equipment manufacturing at $14.584 billion; food manufacturing at $13.293 billion; chemical manufacturing at $12.858 billion; and machinery manufacturing at $8.926 billion.

In 2004, a total of 384,152 people in Tennessee were employed in the state's manufacturing sector, according to the ASM. Of that total, 286,806 were actual production workers. In terms of total employment, the transportation equipment manufacturing industry accounted for the largest portion of all manufacturing employees at 58,023, with 45,837 actual production workers. It was followed by food manufacturing at 36,361 employees (25,980 actual production workers); plastics and rubber products manufacturing at 31,118 employees (24,628 actual production workers); machinery manufacturing at 30,169 employees (22,892 actual production workers); and chemical manufacturing with 25,918 employees (13,339 actual production workers).

ASM data for 2004 showed that Tennessee's manufacturing sector paid $14.808 billion in wages. Of that amount, the transportation equipment manufacturing sector accounted for the largest share at $2.698 billion. It was followed by chemical manufacturing at $1.489 billion; fabricated metal product manufacturing at $1.248 billion; food manufacturing at $1.217 billion; and plastics and rubber products manufacturing at $1.159 billion.

30 COMMERCE

Tennessee has been an important inland commercial center for some 60 years. According to the 2002 Census of Wholesale Trade, Tennessee's wholesale trade sector had sales that year totaling $97.7 billion from 7,566 establishments. Wholesalers of durable goods accounted for 4,886 establishments, followed by nondurable goods wholesalers at 2,166 and electronic markets, agents, and brokers accounting for 514 establishments. Sales by durable goods wholesalers in 2002 totaled $44.2 billion, while wholesalers of nondurable goods saw sales of $42.4 billion. Electronic markets, agents, and brokers in the wholesale trade industry had sales of $11.07 billion.

In the 2002 Census of Retail Trade, Tennessee was listed as having 24,029 retail establishments with sales of $60.1 billion. The leading types of retail businesses by number of establishments were: gasoline stations (3,339); clothing and clothing accessories stores (3,017); motor vehicle and motor vehicle parts dealers (2,974); miscellaneous store retailers (2,783); and food and beverage stores (2,676). In terms of sales, motor vehicle and motor vehicle parts dealers accounted for the largest share of retail sales at $16.2 billion, followed by general merchandise stores at $10.2 billion; food and beverage stores at $7.4 billion; and gasoline stations at $5.5 billion. A total of 304,652 people were employed by the retail sector in Tennessee that year.

Exporters located in Tennessee exported $19.06 billion in merchandise during 2005. Major exports included transportation equipment, chemicals, and non-electric machinery.

31 CONSUMER PROTECTION

The Tennessee Division of Consumer Affairs is a division of the state's Department of Commerce and Insurance. Its mission is to serve and protect consumers from deceptive business practices. The Division's activities include consumer complaint mediation, litigation for violations of the Tennessee Consumer Protection Act, consumer education, investigation, registration of health clubs, and advise the legislature on legislation.

Because the Division of Consumer Affairs is under the state's Department of Commerce, the Tennessee Attorney General's Office has limited authority in regards to consumer affairs, although the office does have a Consumer Advocate and Protection Division. While the Attorney General's Office can initiate civil proceedings, its ability to initiate criminal proceedings is limited and must be done in conjunction with a local district attorney. In addition, the Office's ability to represent the state before state and federal regulatory agencies is also limited, and it has no authority to administer consumer protection and education programs, or to handle formal consumer complaints. However, the Office can exercise broad subpoena powers. In antitrust actions, the Attorney General's Office cannot act on behalf of those consumers who are incapable of acting on their own, but is authorized to: initiate damage actions on behalf of the state in state courts; initiate criminal proceedings; and represent counties, cities and other governmental entities in recovering civil damages under state or federal law.

The offices of the Division of Consumer Affairs and the Consumer Advocate and Protection Division of the Office of the Attorney general are located in Nashville.

32 BANKING

The first bank in Tennessee was the Bank of Nashville, chartered in 1807. Four years later, the Bank of the State of Tennessee was chartered at Knoxville. Branches were established at Nashville, Jonesboro, Clarksville, and Columbia. In 1817, nearly a dozen more banks were chartered in various frontier towns. The Civil War curtailed banking operations, but the industry began again immediately after cessation of hostilities.

As of June 2005, Tennessee had 202 insured banks, savings and loans, and saving banks, in addition to 121 state-chartered and 85 federally chartered credit unions (CUs). Excluding the CUs, the Memphis market area, which includes portions of Mississippi and Arkansas accounted for the largest portion of the state's financial institutions and deposits in 2004, with 52 institutions and $26.946 billion in deposits, followed by the Nashville–Davidson–Murfeesboro market area, with 49 institutions and $25.208 billion in deposits.. As of June 2005, CUs accounted for 11.9 of all assets held by all financial institutions in the state, or some $10.877 billion. Banks, savings and loans, and savings banks collectively accounted for the remaining 88.1% or $80.600 billion in assets held.

The median percentage of past-due/nonaccrual loans to total loans stood at 1.71% as of fourth quarter 2005,down from 1.77% in 2004 and 2.43% in 2003. The median net interest margin (the difference between the lower rates offered to savers and the high-er rates charged on loans) for insured institutions stood at 4.24% as of fourth quarter 2005, up from 4.23% in 2004 and 4.19% in 2003.

Regulation of Tennessee's state-chartered banks and other state-chartered financial institutions is the responsibility of the state's Department of Financial Institutions.

33 INSURANCE

In 2000, 34 property and casualty and 20 life insurance companies had home offices in Tennessee. Some 4.4 million individual life insurance policies worth over $245.8 billion were in force in 2004; total value for all categories of life insurance (individual, group, and credit) was about $421 billion. The average coverage amount is $55,400 per policy holder. Death benefits paid that year totaled at over $1.2 billion.

As of 2003, there were 17 property and casualty and 15 life and health insurance companies domiciled in the state. In 2004, direct premiums for property and casualty insurance totaled over $7.9 billion. That year, there were 17,623 flood insurance policies in force in the state, with a total value of $2.45 billion.

In 2004, 50% of state residents held employment-based health insurance policies, 6% held individual policies, and 28% were covered under Medicare and Medicaid; 14% of residents were uninsured. In 2003, employee contributions for employment-based health coverage averaged at 21% for single coverage and 28% for family coverage. The state offers a three-month health benefits expansion program for small-firm employees in connection with the Consolidated Omnibus Budget Reconciliation Act (COBRA, 1986), a health insurance program for those who lose employment-based coverage due to termination or reduction of work hours.

In 2003, there were over 3.8 million auto insurance policies in effect for private passenger cars. Insurance is not required, but motorists are expected to hold financial responsibility in the event of an accident. Liability limits in the state include bodily injury liability of up to $25,000 per individual and $50,000 for all persons injured in an accident, as well as property damage liability of $10,000. In 2003, the average expenditure per vehicle for insurance coverage was $649.71.

34 SECURITIES

There are no securities exchanges in Tennessee. In 2005, there were 870 personal financial advisers employed in the state and 2,650 securities, commodities, and financial services sales agents. In 2004, there were over 106 publicly traded companies within the state, with over 38 NASDAQ companies, 39 NYSE listings, and 5 AMEX listings. In 2006, the state had seven Fortune 500 companies; Caremark Rx (based in Nashville) ranked first in the state and 60th in the nation with revenues of over $32.9 billion, followed by FedEx (Memphis), HCA–The Healthcare Company (Nashville), UnumProvident (Chattanooga), and Dollar General (Goodlettsville). All five of these top companies are listed on the NYSE.

35 PUBLIC FINANCE

The state budget is prepared annually by the Budget Division of the Tennessee Department of Finance and Administration and submitted by the governor to the legislature every January. The fiscal year (FY) lasts from 1 July through 30 June.

Fiscal year 2006 general funds were estimated at $10.2 billion for resources and $9.8 billion for expenditures. In fiscal year 2004, federal government grants to Tennessee were $9.8 billion.

36 TAXATION

In 2005, Tennessee collected $10,007 million in tax revenues or $1,678 per capita, which placed it 45th among the 50 states in per capita tax burden. The national average was $2,192 per capita. Sales taxes accounted for 61.1% of the total; selective sales taxes, 15.3%; individual income taxes, 1.6%; corporate income taxes, 8.1%; and other taxes, 14.0%.

As of 1 January 2006, Tennessee state income tax was limited to dividends and interest income only. The state taxes corporations at a flat rate of 6.5%.

In 2004, local property taxes amounted to $3,585,440,000 or $608 per capita. The per capita amount ranks the state 41st highest nationally. Tennessee has no state level property taxes.

Tennessee taxes retail sales at a rate of 7%. In addition to the state tax, local taxes on retail sales can reach as much as 2.75%, making for a potential total tax on retail sales of 9.75%. Food purchased for consumption off-premises is taxable, but at a lower rate. The tax on cigarettes is 20 cents per pack, which ranks 48th among the 50 states and the District of Columbia. Tennessee taxes gasoline at 21.4 cents per gallon. This is in addition to the 18.4 cents per gallon federal tax on gasoline.

According to the Tax Foundation, for every federal tax dollar sent to Washington in 2004, Tennessee citizens received $1.30 in federal spending.

37 ECONOMIC POLICY

Since World War II, Tennessee has aggressively sought new business and industry. The Department of Economic and Community Development (ECD) helps prospective firms locate industrial sites in communities throughout the state, and its representatives work with firms in Canada, Europe, and the Far East, as well as with domestic businesses. The department also administers special Appalachian regional programs in 50 counties and directs the state Office of Diversity Business Enterprise.

Tennessee's right-to-work law and relatively weak labor movement constitute important industrial incentives, as well as a low state tax burden. The counties and municipalities, moreover, offer tax exemptions on land, capital improvements, equipment, and machinery.

38 HEALTH

The infant mortality rate in October 2005 was estimated at 8.7 per 1,000 live births. The birth rate in 2003 was 13.5 per 1,000 population. The abortion rate stood at 15.2 per 1,000 women in 2000. In 2003, about 83.4% of pregnant woman received prenatal care beginning in the first trimester. In 2004, approximately 82% of children received routine immunizations before the age of three.

The crude death rate in 2003 was 9.8 deaths per 1,000 population. As of 2002, the death rates for major causes of death (per 100,000 resident population) were: heart disease, 279.9; cancer, 215.9; cerebrovascular diseases, 68.7; chronic lower respiratory diseases, 51.9; and diabetes, 30.2. The mortality rate from HIV in-

fection was 6 per 100,000 population. In 2004, the reported AIDS case rate was at about 13.1 per 100,000 population. In 2002, about 59% of the population was considered overweight or obese. As of 2004, about 26.1% of state residents were smokers, representing the third-highest percentage in the nation (following Kentucky and West Virginia).

In 2003, Tennessee had 125 community hospitals with about 20,300 beds. There were about 813,000 patient admissions that year and 10 million outpatient visits. The average daily inpatient census was about 12,400 patients. The average cost per day for hospital care was $1,187. Also in 2003, there were about 337 cer-

Tennessee—State Government Finances

(Dollar amounts in thousands. Per capita amounts in dollars.)

	AMOUNT	PER CAPITA
Total Revenue	23,920,818	4,059.19
General revenue	20,901,310	3,546.80
Intergovernmental revenue	9,016,698	1,530.07
Taxes	9,529,171	1,617.03
General sales	5,845,206	991.89
Selective sales	1,499,456	254.45
License taxes	1,045,665	177.44
Individual income tax	139,991	23.76
Corporate income tax	694,798	117.90
Other taxes	304,055	51.60
Current charges	1,537,571	260.91
Miscellaneous general revenue	817,870	138.79
Utility revenue	–	–
Liquor store revenue	–	–
Insurance trust revenue	3,019,508	512.39
Total expenditure	22,164,577	3,761.17
Intergovernmental expenditure	5,301,665	899.65
Direct expenditure	16,862,912	2,861.52
Current operation	13,268,720	2,251.61
Capital outlay	1,297,615	220.20
Insurance benefits and repayments	1,566,111	265.76
Assistance and subsidies	548,261	93.04
Interest on debt	182,205	30.92
Exhibit: Salaries and wages	2,979,900	505.67
Total expenditure	22,164,577	3,761.17
General expenditure	20,593,636	3,494.59
Intergovernmental expenditure	5,301,665	899.65
Direct expenditure	15,291,971	2,594.94
General expenditures, by function:		
Education	6,477,758	1,099.23
Public welfare	8,357,217	1,418.16
Hospitals	342,944	58.20
Health	962,310	163.30
Highways	1,545,491	262.26
Police protection	142,127	24.12
Correction	596,095	101.15
Natural resources	224,643	38.12
Parks and recreation	119,821	20.33
Government administration	495,428	84.07
Interest on general debt	182,205	30.92
Other and unallocable	1,147,597	194.74
Utility expenditure	4,830	.82
Liquor store expenditure	–	–
Insurance trust expenditure	1,566,111	265.76
Debt at end of fiscal year	3,580,940	607.66
Cash and security holdings	31,003,166	5,261.02

Abbreviations and symbols: – zero or rounds to zero; (NA) not available; (X) not applicable.

SOURCE: *U.S. Census Bureau, Governments Division, 2004 Survey of State Government Finances,* January 2006.

tified nursing facilities in the state with 37,958 beds and an overall occupancy rate of about 88.3%. In 2004, it was estimated that about 71.5% of all state residents had received some type of dental care within the year. Tennessee had 262 physicians per 100,000 resident population in 2004 and 874 nurses per 100,000 in 2005. In 2004, there were a total of 3,027 dentists in the state.

Tennessee has four medical schools: two in Nashville (Vanderbilt University and Meharry Medical School), one at Johnson City (East Tennessee State University), and one at Memphis (University of Tennessee). The St. Jude Children's Research Hospital is well-know for its ongoing work in developing new treatments for genetic and terminal diseases among children.

With 28% of residents enrolled in Medicaid programs in 2004, Tennessee ranked with California and the District of Columbia as having the second highest percentage of residents on Medicaid (following Maine). About 15% were enrolled in Medicare programs in 2004. Approximately 14% of the state population was uninsured in 2004. In 2003, state health care expenditures totaled $8 million.

39 SOCIAL WELFARE

In 2004, about 168,000 people received unemployment benefits, with the average weekly unemployment benefit at $209. In fiscal year 2005, the estimated average monthly participation in the food stamp program included about 849,703 persons (374,011 households); the average monthly benefit was about $92.35 per person. That year, the total of benefits paid through the state for the food stamp program was about $941.6 million.

Temporary Assistance for Needy Families (TANF), the system of federal welfare assistance that officially replaced Aid to Families with Dependent Children (AFDC) in 1997, was reauthorized through the Deficit Reduction Act of 2005. TANF is funded through federal block grants that are divided among the states based on an equation involving the number of recipients in each state. Tennessee's TANF program is called Families First. In 2004, the state program had 190,000 recipients; state and federal expenditures on this TANF program totaled $165 million in fiscal year 2003.

In December 2004, Social Security benefits were paid to 1,069,600 Tennessee residents. This number included 627,080 retired workers, 112,330 widows and widowers, 171,850 disabled workers, 55,900 spouses, and 102,440 children. Social Security beneficiaries represented 18% of the total state population and 94.2% of the state's population age 65 and older. Retired workers received an average monthly payment of $929; widows and widowers, $843; disabled workers, $862; and spouses, $459. Payments for children of retired workers averaged $472 per month; children of deceased workers, $593; and children of disabled workers, $255. Federal Supplemental Security Income payments in December 2004 went to 160,521 Tennessee residents, averaging $377 a month.

40 HOUSING

In 2004, there were an estimated 2,595,060 housing units in the state, 2,314,688 of which were occupied; 70% were owner-occupied. About 68.4% of all units were single-family, detached homes. Electricity and utility gas were the most common energy sources for heating. It was estimated that 111,374 units lacked telephone service, 11,294 lacked complete plumbing facilities, and 10,036 lacked complete kitchen facilities. The average household had 2.48 members.

In 2004, 44,800 new privately owned housing units were authorized for construction. The median home value was $110,198. The median monthly cost for mortgage owners was $954. Renters paid a median of $564 per month. In September 2005, the state received grants of over $1.6 million from the US Department of Housing and Urban Development (HUD) for rural housing and economic development programs. For 2006, HUD allocated to the state over $26.9 million in community development block grants.

41 EDUCATION

The state assumed responsibility for education in 1873, when the legislature established a permanent school fund and made schools free to all persons between the ages of 6 and 21. In 1917, an eight-year elementary and four-year secondary school system was set up. Thirty years later, enactment of the state sales and use tax enabled state authorities to increase teachers' salaries by about 100% and to provide capital funds for a variety of expanded educational programs. In the early 1980s, Tennessee further improved its educational system by offering incentive pay to its teachers.

The 21st Century Schools Program adopted by the Tennessee General Assembly in 1992 provided K-12 public schools with nearly $1 billion in new state dollars—an increase of 90%. The program repealed 3,700 state rules and regulations, gave communities wide discretion over education decision-making, made local school systems more accountable for results, and funded 5,450 high-tech classrooms in Tennessee's public schools. In 1996/97, Tennessee pioneered a statewide network connecting every public school to museums, libraries, and databases available on the World Wide Web. Tennessee's Literacy 2000 initiative (begun in 1987) improved the adult literacy rate by 24% in its first four years.

In 2004, 82.9% of Tennessee residents age 25 and older were high school graduates; 24.3% had obtained a bachelor's degree or higher. The total enrollment for fall 2002 in Tennessee's public schools stood at 928,000. Of these, 674,000 attended schools from kindergarten through grade eight, and 254,000 attended high school. Approximately 70.7% of the students were white, 25% were black, 2.8% were Hispanic, 1.3% were Asian/Pacific Islander, and 0.2% were American Indian/Alaskan Native. Total enrollment was estimated at 925,000 in fall 2003 and expected to be 929,000 by fall 2014, an increase of 0.1% during the period 2002–14. Expenditures for public education in 2003/04 were estimated at $6.7 billion, or $6,504 per student, the seventh-lowest among the 50 states. There were 87,055 students enrolled in 551 private schools in fall 2003. Since 1969, the National Assessment of Educational Progress (NAEP) has tested public school students nationwide. The resulting report, *The Nation's Report Card*, stated that in 2005, eighth graders in Tennessee scored 271 out of 500 in mathematics compared with the national average of 278.

As of fall 2002, there were 261,899 students enrolled in college or graduate school; minority students comprised 21.4% of total postsecondary enrollment. In 2005 Tennessee had 95 degree-granting institutions. The University of Tennessee system has principal campuses at Knoxville, Memphis, Martin, and Chattanooga. Components of the State University and Community College System of Tennessee include Memphis State University (the largest), Tennessee Technological University at Cookeville, East Tennessee State University at Johnson City, Austin Peay State University at Clarksville, Tennessee State University at Nashville, and Middle Tennessee State University at Murfreesboro, along with 13 two-year community colleges located throughout the state. Well-known private colleges are Vanderbilt University at Nashville, the University of the South at Sewanee, and Rhodes College at Memphis. Vanderbilt has schools of medicine, law, divinity, nursing, business, and education, as well as an undergraduate program. Loan and grant programs are administered by the Tennessee Student Assistance Corporation.

42 ARTS

The Tennessee Arts Commission was created in 1967 and offers several grant opportunities for programs including Arts Education, the Individual Artist Fellowship, and Arts Build Communities. As of 2005, the Greater Memphis Arts Council was the eighth-largest United Arts Fund. Active in promoting the cultural and economic growth of the city, members help to encourage new businesses to relocate in Memphis based on the city's cultural advantages. In 2005, the Tennessee Arts Commission and other Tennessee arts organizations received 19 grants totaling $822,800 from the National Endowment for the Arts.

Humanities Tennessee, founded in 1973, sponsors a number of annual programs. As of 2005, annual programs included the Southern Festival of Books, the Tennessee Young Writers' Workshop, the Tennessee Community History Program, and Letters About Literature. In 2005, the National Endowment for the Humanities contributed $1,461,572 for 25 state programs.

Each of Tennessee's major cities has a symphony orchestra. The best known are the Memphis Symphony and the Nashville Symphony, the latter of which makes its home in the Tennessee Performing Arts Center. The Nashville Symphony began in 1920 as The Symphony Society—a group of amateur and professional musical artists. In 2005, the symphony's Principal Conductor Kenneth Schermerhorn passed away; he had conducted the symphony for over 20 years. Other buildings included in the Tennessee Performing Arts Center are three performing arts theaters and the State Museum. As of 2005, the Tennessee State museum was considered to be one of the largest state museums in the United States. The museum houses permanent collections highlighting the state's history, as well hosts special exhibits such as the 2006 *Old Glory: An American Treasure Comes Home,* an exhibition celebrating the return of the Civil War Old Glory flag to Tennessee after more than 100 years. The major operatic troupes are Nashville Opera, Knoxville Opera, and Opera Memphis. Opera Memphis celebrated 50 years of performing in 2006.

Nashville is known as "Music City, USA," the Grand Ole Opry, Country Music Hall of Fame, Ryman Auditorium, and numerous recording studios are located there. Among the leading art galleries are the Dixon Gallery and Gardens, the Cheekwood Botanical Gardens and Museum of Art in Nashville, the Knoxville Museum of Art, the Hunter Museum of American Art in Chattanooga, and the Brooks Museum of Art in Memphis founded in 1916—the oldest and largest fine arts museum in the state. The Brooks Museum's permanent collection highlights a variety of genres and eras including the Italian Renaissance and Baroque, French Impressionists, and a number of 20th century artists.

There are several state and local festivals reflecting the music and arts of the state. Elvis Week, in August, is celebrated each year in Memphis. Graceland is the site of the annual Elvis Presley Birthday Celebration (January) and Christmas at Graceland. The Dollywood theme park in Pigeon Force, created by singer Dolly Parton, presents several festivals and musical events each year. The Tennessee Association of Craft Artists presents three annual fairs. The Memphis in May International Festival includes the following programs: the Beale Street Music Festival, International Week, the World Championship Barbecue Cooking Contest, and Sunset Symphony (featuring the Memphis Symphony).

43 LIBRARIES AND MUSEUMS

For the fiscal year ending in June 2001, Tennessee had 184 public library systems, with a total of 285 libraries, of which 101 were branches. In that same year, the state's public libraries had 10,080,000 volumes of books and serial publications, and a total circulation of 21,227,000. The system also had 335,000 audio and 299,000 video items, 9,000 electronic format items (CD-ROMs, magnetic tapes, and disks), and two bookmobiles. Libraries and library associations were formed soon after Tennessee became a state. The Dickson Library at Charlotte was founded in 1811, and the Nashville Library Company in 1813. Not until 1854, however, was the first state-maintained library established. Andrew Johnson, the governor, requested a library appropriation of $5,000, telling legislators that he wanted other Tennesseans to have the opportunities that had been denied him.

Today, the institution he founded, the State Library at Nashville, with more than 637,371 volumes, has a renowned collection of state materials and is the repository for state records. In all, there are 16 public library systems in Tennessee. Their combined book stock exceeds 9.6 million volumes, and their total circulation is over 21 million. The largest libraries are the Vanderbilt University Library at Nashville (2,512,072 volumes), Memphis-Shelby County Library (1,938,685), Memphis State University Libraries (1,067,624), University of Tennessee at Knoxville Library (2,013,273), Knoxville-Knox County Library (865,088), and Chattanooga-Hamilton County Library (806,285). In fiscal year 2001, operating income for the state's public library system totaled $75,791,000 and included $438,000 in federal funds and $1,483,000 in state funds.

Tennessee has more than 127 museums and historic sites. The Tennessee State Museum in Nashville displays exhibits on pioneer life, military traditions, evangelical religion, and presidential lore. The Museum of Appalachia, near Norris, attempts an authentic replica of early Appalachian life, with more than 20,000 pioneer relics on display in several log cabins. Displays of solar, nuclear, and other energy technologies are featured at the American Museum of Science and Energy, at Oak Ridge. There are floral collections at the Goldsmith Civic Garden Center in Memphis, and the Tennessee Botanical Gardens and Fine Arts Center in Nashville.

44 COMMUNICATIONS

The first postal service across the state, by stagecoach, began operations in the early 1790s.

As of 2004, 92.8% of Tennessee's occupied housing units had telephones. Additionally, by June of that same year there were 2,337,367 mobile wireless telephone subscribers. In 2003, 54.9% of Tennessee households had a computer and 45.6% had Internet access. By June 2005, there were 464,917 high-speed lines in Tennessee, 414,608 residential and 50,309 for business.

Tennessee had 30 major AM stations and 80 major FM stations in 2005. There were 31 television stations in operation in 2005. In 1999, the Nashville area had 826,090 television households, 63% of which received cable. The Memphis area had 623,110 television homes, 64% of which ordered cable.

About 81,858 Internet domain names were registered in the state as of 2000.

45PRESS

In 2005, there were 14 morning newspapers, 12 evening dailies, and 18 Sunday papers.

The following table lists leading Tennessee newspapers with their approximate daily circulation in 2005:

AREA	NAME	DAILY	SUNDAY
Chattanooga	Times Free Press (m,S)	86,968	99,775
Knoxville	News-Sentinel (m,S)	113,994	153,278
Memphis	Commercial Appeal (m,S)	179,468	235,889
Nashville	Tennessean (m,S)	170,361	238,126

Several dozen trade publications, such as Southern Lumberman, appear in Nashville, the state's major publishing center, where there is also a thriving religious publishing industry.

46ORGANIZATIONS

In 2006, there were over 4,525 nonprofit organizations registered within the state, of which about 3,275 were registered as charitable, educational, or religious organizations.

Nashville is a center for Tennessee cultural and educational organizations. Among them are the American Association for State and Local History, the International Bluegrass Music Association, the Western Music Association, the Country Music Association, the Tennessee Historical Commission, and the Gospel Music Association. The Center for Southern Folklore is based in Memphis. The Tennessee Folklore Society is in Murfreesboro.

Professional and business associations include the American Board of Veterinary Practitioners, the Southern Cotton Association, National Cotton Council of America, the Tennessee Walking Horse Trainers' Association, and National Hardwood Lumber Manufacturing Association.

Several Christian denominations and organizations have their headquarters or major departmental offices in Tennessee. These include AMG International, Church of God World Missions, Gideons International, the National Association of Free Will Baptists, the National Baptist Convention–USA, the Presbyterian Evangelistic Fellowship, the United Methodist Youth Organization, and the World Convention of Churches of Christ.

47TOURISM, TRAVEL, AND RECREATION

The natural beauty of Tennessee, combined with the activities of the Department of Tourist Development, has made tourism a major industry in the state. Tennessee was the first state to create a government department devoted solely to the promotion of tourism. In 2003, Tennessee employed 141,200 people in tourism related jobs.

Leading tourist attractions include Fort Loudoun, built by the British in 1757; the American Museum of Science and Energy at Oak Ridge; the William Blount Mansion at Knoxville; the Beale Street Historic District in Memphis, home of W. C. Handy, the "father of the blues"; Graceland, the Memphis estate of Elvis Presley, the Sun Music Co. which produced Elvis' records, the National Civil Rights Museum; and Opryland USA and the Grand Ole Opry at Nashville. There are three presidential homes—Andrew Johnson's at Greeneville, Andrew Jackson's Hermitage near Nashville, and James K. Polk's at Columbia. Pinson Mounds, near Jackson, offers outstanding archaeological treasures and the remains of an Indian city. Reservoirs and lakes attract thousands of anglers and water sports enthusiasts. The top attractions in 1998 included (with annual attendance records): Dollywood (2,200,000), Tennessee Aquarium (1,150,148), Bristol Motor Sports (1,050,000), Ober Gatlinburg (1,004,659), and Casey Jones Village (840,000). Memphis hosts the Memphis in May Festival which features jazz, barbecue, art and entertainment throughout the month. The Memphis Zoo is one of three zoos in the United States to feature pandas. Memphis is also home to Federal Express.

There are 33 state parks, almost all of which have camping facilities. Altogether, they cover 88,160 acres (35,678 hectares). Among the most visited state parks are the Meeman-Shelby Forest in Shelby County, Montgomery Bell in Dickson County, Cedars of Lebanon in Wilson County, and Natchez Trace in Henderson and Carroll counties. Cherokee National Park is the most visited national park in Tennessee (10,500,000). Extending into North Carolina, the Great Smoky Mountains National Park covers 241,207 acres (97,613 hectares) in Tennessee and receives approximately nine million visitors annually. Dollywood Amusement Park is in Pigeon Forge in the Great Smoky Mountains. Other popular national parks include the TVA's Land Between the Lakes National Historic Park (2,081,053), Cumberland Gap National Historic Park (1,500,000), and Chickamauga-Chattanooga National Military Park (1,022,500).

48SPORTS

Tennessee has three major professional sports teams, the Titans of the National Football League, who relocated to Nashville from Houston before the 1997 season; the Nashville Predators of the National Hockey League, who began play in 1999; and the Memphis Grizzlies, who relocated to Memphis from Vancouver in 2001. Minor league baseball teams play throughout the state including cities such as Chattanooga, Memphis, Elizabethton, Johnson City, Jackson, Kingsport, Knoxville, Greeneville, and Nashville.

Tennessee's colleges and universities provide the major fall and winter sports. The University of Tennessee Volunteers and Vanderbilt University Commodores, in the Southeastern Conference, compete nationally in football, basketball, and baseball. Austin Peay and Tennessee Technological universities belong to the Ohio Valley Conference. The University of Tennessee won the Sugar Bowl in 1943, 1971, 1986, and 1991, the Fiesta Bowl in 1999, and the Florida Citrus Bowl in 1996 and 1997. The Volunteers were named national champions in 1951 and then again in 1999. The University of Tennessee's women's basketball team, the Lady Vols, won National Collegiate Athletic Association (NCAA) titles in 1987, 1989, 1991, 1996, 1997, and 1998. They have won more games than any other NCAA basketball team in the country. Other annual sporting events include the Iroquois steeplechase in Nashville in May and two NASCAR races at the Bristol Motor Speedway, one in March and one in August. Basketball Hall of

Fame member Oscar Robertson and track and field legend Wilma Rudolph were both born and raised in Tennessee.

⁴⁹FAMOUS TENNESSEANS

Andrew Jackson (b.South Carolina, 1767–1845), the seventh president, moved to Tennessee as a young man. He won renown in the War of 1812 and became the first Democratic president in 1828. Jackson's close friend and associate, James Knox Polk (b.North Carolina, 1795–1849), came to Tennessee at the age of 10. He was elected the nation's 11th president in 1844 and served one term. Andrew Johnson (b.North Carolina, 1808–75) also a Democrat, remained loyal to the Union during the Civil War and was elected vice president with Abraham Lincoln in 1864. He became president upon Lincoln's assassination in 1865 and served out his predecessor's second term. Impeached because of a dispute over Reconstruction policies and presidential power, Johnson escaped conviction by one vote in 1868. Albert Gore Jr. (b.Washington, DC, 1948), was elected vice president in 1992 and 1996 on the Democratic ticket with Bill Clinton; Gore, whose father was a prominent US senator from Tennessee, had previously served in the Senate as well.

Supreme Court justices from Tennessee include John Catron (b.Pennsylvania, 1786–1865), Howell Jackson (1832–95), James C. McReynolds (b.Kentucky, 1862–1946), and Edward T. Sanford (1865–1930). Tennesseans who became cabinet officials include Secretary of State Cordell Hull (1871–1955), secretaries of war John Eaton (1790–1856) and John Bell (1797–1869), Secretary of the Treasury George Campbell (b.Scotland, 1769–1848), and attorneys general Felix Grundy (b.Virginia, 1777–1840) and James C. McReynolds.

Other nationally prominent political figures from Tennessee are Cary Estes Kefauver (1903–63), two-term US senator who ran unsuccessfully for vice president in 1956 on the Democratic ticket; Albert Gore Sr. (1907–98), three-term member of the US Senate; and Howard Baker (b.1925), who in 1966 became the first popularly elected Republican senator in Tennessee history. Three Tennesseans have been speaker of the US House of Representatives: James K. Polk, John Bell, and Joseph W. Byrns (1869–1936). Nancy Ward (1738–1822) was an outstanding Cherokee leader, and Sue Shelton White (1887–1943) played a major role in the campaign for women's suffrage.

Tennessee history features several military leaders and combat heroes. John Sevier (b.Virginia, 1745–1815), the first governor of the state, defeated British troops at Kings Mountain in the Revolution. David "Davy" Crockett (1786–1836) was a frontiersman who fought the British with Jackson in the War of 1812. Sam Houston (b.Virginia, 1793–1863) also fought in the War of 1812 and was governor of Tennessee before migrating to Texas. Nathan Bedford Forrest (1821–77) and Sam Davis (1842–63) were heroes of the Civil War. Sergeant Alvin C. York (1887–1964) won the Medal of Honor for his bravery in World War I.

Cordell Hull was awarded the Nobel Peace Prize in 1945 for his work on behalf of the United Nations. In 1971, Earl W. Sutherland Jr. (b.Kansas 1915–75), a biomedical scientist at Vanderbilt University, won a Nobel Prize for his discoveries concerning the mechanisms of hormones. Outstanding educators include Philip Lindsey (1786–1855), a Presbyterian minister and first president of the University of Nashville, and Alexander Heard (b.Georgia, 1917), nationally known political scientist and chancellor of Vanderbilt University.

Famous Tennessee writers are Mary Noailles Murfree (1850–1922), who used the pseudonym Charles Egbert Craddock; influential poet and critic John Crowe Ransom (1888–1974); author and critic James Agee (1909–55), posthumously awarded a Pulitzer Prize for his novel *A Death in the Family;* poet Randall Jarrell (1914–65), winner of two National Book Awards; and Wilma Dykeman (b.1920), novelist and historian. Peter Taylor (Trenton, Tenn., 1917–94) won a Pulitzer in 1987 for *A Summons to Memphis.* Sportswriter Grantland Rice (1880–1954) was born in Murfreesboro.

Tennessee has long been a center of popular music. Musician and songwriter William C. Handy (1873–1958) wrote "St Louis Blues" and "Memphis Blues," among other classics. Bessie Smith (1898?–1937) was a leading blues singer. Elvis Presley (b.Mississippi, 1935–77) fused rhythm-and-blues with country-and-western styles to become one of the most popular entertainers in US history. Other Tennessee-born singers are Dinah Shore (1917–1994), Aretha Franklin (b.1942), and Dolly Parton (b.1946). Morgan Freeman, star of movies including *Driving Miss Daisy,* was born in Memphis in 1937.

⁵⁰BIBLIOGRAPHY

Atkins, Jonathan M. *Parties, Politics, and the Sectional Conflict in Tennessee, 1832–1861.* Knoxville: University of Tennessee Press, 1997.

Ballard, Michael B. *U. S. Grant: The Making of a General, 1861–1863.* Lanham, Md.: Rowman & Littlefield, 2005.

Council of State Governments. *The Book of the States, 2006 Edition.* Lexington, Ky.: Council of State Governments, 2006.

Feeney, Kathy. *Tennessee Facts and Symbols.* Mankato, Minn.: Bridgestone Books, 2000.

Hsiung, David C. *Two Worlds in the Tennessee Mountains: Exploring the Origins of Appalachian Stereotypes.* Lexington: University Press of Kentucky, 1997.

Kosser, Michael. *How Nashville Became Music City, U.S.A.: 50 Years of Music Row.* Milwaukee, Wis.: Hal Leonard, 2006.

Lepa, Jack H. *Breaking the Confederacy: The Georgia and Tennessee Campaigns of 1864.* Jefferson, N.C.: McFarland, 2005.

Lovett, Bobby L. *The Civil Rights Movement in Tennessee: A Narrative History.* Knoxville: University of Tennessee Press, 2005.

Norman, Corrie E., and Don S. Armentrout (eds.). *Religion in the Contemporary South: Changes, Continuities, and Contexts.* Knoxville: University of Tennessee Press, 2005.

Olmstead, Marty. *Hidden Tennessee.* Berkeley, Calif.: Ulysses Press, 1999.

Patterson, Christine P. *Haunting Memories: Echoes and Images of Tennessee's Past.* Knoxville: University of Tennessee Press, 1996.

US Department of Commerce, Economics and Statistics Administration, US Census Bureau. *Tennessee, 2000. Summary Social, Economic, and Housing Characteristics: 2000 Census of Population and Housing.* Washington, D.C.: US Government Printing Office, 2003.

TEXAS

State of Texas

ORIGIN OF STATE NAME: Derived from the Caddo word *tavshas,* meaning "allies" or "friends." **NICK-NAME:** The Lone Star State. **CAPITAL:** Austin. **ENTERED UNION:** 29 December 1845 (28th). **SONG:** "Texas, Our Texas;" "The Eyes of Texas." **MOTTO:** Friendship. **FLAG:** At the hoist is a vertical bar of blue with a single white five-pointed star; two horizontal bars of white and red cover the remainder of the flag. **OFFICIAL SEAL:** A five-pointed star is encircled by olive and live oak branches, surrounded with the words "The State of Texas." **BIRD:** Mockingbird. **FISH:** Guadalupe bass. **FLOWER:** Bluebonnet; prickly pear cactus (plant). **TREE:** Pecan. **GEM:** Topaz. **LEGAL HOLIDAYS:** New Year's Day, 1 January; Confederate Heroes Day, 19 January; Birthday of Martin Luther King Jr., 3rd Monday in January; Presidents' Day, 3rd Monday in February; Texas Independence Day, 2 March: Cesar Cavez Day, 31 March (optional); Good Friday, Friday before Easter, March or April (optional); San Jacinto Day, 21 April; Memorial Day, last Monday in May; Emancipation Day, 19 June; Independence Day, 4 July; Lyndon B. Johnson's Birthday, 27 August; Labor Day, 1st Monday in September; Rosh Hashanah and Yom Kippur, September or October (optional); Veterans' Day, 11 November; Thanksgiving Day, 4th Thursday in November and the day following; Christmas, 24, 25, and 26 December. **TIME:** 6 AM CST = noon GMT.

¹LOCATION, SIZE, AND EXTENT

Located in the west south-central United States, Texas is the largest of the 48 conterminous states. Texas's US rank slipped to second when Alaska entered the Union in 1959.

The total area of Texas is 266,807 sq mi (691,030 sq km), of which land comprises 262,017 sq mi (678,624 sq km) and inland water 4,790 sq mi (12,406 sq km). The state's land area represents 8.8% of the US mainland and 7.4% of the nation as a whole. The state's maximum E–W extension is 801 mi (1,289 km); its extreme N–S distance is 773 mi (1,244 km).

Texas is bordered on the N by Oklahoma and Arkansas (with part of the line formed by the Red River); on the E by Arkansas and Louisiana (with part of the Louisiana line defined by the Sabine River); on the SE by the Gulf of Mexico; on the SW by the Mexican states of Tamaulipas, Nuevo León, Coahuila, and Chihuahua (with the line formed by the Rio Grande); and on the W by New Mexico. The state's geographic center is in McCulloch County, 15 mi (24 km) NE of Brady.

Large islands in the Gulf of Mexico belonging to Texas are Galveston, Matagorda, and Padre. The boundary length of the state totals 3,029 mi (4,875 km), including a general Gulf of Mexico coastline of 367 mi (591 km); the tidal shoreline is 3,359 mi (5,406 km).

²TOPOGRAPHY

Texas's major physiographic divisions are the Gulf Coastal Plain in the east and southeast; the North Central Plains, covering most of central Texas; the Great Plains, extending from west-central Texas up into the panhandle; and the mountainous trans-Pecos area in the extreme west.

Within the Gulf Coastal Plain are the Piney Woods, an extension of western Louisiana that introduces into East Texas for about 125 mi (200 km), and the Post Oak Belt, a flat region of mixed soil that gives way to the rolling prairie of the Blackland Belt, the state's most densely populated region. The Balcones Escarpment (so-called by the Spanish because its sharp profile suggests a balcony), a geological fault line running from the Rio Grande near Del Rio across central Texas, separates the Gulf Coastal Plain and Rio Grande Plain from the North Central Plains and south-central Hill Country, and in so doing, divides East Texas from West Texas, watered Texas from dry Texas, and (culturally speaking) the Old South from the burgeoning West. Sea level at the Gulf of Mexico is the lowest elevation of the state.

The North Central Plains extend from the Blackland Belt to the Cap Rock Escarpment, a natural boundary carved by erosion to heights of nearly 1,000 ft (300 m) in some places. Much of this plains region is rolling prairie, but the dude ranches of the Hill Country and the mineral-rich Burnet-Llano Basin are also found here. West of the Cap Rock Escarpment are the Great Plains, stretching north–south from the Panhandle Plains to the Edwards Plateau, just north of the Balcones Escarpment. Along the western edge of the panhandle and extending into New Mexico is the Llano Estacado (Staked Plains), an extension of the High Plains lying east of the base of the Rocky Mountains.

The trans-Pecos region, between the Pecos River and the Rio Grande, contains the highest point in the state: Guadalupe Peak, with an altitude of 8,749 ft (2,668 m), part of the Guadalupe Range extending southward from New Mexico into western Texas for about 20 mi (32 km). Also in the trans-Pecos region is the Diablo Plateau, which has no runoff to the sea and holds its scant water in lakes that often evaporate entirely. Farther south are the Davis Mountains, with a number of peaks rising above 7,000 ft (2,100 m), and Big Bend country (surrounded on three sides by the Rio Grande), whose canyons sometimes reach depths of nearly 2,000 ft (600 m). The Chisos Mountains, also exceeding 7,000 ft (2,100

m) at some points stand just north and west of the Rio Grande. The mean elevation of the state is approximately 1,700 ft (519 m).

For its vast expanse, Texas boasts few natural lakes. Caddo Lake, which lies in Texas and Louisiana, is the state's largest natural lake, though its present length of 20 mi (32 km) includes waters added by dam construction in Louisiana. Two artificial reservoirs—Amistad (shared with Mexico), near Del Rio, and Toledo Bend (shared with Louisiana) on the Sabine River—have respective storage capacities exceeding 3 million and 4 million acre-ft, and the Sam Rayburn Reservoir (covering 179 sq mi/464 sq km) has a capacity of 2.9 million acre-ft. All together, the state contains close to 200 major reservoirs, eight of which can store more than 1 million acre-ft of water. From the air, Texas looks as well watered as Minnesota, but the lakes are artificial, and much of the soil is dry.

One reason Texas has so many reservoirs is that it is blessed with a number of major river systems, although none is navigable for more than 50 mi (80 km) inland. Starting from the west, the Rio Grande, a majestic stream in some places but a trickling trough in others, imparts life to the Texas desert and serves as the international boundary with Mexico. Its total length of 1,896 mi (3,051 km), including segments in Colorado and New Mexico, makes the Rio Grande the nation's second-longest river, exceeded only by the Missouri-Mississippi river system. The Colorado River is the longest river wholly within the state, extending about 600 mi (970 km) on its journey across central and southeastern Texas to the Gulf of Mexico. Other important rivers include the Nueces, in whose brushy valley the range cattle industry began; the San Antonio, which stems from springs within the present city limits and flows, like most Texas rivers, to the Gulf of Mexico; the Brazos, which rises in New Mexico and stretches diagonally for about 840 mi (1,350 km) across Texas; the Trinity, which serves Fort Worth and Dallas; the San Jacinto, a short river but one of the most heavily trafficked in North America, overlapping the Houston Ship Channel, which connects the Port of Houston with the Gulf; the Neches, which makes an ocean port out of Beaumont; the Sabine, which has the largest water discharge (6,800,000 acre-ft) at its mouth of any Texas river; the Red, forming part of the northern boundary; and the Canadian, which crosses the Texas panhandle from New Mexico to Oklahoma, bringing moisture to the cattle raisers and wheat growers of that region. In all, Texas has about 3,700 identifiable streams, many of which dry up in the summer and flood during periods of rainfall.

Because of its extensive outcroppings of limestone, extending westward from the Balcones Escarpment, Texas contains a maze of caverns. Among the better-known caves are Longhorn Cavern in Burnet County; Wonder Cave, near San Marcos; the Caverns of Sonora, at Sonora; and Jack Pit Cave, in Menard County, which, with 19,000 ft (5,800 m) of passages, is the most extensive cave yet mapped in the state.

About 1 billion years ago, shallow seas covered much of Texas. After the seas receded, the land dropped gradually over millions of years, leaving a thick sediment that was then compressed into a long mountain range called the Ouachita Fold Belt. The sea was eventually restricted to a zone in West Texas called the Permian Basin, a giant evaporation pan holding gypsum and salt deposits hundreds of feet deep. As the mountain chain across central Texas eroded and the land continued to subside, the Rocky Mountains were uplifted, leaving deep cuts in Big Bend country and creating the Llano Estacado. The Gulf of Mexico subsided rapidly, depositing sediment accumulations several thousand feet deep, while salt domes formed over vast petroleum and sulfur deposits. All this geologic activity also deposited quicksilver in the Terlingua section of the Big Bend, built up the Horseshoe Atoll (a buried reef in west-central Texas that is the largest limestone reservoir in the nation), created uranium deposits in southern Texas, and preserved the oil-bearing Jurassic rocks of the northeast.

3 CLIMATE

Texas's great size and topographic variety make climatic description difficult. Brownsville, at the mouth of the Rio Grande, has had no measurable snowfall during all the years that records have been kept, but Vega, in the panhandle, averages 23 in (58 cm) of snowfall per year. Near the Louisiana border, rainfall exceeds 56 in (142 cm) annually, while in parts of extreme West Texas, rainfall averages less than 8 in (20 cm). Average annual precipitation in Dallas is about 33.3 in (84 cm); in El Paso, 8.6 in (21 cm); and in Houston, 47.8 in (121.4 cm).

Generally, a maritime climate prevails along the Gulf coast, with continental conditions inland; the Balcones Escarpment is the main dividing line between the two zones, but they are not completely isolated from each other's influence. Texas has two basic seasons—a hot summer that may last from April through October, and a winter that starts in November and usually lasts until March. When summer ends, the state is too dry for autumn foliage, except in East Texas. Temperatures in El Paso, in the southwest, range from an average January minimum of 31°F (0°C) to an average July maximum of 95°F (35°C); at Amarillo, in the panhandle, from 22°F (-5°C) in January to 91°F (32°C) in July; and at Galveston, on the Gulf, from 48°F (9°C) in January to 88°F (31°C) in August. Perhaps the most startling contrast is in relative humidity, averaging 59% in the morning in El Paso, 73% in Amarillo, and 83% in Galveston. In the Texas panhandle, the average date of the first freeze is 1 November; in the lower Rio Grande Valley, 16 December. The last freeze arrives in the panhandle on 15 April, and in the lower Rio Grande Valley on 30 January. The valley thus falls only six weeks short of having a 12-month growing season while the panhandle approximates the growing season of the upper Midwest.

Record temperatures range from -23°F (-31°C) at Seminole, on 8 February 1933, to 120°F (49°C) at Seymour in north-central Texas on 12 August 1936. The greatest annual rainfall was 109 in (277 cm), measured in 1873 at Clarksville, just below the Red River in northeast Texas; the least annual rainfall, 1.786 in (4.47 cm), was recorded at Wink, near the New Mexico line, in 1956. Thrall, in central Texas, received 38.2 in (97 cm) of rain in 24 hours on 9–10 September 1921. Alvin, in Brazoria County on the Gulf Coast, had 43 in (109 cm) of rain on 25–26 July 1979, a national record for the most rainfall during a 24-hour period. Romero, on the New Mexico border, received a record 65 in (165 cm) of snow in the winter of 1923–24, and Hale Center, near Lubbock, measured 33 in (84 cm) during one storm in February 1956. The highest sustained wind velocity in Texas history, 145 mph (233 km/hr), occurred when Hurricane Carla hit Matagorda and Port Lavaca along the Gulf coast on 11 September 1961.

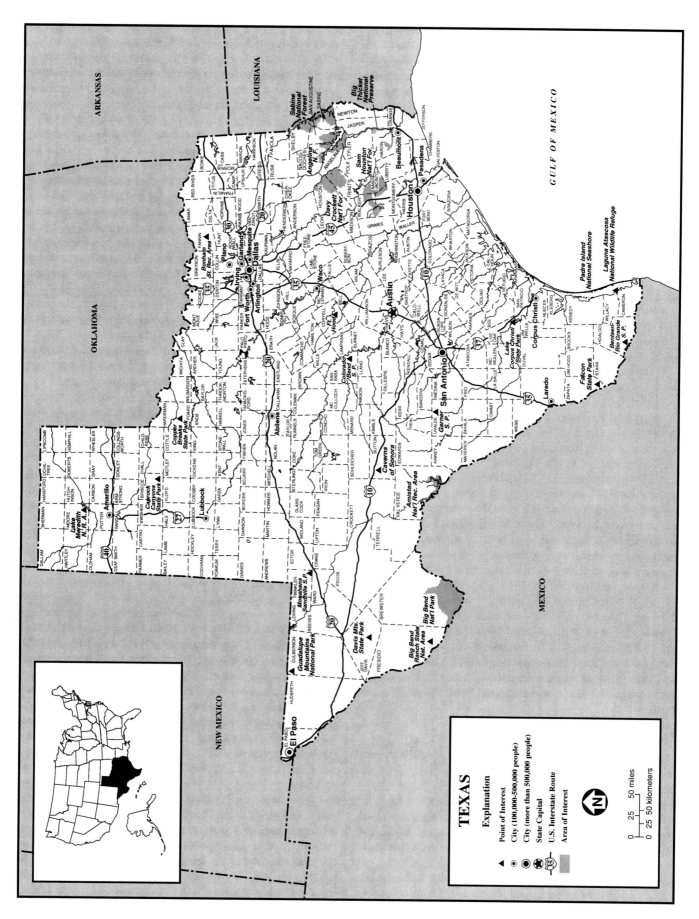

Hurricanes strike the Gulf coast about once every decade, usually in September or October. A hurricane on 19–20 August 1886 leveled the port of Indianola; the town (near present-day Port Lavaca) was never rebuilt. Galveston was the site of the most destructive storm in US history: on 8–9 September 1900, a hurricane blew across the island of 38,000 residents, leaving at least 6,000 dead (the exact total has never been ascertained) and leveling most of the city. A storm of equal intensity hit Galveston in mid-August 1915, but this time, the city was prepared; its new seawall held the toll to 275 deaths and $50 million worth of property damage. Because of well-planned damage-prevention and evacuation procedures, Hurricane Carla—at least as powerful as any previous hurricane—claimed no more than 34 lives.

Texas was not left unscathed by the hurricane season of 2005, which devastated much of the Gulf Coast region, particularly in Louisiana, Mississippi, and Florida. Hurricane Katrina, which made landfall at Buras, Louisiana on 29 August 2005, caused damage to Texas-operated oil production sites in the Gulf of Mexico. This led to the reduction of oil production by 95% during the immediate aftermath of the storm. Thousands of residents from New Orleans were evacuated to locations in Texas as 80% of their city was flooded by the storm and resulting levee damage. A month later, Hurricane Rita made landfall near the Texas–Louisiana border on 24 September 2005 as a Category 3 storm. Two oil refineries in Port Arthur were damaged and extensive flooding occurred in the region. As of early 2006, the estimated cost of damage for Hurricane Rita was about $10 billion in total losses.

Texas also lies in the path of "Tornado Alley," stretching across the Great Plains to Canada. The worst tornado in recent decades struck downtown Waco on 11 May 1953, killing 114 persons, injuring another 597, and destroying or damaging some 1,050 homes and 685 buildings. At least 115 tornadoes—the greatest concentration on record—occurred with Hurricane Beulah during 19–23 September 1967; the 67 tornadoes on 20 September set a record for the largest number of tornadoes on one day in the state.

Floods and droughts have also taken their toll in Texas. The worst flood occurred on 26–28 June 1954, when Hurricane Alice moved inland up the Rio Grande for several hundred miles, dropping 27 in (69 cm) of rain on Pandale above Del Rio. The Rio Grande rose 50 to 60 ft (15–18 m) within 48 hours, as a wall of water 86 ft (26 m) high in the Pecos River canyon fed it from the north. A Pecos River bridge built with a 50-ft (15-m) clearance was washed out, as was the international bridge linking Laredo with Mexico. Periodic droughts afflicted Texas in the 1930s and 1950s.

4 FLORA AND FAUNA

More than 500 species of grasses covered Texas when the Spanish and Anglo-Americans arrived. Although plowing and lack of soil conservation destroyed a considerable portion of this rich heritage, grassy pastureland still covers about two-thirds of the state. Bermuda grass is a favorite ground cover, especially an improved type called Coastal Bermuda, introduced after World War II. The prickly pear cactus is a mixed blessing: like the cedar and mesquite, it saps moisture and inhibits grass growth, but it does retain moisture in periods of drought and will survive the worst dry spells, so (with the spines burned off) it can be of great value to ranchers as cattle feed in difficult times. The bean of the mesquite also provides food for horses and cattle when they have little else to eat, and its wood is a favorite in barbecues and fireplaces.

Texas has more than 20 native trees, of which the catclaw, flowering mimosa, huisache, black persimmon, huajillo, and weeping juniper (unique to the Big Bend) are common only in Texas. Cottonwood grows along streams in almost every part of the state, while cypress inhabits the swamps. The flowering dogwood in East Texas draws tourists to that region every spring, and the largest bois d'arc trees in the United States are grown in the Red River Valley. Probably the most popular shade tree is the American (white) elm, which, like the gum tree, has considerable commercial importance. The magnolia is treasured for its grace and beauty; no home of substance in southeastern Texas would have a lawn without one. Of the principal hardwoods, the white oak is the most commercially valuable, the post oak the most common, and the live oak the most desirable for shade; the pecan is the state tree. Pines grow in two areas about 600 mi (970 km) apart—deep East Texas and the trans-Pecos region. In southeast Texas stands the Big Thicket, a unique area originally covering more than 3 million acres (1.2 million hectares) but now reduced to about one-tenth of that by lumbering. Gonzales County, in south-central Texas, is the home of palmettos, orchids, and other semitropical plants not found anywhere else in the state. Texas wild rice and several cactus species are classified as endangered throughout the state.

Possibly the rarest mammal in Texas is the red wolf, which inhabits the marshland between Houston and Beaumont, one of the most thickly settled areas of the state; owing to human encroachment and possible hybridization with coyotes, the red wolf is steadily disappearing despite efforts by naturalists throughout the United States to save it. On the other hand, Texans claim to have the largest number of white-tailed deer of any state in the Union, an estimated 3 million. Although the Hill Country is the white-tailed deer's natural habitat, the species has been transplanted successfully throughout the state.

Perhaps the most unusual mammal in Texas is the nine-banded armadillo. Originally confined to the Rio Grande border, the armadillo has gradually spread northward and eastward, crossing the Red River into Oklahoma and the Mississippi River into the Deep South. It accomplished these feats of transport by sucking in air until it becomes buoyant and then swimming across the water. The armadillo is likewise notable for always having its young in litters of identical quadruplets. The chief mammalian predators are the coyote, bobcat, and mountain lion.

Texas attracts more than 825 different kinds of birds, with bird life most abundant in the lower Rio Grande Valley and coastal plains. Argument continues as to whether Texas is the last home of the ivory-billed woodpecker, which lives in inaccessible swamps, preferably in cutover timber. Somewhat less rare is the pileated woodpecker, which also inhabits the forested lowlands. Other characteristic birds include the yellow-trimmed hooded warbler, which frequents the canebrakes and produces one of the most melodious songs of any Texas bird; the scissor-tailed flycatcher, known popularly as the scissor-tail; Attwater's greater prairie chicken, now declining because of inadequate protection from hunters and urbanization; the mockingbird, the state bird; and the roadrunner, also known as paisano and chaparral. Rare birds include the Mexican jacana, with a flesh comb and bright yellow-green wings; the white-throated swift, one of the world's fastest flyers; the Texas canyon wren, with a musical range of more than an octave; and the Colima warbler, which breeds only in the Chisos Mountains. In the Arkansas National Wildlife Refuge, along the central Gulf coast, lives the whooping crane, which has long been on the endangered list. Controversy surrounds the golden eagle, protected by federal law but despised by ranchers for allegedly preying on lambs and other young livestock.

Texas has its fair share of reptiles, including more than 100 species of snake, 16 of them poisonous, notably the deadly Texas coral snake. There are 10 kinds of rattlesnake, and some parts of West Texas hold annual rattlesnake roundups. Disappearing with the onset of urbanization are the horned toad, a small iguana-like lizard; the vinegarroon, a stinging scorpion; and the tarantula, a large, black, hairy spider that is scary to behold but basically harmless.

Caddo Lake, a Ramsar Wetland of International Importance, is considered to be the site of the most diverse, native freshwater fish communities in the state. These include the American paddlefish and the American eel. The area contains what is considered to be one of the best examples of a mature bald cypress swampland in the southern states. Inventories of the species found in the wetland include 189 species of trees and shrubs, 75 grasses, 42 woody vines, and 802 herbaceous plants. Animal life includes 216 species of bird, 47 mammal species, and 90 types of reptiles and amphibians.

In addition to providing protection for the animals on federal lists of threatened and endangered species, the state has its own wildlife protection programs. Among the animals classified as non-game (not hunted) and therefore given special consideration are the lesser yellow bat, spotted dolphin, reddish egret, white-tailed hawk, wood stork, Big Bend gecko, rock rattlesnake, Louisiana pine snake, white-lipped frog, giant toad, toothless blindcat, and blue sucker. In April 2006, The US Fish and Wildlife Service listed 28 Texas plant species as threatened or endangered, including ashy dogwood, black lace cactus, large-fruited sand-verbena, South Texas ambrosia, Terlingua creek cats-eye, Texas snowbells, Texas trailing phlox, and Texas wild-rice. In the same report, 62 animal species were listed as threatened or endangered in Texas (up from 43 in 1997), including the Mexican long-nosed bat, Louisiana black bear, bald eagle, ocelot, Mexican spotted owl, Texas blind salamander, Houston toad, black-capped vireo, two species of whale, and five species of turtle.

[5] ENVIRONMENTAL PROTECTION

Conservation in Texas officially began with the creation of a State Department of Forestry in 1915; 11 years later, this body was reorganized as the Texas Forest Service, the name it retains today. The state's Soil Conservation Service was created in 1935.

The scarcity of water is the one environmental crisis every Texan must live with. Much of the state has absorbent soils, a high evaporation rate, vast areas without trees to hold moisture, and a rolling terrain susceptible to rapid runoff. The Texas Water Commission and Water Development Board direct the state's water supply and conservation programs. Various county and regional water authorities have been constituted, as have several water commissions for river systems. Probably the most complete system is that of the three Colorado River authorities—lower, central, and upper. The oldest of these is the Lower Colorado River Authority, created in 1934 by the Texas legislature to "control, store, preserve, and distribute" the waters of the Colorado River and its feeder streams. The authority exercises control over a 10-county area stretching from above Austin to the Gulf coast, overseeing flood control, municipal and industrial water supplies, irrigation, hydroelectric power generation, soil conservation, and recreation.

There are about 7.6 million acres (3 million hectares) of wetlands in the state, accounting for about 4.4% of the total land area. Caddo Lake, in Harrison and Marion Counties, was designated as a Ramsar Wetland of International Importance in 1993. Management for the site is under the Texas Parks and Wildlife Department.

The most powerful conservation agency in Texas is the Railroad Commission. Originally established to regulate railroads, the commission extended its power to regulate oil and natural gas by virtue of its jurisdiction over the transportation of those products by rail and pipeline. In 1917, the state legislature empowered the commission to prevent the waste of oil and gas. The key step in conservation arrived with the discovery of oil in East Texas in 1930. With a national depression in full swing and the price of oil dropping to $1 a barrel, the commission agreed to halt ruinous overproduction, issuing the first proration order in April 1931. In a field composed of hundreds of small owners, however, control was difficult to establish; oil was bootlegged, the commission's authority broke down, Governor Ross S. Sterling declared martial law, and the state's conservation edicts were not heeded until the federal government stepped in to enforce them. As of 2003, the Railroad Commission is comprised of four divisions that oversee the state's oil and gas industry, gas utilities, pipeline and rail safety, safety in the liquefied petroleum gas industry, and coal and uranium mining.

As in other states, hazardous wastes have become an environmental concern in Texas. In 1984, for example, a suit was brought against eight oil and chemical companies, including both Exxon and Shell Oil, alleging that they had dumped hazardous wastes at four sites in Harris County. The agency that oversees compliance with hazardous-waste statutes is the Hazardous and Solid Waste Division of the Texas Water Commission. In 2003, some 261.9 million lb of toxic chemicals were released in the state. That year, Texas ranked third of all the states in the nation for the highest levels of toxic chemicals released (following Alaska and Nevada). In 2003, Texas had 298 hazardous waste sites listed in the US Environment Protection Agency (EPA) database, 43 of which were on the National Priorities List as of 2006, including Crystal City Airport and two Army ammunitions plants (in Texarkana and Karnack). In 2005, the EPA spent over $11.5 million through the Superfund program for the cleanup of hazardous waste sites in the state. The same year, federal EPA grants awarded to the state included $49.2 million to provide loans for wastewater system improvements to municipalities and interstate agencies.

The state has lost about one-half of its original wetlands, which reportedly covered about 5% of the state's total land area in 2003. The three agencies that define wetlands disagree on the total wetlands are in the state, with estimates ranging from about 6 million acres (2.4 million hectares) to 8 million acres (3.2 million hectares).

6 POPULATION

In 1998 Texas overtook New York as the nation's second most populous state. Between 1990 and 2000 Texas's population grew from 16,986,510 to 20,851,820, a gain of 22.8%, and the second-largest increase for the decade among the 50 states. The state had placed fourth in the 1970 census, with a population of 11,196,730, but had surpassed Pennsylvania in 1974. The estimated population as of 2005 was 22,859,968, an increase of 9.6% since 2000. The population is projected to reach 26.5 million by 2015 and 30.8 million by 2025. The population density in 2004 was 86 persons per sq mi.

At the first decennial census of 1850, less than five years after Texas had become a state, the population totaled 212,592. It reached 1,600,000 by the early 1880s (when the state ranked eleventh), passed 4,000,000 during World War I, and jumped to 7,700,000 in 1950. The slowest period of growth occurred during the Depression decade (1930–40) when the population rose only 10%, and the state was surpassed by California. The growth rate ranged between 17% and 27% for each decade from the 1940s through the 1970s; it was 19.4% between 1980 and 1990.

In 1870, only one out of 68 Texans was 65 years of age or older; by 1990, the proportion was one out of 10. In 2004, the median age for Texans was 32.9. In the same year, 27.9% of the populace were under age 18 while 9.9% was age 65 or older.

The largest metropolitan area in 2004 was Dallas–Fort Worth–Arlington with an estimated 5,700,256 people. Close behind was the Houston–Sugar Land–Baytown area, with 5,180,443 residents. Houston, the largest city proper in Texas and fourth-largest city in the United States, had an estimated 2004 population of 2,012,626. San Antonio proper, the eighth-largest city in the United States, had an estimated population of 1,236,249. Next was Dallas (ninth in the nation), with 1,210,393; followed by Austin, 681,804; Fort Worth, 603,337; El Paso, 592,099; Arlington, 359,467; and Corpus Christi, 281,196. With the exception of El Paso, in the far western corner of the trans-Peco region, most of the larger cities are situated along the Gulf coast or on or near an axis that extends north–south from Wichita Falls to Corpus Christi, in the heart of the Blackland Belt.

7 ETHNIC GROUPS

As white settlers pushed toward Texas during the 19th century, many Indian groups moved west and south into the region. The most notable tribes were the Comanche, Wichita, Kiowa, Apache, Choctaw, and Cherokee. Also entering in significant numbers were the Kickapoo and Potawatomi from Illinois, the Delaware and Shawnee from Missouri, the Quapaw from Arkansas, and the Creek from Alabama and Georgia. One of the few Texas tribes that has survived to the present time as an identifiable group is the Alabama-Coushatta, who inhabit a 4,351-acre (1,761-hectare) reservation in Polk County, 90 mi (145 km) northeast of Houston. The Tigua, living in Texas since the 1680s, were recognized by a federal law in 1968 that transferred all responsibility for them to the state of Texas. The two Indian reservations number about 500 persons each. Overall, at the 2000 census, there were 118,362 American Indians living in Texas. In 2004, 0.7% of the state's population was American Indian.

Blacks have been integral to the history of Texas ever since a black Moor named Estevanico was shipwrecked near present-day Galveston in 1528. By 1860, Texas had 182,921 blacks, or 30% of the total population, of whom only 355 were free. Once emancipated, blacks made effective use of the franchise, electing two of their number to the state Senate and nine to the House in 1868. After the return of the Democratic Party to political dominance, however, the power of blacks steadily diminished. Since then, their numbers have grown, but their proportion of the total population has dwindled, although Houston and Dallas were, respectively, about 25% and 26% black at the 2000 census. In 2000, 2,404,566 blacks lived in the state, which ranked second behind New York in the size of its black population. In 2004, 11.7% of the state's population was black.

Hispanics and Latinos, the largest minority in Texas, numbered 6,669,666 in 2000, representing 32% of the population, an increase over 1990, when Texans of Hispanic origin represented 25.5% of the total. In 2004, 34.6% of the population was Hispanic or Latino. Mostly of Mexican ancestry, they are nevertheless a heterogeneous group, divided by history, geography, and economic circumstances. Hispanics have been elected to the state legislature and to the US Congress. In 1980, the Houston independent school district, the state's largest, reported more Hispanic students than Anglos for the first time in its history.

Altogether, Texas has nearly 30 identifiable ethnic groups. Certain areas of central Texas are heavily Germanic and Czech. The first permanent Polish colony in the United States was established at Panna Maria, near San Antonio, in 1854. Texas has one of the largest colonies of Wends in the world, principally at Serbin in central Texas. Significant numbers of Danes, Swedes, and Norwegians have also settled in Texas.

As of 2000, foreign-born Texans numbered 2,899,642 (13.9% of the total population). In the same year, Asians numbered 562,319 (the third-largest Asian population among the 50 states). The 2000 census counted 105,829 Chinese (nearly double the 1990 total of 55,023), 58,340 Filipinos, 129,365 Asian Indians (more than triple the 1990 figure of 40,506), 45,571 Koreans, 17,120 Japanese, and 10,114 Laotians. Of the 134,961 Vietnamese (up from 60,649 in 1990), many were refugees who resettled in Texas beginning in 1975. Pacific Islanders numbered 14,434 in 2000. In 2004, 3.2% of the population was Asian, and 0.1% Pacific Islander. In 2004, 1% of the population reported origin of two or more races.

The term "Anglos" denotes all whites except Spanish-surnamed or Spanish-speaking individuals.

8 LANGUAGES

The Indians of Texas are mostly descendants of the Alabama-Coushatta who came to Texas in the 19th century. The few Indian place-names include Texas itself, Pecos, Waco, and Toyah.

Most of the regional features in Texas English derive from the influx of South Midland and Southern speakers, with a noticeable Spanish flavor from older as well as more recent loans. Settlers from the Gulf Coast states brought such terms as *snap beans* (green beans), the widespread *pail* (here probably of Southern rather the Northern origin), and *carry* (escort), with a 47% frequency in north Texas and 22% in the south. Louisiana *praline*

Texas—Counties, County Seats, and County Areas and Populations

COUNTY	COUNTY SEAT	LAND AREA (SQ MI)	POPULATION (2005 EST.)	COUNTY	COUNTY SEAT	LAND AREA (SQ MI)	POPULATION (2005 EST.)
Anderson	Palestine	1,077	56,408	Edwards	Rocksprings	2,120	1,987
Andrews	Andrews	1,501	12,748	Ellis	Waxahachie	939	133,474
Angelina	Lufkin	807	81,557	El Paso	El Paso	1,014	721,598
Aransas	Rockport	280	24,640	Erath	Stephenville	1,080	34,076
Archer	Archer City	907	9,095	Falls	Marlin	770	17,646
Armstrong	Claude	910	2,173	Fannin	Bonham	895	33,142
Atascosa	Jourdanton	1,218	43,226	Fayette	La Grange	950	22,537
Austin	Bellville	656	26,123	Fisher	Roby	897	4,089
Bailey	Muleshoe	827	6,726	Floyd	Floydada	992	7,174
Bandera	Bandera	793	19,988	Foard	Crowell	703	1,518
Bastrop	Bastrop	895	69,932	Fort Bend	Richmond	876	463,650
Baylor	Seymour	862	3,843	Franklin	Mt. Vernon	294	10,200
Bee	Beeville	880	32,873	Freestone	Fairfield	888	18,800
Bell	Belton	1,055	256,057	Frio	Pearsall	1,133	16,387
Bexar	San Antonio	1,248	1,518,370	Gaines	Seminole	1,504	14,712
Blanco	Johnson City	714	9,110	Galveston	Galveston	399	277,563
Borden	Gail	900	648	Garza	Post	895	5,002
Bosque	Meridian	989	18,053	Gillespie	Fredericksburg	1,061	23,088
Bowie	Boston	891	90,643	Glasscock	Garden City	900	1,327
Brazoria	Angleton	1,407	278,484	Goliad	Goliad	859	7,102
Brazos	Bryan	588	156,305	Gonzales	Gonzales	1,068	19,587
Brewster	Alpine	6,169	9,079	Gray	Pampa	921	21,479
Briscoe	Silverton	887	1,644	Grayson	Sherman	934	116,834
Brooks	Falfurrias	942	7,687	Gregg	Longview	273	115,649
Brown	Brownwood	936	38,664	Grimes	Anderson	799	25,192
Burleson	Caldwell	668	17,238	Guadalupe	Seguin	713	103,032
Burnet	Burnet	994	41,676	Hale	Plainview	1,005	36,233
Caldwell	Lockhart	546	36,523	Hall	Memphis	876	3,700
Calhoun	Port Lavaca	540	20,606	Hamilton	Hamilton	836	8,105
Callahan	Baird	899	13,516	Hansford	Spearman	921	5,230
Cameron	Brownsville	905	378,311	Hardeman	Quanah	688	4,291
Camp	Pittsburg	203	12,238	Hardin	Kountze	898	50,976
Carson	Panhandle	924	6,586	Harris	Houston	1,734	3,693,050
Cass	Linden	937	30,155	Harrison	Marshall	908	63,459
Castro	Dimmitt	899	7,640	Hartley	Channing	1,462	5,450
Chambers	Anahuac	616	28,411	Haskell	Haskell	901	5,541
Cherokee	Rusk	1,052	48,464	Hays	San Marcos	678	124,432
Childress	Childress	707	7,676	Hemphill	Canadian	903	3,422
Clay	Henrietta	1,085	11,287	Henderson	Athens	888	80,017
Cochran	Morton	775	3,289	Hidalgo	Edinburg	1,569	678,275
Coke	Robert Lee	908	3,612	Hill	Hillsboro	968	35,424
Coleman	Coleman	1,277	8,665	Hockley	Levelland	908	22,787
Collin	McKenney	851	659,457	Hood	Granbury	425	47,930
Collingsworth	Wellington	909	2,968	Hopkins	Sulphur Springs	789	33,381
Colorado	Columbus	964	20,736	Houston	Crockett	1,234	23,218
Comal	New Braunfels	555	96,018	Howard	Big Spring	901	32,522
Comanche	Comanche	930	13,709	Hudspeth	Sierra Blanca	4,566	3,295
Concho	Paint Rock	992	3,735	Hunt	Greenville	840	82,543
Cooke	Gainesville	893	38,847	Hutchinson	Stinnett	871	22,484
Coryell	Gatesville	1,057	75,802	Irion	Mertzon	1,052	1,756
Cottle	Paducah	895	1,746	Jack	Jacksboro	920	9,064
Crane	Crane	782	3,837	Jackson	Edna	844	14,339
Crockett	Ozona	2,806	3,934	Jasper	Jasper	921	35,587
Crosby	Crosbyton	898	6,686	Jeff Davis	Ft. Davis	2,258	2,306
Culberson	Van Horn	3,815	2,627	Jefferson	Beaumont	937	247,571
Dallam	Dalhart	1,505	6,174	Jim Hogg	Hebbronville	1,136	5,029
Dallas	Dallas	880	2,305,454	Jim Wells	Alice	867	40,951
Dawson	Lamesa	903	14,256	Johnson	Cleburne	731	146,376
Deaf Smith	Hereford	1,497	18,538	Jones	Anson	931	19,736
Delta	Cooper	278	5,480	Karnes	Karnes City	753	15,351
Denton	Denton	911	554,642	Kaufman	Kaufman	788	89,129
DeWitt	Cuero	910	20,507	Kendall	Boerne	663	28,607
Dickens	Dickens	907	2,646	Kenedy	Sarita	1,389	417
Dimmit	Carrizo Springs	1,307	10,395	Kent	Jayton	878	782
Donley	Clarendon	929	3,889	Kerr	Kerrville	1,107	46,496
Duval	San Diego	1,795	12,578	Kimble	Junction	1,250	4,591
Eastland	Eastland	924	18,393	King	Guthrie	914	307
Ector	Odessa	903	125,339	Kinney	Brackettville	1,359	3,327

Texas—Counties, County Seats, and County Areas and Populations (cont.)

COUNTY	COUNTY SEAT	LAND AREA (SQ MI)	POPULATION (2005 EST.)	COUNTY	COUNTY SEAT	LAND AREA (SQ MI)	POPULATION (2005 EST.)
Kleberg	Kingsville	853	30,757	Roberts	Miami	915	820
Knox	Benjamin	845	3,781	Robertson	Franklin	864	16,192
Lamar	Paris	919	49,644	Rockwall	Rockwall	128	62,944
Lamb	Littlefield	1,013	14,467	Runnels	Ballinger	1,056	10,974
Lampasas	Lampasas	714	19,669	Rusk	Henderson	932	47,971
La Salle	Cotulla	1,517	6,016	Sabine	Hemphill	486	10,416
Lavaca	Hallettsville	971	18,925	San Augustine	San Augustine	524	8,907
Lee	Giddings	631	16,526	San Jacinto	Coldspring	572	24,801
Leon	Centerville	1,078	16,344	San Patricio	Sinton	693	69,209
Liberty	Liberty	1,174	75,141	San Saba	San Saba	1,136	6,076
Limestone	Groesbeck	931	22,763	Schleicher	Eldorado	1,309	2,742
Lipscomb	Lipscomb	933	3,101	Scurry	Snyder	900	16,217
Live Oak	George West	1,057	11,717	Shackelford	Albany	915	3,167
Llano	Llano	939	18,236	Shelby	Center	791	26,346
Loving	Mentone	671	62	Sherman	Stratford	923	3,002
Lubbock	Lubbock	900	252,284	Smith	Tyler	932	190,594
Lynn	Tahoka	888	6,237	Somervell	Glen Rose	188	7,578
McCulloch	Brady	1,071	7,956	Starr	Rio Grande City	1,226	60,941
McLennan	Waco	1,031	224,668	Stephens	Breckenridge	894	9,561
McMullen	Tilden	1,163	883	Sterling	Sterling City	923	1,303
Madison	Madisonville	473	13,167	Stonewall	Aspermont	925	1,372
Marion	Jefferson	385	10,952	Sutton	Sonora	1,455	4,212
Martin	Stanton	914	4,391	Swisher	Tulia	902	7,828
Mason	Mason	934	3,880	Tarrant	Ft. Worth	868	1,620,479
Matagorda	Bay City	1,127	37,849	Taylor	Abilene	917	125,039
Maverick	Eagle Pass	1,287	51,181	Terrell	Sanderson	2,357	996
Medina	Hondo	1,331	43,027	Terry	Brownfield	886	12,419
Menard	Menard	902	2,201	Throckmorton	Throckmorton	912	1,618
Midland	Midland	902	121,371	Titus	Mt. Pleasant	412	29,445
Milam	Cameron	1,019	25,354	Tom Green	San Angelo	1,515	103,611
Mills	Goldthwaite	748	5,237	Travis	Austin	989	888,185
Mitchell	Colorado City	912	9,413	Trinity	Groveton	692	14,363
Montague	Montague	928	19,677	Tyler	Woodville	922	20,617
Montgomery	Conroe	1,047	378,033	Upshur	Gilmer	587	37,881
Moore	Dumas	905	20,348	Upton	Rankin	1,243	3,056
Morris	Daingerfield	256	12,936	Uvalde	Uvalde	1,564	26,955
Motley	Matador	959	1,299	Val Verde	Del Rio	3,150	47,596
Nacogdoches	Nacogdoches	939	60,468	Van Zandt	Canton	855	52,491
Navarro	Corsicana	1,068	48,687	Victoria	Victoria	887	85,648
Newton	Newton	935	14,309	Walker	Huntsville	786	62,735
Nolan	Sweetwater	915	14,878	Waller	Hempstead	514	34,821
Nueces	Corpus Christi	847	319,704	Ward	Monahans	836	10,237
Ochiltree	Perryton	919	9,385	Washington	Brenham	610	31,521
Oldham	Vega	1,485	2,118	Webb	Laredo	3,363	224,695
Orange	Orange	362	84,983	Wharton	Wharton	1,086	41,554
Palo Pinto	Palo Pinto	949	27,478	Wheeler	Wheeler	905	4,799
Panola	Carthage	812	22,997	Wichita	Wichita Falls	606	125,894
Parker	Weatherford	902	102,801	Wilbarger	Vernon	947	13,896
Parmer	Farwell	885	9,754	Willacy	Raymondville	589	20,382
Pecos	Ft. Stockton	4,776	15,859	Williamson	Georgetown	1,137	333,457
Polk	Livingston	1,061	46,640	Wilson	Floresville	807	37,529
Potter	Amarillo	902	119,852	Winkler	Kermit	840	6,690
Presidio	Marfa	3,857	7,722	Wise	Decatur	902	56,696
Rains	Emory	243	11,305	Wood	Quitman	689	40,855
Randall	Canyon	917	110,053	Yoakum	Plains	800	7,408
Reagan	Big Lake	1,173	2,995	Young	Graham	919	18,000
Real	Leakey	697	3,031	Zapata	Zapata	999	13,373
Red River	Clarksville	1,054	13,575	Zavala	Crystal City	1,298	11,796
Reeves	Pecos	2,626	11,638	**TOTALS**		**262,015**	**22,859,968**
Refugio	Refugio	771	7,639				

(pecan patty) is now widespread, but *banquette* (sidewalk) appears only in the extreme southeast corner.

Southern and South Midland terms were largely introduced by settlers from Arkansas, Missouri, and Tennessee; their use ranges from northeast to west, but with declining frequency in the trans-Pecos area. Examples are *clabber cheese* (cottage cheese), *mosquito hawk* (dragonfly), *croker sack* (burlap bag), *mouth harp* (harmonica), *branch* (stream), and *dog irons* (andirons). A dialect survey showed *pallet* (bed on the floor) with a 90% overall frequency; *light bread* (white bread) and *pullybone* (wishbone), each 78%; and *you-all,* more than 80%. General Midland terms also widespread in the state are *sook!* (call to calves), *blinds* (roller shades), *piece* (a certain distance), and *quarter till five* (4:45).

Some terms exhibit uneven distribution. Examples include *mott* (clump of trees) in the south and southwest, *sugan* (a wool-filled comforter for a cowboy's bedroll) in the west, Midland *draw* (dry streambed) in the west and southwest, South Midland *peckerwood* (woodpecker) in most of the state except west of the Pecos, *poke* (paper bag) in the central and northern areas, and *surly* (euphemism for bull) in the west. A curious result of dialect mixture is the appearance of a number of hybrids combining two different dialects, such as *freeseed peach* from *freestone* and *clearseed, fire mantel* and *mantel board* from *fireboard* and *mantel, flapcakes* from *flapjacks* and *pancakes,* and *horse doctor* from *horsefly* and *snake doctor.* The large sandwich is known as a *torpedo* in San Antonio and a *poorboy* in Houston.

In 2000, 13,230,765 Texans—68.8% of the population five years old or older—spoke only English at home, down from 74.6% in 1990.

The following table gives selected statistics from the 2000 Census for language spoken at home by persons five years old and over. The category "African languages" includes Amharic, Ibo, Twi, Yoruba, Bantu, Swahili, and Somali. The category "Other Asian languages" includes Dravidian languages, Malayalam, Telugu, Tamil, and Turkish. The category "Other Indic languages" includes Bengali, Marathi, Punjabi, and Romany. The category "Other Slavic languages" includes Czech, Slovak, and Ukrainian.

LANGUAGE	NUMBER	PERCENT
Population 5 years and over	**19,241,518**	**100.0**
Speak only English	13,230,765	68.8
Speak a language other than English	6,010,753	31.2
Speak a language other than English	**6,010,753**	**31.2**
Spanish or Spanish Creole	5,195,182	27.0
Vietnamese	122,517	0.6
Chinese	91,500	0.5
German	82,117	0.4
French (incl. Patois, Cajun)	62,274	0.3
Tagalog	39,988	0.2
Korean	38,451	0.2
African languages	36,087	0.2
Urdu	32,978	0.2
Arabic	32,909	0.2
Other Asian languages	32,780	0.2
Other Indic languages	24,454	0.1
Hindi	20,919	0.1
Gujarathi	19,140	0.1
Persian	17,558	0.1
Other Slavic languages	15,448	0.1
Japanese	14,701	0.1
Russian	11,574	0.1
Italian	11,158	0.1
Laotian	10,378	0.1

Texas pronunciation is largely South Midland, with such characteristic forms as /caow/, and /naow/ for *cow* and *now* and /dyoo/ for *due,* although /doo/ is now more common in urban areas. In the German settlement around New Braunfels are heard a few loanwords such as *smearcase* (cottage cheese), *krebbel* (doughnut), *clook* (setting hen), and *oma* and *opa* for grandmother and grandfather.

Spanish has been the major foreign-language influence. In areas like Laredo and Brownsville, along the Rio Grande, as many as 90% of the people may be bilingual; in northeast Texas, however,

Spanish is as foreign as French. In the days of the early Spanish ranchers, standard English adopted *hacienda, ranch, burro, canyon,* and *lariat;* in the southwestern cattle country are heard *la reata* (lasso), *remuda* (group of horses), and *resaca* (pond), along with the *acequia* (irrigation ditch), *pilon* (something extra, as a trip), and *olla* (water jar). The presence of the large Spanish-speaking population was a major factor in the passage of the state's bilingual education law, as a result of which numerous school programs in both English and Spanish are now offered; in a ruling issued in January 1981, US District Judge William Wayne Justice ruled that by 1987, the state must expand such programs to cover all Spanish-speaking students. Legislation enacted in 1995 established a requirement for schools with a certain number of students with limited English proficiency to be required to have bilingual and/or English as a second language programs. About one-sixth of all Texas counties—and a great many cities—are named for Mexicans or Spaniards or after place-names in Spain or Mexico.

⁹RELIGIONS

Because of its Spanish heritage, Texas originally was entirely Roman Catholic except for unconverted Indians. Consequently, the early history of Texas is almost identical with that of the Roman Catholic Church in the area. Under the Mexican Republic, the Catholic Church continued as the sole recognized religious body. In order to receive the generous land grants given by the Mexicans, Anglo-American immigrants had to sign a paper saying that they followed the Catholic religion. With an average grant of 4,605 acres (1,864 hectares) as bait, many early Protestants and atheists must have felt little hesitancy about becoming instant Catholics.

The Mexican government was careless about enforcing adherence to the Catholic faith in Texas, however, and many Baptists, Methodists, and Presbyterians drifted in from the east. The Methodist practice of having itinerant ministers range over frontier areas was particularly well suited to the Texas scene and, in 1837, the church hierarchy sent three preachers to the new republic. The first presbytery had been formed by that date and Baptists had organized in Houston by 1840. Swedish and German immigrants brought their Lutheranism with them; the first German Lutheran synod was organized in Houston in 1851.

Geographically, Texas tends to be heavily Protestant in the north and east and Catholic in the south and southwest. In 2004, there were about 6,050,986 Roman Catholics in the state. Leading Protestant denominations and their known adherents in 2000 (unless otherwise indicated) were the Southern Baptist Convention, 3,519,459; the United Methodist Church, 796,306 (in 2004); Churches of Christ, 377,264; the Church of Jesus Christ of Latter-day Saints, 243,957 (in 2006); Assemblies of God, 228,098; the Presbyterian Church USA, 180,315; the Episcopal Church, 177,910; Independent Charismatic Churches, 159,449; the Evangelical Lutheran Church in America, 155,019; Independent Non-Charismatic Churches, 145,249; and the Lutheran Church–Missouri Synod, 140,106. There were an estimated 128,000 Jews, 114,999 Muslims, and about 10,777 adherents to the Baha'i faith. There were about 9.2 million people (44.5% of the population) who were not counted as members of any religious organization.

The Roman Catholic Church has an archdiocese in San Antonio. The Latter-day Saints dedicated a new temple at San Antonio in 2005; there are three other temples in the state.

10 TRANSPORTATION

Texas ranks first among the 50 states in total railroad mileage, highway mileage, and number of airports, and second only to California in motor vehicle registrations and in number of general aviation aircraft.

Transportation has been a severe problem for Texas because of the state's extraordinary size and sometimes difficult terrain; one of the more unusual experiments in US transport history was the use of camels in southwestern Texas during the mid-1800s. The Republic of Texas authorized railroad construction as early as 1836, but the financial panic of 1837 helped kill that attempt. Not until 1853 did the state's first railroad—from Harrisburg (now incorporated into Houston) to Stafford's Point, 20 mi (32 km) to the west—come into service. At the outbreak of the Civil War, 10 railroads were operating, all but two connected with seaports. Although the state legislature in 1852 had offered railroad companies eight sections (5,120 acres/2,072 hectares) of land per mile of road construction and doubled that offer two years later, Texas lacked sufficient capital to satisfy its railroad-building needs until the war was over. The state generally held to the 10,240-acre (4,144-hectare) figure until all grants ceased in 1882. In all, Texas granted more than 50,000 sq mi (130,000 sq km) to railroad companies.

In 1870, Texas had fewer than 600 mi (970 km) of track. Ten years later, it had 3,026 mi (4,870 km). By 1920, there was 16,049 mi (25,828 km) of track in the state. In 1932, railroad trackage peaked with 17,078 mi (27,484 km) of track. By 2003 however, railroad track mileage had dwindled to 14,049 rail mi (22,618 km), with 11,432 mi (18,405 km) of the total being Class I railroad right-of-way. Still, total rail mileage in Texas still ranks higher than in any other state. The state in 2003, was served by 44 railroads, of which there were three Class I carriers: the Burlington Northern Santa Fe; the Kansas City Southern; and the Union Pacific. As of 2006, Amtrak provided passenger train service in Texas via its Sunset Limited (New Orleans–Los Angeles) train from Beaumont through Houston and San Antonio to El Paso, the Texas Eagle (Chicago–San Antonio) train, and its Heartland Flyer (Oklahoma City to Fort Worth) train.

In mid-1983, Dallas-area voters approved the creation of the Dallas Area Rapid Transit system (DART) to serve the city and 13 suburbs. Surface rail routes, running 160 mi (257 km), were to be constructed and bus service doubled at an expense of some $8.9 billion over a 26-year period. As of March 2006, DART operated 45 miles (72.5 km) of surface light rail line. In addition, DART and the Ft. Worth Transportation Authority jointly operated the Trinity Railway Express (TRE), a 35 mile (56 km) light rail line that connects the cities of Dallas and Ft Worth with the Dallas-Ft Worth Regional Airport. Ft. Worth also has the state's only true subway, a one-mi (1.6-km) line from a parking lot to a downtown shipping and office center.

Texas has by far the most road mileage of any state. In 2004, Texas had 303,176 mi (488,113 km) of public roadway The leading interstate highways are I-10 and I-20, respectively linking Houston and the Dallas–Ft.Worth Areas with El Paso in the west, and I-35 and I-45, connecting Dallas–Ft. Worth with, respectively, San Antonio (via Austin) and Galveston (via Houston). There were 14,543,528 licensed drivers in 2004. Registered motor vehicles in 2004 included some 8.621 million automobiles, about 7.851 million trucks of all types, around 284,000 motorcycles, and some 18,000 buses.

River transport did not become commercially successful until the end of the 19th century, when the Houston Ship Channel was dredged along the San Jacinto River and Buffalo Bayou for more than 50 mi (80 km), and another channel was dredged down the Neches River to make a seaport out of Beaumont. With 13 major seaports and many shallow-water ports, Texas has been a major factor in waterborne commerce since the early 1950s. As of 2004, the state of Texas had four ports that ranked among the top 10 busiest ports in the United States. The Port of Houston was the nation's second most active harbor, with 202.047 million tons of cargo handled in 2004. In that same year, the ports of Beaumont, Corpus Christie and Texas City were ranked as the fourth, sixth, and ninth busiest ports, respectively, handling a respective 91.697 million tons, 78.924 million tons and 68.282 million tons of cargo. The Gulf Intracoastal Waterway begins in Brownsville, at the mouth of the Rio Grande, and extends across Texas for 423 mi (681 km) on its way to Florida and its connections with a similar waterway on the Atlantic. In 2004, Texas had 834 mi (1,342 km) of navigable inland waterways. In 2003, waterborne shipments totaled 473.941 million tons.

After American entry into World War I, Texas began to build airfields for training grounds. When the war ended, many US fliers returned to Texas and became civilian commercial pilots, carrying air mail (from 1926), dusting crops, and mapping potential oil fields. In 2005, Texas had a total of 1,913 public and private-use aviation-related facilities. This included 1,435 airports, 470 heliports, and 8 STOLports (Short Take-Off and Landing). Dallas–Ft. Worth International Airport was the state's leading air terminal, with 28,063,035 passengers enplaned in 2004, followed by George Bush Intercontinental/Houston Airport with 17,322,065 enplanements that same year, making them the fourth- and tenth-busiest airports in the United States, respectively. Other major airports in the state in 2004 were: Houston–William P Hobby Airport (3,960,890 enplanements); Austin–Bergstrom International (3,446,564 enplanements); and San Antonio International (3,376,750 enplanements), making them the 46th-, 47th-, and 48th-busiest airports in the United States, respectively.

11 HISTORY

Although a site near Lewisville, in Denton County, contains artifacts that might be more than 37,000 years old, the generally accepted date for the earliest human presence in the region now known as Texas is the Llano civilization, dating from 12,000 years ago. Prehistoric Indians in Texas failed to develop as complex technologies as their neighbors to the west and east. When the first Europeans arrived in the 16th century, the Indians had developed little in the way of pottery or basketry, and had shown little interest in agriculture except in the extreme east and northeast, and possibly west of the Pecos. They were still largely hunter-gatherers on whom the more technologically complex cultures of Mexico and the southeastern United States had little effect.

Along the Gulf coast and overlapping into northeastern Mexico were the Coahuiltecan and Karankawa peoples. They lived in a hostile environment, consuming berries in season, animal dung, spiders, and an occasional deer, bison, or jabalina. In central Texas lived the Tonkawa, who hunted buffalo, slept in tepees, used dogs for hauling, and had a communal structure akin to that of the Plains Indians. Unlike the Karankawa, who were tall, the Tonkawa were of average height, tattooed, and dressed in breechclouts—long for men, short for women. They proved extremely susceptible to European diseases and evidently died out, whereas the Karankawa migrated to northern Mexico.

About two dozen tribes of Caddo in eastern and northeastern Texas were at the time of European penetration the most technologically complex Indians living within the state's present borders. Having developed agriculture, the Caddo were relatively sedentary and village oriented. Those belonging to the Hasinai Confederation called each other *tayshas*, a term that translates as "allies" or "friends." When the Hasinai told Spanish explorers that they were tayshas, the Spaniards wrote the word as Tejas, which in time became Texas. The Caddo lived in the gentle portion of Texas, where woods, wild fruits, and berries abound, and where game was plentiful until the advent of European civilization. Life was so good, in fact, that several members of an expedition under Robert Cavelier, Sieur de la Salle, reaching Matagorda Bay on 15 February 1685, chose to desert to the Caddo rather than remain with their fellow Frenchmen. Henri de Tonti, who entered the region somewhat later, reported that one Caddo tribe had a woman as chief. The Caddo were also unusual in their belief that three women had created the world.

In trans-Pecos Texas, to the west, lived a fourth Indian group, the Jumano, probably descendants of the Pueblo cultures. Some of the Jumano were nomadic hunters in the Davis and Chisos mountains. Others became farmers along the Rio Grande and the lower Rio Conchos, making and using some pottery and raising good crops of corn, beans, squash, and possibly cotton. Probably the successive droughts so common to the region began to thin out their ranks, and the coming of the Spanish removed them from the historical picture altogether.

The first European to enter Texas was Spanish explorer Alonso Alvarez de Pineda, who sailed into the mouth of the Rio Grande in 1519. Basically, the Spanish left the Texas Indians alone for more than 150 years. Sometimes an accident placed Spaniards in Texas, or sometimes they entered by design, but generally, the Spanish looked on Texas as too remote from Florida and the Mexico highlands—where most of their colonizing occurred—for successful settlement. A remarkable episode of this period involves the survivors of the Pánfilo de Narváez expedition, which had been commissioned to occupy the Gulf of Mexico coast from Mexico to Florida. Four shipwrecked men, led by Álvar Nunez Cabeza de Vaca, were washed ashore on a Texas sandbar on 6 November 1528: three were Spaniards, and one was the Moor Estevanico. For eight years, they wandered virtually naked among the Texas Indians, sometimes as slaves and sometimes as free men, alternately blistered by the summer sun and freezing under winter ice storms. Using a deer bone as a needle, Cabeza removed an arrowhead from deep in an Indian's chest—a bit of surgical magic that earned him treatment as a demigod, for a time. Finally, the four Europeans reached the west coast of Mexico, from where Cabeza de Vaca returned home a hero. The other two Spaniards remained in Mexico, but Estevanico joined the Fray Marcos de Niza expedition as a guide, dying at the hands of Pueblo Indians in New Mexico in 1539. The trail he helped blaze through the High Plains of West Texas served as the route for the expedition a year later by Francisco Vásquez de Coronado. The first Texas towns and missions were begun by Spaniards in West Texas, outside present-day El Paso. Ysleta del Sur was founded in 1682, almost a decade before the earliest East Texas missions. But Ysleta was 500 mi (800 km) from anything else resembling a settlement in Texas, and the Spanish considered it a part of New Mexico.

What changed the Spaniards' attitude toward the colonization of Texas was the establishment of Ft. St. Louis by La Salle on the Gulf coast in 1685. Four years later, Capt. Alonso de León, governor of Coahuila, sent out an expedition to expel the French. Father Damien Massanet, a Coahuilan priest, accompanied the León expedition and was charged with establishing a mission near wherever the captain built a fort. During the next several decades these two men and their successors established a string of mission-forts across Texas. After fear of the French presence eased, Spain tended to neglect these establishments. But when the French entered Louisiana in force during the early 18th century, Spanish fears of French expansion were re-ignited. In 1718, the Spanish began to build a mission, San Antonio de Valero, and a fort, San Antonio de Bexar, at the site of the present city of San Antonio. As a halfway post between Mexico and the Louisiana border, San Antonio grew to be Texas's most important city during the Spanish period.

Until the 19th century, the United States showed little interest in Texas. But the purchase of Louisiana Territory from the French by the US government in 1803 made Texas a next-door neighbor, and "filibusters" (military adventurers) began to filter across the border into Spanish territory. The best known is Philip Nolan, an Irish-born intriguer who started spending time in Texas as early as 1790. Ostensibly, he was trading horses with the Indians, but the Spanish associated him with Aaron Burr's schemes to excise the Spanish southwest from its owners. In the summer of 1800, the Spanish governor of Texas, Juan Bautista Elguezábal, ordered that Nolan should be arrested if he returned. In December of that year, Nolan returned with a small force of 20 men and built a fort near Nacogdoches; he was killed fighting the Spanish on 4 March 1801. Nolan is remembered for having drafted the first Anglo-American map of Texas.

In 1810–11, the Mexicans launched their revolution against Spain, and though only an outpost, Texas as a Spanish-Mexican colony was naturally involved. In 1813, Texas formally declared its independence of Spain and its intention of becoming a Mexican state, with its capital at San Antonio. Various Anglo-Americans entered the new state to serve on behalf of Mexico. Pirates also aided the Mexican cause: on Galveston Island, Luis Aury preyed on Spanish shipping, and after 1816, his place was taken by Jean Laffite, who privateered against both Spanish and US shipping until the US Navy drove him out.

The Spanish finally gave up on Mexico in 1821, leaving Texas as a Mexican province with a non-Indian population of about 7,000. The only towns of significant size were Goliad, San Antonio (commonly called Bexar), and Nacogdoches. A year earlier, Moses Austin of Missouri had received permission from Spanish authorities to introduce Anglo-American colonists into Texas, presumably as a barrier against aggression by the United States. When Spanish rule ended, his son, Stephen F. Austin, succeeded his late father as head of the colonization movement, securing permission from the new Mexican government to settle 300 families in the area between the lower Colorado and Brazos rivers. After Austin had settled his "Old Three Hundred" in 1821, he received permission to settle more, and within a decade, his colonists numbered more than 5,000. The Mexicans invested Austin with the responsibilities and privileges of an empresario: authority to run commerce, maintain militia, administer justice, and hand out land titles. Other empresarios made similar arrangements. Green DeWitt, also of Missouri, settled several hundred families farther west and founded the town of Gonzales in 1825. Hayden Edwards received a grant to settle 800 families near Nacogdoches. Mexicans were also permitted to organize colonies. Texas thus began a pattern of growth from the outside that has continued to the present day.

Between 1821 and 1835, the population of non-Indian Texas expanded to between 35,000 and 50,000. Most new settlers were Anglo-Americans who often brought their prejudices against Mexico with them, whether they were from the North or the South. They disliked Mexican culture, Mexican folkways, Mexican justice—and the Protestants among them resented the omnipresence of the Roman Catholic Church. All of these Anglo-American settlers had ties to the United States, and many undoubtedly longed for the time when they would live under the American flag again. The ineptitude of the Mexican government made the situation even worse. In 1826, Hayden Edwards organized the Republic of Fredonia and tried to drive the Mexicans from East Texas, but in the end, he had to flee the province himself. Troubled by the rising spirit of rebellion, the Mexican Congress enacted the Law of 1830, which forbade most immigration and imposed duties on all imports. Anglo-Americans in Texas responded with the same anger that New Englanders had once shown when Britain imposed tax restrictions on the original American colonies.

At first, the Anglo-Texans insisted they were opposing Mexican political excesses, not the Mexican nation. Their hope lay with Gen. Antonio López de Santa Anna, who was leading a liberal revolution against President Anastasio Bustamante. Skirmishes between the Anglo-Texans and Mexican officials remained sporadic and localized until 1833 when Santa Anna became president of Mexico and almost immediately dropped his liberal stance. Texans sent Austin to Mexico City to petition Santa Anna to rescind the Law of 1830, to allow the use of English in public business, and to make Texas (then an appendage of Coahuila) a separate state. After several months in Mexico City, Austin was arrested on his way back to Texas and was imprisoned for a year. When Santa Anna tried to enforce customs collections, colonists at Anahuac, led by William Barret Travis, drove the Mexican officials out of town. Santa Anna's answer was to place Texas under military jurisdiction. When the Mexican military commander, Col. Domingo de Ugartechea, sent his soldiers to Gonzales to take a cannon there from the colonists, the Anglo-Texan civilians drove them off on 2 October 1835, in a battle that is generally considered to mark the start of the Texas Revolution.

On 3 November, a provisional government was formed. It called not for independence but for a return to the liberal Mexican constitution of 1824. Three commissioners, one of them Austin, were sent to Washington, DC, to request aid from the United States. Sam Houston, who only six years earlier had resigned the governorship of Tennessee (when his wife left him) and had come to Texas after stays in Oklahoma and Arkansas, was named commander in chief of the upstart Texas army. Hostilities remained at a standstill until February 1836, when Santa Anna led an army across the Rio Grande. The Mexicans concentrated outside San Antonio at a mission-fort called the Alamo, where 187 or so Texans, commanded by Col. William Barret Travis, had holed up in defense. The Mexicans besieged the Alamo until 6 March, when Santa Anna's forces, now numbering more than 4,000, stormed the fortress. When the battle ended, all the Alamo's defenders, including several native Mexicans, were dead. Among those killed were Travis and two Americans who became legends—James Bowie and Davy Crockett.

Four days before the battle of the Alamo, other Texans gathered at Washington-on-the-Brazos and issued a declaration of independence. As so often happens, a fight that had started on principle—in this case, a constitutional issue—grew into a fight for independence. The men who died at the Alamo believed they were fighting for restoration of the constitution of 1824. But three weeks after the Alamo fell, on 27 March 1836, the Mexicans killed 342 Texans who had surrendered at Goliad, thinking they would be treated as prisoners of war. Coming on the heels of the Alamo tragedy, the "Goliad massacre" persuaded Texans that only total victory or total defeat would solve their problems with Santa Anna. The Texas army under Sam Houston retreated before Santa Anna's oncoming forces, which held a numerical advantage over Houston's of about 1,600 to 800. On 21 April 1836, however, the Texans surprised the Mexicans during their siesta period at San Jacinto (east of present-day Houston). Mexican losses were 630 killed, 280 wounded, and 730 taken prisoner, while the Texans had only 9 killed and 30 wounded. This decisive battle-fought to the cry of "Remember the Alamo, remember Goliad!" freed Texas from Mexico once and for all.

For 10 years, Texas existed as an independent republic, recognized by the United States, Belgium, France, the United Kingdom, the Netherlands, and several German states. Sam Houston, the victorious commander at San Jacinto, became the republic's first nationally elected president. Although Texans are proud of their once-independent status, the fact is that the republic limped along like any new nation, strife-torn and short of cash. It was unable to reach agreement with Mexico on a treaty to clarify the border. Moreover, its original $1-million public debt increased eightfold in a decade, and its paper money depreciated alarmingly. Consequently, when Texas joined the Union on 29 December 1845, the date of the US congressional resolution recognizing the new state (the Lone Star flag, the republic's official banner, was not actually lowered and a governor inaugurated until 19 February 1846), its citizens looked on the action as a rescue. The annexation in great measure provoked the Mexican War, which in turn led to the conclusion of the Treaty of Guadalupe Hidalgo on 2 February 1848. Under the treaty, Mexico dropped its claim to the territory between the Rio Grande and the Nueces River. Later, in accordance with the Compromise of 1850, Texas relinquished, for $10 million, its claim on lands stretching into New Mexico, Colorado, Wyoming, Oklahoma, and Kansas.

With the coming of the Civil War, Texas followed its proslavery southern neighbors out of the Union into the Confederacy; Governor Houston, who opposed secession, was ousted from office. The state saw little fighting, and Texas thus suffered from the war far less than most of the South. The last battle of the war was fought on Texas soil at Palmito Ranch, near Brownsville, on 13

May 1865—more than a month after Gen. Robert E. Lee's surrender at Appomattox Court House in Virginia.

During Reconstruction, Texas was governed briefly by a military occupation force and then by a Republican regime; the so-called carpetbag constitution of 1869, passed during this period, gave the franchise to blacks, a right that the Ku Klux Klan actively sought to deny them. Texas was allowed to rejoin the Union on 30 March 1870. Three years later, Republican Governor Edmund J. Davis was defeated at the polls by Richard Coke, and a Democratic legislature wrote a new constitution, which was approved by the voters in 1876.

While most southern states were economically prostrate, the Texas economy flourished because of the rapid development of the cattle industry. Millions of Texas cattle walked the trails to northern markets, where they were sold for hard cash, providing a bonanza for the state. The widespread use of barbed wire to fence cattle ranches in the 1880s ended the open range and encouraged scientific cattle breeding. By 1900, Texas began to transform its predominantly agricultural economy into an industrial one. This process was accelerated by the discovery of the Spindletop oil field—the state's first gusher—near Beaumont in 1901, and by the subsequent development of the petroleum and petrochemical industries. World War I saw the emergence of Texas as a military training center. The rapid growth of the aircraft industry and other high-technology fields contributed to the continuing industrialization of Texas during and after World War II.

Texas politics remained solidly Democratic during most of the modern era, and the significant political conflict in the state was between the liberal and conservative wings of the Democratic Party. Populist-style reforms were enacted slowly during the governorships of James E. Ferguson—impeached and removed from office during his second term in 1917—and of his wife, Miriam A. "Ma" Ferguson (1925–27, 1933–35), and more rapidly during the two administrations of James V. Allred (1935–39). During the 1960s and 1970s, the Republican Party gathered strength in the state, electing John G. Tower as US senator in 1961 and William P. Clements Jr., as governor in 1978—the first Republicans to hold those offices since Reconstruction. In general, the state's recent political leaders, Democrats was well as Republicans, have represented property interests and taken a conservative line.

On the national level, Texans have been influential since the 1930s, notably through such congressional leaders as US House Speaker Sam Rayburn and Senate Majority Leader Lyndon B. Johnson. Johnson, elected vice president under John F. Kennedy, was riding in the motorcade with the president when Kennedy was assassinated in Dallas on 22 November 1963. The city attained further national notoriety when Kennedy's alleged killer, Lee Harvey Oswald, was shot to death by Jack Ruby, a Dallas nightclub operator, two days later. Johnson served out the remainder of Kennedy's term, was elected to the presidency by a landslide in 1964, and presided over one of the stormiest periods in US history before retiring to his LBJ ranch in 1969. Memorials to him include the Lyndon B. Johnson Library at Austin and Johnson Space Center, headquarters for the US manned spaceflight program, near Houston.

The most prominent Texans on the national scene since Johnson have been Republican George H.W. Bush and his son, George W. Bush. After failing in his bid for the Republican presidential nomi-

nation in 1980, George Bush Sr. became Ronald Reagan's running mate; Reagan and Bush won in 1980 and were reelected in 1984. Bush ran for and won the presidency in 1988, but was defeated in his 1992 bid for re-election by Bill Clinton. Bush's son, George W. Bush, was elected governor of Texas in 1994, succeeding Democrat Ann Richards, the second woman governor in Texas history. In 2000, George W. Bush was elected president in a contested election against then-Vice President Al Gore. He was reelected in 2004, defeating Democrat John Kerry.

Texas benefited from a booming oil industry in the 1970s. The economy grew at an average of 6% a year, more than twice the national average. The boom collapsed in the early 1980s as overproduction caused world oil prices to plummet. The state's annual rate of population growth, 60% of which came from migration, dropped from 4% in 1982 to 1.3% in 1985. By 1986, the state had become a net exporter of population. Scrambling to make up the $100 million in revenues that the government estimated it lost for every $1 dollar decline in the price of a barrel of oil, the government in 1985 imposed or raised fees on everything from vanity license plates to day-care centers. The state also took steps to encourage economic diversification by wooing service, electronics, and high-technology companies to Texas. In the late 1980s, a number of Texas's financial institutions collapsed, brought down by the slump in the oil industry and by unsound real estate loans.

After 1986, oil prices increased, and the state reaped the benefits of diversification efforts spurred by the oil price collapse earlier in the decade. Although the petroleum industry was still the state's leading economic sector in the mid-1990s, high-technology and service sector jobs had played a major role in rebuilding the Texas economy and reversing the population decline of the previous decade. High-tech companies were concentrated in the "Silicon Hills" area surrounding Austin.

In the early 2000s, Texas had the second-largest population of any state, behind California. The high rate of migration into Texas, which accompanied the oil boom, had a profound effect on the state's population distribution and political profile. Newcomers to the state have tended to share the fiscally conservative values of native Texans but take more liberal positions on issues such as abortion, civil rights, and homosexuality. According to the 2000 census, 32% of the Texas population was of Hispanic or Latino origin. By 2004, 34.6% of the population was Hispanic.

On 19 April 1993, the 51-day confrontation between the FBI and the Branch Davidian cult near Waco ended tragically when the group's compound burned to the ground, killing at least 72 persons.

In early 2003, 51 Democratic state representatives fled Texas for Oklahoma to prevent the Republican-dominated state House of Representatives from passing a controversial redistricting plan that would favor Republicans. The tactic worked when the House failed to reach quorum and the redistricting bill died. Eleven state Democratic senators later also fled the state (for New Mexico) in July 2003 to break quorum and thus block a redistricting bill. Republican Governor Rick Perry called special legislative sessions to take up the redistricting measures. In August, the absent senators filed suit in Laredo in *Barrientos v. State of Texas* alleging Republican officials violated the Voting Rights Act by failing to obtain necessary Department of Justice preclearance before changing redistricting practices and procedures and by abandoning the "two-thirds rule" in the Senate: the "two-thirds rule" is regarded as a Senate tradition, which ensure that at least two-thirds of the membership have an interest in debating a measure before it comes to the floor. In September, a three-judge panel in Laredo dismissed all plaintiffs' claims in *Barrientos v. State of Texas*. In October, the Texas legislature passed the mid-decade redistricting plan in favor of the Republicans. Senate Democrats, in *Session v. Perry*, challenged the legality of the plan and filed a motion with the US Supreme Court to stay elections. The Supreme Court in April 2004 reaffirmed the lower court ruling in *Barrientos v. State of Texas*.

On 24 September 2005, Hurricane Rita made landfall as a strong Category 3 storm just east of Sabine Pass, Texas. Some areas received up to 20 inches of rain. This hurricane followed on the heels of Hurricane Katrina, which on 29 August devastated New Orleans, Louisiana, when levees there broke. Damages from Hurricane Rita were estimated at $8 billion. The death toll rose to over 100, but most of the victims died before the hurricane struck, either while preparing for the storm or fleeing from it.

12 STATE GOVERNMENT

Texas has been governed directly under eight constitutions: the Mexican national constitution of 1824, the Coahuila-Texas state constitution of 1827, the independent Republic of Texas constitution of 1836, and the five US state constitutions of 1845, 1861, 1866, 1869, and 1876. This last document, with 432 amendments (through 2005), is the foundation of the state government today. An attempt to replace it with eight propositions that in effect would have given Texas a new constitution was defeated at the polls in November 1975.

The state legislature consists of a Senate of 31 members elected to four-year terms, and a House of Representatives of 150 members elected to two-year terms. The legislature meets on the second Tuesday in January of odd-numbered years for sessions of as many as 140 calendar days; the governor may also call special sessions, each limited to 30 calendar days. Senators and representatives receive the same pay, pursuant to a constitutional amendment of 1975: $7,200 per year (as of 2004, unchanged from 1999) and $124 per diem living expenses (as of 2004) while the legislature is in session. All legislators must be US citizens, qualified voters, and residents of their districts for at least one year. Further, senators are required to be at least 26 years old and to have lived in the state for a minimum of five years. Representatives must be at least 21 and must have lived in the state for at least two years before election.

The state's chief executives are the governor and lieutenant governor, separately elected to four-year terms. Other elected executives, also serving four-year terms, include the attorney general, comptroller, commissioner of agriculture, and commissioner of the general land office. The remaining cabinet members are appointed by the governor, who also appoints members of the many executive boards and commissions. The governor, whose salary was $115,345 as of December 2004 (unchanged from 1999), must be a US citizen, at least 30 years old, and must have resided in the state for at least five years prior to election. A uniquely important executive agency is the Railroad Commission of Texas (RRC). Established in 1891 and consisting of three members elected for six-year terms, the commission regulates the state's railroads, oil and gas production, coal and uranium mining, and trucking industry.

The RRC thus wields extraordinary economic power, and the alleged influence by the regulated industries over the commission has been a major source of political controversy in the state.

To become law, a bill must be approved by a majority of members present and voting in each house, with a quorum of two-thirds of the membership present, and either signed by the governor or left unsigned for 10 days while the legislature is in session or 20 days after it has adjourned. A gubernatorial veto may be overridden by a two-thirds vote of the elected members. Overrides have been rare: the vote in April 1979 by state legislators to override the new Republican governor's veto of a minor wildlife regulation measure affecting only one county was the first successful attempt in 38 years. A constitutional amendment requires a two-thirds vote of the membership of each house and ratification by the voters at the next election.

In order to vote in Texas one must be a US citizen, at least 18 years old, and a resident in the county of registration. Restrictions apply to convicted felons and those declared mentally incompetent by the court.

13 POLITICAL PARTIES

Until recent years, the Democratic Party had dominated politics in Texas. William P. Clements Jr., elected governor in 1978, was the first Republican since Reconstruction to hold that office. No Republican carried Texas in a presidential election until 1928, when Herbert Hoover defeated Democrat Al Smith, a Roman Catholic at a severe disadvantage in a Protestant fundamentalist state. Another Roman Catholic, Democratic presidential candidate John Kennedy, carried the state in 1960 largely because he had a Texan, Lyndon Johnson, on his ticket.

Prior to the Civil War, many candidates for statewide office ran as independents. After a period of Republican rule during Reconstruction, Democrats won control of the statehouse and state legislature in 1873. The major challenge to Democratic rule during the late 19th century came not from Republicans but from the People's Party, whose candidates placed second in the gubernatorial races of 1894, 1896, and 1898, aided by the collapse of the cotton market; imposition of a poll tax in 1902 helped disfranchise the poor white farmers and laborers who were the base of Populist support. The Populists and the Farmers' Alliance probably exercised their greatest influence through a Democratic reformer, Governor James S. Hogg (1891–95), who fought the railroad magnates, secured lower freight rates for farmers and shippers, and curbed the power of large landholding companies. Another Democratic governor, James E. "Farmer Jim" Ferguson, was elected on an agrarian reform platform in 1914 and reelected in 1916, but was impeached and convicted the following year for irregular financial dealings. Barred from holding state office, he promoted the candidacy of his wife, Miriam "Ma" Ferguson, whose first term as governor (1925–27) marked her as a formidable opponent of the Ku Klux Klan. During her second term (1933–35), the state's first New Deal reforms were enacted, and prohibition was repealed. The Fergusons came to represent the more liberal wing of the Democratic Party in a state where liberals have long been in the minority. After the progressive administration of Governor James V. Allred, during which the state's first old-age assistance program was enacted, conservative Democrats, sometimes called "Texas Tories," controlled the state until the late 1970s.

In the November 1994 elections, George W. Bush (son of former President George H. W. Bush), upset Ann Richards to become governor. Bush was reelected in 1998, shortly before announcing his run for the US presidency. In 2000 following his election as president, Bush turned the governor's office over to Republican Rick Perry. Perry was elected in his own right in 2002. Texas is represented in the US Senate by Republican Kay Bailey Hutchison, who was first elected in 1993 to fill the Senate seat vacated by Democrat Lloyd Bentsen, who resigned to become secretary of the treasury in the Clinton administration. In 1994, Hutchinson won reelection to a full term, and she was reelected once again in 2000. Republican John Cornyn was elected to the Senate in 2002. Following the 2002 elections, Texas Democrats held 11 seats in the US House of Representatives and the Republicans 21. As of mid-2005, the Republicans continued to control the state House by a margin of 87 to 63, and they had a majority of 19–12 over the Democrats in the state Senate.

Republican and native son George H.W. Bush captured 56% of the vote in the 1988 presidential election and 41% in the 1992 election. In 2000, his son, George W. Bush, took 59% of the presidential popular vote to Democrat Al Gore's 38%, and Bush went on to become president. In 2004, as an incumbent Bush won 61.2% of the vote to Democratic challenger John Kerry's 38.3%. As of 2004 there were 13,098,000 registered voters in the state; there is no voter registration by party in Texas. The state had 34 electoral votes in the 2004 presidential election, an increase of 2 votes over 2000.

Aside from the Populists, third parties have played a minor role in Texas politics. The Native American (Know-Nothing) Party helped elect Sam Houston governor in 1859. In 1968, George Wallace of the American Independent Party won 19% of the Texas popular vote and in 1992 native son Ross Perot picked up 22% of the vote.

Following passage of the federal Voting Rights Act of 1965, registration of black voters increased to about 11.5% of the total population of voters. Between 1895 and 1967, no black person served as a state legislator. By 1993, however, there were 472 blacks holding elective office. At about the same time. Hispanic elected officials numbered 2,215. Democrat Henry Cisneros, former mayor of San Antonio, served as Secretary of Housing and Urban Development in the Clinton Administration.

14 LOCAL GOVERNMENT

The Texas constitution grants considerable autonomy to local governments. As of 2005, Texas had 254 counties, a number that has remained constant since 1931. Also in 2005, there were 1,196 municipal governments, 1,040 public school districts (down from 8,600 in 1910), and 2,245 special districts.

Each county is governed by a commissioners' court, consisting of commissioners elected by precinct and a county judge or administrator elected at large. Other elected officials generally include a county clerk, attorney, treasurer, assessor-collector, and sheriff.

At the municipal level, cities with populations greater than 5,000 can adopt home rule.

In 2005, local government accounted for about 1,016,476 full-time (or equivalent) employment positions.

15 STATE SERVICES

To address the continuing threat of terrorism and to work with the federal Department of Homeland Security, homeland security in Texas operates under executive order and state statute; a

Texas Presidential Vote by Political Parties, 1948–2004

YEAR	ELECTORAL VOTE	TEXAS WINNER	DEMOCRAT	REPUBLICAN	STATES' RIGHTS DEMOCRAT	PROGRESSIVE	PROHIBITION
1948	23	*Truman (D)	750,700	282,240	106,909	3,764	2,758
					CONSTITUTION		
1952	24	*Eisenhower (R)	969,227	1,102,818	1,563	—	1,983
1956	24	*Eisenhower (R)	859,958	1,080,619	14,591	—	—
1960	24	*Kennedy (D)	1,167,935	1,121,693	18,170	—	3,868
1964	25	*Johnson (D)	1,663,185	958,566	5,060	—	—
					AMERICAN IND.		
1968	25	Humphrey (D)	1,266,804	1,227,844	584,269	—	—
					AMERICAN	SOC. WORKERS	
1972	26	*Nixon (R)	1,154,289	2,298,896	6,039	8,664	—
1976	26	*Carter (D)	2,082,319	1,953,300	11,442	1,723	—
					LIBERTARIAN		
1980	26	*Reagan (R)	1,881,147	2,510,705	37,643	—	—
1984	29	*Reagan (R)	1,949,276	3,433,428	—	—	—
						NEW ALLIANCE	
1988	29	*Bush (R)	2,352,748	3,036,829	30,355	7,208	—
						POPULIST/AMERICA FIRST	IND. (Perot)
1992	32	Bush (R)	2,281,815	2,496,071	19,699	505	1,354,781
1996	32	Dole (R)	2,549,683	2,736,167	20,256	—	378,537
						GREEN	IND. (Buchanan)
2000	32	*Bush, G. W. (R)	2,433,746	3,799,639	23,160	137,994	12,394
						WRITE-IN (Nader)	WRITE-IN (Peroutka)
2004	34	*Bush, G. W. (R)	2,832,704	4,526,917	38,787	9,159	1,636

*Won US presidential election.

homeland security director oversees the state's homeland security activities.

The Texas Commission on Environmental Quality is responsible for environmental protection. The Department of Housing and Community Affairs helps to provide shelter for all citizens. The Ethics Commission promotes individual participation and confidence in governmental processes by enforcing and administering applicable laws and by providing public official conduct information.

Educational services in the public schools are administered by the Texas Education Agency, which is run by a commissioner of education appointed by an elected State Board of Education. The Higher Education Coordinating Board, consisting of appointed members, oversees public higher education. Transportation facilities are regulated by the Department of Transportation and the Texas Railroad Commission.

Health and welfare services are offered by the Department of Family and Protective Services, the Department of Aging and Disability Services, the Council for Developmental Disabilities, Texas Health and Human Services, the Health and Human Services Commission, and the Department of State Health Services. Public protection is the responsibility of the National Guard, Texas Department of Criminal Justice, and Texas Youth Commission, which maintains institutions for juvenile offenders. Labor services are provided by the Texas Workforce Investment Council and the Department of Licensing and Regulation. Other departments deal with public safety, banking, and agriculture.

16 JUDICIAL SYSTEM

The Texas judiciary is comprised of a supreme court, a state court of criminal appeals, 14 courts of appeals, and more than 380 district courts.

The highest court is the Supreme Court, consisting of a chief justice and eight justices, who are popularly elected to staggered six-year terms. The Court of Criminal Appeals, which has final jurisdiction in most criminal cases, consists of a presiding judge and eight judges, who are also elected to staggered six-year terms.

Justices of the courts of appeals, numbering 80 in 1999, are elected to six-year terms and sit in 14 judicial districts; each court has a chief justice and at least two associate justices. There were 27 district court judges in 1999, each elected to a four-year term. County, justice of the peace, and municipal courts handle local matters.

As of 31 December 2004, a total of 168,105 prisoners (the highest in the United States) were held in Texas's state and federal prisons, an increase from 166,911 of 0.7% from the previous year. As of year-end 2004, a total of 13,958 inmates were female, up from 13,487 or 3.5% from the year before. Among sentenced prisoners (one year or more), Texas had an incarceration rate of 694 per 100,000 population in 2004 (the second-highest in the United States, below Louisiana).

According to the Federal Bureau of Investigation, Texas in 2004, had a violent crime rate (murder/nonnegligent manslaughter; forcible rape; robbery; aggravated assault) of 540.5 reported incidents per 100,000 population, or a total of 121,554 reported incidents. Crimes against property (burglary; larceny/theft; and motor vehicle theft) in that same year totaled 1,010,702 reported incidents or 4,494 reported incidents per 100,000 people. Texas

has a death penalty, of which lethal injection is the sole method of execution. From 1976 through 5 May 2006, the state has carried out 363 executions (highest in the United States); 19 inmates were executed in 2005 and 8 in 2006 (as of 5 May). As of 1 January 2006, Texas had 409 inmates on death row.

In 2003, Texas spent $2,164,257,669 on homeland security, an average of $101 per state resident.

17 ARMED FORCES

In few states do US military forces and defense-related industries play such a large role as in Texas, which as of 2004 had 109,760 active-duty military personnel and 39,385 civilian personnel employed at major US military bases, second to California in defense personnel. Also in 2004, Texas received prime defense contract awards worth more than $21 billion, third-largest awards in the United States after California and Virginia, first and second, respectively. Texas was also third in that nation in defense payroll outlays of $11.08 billion, after Virginia, first with $15.9 billion, and California, second with $15.0 billion.

Ft. Sam Houston, at San Antonio, is headquarters of the US 5th Army Recruiting Brigade and home to the 4th Infantry Division, the most lethal, modern, and deployable heavy division in the world. It is also the headquarters of the US Army Health Services Command and the site of the Academy of Health Sciences, the largest US military medical school, enrolling more than 25,000 officers and enlisted personnel. Ft. Bliss, at El Paso, is the home of the US Army Air Defense Artillery Center. Ft. Hood, near Killeen, is headquarters of the 3rd Army Corps and other military units. It is the state's single largest defense installation and Ft. Hood is the only post in the United States capable of stationing and training two Armored Divisions.

Four principal Air Force bases are located near San Antonio: Brooks, Kelly, Lackland, and Randolph. Other major air bases are Dyess (Abilene); Goodfellow (San Angelo); Laughlin (Del Rio); and Sheppard (Wichita Falls). All US-manned space flights are controlled from the Lyndon B. Johnson Space Center, operated by the National Aeronautics and Space Administration. Naval air training stations are located at Corpus Christi, Dallas, and Kingsville. The Inactive Ships Maintenance Facility, at Orange, was home port for some of the US Navy's "mothball fleet" from 1945 to 1975 when it was closed.

Texas was a major military training center during World War II, when about one out of every 10 soldiers was trained there. Some 750,000 Texans served in the US armed forces during that war; the state's war dead numbered 23,022. Military veterans living in the state in 2003 totaled 1,681,748, including 194,173 who served in World War II; 154,449 during the Korean conflict; 517,031 during the Vietnam era; and 322,909 during the Gulf War. Expenditures on Texas veterans totaled nearly $5.0 billion in 2004.

The Texas Army National Guard has dual status as a federal and state military force. The Texas State Guard is an all-volunteer force available either to back up National Guard units or to respond to local emergencies.

The famous Texas Rangers, a state police force first employed in 1823 (though not formally organized until 1835) to protect the early settlers, served as scouts for the US Army during the Mexican War. Many individual rangers fought with the Confederacy in the Civil War; during Reconstruction, however, the rangers were used to enforce unpopular carpetbagger laws. Later, the rangers put down banditry on the Rio Grande. The force was reorganized in 1935 as a unit of the Department of Public Safety and is now called on in major criminal cases, helps control mob violence in emergencies, and sometimes assists local police officers. The Texas Rangers have been romanticized in fiction and films, but one of their less glamorous tasks has been to intervene in labor disputes on the side of management. In 2004, the Texas Department of Public Safety employed 3,407 full-time sworn officers.

18 MIGRATION

Estimates of the number of Indians living in Texas when the first Europeans arrived range from 30,000 to 130,000. Eventually, they all were killed, fled southward or westward, or were removed to reservations. The first great wave of white settlers, beginning in 1821, came from nearby southern states, particularly Tennessee, Alabama, Arkansas, and Mississippi; some of these newcomers brought their black slaves to work in the cotton fields. During the 1840s, a second wave of immigrants arrived directly from Germany, France, and eastern Europe.

Interstate migration during the second half of the 19th century was accelerated by the Homestead Act of 1862 and the westward march of the railroads. Particularly notable since 1900 has been the intrastate movement from rural areas to the cities; this trend was especially pronounced from the end of World War II, when about half the state's population was rural, to the late 1970s, when nearly four out of every five Texans made their homes in metropolitan areas.

Texas's net gain from migration between 1940 and 1980 was 1,821,000, 81% of that during the 1970–80 period. A significant proportion of postwar immigrants were seasonal laborers from Mexico, remaining in the United States either legally or illegally. By 1990, Texas had a foreign-born population of 1,524,436, representing 9% of the total. During 1980–83, Texas had the highest net migration gain—922,000—in the nation. From 1985 to 1990, the net gain from migration was 36,700. Between 1990 and 1998, the state had net gains of 541,000 in domestic migration and 656,000 in international migration. In 1996, the state's foreign-born population was 2,081,000, or 11% of the total population. In 1998, 44,428 foreign immigrants arrived in Texas, the fourth-highest total among the states. Of that total, the greatest number of immigrants (22,956) came from Mexico. Between 1990 and 1998, Texas's overall population increased 16.3%. In the period 2000–05, net international migration was 663,161 and net internal migration was 218,722, for a net gain of 881,883 people.

19 INTERGOVERNMENTAL COOPERATION

The Texas Commission on Interstate Cooperation represents Texas before the Council of State Governments. Texas is a member of the Interstate Mining Compact Commission and Interstate Oil and Gas Compact Commission. The state also belongs to the Gulf States Marine Fisheries Commission, South Central Interstate Forest Fire Protection Compact, Southern States Energy Board, and Southern Regional Education Board, and to accords apportioning the waters of the Canadian, Pecos, Red River, Pecos, and Sabine rivers and the Rio Grande. During fiscal year 2005, Texas received $22.347 billion in federal grants (third largest after California and New York). In fiscal year 2006, Texas received an esti-

mated $23.000 billion in federal grants, and an estimated $23.782 billion in fiscal year 2007.

20 ECONOMY

Traditionally, the Texas economy has been dependent on the production of cotton, cattle, timber, and petroleum. In recent years, cotton has declined in importance, cattle ranchers have suffered financial difficulties because of increased production costs, and lumber production has remained relatively stable. In the 1970s, as a result of rising world petroleum prices, oil and natural gas emerged as by far the state's most important resource. The decades since World War II have also witnessed a boom in the electronics, computer, transport equipment, aerospace, and communications industries, which has placed Texas second only to California in manufacturing among all the states of the Sunbelt region. Between 1972 and 1982, the Texas economy grew 6% a year, twice the national average, led by a booming oil industry. Other factors that contributed to the Lone Star State's robust economy in the early 1980s were a plentiful labor market, high worker productivity, diversification of new industries, and less restrictive regulation of business activities than in most other states. The result was a steady increase in industrial production, construction values, retail sales, and personal income, coupled with a relatively low rate of unemployment. In 1982, however, Texas began to be affected by the worldwide recession. Lower energy demand, worldwide overproduction of oil, and the resulting fall in prices, caused a steep decline in the state's petroleum industry. Unemployment in Texas jumped from 6.9% in 1982 to 8% in 1983, a period during which the national rate fell 0.1%. Much of this unemployment was among persons who came to Texas seeking jobs, particularly from northern industrial states. The rise and fall of the oil industry's fortunes affected other industries as well. Thousands of banks that had speculated in real estate in the early eighties, saw many of their investments become worthless, and numerous banks were declared insolvent.

In the wake of the oil-centered recession, Texas began attempts to diversify. The state government has successfully wooed high-tech industries to locate in Texas. The percentage of economic activity contributed by the oil and gas extraction industry dropped from about 20% to 6% between 1980 and 2000. Electronics, telecommunications, food processing, services and retail trade, on the other hand, saw substantial growth in the 1990s. While output from oil and gas extraction increased 7.4% between 1997 and 2001, output from general services rose 35.4%, while output from financial services rose 32.5%; with retail and wholesale trade rising 30.7%, transportation and public utilities by 26.4%, and from government by 24%. In the recession and slowdown of 2001 and 2002, employment growth in Texas followed the national trends, remaining negative through the end of 2002. Shortfalls in state revenues flowing, particularly from the collapse of capital gains income, faced the state government with a serious budget deficit. However, higher oil prices following a Venezuelan oil strike, the US-led invasion of Iraq and rising tensions with Iran have benefited the Texas economy.

In 2004, Texas's gross state product (GSP) was $884.136 billion, of which manufacturing (durable and nondurable goods) accounted for the largest share at $106.749 billion or 12% of GSP, followed by the real estate sector at $90.670 billion (10.2% of GSP), and mining at $56.971 billion (6.4% of GSP). In that same year, there were an estimated 1,787,607 small businesses in Texas. Of the 404,683 businesses that had employees, an estimated total of 399,323 or 98.7% were small companies. An estimated 54,098 new businesses were established in the state in 2004, up 2.7% from the year before. Business terminations that same year came to 55,792, up 0.6% from 2003. There were 3,094 business bankruptcies in 2004, down 1.9% from the previous year. In 2005, the state's personal bankruptcy (Chapter 7 and Chapter 13) filing rate was 407 filings per 100,000 people, ranking Texas as the 37th highest in the nation.

21 INCOME

In 2005 Texas had a gross state product (GSP) of $982 billion which accounted for 7.9% of the nation's gross domestic product and placed the state at number 2 in highest GSP among the 50 states and the District of Columbia.

According to the Bureau of Economic Analysis, in 2004 Texas had a per capita personal income (PCPI) of $30,732. This ranked 29th in the United States and was 93% of the national average of $33,050. The 1994–2004 average annual growth rate of PCPI was 4.3%. Texas had a total personal income (TPI) of $690,587,968,000, which ranked third in the United States and reflected an increase of 6.1% from 2003. The 1994–2004 average annual growth rate of TPI was 6.3%. Earnings of persons employed in Texas increased from $536,483,781,000 in 2003 to $571,564,011,000 in 2004, an increase of 6.5%. The 2003–04 national change was 6.3%.

The US Census Bureau reports that the three-year average median household income for 2002 to 2004 in 2004 dollars was $41,275 compared to a national average of $44,473. During the same period an estimated 16.4% of the population was below the poverty line as compared to 12.4% nationwide.

22 LABOR

According to the Bureau of Labor Statistics (BLS), in April 2006 the seasonally adjusted civilian labor force in Texas 11,390,900, with approximately 578,700 workers unemployed, yielding an unemployment rate of 5.1%, compared to the national average of 4.7% for the same period. Preliminary data for the same period placed nonfarm employment at 9,928,100. Since the beginning of the BLS data series in 1976, the highest unemployment rate recorded in Texas was 9.3% in October 1986. The historical low was 4.3% in January 2001. Preliminary nonfarm employment data by occupation for April 2006 showed that approximately 5.9% of the labor force was employed in construction; 9.1% in manufacturing; 20.4% in trade, transportation, and public utilities; 6.3% in financial activities; 12.1% in professional and business services; 12.2% in education and health services; 9.2% in leisure and hospitality services; and 17.1% in government.

Organized labor has never been able to establish a strong base in Texas, and a state right-to-work law continues to make unionization difficult. The earliest national union, the Knights of Labor, declined in Texas after failing to win a strike against the railroads in 1886 when the Texas Rangers served as strike breakers. That same year, the American Federation of Labor (AFL) began to organize workers along craft lines. One of the more protracted and violent disputes in Texas labor history occurred in 1935 when longshoremen struck Gulf coast ports for 62 days. The Congress of

Industrial Organizations (CIO) succeeded in organizing oil-field and maritime workers during the 1930s.

The BLS reported that in 2005, a total of 506,000 of the state's 9,485,000 employed wage and salary workers were formal members of a union. This represented 5.3% of those so employed, up from 5% in 2004, but still below the national average of 12%. Overall in 2005, a total of 590,000 workers (6.2%) in Texas were covered by a union or employee association contract, which includes those workers who reported no union affiliation.

As of 1 March 2006, Texas had a state-mandated minimum wage rate of $5.15 per hour. In 2004, women in the state accounted for 44.6% of the employed civilian labor force.

23 AGRICULTURE

Texas ranked second among the 50 states in agricultural production in 2005, with farm marketings totaling nearly $16.9 billion (7.2% of US total); crops accounted for 33% of the total. Texas leads the nation in output of cotton, grain sorghum, hay, watermelons, cabbages, and spinach.

Since 1880, Texas has been the leading producer of cotton (producing both Upland and American-Pima), which accounted for 33% of total US production and 9.4% of the state's farm marketings in 2004. After 1900, Texas farmers developed bumper crops of wheat, corn, and other grains by irrigating dry land and transformed the "great Sahara" of West Texas into one of the nation's foremost grain-growing regions. Texans also grow practically every vegetable suited to a temperate or semitropical climate. Since World War II, farms have become fewer and larger, more specialized in raising certain crops and meat animals, more expensive to operate, and far more productive.

About 130 million acres (52.6 million hectares) are devoted to farms and ranches, representing more than three-fourths of the state's total area. The number of farms declined from 420,000 in 1940 to fewer than 185,000 in 1978, but rose to 229,000 in 2004. The average farm was valued at $855 per acre in 2004.

Productive farmland is located throughout the state. Grains are grown mainly in the temperate north and west, and vegetables and citrus fruits in the subtropical south. Cotton has been grown in all sections, but in recent years, it has been extensively cultivated in the High Plains of the west and the upper Rio Grande Valley. Grain sorghum, wheat, corn, hay, and other forage crops are raised in the north-central and western plains regions. Rice is cultivated along the Gulf coast, and soybeans are raised mainly in the High Plains and Red River Valley.

Major crops in 2004 included: upland cotton, 5.35 million acres produced 7.5 million bales (valued at $1.53 billion); wheat, 3.5 million acres produced 108.5 million bushels (valued at $363.5 million); hay, 5.35 million acres produced 12.3 million (valued at $833.6 million); sorghum, grain, 2.1 million acres produced 127.1 million bushels (valued at $288.3 million); corn, 1.7 million acres produced 233.5 million bushels (valued at $595.5 million); rice, 218,000 acres produced 14,690 hundred weight (valued at $120.5 million); vegetables, fresh, 93,500 acres produced 1,010,460 tons (valued at $366.2 million); soybeans, 290,000 acres produced 86 million bushels (valued at $50.5 million).

The major vegetables and fruits, in terms of value, are onions, cabbages, watermelons, carrots, potatoes, cantaloupes, green peppers, honeydew melons, spinach, cucumbers, and lettuce. Cottonseed, barley, oats, peanuts, pecans, sugar beets, sugarcane, and sunflowers are also produced in commercial quantities.

The total value of farmland and buildings alone was estimated at $111.1 billion in 2004, higher than any other state.

About 11.8% of cropland was irrigated in 2002, primarily in the High Plains; other areas dependent on irrigation included the lower Rio Grande Valley and the trans-Pecos region. Approximately 80% of the irrigated land is supplied with water pumped from wells. Because more than half of the state's irrigation pumps are fueled by natural gas, the cost of irrigation increased significantly as gas prices rose during the 1970s.

24 ANIMAL HUSBANDRY

About two-thirds of cattle fattened for market are kept in feedlots located in the Texas panhandle and northwestern plains. In 2005, Texas ranked first in number of cattle and calves with an estimated 13.8 million, valued at $10.8 billion. During 2004, Texas farms had around 980,000 hogs and pigs, valued at $86.2 million. In 2003, Texas's production of sheep and lambs was second after California at 61.9 million lb (28.1 million kg), valued at $50.7 million; shorn wool production was an estimated 5.6 million lb (2.5 million kg) in 2004.

About 90% of the dairy industry is located in eastern Texas. In 2003, milk production was around 5.6 billion lb (2.5 billion kg) from 319,000 milk cows. Poultry production included 2.95 billion lb (1.4 billion kg) of broilers, valued at around $1.03 billion, and 4.8 billion eggs were produced, valued at $310 million.

Breeding of Palominos, Arabians, Appaloosas, Thoroughbreds, and quarter horses is a major industry in Texas. The animals are most abundant in the most heavily populated areas, and it is not unusual for residential subdivisions of metropolitan areas to include facilities for keeping and riding horses.

25 FISHING

In 2004, the commercial catch was about 85.6 million lb (38.9 million kg), valued at $166.2 million. Brownsville-Port Isabel ranked 14th in the nation in ports bringing in the most valuable catches, with receipts of $40.3 million. Other high value ports included Port Arthur (16th), Galveston (20th), and Palacios (25th).

The most important catch was shrimp. In 2004, Texas had the second largest shrimp catch in the nation with 70.1 million lb (31.9 million kg). Other commercial shellfish include blue crabs and oysters. Species of saltwater fish with the greatest commercial value are yellowfin tuna, red snapper, swordfish, and flounder. Texas had 93 fish processing and wholesale plants employing 2,262 people in 2003.

Early in 1980, the US government banned shrimp fishing for 45 days, effective in the summer of 1981, in order to conserve shrimp supplies. Texas has since continued to close the Gulf to shrimping from about 1 June to 15 July.

In 2005, Texas had 62 catfish farms covering 1,030 acres (417 hectares) with sales of $3.5 million, and a 2006 inventory of 10.1 million fingerlings and 2.1 million stocker-sized fish. The state manages fish stocks and habitats to maintain 40.4 million freshwater and 14.5 million marine angler days per year. There are three national fish hatcheries in the state (Uvalde, Inks Dam, and San Marcos). In 2004, Texas issued 1,632,016 sport fishing licenses, more than any other state. Among the most sought-after native freshwater fish are large-mouth and white bass, crappie, sunfish, and catfish.

26 FORESTRY

Texas forestland in 2003 covered 17,149,000 acres (6,940,000 hectares), representing 2.3% of the US total and over 10% of the state's land area. Commercial timberland comprised 11,774,000 acres (4,765,000 hectares), of which about 90% was privately owned. Timberlands managed by the federal government covered 794,000 acres (321,000 hectares). Most forested land, including practically all commercial timberland, is located in the Piney Woods region of east Texas.

In 2004, Texas timberlands yielded 1.79 billion board ft of lumber (88% softwood), tenth in the United States. Primary forest products manufactured include plywood, waferboard, and pulpwood. Texas wood-treating plants process utility poles, crossties, lumber, and fence posts.

The Texas Forest Service, a member of the Texas A&M University System, provides direct, professional forestry assistance to private landowners, manages several state and federal reforestation and forest stewardship incentives programs, coordinates pest control activities, and assists in protecting against wildfires statewide. In addition, the state agency has an urban and community forestry program, forest products laboratory, two tree nurseries, and a genetics laboratory.

As of 2005 there were four national forests in Texas—Angelina, Davy Crockett, Sabine, and Sam Houston—with a total area of 641,574 acres (259,645 hectares). Texas also has five state forests: the E. O. Siecke, W. Goodrich Jones, I. D. Fairchild, John Henry Kirby, and Paul N. Masterson Memorial State Forests.

27 MINING

According to preliminary data from the US Geological Survey (USGS), the estimated value of nonfuel mineral production by Texas in 2003 was valued at around $2 billion, a decrease from 2002 of about 3%. The USGS data ranked Texas as fourth among the 50 states by the total value of its nonfuel mineral production, accounting for over 5% of total US output.

In descending order of value, according to preliminary data for 2003, cement (portland and masonry), crushed stone, construction sand and gravel, lime and salt were the state's top nonfuel minerals. Collectively, these five commodities accounted for around 93% of all nonfuel mineral output, by value, with cement alone accounting for almost 39% of all nonfuel mineral production by the state. Nationally, in descending order of value, Texas in 2003 was the nation's leading producer of crushed stone, second in the production of portland cement, construction sand and gravel, salt, common clays, gypsum, talc, and zeolites. The state was also second (out of two states) in the production of crude helium, ball clay (out of four), and second in the production of brucite (out of two).

The preliminary data for 2003 showed production of portland cement at 10.6 million metric tons, with an estimated value of $753 million, while crushed stone output, that same year, totaled 104 million metric tons, and was valued at $504 million. Construction sand and gravel production in 2003 totaled 78 million metric tons and was valued at $394 million, while lime output totaled 1.58 million metric tons, with a value of $104 million. Salt output in 2003 was put at 8.47 million metric tons, and was valued at $99.3 million.

In 2003, Texas also produced fuller's earth, kaolin, and dimension stone.

²⁸ENERGY AND POWER

Texas is an energy-rich state. Its vast deposits of petroleum and natural gas liquids account for nearly 30% of US proved liquid hydrocarbon reserves. Texas is also the largest producer and exporter of oil and natural gas to other states, and it leads the United States in electric power production.

As of 2003, Texas had 210 electrical power service providers, of which 72 were publicly owned and 68 were cooperatives. Of the remainder, 53 were investor owned, and 17 were owners of independent generators that sold directly to customers. As of that same year there were 10,114,100 retail customers. Of that total, 7,046,095 received their power from investor-owned service providers. Cooperatives accounted for 1,568,284 customers, while publicly owned providers had 1,499,968 customers. There were 23 independent generator or "facility" customers.

Total net summer generating capability by the state's electrical generating plants in 2003 stood at 99.593 million kW, with total production that same year at 379.199 billion kWh. Of the total amount generated, 22.9% came from electric utilities, with the remaining 77.1% coming from independent producers and combined heat and power service providers. The largest portion of all electric power generated, 184.911 billion kWh (48.8%), came from natural gas fired plants, with coal-fired plants in second place at 146.989 billion kWh (38.8%) and nuclear fueled plants in third at 33.437 billion kWh (8.8%). Other renewable power sources, plants using other types of gases, petroleum fired plants, hydroelectric facilities and "other" types of generating plants accounted for the remaining output.

As of 2006, the state had four nuclear reactors in operation: two at the Comanche Peak plant in Somervell County; and two at the South Texas plant (the largest commercial reactors in the United States) near Bay City.

The state's first oil well was drilled in 1866 at Melrose in East Texas, and the first major oil discovery was made in 1894 at Corsicana, northwest of Melrose, in Navarro County. The famous Spindletop gusher, near Beaumont, was tapped on 10 January 1901. Another great oil deposit was discovered in the panhandle in 1921, and the largest of all, the East Texas field, in Rusk County, was opened in 1930. Subsequent major oil discoveries were made in West Texas, starting in Scurry County in 1948. Thirty years later, the state's crude-oil production exceeded 1 billion barrels. In 1983, production was 908.2 million barrels, averaging 2.5 million barrels per day. Production in 1999 was 449.2 million barrels (including over 1 million barrels from offshore wells), averaging 1.23 million barrels per day.

As of 2004, Texas had proven crude oil reserves of 4,613 million barrels, or 22% of all proven US reserves, while output that same year averaged 1,073,000 barrels per day. Including federal offshore domains, the state that year ranked second (first excluding federal offshore) in both proven reserves and production among the 31 producing states. In 2004 Texas had 151,653 producing oil wells and accounted for 20% of all US production. As of 2005, the state's 26 refineries had a combined crude oil distillation capacity of 4,627,611 barrels per day.

In 2004, Texas had 72,237 producing natural gas and gas condensate wells. In that same year, marketed gas production (all gas produced excluding gas used for repressuring, vented and flared, and nonhydrocarbon gases removed) totaled 5,067.315 billion cu ft (143.91 billion cu m). As of 31 December 2004, proven reserves of dry or consumer-grade natural gas totaled 49,955 billion cu ft (1,418.7 billion cu m).

Texas in 2004, had 13 producing coal mines, all of which were surface operations. Coal production that year totaled 45,863,000 short tons, down from 47,517,000 short tons in 2003. Recoverable coal reserves in 2004 totaled 546 million short tons. One short ton equals 2,000 lb (0.907 metric tons).

²⁹INDUSTRY

Before 1900, Texas had an agricultural economy based, in the common phrase, on "cotton, cows, and corn." When the first US Census of Manufactures was taken in Texas in 1849, there were only 309 industrial establishments, with 1,066 wage earners; payrolls totaled $322,368, and the value added by manufacture was a mere $773,896. The number of establishments increased tenfold by 1899, when the state had 38,604 wage earners and a total value added of $38,506,130. During World War II, the value added passed the $1-billion mark, and by 1982, the total was $53.4 billion.

According to the US Census Bureau's Annual Survey of Manufactures (ASM) for 2004, the state's manufacturing sector covered some 21 product subsectors. The shipment value of all products manufactured in the state that same year was $385.534 billion. Of that total, petroleum and coal products manufacturing accounted for the largest share at $91.303 billion. It was followed by chemical manufacturing at $90.169 billion; computer and electronic product manufacturing at $41.537 billion; food manufacturing at $31.430 billion; and transportation equipment manufacturing at $24.747 billion.

In 2004, a total of 773,506 people in Texas were employed in the state's manufacturing sector, according to the ASM. Of that total, 525,332 were actual production workers. In terms of total employment, the fabricated metal product manufacturing industry accounted for the largest portion of all manufacturing employees with 98,407 (74,214 actual production workers). It was followed by food manufacturing, with 82,594 (62,350 actual production workers); computer and electronic product manufacturing, with 72,604 (33,125 actual production workers); machinery manufacturing, with 70,968 (42,913 actual production workers); and transportation equipment manufacturing, with 70,871 (40,627 actual production workers).

ASM data for 2004 showed that Texas's manufacturing sector paid $33.559 billion in wages. Of that amount, the computer and electronic product manufacturing sector accounted for the largest share at $4.435 billion. It was followed by chemical manufacturing at $4.062 billion; transport equipment manufacturing at $3.888 billion; fabricated metal product manufacturing at $3.639 billion; and machinery manufacturing at $3.143 billion.

30 COMMERCE

According to the 2002 Census of Wholesale Trade, Texas's wholesale trade sector had sales that year totaling $397.4 billion from 31,832 establishments. Wholesalers of durable goods accounted for 20,192 establishments, followed by nondurable goods wholesalers at 9,493 and electronic markets, agents, and brokers accounting for 2,147 establishments. Sales by durable goods wholesalers in 2002 totaled $183.4 billion, while wholesalers of nondurable goods saw sales of $177.9 billion. Electronic markets, agents, and brokers in the wholesale trade industry had sales of $36.06 billion.

Texas ranked second among the 50 states in wholesale trade in 2002. The leading wholesaling centers are the Houston, Dallas-Ft. Worth, San Antonio, El Paso, Lubbock, Midland, Amarillo, Austin, and Corpus Christi metropolitan areas.

In the 2002 Census of Retail Trade, Texas was listed as having 75,703 retail establishments with sales of $228.6 billion. The leading types of retail businesses by number of establishments were: gasoline stations (10,610); clothing and clothing accessories stores (10,275); motor vehicle and motor vehicle parts dealers (9,319); food and beverage stores (8,903); and miscellaneous store retailers (8,216). In terms of sales, motor vehicle and motor vehicle parts stores accounted for the largest share of retail sales at $67.4 billion, followed by general merchandise stores at $35.6 billion; food and beverage stores at $32.3 billion; gasoline stations at $20.3 billion; and building material/garden equipment and supplies dealers at $16.2 billion. A total of 1,026,326 people were employed by the retail sector in Texas that year. The state also ranked second behind California in retail sales in 2002.

Foreign exports through Texas during 2005 totaled $128.7 billion. The leading items shipped through Texas ports to foreign countries were grains, chemicals, fertilizers, and petroleum refinery products; principal imports included crude petroleum, minerals and metals (especially aluminum ores), liquefied gases, motor vehicles, bananas, sugar, and molasses. Texas ranked first among the 50 states in 2005 as an exporter of goods produced in the state.

31 CONSUMER PROTECTION

The Attorney General's Consumer Protection Division protects consumers and the legitimate business community by filing civil lawsuits under the Deceptive Trade Practices Act (DTPA) and other related statutes. The division is best known for its work in traditional areas of consumer protection litigation such as false and deceptive advertising, defective merchandise, and home or appliance repair scams, for example.

The attorney general's litigation activities are supplemented by a highly effective mediation program that is available to Texas consumers who have complaints amenable to informal resolution. The Consumer Protection Division also disseminates a wide range of public information materials to educate consumers about their rights, alert them to trends in deceptive or unfair business practices, and prevent losses due to fraud before they occur. Over the years, the division has succeeded in winning funds for consumer education as part of the settlement of consumer protection litigation.

When dealing with consumer protection issues, the state's Attorney General's Office can initiate civil proceedings but can only initiate criminal proceedings under specific statutes for specific crimes. The office can represent the state before state and federal regulatory agencies, administer consumer protection and education programs, and handle formal consumer complaints. However its exercise of subpoena powers is limited. In antitrust actions, the Attorney General's Office can act on behalf of those consumers who are incapable of acting on their own and initiate damage actions on behalf of the state in state courts and represent counties, cities and other governmental entities in recovering civil damages under state or federal law, but the Office has no power to initiate criminal proceedings in an antitrust case.

The state's Office of the Attorney General has regional offices in Austin, Dallas, El Paso, Houston, Lubbock, McAllen, San Antonio. There is a county government consumer affairs office under the District Attorney's Office in Houston, and the city of Dallas also has its own consumer affairs office located within the city's Department of Environmental and Health services.

32 BANKING

Texas has the second highest number of banks in the nation, behind Illinois. As of June 2005, Texas had 677 insured banks, savings and loans, and saving banks, in addition to 231 state-chartered and 407 federally chartered credit unions (CUs). Excluding the CUs, the Dallas-Fort Worth market area accounted for the largest portion of the state's financial institutions and deposits in 2004, with 176 institutions and $113.409 billion in deposits. As of June 2005, CUs accounted for 18% of all assets held by all financial institutions in the state, or some $49.146 billion. Banks, savings and loans, and savings banks collectively accounted for the remaining 72% or $224.280 billion in assets held.

Banking was illegal in the Texas Republic and under the first state constitution, reflecting the widespread fear of financial speculation like that which had caused the panic of 1837. Because both the independent republic and the new state government found it difficult to raise funds or obtain credit without a banking system, they were forced to borrow money from merchants, thus permitting banking functions and privileges despite the constitutional ban. A formal banking system was legalized during the latter part of the 19th century.

The median percentage of past-due/nonaccrual loans to total loans stood at 1.51% as of fourth quarter 2005, down from 1.77% in 2004 and 2.04% in 2003. The median net interest margin (the difference between the lower rates offered savers and the higher rates charged to loans) for the state's insured institutions stood at 4.50% in fourth quarter 2005, up from 4.22% in 2004 and 4.21% in 2003.

Regulation of Texas's state-chartered banks and other state-chartered financial institutions is the responsibility of the Finance Commission of Texas's Department of Banking, Savings and Loan Department, and the Office of Consumer Credit.

33 INSURANCE

The industry's most recent state-by-state comparison (year-end 2003) showed Texas ranked second (behind Arizona) in number of domestic life and health insurance companies with 165, and first in the number of domestic property and casualty companies with 238. In 2004, direct premiums for property and casualty insurance totaled over $32.2 billion. That year, there were 459,522 flood insurance policies in force in the state, with a total value of $84 billion. There were 113,443 beach and windstorm plans in force with a value of about $30 billion. About $22.7 billion of coverage was held through FAIR plans, which are designed to offer coverage for some natural circumstances, such as wind and hail, in high risk areas.

In 2004, there were 10.8 million individual life insurance policies in force in Texas with a total value of $839.3 billion; total value for all categories of life insurance (individual, group, and credit) was over $1.4 trillion. The average coverage amount is $77,600 per policy holder. Death benefits paid that year totaled $3.69 billion.

In 2004, 48% of state residents held employment-based health insurance policies, 4% held individual policies, and 21% were covered under Medicare and Medicaid; 25% of residents were uninsured. Texas has the highest percentage of uninsured residents of all the fifty states; the national average is 16%. In 2003, employee contributions for employment-based health coverage averaged at 16% for single coverage and 27% for family coverage. The state offers a six-month health benefits expansion program for small-firm employees in connection with the Consolidated Omnibus Budget Reconciliation Act (COBRA, 1986), a health insurance program for those who lose employment-based coverage due to termination or reduction of work hours.

Motorists are required to maintain auto insurance coverage that includes a minimum of bodily injury liability of up to $20,000 per individual and $40,000 for all persons injured in an accident, as well as property damage liability of $15,000. In 2003, the average expenditure per vehicle for insurance coverage was about $837.40.

The insurance industry is regulated by the Texas Department of Insurance. TDI is headed by the commissioner of insurance, who is appointed by the governor and confirmed by the state Senate for two-year terms beginning 1 February of odd-numbered years.

[34] SECURITIES

There are no securities exchanges in Texas. In 2005, there were 5,060 personal financial advisers employed in the state and 14,170 securities, commodities, and financial services sales agents. In 2004, there were over 729 publicly traded companies within the state, with over 213 NASDAQ companies, 211 NYSE listings, and 56 AMEX listings. In 2006, the state had 56 Fortune 500 companies, including 8 in the Fortune 100; Exxon Mobil (based in Irving), ranked first in the state and the nation with revenues of over $339.9 billion, followed by ConocoPhillips (Houston, sixth in the nation), Valero Energy (San Antonio, 15th in the nation), Marathon Oil (Houston, 23rd in the nation), and Dell Computers (Round Rock, 25th in the nation). Dell is listed on NASDAQ; the other top four companies are listed on the NYSE. A total of 102 companies are listed on the Fortune 1,000.

The State Securities Board, established in 1957, oversees the issuance and sale of stocks and bonds in Texas.

[35] PUBLIC FINANCE

The Texas budget operates on a "pay as you go" basis in that expenditures cannot exceed revenues during the budget cycle. The state's budget period runs on a biennial basis from 1 September of

each odd-numbered year to 31 August of the following odd-numbered year.

The state legislature meets from approximately January to May every odd-numbered year and writes a budget for the next two years. The appropriations committee in the House, and the finance committee in the Senate are responsible for budget development. The primary legislative entity responsible for oversight of the budget when the legislature is not in session is the 10-member legislative budget board. Chaired by the lieutenant governor, the board prepares the initial budget that will be considered by the legislature.

Texas—State Government Finances

(Dollar amounts in thousands. Per capita amounts in dollars.)

	AMOUNT	PER CAPITA
Total Revenue	90,570,423	4,030.37
General revenue	71,567,893	3,184.76
Intergovernmental revenue	25,639,654	1,140.96
Taxes	30,751,860	1,368.45
General sales	15,460,221	687.98
Selective sales	9,160,557	407.64
License taxes	4,083,148	181.70
Individual income tax	–	–
Corporate income tax	–	–
Other taxes	2,047,934	91.13
Current charges	7,027,396	312.72
Miscellaneous general revenue	8,148,983	362.63
Utility revenue	–	–
Liquor store revenue	–	–
Insurance trust revenue	19,002,530	845.61
Total expenditure	77,338,118	3,441.53
Intergovernmental expenditure	17,032,016	757.92
Direct expenditure	60,306,102	2,683.61
Current operation	40,686,513	1,810.54
Capital outlay	7,429,464	330.61
Insurance benefits and repayments	9,667,420	430.20
Assistance and subsidies	1,481,676	65.93
Interest on debt	1,041,029	46.33
Exhibit: Salaries and wages	11,861,335	527.83
Total expenditure	77,338,118	3,441.53
General expenditure	67,660,579	3,010.88
Intergovernmental expenditure	17,032,016	757.92
Direct expenditure	50,628,563	2,252.96
General expenditures, by function:		
Education	27,312,446	1,215.40
Public welfare	18,613,103	828.28
Hospitals	2,929,885	130.38
Health	1,302,365	57.96
Highways	5,828,707	259.38
Police protection	465,109	20.70
Correction	2,972,593	132.28
Natural resources	893,598	39.76
Parks and recreation	120,673	5.37
Government administration	1,572,677	69.98
Interest on general debt	1,041,029	46.33
Other and unallocable	4,608,394	205.07
Utility expenditure	10,119	.45
Liquor store expenditure	–	–
Insurance trust expenditure	9,667,420	430.20
Debt at end of fiscal year	22,925,515	1,020.18
Cash and security holdings	197,828,786	8,803.35

Abbreviations and symbols: – zero or rounds to zero; (NA) not available; (X) not applicable.

SOURCE: *U.S. Census Bureau, Governments Division, 2004 Survey of State Government Finances*, January 2006.

The governor's office of budget and planning also prepares a budget for the Legislature's consideration. The governor has line-item veto authority over the budget and must sign the appropriations bill before it becomes law. The comptroller of public accounts must also sign the bill certifying that sufficient revenue will be available to fund the budget.

After running large budget surpluses in the early 1980s, the state experienced several years of budget shortfalls in the wake of falling oil prices. As the state's economy has diversified, the budget has shown greater ability to withstand minor economic fluctuations.

Fiscal year (FY) 2006 general funds were estimated at $35.7 billion for resources and $32.2 billion for expenditures. In fiscal year 2004, federal government grants to Texas were $27.7 billion.

In the fiscal year 2007 federal budget, Texas was slated to receive $22 million (a $4 million increase over fiscal year 2006) for the Army Corps of Engineers' urban flood damage reduction project in Sims Bayou; $20 million for the upgrade and expansion of the Ysleta Border Station in El Paso; $13 million to expand the national cemetery in Dallas/Fort Worth; and $7.5 million for additional design and construction funds for a new border station at the proposed international bridge in McAllen.

³⁶TAXATION

In 2005, Texas collected $32,785 million in tax revenues or $1,434 per capita, which placed it 49th among the 50 states in per capita tax burden. The national average was $2,192 per capita. Sales taxes accounted for 49.9% of the total; selective sales taxes, 29.0%; and other taxes, 21.2%.

As of 1 January 2006, Texas had no state income tax, a distinction it shared with Wyoming, Washington, Nevada, Florida, Alaska, and South Dakota.

In 2004, local property taxes amounted to $28,176,329,000 or $1,254 per capita. The per capita amount ranks the state 13th highest nationally. Texas has no state level property taxes.

Texas taxes retail sales at a rate of 6.25%. In addition to the state tax, local taxes on retail sales can reach as much as 2%, making for a potential total tax on retail sales of 8.25%. Food purchased for consumption off-premises is tax exempt. The tax on cigarettes is 41 cents per pack, which ranks 40th among the 50 states and the District of Columbia. Texas taxes gasoline at 20 cents per gallon. This is in addition to the 18.4 cents per gallon federal tax on gasoline.

According to the Tax Foundation, for every federal tax dollar sent to Washington in 2004, Texas citizens received $0.94 in federal spending.

³⁷ECONOMIC POLICY

Texas state government has historically been pro business: regulation is less restrictive than in many states, and there is no corporate income tax. The state government actively encourages outside capital investment in Texas industries, and the state's industrial productivity has produced a generally high return on investment.

Texas Economic Development (TXED) (formerly the Texas Industrial Commission) helps businesses locate or expand their operations in the state. Its stated mission is to market Texas and assist communities to maximize their economic development opportunities. The main divisions within TXED are Business Devel-opment and Tourism. A private organization, the Texas Industrial Development Council, in Bryan, also assists new and developing industries.

Texas announced in 2004 it would put more focus on courting businesses within the technology sector through the establishment of the Texas Emerging Technology Fund (TETF), an outgrowth of the Texas Enterprise Fund (TEF) program. Targeted industries range from nanotechnology to environmental sciences.

³⁸HEALTH

The infant mortality rate in October 2005 was estimated at 6.2 per 1,000 live births. The birth rate in 2003 was 17.2 per 1,000 population, the second-highest rate in the country for that year (following Utah). The abortion rate stood at 18.8 per 1,000 women in 2000. In 2003, about 80.9% of pregnant woman received prenatal care beginning in the first trimester. In 2004, approximately 73% of children received routine immunizations before the age of three.

The crude death rate in 2003 was 7 deaths per 1,000 population. As of 2002, the death rates for major causes of death (per 100,000 resident population) were: heart disease, 199.5; cancer,156.9; cerebrovascular diseases, 48.4; chronic lower respiratory diseases, 35.4; and diabetes, 26. The mortality rate from HIV infection was 4.9 per 100,000 population. In 2004, the reported AIDS case rate was at about 14.7 per 100,000 population. In 2002, about 58.8% of the population was considered overweight or obese. As of 2004, about 20.4% of state residents were smokers.

In 2003, Texas had 414 community hospitals with about 57,300 beds, the highest numbers in the nation. There were about 2.5 million patient admissions that year and 32.3 million outpatient visits. The average daily inpatient census was about 36,400 patients. The average cost per day for hospital care was $1,482. Also in 2003, there were about 1,143 certified nursing facilities in the state with 121,548 beds and an overall occupancy rate of about 72%. In 2004, it was estimated that about 61.3% of all state residents had received some type of dental care within the year. Texas had 219 physicians per 100,000 resident population in 2004 and 656 nurses per 100,000 in 2005. In 2004, there were a total of 10,559 dentists in the state.

There are 8 medical schools, 2 dental colleges, and 64 schools of nursing in the state. The University of Texas has medical colleges at Dallas, Houston, Galveston, San Antonio, and Tyler. The University of Texas Cancer Center at Houston is one of the nation's major facilities for cancer research. Houston is also noted as a center for cardiovascular surgery. On 3 May 1968, Houston surgeon Denton Cooley performed the first human heart transplant in the United States.

In 2005, University of Texas, M.D. Anderson Cancer Center in Houston ranked as the second best hospital in the nation for cancer care by *U.S. News & World Report*. In the same report, the Texas Heart Institute at St. Luke's Episcopal Hospital in Houston was ranked eight in the nation for best care in heart disease and heart surgery. Texas Children's Hospital in Houston ranked fourth for best reputation in pediatric care.

About 17% of state residents were enrolled in Medicaid programs in 2003; 11% were enrolled in Medicare programs in 2004. Approximately 25% of the state population was uninsured in 2004;

this was the highest percentage of uninsured residents in the nation. In 2003, state health care expenditures totaled $25.3 million.

³⁹SOCIAL WELFARE

In 2004, about 422,000 people received unemployment benefits, with the average weekly unemployment benefit at $259. In fiscal year 2005, the estimated average monthly participation in the food stamp program included about 2,451,197 persons (943,506 households); the average monthly benefit was about $90.41 per person. That year, the total of benefits paid through the state for the food stamp program was over $2.6 billion. the highest total in the nation.

Temporary Assistance for Needy Families (TANF), the system of federal welfare assistance that officially replaced Aid to Families with Dependent Children (AFDC) in 1997, was reauthorized through the Deficit Reduction Act of 2005. TANF is funded through federal block grants that are divided among the states based on an equation involving the number of recipients in each state. Texas's TANF cash assistance program, run by the Department of Human Services, is called Texas Works; the work program, run by the Texas Workforce Commission, is called Choices. In 2004, the state program had 250,000 recipients; state and federal expenditures on this TANF program totaled $405 million in fiscal year 2003.

In December 2004, Social Security benefits were paid to 2,864,870 Texans. This number included 1,714,830 retired workers, 334,150 widows and widowers, 347,010 disabled workers, 203,650 spouses, and 265,130 children. Social Security beneficiaries represented 12.7% of the total state population and 89.7% of the state's population age 65 and older. Retired workers received an average monthly payment of $930; widows and widowers, $870; disabled workers, $884; and spouses, $452. Payments for children of retired workers averaged $424 per month; children of deceased workers, $604; and children of disabled workers, $253. Federal Supplemental Security Income payments in December 2004 went to 472,347 Texas residents, averaging $362 a month. An additional $51,000 of state-administered supplemental payments were distributed to 10,371 residents.

⁴⁰HOUSING

The variety of Texas architectural styles reflects the diversity of the state's topography and climate. In the early settlement period, Spanish-style adobe houses were built in southern Texas. During the 1840s, Anglo-American settlers in the east erected primitive log cabins. These were later replaced by "dog-run" houses, consisting of two rooms linked by an open passageway covered by a gabled roof, so-called because pet dogs slept in the open, roofed shelter, as did occasional overnight guests. During the late 19th century, southern-style mansions were built in East Texas, and the familiar ranch house, constructed of stone and usually stuccoed or whitewashed, with a shingle roof and a long porch, proliferated throughout the state; the modern ranch house in southwestern Texas shows a distinct Mexican-Spanish influence. Climate affects such modern amenities as air conditioning: a new house in the humid eastern region is likely to have a refrigeration-style cooler,

while in the dry west and south, an evaporating "swamp cooler" is the more common means of making hot weather bearable.

In 2004, Texas had an estimated 8,846,728 housing units, of which 7,790,853 were occupied; 65.1% were owner-occupied. That year, Texas had the second-highest number of housing units in the nation (following California). About 64.5% of all units were single-family, detached homes. About 63% of all units were built between 1950 and 1989. Electricity and utility gas were the most common energy sources for heating. It was estimated that 492,782 units lacked telephone service, 36,697 lacked complete plumbing facilities, and 47,643 lacked complete kitchen facilities. The average household had 2.81 members.

In 2004, 188,800 new privately owned housing units were authorized for construction. The median home value was $99,858. The median monthly cost for mortgage owners was $1,166. Renters paid a median of $648 per month. In September 2005, the state received grants of over $2.4 million from the US Department of Housing and Urban Development (HUD) for rural housing and economic development programs. For 2006, HUD allocated to the state over $73.2 million in community development block grants (CDBG). Dallas was also awarded about $18.4 million in CDBG monies, Houston was awarded over $30.7 million, and San Antonio was awarded over $14.8 million. Also in 2006, HUD offered an additional $74.5 million to the state in emergency funds to rebuild housing that was destroyed by Hurricanes Katrina, Rita, and Wilma in late 2005.

⁴¹EDUCATION

Although public instruction began in Texas as early as 1746, education was slow to develop during the period of Spanish and Mexican rule. The legislative foundation for a public school system was laid by the government of the Republic of Texas during the late 1830s, but funding was slow in coming. After annexation, in 1846, Galveston began to support free public schools, and San Antonio had at least four free schools by the time a statewide system of public education was established in 1854. Free segregated schooling was provided for black children beginning in the 1870s, but their schools were ill-maintained and underfinanced. School desegregation was accomplished during the 1960s, nonviolently for the most part.

In 2004, 78.3% of the population 25 years old and over had completed four years of high school, significantly lower than the national average of 84%. Some 24.5% had four or more years of college. The total enrollment for fall 2002 in Texas public schools stood at 4,260,000. Of these, 3,080,000 attended schools from kindergarten through grade eight, and 1,180,000 attended high school. Approximately 38.7% of the students were white, 14.3% were black, 43.8% were Hispanic, 2.9% were Asian/Pacific Islander, and 0.3% were American Indian/Alaskan Native. Total enrollment was estimated at 4,277,000 in fall 2003 and expected to be 4,923,000 by fall 2014, an increase of 15.6% during the period 2002–14. Expenditures for public education in 2003/04 were estimated at $38 billion. In fall 2003 there were 220,206 students enrolled in 1,282 private schools. Since 1969, the National Assessment of Educational Progress (NAEP) has tested public school students nationwide. The resulting report, *The Nation's Report Card,* stated that in 2005, eighth graders in Texas scored 281 out of 500 in mathematics compared with the national average of 278.

As of fall 2002, there were 1,152,369 students enrolled in college or graduate school; minority students comprised 41.3% of total postsecondary enrollment. In 2005 Texas had 208 degree-granting institutions. Institutions of higher education include 42 public four-year colleges and universities, 69 public two-year college campuses, and 51 nonprofit, private four-year schools. The leading public universities are Texas A&M (College Station), which opened in 1876, and the University of Texas (Austin), founded in 1883. Each institution is now the center of its own university system, including campuses in several other cities. Oil was discovered on lands owned by the University of Texas in 1923, and beginning in 1924, the university and Texas A&M shared more than $1 billion in oil-related rentals and royalties. Other state-supported institutions include the University of Houston and Texas Tech University (Lubbock).

The first private college in Texas was Rutersville, established by a Methodist minister in Fayette County in 1840. The oldest private institution still active in the state is Baylor University (1845), at Waco. Other major private universities include Hardin-Simmons (Abilene), Rice (Houston), Southern Methodist or SMU (Dallas), and Texas Christian, or TCU (Ft. Worth). Well-known black-oriented institutions of higher learning include Texas Southern University in Houston and Prairie View A&M University.

Tuition charges to Texas colleges are among the lowest in the nation. The Texas Guaranteed Student Loan Corporation administers a guaranteed-loan program and tuition equalization grants for students in need.

42ARTS

In 2005, the Texas Commission on the Arts (TCA) and other Texas arts organizations received 91 grants totaling $2,751,200 from the National Endowment for the Arts (NEA); in 2006 TCA celebrated its 40th anniversary. Humanities Texas, formerly the Texas Council for the Humanities was established in 1965. In 2005, the National Endowment for the Humanities contributed $3,677,357 for 47 state programs. The state and private sources also provide funding to the Commission and other arts organizations. Both the Texas Museums Association and Texas Responds—a grant program for Texas library services and programs—provided aid for hurricane victims affected by hurricanes Katrina and Rita in 2005.

Although Texas has never been regarded as a leading cultural center, the arts have a long history in the state. The cities of Houston and Matagorda each had a theater before they established churches, and the state's first theater was active in Houston as early as 1838. Stark Young founded the Curtain Club acting group at the University of Texas in Austin in 1909 and the little-theater movement began in that city in 1921. As of 2005, the arts flourished at Houston's Theater District, Jones Hall for the Performing Arts, and Alley Theater, as well as at the Dallas Theater Center, and Theater Three. The Dallas theater company, run by the groundbreaking artist, Margo Jones had a national reputation. After her death in 1955 other companies were founded such as the Texas Repertory Theater Company in Houston. During the late 1970s, Texas also emerged as a center for motion picture production. The city of Austin has since become the host for the Austin Film Festival and the South by Southwest (SXSW) Film festival and SXSW Music and Media Conference and Festival.

Texas has five major symphony orchestras—the Dallas Symphony (performing in the Myerson Symphony Center since 1989), Houston Symphony, San Antonio Symphony, Austin Symphony, and Fort Worth Symphony—and 25 orchestras in other cities. The Houston Grand Opera performs at Jones Hall, and in 1999 received a National Endowment for the Arts Access grant to provide free outdoor performances and artist residencies.

Several cities have resident dance companies, including Abilene, Amarillo, Denton, Galveston, Garland, Longview, Lubbock, Midland-Odessa, and Pampa. The ballet groups in Fort Worth, Austin, and Corpus Christi are notable. As of 2005, the Houston Ballet, founded in 1955, was the fifth-largest ballet company in the United States.

Popular music in Texas stems from early Spanish and Mexican folk songs, Negro spirituals, cowboy ballads, and German-language songfests. Texans pioneered a kind of country and western music that is more outspoken and direct than Nashville's commercial product, and a colony of country-rock songwriters and musicians were active in the Austin area during the 1970s. Texans of Mexican ancestry have also fashioned a Latin-flavored music ("Tejano") that is as distinctly "Tex-Mex" as the state's famous chili. The Texas Talent Musicians Association (TTMA) holds the annual Tejano Music Awards in San Antonio.

There are a number of groups for writers and storytellers, including the Writers' League of Texas and the Tejas Storytelling Association. In 2005 the Texas Storytelling Association celebrated the 20th anniversary of the Texas Storytelling Festival and in 2006 the Writers' League of Texas celebrated its 25th anniversary. In 2000, the National Center for Children's Illustrated Literature (chartered in 1997) opened in Abilene. Besides sponsoring its own museum of illustrated works, the Center provides educational programs and exhibits for teachers and other display venues.

43LIBRARIES AND MUSEUMS

In 2001, Texas had 540 public library systems, with a total of 825 libraries, of which there were 285 branches. In that same year, the Texas public library system had 35,725,000 volumes of books and serial publications, and a total circulation of 81,505,000. The system also had 1,350,000 audio and 1,139,000 video items, 100,000 electronic format items (CD-ROMs, magnetic tapes, and disks), and 15 bookmobiles. Funding for public libraries in Texas comes from local cities, counties, school districts, and state and federal sources, with additional funding from donations, gifts, and corporate and foundation grants. In fiscal year 2001,operating income for the state's public library system totaled $319,354,000 and included $3,129,000 in federal grants, and $1,672,000 in state grants.

The largest municipal libraries in Texas include the Houston Public Library with 4,573,356 volumes, and the Dallas Public Library with 2,568,852 volumes. The University of Texas at Austin, noted for outstanding collections in the humanities and in Latin American studies, had over seven million volumes in 1998. The Lyndon B. Johnson Presidential Library is also located in Austin, as is the Lorenzo de Zavala State Archives and Library Building. Other notable academic libraries include those of Texas A&M University, with over two million volumes, and the University of Houston, Rice University, Southern Methodist University, and

Texas Tech University, all with collections of over one million volumes.

Among the state's 389 museums are Austin's Texas Memorial Museum; the Dallas Museum of Fine Arts and the Dallas Museum of Art; and the Amon Carter Museum of Western Art, the Ft. Worth Art Museums, and Kimbell Art Museum, all in Ft. Worth. Houston has the Museum of Fine Arts, Contemporary Arts Museum, and at least 30 galleries. Both Dallas-Ft. Worth and Houston have become major centers of art sales.

National historic sites in Texas are Ft. Davis (Jeff Davis County), President Johnson's boyhood home and Texas White House (Blanco and Gillespie counties), and the San Jose Mission (San Antonio). Other historic places include the Alamo, Dwight D. Eisenhower's birthplace at Denison, the Sam Rayburn home in Bonham, and the John F. Kennedy memorials in Dallas. A noteworthy prehistoric Indian site is the Alibates Flint Quarries National Monument, located in Potter County and accessible by guided tour.

44COMMUNICATIONS

In 2004, 91.8% of the occupied housing units in Texas had telephones. In addition, by June of that same year there were 12,091,134 mobile wireless telephone subscribers. In 2003, 59.0% of Texas households had a computer and 51.8% had Internet access. By June 2005, there were 2,989,919 high-speed lines in Texas, 2,737,826 residential and 252,093 for business.

Dallas was one of Western Union's first US communications satellite stations, and it leads the state as a center for data communications. The state has not always been in the communications vanguard, however. Texas passed up a chance to make a handsome profit from the invention of the telegraph when, in 1838, inventor Samuel F. B. Morse offered his newfangled device to the republic as a gift. When the Texas government neglected to respond, Morse withdrew the offer.

Texas had 298 major radio stations (73 AM, 225 FM) in 2005 and 87 major television stations. The state's first radio station, WRR, was established by the city of Dallas in 1920. The first television station, WBAP, began broadcasting in Ft. Worth in 1948. In 1999, the Dallas-Fort Worth area has 2,018,120 television households, only 51% receiving cable; the Houston area has 1,712,060 television households, 58% with cable; and the San Antonio area has 684,730 television homes, 66% with cable.

Approximately 439,135 Internet domain names were registered with the state in the year 2000; the third most of any state.

45PRESS

The first newspaper in Texas was a revolutionary Spanish-language sheet published in May 1813 at Nacogdoches. Six years later, the *Texas Republican* was published by Dr. James Long in the same city. In 1835, the *Telegraph and Texas Register* became the official newspaper of the Texas Republic and it continued to publish until 1877. The first modern newspaper was the *Galveston News* (1842), a forerunner of the *Dallas Morning News* (1885).

In 2005, Texas had 49 morning dailies, 36 evening dailies, and 78 Sunday papers. Texas had the second-largest number of daily newspapers in the country in 2005 (second to California). In 2004, the Houston *Chronicle* and the Dallas *Morning News* were ranked as the ninth- and tenth-largest daily newspapers nationwide.

The newspapers with the largest daily circulations (2005 est.) were as follows:

AREA	NAME	DAILY	SUNDAY
Austin	*American-Statesman* (m,S)	177,926	226,766
Dallas	*Morning News* (m,S)	519,014	755,912
Fort Worth	*Star-Telegram* (m,S)	258,489	326,803
Houston	*Chronicle* (m,S)	554,783	737,580
San Antonio	*Express-News* (m,S)	270,067	356,680

In 2005, there were 491 weekly newspapers with a total circulation of 2,545,596. Of these, the paid weekly *Park City News* of Highland Park ranked seventh in the United States with a circulation of 51,000. Two free weeklies, the McAllen Valley *Town Crier* and the San Antonio *North Side Recorder-Times,* ranked ninth (104,037) and fourteenth (83,700), respectively, by circulation in the United States. The *Texas Almanac,* a comprehensive guide to the state, has been issued at regular intervals since 1857 by the A.H. Belo Corp., publishers of the *Dallas Morning News.* Leading magazines include the *Texas Monthly* and *Texas Observer,* both published in Austin.

46ORGANIZATIONS

In 2006, there were over 14,665 nonprofit organizations registered within the state, of which about 10,292 were registered as charitable, educational, or religious organizations. Irving is the home of one of the nation's largest organizations, the Boy Scouts of America.

Important medical groups are the American Heart Association, the National Association for Retarded Citizens, the American Academy of Nurse Practitioners, the American Pediatric Society, the American Organ Transplant Association, the American Board of Obstetrics and Gynecology, and the American Board of Otolaryngology. The National Temperance and Prohibition Council is in Richardson.

Other professional associations include the American Engineering Association, the Working Ranch Cowboys Association, and the National Athletic Trainers' Association. The Association of Space Explorers., based in Houston, is an international professional organization for astronauts who have made at least one orbit around the Earth.

Among the many organizations devoted to horse breeding are the American Quarter Horse Association, Amarillo, the National Cutting Horse Association, and American Paint Association. Ft. Worth is the home of the Texas Longhorn Breeders Association of America.

The scholarly organization American Mensa is based in Arlington. National and state arts and cultural organizations include the American Association of Community Theatre, the American Cowboy Culture Association, the American Indian Arts Council, the Texas Folklore Society, the Texas International Theatrical Arts Society, the Texas Historical Foundation, and the Writers' League of Texas. National sports organizations based in Texas include the United States Professional Tennis Association and the United States Youth Soccer Association.

47TOURISM, TRAVEL, AND RECREATION

In 2004, the state hosted over 180 million visitors with direct travel spending at $44.4 billion, an all-time high. The industry supported 500,000 jobs with $13 million in payroll. Marketing for tourism and travel to Texas is the responsibility of Texas Economic Development Market Texas Tourism. Dallas-Ft. Worth, San Antonio, and Austin are the cities most frequently visited.

Each of the state's seven major tourist regions offers outstanding attractions. East Texas has one of the state's oldest cities, Nacogdoches, with the nation's oldest public thoroughfare and a reconstruction of the Old Stone Fort, a Spanish trading post dating from 1779. Jefferson, an important 19th-century inland port, has many old homes, including Excelsior House. Tyler, which bills itself as the "rose capital of the world," features a 28-acre (11-hectare) municipal rose garden and puts on a Rose Festival each October. The Gulf Coast region of southeastern Texas offers the Lyndon B. Johnson Space Center, the Astrodome sports stadium, and adjacent Astroworld amusement park, and a profusion of museums, galleries, and shops, all in metropolitan Houston; Spindletop Park, in Beaumont, commemorates the state's first great oil gusher; Galveston's sandy beaches, deep-sea fishing, and Sea-Arama Marineworld; and the Padre Island National Seashore.

To the north, the Dallas-Ft. Worth metropolitan area (including Arlington) has numerous cultural and entertainment attractions, including the Six Flags Over Texas amusement park and the state fair held in Dallas each October. Old Abilene Town amusement park, with its strong western flavor, is also popular with visitors. The Hill Country of south-central Texas encompasses many tourist sites, including the state capitol in Austin, Waco's Texas Ranger Museum (Ft. Fisher), the Lyndon B. Johnson National Historic Site, and frontier relics in Bastrop and Bandera. The Lyndon Baines Johnson Presidential Library is in Austin and the George H.W. Bush Presidential Library is in College Station.

South Texas has the state's most famous historic site—the Alamo, in San Antonio. The Rio Grande Valley Museum, at Harlingen, is popular with visitors, as is the King Ranch headquarters in Kleberg County. The Great Plains region of the Texas panhandle offers Palo Duro Canyon—Texas's largest state park covering 16,402 acres (6,638 hectares) in Armstrong and Randall counties; the Prairie Dog Town at Lubbock; Old West exhibits at Matador; and the cultural and entertainment resources of Amarillo. In the extreme northwestern corner of the panhandle is the XIT Museum, recalling the famous XIT Ranch, at one time the world's largest fenced ranch, which formerly covered more than 3 million acres (1.2 million hectares). Outstanding tourist sites in the far west are the Big Bend and Guadalupe Mountains national parks, the Jersey Lilly Saloon and Judge Roy Bean visitor center in Langtry, and metropolitan El Paso. Texas also has the Great Texas Coastal Birding Trail with 624 mi (1,040 km) of coastline viewing.

Texas's park system includes Palo Duro Canyon, Big Creek (Ft. Bend County), Brazos Island (Cameron County), Caddo Lake (Harrison County), Dinosaur Valley (Somervell County), Eisenhower (Grayson County), Galveston Island, and Longhorn Cavern (Burnet County). State historical parks include San Jacinto Battleground (east Harris County), Texas State Railroad (Anderson and Cherokee counties), and Washington-on-the-Brazos (Washington County). Hunting and fishing are extremely popular in Texas. White-tailed deer are hunted as a way of cutting the wildlife population; thousands of jabalina and wild turkeys are shot annually.

48 SPORTS

Texas has 11 major professional sports teams: the Texas Rangers and Houston Astros of Major League Baseball; the Dallas Cowboys and Houston Texans of the National Football League; the Dallas Stars of the National Hockey League; the Houston Rockets, San Antonio Spurs, and Dallas Mavericks of the National Basketball Association; the Houston Comets and San Antonio Silver Stars of the Women's National Basketball Association, and the FC Dallas, formerly the Dallas Burn, of Major League Soccer. The Cowboys are, by far, the most consistently successful of Texas's teams. They have won the Super Bowl five times—in 1972, 1978, 1993, 1994, and 1996. They have appeared in it and lost an additional three times. The Houston Rockets won consecutive NBA Championships in 1994 and 1995. Houston lost the Oilers of the NFL, who moved to Tennessee after the 1996 season. However, an expansion team, the Texans, replaced them and began NFL play in 2002. Texas is also home to many minor league baseball and hockey teams.

Pari-mutuel betting on horse races was legalized in Texas in the early 1990s, and thoroughbred tracks are open near Houston and Dallas. Quarter-horse racing is also popular and rodeo is a leading spectator sport. Participant sports popular with Texans include hunting, fishing, horseback riding, boating, swimming, tennis, and golf. State professional and amateur golf tournaments are held annually, as are numerous rodeos. The Texas Sports Hall of Fame was organized in 1951; new members are selected each year by a special committee of the Texas Sports Writers Association.

There are a plethora of colleges and universities in Texas, with many elite teams in football, basketball, and baseball. The University of Texas Longhorns are traditionally strong in football, having captured four national championships (1963, 1969, 1970, 2005) and made over 40 bowl game appearances. They also have a very solid baseball program. Texas A&M University in College Station also has an elite football program. Their team earned a national championship in 1939 and won 18 conference titles in the now-defunct Southwestern Conference. In 1998 the Aggies won the Big Twelve Conference title. Texas Tech's women's basketball team has been consistently ranked as a top team in the national polls. Baylor and Rice Universities, of the Big Twelve Conference and Western Athletic Conference, respectively, both field outstanding baseball teams. The teams are traditionally ranked high in the national polls. The Rice Owls won the 2003 College World Series.

Two NASCAR Nextel Cup races, the Samsung/Radio Shack 500 and the Dickies 500, and two NASCAR Busch Grand National series races, the O'Reilly 300 and the O'Reilly Challenge, are held each year at the Texas Motor Speedway in Fort Worth.

49 FAMOUS TEXANS

Two native sons of Texas have served as president of the United States. Dwight D. Eisenhower (1890–1969), the 34th president, was born in Denison, but his family moved to Kansas when he was two years old. Lyndon Baines Johnson (1908–73), the 36th president, was the only lifelong resident of the state to serve in that office. Born near Stonewall, he occupied center stage in state and national politics for a third of a century as US representative, Democratic majority leader of the US Senate, and vice president under John F. Kennedy, before succeeding to the presidency after Kennedy's assassination. Reelected by a landslide, Johnson accomplished much of his Great Society program of social reform but saw his power and popularity wane because of the war in Viet Nam. His wife, Claudia Alta Taylor "Lady Bird" Johnson (b.1912), was influential in environmental causes as First Lady.

Texas's other native vice president was John Nance Garner (1868–1967), former speaker of the US House of Representatives. George Bush (b.Massachusetts, 1924), who founded his own oil development company and has served in numerous federal posts, was elected vice president in 1980 on the Republican ticket and reelected in 1984, then elected to the presidency in 1988. Tom C. Clark (1899–1977) served as an associate justice on the US Supreme Court from 1949 to 1967; he stepped down when his son Ramsey (b.1927) was appointed US attorney general, a post the elder Clark had also held.

Another prominent federal officeholder from Texas was Jesse H. Jones (1874–1956), who served as chairman of the Reconstruction Finance Corporation and secretary of commerce under Franklin D. Roosevelt. Oveta Culp Hobby (1905–95), publisher of the *Houston Post,* became the first director of the Women's Army Corps (WAC) during World War II and the first secretary of the Department of Health, Education, and Welfare under President Eisenhower. John Connally (1917–1993), a protégé of Lyndon Johnson's, served as secretary of the US Navy under Kennedy and, as governor of Texas, was wounded in the same attack that killed the president; subsequently, he switched political allegiance, was secretary of the treasury under Richard Nixon, and had been active in Republican Party politics. Other federal officials from Texas include "Colonel" Edward M. House (1858–1938), principal advisor to President Wilson, and Leon Jaworski (1905–82), the Watergate special prosecutor whose investigations led to President Nixon's resignation. Lloyd Bentsen, a senator and a secretary of the treasury, was born 11 February 1921 in Mission, Texas.

The state's most famous legislative leader was Sam Rayburn (1882–1961), who served the longest tenure in the nation's history as speaker of the US House of Representatives—17 years in three periods between 1940 and 1961. James Wright (b.1922) was Democratic majority leader of the House in the 1970s and early 1980s, and Barbara C. Jordan (1936–96) won national attention as a forceful member of the House Judiciary Committee during its impeachment deliberations in 1974.

Famous figures in early Texas history include Moses Austin (b.Connecticut, 1761–1821) and his son, Stephen F. Austin (b.Virginia, 1793–1836), often called the "father of Texas." Samuel "Sam" Houston (b.Virginia, 1793–1863), adopted as a youth by the Cherokee, won enduring fame as commander in chief of the Texas revolutionary army, as president of the Texas Republic, and as the new state's first US senator; earlier in his career, he had been governor of Tennessee. Mirabeau Bonaparte Lamar (b.Georgia, 1798–1859), the second president of the republic, founded the present state capital (now called Austin) in 1839. Anson Jones (b.Massachusetts, 1798–1858) was the last president of the republic.

Noteworthy state leaders include John H. Reagan (b.Tennessee, 1818–1905), postmaster general for the Confederacy; he dominated Texas politics from the Civil War to the 1890s, helping to write the state constitutions of 1866 and 1875, and eventually becoming chairman of the newly created Texas Railroad Commission.

The most able Texas governor was probably James Stephen Hogg (1851–1906), the first native-born Texan to hold that office. Another administration with a progressive record was that of Governor James V. Allred (1899–1959), who served during the 1930s. In 1924 Miriam A. "Ma" Ferguson (1875–1961) became the first woman to be elected governor of a state, and she was elected again in 1932. With her husband, Governor James E. Ferguson (1871–1944), she was active in Texas politics for nearly 30 years. Texas military heroes include Audie Murphy (1924–71), the most decorated soldier of World War II (and later a film actor), and Admiral of the Fleet Chester W. Nimitz (1885–1966).

Figures of history and legend include James Bowie (b.Kentucky, 1796?–1836), who had a reputation as a brawling fighter and wheeler-dealer until he died at the Alamo: he is popularly credited with the invention of the bowie knife. David "Davy" Crockett (b.Tennessee, 1786–1836) served three terms as a US representative from Tennessee before departing for Texas; he, too, lost his life at the Alamo. Among the more notorious Texans was Roy Bean (b.Kentucky, 1825–1903), a judge who proclaimed himself "the law west of the Pecos." Gambler, gunman, and desperado John Wesley Hardin (1853–95) boasted that he "never killed a man who didn't deserve it." Bonnie Parker (1910–34) and Clyde Barrow (1909–34), second-rate bank robbers and murderers who were shot to death by Texas lawmen, achieved posthumous notoriety through the movie *Bonnie and Clyde* (1967).

Many Texas businessmen have profoundly influenced the state's politics and lifestyle. Clint Murchison (1895–1969) and Sid Richardson (1891–1959) made great fortunes as independent oil operators and spread their wealth into other enterprises: Murchison became owner-operator of the successful Dallas Cowboys professional football franchise, and Richardson, through the Sid Richardson Foundation, aided educational institutions throughout the Southwest. Oilman H(aroldson) L(afayette) Hunt (b.Illinois, 1889–1974), reputedly the wealthiest man in the United States, was an avid supporter of right-wing causes. Howard Hughes (1905–79), an industrialist, aviation pioneer, film producer, and casino owner, became a fabulously wealthy eccentric recluse in his later years. Stanley Marcus (1905–2002), head of the famous specialty store Neiman-Marcus, became an arbiter of taste for the world's wealthy and fashionable men and women. Rancher Richard King (b.New York, 1825–85) put together the famed King Ranch, the largest in the United States at his death. Charles Goodnight (b.Illinois, 1836–1929) was an outstanding cattleman. H. Ross Perot, billionaire computer software developer and independent presidential candidate in 1992 and 1996, was born 27 June 1930 in Dallas.

Influential Texas historians include folklorist John A. Lomax (b.Mississippi, 1867–1948); Walter Prescott Webb (1888–1963), whose books *The Great Plains* and *The Great Frontier* helped shape American thought; and J. Frank Dobie (1888–1964), well-known University of Texas educator and compiler of Texas folklore. Dan Rather (b.1931) has earned a nationwide reputation as a television reporter and anchorman. Frank Buck (1884–1950), a successful film producer, narrated and appeared in documentaries showing his exploits among animals.

William Sydney Porter (b.North Carolina, 1862–1910) apparently embezzled funds from an Austin bank, escaped to Honduras, but returned to serve a three-year jail term—during which time he began writing short stories, later published under the pen name

O. Henry. Katherine Anne Porter (1890–1980) also won fame as a short-story writer. Fred Gipson (1908–73) wrote *Hound Dog Man* and *Old Yeller,* praised by critics as a remarkable evocation of a frontier boy's viewpoint. Two novels by Larry McMurtry (b.1936), *Horsemen, Pass By* (film title, *Hud*) and *The Last Picture Show,* became significant motion pictures. Robert Rauschenberg (b.1925) is a leading contemporary painter. Elisabet Ney (b.Germany, 1833–1907), a sculptor, came to Texas with a European reputation and became the state's first determined feminist; she wore pants in public, and seldom passed up an opportunity to transgress Texans' Victorian mores. E. Donnall Thomas, 1990 co-recipient of the Nobel Prize in medicine, was born 15 March 1920 in Mart, Texas.

Prominent Texans in the entertainment field include Mary Martin (1913–1990), who reigned over the New York musical comedy world for two decades; her son, Larry Hagman (b.1931), star of the *Dallas* television series; actress Debbie Reynolds (b.1931); movie director King Vidor (1894–1982); and Joshua Logan (1903–1988), director of Broadway plays and Hollywood movies. Texans who achieved national reputations with local repertory companies were Margo Jones (1912–55) and Nina Vance (1914–80), who founded and directed theater groups in Dallas and Houston, respectively; and Preston Jones (1936–79), author of *A Texas Trilogy* and other plays.

Among Texas-born musicians, Tina Turner (b.1941) is a leading rock singer, as was Janis Joplin (1943–70). Willie Nelson (b.1933) wedded progressive rock with country music to start a new school of progressive "outlaw" music. Bob Wills (b.Oklahoma, 1905–75) was the acknowledged king of western swing. Musicians Trini Lopez (b.1937), Freddy Fender (Baldemar Huerta, b.1937), and Johnny Rodriguez (b.1951) have earned popular followings based on their Mexican-American music. Charlie Pride (b.Mississippi, 1938) became the first black country-western star. Other country-western stars born in Texas are Waylon Jennings (1937–2002) and Kenny Rogers (b.1938). In the jazz field, pianist Teddy Wilson (1912–86) was a member of the famed Benny Goodman trio in the 1930s. Trombonist Jack Teagarden (1905–64) and trumpeter Harry James (1916–83) have also been influential.

The imposing list of Texas athletes is headed by Mildred "Babe" Didrikson Zaharias (1913–56), who gained fame as an All-American basketball player in 1930, won two gold medals in track and field in the 1932 Olympics, and was the leading woman golfer during the 1940s and early 1950s. Another Texan, John Arthur "Jack" Johnson (1878–1946), was boxing's first black heavyweight champion. Texans who won fame in football include quarterbacks Sammy Baugh (b.1914), Don Meredith (b.1938), and Roger Staubach (b.Ohio, 1942); running back Earl Campbell (b.1955); and coaches Dana X. Bible (1892–1980). Darrell Royal (b.Oklahoma, 1924), and

Thomas Wade "Tom" Landry (1924–2000). Tim Brown (b.Dallas, Texas 1966), a wide receiver in the NFL, won the Heisman Trophy in 1987 as a member of the Fighting Irish of Notre Dame. Among other Texas sports greats are baseball Hall of Famers Tris Speaker (1888–1958) and Rogers Hornsby (1896–1963); golfers Ben Hogan (1912–97), Byron Nelson (b.1912), and Lee Trevino (b.1939); auto racing driver A(nthony) J(oseph) Foyt (b.1935); and jockey William Lee "Willie" Shoemaker (1931–2003). Nolan Ryan, pitching giant, was born 31 January 31 1947 in Refugio, Texas.

50 BIBLIOGRAPHY

Cartwright, Gary. *Turn Out the Lights: Chronicles of Texas in the 80s and 90s.* Austin: University of Texas Press, 2000.

Chipman, Donald E. *Spanish Texas, 1519-1821.* Austin: University of Texas Press, 1992.

Council of State Governments. *The Book of the States, 2006 Edition.* Lexington, Ky.: Council of State Governments, 2006.

Haley, James L. *Passionate Nation: The Epic History of Texas.* New York: Free Press, 2006.

James, Gary. *The Texas Guide.* Golden, Colo.: Fulcrum Pub., 2000.

Jones, C. Allan. *Texas Roots: Agriculture and Rural Life before the Civil War.* College Station: Texas A&M University Press, 2005.

Lack, Paul D. *The Texas Revolutionary Experience: A Political and Social History, 1835-1836.* College Station: Texas A&M University Press, 1992.

Powell, Mary Jo. *Texas.* New York: Interlink Books, 2004.

Preston, Thomas. *Great Plains: North Dakota, South Dakota, Nebraska, Kansas, Oklahoma, and Texas.* Vol. 4 in *The Double Eagle Guide to 1,000 Great Western Recreation Destinations.* Billings, Mont.: Discovery Publications, 2003.

Rees, Amanda (ed.). *The Great Plains Region.* Vol. 1 in *The Greenwood Encyclopedia of American Regional Cultures.* Westport, Conn.: Greenwood Press, 2004.

Reseńdez, Andreś. *Changing National Identities at the Frontier: Texas and New Mexico, 1800–1850.* New York: Cambridge University Press, 2005.

Teitelbaum, Michael. *Texas, 1527-1836.* Washington, D.C.: National Geographic, 2005.

US Department of Commerce, Economics and Statistics Administration, US Census Bureau. *Texas, 2000. Summary Social, Economic, and Housing Characteristics: 2000 Census of Population and Housing.* Washington, D.C.: US Government Printing Office, 2003.

UTAH

State of Utah

ORIGIN OF STATE NAME: Named for the Ute Indians. **NICKNAME:** The Beehive State. **CAPITAL:** Salt Lake City. **ENTERED UNION:** 4 January 1896 (45th). **SONG:** "Utah, We Love Thee;" "Utah, This is the Place." **MOT-TO:** Industry. **COAT OF ARMS:** In the center, a shield flanked by American flags shows a beehive with the state motto and six arrows above, sego lilies on either side, and the numerals "1847" (the year the Mormons settled in Utah) below. Perched atop the shield is an American eagle. **FLAG:** Inside a thin gold circle, the coat of arms and the year of statehood are centered on a blue field, fringed with gold. **OFFICIAL SEAL:** The coat of arms with the words "The Great Seal of the State of Utah 1896" surrounding it. **BIRD:** California sea gull. **FISH:** Bonneville cutthroat trout. **FLOWER:** Sego lily. **TREE:** Blue spruce. **GEM:** Topaz. **LEGAL HOLIDAYS:** New Year's Day, 1 January; Birthday of Martin Luther King Jr., 3rd Monday in January; Washington and Lincoln Day, 3rd Monday in February; Memorial Day, last Monday in May; Independence Day, 4 July; Pioneer Day, 24 July; Labor Day, 1st Monday in September; Columbus Day, 2nd Monday in October; Veterans' Day, 11 November; Thanksgiving Day, 4th Thursday in November; Christmas Day, 25 December. **TIME:** 5 AM MST = noon GMT.

¹LOCATION, SIZE, AND EXTENT

Located in the Rocky Mountain region of the western United States, Utah ranks 11th in size among the 50 states.

The area of Utah totals 84,899 sq mi (219,899 sq km), of which land comprises 82,073 sq mi (212,569 sq km) and inland water 2,826 sq mi (7,320 sq km). Utah extends 275 mi (443 km) E–W and 345 mi (555 km) N–S.

Utah is bordered on the N by Idaho; on the NE by Wyoming; on the E by Colorado; and on the S by Arizona (with the two borders joined at Four Corners); and on the W by Nevada. The total boundary length of Utah is 1,226 mi (1,973 km). The state's geographic center is in Sanpete County, 3 mi (5 km) N of Manti.

²TOPOGRAPHY

The eastern and southern two-thirds of Utah belong to the Colorado Plateau, a region characterized by deep river canyons; erosion has carved much of the plateau into buttes and mesas. The Rocky Mountains are represented by the Bear River, Wasatch, and Uinta ranges in the north and northeast. These ranges, rising well above 10,000 ft (3,000 m), hold the highest point in Utah—Kings Peak in the Uintas—at an altitude of 13,528 ft (4,126 m). The mean elevation of the state is approximately 6,100 ft (1,861 m).

The arid, sparsely populated Great Basin dominates the western third of the state. Drainage in this region does not reach the sea, and streams often disappear in the dry season. To the north are the Great Salt Lake, a body of hypersaline water, and the Great Salt Lake Desert (containing the Bonneville Salt Flats), both remnants of a vast prehistoric lake that covered the region during the last Ice Age. The lowest point in Utah—2,000 ft (610 m) above sea level—occurs at Beaverdam Creek in Washington County, in the southwest corner of the state.

The western edge of the Wasatch Range, or Wasatch Front, holds most of Utah's major cities. It also attracts the greatest rain-fall and snowfall, particularly in the north. Two regions rich in fossil fuels are the Kaiparowits Plateau, in southern Utah, and the Overthrust Belt, a geologic structural zone underlying the north-central part of the state.

The largest lake is the Great Salt Lake, which at the end of 1984 covered 2,250 sq mi (5,827 sq km) and was 34% larger than in 1976. In 1984, as a result of increased precipitation, the lake rose to 4,209.25 ft (1,283 m) above sea level, its highest level since 1877; the lake has been rising steadily since 1963, causing severe flooding, and its waters, diluted by runoff, have lost some salinity. Other major bodies of water are Utah Lake, Bear Lake (shared with Idaho), and Lake Powell, formed by the Glen Canyon Dam on the Colorado River. Other important rivers include the Green, flowing into the Colorado; the Sevier, which drains central and southern Utah; and the Bear, which flows into the Great Salt Lake.

³CLIMATE

The climate of Utah is generally semiarid to arid. Temperatures are favorable along the Wasatch Front, where there are relatively mild winters. At Salt Lake City, the normal daily average temperature is 52°F (11°C), ranging from 28°F (-2°C) in January to 78°F (26°C) in July. The record high temperature, 117°F (47°C), was set at St. George on 5 July 1985; the record low temperature, -69°F (-56°C), in Peter's Sink, on 1 February 1985. The average annual precipitation varies from less than 5 in (12.7 cm) in the west to over 40 in (102 cm) in the mountains, with Salt Lake City receiving about 15.6 in (39 cm) per year. The annual snowfall for the state is about 59 in (150 cm) and remains on the higher mountains until late summer.

⁴FLORA AND FAUNA

Botanists have recognized more than 4,000 floral species in Utah's six major life zones. Common trees and shrubs include four species of pine and three of juniper; aspen, cottonwood, maple, hawthorn, and chokecherry also flourish, along with the Utah oak, Joshua tree, and blue spruce (the state tree). Among Utah's wildflowers are sweet William and Indian paintbrush; the sego lily is the state flower. In April 2006, 24 of Utah's plant species were classified as threatened or endangered by the US Fish and Wildlife Service, including five species (San Rafael, Siler pincushion, Wright fishhook, Uinta Basin hookless, and Winkler) of cactus, dwarf bear-poppy, five species (Shivwitz, Deseret, Holmgren, heliotrope, and Welsh's) of milk-vetch, and autumn buttercup.

Mule deer are the most common of Utah's large mammals; other mammals include pronghorn antelope, Rocky Mountain bighorn sheep, lynx, grizzly and black bears, and white- and black-tailed jackrabbits. Among native bird species are the great horned owl, plain titmouse, and water ouzel; the golden eagle and great white pelican are rare species; and the sea gull (the state bird) is a spring and summer visitor from the California coast. The pygmy rattler is found in southwest Utah, and the Mormon cricket is unique to the state.

In April 2006, 16 animal species (vertebrates and invertebrates) were listed as threatened or endangered in Utah. Among them were the bald eagle, Utah prairie dog, three species (bonytail, humpback, and Virgin River) of chub, two species of sucker, southwestern willow flycatcher, and woundfin. Many birds and fish have been killed or imperiled by the inundation of freshwater marshes with salt water from the flooding Great Salt Lake.

[5] ENVIRONMENTAL PROTECTION

Divisions of the Department of Natural Resources oversee water and mineral resources, parks and recreation, state lands and forests, and wildlife. The Department of Agriculture is concerned with soil conservation and pesticide control. The Department of Environmental Quality has separate divisions dealing with air quality, drinking water systems, water quality, and regulation of water pollution, radioactive, hazardous, and solid wastes.

Air pollution is a serious problem along the Wasatch Front where 70% of the state's population resides. Automobiles are a major contributor to the high levels of ozone and carbon monoxide impacting the communities in the Salt Lake, Weber, and Utah counties. Also of considerable concern is the quality of drinking water. Other environmental issues of concern in the state are transportation safety of hazardous materials, chemical warfare agent storage and disposal, a proposed nuclear fuel storage site in the western part of the state (which, as of March 2003 had been approved despite widespread protests against it, but had not yet built), and interstate transportation of hazardous waste for disposal. In 2003, 242 million lb of toxic chemicals were released in the state.

Another environmental problem is the pollution of Great Salt Lake by industrial waste. In 1996, the lake and its surrounding wetlands were designated a Hemispheric Reserve in the Western Hemisphere Shorebird Reserve Network. The move was taken in recognition of the area's importance to migratory waterfowl and shorebirds.

In 2003, Utah had 197 hazardous waste sites listed in the US Environment Protection Agency (EPA) database, 14 of which were on the National Priorities List as of 2006, including Hill Air Force Base. As of 2003, Utah's Carbon County was home to the second-largest landfill in the United States. In 2005, the EPA spent over $33.9 million through the Superfund program for the cleanup of hazardous waste sites in the state. The same year, federal EPA grants awarded to the state included $8.2 million for the drinking water state revolving fund and $5.6 million for the clean water revolving fund. Other grants included $1.3 million for implementation of the Utah Nonpoint Source Water Pollution Control Program.

[6] POPULATION

Utah ranked 34th in population in the United States with an estimated total of 2,469,585 in 2005, an increase of 10.6% since 2000. Between 1990 and 2000, Utah's population grew from 1,722,850 to 2,233,169, an increase of 29.6%, the fourth-highest percentage gain in the decade among the 50 states. The population is projected to reach 2.78 million by 2015 and 3.2 million by 2025. The population density in 2004 was 29.1 persons per sq mi (11.2 persons per sq km).

Because of the state's consistently high birthrate, Utahans tend to be much younger than the US population as a whole. In 2004, the median age was 28 (compared with the US average of 36.2). In the same year, about 9.7% of state residents were under 5 years of age, and about 31% were younger than 18 years of age (compared with the national average of 25%); only 8.7% of the populace was age 65 or older.

Nearly 90% of all Utahans live in cities and towns, mostly along the Wasatch Front. Salt Lake City is Utah's most populous urban center, with an estimated 2004 population of 178,605 in the city proper and an estimated 1,018,826 in its metropolitan region. Other major cities with large populations include Provo, Ogden, and Orem. The Ogden-Clearfield metropolitan area had an estimated population of 477,455 in 2004 and the Provo-Orem metropolitan area had an estimated population of 412,361.

[7] ETHNIC GROUPS

Hispanics and Latinos constitute the largest ethnic minority in Utah, with an estimated 2000 population of 201,559 or 9% of the total, up from 6.8% in 1990. That percentage had increased to 10.6% by 2004.

American Indians are the third-largest minority group in Utah, numbering an estimated 29,684 in 2000, up from 24,000 in 1990. In 2004, American Indians accounted for 1.3% of the population. Indian lands covered 2,331,000 acres (943,000 hectares) in 1982, all but 35 acres (14 hectares) of which were tribal landholdings. The Uintah and Ouray Indian reservation, in the northeast (2000 population 19,182), and the Navaho Indian reservation, in the southeast, are the largest. Far smaller are the Skull Valley and Goshute reservations, in the west.

About 37,108 Asians resided in the state as of 2000, including 8,045 Chinese, 6,186 Japanese, and 5,968 Vietnamese. Pacific Islanders numbered 15,145. In 2004, Asians accounted for 1.9% of the population, and Pacific Islanders 0.7%. Utah also had an estimated black population of 17,657 as of 2000, up from 12,000 in 1990. In 2004, blacks accounted for 0.9% of the state's population. Until 1978, blacks were denied full church membership as Mormons. In 2004, 1.3% of the population reported origin of two or more races.

Utah had 158,664 residents who were foreign born, or 7.1% of the population, up from 58,600 in 1990. Among persons report-

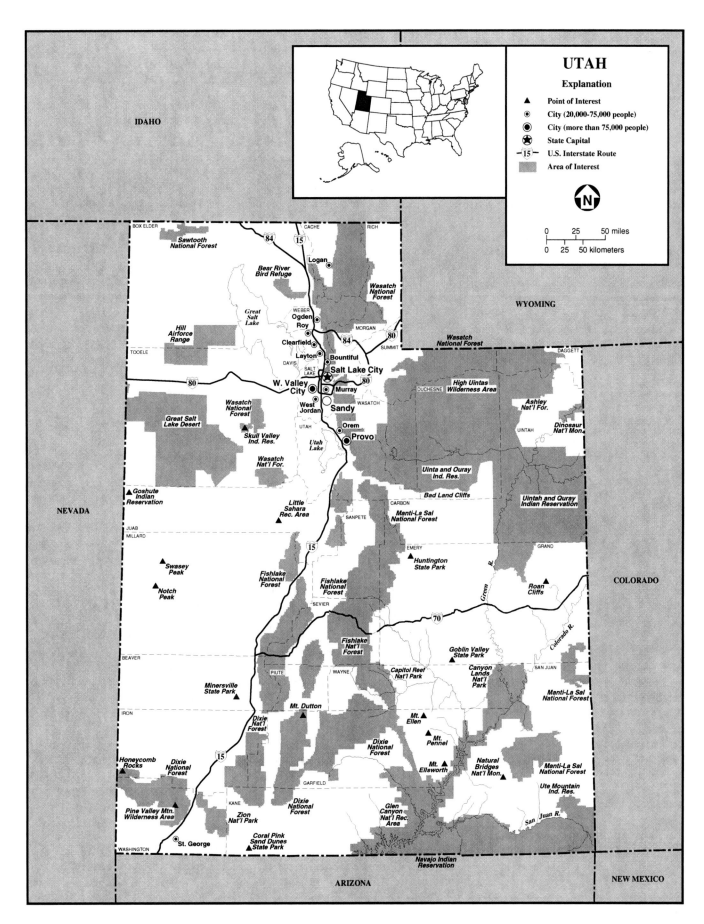

UTAH

Explanation

▲ Point of Interest
⊙ City (20,000–75,000 people)
◉ City (more than 75,000 people)
★ State Capital
—15— U.S. Interstate Route
▨ Area of Interest

IDAHO

NEVADA

WYOMING

COLORADO

ARIZONA

NEW MEXICO

BOX ELDER
CACHE
RICH

Sawtooth
National Forest

Bear River
Bird Refuge

Logan

Wasatch
National
Forest

Great
Salt
Lake

Hill
Airforce
Range

WEBER
Ogden
Roy

Clearfield

Layton

Bountiful

DAVIS

SALT
LAKE

Salt Lake City

W. Valley
City

Murray

West
Jordan

Sandy

Orem

Provo

TOOELE

Wasatch
National
Forest

Skull Valley
Ind. Res.

Wasatch
Nat'l For.

Utah
Lake

UTAH

WASATCH

MORGAN

SUMMIT

Wasatch
National Forest

DAGGETT

High Uintas
Wilderness Area

DUCHESNE

Ashley
Nat'l For.

Dinosaur
Nat'l Mon.

UINTAH

Uinta and Ouray
Ind. Res.

Great Salt
Lake Desert

Goshute
Indian
Reservation

Little
Sahara
Rec. Area

Bad Land Cliffs

Uintah and Quray
Indian Reservation

JUAB
MILLARD

Swasey
Peak

Notch
Peak

Fishlake
National
Forest

Fishlake
National
Forest

CARBON

Manti-La Sal
National Forest

SANPETE

EMERY

Huntington
State Park

GRAND

Green R.

Roan
Cliffs

Colorado R.

SEVIER

70

Fishlake
Nat'l
Forest

Goblin Valley
State Park

San Juan

BEAVER

Minersville
State Park

PIUTE

Mt. Dutton

WAYNE

Capitol Reef
Nat'l Park

Canyon
Lands
Nat'l
Park

SAN JUAN

Manti-La Sal
National Forest

IRON

Dixie
Nat'l
Forest

Mt.
Ellen

Dixie
National
Forest

Mt.
Pennel

Mt.
Ellsworth

Natural
Bridges
Nat'l Mon.

Manti-La Sal
National Forest

Honeycomb
Rocks

Dixie
National
Forest

GARFIELD

Glen
Canyon
Nat'l Rec.
Area

Ute Mountain
Ind. Res.

Pine Valley Mtn.
Wilderness Area

KANE

Dixie
National
Forest

San Juan R.

St. George

Zion
Nat'l Park

Coral Pink
Sand Dunes
State Park

WASHINGTON

Navajo Indian
Reservation

0   25   50 miles
0 25 50 kilometers

N

ing at least one specific ancestry in 2000, 647,987 persons claimed English descent, 258,496 German, 163,048 Danish, 144,713 Irish, and 94,911 Swedish.

8LANGUAGES

Forebears of the Ute, Goshute, and Paiute contributed to English only a few place-names, such as Utah itself, Uinta (and Uintah), Wasatch, and Tavaputs.

Utah English is primarily that merger of Northern and Midland carried west by the Mormons, whose original New York dialect later incorporated features from southern Ohio and central Illinois. Conspicuous in Mormon speech in the central valley, although less frequent now in Salt Lake City, is a reversal of vowels, so that *farm* and *barn* sound like *form* and *born* and, conversely, *form* and *born* sound like *farm* and *barn*.

In 2000, 87.5% of all state residents five years of age or older spoke only English at home; this was a decrease from 92.2% in 1990.

The following table gives selected statistics from the 2000 Census for language spoken at home by persons five years old and over. The category "Other Pacific Island languages" includes Chamorro, Hawaiian, Ilocano, Indonesian, and Samoan.

LANGUAGE	NUMBER	PERCENT
Population 5 years and over	**2,023,875**	**100.0**
Speak only English	1,770,626	87.5
Speak a language other than English	253,249	12.5
Speak a language other than English	**253,249**	**12.5**
Spanish or Spanish Creole	150,244	7.4
German	12,095	0.6
Navajo	9,373	0.5
Other Pacific Island languages	8,998	0.4
French (incl. Patois, Cajun)	7,905	0.4
Chinese	7,093	0.4
Portuguese or Portuguese Creole	5,715	0.3
Vietnamese	5,202	0.3
Japanese	5,032	0.2

9RELIGIONS

The dominant religious group in Utah, accounting for 66% of the entire state population in 2000, was the Church of Jesus Christ of Latter-day Saints, popularly known as the Mormons. The church was founded by Joseph Smith Jr., in 1830, the same year he published the Book of Mormon, the group's sacred text. The Mormon's arrival in Utah climaxed a long pilgrimage that began in New York State and led westward to Missouri, then back to Illinois (where Smith was lynched), and finally across Iowa, Nebraska, and Wyoming to Salt Lake City in 1847.

The Mormon Church and its leadership continue to play a central role in the state's political, economic, and cultural institutions. Among other assets in the state, the church owns Zion Cooperative Mercantile Institute (the largest department store in Salt Lake City), one of the leading newspapers, one television station, and holdings in banks, insurance companies, and real estate. The Salt Lake City Temple on Temple Square has nearly 5 million visitors each year; as of 2006, there were 10 other temples throughout the state. Brigham Young University, named for the second president of the Mormon Church, was established by the church in Provo in 1875.

In 2006, the Church of Latter-day Saints reported a statewide membership of 1,720,434 in 4,307 congregations. The next largest Christian groups include Roman Catholics, with 150,000 members in 2004 and Southern Baptists, with 13,258 members in 2000. In 2000, there were an estimated 4,500 Jews and 3,645 Muslims in the state. About 25.3% of the population did not specify a religious affiliation.

10TRANSPORTATION

Utah, where the golden spike was driven in 1869 to mark the completion of the first transcontinental railroad, had 2,067 rail mi (3,327 km) of track in 2003. The state is served by six railroads, of which two are Class I railroads: the Burlington Northern Santa Fe; and the Union Pacific. As of 2006, Amtrak provided east–west passenger service via its California Zephyr train to Salt Lake City, Provo, Helper, and Green River.

The Utah Transit Authority, created in 1970, provides bus service for Salt Lake City, Provo, and Ogden. In 2004, Utah had 42,710 mi (68,763 km) of public roads and streets. In that same year, there were 2.100 million registered motor vehicles in the state and 1,582,599 licensed drivers. The main east–west and north–south routes (I-80 and I-15, respectively) intersect at Salt Lake City.

In 2005, Utah had a total of 143 public and private-use aviation-related facilities. This included 99 airports and 44 heliports. By far the busiest was Salt Lake City International Airport, with 8,884,880 passengers enplaned in 2004.

11HISTORY

Utah's historic Indian groups are primarily Shoshonean: the Ute in the eastern two-thirds of the state, the Goshute of the western desert, and the Southern Paiute of southwestern Utah. The Athapaskan-speaking Navaho of southeastern Utah migrated from western Canada, arriving not long before the Spaniards. The differing lifestyles of each group remained essentially unchanged until the introduction of the horse by the Spanish sometime after 1600. White settlement from 1847 led to two wars between whites and Indians—the Walker War of 1853–54 and the even more costly Black Hawk War of 1865–68—resulting finally in the removal of many Indians to reservations.

Mexicans and Spaniards are the first non-Indians known to have entered Utah, with Juan María Antonio Rivera reportedly arriving near present-day Moab as early as 1765. In July 1776, a party led by two Franciscan priests, Francisco Atanasio Domínguez and Silvestre Vélez de Escalanta, entered Utah from the east, traversed the Uinta basin, crossed the Wasatch Mountains, and visited the Ute encampment at Utah Lake. Trade between Santa Fe, the capital of the Spanish province of New Mexico, and the Indians of Utah was fairly well established by the early 1800s.

Until 1848, the 1,200-mi (1,900-km) Spanish Trail, the longest segment of which lies in Utah, was the main route through the Southwest. Following this trail, mountain men competing for fur explored vast areas of the American West, including most of Utah's rivers and valleys. In the 1840s, Utah was traversed by California-bound settlers and explorers, the most notable being John C. Frémont.

When Joseph Smith Jr., founder of the Church of Jesus Christ of Latter-day Saints (Mormons), was lynched at Carthage, Ill., in June 1844, Brigham Young and other Mormon leaders decided to move west. By April 1847, the pioneer company of Mormons, including three blacks, was on its way to Utah, the reports of Frémont having influenced their choice of the Great Basin as a refuge. Advance scouts entered the Salt Lake Valley on 22 July, and the rest of the company two days later. Planting and irrigation were begun immediately. Natural resources were regarded as community property, and the church organization served as the first government.

After the Treaty of Guadalupe-Hidalgo (1848) gave the US title to much of the Southwest, the Mormons established the provisional state of Deseret. Congress refused to admit Deseret to the Union, choosing instead to create Utah Territory "with or without slavery." The territory encompassed, in addition to present-day Utah, most of Nevada and parts of Wyoming and Colorado; land cessions during the 1860s left Utah with its present boundaries.

The territorial period lasted for 46 years, marked by immigration, growth, and conflict. Reports that Utahns were in rebellion against federal authority led President James Buchanan to send an expeditionary force under Albert Sidney Johnston to Utah in 1857. On 11 September, Mormon militiamen and their Indian allies, caught up in an atmosphere of war hysteria, massacred some 120 California-bound migrants at Mountain Meadows—the darkest event in Utah history and the only major disaster of the so-called Utah War. Peace was attained in June 1858, and Alfred Cumming assumed civil authority, replacing Brigham Young as territorial governor. Cumming's appointment signaled the beginning of prolonged hostility between Mormon leaders and federal authorities.

Almost 98% of Utah's total population was Mormon until after 1870, and the Mormon way of life dominated politics, economics, and social and cultural activities. As church president, Brigham Young remained the principal figure in the territory until his death in 1877. He contracted in 1868 with the Union Pacific to lay part of the track for the transcontinental railroad in Utah, and on 10 May 1869, the Central (now Southern) Pacific and Union Pacific were joined at Promontory. During the 1870s, new rail lines connected many settlements with the capital, Salt Lake City, spurring commerce and mining. Young had discouraged mining until agriculture and manufacturing were firmly established. Not until 1863, with the rediscovery of silver-bearing ore in Bingham Canyon, did the boom in precious metals begin. Those connected with mining, mostly non-Mormons, began to exert influence in the territory's business, politics, and social life.

Several factors made the non-Mormon minority fearful of Mormon domination: communitarian economic practices, lack of free public schools, encouragement of immigration of Mormon converts, church authoritarianism, and the mingling of church and state. But the most sensational reason was the Mormon practice of polygamy. Congress passed the Anti-Bigamy Act in 1862, but it was generally not enforced. After the Edmunds Act of 1882 was upheld by the US Supreme Court, arrests for polygamy greatly increased. Finally, in 1887, the Edmunds-Tucker Act dissolved the Mormon Church as a corporate entity, thereby threatening the survival of all Mormon institutions.

In fall 1890, Mormon president Wilford Woodruff issued a manifesto renouncing the practice of polygamy. The following year, the Republican and Democratic parties were organized in Utah, effectively ending political division along religious lines. A constitutional convention was held in 1895, and statehood became a reality on 4 January 1896. The new state constitution provided for an elected governor and a bicameral legislature, and restored the franchise to women, a privilege they had enjoyed from 1870 until 1887, when the Edmunds-Tucker Act had disfranchised Utah women and polygamous men.

The early 20th century saw further growth of the mineral industry. Many of those who came to mine copper and coal were foreign immigrants. Militant union activity had begun slowly during the 1890s, until an explosion that killed 200 miners at Scofield on 1 May 1900 dramatized the plight of the miners and galvanized radical organizers in the state. It was in Utah in 1915 that a Swedish miner and songwriter named Joe Hill, associated with the Industrial Workers of the World ("Wobblies"), was executed for the murder of a Salt Lake City grocer and his son, a case that continues to generate controversy because of the circumstantial quality of the evidence against him.

Gradually, modern cities emerged, along with power plants, interurban railroads, and highways. By 1920, nearly half the population lived along the Wasatch Front. The influx of various ethnic groups diversified the state's social and cultural life, and the proportion of Mormons in the total population declined to about 68% in 1920.

Utah businesses enjoyed the postwar prosperity of the 1920s. On the other hand, mining and agriculture were depressed throughout the 1920s and 1930s, decades marked by increased union activity, particularly in the coal and copper industries. The depression of the 1930s hit Utah especially hard. Severe droughts hurt farmers in 1931 and 1934, and high freight rates limited the expansion of manufacturing. With the coming of World War II, increased demand for food revived Utah's agriculture, and important military installations and war-related industries brought new jobs to the state.

In the years after World War II, the state's population more than doubled, while per capita income declined relative to the national average—both trends indicative of a very high birthrate. Politics generally reflect prevailing Mormon attitudes and tend to be conservative. The state successfully opposed plans for storing nerve gas bombs in Utah and for the location in the western desert of an MX missile racetrack system. In 1967 work began on the Central Utah Project, a dam and irrigation program still under way in the early 2000s and intended to assure an adequate water supply for the state through the year 2020.

Utah had one of the nation's fastest growing economies in the 1990s and one of its lowest rates of unemployment. The state's leading industry was the manufacture of transport equipment, including aircraft parts and parts for missiles and rockets. At the beginning of the 21st century, Utahns were divided over the issue of protecting the state's natural areas from residential and commercial development.

Salt Lake City was the site of the 2002 Winter Olympic Games. The selection of Salt Lake City as the site for the games was controversial and mired in a scandal that broke in 1998, as bid leaders for Salt Lake City's selection were charged with bribing International Olympic Committee officials in exchange for their support of Salt Lake City's bid. Ten International Olympic Committee members either resigned or were expelled as a result of the scandal. The 2002 Winter Olympics generated $56 million in profits.

Governor Michael O. Leavitt became the second Utah governor to be elected to a third term in 2000. He was responsible for cutting income and property taxes, and pledged to balance Utah's budget without raising taxes. Leavitt maintained economic prosperity would be achieved through reforming Utah's education system, including adopting a competency standard for high school graduation. In August 2003, President George W. Bush nominated Leavitt to become administrator of the Environmental Protection Agency; he took office that October. Bush then chose Leavitt in December 2004 to become Secretary of the Department of Health and Human Services; he was inaugurated in January 2005.

Wildfires and serious drought conditions plagued Utah in the early 2000s. By 2005, however, the Utah Center for Climate and Weather had declared Utah's six-year drought to be over.

12 STATE GOVERNMENT

The state legislature, as established in the constitution of 1896, consists of a 29-member Senate and a 75-seat House of Representatives; senators serve for four years, representatives for two. Annual sessions begin in January and are limited to 45 calendar days. Legislators must be at least 25 years old, US citizens, state residents for at least three years, district residents for at least six months, and qualified voters in their districts. In 2004 legislators received a per diem salary of $120 during regular sessions.

The chief executive officers, all elected for four-year terms, include the governor, lieutenant governor (who also serves as secretary of state), attorney general, treasurer, and auditor. The governor must be at least 30 years old, a qualified voter, and must have been a state resident and citizen for at least five years. The governor and lieutenant governor are jointly. As of December 2004, the governor's salary was $101,600.

A bill passed by the legislature becomes law if signed by the governor, if left unsigned by the governor for 60 days after it has adjourned, or if passed over the governor's veto by two-thirds of the elected members of each house.

Amending the constitution requires a two-thirds vote of the legislature and ratification by majority vote at the next general election. The Utah Constitutional Revision Commission has been a permanent commission since 1977, recommending and drafting proposed constitutional changes. In 2002 voters approved the Commission's recommended constitution changes regarding taxation and state revenue. In 1994 Utah's voters approved constitutional amendment dealings with the rights of crime victims. The state's constitution had been amended 106 times by January 2005.

Voters must be US citizens, at least 18 years old, and have been residents of the state 30 days prior to election day. Restrictions apply to those convicted of certain crimes and to those judged by the court as mentally incompetent to vote.

13 POLITICAL PARTIES

The Republican and Democratic parties are the state's leading political groups. Though there is no party registration in the state, Utah's voting record shows its voters to be heavily Republican. In the elections of 2000, Orrin Hatch was reelected to a fifth term in the US Senate. Utah's other US senator, Republican Robert F. Bennett, was last reelected in 2004. In the 2004 elections, voters sent two Republicans and one Democrat to Washington as their delegation in the US House. At the state level, Republicans continued to dominate the Assembly, with 56 members to the Democrats' 19; while the state Senate had 21 Republicans and 8 Democrats. Republican governor Michael O. Leavitt was first elected in 1992

Utah Presidential Vote by Major Political Parties, 1948–2004

YEAR	ELECTORAL VOTE	UTAH WINNER	DEMOCRAT	REPUBLICAN
1948	4	*Truman (D)	149,151	124,402
1952	4	*Eisenhower (R)	135,364	194,190
1956	4	*Eisenhower (R)	118,364	215,631
1960	4	Nixon (R)	169,248	205,361
1964	4	*Johnson (D)	219,628	181,785
1968	4	*Nixon (R)	156,665	238,728
1972	4	*Nixon (R)	126,284	323,643
1976	4	Ford (R)	182,110	337,908
1980	4	*Reagan (R)	124,266	439,687
1984	5	*Reagan (R)	155,369	469,105
1988	5	*Bush (R)	207,343	428,442
1992**	5	Bush (R)	183,429	322,632
1996**	5	Dole (R)	221,633	361,911
2000	5	*Bush, G. W. (R)	203,053	515,096
2004	5	*Bush, G. W. (R)	241,199	663,742

*Won US presidential election.
**IND. candidate Ross Perot received 203,400 votes in 1992 and 66,461 votes in 1996.

and secured a third term in the 2000 election. In November 2003, he resigned to become the head of the Environmental Protection Agency, and Lt. Gov. Olene Walker became governor. Jon Huntsman, Jr. was elected governor in 2004.

In November 2000, true to form, Utahns cast 67% of their presidential votes for Republican George W. Bush; 26% for Democrat Al Gore; and 5% for Green Party candidate Ralph Nader. In 2004, incumbent President Bush won even greater support, at 71% of the vote to Democratic challenger John Kerry's 26.4%. In 2004 there were 1,278,000 registered voters; there is no party registration in the state. The state had five electoral votes in the 2004 presidential election.

14 LOCAL GOVERNMENT

Utah has 29 counties, governed by elected commissioners. Other elected county officials include clerk-auditor, sheriff, assessor, recorder, treasurer, county attorney, and surveyor. Counties are the most powerful form of local government, having administrative, judicial, and financial authority. They also are responsible for law enforcement, education, and welfare.

There were 236 municipal governments in 2005. Larger cities were run by an elected mayor and two commissioners while smaller communities were governed by mayor and city council. Nevertheless, the state's largest municipality, Salt Lake City, adopted the mayor-council system. Additionally, the state had 40 public school districts and 300 special districts in 2005.

In 2005, local government accounted for about 78,549 full-time (or equivalent) employment positions.

15 STATE SERVICES

To address the continuing threat of terrorism and to work with the federal Department of Homeland Security, homeland security in Utah operates under state statute; the public safety director is designated as the state homeland security advisor.

The Office of Education is responsible for public instruction, and the Utah State Board of Regents oversees the state college and university system. Highways and airports are the responsibility of the Department of Transportation.

The Department of Commerce supports economic and technological development programs in the state. Agencies dealing with the elderly, disabled, family services, mental health, assistance payments, and youth corrections are under the Department of Human Services. The Department of Health oversees public health and health care for the indigent. Other state departments deal with natural resources, business, labor, agriculture, corrections, and public safety.

[16]JUDICIAL SYSTEM

Utah's highest court is the Supreme Court, consisting of a chief justice and four other justices, each serving a 10-year term. As of 1999 there were 37 district court judges, each one serving a 6-year term. Supreme court justices and district court judges are appointed by the governor with the consent of the state Senate. Appointments must be ratified by the voters at the next general election. In 1984, to ease the supreme court's caseload, residents approved a constitutional amendment allowing the legislature to create an intermediate court.

As of 31 December 2004, a total of 5,989 prisoners were held in Utah's state and federal prisons, an increase from 5,763 of 2.5% from the previous year. As of year-end 2004, a total of 510 inmates were female, up from 427 or 19.4% from the year before. Among sentenced prisoners (one year or more), Utah had an incarceration rate of 246 per 100,000 population in 2004.

According to the Federal Bureau of Investigation, Utah in 2004, had a violent crime rate (murder/nonnegligent manslaughter; forcible rape; robbery; aggravated assault) of 236 reported incidents per 100,000 population, or a total of 5,639 reported incidents. Crimes against property (burglary; larceny/theft; and motor vehicle theft) in that same year totaled 97,607 reported incidents or 4,085.6 reported incidents per 100,000 people. Utah has a death penalty, of which lethal injection is the sole method of execution. However, those inmates sentenced to death prior to the passage of legislation banning the firing squad may still opt for that method of execution. From 1976 through 5 May 2006, the state carried out six executions, the last of which was in October 1999. As of 1 January 2006, Utah had nine inmates on death row.

In 2003, Utah spent $47,120,361 on homeland security, an average of $20 per state resident.

[17]ARMED FORCES

In 2004, there were 5,756 active-duty military personnel and 14,715 civilian personnel stationed in Utah, the majority of whom were at Hill Air Force Base near Ogden and, in the Great Salt Lake Desert, Tooele Army Depot. Dugway Proving Ground—where nerve gas tests have been conducted—and the USAF Utah Test and Training Range are near the Nevada line. State firms were awarded more than $1.87 billion in federal contracts during the same year. In addition, there was another $1.54 billion in payroll outlays by the Department of Defense in the state.

In 2003, there were 151,129 veterans living in Utah, of whom 21,934 were veterans of World War II, 17,133 of the Korean conflict, 44,416 of the Vietnam era, and 25,822 of the Persian Gulf War. In 2004, the Veterans Administration expended more than

$369 million in pensions, medical assistance, and other major veterans' benefits.

As of 31 October 2004, the Utah Highway Patrol employed 387 full-time sworn officers.

[18]MIGRATION

After the initial exodus of Latter-day Saints from the eastern United States to Utah, Mormon missionaries attracted other immigrants to the state, and some 90,000 foreign converts arrived between 1850 and 1905. Many non-Mormons were recruited from overseas to work in the mines, especially during the early 20th century. Utah had a net gain from migration of 176,000 between 1940 and 1985. From 1985 to 1990, there was a net loss from migration of 10,500. Between 1990 and 1998, the state had net gains of 86,000 in domestic migration and 27,000 in international migration. In 1998, some 3,360 foreign immigrants arrived in Utah; of these, 1,035 came from Mexico. The state's population increased 21.9% between 1990 and 1998, making it the fourth-fastest growing state in the nation. In the period 2000–05, net international migration was 49,995 and net internal migration was -33,822, for a net gain of 16,173 people.

[19]INTERGOVERNMENTAL COOPERATION

Utah participates in several regional agreements, including the Bear River Compact (with Idaho and Wyoming), Colorado River Compact, and the Upper Colorado River Basin Compact. The state is also a signatory to the Interstate Oil and Gas Compact, Western Interstate Corrections Compact, Western Interstate Commission for Higher Education, and Western Interstate Energy Compact. Federal grants in fiscal year 2005 amounted to $2.107 billion, an estimated $2.144 billion in fiscal year 2006, and an estimated $2.252 billion in fiscal year 2007.

[20]ECONOMY

Trade replaced government as the leading employer in Utah in 1980. Nearly 14% of personal income in the state was derived from government sources in 1995, a proportion that increased to 14.7% by 1997. With more than 70% of Utah's land under US control and some 37,750 civilian workers on federal payrolls—and others employed by defense industries or the military—the federal presence in Utah is both a major economic force and a controversial political issue. On one hand, elected officials have sought federal funds for mammoth reclamation and power projects. On the other hand, they resent many federal programs concerned with social welfare, land use, or environmental protection. Employment in the 1990s shifted away from agriculture, mining, transportation, and communications toward government, trade, and service occupations, and to a much lesser extent, manufacturing. Utah suffered disproportionately from cuts in the federal military budget in the early nineties, but from 1997 to 2001, output from the government sector increased 27%, including a 30.7% increase from federal operations, civilian and military. Even stronger growth was shown in other service sectors, with financial services up 55%, and general services up 33.8%. Output from Utah's manufacturing sector increased 18% between 1997 and 2000, increasing its share in the gross state product from 14.1% to 15.6%. However, it plummeted 11.7% in the national recession and slowdown of 2001, reducing its share in total state output to 11.5%. In

2002, Utah ranked seventh in the nation in job losses. Construction jobs were down 7%, in part because of the end of work for the 2002 Winter Olympics that were held in Utah. Manufacturing jobs in December 2002 were down 3.2% year-on-year, and the loss of high-paying jobs in high-tech and venture capital fields was seriously impacting personal income in the state. As of September 2002, personal bankruptcy filings had increased 15% over the year before, as Utah continued to have among the highest foreclosure and bankruptcy rates in the country.

In 2004, Utah's gross state product (GSP) was $82.611 billion, of which the real estate sector accounted for the largest share at $10.101 billion or 12.2% of GSP, followed by manufacturing (durable and nondurable goods) at $8.567 billion (10.3% of GSP), and professional and technical services at $4.917 billion (5.9% of GSP). In that same year, there were an estimated 203,468 small businesses in Utah. Of the 61,118 businesses that had employees, an estimated total of 59,025 or 96.6% were small companies. An estimated 11,357 new businesses were established in the state in 2004, up 6.6% from the year before. Business terminations that same year came to 11,579, up 11.9% from 2003. There were 440 business bankruptcies in 2004, down 15.2% from the previous year. In 2005, the state's personal bankruptcy (Chapter 7 and Chapter 13) filing rate was 931 filings per 100,000 people, ranking Utah as the fourth-highest in the nation.

21 INCOME

In 2005 Utah had a gross state product (GSP) of $90 billion which accounted for 0.7% of the nation's gross domestic product and ranked the state 33rd among the 50 states and the District of Columbia.

According to the Bureau of Economic Analysis, in 2004 Utah had a per capita personal income (PCPI) of $26,603. This ranked 47th in the United States and was 80% of the national average of $33,050. The 1994–2004 average annual growth rate of PCPI was 4.2%. Utah had a total personal income (TPI) of $64,398,905,000, which ranked 35th in the United States and reflected an increase of 6.8% from 2003. The 1994–2004 average annual growth rate of TPI was 6.5%. Earnings of persons employed in Utah increased from $49,557,449,000 in 2003 to $53,256,554,000 in 2004, an increase of 7.5%. The 2003–04 national change was 6.3%.

The US Census Bureau reports that the three-year average median household income for 2002–04 in 2004 dollars was $50,614 compared to a national average of $44,473. During the same period an estimated 9.6% of the population was below the poverty line as compared to 12.4% nationwide.

22 LABOR

According to the Bureau of Labor Statistics (BLS), in April 2006 the seasonally adjusted civilian labor force in Utah 1,314,200, with approximately 46,200 workers unemployed, yielding an unemployment rate of 3.5%, compared to the national average of 4.7% for the same period. Preliminary data for the same period placed nonfarm employment at 1,185,100. Since the beginning of the BLS data series in 1976, the highest unemployment rate recorded in Utah was 9.7% in March 1983. The historical low was 3% in April 1997. Preliminary nonfarm employment data by occupation for April 2006 showed that approximately 7.5% of the labor force was employed in construction; 10.1% in manufacturing; 19.5% in trade, transportation, and public utilities; 5.8% in financial activities; 13% in professional and business services; 11.2% in education and health services; 8.9% in leisure and hospitality services; and 17.3% in government.

The BLS reported that in 2005, a total of 51,000 of Utah's 1,035,000 employed wage and salary workers were formal members of a union. This represented 4.9% of those so employed, down from 5.8% in 2004, and well below the national average of 12%. Overall in 2005, a total of 63,000 workers (6.1%) in Utah were covered by a union or employee association contract, which includes those workers who reported no union affiliation. Utah is one of 22 states with a right-to-work law.

As of 1 March 2006, Utah had a state-mandated minimum wage rate of $5.15 per hour. In 2004, women in the state accounted for 44.5% of the employed civilian labor force.

23 AGRICULTURE

Despite a dry climate and unpromising terrain, Utah ranked 37th in the United States in value of farm marketings in 2005, with $1.25 billion. Crops accounted for $292 million; livestock and livestock products for $961 million. The first pioneers in Utah settled in fertile valleys near streams, which were diverted for irrigation. Modern Utah farmers and ranchers practice comprehensive soil and water conservation projects to help maximize crop yields and protect the natural resources. A farmland preservation movement is under way to protect valuable food-producing land from urban sprawl. In 2004 there were some 15,300 farms and ranches, covering 11,600,000 acres (4,700,000 hectares). The chief crops in 2004 were hay, 2.5 million tons; wheat, 5.8 million bushels; and tart cherries, 22 tons.

24 ANIMAL HUSBANDRY

Livestock and livestock products accounted for 77% of Utah's agricultural income in 2004. In 2005, there were an estimated 860,000 cattle and calves, valued at nearly $808.4 million, on Utah farms and ranches. During 2004, hogs and pigs numbered 690,000 and were valued at around $75.9 million. Utah farms produced 20.4 million lb of sheep and lambs in 2003, and an estimated 2.25 million lb (1 million kg) of shorn wool in 2004. Dairy farms had around 91,000 milk cows, which produced 1.62 billion lb (0.74 billion kg) of milk.

25 FISHING

Fishing in Utah is for recreation only. The state maintains egg-taking facilities at Bear Lake, Swan Creek, St. Charles, and Big Spring Creek to support 5.2 million angler days annually. There are two national fish hatcheries in the state (Ouray and Jones Hole). Fish restoration projects seek to recover razorback sucker and cutthroat trout. In 2004, Utah issued 373,834 sport fishing licenses.

26 FORESTRY

In 2004, Utah had 15,173,000 acres (6,141,000 hectares) of forestland. In 2004, 8,189,000 acres (3,314,000 hectares) were in the state's six national forests—Ashley, Dixie, Fishlake, Manti-La Sal, Uinta, and Wasatch-Cache. Only 2,746,000 acres (1,111,000 hectares) were private commercial timberland in 2004. In the same year, lumber production was 57 million board feet.

²⁷MINING

According to preliminary data from the US Geological Survey (USGS), the estimated value of nonfuel mineral production by Utah in 2003 was $1.26 billion, an increase from 2002 of about 2%. The USGS data ranked Utah as ninth among the 50 states by the total value of its nonfuel mineral production, accounting for over 3% of total US output.

According to the preliminary data for 2003, the production of metals were the state's top nonfuel minerals sector, accounting for some 59% of all nonfuel minerals output, of which copper accounted for over 60% of all metals produced. By descending order of value, magnesium metal was the state's top nonfuel mineral, followed by beryllium concentrates. Nationally, Utah was second in the production of copper, magnesium compounds and potash, third in the production of gold and molybdenum concentrates, fourth in phosphate rock and silver, and sixth in the output of salt. The state also ranked third in perlite.

Preliminary data for 2003, showed salt production totaling 2.2 million metric tons, with a value of $112 million, while the output of construction sand and gravel, that same year, totaled 26.5 million metric tons, with a value of $101 million. Crushed stone production in 2003 stood at 8 million metric tons, and was worth $40 million. Utah in 2003 produced 2.5 million metric tons of beryllium contrates, which were valued at $ million.

Utah was also the only US source of mined beryllium during the year. The largest operating beryllium mine in the world is in Juab County, located at Spor Mountain. Utah was also a producer of portland cement and lime.

²⁸ENERGY AND POWER

As of 2003, Utah had 52 electrical power service providers, of which 41 were publicly owned and nine were cooperatives. Of the remainder, one was investor owned, and one was federally operated. As of that same year there were 929,903 retail customers. Of that total, 699,483 received their power from investor-owned service providers. Cooperatives accounted for 33,957 customers, while publicly owned providers had 196,459 customers. There were four federal customers.

Total net summer generating capability by the state's electrical generating plants in 2003 stood at 5.798 million kW, with total production that same year at 38.023 billion kWh. Of the total amount generated, 98.7% came from electric utilities, with the remainder coming from independent producers and combined heat and power service providers. The largest portion of all electric power generated, 35.978 billion kWh (94.6%), came from coal-fired plants, with natural gas fueled plants in second place at 1.385 billion kWh (3.6%) and hydroelectric plants in third at 421.339 million kWh (1.1%). Other renewable power sources and petroleum fired plants accounted for the remaining production.

As of 2004, Utah had proven crude oil reserves of 215 million barrels, or 1% of all proven US reserves, while output that same year averaged 40,000 barrels per day. Including federal offshore domains, the state that year ranked 13th (12th excluding federal offshore) in proven reserves and 14th (13th excluding federal offshore) in production among the 31 producing states. In 2004 Utah had 2,143 producing oil wells and accounted for 1% of all US production. As of 2005, the state's five refineries had a combined crude oil distillation capacity of 167,350 barrels per day.

In 2004, Utah had 3,657 producing natural gas and gas condensate wells. In that same year, marketed gas production (all gas produced excluding gas used for repressuring, vented and flared, and nonhydrocarbon gases removed) totaled 277.969 billion cu ft (7.89 billion cu m). As of 31 December 2004, proven reserves of dry or consumer-grade natural gas totaled 3,866 billion cu ft (109.79 billion cu m).

Utah is the only coal-producing state whose entire production comes from underground mines. In 2004, there were 13 producing coal mines in the state. Coal production that year totaled 21,746,000 short tons, down from 23,044,000 short tons in 2003. Recoverable coal reserves in 2004 totaled 317 million short tons. One short ton equals 2,000 lb (0.907 metric tons).

²⁹INDUSTRY

Utah's diversified manufacturing is concentrated geographically in Salt Lake City, Weber, Utah, and Cache counties.

According to the US Census Bureau's Annual Survey of Manufactures (ASM) for 2004, Utah's manufacturing sector covered some 16 product subsectors. The shipment value of all products manufactured in the state that same year was $29.588 billion. Of that total, food manufacturing accounted for the largest share at $4.369 billion. It was followed by transportation equipment manufacturing at $3.210 billion; miscellaneous manufacturing at $3.123 billion; computer and electronic product manufacturing at $2.704 billion; and primary metal manufacturing at $2.540 billion.

In 2004, a total of 107,362 people in Utah were employed in the state's manufacturing sector, according to the ASM. Of that total, 72,810 were actual production workers. In terms of total employment, the miscellaneous manufacturing industry accounted for the largest portion of all manufacturing employees with 16,401 (10,632 actual production workers). It was followed by food manufacturing, with 14,440 (10,624 actual production workers); computer and electronic product manufacturing, with 11,804 (5,674 actual production workers); transportation equipment manufacturing, with 10,773 (7,204 actual production workers); and fabricated metal product manufacturing, with 10,016 (7,282 actual production workers).

ASM data for 2004 showed that Utah's manufacturing sector paid $4.202 billion in wages. Of that amount, the computer and electronic product manufacturing sector accounted for the largest share at $627.344 million. It was followed by miscellaneous manufacturing at $569.037 million; transport equipment manufacturing at $514.227 million; food manufacturing at $437.197 million; and fabricated metal product manufacturing at $410.073 million.

³⁰COMMERCE

According to the 2002 Census of Wholesale Trade, Utah's wholesale trade sector had sales that year totaling $22.9 billion from 3,369 establishments. Wholesalers of durable goods accounted for 2,111 establishments, followed by nondurable goods wholesalers at 988 and electronic markets, agents, and brokers accounting for 270 establishments. Sales by durable goods wholesalers in 2002 totaled $10.07 billion, while wholesalers of nondurable goods saw sales of $9.2 billion. Electronic markets, agents, and brokers in the wholesale trade industry had sales of $3.5 billion.

In the 2002 Census of Retail Trade, Utah was listed as having 8,135 retail establishments with sales of $23.6 billion. The leading types of retail businesses by number of establishments were: motor vehicle and motor vehicle parts dealers (1,110); clothing and clothing accessories stores (1,038); miscellaneous store retailers (902); and gasoline stations (884). In terms of sales, motor vehicle and motor vehicle parts dealers accounted for the largest share of retail sales at $6.4 billion, followed by general merchandise stores at $3.8 billion; food and beverage stores at $3.2 billion; and gasoline stations at $2.1 billion. A total of 121,745 people were employed by the retail sector in Utah that year.

Foreign exports of Utah's manufactured goods totaled $6.05 billion in 2005.

31 CONSUMER PROTECTION

Consumer protection issues in Utah are primarily handled by the Division of Consumer Protection and the Committee of Consumer Services, both of which are under the state's Department of Commerce, although the Office of the Attorney General does have limited consumer protection responsibilities through its Commercial Enforcement Division.

The Consumer Protection Division investigates and mediates complaints and allegations of unfair, deceptive, or fraudulent business practices. It also conducts ongoing consumer education programs to teach consumers how to recognize consumer fraud and how to avoid becoming a victim. The right's division supplies attorneys for subsequent legal action. The Committee of Consumer Services is the state's consumer advocate regarding utility matters, representing the state's residential, small commercial and agricultural users of electricity, natural gas, and telephone services before the Utah Public Service Commission.

The Commercial Enforcement Division of the Office of the Attorney General is charged with protecting Utah's consumers, specifically in the areas of enforcing federal and state antitrust laws, handling cybercrime, enforcing laws to protect consumers from fraud, identity fraud, and ensuring against Medicaid fraud, as well as consumer related issues associated with the national tobacco settlement, access to government records and with the Health insurance Portability and Accountability Act.

When dealing with consumer protection issues, the state's Attorney General's Office has exclusive authority to file civil proceedings and to represent the state before regulatory agencies. The office can also file criminal proceedings, but has no authority to administer consumer education programs. In addition, the Attorney General's Office can only handle legal issues regarding the administration of formal consumer complaints, and has only limited subpoena powers. In antitrust actions, the Attorney General's Office can only offer legal opinions regarding the state's ability to act on behalf of those consumers who are incapable of acting on their own, and on the representation of counties, cities and other governmental entities in the recovering of civil damages under state or federal law. However, the office can initiate damage actions on behalf of the state in state courts and initiate criminal proceedings.

The offices of the Division of Consumer Protection are located in Salt Lake City.

32 BANKING

As of June 2005, Utah had 68 insured banks, savings and loans, and saving banks, plus 66 state-chartered and 50 federally chartered credit unions (CUs). Excluding the CUs, the Salt Lake City market area accounted for the largest portion of the state's financial institutions and deposits in 2004, with 58 institutions and $101.616 billion in deposits. As of June 2005, CUs accounted for 4.5% of all assets held by all financial institutions in the state, or some $9.792 billion. Banks, savings and loans, and savings banks collectively accounted for the remaining 95.5% or $207.630 billion in assets held.

The median net interest margin (the difference between the lower rates offered savers and the higher rates charged on loans was 6.09% as of fourth quarter 2005, up from 5.13% in 2004 and 5.26% in 2003. The median percentage of past-due/nonaccrual loans to total loans was 1.45% as of fourth quarter 2005, down from 2.17% in 2004 and 2.82% in 2003.

Regulation of Utah's state-chartered banks and other state-chartered financial institutions is the responsibility of the Utah department of Financial Institutions.

33 INSURANCE

Utahans held some 797,000 individual life insurance policies in 2004 with a total value of about $106 billion; total value for all categories of life insurance (individual, group, and credit) was over $144.9 billion. The average coverage amount is $133,200 per policy holder. Death benefits paid that year totaled $381.2 million.

As of 2003, there were 7 property and casualty and 17 life and health insurance companies domiciled in the state. In 2004, direct premiums for property and casualty insurance totaled over $2.89 billion. That year, there were 2,862 flood insurance policies in force in the state, with a total value of $452 million.

In 2004, 62% of state residents held employment-based health insurance policies, 7% held individual policies, and 17% were covered under Medicare and Medicaid; 13% of residents were uninsured. In 2003, employee contributions for employment-based health coverage averaged at 19% for single coverage and 28% for family coverage. The state offers a six-month health benefits expansion program for small-firm employees in connection with the Consolidated Omnibus Budget Reconciliation Act (COBRA, 1986), a health insurance program for those who lose employment-based coverage due to termination or reduction of work hours.

In 2003, there were over 1.5 million auto insurance policies in effect for private passenger cars. Required minimum coverage includes bodily injury liability of up to $25,000 per individual and $50,000 for all persons injured in an accident, as well as property damage liability of $15,000. Personal injury protection is also required. In 2003, the average expenditure per vehicle for insurance coverage was $732.35.

34 SECURITIES

There are no securities exchanges in Utah. In 2005, there were 800 personal financial advisers employed in the state. In 2004, there were over 127 publicly traded companies within the state, with over 33 NASDAQ companies, 7 NYSE listings, and 2 AMEX listings. In 2006, the state had two Fortune 500 companies; Huntsman Corp. ranked first in the state and 172nd in the nation with revenues of over $12.9 billion, followed by Autoliv at 351st in the nation with revenues of $6.2 billion. Both companies were listed on the NYSE. Questar, Zions Bancorp, and SkyWest are listed on the Fortune 1,000.

35 PUBLIC FINANCE

The annual budget is prepared by the State Budget Office and submitted by the governor to the legislature for amendment and approval. The fiscal year (FY) runs from 1 July through 30 June.

Fiscal year 2006 general funds were estimated at $4.4 billion for resources and $4.4 billion for expenditures. In fiscal year 2004, federal government grants to Utah were $2.9 billion

In the fiscal year 2007 federal budget, Utah was slated to receive: $39.8 million in State Children's Health Insurance Program (SCHIP) funds to help the state provide health coverage to low-income, uninsured children who do not qualify for Medicaid. This funding is a 23% increase over fiscal year 2006; and $10 million for the HOME Investment Partnership Program to help Utah fund a wide range of activities that build, buy, or rehabilitate affordable housing for rent or homeownership, or provide direct rental assistance to low-income people. This funding is a 12% increase over fiscal year 2006.

36 TAXATION

In 2005, Utah collected $4,686 million in tax revenues or $1,897 per capita, which placed it 38th among the 50 states in per capita tax burden. The national average was $2,192 per capita. Sales taxes accounted for 36.5% of the total, selective sales taxes 13.2%, individual income taxes 41.1%, corporate income taxes 4.0%, and other taxes 5.1%.

As of 1 January 2006, Utah had six individual income tax brackets ranging from 2.30% to 7.0%. The state taxes corporations at a flat rate of 5.0%.

In 2004, local property taxes amounted to $1,668,988,000 or $689 per capita. The per capita amount ranks the state 39th nationally. Utah has no state level property taxes.

Utah taxes retail sales at a rate of 4.75%. In addition to the state tax, local taxes on retail sales can reach as much as 2.25%, making for a potential total tax on retail sales of 7%. Food purchased for consumption off-premises is taxable. The tax on cigarettes is 69.5 cents per pack, which ranks 29th among the 50 states and the District of Columbia. Utah taxes gasoline at 24.5 cents per gallon. This is in addition to the 18.4 cents per gallon federal tax on gasoline.

According to the Tax Foundation, for every federal tax dollar sent to Washington in 2004, Utah citizens received $1.14 in federal spending.

37 ECONOMIC POLICY

The economic development of Utah has been dominated by two major forces: the relatively closed system of the original Mormon settlers and the more wide-open, speculative ventures of the state's later immigrants. The Mormons developed agriculture, industry, and a cooperative exchange system that excluded non-Mormons. The church actively opposed mining, and it was mostly with non-

Mormon capital, by non-Mormon foreign immigrants, that the state's mineral industry was developed.

In the 1990s, these conflicts were supplanted by a widespread fiscal conservatism that supports business activities and opposes expansion of government social programs at all levels. One Utah politician, J. Bracken Lee, who served as governor from 1949 to 1957, and as mayor of Salt Lake City from 1960–72, became nationally famous for his call to repeal the federal income tax.

Until 2005, Department of Community and Economic Development was the state agency responsible for the expansion of tourism and industry. Effective 1 July 2005, the Division of Busi-

Utah—State Government Finances

(Dollar amounts in thousands. Per capita amounts in dollars.)

	AMOUNT	PER CAPITA
Total Revenue	13,167,850	5,439.01
General revenue	9,560,033	3,948.80
Intergovernmental revenue	2,877,849	1,188.70
Taxes	4,195,962	1,733.15
General sales	1,560,902	644.73
Selective sales	581,338	240.12
License taxes	156,999	64.85
Individual income tax	1,692,035	698.90
Corporate income tax	145,005	59.89
Other taxes	59,683	24.65
Current charges	1,853,528	765.60
Miscellaneous general revenue	632,694	261.34
Utility revenue	–	–
Liquor store revenue	141,859	58.60
Insurance trust revenue	3,465,958	1,431.62
Total expenditure	10,794,264	4,458.60
Intergovernmental expenditure	2,112,921	872.75
Direct expenditure	8,681,343	3,585.85
Current operation	6,224,862	2,571.19
Capital outlay	1,001,804	413.80
Insurance benefits and repayments	937,202	387.11
Assistance and subsidies	331,187	136.80
Interest on debt	186,288	76.95
Exhibit: Salaries and wages	2,029,544	838.31
Total expenditure	10,794,264	4,458.60
General expenditure	9,752,869	4,028.45
Intergovernmental expenditure	2,112,921	872.75
Direct expenditure	7,639,948	3,155.70
General expenditures, by function:		
Education	4,335,952	1,790.98
Public welfare	1,992,986	823.21
Hospitals	505,963	208.99
Health	304,254	125.67
Highways	817,113	337.51
Police protection	114,615	47.34
Correction	275,912	113.97
Natural resources	172,767	71.36
Parks and recreation	41,745	17.24
Government administration	571,909	236.23
Interest on general debt	186,288	76.95
Other and unallocable	433,365	179.00
Utility expenditure	–	–
Liquor store expenditure	104,193	43.04
Insurance trust expenditure	937,202	387.11
Debt at end of fiscal year	4,962,141	2,049.62
Cash and security holdings	19,472,625	8,043.22

Abbreviations and symbols: – zero or rounds to zero; (NA) not available; (X) not applicable.

SOURCE: *U.S. Census Bureau, Governments Division, 2004 Survey of State Government Finances*, January 2006.

ness and Economic Development (DBED) and the Division of Travel Development became part of the new Governor's Office of Economic Development. Programs that are part of the governor's economic include tourism, corporate site selection, rural development, film, science and technology, and international business development. Also created in 2005 was the Department of Community and Culture, which administers programs for volunteers, the Division of Housing and Community Development, the Division of Indian Affairs, the Martin Luther King Jr. Commission, the Office of Museum Services, the Utah Office of Ethnic Affairs, the Utah Arts Council, the Utah Citizens Corps, the Division of Utah State History, and the Utah State Library.

[38] HEALTH

Health conditions in Utah are exceptionally good. The infant mortality rate in October 2005 was estimated at 4.4 per 1,000 live births, the lowest rate in the country for that year. The birth rate in 2003 was the highest in the nation at 21.2 per 1,000 population. The abortion rate stood at 6.6 per 1,000 women in 2000. In 2003, about 80.3% of pregnant woman received prenatal care beginning in the first trimester. In 2004, approximately 71% of children received routine immunizations before the age of three; this was the second-lowest rate in the nation for immunizations (above Nevada).

The crude death rate in 2003 was 5.7 deaths per 1,000 population. As of 2002, the death rates for major causes of death (per 100,000 resident population) were: heart disease, 128.5; cancer, 102.6; cerebrovascular diseases, 39; chronic lower respiratory diseases, 26; and diabetes, 22. The mortality rate from HIV infection was unavailable that year. In 2004, the reported AIDS case rate was at about 3.3 per 100,000 population. In 2002, about 52.1% of the population was considered overweight or obese. As of 2004, about 10.5% of state residents were smokers, the lowest percentage of the 50 states.

In 2003, Utah had 42 community hospitals with about 4,400 beds. There were about 215,000 patient admissions that year and 4.5 million outpatient visits. The average daily inpatient census was about 2,500 patients. The average cost per day for hospital care was $1,654. Also in 2003, there were about 90 certified nursing facilities in the state with 7,438 beds and an overall occupancy rate of about 71.3%. In 2004, it was estimated that about 72.3% of all state residents had received some type of dental care within the year. Utah had 215 physicians per 100,000 resident population in 2004 and 630 nurses per 100,000 in 2005. In 2004, there was a total of 1,573 dentists in the state.

About 12% of state residents were enrolled in Medicaid programs in 2003; 9% were enrolled in Medicare programs in 2004. Approximately 13% of the state population was uninsured in 2004. In 2003, state health care expenditures totaled $1.5 million.

[39] SOCIAL WELFARE

In 2004, about 45,000 people received unemployment benefits, with the average weekly unemployment benefit at $266. In fiscal year 2005, the estimated average monthly participation in the food stamp program included about 133,263 persons (53,162 households); the average monthly benefit was about $88.31 per person.

That year, the total of benefits paid through the state for the food stamp program was about $141.2 million.

Temporary Assistance for Needy Families (TANF), the system of federal welfare assistance that officially replaced Aid to Families with Dependent Children (AFDC) in 1997, was reauthorized through the Deficit Reduction Act of 2005. TANF is funded through federal block grants that are divided among the states based on an equation involving the number of recipients in each state. Utah's TANF program is called the Family Employment Program (FEP). In 2004, the state program had 23,000 recipients; state and federal expenditures on this TANF program totaled $56 million in fiscal year 2003.

In December 2004, Social Security benefits were paid to 262,330 Utah residents. This number included 171,520 retired workers, 22,770 widows and widowers, 27,120 disabled workers, 17,420 spouses, and 23,500 children. Social Security beneficiaries represented 11% of the total state population and 91.5% of the state's population age 65 and older. Retired workers received an average monthly payment of $959; widows and widowers, $954; disabled workers, $886; and spouses, $498. Payments for children of retired workers averaged $494 per month; children of deceased workers, $642; and children of disabled workers, $267. Federal Supplemental Security Income payments in December 2004 went to 21,646 Utah residents, averaging $394 a month.

[40] HOUSING

In 2004, there were an estimated 848,737 housing units in Utah, of which 780,029 were occupied; 69.7% were owner-occupied. About 67.4% of all units were single-family, detached homes. Utility gas was the most common energy source for heating. It was estimated that 20,431 units lacked telephone services, 2,612 lacked complete plumbing facilities, and 3,489 lacked complete kitchen facilities. The average household had 3.01 members, the highest average in the nation.

In 2004, 24,300 new privately owned housing units were authorized for construction. The median home value was $157,275. The median monthly cost for mortgage owners was $1,164. Renters paid a median of $662 per month. In September 2005, the state received grants of $550,000 from the US Department of Housing and Urban Development (HUD) for rural housing and economic development programs. For 2006, HUD allocated to the state over $6.5 million in community development block grants.

[41] EDUCATION

In 2004, 91% of Utah residents had graduated from high school, significantly higher than the national average of 84%. Some 30.8% had four or more years of college, surpassing the national average of 26%.

The total enrollment for fall 2002 in Utah's public schools stood at 489,000. Of these, 343,000 attended schools from kindergarten through grade eight, and 147,000 attended high school. Approximately 83.4% of the students were white, 1.1% were black, 11% were Hispanic, 2.9% were Asian/Pacific Islander, and 1.5% were American Indian/Alaskan Native. Total enrollment was estimated at 489,000 in fall 2003 and expected to be 562,000 by fall 2014, an increase of 14.9% during the period 2002–14. Expenditures for public education in 2003/04 were estimated at $3 billion or $5,008 per student, the lowest among the 50 states. There were

15,907 students enrolled in 108 private schools in fall 2003. Since 1969, the National Assessment of Educational Progress (NAEP) has tested public school students nationwide. The resulting report, *The Nation's Report Card,* stated that in 2005 eighth graders in Utah scored 279 out of 500 in mathematics compared with the national average of 278.

As of fall 2002, there were 178,932 students enrolled in college or graduate school; minority students comprised 8% of total post-secondary enrollment. In 2005 Utah had 28 degree-granting institutions. Major public institutions include the University of Utah; Utah State University; and Weber State College. Brigham Young University (Provo), founded in 1875 and affiliated with the Latter-day Saints, is the main private institution.

42ARTS

The Utah Arts Council (UAC) was founded in 1899 as the Utah Art Institute, only three years after it achieved statehood. UAC sponsors exhibitions, artists in the schools, rural arts and folk arts programs, and statewide arts competitions in cooperation with arts organizations throughout the state. In addition, the partially state-funded Utah Arts Festival has been held each year, since 1984, in Salt Lake City. In 2006, the Utah Arts Festival celebrated its 30th anniversary.

In 2005, the Utah Arts Council and other Utah arts organizations received 20 grants totaling $1,071,800 from the National Endowment for the Arts. The Utah Humanities Council was established in 1975 and promotes several literacy and history-related programs and exhibits. In 2005, the National Endowment for the Humanities contributed $1,109,314 for eight state programs. In addition, the state and private sources provide substantial contributions to the arts.

Music has a central role in Utah's cultural life. The Mormon Tabernacle Choir has won world renown, and Ballet West is ranked among the nation's leading dance companies. The Utah Symphony (Salt Lake City), founded in 1940, has also gained a national reputation. The Utah Symphony works with the Utah State Office of Education to bring concerts to schools throughout the state; as of 2006 the symphony performed for over 80,000 students each year. Opera buffs enjoy the Utah Opera Company, founded in 1976.

Kenneth Brewer was named Utah's poet laureate in 2003; he later died in March 2006. His books include *The Place In Between* (1998), *Lake's Edge* (1997), *Hoping for All, Dreading Nothing* (1994), and his final title, *Whale Song: A Poet's Journey Into Cancer* (2006)—it includes poems that were written after he was diagnosed with cancer.

Utah has several art museums and galleries, including Utah State University's Nora Eccles Harrison Museum in Logan and the LDS Church Museum of Art and History in Salt Lake City. Other major facilities are the Brigham Young University Art Museum Collection, Provo and the Springville Art Museum. The Museum of Fine Arts of the University of Utah (Salt Lake City) houses a diverse permanent collection that includes but is not limited to, African Art, German Art, American Art, Flemish Art, Japanese Art and Scottish Art.

Living Traditions: A Celebration of Salt Lake's Folk and Ethnic Arts is an annual festival that takes place on the weekend before Memorial Day. As of 2005, the three-day event attracted over 45,000 people with continuous music and dance on two stages, as well as crafts demonstrations and sales that incorporate the cultural traditions of the state. The Sundance Institute, founded by Robert Redford in 1981, presents the annual Sundance Film Festival, which is widely regarded as one of the nation's most influential gatherings for independent filmmakers. The Sundance Institute celebrated its 25th anniversary in 2006 and the 22nd annual Sundance Film Festival.

43LIBRARIES AND MUSEUMS

In December 2001, Utah had 70 public library systems, with a total of 107 libraries, of which there were 56 branches. For that same year, the systems had a combined 6,064,000 volumes of books and serial publications, and a total circulation of 24,592,000. The system also had 371,000 audio and 253,000 video items, 25,000 electronic format items (CD-ROMs, magnetic tapes, and disks), and 25 bookmobiles. The Salt Lake County library system had 1,765,295 volumes (not including Salt Lake City, whose system has 704,123 volumes). The Weber County system (including Ogden) has 382,024. The leading academic libraries are the University of Utah (Salt Lake City), 2,350,297, and Brigham Young University (Provo), 2,500,849. Other collections are the Latter-day Saints' Library-Archives and the Utah State Historical Society Library, both in Salt Lake City.

During 2000, Utah had at least 60 museums, notably the Utah Museum of Natural History and Utah Museum of Fine Arts, Salt Lake City; Hill Aerospace Museum near Ogden; College of Eastern Utah Prehistoric Museum, Price; and Museum of Peoples and Cultures, Provo. Some homes are maintained as museums, including Beehive House and Wheeler Historic Farm, Salt Lake City, and Brigham Young's Winter Home, St. George. In fiscal year 2001, operating income for the state's public library system was $56,915,000 and included $354,000 in federal funds, and $908,000 in state funds.

44COMMUNICATIONS

In 2004, 96.3% of Utah's occupied houses had telephones. Additionally, by June of that same year there were 1,229,029 mobile wireless telephone subscribers. In 2003, 74.1% of Utah households had a computer and 62.6% had Internet access. By June 2005, there were 261,135 high-speed lines in Utah, 231,418 residential and 29,717 for business.

A total of 45 major radio stations broadcast in Utah in 2005; 14 were AM stations, 31 FM. There were 8 major television stations in 2005. The Salt Lake City area had 720,860 television households, 53% ordering cable in 1999. In the year 2000, Utah had registered 64,217 Internet domain names.

45PRESS

In 2005, Utah had six daily newspapers and six Sunday papers. The following table shows leading daily newspapers as of 2005:

AREA	NAME	DAILY	SUNDAY
Ogden	*Standard-Examiner* (m,S)	60,844	63,649
Provo	*Daily Herald* (m,S)	42,744	34,324
Salt Lake City	*Desert News* *(m,S)	72,008	73,601
	Tribune *(m,S)	133,025	152,859

*operated by Newspaper Agency Corp.

46 ORGANIZATIONS

In 2006, there were over 1,140 nonprofit organizations registered within the state, of which about 817 were registered as charitable, educational, or religious organizations. Salt Lake City is the world headquarters of the Church of Jesus Christ of Latter-day Saints (Mormon). The city is also home to the Mental Retardation Association of America, the National Energy Foundation, and Executive Women International.

The Utah Arts Council and the Utah State Historical Society are primary organizations for promoting arts and culture in the state. The organization Artists of Utah was founded in 2001. Offices for the Sundance Institute, a resource center for independent filmmakers, are in Salt Lake City. The national office of the US Ski and Snowboarding Association is in Park City. The Southern Utah Wilderness Alliance and Ride With respect are state environmental and conservation associations.

47 TOURISM, TRAVEL, AND RECREATION

In 2003, some 16.9 million visitors traveled to Utah, down 1.3% over the 17.5 million visitors spending a total of approximately $4.15 billion in 2002, the year Salt Lake City hosted the Olympic Games. In 2003, 83% of all trips were made by residents within the state and by those traveling from California, Idaho, Nevada, Colorado, Texas, Wyoming, and Washington. International visitors accounted for 3.1% of all travel to the state. The top international markets were Canada, Germany, the United Kingdom, and France. Also in 2002, nearly 5.8 million visitors came to state parks and 5.2 million came to national parks. Skier visits totaled 3 million. In 2003, The industry supported some 130,000 jobs.

The top five tourist attractions in 2002 (by attendance) were Temple Square (5–7 million), Zion National Park (2.6 million), Glen Canyon National Recreation Center (2.1 million), Wasatch Mountain State Park (1.2 million), and Lagoon Amusement Park (1.1 million). Pioneer Trail State Park and Hogle Zoological Gardens are leading attractions of Salt Lake City, about 11 mi (18 km) east of the Great Salt Lake. At the Bonneville Salt Flats, experimental automobiles have set world land-speed records. Utah considers itself the ice cream capital of the world; the state's well-known Blue Bunny ice cream parlor is in St. George.

Utah has 41 state parks, 5 national parks (Zion, Bryce, Arches, Canyonlands, and Capitol Reef), and 8 national monuments. Mountain and rock climbing, skiing, fishing, and hunting are major forms of recreation.

48 SPORTS

Utah has two major professional sports teams, both located in Salt Lake City: the Utah Jazz of the National Basketball Association (NBA), which moved from New Orleans at the close of the 1979 season, and Real Salt Lake of Major League Soccer. The Jazz, led by John Stockton and Karl Malone, advanced to the NBA Finals for the first time in 1997, but lost to the Chicago Bulls. The Jazz again advanced to the Finals in 1998, but were again defeated by the Chicago Bulls in Michael Jordan's last game. Utah hosted the Starzz of the Women's National Basketball Association (WNBA) until the team's relocation to San Antonio prior to the 2003 season. Basketball is also popular at the college level. The University of Utah's Running Utes have had great success in the recent past and won the National Collegiate Athletic Association (NCAA) championship back in 1944 and the National Invitation Tournament in 1947, while the Cougars of Brigham Young won National Invitational Tournament titles in 1951 and 1966, and were named college football's national champions in 1984. Salt Lake City is also home to minor league baseball and hockey teams.

Other annual sporting events include the Easter Jeep Sandhill Climb in Moab, the Ute Stampede (a rodeo) in Nephi in July, and various skiing events at Utah's world-class resort in Park City. Salt Lake City hosted the Winter Olympics in 2002.

49 FAMOUS UTAHNS

George Sutherland (b.England, 1862–1942) capped a long career in Utah Republican politics by serving as an associate justice of the US Supreme Court (1922–38). Other important federal officeholders from Utah include George Dern (b.Nebraska, 1872–1936), President Franklin D. Roosevelt's secretary of war from 1933 to 1936; Ezra Taft Benson (Idaho, 1899–1994), a high official of the Mormon Church and President Dwight Eisenhower's secretary of agriculture; and Ivy Baker Priest (1905–75), US treasurer during 1953–61. Prominent in the US Senate for 30 years was Republican tariff expert Reed Smoot (1862–1941), also a Mormon Church official. The most colorful politician in state history. J(oseph) Bracken Lee (1899–1996), was mayor of Price for 12 years before serving as governor during 1949–57 and mayor of Salt Lake City during 1960–72. Jacob "Jake" Garn (b.1932), first elected to the US Senate in 1974, was launched into space aboard the space shuttle in 1985.

The dominant figure in Utah history is undoubtedly Brigham Young (b.Vermont, 1801–77), the great western colonizer. As leader of the Mormons for more than 30 years, he initiated white settlement of Utah in 1847 and, until his death, exerted almost complete control over life in the territory. Other major historical figures include Eliza R. Snow (b.Massachusetts, 1804–87), Mormon women's leader; Wakara, anglicized Walker (c.1808–55), the foremost Ute leader of the early settlement period; Colonel Patrick Edward Conner (b.Ireland, 1820–91), founder of Camp Douglas and father of Utah mining; George Q. Cannon (b.England, 1827–1901), editor, businessman, political leader, and a power in the Mormon Church for more than 40 years; and Lawrence Scanlan (b.Ireland, 1843–1915), first Roman Catholic bishop of Salt Lake City, founder of schools and a hospital.

Utah's most important scientist is John A. Widtsoe (b.Norway, 1872–1952), whose pioneering research in dryland farming revolutionized agricultural practices. Noted inventors are gunsmith John M. Browning (1855–1926) and television innovator Philo T. Farnsworth (1906–71). Of note in business are mining entrepreneurs David Keith (b.Canada, 1847–1918), Samuel Newhouse (b.New York, 1853–1930), Susanna Emery-Holmes (b.Missouri, 1859–1942), Thomas Kearns (b.Canada, 1862–1918), and Daniel C. Jackling (b.Missouri, 1869–1956). Labor leaders include William Dudley "Big Bill" Haywood (1869–1928), radical Industrial Workers of the World organizer, and Frank Bonacci (b.Italy, 1884–1954), United Mine Workers of America organizer.

Utah's artists and writers include sculptors Cyrus E. Dallin (1861–1944) and Mahonri M. Young (1877–1957), painter Henry L. A. Culmer (b.England, 1854–1914), author-critic Bernard A. DeVoto (1897–1955), poet-critic Brewster Ghiselin (b.Missouri,

1903), folklorist Austin E. Fife (b.Idaho, 1909–86), and novelists Maurine Whipple (1904–92), Virginia Sorensen (b.1912–91), and Edward Abbey (b.1927–1989).

Actors from Utah are Maude Adams (1872–1953), Robert Walker (1918–1951, Loretta Young (1913–2000), Laraine Day (b.1920). Donald "Donny" Osmond (b.1957) and his sister Marie (b.1959) are Utah's best-known popular singers. Emma Lucy Gates Bowen (1880–1951), an opera singer, founded her own traveling opera company, and William F. Christensen (1902–2001) founded Ballet West. Maurice Abravanel (b.Greece, 1903–1993) conducted the Utah Symphony for many years. Other musicians of note include jazz trumpeter Ernest Loring "Red" Nichols (1905–1965).

Sports figures include former world middleweight boxing champion Gene Fullmer (b.1931), former Los Angeles Rams tackle Merlin Olsen (b.1940), and NFL quarterback Steve Young (b.1961) of the San Francisco 49ers.

⁵⁰BIBLIOGRAPHY

Arrington, Leonard J., and Davis Bitton. *The Mormon Experience: A History of the Latter-day Saints.* 2nd ed. Urbana: University of Illinois Press, 1992.

Busby, Mark (ed.). *The Southwest.* Vol. 8 in *The Greenwood Encyclopedia of American Regional Cultures.* Westport, Conn.: Greenwood Press, 2004.

Council of State Governments. *The Book of the States, 2006 Edition.* Lexington, Ky.: Council of State Governments, 2006.

McPherson, Robert S. *Navajo Land, Navajo Culture: The Utah Experience in the Twentieth Century.* Norman: University of Oklahoma Press, 2001.

Parzybok, Tye W. *Weather Extremes in the West.* Missoula, Mont.: Mountain Press, 2005.

Preston, Thomas. *Intermountain West: Idaho, Nevada, Utah, and Arizona.* Vol. 2 of *The Double Eagle Guide to 1,000 Great Western Recreation Destinations.* 2nd ed. Billings, Mont.: Discovery Publications, 2003.

Smart, William B., and Donna T. Smart (eds.). *Over the Rim: the Parley P. Pratt Exploring Expedition to Southern Utah, 1849–50.* Logan: Utah State University Press, 1999.

Stanley, David (ed.). *Folklore in Utah: A History and Guide to Resources.* Logan: Utah State University Press, 2004.

Topping, Gary. *Utah Historians and the Reconstruction of Western History.* Norman: University of Oklahoma Press, 2003.

US Department of Commerce, Economics and Statistics Administration, US Census Bureau. *Utah, 2000. Summary Social, Economic, and Housing Characteristics: 2000 Census of Population and Housing.* Washington, D.C.: US Government Printing Office, 2003.

Utah History Encyclopedia. Salt Lake City: University of Utah Press, 1994.

Verdoia, Ken. *Utah: The Struggle for Statehood.* Salt Lake City: University of Utah Press, 1996.

Watkins, Tom H. *The Redrock Chronicles: Saving Wild Utah.* Baltimore, Md.: Johns Hopkins University Press, 2000.

Webb, Robert H. *Cataract Canyon: A Human and Environmental History of the Rivers in Canyonlands.* Salt Lake City: University of Utah Press, 2004.

VERMONT

State of Vermont

ORIGIN OF STATE NAME: Derived from the French words *vert* (green) and *mont* (mountain). **NICKNAME:** The Green Mountain State. **CAPITAL:** Montpelier. **ENTERED UNION:** 4 March 1791 (14th). **SONG:** "Hail Vermont." **MOTTO:** Freedom and Unity. **COAT OF ARMS:** Rural Vermont is represented by a pine tree in the center, three sheaves of grain on the left, and a cow on the right, with a background of fields and mountains. A deer crests the shield. Below are crossed pine branches and the state name and motto. **FLAG:** The coat of arms on a field of dark blue. **OFFICIAL SEAL:** Bisecting Vermont's golden seal is a row of wooded hills above the state name. The upper half has a spearhead, pine tree, cow, and two sheaves of wheat, while two more sheaves and the state motto fill the lower half. **BIRD:** Hermit thrush. **FISH:** Brook trout (cold water) and walleye pike (warm water). **FLOWER:** Red clover. **TREE:** Sugar maple. **LEGAL HOLIDAYS:** New Year's Day, 1 January; Birthday of Martin Luther King Jr., 3rd Monday in January; Presidents' Day, 3rd Monday in February; Town Meeting Day, 1st Tuesday in March; Memorial Day, last Monday in May; Independence Day, 4 July; Bennington Battle Day, 16 August; Labor Day, 1st Monday in September; Veterans' Day, 11 November; Thanksgiving Day, 4th Thursday in November and the day following; Christmas Day, 25 December. **TIME:** 7 AM EST = noon GMT.

¹LOCATION, SIZE, AND EXTENT

Situated in the northeastern United States, Vermont is the second-largest of the six New England states, and ranks 43rd in size among the 50 states.

Vermont's total area of 9,614 sq mi (24,900 sq km) consists of 9,249 sq mi (23,955 sq km) of land and 365 sq mi (945 sq km) of inland water. Vermont's maximum E–W extension is 90 mi (145 km); its maximum N–S extension is 158 mi (254 km). The state resembles a wedge, wide and flat at the top and narrower at the bottom.

Vermont is bordered on the N by the Canadian province of Quebec; on the E by New Hampshire (separated by the Connecticut River); on the S by Massachusetts; and on the W by New York (with part of the line passing through Lake Champlain and the Poultney River).

The state's territory includes several islands and the lower part of a peninsula jutting south into Lake Champlain from the Canadian border, collectively called Grand Isle County. Vermont's total boundary length is 561 mi (903 km). Its geographic center is in Washington County, 3 mi (5 km) E of Roxbury.

²TOPOGRAPHY

The Green Mountains are the most prominent topographic region in Vermont. Extending north–south from the Canadian border to the Massachusetts state line, the Green Mountains contain the state's highest peaks, including Mansfield, 4,393 ft (1,340 m), the highest point in Vermont; Killington, 4,235 ft (1,293 m); and Elbow Mountain (Warren), 4,135 ft (1,260 m). A much lower range, the Taconic Mountains, straddles the New York-Vermont border for about 80 mi (129 km). To their north is the narrow Valley of Vermont; farther north is the Champlain Valley, a lowland about 20 mi (32 km) wide between Lake Champlain—site of the state's lowest point, 95 ft (29 m) above sea level—and the Green Moun-

tains. The Vermont piedmont is a narrow corridor of hills and valleys stretching about 100 mi (161 km) to the east of the Green Mountains. The Northeast Highlands consist of an isolated series of peaks near the New Hampshire border. The mean elevation of the state is approximately 1,000 ft (305 m).

Vermont's major inland rivers are the Missisquoi, Lamoille, and Winooski. The state includes about 66% of Lake Champlain on its western border and about 25% of Lake Memphremagog on the northern border.

³CLIMATE

Burlington's normal daily average temperature is 45°F (7°C), ranging from 18°F (-7°C) in January to 70°F (21°C) in July. Winters are generally colder and summer nights cooler in the higher elevations of the Green Mountains. The record high temperature for the state is 105°F (41°C), registered at Vernon on 4 July 1911; the record low, -50°F (-46°C), at Bloomfield, 30 December 1933. Burlington's average annual precipitation of about 34 in (86 cm) is less than the statewide average of about 40 in (102 cm). Annual snowfall in Burlington is 76.9 in (195 cm); elsewhere in the state snowfall ranges from 55 to 65 in (140–165 cm) in the lower regions, and from 100 to 125 in (254–318 cm) in the mountain areas.

⁴FLORA AND FAUNA

Common trees of Vermont are the commercially important sugar maple (the state tree), the butternut, white pine, and yellow birch. Other recognized flora include 15 types of conifer, 130 grasses, and 192 sedges. Two plant species, Jesup's milk-vetch and Northeastern bulrush, were endangered in 2006.

Native mammalian species include white-tailed deer, coyote, red fox, and snowshoe hare. Several species of trout are prolific. Characteristic birds include the raven (Corvus corax), gray or Canada jay, and saw-whet owl. In 2006, the US Fish and Wildlife

Service listed six animal species (vertebrates and invertebrates) as threatened or endangered in Vermont, including the Indiana bat, dwarf wedgemussel, and bald eagle.

5 ENVIRONMENTAL PROTECTION

All natural resource regulation, planning, and operation are coordinated by the Department of Environmental Conservation. The state is divided into 14 soil and water conservation districts operated by local landowners with the assistance of the state Natural Resources Conservation Council. Several dams on the Winooski and Connecticut river's drainage basins help control flooding.

Legislation enacted in 1972 bans the use of throwaway beverage containers in Vermont, in an effort to reduce roadside litter. Billboards were banned in 1968. In the 1980s and early 1990s, the effects of acid rain became a source of concern in Vermont, as in the rest of the Northeast. In 2003, 0.3 million lb of toxic chemicals were released in the state. That year, Vermont ranked as having the least amount of toxic chemical releases of all 50 states.

By some estimates as much as 35% of Vermont's wetlands have been lost since colonization. As of 2002, about 4% of the state was designated as wetlands, and the government has established the Vermont Wetlands Conservation Strategy.

In 2003, Vermont had 56 hazardous waste sites listed in the US Environment Protection Agency (EPA) database, 11 of which were on the National Priorities List as of 2006, including the Pine Street Canal in Burlington and the Ely Copper Mine. In 2005, the EPA spent over $4.4 million through the Superfund program for the cleanup of hazardous waste sites in the state. The same year, federal EPA grants awarded to the state included $6.4 million for the clean water state revolving fund.

6 POPULATION

Vermont ranked 49th in population in the United States with an estimated total of 623,050 in 2005, an increase of 2.3% since 2000. Between 1990 and 2000, Vermont's population grew from 562,758 to 608,827, an increase of 8.2%. The population is projected to reach 673,169 by 2015 and 703,288 by 2025. The population density in 2004 was 67.2 persons per sq mi.

In 2004, the median age for Vermont residents was 40.4. In the same year, 21.7% of the populace were under age 18 while 13% was age 65 or older. The rural population increased 12% between 1970 and 1980; in the 1990s, Vermont had the highest percentage of rural dwellers in all states.

Vermont cities with the largest populations, all under 100,000, include Burlington, Rutland, and Montpelier. The Burlington–South Burlington metropolitan area had an estimated population of 204,485 in 2004.

7 ETHNIC GROUPS

There were 53,835 residents reporting French Canadian ancestry in 2000. These Vermonters are congregated chiefly in the northern counties and in such urban centers as Burlington, St. Albans, and Montpelier. Italians make up 6.4% of the population reporting at least one specific ancestry group. The foreign born numbered 23,245—3.8% of the population—in 2000. In 2000, Hispanics and Latinos numbered 5,504, just under 1% of the total. That percentage remained roughly the same in 2004.

The 1990 census counted few non-Caucasians. There were 5,217 Asians, 3,063 blacks, and 2,420 American Indians. In 2004, 1% of the population was Asian, 0.6% black, 0.4% American Indian, and 1.1% reported origin of two or more races.

8 LANGUAGES

A few place-names and very few Indian-language speakers remain as evidence of the early Vermont presence of the Algonkian Mohawk tribe and of some Iroquois in the north. Vermont English, although typical of the Northern dialect, differs from that of New Hampshire in several respects, including retention of the final /r/ and use of *eavestrough* in place of eavespout.

In 2000, 540,767 Vermonters—94.1% of the population age five and over—spoke only English at home. The percent of the population who spoke only English at home remained constant from 1990 to 2000.

The following table gives selected statistics from the 2000 Census for language spoken at home by persons five years old and over. The category "Scandinavian languages" includes Danish, Norwegian, and Swedish.

LANGUAGE	NUMBER	PERCENT
Population 5 years and over	**574,842**	**100.0**
Speak only English	540,767	94.1
Speak a language other than English	34,075	5.9
Speak a language other than English	**34,075**	**5.9**
French (incl. Patois, Cajun)	14,624	2.5
Spanish or Spanish Creole	5,791	1.0
German	2,612	0.5
Serbo-Croatian	1,600	0.3
Italian	1,198	0.2
Polish	977	0.2
Vietnamese	812	0.1
Chinese	782	0.1
Russian	554	0.1
Scandinavian languages	415	0.1

9 RELIGIONS

From the early days of settlement to the present, Congregationalists (now called the United Church of Christ) have played a dominant role in the state. They were the largest Protestant denomination in the state in 2000, with 21,597 known adherents. Other major Protestant groups include the United Methodists, 19,000; Episcopalians, 9,163; and American Baptists, 8,352. The largest single religious organization in Vermont is the Roman Catholic Church, with 149,154 members in 2004. There is a small Jewish population (estimated at 5,810 in 2000), most of whom live in Burlington. Over 370,000 people (about 60.9% of the population) were not counted as members of any religious organization.

Vermont was the birthplace of both Joseph Smith and Brigham Young, founders of the Church of Jesus Christ of Latter-day Saints. The state had 4,150 Mormons in 2006.

10 TRANSPORTATION

Vermont's first railroad, completed in 1849, served more as a link to Boston than as an intrastate line. It soon went into receivership, as did many other early state lines. From a high of nearly 1,100 mi (1,770 km) of track in 1910, trackage shrank to 562 rail mi (904 km) in 2003, none of it Class I line. As of that year, eight railroads

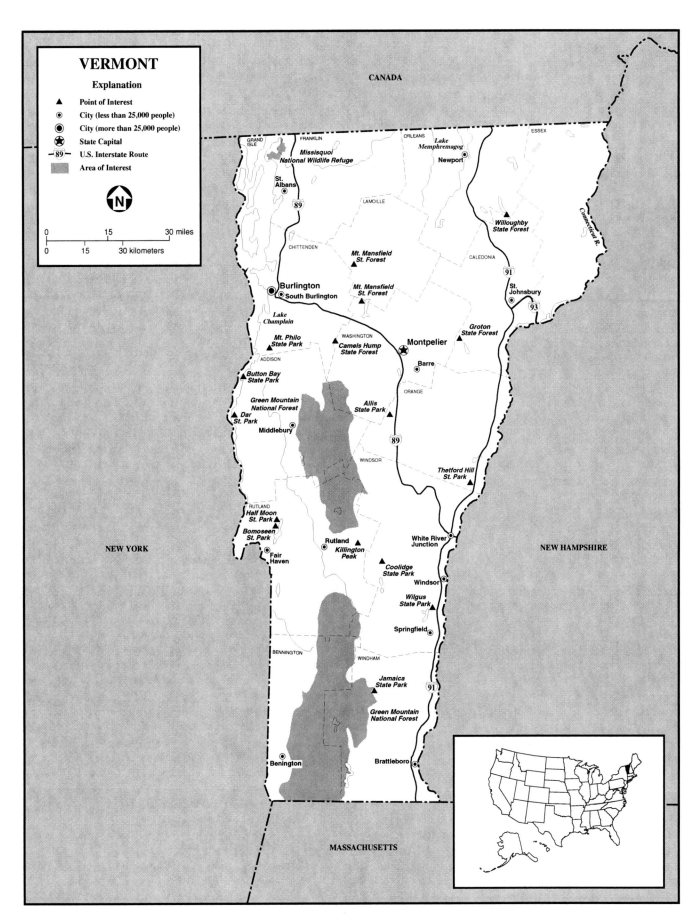

VERMONT

Explanation

▲ Point of Interest
⊙ City (less than 25,000 people)
◉ City (more than 25,000 people)
✪ State Capital
―⟨89⟩― U.S. Interstate Route
▨ Area of Interest

N

0 — 15 — 30 miles
0 — 15 — 30 kilometers

CANADA

GRAND ISLE

FRANKLIN

ORLEANS

Lake Memphremagog

Newport

ESSEX

Missisquoi National Wildlife Refuge

St. Albans

⟨89⟩

LAMOILLE

Willoughby State Forest

CHITTENDEN

Mt. Mansfield St. Forest

CALEDONIA

⟨91⟩

Burlington
South Burlington

Mt. Mansfield St. Forest

St. Johnsbury
⟨93⟩

Lake Champlain

WASHINGTON

Groton State Forest

Connecticut R.

Mt. Philo State Park

Camels Hump State Forest

Montpelier

ADDISON

Barre

Button Bay State Park

Green Mountain National Forest

Allis State Park

ORANGE

Dar St. Park

⟨89⟩

Middlebury

WINDSOR

Thetford Hill St. Park

RUTLAND

Half Moon St. Park

Bomoseen St. Park

Rutland

Killington Peak

White River Junction

NEW HAMPSHIRE

NEW YORK

Fair Haven

Coolidge State Park

Windsor

Wilgus State Park

BENNINGTON

Springfield

WINDHAM

Jamaica State Park

⟨91⟩

Green Mountain National Forest

Benington

Brattleboro

MASSACHUSETTS

were operating within the state. Glass and stone products were the top commodities shipped by rail that originated within the state, while lumber and wood products were the top commodities shipped by rail that terminated within Vermont that same year. In 2006, Amtrak provided passenger service to 11 stations in the state via its Ethan Allen (Rutland to New York City) train and its Vermonter (St. Albans to New York City to Washington DC) train.

There were 14,368 mi (23,132 km) of public streets, roads, and highways in 2004. In that same year, there were some 540,000 motor vehicles registered in the state, while there were 550,462 licensed drivers.

In 2005, Vermont had a total of 87 public and private-use aviation-related facilities. This included 61 airports, 20 heliports, 3 STOLports (Short Take-Off and Landing), and 3 seaplane bases. Burlington International Airport is the state's major air terminal. In 2004 the airport handled 627,423 enplanements.

[11]HISTORY

Vermont has been inhabited continuously since about 10,000 BC. Archaeological finds suggest the presence of a pre-Algonkian group along the Otter River. Algonkian-speaking Abnaki settled along Lake Champlain and in the Connecticut Valley, and Mahican settled in the southern counties between AD 1200 and 1790. In 1609, Samuel de Champlain crossed the lake that now bears his name, becoming the first European explorer of Vermont. From the 1650s to the 1760s, French, Iroquois Indians from New York, Dutch, and English passed through the state over trails connecting Montreal with Massachusetts and New York. However, few settled there. In 1666 the French built and briefly occupied Ft. Ste. Anne on Isle La Motte, and in 1690 there was a short-lived settlement at Chimney Point. Ft. Dummer, built in 1724 near present-day Brattleboro, was the first permanent settlement.

Governor Benning Wentworth of New Hampshire, claiming that his colony extended as far west as did Massachusetts and Connecticut, had granted 131 town charters in the territory by 1764. In that year, the crown declared that New York's northeastern boundary was the Connecticut River. Owners of New Hampshire titles, fearful of losing their land, prevented New York from enforcing its jurisdiction. The Green Mountain Boys, organized by Ethan Allen in 1770–71, scared off the defenseless settlers under New York title and flouted New York courts.

Shortly after the outbreak of the Revolutionary War, Ethan Allen's men helped capture Ft. Ticonderoga, and for two years frontiersmen fought in the northern theater. On 16 August 1777, after a skirmish at Hubbardton, a Vermont contingent routed German detachments sent by British General Burgoyne toward Bennington—a battle that contributed to the general's surrender at Saratoga, New York. There were several British raids on Vermont towns during the war.

Vermont declared itself an independent republic with the name "New Connecticut" in 1777, promulgated a constitution abolishing slavery and providing universal manhood suffrage, adopted the laws of Connecticut, and confiscated Tory lands. Most Vermonters preferred to join the United States, but the dominant Allen faction, with large holdings in the northwest, needed free trade with Canada, even at the price of returning to the British Empire. Political defeat of the Allen faction in 1789 led to negotiations that settled New York's claims and secured Vermont's admission to the Union on 4 March 1791.

With 30,000 people in 1781 and nearly 220,000 in 1810, Vermont was a state of newcomers spread evenly over the hills in self-sufficient homesteads. Second-generation Vermonters developed towns and villages with water-powered mills, charcoal-fired furnaces, general stores, newspapers, craft shops, churches, and schools. Those who ran these local institutions tended to be Congregationalist in religion and successively Federalist, Whig, and Republican in party politics. Dissidents in the early 1800s included minority Protestants suffering legal and social discrimination, hardscrabble farmers, and Jacksonian Democrats.

Northwestern Vermonters smuggled to avoid the US foreign trade embargo of 1808, and widespread trade continued with Canada during the War of 1812. In September 1814, however, Vermont soldiers fought in the Battle of Plattsburgh, New York, won by Thomas Macdonough's fleet built at Vergennes the previous winter. The Mexican War (1846–48) was unpopular in the state, but Vermont, which had strongly opposed slavery, was an enthusiastic supporter of the Union during the Civil War.

The opening of the Champlain-Hudson Canal in 1823, and the building of the early railroad lines in 1846–53, made Vermont more vulnerable to western competition, caused the demise of many small farms and businesses, and stimulated emigration. The remaining farmers' purchasing power steadily increased as they held temporary advantages in wool, then in butter and cheese-making, and finally in milk production. The immigration of the Irish and French Canadians stabilized the population, and the expansion of light industry bolstered the economy.

During the 20th century, and especially after World War II, autos, buses, trucks, and planes took over most passengers and much freight from the railroads. Manufacturing, especially light industry, prospered in valley villages. Vermont's picturesque landscape began to attract city buyers of second homes. Still rural in population distribution, Vermont became increasingly suburban in outlook, as new highways made the cities and hills mutually accessible, and the state absorbed an influx of young professionals from New York and Massachusetts. Tourism thrived, especially in the Green Mountains and other ski resort areas. Longtime Vermonters, accustomed to their state's pristine beauty, were confronted in the 1980s with the question of how much development was necessary for the state's economic health. The newcomers changed the political landscape as well. Whereas Vermont had long been dominated by the Republican Party, by the mid-1980s fully a third of the electorate voted Democratic. The Democratic presidential candidate carried Vermont in the 1988, 1992, 1996, 2000, and 2004 elections. In 1990, Vermont elected as its sole Congressional representative a democratic socialist, Bernie Sanders, who called for reduced limits on campaign spending, a sharply progressive income tax, national health care, and 50% cuts in military spending over five years. Sanders was reelected in 2004.

In the early 1990s Vermont had the nation's highest percentage of women in its state legislature. With two-thirds of its population living in towns of 2,500 or fewer, it was the nation's most rural state. In 1993 Vermont passed legislation barring smoking in all public buildings, including most restaurants and hotels.

Governor James H. Douglas, a Republican elected in 2002, pledged to create jobs and provide economic security to the state.

He also emphasized higher education, and transportation spending. Douglas announced a substance abuse and interdiction program for Vermont's correctional facilities that would include random drug testing, including for those inmates out on furlough. Douglas was reelected to a second two-year term in 2004. In April 2005, Senator Jim Jeffords of Vermont, an independent who caucuses with the Democrats, announced he would not seek reelection in 2006. Speculation was raised as to whether or not Douglas would vie with Congressman Bernie Sanders for Jeffords's seat, but Douglas later debunked this notion and declared he would seek reelection as governor in 2006.

12 STATE GOVERNMENT

A constitution establishing Vermont as an independent republic was adopted in 1777. The constitution that governs the state today became effective on 9 July 1793. By January 2005, that document had been amended 53 times.

The General Assembly consists of a 150-member House of Representatives and a 30-member Senate. All legislators are elected to two-year terms. Regular sessions begin in January and are not formally limited in length. Legislators must be US citizens, at least 18 years old and residents of the state for at least two years and of their districts for at least one year. In 2003 the legislative salary was $589 per week during session.

State elected officials are the governor and lieutenant governor (elected separately), treasurer, secretary of state, auditor of accounts, and attorney general, all of whom serve two-year terms. A governor must be at least 18 years of age and have been a state citizen for one year and a state resident for at least four years prior to election. As of December 2004, the governor's salary was $133,162.

All bills require a majority vote in each house for passage. Bills can be vetoed by the governor, and vetoes can be overridden by a two-thirds vote of those present in each legislative house. If the governor neither vetoes nor signs a bill within five days of receiving it, it becomes law. If the legislature has adjourned, an unsigned bill dies after three days. A constitutional amendment must first be passed by a two-thirds vote in the Senate, followed by a majority in the House during the same legislative session. It must then receive majority votes in both houses before it can be submitted to the voters for approval. Amendments may only be submitted every four years.

Voters must be US citizens, at least 18 years old, and state residents.

13 POLITICAL PARTIES

The Republican Party, which originally drew strength from powerful abolitionist sentiment, gained control of Vermont state offices in 1856 and for more than 100 years dominated state politics. No Democrat was elected governor from 1853 until 1962.

In 1984, Democrat Madeleine M. Kunin was elected as Vermont's first woman governor and only the third Democratic governor in the state's history. Kunin served as governor for three terms, followed in 1990 by Republican Richard Snelling. When Snelling died in office in August 1991, Lieutenant Governor Howard Dean, a Democrat, became governor. Dean was elected to full two-year terms in November 1992, 1994, 1996, 1998, and 2000. (The state has no term limit for the office of governor.) Dean an-

Vermont Presidential Vote by Major Political Parties, 1948–2004

YEAR	ELECTORAL VOTE	VERMONT WINNER	DEMOCRAT	REPUBLICAN
1948	3	Dewey (R)	45,557	75,926
1952	3	*Eisenhower (R)	43,355	109,717
1956	3	*Eisenhower (R)	42,549	110,390
1960	3	Nixon (R)	69,186	98,131
1964	3	*Johnson (D)	108,127	54,942
1968	3	*Nixon (R)	70,255	85,142
1972	3	*Nixon (R)	68,174	117,149
1976	3	Ford (R)	77,798	100,387
1980	3	*Reagan (R)	81,891	94,598
1984	3	*Reagan (R)	95,730	135,865
1988	3	*Bush (R)	115,775	124,331
1992**	3	*Clinton (D)	133,592	88,122
1996**	3	*Clinton (D)	137,894	80,352
2000	3	Gore (D)	149,022	119,775
2004	3	Kerry (D)	184,067	121,180

*Won US presidential election.
**IND. candidate Ross Perot received 65,991 votes in 1992 and 31,024 votes in 1996.

nounced in 2001 that he would not seek reelection in 2002, and in May 2002, became the first candidate to enter the race for the Democratic nomination for president in 2004. Republican James Douglas was elected governor of Vermont in 2002.

Vermont's delegation to the US House of Representatives consists of one Independent. In mid-2005, Democrats controlled the state Senate, with 21 seats out of 30. In the state House of Representatives, the Democrats held 83 seats; the Republicans had 60; and Independents had 7. Following the 2004 election, Vermont had one Independent US senator, James Jeffords, elected in 1988 as a Republican and reelected in 2000 (he switched party affiliation from the Republican Party to independent status in 2001), and one Democratic senator, Patrick Leahy, who was elected to his sixth term in 2004.

Vermont has often shown its independence in national political elections. In 1832, it was the only state to cast a plurality vote for the Anti-Masonic presidential candidate, William Wirt; in 1912, the only state besides Utah to vote for William Howard Taft; and in 1936, the only state besides Maine to prefer Alf Landon to Franklin D. Roosevelt. In 2000, Vermonters gave 51% of their presidential vote to Democratic candidate Al Gore; 41% to Republican George W. Bush; and 7% to Green Party candidate Ralph Nader. In 2004, Democrat John Kerry won 59% to Bush's 39%. In 2004, there were 419,000 registered voters; there is no party registration in the state. The state had three electoral votes in the 2004 presidential election.

14 LOCAL GOVERNMENT

As of 2005, there were 14 counties, 47 municipal governments, 288 public school districts, and 152 special districts. In 2002, there were 237 townships. County officers, operating out of shire towns (county seats), include the probate courts judge, assistant judges of the county court, county clerk, state's attorney, high bailiff, treasurer, and sheriff. All cities have mayor-council systems. Towns are governed by selectmen, who serve staggered terms. Larger towns also have town managers. The town meeting remains an important part of government in the state: citizens gather on the first Tuesday in March each year to discuss municipal issues and elect local officials.

In 2005, local government accounted for about 25,068 full-time (or equivalent) employment positions.

[15] STATE SERVICES

To address the continuing threat of terrorism and to work with the federal Department of Homeland Security, homeland security in Vermont operates under executive order; the public safety director/secretary is designated as the state homeland security advisor.

Vermont's Department of Education oversees public elementary, secondary, higher education, and adult education programs. The Agency of Transportation includes the Department of Motor Vehicles, Transportation Board, and Hazardous Materials Committee. The Agency of Human Services coordinates programs for nursing homes, veterans' affairs, social welfare, employment and training, health, corrections, and parole. The Department of Housing and Community Affairs and the Agency of Commerce and Community Development administer federal housing programs and offers aid to localities. Other departments specialize in the areas of: personnel, natural resources, aging, agriculture, labor and industry, libraries, and liquor control.

[16] JUDICIAL SYSTEM

Vermont's highest court is the Supreme Court, which consists of a chief justice and four associate justices. Other courts include the superior, district, family, and environmental courts, with a total of 497 judges. All judges are appointed by the governor to six-year terms, subject to Senate confirmation, from a list of qualified candidates prepared by the Judicial Nominating Board, which includes representatives of the governor, the legislature, and the Vermont bar. There are also 318 associate judges and 50 permissive associate judges.

As of 31 December 2004, a total of 1,968 prisoners were held in Vermont's state and federal prisons, an increase from 1,944 of 1.2% from the previous year. As of year-end 2004, a total of 143 inmates were female, up from 135 or 5.9% from the year before. Among sentenced prisoners (one year or more), Vermont had an incarceration rate of 233 per 100,000 population in 2004.

According to the Federal Bureau of Investigation, Vermont in 2004, had a violent crime rate (murder/nonnegligent manslaughter; forcible rape; robbery; aggravated assault) of 112 reported incidents per 100,000 population (the third-lowest in the United States), or a total of 696 reported incidents. Crimes against property (burglary; larceny/theft; and motor vehicle theft) in that same year totaled 14,343 reported incidents or 2,308.2 reported incidents per 100,000 people. Vermont has no death penalty. The state's last execution took place in 1954.

In 2003, Vermont spent $60,914,924 on homeland security, an average of $95 per state resident.

[17] ARMED FORCES

In 2004, there were 60 active-duty military personnel and 613 civilian personnel stationed in Vermont. Also in 2004, the government awarded almost $452 million in defense contracts to Ver-

mont firms, and defense payroll outlays were $140 million, the lowest in the nation.

In 2003, there were 57,802 veterans living in Vermont, of which 7,823 served in World War II; 6,808 in the Korean conflict; 18,371 during the Vietnam era; and 6,589 during the Gulf War. In 2004, the Veterans Administration expended more than $159 million in pensions, medical assistance, and other major veterans' benefits.

In 2004, the Vermont State Police employed 302 full-time sworn officers.

[18] MIGRATION

The earliest Vermont settlers were farmers from southern New England and New York; most were of English descent although some Dutch settlers moved to Vermont from New York. French Canadians came beginning in the 1830s; by 1850, several thousand had moved into Vermont. As milling, quarrying, and mining grew during the 19th century, other Europeans arrived—small groups of Italians and Scots in Barre, and Poles, Swedes, Czechs, Russians, and Austrians in the Rutland quarry areas. Irish immigrants built the railroads in the mid-19th century. Steady out-migrations during the 19th and early 20th centuries kept population increases down, and in the decades 1910–20 and 1930–40, the population dropped. During the 1960s, the population of blacks more than doubled, though they still accounted for only 0.34% of the population in 1990. Between 1970 and 1983, 45,000 migrants settled in Vermont. From 1985 to 1990, Vermont had a net gain from migration of nearly 21,400. Falling from 33.8% in 1980, Vermont's urban population in 1990 was the lowest among the states at 32.2% and fell further to 27.7% in 1996. Between 1990 and 1998, the state had net gains of 5,000 in domestic migration and 4,000 in international migration. In 1998, Vermont admitted 513 foreign immigrants. Between 1990 and 1998, Vermont's overall population increased 5%. In the period 2000–05, net international migration was 4,359 and net internal migration was 3,530, for a net gain of 7,889 people.

[19] INTERGOVERNMENTAL COOPERATION

Vermont participates in New England compacts on corrections, higher education, water pollution control, police, and radiological health protection. The state also takes part in the Connecticut River Valley Flood Control Compact, Connecticut River Atlantic Salmon Compact, Interstate Pest Control Compact, and Northeastern Forest Fire Protection Compact. The state has several agreements with New Hampshire regarding schools, and sewage and waste disposal. Federal grants to Vermont amounted to $1.019 billion in fiscal year 2005, fifth-lowest of all the states (Wyoming received the least amount of federal aid). In fiscal year 2006, Vermont received an estimated $1.053 billion in federal grants, and an estimated $1.080 billion in fiscal year 2007.

[20] ECONOMY

During its early years of statehood, Vermont was overwhelmingly agricultural, with beef cattle, sheep, and dairying contributing greatly to the state's income. After World War II, agriculture was replaced by manufacturing and tourism as the backbone of the economy. Durable goods manufacturing (primarily electronics and machine parts), construction, wholesale and retail trade, and other service industries have shown the largest growth in employment during the 1990s. Vermont's economy was little impacted by the national recession in 2001, as the growth rate of its gross state product, which had accelerated from 5.1% in 1998 to 5.3% in 1999, to 5.6% in 2000, actually improved to 5.7% in 2001. The main negative effect was an unexpected shortfall in tax revenues that followed the abrupt collapse in capital gains income, presenting Vermont, as with most states, with a state budget crisis. Payroll employment did decline, but the trough was reached by April 2002, and despite layoffs by IBM in late 2002, the state economy registered net job gains in fall 2002. Per capita income grew in the first half of 2002, and Vermont's bankruptcy rate was the lowest in New England.

In 2004, Vermont's gross state product (GSP) was $21.921 billion, of which manufacturing (durable and nondurable goods) accounted for the largest share at $2.954 billion or 13.4% of GSP, followed by the real estate sector at $2.760 billion (12.5% of GSP), and healthcare and social assistance at $2.025 billion (9.2% of GSP). In that same year, there were an estimated 74,957 small businesses in Vermont. Of the 21,335 businesses that had employees, an estimated total of 20,649 or 96.8% were small companies. An estimated 2,322 new businesses were established in the state in 2004, up 9.4% from the year before. Business terminations that same year came to 2,578, down 0.2% from 2003. There were 85 business bankruptcies in 2004, up 9% from the previous year. In 2005, the state's personal bankruptcy (Chapter 7 and Chapter 13) filing rate was 296 filings per 100,000 people, ranking Vermont as the 49th highest in the nation.

21 INCOME

In 2005 Vermont had a gross state product (GSP) of $23 billion which accounted for 0.2% of the nation's gross domestic product and placed the state at number 51 in highest GSP among the 50 states and the District of Columbia.

According to the Bureau of Economic Analysis, in 2004 Vermont had a per capita personal income (PCPI) of $31,780. This ranked 24th in the United States and was 96% of the national average of $33,050. The 1994–2004 average annual growth rate of PCPI was 4.6%. Vermont had a total personal income (TPI) of $19,742,824,000, which ranked 49th in the United States and reflected an increase of 5.8% from 2003. The 1994–2004 average annual growth rate of TPI was 5.3%. Earnings of persons employed in Vermont increased from $13,759,886,000 in 2003 to $14,628,555,000 in 2004, an increase of 6.3%. The 2003–04 national change was 6.3%.

The US Census Bureau reports that the three-year average median household income for 2002–04 in 2004 dollars was $45,692 compared to a national average of $44,473. During the same period an estimated 8.8% of the population was below the poverty line as compared to 12.4% nationwide.

22 LABOR

According to the Bureau of Labor Statistics (BLS), in April 2006 the seasonally adjusted civilian labor force in Vermont 360,300, with approximately 12,000 workers unemployed, yielding an unemployment rate of 3.3%, compared to the national average of 4.7% for the same period. Preliminary data for the same period placed nonfarm employment at 307,100. Since the beginning of the BLS data series in 1976, the highest unemployment rate re-

corded in Vermont was 9% in June 1976. The historical low was 2.2% in March 2000. Preliminary nonfarm employment data by occupation for April 2006 showed that approximately 5.5% of the labor force was employed in construction; 11.9% in manufacturing; 19.5% in trade, transportation, and public utilities; 4.2% in financial activities; 7.2% in professional and business services; 17.9% in education and health services; 10.6% in leisure and hospitality services; and 17.3% in government.

The BLS reported that in 2005, a total of 31,000 of Vermont's 287,000 employed wage and salary workers were formal members of a union. This represented 10.8% of those so employed, up from 9.8% in 2004, but still below the national average of 12%. Overall in 2005, a total of 37,000 workers (13%) in Vermont were covered by a union or employee association contract, which includes those workers who reported no union affiliation. Vermont is one of 28 states that does not have a right-to-work law.

As of 1 March 2006, Vermont had a state-mandated minimum wage rate of $7.25 per hour, which applied to employers with two or more employees. Beginning 1 January 2007, Vermont's state minimum wage rate was scheduled to be adjusted annually by either 5%, the percent increase of the Consumer Price Index, or the city average. In 2004, women in the state accounted for 47.9% of the employed civilian labor force.

23 AGRICULTURE

Although Vermont is one of the nation's most rural states, its agricultural income was only $561 million in 2005, 41st among the 50 states. More than 85% of that came from livestock and livestock products, especially dairy products. The leading crops in 2004 were corn for silage, 1,755,000 tons; hay, 384,000 tons; and apples, 44.5 million lb.

24 ANIMAL HUSBANDRY

The merino sheep and the Morgan horse (a breed developed in Vermont) were common sights on pastures more than a century ago, but today they have been for the most part replaced by dairy cattle. In 2003, Vermont dairy farms had around 149,000 milk cows that produced 2.64 billion lb (1.2 billion kg) of milk. In 2005, the state had an estimated 275,000 cattle and calves, valued at $357.5 million.

25 FISHING

Sport fishermen can find ample species of trout, perch, walleye pike, bass, and pickerel in Vermont's waters, many of which are stocked by the Department of Fish and Game. There are two national fish hatcheries in the state (Pittsford and White River). In 2004, the state issued 121,701 sport fishing licenses. There is very little commercial fishing.

26 FORESTRY

The Green Mountain State is covered by 4,628,000 acres (1,873,000 hectares) of forestland—78% of the state's total land area—much of it owned or leased by lumber companies. In 2004, lumber production totaled 183 million board ft.

The largest forest reserve in Vermont is the Green Mountain National Forest, with 391,862 acres (158,587 hectares) in 2005, managed by the US Forest Service.

27 MINING

According to preliminary data from the US Geological Survey (USGS), the estimated value of nonfuel mineral production by Vermont in 2003 was $73 million, an increase from 2002 of over 3%.

According to the preliminary data for 2003, dimension stone was the state's top nonfuel minerals by value, accounting for around 40% of the state's publishable nonfuel mineral output, by value. Nationally by volume, Vermont ranked third in the production of talc and fourth in the production of dimension stone.

Preliminary data in 2003 showed that Vermont produced 98,000 metric tons of dimension stone, which was valued at $29 million. In that same year, the state produced 4.6 million metric tons of crushed stone, valued at $22.8 million, and 4.7 million metric tons of construction sand and gravel, valued at $21.2 million. Granite is quarried near Barre, and slate is found in the Southwest. The West Rutland-Proctor area has the world's largest marble reserve, the Danby quarry.

28 ENERGY AND POWER

Because of the state's lack of fossil fuel resources, utility bills are higher in Vermont than in most states. As of 2003, Vermont had 22 electrical power service providers, of which 15 were publicly owned and two were cooperatives. Of the remainder, four were investor owned, and one was the owner of an independent generator that sold directly to customers. As of that same year there were 317,126 retail customers. Of that total, 238,957 received their power from investor-owned service providers. Cooperatives accounted for 26,265 customers, while publicly owned providers had 51,903 customers. There was only one independent generator or "facility" customer.

Total net summer generating capability by the state's electrical generating plants in 2003 stood at 997 MW, with total production that same year at 6.027 billion kWh. Of the total amount generated, 10.4% came from electric utilities, with the remaining 89.6% coming from independent producers and combined heat and power service providers. The largest portion of all electric power generated, 4.444 billion kWh (73.7%), came from nuclear power plants, with hydroelectric plants in second place at 1.154 billion kWh (19.1%). Other renewable power sources accounted for 6.7% of all power generated, with petroleum fired plants accounting for the remainder.

As of 2006, the Vermont Yankee nuclear power plant in Windham County was the state's sole operating nuclear power station.

Vermont has no proven reserves or production of crude oil or natural gas. There are no refineries in the state.

29 INDUSTRY

According to the US Census Bureau's Annual Survey of Manufactures (ASM) for 2004, Vermont's manufacturing sector covered some 13 product subsectors. The shipment value of all products manufactured in the state that same year was $9.911 billion. Of that total, computer and electronic product manufacturing accounted for the largest share at $3.943 billion. It was followed by food manufacturing at $1.579 billion; fabricated metal product manufacturing at $775.845 million; machinery manufacturing at $477.558 million; and wood product manufacturing at $416.521 million.

In 2004, a total of 38,341 people in Vermont were employed in the state's manufacturing sector, according to the ASM. Of that total, 24,379 were actual production workers. In terms of total employment, the computer and electronic product manufacturing industry accounted for the largest portion of all manufacturing employees at 8,799, with 3,441 actual production workers. It was followed by fabricated metal product manufacturing at 4,407 employees (2,778 actual production workers); food manufacturing at 3,790 employees (2,462 actual production workers); machinery manufacturing at 3,097 employees (1,983 actual production workers);and furniture and related product manufacturing with 2,396 employees (1,896 actual production workers).

ASM data for 2004 showed that Vermont's manufacturing sector paid $1.687 billion in wages. Of that amount, the computer and electronic product manufacturing sector accounted for the largest share at $513.080 million. It was followed by fabricated metal product manufacturing at $228.640 million; machinery manufacturing at $143.549 million; and food manufacturing at $123.967 million.

30 COMMERCE

According to the 2002 Census of Wholesale Trade, Vermont's wholesale trade sector had sales that year totaling $1.6 billion from 869 establishments. Wholesalers of durable goods accounted for 519 establishments, followed by nondurable goods wholesalers at 303 and electronic markets, agents, and brokers accounting for 47 establishments. Sales by durable goods wholesalers in 2002 totaled $1.6 billion, while wholesalers of nondurable goods saw sales of $3.1 billion. Electronic markets, agents, and brokers in the wholesale trade industry had sales of $328.6 million.

In the 2002 Census of Retail Trade, Vermont was listed as having 3,946 retail establishments with sales of $7.6 billion. The leading types of retail businesses by number of establishments were: food and beverage stores (595); gasoline stations (479); miscellaneous store retailers (451); motor vehicle and motor vehicle parts dealers (435); and clothing and clothing accessories stores (388). In terms of sales, motor vehicle and motor vehicle parts dealers accounted for the largest share of retail sales at $1.9 billion, followed by food and beverage stores at $1.3 billion; gasoline stations at $797.6 million; and building material/garden equipment and supplies dealers at $757.3 million. A total of 40,105 people were employed by the retail sector in Vermont that year.

Foreign exports of Vermont manufacturers were estimated at $4.2 billion for 2005.

31 CONSUMER PROTECTION

The Consumer Protection Division of the Attorney General's Office handles most consumer complaints, while the Vermont Public Service Department's Consumer Affairs Division monitors utility rates, and the Agency of Human Services' Department of Aging and Disabilities protects the rights of the state's senior citizens and adults with physical disabilities.

When dealing with consumer protection issues, the state's Attorney General's Office can initiate civil and criminal proceedings; represent the state before state and federal regulatory agencies; administer consumer protection and education programs; handle formal consumer complaints; and exercise broad subpoena powers. In antitrust actions, the Attorney General's Office can act on behalf of those consumers who are incapable of acting on their own; initiate damage actions on behalf of the state in state courts; and initiate criminal proceedings. However, the office cannot represent counties, cities and other governmental entities in recovering civil damages under state or federal law.

The Office of the Attorney General's Consumer Assistance Program has offices in Burlington and Montpelier.

32 BANKING

As of June 2005, Vermont had 19 insured banks, savings and loans, and saving banks, plus 26 state-chartered and eight federally chartered credit unions (CUs). Excluding the CUs, the Burlington-South Burlington market area accounted for the largest portion of the state's financial institutions and deposits in 2004, with 10 institutions and $3.511 billion in deposits. As of June 2005, CUs accounted for 17.3% of all assets held by all financial institutions in the state, or some $1.660 billion. Banks, savings and loans, and savings banks collectively accounted for the remaining 82.7% or $7.960 billion in assets held.

The median percentage of past-due/nonaccrual loans to total loans was 1.08% as of fourth quarter 2005, down from 1.46% in 2004 and 2.01% in 2003. Regulation of Vermont's state-chartered banks and other state-chartered financial institutions is the responsibility of the Banking Division of the Department of Banking, Insurance, Securities and Healthcare Administration.

33 INSURANCE

In 2004, there were 324,000 individual life insurance policies in force in Vermont with a total value of about $24.7 billion; total value for all categories of life insurance (individual, group, and credit) was over $38.5 billion. The average coverage amount is $76,400 per policy holder. Death benefits paid that year totaled $112.8 million.

In 2003, there were 16 property and casualty and 2 life and health insurance companies domiciled in the state. In 2003, direct premiums for property and casualty insurance totaled over $1 billion. That year, there were 2,969 flood insurance policies in force in the state, with a total value of $379 million.

In 2004, 52% of state residents held employment-based health insurance policies, 5% held individual policies, and 31% were covered under Medicare and Medicaid; 10% of residents were uninsured. In 2003, employee contributions for employment-based health coverage averaged at 18% for single coverage and 21% for family coverage. The state offers a six-month health benefits expansion program for small-firm employees in connection with the Consolidated Omnibus Budget Reconciliation Act (COBRA, 1986), a health insurance program for those who lose employment-based coverage due to termination or reduction of work hours.

In 2003, there were 460,571 auto insurance policies in effect for private passenger cars. Required minimum coverage includes bodily injury liability of up to $25,000 per individual and $50,000 for all persons injured in an accident, as well as property damage liability of $10,000. Uninsured and underinsured motorist coverage are also required. In 2003, the average expenditure per vehicle for insurance coverage was $683.07.

34 SECURITIES

There are no stock or commodity exchanges in Vermont. In 2005, there were 250 personal financial advisers employed in the state and 360 securities, commodities, and financial services sales agents. The state is home to 14 NASDAQ companies, and has incorporated 4 NYSE-listed companies: Bluegreen Corp., Central Vermont Public Services Corp., Chittenden Corp., and Green Mountain Power Company.

35 PUBLIC FINANCE

The budgets for two fiscal years are submitted by the governor to the General Assembly for approval during its biennial session. The fiscal year (FY) runs from 1 July to 30 June.

Fiscal year 2006 general funds were estimated at $1.1 billion for resources and $1.0 billion for expenditures. In fiscal year 2004, federal government grants to Vermont were $1.4 billion.

In the fiscal year 2007 federal budget, Vermont was slated to receive: $5.9 million in State Children's Health Insurance Program (SCHIP) funds to help the state provide health coverage to low-income, uninsured children who do not qualify for Medicaid. This funding is a 23% increase over fiscal year 2006; and $4.5 million for the HOME Investment Partnership Program to help Vermont fund a wide range of activities that build, buy, or rehabilitate affordable housing for rent or homeownership, or provide direct rental assistance to low-income people. This funding is an 11% increase over fiscal year 2006.

On 5 January 2006 the federal government released $100 million in emergency contingency funds targeted to the areas with the greatest need, including $680,000 for Vermont.

36 TAXATION

In 2005, Vermont collected $2,243 million in tax revenues or $3,600 per capita, which placed it first among the 50 states in per capita tax burden. The national average was $2,192 per capita. Property taxes accounted for 33.2% of the total, sales taxes 13.9%, selective sales taxes 20.8%, individual income taxes 22.3%, corporate income taxes 3.1%, and other taxes 6.7%.

As of 1 January 2006, Vermont had five individual income tax brackets ranging from 3.6% to 9.5%. The state taxes corporations at rates ranging from 7.0 to 8.9% depending on tax bracket.

In 2004, state and local property taxes amounted to $950,456,000 or $1,531 per capita. The per capita amount ranks the state eighth-highest nationally. Local governments collected $502,253,000 of the total and the state government $448,203,000.

Vermont taxes retail sales at a rate of 6%. In addition to the state tax, local taxes on retail sales can reach as much as 1%, making for a potential total tax on retail sales of 7%. Food purchased for consumption off-premises is tax exempt. The tax on cigarettes is 119 cents per pack, which ranks 15th among the 50 states and the District of Columbia. Vermont taxes gasoline at 20 cents per gallon. This is in addition to the 18.4 cents per gallon federal tax on gasoline.

According to the Tax Foundation, for every federal tax dollar sent to Washington in 2004, Vermont citizens received $1.12 in federal spending.

Vermont—State Government Finances

(Dollar amounts in thousands. Per capita amounts in dollars.)

	AMOUNT	PER CAPITA
Total Revenue	4,302,590	6,928.49
General revenue	3,794,824	6,110.83
Intergovernmental revenue	1,314,916	2,117.42
Taxes	1,766,719	2,844.96
General sales	256,958	413.78
Selective sales	430,637	693.46
License taxes	98,758	159.03
Individual income tax	429,817	692.14
Corporate income tax	62,228	100.21
Other taxes	488,321	786.35
Current charges	365,920	589.24
Miscellaneous general revenue	347,269	559.21
Utility revenue	–	–
Liquor store revenue	35,279	56.81
Insurance trust revenue	472,487	760.85
Total expenditure	3,913,616	6,302.12
Intergovernmental expenditure	981,307	1,580.20
Direct expenditure	2,932,309	4,721.91
Current operation	2,313,956	3,726.18
Capital outlay	155,818	250.91
Insurance benefits and repayments	199,843	321.81
Assistance and subsidies	123,631	199.08
Interest on debt	139,061	223.93
Exhibit: Salaries and wages	623,120	1,003.41
Total expenditure	3,913,616	6,302.12
General expenditure	3,676,138	5,919.71
Intergovernmental expenditure	981,307	1,580.20
Direct expenditure	2,694,831	4,339.50
General expenditures, by function:		
Education	1,482,438	2,387.18
Public welfare	1,015,398	1,635.10
Hospitals	14,579	23.48
Health	92,467	148.90
Highways	253,779	408.66
Police protection	69,078	111.24
Correction	93,827	151.09
Natural resources	84,449	135.99
Parks and recreation	12,714	20.47
Government administration	135,824	218.72
Interest on general debt	139,061	223.93
Other and unallocable	282,524	454.95
Utility expenditure	2,753	4.43
Liquor store expenditure	34,882	56.17
Insurance trust expenditure	199,843	321.81
Debt at end of fiscal year	2,537,139	4,085.57
Cash and security holdings	5,237,854	8,434.55

Abbreviations and symbols: – zero or rounds to zero; (NA) not available; (X) not applicable.

SOURCE: *U.S. Census Bureau, Governments Division, 2004 Survey of State Government Finances*, January 2006.

37 ECONOMIC POLICY

Incentives for industrial expansion include state and municipally financed industrial sites; state employment development and training funds; revenue bond financing; tax credits for investment in research and development and in capital equipment; loans and loan guarantees for construction and equipment; and financial incentives for locating plants in areas of high unemployment. There are also exemptions from inventory taxes and sales tax on new equipment and raw materials. Major economic development initiatives by the state include streamlining the environmental permit process, funding for workforce development, an aggressive business recruitment campaign, infrastructural improvements, increased financial incentives for business, and a phase out of the corporate income tax. In the mid-2000s, Vermont posted one of the lowest unemployment rates in the country, and was engaged in creating a number of programs to help maintain and create new job opportunities for residents. One such program that has proven successful is the Vermont Department of Economic Development's Vermont Training Program (VEP), which encourages expansion among industrial companies by providing training through individually tailored programs: the state covers as much as 50% of the training costs.

38 HEALTH

The infant mortality rate in October 2005 was estimated at 5.3 per 1,000 live births. The birth rate in 2003 was 10.6 per 1,000 population, the lowest rate in the country. The abortion rate stood at 12.7 per 1,000 women in 2000. In 2003, about 90.6% of pregnant woman received prenatal care beginning in the first trimester. In 2004, approximately 85% of children received routine immunizations before the age of three.

The crude death rate in 2003 was 8.3 deaths per 1,000 population. As of 2002, the death rates for major causes of death (per 100,000 resident population) were: heart disease, 222.2; cancer, 198.5; cerebrovascular diseases, 54.3; chronic lower respiratory diseases, 44.8; and diabetes, 28.2. The mortality rate from HIV infection was unavailable that year. In 2004, the reported AIDS case rate was at about 2.7 per 100,000 population, one of the lowest rate in the nation. In 2002, about 52.1% of the population was considered overweight or obese. As of 2004, about 19.9% of state residents were smokers.

In 2003, Vermont had 14 community hospitals with about 1,500 beds. There were about 52,000 patient admissions that year and 2.2 million outpatient visits. The average daily inpatient census was about 900 patients. The average cost per day for hospital care was $1,148. Also in 2003, there were about 43 certified nursing facilities in the state with 3,582 beds and an overall occupancy rate of about 92.7%. In 2004, it was estimated that about 74.3% of all state residents had received some type of dental care within the year. Vermont had 363 physicians per 100,000 resident population in 2004 and 892 nurses per 100,000 in 2005. In 2004, there were a total of 348 dentists in the state.

About 26% of state residents were enrolled in Medicaid programs in 2003; 15% were enrolled in Medicare programs in 2004. Approximately 10% of the state population was uninsured in 2004. In 2003, state health care expenditures totaled $847,000.

39 SOCIAL WELFARE

In 2004, about 23,000 people received unemployment benefits, with the average weekly unemployment benefit at $256. In fiscal year 2005, the estimated average monthly participation in the food stamp program included about 45,218 persons (22,355 households); the average monthly benefit was about $82.93 per person. That year, the total of benefits paid through the state for the food stamp program was about $44.9 million.

Temporary Assistance for Needy Families (TANF), the system of federal welfare assistance that officially replaced Aid to Families with Dependent Children (AFDC) in 1997, was reauthorized through the Deficit Reduction Act of 2005. TANF is funded through federal block grants that are divided among the states based on an equation involving the number of recipients in each state. Vermont's TANF cash assistance program is called Aid to Needy Families with Children (ANFC); the work program is called Reach Up. In 2004, the state program had 12,000 recipients; state and federal expenditures on this TANF program totaled $42 million in fiscal year 2003.

In December 2004, Social Security benefits were paid to 110,180 Vermont residents. This number included 70,220 retired workers, 10,040 widows and widowers, 15,210 disabled workers, 5,710 spouses, and 9,000 children. Social Security beneficiaries represented 17.7% of the total state population and 95.9% of the state's population age 65 and older. Retired workers received an average monthly payment of $945; widows and widowers, $897; disabled workers, $848; and spouses, $452. Payments for children of retired workers averaged $455 per month; children of deceased workers, $640; and children of disabled workers, $243. Federal Supplemental Security Income payments in December 2004 went to 12,915 Vermont residents, averaging $387 a month.

⁴⁰HOUSING

As rustic farmhouses gradually disappear, modern units (many of them vacation homes for Vermonters and out-of-staters) are being built to replace them. In 2004, there were an estimated 304,291 housing units in Vermont (one of the lowest housing stocks in the country), 249,590 of which were occupied; 73.3% were owner-occupied. About 66.3% of all units were single-family, detached homes. About 30% of all housing was built in 1939 or earlier. Fuel oil was the most common energy source for heating. It was estimated that 6,112 units lacked telephone service, 1,634 lacked complete plumbing facilities, and 1,495 lacked complete kitchen facilities. The average household had 2.41 members.

In 2004, 3,600 new privately owned housing units were authorized for construction. The median home value was $154,318. The median monthly cost for mortgage owners was $1,174. Renters paid a median of $674 per month. In 2006, the state received over $7.4 million in community development block grants from the US Department of Housing and Urban Development (HUD)

⁴¹EDUCATION

In 2004, 90.8% of Vermont residents age 25 and older were high school graduates. Some 34.2% had obtained a bachelor's degree or higher, surpassing the national average of 26%.

The total enrollment for fall 2002 in Vermont's public schools stood at 100,000. Of these, 68,000 attended schools from kindergarten through grade eight, and 32,000 attended high school. Approximately 95.9% of the students were white, 1.2% were black, 0.8% were Hispanic, 1.5% were Asian/Pacific Islander, and 0.6% were American Indian/Alaskan Native. Total enrollment was estimated at 98,000 in fall 2003 and expected to be 85,000 by fall 2014, a decline of 15.2% during the period 2002–14. Expenditures for public education in 2003/04 were estimated at $1.19 billion or $11,128 per student, the fourth-highest among the 50 states. There were 12,218 students enrolled in 123 private schools. Since 1969, the National Assessment of Educational Progress (NAEP) has tested public school students nationwide. The resulting report, *The Nation's Report Card,* stated that in 2005, eighth graders in

Vermont scored 287 out of 500 in mathematics compared with the national average of 278.

As of fall 2002, there were 36,537 students enrolled in college or graduate school; minority students comprised 6.2% of total post-secondary enrollment. In 2005 Vermont had 27 degree-granting institutions. The state college system includes colleges at Castleton, Johnson, and Lyndonville, a technical college at Randolph Center, and the Community College of Vermont system with 12 branch campuses. The University of Vermont (Burlington) is a state-supported institution combining features of both a private and a state facility. Founded in 1791, it is the oldest higher educational institution in the state.

Notable private institutions include Bennington College, Champlain College (Burlington), Landmark College (Putney) serving students with ADHD and learning disabilities, Marlboro College (Marlboro), and Norwich University (Northfield), the oldest private military college in the United States. The School for International Training (Brattleboro) is the academic branch of the Experiment in International Living, a student exchange program. Other notable institutions include St. Michael's College (Winooski) and Trinity College (Burlington).

The Vermont Student Assistance Corporation offers scholarships, incentive grants, and guaranteed loans for eligible Vermont students.

⁴²ARTS

The Vermont Arts Council was founded in 1964. In 2005, the Arts Council and other Vermont arts organizations received 15 grants totaling $873,800 from the National Endowment for the Arts. The Vermont Humanities Council (VHC), founded in 1974, supports a number of literacy and history-related programs, as well as sponsors annual Humanities Camps at schools throughout the state. As of 2005 VHC offered literacy programs that included "Connections," a program geared towards teen parents and new adult readers and "Never Too Early," a program designed to teach childcare providers and parents techniques to stimulate reading. In 2005, the National Endowment for the Humanities contributed $1,180,125 for 15 state programs.

The Vermont State Crafts Centers at Frog Hollow (Middlebury), Burlington, and Manchester display the works of Vermont artisans. The Vermont Symphony Orchestra, in Burlington, makes extensive statewide tours including visits to several schools to promote music education. During the 2004/05 season the orchestra reached approximately 27,000 students within 193 schools. Marlboro College is the home of the summer Marlboro Music Festival, co-founded by famed pianist Rudolf Serkin, who directed the festival from 1952 to 1992. Among the summer theaters in the state are those at Dorset and Weston and the University of Vermont Shakespeare Festival. The Middlebury College Bread Loaf Writers' Conference, founded in 1926, meets each August in Ripton. The conference expected to host over 200 writers in 2006.

The Flynn Center for the Performing Arts in Burlington serves as a major performance center for the area. It is home to the Lyric Theater Company, the Vermont Symphony Orchestra, the Vermont Stage Company, and the Burlington Discover Jazz Festival. In 2005, the Flynn Center celebrated 75 years of history and 25 years of performance. Other musical performance and education venues include the Vermont Jazz Center in Brattleboro and the

Vergennes Opera House, which presents concerts, films, dance, and theater presentations, and various literary readings, as well as operas.

⁴³LIBRARIES AND MUSEUMS

In June 2001, Vermont had 188 public library systems, with a total of 190 libraries, of which there were three branches. For that same year, the state's public libraries held 2,731,000 volumes of books and serial publications, and had a combined circulation of 3,842,000. The system also had 78,000 audio and 655,000 video items, 3,000 electronic format items (CD-ROMs, magnetic tapes, and disks), and eight bookmobiles. The largest academic library was at the University of Vermont, with a book stock of 1,112,121, and 4,808 periodical subscriptions. In fiscal year 2001, operating income for the state's public library system totaled $13,408,000 and included $9,323,000 from local sources and $40,000 from state sources. Operating expenditures that year came to $13,921,000 of which 64.8% was spent on staff, and 13.9% on the collection.

Vermont has 89 museums and more than 65 historic sites. Among them are the Bennington Museum, with its collection of Early American glass, pottery, furniture, and Grandma Moses paintings, and the Art Gallery–St. Johnsbury Athenaeum, featuring 19th-century American artists. The Shelburne Museum, housed in restored Early American buildings, contains collections of American primitives and Indian artifacts. The Vermont Museum, in Montpelier, features historical exhibits concerning Indians, the Revolutionary War, rural life, and railroads and industry. Old Constitution House in Windsor offers exhibits on Vermont history.

⁴⁴COMMUNICATIONS

In 2004, about 95.9% of all occupied homes had telephones. In 2003, 65.5% of Vermont households had a computer and 58.1% had Internet access. By June 2005, there were 82,259 high-speed lines in Vermont, 76,895 residential and 5,364 for business. There were 5 major AM and 19 major FM radio stations and seven television stations in operation in 2005.

⁴⁵PRESS

In 2005, there were eight daily papers and three Sunday papers. A leading daily in 2005 was the *Burlington Free Press* (48,524 mornings, 56,850 Sundays). *Vermont Life* magazine founded in 1946 is published quarterly. The paid circulation in 2005 was 57,244. *Vermont Life* is considered one of America's leading regional magazines, winning over 95 national and international magazine awards since 1990.

⁴⁶ORGANIZATIONS

In 2006, there were over 1,590 nonprofit organizations registered within the state, of which about 1,179 were registered as charitable, educational, or religious organizations.

Associations headquartered in Vermont largely reflect the state's agricultural interests. Among these are the National Association for Gardening, the American Chestnut Foundation, the Holstein Association USA, the Composting Association of Vermont, and the Vermont Maple Industry Council, and the International Maple Syrup Institute. Professional associations are available for many fields. The Vermont Arts Council is located in Montpelier.

There are several local arts organizations and historical societies as well. The Bread Loaf Writers Conference, based at Middlebury College, sponsors educational programs that attract writers from across the country.

⁴⁷TOURISM, TRAVEL, AND RECREATION

With the building of the first ski slopes in the 1930s (Woodstock claims the first ski area in the United States) and the development of modern highways, tourism became a major industry in Vermont. In 2001, direct spending from 13.9 million visitors totaled $2.84 billion, or 13% of the entire Vermont economy. Over 30% of all trips were day trips. The tourism and travel industry supports 63,279 jobs (21% of all jobs in the state.

Summer and fall are the most popular seasons for visitors. Fall foliage trips account for 28% of all travel. In the winter, the state's ski areas offer some of the finest skiing in the East. About 11,000 Vermonters work at a Vermont ski area. There are 52 state parks and over 100 campgrounds in the state. Historical sites, including several Revolutionary War battlefields, are popular attractions and shopping, particularly for Vermont-made products such as maple syrup, is a major activity for all visitors. Vermont has tours of the maple syrup industry. Bennington is the site of the Bennington Battle Monument and President Calvin Coolidge's homestead is in Plymouth. Vermont hosts an annual Mozart Festival from mid-July to mid-August.

⁴⁸SPORTS

Vermont has no major professional sports teams. A single-A minor league baseball team, the Vermont Lake Monsters, plays in Burlington. Skiing is, perhaps, the most popular participation sport, and Vermont ski areas have hosted national and international ski competitions in both Alpine and Nordic events. World Cup races have been run at Stratton Mountain, and the national cross-country championships have been held near Putney. Famous skiers Billy Kidd and Andrea Mead Lawrence, both Olympic medalists, grew up in Vermont and trained in the state.

⁴⁹FAMOUS VERMONTERS

Two US presidents, both of whom assumed office upon the death of their predecessors, were born in Vermont. Chester Alan Arthur (1829–86) became the 21st president after James A. Garfield's assassination in 1881 and finished his term. A machine politician, Arthur became a civil-service reformer in the White House. Calvin Coolidge (1872–1933), 28th president, was born in Plymouth Notch but pursued a political career in Massachusetts. Elected vice president in 1920, he became president on the death of Warren G. Harding in 1923 and was elected to a full term in 1924.

Other federal officeholders have included Matthew Lyon (1750–1822), a US representative imprisoned under the Sedition Act and reelected from a Vergennes jail; Jacob Collamer (1791–1865), who, after serving three terms in the US House, was US postmaster general and then a US senator; Justin Smith Morrill (1810–98), US representative and senator who sponsored the Morrill tariff in 1861 and the Land Grant College Act in 1862; Levi Parsons Morton (1824–1920), Benjamin Harrison's vice president from 1889 to 1893; George Franklin Edmunds (1828–1919), a US senator who helped draft the Sherman Antitrust Act; Redfield Proctor (1831–1908), secretary of war, US senator, state governor, and the founder of a marble company; John Garibaldi Sargent (1860–1939), Coolidge's attorney general; Warren Robinson Austin (1877–1963), US senator and head of the US delegation to the UN; and George David Aiken (1892–1984), US senator from 1941 to 1977.

Important state leaders were Thomas Chittenden (1730–97), leader of the Vermont republic and the state's first governor; Ethan Allen (1738–89), a frontier folk hero, leader of the Green Mountain Boys, and presenter of Vermont's claim to independence to the US Congress in 1778; Ira Allen (1751–1814), the brother of Ethan, who led the fight for statehood; Cornelius Peter Van Ness (b.New York, 1782–1852), who served first as Vermont chief justice and then as governor; and Erastus Fairbanks (1792–1864), a governor and railroad promoter.

Vermont's many businessmen and inventors include Thaddeus Fairbanks (1796–1886), inventor of the platform scale; Thomas Davenport (1802–51), inventor of the electric motor; plow and tractor manufacturer John Deere (1804–86); Elisha G. Otis (1811–61), inventor of a steam elevator and elevator safety devices; and Horace Wells (1815–48), inventor of laughing gas. Educator John Dewey (1859–1952) was born in Burlington. Donald James Cram (1919–2001), a professor of chemistry at the University of California at Los Angeles, was awarded a Nobel Prize in chemistry in 1987.

Robert Frost (b.California, 1874–1963) maintained a summer home near Ripton, where he helped found Middlebury College's Bread Loaf Writers' Conference. He was named poet laureate of Vermont in 1961. In 1992, Louise Gluck became the first Vermont woman to win a Pulitzer Prize for poetry. A famous Vermont performer is crooner and orchestra leader Rudy Vallee (Hubert Prior Rudy Vallee, 1901–1986).

50 BIBLIOGRAPHY

Council of State Governments. *The Book of the States, 2006 Edition.* Lexington, Ky.: Council of State Governments, 2006.

Davis, Allen Freeman. *Postcards from Vermont: A Social History, 1905–1945.* Hanover, N.H.: University Press of New England, 2002.

Husher, Helen. *Off the Leash: Subversive Journeys Around Vermont.* Woodstock, Vt.: Countryman Press, 1999.

Klyza, Christopher McGrory, and Stephen C. Trombulak. *The Story of Vermont: A Natural and Cultural History.* Hanover, N.H.: University Press of New England, 1999.

Sherman, Michael. *Freedom and Unity: A History of Vermont.* Barre: Vermont Historical Society, 2004.

———, and Jennie Versteeg (eds.). *We Vermonters: Perspectives on the Past.* Montpelier: Vermont Historical Society, 1992.

Sletcher, Michael (ed.). *New England.* Vol. 4 in *The Greenwood Encyclopedia of American Regional Cultures.* Westport, Conn.: Greenwood Press, 2004.

US Department of Commerce, Economics and Statistics Administration, US Census Bureau. *Vermont, 2000. Summary Social, Economic, and Housing Characteristics: 2000 Census of Population and Housing.* Washington, D.C.: US Government Printing Office, 2003.

VIRGINIA

Commonwealth of Virginia

ORIGIN OF STATE NAME: Named for Queen Elizabeth I of England, the "Virgin Queen." **NICKNAME:** The Old Dominion. **CAPITAL:** Richmond. **ENTERED UNION:** 25 June 1788 (10th). **SONG:** "Carry Me Back to Old Virginia" was formally retired from use in 1997 but has not yet been replaced. **MOTTO:** *Sic semper tyrannis* (Thus ever to tyrants). **FLAG:** On a blue field, the state seal is centered on a white circle. **OFFICIAL SEAL:** OBVERSE: the Roman goddess Virtus, dressed as an Amazon and holding a sheathed sword in one hand and a spear in the other, stands over the body of Tyranny, who is pictured with a broken chain in his hand and a fallen crown nearby. The state motto appears below, the word "Virginia" above, and a border of Virginia creeper encircles the whole. REVERSE: the Roman goddesses of Liberty, Eternity, and Fruitfulness, with the word "Perseverando" (by persevering) above. **BIRD:** Cardinal. **FLOWER:** Dogwood. **TREE:** Dogwood. **LEGAL HOLIDAYS:** New Year's Day, 1 January; Lee-Jackson Day, 13 January; Birthday of Martin Luther King Jr., 3rd Monday in January; Washington's Birthday, 3rd Monday in February; Memorial Day, last Monday in May; Independence Day, 4 July; Labor Day, 1st Monday in September; Columbus Day, 2nd Monday in October; Veterans' Day, 11 November; Thanksgiving Day, 4th Thursday in November and the day following; Christmas Day, 25 December. **TIME:** 7 AM EST = noon GMT.

¹LOCATION, SIZE, AND EXTENT

Situated on the eastern seaboard of the United States, Virginia is the fourth-largest of the South Atlantic states and ranks 36th in size among the 50 states.

The total area of Virginia is 40,767 sq mi (105,586 sq km), of which land occupies 39,704 sq mi (102,833 sq km) and inland water 1,063 sq mi (2,753 sq km). Virginia extends approximately 440 mi (710 km) E–W, but the maximum point-to-point distance from the state's noncontiguous Eastern Shore to the western extremity is 470 mi (756 km). The maximum N–S extension is about 200 mi (320 km).

Virginia is bordered on the NW by West Virginia; on the NE by Maryland and the District of Columbia (with the line passing through the Potomac River and Chesapeake Bay); on the E by the Atlantic Ocean; on the S by North Carolina and Tennessee; and on the W by Kentucky. The state's geographic center is in Buckingham County, 5 mi (8 km) SW of the town of Buckingham.

Virginia's offshore islands in the Atlantic include Chincoteague, Wallops, Cedar, Parramore, Hog, Cobb, and Smith. The boundaries of Virginia, including the Eastern Shore at the tip of the Delmarva Peninsula, total 1,356 mi (2,182 km), of which 112 mi (180 km) is general coastline; the tidal shoreline extends 3,315 mi (5,335 km).

²TOPOGRAPHY

Virginia consists of three principal physiographic areas: the Atlantic Coastal Plain, or Tidewater; the Piedmont Plateau, in the central section; and the Blue Ridge and Allegheny Mountains of the Appalachian chain, in the west and northwest.

The long, narrow Blue Ridge rises sharply from the piedmont, reaching a maximum elevation of 5,729 ft (1,747 m) at Mt. Rogers, the state's highest point. Between the Blue Ridge and the Allegheny Mountains of the Appalachian chain in the northwest lies the Valley of Virginia, consisting of transverse ridges and six separate valleys. The floors of these valleys ascend in altitude from about 300 ft (90 m) in the northern Shenandoah Valley to 2,400 ft (730 m) in the Powell Valley. The Alleghenies average 3,000 ft (900 m) in height. The mean elevation of the state is approximately 950 ft (290 m).

The Piedmont, shaped roughly like a triangle, varies in width from 40 mi (64 km) in the far north to 180 mi (290 km) in the extreme south. Altitudes in this region range from about 300 ft (90 m) at the fall line in the east to a maximum of about 1,000 ft (300 m) at the base of the Blue Ridge in the southwest. The Tidewater, which declines gently from the fall line to sea level (the lowest point of the state), is divided by four long peninsulas cut by the state's four principal rivers—the Potomac, Rappahannock, York, and James—and the Chesapeake Bay. On the opposite side of the bay is Virginia's low-lying Eastern Shore, the southern tip of the Delmarva Peninsula. The Tidewater has many excellent harbors, notably the deep Hampton Roads estuary. Also in the southeast lies the Dismal Swamp, a drainage basin that includes Lake Drummond, about 7 mi (11 km) long and 5 mi (8 km) wide near the North Carolina border. Other major lakes in Virginia are Smith Mountain—at 31 sq mi (80 sq km) the largest lake wholly within the state—Claytor, and South Holston. The John H. Kerr Reservoir, covering 76 sq mi (197 sq km), straddles the Virginia–North Carolina line.

³CLIMATE

A mild, humid coastal climate is characteristic of Virginia. Temperatures, most equable in the Tidewater, become increasingly cooler with the rising altitudes as one moves westward. The normal daily average temperature at Richmond is about 58°F (14°C), ranging from 38°F (3°C) in January to 78°F (25°C) in July. The record high, 110°F (43°C), was registered at Balcony Falls (near

Glasgow) on 15 July 1954; the record low, -30°F (-34°C), was set at Mountain Lake on 22 January 1985. The frost-free growing season ranges from about 140 days in the mountains of the extreme west to over 250 in the Norfolk area.

Annual precipitation at Richmond averages about 42.7 in (108 cm); at Norfolk, annual precipitation averages 44.8.7 in (113 cm) per year. The average annual snowfall amounts to nearly 13.9 in (35 cm) at Richmond but only 7.4 in (18 cm) at Norfolk.

⁴FLORA AND FAUNA

Native to Virginia are 12 varieties of oak, 5 of pine, and 2 each of walnut, locust, gum, and popular. Pines predominate in the coastal areas, with numerous hardwoods on slopes and ridges inland; isolated stands of persimmon, ash, cedar, and basswood can also be found. Characteristic wild flowers include trailing arbutus, mountain laurel, and diverse azaleas and rhododendrons. In 2006, the US Fish and Wildlife Service listed 14 plant species as threatened or endangered in Virginia, including the Virginia roundleaf birch, Virginia sneezeweed, Northeastern bulrush, and small whorled pogonia.

Among indigenous mammalian species are white-tailed (Virginia) deer, elk, black bear, bobcat, woodchuck, raccoon, opossum, nutria, red and gray foxes, and spotted and striped skunks, along with several species each of moles, shrews, bats, squirrels, deermice, rats, and rabbits; the beaver, mink, and river otter, once thought to be endangered, have returned in recent decades. Principal game birds include the ruffed grouse (commonly called pheasant in Virginia), wild turkey, bobwhite quail, mourning dove, woodcock, and Wilson's snipe. Tidal waters abound with croaker, hogfish, gray and spotted trout, and flounder; bass, bream, bluegill, sunfish, perch, carp, catfish, and crappie live in freshwater ponds and streams. Native reptiles include such poisonous snakes as the northern copperhead, eastern cottonmouth, and timber rattler.

In April 2006, 47 animal species were listed as threatened or endangered in Virginia, including the puma; Indiana, gray, and Virginia big-eared bats; bald eagle; red-cockaded woodpecker; Virginia fringed mountain snail; Lee County cave isopod; four species of pearly mussel; three species of pigtoe; tan riffleshell; and three species of whale. At least one-fourth of the rare or endangered species in the state are found in the Dismal Swamp.

⁵ENVIRONMENTAL PROTECTION

The Virginia Department of Environmental Quality (DEQ), established in 1993, is under the jurisdiction of the Secretary of Natural Resources. The mission of the DEQ is to protect the environment of Virginia in order to promote the health and well-being of the citizens of the Commonwealth. The DEQ administers state and federal environmental programs; issues environmental permits and ensures compliance with regulations; and coordinates planning among Virginia's environmental programs. The DEQ provides staff support to assist the State Water Control Board in administering the federal Clean Water Act and enforcing state laws to improve the quality of surface water and groundwater for aquatic life and human health; the State Air Pollution Control Board in administering the federal Clean Air Act and enforcing state laws and regulations to improve air quality; and the Waste Management Board in administering waste management programs created by legislation such as the Resource Conservation and Recovery Act and the Virginia Waste Management Act.

In 2002, Virginia waste treatment facilities received about 12% less total solid waste (municipal solid waste, construction and demolition debris, sludge and other types of waste), or about 824,000 tons less that they received in 2001.

The Commission of Game and Inland Fisheries manages land wildlife and freshwater fish resources, while the Marine Resources Commission manages the wetlands, commercial fishery resources, and the use of the marine environment in the Tidewater area. About 1 million acres (404,685 hectares) of wetlands are found in the state. These areas are generally regulated by the Virginia Water Protection Permit. The Chesapeake Bay Estuarine Complex, the largest estuary and most important wetland in the United States, was designated as a Ramsar Wetland of International Importance in 1987.

Virginia has implemented programs to improve air quality in the Northern Virginia, Richmond, and Hampton Roads regions; to enhance water quality monitoring for streams and lakes statewide; to continue restoration efforts for the Chesapeake Bay; and to promote voluntary cleanups of contaminated industrial sites.

In 2003, Virginia had 250 hazardous waste sites listed in the US Environment Protection Agency (EPA) database, 29 of which were on the National Priorities List as of 2006, including the Langley Air Force Base and NASA Langley Research Center, The Marine Corps Combat Development Command in Quantico, the Naval Surface Warfare Center, Norfolk Naval Shipyards. Also in 2003, 74.2 million lb of toxic chemicals were released in the state. In 2005, the EPA spent over $3.4 million through the Superfund program for the cleanup of hazardous waste sites in the state. The same year, federal EPA grants awarded to the state included $22 million for the wastewater revolving loan fund and $11.4 million for the drinking water revolving fund.

⁶POPULATION

Virginia ranked 12th in population in the United States with an estimated total of 7,567,465 in 2005, an increase of 6.9% since 2000. Between 1990 and 2000, Virginia's population grew from 6,187,358 to 7,078,515, an increase of 14.4%. The population is projected to reach 8.4 million by 2015 and 9.3 million by 2025. The population density in 2004 was 188.5 persons per sq mi. In 2004 the median age was 36.9. Persons under 18 years old accounted for 24.2% of the population while 11.4% was age 65 or older.

From the outset, Virginia was the most populous of the English colonies, with a population that doubled every 25 years and totaled more than 100,000 by 1727. By 1790, the time of the first US census, Virginia's population of 821,287 was about 21% of the US total and almost twice that of second-ranked Pennsylvania. Although surpassed by New York State at the 1820 census, Virginia continued to enjoy slow but steady growth until the Civil War. During the 1860s, the loss of its western counties (which became the new state of West Virginia) and wartime devastation caused a decline of 23%. The population passed the 2 million mark in 1910, and the number of Virginians doubled between 1920 and 1970. The population growth rates for the five decades following 1940 were 23.9%, 19.5%, 17.2%, 15%, and 15.7%, in each case above the US average.

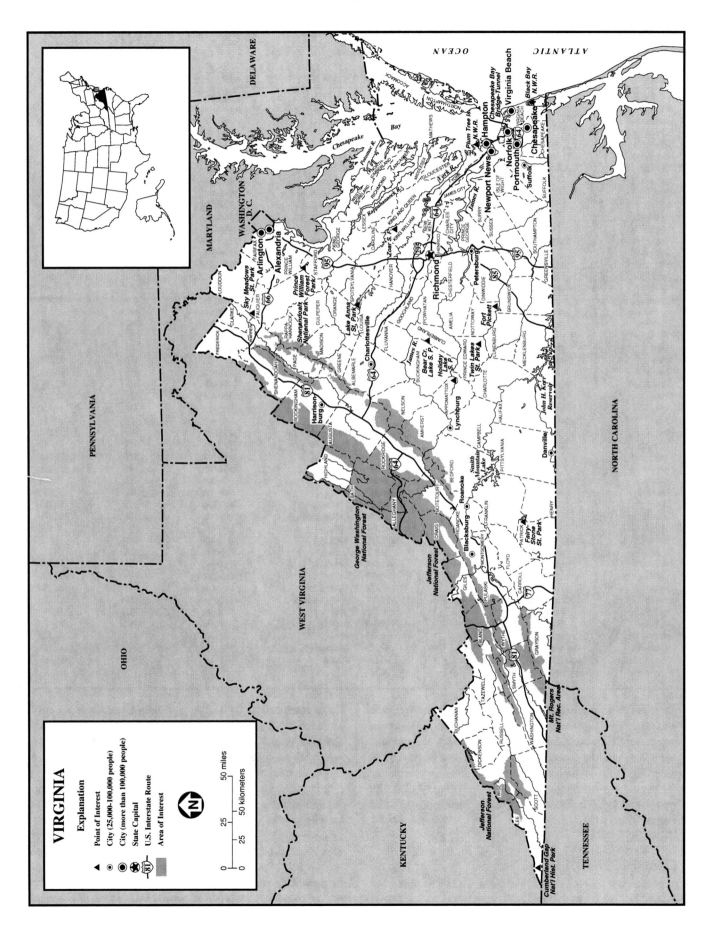

Virginia—Counties, County Seats, and County Areas and Populations

COUNTY	COUNTY SEAT	LAND AREA (SQ MI)	POPULATION (2005 EST.)	COUNTY	COUNTY SEAT	LAND AREA (SQ MI)	POPULATION (2005 EST.)
Accomack	Accomac	476	39,424	King William	King William	278	14,732
Albemarle	Charlottesville	725	90,717	Lancaster	Lancaster	133	11,593
Alleghany	Covington	446	16,715	Lee	Jonesville	437	23,686
Amelia	Amelia	357	12,273	Loudoun	Leesburg	521	255,518
Amherst	Amherst	478	32,134	Louisa	Louisa	497	30,020
Appomattox	Appomattox	336	13,967	Lunenburg	Lunenburg	432	13,194
Arlington	Arlington	26	195,965	Madison	Madison	322	13,398
Augusta	Staunton	989	69,725	Mathews	Mathews	87	9,194
Bath	Warm Springs	537	4,937	Mecklenburg	Boydton	616	32,529
Bedford	Bedford	747	65,286	Middlesex	Saluda	134	10,493
Bland	Bland	359	6,943	Montgomery	Christiansburg	390	84,303
Botetourt	Fincastle	545	32,027	Nelson	Lovingston	475	15,101
Brunswick	Lawrenceville	563	17,920	New Kent	New Kent	213	16,107
Buchanan	Grundy	504	24,755	Northampton	Eastville	226	13,548
Buckingham	Buckingham	583	16,058	Northumberland	Heathsville	185	12,874
Campbell	Rustburg	505	52,339	Nottoway	Nottoway	317	15,560
Caroline	Bowling Green	536	25,563	Orange	Orange	342	30,246
Carroll	Hillsville	478	29,438	Page	Luray	313	23,831
Charles City	Charles City	181	7,119	Patrick	Stuart	481	19,209
Charlotte	Charlotte	476	12,404	Pittsylvania	Chatham	995	61,854
Chesterfield	Chesterfield	434	288,876	Powhatan	Powhatan	261	26,598
Clarke	Berryville	178	14,205	Prince Edward	Farmville	354	20,455
Craig	New Castle	330	5,154	Prince George	Prince George	266	36,725
Culpeper	Culpeper	382	42,530	Prince William	Manassas	3,392	348,588
Cumberland	Cumberland	300	9,378	Pulaski	Pulaski	318	35,081
Dickenson	Clintwood	331	16,243	Rappahannock	Washington	267	7,271
Dinwiddie	Dinwiddie	507	25,391	Richmond	Warsaw	193	9,114
Essex	Tappahannock	263	10,492	Roanoke	Salem	251	88,172
Fairfax	Fairfax	393	1,006,529	Rockbridge	Lexington	603	21,242
Fauquier	Warrenton	651	64,997	Rockingham	Harrisonburg	865	71,251
Floyd	Floyd	381	14,649	Russell	Lebanon	479	28,949
Fluvanna	Palmyra	290	24,751	Scott	Gate City	536	22,962
Franklin	Rock Mount	683	50,345	Shenandoah	Woodstock	512	39,184
Frederick	Winchester	415	69,123	Smyth	Marion	452	32,640
Giles	Pearisburg	362	17,098	Southampton	Courtland	603	17,585
Gloucester	Gloucester	225	37,787	Spotsylvania	Spotsylvania	404	116,549
Goochland	Goochland	281	19,360	Stafford	Stafford	271	117,874
Grayson	Independence	446	16,366	Surry	Surry	281	7,013
Greene	Standardsville	157	17,418	Sussex	Sussex	496	12,071
Greensville	Emporia	300	11,088	Tazewell	Tazewell	522	44,795
Halifax	Halifax	816	36,284	Warren	Front Royal	219	35,556
Hanover	Hanover	468	97,426	Washington	Abingdon	578	52,085
Henrico	Richmond	238	280,581	Westmoreland	Montross	250	17,227
Henry	Martinsville	283	56,501	Wise	Wise	405	41,997
Highland	Monterey	416	2,475	Wythe	Wytheville	460	28,421
Isle of Wight	Isle of Wight	319	33,417	York	Yorktown	122	61,758
James City	Williamsburg	153	57,525	Independent Cities		1,605	2,400,181
King and Queen	King and Queen	317	6,796	**TOTALS**		42,705	7,567,465
King George	King George	180	20,637				

In the 1990s, approximately three-fourths of all Virginians lived in metropolitan areas, the largest of which in 2004 was the Norfolk–Virginia Beach–Newport News area, with an estimated 1,644,250 people; the Richmond metropolitan area had 1,154,317 people. Virginia's most populous cities proper with their estimated 2004 populations are Virginia Beach, 440,098; Norfolk, 237,835; Chesapeake, 214,725; Richmond, 192,494; Arlington, 186,117; Newport News, 181,913; Hampton, 145,951; and Alexandria, 128,206.

7 ETHNIC GROUPS

When the first federal census was taken in 1790, more than 306,000 blacks—of whom only 12,000 were free—made up more than one-third of Virginia's total population. After emancipation, blacks continued to be heavily represented, accounting in 1870 for 512,841 (42%) of the 1,225,163 Virginians. Blacks numbered 1,390,293 in 2000, and their proportion of the total estimated population was 19.6%. That percentage had increased slightly, to 19.9%, by 2004.

In 2000, Virginia had 329,540 Hispanic and Latino residents, chiefly Mexicans and Salvadorans. In 2004, 5.7% of the population was Hispanic or Latino. The 2000 census counted some 261,025 Asians, including 47,609 Filipinos, 45,279 Koreans, 36,966 Chinese, 37,309 Vietnamese, 48,815 Asian Indians, and 9,080 Japanese. In 2000, Pacific Islanders numbered 3,946. In 2004, 4.4% of the population was Asian and 0.1% Pacific Islander. Equal to the national average, 1.5% reported origin of more than one race. An estimated 570,279 Virginians—8.1% of all state residents—were of foreign birth in 2000, compared with 177,000 in 1980. The Native American population, including Eskimos and Aleuts, numbered 21,172 in 2000. In 2004, 0.3% of the population was American Indian or Alaskan Native.

8 LANGUAGES

English settlers encountered members of the Powhatan Indian confederacy, speakers of an Algonkian language, whose legacy includes such place-names as Roanoke and Rappahannock.

Although the expanding suburban area south of the District of Columbia has become dialectically heterogeneous, the rest of the state has retained its essentially Southern speech features. Many dialect markers occur statewide, but subregional contrasts distinguish the South Midland of the Appalachians from the Southern of the piedmont and Tidewater. General are *batter bread* (a soft corn cake), *batter cake* (pancake), *comfort* (tied and filled bed cover), and *polecat* (skunk). Widespread pronunciation features include *greasy* with a /z/ sound; *yeast* and *east* as sound-alikes, *creek* rhyming with *peek*, and *can't* with *paint; coop* and *bulge* with the vowel of *book;* and *forest* with an /ah/ sound.

The Tidewater is set off by *creek* meaning a saltwater inlet, *fishing worm* for earthworm, and fog as /fahg/. Appalachian South Midland has *redworm* for earthworm, *fog* as /fawg/, *wash* as /wawsh/, *Mary* and *merry* as sound-alikes, and *poor* with the vowel of *book*. The Richmond area is noted also for having two variants of the long /i/ and /ow/ diphthongs as they occur before voiceless and voiced consonants, so that the vowel in the noun *house* is quite different from the vowel in the verb *house,* and the vowel in *advice* differs from that in *advise*. The Tidewater exhibits similar features.

In 2000, Virginia residents five years of age and over who spoke only English at home numbered 5,884,075, or 88.9% of the total population, down from 92.7% in 1990.

The following table gives selected statistics from the 2000 Census for language spoken at home by persons five years old and over. The category "African languages" includes Amharic, Ibo, Twi, Yoruba, Bantu, Swahili, and Somali. The category "Other Indic languages" includes Bengali, Marathi, Punjabi, and Romany. The category "Other Asian languages" includes Dravidian languages, Malayalam, Telugu, Tamil, and Turkish.

LANGUAGE	NUMBER	PERCENT
Population 5 years and over	**6,619,266**	**100.0**
Speak only English	5,884,075	88.9
Speak a language other than English	735,191	11.1
Speak a language other than English	**735,191**	**11.1**
Spanish or Spanish Creole	316,274	4.8
French (incl. Patois, Cajun)	40,117	0.6
Korean	39,636	0.6
Tagalog	33,598	0.5
German	32,736	0.5
Vietnamese	31,918	0.5
Chinese	29,837	0.5
Arabic	25,984	0.4
African languages	21,164	0.3
Persian	19,199	0.3
Urdu	15,250	0.2
Other Indic languages	13,767	0.2
Other Asian languages	12,115	0.2
Hindi	11,947	0.2
Italian	10,099	0.2

9 RELIGIONS

The Anglican Church (later the Episcopal Church), whose members founded and populated Virginia Colony in the early days, was the established church during the colonial period. The first dissenters to arrive were Scotch-Irish Presbyterians in the late 17th century; they were followed by large numbers of German Lutherans, Welsh Baptists, and English Quakers, who settled in the Valley of Virginia in the early 18th century. The General Assembly's adoption in 1785 of the Virginia Statute for Religious Freedom, drafted by Thomas Jefferson, disestablished the Episcopal Church and made religious toleration the norm in Virginia. Although the Episcopal and Presbyterian churches retained the allegiance of the landed gentry during the 19th century, the Methodists and Baptists became the largest church groups in the state.

Protestant denominations combined had the greatest number of known adherents in 2000. That year, the leading group was the Southern Baptist Convention, with 774,673 adherents. The United Methodist Church is considered to be the second-largest denomination in the state, with 343,580 members reported in 2003. Other major denominations in 2000 included the Presbyterian Church USA, 135,435 members, and the Episcopal Church, 126,874. In 2004, there were about 603,190 Roman Catholics in the state. The Jewish population in 2000 was estimated at 76,140 and there were an estimated 51,021 Muslims. Over 4.1 million people (about 58.4% of the population) were not counted as members of any religious organization.

Headquarters for the Baptist World Alliance are located in Falls Church.

10 TRANSPORTATION

Virginia has one of the nation's most extensive highway systems, one of the leading ports—Hampton Roads—and two of the nation's busiest air terminals.

Virginia was a leader in early railroad development. Rail lines were completed between Richmond and Fredericksburg in 1836, from Portsmouth to Roanoke in 1837, and from Richmond to Washington, DC, in 1872. Virginia's 1,290 mi (2,076 km) of track formed a strategic supply link for both the Confederate and Union armies during the Civil War. Railroads remained the primary system of transportation until the rise of the automobile in the 1920s. As of 2003, there were nine railroads operating in the state, with a combined track mileage of 3,428 mi (5,519 km). Of these, two were Class I railways with a combined trackage of 3,184 rail mi (5,126 km). The two Class I railroads were CSX, and Norfolk Southern. As of 2006, Amtrak passenger trains served 18 communities in Virginia providing north–south and east–west services.

Virginia's road network, at first built mainly for hauling tobacco to market, had expanded across the Blue Ridge by 1782, to the Cumberland Gap by 1795, and into the Shenandoah Valley by means of the Valley Turnpike in 1840. As of 2004, Virginia had 71,534 mi (115,169 km) of public roads, some 6.486 million registered vehicles, and 5,112,523 licensed drivers. Major interstate highways are I-95 extending north–south from Washington, DC, via Richmond to the North Carolina border (and, eventually, to Florida); I-81, connecting northern Virginia with the southwest; and I-64, linking the Hampton Roads area with West Virginia via Clifton Forge and Covington in the west. The 18-mi (29-km)

Chesapeake Bay Bridge-Tunnel, completed in 1964, connects the Eastern Shore with the southeastern mainland. Popular scenic highways include the Blue Ridge Parkway, Colonial National Historical Parkway, and George Washington Memorial Parkway.

Virginia's District of Columbia suburbs are linked to the nation's capital by the Washington Metropolitan Area Transit Authority's bus and rail systems. Norfolk, Newport News-Hampton, and Richmond have extensive bus systems.

Virginia's Hampton Roads has one of the largest and strongest commercial port complexes in the world. Three state-owned general cargo marine terminals: Newport News Marine Terminal; Norfolk International Terminals; and Portsmouth Marine Terminal, share the harbor with more than 20 privately owned bulk terminals. The Hampton Roads harbor has the greatest volume of total tonnage on the US east coast and leads the world in coal exports. In 2004, the Port of Hampton Roads handled 48.446 million tons of cargo, making it the 15th-busiest port in the United States. Located on a naturally deep, ice-free harbor, 18 mi (29 km) from the open sea, Virginia's ports have the largest landside intermodal facilities on the US east coast. Each general cargo terminal in the port has on-site rail connections that offer single and double-stack train service from the docks. Virginia's mid-Atlantic location and transportation infrastructure offer users of the port access to two-thirds of the US population within 24 hours. In addition to the marine terminals, the Virginia Inland Port (VIP) terminal, just west of Washington, DC, in Front Royal, Virginia, offers daily rail service to the marine terminals in Hampton Roads and allows direct access to the international trade routes of the 75 international shipping lines calling at the ports. In addition to the movement of international export and import cargo, the VIP is a full-service domestic rail ramp for Norfolk Southern's domestic service. In 2003, waterborne shipments totaled 50.033 million tons. As of 2004, Virginia had 674 mi (1,085 km) of navigable inland waterways.

In 2005, Virginia had a total of 429 public and private-use aviation-related facilities. This included 291 airports, 130 heliports, 3 STOLports (Short Take-Off and Landing), and 4 seaplane bases. Dulles International Airport located in the Washington, DC, suburb of Chantilly is the state's main airport, with 10,961,614 passengers enplaned in 2004, followed by Ronald Reagan Washington National in Arlington with 7,661,532 enplanements in that same year, making these two airports the 21st- and 30th-busiest airports in the United States, respectively. Other major airports in the state were Norfolk International, with 1,895,472 enplanements and Richmond International with 1,251,406 enplanements in 2004.

11 HISTORY

Distinctively fluted stone points found at Flint Run in Front Royal and at the Williamson Site in Dinwiddie County testify to the presence in what is now the Commonwealth of Virginia of nomadic Paleo-Indians after 8000 BC. Climatic changes and the arrival of other Indian groups about 3500 BC produced the Archaic Culture, which lasted until about AD 500. These Indians apparently were great eaters of oysters, and shell accumulations along riverbanks mark their settlement sites. The Woodland Period (AD 500–1600) marked the Indians' development of the bow and arrow and sophisticated pottery. At the time of English contact, early in the 17th century, Tidewater Virginia was occupied principally by Algonkian-speakers, planters as well as hunters and fishers, who lived in pole-framed dwellings forming small, palisaded towns. The piedmont area was the home of the Manahoac, Monacan, and Tutelo, all of Siouan stock. Cherokee lived in Virginia's far southwestern triangle.

The first permanent English settlement in America was established at Jamestown on 13 May 1607 in the new land named Virginia in honor of Elizabeth I, the "Virgin Queen." The successful settlement was sponsored by the London Company (also known as the Virginia Company), a joint-stock venture chartered by King James I in 1606. The charter defined Virginia as all of the North American coast between 30° and 45°N and extending inland for 50 mi (80 km). A new royal charter in 1609 placed Virginia's northern and southern boundaries at points 200 mi (320 km) north and south of Point Comfort, at the mouth of the James River, and extended its territory westward to the Pacific; a third charter issued in 1612 pushed Virginia eastward to embrace the Bermuda Islands. Thus, Virginia at one time stretched from southern Maine to California and encompassed all or part of 42 of the present 50 states, as well as Bermuda and part of the Canadian province of Ontario.

Upon landing at Jamestown, the 100 or more male colonists elected from among 12 royally approved councillors a governor and captain general, Edward Maria Wingfield. Much internal strife, conflict with the Indians, and a "starving time" that reduced the settlers to eating their horses caused them to vote to leave the colony in 1610, but just as they were leaving, three supply ships arrived; with them came Thomas West, Baron De La Warr (Lord Delaware), who stayed to govern the Virginia Colony until 1611. Finally, however, it was the energy, resourcefulness, and military skill of Captain John Smith that saved the colony from both starvation and destruction by the Indians. He also charted the coast and wrote the first American book, *A True Relation,* which effectively publicized English colonization of the New World.

Smith's chief Algonkian adversary was Powhatan, emperor of a confederacy in eastern Virginia that bore his name. Although Smith was taken prisoner by Powhatan, he was able to work out a tenuous peace later cemented by the marriage in 1614 of the emperor's favorite daughter, Pocahontas, to John Rolfe, a Jamestown settler who founded the colonial tobacco industry.

Three events marked 1619 as a red-letter year in Virginia history. First, women were sent to the colony in large numbers. Any man marrying one of a shipment of 90 "young maids" had to pay 120 lb of tobacco for the cost of her transportation. The women were carefully screened for respectability, and none had to marry if she did not find a man to her liking. The second key event was the arrival in Jamestown of the first blacks, probably as indentured servants, a condition from which slavery in the colony evolved (the first legally recognized slaveholder, in the 1630s, was Anthony Johnson, himself black). The third and most celebrated event of 1619 was the convening in Jamestown of the first representative assembly in the New World, consisting of a council chosen by the London Company and a House of Burgesses elected by the colonists. Thus, self-government through locally elected representatives became a reality in America and an important precedent for the English colonies.

King James I, for whom the colonial capital was named, was at first content with colonization under the London Company's direction. But in 1624, he charged the company with mismanagement and revoked its charter. Virginia remained a royal colony until 1776, although royal governors such as Sir Francis Wyatt and Sir George Yeardley continued to convoke the General Assembly without the Crown's assent. A serious challenge to self-government came in 1629–35 with Governor John Harvey's "executive offenses"—including the knocking out of a councillor's teeth and the detaining of a petition of protest to the king—which sparked a rebellion led by Dr. John Pott. Harvey was bloodlessly deposed by the council, which turned, significantly, to the House of Burgesses for confirmation of the action the council had taken.

Despite serious setbacks because of Indian massacres in 1622 and 1644, the colony's population expanded rapidly along the James, York, Rappahannock, and Potomac rivers, and along the Eastern Shore. In 1653, the General Assembly attempted to collect taxes from the Eastern Shore although that area had no legislative representation. At a mass meeting, Colonel Thomas Johnson urged resistance to taxation without representation. The resulting Northampton Declaration embodied this principle, which would provide the rallying cry for the American Revolution; the immediate result was the granting of representation to the Eastern Shore.

Virginia earned the designation Old Dominion through its loyalty to the Stuarts during England's Civil War, but the superior military and naval forces of Oliver Cromwell compelled submission to parliamentary commissioners in 1652. In the eight years that followed, the House of Burgesses played an increasingly prominent role. Colonial governors, while at least nominally Puritan, usually conducted affairs with an easy tolerance that did not mar Virginia's general hospitality to refugee Cavaliers from the mother country.

With the restoration of the royal family in 1660, Sir William Berkeley, an ardent royalist who had served as governor before the colony's surrender to the Commonwealth, was returned to that office. In his first administration, his benign policies and appealing personality had earned him great popularity, but during his second term, his dictatorial and vindictive support of royal prerogatives made him the most hated man in the colony. When he seemed unable to defend the people against Indian incursions in 1676, they sought a general of their own. They found him in young Nathaniel Bacon, a charismatic planter of great daring and eloquence, whose leadership attracted many small planters impatient by this time with the privileged oligarchy directing the colony. Bacon's war against the Indians became a populist-style revolt against the governor, who fled to the Eastern Shore, and reform legislation was pushed by the burgesses. Berkeley regained control of the capital briefly, only to be defeated by Bacon's forces; but Jamestown was burned by the retreating Bacon, who died of fever shortly afterward. Berkeley's subsequent return to power was marked by so many hangings of offenders that the governor was summoned to the court of Charles II to answer for his actions. Bacon's Rebellion was cited as a precedent when the colonies waged war against George III a century later.

The 17th century closed on a note of material and cultural progress with the gubernatorial administration of Francis Nicholson. The College of William and Mary, the second institution of higher learning in America, was chartered in 1693, and Middle Planta-tion (renamed Williamsburg in 1722), the site of the college, became the seat of government when the capital was moved from Jamestown in 1699. The new capital remained small, although it was crowded when the legislature was in session. A new era of cultural and economic progress dawned with the administration of Alexander Spotswood (1710–22), sometimes considered the greatest of Virginia's colonial governors. He discouraged the colony's excessively heavy dependence on a single crop, tobacco; promoted industry, especially ironwork; took a humane interest in blacks and Indians' strengthened fortification; ended the depredations of the notorious pirate Edward Teach, better known as Blackbeard; and, by leading his "Knights of the Golden Horseshoe" across the Blue Ridge, dramatized the opening of the transmontane region.

In the decades that followed, eastern Virginians moving into the Valley of Virginia were joined by Scotch-Irish and Germans moving southward from Maryland and Pennsylvania. Virginians caught up in western settlement lost much of their awe of the mother country during the French and Indian War (1756–63). A young Virginia militiaman, Colonel George Washington, gave wise but unheeded advice to Britain's Major General Edward Braddock before the Battle of Monongahela, and afterward emerged as the hero of that action.

Virginia, acting independently and with other colonies, repeatedly challenged agents of the Crown. In 1765, the House of Burgesses, swept by the eloquence of Patrick Henry, adopted five resolutions opposing the Stamp Act, through which the English Parliament had sought to tax the colonists for their own defense. In 1768, Virginia joined Massachusetts in issuing an appeal to all the colonies for concerted action. The following year, Virginia initiated a boycott of British goods in answer to the taxation provisions of the hated Townshend Acts. In 1773, the Old Dominion became the first colony to establish an intercolonial Committee of Correspondence. And it joined the other colonies at the First Continental Congress, which met in Philadelphia in 1774 and elected Virginia's Peyton Randolph president.

Virginia was the first colony to instruct its delegates to move for independence at the Continental Congress of 1776. The congressional resolution was introduced by one native son, Richard Henry Lee, and the Declaration of Independence was written by another, Thomas Jefferson. In the same year, Virginians proclaimed their government a commonwealth and adopted a constitution and declaration of rights, prepared by George Mason. The declaration became the basis for the Bill of Rights in the US Constitution. Virginians were equally active in the Revolutionary War. George Washington was commander in chief of the Continental Army, and other outstanding Virginia officers were George Rogers Clark, Hugh Mercer, Henry "Light Horse Harry" Lee, William Campbell, Isaac Shelby, and an adopted son, Daniel Morgan. In addition, the greatest American naval hero was a Scottish-born Virginian, John Paul Jones. Virginia itself was a major battlefield, and it was on Virginia soil, at Yorktown on 19 October 1781, that British General Charles Cornwallis surrendered to Washington, effectively ending the war.

During the early federal period, Virginia's leadership was as notable as it had been during the American Revolution. James Madison is honored as the "father of the Constitution," and Washington, who was president of the constitutional convention, became the first US president in 1789. Indeed, Virginians occupied the presidency for all but four of the nation's first 28 years. Far more influential than most presidents was another Virginian, John Marshall, who served as US chief justice for 34 years, beginning in 1801.

During the first half of the 19th century, Virginians became increasingly concerned with the problem of slavery. From the early 1700s, the General Assembly had repeatedly prohibited the importation of slaves, only to be overruled by the Crown, protecting the interests of British slave traders. In 1778, no longer subject to royal veto, the legislature provided that any slave brought into the state would automatically be freed upon arrival. (There was no immediate legal termination of the bondage of those already enslaved, or of their offspring.) The number of free blacks grew tenfold by 1810, and though some became self-supporting farmers and artisans, many could find no employment. Fearing that unhappy free blacks might incite those who were still slaves to rebellion, the General Assembly in 1806 decreed that each slave emancipated in due course must then leave Virginia within a year or after reaching the age of 21. Nat Turner's slave revolt—which took the lives of at least 55 white men, women, and children in Southampton County in 1831—increased white fears of black emancipation. Nevertheless, legislation to end slavery in Virginia failed adoption by only seven votes the following year.

The slavery controversy did not consume all Virginians' energies in the first half of the 19th century, an era that saw the state become a leading center of scientific, artistic, and educational advancement. But this era ended with the coming of the Civil War, a conflict about which many Virginians had grave misgivings. Governor John Letcher was a Union man, and most of the state's top political leaders hoped to retain the federal tie. Even after the formation at Montgomery, Alabama, of the Confederate States of America, Virginia initiated a national peace convention in Washington, DC, headed by a native son and former US president, John Tyler. A statewide convention, assembled in Richmond in April 1861, adopted an ordinance of secession only after President Abraham Lincoln sought to send troops across Virginia to punish the states that had already seceded and called upon the commonwealth to furnish soldiers for that task. Virginia adopted secession with some regret and apprehension but with no agonizing over constitutional principles, for in ratifying the Constitution the state had reserved the right to secede. Shortly afterward, Richmond, the capital of Virginia since 1780, became the capital of the Confederacy. It was also the home of the Tredegar Ironworks, the South's most important manufacturer of heavy weaponry.

Robert E. Lee, offered field command of the Union armies, instead resigned his US commission in order to serve his native state as commander of the Army of Northern Virginia and eventually as chief of the Confederate armies. Other outstanding Virginian generals included Thomas Jonathan "Stonewall" Jackson, J. E. B. "Jeb" Stuart, Joseph E. Johnston, and A. P. Hill. Besides furnishing a greater number of outstanding Confederate generals than any other state, the Old Dominion supplied some of the Union's military leaders, George H. Thomas, the "Rock of Chickamauga," among them. More than 30 Virginians held the rank of brigadier general or major general in the federal forces.

Virginia became the principal battlefield of the Civil War, the scene of brilliant victories won by General Lee's army at Bull Run (about 30 mi/48 km southwest of Washington, DC), Fredericksburg, and Chancellorsville (Spotsylvania County). But the overwhelming numbers and industrial and naval might of the Union compelled Lee's surrender at Appomattox on 9 April 1865. Virginia waters were the scene of one of the most celebrated naval engagements in world history, the first battle of the ironclads, when the USS Monitor and CSS Virginia (Merrimac), rebuilt in the Portsmouth Shipyard, met at Hampton Roads. The war cost Virginia one-third of its territory when West Virginia was admitted to the Union as a separate state on 20 June 1863. Richmond was left in ruins, and agriculture and industry throughout the commonwealth were destroyed. Union General Philip H. Sheridan's systematic campaign of demolition in the Shenandoah Valley almost made good his boast that a crow flying over the valley would have to carry its own rations.

In 1867, Virginia was placed under US military rule. A constitutional convention held in Richmond under the leadership of carpetbaggers and scalawags drafted a constitution that disqualified the overwhelming majority of white Virginians from holding office and deprived about 95% of them of the right to vote. In this crisis, a compromise was negotiated under which white Virginians would accept Negro suffrage if they themselves were permitted to vote and hold office. The amended constitution, providing for universal manhood suffrage, was adopted in 1869, and Virginia was readmitted to the Union on 26 January 1870.

Although the bankrupt state was saddled with a debt of more than $45 million, the Conservative Democrats undertook repayment of the entire debt, including approximately one-third estimated to be West Virginia's share. Other Democrats, who came to be known as Readjusters, argued that the commonwealth could not provide education and other essential services to its citizens unless it disclaimed one-third of the debt and reached a compromise with creditors concerning the remainder. William Mahone, a railroad president and former Confederate major general, engineered victory for the Readjusters in 1880 with the aid of the Republicans. His election to the US Senate that year represented another success for the Readjuster-Republican coalition, which was attentive to the needs of both blacks and underprivileged whites.

Throughout the 1880s and 1890s, life in public places in Virginia continued in an unsegregated fashion that sometimes amazed visitors from northern cities. As the 19th century neared an end, however, Virginia moved toward legal separation of the races. In 1900, the General Assembly by a one-vote majority enacted segregation on railroad cars. The rule became applicable the following year to streetcars and steamboats. In 1902, the Virginia constitutional convention enacted a literacy test and poll tax that effectively reduced the black vote to negligible size.

Two decades later, just when the Old Dominion seemed permanently set in the grooves of conservatism, two liberals, each with impeccable old-line backgrounds, found themselves battling for the governorship in a Democratic primary campaign that changed the course of Virginia's political history. Harry F. Byrd defeated G. Walter Mapp in the election of 1925 and immediately after taking office launched the state on an era of reform. In a whirlwind 60 days, the General Assembly revised the tax system, revised balloting procedures, and adopted measures to lure industry to Virginia. The Anti-Lynch Act of 1927 made anyone present at the scene of a lynching who did not intervene guilty of murder; there has not been a lynching in Virginia since its passage. Byrd also reorganized the state government, consolidating nearly 100 agencies into 14 departments. Later, as US Senator, Byrd became so renowned as a conservative that many people forgot his earlier career as a fighting liberal.

Following the depression of the 1930s, Virginia became one of the most prosperous states of the Southeast. It profited partly from national defense contracts and military and naval expansion, but also from increased manufacturing and from what became one of the nation's leading tourist industries. Few states made so great a contribution as Virginia to the US effort in World War II. More than 300,000 Virginians served in the armed forces; 9,000 lost their lives, and 10 were awarded the Medal of Honor. Virginians were proud of the fact that General George C. Marshall was a Virginia resident and a graduate of Virginia Military Institute, and even delighted in the knowledge that both General Dwight D. Eisenhower, commander in the European theater, and General Douglas MacArthur, commander in the Pacific, were sons of Virginia mothers.

The postwar period brought many changes in the commonwealth's public life. During the first administration of Governor Mills E. Godwin Jr. (1966–70), the state abandoned its strict pay-as-you-go fiscal policy, secured an $81-million bond issue, and enacted a sales tax. Much of the increased revenue benefited the public school system; funding for the four-year colleges was greatly expanded, and a system of low-tuition community colleges was instituted.

In 1970, A. Linwood Holton Jr., became the first Republican governor of Virginia since 1874. Pledging to "make today's Virginia a model in race relations," Holton increased black representation on state boards and in the higher echelons of government. He reversed the policies of his immediate predecessors, who had generally met the US Supreme Court's desegregation ruling in 1954 with a program of massive resistance, eschewing violence but adopting every legal expedient to frustrate integration. By the mid-1970s, public school integration in Virginia had been achieved to a degree not yet accomplished in many northern states.

The northeast and Virginia Beach/Norfolk area of Virginia boomed in the early 1980s, spurred by an expansion of federal jobs and a national military build-up. The population in Virginia Beach grew by 50% between 1980 and 1990. Non-agricultural employment rose by 29% between 1980 and 1988. The economies of rural parts of the state to the west and south, however, remained stagnant.

In the late 1980s, Virginia was hit by a recession. Douglas Wilder, the nation's first black governor and a moderate Democrat, responded to a significant shortfall in state revenues by refusing to raise taxes and by insisting on maintaining a $200 million reserve fund. Instead, Wilder reduced the budgets and staff of state services and of the state's college and university system. Wilder's cuts created particular hardship for the less affluent counties that relied heavily on state aid for their funding of schools, libraries, and road maintenance. Wilder, limited by law to one term in office, was succeeded in 1993 by conservative Republican Richard Allen. In 1994, nationwide attention was focused on the US Senate race in which the Democratic incumbent, Charles S. Robb, defeated Republican challenger Oliver North, known for his role in the Iran-contra affair of the 1980s.

In the mid-1990s Virginia's economy was strong, thanks to its diversified base of agriculture, manufacturing, and service industries (the latter dominated by federal government employment). Pollution from industry and agricultural chemicals remained a significant concern, and the state was investing in cleanup efforts in the Chesapeake Bay.

In 1994, the Walt Disney Company abandoned its much-publicized plan to build a history theme park, "Disney's America," in Virginia, following strong opposition from residents, environmentalists, and historians.

Virginia was in the midst of its worst state revenue performance in 40 years in 2003. To help it overcome massive budget deficits, the state cut funding for higher education by more than 25% over the previous two years. Nearly all state universities raised tuition in response. Despite this fact, the State Council of Higher Education said Virginia needed to come up with an additional $350 million per year to maintain the quality of its public higher education system.

In November 2005, Democratic Lt. Governor Tim Kaine defeated Republican nominee Jerry Kilgore to become governor of Virginia. Whether justified or not, the vote—along with Senator Jon Corzine's defeat of Republican nominee Doug Forrester for governor of New Jersey—was seen to be a referendum on President George W. Bush's stewardship of the nation.

12 STATE GOVERNMENT

Since 1776, Virginia has had six constitutions, all of which have expanded the power of the executive branch. The last constitution, framed in 1970 and effective 1 July 1971, governs the state today. As of January 2005, this document had been amended 40 times.

The General Assembly consists of a 40-member Senate, elected to four-year terms, and a 100-member house of delegates, serving for two-year terms. Senators and delegates must be US citizens, at least 21 years old, state residents for at least one year, district residents, and qualified voters. The assembly convenes annually on the second Wednesday in January for 60-day sessions in even-numbered years and 30-day sessions in odd-numbered years, with an option to extend the annual session for a maximum of 30 days or declare a special session by two-thirds vote of each house. In 2004 legislative salaries were $18,000 for state senators and $17,640 for delegates, unchanged from 1999.

The governor and lieutenant governor (elected separately), and attorney general, all serving four-year terms, are the only officials elected statewide. Elections for these offices are held in odd-numbered years, following presidential elections. The governor, who must be at least 30 years old, a US citizen, and a state resident and qualified voter for five years, may not serve two successive terms. As of December 2004, the governor's salary was $124,855. Most state officials—including the secretaries of administration and finance, commerce and resources, education, human resources, public safety, and transportation—are appointed by the governor but must be confirmed by both houses of the legislature.

Bills become law when signed by the governor or left unsigned for seven days (including Sundays) while the legislature is in session; a bill dies if left unsigned for 30 days after the legislature has adjourned. A two-thirds majority of those present in each house is needed to override a gubernatorial veto. The constitution may be amended by constitutional convention or by a majority vote of two sessions of the General Assembly; ratification by the electorate is required.

Voters must be US citizens, at least 18 years old, and residents of their voting precinct. Restrictions apply to convicted felons and those declared mentally incompetent by the court.

¹³POLITICAL PARTIES

Virginia has exercised a unique role in US politics as the birthplace not only of representative government but also of one of America's two major parties. The modern Democratic Party traces its origins to the original Republican Party (usually referred to as the Democratic-Republican Party, or the Jeffersonian Democrats), led by two native sons of Virginia, Thomas Jefferson and James Madison. Virginians have also been remarkably influential in the political life of other states: a survey published in 1949 showed that 319 Virginia natives had represented 31 other states in the US Senate and House of Representatives.

From the end of Reconstruction through the 1960s, conservative Democrats dominated state politics, with few exceptions. Harry F. Byrd was the state's Democratic political leader for 40 years, first as a reform governor (1926–30) and then as a conservative senator (1933–95). During the 1970s, Virginians, still staunchly conservative, turned increasingly to the Republican Party, whose presidential nominees carried the state in every election from 1952 through 1984, except for 1964. Linwood Holton, the first Republican governor since Reconstruction, was elected in 1969. His Republican successor, Mills E. Godwin Jr., the first governor since the Civil War to serve more than one term, had earlier won election as a Democrat. The election in 1977 of another Republican, John N. Dalton, finally proved that Virginia had become a two-party state. In 1981, however, the governorship was won by Democrat Charles S. Robb, who appointed a record number of blacks and women to state offices. Robb, prohibited by law from seeking a consecutive second term, was succeeded by Democrat Gerald L. Baliles in 1985 when Virginians also elected L. Douglas Wilder as lieutenant governor and Mary Sue Terry as attorney general. Wilder became the highest-ranking black state official in the United States, and Terry was the first woman to win a statewide office in Virginia. Wilder was elected governor in 1989, followed by Republican George Allen in 1993. Another Republican, James S. Gilmore III, was elected to the office in the 1997 election. Democrats Mark Warner and Tim Kaine were elected governor in 2001 and 2005, respectively.

Former governor Robb won election to the US Senate in 1988 and reelection in 1994 when he was opposed by Republican Oliver North, a former Marine and Reagan White House aide who gained fame for his role in the Iran-contra affair. Republican George F. Allen won the seat in 2000. Senior Senator John Warner, a Republican, was elected to a fifth term in 2002.

After the 2004 elections, Virginia's delegation to the US House of Representatives consisted of three Democrats and eight Republicans. As of the 2005 state legislative elections, control of the state Senate and house was in the hands of the Republicans. Republicans controlled the state House, 58–39, with 3 independents; the state Senate was split 24–16, Republicans to Democrats.

Virginia Presidential Vote by Political Parties, 1948–2004

YEAR	ELECTORAL VOTE	VIRGINIA WINNER	DEMOCRAT	REPUBLICAN	STATES' RIGHTS DEMOCRAT	PROGRESSIVE	SOCIALIST	SOCIALIST LABOR
1948	11	*Truman (D)	200,786	172,070	43,393	2,047	726	234
1952	12	*Eisenhower (R)	268,677	349,037	—	—	504	1,160
					CONSTITUTION			
1956	12	*Eisenhower (R)	267,760	386,459	42,964	—	444	351
					VA. CONSERVATIVE			
1960	12	Nixon (R)	362,327	404,521	4,204	—	—	397
1964	12	*Johnson (D)	558,038	481,334`	—	—	—	2,895
					AMERICAN IND.		PEACE AND FREEDOM	
1968	12	*Nixon (R)	442,387	590,319	320,272	—	1,680	4,671
					AMERICAN			
1972	12	*Nixon (R)	438,887	988,493	19,721	—	—	9,918
						LIBERTARIAN	US LABOR	SOC. WORKERS
1976	12	Ford (R)	813,896	836,554	16,686	4,648	7,508	17,802
							CITIZENS	
1980	12	*Reagan (R)	752,174	989,609	—	12,821	**14,024	1,9861
1984	12	*Reagan (R)	796,250	1,337,078	—	—	—	—
					NEW ALLIANCE			
1988	12	*Bush (R)	859,799	1,309,162	14,312	8,336	—	—
							IND. (Perot)	IND. (laRouche)
1992	13	Bush (R)	1,038,650	1,150,517	3,192	5,730	348,639	11,937
1996	13	Dole (R)	1,091,060	1,138,350	—	9,174	159,861	—
					GREEN			
2000	13	*Bush, G. W. (R)	1,217,290	1,437,490	59,398	15,198	—	—
					WRITE-IN (Nader)		CONSTITUTION (Peroutka)	WRITE-IN (Cobb)
2004	13	*Bush, G. W. (R)	1,454,742	1,716,959	2,393	11,032	10,161	104

*Won US presidential election.
**Candidates of the nationwide Citizens and Socialist Workers parties were listed as independents on the Virginia ballot; another independent, John Anderson, won 95,418 votes.

In 2000, Republican George W. Bush won 52% of the presidential vote; Democrat Al Gore received 45%; and Green Party candidate Ralph Nader garnered 2%. In 2004, incumbent Bush won 54% over Democratic challenger John Kerry's 45%. In 2004 there were 4,528,000 registered voters; there is no party registration in the state. The state had 13 electoral votes in the 2004 presidential election.

14 LOCAL GOVERNMENT

As of 2005, Virginia had 125 counties and 229 municipal governments, as well as 196 special districts and 135 school districts.

During the colonial period, most Virginians lived on plantations and were reluctant to form towns. In 1705, the General Assembly approved the formation of 16 "free boroughs." Although only Jamestown, Williamsburg, and Norfolk chose at that time to avail themselves of the option and become independent municipalities, their decision laid the foundation for the independence of Virginia's present-day cities from county government. In 1842, Richmond became the commonwealth's first charter city. Cities elect their own officials (typically including council members and city managers), levy their own taxes, and are unencumbered by county obligations. Incorporated towns, on the other hand, remain part of the counties.

In general, counties are governed by elected boards of supervisors, with a county administrator or executive handling day-to-day affairs; other typical county officials are the clerk of the circuit court (chief administrator of the court), the county treasurer, the commissioner of the revenue, the commonwealth's attorney, and the sheriff. Incorporated towns have elected mayors and councils.

In 2005, local government accounted for about 298,240 full-time (or equivalent) employment positions.

15 STATE SERVICES

To address the continuing threat of terrorism and to work with the federal Department of Homeland Security, homeland security in Virginia operates under executive order and state statute; a special assistant to the governor is designated as the state homeland security advisor.

Under the jurisdiction of the secretary of education are the Department of Education, which administers the public school system, and the State Council of Higher Education, which coordinates the programs of the state-controlled colleges and universities. The secretary of transportation oversees the Department of Transportation, Department of Rail and Public Transportation, Department of Aviation, Virginia Port Authority, Department of Motor Vehicles, the Motor Vehicle Dealer Board. The Virginia National Guard falls under the authority of the Department of Military Affairs.

Within the purview of the secretary of health and human resources are the Department of Health; Department of Mental Health, Mental Retardation, and Substance Abuse Services; Department of Health Professions, Department of Social Services, and Department of Rehabilitative Services, as well as special offices dealing with problems that affect women, children, the elderly, and the disabled. The departments of State Police, Corrections, Criminal Justice Services, Fire Programs, and Alcoholic Beverage Control are under the aegis of the secretary of public safety.

The secretary of commerce and trade oversees the departments of Housing and Community Development, Labor and Industry, Business Assistance, the Department of Mines, Minerals, and Energy, and the Tourism Corporation, as well as a profusion of boards, councils, offices, divisions, and commissions. The secretary of administration exercises jurisdiction over budgeting, telecommunications, accounting, computer services, taxation, the state treasury, records, and personnel, as well as over the State Board of Elections. Regulatory functions are concentrated in the quasi-independent State Corporation Commission, consisting of three commissioners elected by the legislature to staggered six-year terms. The commission regulates all public utilities; licenses banks, savings and loan associations, credit unions, and small loan companies; enforces motor carrier and certain aviation laws and sets railroad rates; supervises the activities of insurance companies; and enforces laws governing securities and retail franchising. Natural resources are protected by the Department of Environmental Quality, the Department of Forestry, and the Department of Game and Inland Fisheries.

16 JUDICIAL SYSTEM

The highest judicial body in the commonwealth is the Supreme Court, consisting of a chief justice and six other justices elected to 12-year terms by the General Assembly. The court of appeals has ten judges serving 8-year terms. The state is divided into 31 judicial circuits/districts. Each city and county has a circuit court, a general district court, and a juvenile and domestic relations district court. Circuit court judges are elected by the legislature for eight-year terms. General district courts hear all misdemeanors, including civil cases involving $1,000 or less, and have concurrent jurisdiction with the circuit courts in claims involving $1,000 to $15,000. General district courts also hold preliminary hearings concerning felony cases. Each of the 31 judicial districts has a juvenile and a domestic relations court, with judges elected by the General Assembly to six-year terms. Each city or county has at least one local magistrate.

As of 31 December 2004, a total of 35,564 prisoners were held in Virginia's state and federal prisons, an increase from 35,067 of 1.4% from the previous year. As of year-end 2004, a total of 2,706 inmates were female, up from 2,681 or 0.9% from the year before. Among sentenced prisoners (one year or more), Virginia had an incarceration rate of 473 per 100,000 population in 2004.

According to the Federal Bureau of Investigation, Virginia in 2004, had a violent crime rate (murder/nonnegligent manslaughter; forcible rape; robbery; aggravated assault) of 275.6 reported incidents per 100,000 population, or a total of 20,559 reported incidents. Crimes against property (burglary; larceny/theft; and motor vehicle theft) in that same year totaled 199,668 reported incidents or 2,676.6 reported incidents per 100,000 people. Virginia has a death penalty which allows prisoners to choose either lethal injection or electrocution. From 1976 through 5 May 2006, the state has carried out 95 executions (the second-highest in the United States, after Texas), of which the most recent execution took place in 2006 (prior to May 5). There were no executions in 2005 As of 1 January 2006, Virginia had 22 inmates on death row.

In 2003, Virginia spent $1,958,536,955 on homeland security, an average of $267 per state resident.

17ARMED FORCES

In 2004, there were 90,088 active-duty military personnel and 78,792 civilian personnel stationed in Virginia. The Hampton Roads area, one of the nation's major concentrations of military facilities, includes Langley Air Force Base in Hampton, the Norfolk naval air station and shipyard, the naval air station at Virginia Beach, the Marine Corps air facility and command and staff college at Quantico, and Forts Eustis, Belvoir, and Lee. Langley hosts the 1st Fighter Wing which operates and maintains one of the largest fighter bases in Air Combat Command. The wing flies the F-15 Eagle. Norfolk is the home base of the Atlantic Fleet, and several major army and air commands are in Virginia. Virginia's major defense establishments also include an army base at Arlington. Also, located there is Arlington National Cemetery established by Brig. Gen. Montgomery C. Meigs for use as a military cemetery on June 15, 1864.

In 2004, Virginia firms received more than $23.5 billion in defense contracts, second to California. In addition, Virginia had the highest defense payroll outlays in the United States, $15.99 billion, highest in both civilian pay and military active duty pay.

In 2003, there were 750,950 veterans of US military service living in Virginia. Of these, 70, 802 saw service in World War II; 60,921 during the Korean conflict; 216,388 during the Vietnam era; and 168,444 during the Persian Gulf War. Veterans' benefits allocated to Virginia totaled more than $1.7 billion in 2004.

As of 31 October 2004, the Virginia State Police employed 1,840 full-time sworn officers.

18MIGRATION

Virginia's earliest European immigrants were English—only a few hundred at first, but 4,000 between 1619 and 1624, of whom fewer than 1,200 survived epidemics and Indian attacks. Despite such setbacks, Virginia's population increased, mostly by means of immigration, from about 5,000 in 1634 to more than 15,000 in 1642, including 300 blacks. Within 30 years, the population had risen to more than 40,000, including 2,000 blacks. In the late 17th and early 18th centuries, immigrants came not only from England but also from Scotland, Wales, Ireland, Germany, France, the Netherlands, and Poland. In 1701, about 500 French Huguenots fled Catholic France to settle near the present site of Richmond, and beginning in 1714, many Germans and Scotch-Irish moved from Pennsylvania into the Valley of Virginia.

By the early 19th century, Virginians were moving westward into Kentucky, Ohio, and other states; the 1850 census showed that 388,000 former Virginians (not including the many thousands of slaves sold to other states) were living elsewhere. Some of those who left—Henry Clay, Sam Houston, Stephen Austin—were among the most able men of their time. The Civil War era saw the movement of thousands of blacks to northern states, a trend that accelerated after Reconstruction and again after World War I. Since 1900, the dominant migratory trend has been intrastate, from farm to city. Urbanization has been most noticeable since World War II in the Richmond and Hampton Roads areas. At the same time, the movement of middle-income Virginians to the suburbs and increasing concentrations of blacks in the central cities have been evident in Virginia as in other states. During the 1980s, the urban population grew from 66% to 69.4% of the total population; during the 1990s it reached 77.9%.

Between 1940 and 1970, Virginia enjoyed a net gain from migration of 325,000. In the 1970s, the net gain was 239,000, and during 1985–90, 377,000 (fourth highest among the states for that period). Between 1990 and 1998, Virginia had net gains of 68,000 in domestic migration and 131,000 in international migration. In 1996, 372,000, or about 6%, of the state's population was foreign-born. In 1998, 15,686 foreign immigrants arrived in Virginia, the ninth-highest total of any state. Of that total, 1,509 came from El Salvador, 921 from the Philippines, and 910 from India. Between 1990 and 1998, Virginia's overall population increased 9.7%. In the period 2000–05, net international migration was 139,977 and net internal migration was 103,521, for a net gain of 243,498 people.

19INTERGOVERNMENTAL COOPERATION

Regional bodies in which Virginia participates include the Atlantic States Marine Fisheries Commission, Ohio River Valley Water Sanitation Commission, Southern Growth Policies Board, Southern States Energy Board, Southeastern Forest Fire Protection Compact, Ohio River Basin Commission, Mid-Atlantic Fishery Management Council, Southern Regional Education Board, Appalachian Regional Commission, Potomac River Fisheries Commission (with Maryland) and Washington Metropolitan Area Transit Authority. The Delmarva Advisory Council, representing Delaware, Maryland, and Virginia, works with local organizations on the Delmarva Peninsula to develop and implement economic improvement programs. The state also has a number of border compacts, including ones with Maryland, West Virginia, District of Columbia, Kentucky, Maryland, North Carolina, and Tennessee. In fiscal year 2005, Virginia received federal grants worth $5.269 billion, an estimated $5.495 billion in fiscal year 2006, and an estimated $5.744 billion in fiscal year 2007.

20ECONOMY

Early settlements in Virginia depended on subsistence farming of native crops such as corn and potatoes. Tobacco, the leading export crop during the colonial era, was joined by cotton during the early statehood period. Although cotton was never "king" in Virginia, as it was in many other southern states, the sale of slaves to Deep South plantations was an important source of income for Virginians, especially during the 1830s, when some 118,000 slaves were exported for profit. Eventually, a diversified agriculture developed in the piedmont and the Shenandoah Valley. Manufacturing became significant during the 19th century, with a proliferation of cotton mills, tobacco-processing plants, ironworks, paper mills, and shipyards.

Services, trade, and government are important economic sectors today. Because of Virginia's extensive military installations and the large number of Virginia residents working for the federal government in the Washington DC metropolitan area, the federal government plays a larger role in the state's economy than in any other except Hawaii. The industries that experienced the most growth in the 1990s were printing, transportation equipment, electronic and other electrical equipment. Between 1992 and 2000, job growth in Virginia averaged 2.7% a year, and in northern Virginia, the rate was 4% a year. The state's economy as a whole grew briskly, averaging 7.13% a year from 1998 to 2000. However, the high concentration of high-technology industries in Virginia, the two largest being computer and data processing services, and electronic equipment, meant that the collapse of the dot.com bubble in the national recession of 2001 would have negative impacts, despite counter-cyclical increases in government spending. The growth rate moderated to 4.7% in 2001, employment contracted., and for 2000/01 tax revenues, growth fell by more than half. By November 2002 employment was still 1.5% below the peak reached in March 2001. Tax revenues in 2001/02 declined 4%, facing the state with a billion dollar deficit after successive years of budget surpluses.

In 2004, Virginia's gross state product (GSP) was $329.332 billion, of which the real estate sector accounted for the largest share at $40.274 billion or 12.2% of GSP, followed by manufacturing (durable and nondurable goods) at $38.345 billion (11.6% of GSP) and professional and technical services at $33.911 billion (10.2% of GSP). In that same year, there were an estimated 567,830 small businesses in Virginia. Of the 172,785 businesses that had employees, an estimated total of 169,053 or 97.8% were small companies. An estimated 24,134 new businesses were established in the state in 2004, up 9.4% from the year before. Business terminations that same year came to 19,919, down 3% from 2003. There were 750 business bankruptcies in 2004, down 21.5% from the previous year. In 2005, the state's personal bankruptcy (Chapter 7 and Chapter 13) filing rate was 583 filings per 100,000 people, ranking Virginia 22nd in the nation.

21 INCOME

In 2005 Virginia had a gross state product (GSP) of $353 billion which accounted for 2.8% of the nation's gross domestic product and placed the state at number 11 in highest GSP among the 50 states and the District of Columbia.

According to the Bureau of Economic Analysis, in 2004 Virginia had a per capita personal income (PCPI) of $36,160. This ranked ninth in the United States and was 109% of the national average of $33,050. The 1994–2004 average annual growth rate of PCPI was 4.5%. Virginia had a total personal income (TPI) of $270,521,697,000, which ranked 10th in the United States and reflected an increase of 7.7% from 2003. The 1994–2004 average annual growth rate of TPI was 5.8%. Earnings of persons employed in Virginia increased from $196,522,936,000 in 2003 to $213,341,529,000 in 2004, an increase of 8.6%. The 2003–04 national change was 6.3%.

The US Census Bureau reports that the three-year average median household income for 2002–04 in 2004 dollars was $53,275 compared to a national average of $44,473. During the same period an estimated 9.8% of the population was below the poverty line as compared to 12.4% nationwide.

22 LABOR

According to the Bureau of Labor Statistics (BLS), in April 2006 the seasonally adjusted civilian labor force in Virginia 4,013,400, with approximately 134,100 workers unemployed, yielding an unemployment rate of 3.3%, compared to the national average of 4.7% for the same period. Preliminary data for the same period placed nonfarm employment at 3,724,800. Since the beginning of the BLS data series in 1976, the highest unemployment rate recorded in Virginia was 7.8% in January 1983. The historical low was 2.2% in January 2001. Preliminary nonfarm employment data

by occupation for April 2006 showed that approximately 7% of the labor force was employed in construction; 7.9% in manufacturing; 17.8% in trade, transportation, and public utilities; 5.2% in financial activities; 8.9% in professional and business services; 10.7% in education and health services; 8.9% in leisure and hospitality services; and 17.9% in government.

Although the state has no equal-employment statute, an equal-pay law does prohibit employers from wage discrimination on the basis of sex, and the Virginia Employment Contracting Act established as state policy the elimination of racial, religious, ethnic, and sexual bias in the employment practices of government agencies and contractors. The labor movement has grown slowly, partly because of past practices of racial segregation that prevented workers from acting in concert.

The BLS reported that in 2005, a total of 165,000 of Virginia's 3,406,000 employed wage and salary workers were formal members of a union. This represented 4.8% of those so employed, down from 5.3% in 2004, and well below the national average of 12%. Overall in 2005, a total of 211,000 workers (6.2%) in Virginia were covered by a union or employee association contract, which included those workers who reported no union affiliation. Virginia is one of 22 states with a right-to-work law.

As of 1 March 2006, Virginia had a state-mandated minimum wage rate of $5.15 per hour. In 2004, women in the state accounted for 47.4% of the employed civilian labor force.

23 AGRICULTURE

Virginia ranked 31st among the 50 states in 2005 with farm marketings of more than $2.6 billion. The commonwealth is an important producer of tobacco, soybeans, peanuts, cotton, tomatoes, potatoes, and peaches. There were an estimated 47,500 farms in 2004, covering 8.6 million acres (3.5 million hectares).

The Tidewater is an important farming region, as it has been since the early 17th century. Crops grown include corn, wheat, tobacco, cotton, peanuts and truck crops. Truck crops and soybeans are cultivated on the Eastern Shore. The piedmont is known for its apples and other fruits, while the Shenandoah Valley is one of the nation's main apple growing regions. In 2004, Virginia ranked fourth among states in tobacco, seventh in peanuts, and sixth in apples. In 2004, greenhouse/nursery products accounted for 8.7% of farm receipts.

24 ANIMAL HUSBANDRY

In 2005, Virginia farms and ranches had 1.6 million cattle and calves, valued at $1.26 billion. During 2004, the state had around 375,000 hogs and pigs, valued at $32.6 million. The state produced 3.5 million lb (1.6 million kg) of sheep and lambs in 2003, and an estimated 226,000 lb of shorn wool in 2004.

Dairy farmers produced 1.73 billion lb (0.79 billion kg) of milk from 113,000 milk cows in 2003. That same year, poultry farmers produced 744 million eggs, worth around $73.2 million; 492.2 million lb (223.7 million kg) of turkey, worth almost $177.2 million; 1.3 billion lb (590 million kg) of broilers, valued at $441.7 million; and 21.7 million lb (9.9 million kg) of chicken sold for over $1.5 million.

[25] FISHING

The relative importance of Chesapeake Bay and Atlantic fisheries to Virginia's economy has lessened considerably in recent decades, although the state continues to place high in national rankings. In 2004, Virginia's commercial fish landings totaled 481.6 million lb (218.9 million kg), ranking the state third in the nation for volume of landings. The catch was worth $160.3 million. Landings at the Reedville port totaled over 400.5 million lb (182 million kg), the second highest volume of all US ports. The port at Hampton Road Area ranked third in the nation in catch value with $100.6 million. The bulk of the catch consists of shellfish such as crabs, scallops, and clams, and finfish such as flounder and menhaden. The sea scallop catch in 2004 was at 19.6 million lb (8.9 million kg), the second largest in the nation (after Massachusetts).

In 2003, there were 28 processing and 57 wholesale plants in the state, with about 1,801 employees. In 2001, the commercial fishing fleet had 261 vessels.

Both saltwater and freshwater fish are avidly sought by sport fishermen. A threat to Virginia fisheries has been the chemical and oil pollution of the Chesapeake Bay and its tributaries. In 2004, the state issued 619,853 fishing licenses. The Harrison Lake National Fish Hatchery is located in Charles City.

[26] FORESTRY

As of 2004, Virginia had 15,844,000 acres (6,412,000 hectares) of forestland, representing more than 63% of the state's land area and 2.1% of all US forests. Virtually every county has some commercial forestland and supports a wood products industry. In 2004, 1,474 million board feet of lumber were produced.

Reforestation programs initiated by the Division of Forestry in 1971 have paid landowners to plant pine seedlings, and state-funded tree nurseries produce 60–70 million seedlings annually. The Division of Forestry's tree seed orchards have developed improved strains of loblolly, shortleaf, white, and Virginia pine for planting in cutover timberland.

For recreational purposes, there were 2.7 million acres (1.1 million hectares) of forested public lands in 2004, including Shenandoah National Park, Washington and Jefferson National Forests, 24 state parks, and eight state forests.

[27] MINING

According to preliminary data from the US Geological Survey (USGS), the estimated value of nonfuel mineral production by Virginia in 2003 was $727 million, an increase from 2002 of about 5%. The USGS data ranked Virginia as 19th among the 50 states by the total value of its nonfuel mineral production, accounting for almost 2% of total US output.

According to the preliminary data for 2003, crushed stone was the state's top raw nonfuel mineral, by value, accounting for around 59% of Virginia's total nonfuel mineral output, and was followed by cement (portland and masonry), construction sand and gravel, and lime. Collectively, these four commodities accounted for around 86% of all nonfuel mineral output, by value. Virginia in 2003 was the only state to mine kyanite, while it ranked (by value) second in the production of feldspar, zirconium concentrates, and titanium. Virginia was also second (out of two states) in the pro-

duction of vermiculite and was fourth in the output of iron oxide pigments.

The preliminary data for 2003 showed crushed stone output at 63 million metric tons, with a value of $428 million, with construction sand and gravel production that same year as totaling 11.1 million metric tons, with a value of $63.8 million. Kyanite production in 2003 was estimated at 90,000 metric tons, with a value of $13.4 million.

Virginia in 2003 also produced dimension stone and common clays.

[28] ENERGY AND POWER

As of 2003, Virginia had 39 electrical power service providers, of which 16 were publicly owned and 13 were cooperatives. Of the remainder, five were investor owned, one was federally operated, one was the owner of an independent generator that sold directly to customers, one was an energy-only supplier and two were delivery-only providers. As of that same year there were 3,301,904 retail customers. Of that total, 2,728,215 received their power from investor-owned service providers. Cooperatives accounted for 411,861 customers, while publicly owned providers had 159,588 customers. There was only one federal customer, one independent generator or "facility" customer, and 2,238 energy-only supplier customers. There was no data on the number of delivery-only customers.

Total net summer generating capability by the state's electrical generating plants in 2003 stood at 21.257 million kW, with total production that same year at 75.309 billion kWh. Of the total amount generated, 82.1% came from electric utilities, with the remainder coming from independent producers and combined heat and power service providers. The largest portion of all electric power generated, 37.093 billion kWh (49.3%), came from coal-fired plants, with nuclear generating plants in second place at 24.816 billion kWh (33%) and petroleum fueled plants in third at 5.780 billion kWh (7.7%). Other renewable power sources, natural gas fueled plants, hydroelectric and pumped storage facilities accounting for the remaining generation.

As of 2006, Virginia had two nuclear power plants: the North Anna plant in Louisa County; and the Surry plant near Williamsburg.

As of 2004, Virginia had proven crude oil reserves of less than 1% of all proven US reserves, while output that same year averaged 52 barrels per day. Including federal offshore domains, the state that year ranked 32nd (31st excluding federal offshore) in production among the 31 producing states. In 2004 Virginia had 10 producing oil wells and accounted for under 1% of all US production. As of 2005, the state's single crude oil refinery at Yorktown had a distillation capacity of 58,600 barrels per day.

The state is supplied with natural gas by three major interstate pipeline companies. Liquefied natural gas plants operate in Chesapeake, Roanoke, and Lynchburg, and a synthetic gas plant is in service at Chesapeake. There is underground natural gas storage facilities in Scott and Washington Counties and in Saltville.

In 2004, Virginia had 3,870 producing natural gas and gas condensate wells. In that same year, the production of dry or consumer-grade natural gas totaled 152.495 billion cu ft (4.33 billion cu m). As of 31 December 2004, proven reserves of dry natural gas totaled 1,742 billion cu ft (49.47 billion cu m).

Virginia in 2004 had 123 producing coal mines, 46 of which were surface operations and 77 were underground. Coal production that year totaled 31,420,000 short tons, down from 31,596,000 short tons in 2003. Of the total produced in 2004, underground mines accounted for 20,437,000 short tons. All of the coal produced was bituminous. Recoverable coal reserves in 2004 totaled 250 million short tons. One short ton equals 2,000 lb (0.907 metric tons).

29 INDUSTRY

Beginning with the establishment of a glass factory at Jamestown in 1608, manufacturing grew slowly during the colonial era to include flour mills and, by 1715, an iron foundry. During the 19th century, the shipbuilding industry flourished, and many cotton mills, tanneries, and ironworks were built. Light industries producing a wide variety of consumer goods developed later.

Richmond is a principal industrial area for tobacco processing, paper and printing, clothing, and food products. Nearby Hopewell is a locus of the chemical industry. Newport News, Hampton, and Norfolk are centers for shipbuilding and the manufacture of other transportation equipment. In the western part of the state, Lynchburg is a center for electrical machinery, metals, clothing, and printing, and Roanoke for food, clothing, and textiles. In the south, Martinsville has a concentration of furniture and textile-manufacturing plants, and textiles are also dominant in Danville.

According to the US Census Bureau's Annual Survey of Manufactures (ASM) for 2004, Virginia's manufacturing sector covered some 19 product subsectors. The shipment value of all products manufactured in the state that same year was $87.842 billion. Of that total, beverage and tobacco product manufacturing accounted for the largest share at $12.856 billion. It was followed by transportation equipment manufacturing at $12.211 billion; food manufacturing at $10.007 billion; chemical manufacturing at $7.864 billion; and plastics and rubber products manufacturing at $4.864 billion.

In 2004, a total of 284,076 people in Virginia were employed in the state's manufacturing sector, according to the ASM. Of that total, 206,060 were actual production workers. In terms of total employment, the transportation equipment manufacturing industry accounted for the largest portion of all manufacturing employees, with 38,533 (27,606 actual production workers). It was followed by food manufacturing, with 30,982 (23,946 actual production workers); plastics and rubber products manufacturing, with 20,032 (15,772 actual production workers); wood product manufacturing, with 18,753 (14,802 actual production workers); and furniture and related product manufacturing, with 17,633 (14,738 actual production workers).

ASM data for 2004 showed that Virginia's manufacturing sector paid $11.915 billion in wages. Of that amount, the transportation equipment manufacturing sector accounted for the largest share at $1.836 billion. It was followed by computer and electronic product manufacturing at $1.222 million; food manufacturing at $936.758 million; chemical manufacturing at $920.204 million; and plastics and rubber products manufacturing at $804.629 million.

30 COMMERCE

According to the 2002 Census of Wholesale Trade, Virginia's wholesale trade sector had sales that year totaling $69.2 billion from 7,712 establishments. Wholesalers of durable goods accounted for 4,990 establishments, followed by nondurable goods wholesalers at 2,182 and electronic markets, agents, and brokers accounting for 540 establishments. Sales by durable goods wholesalers in 2002 totaled $33.8 billion, while wholesalers of nondurable goods saw sales of $27.06 billion. Electronic markets, agents, and brokers in the wholesale trade industry had sales of $8.3 billion.

In the 2002 Census of Retail Trade, Virginia was listed as having 28,914 retail establishments with sales of $80.5 billion. The leading types of retail businesses by number of establishments were: clothing and clothing accessories stores (3,924); gasoline stations (3,623); food and beverage stores (3,383); and miscellaneous store retailers (3,313). In terms of sales, motor vehicle and motor vehicle parts dealers accounted for the largest share of retail sales at $20.1 billion, followed by general merchandise stores at $12.5 billion; food and beverage stores at $11.8 billion; and gasoline stations at $7.8 billion. A total of 401,921 people were employed by the retail sector in Virginia that year.

Virginia is a major container shipping center, with almost all shipments handled through the Hampton Roads estuary. Coal is the leading exported commodity and residual fuel oil the principal import. Exports of goods originating within Virginia totaled $12.2 billion in 2005.

31 CONSUMER PROTECTION

Consumer protection issues are generally the responsibility of the state's Office of Consumer Affairs, which is under the Department of Agriculture and Consumer Services, although the Office of the Attorney General does have limited authority to act on consumer protection issues. The Department of Agriculture and Consumer Affairs regulates food processors and handlers, product labeling, the use of pesticides, and product safety, and through its Office of Consumer Affairs is also responsible for the enforcement of consumer protection laws as well as acting as the central clearinghouse for consumer complaints in Virginia.

When dealing with consumer protection issues, the state's Attorney General's Office can initiate civil proceedings and to a limited extent, criminal proceedings. The office can represent the state before state and federal regulatory agencies, but can only offer legal opinions regarding the administration of consumer protection and education programs and in the handling of formal consumer complaints. In consumer matters the Attorney General's Office has limited subpoena powers. In antitrust actions, the Attorney General's Office can act on behalf of those consumers who are incapable of acting on their own; initiate damage actions on behalf of the state in state courts; initiate criminal proceedings; and represent counties, cities and other governmental entities in recovering civil damages under state or federal law.

The offices of the state's Office of Consumer Affairs, and the Antitrust and Consumer Litigation Section of the Attorney General's Office are located in Richmond. County government consumer affairs offices are located in the cities of Arlington and Fairfax. City government consumer protection offices are located in Alexandria and Virginia Beach.

32 BANKING

As of June 2005, Virginia had 140 insured banks, savings and loans, and saving banks, in addition to 61 state-chartered and 161 federally chartered credit unions (CUs). Excluding the CUs, the Washington-Arlington-Alexandria market area, which includes portions of Maryland, West Virginia and the District of Columbia, accounted for the largest portion of the state's financial institutions and deposits in 2004, with 103 institutions and $130.985 billion in deposits, followed by the Richmond market area with 36 institutions and $33.475 billion in deposits. As of June 2005, CUs accounted for 16.1% of all assets held by all financial institutions in the state, or some $48.182 billion. Banks, savings and loans, and savings banks collectively accounted for the remaining 83.9% or $250.480 billion in assets held.

The median net interest margin (the difference between the lower rates offered to savers and the higher rates charged on loans) as of fourth quarter 2005 stood at 4.25%, up from 3.94% in 2004 and 3.95% in 2003. The median percentage of past-due/nonaccrual loans to total loans in fourth quarter 2005 stood at 0.99%, down from 1% in 2004 and 1.52% in 2003.

Regulation of Virginia's state-chartered banks and other state-chartered financial institutions is the responsibility of the State Corporation Commission's Bureau of Financial Institutions.

33 INSURANCE

Virginians held over 4.5 million individual life insurance policies worth over $338.8 billion in 2004; total value for all categories of life insurance (individual, group, and credit) was over $597 billion. The average coverage amount is $73,800 per policy holder. Death benefits paid that year totaled $1.6 billion.

As of 2003, there were 19 property and casualty and 14 life and health insurance companies domiciled in the state. In 2004, direct premiums for property and casualty insurance totaled over $9.8 billion. That year, there were 84,492 flood insurance policies in force in the state, with a total value of $14.2 billion. About $3.6 billion of coverage was held through FAIR plans, which are designed to offer coverage for some natural circumstances, such as wind and hail, in high risk areas.

In 2004, 59% of state residents held employment-based health insurance policies, 7% held individual policies, and 19% were covered under Medicare and Medicaid; 14% of residents were uninsured. In 2003, employee contributions for employment-based health coverage averaged at 19% for single coverage. The employee contribution rate of 30% for family coverage is one of the highest averages among the fifty states. The state does not offer a health benefits expansion program in connection with the Consolidated Omnibus Budget Reconciliation Act (COBRA, 1986), a health insurance program for those who lose employment-based coverage due to termination or reduction of work hours.

In 2003, there were over 5.6 million auto insurance policies in effect for private passenger cars. Required minimum coverage includes bodily injury liability of up to $25,000 per individual and $50,000 for all persons injured in an accident, as well as property damage liability of $20,000. Uninsured motorist coverage is also required. In 2003, the average expenditure per vehicle for insurance coverage was $657.37.

34 SECURITIES

There are no securities exchanges in Virginia. In 2005, there were 3,130 personal financial advisers employed in the state and 5,060 securities, commodities, and financial services sales agents. In 2004, there were over 215 publicly traded companies within the state, with over 83 NASDAQ companies, 47 NYSE listings, and 10 AMEX listings. In 2006, the state 18 Fortune 500 companies; Sprint Nextel (based in Reston) ranked first in the state and 59th in the nation with revenues of over $34.6 billion, followed by General Dynamics (Falls Church), Dominion Resources (Richmond), Capital One Financial (McLean), and Smithfield Foods (Smithfield). All of these top five companies are listed on the NYSE.

35 PUBLIC FINANCE

Virginia's resources are divided equally into two portions: the general fund (which comes from general state taxes), and the non-general fund (which is used for set purposes). Total general funds for fiscal year 2002 were over $12 billion, 64% from individual income taxes, 20% from sales taxes, and 4% from corporate taxes. The governor's fiscal year 2000–02 budget emphasized a property tax phase-out.

Fiscal year 2006 general funds were estimated at $15.8 billion for resources and $15.2 billion for expenditures. In fiscal year 2004, federal government grants to Virginia were $7.9 billion.

36 TAXATION

In 2005, Virginia collected $15,919 million in tax revenues or $2,104 per capita, which placed it 26th among the 50 states in per capita tax burden. The national average was $2,192 per capita. Property taxes accounted for 0.1% of the total, sales taxes 19.4%, selective sales taxes 15.0%, individual income taxes 52.5%, corporate income taxes 3.8%, and other taxes 9.2%.

As of 1 January 2006, Virginia had four individual income tax brackets ranging from 2.0% to 5.75%. The state taxes corporations at a flat rate of 6.0%.

In 2004, state and local property taxes amounted to $7.8 billion or $1,031 per capita. The per capita amount ranks the state 21st nationally. Local governments collected $7,694,442,000 of the total and the state government $20,778,000.

Virginia taxes retail sales at a rate of 4%. In addition to the state tax, local taxes on retail sales can reach as much as 1%, making for a potential total tax on retail sales of 5%. Food purchased for consumption off-premises is taxable, but at a lower rate. The tax on cigarettes is 30 cents per pack, which ranks 45th among the 50 states and the District of Columbia. Virginia taxes gasoline at 17.5 cents per gallon. This is in addition to the 18.4 cents per gallon federal tax on gasoline.

According to the Tax Foundation, for every federal tax dollar sent to Washington in 2004, Virginia citizens received $1.66 in federal spending, which ranks the state seventh nationally.

37 ECONOMIC POLICY

The state government actively promotes a pro-business climate. Conservative traditions, low tax rates, low wage rates, a weak labor movement, and excellent access to eastern and overseas markets are the general incentives for companies to relocate into Virginia. Five duty-free foreign trade zones have been established in Virginia.

The Virginia Economic Development Partnership extends low-interest loans to creditworthy companies to purchase land, buildings, and machinery if conventional financing is not available. The state also issues revenue bonds to finance industrial projects—a

Virginia—State Government Finances

(Dollar amounts in thousands. Per capita amounts in dollars.)

	AMOUNT	PER CAPITA
Total Revenue	35,739,829	4,777.41
General revenue	27,971,743	3,739.04
Intergovernmental revenue	6,237,933	833.84
Taxes	14,233,065	1,902.56
General sales	2,977,401	398.00
Selective sales	2,234,662	298.71
License taxes	613,910	82.06
Individual income tax	7,422,071	992.12
Corporate income tax	422,119	56.43
Other taxes	562,902	75.24
Current charges	4,472,170	597.80
Miscellaneous general revenue	3,028,575	404.84
Utility revenue	–	–
Liquor store revenue	407,574	54.48
Insurance trust revenue	7,360,512	983.89
Total expenditure	30,370,027	4,059.62
Intergovernmental expenditure	8,819,067	1,178.86
Direct expenditure	21,550,960	2,880.76
Current operation	15,602,380	2,085.60
Capital outlay	1,772,815	236.98
Insurance benefits and repayments	2,383,042	318.55
Assistance and subsidies	1,070,788	143.13
Interest on debt	721,935	96.50
Exhibit: Salaries and wages	6,831,680	913.20
Total expenditure	30,370,027	4,059.62
General expenditure	27,618,308	3,691.79
Intergovernmental expenditure	8,819,067	1,178.86
Direct expenditure	18,799,241	2,512.93
General expenditures, by function:		
Education	10,308,063	1,377.90
Public welfare	5,618,854	751.08
Hospitals	1,966,021	262.80
Health	724,350	96.83
Highways	2,477,512	331.17
Police protection	549,489	73.45
Correction	1,215,898	162.53
Natural resources	181,365	24.24
Parks and recreation	77,446	10.35
Government administration	1,005,575	134.42
Interest on general debt	721,935	96.50
Other and unallocable	2,771,800	370.51
Utility expenditure	18,759	2.51
Liquor store expenditure	349,918	46.77
Insurance trust expenditure	2,383,042	318.55
Debt at end of fiscal year	15,314,018	2,047.05
Cash and security holdings	57,642,635	7,705.20

Abbreviations and symbols: – zero or rounds to zero; (NA) not available; (X) not applicable.

SOURCE: *U.S. Census Bureau, Governments Division, 2004 Survey of State Government Finances,* January 2006.

popular method of financing because the return to investors is tax-free. The bonds are issued for small as well as large companies and may be used to finance the installation of pollution control equipment. Localities allow total or partial tax exemptions for such equipment and for certified solar energy devices. The Virginia Small Business Financing Authority's loan guarantee program helps small companies obtain working capital by guaranteeing up to $150,000 of a bank loan.

Counties, cities, and incorporated towns may form local industrial development authorities to finance industrial projects and various other facilities, and may issue their own revenue bonds to cover the cost of land, buildings, machinery, and equipment. The authority's lease of the property normally includes an option to buy at a nominal price on the expiration of the lease. In addition, some 110 local development corporations have been organized. The Virginia Department of Housing and Community Development offers grants for projects which will generate employment in economically depressed areas, and the Virginia Coalfield Economic Development Authority extends loans to new or growing companies in southwestern Virginia. For minority-owned entrepreneurships, Virginia maintains the Office of Minority Business Enterprise to give advice on special problems. With Delaware, Maryland, and Washington, DC, Virginia has been recognized as part of an international life sciences hub, dubbed the BioCapital hub. Virginia companies and agencies have participated in bioscience "hotbed" campaigns, concerted efforts by groups made up of government development agencies, pharmaceutical and bioscience companies, research institutes, universities, and nonprofits to attract capital, personnel and resources to develop a life sciences cluster.

In 2006, the US Chamber of Commerce ranked all 50 states on legal fairness towards business. The chamber found Virginia to be one of five states with the best legal environment for business. The other four were Iowa, Nebraska, Connecticut, and Delaware.

38 HEALTH

The infant mortality rate in October 2005 was estimated at 7.4 per 1,000 live births. The birth rate in 2003 was 13.7 per 1,000 population. The abortion rate stood at 18.1 per 1,000 women in 2000. In 2003, about 85.3% of pregnant woman received prenatal care beginning in the first trimester. In 2004, approximately 81% of children received routine immunizations before the age of three.

The crude death rate in 2003 was 7.9 deaths per 1,000 population. As of 2002, the death rates for major causes of death (per 100,000 resident population) were: heart disease, 205; cancer, 186.5; cerebrovascular diseases, 54.3; chronic lower respiratory diseases, 37.7; and diabetes, 21.4. The mortality rate from HIV infection was 3.6 per 100,000 population. In 2004, the reported AIDS case rate was at about 10.7 per 100,000 population. In 2002, about 56.4% of the population was considered overweight or obese. As of 2004, about 20.8% of state residents were smokers.

In 2003, Virginia had 84 community hospitals with about 17,200 beds. There were about 758,000 patient admissions that year and 11.2 million outpatient visits. The average daily inpatient census was about 12,000 patients. The average cost per day for hospital care was $1,277. Also in 2003, there were about 278 certified nursing facilities in the state with 31,472 beds and an overall occupancy rate of about 87.7%. In 2004, it was estimated that about 73.5% of all state residents had received some type of dental care within the year. Virginia had 264 physicians per 100,000 resident population in 2004 and 712 nurses per 100,000 in 2005. In 2004, there were a total of 4,395 dentists in the state.

About 10% of state residents were enrolled in Medicaid programs in 2003; 13% were enrolled in Medicare programs in 2004. Approximately 14% of the state population was uninsured in 2004. In 2003, state health care expenditures totaled $5.4 million.

[39] SOCIAL WELFARE

In 2004, about 126,000 people received unemployment benefits, with the average weekly unemployment benefit at $240. In fiscal year 2005, the estimated average monthly participation in the food stamp program included about 488,481 persons (215,817 households); the average monthly benefit was about $85.25 per person. That year, the total of benefits paid through the state for the food stamp program was about $499.7 million.

Temporary Assistance for Needy Families (TANF), the system of federal welfare assistance that officially replaced Aid to Families with Dependent Children (AFDC) in 1997, was reauthorized through the Deficit Reduction Act of 2005. TANF is funded through federal block grants that are divided among the states based on an equation involving the number of recipients in each state. Virginia's TANF program is called VIEW (Virginia Initiative for Employment, Not Welfare). In 2004, the state program had 27,000 recipients; state and federal expenditures on this TANF program totaled $129 million in fiscal year 2003.

In December 2004, Social Security benefits were paid to 1,114,210 Virginians. This number included 693,350 retired workers, 111,370 widows and widowers, 155,830 disabled workers, 58,240 spouses, and 95,420 children. Social Security beneficiaries represented 14.9% of the total state population and 91.1% of the state's population age 65 and older. Retired workers received an average monthly payment of $940; widows and widowers, $860; disabled workers, $898; and spouses, $474. Payments for children of retired workers averaged $492 per month; children of deceased workers, $645; and children of disabled workers, $273. Federal Supplemental Security Income payments in December 2004 went to 134,531 Virginia residents, averaging $375 a month. An additional $1.7 million of state-administered supplemental payments were distributed to 6,301 residents.

[40] HOUSING

In 2004, Virginia had an estimated 3,116,827 housing units, 2,846,417 of them occupied; 69.2% were owner-occupied. About 62.7% of all units were single-family, detached homes. Electricity and utility gas were the most common energy sources for heating. It was estimated that 118,489 units lacked telephone service, 8,701 lacked complete plumbing facilities, and 8.175 lacked complete kitchen facilities. The average household had 2.54 members.

In 2004, 63,200 new privately owned housing units were authorized for construction. The median home value was $179,191. The median monthly cost for mortgage owners was $1,323. Renters paid a median of $757 per month. In 2006, the state received over $19.5 million in community development block grants from the US Department of Housing and Urban Development (HUD).

[41] EDUCATION

Although Virginia was the first English colony to found a free school (1634), the state's public school system developed very slowly. Thomas Jefferson proposed a system of free public schools as early as 1779, but it was not until 1851 that such a system was established—for whites only. Free schools for blacks were founded after the Civil War, but they were poorly funded. Opposition by white Virginians to the US Supreme Court's desegregation order in 1954 was marked in certain communities by public school closings and the establishment of all-white private schools. In Prince Edward County, the most extreme case, the school board abandoned public education and left black children without schools from 1959 to 1963. By the 1970s, however, school integration was an accomplished fact throughout the commonwealth.

In 2004, 88.4% of all state residents 25 years of age or older were high school graduates, and 33.1% had four or more years of college.

The total enrollment for fall 2002 in Virginia's public schools stood at 1,177,000. Of these, 832,000 attended schools from kindergarten through grade eight, and 346,000 attended high school. Approximately 61.3% of the students were white, 26.8% were black, 6.6% were Hispanic, 4.7% were Asian/Pacific Islander, and 0.5% were American Indian/Alaskan Native. Total enrollment was estimated at 1,186,000 in fall 2003 and expected to be 1,202,000 by fall 2014, an increase of 2.1% during the period 2002–14. Expenditures for public education in 2003/04 were estimated at $11.25 billion. There were 104,304 students enrolled in 604 private schools in fall 2003. Since 1969, the National Assessment of Educational Progress (NAEP) has tested public school students nationwide. The resulting report, *The Nation's Report Card,* stated that in 2005 eighth graders in Virginia scored 284 out of 500 in mathematics compared with the national average of 278.

As of fall 2002, there were 404,966 students enrolled in college or graduate school; minority students comprised 27.6% of total postsecondary enrollment. In 2005 Virginia had 104 degree-granting institutions including, 15 public four-year schools, 24 public two-year schools, and 32 nonprofit, private four-year schools. Virginia has had a distinguished record in higher education since the College of William and Mary was founded at Williamsburg (then called Middle Plantation) in 1693, especially after Thomas Jefferson established the University of Virginia at Charlottesville in 1819. In addition to the University of Virginia and the College of William and Mary, public state-supported institutions include Virginia Polytechnic Institute and State University, Blacksburg; Virginia Commonwealth University, Richmond; Virginia Military Institute, Lexington; Old Dominion University, Norfolk; and George Mason University, Fairfax. Well-known private institutions include the Hampton Institute, Hampton; Randolph-Macon College, Ashland; University of Richmond; Sweet Briar College, Sweet Briar; and Washington and Lee University, Lexington. Tuition assistance grants and scholarships are provided through the State Council of Higher Education, while the Virginia Student Assistance Authority provides guaranteed student loans.

[42] ARTS

The Virginia Commission for the Arts was founded in 1968 and is comprised of 13 commissioners appointed by the governor for five-year terms. In 2005, the Virginia Commission for the Arts and other Virginia arts organizations received 32 grants totaling $1,197,200 from the National Endowment for the Arts. The Virginia Foundation for the Humanities (VFH) was established in 1974; as of 2005 VFH had sponsored over 40,000 humanities programs. In 2005, the National Endowment for the Humanities contributed $4,267,066 for 46 state programs.

Richmond, Norfolk, and the northern Virginia metropolitan area are the principal centers for the creative and the performing arts in Virginia, although the arts flourish throughout the state. Richmond's Landmark Theater (formerly known as The Mosque) has been the scene of concerts by internationally famous orchestras and soloists for generations. As of 2005, Richmond's Landmark Theater had the largest proscenium stage on the East Coast. The Barksdale Theatre and its repertory company presents a variety of performances at both Willow Lawn and Hanover Tavern. The 2005/06 season performances included *The Syringa Tree, The Full Monty,* and *Barefoot in the Park.*

In Norfolk, the performing arts are strikingly housed in Scope, a large auditorium designed by Pier Luigi Nervi; Chrysler Hall, an elegant structure with gleaming crystal; and the Wells Theatre, an ornate building that has hosted such diverse performers as John Philip Sousa, Will Rogers, and Fred Astaire. The internationally recognized Virginia Opera Association is housed in the Harrison Opera House. As of 2004, the Virginia Opera's Education and Outreach program reached more than 200,000 students and community members annually.

The Wolf Trap Foundation, in northern Virginia, provides theatrical, operatic, and musical performances featuring internationally celebrated performers. The College of William and Mary's Phi Beta Kappa Hall in Williamsburg is the site of the Virginia Shakespeare Festival, an annual summer event inaugurated in 1979. Abingdon is the home of the Barter Theatre (1933), the first state-supported theatre in the United States, whose alumni include Ernest Borgnine and Gregory Peck. This repertory company has performed widely in the United States and at selected sites abroad. The 2006 season included performances of *Romeo and Juliet, Thoroughly Modern Millie, Robin Hood,* and *The Lion, The Witch, and The Wardrobe.*

There are orchestras in Alexandria, Arlington, Fairfax, Lynchburg, Petersburg, and Roanoke. Richmond is home to the Richmond Ballet, Richmond Choral Society, Richmond Jazz Society, Richmond Philharmonic, and the Richmond Symphony. The Virginia Symphony, founded in 1920, has been recognized as one of the nation's leading regional symphony orchestras. The symphony provides an education and outreach program; as of 2005 it offered programs such as "The Peanut Butter and Jam Family Series," "Young People's Concerts," and "Beethoven Play-Along."

The annual Virginia Arts Festival has drawn national attention since its inception in 1997. In 2004, the festival presented 134 performances of music, theater, and dance in 32 days and more than 22,000 students and 1,546 artists participated. The annual Shenandoah Valley Music Festival, established in 1963, is held in Orkney Springs and features arts and crafts presentations as well as musical performances.

In 2004 former US Poet Laureate (1993–1995), Rita Dove, was named Poet Laureate of the Commonwealth of Virginia. Her books of poetry include *American Smooth* (2004), *On the Bus with Rosa Parks* (1999), *Mother Love* (1995), Pulitzer Prize-winning *Thomas and Beulah* (1986), and *The Yellow House on the Corner* (1980). She has also published a book of short stories, *Fifth Sunday* (1985) and a novel, *Through the Ivory Gate* (1992).

43 LIBRARIES AND MUSEUMS

For the fiscal year ending in June 2001, Virginia had 90 public library systems, with a total of 338 libraries, of which 259 were branches. In that same year, they had a combined 18,659,000 volumes of books and serial publications one their shelves, and had a combined circulation of 63,075,000. The system also had 810,000 audio and 448,000 video items, 13,000 electronic format items (CD-ROMs, magnetic tapes, and disks), and 35 bookmobiles. The

Virginia State Library in Richmond and the libraries of the University of Virginia (Charlottesville) and the College of William and Mary (Williamsburg) have the personal papers of such notables as Washington, Jefferson, Madison, Robert E. Lee, William H. McGuffey, and William Faulkner. The University of Virginia also has an impressive collection of medieval illuminated manuscripts, and the library of colonial Williamsburg has extensive microfilms of British records. In fiscal year 2001, operating income for the state's public library system totaled $199,658,000 and included $1,384,000 in federal funds and $21,181,000 in state funding.

There were 260 museums in 1996–97. In Richmond, the Virginia Museum of Fine Arts, the first state museum of art in the United States, has a collection that ranges from ancient Egyptian artifacts to mobile jewelry by Salvador Dali. The Science Museum of Virginia has a 280-seat planetarium that features a simulated excursion to outer space. Other museums in Richmond are Wilton, the Randolphs' handsome 18th-century mansion, and the Maymont and Wickham-Valentine houses, elaborate 19th-century residences; Agecroft Hall and Virginia House, Tudor manor houses that were moved from England, are also open to the public. Norfolk has the Chrysler Museum, with its famous glassware collection; Myers House, an early Federal period home with handsome art and furnishings; and the Hermitage Foundation Museum, noted for its Oriental art. The Mariners Museum in Newport News has a superb maritime collection, and the much smaller but quite select exhibits of the Portsmouth Naval Shipyard Museum are also notable. Perhaps the most extensive "museum" in the United States is Williamsburg's mile-long Duke of Gloucester Street, with such remarkable restorations as the Christopher Wren Building of the College of William and Mary, Bruton Parish Church, the Governor's Palace, and the colonial capital.

More historic sites are maintained as museums in Virginia than in any other state. These include Washington's home at Mt. Vernon (Fairfax County), Jefferson's residence at Monticello (Charlottesville), and James River plantation houses such as Berkeley, Shirley, Westover, Sherwood Forest, and Carter's Grove. The National Park Service operates a visitors' center at Jamestown.

44 COMMUNICATIONS

The state's communications network has expanded steadily since the first postal routes were established in 1738. Airmail service from Richmond to New York and Atlanta began in 1928.

In 2004, 94.0% of Virginia's occupied housing units had telephones. Additionally, by June of that same year there were 4,392,319 mobile wireless telephone subscribers. In 2003, 66.8% of Virginia households had a computer and 60.3% had Internet access. By June 2005, there were 1,134,059 high-speed lines in Virginia, 1,022,318 residential and 111,741 for business.

In 2005, broadcasters operated 23 major AM radio stations and 82 major FM stations. In the same year, Virginia had 26 major television stations. The Norfolk-Portsmouth-Newport News area had 629,100 television households, 76% of which ordered cable in 1999. Approximately 187,445 Internet domain names were registered with the state in the year 2000.

45 PRESS

Although the Crown forbade the establishment of a printing press in Virginia Colony, William Parks was publishing the *Virginia Gazette* at Williamsburg in 1736. Three newspapers were published regularly during the Revolutionary period, and in 1780 the General Assembly declared that the press was "indispensable for the right information of the people and for the public service." The oldest continuously published Virginia daily, tracing its origins to 1784, is the *Alexandria Gazette*. The first Negro newspaper, *The True Southerner*, was started by a white man in 1865; several weeklies published and edited by blacks began soon after. By 1900 there were 180 newspapers in the state, but the number has declined drastically since then because of fierce competition, mergers, and rising costs.

USA Today, the nation's largest daily newspaper in 2004 with a circulation of 2,220,863, is based in Arlington, Virginia. In 2002, the Arlington *Journal* and the Fairfax *Journal* merged to form the *Northern Virginia Journal*. In 2005, Virginia had 21 morning dailies, 4 evening, and 17 Sunday papers.

Leading dailies and their approximate circulation rates in 2005 were:

AREA	NAME	DAILY	SUNDAY
Alexandria	*Northern Virginia Journal* (m,S)	62,910	386,000
Arlington	*USA Today* (m)	2,665,815	
Newport News	*Daily Press* (m,S)	91,307	112,955
Norfolk	*Virginian-Pilot* (m,S)	200,055	234,508
Richmond	*Times–Dispatch* (m,S)*	184,950	225,293
Roanoke	*Times* (m,S)	96,687	108,564

*Absorbed Richmond's *News Leader* in 1992.

The newspaper group, Gannett Co, Inc, is based in Virginia. This group owns about 90 daily newspapers nationwide, including *USA Today*, as well as over 1,000 non-daily papers and shoppers bulletins. Gannett's UK subsidiary, Newsquest plc, publishes 17 daily newspapers and more than 300 non-daily publications.

⁴⁶ORGANIZATIONS

In 2006, there were over 8,990 nonprofit organizations registered within the state, of which about 6.072 were registered as charitable, educational, or religious organizations.

Service and educational groups headquartered in the state include the United Way of America, American Astronautical Society, American Society for Horticultural Science, and American Geological Institute, all located in Alexandria; and the National Honor Society, Music Educators National Conference, and National Art Education Association, located in Reston. Art and cultural organizations include Army Historical Foundation, the Association for the protection of Virginia Antiquities, the Chesapeake and Ohio Historical Society, the Folk Art Society of America, and the Virginia Historical Society.

Veterans' organizations include the Veterans of World War I of the USA and the Retired Officers Association, Alexandria, and the Military Order of the Purple Heart, Springfield. The United Daughters of the Confederacy has national offices in Richmond. Among the business and professional groups based in Virginia are the American Academy of Audiology, the American Physical Therapy Association, and the American Chiropractic Association.

Sports societies headquartered in the state include the American Canoe Association, the United States Parachute Association, and the Boat Owners Association of the United States. The headquarters of the National Rifle Association are in Fairfax. Environmental and conservation associations include, Nature Conservancy, the American Bird Conservancy, and the American Seed Tree Association.

Other groups operating out of Virginia include the National Sojourners, National Alliance of Senior Citizens, and the Association of Former Intelligence Officers.

⁴⁷TOURISM, TRAVEL, AND RECREATION

In 2004, travelers spent over $15 billion in Virginia on day trips and overnight stays. The tourism and travel industry is the state's third-largest employer, supporting over 203,000 jobs. Attractions in the coastal region alone include the Jamestown (the first permanent English settlement in America) and Yorktown historic sites (Jamestown will celebrate its 400 anniversary in 2006–07), the Williamsburg restoration, and the homes of George Washington and Robert E. Lee. Also featured are the National Aeronautics and Space Administration's Langley Research Center, Assateague Island National Seashore, and the resort pleasures of Virginia Beach.

The interior offers numerous Civil War Sites, including Appomattox; Thomas Jefferson's Monticello as well as The University of Virginia, founded by Jefferson; Booker T. Washington's birthplace near Smith Mountain Lake; and the historic cities of Richmond, Petersburg, and Fredericksburg. Visitors can also tour nearby Civil War battlefields and cemeteries. In the west, the Blue Ridge Parkway and Shenandoah National Park, traversed by the breathtaking Skyline Drive, are favorite tourist destinations, as are Cumberland Gap and, in the Lexington area, the Natural Bridge, the home of Confederate General Thomas "Stonewall" Jackson, the George C. Marshall Library and Museum, and the Virginia Military Institute. A number of historic sites in Arlington and Alexandria attract many visitors to the Washington, D.C, area. The colonial city of Williamsburg attracts visitors to its historic pre-Revolutionary sites. Nearby are the James River Plantation homes.

The state's many recreation areas include state parks, national forests, a major national park, scenic parkways, and thousands of miles of hiking trails and shoreline. Some of the most-visited sites are Mt. Rogers National Recreational Area, Prince William Forest Park, Chincoteague National Wildlife Refuge (where wild ponies are rounded up each year), and the Kerr Reservoir. Part of the famous Appalachian Trail winds through Virginia's Blue Ridge and Appalachian mountains. Virginia has more than 1,500 mi (2,400 km) of well-stocked trout streams.

⁴⁸SPORTS

Although Virginia has no major professional sports teams, it does support two Triple-A baseball teams: the Richmond Braves and Norfolk Tides. Other minor league baseball teams play in Bristol, Danville, Lynchburg, Pulaski, Salem, Martinsville, and Woodbridge. There is also minor league hockey in Richmond and Norfolk.

In collegiate sports, the University of Virginia belongs to the Atlantic Coast Conference, and the Virginia Military Institute competes in the Southern Conference. Virginia won college basketball's National Invitational Tournament (NIT) in 1980 and 1992; Virginia Tech won the NIT in 1973 and has appeared in thirteen consecutive postseason college football bowl games.

Stock car racing is also popular in the state. The Richmond International Raceway and Martinsville Speedway host four NASCAR Nextel Cup races each year.

Participant sports popular with Virginians include tennis, golf, swimming, skiing, boating, and water skiing. The state has at least 180 public and private golf courses.

Among the many notable persons that call Virginia their home, several are legendary athletes—tennis great Arthur Ashe, football's Fran Tarkenton, and golf's Sam Snead all were born and raised in the state.

⁴⁹FAMOUS VIRGINIANS

Virginia is the birthplace of eight US presidents and many famous statesmen, noted scientists, influential educators, distinguished writers, and popular entertainers.

The first president of the United States, George Washington (1732–99), also led his country's armies in the Revolutionary War and presided over the convention that framed its Constitution. Washington—who was unanimously elected president in 1789 and served two four-year terms, declining a third—was not, as has sometimes been assumed, a newcomer to politics: his political career began at the age of 27 with his election to the House of Burgesses.

Thomas Jefferson (1743–1826), the nation's third president, offered this as his epitaph: "author of the Declaration of Independence and the Virginia Statute for Religious Freedom, and father of the University of Virginia." After serving as secretary of state under Washington and vice president under John Adams, he was elected president of the United States in 1800 and reelected in 1804. Honored now as a statesman and political thinker, Jefferson was also a musician and one of the foremost architects of his time, and he has been called the first American archaeologist.

Jefferson's successor, James Madison (1751–1836), actually made his most important contributions before becoming chief executive. As a skillful and persistent negotiator throughout the Constitutional Convention of 1787, he earned the designation "father of the Constitution"; then, as coauthor of the Federalist papers, he helped produce a classic of American political philosophy. He was more responsible than any other statesman for Virginia's crucial ratification vote. Secretary of State during Jefferson's two terms, Madison occupied the presidency from 1809 to 1817.

Madison was succeeded as president in 1817 by James Monroe (1758–1831), who was reelected to a second term starting in 1821. Monroe—who had served as governor, US senator, minister to France, and secretary of state—is best known for the Monroe Doctrine, which has been US policy since his administration. William Henry Harrison (1773–1841) became the ninth president in 1841 but died of pneumonia one month after his inauguration; he had been a governor of Indiana Territory, a major general in the War of 1812, and a US representative and senator from Indiana. Harrison was succeeded by Vice President John Tyler (1790–1862), a native and resident of Virginia, who established the precedent that, upon the death of the president, the vice president inherits the title as well as the duties of the office.

Another native of Virginia, Zachary Taylor (1784–1850), renowned chiefly as a military leader, became the 12th US president in 1849 but died midway through his term. The eighth Virginia-born president, (Thomas) Woodrow Wilson (1856–1924), became the 28th president of the United States in 1913 after serving as governor of New Jersey.

John Marshall (1755–1835) was the third confirmed chief justice of the United States and is generally regarded by historians as the first great American jurist, partly because of his establishment of the principle of judicial review. Five other Virginians—John Blair (1732–1800), Bushrod Washington (1762–1829), Philip P. Barbour (1783–1841), Peter V. Daniel (1784–1860), and Lewis F. Powell Jr. (1907–98)—have served as associate justices.

George Washington's cabinet included two Virginians, Secretary of State Jefferson and Attorney General Edmund Randolph (1753–1813), who, as governor of Virginia, had introduced the Virginia Plan—drafted by Madison and calling for a House of Representatives elected by the people and a Senate elected by the House—at the Constitutional Convention of 1787. Among other distinguished Virginians who have served in the cabinet are James Barbour (1775–1842), secretary of war; John Y. Mason (1799–1859), secretary of the Navy and attorney general; Carter Glass (1858–1946), secretary of the treasury, author of the Federal Reserve System, and US senator for 26 years; and Claude Augustus Swanson (1862–1939), secretary of the Navy and earlier, state governor and US senator.

Other prominent US senators from Virginia include Richard Henry Lee (1732–94), former president of the Continental Congress; James M. Mason (b.District of Columbia, 1798–1871), who later was commissioner of the Confederacy to the United Kingdom and France; John W. Daniel (1842–1910), a legal scholar and powerful Democratic Party leader; Thomas S. Martin (1847–1919), US Senate majority leader; Harry F. Byrd (1887–1966), governor of Virginia from 1926 to 1930 and US senator from 1933 to 1965; and Harry F. Byrd Jr. (b.1914), senator from 1965 to 1982. In 1985, Virginia was represented in the Senate by Republican John W. Warner (b.District of Columbia, 1927), former secretary of the Navy, and Republican Paul S. Trible Jr. (b.Maryland, 1946), a US representative from 1976 to 1982.

Some native-born Virginians have become famous as leaders in other nations. Joseph Jenkins Roberts (1809–76) was the first president of the Republic of Liberia, and Nancy Langhorne Astor (1879–1964) was the first woman to serve in the British House of Commons.

Virginia's important colonial governors included Captain John Smith (b.England, 1580?–1631), Sir George Yeardley (b.England, 1587?–1627), Sir William Berkeley (b.England, 1606–77), Alexander Spotswood (b.Tangier, 1676–1740), Sir William Gooch (b.England, 1681–1751), and Robert Dinwiddie (b.Scotland, 1693–1770).

Virginia signers of the Declaration of Independence, besides Jefferson and Richard Henry Lee, were Carter Braxton (1736–97); Benjamin Harrison (1726?–1791), father of President William Henry Harrison; Francis Lightfoot Lee (1734–97); Thomas Nelson Jr. (1738–89); and George Wythe (1726–1806). Wythe is also famous as the first US law professor and the teacher, in their student days, of Presidents Jefferson, Monroe, and Tyler, and Chief Justice Marshall. Virginia furnished both the first president of the Continental Congress, Peyton Randolph (1721–75), and the last, Cyrus Griffin (1748–1810).

Other notable Virginia governors include Patrick Henry (1736–99), the first governor of the commonwealth, though best remembered as a Revolutionary orator; Westmoreland Davis (1859–1942); Andrew Jackson Montague (1862–1937); and Mills E. Goodwin Jr. (b.1914). A major historical figure who defies classification is Robert "King" Carter (1663–1732), greatest of the Virginia land barons, who also served as acting governor of Virginia and rector of the College of William and Mary.

Chief among Virginia's great military and naval leaders besides Washington and Taylor are John Paul Jones (b.Scotland, 1747–92); George Rogers Clark (1752–1818); Winfield Scott (1786–1866); Robert E. Lee (1807–70), the Confederate commander who earlier served in the Mexican War and as superintendent of West Point; Joseph E. Johnston (1807–91); George H. Thomas (1816–70); Thomas Jonathan "Stonewall" Jackson (1824–63); James Ewell Brown "Jeb" Stuart (1833–64); and George C. Marshall (b.Pennsylvania, 1880–1959). Virginians' names are also written high in the history of exploration. Daniel Boone (b.Pennsylvania, 1734–1820), who pioneered in Kentucky and Missouri, was once a member of the Virginia General Assembly. Meriwether Lewis (1774–1809) and William Clark (1770–1838), both native Virginians, led the most famous expedition in US history, from St. Louis to the Pacific coast (1804–6). Richard E. Byrd (1888–1957) was both an explorer of Antarctica and a pioneer aviator.

Woodrow Wilson and George C. Marshall both received the Nobel Peace Prize, in 1919 and 1953, respectively. Distinguished Virginia-born scientists and inventors include Matthew Fontaine Maury (1806–73), founder of the science of oceanography; Cyrus H. McCormick (1809–84), who perfected the mechanical reaper; and Dr. Walter Reed (1851–1902) who proved that yellow fever was transmitted by a mosquito. Among educators associated with the state are William H. McGuffey (b.Pennsylvania, 1800–1873), a University of Virginia professor who designed and edited the most famous series of school readers in American history; and Booker T. Washington (1856–1915), the nation's foremost black educator.

William Byrd II (1674–1744) is widely acknowledged to have been the most graceful writer in English America in his day, and Jefferson was a leading prose stylist of the Revolutionary period. Edgar Allen Poe (b.Massachusetts, 1809–49), who was taken to Richmond at the age of three and later educated at the University of Virginia, was the father of the detective story and one of America's great poets and short-story writers. Virginia is the setting of historical romances by three natives: John Esten Cooke (1830–86), Thomas Nelson Page (1853–1922), and Mary Johnston (1870–1936). Notable 20th-century novelists born in Virginia include Willa Cather (1873–1947), Ellen Glasgow (1874–1945), and James Branch Cabell (1879–1958). Willard Huntington Wright (1888–1939), better known as S. S. Van Dine, wrote many detective thrillers. Twice winner of the Pulitzer Prize for biography and often regarded as the greatest American master of that genre was Douglas Southall Freeman (1886–1953). Other important historians were Lyon Gardiner Tyler (1853–1935), son of President Tyler and also an eminent educator; Philip A. Bruce (1856–1933); William Cabell Bruce (1860–1946); Virginius Dabney (1901–95); and Alf J. Mapp Jr. (b.1925). Some contemporary Virginia authors are poet Guy Carleton Drewry (1901–91); television writer-producer Earl Hamner (b.1923); novelist William Styron (b.1925); and journalists Virginia Moore (1903–1993) and Tom Wolfe (Thomas Kennerly Wolfe Jr., b. 1931).

Celebrated Virginia artists include sculptors Edward V. Valentine (1838–1930) and Moses Ezekiel (1844–1917), and painters George Caleb Bingham (1811–79) and Jerome Myers (1867–1940). A protégé of Jefferson's, Robert Mills (b.South Carolina, 1781–1855), designed the Washington Monument.

The roster of Virginians prominent in the entertainment world includes Bill "Bojangles" Robinson (1878–1949), Francis X. Bushman (1883–1966), Freeman Gosden (1899–1982), Randolph Scott (1903–1987), Joseph Cotten (1905–94), Margaret Sullavan (1911–60), John Payne (1912–1989), George C. Scott (1927–99), Shirley MacLaine (b.1934), and Warren Beatty (b.1938).

Outstanding musical performers include John Powell (1882–1963), whose fame as a pianist once equaled his prominence as a composer. Virginia's most eminent contemporary composer is Thea Musgrave (b.Scotland, 1928). Popular musical stars include Kathryn Elizabeth "Kate" Smith (1907–1986), Pearl Bailey (1918–1990), Ella Fitzgerald (1918–1996), June Carter (1929–2003), Roy Clark (b.1933), and Wayne Newton (b.1942).

The Old Dominion's sports champions include golfers Bobby Cruickshank (1896–1975), Sam Snead (1912–2002), and Chandler Harper (1914–2004); tennis star Arthur Ashe (1943–1993); football players Clarence "Ace" Parker (b.1912), Bill Dudley (b.1921), and Francis "Fran" Tarkenton (b.1940); and baseball pitcher Eppa Rixey (1891–1963). At age 15, Olympic swimming champion Melissa Belote (b.1957) won three gold medals. Helen Chenery "Penny" Tweedy (b.1922) is a famous breeder and racer of horses from whose stables have come Secretariat and other champions. Equestrienne Jean McLean Davis (b.1929) won 65 world championships.

⁵⁰BIBLIOGRAPHY

Council of State Governments. *The Book of the States, 2006 Edition.* Lexington, Ky.: Council of State Governments, 2006.

Dabney, Virginius. *Richmond: The Story of a City.* Rev. and enl. ed. Charlottesville: University Press of Virginia, 1990.

Diversity and Accommodation: Essays on the Cultural Composition of the Virginia Frontier. Knoxville: University of Tennessee Press, 1997. (orig. 1964).

Ferris, William (ed.). *The South.* Vol. 7 in *The Greenwood Encyclopedia of American Regional Cultures.* Westport, Conn.: Greenwood Press, 2004.

Goodwin, Bill. *Virginia.* London: Frommers/Transworld, 2000.

Holzer, Harold, and Tim Mulligan (eds.). *The Battle of Hampton Roads: New Perspectives on the USS Monitor and CSS Virginia.* New York: Fordham University Press, 2005.

Horn, James P. P. *A Land as God Made It: Jamestown and the Birth of America.* New York: Basic Books, 2005.

Mapp, Alf J. Jr. *Frock Coats and Epaulets: The Men Who Led the Confederacy.* Lanham, Md.: Madison Books, 1996.

Pratt, Robert A. *The Color of their Skin: Education and Race in Richmond, Virginia, 1954-89.* Charlottesville: University Press of Virginia, 1992.

Ragsdale, Bruce A. *A Planters' Republic: The Search for Economic Independence in Revolutionary Virginia.* Madison, Wis.: Madison House, 1996.

Rosen, Daniel. *New Beginnings: Jamestown and the Virginia Colony, 1607-1699.* Washington, D.C.: National Geographic, 2005.

Saffell, William Thomas Roberts. *Records of the Revolutionary War: Containing the Military and Financial Correspondence of Distinguished Officers.* Bowie, Md.: Heritage Books, 1999.

WASHINGTON

State of Washington

ORIGIN OF STATE NAME: Named for George Washington. **NICKNAME:** The Evergreen State. **CAPITAL:** Olympia. **ENTERED UNION:** 11 November 1889 (42nd). **SONG:** "Washington, My Home." **MOTTO:** *Alki* (Chinook for "By and by"). **FLAG:** The state seal centered on a dark green field. **OFFICIAL SEAL:** Portrait of George Washington surrounded by the words "The Seal of the State of Washington 1889." **BIRD:** Willow goldfinch. **FISH:** Steelhead trout. **FLOWER:** Coast rhododendron. **TREE:** Western hemlock. **LEGAL HOLIDAYS:** New Year's Day, 1 January; Birthday of Martin Luther King Jr., 3rd Monday in January; Presidents' Day, 2nd Monday in February; Memorial Day, last Monday in May; Independence Day, 4 July; Labor Day, 1st Monday in September; Veterans' Day, 11 November; Thanksgiving Day, 4th Thursday in November and the day following; Christmas Day, 25 December. **TIME:** 4 AM PST = noon GMT.

¹LOCATION, SIZE, AND EXTENT

Located on the Pacific coast of the northwestern United States, Washington ranks 20th in size among the 50 states.

The total area of Washington is 66,582 sq mi (176,477 sq km), of which land takes up 66,511 sq mi (172,263 sq km) and inland water 1,627 sq mi (4,214 sq km). The state extends about 360 mi (580 km) E–W and 240 mi (390 km) N–S.

Washington is bounded on the N by the Canadian province of British Columbia (with the northwestern line passing through the Juan de Fuca Strait and the Haro and Georgia straits); on the E by Idaho (with the line in the southwest passing through the Snake River); on the s by Oregon (with most of the line defined by the Columbia River); and on the w by the Pacific Ocean.

Islands of the San Juan group, lying between the Haro and Rosario straits, include Orcas, San Juan, and Lopez; Whidbey is a large island in the upper Puget Sound. The state's boundary length totals 1,099 mi (1,769 km), including 157 mi (253 km) of general coastline; the tidal shoreline extends 3,026 mi (4,870 km). Washington's geographic center is in Chelan County, 10 mi (16 km) wsw of Wenatchee.

²TOPOGRAPHY

Much of Washington is mountainous. Along the Pacific coast are the Coast Ranges extending northward from Oregon and California. This chain forms two groups: the Olympic Mountains in the northwest, mainly on the Olympic Peninsula between the Pacific Ocean and Puget Sound, and the Willapa Hills in the southwest. The highest of the Olympic group is Mt. Olympus, at 7,965 ft (2,428 m). About 100 mi (160 km) inward from the Pacific coast is the Cascade Range, extending northward from the Sierra Nevada in California. This chain, 50–100 mi (80–100 km) wide, has peaks generally ranging up to 10,000 ft (3,000 m), except for such volcanic cones as Mt. Adams, Mt. Baker, Glacier Peak, Mt. St. Helen's,

and Mt. Rainier, which at 14,410 ft (4,395 m) is the highest peak in the state. The mean elevation of the state is approximately 1,700 ft (519 m). Sea level at the Pacific Coast is the lowest elevation.

Between the Coast and Cascade ranges lies a long, troughlike depression—the Western Corridor—where most of Washington's major cities are concentrated. The northern section of this lowland is carved by Puget Sound, a complex, narrow arm of the Pacific wending southward for about 80 mi (130 km) and covering an area of 561 sq mi (1,453 sq km). Of all the state's other major regions, only south-central Washington, forming part of the Columbia Plateau, is generally flat.

The Cascade volcanoes were dormant, for the most part, during the second half of the 19th century and most of the 20th. Early in 1980, however, Mt. St. Helen's began to show ominous signs of activity. On 18 May, the volcano exploded, blasting more than 1,300 ft (400 m) off a mountain crest that had been 9,677 ft (2,950 m) high. Tremendous plumes of steam and ash were thrust into the stratosphere, where prevailing winds carried volcanic dust thousands of miles eastward. The areas immediately surrounding Mt. St. Helen's were deluged with ash and mudflows, choking local streams and lakes, particularly Spirit Lake. About 150 sq mi (388 sq km) of trees and brush were destroyed; the ash fall also damaged crops in neighboring agricultural areas and made highway travel extremely hazardous. The eruption left 57 people dead or missing. Eruptions of lesser severity followed the main outburst; the mountain continued to pose a serious danger to life in the area as the estimated cost of the damage to property, crops, and livestock approached $3 billion. Another minor eruption, on 14 May 1984, shot ash 4 mi (6 km) high and caused a small mudflow down the mountain's flanks, but no injuries or other damage occurred. East of the Cascade Range, much of Washington is a plateau underlain by ancient basalt lava flows. In the northeast are the Okanogan Highlands; in the southeast, the Blue Mountains and the Palouse Hills. All these uplands form extensions of the Rocky Mountain system.

Among Washington's numerous rivers, the longest and most powerful is the Columbia, entering Washington from Canada in the northeast corner and flowing for more than 1,200 mi (1,900 km) across the heart of the state and then along the Oregon border to the Pacific. In average discharge, the Columbia ranks second only to the Mississippi, with 262,000 cu ft (7,400 cu m) per second. Washington's other major river, the Snake, enters the state from Idaho in the southeast and flows generally westward, meeting the Columbia River near Pasco.

Washington has numerous lakes, of which the largest is the artificial Franklin D. Roosevelt Lake, covering 123 sq mi (319 sq km). Washington has some 90 dams, providing water storage, flood control, and hydroelectric power. One of the largest and most famous dams in the United States is Grand Coulee on the upper Columbia River, measuring 550 ft (168 m) high and 4,173 ft (1,272 m) long, with a storage capacity of more than 9.7 million acre-ft (11,960 cu m).

3 CLIMATE

The Cascade Mountains divide Washington not only topographically but also climatically. Despite its northerly location, western Washington is as mild as the middle and southeastern Atlantic coast; it is also one of the rainiest regions in the world. Eastern Washington, on the other hand, has a much more continental climate, characterized by cold winters, hot summers, and sparse rainfall. Since the prevailing winds are from the west, the windward (western) slopes of the state's major mountains intercept most of the atmospheric moisture and precipitate it as rain or snow. Certain coastal areas, receiving more than 200 in (500 cm) of rain a year, support dense stands of timber in a temperate rain forest. But in the dry southeastern quadrant, there are sagebrush deserts.

Average January temperatures in western Washington range from a minimum of 20°F (-7°C) on the western slope of the Cascades to a maximum of 48°F (9°C) along the Pacific coast; July temperatures range from a minimum of 44°F (7°C) on the western slope of the Cascades to a maximum of 80°F (27°C) in the foothills. In the east the temperature ranges are much more extreme: in January, from 8°F (-13°C) in the northeastern Cascades to 40°F (4°C) on the southeastern plateau; in July, from 48°F (9°C) on the eastern slope of the Cascades to 92°F (33°C) in the south-central portion of the state. The normal daily average temperature in Seattle is 53°F (11°C), ranging from 41°F (5°C) in January to 65°F (18°C) in July; Spokane averages 48°F (8°C), ranging from 26°F (-3°C) in January to 69°F (20°C) in July. The lowest temperature ever recorded in the state is -48°F (-44°C), set at Mazama and Winthrop on 30 December 1968; the highest, at Ice Harbor Dam on 5 August 1961, was 118°F (48°C).

In Seattle average annual precipitation is about 34 in (86 cm), falling most heavily from October through March; in the same period, Spokane receives an average of only 16.9 in (42 cm) annually, more than half of that from November through February. Snowfall in Seattle averages 7.1 in (18 cm) annually; in Spokane, 50.4 in (128 cm). Paradise Ranger Station holds the North American record for the most snowfall in one season, when 1,122 in (2,850 cm) of snow fell during the winter of 1971–72. High mountain peaks, such as Mt. Adams, Mt. Baker, and Mt. Rainier, have permanent snowcaps or snowfields of up to 100 ft (30 m) deep.

4 FLORA AND FAUNA

More than 1,300 plant species have been identified in Washington. Sand strawberries and beach peas are found among the dunes while fennel and spurry grow in salt marshes; greasewood and sagebrush predominate in the desert regions of the Columbia Plateau. Conifers include Sitka spruce, Douglas fir, western hemlock, and Alaska cedar; big-leaf maple, red alder, black cottonwood, and western yew are among the characteristic deciduous trees. Wild flowers include the deerhead orchid and wake-robin; the western rhododendron is the state flower. In April 2006, nine plant species were listed as threatened or endangered by the US Fish and Wildlife Service, including golden paintbrush, Nelson's checker-mallow, Kincaid's lupine, Spalding's catchfly, Ute ladies' tresses, water howelia, Bradshaw's desert-parsley, showy stickseed, Wenatchee and Mountains checkermallow.

Forest and mountain regions support Columbia black-tailed and mule deer, elk, and black bear; the Roosevelt elk, named after President Theodore Roosevelt, is indigenous to the Olympic Mountains. Other native mammals are the Canadian lynx, red fox, and red western bobcat. Smaller native mammals—western fisher, raccoon, muskrat, porcupine, marten, and mink—are plentiful. The whistler (hoary) marmot is the largest rodent. Game birds include the ruffed grouse, bobwhite quail, and ring-necked pheasant. Sixteen varieties of owl have been identified; other birds of prey include the prairie falcon, sparrow hawk, and golden eagle. The bald eagle is more numerous in Washington than in any other state except Alaska. Washington is also a haven for marsh, shore, and water birds.

Various salmon species thrive in coastal waters and along the Columbia River, and the octopus, hair seal, and sea lion inhabit Puget Sound. Many of the state's wetlands (covering about 2% of the land area) serve as nurseries and feeding sites for steelhead trout as well as salmon.

Animals driven away from the slopes of Mt. St. Helen's by the volcanic eruption in 1980 have largely returned; more than 25 species of mammals and over 100 species of birds have been observed inhabiting the mountain again. The number of elk and deer in the vicinity was roughly the same as prior to the eruption although the mountain goat population reportedly had been killed off. Earlier, on 17 August 1982, the Mt. St. Helen's National Volcanic Monument was created by an act of Congress; it includes about 110,000 acres (44,500 hectares) of the area that had been devastated by the original eruption.

In April 2006, 27 animal species (vertebrates and invertebrates) were listed as threatened or endangered in Washington, including the Columbian white-tailed deer, woodland caribou, short-tailed albatross, brown pelican, pygmy rabbit, humpback whale, eight species of salmon, and two species (green and leatherback) of sea turtle.

5 ENVIRONMENTAL PROTECTION

The mission of the Department of Ecology (established in 1970) is to protect, preserve, and enhance Washington's environment and promote the wise management of its air, land, and water for the benefit of current and future generations. To fulfill this mission,

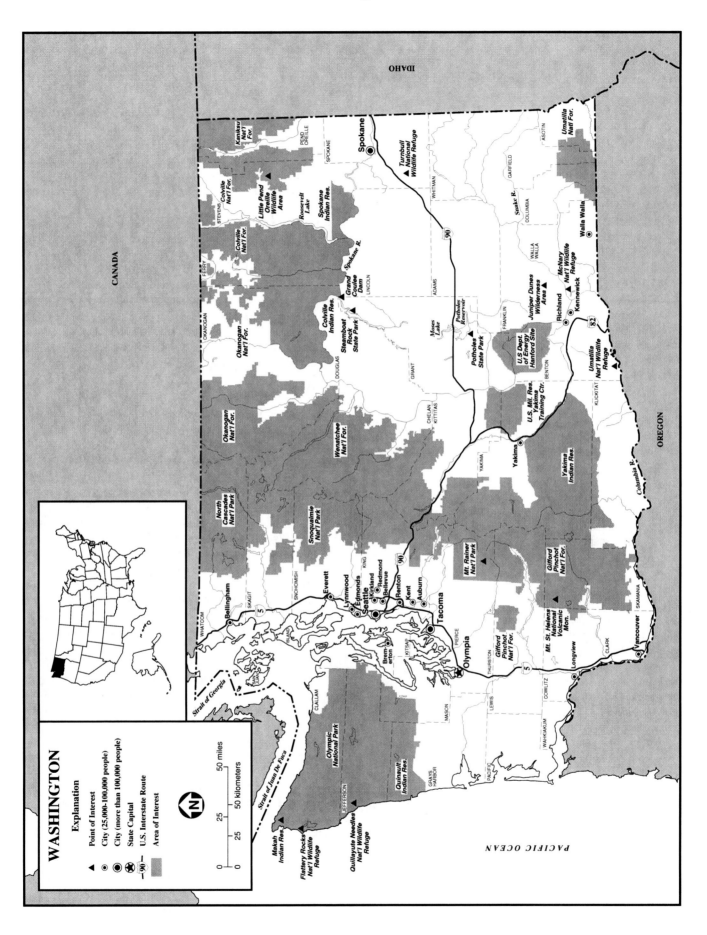

the Department of Ecology: administers permit and authorization programs which ensure that pollutant discharges, waste management and cleanup, and resource uses are properly controlled; provides technical assistance on pollution control or resource development issues; and provides financial assistance through grant and loan programs to local governments for waste water and solid waste facilities. The Department of Ecology also reviews federal and state actions and plans for consistency with state laws and regulations for natural resource protection, maintains an ongoing program to monitor the quality of air and water resources, hazardous waste management, and toxic and nuclear cleanup actions; and reviews local government-permitting actions relating to the state's shorelands and to solid waste facilities. Furthermore, the Department of Ecology directly administers an automobile inspection program for the Seattle, Vancouver (Washington), and Spokane areas, an Estuarine Sanctuary program at Padilla Bay, the Conservation Corps employment program, and the Youth Corps litter control program.

Among other state agencies with environmental responsibilities are the State Conservation Commission, Environmental Hearings Office, State Parks and Recreation Commission, Department of Health, Department of Fish and Wildlife, and Department of Natural Resources.

Principal air pollutants in the state are particulate emissions, carbon monoxide, hydrocarbons, lead, and dioxides of nitrogen. Fuel combustion and industrial processes are responsible for most of the first two pollutants, transportation (especially the automobile) for most of the last four. Significant progress has been made since 1988 in reducing the amount of pollutants released to the air. In 1988, the total number of days air quality did not meet health standards was 25. In 1994, the total number of days was 15, and by 1999, the total had been reduced to seven days. In 1990, more than two million people were exposed to air that violated federal standards, but by 1999, the number had been reduced to 112,000.

More than 6,500 sites in Washington are suspected or confirmed to be contaminated with toxic chemicals. At the Hanford Nuclear Site alone, contamination includes 1,500 places where radioactive and chemical wastes were disposed to the soil. From 1990—2002, cleanup was completed (or nearly completed) at a majority of the high-priority sites. In 2003, 22.9 million lb of toxic chemicals were released in the state.

Washington state has one of the highest overall recycling rates in the United States. In the mid-1980s, Bellingham began the state's first curbside recycling collection program. Seattle soon started its own program after being forced to close a municipal landfill and facing fierce opposition to construction of a garbage incinerator. In 1989, the state legislature passed the Waste-Not Washington Act, which defined a clear solid-waste management strategy and set a recycling goal of 50%; while this had not been achieved as of 2003, the rate of 40% was reported in 1995, with 37% reported for 2001. (The national average is 30%.) In 2003, Washington had 236 hazardous waste sites listed in the US Environment Protection Agency (EPA) database, 46 of which were on the National Priorities List as of 2006, including the Bangor Naval Submarine Base, Fairchild Air Force Base, and the Seattle Municipal Landfill. In 2005, the EPA spent over $4.8 million through the Superfund program for the cleanup of hazardous waste sites in the state. The same year, federal EPA grants awarded to the state included

$18.7 million for the clean water state revolving fund. A grant of $208,400 was awarded for assessment and response to the problem of declining oxygen levels in the Hood Canal.

6 POPULATION

Washington ranked 14th in population in the United States with an estimated total of 6,287,759 in 2005, an increase of 6.7% since 2000. Between 1990 and 2000, Washington's population grew from 4,866,692 to 5,894,121, an increase of 21.1%, making it one of the nation's 10 fastest-growing states. The population is projected to reach 6.9 million by 2015 and 7.9 million by 2025. The population density in 2004 was 93.2 persons per sq mi. In 2004 the median age was 36.4. Persons under 18 years old accounted for 24% of the population while 11.3% was age 65 or older.

Most Washingtonians live in the Western Corridor, a broad strip in western Washington running north–south between the Coast and Cascade ranges. The leading city in the Western Corridor is Seattle, with an estimated 2004 population of 571,480. Other leading cities with their 2004 population estimates are Spokane, 196,721; Tacoma, 196,094; Vancouver, 155,053; and Bellevue, 116,914. The Seattle-Tacoma-Bellevue metropolitan area had an estimated 2004 population of 3,166,828.

7 ETHNIC GROUPS

Washington is ethnically and racially heterogeneous. As of 2000, foreign-born Washingtonians made up 10.4% of the state's population (614,457), up from 6.6% in 1990. The largest minority group consists of Hispanics and Latinos, numbering 441,509, or 7.5% of the state population, according to the 2000 census, more than double the 1990 figure of 215,000. In 2004, 8.5% of the total population was Hispanic or Latino. Most of the state's Spanish-speaking residents have arrived since World War II. Black Americans numbered 190,267 in 2000. In 2004, 3.5% of the population was black. Black immigration dates largely from World War II and postwar recruitment for defense-related industries.

Japanese-Americans have been farmers and small merchants in Washington throughout the 20th century. During World War II, the Nisei (Japanese Americans) of Washington were deported to internment camps. Chinese-Americans, imported as laborers in the mid-1800s, endured a wave of mob violence during the 1880s. As of 2000, the Asian population was estimated at 322,335, up from 281,000 in 1996. According to the 1990 census, there were 65,373 Filipinos, 35,985 Japanese, 59,914 Chinese, 46,880 Koreans, and 46,149 Vietnamese, up from 17,004 in 1990. Pacific Islanders numbered 23,953 in 2000, including 8,049 Samoans and 4,883 native Hawaiians. Immigration from Southeast Asia was an important demographic factor during the late 1970s and early 1980s. In 2004, 6.3% of the population was Asian, and 0.5% Native Hawaiian or other Pacific Islander.

There were 93,301 American Indians, Eskimos, and Aleuts living in Washington in 2000, the eighth-highest total in the nation. In 2004, 1.6% of the population was American Indian or Alaskan Native. Indian lands in the state cover some 2.5 million acres (1 million hectares). The Yakama reservation had a population of 31,799 in 2000. A dispute developed in the 1970s over Indian fishing rights in the Puget Sound area; a decision in 1974 by US District Judge George Boldt that two 120-year-old treaties guaranteed the Indians 50% of the salmon catch in certain rivers was essentially upheld by the US Supreme Court in 1979.

In 2004, 2.9% of the population reported origin of two or more races.

8 LANGUAGES

Early settlers took from Chinook jargon some words like *potlatch* (gift-dispensing feast), *skookum* (strong), and *tillicum* (friend). Other language influences came from the many Indian tribes inhabiting Washington, especially such place-names as Chehalis, Walla Walla, Puyallup, Humptulips, and Spokane. Northern and Midland dialects dominate, with Midland strongest in eastern Washington and the Bellingham area, Northern elsewhere. In the urban areas, minor eastern variants have been lost; in rural sections, however, older people have preserved such terms as *johnnycake* (corn bread) and *mouth organ* (harmonica). One survey showed Northern *quarter* to dominant in the state with 81%, with Midland *quarter till* having only a 5% response; Northern *angleworm* (earthworm) had 63%, but Midland *fishworm* and *fishing worm* only 17%. The north coast of the Olympic Peninsula, settled by New Englanders who sailed around Cape Horn, retains New England /ah/ in *glass* and *aunt*. In Seattle, *fog* and *frog* are Midland /fawg/ and /frawg/, but *on* is Northern /ahn/; *cot* and *caught* sound alike, as in Midland; but the final /y/, as in *city* and *pretty,* has the Northern /ee/ sound rather than the Midland short /i/ as in pit.

In 2000, English was the language spoken at home by 86% of Washington residents five years old and older, down from 91% in 1990.

The following table gives selected statistics from the 2000 Census for language spoken at home by persons five years old and over. The category "Other Pacific Island languages" includes Chamorro, Hawaiian, Ilocano, Indonesian, and Samoan. The category "Other Slavic languages" includes Czech, Slovak, and Ukrainian. The category "African languages" includes Amharic, Ibo, Twi, Yoruba, Bantu, Swahili, and Somali. The category "Scandinavian languages" includes Danish, Norwegian, and Swedish.

LANGUAGE	NUMBER	PERCENT
Population 5 years and over	**5,501,398**	**100.0**
Speak only English	4,730,512	86.0
Speak a language other than English	770,886	14.0
Speak a language other than English	**770,886**	**14.0**
Spanish or Spanish Creole	321,490	5.8
Chinese	48,459	0.9
Tagalog	41,674	0.8
Vietnamese	39,829	0.7
German	39,702	0.7
Korean	39,522	0.7
Russian	31,339	0.6
Japanese	24,055	0.4
French (incl. Patois, Cajun)	22,385	0.4
Other Pacific Island languages	16,199	0.3
Other Slavic languages	15,596	0.3
Mon-Khmer, Cambodian	14,559	0.3
African languages	12,420	0.2
Scandinavian languages	10,695	0.2

9 RELIGIONS

First settled by Protestant missionaries, Protestant denominations were only slightly predominant among the religiously active population in 2000. The leading denominations that year were the Church of Jesus Christ of Latter-day Saints (Mormon), 178,000;

Assemblies of God, 105,692; the Evangelical Lutheran Church in America, 127,854; the United Methodist Church, 76,648; and the Presbyterian Church USA, 74,338. In 2004, there were 705,732 Roman Catholics in the state, with about 550,450 belonging to the archdiocese of Seattle. In 2000, there were an estimated 43,500 Jews, and about 15,550 Muslims. Over 3.9 million people (about 67% of the population) were not counted as members of any religious organization.

Aglow International, a Christian women's organization, has its worldwide headquarters in Edmonds. The US office of the World Evangelical Alliance is located in Seattle.

10 TRANSPORTATION

As of 2003, the state of Washington had 3,576 rail mi (5,757 km) of railroad lines. In that same year, farm products were the top commodities carried by rail that terminated in the state, while mixed freight was the top commodity carried by rail that originated in the state. Washington is served by a total of 19 railroads, of which two are Class I lines. As of 2006, Amtrak provided service from Seattle down the coast to Los Angeles, and eastward via Spokane to St. Paul, Minnesota, and Chicago.

As of 2004, Washington had 81,216 mi (130,757 km) of public highways, roads, and streets. Principal interstate highways include I-90, connecting Spokane and Seattle, and I-5, proceeding north–south from Vancouver in British Columbia through Seattle and Tacoma to Vancouver, Washington, and Portland, Oregon. In 2004, the state had 4,504,581 licensed drivers and some 5.623 million registered motor vehicles, including around 3.013 million automobiles.

Washington's principal ports include Seattle, Tacoma, and Anacortes, all part of the Puget Sound area and belonging to the Seattle Customs District. The Ports of Longview, Kalama, and Vancouver, along the Columbia River, are considered part of the Portland (Oregon) Customs District. In 2004, the Port of Seattle handled 23.501 million tons of cargo, while Tacoma handled 26.282 million tons, making them the 37th- and the 30th-busiest ports in the United States, respectively. State-operated ferry systems transported more than 13 million passengers and over 10 million vehicles across Puget Sound annually in the mid-1990s. In 2003, waterborne shipments totaled 106.489 million tons. In 2004, the state of Washington had 1,057 mi (1,701 km) of navigable inland waterways.

In 2005, the state of Washington had a total of 493 public and private-use aviation-related facilities. This included 336 airports, 138 heliports, three STOLports (Short Take-Off and Landing), and 16 seaplane bases. Seattle-Tacoma (SEATAC) International Airport is by far the busiest in the state, with 14,092,285 passengers enplaned in 2004, making it the 16th busiest airport in the United States.

11 HISTORY

The region now known as the State of Washington has been inhabited for at least 9,000 years, the first Americans having crossed the Bering Strait from Asia and entered North America via the Pacific Northwest. Their earliest known remains in Washington—burned bison bones and a human skeleton—date from approximately

7000 BC. Clovis points, a type of arrowhead, have been unearthed and determined to be approximately 30,000 years old.

The Cascades impeded communications between coastal Indians and those of the eastern plateau, and their material cultures evolved somewhat differently. Coastal Indians—belonging mainly to the Nootkin and Salishan language families—lived in a land of plenty, with ample fish, shellfish, roots, and berries. Timber was abundant for the construction of dugout canoes, villages with wooden dwellings, and some stationary wooden furniture. Warfare between villages was fairly common, with the acquisition of slaves the primary objective. The coastal Indians also emphasized rank based on wealth, through such institutions as the potlatch, a gigantic feast with extravagant exchanges of gifts. The plateau (or "horse") Indians, on the other hand, paid little attention to class distinctions. Social organization was simpler and intertribal warfare less frequent than on the coast. After the horse reached Washington around 1730, the plateau tribes (mainly of the Shahaptian language group) became largely nomadic, traveling long distances in search of food. Housing was portable, often taking the form of skin or mat teepees. In winter, circular pit houses were dug for protection from the wind and snow.

The first Europeans known to have sailed along the Washington coast were 18th-century Spaniards; stories of earlier voyages to the area by Sir Francis Drake in 1579 and Juan de Fuca in 1592 are largely undocumented. In 1774, Juan Pérez explored the northwestern coastline to the southern tip of Alaska; an expedition led by Bruno Heceta and his assistant, Juan Francisco de la Bodega y Quadra, arrived a year later. Men from this expedition made the first known landing on Washington soil, at the mouth of the Hoh River, but the venture ended in tragedy when the Indians seized the landing boat and killed the Spaniards.

English captain James Cook, on his third voyage of exploration, arrived in the Pacific Northwest in 1778 while searching for a northwest passage across America. He was the first of numerous British explorers and traders to be attracted by the luxuriant fur of the sea otter. Cook was followed in 1792 by another Englishman, George Vancouver, who mapped the Pacific coast and the Puget Sound area. In the same year, an American fur trader and explorer, Captain Robert Gray, discovered the mouth of the Columbia River. As the maritime fur trade began to prosper, overland traders moved toward the Northwest, the most active organizations being the British Hudson's Bay Company and the Canadian North West Company.

American interest in the area also increased. Several US maritime explorers had already visited the Northwest when President Thomas Jefferson commissioned an overland expedition to inspect the territory acquired from France through the Louisiana Purchase (1803). That expedition, led by Meriwether Lewis and William Clark, first sighted the Pacific Ocean in early November 1805 from the north bank of the Columbia River in what is now Pacific County. In time, as reports of the trip became known, a host of British and American fur traders followed portions of their route to the Pacific coast, and the interest of missionaries was excited. In 1831, a delegation visited Clark in St. Louis, Missouri, where he was then superintendent of Indian affairs, to persuade him to send teachers who could instruct the Indians in the Christian religion. When news of the visit became known, there was an immediate response from the churches.

The first missionaries to settle in Washington were Marcus and Narcissa Whitman, representing the Protestant American Board of Missions; their settlement, at Waiilatpu in southeastern Washington (near present-day Walla Walla), was established in 1836. Although the early Protestant missions had scant success in converting the Indians, the publicity surrounding their activities encouraged other Americans to journey to the Pacific Northwest, and the first immigrant wagons arrived at Waiilatpu in 1840. The Indian population became increasingly hostile to the missionaries, however, and on 29 November 1847, Marcus and Narcissa Whitman and 12 other Americans were massacred.

As early as 1843, an American provisional government had been established, embracing the entire Oregon country and extending far into the area that is now British Columbia, Canada. Three years later, after considerable military and diplomatic maneuvering, a US-Canada boundary along the 49th parallel was established by agreement with the British. Oregon Territory, including the present state of Washington, was organized in 1848. In the early 1850s, residents north of the Columbia River petitioned Congress to create a separate "Columbia Territory." The new territorial status was granted in 1853, but at the last minute the name of the territory (which embraced part of present-day Idaho) was changed to Washington.

President Franklin Pierce appointed Isaac I. Stevens as the first territorial governor. Stevens, who served at the same time as a US superintendent of Indian affairs, negotiated a series of treaties with the Northwest Indian tribes, establishing a system of reservations. Although the Indian situation had long been tense, it worsened after the treaties were concluded, and bloody uprisings by the Yakima, Nisqualli, and Cayuse were not suppressed until the late 1850s. Court battles over fishing rights spelled out in those treaties were not substantially resolved until 1980.

On the economic front, discoveries of gold in the Walla Walla area, in British Columbia, and in Idaho brought prosperity to the entire region. The completion in 1883 of the Northern Pacific Railroad line from the eastern United States to Puget Sound encouraged immigration, and Washington's population, only 23,955 in 1870, swelled to 357,232 by 1890. In the political sphere, Washington was an early champion of women's suffrage. The territorial legislature granted women the vote in 1883; however, the suffrage acts were pronounced unconstitutional in 1887.

Cattle and sheep raising, farming, and lumbering were all established by the time Washington became the 42d state in 1889. The Populist movement of the 1890s found fertile soil in Washington, and the financial panic of 1893 further stimulated radical labor and Granger activity. In 1896, the Fusionists—a coalition of Populists, Democrats, and Silver Republicans—swept the state. The discovery of gold in the Klondike, for which Seattle was the primary departure point, helped dim the Fusionists' prospects, and for the next three decades the Republican Party dominated state politics.

In 1909 Seattle staged the Alaska-Yukon-Pacific Exposition, celebrating the Alaska gold rush and Seattle's new position as a major seaport. World War I brought the state several major new military installations, and the Puget Sound area thrived as a shipbuilding center. The war years also saw the emergence of radical labor activities, especially in the shipbuilding and logging industries. Seattle was the national headquarters of the Industrial Workers of the World (IWW) and became, in 1919, the scene of the first general strike in the United States, involving about 60,000 workers. The towns of Centralia and Everett were the sites of violent conflict between the IWW and conservative groups.

Washington's economy was in dire straits during the depression of the 1930s, when the market for forest products and field crops tumbled. The New Deal era brought numerous federally funded public works projects, notably the Bonneville and Grand Coulee dams on the Columbia River, providing hydroelectric power for industry and water for the irrigation of desert lands. Eventually, more than one million acres (400,000 hectares) were reclaimed for agricultural production. During World War II, Boeing led the way in establishing the aerospace industry as Washington's primary employer. Also during the war, the federal government built the Hanford Reservation nuclear research center; the Hanford plant was one of the major contractors in the construction of the first atomic bomb and later became a pioneer producer of atomic-powered electricity.

In 1962, "Century 21," the Seattle World's Fair, again promoted the area as the Alaska-Yukon-Pacific Exposition had a half-century earlier. The exhibition left Seattle a number of buildings—including the Space Needle and Coliseum—that have since been converted into a civic and performing arts center. The 1960s and 1970s, a period of rapid population growth (with Seattle and the Puget Sound area leading the way), also witnessed an effort by government and industry to reconcile the needs of an expanding economy with an increasing public concern for protection of the state's unique natural heritage. An unforeseen environmental hazard emerged in May 1980 with the eruption of Mt. St. Helens and the resultant widespread destruction.

Washington experienced a deep recession in 1979. The industries of logging and lumber, which lost market share to mills in the Southeast and in Canada, were particularly hard hit. Employment in wood products dropped 30% between 1978 and 1982. Nuclear waste also became an issue with the publication of a study in 1985 claiming that plutonium produced at the Hanford bomb fuel facility had leaked into the nearby Columbia River. This claim was confirmed in 1990 by the federal government, which, together with the state, started a cleanup program. The state's economy, strengthened by the expansion of Microsoft Corporation, Boeing, and Weyerhauser Paper in the 1980s, was still hampered by falling agricultural prices and weakness in the timber industry.

Speaker of the House Tom Foley, a Democrat and 30-year Congressional veteran, lost his House seat in the 1994 mid-term elections in which Republicans prevailed in seven of the state's nine Congressional districts.

Washingtonian Gary Locke, a Democrat, was elected the nation's first governor of Chinese heritage in 1996; he won reelection in 2000. Under his administration, the state raised education spending by $1 billion. Locke also signed a welfare reform bill that reduced the number of recipients by one-third. Locke chose not to run for a third term. Christine Gregoire, former Washington attorney general, was elected governor in 2004. In 2005, Gregoire announced Washington's six regional salmon recovery plans were submitted to the federal government. The first listings of salmon in Washington under the federal Endangered Species Act were made in 1991, and within eight years more than 75% of the state had salmon populations listed.

12 STATE GOVERNMENT

Washington's constitution of 1889, as amended (95 times as of January 2005), continues to govern the state today. The legislative branch consists of a Senate of 49 members elected to four-year terms, and a House of Representatives with 98 members serving two-year terms. Legislators assemble annually in January, meeting for a maximum of 105 calendar days in odd-numbered years and 60 calendar days in even-numbered years. Special sessions, which are limited to 30 calendar days, may be called by a two-thirds vote of the members in each house. Legislators must be US citizens at least 18 years old and qualified voters in their districts. The legislative salary in 2004 was $34,227.

Executives elected statewide are the governor and lieutenant governor (who run separately), secretary of state, treasurer, attorney general, auditor, superintendent of public education, and officers of insurance and public land. The governor and lieutenant governor and serve four-year terms. Candidates for these offices must be US citizens, qualified voters, state residents, and at least 18 years old. As of December 2004, the governor's salary was $139,087.

A bill becomes law if passed by a majority of the elected members of each house and then signed by the governor or left unsigned for five days while the legislature is in session or 20 days after it has adjourned. A two-thirds vote of members present in each house is sufficient to override a gubernatorial veto. Constitutional amendments require a two-thirds vote of the legislature and ratification by the voters at the next general election.

Voters in Washington must be US citizens, at least 18 years old, and residents of the state, their county, and their precinct for at least 30 days prior to election day. Restrictions apply to those convicted of certain crimes and to those judged by the court as mentally incompetent to vote.

13 POLITICAL PARTIES

Washington never went for a full-fledged Democrat in a presidential election until 1932, when Franklin D. Roosevelt won the first of four successive victories in the state. Until then, Washington had generally voted Republican, the lone exceptions being 1896, when the state's Populist voters carried Washington for William Jennings Bryan, and 1912, when a plurality of the voters chose Theodore Roosevelt on the Progressive ticket.

The rise of the Democratic Party after World War II was linked to the careers of two US senators—Henry Jackson, who held his seat from 1953 until his death in 1983, and Warren Magnuson, defeated in 1980 after serving since 1945.

During the 1970s and 1980s the state tended to favor Republicans in presidential elections, but Democrats more than held their own in other contests. Washingtonians elected a Democratic governor, Dixy Lee Ray, in 1976, but in 1980 they chose a Republican, John Spellman; in 1984, they returned to the Democratic column, electing Booth Gardner. Mike Lowry, also a Democrat, was elected governor in 1992. He was succeeded, in 1997, by fellow Democrat Gary Locke. Locke was reelected in 2000, but in 2003, announced he would not seek reelection in 2004. Democrat Christine Gregoire won the office in 2004.

In November 2000, Democrat Maria Cantwell was elected to the US Senate. Washington's other senator, Democrat Patty Murray, was elected to a third term in 2004. A stunning Republican victory in the 1994 mid-term elections saw, for the first time since 1860, a sitting Speaker of the US House of Representatives, Thomas S. Foley, lose his seat in the House. The winner was a little-known Republican, George Nethercutt, who called for change and received support from conservative national talk show hosts and former presidential candidate Ross Perot. Nethercutt was reelected in 1996, 1998, 2000, and 2002. Following the 2004 elections, three of Washington's nine US Representatives were Republicans; the other six were Democrats. There were 23 Republicans and 26 Democrats serving in the state Senate, and 55 Democrats and 43 Republicans in the state House in mid-2005.

Democratic candidate Al Gore received 50% of Washington's popular vote in the 2000 presidential election; Republican George W. Bush received 45%, and Green Party candidate Ralph Nader garnered 4%. In 2004, Democrat John Kerry won 53% of the vote to 46% for the incumbent Bush. In 2004 there were 2,884,000 registered voters; there is no party registration in the state. The state had 11 electoral votes in the 2004 presidential election.

¹⁴LOCAL GOVERNMENT

As of 2005, Washington had 39 counties, 279 municipal governments, 296 public school districts, and 1,173 special districts, including public utility, library, port, water, hospital, cemetery, and sewer districts.

Counties may establish their own institutions of government by charter; otherwise, the chief governing body is an elected board of commissioners. Other elected officials generally include the sheriff, prosecuting attorney, coroner, auditor, treasurer, and clerk. Cities and towns are governed under the mayor-council or coun-

cil-manager systems. Larger cities, Seattle among them, generally have their own charters and elected mayors.

In 2005, local government accounted for about 212,591 full-time (or equivalent) employment positions.

¹⁵STATE SERVICES

To address the continuing threat of terrorism and to work with the federal Department of Homeland Security, homeland security in Washington operates under the authority of the governor; the adjutant general is designated as the state homeland security advisor.

The Public Disclosure Commission, consisting of five members appointed by the governor and confirmed by the Senate, provides disclosure of financial data in connection with political campaigns, lobbyists' activities, and the holdings of elected officials and candidates for public office. Each house of the legislature has its own board of ethics.

Public education in Washington is governed by a Board of Education and superintendent of public instruction; the Higher Education Coordinating Board coordinates the state's higher educational institutions. The Department of Transportation oversees the construction and maintenance of highways, bridges, and ferries and assists locally owned airports.

The Department of Social and Health Services, the main human resources agency, oversees programs for adult corrections, juvenile rehabilitation, public and mental health, Medicaid, nursing homes, income maintenance, and vocational rehabilitation. Also involved in human resources activities are the Human Rights Commission, Department of Labor and Industries, Employment Security Department, and the Department of Veterans Affairs.

Washington Presidential Vote by Political Parties, 1948–2004

YEAR	ELECTORAL VOTE	WASHINGTON WINNER	DEMOCRAT	REPUBLICAN	PROGRESSIVE	SOCIALIST	PROHIBITION	SOC. LABOR	CONSTITUTION
1948	8	*Truman (D)	476,165	386,315	31,692	3,534	6,117	1,113	—
1952	9	*Eisenhower (R)	492,845	599,107	2,460	—	—	633	7,290
1956	9	*Eisenhower (R)	523,002	620,430	—	—	—	7,457	
1960	9	Nixon (R)	599,298	629,273	—	—	—	10,895	1,401
1964	9	*Johnson (D)	779,699	470,366	—	—	—	7,772	—
					PEACE AND FREEDOM		**AMERICAN IND.**		
1968	9	Humphrey (D)	616,037	588,510	1,669	—	96,900	491	—
					PEOPLE'S	**LIBERTARIAN**			**AMERICAN**
1972	9	*Nixon (R)	568,334	837,135	2,644	1,537	—	1,102	58,906
1976	9	Ford (R)	717,323	777,732	1,124	5,042	8,585	—	5,046
					CITIZENS			**SOC. WORKERS**	
1980	9	*Reagan (R)	650,193	865,244	9,403	29,213	—	1,137	—
1984	9	*Reagan (R)	807,352	1,051,670	1,891	8,844	—	—	—
					NEW ALLIANCE		**WORKER'S**		
1988	9	Dukakis (D)	933,516	903,835	3,520	17,240	1,440	1,290	—
					IND. (Perot)		**TAXPAYERS**	**NATURAL LAW**	**POPULIST**
1992	11	*Clinton (D)	993,037	731,234	541,780	7,533	2,354	2,456	4,854
							IND. (Nader)		
1996	11	*Clinton (D)	1,123,323	840,712	201,003	12,522	60,322	—	—
					FREEDOM (Buchanan)		**GREEN (Nader)**		
2000	11	Gore (D)	1,247,652	1,108,864	7,171	13,135	103,002	2,927	—
					CONSTITUTION (Peroutka)		**IND. (Nader)**	**GREEN (Cobb)**	**WORKERS (Parker)**
2004	11	Kerry (D)	1,510,201	1,304,894	3,922	11,955	23,283	2,974	1,077

*Won US presidential election.

Public protection services are provided by the Washington State Patrol, the Division of Emergency Management (civil defense), and the Military Department (Army and Air National Guard).

16 JUDICIAL SYSTEM

The state's highest court, the Supreme Court, consists of nine justices serving six-year terms. Three justices are elected by nonpartisan ballot in each even-numbered year. The Chief Justice is elected to a four-year term by members of the court. The courts' senior judge holds the title of associate chief justice. Appeals of superior court decisions are usually heard in the court of appeals, whose 21 judges are elected to staggered six-year terms. The superior courts are the state's felony trial courts. There are 176 district and municipal courts; they hear traffic and misdemeanor matters.

As of 31 December 2004, a total of 16,614 prisoners were held in the state of Washington's state and federal prisons, an increase from 16,148 of 2.9% from the previous year. As of year-end 2004, a total of 1,330 inmates were female, up from 1,288 or 3.3% from the year before. Among sentenced prisoners (one year or more), the state of Washington had an incarceration rate of 264 per 100,000 population in 2004.

According to the Federal Bureau of Investigation, Washington state in 2004, had a violent crime rate (murder/nonnegligent manslaughter; forcible rape; robbery; aggravated assault) of 343.8 reported incidents per 100,000 population, or a total of 21,330 reported incidents. Crimes against property (burglary; larceny/theft; and motor vehicle theft) in that same year totaled 300,837 reported incidents or 4,849.2 reported incidents per 100,000 people. Washington has a death penalty which allows the condemned the option of lethal injection or hanging. From 1976 through 5 May 2006, the state has carried out four executions, the most recent taking place in August 2001. As of 1 January 2006, Washington had 10 inmates on death row.

In 2003, the state of Washington spent $381,988,278 on homeland security, an average of $61 per state resident.

17 ARMED FORCES

In 2004, there were 37,906 active-duty military personnel and 23,433 civilian personnel stationed in Washington, nearly half of whom were at Fort Lewis near Tacoma. Other chief facilities in Washington include a Trident nuclear submarine base at Bangor, Whidbey Island Naval Air Station, McChord Air Force Base (Tacoma), and Fairchild Air Force Base (Airway Heights). In 2004, federal defense contract awards totaled more than $3.3 billion, and defense payroll outlays were $5.3 billion.

In 2003, there were 632,929 veterans living in Washington, of whom 69,756 saw service during World War II; 55,166 in the Korean conflict; 205,783 during the Vietnam era; and 109,183 in the Persian Gulf War. In 2004, the Veterans Administration expended more than $1.6 billion in pensions, medical assistance, and other major veterans' benefits.

In 2004, the Washington State Patrol employed 1,054 full-time sworn officers.

18 MIGRATION

The first overseas immigrants to reach Washington were Chinese laborers, imported during the 1860s; Chinese continued to arrive into the 1880s, when mob attacks on Chinese homes forced the territorial government to put Seattle under martial law and call in federal troops to restore order. The 1870s and 1880s brought an influx of immigrants from western Europe—especially Germany, Scandinavia, and the Netherlands—and from Russia and Japan.

In recent decades, Washington has benefited from a second migratory wave even more massive than the first. From 1970 to 1980, the state ranked seventh among the states in net migration with a gain of 719,000. From 1985 to 1990, the net migration gain was 317,832 (sixth among the states). Many of those new residents were drawn from other states by Washington's defense- and trade-related industries. In addition, many immigrants from Southeast Asia arrived during the late 1970s. Between 1990 and 1998, Washington had net gains of 374,000 in domestic migration and 121,000 in international migration. In 1996, the foreign-born population totaled 386,000, or 7% of the state's total population. In 1998, 16,920 immigrants from foreign countries entered Washington, the seventh-highest total of any state for that year. Of that total, 4,129 came from Mexico, 1,159 from the Philippines, and 940 from Vietnam. In the period 2000–05, net international migration was 134,242 and net internal migration was 80,974, for a net gain of 215,216 people.

19 INTERGOVERNMENTAL COOPERATION

Washington participates in the Columbia River Gorge Compact (with Oregon), Pacific States Marine Fisheries Commission, Western Interstate Corrections Compact, Western Interstate Energy Compact, Western Interstate Commission for Higher Education, Northwest Power and Conservation Council (with Idaho, Montana, and Oregon), Interstate Compact for the Supervision of Parolees and Probationers, Agreement on Qualification of Educational Personnel, Interstate Compact on Placement of Children, Multistate Tax Compact, and Driver License Compact, among other interstate bodies. The state has one boundary compact with Oregon. Federal grants in fiscal year 2001 totaled over $6.7 billion. Mirroring a national trend, that figure declined to $6.213 billion in fiscal year 2005, an estimated $6.232 billion in fiscal year 2006, and an estimated $6.414 billion in fiscal year 2007.

20 ECONOMY

The mainstays of Washington's economy are services, financial institutions, manufacturing (especially aerospace equipment, shipbuilding, food processing, and wood products), agriculture, lumbering, and tourism. Between 1971 and 1984, employment increased in such sectors as lumber and wood products, metals and machinery, food processing, trade, services, and government, while decreasing in aerospace, which remains, nevertheless, the state's single leading industry. The eruption of Mt. St. Helens in 1980 had an immediate negative impact on the forestry industry, already clouded by a slowdown in housing construction, crop growing, and the tourist trade. Foreign trade, especially with Canada and Japan, was an important growth sector during the 1990s. Leading manufacturers have been the Boeing Aerospace Co. and Microsoft, Inc, although Boeing moved its headquarters to Chicago in 2001. In the 1990s, state economic growth was robust, with annual rates soaring to 9.6% in 1998 and 8.6% in 1999, before moderating to 4.6% in 2000. However, the driving forces in Washington's economy, the high-tech computer and aerospace sectors, became the main source of its troubles after the collapse of the dot.com bubble on the stock market in 2001 and after the terrorist attacks on the United States on 11 September 2001. Growth fell to 2.2% in 2001, and by the end of 2002, all sectors except government and financial services (including insurance and real estate) had lost jobs. In December 2002, Washington's unemployment rate of 6.8% was higher than all states except its neighbor, Oregon, and Alaska. Already having problems before 9/11, Boeing cut its workforce 18% in 2002, announcing plans to cut more jobs and/or relocate its operations out of Washington. In addition, Spokane continued to suffer the adverse effects of the bankruptcy of Kaiser Aluminum. But it was the job losses in the high-paid dot. com, high-tech, and aerospace sectors that had disproportionate impacts on personal income in Washington.

In 2004, Washington's gross state product (GSP) was $261.546 billion, of which the real estate sector accounted for the largest share at $38.797 billion or 14.8% of GSP, followed by manufacturing (durable and nondurable goods) at $22.955 billion (8.7% of GSP), and health care and social assistance at $17.182 billion (6.5% of GSP). In that same year, there were an estimated 529,863 small businesses in the state of Washington. Of the 198,635 businesses that had employees, an estimated total of 194,951 or 98.1% were small companies. An estimated 31,955 new businesses were established in the state in 2004, down 11.6% from the year before. Business terminations that same year came to 47,141, up 33.4% from 2003. There were 665 business bankruptcies in 2004, down 9.8% from the previous year. In 2005, the state's personal bankruptcy (Chapter 7 and Chapter 13) filing rate was 656 filings per 100,000 people, ranking the state of Washington as the 16th highest in the nation.

21 INCOME

In 2005 Washington had a gross state product (GSP) of $269 billion which accounted for 2.2% of the nation's gross domestic product and placed the state at number 14 in highest GSP among the 50 states and the District of Columbia.

According to the Bureau of Economic Analysis, in 2004 Washington had a per capita personal income (PCPI) of $35,041. This ranked 13th in the United States and was 106% of the national average of $33,050. The 1994–2004 average annual growth rate of PCPI was 4.3%. Washington had a total personal income (TPI) of $217,503,197,000, which ranked 15th in the United States and reflected an increase of 7.9% from 2003. The 1994–2004 average annual growth rate of TPI was 5.8%. Earnings of persons employed in Washington increased from $157,846,074,000 in 2003 to $167,346,671,000 in 2004, an increase of 6.0%. The 2003–04 national change was 6.3%.

The US Census Bureau reports that the three-year average median household income for 2002 to 2004 in 2004 dollars was $48,688 compared to a national average of $44,473. During the same period an estimated 11.7% of the population was below the poverty line as compared to 12.4% nationwide.

22 LABOR

According to the Bureau of Labor Statistics (BLS), in April 2006 the seasonally adjusted civilian labor force in Washington 3,346,700, with approximately 157,700 workers unemployed, yielding an unemployment rate of 4.7%, compared to the national average of 4.7% for the same period. Preliminary data for the same period placed nonfarm employment at 2,859,000. Since the beginning of the BLS data series in 1976, the highest unemployment rate recorded in Washington was 12.2% in November 1982. The historical low was 4.6% in March 2006. Preliminary nonfarm employment data by occupation for April 2006 showed that approximately 6.7% of the labor force was employed in construction; 9.9% in manufacturing; 19% in trade, transportation, and public utilities; 5.5% in financial activities; 11.6% in professional and business services; 11.8% in education and health services; 9.5% in leisure and hospitality services; and 18.4% in government.

Although state and federal authorities suppressed radical labor activities in the mines around the turn of the century, in the logging camps during World War I, and in Seattle in 1919, the impulse to unionize remained strong in Washington. The state's labor force is still one of the most organized in the United States although (in line with national trends) the unions' share of the non-farm work force declined from 45% in 1970 to 34% in 1980.

The BLS reported that in 2005, a total of 523,000 of Washington's 2,746,000 employed wage and salary workers were formal members of a union. This represented 19.1% of those so employed, down slightly from 19.3% in 2004, but still well above the national average of 12%. Overall in 2005, a total of 559,000 workers (20.4%) in Washington were covered by a union or employee association contract, which includes those workers who reported no union affiliation. Washington is one of 28 states that do not have a right-to-work law.

As of 1 March 2006, Washington had a state-mandated minimum wage of $7.63 per hour. As of 1 January 2001, the state's minimum wage rate is required to be annually adjusted for inflation based upon the consumer price index for urban and clerical wage earners for the previous year. In 2004, women in the state accounted for 46% of the employed civilian labor force.

23 AGRICULTURE

Orchard and field crops dominate Washington's agricultural economy, which yielded nearly $5.7 billion in farm marketings in 2005, 13th among the 50 states. Fruits and vegetables are raised in the humid and irrigated areas of the state while wheat and other grains grow in the drier central and eastern regions.

Washington is the nation's leading producer of apples. The estimated 2004 crop, representing 58% of the US total, totaled 5.9 million tons. Among leading varieties, delicious apples ranked first, followed by golden delicious and winesap. The state also ranked first in production of hops, red raspberries, pears, and cherries; and second in grapes and apricots. Other preliminary crop figures for 2004 included wheat, 143.5 million bushels, valued at $518.6 million; potatoes, 93,810,000 hundredweight, $453.3 million; barley, 17.2 million bushels, $33.4 million; and corn for grain, 21 million bushels, $60.9 million. Sugar beets, peaches, and various seed crops are also grown in Washington.

24 ANIMAL HUSBANDRY

In 2005, Washington's farms and ranches had 1.08 million cattle and calves, valued at $1.2 billion. During 2004, the state had approximately 26,000 hogs and pigs, valued at $3.1 million. The state produced 4.6 million lb (2.1 million kg) of sheep and lambs in 2003, which brought in $4.7 million in gross income.

Washington dairy farmers had 245,000 milk cows that produced 5.58 billion lb (2.5 billion kg) of milk in 2003. Poultry farmers sold 8.2 million lb (3.7 million kg) of chicken, and produced 1.31 billion eggs, valued at $70.4 million.

25 FISHING

In 2004, Washington's commercial fish catch was 454.7 million lb (206.7 million kg) valued at approximately $175 million, representing the fourth largest catch in quantity and the fifth highest in value nationwide. Oyster landings in 2004 amounted to over 9.5 million lb (4.3 million kg), 82% of the Pacific region's total. Most production of farm-raised oysters occurs in Washington although there are some smaller operations in the other Pacific coastal states. The dungeness crab catch reached 14.9 million lb (6.8 million kg), the largest in the nation. The salmon catch was marked as the second largest in the nation with 26.9 million lb (12.3 million kg) valued at $16.6 million.

Westport, Ilwaco-Chinook, and Bellingham are the major ports. In 2003, there were 67 processing and 146 wholesale plants in the state, with about 4,537 employees. In 2002, the commercial fishing fleet had 329 boats and 695 vessels.

In 2004, 59 trout farms sold 4 million lb (1.8 million kg), valued at nearly $4 million. In 2004, Washington issued 691,191 fishing licenses. There are ten national fish hatcheries in the state.

26 FORESTRY

Washington's forests, covering 21,300,000 acres (8,620,000 hectares), are an important commercial and recreational resource. Some 17,347,000 acres (7,020,000 hectares) are classified as commercial forestland. The largest federal forests are Wenatchee, Mt. Baker–Snoqualmie, and Okanogan.

Forest production is one of Washington's major manufacturing industries. In 2004, lumber production totaled 5.23 billion board ft (second in the United States), 10.6% of national production.

Restrictions on federal timberlands to protect the Northern spotted owl, which became effective in late 1990, reflect diverse public demands on forest values. The regulations impact Washington's forest industry and forest-based employment due to the sharp decline of federal timber supply. However, this scarcity of timber created by forest preservation practices will enhance the value of the state's timber resource. This will spur the trend toward more efficient wood use and higher value-added products.

Public ownership accounts for about 56% of Washington's forest, with the remaining 44% owned by the forest industry and other private owners. Lumber and plywood, logs for export, various chip products, pulp logs, and shakes and shingles are leading forest commodities. The largest forest industry company is Weyerhauser, with headquarters in Tacoma.

Since 1975, more acres have been planted or seeded than have been cut down. Washington's forest-fire control program covers some 12.5 million acres (5.1 million hectares). Leading causes of forest fires in lands under the jurisdiction of the Department of Natural Resources are (in order of frequency) burning debris, lightning, recreation, children, smokers, incendiary logging, and railroad operations.

27 MINING

According to preliminary data from the US Geological Survey (USGS), the estimated value of nonfuel mineral production by Washington in 2003 was $430 million, a decrease from 2002 of about 1.5%. The USGS data ranked the state of Washington as 31st among the 50 states by the total value of its nonfuel mineral production, accounting for over 1% of total US output.

According to the preliminary data for 2003, construction sand and gravel, portland cement, crushed stone and diatomite were the state's top nonfuel minerals by value. Collectively, these four commodities accounted for around 95% of all nonfuel mineral output, followed by lime and industrial sand and gravel. Nationally by volume, Washington in 2003, was second (among two states) in the production of olivine, fourth (among four) in diatomite, and seventh in the output of construction sand and gravel.

Preliminary figures for 2003 showed that 42 million metric tons of construction sand and gravel valued at $218 million were produced, with crushed stone output at 13.4 million metric tons, and with a value of $79.1 million.

The 2003 data showed no output of gold and silver.

28 ENERGY AND POWER

As of 2003, the state of Washington had 68 electrical power service providers, of which 41 were publicly owned and 18 were cooperatives. Of the remainder, three were investor owned, one was federally operated, one was the owner of an independent generator that sold directly to customers, three were energy-only suppliers and one was a delivery-only provider. As of that same year there were 2,895,063 retail customers. Of that total, 1,302,818 received their power from investor-owned service providers. Cooperatives accounted for 145,935 customers, while publicly owned providers had 1,446,284 customers. There were nine federal customers, one independent generator or "facility" customer, and 16 energy-only supplier customers. There was no data on the number of delivery-only providers.

Total net summer generating capability by the state's electrical generating plants in 2003 stood at 27.689 million kW, with total production that same year at 100.094 billion kWh. Of the total amount generated, 82.1% came from electric utilities, with the remainder coming from independent producers and combined heat and power service providers. The largest portion of all electric power generated, 71.756 billion kWh (71.7%), came from hydroelectric facilities, with coal-fired plants in second place at 11.089 billion kWh (11.1%) and nuclear fueled plants in third at 7.614 billion kWh (7.6%). Other renewable power sources accounted for 2.2% of all power generated, with natural gas fired plants at 7.1%. Petroleum fueled plants and generating facilities using other types of gasses accounted for the remaining output.

As of 2006, Washington had one operating nuclear plant, the single-unit Columbia Generating Station in Benton County.

Washington in 2004, had only one producing coal mine, a surface mining operation. Coal production that year totaled 5,653,000 short tons, down from 6,232,000 short tons in 2003. One short ton equals 2,000 lb (0.907 metric tons). Almost all of the coal mined in the state was burned to generate electricity.

As of 2005, Washington had five petroleum refineries with combined production of 616,150 barrels per day. However, the state has no proven reserves or production of crude oil and natural gas.

Washington is one of the beneficiaries of the hydropower system owned by various federal entities and marketed by Bonneville Power Administration. While this results in both low power costs and the lowest power-related air emissions per capita of any state, there are associated responsibilities to ensure protection and preservation of fish.

29 INDUSTRY

The 1990s were Washington's busiest years in terms of technology company start-ups. Software and computer-related businesses accounted for most of the activity but more traditional manufacturing companies were also emerging. Computers, software, and related activities make up the largest single portion of Washington's technology companies although manufacturing of all types is strong in the state.

Washington technology companies cross borders and many are world leaders. Boeing's commercial airplane unit is one of the nation's leading exporters. Microsoft has offices around the world and its products are in use on every continent. However, even small firms benefit from foreign trade and over half of Washington's technology companies are in overseas markets. Aerospace/transportation equipment is the largest industry in Washington state, dominated primarily by Boeing.

The state's biotechnology firms are growing at a phenomenal rate, but many are still in the research and development stage. More than two-thirds are developing products for human health care. Most of the firms not focused on medical treatment are developing products and processes for the state's natural resource sectors: agriculture, food processing, forestry, veterinary medicine, marine industries, and environmental waste cleanup and management.

Washington state is one of the leading film-production states in the United States. Film and video have grown to represent at least a $100- million-a-year industry. Washington state has thousands of film and video businesses which provide jobs for thousands of state residents. Washington film companies make feature films, television movies, TV series or episodes, TV commercials, documentaries, industrial films, and music videos. Out-of-state producers shoot over 100 film and video projects in Washington annually.

According to the US Census Bureau's Annual Survey of Manufactures (ASM) for 2004, Washington's manufacturing sector covered some 19 product subsectors. The shipment value of all products manufactured in the state that same year was $77.664 billion. Of that total, transportation equipment manufacturing accounted for the largest share at $22.700 billion. It was followed by petroleum and coal products manufacturing at $9.751 billion; food manufacturing at $9.539 billion; and computer and electronic product manufacturing at $7.760 billion.

In 2004, a total of 242,483 people in Washington were employed in the state's manufacturing sector, according to the ASM. Of that total, 153,825 were actual production workers. In terms of total employment, the transportation equipment manufacturing industry accounted for the largest portion of all manufacturing employees, with 48,967 (22,164 actual production workers). It was followed by food manufacturing, with 35,817 (27,614 actual production workers); computer and electronic product manufacturing, with 28,726 (9,116 actual production workers); fabricated metal product manufacturing, with 19,101 (14,053 actual production workers); and wood product manufacturing, with 18,796 (15,898 actual production workers).

ASM data for 2004 showed that Washington's manufacturing sector paid $11.179 billion in wages. Of that amount, the transportation equipment manufacturing sector accounted for the largest share at $2.899 billion. It was followed by computer and electronic product manufacturing at $1.814 billion; food manufacturing at $1.123 billion; fabricated metal product manufacturing at $743.488 million; and wood product manufacturing at $691.973 million.

30 COMMERCE

According to the 2002 Census of Wholesale Trade, Washington's wholesale trade sector had sales that year totaling $84.6 billion from 9,670 establishments. Wholesalers of durable goods accounted for 5,731 establishments, followed by nondurable goods wholesalers at 3,080 and electronic markets, agents, and brokers accounting for 859 establishments. Sales by durable goods wholesalers in 2002 totaled $36.2 billion, while wholesalers of nondurable goods saw sales of $38.3 billion. Electronic markets, agents, and brokers in the wholesale trade industry had sales of $10.1 billion.

In the 2002 Census of Retail Trade, Washington was listed as having 22,564 retail establishments with sales of $65.2 billion. The leading types of retail businesses by number of establishments were: miscellaneous store retailers (3,091); food and beverage stores (2,982); motor vehicle and motor vehicle parts dealers (2,712); clothing and clothing accessories stores (2,434); and gasoline stations (2,104). In terms of sales, motor vehicle and motor vehicle parts stores accounted for the largest share of retail sales at $15.5 billion, followed by food and beverage stores at $11.1 billion; general merchandise stores at $10.4 billion; and nonstore retailers at $5.4 billion. A total of 296,507 people were employed by the retail sector in Washington that year.

In 2005, exports of goods originating from the state had a value of $37.9 billion, fourth in the United States. The leading exports were aircraft and aircraft parts, machinery, lumber and logs, fish and fish products, grains, motor vehicles and parts, fruits and vegetables, wood pulp, and paper products.

31 CONSUMER PROTECTION

Consumer protection issues in the state of Washington are primarily the responsibility of the Office of the Attorney General, which enforces the state's 1961 Consumer Protection Act through its Consumer Protection Division. The division investigates consumer complaints and, when necessary, seeks court action in connection with retail sales abuses, unfair automobile sales techniques, false advertising, and other fraudulent or deceptive practices, which can involve the recovery of refunds, costs and penalties. The division also seeks to resolve consumer issues through the notification of businesses of written complaints and through mediation. It also provides information to the public on consumer rights, as well as on fraudulent and predatory business activities, and issues alerts when illegal or fraudulent practices target consumers.

Consumer protection is also handled by the state's Department of Agriculture which involves food inspection and labeling, sanitary food handling and storage, and accurate weights and measures.

When dealing with consumer protection issues, the state's Attorney General's Office can initiate civil but not criminal proceedings. The office, through its Public Counsel Unit, appears and represents the public before the state's Utilities and Transportation Commission. The Attorney General's Office also administers consumer protection and education programs, handles formal consumer complaints, and can exercise broad subpoena powers. In antitrust actions, the Attorney General's Office can act on behalf of those consumers who are incapable of acting on their own; initiate damage actions on behalf of the state in state courts; and represent counties, cities and other governmental entities in recovering civil damages under state or federal law.

The Attorney General's Office has its main location in Olympia, with regional offices in Bellingham, Kennewick, Seattle, Spokane, Tacoma, and Vancouver

[32]BANKING

As of June 2005, the state of Washington had 100 insured banks, savings and loans, and saving banks, in addition to 79 state-chartered and 59 federally chartered credit unions (CUs). Excluding the CUs, the Seattle-Tacoma-Bellevue market area accounted for the largest portion of the state's financial institutions and deposits in 2004, with 78 institutions and $58.440 billion in deposits. As of June 2005, CUs accounted for 27.3% of all assets held by all financial institutions in the state, or some $20.562 billion. Banks, savings and loans, and savings banks collectively accounted for the remaining 72.7% or $54.890 billion in assets held.

The state in 2001/02 was experiencing its worst recession since 1980/81. The weak economy caused demand for commercial property to weaken: office and industrial vacancy rates rose sharply from 2000 to 2003, particularly in the Seattle area. However, low interest rates caused a rise in housing prices. But loan delinquency ratios for commercial real estate (CRE) increased in 2002.

The median return on assets (ROA—the measure of earnings in relation to all resources) among insured banks headquartered in Washington improved in the fourth quarter of 2005 to 1.13%up from 1.05% in 2004and 1.06% in 2003. The median net interest margin (the difference between the lower rates offered to savers and the higher rates charged on loans) as of fourth quarter 2005 stood at 4.98%, up from 4.68% in 2004 and 4.59% in 2003.

Regulation of state-chartered banks and other state-chartered financial institutions in the state of Washington is the responsibility of the Department of Financial Institutions.

[33]INSURANCE

Washingtonians held over 1.9 million individual life insurance policies with a total face value of about $235 billion in 2001. Total value for all categories of life insurance (individual, group, and credit) was $409.8 billion. The average coverage amount is $119,000 per policy holder. Death benefits paid that year totaled $912 million.

As of 2003, there were 26 property and casualty and 12 life and health insurance companies domiciled in the state. In 2004, direct premiums for property and casualty insurance totaled over $8.3 billion. That year, there were 29,043 flood insurance policies in force in the state, with a total value of $4.6 billion. About $44.4 million of coverage was held through FAIR plans, which are designed to offer coverage for some natural circumstances, such as wind and hail, in high risk areas.

The Office of the Insurance Commissioner and State Fire Marshal regulates insurance company operations, reviews insurance policies and rates, and examines and licenses agents, and brokers. It also conducts fire safety inspections in hospitals, nursing homes, and other facilities, investigates fires of suspicious origin, and regulates the manufacture, sale, and public display of fireworks.

In 2004, 54% of state residents held employment-based health insurance policies, 5% held individual policies, and 24% were covered under Medicare and Medicaid; 14% of residents were uninsured. In 2003, employee contributions for employment-based health coverage averaged at 11% for single coverage and 22% for family coverage. The state does not offer a health benefits expansion program in connection with the Consolidated Omnibus Budget Reconciliation Act (COBRA, 1986), a health insurance program for those who lose employment-based coverage due to termination or reduction of work hours.

In 2003, there were over 4 million auto insurance policies in effect for private passenger cars. Required minimum coverage includes bodily injury liability of up to $25,000 per individual and $50,000 for all persons injured in an accident, as well as property damage liability of $10,000. In 2003, the average expenditure per vehicle for insurance coverage was $824.46.

[34]SECURITIES

The Spokane Stock Exchange (founded 1897), which specialized in mining stocks, ceased operations in 1991. In 2005, there were 2,440 personal financial advisers employed in the state and 4,780 securities, commodities, and financial services sales agents. In 2004, there were over 194 publicly traded companies within the state, with over 95 NASDAQ companies, 18 NYSE listings, and 3 AMEX listings. In 2006, the state had nine Fortune 500 companies; Costco Wholesale in Issaquah (NASDAQ) ranked first in the state and 28th in the nation with revenues of over $52.9 billion, followed by Microsoft in Redmond (NASDAQ), Weyerhauser in Federal Way (NYSE), Washington Mutual in Seattle (NYSE), Paccar in Bellevue (NASDAQ), and Amazon.com in Seattle (NASDAQ).

[35]PUBLIC FINANCE

Washington's biennial budget is prepared by the Office of Financial Management and submitted by the governor to the legislature for amendment and approval. The fiscal year (FY) runs from 1 July through 30 June.

Fiscal year 2006 general funds were estimated at $13.8 billion for resources and $12.7 billion for expenditures. In fiscal year 2004, federal government grants to Washington were $9.0 billion

Washington—State Government Finances

(Dollar amounts in thousands. Per capita amounts in dollars.)

	AMOUNT	PER CAPITA
Total Revenue	35,085,947	5,652.64
General revenue	25,201,752	4,060.21
Intergovernmental revenue	6,953,519	1,120.27
Taxes	13,895,346	2,238.66
General sales	8,423,160	1,357.04
Selective sales	2,441,440	393.34
License taxes	686,564	110.61
Individual income tax	–	–
Corporate income tax	–	–
Other taxes	2,344,182	377.67
Current charges	2,887,154	465.14
Miscellaneous general revenue	1,465,733	236.14
Utility revenue	–	–
Liquor store revenue	418,142	67.37
Insurance trust revenue	9,466,053	1,525.06
Total expenditure	32,510,057	5,237.64
Intergovernmental expenditure	6,911,826	1,113.55
Direct expenditure	25,598,231	4,124.09
Current operation	16,051,105	2,585.97
Capital outlay	2,577,797	415.30
Insurance benefits and repayments	5,124,437	825.59
Assistance and subsidies	1,091,294	175.82
Interest on debt	753,598	121.41
Exhibit: Salaries and wages	5,405,207	870.82
Total expenditure	32,510,057	5,237.64
General expenditure	27,010,041	4,351.55
Intergovernmental expenditure	6,911,826	1,113.55
Direct expenditure	20,098,215	3,237.99
General expenditures, by function:		
Education	11,211,187	1,806.22
Public welfare	6,422,900	1,034.78
Hospitals	1,376,974	221.84
Health	1,349,741	217.45
Highways	2,000,672	322.33
Police protection	243,188	39.18
Correction	796,810	128.37
Natural resources	608,622	98.05
Parks and recreation	105,935	17.07
Government administration	617,982	99.56
Interest on general debt	753,598	121.41
Other and unallocable	1,522,432	245.28
Utility expenditure	25,072	4.04
Liquor store expenditure	350,507	56.47
Insurance trust expenditure	5,124,437	825.59
Debt at end of fiscal year	15,773,698	2,541.28
Cash and security holdings	66,903,572	10,778.73

Abbreviations and symbols: – zero or rounds to zero; (NA) not available;
(X) not applicable.

SOURCE: *U.S. Census Bureau, Governments Division, 2004 Survey of State Government Finances*, January 2006.

In the fiscal year 2007 federal budget, Washington was slated to receive: $38.2 million for seismic corrections and improvements to a veterans nursing home facility in American Lake; and $15 million to deepen the Columbia River Channel.

36 TAXATION

In 2005, Washington collected $14,840 million in tax revenues or $2,360 per capita, which placed it 17th among the 50 states in per capita tax burden. The national average was $2,192 per capita. Property taxes accounted for 10.7% of the total, sales taxes 61.6%, selective sales taxes 16.8%, and other taxes 10.8%.

As of 1 January 2006, Washington had no state income tax, a distinction it shared with Wyoming, Alaska, Nevada, Florida, Alaska, and South Dakota.

In 2004, state and local property taxes amounted to $6.4 billion or $1,029 per capita. The per capita amount ranks the state 22nd highest nationally. Local governments collected $4,859,729,000 of the total and the state government $1,526,617,000.

Washington taxes retail sales at a rate of 6.50%. In addition to the state tax, local taxes on retail sales can reach as much as 2.40%, making for a potential total tax on retail sales of 8.90%. Food purchased for consumption off-premises is tax exempt. The tax on cigarettes is 202.5 cents per pack, which ranks third among the 50 states and the District of Columbia. Washington taxes gasoline at 31 cents per gallon. This is in addition to the 18.4 cents per gallon federal tax on gasoline.

According to the Tax Foundation, for every federal tax dollar sent to Washington in 2004, Washington citizens received $0.88 in federal spending.

37 ECONOMIC POLICY

The Department of Community, Trade, and Economic Development seeks to promote a healthy state economy and to expand markets for Washington's products. The state has no corporate or personal income tax and no tax on interest, dividends, or capital gains. The department offers a tax credit program for companies that expand or locate in high unemployment areas and issues industrial development bonds with federal tax-exempt status for new capital construction. It extends loans to projects in distressed and timber-dependent areas and offers low interest loans to small and medium-sized Washington State forest products companies. The state helps communities finance infrastructure improvements to retain existing businesses or to attract new companies and provides special services for small and minority-owned enterprises. In an effort to encourage international trade, Washington has created nine foreign trade zones. Washington has foreign offices in China (Guangzhou and Shanghai), Germany, Japan, Mexico, South Korea, and Taiwan. Other initiatives include workshops sponsored by the Small Business Development Center on starting and expanding small businesses in the state.

38 HEALTH

The infant mortality rate in October 2005 was estimated at 5.4 per 1,000 live births. The birth rate in 2003 was 13.1 per 1,000 population. The abortion rate stood at 20.3 per 1,000 women in 2000. In 2003, about 74% of pregnant woman received prenatal care beginning in the first trimester. In 2004, approximately 78% of children received routine immunizations before the age of three.

The crude death rate in 2003 was 7.5 deaths per 1,000 population. As of 2002, the death rates for major causes of death (per 100,000 resident population) were: heart disease, 183.6; cancer, 178.9; cerebrovascular diseases, 61.8; chronic lower respiratory diseases, 44.8; and diabetes, 24.6. The mortality rate from HIV infection was 2 per 100,000 population. In 2004, the reported AIDS case rate was at about 7.2 per 100,000 population. In 2002, about 56.7% of the population was considered overweight or obese. As of 2004, about 19.1% of state residents were smokers.

In 2003, Washington had 85 community hospitals with about 11,200 beds. There were about 516,000 patient admissions that year and 10.3 million outpatient visits. The average daily inpatient census was about 6,800 patients. The average cost per day for hospital care was $1,827. Also in 2003, there were about 260 certified nursing facilities in the state with 23,713 beds and an overall occupancy rate of about 84.2%. In 2004, it was estimated that about 71% of all state residents had received some type of dental care within the year. Washington had 266 physicians per 100,000 resident population in 2004 and 762 nurses per 100,000 in 2005. In 2004, there was a total of 4,255 dentists in the state.

In 2005, University of Washington Medical Center in Seattle ranked ninth on the Honor Roll of Best Hospitals 2005 by *U.S. News & World Report.* In the same report, the Children's Hospital and regional Medical Center in Seattle ranked among the top 20 for best pediatric care.

About 19% of state residents were enrolled in Medicaid programs in 2003; 13% were enrolled in Medicare programs in 2004. Approximately 14% of the state population was uninsured in 2004. In 2003, state health care expenditures totaled $7.7 million.

39 SOCIAL WELFARE

In 2004, about 208,000 people received unemployment benefits, with the average weekly unemployment benefit at $310. In fiscal year 2005, the estimated average monthly participation in the food stamp program included about 508,472 persons (250,788 households); the average monthly benefit was about $88.34 per person. That year, the total of benefits paid through the state for the food stamp program was about $539 million.

Temporary Assistance for Needy Families (TANF), the system of federal welfare assistance that officially replaced Aid to Families with Dependent Children (AFDC) in 1997, was reauthorized through the Deficit Reduction Act of 2005. TANF is funded through federal block grants that are divided among the states based on an equation involving the number of recipients in each state. Washington's TANF program is called WorkFirst. In 2004, the state program had 137,000 recipients; state and federal expenditures on this TANF program totaled $269 million in fiscal year 2003.

In December 2004, Social Security benefits were paid to 913,040 Washington residents. This number included 599,710 retired workers, 82,920 widows and widowers, 114,140 disabled workers, 52,750 spouses, and 63,520 children. Social Security beneficiaries represented 14.7% of the total state population and 93.2% of the state's population age 65 and older. Retired workers received an average monthly payment of $993; widows and widowers, $964; disabled workers, $906; and spouses, $505. Payments for children of retired workers averaged $518 per month; children of deceased workers, $679; and children of disabled workers, $288. Federal Supplemental Security Income payments in December 2004 went to 111,895 Washington residents, averaging $423 a month. An additional $10,000 of state-administered supplemental payments were distributed to 20 residents.

40 HOUSING

In 2004, there were an estimated 2,606,623 housing units in Washington, 2,416,301 of which were occupied; 64.1% were owner-occupied. About 62.1% of all units were single-family, detached homes. Electricity was the most common energy source for heating. It was estimated that 84,890 units lacked telephone service, 10,663 lacked complete plumbing, and 15,987 lacked complete kitchen facilities. The average household had 2.51 members.

In 2004, 50,100 new privately owned housing units were authorized for construction. The median home value was $204,719. The median monthly cost for mortgage owners was $1,389. Renters paid a median of $727 per month. In 2006, the state received over $15.5 million in community development block grants from the US Department of Housing and Urban Development (HUD).

41 EDUCATION

As of 2004, 89.7% of Washingtonians 25 years of age or older were high school graduates, and 29.9% had four or more years of college.

The total enrollment for fall 2002 in Washington's public schools stood at 1,015,000. Of these, 697,000 attended schools from kindergarten through grade eight, and 318,000 attended high school. Approximately 71.5% of the students were white, 5.7% were black, 12.3% were Hispanic, 7.9% were Asian/Pacific Islander, and 2.7% were American Indian/Alaskan Native. Total enrollment was estimated at 1,011,000 in fall 2003 and expected to be 1,057,000 by fall 2014, an increase of 4.1% during the period 2002–14. Expenditures for public education in 2003/04 were estimated at $8.98 billion. In fall 2003, there were 78,746 students enrolled in 556 privates schools. Since 1969, the National Assessment of Educational Progress (NAEP) has tested public school students nationwide. The resulting report, *The Nation's Report Card,* stated that in 2005, eighth graders in Washington scored 285 out of 500 in mathematics compared with the national average of 278.

As of fall 2002, there were 338,820 students enrolled in college or graduate school; minority students comprised 20.1% of total postsecondary enrollment. In 2005 Washington had 81 degree-granting institutions including 11 public 4-year institutions, 35 public 2-year institutions, and 21 nonprofit private 4-year institutions. The largest institutions are the University of Washington (Seattle), founded in 1861, and Washington State University (Pullman). Other public institutions include the following: Eastern Washington University (Cheney); Central Washington University (Ellensburg); Western Washington University (Bellingham); and Evergreen State College (Olympia). Private institutions include Gonzaga University (Spokane); Pacific Lutheran University (Tacoma); Seattle University; Seattle Pacific College; University of Puget Sound (Tacoma); Walla Walla College; and Whitworth College (Spokane).

42 ARTS

The Washington State Arts Commission (WSAC) was established in 1961 and is governed by 19 citizens appointed by the governor and 4 legislators. In 2005, WSAC and other Washington arts organizations received 66 grants totaling $2,077,200 from the National Endowment for the Arts. Humanities Washington was founded in 1973. In 2005, the National Endowment for the Humanities contributed $1,194,718 for 17 state programs. Contributions to the arts also come from state and private sources.

The focus of professional performance activities in Washington is Seattle Center, home of the Seattle Children's Theater, Pacific Northwest Ballet Company, and Seattle Repertory Theater.

The Seattle Opera Association (founded 1964), which also performs there throughout the year, is one of the nation's leading opera companies, offering five operas each season and presenting Richard Wagner's "Ring" cycle. Tacoma and Spokane have notable local orchestras.

The Seattle Cherry Blossom and Japanese Cultural Festival has been a popular community event since its inception in 1975. The annual Diwali Festival, also in Seattle, is sponsored in part by the regional Society for the Confluence of Festivals in India (SCFI) and the Washington State Arts Commission. It includes performances of traditional dance, music, and drama, as does the Hmong New Year Celebration, another popular cultural event in Seattle.

Among Washington's many museums, universities, and other organizations exhibiting works of art on a permanent or periodic basis are the Seattle Art Museum, with its Modern Art Pavilion, and the Henry Art Gallery of the University of Washington at Seattle. The Seattle Art Museum was scheduled to unveil its Olympic Sculpture Park—a nine-acre site adjoining the city's Myrtle Edwards Park and designated to showcase sculptures, video projections, temporary installations, and loaned artwork—in fall 2006. The museum was also expected to complete an expansion project for their downtown center in 2007. Others include the Washington State University Museum of Art at Pullman; the Whatcom Museum of History and Art (Bellingham); the Tacoma Art Museum; the State Capital Museum (Olympia); and the Cheney Cowles Memorial Museum of the Eastern Washington State Historical Society (Spokane).

43 LIBRARIES AND MUSEUMS

In 2001, the state of Washington had 65 public library systems, with a total of 320 libraries, of which 265 were branches. In that same year, the systems held a combined 17,003,000 volumes of books and serial publications, and had a combined circulation of 56,298,000. The system also had 923,000 audio and 671,000 video items, 30,000 electronic format items (CD-ROMs, magnetic tapes, and disks), and 19 bookmobiles. Of Washington's 39 counties, 27 were served by the state's 21 county and multi-county libraries. In 2001, operating income for the state's public library system totaled $233,162,000 and included $220,927 from local sources and $1,489,000 from state sources.

The leading public library system is the Seattle Public Library, with 25 branches and 1,892,067 volumes in 1998. The principal academic libraries are at the University of Washington (Seattle) and Washington State University (Pullman), with 5,820,230 and 1,966,516 volumes, respectively. Olympia is the home of the Washington State Library, with a collection of 339,194 books and more than one million documents.

Washington has 160 museums and historic sites. The Washington State Historical Society Museum (Tacoma) features Native American and other pioneer artifacts; the State Capitol Museum (Olympia) and Cheney Cowles Memorial Museum (Spokane) also have important historical exhibits, as do the Thomas Burke Memorial Washington State Museum (Seattle) and the Pacific Northwest Indian Center (Spokane). Mt. Rainier National Park displays zoological, botanical, geological, and historical collections. The Pacific Science Center (Seattle) concentrates on aerospace technology; the Seattle Aquarium is a leading attraction of Waterfront Park. Also in Seattle is Woodland Park Zoological Gardens, while Tacoma has the Point Defiance Zoo and Aquarium.

44 COMMUNICATIONS

As of 2004, 95.5% of Washington's households had telephones. In addition, by June of that same year there were 3,567,896 mobile wireless telephone subscribers. In 2003, 71.4% of Washington households had a computer and 62.3% had Internet access. By June 2005, there were 1,000,634 high-speed lines in Washington, 900,741 residential and 99,893 for business. During 2005, Washington had 146 major radio stations—51 AM, 95 FM—and 19 major television stations. In 1999, the Seattle-Tacoma area had 1,591,100 television households, 74% of which ordered cable. About 206,961 Internet domain names were registered in the state as of 2000.

45 PRESS

In 2005, Washington had 15 morning newspapers, 8 evening dailies, and 17 Sunday papers.

The following table shows the leading newspapers with their approximate 2005 circulations:

AREA	NAME	DAILY	SUNDAY
Seattle	*Post-Intelligencer* (m,S)	145,964	462,920*
	Times (m,S)	231,051	462,920*
Spokane	*Spokesman–Review* (m,S)	120,785	129,607
Tacoma	*News Tribune* (m,S)	127,928	142,876

*Sunday edition is a combination of *Post-Intelligencer* and *Times*.

46 ORGANIZATIONS

In 2006, there were over 5,550 nonprofit organizations registered within the state, of which about 3,902 were registered as charitable, educational, or religious organizations.

Professional and business associations with headquarters in Washington include the APA–The Engineered Wood Association, the Center for the Defense of Free Enterprise, the Northwest Mining Association, Northwest Fisheries Association, the Northwest Horticultural Council, and Hop Growers of America. There are several local art, cultural, and historical societies.

The Citizens Committee for the Right to Keep and Bear Arms is based in Bellevue. The International Association for the Study of Pain is based in Seattle. The national offices of the Freedom Socialist Party are based in Seattle.

47 TOURISM, TRAVEL, AND RECREATION

Seattle Center—featuring the 605-ft (184-m) Space Needle tower, Opera House, and Pacific Science Center—helps make Washington's largest city one of the most exciting on the West Coast. Nevertheless, scenic beauty and opportunities for outdoor recreation are Washington's principal attractions for tourists from out of the state. Although Washington state was only settled in the mid-19th century, there are over 11,000 documented archaeological sites. There are caves, petroglyphs and the burial site of the 9,300 year old Kennewick Man.

Mt. Rainier National Park, covering 235,404 acres (95,265 hectares), encompasses not only the state's highest peak but also the most extensive glacial system in the conterminous United States. Glaciers, lakes, and mountain peaks are also featured at North Cascades National Park (504,780 acres/204,278 hectares), while

Olympic National Park (908,720 acres/367,747 hectares) is famous as the site of Mt. Olympus and for its dense rain forest and rare elk herds. Deception Pass is another popular park. Washington also offers two national historic parks (San Juan Island and part of Klondike Gold Rush), two national historic sites (Fort Vancouver and the Whitman Mission), and three national recreation areas (Coulee Dam, Lake Chelan, and Ross Lake). Washington state has areas of high desert, rain forests, mountains, and rivers. There are over 120 state parks.

Tourism is the fourth-largest industry in Washington state, after aerospace/transportation equipment, agriculture, and timber. Travelers pumped more than $11.2 billion into the economy in 2003 on overnight and day trips in Washington. The industry supplies over 126,800 jobs in the state annually. Washington has been consistently ranked among the nation's top 10 tourist destination states and attracts a significant proportion of the nation's international visitors.

48 SPORTS

Washington is home to four major professional sports teams, all of which play in Seattle. The Mariners of Major League Baseball (MLB); the Seahawks of the National Football League (NFL); the Storm of the Women's National Basketball Association (WNBA); and the Supersonics of the National Basketball Association (NBA). The Supersonics won the NBA Championship in 1979. The Storm won the WNBA Championship in 2004. The Mariners reached the American League Championship Series in 1995. In collegiate sports, the Huskies of the University of Washington won the Rose Bowl in 1960, 1961, 1978, 1982, and 1992. Skiing, boating, and hiking are popular participant sports.

Other annual sporting events include outboard hydroplane races in Electric City in June and the Ellensburg Rodeo in September.

49 FAMOUS WASHINGTONIANS

Washington's most distinguished public figure was US Supreme Court Justice William O. Douglas (b.Minnesota, 1898–1980), who grew up in Yakima and attended Whitman College in Walla Walla. In addition to his 37-year tenure on the Court, an all-time high, Douglas was the author of numerous legal casebooks as well as 27 other volumes on various subjects. Other federal officeholders from Washington include Lewis B. Schwellenbach (b.Wisconsin, 1894–1948), secretary of labor under Harry Truman, and Brockman Adams (b.Georgia, 1927–2004), secretary of transportation under Jimmy Carter. Serving in the US Senate from 1945 to 1981), Warren G. Magnuson (Minnesota, 1905–89) held the chairmanship of the powerful Appropriations Committee. A fellow Democrat, Henry M. "Scoop" Jackson (1912–83) was first elected to the House in 1940 and to the Senate in 1952. Influential on the Armed Services Committee, Jackson ran unsuccessfully for his party's presidential nomination in 1976. William E. Boeing (b.Michigan, 1881–1956) pioneered Washington's largest single industry, aerospace technology.

Notable governors include Isaac I. Stevens (b.Massachusetts, 1818–62), Washington's first territorial governor; after serving as Washington's territorial representative to Congress, he died in the Civil War. Elisha P. Ferry (b.Michigan, 1825–95), territorial governor from 1872 to 1880, was elected as Washington's first state governor in 1889. John R. Rogers (b.Maine, 1838–1901), Washington's only Populist governor, was also the first to be elected for a second term. Clarence D. Martin (1886–1955) was governor during the critical New Deal period. Daniel J. Evans (b.1925) is the youngest man ever elected governor of Washington and also is the only one to have served three consecutive terms (1965–77).

Dixy Lee Ray (1914–93), governor from 1977 to 1981 and the only woman governor in the state's history, was a former head of the federal Atomic Energy Commission and a staunch advocate of nuclear power. Other notable women were Emma Smith DeVoe (b.New Jersey, 1848–1927), a leading proponent of equal suffrage, and Bertha Knight Landes (b.Massachusetts, 1868–1943), elected mayor of Seattle in 1926; Landes, the first woman to be elected mayor of a large US city, was also an outspoken advocate of moral reform in municipal government.

Thomas Stephen Foley, former Speaker of the House, was born on 6 March 1929 in Spokane.

Several Washington Indians attained national prominence. Seattle (1786–1866) was the first signer of the Treaty of Point Elliott, which established two Indian reservations; the city of Seattle is named for him. Kamiakin (b.Idaho, c.1800–80) was the leader of the Yakima tribe during the Indian Wars of 1855, and Leschi (d.1858) was chief of the Nisqualli Indians and commanded the forces west of the Cascades during the 1855 uprising; Leschi was executed by the territorial government after the uprising was suppressed.

Washington authors have made substantial contributions to American literature. Mary McCarthy (1912–1989) was born in Seattle, and one of her books, *Memories of a Catholic Girlhood* (1957), describes her early life there. University of Washington professor Vernon Louis Parrington (b.Illinois, 1871–1929) was the first Washingtonian to win a Pulitzer Prize (1928), for his monumental *Main Currents in American Thought*. Another University of Washington faculty member, Theodore Roethke (b.Michigan, 1908–63), won the Pulitzer Prize for poetry in 1953. Seattle-born Audrey May Wurdemann (1911–60) was awarded a Pulitzer Prize for poetry in 1934 for *Bright Ambush*. Max Brand (Frederick Schiller Faust, 1892–1944) wrote hundreds of Western novels. Norman Ramsey (b.Washington, 1915) 1989 Nobel Prize recipient for physics. Hans Georg Dehmelt (b.Germany, 1922) was a recipient of the 1989 Nobel Prize for physics as a member at the University of Washington. George Herbert Hitchings, Nobel Prize winner in medicine 1988, was born April 18, 1905 in Hoquiam, Washington.

Singer-actor Harry Lillis "Bing" Crosby (1904–77), born in Tacoma, remained a loyal alumnus of Spokane's Gonzaga University. Modern dance choreographers Merce Cunningham (b.1919) and Robert Joffrey (1930–88) are both Washington natives. Photographer Edward S. Curtis (b.Wisconsin, 1868–1952) did most of the work on the North American Indian series while residing in Seattle. Modern artists Mark Tobey (b.Wisconsin, 1890–1976) spent much of his productive life in Seattle, and Robert Motherwell (1915–91) was born in Aberdeen. Washington's major contribution to popular music is rock guitarist Jimi Hendrix (1943–70).

50 BIBLIOGRAPHY

Allerfeldt, Kristofer. *Race, Radicalism, Religion, and Restriction: Immigration in the Pacific Northwest, 1890–1924*. Westport, Conn.: Praeger, 2003.

Asher, Brad. *Beyond the Reservation: Indians, Settlers, and the Law in Washington Territory, 1853–1889.* Norman: University of Oklahoma Press, 1999.

Blair, Karen J. *Northwest Women: An Annotated Bibliography of Sources on the History of Oregon and Washington Women, 1787–1970.* Pullman: Washington State University Press, 1997.

Council of State Governments. *The Book of the States, 2006 Edition.* Lexington, Ky.: Council of State Governments, 2006.

DeGrove, John Melvin. *Planning Policy and Politics: Smart Growth and the States.* Cambridge, Mass.: Lincoln Institute of Land Policy, 2005.

Goggans, Jan (ed.). *The Pacific Region.* Vol. 5 in *The Greenwood Encyclopedia of American Regional Cultures.* Westport, Conn.: Greenwood Press, 2004.

Mapes, Lynda. *Washington: the Spirit of the Land.* Stillwater, Minn.: Voyageur Press, 1999.

Parzybok, Tye W. *Weather Extremes in the West.* Missoula, Mont.: Mountain Press, 2005.

Preston, Thomas. *Pacific Coast: Washington, Oregon, California.* 2nd ed. Vol. 1 in *The Double Eagle Guide to 1,000 Great Western Recreation Destinations.* Billings, Mont.: Discovery Publications, 2003.

Riley, Gail Blasser. *Volcano!: The 1980 Mount St. Helens Eruption.* New York: Bearport, 2006.

Seeberger, Edward D. *Sine Die: A Guide to the Washington State Legislative Process.* Seattle: Washington State University Press, 1997.

US Department of Commerce, Economics and Statistics Administration, US Census Bureau. *Washington, 2000. Summary Social, Economic, and Housing Characteristics: 2000 Census of Population and Housing.* Washington, D.C.: US Government Printing Office, 2003.

The Washington Almanac. Portland, Or.: WestWinds Press, 1999.

WEST VIRGINIA

State of West Virginia

ORIGIN OF STATE NAME: The state was originally the western part of Virginia. **NICKNAME:** The Mountain State. **CAPITAL:** Charleston. **ENTERED UNION:** 20 June 1863 (35th). **SONG:** "The West Virginia Hills;" "West Virginia, My Home Sweet Home;" "This Is My West Virginia." **MOTTO:** *Montani semper liberi* (Mountaineers are always free). **COAT OF ARMS:** A farmer stands to the right and a miner to the left of a large ivy-draped rock bearing the date of the state's admission to the Union. In front of the rock are two hunters' rifles upon which rests a Cap of Liberty. The state motto is beneath and the words "State of West Virginia" above. **FLAG:** The flag has a white field bordered by a strip of blue, with the coat of arms in the center, wreathed by rhododendron leaves; across the top of the coat of arms are the words "State of West Virginia." **OFFICIAL SEAL:** The same as the coat of arms. **BIRD:** Cardinal. **FISH:** Brook trout. **FLOWER:** Rhododendron. **TREE:** Sugar maple. **LEGAL HOLIDAYS:** New Year's Day, 1 January; Birthday of Martin Luther King Jr., 3rd Monday in January; Presidents' Day, 3rd Monday in February; Memorial Day, last Monday in May; West Virginia Day, 20 June; Independence Day, 4 July; Labor Day, 1st Monday in September; Columbus Day, 2nd Monday in October; Veterans' Day, 11 November; Thanksgiving Day, 4th Thursday in November and the day following; Christmas Day, 25 December. **TIME:** 7 AM EST = noon GMT.

¹LOCATION, SIZE, AND EXTENT

Located in the eastern United States, in the South Atlantic region, West Virginia ranks 41st in size among the 50 states.

The area of West Virginia totals 24,231 sq mi (62,758 sq km), including 24,119 sq mi (62,468 sq km) of land and 112 sq mi (290 sq km) of inland water. The state extends 265 mi (426 km) E–W; its maximum N–S extension is 237 mi (381 km). West Virginia is one of the most irregularly shaped states in the United States, with two panhandles of land—the northern, narrower one separating parts of Ohio and Pennsylvania, and the eastern panhandle separating parts of Maryland and Virginia.

West Virginia is bordered on the N by Ohio (with the line formed by the Ohio River), Pennsylvania, and Maryland (with most of the line defined by the Potomac River); on the E and s by Virginia; and on the W by Kentucky and Ohio (with the line following the Ohio, Big Sandy, and Tug Fork rivers).

The total boundary length of West Virginia is 1,180 mi (1,899 km). The geographical center of the state is in the Elk River Public Hunting Area in Braxton County, 4 mi (6 km) E of Sutton.

²TOPOGRAPHY

West Virginia lies within two divisions of the Appalachian Highlands. Most of the eastern panhandle, which is crossed by the Allegheny Mountains, is in the Ridge and Valley region. The remainder, or more than two-thirds of the state, is part of the Allegheny Plateau, to the west of a bold escarpment known as the Allegheny Front, and tilts toward the Ohio River.

The mean elevation of West Virginia is 1,500 ft (458 m), higher than any other state east of the Mississippi River. Its highest point, Spruce Knob, towers 4,861 ft (1,483 m) above sea level. Major lowlands lie along the rivers, especially the Potomac, Ohio, and

Kanawha. A point on the Potomac River near Harpers Ferry has the lowest elevation, only 240 ft (73 m) above sea level. West Virginia has no natural lakes.

Most of the eastern panhandle drains into the Potomac River. The Ohio and its tributaries—the Monongahela, Little Kanawha, Kanawha, Guyandotte, and Big Sandy—drain most of the Allegheny Plateau section. Subterranean streams have carved out numerous caverns—including Seneca Caverns, Smoke Hole Caverns, and Organ Cave—from limestone beds.

During the Paleozoic era, when West Virginia was under water, a 30,000-ft (9,000-m) layer of rock streaked with rich coal deposits was laid down over much of the state. Alternately worn down and uplifted during succeeding eras, most of West Virginia is thus a plateau where rivers have carved deep valleys and gorges and given the land a rugged character.

³CLIMATE

West Virginia has a humid continental climate, with hot summers and cool to cold winters. The climate of the eastern panhandle is influenced by its proximity to the Atlantic slope and is similar to that of nearby coastal areas. Mean annual temperatures vary from 56°F (13°C) in the southwest to 48°F (9°C) at higher elevations. The yearly average is 53°F (12°C). The highest recorded temperature, 112°F (44°C), was at Martinsburg on 10 July 1936; the lowest, -37°F (-38°C), at Lewisburg on 30 December 1917.

Prevailing winds are from the south and west, and seldom reach hurricane or tornado force. In Charleston, average annual precipitation is about 42.9 in (108 cm) and is slightly heavier on the western slopes of the Alleghenies. Accumulations of snow may vary from about 20 in (51cm) in the western sections to more than 50 in (127 cm) in the higher mountains.

4 FLORA AND FAUNA

With its varied topography and climate, West Virginia provides a natural habitat for more than 3,200 species of plants in three life zones: Canadian, Alleghenian, and Carolinian. Oak, maple, poplar, walnut, hickory, birch, and such softwoods as hemlock, pine, and spruce are the common forest trees. Rhododendron, laurel, dogwood, redbud, and pussy willow are among the more than 200 flowering trees and shrubs. Rare plant species include the box huckleberry, Guyandotte beauty, and Kate's mountain clover. The Cranberry Glades, an ancient lake bed similar to a glacial bog, contains the bog rosemary and other plant species common in more northern climates. In April 2006, six plant species were listed as threatened or endangered by the US Fish and Wildlife Service, including shale barren rock-cress, harperella, northeastern bulrush, running buffalo clover, Virginia spirea, and small whorled pogonia.

West Virginia fauna includes at least 56 species and subspecies of mammals and more than 300 types of birds. The gray wolf, puma, elk, and bison of early times have disappeared. The white-tailed (Virginia) deer and the black bear (both protected by the state) as well as the wildcat are still found in the deep timber of the Allegheny ridges; raccoons, skunks, woodchucks, opossums, gray and red foxes, squirrels, and cottontail rabbits remain numerous. Common birds include the cardinal, tufted titmouse, brown thrasher, scarlet tanager, catbird, and a diversity of sparrows, woodpeckers, swallows, and warblers. Major game birds are the wild turkey, bobwhite quail, and ruffed grouse; hawks and owls are the most common birds of prey. Notable among more than 100 species of fish are smallmouth bass, rainbow trout, and brook trout (the state fish). The copperhead and rattlesnake are both numerous and poisonous. In April 2006, 13 animal species (vertebrates and invertebrates) were listed as threatened or endangered in West Virginia, including the bald eagle, three species (gray, Indiana, and Virginia big-eared) of bat, fanshell, flat-spired three-toothed snail, and the Cheat Mountain salamander.

5 ENVIRONMENTAL PROTECTION

Major responsibility for environmental protection in West Virginia rests with the Division of Environmental Protection (DEP). The DEP was established in October 1991 and became West Virginia's leading environmental agency in July 1992, with the consolidation of the state's major environmental regulatory programs. Today, the DEP is responsible for the oversight of the state's Abandoned Mine Lands, Air Quality, Mining and Reclamation, Oil and Gas, Waste Management, and Water Resources programs. A new DEP program is the Office of Environmental Advocate. The office was created to improve public access and input into DEP functioning.

Environmental issues confronting the state of West Virginia include the restoration of about 2,000 mi (3,218 km) of streams that are being impacted by acid mine damage. To combat the problem, the state has created a Stream Restoration program, which is using a variety of treatment methods, including limestone drum technology, to improve water quality. The first treatment station is under construction in the Blackwater River watershed, with plans to construct a second station in the Middlefork River watershed. The state is in the midst of an initiative that focuses on better planning and management of West Virginia's five major watersheds. In 1996, less than 1% of West Virginia's land was designated wetlands.

The proper disposal of solid waste had been addressed through requirements for landfills to meet environmental safety standards by the end of 1994 or face closure. West Virginia also mandates that cities with populations of 10,000 or more develop recycling programs. In 2003, 102.2 million lb of toxic chemicals were released in the state. Also in 2003, West Virginia had 154 hazardous waste sites listed in the US Environment Protection Agency (EPA) database, nine of which were on the National Priorities List as of 2006, including the Allegany Ballistics Laboratory of the US Navy. In 2005, the EPA spent over $1.3 million through the Superfund program for the cleanup of hazardous waste sites in the state. The same year, federal EPA grants awarded to the state included $2 million for projects involving water quality protection and control through nonpoint source program management.

6 POPULATION

West Virginia ranked 37th in population in the United States with an estimated total of 1,816,856 in 2005, an increase of 0.5% since 2000. Between 1990 and 2000, West Virginia's population grew from 1,793,477 to 1,808,344, an increase of 0.8%. The population is projected to decline to 1.76 million by 2025. The population density in 2004 was 75.4 persons per sq mi.

In 2004 the median age was 40.3, compared to the US average of 36.2. Persons under 18 years old accounted for 21.2% of the population (the national average was 25%) while 15.3% was age 65 or older (national average 12.4%).

The state's population grew rapidly in the 1880s and 1890s, as coal mining, lumbering, and railroads expanded to meet the needs of nearby industrial centers, but the pace of expansion slowed in the early 20th century. The population peaked at 2,005,552 in 1950; then mass unemployment, particularly in the coal industry, caused thousands of families to migrate to Midwestern cities. An upswing began in the 1970s.

West Virginia's major cities all have populations of less than 100,000. However, the Charleston metropolitan area had an estimated 2004 population of 307,763. The Huntington-Ashland metropolitan region, which includes parts of eastern Kentucky and southern Ohio, had an estimated population of 287,038 the same year.

7 ETHNIC GROUPS

Nearly all Indian inhabitants had left the state before the arrival of European settlers. In the 2000 census, about 3,606 Indians were counted. In 2004, 0.2% of the population was American Indian.

The 57,232 blacks in the state in 2000 constituted about 3.2% of the population. That percentage remained unchanged in 2004. The majority lived in industrial centers and coal-mining areas. Only 19,390 West Virginians, or 1.1% of the population, were foreign born in 2000. In 2000, there were 12,279 Hispanics and Latinos, representing 0.7% of the total population. In 2004, Hispanics or Latinos accounted for 0.8% of the total population. In 2000, there were 9,434 persons of Asian origin. In 2004, 0.6% of the population was Asian. In 2004, 0.8% of the population reported origin of two or more races. Persons reporting at least one specific an-

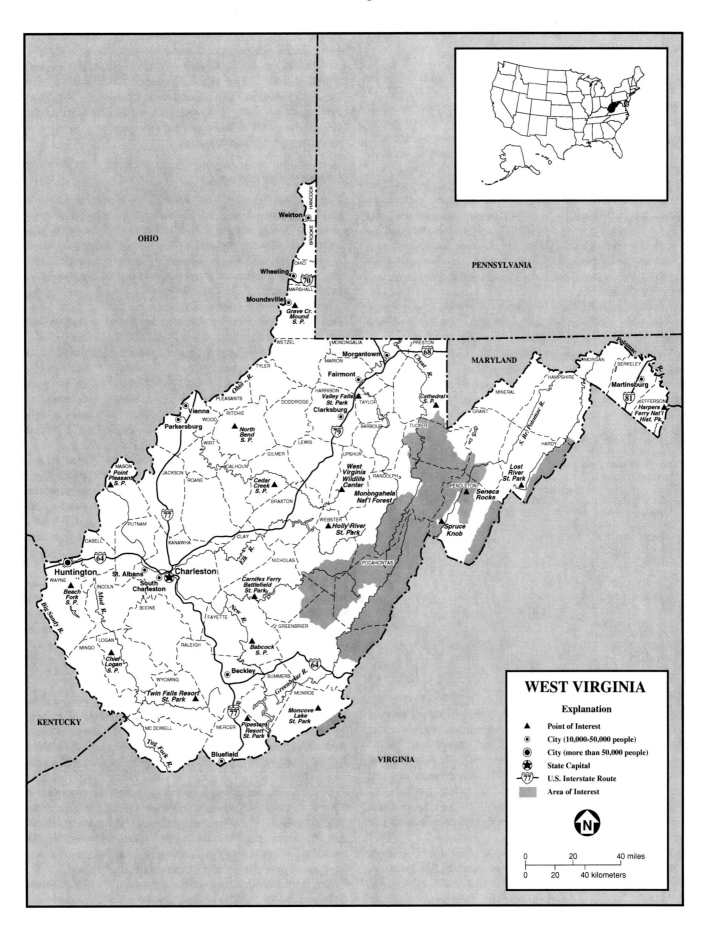

WEST VIRGINIA

Explanation

▲ Point of Interest

⊙ City (10,000-50,000 people)

◉ City (more than 50,000 people)

★ State Capital

77 U.S. Interstate Route

▓ Area of Interest

cestry group in 2000 included 176,297 English, 253,388 Germans, 198,473 Irish, and 37,837 Dutch.

8 LANGUAGES

With little foreign immigration and with no effect from the original Iroquois and Cherokee Indians, West Virginia maintains Midland speech. There is a secondary contrast between the northern half and the southern half, with the former influenced by Pennsylvania and the latter by western Virginia.

The basic Midland speech sounds the /r/ after a vowel as in *far* and *short*, and has /kag/ for *keg*, /greezy/ for *greasy*, *sofy* instead of *sofa*, and *nicker* in place of neigh. The northern part has /yelk/ for *yolk*, /loom/ for *loam*, an /ai/ diphthong so stretched that *sat* and *sight* sound very much alike, *run* for creek, and *teeter(totter)* for seesaw. The southern half pronounces *here* and *hear* as /hyeer/, *aunt* and *can't* as /aint/ and /kaint/, and uses *branch* for creek, and *tinter* for teeter.

In 2000, 1,661,036 West Virginians—97.3% of the population five years of age or over (virtually unchanged since 1990)—spoke only English at home.

The following table gives selected statistics from the 2000 Census for language spoken at home by persons five years old and over. The category "Other Indic languages" includes Bengali, Marathi, Punjabi, and Romany. The category "Other Asian languages" includes Dravidian languages, Malayalam, Telugu, Tamil, and Turkish.

LANGUAGE	NUMBER	PERCENT
Population 5 years and over	**1,706,931**	**100.0**
Speak only English	1,661,036	97.3
Speak a language other than English	45,895	2.7
Speak a language other than English	**45,895**	**2.7**
Spanish or Spanish Creole	17,652	1.0
French (incl. Patois, Cajun)	5,693	0.3
German	5,040	0.3
Italian	2,815	0.2
Chinese	1,634	0.1
Arabic	1,563	0.1
Japanese	1,135	0.1
Tagalog	970	0.1
Greek	912	0.1
Other Indic languages	806	0.0
Other Asian languages	784	0.0
Polish	763	0.0
Korean	581	0.0

9 RELIGIONS

Throughout its history, the religiously active population in West Virginia has been overwhelmingly Protestant. Most settlers before the American Revolution were Anglicans, Presbyterians, Quakers, or members of German sects, such as Lutherans, German Reformed, Dunkers, and Mennonites. The Great Awakening had a profound effect on these settlers and they avidly embraced its evangelism, emotionalism, and emphasis on personal religious experience. Catholics were mostly immigrants from Ireland and southern and eastern Europe.

The major Protestant denominations and the number of their adherents (in 2000 except as indicated) include the American Baptist Churches USA, 108,087; the United Methodist Church, 105,879 (in 2004); the Southern Baptist Convention, 43,606; and the Presbyterian Church USA, 28,467. In 2002, the Southern Baptist Convention reported 967 newly baptized members in the state. Other fundamentalist denominations included the Churches of Christ, 24,143; the Church of God (Cleveland, Tennessee), 21,657; and the Church of the Nazarene, 21,389. In 2004, there were about 100,648 Roman Catholics in the state. In 2000, there were an estimated 2,400 Jews and 1,528 Muslims. Over 1.1 million people (about 64% of the population) were not counted as members of any religious organization.

10 TRANSPORTATION

West Virginia has long been plagued by inadequate transportation. The first major pre–Civil War railroad line was the Baltimore and Ohio (B&O), completed to Wheeling in 1852. Later railroads, mostly built between 1880 and 1917 to tap rich coal and timber resources, also helped open up interior regions to settlement. Today, the railroads still play an important part in coal transportation. In 2003, CSX and Norfolk Southern were the state's Class I operators. In the same year, total rail mileage was 2,489 mi (4,007 km). Coal was the top commodity carried by rail that terminated and originated within the state that year. As of 2006, Amtrak provided east–west passenger service (Washington DC to Chicago) to 10 communities in the state.

In 2004, there were 37,011 mi (59,587 km) of public roads under the state system The West Virginia Turnpike was completed from Charleston to Princeton in 1955. There were some 1.3 million registered motor vehicles in the state in 2003 and 1,292,036 licensed drivers in 2004.

Major navigable inland rivers are the Ohio, Kanawha, and Monongahela. Each has locks and dams. West Virginia is home to the Port of Huntington-Tristate, the largest inland river port in the United States. Located on the Ohio River, the port handled 77.307 million tons of cargo in 2004, making it the eighth-busiest port in the United States. In 2003, waterborne shipments totaled 73.326 million tons. In 2004, West Virginia had 682 mi (1,098 km) of navigable inland waterways.

In 2005, West Virginia had a total of 126 public and private-use aviation-related facilities. This included 75 airports, 40 heliports, 1 STOLport (Short Take-Off and Landing), and 10 seaplane bases. Yeager Airport in Charleston is the state's main air terminal. In 2004, the airport had 292,054 passenger enplanements.

11 HISTORY

Paleo-Indian cultures in what is now West Virginia existed some 15,000 years ago, when hunters pursued buffalo and other large game. About 7000 BC, they were supplanted by Archaic cultures, marked by pursuit of smaller game. Woodland (Adena) cultures, characterized by mound-building and agriculture, prevailed after about 1000 BC.

By the 1640s, the principal Indian claimants, the Iroquois and Cherokee, had driven out older inhabitants and made the region a vast buffer land. When European settlers arrived only a few Shawnee, Tuscarora, and Delaware Indian villages remained, but the area was still actively used as hunting and warring grounds, and European possession was hotly contested.

The fur trade stimulated early exploration. In 1671, Thomas Batts and Robert Fallam explored New River and gave England a claim to the Ohio Valley, to which most of West Virginia belongs.

France also claimed the Ohio Valley by virtue of an alleged visit by Robert Cavelier, Sieur de la Salle, in 1669. England eventually prevailed as a result of the French and Indian War.

Unsubstantiated tradition credits Morgan Morgan, who moved to Bunker Hill in 1731, with the first settlement in the state. By 1750, several thousand settlers were living in the eastern panhandle. In 1769, following treaties with the Iroquois and Cherokee, settlers began to occupy the Greenbrier, Monongahela, and upper Ohio valleys, and movement into other interior sections continued into the Revolutionary War, although wars with Indians occurred sporadically until the 1790s. The area that is now West Virginia was part of Virginia at the time of that state's entry into the Union, 25 June 1788.

Serious differences between eastern and western Virginia developed after the War of 1812. Eastern Virginia was dominated by a slaveholding aristocracy, while small diversified farms and infant industries predominated in western Virginia. Westerners bristled under property qualifications for voting, inadequate representation in the Virginia legislature, and undemocratic county governments, as well as poor transportation, inadequate schools, inequitable taxes, and economic retardation. A constitutional convention in 1829–30 failed to effect changes, leaving the westerners embittered. Another convention in 1850–51 met the west's political demands but exacerbated economic differences.

When Virginia seceded from the Union in 1861, western counties remaining loyal to the Union set up the Reorganized Government and consented to the separation of present-day West Virginia from Virginia. After approval by Congress and President Lincoln, West Virginia entered the Union on 20 June 1863 as the 35th state. West Virginia won control over Jefferson and Berkeley counties in the eastern panhandle in 1871, giving it a greater share of the Baltimore and Ohio Railroad lines in the state.

Both Bourbon Democratic and Republican governors after the Civil War sought to improve transportation, foster immigration, and provide tax structures attractive to business. Industrialists such as Democrats Henry Gassaway Davis and Johnson N. Camden, who amassed fortunes in coal, oil, railroads, and timber, sat in the US Senate and dominated party affairs in West Virginia. Similarly, industrialists Nathan Goff Jr., and Stephen B. Elkins—Davis's son-in-law—wielded preponderant influence in the Republican Party from the 1870s until 1911. Native industrialists often collaborated with eastern interests to give the state a colonial economy dominated by absentee owners. Although Republican governors of the early 20th century were dominated by Elkins, they were attuned to Progressive ideas and were instrumental in the adoption of the direct primary, safety legislation for the coal mines, revision of corporate tax laws, and improvements in highways and education.

The Great Depression of the 1930s, from which West Virginia suffered acutely, ushered in a Democratic era. West Virginians embraced the New Deal and Fair Deal philosophies of presidents Franklin D. Roosevelt and Harry S Truman.

World Wars I and II produced significant changes in West Virginia, particularly through stimulation of chemical, steel, and textile industries in the Kanawha and Ohio valleys and the eastern panhandle. These industries lessened the state's dependence on extractive industries, historically the backbone of its economy, and gave cities and towns a more cosmopolitan character.

Overshadowing the economic diversification was the plight of the coal-mining areas, where, after World War II, mechanization and strip-mining displaced thousands of miners and resulted in a large exodus to other states. By 1960, West Virginia was considered one of the most economically depressed areas of the country, primarily because of conditions in the mining regions. The antipoverty programs of the Kennedy and Johnson administrations provided some relief, but much of it was temporary, as was a brief upsurge in coal mining during the late 1970s.

Over the last several decades, West Virginia's manufacturing and mining sectors have shrunk dramatically. Automation, foreign competition, and the recession of the early 1980s caused employment in steel, glass, and chemical manufacturing and in coal mining to drop by a third between 1979 and 1985, when the state had the highest rate of unemployment in the nation.

West Virginia's economy improved in the 1990s. Coal and timber production expanded, and trade and tourism were boosted by the completion of Interstate Highway 64 in 1988. The state won a number of federal projects (including the FBI's fingerprint identification division), aided by the tenure of Democrat Robert C. Byrd as chairman of the US Senate Appropriations Committee from 1988 to 1995 and from 2001 to 2003. Byrd remained ranking member on the committee as of 2005.

In 2003, Democratic governor Bob Wise called for a special session of the legislature to prevent the state Workers' Compensation Fund from going bankrupt. The system provides medical care and cash benefits for workers injured on the job. Democrat Joe Manchin III was elected the state's governor in November 2004 after Wise decided not to run for reelection. Manchin's election marked the first time two persons of the same political party have followed one another in the governor's office since 1964.

12 STATE GOVERNMENT

Since becoming a state, West Virginia has had two constitutions. The first, adopted in 1863, served until 1872, when the present constitution was adopted. As of January 2005, 71 amendments to this constitution had become law.

The legislature consists of a Senate with 34 members and a house of delegates with 100 members. Senators and delegates must be at least 25 and 18 years old, respectively. All legislators must be qualified voters, state citizens, and residents of their districts for at least one year before taking their seats. In addition, delegates must have been US citizens for at least one year, and a one-year resident of the state. Senators must be US citizens for at least five years, and five-year residents of their state. Senators are elected to staggered four-year terms, and delegates serve for two years. The legislature meets annually in 60-day sessions, beginning in January. Special sessions may be called by a petition signed by three-fifths of the members of each house. The legislative salary in 2004 was $15,000, unchanged from 1999.

Elected officials of the executive branch of government are the governor, secretary of state, auditor, attorney general, commissioner of agriculture, and treasurer, all elected for four-year terms. The governor, who may serve no more than two terms in succession, must be at least 30 years old, a registered voter, a citizen of the state for at least five years, and a resident for at least one. His successor is the president of the Senate (there is no lieutenant governor). As of December 2004, the governor's salary was $90,000.

Bills passed by the legislature become law when signed by the governor or left unsigned for five days when the legislature is in session (or 15 days after it has adjourned). Bills vetoed by the governor become law if passed again by a majority of the elected members of each house. Either house may propose an amendment to the state constitution. If both houses approve it by a two-thirds majority, it is submitted to the voters at the next regular election or at a special election for adoption by majority vote.

Voters in West Virginia must live in the state, be US citizens, and at least 18 years old. Restrictions apply to those convicted of certain crimes and to those judged by the court as mentally incompetent to vote.

13 POLITICAL PARTIES

The Republican Party presided over the birth of West Virginia, but the Democrats have generally been in power for the past five decades. In 1940, a strong New Deal faction, headed by Matthew M. Neely and supported by organized labor, formed the "state-house machine," which became a dominant factor in state politics. Only two Republicans, Cecil H. Underwood (1957–61, 1997–2001) and Arch Moore Jr. (1969–77, 1985–89), have been governor since 1933. Underwood was elected in 1996, having vacated the office 35 years earlier. Democrat Bob Wise unseated Underwood in 2000. Underwood did not seek a second term; in 2004 Democrat Joe Manchin III was elected.

Democratic senator Robert C. Byrd, first elected in 1958, was reelected to his eighth term in 2000. Democratic senator John D. "Jay" Rockefeller IV, first elected in 1984, was reelected to his fourth term in 2002. Following the 2004 elections, West Virginia sent two Democrats and one Republican to the US House of Representatives. As of mid-2005, Democrats controlled both the state House and state Senate. There were 21 Democrats and 13 Republicans in the state Senate, and 68 Democrats and 32 Republicans in the state House.

West Virginia Presidential Vote by Major Political Parties, 1948–2004

YEAR	ELECTORAL VOTE	W. VA. WINNER	DEMOCRAT	REPUBLICAN
1948	8	*Truman (D)	429,188	316,251
1952	8	Stevenson (D)	453,578	419,970
1956	8	*Eisenhower (R)	381,534	449,297
1960	8	*Kennedy (D)	441,786	395,995
1964	7	*Johnson (D)	538,087	253,953
1968	7	Humphrey (D)	374,091	307,555
1972	6	*Nixon (R)	277,435	484,964
1976	6	*Carter (D)	435,914	314,760
1980	6	Carter (D)	367,462	334,206
1984	6	*Reagan (R)	328,125	405,483
1988	6	Dukakis (D)	341,016	310,065
1992**	5	*Clinton (D)	331,001	241,974
1996**	5	*Clinton (D)	327,812	233,946
2000	5	*Bush, G. W. (R)	295,497	336,475
2004	5	*Bush, G. W. (R)	326,541	423,778

*Won US presidential election.
**IND. candidate Ross Perot received 108,829 votes in 1992 and 71,639 in 1996.

Republican presidential candidates carried West Virginia in 1956, 1972, 1984, 2000, and 2004. In 2000, Republican George W. Bush received 52% of the popular vote to Democrat Al Gore's 46%; Green Party candidate Ralph Nader garnered 2% of the vote. In 2004, Bush again won the state, with 56% of the vote to Democrat John Kerry's 43%. In 2004 there were 1,169,000 registered voters. In 1998, 63% of registered voters were Democratic, 29% Republican, and 8% unaffiliated or members of other parties. The state had five electoral votes in the 2004 presidential election.

14 LOCAL GOVERNMENT

As of 2005, West Virginia had 55 counties, 234 municipal governments, 55 school districts, and 342 special districts. The chief county officials are the three commissioners, elected for six-year terms, who serve on the county court; the sheriff, assessor, county clerk, and prosecuting attorney, elected for four-year terms; and the five-member board of education, elected for six-year terms. The sheriff is the principal peace officer but also collects taxes and disburses funds of the county court and board of education. The cities, towns, and villages are divided into classes according to population. They are run by mayor and council or by council and city manager.

In 2005, local government accounted for about 60,712 full-time (or equivalent) employment positions.

15 STATE SERVICES

To address the continuing threat of terrorism and to work with the federal Department of Homeland Security, homeland security in West Virginia operates under the authority of the governor; the public safety director/secretary was designated as the state homeland security advisor.

The Department of Education determines policy for public elementary and secondary schools, and the West Virginia Higher Education Policy Commission governs the state's colleges and universities. The Department of Transportation is responsible for construction and operation of state roads. Services of the Department of Health and Human Resources center around treatment of alcoholism and drug abuse, mental health, environmental health services, maternal and child care, family planning, and control of communicable diseases, along with a variety of economic, medical, and social services.

In the area of public protection, the Department of Public Safety enforces criminal and traffic laws, the Division of Homeland Security and Emergency Management oversees civil defense and other emergency activities, and the Department of Corrections oversees prisons and other such facilities. The Public Service Commission regulates utilities. The Housing Development Fund concentrates on housing for low- and middle-income families and the elderly. The Department of Environmental Protection has the major responsibility for protection of forests, wildlife, water, and other resources, for reclamation projects, and for operation of state parks and recreational facilities.

Responsibility in labor matters is shared by the Division of Labor, Bureau of Employment Programs, Office of Miners' Health, Safety, and Training, and BrickStreet (workers' compensation plan).

[16]JUDICIAL SYSTEM

The highest court in West Virginia, the Supreme Court of Appeals, has five justices, including the chief justice, elected for 12-year terms. The court has broad discretionary appellate jurisdiction in both civil and criminal cases, and original jurisdiction in certain other cases.

West Virginia's general trial court is the circuit court, with 156 judges in 1999. Each circuit serves from one to four counties and has jurisdiction over civil cases in amounts that exceed $300 and criminal cases. Circuit courts also have jurisdiction over juveniles, domestic relations, and certain administrative appeals. Family law specialists conduct most domestic relations hearings.

Local courts include the county magistrate and municipal courts. Magistrate courts have original jurisdiction in criminal matters but may not convict or sentence in felony cases. All judges down to the magistrate level are popularly elected by partisan ballot. Municipal, police, or mayor's courts have authority to enforce municipal ordinances. Unlike other courts, these are not part of the unified court system. Appeals from municipal and magistrate courts are to circuit courts, and from circuit courts are to the supreme court.

As of 31 December 2004, a total of 5,067 prisoners were held in West Virginia's state and federal prisons, an increase from 4,758 of 2.5% from the previous year. As of year-end 2004, a total of 4,589 inmates were female, up from 405 or 13.3% from the year before. Among sentenced prisoners (one year or more), West Virginia had an incarceration rate of 277 per 100,000 population in 2004.

According to the Federal Bureau of Investigation, West Virginia in 2004, had a violent crime rate (murder/nonnegligent manslaughter; forcible rape; robbery; aggravated assault) of 271.2 reported incidents per 100,000 population, or a total of 4,924 reported incidents. Crimes against property (burglary; larceny/theft; and motor vehicle theft) in that same year totaled 45,497 reported incidents or 2,506.2 reported incidents per 100,000 people. West Virginia abolished its death penalty in 1965.

In 2003, West Virginia spent $76,290,914 on homeland security, an average of $41 per state resident.

[17]ARMED FORCES

In 2004, there were 503 active duty military personnel and 1,810 civilian personnel stationed in West Virginia. The state has no military bases, academies, or training facilities. The Naval Telecommunications Station, Sugar Grove, operated by the National Security Agency is the main receiving facility for the Navy's global high-frequency radio communications and for point-to-point circuits destined for Washington, DC, and has been mentioned as a site that intercepts all international communications entering the Eastern United States.

In 2004, defense contracts awarded West Virginia totaled about $279 million, and defense payroll outlays were $410 million.

In 2003, there were 188,101 veteran living in West Virginia, of whom 27,900 served in World War II; 23,322 in the Korean conflict; 59,857 in the Vietnam era; and 24,626 in the Gulf War. In 2004, the Veterans Administration expended more than $747 million in pensions, medical assistance, and other major veterans' benefits.

As of 31 October 2004, the West Virginia State Police employed 649 full-time sworn officers.

[18]MIGRATION

West Virginia has considerable national and ethnic diversity. Settlers before the Civil War consisted principally of English, German, Scotch-Irish, and Welsh immigrants, many of whom came by way of Pennsylvania. A second wave of immigration from the 1880s to the 1920s brought thousands of Italians, Poles, Austrians, and Hungarians to the coal mines and industrial towns, which also attracted many blacks from the South. In 1980, 79% of the residents of the state were born in West Virginia (fourth highest among states).

Between 1950 and 1970, West Virginia suffered a 13% loss in population, chiefly from the coal-mining areas; but between 1970 and 1980, population rose by almost 12%. According to federal estimates, the state had a net migration gain of 71,000 in the 1970s and a net migration loss of about 81,000 in the 1980s. Between 1990 and 1998, West Virginia had net gains of 8,000 in domestic migration and 3,000 in international migration. In 1998, the state admitted 375 foreign immigrants. Between 1990 and 1998, the state's overall population increased by 1%. In the period 2000–05, net international migration was 3,691 and net internal migration was 10,518, for a net gain of 14,209 people.

[19]INTERGOVERNMENTAL COOPERATION

The West Virginia Commission on Interstate Cooperation participates in the Council of State Governments. West Virginia is a member of some 30 regional compacts, including the Ohio River Valley Water Sanitation and Potomac River Basin compacts, Interstate Mining Compact Commission, Wheeling Creek Watershed Protection and Flood Prevention Commission, Ohio River Basin Commission, Appalachian Regional Commission, Jennings Randolph Lake Project Compact, Southern Regional Education Board, Southern States Energy Board, and Southern Governors' Association. In fiscal year 2005, federal grants to West Virginia totaled $2.960 billion, an estimated $2.861 billion in fiscal year 2006, and an estimated $3.045 billion in fiscal year 2007.

[20]ECONOMY

Agriculture was the backbone of West Virginia's economy until the 1890s, when extractive industries (including coal, oil, natural gas, and timber) began to play a major role. World War I stimulated important secondary industries, such as chemicals, steel, glass, and textiles. The beauty of West Virginia's mountains and forests attracted an increasing number of tourists in the 1990s, but the state's rugged topography and relative isolation from major markets continued to hamper its economic development. West Virginia did not participate substantially in the high-tech boom of the 1990s, and the long-term decline of its critical coal mining sector continued. From 1997 to 2000, output from the general services and retail trade sectors grew 19% and 13.6%, respectively, while coal mining declined 17.6%, trends that meant the loss of coal mining jobs paying more than $53,000 a year and the increase in service jobs paying $14,000 to $24,000 annually. Output from the manufacturing sector fell at the same rate as mining output

(17.6%) from 1997 to 2000, although from a high base ($6.5 billion in 1997 vs. $2.4 billion from coal mining). Overall growth was sluggish in the late 1990s, reaching 3.8% in 1999 (up from 1.9% in 1998), but falling to 0.1% in 2000. In 2001, growth actually improved to 3.5%, including a 13.8% jump in output from coal mining. However, by 2002, the national economic slowdown had begun to impact West Virginia's employment, and by October 2002, there was a year-on-year losses in jobs in every state economic sector except services and government (a sector that grew 24.5% 1997 to 2001). The overall decline in employment was 0.7%, ahead of the national average of 0.4%.

In 2004, West Virginia's gross state product (GSP) was $49.454 billion, of which manufacturing (durable and nondurable goods) accounted for the largest share at $5.469 billion or 11% of GSP, followed by health care and social assistance at $4.757 billion (9.6% of GSP), and the real estate sector at $4.598 billion (9.2% of GSP). In that same year, there were an estimated 119,806 small businesses in West Virginia. Of the 36,830 businesses that had employees, an estimated total of 35,621 or 96.7% were small companies. An estimated 3,937 new businesses were established in the state in 2004, down 4.6% from the year before. Business terminations that same year came to 5,136, down 7.5% from 2003. There were 247 business bankruptcies in 2004, down 14.8% from the previous year. In 2005, the state's personal bankruptcy (Chapter 7 and Chapter 13) filing rate was 600 filings per 100,000 people, ranking West Virginia 20th in the nation.

21 INCOME

In 2005 West Virginia had a gross state product (GSP) of $54 billion which accounted for 0.4% of the nation's gross domestic product and placed the state at number 41 in highest GSP among the 50 states and the District of Columbia.

According to the Bureau of Economic Analysis, in 2004 West Virginia had a per capita personal income (PCPI) of $25,792. This ranked 50th in the United States and was 78% of the national average of $33,050. The 1994–2004 average annual growth rate of PCPI was 4.1%. West Virginia had a total personal income (TPI) of $46,749,648,000, which ranked 39th in the United States and reflected an increase of 5.3% from 2003. The 1994–2004 average annual growth rate of TPI was 4.1%. Earnings of persons employed in West Virginia increased from $29,740,318,000 in 2003 to $31,612,176,000 in 2004, an increase of 6.3%. The 2003–04 national change was 6.3%.

The US Census Bureau reports that the three-year average median household income for 2002–04 in 2004 dollars was $32,589 compared to a national average of $44,473. During the same period an estimated 16.1% of the population was below the poverty line as compared to 12.4% nationwide.

22 LABOR

According to the Bureau of Labor Statistics (BLS), in April 2006 the seasonally adjusted civilian labor force in West Virginia 813,700, with approximately 33,600 workers unemployed, yielding an unemployment rate of 4.1%, compared to the national average of 4.7% for the same period. Preliminary data for the same period placed nonfarm employment at 754,200. Since the beginning of the BLS data series in 1976, the highest unemployment rate recorded in West Virginia was 18.2% in March 1983. The historical low was 3.8% in January 2006. Preliminary nonfarm employment data by occupation for April 2006 showed that approximately 5.1% of the labor force was employed in construction; 8.1% in manufacturing; 18.6% in trade, transportation, and public utilities; 4% in financial activities; 7.8% in professional and business services; 15.3% in education and health services; 9.3% in leisure and hospitality services; and 19% in government.

Important milestones in the growth of unionism were the organization of the state as District 17 of the United Mine Workers of America (UMWA) in 1890 and the formation of the State Federation of Labor in 1903. The coal miners fought to gain union recognition by coal companies, and instances of violence were not uncommon in the early 1900s. Wages, working conditions, and benefits for miners improved rapidly after World War II. Membership in unions in 1980 was 222,000, or 34% of the work force, compared to 47% in 1970, an indication of the UMWA's waning strength.

The BLS reported that in 2005, a total of 99,000 of West Virginia's 688,000 employed wage and salary workers were formal members of a union. This represented 14.4% of those so employed, up from 14.2% in 2004, and above the national average of 12%. Overall in 2005, a total of 107,000 workers (15.5%) in West Virginia were covered by a union or employee association contract, which includes those workers who reported no union affiliation. West Virginia is one of 28 states that does not have a right-to-work law.

As of 1 March 2006, West Virginia had a state-mandated minimum wage rate of $5.15 per hour, which was applied to those employers with six or more employees at any one location. In 2004, women in the state accounted for 46.7% of the employed civilian labor force.

23 AGRICULTURE

With estimated farm marketings of $429 million ($348 million from livestock and poultry), West Virginia ranked 46th among the 50 states in 2005. Poultry, meat animals, and dairy dominate the farm economy in the Mountain State.

Until about 1890 small, diversified farms were dominant, but, as in other states, farms have grown larger and the farm population has dropped. In 2004, the state had 3,600,000 acres (1,457,000 hectares), or 23% of its land, devoted to farming. Its 20,800 farms averaged 173 acres (70 hectares) in size. Major farm sections are the eastern panhandle, a tier of counties along the Virginia border, the upper Monongahela Valley, and the Ohio Valley. Leading crops produced in 2004 were hay, 1,062,000 tons; corn for grain, 3,799,000 bushels; corn for silage, 306,000 tons; commercial apples, 86,000,000 lb; and tobacco, 1,690,000 lb.

24 ANIMAL HUSBANDRY

In 2005, there were an estimated 405,000 cattle and calves, valued at $315.9 million. During 2004, the state had 10,000 hogs and pigs, valued at around $1.1 million. During 2003, poultry farmers produced 357 million lb (162 million kg) of broilers valued at $121.5 million, and 92 million lb of turkey, valued at $33.1 million. The dairy industry yielded 222 million lb (101 million kg) of milk and 270 million eggs.

25 FISHING

West Virginia fishing has little commercial importance. In 2004, there were 34 trout farms, selling 378,000 lb (172,000 kg) of fish. In 2004, the state issued 269,727 sport fishing licenses. The White Sulphur Springs National Fish Hatchery is located within the state. There are two state hatcheries.

26 FORESTRY

In 2004, West Virginia had four-fifths, or 12.1 million acres (4.9 million hectares), of its land area in forestland and, of this, 11.9 million acres (4.8 million hectares) are classified as timberland.

Despite increasing production of wood and paper products, West Virginia's total softwood and hardwood inventory has more than doubled since 1953. Sawtimber volumes average 6,500 board feet per acre. About 92% of West Virginia forest species are hardwoods, with approximately 77% of the timberland being of the oak-hickory forest type. In all, West Virginia's forests contain more than 100 species of trees.

During the early 1900s, West Virginia became a lumbering giant. From 1908 to 1911, some 1,500 mills produced up to 1.5 billion board ft of lumber annually to feed the nation's needs. By 1920, the state was first in the production of cherry and chestnut lumber and 13th in total production. After the extensive logging and resulting debris came forest fires which devastated the remaining forest resource and caused extensive soil erosion. In the early 1930s, a cooperative fire prevention program was initiated in the state and later in the early 1950s, an educational and forestry technical assistance program was created to help forest landowners manage and protect their forests. The maturing forests of West Virginia languished in their contribution to the state's economy until the 1980s when annual production, which had averaged around 350 to 450 million board ft per year, began to increase significantly.

Production increased to 600 million board ft in 1988, and 701 million board ft by 2004, with over 300 mills and manufacturing facilities. Employment in the forest industry is second only to the chemical and primary metal manufacturing industries. However, it is estimated that growth still exceeded removals by a ratio of 1.34 to 1.

The state is encouraging the professional management of its forests so they will continue to produce a sustained array of benefits, such as wood products, jobs, clean water, oxygen, scenery, and diverse recreational opportunities like hunting, hiking, and tourism.

27 MINING

According to preliminary data from the US Geological Survey (USGS), the estimated value of nonfuel mineral production by West Virginia in 2003 was $168 million, which was only a marginal increase over 2002.

According to preliminary USGS data for 2003, crushed stone was the state's top nonfuel mineral by value, accounting for about 39% of all nonfuel mineral output, and was followed by cement (portland and masonry), industrial sand and gravel, lime and salt. Collectively, these five commodities accounted for around 95% of all nonfuel mineral output, by value. By volume, West Virginia in 2003 was the nation's ninth leading producer of salt.

Preliminary data for 2003 showed crushed stone production as totaling 14.8 million metric tons, with a value of $65.9 million, while construction sand and gravel that year at 1.6 million metric tons, with a value of $8 million.

All of West Virginia's mines in 2003 produced either coal or industrial minerals. No metals were mined in the state. Although raw steel and primary aluminum were produced in that year, materials were acquired from other states or foreign sources. West Virginia ranked 11th out of 12 primary aluminum producing states.

28 ENERGY AND POWER

West Virginia has long been an important supplier of energy in the form of electric power and fossil fuels. As of 2003, West Virginia had 17 electrical power service providers, of which two were publicly owned and three were cooperatives. Of the remainder, 11 were investor owned, and one was the owner of an independent generator that sold directly to customers. As of that same year there were 974,510 retail customers. Of that total, 961,675 received their power from investor-owned service providers. Cooperatives accounted for 9,318 customers, while publicly owned providers had 3,516 customers. There was only one independent generator or "facility" customer.

Total net summer generating capability by the state's electrical generating plants in 2003 stood at 16.124 million kW, with total production that same year at 94.711 billion kWh. Of the total amount generated, 67.6% came from electric utilities, with the remainder coming from independent producers and combined heat and power service providers. The largest portion of all electric power generated, 92.468 billion kWh (97.6%), came from coal-fired plants, with hydroelectric plants in second place at 1.356 billion kWh (1.4%). Other renewable power sources, petroleum and natural gas fired plants, and plants using other types of gases accounted for the remaining output.

Major coal-mining regions lie within a north–south belt some 60 mi (97 km) wide through the central part of the state and include the Fairmount, New River-Kanawha, Pocahontas, and Logan-Mingo fields. West Virginia in 2004, had 261 producing coal mines, 109 of which were surface mines and 152 were underground. Coal production that year totaled 147,993,000 short tons, up from 139,711,000 short tons in 2003. Of the total produced in 2004, underground mines accounted for the largest share of production at 90,932,000 short tons. In 2004, West Virginia's output of coal was exceeded only by Wyoming. Recoverable coal reserves that year totaled 1.51 billion short tons. One short ton equals 2,000 lb (0.907 metric tons).

As of 2004, West Virginia had proven crude oil reserves of 11 million barrels, or under 1% of all proven US reserves, while output that same year averaged 4,000 barrels per day. Including federal offshore domains, the state that year ranked 25th (24th excluding federal offshore) in proven reserves and 26th (25th excluding federal offshore) in production among the 31 producing states. In 2004 West Virginia had 6,037 producing oil wells and accounted for less than 1% of all US production. As of 2005, the state's sole refinery had a crude oil distillation capacity of 19,400 barrels per day.

In 2004, West Virginia had 47,117 producing natural gas and gas condensate wells. In that same year, marketed gas production (all gas produced excluding gas used for repressuring, vented and flared, and nonhydrocarbon gases removed) totaled 187.723 billion cu ft (5.33 billion cu m). As of 31 December 2004, proven reserves of dry or consumer-grade natural gas totaled 3,306 billion cu ft (93.89 billion cu m).

²⁹INDUSTRY

Major industrial areas are the Kanawha, Ohio, and Monongahela valleys and the eastern panhandle. The largest industrial corporations with headquarters in West Virginia are Weirton Steel and Wheeling-Pittsburgh. Other major industrial companies with operations in West Virginia include E. I. du Pont de Nemours, Union Carbide, Ravenswood Aluminum, and Rhone Poulenc.

According to the US Census Bureau's Annual Survey of Manufactures (ASM) for 2004, West Virginia's manufacturing sector covered some 14 product subsectors. The shipment value of all products manufactured in the state that same year was $20.578 billion. Of that total, chemical manufacturing accounted for the largest share at $6.325 billion. It was followed by primary metal manufacturing at $3.379 billion; transportation equipment manufacturing at $2.538 billion; wood product manufacturing at $1.795 billion; and fabricated metal product manufacturing at $1.662 billion.

In 2004, a total of 63,094 people in West Virginia were employed in the state's manufacturing sector, according to the ASM. Of that total, 47,549 were actual production workers. In terms of total employment, the chemical manufacturing industry accounted for the largest portion of all manufacturing employees at 10,101, with 6,121 actual production workers. It was followed by primary metal manufacturing at 9,081 employees (7,110 actual production workers);wood product manufacturing at 8,782 employees (7,692 actual production workers); fabricated metal product manufacturing at 6,520 employees (5,157 actual production workers); and food manufacturing with 4,433 employees (3,105 actual production workers).

ASM data for 2004 showed that West Virginia's manufacturing sector paid $2.651 billion in wages. Of that amount, the chemical manufacturing sector accounted for the largest share at $648.063 million. It was followed by primary metal manufacturing at $535.129 million; wood product manufacturing at $251.845 million; fabricated metal product manufacturing at $226.838 million; and transportation equipment manufacturing at $203.334 million.

³⁰COMMERCE

According to the 2002 Census of Wholesale Trade, West Virginia's wholesale trade sector had sales that year totaling $10.9 billion from 1,699 establishments. Wholesalers of durable goods accounted for 1,162 establishments, followed by nondurable goods wholesalers at 486 and electronic markets, agents, and brokers accounting for 50 establishments. Sales by durable goods wholesalers in 2002 totaled $5.1 billion, while wholesalers of nondurable goods

saw sales of $5.3 billion. Electronic markets, agents, and brokers in the wholesale trade industry had sales of $426.5 million.

In the 2002 Census of Retail Trade, West Virginia was listed as having 7,454 retail establishments with sales of $16.7 billion. The leading types of retail businesses by number of establishments were: gasoline stations (1,212); motor vehicle and motor vehicle parts dealers (1,010); food and beverage stores (873); miscellaneous store retailers (863); and clothing and clothing accessories stores (646). In terms of sales, motor vehicle and motor vehicle parts dealers accounted for the largest share of retail sales at $4.2 billion, followed by general merchandise stores at $3.1 billion; food and beverage stores at $2.1 billion; and gasoline stations at $2.06 billion. A total of 89,340 people were employed by the retail sector in West Virginia that year.

In 2005, exports of goods originating from the state had a value of $3.1 billion.

³¹CONSUMER PROTECTION

The state Attorney General Office's, Division of Consumer Protection and Antitrust, is empowered to investigate, arbitrate, and litigate complaints by consumers alleging unfair and deceptive trade practices, and violations of the West Virginia Consumer Credit and Protection Act, the West Virginia Antitrust Act, and the Preneed Funeral Contracts Act. There are five assistant attorneys general assigned to defend these laws.

The Public Service Commission, consisting of three members, regulates rates, charges, and services of utilities and common carriers. Since 1977, it has included one member who is supposed to represent the "average" wage earner.

When dealing with consumer protection issues, the state's Attorney General's Office can initiate civil but not criminal proceedings; represent the state before state and federal regulatory agencies; administer consumer protection and education programs; handle formal consumer complaints; and exercise broad subpoena powers. In antitrust actions, the Attorney General's Office can act on behalf of those consumers who are incapable of acting on their own; initiate damage actions on behalf of the state in state courts; and represent counties, cities and other governmental entities in recovering civil damages under state or federal law. However, the Office cannot initiate criminal proceedings over antitrust actions.

The office of the Consumer Protection Division of the Office of the Attorney General is located in Charleston.

³²BANKING

As of June 2005, West Virginia had 71 insured banks, savings and loans, and saving banks, in addition to 7 state-chartered and 110 federally chartered credit unions (CUs). Excluding the CUs, as of 2004, the Charleston market area ranked first for its portion of financial institution deposits in the state with $4.404 billion and second in the number of financial institutions. The Huntington-Ashland market area in that same year was first in the number of financial institutions at 25, and was second by the volume of deposits at $3.566 billion. As of June 2005, CUs accounted for 9.8% of all assets held by all financial institutions in the state, or some $2.234 billion. Banks, savings and loans, and savings banks collectively accounted for the remaining 90.2% or $20.560 billion in assets held.

The state's insured banks median return on assets (ROA) ratio (the measure of earnings in relation to all resources) was unchanged in 2005 compared to 2004, at 0.96%, but up from 0.92% for 2003. The median net interest margin (the difference between the lower rates offered to savers and the higher rates charged on loans) stood at 4.30% in fourth quarter 2005, up from 4.23% for all of 2004 and 4.12% for all of 2003.

West Virginia—State Government Finances

(Dollar amounts in thousands. Per capita amounts in dollars.)

	AMOUNT	PER CAPITA
Total Revenue	11,633,343	6,416.63
General revenue	9,638,139	5,316.13
Intergovernmental revenue	3,306,193	1,823.60
Taxes	3,749,013	2,067.85
General sales	1,021,365	563.36
Selective sales	1,071,888	591.22
License taxes	179,107	98.79
Individual income tax	1,068,212	589.20
Corporate income tax	181,515	100.12
Other taxes	226,926	125.17
Current charges	1,343,207	740.88
Miscellaneous general revenue	1,239,726	683.80
Utility revenue	330	.18
Liquor store revenue	59,803	32.99
Insurance trust revenue	1,935,071	1,067.33
Total expenditure	9,879,217	5,449.10
Intergovernmental expenditure	1,942,069	1,071.19
Direct expenditure	7,937,148	4,377.91
Current operation	5,574,720	3,074.86
Capital outlay	746,595	411.80
Insurance benefits and repayments	1,257,883	693.81
Assistance and subsidies	167,482	92.38
Interest on debt	190,468	105.06
Exhibit: Salaries and wages	1,343,106	740.82
Total expenditure	9,879,217	5,449.10
General expenditure	8,555,271	4,718.85
Intergovernmental expenditure	1,942,069	1,071.19
Direct expenditure	6,613,202	3,647.66
General expenditures, by function:		
Education	2,939,679	1,621.44
Public welfare	2,294,466	1,265.56
Hospitals	72,782	40.14
Health	287,709	158.69
Highways	948,901	523.39
Police protection	58,552	32.30
Correction	182,906	100.89
Natural resources	185,025	102.05
Parks and recreation	56,547	31.19
Government administration	444,431	245.14
Interest on general debt	190,468	105.06
Other and unallocable	893,805	493.00
Utility expenditure	14,800	8.16
Liquor store expenditure	51,263	28.28
Insurance trust expenditure	1,257,883	693.81
Debt at end of fiscal year	4,745,387	2,617.42
Cash and security holdings	12,389,391	6,833.64

Abbreviations and symbols: – zero or rounds to zero; (NA) not available; (X) not applicable.

SOURCE: U.S. Census Bureau, Governments Division, 2004 Survey of State Government Finances, January 2006.

Regulation of West Virginia's state-chartered banks and other state-chartered financial institutions is the responsibility of the West Virginia Division of Banking.

33 INSURANCE

As of 2003, there were four property and casualty companies and one life and health insurance company domiciled in the state. In 2003, direct premiums for property and casualty insurance totaled $2.3 billion. That year, there were 21,424 flood insurance policies in force in the state, at a total value of $1.8 billion. About $47 million of coverage was held through FAIR plans, which are designed to offer coverage for some natural circumstances, such as wind and hail, in high risk areas.

In 2004, there were about 1.1 million individual life insurance policies in force with a total value of $43.7 billion; total value for all categories of life insurance (individual, group, and credit) was $80.3 billion. The average coverage amount is $39,600 per policy holder. Death benefits paid that year totaled $308.2 million.

In 2004, 47% of state residents held employment-based health insurance policies, 3% held individual policies, and 32% were covered under Medicare and Medicaid; 17% of residents were uninsured. In 2003, employee contributions for employment-based health coverage averaged at 14% for single coverage and 17% for family coverage. The state offers an 18-month health benefits expansion program for small-firm employees in connection with the Consolidated Omnibus Budget Reconciliation Act (COBRA, 1986), a health insurance program for those who lose employment-based coverage due to termination or reduction of work hours.

In 2003, there were over 1.2 million auto insurance policies in effect for private passenger cars. Required minimum coverage includes bodily injury liability of up to $20,000 per individual and $40,000 for all persons injured in an accident, as well as property damage liability of $10,000 and uninsured motorist coverage. In 2003, the average expenditure per vehicle for insurance coverage was $841.95.

34 SECURITIES

There are no securities exchanges in West Virginia. In 2005, there were 220 personal financial advisers employed in the state and 390 securities, commodities, and financial services sales agents. In 2004, there were over 21 publicly traded companies within the state, with over eight NASDAQ companies and three AMEX listings. In 2006, the state had one Fortune 1,000 company; Wheeling Pittsburgh, based in Wheeling and listed on NASDAQ, ranked 943rd in the nation with revenues of over $1.5 billion.

35 PUBLIC FINANCE

The state constitution requires the governor to submit to the legislature within 10 days after the opening of a regular legislative session a budget for the ensuing fiscal year (FY) which runs 1 July through 30 June.

Fiscal year 2006 general funds were estimated at $3.9 billion for resources and $3.8 billion for expenditures. In fiscal year 2004, federal government grants to West Virginia were $3.7 billion.

In the fiscal year 2007 federal budget, West Virginia was slated to receive $35 million to build a Department of Veterans Affairs data center in Martinsburg.

36 TAXATION

In 2005, West Virginia collected $4,301 million in tax revenues or $2,367 per capita, which placed it 16th among the 50 states in per capita tax burden. The national average was $2,192 per capita. Property taxes accounted for 0.1% of the total, sales taxes 25.5%, selective sales taxes 24.6%, individual income taxes 27.2%, corporate income taxes 10.8%, and other taxes 11.8%.

As of 1 January 2006, West Virginia had five individual income tax brackets ranging from 3.0% to 6.5%. The state taxes corporations at a flat rate of 9.0%.

In 2004, state and local property taxes amounted to $979,034,000 or $540 per capita. The per capita amount ranks the state 44th highest nationally. Local governments collected $975,664,000 of the total and the state government $3,370,000.

West Virginia taxes retail sales at a rate of 6%. Food purchased for consumption off-premises is taxable. The tax on cigarettes is 55 cents per pack, which ranks 35th among the 50 states and the District of Columbia. West Virginia taxes gasoline at 27 cents per gallon. This is in addition to the 18.4 cents per gallon federal tax on gasoline.

According to the Tax Foundation, for every federal tax dollar sent to Washington in 2004, West Virginia citizens received $1.83 in federal spending, which ranks West Virginia third-highest nationally.

37 ECONOMIC POLICY

The West Virginia Development Office supports business and industry in the state and assists new companies with site location and employee training programs as well as with the construction of plants and access roads and the provision of essential services. The West Virginia Economic Development Authority may make loans of up to 45% of the costs of land, buildings, and equipment at low interest rates for a normal term of 15 years. Tax incentives include a credit of 10% on industrial expansion and revitalization, applicable to the business and occupations tax over a 10-year period. The Development Office helps small business by investing in venture capital companies and by offering loans for venture capital purposes. In 2006, West Virginia has trade offices in Munich, Germany and Nagoya, Japan. Workforce development has been one important focus for economic development in the state.

38 HEALTH

The infant mortality rate in October 2005 was estimated at 8.2 per 1,000 live births. The birth rate in 2003 was 11.5 per 1,000 population. The abortion rate stood at 6.8 per 1,000 women in 2000. In 2003, about 85.8% of pregnant woman received prenatal care beginning in the first trimester. In 2004, approximately 87% of children received routine immunizations before the age of three.

The crude death rate in 2003 of 11.8 deaths per 1,000 population was the highest rate in the nation. West Virginia also had the highest mortality rates in the nation for heart disease, cancer, chronic lower respiratory diseases and diabetes. As of 2002, the death rates for major causes of death (per 100,000 resident population) were: heart disease, 343.5; cancer, 258.2; cerebrovascular diseases, 69.9; chronic lower respiratory diseases, 68.2; and diabetes, 47. The mortality rate from HIV infection was 1.1 per 100,000 population, the second-lowest rate in the nation after Iowa. In 2004, the reported AIDS case rate was at about 5.1 per 100,000 population. In 2002, about 61.2% of the population was considered overweight or obese, representing the highest percentage in the nation. As of 2004, about 26.9% of state residents were smokers, representing the second-highest percentage in the nation, after Kentucky.

In 2003, West Virginia had 57 community hospitals with about 7,800 beds. There were about 296,000 patient admissions that year and 5.8 million outpatient visits. The average daily inpatient census was about 4,800 patients. The average cost per day for hospital care was $993. Also in 2003, there were about 136 certified nursing facilities in the state with 11,152 beds and an overall occupancy rate of about 89.3%. In 2004, it was estimated that about 62.5% of all state residents had received some type of dental care within the year. West Virginia had 254 physicians per 100,000 resident population in 2004 and 861 nurses per 100,000 in 2005. In 2004, there was a total of 844 dentists in the state.

Medical education is provided by medical schools at West Virginia University and Marshall University and at the West Virginia School of Osteopathic Medicine.

About 20% of state residents were enrolled in Medicaid programs in 2003. In 2004, 19% were enrolled in Medicare programs; this percentage was the highest in the nation. Approximately 17% of the state population was uninsured in 2004. In 2003, state health care expenditures totaled $2.2 million.

39 SOCIAL WELFARE

Although rich in natural resources, West Virginia is a generally poor state. In 2004, about 44,000 people received unemployment benefits, with the average weekly unemployment benefit at $219. In fiscal year 2005, the estimated average monthly participation in the food stamp program included about 262,442 persons (114,038 households); the average monthly benefit was about $81.94 per person. That year, the total of benefits paid through the state for the food stamp program was about $258 million.

Temporary Assistance for Needy Families (TANF), the system of federal welfare assistance that officially replaced Aid to Families with Dependent Children (AFDC) in 1997, was reauthorized through the Deficit Reduction Act of 2005. TANF is funded through federal block grants that are divided among the states based on an equation involving the number of recipients in each state. West Virginia's TANF program is called West Virginia Works. In 2004, the state program had 36,000 recipients; state and federal expenditures on this TANF program totaled $88 million in fiscal year 2003.

In December 2004, Social Security benefits were paid to 407,460 West Virginians. This number included 205,770 retired workers, 54,610 widows and widowers, 76,340 disabled workers, 31,890 spouses, and 38,850 children. Social Security beneficiaries represented 22.6% of the total state population and 92.2% of the state's population age 65 and older. Retired workers received an average monthly payment of $943; widows and widowers, $858; disabled workers, $936; and spouses, $443. Payments for children of retired workers averaged $447 per month; children of deceased workers, $616; and children of disabled workers, $268. Federal Supplemental Security Income payments in December 2004 went to 75,982 West Virginia residents, averaging $401 a month.

40 HOUSING

In 2004, West Virginia had an estimated 866,944 housing units, 736,954 of which were occupied; 74% were owner-occupied (the third-highest percentage of owner-occupied units in the nation, following Minnesota and Michigan). About 70.2% of all units were single-family, detached homes; 16% were mobile homes. Utility gas and electricity were the most common energy sources for heating. It was estimated that 44,343 units lacked telephone service, 3,995 lacked complete plumbing facilities, and 4,267 lacked complete kitchen facilities. The average household had 2.40 members.

In 2004, 5,700 new privately owned housing units were authorized for construction. The median home value was $81,826, one of the lowest in the country. The median monthly cost for mortgage owners was $769, representing the lowest rate in the country. Renters paid a median of $461 per month, which was also the lowest rate in the nation. In September 2005, the state received grants of $400,000 from the US Department of Housing and Urban Development (HUD) for rural housing and economic development programs. For 2006, HUD allocated to the state over $17 million in community development block grants.

41 EDUCATION

In 2004, 80.9% of adult West Virginians were high school graduates, below the national average of 84%. Only 15.3% had completed four or more years of college, also well below the national average of 26%.

The total enrollment for fall 2002 in West Virginia's public schools stood at 282,000. Of these, 197,000 attended schools from kindergarten through grade eight, and 82,000 attended high school. Approximately 94.1% of the students were white, 4.6% were black, 0.5% were Hispanic, 0.6% were Asian/Pacific Islander, and 0.1% were American Indian/Alaskan Native. Total enrollment was estimated at 279,000 in fall 2003 and expected to be 255,000 by fall 2014, a decline of 9.8% during the period 2002–14. Expenditures for public education in 2003/04 were estimated at $2.6 billion. There were 14,397 students enrolled in 166 private schools in fall 2003. Since 1969, the National Assessment of Educational Progress (NAEP) has tested public school students nationwide. The resulting report, *The Nation's Report Card,* stated that in 2005, eighth graders in West Virginia scored 269 out of 500 in mathematics compared with the national average of 278.

As of fall 2002, there were 93,723 students enrolled in college or graduate school; minority students comprised 7.2% of total postsecondary enrollment. In 2005 West Virginia had 40 degree-granting institutions including 12 public 4-year schools, 6 public 2-year schools and 10 nonprofit private 4-year schools. The state supports West Virginia University, Marshall University, and the West Virginia College of Graduate Studies (all offering graduate work), as well as three medical schools.

42 ARTS

The West Virginia Commission on the Arts was established in 1967 and is part of the West Virginia Division of Culture and History. In 2005, the commission and other West Virginia arts organizations received eight grants totaling $637,900 from the National Endowment for the Arts. In 2005, the National Endowment for the Humanities contributed $578,176 for six state programs. Contributions to the arts also come from state and private sources.

West Virginia is known for the quilts, pottery, and woodwork of its mountain artisans. The Huntington Museum of Art, the Avampato Discovery Museum at the Clay Center (formerly the Sunrise Museum), and Oglebay Park in Wheeling are major art centers. The Avampato Discovery Museum was initially accredited by the American Association of Museums (AAM) in 1976 and has maintained that status as of 2003. The museum features both art and science exhibits and, since their relocation in July 2004 to the Clay Center, the museum has hosted almost 300,000 guests.

Other musical attractions include the West Virginia Symphony Orchestra in Charleston, the Charleston Ballet, Charleston Light Opera Guild, the Wheeling Symphony, and a country music program at Wheeling. The Charleston Stage Company and the Children's Theater of Charleston are also popular. As of 2005, the Charleston Light Opera Guild (founded in 1949) has produced over 150 musical theater shows. The Mountain State Art and Craft Fair is held each summer at Ripley. FestivALL Charleston began in 2005 and was designed to become an annual celebration of the arts.

43 LIBRARIES AND MUSEUMS

In 2001, West Virginia had 97 public library systems, with a total of 177 libraries, of which there were 80 branches. In that same year, the systems had a combined 4,920,000 volumes of books and serial publications, and a combined circulation of 7,868,000. The system also had 151,000 audio and 126,000 video items, 11,000 electronic format items (CD-ROMs, magnetic tapes, and disks), and seven bookmobiles. The largest was the Kanawha County Public Library system at Charleston, with 628,308 volumes. Of college and university libraries, the largest collection was at West Virginia University. In fiscal year 2001, operating income for the state's public library system totaled $26,844,000 and included $336,000 from federal sources and $8,302,000 from state sources.

There were 51 museums in 2000, including the State Museum and the Sunrise Museum in Charleston, and Oglebay Institute-Mansion Museum in Wheeling. Point Pleasant marks the site of a battle between colonists and Indians, and Harpers Ferry is the site of John Brown's raid. Wheeling is the location of the Oglebay's Good Children's Zoo.

44 COMMUNICATIONS

In 2004, 93.2% of West Virginian homes had telephones. Additionally, by June of that same year there were 713,657 mobile wireless telephone subscribers. In 2003, 55.0% of West Virginia households had a computer and 47.6% had Internet access. By June 2005, there were 178,242 high-speed lines in West Virginia, 166,454 residential and 11,788 for business. In 2005, broadcasting facilities included 9 major AM and 46 major FM radio stations, and 13 major television stations. Approximately 13,062 Internet domain names were registered in the state as of 2000.

45 PRESS

In 2005 West Virginia had 20 daily newspapers and 12 Sunday newspapers.

The following table shows leading West Virginia newspapers with their approximate 2002 circulations:

AREA	NAME	DAILY	SUNDAY
Charleston	*Gazette* (m,S)	68,975	84,676*
	Daily Mail (e,S)	68,975	84,676*
Huntington	*Herald–Dispatch* (m,S)	29,323	35,492
Wheeling	*Intelligencer/News Register* (m,e,S)	33,644	39,696

*The Sunday edition is a combination of the *Gazette* and the *Daily Mail*.

46 ORGANIZATIONS

In 2006, there were over 2,300 nonprofit organizations registered within the state, of which about 1,421 were registered as charitable, educational, or religious organizations.

The West Virginia Coal Association is one of several statewide labor, business, and professional associations. The Black Lung Association promotes safe working conditions in coalmines and benefits for disabled miners. The Appalachian Studies Association is based in Huntington. The Hereditary Order of the Families of the Presidents and First Ladies of America, based in Sutton, was established in 2003. There are city and county historical societies throughout the state. Some counties also sponsor arts councils. The Cacapon Institute and the Ohio Valley Environmental Coalition are regional environmental conservation organizations. The headquarters of the Appalachian Trail Conference is in Harpers Ferry and the American Association of Zoological Parks and Aquariums is in Oglebay.

47 TOURISM, TRAVEL, AND RECREATION

In 2004, tourists spent $3.4 billion on visits to the state; in 2002, almost 23.9 million travelers visited West Virginia, representing an increase of 8.5% from 2000, with some 14.19 million visitors making day trips. Travel spending has increased every year since 2000. Tourism supports an estimated 41,000 jobs and generates $766 million in state taxes. About 250,000 whitewater rafting enthusiasts raft West Virginia waters each year, and more than 750,000 skiers venture down the slopes of the Appalachian Mountains.

Major attractions are Harpers Ferry National Historical Park, New River Gorge National River, the Naval Telecommunications Station at Sugar Grove, and White Sulphur Springs, a popular mountain golfing resort. Mountaineer casinos, with over 3,200 slot machines, attract many visitors also.

Nearly 80% of the state is covered by forest. Among the 37 state parks and state forests are Cass Scenic Railroad, which includes a restoration of an old logging line, and Prickett's Fort, with recreations of pioneer life.

48 SPORTS

No major professional teams are based in West Virginia, but there are minor league baseball teams in Charleston, Bluefield, and Princeton, and there is minor league hockey in Wheeling. West Virginia University's basketball team won a National Invitation Tournament championship in 1942 and was National Collegiate Athletic Association (NCAA) Division I runner-up in 1959. In football, West Virginia produced a string of national contenders in the late 1980s and early 1990s. West Virginia won the Peach Bowl in 1981 and played for the national championship in the 1989 Fiesta Bowl, which they lost to Notre Dame. Marshall University has also risen to the elite among college football teams, having secured a string of several Mid-American Conference champions and having won five straight bowl game appearances from 1998 to 2002.

Horse-racing tracks operate in Chester and Charles Town. Greyhound races are run in Wheeling and Charleston. Other popular sports are skiing and white-water rafting.

Professional athletes born in West Virginia include George Brett, Mary Lou Retton, and Jerry West.

49 FAMOUS WEST VIRGINIANS

Among West Virginians who have served in presidential cabinets are Nathan Goff Jr. (1843–1920), navy secretary; William L. Wilson (1843–1900), postmaster general; John Barton Payne (1855–1935), interior secretary; and Newton D. Baker (1871–1937), secretary of war during World War I. Lewis L. Strauss (1896–1974) was commerce secretary and chairman of the Atomic Energy Commission, and Cyrus R. Vance (1917–2002) served as secretary of state. John W. Davis (1873–1955), an ambassador to Great Britain, ran as the Democratic presidential nominee in 1924. Prominent members of the US Senate have included Matthew M. Neely (1874–1958), who was also governor, Harley M. Kilgore (1893–1956), and Robert C. Byrd (b.1917).

Thomas J. "Stonewall" Jackson (1824–63) was a leading Confederate general during the Civil War. Brigadier General Charles E. "Chuck" Yeager (b.1923), a World War II ace, became the first person to fly faster than the speed of sound.

Major state political leaders, all governors (though some have held federal offices), have been E. Willis Wilson (1844–1905), Henry D. Hatfield (1875–1962), Arch A. Moore Jr. (b.1923), and John D. "Jay" Rockefeller IV (b.New York, 1937).

The state's only Nobel Prize winner has been Pearl S. Buck (Pearl Sydenstricker, 1893–1973), who won the Nobel Prize for literature for her novels concerning China. Alexander Campbell (b.Ireland, 1788–1866), with his father, founded the Disciples of Christ Church and was president of Bethany College in West Virginia. Major labor leaders have included Walter Reuther (1907–70), president of the United Automobile Workers, and Arnold Miller (1923–85), president of the United Mine Workers.

Musicians include George Crumb (b.1929), a Pulitzer Prize-winning composer, and opera singers Eleanor Steber (1916–90) and Phyllis Curtin (b.1922). Melville Davisson Post (1871–1930) was a leading writer of mystery stories. Important writers of the modern period include Mary Lee Settle (1918–2005) and John Knowles (1926–2001). Jerry West (b.1938) was a collegiate and professional basketball star, and a pro coach after his playing days ended; Rod Hundley (b.1934) and Hal Greer (b.1936) also starred in the National Basketball Association. Mary Lou Retton (b.1968) won a gold medal in gymnastics at the 1984 Olympics. Another West Virginian of note is Anna Jarvis (1864–1948), founder of Mother's Day.

⁵⁰BIBLIOGRAPHY

Brisbin, Richard A. Jr., et al. (eds.). *West Virginia Politics and Government.* Lincoln: University of Nebraska Press, 1996.

Council of State Governments. *The Book of the States, 2006 Edition.* Lexington, Ky.: Council of State Governments, 2006.

Duda, Mark Damian. *West Virginia Wildlife Viewing Guide.* Helena, Mont.: Falcon, 1999.

Lesser, W. Hunter. *Rebels at the Gate: Lee and McClellan on the Front Line of a Nation Divided.* Naperville, Ill.: Sourcebooks, 2004.

Lilly, John (ed.). *Mountains of Music: West Virginia Traditional Music from Goldenseal.* Urbana: University of Illinois Press, 1999.

Rice, Otis K. *West Virginia: A History.* 2nd ed. Lexington: University of Kentucky Press, 1993.

Shogan, Robert. *The Battle of Blair Mountain: The Story of America's Largest Labor Uprising.* Boulder, Colo.: Westview Press, 2004.

Thomas, Jerry Bruce. *An Appalachian New Deal: West Virginia in the Great Depression.* Lexington: The University Press of Kentucky, 1998.

US Department of Commerce, Economics and Statistics Administration, US Census Bureau. *West Virginia, 2000. Summary Social, Economic, and Housing Characteristics: 2000 Census of Population and Housing.* Washington, D.C.: US Government Printing Office, 2003.

WISCONSIN

State of Wisconsin

ORIGIN OF STATE NAME: Probably from the Ojibwa word *wishkonsing,* meaning "place of the beaver." **NICKNAME:** The Badger State. **CAPITAL:** Madison. **ENTERED UNION:** 29 May 1848 (30th). **SONG:** "On, Wisconsin!" **MOTTO:** Forward. **COAT OF ARMS:** Surrounding the US shield is the shield of Wisconsin, which is divided into four parts symbolizing agriculture, mining, navigation, and manufacturing. Flanking the shield are a sailor, representing labor on water; and a yeoman or miner, representing labor on land. Above is a badger and the state motto; below, a horn of plenty and a pyramid of pig lead. **FLAG:** A dark-blue field, fringed in yellow on three sides, surrounds the state coat of arms on each side, with "Wisconsin" in white letters above the coat of arms and '1848' below. **OFFICIAL SEAL:** Coat of arms surrounded by the words "Great Seal of the State of Wisconsin" and 13 stars below. **BIRD:** Robin. **FISH:** Muskellunge. **FLOWER:** Wood violet. **TREE:** Sugar maple. **LEGAL HOLIDAYS:** New Year's Day, 1 January; Birthday of Martin Luther King Jr., 3rd Monday in January; Presidents' Day, 3rd Monday in February; Good Friday, Friday before Easter, March or April; Memorial Day, last Monday in May; Independence Day, 4 July; Labor Day, 1st Monday in September; Primary Day, 2nd Tuesday in September in even-numbered years; Columbus Day, 2nd Monday in October; Election Day, 2nd Tuesday in November in even-numbered years; Veterans' Day, 11 November; Thanksgiving Day, 4th Thursday in November; Christmas Day, 25 December. **TIME:** 6 AMCST = noon GMT.

¹LOCATION, SIZE, AND EXTENT

Located in the eastern north-central United States, Wisconsin ranks 26th in size among the 50 states.

The total area of Wisconsin is 56,153 sq mi (145,436 sq km), of which 54,426 sq mi (140,963 sq km) is land and 1,727 sq mi is (4,473 sq km) inland water. The state extends 295 mi (475 km) E–W and 320 mi (515 km) N–S.

Wisconsin is bordered on the N by Lake Superior and the state of Michigan (with the northeastern boundary formed by the Menominee River); on the E by Lake Michigan; on the S by Illinois; and on the W by Iowa and Minnesota (with the line defined mainly by the Mississippi and St. Croix rivers).

Important islands belonging to Wisconsin are the Apostle Islands in Lake Superior, and Washington Island in Lake Michigan. The state's boundaries have a total length of 1,379 mi (2,219 km). Wisconsin's geographic center is in Wood County, 9 mi (14 km) SE of Marshfield.

²TOPOGRAPHY

Wisconsin can be divided into four main geographical regions, each covering roughly one-quarter of the state's land area. The most highly elevated of these is the Superior Upland, below Lake Superior and the border with Michigan. It has heavily forested rolling hills but no high mountains. Elevations range from about 700 ft (200 m) to slightly under 2,000 ft (600 m). A second upland region, called the Driftless Area, has a more rugged terrain, having been largely untouched by the glacial drifts that smoothed out topographical features in other parts of the state. Elevations here reach more than 1,200 ft (400 m). The third region is a large, crescent-shaped plain in central Wisconsin; its unglaciated portion is a sandstone plain, broken by rock formations that from a distance appear similar to the buttes and mesas of Colorado. Finally, in the east and southeast along Lake Michigan lies a large, glaciated lowland plain, fairly smooth in the Green Bay-Winnebago area but more irregular on the Door Peninsula and in the south.

Wisconsin's mean altitude is 1,050 ft (320 m), with elevations generally higher in the north. The Gogebic Range, extending westward from Michigan's Upper Peninsula into northern Wisconsin, was an important center of iron mining in the early days of statehood. Timms Hill, in north-central Wisconsin, is the state's highest point, at 1,951 ft (595 m). The lowest elevation is 579 ft (177 m), along the Lake Michigan shoreline.

There are well over 8,000 lakes in Wisconsin. Lakes Michigan and Superior form part of the northern and eastern borders; the Wisconsin mainland has at least 575 mi (925 km) of lakeshore and holds jurisdiction over 10,062 sq mi (26,061 sq km) of lake waters. By far, the largest inland lake is Lake Winnebago, in eastern Wisconsin, covering an area of 215 sq mi (557 sq km).

The Mississippi River, which forms part of the border with Minnesota and the entire border with Iowa, is the main navigable river. The major river flowing through the state is the Wisconsin, which follows a south-southwest course for 430 mi (692 km) before meeting the Mississippi at the Iowa border. Other tributaries of the Mississippi are the St. Croix River, also part of the Minnesota border, and the Chippewa and Black rivers. Located on the Black River are Big Manitou Falls, at 165 ft (50 m) the highest of the state's many waterfalls. Waters from the Fox River and its major tributary, the Wolf, flow into Green Bay and then into Lake Michigan, as does the Menominee, which is part of the Michigan state line.

Except in the Driftless Area, glaciation smoothed out many surface features, gouged out new ones, and left deposits of rock and soil creating distinctively shaped hills and ridges. Oval mounds, called drumlins, are still scattered over the southeast; and moraines, formed by deposits left at the edges of glaciers, are a prominent feature of eastern, central, and northwestern Wisconsin. In one section, called the Dells, the Wisconsin River has cut a gorge through 8 mi (13 km) of sandstone, creating caves and interesting rock formations.

3 CLIMATE

Wisconsin has a continental climate. Summers are warm and winters very cold, especially in the upper northeast and north-central lowlands, where the freeze-free (growing) season is around 80 days. The average annual temperature ranges from 39°F (4°C) in the north to about 50°F (10°C) in the south. At Danbury, in the northwest, the average January daily temperature is about 8°F (-13°C), and the average July daily temperature 68.6°F (20°C); at Racine, in the southeast, these figures are 19.4°F (-7°C) and 71°F (21°C), respectively. Milwaukee has average daily temperatures ranging from 13°F (-10°C) to 27°F (-2°C) in January and from 62°F (16°C) to 79°F (26°C) in July. The lowest temperature ever recorded in Wisconsin was -55°F (-48.3°C), at Couderay on 4 February 1996; the highest, 114°F (46°C), at Wisconsin Dells on 13 July 1936.

Annual precipitation in the state ranges from about 34 in (86 cm) for parts of the northwest to about 28 in (71 cm) in the south-central region and the areas bordering Lake Superior and Lake Michigan. In Milwaukee average annual precipitation is about 32.2 in (81 cm); March, April, and May are the rainiest months in Milwaukee. Milwaukee's annual snowfall averages 47 in (118 cm); the average wind speed is 12 mph (19 km/hr).

4 FLORA AND FAUNA

Common trees of Wisconsin include four oaks—bur, black, white, and red—along with black cherry and hickory. Jack, red, and white pine, yellow birch, eastern hemlock, mountain maple, moosewood, and leatherwood grow in the north, with black spruce, black ash, balsam fir, and tamarack concentrated in the northern lowlands. Characteristic of southern Wisconsin's climax forests are sugar maple (the state tree), white elm, basswood, and ironwood, with silver maple, black willow, silver birch, and cottonwood on low, moist land. Prairies are thick with grasses; bogs and marshes are home to white and jack pines and jack oak. Forty-five varieties of orchid have been identified, as well as 20 types of violet, including the wood violet (the state flower). In April 2006, six plant species were listed as threatened by the US Fish and Wildlife Service, including the eastern prairie fringed orchid, prairie bush-clover, dwarf lake iris, Pitcher's thistle, Fassett's locoweed, and northern wild monkshood.

White-tailed deer, black bear, woodchuck, snowshoe hare, chipmunk, and porcupine are mammals typical of forestlands. The striped skunk, red and gray foxes, and various mice are characteristic of upland fields while wetlands harbor such mammals as the muskrat, mink, river otter, and water shrew. The badger, dwelling in grasslands and semi-open areas, is rarely seen today. Game birds include the ring-necked pheasant, bobwhite quail, Hungarian partridge, and ruffed grouse; among 336 bird species native to Wisconsin are 42 kinds of waterfowl and 6 types of shorebird that are also hunted. Reptiles include 23 varieties of snake, 13 types of turtle, and 4 kinds of lizard. Muskellunge (the state fish), northern pike, walleye, and brook trout are native to Wisconsin waterways.

In 2006, eight animal species were listed as threatened or endangered in Wisconsin, including the bald eagle, Karner blue butterfly, Hine's emerald dragonfly, Higgins eye pearly mussel, piping plover, and Canadian lynx. The Bureau of Endangered Resources in the Department of Natural Resources develops programs designed to aid the recovery of threatened or endangered flora and fauna.

5 ENVIRONMENTAL PROTECTION

Conservation has been a concern in Wisconsin for more than a century. In 1867, a legislative commission reported that depletion of the northern forests by wasteful timber industry practices and frequent forest fires had become an urgent problem, partly because it increased the hazards of flooding. In 1897, a forestry warden was appointed and a system of fire detection and control was set up. A reforestation program was instituted in 1911; at about the same time, the state university began planting rows of trees in plains areas to protect soil from wind erosion, a method that was widely copied in other states. Fish and game wardens were appointed in the 1880s. In 1927, the state began a program to clean its waters of industrial wastes, caused especially by pulp and paper mills and canneries. The legislature enacted a comprehensive antipollution program in 1966.

The present Department of Natural Resources (DNR), organized in 1967, brings together conservation and environmental protection responsibilities. The department supervises air, water, and solid-waste pollution control programs and deals with the protection of forest, fish, and wildlife resources.

Southeastern Wisconsin has experienced serious air quality problems since the 1970s. Reductions in industrial emissions have been offset by increases in emissions from transportation sources and consumer products. In 2002, the US Environmental Protection Agency implemented new requirements for reporting air quality, and the DNR developed procedures to help corporations comply.

Since water pollution became a serious problem in the 1920s, pulp and paper mills, cheese factories, and canneries have taken major steps to control and prevent harmful water pollution. Communities built new or upgraded existing sewage treatment plants to reduce the flow of sewage into rivers and streams. Pulp and paper mills spent millions of dollars to reduce suspended solids and other pollutants in their industrial effluent. Water quality and fisheries visibly improved, but problems caused by persistent toxic chemicals, such as PCBs (polychlorinated biphenyls) and mercury, arose that had to be addressed next. In the 1980s, the state identified five Areas of Concern on Lakes Michigan and Superior where toxic pollutants harmed fish or wildlife or impaired human use of the waterways. Efforts are underway to identify sources of contamination and cleanup options at these sites and inland areas suffering similar problems. Regulations controlling the discharge of toxic substances from both water and air were passed in the late 1980s, and water quality improved significantly by 2000. In 2003, 50.8 million lb of toxic chemicals were released in the state.

Contaminated stormwater and run-off from agriculture, development, and other sources remain the most serious threats to Wisconsin's lakes, rivers, and streams. The state adopted rules to limit stormwater contamination in large municipalities, construc-

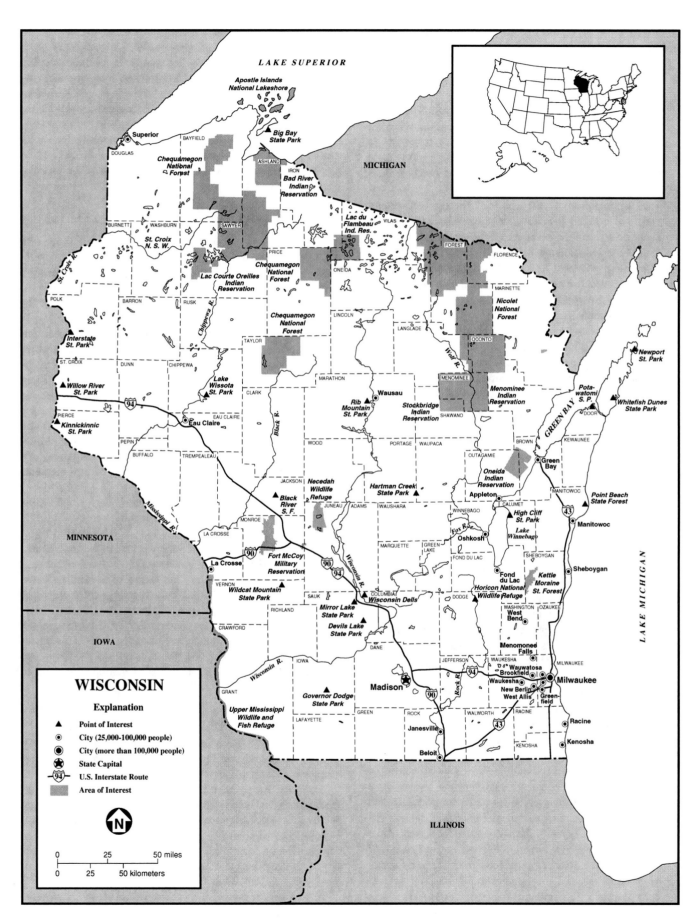

LAKE SUPERIOR

Apostle Islands
National Lakeshore

Superior

MICHIGAN

Big Bay
State Park

BAYFIELD

DOUGLAS

ASHLAND

IRON

Chequamegon
National
Forest

Bad River
Indian
Reservation

BURNETT

WASHBURN

SAWYER

Lac du
Flambeau
Ind. Res.

VILAS

St. Croix
N. S. W.

PRICE

FOREST

FLORENCE

POLK

BARRON

RUSK

Lac Courte Oreilles
Indian
Reservation

Chequamegon
National
Forest

ONEIDA

MARINETTE

Nicolet
National
Forest

LINCOLN

LANGLADE

OCONTO

Chequamegon
National
Forest

TAYLOR

Interstate
St. Park

ST. CROIX

DUNN

CHIPPEWA

Willow River
St. Park

CLARK

MARATHON

Wolf R.

MENOMINEE

Menominee
Indian
Reservation

Newport
St. Park

Lake
Wissota
St. Park

Wausau

Rib
Mountain
St. Park

Stockbridge
Indian
Reservation

SHAWANO

GREEN BAY

DOOR

Pota-
watomi
S. P.

Whitefish Dunes
State Park

PIERCE

Kinnickinnic
St. Park

Eau Claire

EAU CLAIRE

Black R.

PEPIN

WOOD

PORTAGE

WAUPACA

BROWN

KEWAUNEE

BUFFALO

TREMPEALEAU

JACKSON

Necedah
Wildlife
Refuge

Hartman Creek
State Park

OUTAGAMIE

Oneida
Indian
Reservation

Green
Bay

Appleton

MANITOWOC

Point Beach
State Forest

MINNESOTA

Black
River
S. F.

JUNEAU

ADAMS

WAUSHARA

CALUMET

High Cliff
St. Park

Lake
Winnebago

Manitowoc

MONROE

LA CROSSE

MARQUETTE

GREEN
LAKE

WINNEBAGO

Oshkosh

Fox R.

SHEBOYGAN

Sheboygan

La Crosse

VERNON

Wildcat Mountain
State Park

Fort McCoy
Military
Reservation

SAUK

Wisconsin R.

COLUMBIA

FOND DU LAC

Fond
du Lac

Horicon National
Wildlife Refuge

Kettle
Moraine
St. Forest

RICHLAND

Mirror Lake
State Park

Wisconsin Dells

DODGE

WASHINGTON

OZAUKEE

West
Bend

LAKE MICHIGAN

CRAWFORD

Devils Lake
State Park

DANE

Menomonee
Falls

WAUKESHA

MILWAUKEE

IOWA

IOWA

Wisconsin R.

Madison

Rock R.

JEFFERSON

Wauwatosa
Brookfield

Waukesha

New Berlin

West Allis

Milwaukee

Green-
field

GRANT

Governor Dodge
State Park

GREEN

ROCK

WALWORTH

RACINE

Racine

Upper Mississippi
Wildlife and
Fish Refuge

LAFAYETTE

Janesville

Beloit

KENOSHA

Kenosha

ILLINOIS

WISCONSIN

Explanation

▲ Point of Interest

◉ City (25,000-100,000 people)

◉ City (more than 100,000 people)

★ State Capital

94 U.S. Interstate Route

Area of Interest

N

0   25   50 miles

0   25   50 kilometers

tion sites over five acres, and 10,000 industrial facilities. The DNR also formed a citizen advisory committee in 1994 to overhaul the state's animal waste regulations; new rules to control polluted run-off from agricultural, non-agricultural, and transportation sources went into effect 1 October 2002.

Wetland protection regulations were upgraded in the late 1980s, and in 1991 the state became the first in the nation to legislate wetlands protection. Wisconsin has a Wetlands Restoration program administered by the US Department of Agriculture Natural Resources Conservation Service (NRCS) and the US Fish and Wildlife Service (FWS) with assistance from DNR. Between 1992 and 1998, approximately 11,312 acres (4,578 hectares) of wetlands were restored, bringing the total amount of wetland area to about 5 million acres (2 million hectares), or 15% of the told land area. Horicon Marsh was designated as a Ramsar Wetland of International Importance in 1990. It is considered to be one of the largest intact freshwater wetlands in the nation and among the largest cat-tail marshes in the world. The site is primarily managed through the National Wildlife Refuge program.

Wisconsin passed a comprehensive groundwater protection law in 1984 to safeguard underground water supplies that serve two-thirds of the state's population. The law requires identification and cleanup of groundwater-damaging contamination sources, such as abandoned, leaking landfills; underground gasoline storage tanks; and illegal, hazardous waste dumps. The law also requires the state to establish groundwater protection and enforcement standards for various substances. Wisconsin has identified over 16,000 contamination sites that must be cleaned up to prevent environmental contamination and safety hazards. Over one-third of these sites have been cleaned up and no further action is deemed necessary.

In 1996, Wisconsin began administering a new program whereby owners of contaminated property could petition the state for cleanup waivers if they were able to demonstrate that contamination was being cleaned up by natural processes. Property owners would then be able to redevelop within strict guidelines and monitoring. By mid-1997, 51 properties had applied for such liability releases, 30 of which were approved.

Bacterial contamination of Wisconsin drinking water supplies did not pose much of a problem in the state until 1993 when 400,000 Milwaukee residents became ill from inadequately treated water drawn from Lake Michigan. The water was found to contain the protozoan Cryptosporidium. Water treatment procedures were changed immediately at 21 community drinking water treatment plants that drew water from the Great Lakes. The state also began a two-year Cryptosporidium monitoring effort to determine the presence and distribution of this protozoan in state waterways.

In the 1980s, more than 800 landfills in the state closed because they could not meet new federal environmental protection requirements. To ease the burden on the state's remaining landfills, Wisconsin passed a comprehensive waste reduction and recycling law, 1989 Wisconsin Act 335. The law required local units of government to set up effective programs to recycle more than 11 different items by 1995. State grants collected from a tax on businesses were awarded to local governments to aid in setting up local recycling programs. The legislature is expected to decide a permanent funding mechanism in a future legislative session.

In 2003, Wisconsin had 163 hazardous waste sites listed in the US Environment Protection Agency (EPA) database, 37 of which were on the National Priorities List as of 2006, including the Eau Claire Municipal Well Field. In 2005, the EPA spent over $2.2 million through the Superfund program for the cleanup of hazardous waste sites in the state. In 2004, federal EPA grants awarded to the state included $16 million to provide assistance to the improvement of public water systems and $29.1 million to offer loan assistance for water pollution control projects. One of the largest EPA grants awarded to the state in 2005 was $2.5 million for nonpoint source implementation programs.

⁶POPULATION

Wisconsin ranked 20th in population in the United States with an estimated total of 5,536,201 in 2005, an increase of 3.2% since 2000. Between 1990 and 2000, Wisconsin's population grew from 4,891,769 to 5,363,675, an increase of 9.6%. The population is projected to reach 5.8 million by 2015 and 6.08 million by 2025. The population density in 2004 was 101.5 persons per sq mi.

During the 18th and early 19th centuries, the area that is now Wisconsin was very sparsely settled by perhaps 20,000 Indians and a few hundred white settlers, most of them engaged in the fur trade. With the development of lead mining, the population began to expand, reaching a total of 30,945 (excluding Indians) by 1840. During the next two decades, the population increased rapidly to 775,881, as large numbers of settlers from the East and German, British, and Scandinavian immigrants arrived. Subsequent growth has been steady, if slower. In the late 19th century, industry expanded and, by 1930, the population became predominantly urban.

In 2004, the median age for Wisconsinites was 37.5. In the same year, 23.7% of the State's residents were under age 18 while 13% were age 65 or older.

The majority of Wisconsinites live in urban areas, most of them in the heavily urbanized southeastern region. Milwaukee, the largest city in Wisconsin and the 22nd largest in the United States, had a population of 583,624 in 2004. Other large cities, with their 2004 population estimates, were Madison, 220,332, and Green Bay, 101,100. The Milwaukee–Waukesha–West Allis metropolitan area had an estimated population of 1,515,738 in 2004. The Madison metropolitan area had 531,766 residents and the Green Bay metropolitan area had 295,473. The Racine metropolitan area had 194,188 residents.

⁷ETHNIC GROUPS

As early as 1839, Wisconsin attracted immigrants from Norway, Sweden, Denmark, and Finland, soon to be followed by large numbers of Germans and Irish. In 1850, the greatest number of foreign-born persons were English-speaking, but within a decade, the Germans had eclipsed them. Industrial development brought Belgians, Greeks, Hungarians, Lithuanians, Italians, and especially Poles, who continued to come steadily until the restriction of immigration in the early 1920s; in the 1930 census, Poles were the largest foreign-born group. In 2000, foreign-born residents numbered 193,751 (3.6% of the total).

Black Americans were in the region as early as 1822. Before World War I, however, there were no more than 3,000 blacks. Migration during and after that war brought the number to 10,739 by 1930; by 1990, blacks were the largest racial minority in the state, numbering 245,000 (5% of Wisconsin's population). As of 2000, the black population was 304,460, or 5.7% of the state total. That percentage increased to 5.9% in 2004. Most black Wisconsinites live in Milwaukee, which was 37% black in 2000.

The Asian population in 2000 was 88,763. In that year Wisconsin had 33,791 Hmong (the nation's third-largest Hmong community), 11,184 Chinese, 6,800 Koreans, 5,158 Filipinos, and 4,469 Laotians. Pacific Islanders numbered 1,630. In 2004, 1.9% of the population was Asian. As of 2000, there were 192,921 Hispanics and Latinos (3.6% of the total population), of whom 126,719 were of Mexican ancestry and 30,267 of Puerto Rican descent. In 2004, 4.3% of the population was Hispanic or Latino. That year, 1% of the population reported origin of two or more races.

Wisconsin had an estimated 47,228 American Indians in 2000, up from 39,000 American Indians in 1990. In 2004, 0.9% of the population was American Indian or Alaskan Native. The principal tribes are Oneida, Menominee, Ojibwa (Chippewa), and Winnebago. There were 11 reservations, the largest being that of the Menominee, which comprised Menominee County (345 sq mi, 896 sq km) and had a population of 3,225 in 2000. Indian reservations covered 634 sq mi (1,642 sq km).

[8]LANGUAGES

Early French and English fur traders found in what is now Wisconsin several Indian tribes of the Algonkian family: Ojibwa along Lake Superior, Sauk in the northeast, Winnebago and Fox south of them, and Kickapoo in the southwest. Numerous Indian place-names include Antigo, Kaukauna, Kewaunee, Menomonie, Oshkosh, Wausau, and Winnebago.

The following table gives selected statistics from the 2000 Census for language spoken at home by persons five years old and over. The category "Other West Germanic languages" includes Dutch, Pennsylvania Dutch, and Afrikaans. The category "Scandinavian languages" includes Danish, Norwegian, and Swedish. The category "Other Native North American languages" includes Apache, Cherokee, Choctaw, Dakota, Keres, Pima, and Yupik.

LANGUAGE	NUMBER	PERCENT
Population 5 years and over	**5,022,073**	**100.0**
Speak only English	4,653,361	92.7
Speak a language other than English	368,712	7.3
Speak a language other than English	**368,712**	**7.3**
Spanish or Spanish Creole	168,778	3.4
German	48,409	1.0
Miao, Hmong	30,569	0.6
French (incl. Patois, Cajun)	14,970	0.3
Polish	12,097	0.2
Chinese	7,951	0.2
Italian	6,774	0.1
Other West Germanic languages	5,870	0.1
Scandinavian languages	5,651	0.1
Russian	5,362	0.1
Serbo-Croatian	4,988	0.1
Other Native North American languages	4,210	0.1
Arabic	4,088	0.1
Korean	4,075	0.1

In 2000, 92.7% (down from 94.2% in 1990) of the state population five years old and older spoke only English in the home.

Wisconsin English is almost entirely Northern, like that of the areas that provided Wisconsin's first settlers—Michigan, northern Ohio, New York State, and western New England. Common are the Northern *pail, comforter* (tied and filled bed cover), *sick to the stomach, angleworm* (earthworm), *skip school* (play truant), and *dove* as the past of *dive*. Pronunciation features are *fog, frog,* and *on* with the vowel sound /ah/; and *orange, forest,* and *foreign* with the / aw/ vowel sound. Northern *fried cakes* is now yielding to *doughnuts,* and *johnnycake* is giving way to *corn bread*. Milwaukee has *sick in the stomach* and is known for the localism *bubbler* (drinking fountain). A small exception to Northern homogeneity is the cluster of South Midland terms brought by Kentucky miners to the southwestern lead-mining district, such as *dressing* (sweet sauce for a pudding), *eaves spout* as a blend of *eavestrough* and Midland *spouting, branch* for stream, and *fishworm* for earthworm.

[9]RELIGIONS

The first Catholics to arrive were Jesuit missionaries seeking to convert the Huron Indians in the 17th century. Protestant settlers and missionaries of different sects, including large numbers of German Lutherans, came during the 19th century, along with Protestants from the east. Jews settled primarily in the cities.

These groups often had conflicting aims. Evangelical sects favored strict blue laws and temperance legislation, which was enacted in many communities. The use of Protestant prayers and the King James Bible in public schools was another source of public discord until these practices were declared unconstitutional by the state supreme court in 1890. A constitutional amendment allowing parochial school students to ride in public school buses was defeated in 1946, amid great controversy; 19 years later, however, it was enacted with little opposition. By that time, religious conflicts appeared to be on the decline.

In 2004, there were 1,658,478 Roman Catholics in Wisconsin; with about 731,516 members belonging to the archdiocese of Milwaukee. As of 2000, Lutherans make up the largest Protestant group, though they are divided in denominations: the Evangelical Lutheran Church in American, 463,432 in 2000; the Lutheran Church—Missouri Synod, 241,306; and the Wisconsin Evangelical Lutheran Synod, 241,306. Other leading Protestant groups include the United Methodists, with 95,589 members in 2004, and the United Church of Christ, with 62,521 members in 2005. There were an estimated 28,230 Jews in 2000, primarily in the Milwaukee area. The Muslim population had about 7,796 members. Though still relatively small in total membership, the Salvation Army reported growth from 2,574 members in 1990 to 12,951 members in 2000, a difference of 403%. In a 2000 report, over 2.1 million people (about 39% of the population) were not counted as members of any religious organization.

The US office of the Catholic Apostleship of Prayer is located in Milwaukee. The headquarters of the InterVarsity Christian Fellowship/USA, an evangelical Christian program directed toward college students, is based in Madison. The offices of the National Association of Congregational Christian Churches are based in Oak Creek. The Seventh Day Baptist General Conference of the United States and Canada is based in Janesville.

¹⁰TRANSPORTATION

Wisconsin's first rail line was built across the state, from Milwaukee to Prairie du Chien, in the 1850s. Communities soon began vying with one another to be included on proposed railroad routes. Several thousand farmers mortgaged property to buy railroad stock; the state had to rescue them from ruin when companies went bankrupt. By the late 1860s, two railroads, the Chicago and North Western, and the Chicago, Milwaukee, and St. Paul, had become dominant in the state. However, Chicago emerged as the major rail center of the Midwest because of its proximity to eastern markets. In 1920, there were 35 railroads operating on 11,615 mi (18,700 km) of track. By 2003, there were just 10 railroads operating on 4,167 rail mi (6,708 km) of track, of which 3,462 mi (5,573 km) was operated by Class I lines. Nonmetallic minerals were the top commodities carried by rail that originated within the state in 2003, while coal was the top commodity carried by rail that terminated within Wisconsin. As of 2006, Amtrak provided passenger rail service to 10 stations in Wisconsin via its north–south Hiawatha (Milwaukee to Chicago) train and east–west service via its Empire Builder (Chicago to Seattle/Portland) train.

As of 2004, Wisconsin had 113,699 mi (183,055 km) of public roadway. The private passenger vehicle continues to be the dominant mode of travel. In that same year, Wisconsin had 3,910,188 licensed drivers and some 4.868 million registered vehicles (2.575 million automobiles and 2.051 million trucks of all types).

Public transit includes large bus systems in Milwaukee and Madison. In the mid-1990s, Milwaukee County Transit System transported more than 60 million passengers annually, and Madison Metro annually transported more than 9.9 million passengers.

The opening of the St. Lawrence Seaway in 1959 allowed oceangoing vessels access to Wisconsin via the Great Lakes but failed to stimulate traffic to the extent anticipated. Overall, the state has 15 cargo-handling ports. The port of Superior (shared with Duluth, Minnesota) on Lake Superior is the busiest of all US Great Lakes ports. Its chief commodities are iron ore and coal. In 2004, the Port of Duluth/Superior handled 45.392 million tons of cargo, making it the 19th-busiest port in the United States. Other important Wisconsin ports, all on Lake Michigan, are Milwaukee, Green Bay, Port Washington, Oak Creek, Manitowoc, and Sturgeon Bay. Coal is the chief commodity. The Port of Milwaukee in 2004, handled 3.155 million tons of cargo. On the Mississippi River, Prairie du Chien and La Crosse are the main ports. Ferry service across Lake Michigan is offered from Manitowoc to Ludington, Michigan. In 2003, waterborne shipments totaled 33.546 million tons. In 2004, Wisconsin had 231 mi (371 km) of navigable inland waterways.

In 2005, Wisconsin had a total of 565 public and private-use aviation-related facilities. This included 459 airports, 89 heliports, and 17 seaplane bases. Milwaukee's General Mitchell International Airport is the state's main air terminal, with 3,302,604 enplanements in 2004.

¹¹HISTORY

The region that is now Wisconsin has probably been inhabited since the end of the glacial period, 10,000 years ago. Some of the earliest inhabitants were ancestors of the Menominee; these early immigrants from the north built burial mounds, conical ones at first, then large effigy mounds shaped like different animals. Other peoples arrived from the south and east, including ancestors of the Winnebago Indians (about AD 1400) and a tribe that built flattop earthen pyramids. During the 17th century, the Ojibwa, Sauk, Fox, Potawatomi, Kickapoo, and other tribes came to Wisconsin. These tribes engaged in agriculture, hunting, and fishing, but with the arrival of Europeans, they became increasingly dependent on the fur trade—a dependence that had serious economic consequences when the fur trade declined in the early 19th century.

The first European believed to have reached Wisconsin was Jean Nicolet, who in 1634 landed on the shores of Green Bay while in the service of Samuel de Champlain. Two decades later, Médard Chouart des Groseilliers and Pierre Esprit Radisson, both fur traders, explored northern Wisconsin; in 1673, the Jesuit priest Jacques Marquette and the explorer Louis Jolliet crossed the whole area that is now Wisconsin, via the Fox and Wisconsin rivers, on their way to the Mississippi. Other Jesuits established missions, and French fur traders opened up posts. The French were succeeded by the British after the French and Indian War (the British ruled Wisconsin as part of Quebec Province from 1774 to 1783). Although ceded to the United States in 1783, it remained British in all but name until 1816, when the United States built forts at Prairie du Chien and Green Bay.

Under the Ordinance of 1787, Wisconsin became part of the Northwest Territory; it was subsequently included in the Indiana Territory, the Territory of Illinois, and then the Michigan Territory. In the early 1820s, lead mining brought an influx of white settlers called "Badgers." Indian resistance to white expansion collapsed after the 1832 Black Hawk War, in which Sauk and Fox Indians fleeing from Illinois were defeated and massacred by white militia near the site of present-day La Crosse, at the Battle of Bad Axe. Subsequently, the Winnebago and other tribes were removed to reservations outside the state, while the Ojibwa, Menominee, and some eastern tribes were among those resettled in reservations inside Wisconsin.

The Wisconsin Territory was formed in 1836. Initially it included all of Iowa and Minnesota, along with a portion of the Dakotas, but in 1838, these areas became part of a newly organized Iowa Territory. The 1830s also saw the beginning of a land boom, fueled by migration of Yankees from New England and southerners who moved to the lead-mining region of southwestern Wisconsin. The population and economy began to expand rapidly. Wisconsin voters endorsed statehood in 1846, and Congress passed enabling legislation that year. After a first constitution was rejected by the voters, a revised document was adopted on 13 March 1848, and on 29 May, President James K. Polk signed the bill that made Wisconsin the 30th state.

Transportation and industry did not develop as rapidly as proponents of statehood had expected. A canal was opened at the portage between the Fox and Wisconsin rivers in 1851, but the waterway was not heavily used. Railroads encountered difficulties in gaining financing, then suffered setbacks in the panic of 1857.

Wisconsinites took a generally abolitionist stand, and it was in Wisconsin—at Ripon, on 28 February 1854—that the Republican Party was formally established in the state. The new party developed an efficient political machine and later used much of its influence to benefit the railroads and lumber industry, both of which grew in importance in the decade following the Civil War. In that war, 96,000 Wisconsin men fought on the Union side, and 12,216 died. During the late 19th century, Wisconsin was generally prosperous; dairying, food processing, and lumbering emerged as major industries, and Milwaukee grew into an important industrial center.

Wisconsin took a new political turn in the early 20th century with the inauguration of Republican Robert "Fighting Bob" La Follette as governor and the dawning of the Progressive Era. An ardent reformer, La Follette fought against conservatives within his own party. In 1903, the legislature, under his prodding, passed a law providing for the nation's first direct statewide primary; other measures that he championed during his tenure as governor (1901–06) provided for increased taxation of railroads, regulation of lobbyists, creation of a civil service, and establishment of a railroad commission to regulate intrastate rates.

La Follette was also a conspicuous exponent of what came to be called the "Wisconsin idea": governmental reform guided by academic experts and supported by an enlightened electorate. Around the time he was governor, the philosophy of reform was energetically promoted at the University of Wisconsin (which had opened at Madison, the state capital, in 1849), and many professors were drafted to serve on government commissions and boards. In 1901, Wisconsin became the first state to establish a legislative reference bureau, intended to help lawmakers shape effective, forward-looking measures.

After La Follette left the governor's office to become a US senator, his progressivism was carried on by Republican governors James O. Davidson (1906–11) and especially by Francis E. McGovern (1911–15). During one session in 1911, legislators enacted the first state income tax in the United States and one of the first workers' compensation programs. Other legislation passed during the same year sought to regulate the insurance business and the use of water power, create forest reserves, encourage farmer cooperatives, limit and require disclosure of political campaign expenditures, and establish a board of public affairs to recommend efficiency measures for state and local governments. This outburst of activity attracted national attention, and many states followed in Wisconsin's footsteps.

While serving as US Senator (1906–25), La Follette opposed involvement in World War I and was one of only six Senators to vote against US entry into the war; as a result, he was censured by the state legislature and the faculty of the University of Wisconsin, and there was a move to expel him from the Senate. His renomination and reelection in 1922 served to vindicate him, however, and he carried Wisconsin when he ran in 1924 for president on the national League for Progressive Political Action ticket.

After his death in 1925, the reform tradition continued in Wisconsin. A pioneering old-age pension act was passed in 1925; seven years later, Wisconsin enacted the nation's first unemployment compensation act, with the encouragement of La Follette's son Philip, then serving his first term as governor. When Wisconsin went Democratic in November 1932, turning Philip out of office, he and his brother, Robert Jr., a US Senator, temporarily left the state Republican organization and in 1934 formed a separate Progressive Party; that party, with the support of President Franklin Roosevelt and the Socialists, swept the 1934 elections and returned both brothers to office. During his second and third terms as governor, Philip La Follette successfully pressed for the creation of state agencies to develop electric power, arbitrate labor disputes, and set rules for fair business competition; his so-called Little New Deal corresponded to the New Deal policies of the Roosevelt administration.

After World War II, the state continued a trend toward increased urbanization, and its industries prospered. The major figure on the national scene in the postwar era was Senator Joseph R. McCarthy, who served 10 years in the Senate, launching unsubstantiated attacks in the early 1950s on alleged communists and other subversives in the federal government. After McCarthy's censure by the US Senate in 1954 and death in 1957, the Progressive tradition began to recover strength, and the liberal Democratic Party grew increasingly influential in state politics. There was student unrest at the University of Wisconsin during the 1960s and early 1970s, and growing discontent among Milwaukee's black population. A major controversy in the 1970s concerned a court-ordered busing plan, implemented in 1979, aimed at decreasing racial imbalances in Milwaukee's public schools. In 1984, the Milwaukee school board filed suit in federal court, charging that the policies of the state and suburban schools had resulted in an unconstitutionally segregated school system that restricted blacks to city schools. Two years later, the city school board and nine suburban districts agreed on a plan by which minority students from the city would transfer voluntarily to the nine suburbs, and suburban students would attend Milwaukee schools.

Wisconsin's economy, with its strong manufacturing and agricultural sectors, remained sound throughout the 1980s and into the 1990s. The dairy industry, traditionally a mainstay of the economy, was linked to two different environmental issues. The first was the 1993 contamination of Milwaukee's drinking water with harmful bacteria that made thousands of people sick and killed some of them. Some claimed that the organisms had come from agricultural runoff containing animal wastes. The second issue was the use of bovine growth hormone to bolster milk production.

Flooding of the Mississippi River in 1993 caused massive damage in Wisconsin. Forty-seven counties were declared federal disaster areas; four people were killed; and financial losses totaled $900 million.

In 2003, Wisconsin faced a $3.2 billion two-year budget deficit, the largest deficit in Wisconsin's history. Governor Jim Doyle, elected in 2002, became the first Democratic governor to be elected in Wisconsin in 16 years. Doyle, who advocated abortion rights, gun control, and environmental protection, was at odds with the Republican-controlled state legislature over issues of state spending on health care and public education, and on raising taxes. Doyle promised to counteract the budget shortfall with deep spending cuts, which might threaten local services. He managed to balance the budget, while holding the line on taxes, and as a result, state taxes as a percentage of income were by 2005 the lowest in 34 years in the state. In 2005, Doyle announced his "KidsFirst" plan, an agenda to invest in Wisconsin's children, starting with the early years of life. He also implemented a "GrowWisconsin" agenda, to create jobs in the state. He is an advocate of providing citizens with access to safe, affordable prescription drugs from Canada.

12 STATE GOVERNMENT

Wisconsin's first constitutional convention, meeting in Madison in October 1846, was marked by controversy between conservative Whigs and allied Democrats on the one hand, and progressive Democrats with a constituency made up of miners, farmers, and immigrants on the other. The latter, who favored the popular election of judges and exemption of homesteads from seizure for debt, among other provisions, carried the day, but this version of the constitution failed to win ratification. A second constitutional convention, convened in December 1847, agreed on a new draft which made few major changes. This document, ratified by the electorate in 1848 and amended 133 times (two of which were subsequently nullified by the courts) as of January 2005, remains in effect today.

The Wisconsin legislature consists of a Senate with 33 members elected for four-year terms, and an assembly of 99 representatives elected for two-year terms. Legislators must be state residents for one year prior to election, and residents of their districts at least 10 days before the election. Voters elect an assembly and half the Senate membership in even-numbered years. Legislators must be US citizens, at least 18 years old, qualified voters in their districts, and residents of the state for at least one year. Regular legislative sessions begin in January; session schedules are determined biennially (in odd-numbered years) by joint resolution. Each house elects its own presiding officer and other officers from among its members. The legislative salary in 2004 was $45,569.

There are six elected state officers: governor and lieutenant governor (elected jointly), secretary of state, state treasurer, attorney general, and superintendent of public instruction. Since 1970, all have been elected for four-year terms. The governor and lieutenant governor must be US citizens, qualified voters, and state residents. As of December 2004, the governor's salary was $131,768. As the chief executive officer, the governor exercises authority by the power of appointment, by presenting a budget bill and major addresses to the legislature, and by the power to veto bills and call special legislative sessions.

A bill may be introduced in either house of the legislature, but must be passed by both houses to become law. The governor has six days (Sundays excluded) to sign or veto a measure. If the governor fails to act and the legislature is still in session, the bill automatically becomes law. (If the legislature has adjourned, a bill automatically dies after six days unless the governor acts on it.) Gubernatorial vetoes can be overridden by a two-thirds majority of those present in each house. Constitutional amendments may be introduced in either house. They must be approved by a simple majority of both houses in two legislatures and then ratified by a majority of the electorate at a subsequent election.

Voters must be US citizens, at least 18 years old, and must have resided in the state for at least 10 days before the election. (The residency requirement is waived in voting for US president and vice-president.) Restrictions apply to those convicted of certain crimes and to those judged by the court as mentally incompetent to vote.

13 POLITICAL PARTIES

The Democratic Party dominated politics until the late 1850s; then the newly founded Republican Party held sway for almost

Wisconsin Presidential Vote by Political Party, 1948–2004

YEAR	ELEC. VOTE	WISCONSIN WINNER	DEMOCRAT	REPUBLICAN	PROGRESSIVE	SOCIALIST	SOC. WORKERS	SOCIALIST LABOR
1948	12	*Truman (D)	647,310	590,959	25,282	12,547	—	399
1952	12	*Eisenhower (R)	622,175	979,744	2,174	1,157	1,350	770
					CONSTITUTION			
1956	12	*Eisenhower (R)	586,768	954,844	6,918	754	564	710
1960	12	Nixon (R)	830,805	895,175	—	—	1,792	1,310
1964	12	*Johnson (D)	1,050,424	638,495	—	—	1,692	1,204
1968	12	*Nixon (R)	748,804	809,997	—	—	1,222	1,338
					AMERICAN IND.	AMERICAN		
1972	11	*Nixon (R)	810,174	989,430	127,835	47,525	—	998
						SOCIALIST		LIBERTARIAN
1976	11	*Carter (D)	1,040,232	1,004,967	8,552	4,298	1,691	3,814
							CITIZENS	
1980	11	*Reagan (R)	981,584	1,088,845	**1,519	—	7,767	29,135
1984	11	*Reagan (R)	995,740	1,198,584	—	—	—	4,883
					POPULIST	SOC. WORKERS	NEW ALLIANCE	
1988	11	Dukakis (D)	1,126,794	1,047,499	3,056	2,574	1,953	5,157
						IND. (Perot)	TAXPAYERS	
1992	11	*Clinton (D)	1,041,066	930,855	2,311	544,479	1,772	2,877
							IND. (Nader)	
1996	11	*Clinton (D)	1,071,971	845,029	—	227,339	28,723	7,929
					CONSTITUTION	IND. (Buchanan)	GREEN (Nader)	
2000	11	Gore (D)	1,242,987	1,237,279	2,042	11,471	94,070	6,640
						SOC. PARTY OF WI. (Brown)	WI. GREENS (Cobb)	BETTER LIFE (Nader)
2004	10	Kerry (D)	1,489,504	1,478,120	471	2,661	16,390	6,464

*Won US presidential election.
Listed as **CONSTITUTION Party on Wisconsin ballot.

100 years. More recently, the parties remain relatively even in power at both the national and state levels.

Jacksonian democracy was strong in Wisconsin in the early days, and until 1856 all territorial and state governors were Democrats, except for one Whig. In 1854, however, a coalition of Whigs, antislavery Democrats, and Free Soilers formed a Republican Party in the state—a key event in the establishment of the national Republican Party. Republicans quickly gained control of most elective offices; from 1856 to 1959 there were only three Democratic governors. The Republican Party was dominated in the late 19th century by conservatives, who were sympathetic to the railroads and the lumbering industry but whose stands on pensions and jobs for Union veterans and ability to win federal funds for the state attracted support from farmers and small business. Then, in the 1890s, Progressives within the party, led by Robert La Follette, began a successful battle for control that culminated in La Follette's election as governor in 1900.

The La Follette brand of progressivism remained strong in the state, although not always under the umbrella of Republicanism. In 1924, La Follette ran for president on the Progressive ticket; 10 years later, his sons, Robert and Philip, also broke away from the GOP, to head a Progressive Party slate. However, their newly organized national third party faded and folded when Philip La Follette failed to be reelected governor, and World War II made isolationism unpopular. The Progressives rejoined the GOP in 1946.

Socialist parties have won some success in Wisconsin's political history. Socialists worked with progressive Republicans at the state level to pass important legislation in the early 20th century. In 1910, the Socialists scored two major political victories in Wisconsin: Emil Seidel was elected mayor of Milwaukee, becoming the first Socialist mayor of a major US city, and Victor Berger became the first Socialist ever elected to Congress. The state does not require voters to register. There were 3,045,730 voters registered in the state in 2002, however; 2,997,000 voters cast ballots in the 2004 presidential election.

Wisconsin's senators, both Democrats, are Herb Kohl, reelected in 2000 and Russell Feingold, reelected in 2004. Wisconsin's US House delegation consists of four Republicans and four Democrats following 2004 elections. In mid-2005, there were 19 Republicans and 14 Democrats in the state Senate, and 39 Democrats and 60 Republicans in the state Assembly. Wisconsin's former Republican governor, Tommy Thompson, who was reelected to an unprecedented fourth four-year term in 1998, was named President George W. Bush's Secretary of Health and Human Services in 2001, a post he held until January 2005. Republican Scott McCallum, began his first term as governor in 2001; he lost his bid for a second term to Democrat Jim Doyle in the 2004 election. Doyle became governor in 2005.

In the 2000 presidential election, Democrat Al Gore beat Republican George W. Bush by a mere 5,396 votes in Wisconsin; Green Party candidate Ralph Nader received 4% of the vote. In 2004, Democratic challenger John Kerry won 49.8% of the vote to incumbent President George W. Bush's 49.4%. The state had 10 electoral votes in the 2004 presidential election, a decrease of 1 vote over 2000.

¹⁴LOCAL GOVERNMENT

Wisconsin had 72 counties, 585 municipal governments, and 431 public school districts. There were also 684 special districts, each providing a certain local service, such as sewerage or fire fighting, usually across municipal lines. In 2002, there were 1,265 townships.

Each county is governed by a board of supervisors (which in the most populous counties has more than 40 members), generally elected for two-year terms. Some counties have elected county executives, serving four-year terms; several others have an appointed administrator or similar official. County officials can include district attorneys, sheriffs, clerks, treasurers, coroners, registers of deeds, and surveyors.

Towns are civil subdivisions of counties equivalent to townships in other states. Each town is a unit of 6 sq mi (16 sq km) marked off for governmental purposes. Wisconsin towns are generally small units with populations under 2,500. Each town is governed by a board of supervisors elected every two years; a town supervisor carries out policies set at an annual town meeting. Cities and villages have home-rule powers limited by legislative review. Most cities are governed by a mayor-council system: a small percentage of cities have a council-manager system, which was first authorized in Wisconsin in 1923. Executive power in a village is vested in an elected president who presides over an elected board but has no veto power.

The state is home to six Native American nations represented by 11 tribal governments.

In 2005, local government accounted for about 223,523 full-time (or equivalent) employment positions.

¹⁵STATE SERVICES

To address the continuing threat of terrorism and to work with the federal Department of Homeland Security, homeland security in Wisconsin operates under the authority of state statute; the adjutant general is designated as the state homeland security advisor.

A six-member Ethics Board, appointed by the governor, administers an ethics code for public officials and employees and investigates complaints against them. The board may refer cases for criminal prosecution.

The Department of Public Instruction administers public elementary and secondary education in the state, and the Board of Regents of the University of Wisconsin System has jurisdiction over all public higher education. The Wisconsin Technical College System supervises the state's 16 technical colleges.

The Transportation Department plans, constructs, and maintains highways and licenses motor vehicles and drivers. Physical and mental health, corrections, public and medical assistance, service to the aged, children's services, and vocational rehabilitation fall within the purview of the Department of Health and Family Services. The Office of Employment Relations enforces antidiscrimination laws in employment as well as minimum standards for wages and working conditions, provides training for the unemployed and disadvantaged, and sets safety standards for buildings.

Public protection in general is provided by the Department of Justice, which is responsible for investigating crimes of statewide magnitude and offering technical assistance to local law enforcement agencies. Regulations to protect consumers are administered and enforced by the Trade and Consumer Protection Division of the Department of Agriculture, Trade, and Consumer Protection, in cooperation with the Justice Department. The Army and Air National Guard are under the Department of Military Affairs.

The Department of Commerce has responsibilities in the areas of community, economic, and housing development, promotion of trade and tourism, and small and minority business assistance.

[16]JUDICIAL SYSTEM

The judicial branch is headed by a supreme court, consisting of seven justices, elected statewide on a nonpartisan basis for terms of 10 years. Vacancies are filled by gubernatorial appointment until an open election day becomes available. The justice with the greatest seniority serves as chief justice. The supreme court, which is the final authority on state constitutional questions, hears appeals at its own discretion and has original jurisdiction in limited areas.

The state's next-highest court is the Court of Appeals, established by constitutional amendment in 1977. Its 16 judges are elected by district on a nonpartisan basis and serve staggered six-year terms. Vacancies are filled by the governor until a successor is elected. Judges sit in panels of three for most cases, although some cases can be heard by a single judge. Decisions by the court of appeals may be reviewed by the supreme court.

Circuit courts are the trial court of general jurisdiction, which also hears appeals from municipal courts. Circuit court boundaries coincide with county boundaries, except that three judicial circuits comprise two counties each; thus, there are 69 judicial circuits. Trial judges are elected by district on a nonpartisan basis for six-year terms. All justices at the circuit court level or higher must have at least five years' experience as practicing attorneys and be less than 70 years old in order to qualify for office. Vacancies are filled by the governor until a successor is elected.

Wisconsin's 200 municipal courts have jurisdiction over local matters. Municipal judges are elected for terms of two or four years, generally serve on a part-time basis, and need not be attorneys.

As of 31 December 2004, a total of 22,966 prisoners were held in Wisconsin's state and federal prisons, an increase from 22,604 of 1.6% from the previous year. As of year-end 2004, a total of 1,387 inmates were female, down from 1,405 or 1.3% from the year before. Among sentenced prisoners (one year or more), Wisconsin had an incarceration rate of 390 per 100,000 population in 2004.

According to the Federal Bureau of Investigation, Wisconsin in 2004, had a violent crime rate (murder/nonnegligent manslaughter; forcible rape; robbery; aggravated assault) of 209.6 reported incidents per 100,000 population, or a total of 11,548 reported incidents. Crimes against property (burglary; larceny/theft; and motor vehicle theft) in that same year totaled 146,710 reported incidents or 2,663.1 reported incidents per 100,000 people. Wisconsin has no death penalty.

In 2003, Wisconsin spent $87,417,174 on homeland security, an average of $16 per state resident.

[17]ARMED FORCES

In 2004, there were 502 active-duty military personnel and 2,847 civilian personnel stationed in Wisconsin. Prime military contracts amounted to more than $1.7 billion in the same fiscal year, and total defense payroll outlays were $647 million.

A total of 3,932 Wisconsinites were killed in World War I; 7,980 in World War II; 800 in Korea; and 1,142 in Vietnam. In 2003, there were 474,594 veterans were living in Wisconsin. Of these, 69,671 saw service in World War II; 58,649 in the Korean conflict; 145,970 in the Vietnam era; and 61,028 in the Persian Gulf War. Wisconsin veterans received benefits of over $1.1 billion in 2004.

In 2004, the Wisconsin State Patrol employed 492 full-time sworn officers.

[18]MIGRATION

Until the early 19th century, Wisconsin was inhabited mainly by Indians; the French and British brought few permanent settlers. In the 1820s, southerners began to arrive from the lower Mississippi, and in the 1830s easterners poured in from New York, Ohio, Pennsylvania, and New England.

Foreign immigrants began arriving in the 1820s, either directly from Europe or after temporary settlement in eastern states. Most of the early immigrants were from Ireland and England. Germans also came in large numbers, especially after the Revolution of 1848, and by 1860 they were predominant in the immigrant population, which was proportionately larger than in any other state except California. The state soon became a patchwork of ethnic communities—Germans in the counties near Lake Michigan, Norwegians in southern and western Wisconsin, Dutch in the lower Fox Valley and near Sheboygan, and other groups in other regions.

After the Civil War, and especially in the 1880s, immigration reached new heights, with Wisconsin receiving a large share of Germans and Scandinavians. The proportion of Germans declined, however, as new immigrants arrived from Finland, Russia and from southern and eastern Europe, especially Poland, before World War I. Despite this overseas immigration, Wisconsin suffered a net population loss from migration beginning in 1900 as Wisconsinites moved to other states. Between 1970 and 1983 alone, this loss totaled 154,000. From 1985 to 1990, the net loss from migration amounted to 3,150. Between 1990 and 1998, Wisconsin had net gains of 84,000 in domestic migration and 21,000 in international migration. In 1998, 3,724 foreign immigrants arrived in Wisconsin; of these, the greatest number (680) came from Mexico. The state's overall population increased 6.8% between 1990 and 1998.

A significant trend since 1970 has been the decline in population in Milwaukee and other large cities; at the same time, suburbs have continued to grow, as have many other areas, especially in parts of northern Wisconsin. In the period 2000–05, net international migration was 46,106 and net internal migration was 14,595, for a net gain of 60,701 people.

[19]INTERGOVERNMENTAL COOPERATION

The Commission on Interstate Cooperation represents the state in its dealings with the Council of State Governments. Wisconsin also participates in the Education Commission of the States,

Great Lakes Commission, Midwest Interstate Low-Level Radioactive Waste Compact Commission, and Mississippi River Parkway Commission. In 1985, Wisconsin, seven other Great Lakes states, and the Canadian provinces of Quebec and Ontario signed the Great Lakes Compact to protect the lakes' water reserves. In fiscal year 2001, Wisconsin received over $5.8 billion in federal grants. Mirroring a national trend, that figure declined to $5.547 billion in fiscal year 2005, an estimated $5.418 billion in fiscal year 2006, and an estimated 5.600 in fiscal year 2007.

²⁰ECONOMY

With the coming of the first Europeans, fur trading became a major economic activity. As more settlers arrived, agriculture prospered. Although farming—preeminently dairying—remains important, manufacturing is the mainstay of today's economy. Wisconsin's industries are diversified, with nonelectrical machinery and food products the leading items. Other important industries are paper and pulp products, transportation equipment, electrical and electronic equipment, and fabricated metals. Economic growth has been concentrated in the southeast. There, soils and climate are favorable for agriculture. A skilled labor force is available to industry, and capital, transportation, and markets are most readily accessible.

As happened to the country at large, Wisconsin in 1981–82 experienced the worst economic slump since the Great Depression, with the unemployment rate rising to 11.7% in late 1982. Manufacturing was hard hit, and the loss of jobs in this sector was considered permanent. Nevertheless, manufacturing has remained Wisconsin's dominant sector, accounting for 27% of total state output in 1997, and growing close to 2.7% a year from 1997 to 2000, before falling 2.9% in the national recession of 2001. The strongest growth in the period, as in most of the country, was in various service categories such as general services, financial services, government, trade and the transportation and utilities sectors, all up more than 20% from 1997 to 2001. The diversity of Wisconsin's economy moderated the impact of the national recession that began in 2001 and 2002. By the end of 2002, the rebound of employment in the state was outpacing that of the nation overall.

In 2004, Wisconsin's gross state product (GSP) was $211.616 billion, of which manufacturing (durable and nondurable goods) contributed the biggest share at $47.685 billion or 22.5% of GSP, followed by the real estate sector at $23.778 billion (11.2% of GSP), and health care and social assistance at $16.968 billion (8% of GSP). In that same year, there were an estimated 406,766 small businesses in Wisconsin. Of the 125,888 businesses that had employees, an estimated total of 123,349 or 98% were small companies. An estimated 13,093 new businesses were established in the state in 2004, up 5.6% from the year before. Business terminations that same year came to 12,711, up 0.7% from 2003. There were 742 business bankruptcies in 2004, up 2.8% from the previous year. In 2005, the state's personal bankruptcy (Chapter 7 and Chapter 13) filing rate was 506 filings per 100,000 people, ranking Wisconsin as the 26th highest in the nation.

²¹INCOME

In 2005 Wisconsin had a gross state product (GSP) of $218 billion which accounted for 1.8% of the nation's gross domestic product

and placed the state at number 19 in highest GSP among the 50 states and the District of Columbia.

According to the Bureau of Economic Analysis, in 2004 Wisconsin had a per capita personal income (PCPI) of $32,166. This ranked 22nd in the United States and was 97% of the national average of $33,050. The 1994–2004 average annual growth rate of PCPI was 4.2%. Wisconsin had a total personal income (TPI) of $177,026,243,000, which ranked 18th in the United States and reflected an increase of 5.5% from 2003. The 1994–2004 average annual growth rate of TPI was 4.9%. Earnings of persons employed in Wisconsin increased from $127,965,881,000 in 2003 to $135,601,941,000 in 2004, an increase of 6.0%. The 2003–04 national change was 6.3%.

The US Census Bureau reports that the three-year average median household income for 2002–04 in 2004 dollars was $47,220 compared to a national average of $44,473. During the same period an estimated 10.2% of the population was below the poverty line as compared to 12.4% nationwide.

²²LABOR

According to the Bureau of Labor Statistics (BLS), in April 2006 the seasonally adjusted civilian labor force in Wisconsin 3,079,600, with approximately 147,200 workers unemployed, yielding an unemployment rate of 4.8%, compared to the national average of 4.7% for the same period. Preliminary data for the same period placed nonfarm employment at 2,873,300. Since the beginning of the BLS data series in 1976, the highest unemployment rate recorded in Wisconsin was 11.8% in January 1983. The historical low was 2.9% in April 1999. Preliminary nonfarm employment data by occupation for April 2006 showed that approximately 4.7% of the labor force was employed in construction; 17.6% in manufacturing; 18.9% in trade, transportation, and public utilities; 5.5% in financial activities; 9.3% in professional and business services; 13.7% in education and health services; 9.2% in leisure and hospitality services; and 14.3% in government.

Labor began to organize in the state after the Civil War. The Knights of St. Crispin, a shoemakers' union, grew into what was at that time the nation's largest union, before it collapsed during the Panic of 1873. In 1887, unions of printers, cigarmakers, and iron molders organized the Milwaukee Federated Trades Council, and in 1893 the Wisconsin State Federation of Labor was formed. A statewide union for public employees was established in 1932. In 1977, the state's legislature granted public employees (except public safety personnel) the right to strike, subject to certain limitations.

The BLS reported that in 2005, a total of 410,000 of Wisconsin's 3,551,000 employed wage and salary workers were formal members of a union. This represented 16.1% of those so employed, up slightly from 16% in 2004, well above the national average of 12%. Overall in 2005, a total of 438,000 workers (17.2%) in Wisconsin were covered by a union or employee association contract, which includes those workers who reported no union affiliation. Wisconsin is one of 28 states that did not have a right-to-work law.

As of 1 March 2006, Wisconsin had a state-mandated minimum wage rate of $5.70 per hour. In 2004, women in the state accounted for 47.6% of the employed civilian labor force.

[23]AGRICULTURE

Farm marketings in 2005 amounted to $6.6 billion, 10th among the 50 states; nearly $4.9 billion in farm marketings came from dairy products and livestock. Wisconsin led the United States in 2004 in the production of snap beans for processing, cranberries, processing beets, corn for silage, and cabbage for kraut. It also ranked third for oat production and sweet corn for processing, peas, and carrots for processing, fourth in oats and fall potatoes, fifth in tart cherries, seventh in alfalfa hay, and ninth in corn for grain.

In the early years, Wisconsin developed an agricultural economy based on wheat, some of which was exported to eastern states and overseas via the port of Milwaukee. Farmers also grew barley and hops, finding a market for these products among early Milwaukee brewers. After the Civil War, soil exhaustion and the depredations of the chinch bug forced farmers to turn to other crops, including corn, oats, and hay, which could be used to feed hogs, sheep, cows, and other livestock.

Although agricultural income has continued to rise in recent years and the average size of farms has increased, farm acreage and the number of farms have declined. In 2004 there were 15.5 million acres (6.3 million hectares) of land in farms, nearly 50% of the total land area, distributed among 76,500 farms, a decline of 4,600 from 1986. Farmland is concentrated in the southern two-thirds of the state, especially in the southeast. Potatoes are grown mainly in central Wisconsin, cranberries in the Wisconsin River Valley, and cherries in the Door Peninsula.

Leading field crops (in bushels) in 2004 were corn for grain, 353,600,000; oats 13,650,000; wheat, 12,852,000; and barley, 1,650,000. About 4,880,000 tons of dry hay and 13,300,000 tons of corn for silage were harvested that year. Potato production was 30,450,000 hundredweight. In 2004, Wisconsin farmers produced for processing 511,220,000 hundredweight of sweet corn, 322,640 tons of snap beans, 54,500 tons of green peas, 3,480,000 barrels of cranberries, and 6.7 tons of tart cherries, and 302,000 lb (137,000 kg) of spearmint and peppermint for oil. Some 30,180 tons of cucumber pickles and 630,000 hundredweight of cabbage were produced in 2004.

[24]ANIMAL HUSBANDRY

Aided by the skills of immigrant cheesemakers and by the encouragement of dairy farmers who emigrated from New York—especially by the promotional effort of the agriculturist and publisher William D. Hoard—Wisconsin turned to dairying in the late 19th century. In 2003, Wisconsin ranked second (after California) in the number of milk cows with 1.26 million milk cows which produced over 22.2 billion lb (10 billion kg) of milk. Dairy farms are prominent in nearly all regions, but especially in the Central Plains and Western Uplands. Wisconsin ranchers also raise livestock for meat production. In 2004, dairy products accounted for 53.7% of total farm receipts; cattle and calves, 11.7%.

In 2005, the state had 3.35 million cattle and calves, valued at $4 billion. During 2004, Wisconsin farms had about 430,000 hogs and pigs, valued at $38.7 million. Poultry farmers sold 12.3 million lb (5.6 million kg) of chicken in 2003. Also during 2003, there were 1.1 billion eggs produced, valued at $55.6 million. Wisconsin was also the leading producer of mink pelts in 2004, at 706,300.

[25]FISHING

In 2004, Wisconsin ranked third among the Great Lakes states in the quantity of its commercial fishing, with 3.9 million lb (1.8 million kg) valued at $3.1 million. In 2001, the commercial fishing fleet had 18 boats and 78 vessels. Walleye, perch, and lake trout are primary Great Lakes fish species.

In 2004, there were 61 trout farms, with sales of nearly $1.5 million. The muskellunge is the premier game fish of Wisconsin's inland waters; Coho and Chinook salmon, introduced to Lake Michigan, now thrive there. The largest concentration of lake sturgeon in the United States is in Lake Winnebago. In 2004, the state issued 1,391,173 fishing licenses. There are 16 state fish hatcheries and 2 national hatcheries in the state.

[26]FORESTRY

Wisconsin was once about 85% forested. Although much of the forest was depleted by forest fires and wasteful lumber industry practices, vast areas reseeded themselves naturally, and more than 820,000 acres (332,000 hectares) have been replanted. In 2004, Wisconsin had 15,965,000 acres (6,461,000 hectares) of forest, covering 46% of the state's land area; 70% of all forestlands are privately owned. Hardwoods make up over 80% of the sawtimber. The most heavily forested region is in the north. The timber industry reached its peak in the late 19th century. In 2004, lumber production totaled 539 million board feet.

Wisconsin's woods have recreational as well as commercial value. Two national forests—Chequamegon and Nicolet, both located in northern Wisconsin—cover 1,527,300 acres (618,098 hectares). The 10 state forests cover 471,329 acres (190,741 hectares).

Forest management and fire control programs are directed by the Department of Natural Resources. The US Forest Service operates a Forest Products Laboratory at Madison, in cooperation with the University of Wisconsin.

[27]MINING

According to preliminary data from the US Geological Survey (USGS), the estimated value of nonfuel mineral production by Wisconsin in 2003 was $405 million, an increase from 2002 of over 3%. The USGS data ranked Wisconsin as 32nd among the 50 states by the total value of its nonfuel mineral production, accounting for over 1% of total US output.

According to the preliminary data for 2003, crushed stone, and construction sand and gravel were the state's top nonfuel minerals, accounting for around 40% and 39%, respectively, of all nonfuel mineral output, by value. These were followed by lime (more than 9% by value); industrial sand and gravel (around 8% by value); and dimension stone (over 3% by value). By volume, Wisconsin in 2003, was the nation's fourth largest producer of dimension stone; eighth largest in construction sand and gravel; and fifth in peat and in industrial sand and gravel.

Preliminary data for 2003 showed crushed stone production at 38 million metric tons, with a value of $163 million, while construction sand and gravel output that same year stood at 39.1 million metric tons, and was valued at $156 million. Industrial sand and gravel production in 2003 totaled 38 million metric tons, and was valued at $32.7 million. Lime output that year came to 640,000 metric tons, and had a value of $38.4 million.

28 ENERGY AND POWER

As of 2003, Wisconsin had 125 electrical power service providers, of which 82 were publicly owned and 25 were cooperatives. Of the remainder, 12 were investor owned, and six were owners of independent generators that sold directly to customers. As of that same year there were 2,753,247 retail customers. Of that total, 2,262,424 received their power from investor-owned service providers. Cooperatives accounted for 236,036 customers, while publicly owned providers had 254,781 customers. There were six independent generator or "facility" customers.

Total net summer generating capability by the state's electrical generating plants in 2003 stood at 14.309 million kW, with total production that same year at 60.122 billion kWh. Of the total amount generated, 93.3% came from electric utilities, with the remainder coming from independent producers and combined heat and power service providers. The largest portion of all electric power generated, 41.717 billion kWh (69.4%), came from coal-fired plants, with nuclear generation in second place at 12.215 billion kWh (20.3%) and natural gas fueled plants in third at 2.478 billion kWh (4.1%). Other renewable power sources accounted for 2.3% of all power generated, with hydroelectric at 3.1%, and petroleum fired plants at 0.8%.

The state's first hydroelectric plant was built at Appleton in 1882, with many others built later, especially along the Wisconsin River. Because Wisconsin itself has no coal, oil, or natural gas resources, the state has been active in developing alternative energy resources to increase its energy independence. Biomass energy is being developed for the production of ethanol; and waste wood is being used for utility generation and as fuel in industrial processes. Hydropower is a significant source of electricity generation in the paper industry and for electric utility generation.

As of 2006, Wisconsin had two nuclear power stations; the Point Beach station operated by Wisconsin Electric Power Company near Two Rivers and Manitowoc; and the Kewaunee plant, operated by the Wisconsin Public Service Co in Carlton.

Wisconsin has no proven reserves or production of crude oil or natural gas. As of 2005, the state's only crude oil refinery had a distillation capacity of 33,000 barrels per day.

29 INDUSTRY

Industrial activity is concentrated in the southeast, especially the Milwaukee metropolitan area. Milwaukee however, has lost some of its luster as a brewery center, as a number of breweries have ceased operations there.

According to the US Census Bureau's Annual Survey of Manufactures (ASM) for 2004, Wisconsin's manufacturing sector covered some 20 product subsectors. The shipment value of all products manufactured in the state that same year was $136.676 billion. Of that total, food manufacturing accounted for the largest share at $24.600 billion. It was followed by transportation equipment manufacturing at $19.702 billion; machinery manufacturing at $14.744 billion; paper manufacturing at $12.765 billion; and fabricated metal product manufacturing at $11.289 billion.

In 2004, a total of 476,794 people in Wisconsin were employed in the state's manufacturing sector, according to the ASM. Of that total, 344,680 were actual production workers. In terms of total employment, the fabricated metal product manufacturing industry accounted for the largest portion of all manufacturing employees, with 62,051 (46,048 actual production workers). It was followed by machinery manufacturing, with 60,111 (37,179 actual production workers); food manufacturing, with 59,750 (47,137 actual production workers); transportation equipment manufacturing, with 36,790 (28,314 actual production workers); and printing and related support activities, with 33,849 (25,226 actual production workers).

ASM data for 2004 showed that Wisconsin's manufacturing sector paid $19.808 billion in wages. Of that amount, the machinery manufacturing sector accounted for the largest share at $2.895 billion. It was followed by fabricated metal product manufacturing at $2.486 billion; food manufacturing at $2.080 billion; and transport equipment manufacturing at $1.808 billion.

30 COMMERCE

According to the 2002 Census of Wholesale Trade, Wisconsin's wholesale trade sector had sales that year totaling $68.5 billion from 7,557 establishments. Wholesalers of durable goods accounted for 4,617 establishments, followed by nondurable goods wholesalers at 2,311 and electronic markets, agents, and brokers accounting for 629 establishments. Sales by durable goods wholesalers in 2002 totaled $26.9 billion, while wholesalers of nondurable goods saw sales of $33.6 billion. Electronic markets, agents, and brokers in the wholesale trade industry had sales of $7.9 billion.

In the 2002 Census of Retail Trade, Wisconsin was listed as having 21,360 retail establishments with sales of $59.9 billion. The leading types of retail businesses by number of establishments were: motor vehicle and motor vehicle parts dealers (2,776); gasoline stations (2,667); miscellaneous store retailers (2,564); clothing and clothing accessories stores (2,268); and food and beverage stores (2,205). In terms of sales, motor vehicle and motor vehicle parts stores accounted for the largest share of retail sales at $15.5 billion, followed by general merchandise stores at $8.8 billion; food and beverage stores at $8.1 billion; gasoline stations at $5.95 billion; and building material/garden equipment and supplies dealers at $5.92 billion. A total of 311,730 people were employed by the retail sector in Wisconsin that year.

The state engages in foreign as well as domestic trade through the Great Lakes ports of Superior-Duluth, Milwaukee, Green Bay, and Kenosha. Iron ore and grain are shipped primarily from Superior-Duluth, while Milwaukee handles the heaviest volume of general merchandise. Wisconsin exported $14.9 billion in goods (18th in the United States) in 2005. Greater Milwaukee is a foreign-trade zone where goods can enter duty-free under certain conditions.

31 CONSUMER PROTECTION

Consumer protection in Wisconsin is not the responsibility of a single, dedicated agency, office or department. The administration of the state's laws governing product safety and trade practices is the responsibility of the Trade and Consumer Protection Division of the state's Department of Agriculture, Trade and Consumer Protection, which monitors food production, inspects meat, and administers grading programs. The Trade and Consumer Protection Division in turn, acts in cooperation with the state's Department of Justice through its Consumer Protection Unit, which litigates cases involving deceptive and fraudulent business practices that have been referred to it by other state agencies. Consumer protection in financial matters is handled by the Office of the Commissioner of Banking, which administers laws governing consumer credit, while the Department of Transportation's Motor Vehicles Division investigates complaints from buyers of new and used automobiles.

When dealing with consumer protection issues, the Wisconsin Department of Justice's Attorney General's Office can initiate civil and criminal proceedings; represent the state before state and federal regulatory agencies; administer consumer protection and education programs; handle formal consumer complaints; and exercise broad subpoena powers. In antitrust actions, the Attorney General's Office can act on behalf of those consumers who are incapable of acting on their own; initiate damage actions on behalf of the state in state courts; initiate criminal proceedings; and represent other governmental entities in recovering civil damages under state or federal law.

The Department of Agriculture, Trade and Consumer Protection has its main office in Madison, but also has regional offices in Green Bay and Milwaukee. There is also a county government consumer affairs office in Racine.

32 BANKING

As of June 2005, Wisconsin had 303 insured banks, savings and loans, and saving banks, in addition to 282 state-chartered and 2 federally chartered credit unions (CUs). Excluding the CUs, the Milwaukee-Waukesha-West Allis market area accounted for the largest portion of the state's financial institutions and deposits in 2004, with 63 institutions and $40.172 billion in deposits, followed by the Madison market area with 48 institutions and $10.944 billion in deposits. As of June 2005, CUs accounted for 10.9% of all assets held by all financial institutions in the state, or some $14.838 billion. Banks, savings and loans, and savings banks collectively accounted for the remaining 89.1% or $121.910 billion in assets held.

The Office of the Commissioner of Banking licenses and charters banks, loan and collection companies, and currency exchanges. The Office of the Commissioner of Savings and Loan supervises state-chartered savings and loan associations. The Office of the Commissioner of Credit Unions enforces laws relating to state-chartered credit unions.

33 INSURANCE

In 2004, there were 3.4 million individual life insurance policies in force with a total value of about $248 billion; total value for all categories of life insurance (individual, group, and credit) was about $388.7 billion. The average coverage amount is $72,800 per policy holder. Death benefits paid that year totaled $1 billion.

As of 2003, there were 182 property and casualty and 31 life and health insurance companies domiciled in the state. In 2004, direct premiums for property and casualty insurance totaled $7.8 billion.

That year, there were 12,861 flood insurance policies in force in the state, with a total value of $1.5 billion.

The Office of the Commissioner of Insurance licenses insurance agents, enforces state and federal regulations, responds to consumer complaints, and develops consumer education programs and literature. The office also operates the State Life Insurance Fund, which sells basic life insurance (maximum $10,000) to state residents; and the Local Government Property Insurance Fund, which insures properties of local government units on an optional basis.

In 2004, 59% of state residents held employment-based health insurance policies, 5% held individual policies, and 24% were covered under Medicare and Medicaid; 11% of residents were uninsured. In 2003, employee contributions for employment-based health coverage averaged at 22% for single coverage and 24% for family coverage. The state offers an 18-month health benefits expansion program for small-firm employees in connection with the Consolidated Omnibus Budget Reconciliation Act (COBRA, 1986), a health insurance program for those who lose employment-based coverage due to termination or reduction of work hours.

In 2003, there were over 3.5 million auto insurance policies in effect for private passenger cars. While liability coverage is not mandatory, motorists are expected to accept financial responsibility in the event of an accident. Minimum liability limits include bodily injury liability of up to $25,000 per individual and $50,000 for all persons injured in an accident, as well as property damage liability of $10,000. Uninsured motorist coverage is available in the state. In 2003, the average expenditure per vehicle for insurance coverage was $620.44.

34 SECURITIES

Wisconsin has no securities exchanges. In 2005, there were 1,940 personal financial advisers employed in the state and 3,800 securities, commodities, and financial services sales agents. In 2004, there were over 90 publicly traded companies within the state, with over 35 NASDAQ companies, 29 NYSE listings, and 4 AMEX listings. In 2006, the state had ten Fortune 500 companies; Johnson Controls ranked first in the state and 75th in the nation with revenues of over $28 billion, followed by Northwestern Mutual, Manpower, Kohl's, and WPS Resources.

The sale of securities is regulated by the Department of Financial Institutions, Division of Securities.

35 PUBLIC FINANCE

Budget estimates are prepared by departments and sent to the governor or governor-elect in the fall of each even-numbered year. The following January, the governor presents a biennial budget to the legislature, which passes a budget bill, often after many amendments. Most appropriations are made separately for each year of the biennium. The fiscal year (FY) begins 1 July. Expenditures by state and local governments alike have risen dramatically since 1960. At one time, the state was constitutionally prohibited from borrowing money. This provision was at first circumvented

Wisconsin—State Government Finances

(Dollar amounts in thousands. Per capita amounts in dollars.)

	AMOUNT	PER CAPITA
Total Revenue	34,753,272	6,314.18
General revenue	23,933,776	4,348.43
Intergovernmental revenue	6,831,514	1,241.19
Taxes	12,638,266	2,296.20
General sales	3,899,395	708.47
Selective sales	1,721,642	312.80
License taxes	811,548	147.45
Individual income tax	5,251,190	954.07
Corporate income tax	681,990	123.91
Other taxes	272,501	49.51
Current charges	2,660,736	483.42
Miscellaneous general revenue	1,803,260	327.63
Utility revenue	–	–
Liquor store revenue	–	–
Insurance trust revenue	10,819,496	1,965.75
Total expenditure	28,577,240	5,192.09
Intergovernmental expenditure	9,285,137	1,686.98
Direct expenditure	19,292,103	3,505.11
Current operation	12,335,594	2,241.21
Capital outlay	1,781,247	323.63
Insurance benefits and repayments	3,781,755	687.09
Assistance and subsidies	571,629	103.86
Interest on debt	821,878	149.32
Exhibit: Salaries and wages	3,462,527	629.09
Total expenditure	28,577,240	5,192.09
General expenditure	24,789,046	4,503.82
Intergovernmental expenditure	9,285,137	1,686.98
Direct expenditure	15,503,909	2,816.84
General expenditures, by function:		
Education	9,045,030	1,643.36
Public welfare	5,908,896	1,073.56
Hospitals	799,711	145.30
Health	644,461	117.09
Highways	1,678,313	304.93
Police protection	121,120	22.01
Correction	918,706	166.92
Natural resources	555,771	100.98
Parks and recreation	55,244	10.04
Government administration	614,390	111.63
Interest on general debt	821,878	149.32
Other and unallocable	3,625,526	658.71
Utility expenditure	6,439	1.17
Liquor store expenditure	–	–
Insurance trust expenditure	3,781,755	687.09
Debt at end of fiscal year	17,727,318	3,220.81
Cash and security holdings	83,020,637	15,083.69

Abbreviations and symbols: – zero or rounds to zero; (NA) not available; (X) not applicable.

SOURCE: *U.S. Census Bureau, Governments Division, 2004 Survey of State Government Finances,* January 2006.

by the use of private corporations and then, in 1969, eliminated by constitutional amendment.

Fiscal year 2006 general funds were estimated at $12.7 billion for resources and $12.4 billion for expenditures. In fiscal year 2004, federal government grants to Wisconsin were $7.4 billion.

In the fiscal year 2007 federal budget, Wisconsin was slated to receive: $32.5 million for a new Department of Veterans Affairs spinal-cord injury center in Milwaukee; and $5.6 million for the repair or replacement of the windows and doors at the historic US Federal Building and Courthouse in Milwaukee.

³⁶TAXATION

In 2005, Wisconsin collected $13,452 million in tax revenues or $2,430 per capita, which placed it 13th among the 50 states in per capita tax burden. The national average was $2,192 per capita. Property taxes accounted for 0.8% of the total, sales taxes 30.0%, selective sales taxes 15.2%, individual income taxes 40.6%, corporate income taxes 5.8%, and other taxes 7.4%.

As of 1 January 2006, Wisconsin had four individual income tax brackets ranging from 4.6% to 6.75%. The state taxes corporations at a flat rate of 7.9%.

In 2004, state and local property taxes amounted to $7.5 billion or $1,350 per capita. The per capita amount ranks the state 11th highest nationally. Local governments collected $7,324,843,000 of the total and the state government $104,158,000.

Wisconsin taxes retail sales at a rate of 5%. In addition to the state tax, local taxes on retail sales can reach as much as 0.60%, making for a potential total tax on retail sales of 5.60%. Food purchased for consumption off-premises is tax exempt. The tax on cigarettes is 77 cents per pack, which ranks 28th among the 50 states and the District of Columbia. Wisconsin taxes gasoline at 32.9 cents per gallon. This is in addition to the 18.4 cents per gallon federal tax on gasoline.

According to the Tax Foundation, for every federal tax dollar sent to Washington in 2004, Wisconsin citizens received $0.82 in federal spending.

³⁷ECONOMIC POLICY

The state seeks to promote the relocation of new industries to Wisconsin, as well as the expansion of existing ones, by providing advice and assistance through the Wisconsin Commerce Development and some 280 local development corporations. It supports businesses that promise to substantially improve the economy of a community or the state; extends loans to small businesses; helps with the training or retraining of employees; and offers financial assistance for applied research that results in a new product or production process. To revitalize economically depressed areas, the state provides tax benefits to businesses locating or expanding operations in such areas and helps finance local economic development projects. Communities are authorized to issue tax-exempt bonds to enable industries to finance new equipment. In addition, all machinery and equipment used in goods production is tax-exempt under state law. In 2006, the Commerce Department contained seven main operating divisions: the Administrative Services Division, the Business Development Division, the Community Development Division, the Environmental and Regulatory Services Division, the International and Export Development Division, the Office of the Secretary, and the Buildings and Safety Division. The Bureau of Minority Business Development also operates.

³⁸HEALTH

The infant mortality rate in October 2005 was estimated at 6.4 per 1,000 live births. The birth rate in 2003 was 12.8 per 1,000 population. The abortion rate stood at 9.6 per 1,000 women in 2000. In 2003, about 84.9% of pregnant woman received prenatal care be-

Wisconsin

ginning in the first trimester. In 2004, approximately 83% of children received routine immunizations before the age of three.

The crude death rate in 2003 was 8.4 deaths per 1,000 population. As of 2002, the death rates for major causes of death (per 100,000 resident population) were: heart disease, 237.5; cancer, 199; cerebrovascular diseases, 63.9; chronic lower respiratory diseases, 42.9; and diabetes, 24.9. The mortality rate from HIV infection was 1.4 per 100,000 population. In 2004, the reported AIDS case rate was at about 3.2 per 100,000 population. In 2002, about 55.5% of the population was considered overweight or obese. As of 2004, about 21.9% of state residents were smokers.

In 2003, Wisconsin had 121 community hospitals with about 14,800 beds. There were about 588,000 patient admissions that year and 11.8 million outpatient visits. The average daily inpatient census was about 9,200 patients. The average cost per day for hospital care was $1,282. Also in 2003, there were about 408 certified nursing facilities in the state with 42,644 beds and an overall occupancy rate of about 85.6%. In 2004, it was estimated that about 77.5% of all state residents had received some type of dental care within the year. Wisconsin had 262 physicians per 100,000 resident population in 2004 and 856 nurses per 100,000 in 2005. In 2004, there was a total of 3,055 dentists in the state.

Medical degrees are granted by the University of Wisconsin at Madison and by the Medical College of Wisconsin (formerly part of Marquette University). The Division of Health, a branch of the State Department of Health and Social Services, has responsibility for planning and supervising health services and facilities, enforcing state and federal regulations, administering medical assistance programs, and providing information to the public.

About 17% of state residents were enrolled in Medicaid programs in 2003; 15% were enrolled in Medicare programs in 2004. Approximately 11% of the state population was uninsured in 2004. In 2003, state health care expenditures totaled $5.3 million.

39 SOCIAL WELFARE

In 2004, about 269,000 people received unemployment benefits, with the average weekly unemployment benefit at $251. In fiscal year 2005, the estimated average monthly participation in the food stamp program included about 345,748 persons (143,459 households); the average monthly benefit was about $76.39 per person, which was the lowest average benefit in the nation. That year, the total of benefits paid through the state for the food stamp program was about $316.9 million.

Temporary Assistance for Needy Families (TANF), the system of federal welfare assistance that officially replaced Aid to Families with Dependent Children (AFDC) in 1997, was reauthorized through the Deficit Reduction Act of 2005. TANF is funded through federal block grants that are divided among the states based on an equation involving the number of recipients in each state. Wisconsin's TANF program is called Wisconsin Works (W-2). In 2004, the state program had 54,000 recipients; state and federal expenditures on this TANF program totaled $109 million in fiscal year 2003.

In December 2004, Social Security benefits were paid to 937,490 Wisconsin residents. This number included 629,930 retired workers, 89,810 widows and widowers, 103,460 disabled workers,

49,000 spouses, and 65,290 children. Social Security beneficiaries represented 17.1% of the total state population and 96.8% of the state's population age 65 and older. Retired workers received an average monthly payment of $979; widows and widowers, $952; disabled workers, $894; and spouses, $493. Payments for children of retired workers averaged $525 per month; children of deceased workers, $659; and children of disabled workers, $260. Federal Supplemental Security Income payments in December 2004 went to 90,026 Wisconsin residents, averaging $386 a month. An additional $9.6 million of state-administered supplemental payments were distributed to 95,173 residents.

40 HOUSING

In 2004, there were an estimated 2,463,802 housing units, 2,172,924 of which were occupied; 69.9% were owner-occupied. About 65.2% of all units were single-family, detached homes. Rural areas had a higher proportion of deficient housing than urban areas, and substandard conditions were three times as common in units built before 1939, which account for about 21% of the existing housing stock. In 2004, utility gas was the most common energy source for heating. It was estimated that 97,491 units lacked telephone service, 9,105 lacked complete plumbing facilities, and 9,348 lacked complete kitchen facilities. The average household had 2.46 members.

In 2004, 40,000 new privately owned housing units were authorized for construction. The median home value was $137,727. The median monthly cost for mortgage owners was $1,155. Renters paid a median of $609 per month. In 2006, the state received over $28.4 million in community development block grants from the US Department of Housing and Urban Development (HUD).

The Department of Veterans Affairs makes home loans to veterans. The Housing Finance Authority, created by the legislature in 1971, raises money through the sale of tax-exempt bonds and makes loans directly or indirectly to low- and moderate-income home buyers. Wisconsin's state building code, developed in 1913 to cover construction of all dwellings with three or more units, was revised in the late 1970s to cover new one- and two-family dwellings. Local housing codes prescribing standards for structural upkeep and maintenance in existing buildings are in force in all large cities and in many smaller cities and villages.

41 EDUCATION

Wisconsin has a tradition of leadership in education. The state's constitution, adopted in 1848, provided for free public education; however, there was no state tax for schools until 1885. A compulsory education law was passed in 1879 and strengthened in 1903 and 1907. The first kindergarten in the United States was established in Watertown, Wisconsin, in 1856.

General public elementary and secondary education is administered under the overall supervision of the Department of Public Instruction, which is headed by a state superintendent elected on a nonpartisan basis. As of 2004, 88.8% of all Wisconsinites 25 years or older had completed high school, above the national average of 84%. Some 25.6% had obtained a bachelor's degree or higher.

The total enrollment for fall 2002 in Wisconsin's public schools stood at 881,000. Of these, 592,000 attended schools from kindergarten through grade eight, and 290,000 attended high school. Approximately 78.8% of the students were white, 10.5% were black, 5.8% were Hispanic, 3.4% were Asian/Pacific Islander, and 1.4% were American Indian/Alaskan Native. Total enrollment was estimated at 871,000 in fall 2003 and expected to be 847,000 by fall 2014, a decline of 3.9% during the period 2002–14. Expenditures for public education in 2003/04 were estimated at $9 billion. There were 134,474 students enrolled in 1,041 private schools in fall 2003. Since 1969, the National Assessment of Educational Progress (NAEP) has tested public school students nationwide. The resulting report, *The Nation's Report Card,* stated that in 2005 eighth graders in Wisconsin scored 285 out of 500 in mathematics compared with the national average of 278.

As of fall 2002, there were 329,443 students enrolled in college or graduate school; minority students comprised 10.9% of total postsecondary enrollment. In 2005 Wisconsin had 68 degree-granting institutions. The University of Wisconsin (UW) system is comprised of 13 degree-granting campuses, 13 two-year centers, and the University of Wisconsin-Extension, which has outreach and continuing education activities on all 26 UW campuses and in all 72 Wisconsin counties. All 13 universities award bachelor's and master's degrees. University of Wisconsin-Madison and University of Wisconsin-Milwaukee also confer doctoral degrees. UW-Madison, one of the world's largest and most respected institutions of higher learning, was chartered by the state's first legislature in 1848. UW-Milwaukee is the system's second-largest campus. The 11 other universities are Eau Claire, Green Bay, La Crosse, Oshkosh, Parkside (at Kenosha-Racine), Platteville, River Falls, Stevens Point, Stout (at Menomonie), Superior, and Whitewater.

Wisconsin's private institutions of higher education encompass a broad range of schools. There were 35 private 4-year institutions in 2005, including such leading institutions as Marquette University, Lawrence University, Ripon College, and Beloit College. Wisconsin also has a system of technical colleges, the Wisconsin Technical College System. In 1911, the legislature enacted the first system of state support for vocational, technical, and adult education in the nation. The system includes 16 technical colleges with 47 campuses, each governed by a local board. At the same time, each college is part of a statewide system governed by an independent board.

42 ARTS

The Wisconsin Arts Board, consisting of 15 members appointed by the governor for three-year terms, aids artists and performing groups and assists communities in developing arts programs. In 2005, the Wisconsin Arts Board and other Wisconsin arts organizations received 22 grants totaling $1,013,400 from the National Endowment for the Arts. The Wisconsin Humanities Council, founded in 1972, offers series of book discussions. In 2005, the National Endowment for the Humanities contributed $2,188,896 for 21 state programs. State and private sources contribute funding to supplement federal assistance.

Wisconsin offers numerous facilities for drama, music, and other performing arts, including Marcus Center for the Performing Arts Center in Milwaukee and the Alliant Energy Center in Madison. Milwaukee hosts the Milwaukee Repertory Theater (The Rep),

which celebrated its 50th season in 2003/04. There are many other theater groups around the state. Summer plays are performed at a unique garden theater at Fish Creek in the Door Peninsula. The Door County Folk Festival is held annually in July and hosts numerous folk dancing workshops, children's activities, and singing workshops; in 2006 the festival marked its 27th season.

The Pro Arte Quartet in Madison, founded in 1912, and the Fine Arts Quartet in Milwaukee have been sponsored by the University of Wisconsin, which has also supported many other musical activities. The Fine Arts Quartet celebrated its 60th anniversary in 2006. Milwaukee is the home of the Great Lakes Opera Company, the Milwaukee Ballet Company, and the Milwaukee Symphony. Madison is home to the Madison Symphony, the Madison Opera, and the Wisconsin Chamber Orchestra.

43 LIBRARIES AND MUSEUMS

In 2001, the state of Wisconsin had 379 public library systems, with a total of 455 libraries, of which there were 79 branches. In that same year, the public library system had a combined total of 18,647,00 volumes of books and serial publications, and a total circulation of 49,768,000. The system also had 844,000 audio and 857,000 video items, 46,000 electronic format items (CD-ROMs, magnetic tapes, and disks), and 11 bookmobiles. The Milwaukee Public Library, founded in 1878, maintained 12 branches and had 2,504,461 bound volumes as of 1998; the Madison Public Library had seven branches and over 815,686 volumes. The largest academic library is that of the University of Wisconsin at Madison, with six million bound volumes. The best-known special library is that of the State Historical Society of Wisconsin at Madison, with 3.6 million books and over 60,000 cu ft (1,700 cu m) of government publications and documents. In 2001, operating income for the state's public library system was $166,870,000 and included $5,311,000 in state funding and $149,637,000 in local funding.

Wisconsin had 208 museums and historical sites in 2000. The State Historical Society maintains a historical museum in Madison and other historical sites and museums around the state. The Milwaukee Public Museum contains collections on history, natural history, and art. The Milwaukee Art Center, founded in 1888, a major museum of the visual arts, emphasizes European works of the 17th to 19th centuries. The Madison Art Center, founded in 1901, has European, Japanese, Mexican, and American paintings and sculpture, as well as 17th-century Flemish tapestries. The Charles Allis Art Library in Milwaukee, founded in 1947, houses collections of Chinese porcelains, French antiques, and 19th-century American landscape paintings. Other leading art museums include the Elvehjem Museum of Art in Madison and the Theodore Lyman Wright Art Center at Beloit College.

The Circus World Museum at Baraboo occupies the site of the original Ringling Brothers Circus. Other museums of special interest include the Dard Hunter Paper Museum (Appleton), the National Railroad Museum (Green Bay), and the Green Bay Packer Hall of Fame. More than 500 species of animals are on exhibit at the Milwaukee County Zoological Park; Madison and Racine also have zoos. Historical sites in Wisconsin include Villa Louis, a fur trader's mansion at Prairie du Chien; the Old Wade House in Greenbush; Old World Wisconsin, an outdoor ethnic museum near Eagle; Pendarvis, focusing on lead mining at Mineral Point; and the Taliesin estate of architect Frank Lloyd Wright, in Spring Green.

44 COMMUNICATIONS

About 95.5% of the state's households had telephones in 2004. In addition, by June of that same year there were 2,831,645 mobile wireless telephone subscribers. In 2003, 63.8% of Wisconsin households had a computer and 57.4% had Internet access. By June 2005, there were 732,706 high-speed lines in Wisconsin, 682,073 residential and 50,633 for business. In 2005 there were 34 major AM and 99 major FM radio stations. The state also had 28 major television stations. The Milwaukee area had 815,640 television households, 63% of which subscribed to cable in 1999. A total of 77,862 Internet domain names were registered within the state in the year 2000.

45 PRESS

The state's first newspaper was the *Green Bay Intelligencer*, founded in 1833. Some early papers were put out by rival land speculators who used them to promote their interests. Among these was the *Milwaukee Sentinel*, launched in 1837 and a major daily newspaper today. As immigrants poured in from Europe in succeeding decades, German, Norwegian, Polish, Yiddish, and Finnish papers sprang up. Wisconsin journalism has a tradition of political involvement. The *Milwaukee Leader*, founded as a Socialist daily by Victor Berger in 1911, was denied the use of the US mails because it printed antiwar articles; the *Madison Capital Times*, still important today, also started as an antiwar paper. Founded in 1882 by Lucius Nieman, the *Milwaukee Journal* (now known as the *Milwaukee Journal Sentinel*), won a Pulitzer Prize in 1919 for distinguished public service and remains the state's largest-selling and most influential newspaper.

In 2005, Wisconsin had 11 morning papers, 24 evening papers, and 18 Sunday papers.

The following table shows leading dailies with their approximate 2005 circulations:

AREA	NAME	DAILY	SUNDAY
Green Bay	*Press–Gazette* (m,S)	68,944	83,395
Madison	*Wisconsin State Journal* (m,S)	101,639	152,943
Milwaukee	*Journal Sentinel* (m,S)	227,387	435,127

As of 2005 there were also 223 weekly newspapers, as well as some 300 periodicals directed to a wide variety of special interests. Among the largest are *Hoard's Dairyman*, founded by William D. Hoard in 1885, with a 81,133 paid subscribers in 2005; it is the only paid dairy publication in the United States. Kalmbach Publishing Co. located in Brookfield originally published rail magazines, *Model Railroader, Trains, Classic Toy Trains, Garden Railways* and *Classic Trains*, and later diversified with *Birder's World, Scale Auto,* and *Bead&Button, BeadStyle* and *Art Jewelry, The Writer,* and *American Snowmobiler*. Other publications are *Bowling Magazine, Coin Prices, Coin,* and *Old Cars Weekly*. Other notable periodicals are the *Wisconsin Magazine of History*, published quarterly in Madison by the state historical society; and *Wisconsin Trails*, another quarterly, also published in Madison.

46 ORGANIZATIONS

In 2006, there were over 8,188 nonprofit organizations registered within the state, of which about 5,639 were registered as charitable, educational, or religious organizations.

The Wisconsin Historical Society, founded in 1846, is one of the largest organizations of its kind. It has a museum, a library, and research collections in Madison and is a prominent publisher of historical articles and books. The Wisconsin Arts Board is also in Madison. There are several city and county historical societies throughout the state as well.

National organizations based in Wisconsin include the United States Bowling Congress, American Society of Agronomy, Crop Science Society of America, Experimental Aircraft Association, Inter-Varsity Christian Fellowship, the John Birch Society, the National Association of Congregational Christian Churches, the Seventh Day Baptist General Conference, the National Funeral Directors Association, the United States Curling Association, and World Council of Credit Unions.

The Purebred Dairy Cattle Association is a national agricultural organization. State agricultural organizations include the Wisconsin Cheesemakers' Association, the Wisconsin Dairy Products Association, the Wisconsin Apple Growers Association, the Wisconsin Christmas Trees Producers, and the Wisconsin Berry Growers Association. There are professional organizations for a variety of professions. The Natural Heritage Land Trust and the North American Lake Management Society are local conservation groups.

47 TOURISM, TRAVEL, AND RECREATION

Wisconsin had estimated tourism revenues of $11.7 billion in 2004, reflecting a 2% increase over the previous year. Tourism supports 309,000 jobs in the state.

The state has ample scenic attractions and outdoor recreational opportunities. There are over 33 state parks. In addition to the famous Wisconsin Dells gorge, visitors are attracted to the Cave of the Mounds at Blue Mounds, the sandstone cliffs along the Mississippi River, the rocky Lake Michigan shoreline of the Door Peninsula, the lakes and forests of the Rhinelander and Minocqua areas in the north, and Lake Geneva, a resort, in the south. Several areas in southern and northwestern Wisconsin, preserved by the state as the Ice Age National Scientific Reserve, still exhibit drumlins, moraines, and unusual geological formations. The town of Hayward hosts the Freshwater Fishing Hall of Fame. Hank Aaron State Trail is named for the Milwaukee baseball star. Wisconsin hosts the World's Championship Snowmobile Derby in Eagle River. There are 43 auto race tracks. The Milwaukee Mile is the oldest racetrack in the world. Spring Green is the home of Frank Lloyd Wright's home, Taliesin. America's largest waterpark, Noah's Ark, is located in the Wisconsin Dells.

There are three national parks in Wisconsin: Apostle Islands National Lakeshore, on Lake Superior, and the St. Croix and Lower St. Croix scenic riverways. There are 48 state parks, covering 65,483 acres (26,193 hectares).

48 SPORTS

Wisconsin has three major professional sports teams: the Milwaukee Brewers of Major League Baseball (MLB), the Green Bay Packers of the National Football League (NFL), and the Milwaukee Bucks of the National Basketball Association (NBA). The Brewers won the American League Pennant in 1982 but lost the World Series to St. Louis. The Brewers have since been realigned and now play in the National League. The Packers won five league championships prior to the establishment of the Super Bowl and then won Super Bowls I, II, and XXXI in 1967, 1968, and 1997, respectively. The Bucks won the NBA championship in 1971. Milwaukee is the site of the Greater Milwaukee Open in professional golf. There are also numerous minor league baseball, basketball, and hockey teams in the state.

The University of Wisconsin Badgers compete in the Big Ten Conference. Badger ice hockey teams won the National Collegiate Athletic Association (NCAA) championship in 1973, 1977, 1981, 1983, 1990, and 2006. In football, they won the Rose Bowl in 1994, 1999, and 2000 after losing their first three appearances, in 1953, 1960, and 1963. Overall, they have eight bowl game victories. The basketball team from Marquette University in Milwaukee won the NCAA Division I title in 1977 and the National Invitation Tournament championship in 1970. They advanced to the NCAA Final Four in 2003.

Other annual sporting events include ski jumping tournaments in Iola, Middleton, and Wetsby; the World Championship Snowmobile Derby in Eagle River in January; the American Birkebeiner Cross-Country Race at Cable and Hayward in February; and the Great Wisconsin Dells Balloon Race in the Dells. Famous athletes native to Wisconsin include Eric Heiden, Elroy (Crazy Legs) Hirsch, and Chris Witty.

49 FAMOUS WISCONSINITES

Wisconsinites who have won prominence as federal judicial or executive officers include Jeremiah Rusk (b.Ohio, 1830–93), a Wisconsin governor selected as the first head of the Agriculture Department in 1889; William F. Vilas (b.Vermont, 1840–1908), who served as postmaster general under Grover Cleveland; Melvin Laird (b.Nebraska, 1922–92), a congressman who served as secretary of defense from 1969–73; and William Rehnquist (1924–2005), named to the Supreme Court in 1971 and the 16th Chief Justice from 1986-2005.

The state's best-known political figures achieved nationwide reputations as members of the US Senate. John C. Spooner (b.Indiana, 1843–1919) won distinction as one of the inner circle of Senate conservatives before he retired in 1907 amid an upsurge of Progressivism within his party. Robert La Follette (1855–1925) embodied the new wave of Republican Progressivism—and, later, isolationism—as governor and in the Senate. His sons, Robert Jr. (1895–1953), and Philip (1897–1965), carried on the Progressive tradition as US senator and governor, respectively. Joseph R. McCarthy (1908–57) won attention in the Senate and throughout the nation for his anti-communist crusade. William Proxmire (b.Illinois, 1915–2005), a Democrat, succeeded McCarthy in the Senate and eventually became chairman of the powerful Senate Banking Committee. Representative Henry S. Reuss (1912–2002), also a Democrat, served in the House for 28 years and was chairman of the Banking Committee. Democrat Clement Zablocki (1912–83), elected to the House in 1948, was chairman of the Foreign Affairs Committee. Victor L. Berger (b.Transylvania, 1860–1929), a founder of the Social-Democratic Party, was first elected to the House in 1910; during World War I, he was denied his seat and prosecuted because of his antiwar views.

Besides the La Follettes, other governors who made notable contributions to the state include James D. Doty (b.New York, 1799–1865), who fought to make Wisconsin a separate territory and became the territory's second governor; William D. Hoard (b.New York, 1836–1918), a tireless promoter of dairy farming, as both private citizen and chief executive; James O. Davidson (b.Norway, 1854–1922), who attempted to improve relations between conservatives and progressives; Francis E. McGovern (1866–1946), who pushed through the legislature significant social and economic reform legislation; and Walter J. Kohler (1875–1940), an industrialist who, as governor, greatly expanded the power of the office.

Prominent figures in the state's early history include the Jesuit Jacques Marquette (b.France, 1637–75) and the explorer Louis Jolliet (b.Canada, 1645–1700); and the Sauk Indian leader Black Hawk (b.Illinois, 1767–1838), who was defeated in the Battle of Bad Axe. John Bascom (b.New York, 1827–1911) was an early president of the University of Wisconsin. Charles Van Hise (1857–1918), a later president, promoted the use of academic experts as government advisers; John R. Commons (b.Ohio, 1862–1945), an economist at the university, drafted major state legislation. Philetus Sawyer (b.Vermont, 1816–1900), a prosperous lumberman and US senator, led the state Republican Party for 15 years, before Progressives won control. Carl Schurz (b.Germany, 1829–1906) was a prominent Republican Party figure in the years immediately before the Civil War. Lucius W. Nieman (1857–1935) founded the *Milwaukee Journal,* and Edward P. Allis (b.New York, 1824–89) was an important iron industrialist.

Wisconsin was the birthplace of several Nobel Prize winners, including Herbert S. Gasser (1888–1963), who shared a 1944 Nobel Prize for research into nerve impulses; William P. Murphy (1892–1987), who shared a 1934 prize for research relating to anemia; John Bardeen (1908–91), who shared the physics award in 1956 for his contribution to the development of the transistor; and Herbert A. Simon (1916–2001), who won the 1978 prize in economics. Stephen Babcock (b.New York, 1843–1931) was an agricultural chemist who did research important to the dairy industry. In addition, Wisconsin was the birthplace of the child psychologist Arnold Gesell (1880–1961), and of naturalist and explorer Chapman Andrews (1884–1960). John Muir (b.Scotland, 1838–1914), another noted naturalist and explorer, lived in Wisconsin in his youth. Conservationist Aldo Leopold (1887–1948) taught at the University of Wisconsin and wrote *A Sand County Almanac.*

Frederick Jackson Turner (1861–1932), historian of the American frontier, was born in Wisconsin, as were the economist and social theorist Thorstein Veblen (1857–1929) and the diplomat and historian George F. Kennan (1904–2005). Famous journalists include news commentator H. V. Kaltenborn (1878–1965), award-winning sports columnist Red Smith (Walter Wellesley Smith, 1905–82), and television newsman Tom Snyder (b.1936).

Thornton Wilder (1897–1975), a novelist and playwright best known for *The Bridge of San Luis Rey* (1927), *Our Town* (1938), and *The Skin of Our Teeth* (1942), each of which won a Pulitzer Prize, heads the list of literary figures born in the state. Hamlin Garland (1860–1940), a novelist and essayist, was also a native, as were the poet Ella Wheeler Wilcox (1850–1919) and the novelist and playwright Zona Gale (1874–1938). The novelist Edna Ferber (b.Michigan, 1887–1968) spent her early life in the state.

Wisconsin is the birthplace of architect Frank Lloyd Wright (1869–1959) and the site of his famous Taliesin estate (Spring Green), Johnson Wax Co. headquarters (Racine), and first Unitarian Church (Madison). The artist Georgia O'Keefe (1887–1986) was born in Sun Prairie. Wisconsin natives who have distinguished themselves in the performing arts include Alfred Lunt (1893–1977), Frederic March (Frederick Bickel, 1897–1975), Spencer Tracy (1900–1967), Agnes Moorehead (1906–74), and Orson Welles (1915–85). Magician and escape artist Harry Houdini (Ehrich Weiss, b.Hungary, 1874–1926) was raised in the state, and piano stylist Liberace (Wlad Ziu Valentino Liberace, 1919–1987) was born there. Speed skater Eric Heiden (b.1958), a five-time Olympic gold medalist in 1980, is another Wisconsin native.

50 BIBLIOGRAPHY

Council of State Governments. *The Book of the States, 2006 Edition.* Lexington, Ky.: Council of State Governments, 2006.

Davenport, Don. *Natural Wonders of Wisconsin: Exploring Wild and Scenic Places.* Lincolnwood, Ill.: Country Roads Press, 1999.

Erickson, Sue. *Ojibwe Treaty Rights: Understanding and Impact.* 4th ed. Odanah, Wis.: Great Lakes Indian Fish & Wildlife Commission, 2004.

John, Tim. *The Miller Beer Barons: The Frederick J. Miller Family and Its Brewery.* Oregon, Wis.: Badger Books, 2005.

Klement, Frank L. *Wisconsin in the Civil War: The Home Front and the Battle Front, 1861–1865.* Madison: State Historical Society of Wisconsin, 1997.

Pederson, Jane Marie. *Between Memory and Reality: Family and Community in Rural Wisconsin, 1870–1970.* Madison: University of Wisconsin Press, 1992.

Reading, William H. *Wisconsin Timber Industry [microform]: An Assessment of Timber Product Output and Use, 1999.* St. Paul, Minn.: U.S. Dept. of Agriculture, Forest Service, North Central Research Station, 2003.

Risjord, Norman K. *Wisconsin: The Story of the Badger State.* Madison: Wisconsin Trails, 1995.

Strohschank, Johannes. *The Wisconsin Office of Emigration, 1852–1855, and Its Impact on German Immigration to the State.* Madison: Max Kade Institute for German-American Studies, University of Wisconsin, 2005.

Thomas, Stacy. *Guarding Door County: Lighthouses and Life-saving Stations.* Charleston, S.C.: Arcadia, 2005.

US Department of Commerce, Economics and Statistics Administration, US Census Bureau. *Wisconsin, 2000. Summary Social, Economic, and Housing Characteristics: 2000 Census of Population and Housing.* Washington, D.C.: US Government Printing Office, 2003.

Yatzeck, Richard. *Hunting the Edges.* Madison: University of Wisconsin Press, 1999.

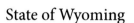

WYOMING

State of Wyoming

ORIGIN OF STATE NAME: Derived from the Delaware Indian words *maugh-wau-wa-ma,* meaning "large plains." **NICKNAME:** The Equality State; The Cowboy State. **CAPITAL:** Cheyenne. **ENTERED UNION:** 10 July 1890 (44th). **SONG:** "Wyoming." **MOTTO:** Equal Rights. **FLAG:** A blue field with a white inner border and a red outer border (symbolizing, respectively, the sky, purity, and the Native Americans) surrounds a bison with the state seal branded on its side. **OFFICIAL SEAL:** A female figure holding the banner "Equal Rights" stands on a pedestal between pillars topped by lamps symbolizing the light of knowledge. Two male figures flank the pillars, on which are draped banners that proclaim "Livestock," "Grain," "Mines," and "Oil." At the bottom is a shield with an eagle, star, and Roman numerals XLIV, flanked by the dates 1869 and 1890. The whole is surrounded by the words "Great Seal of the State of Wyoming." **BIRD:** Western meadowlark. **FISH:** Cutthroat trout. **FLOWER:** Indian paintbrush. **TREE:** Cottonwood. **GEM:** Jade. **LEGAL HOLIDAYS:** New Year's Day, 1 January; Birthday of Martin Luther King Jr. and Wyoming Equality Day, 3rd Monday in January; Presidents' Day, 3rd Monday in February; Memorial Day, last Monday in May; Independence Day, 4 July; Labor Day, 1st Monday in September; Veterans' Day, 11 November; Thanksgiving Day, 4th Thursday in November; Christmas Day, 25 December. Special observances are made on Arbor Day, last Monday in April; Native American Day, 2nd Friday in May; Juneteenth, 3rd Saturday in June;Birthday of Nellie Tayloe Ross, 29 November; Pearl Harbor Remembrance Day, 7 December; Wyoming Day, 10 December. **TIME:** 5 AM MST = noon GMT.

¹LOCATION, SIZE, AND EXTENT

Located in the Rocky Mountain region of the northwestern United States, Wyoming ranks ninth in size among the 50 states.

The total area of Wyoming is 97,809 sq mi (253,325 sq km), of which land comprises 96,989 sq mi (251,201 sq km) and inland water 820 sq mi (2,124 sq km). Shaped like a rectangle, Wyoming has a maximum E–W extension of 365 mi (587 km); its extreme distance N–S is 265 mi (426 km).

Wyoming is bordered on the N by Montana; on the E by South Dakota and Nebraska; on the s by Colorado and Utah; and on the w by Utah, Idaho, and Montana. The boundary length of Wyoming totals 1,269 mi (2,042 km). The state's geographic center lies in Fremont County, 58 mi (93 km) ENE of Lander.

²TOPOGRAPHY

The eastern third of Wyoming forms part of the Great Plains; the remainder belongs to the Rocky Mountains. Much of western Wyoming constitutes a special geomorphic province known as the Wyoming Basin. It represents a westward extension of the Great Plains into the Rocky Mountains, separating the Middle and Southern Rockies. Extending diagonally across the state from northwest to south is the Continental Divide, which separates the generally eastward-flowing drainage system of North America from the westward-flowing drainage of the Pacific states.

Wyoming's mean elevation is 6,700 ft (2,044 m), second only to Colorado's among the 50 states. Gannett Peak, in western Wyoming, at 13,804 ft (4,210 m), is the highest point in the state. With the notable exception of the Black Hills in the northeast, the eastern portion of Wyoming is generally much lower. The lowest point in the state—3,099 ft (945 m)—occurs in the northeast, on the Belle Fourche River.

Wyoming's largest lake—Yellowstone—lies in the heart of Yellowstone National Park. In Grand Teton National Park to the south are two smaller lakes, Jackson and Jenny. All but one of Wyoming's major rivers originate within its boundaries and flow into neighboring states. The Green River flows into Utah; the Yellowstone, Big Horn, and Powder rivers flow into Montana; the Snake River, into Idaho; the Belle Fourche and Cheyenne rivers, into South Dakota; and the Niobrara and Bear rivers, into Nebraska. The lone exception, the North Platte River, enters Wyoming from Colorado and eventually exits into Nebraska.

³CLIMATE

Wyoming is generally semiarid, with local desert conditions. Normal daily temperatures in Cheyenne range from 15°F (-9°C) to 38°F (3°C) in January, and 54°F (12°C) to 83°F (28°C) in July. The record low temperature, -66°F (-54°C), was set 9 February 1933 at Riverside; the record high, 114°F (46°C), 12 July 1900 at Basin. In Cheyenne, average annual precipitation is about 14.5 in (36 cm) a year, most of that falling between April and September; the snowfall in Cheyenne averages 51.2 in (130 cm) annually.

⁴FLORA AND FAUNA

Wyoming has more than 2,000 species of ferns, conifers, and flowering plants. Prairie grasses dominate the eastern third of the state; desert shrubs, primarily sagebrush, cover the Great Basin in the west. Rocky Mountain forests consist largely of pine, spruce, and fir. In April 2006, three species were listed as threatened by the US Fish and Wildlife Service, including Colorado butterfly plant,

Ute ladies' tresses, and desert yellowhead; no plant species were listed as endangered.

The mule deer is the most abundant game mammal; others include the white-tailed deer, pronghorn antelope, elk, and moose. The jackrabbit, antelope, and raccoon are plentiful. Wild turkey, bobwhite quail, and several grouse species are leading game birds; more than 50 species of non-game birds also inhabit Wyoming all year long. There are 78 species of fish, of which rainbow trout is the favorite game fish. In April 2006, nine Wyoming animal species (vertebrates and invertebrates) were listed as threatened or endangered, including the black-footed ferret, grizzly bear, razorback sucker, Kendall Warm Springs dace, and Wyoming toad.

5 ENVIRONMENTAL PROTECTION

The Environmental Quality Council, a seven-member board appointed by the governor, hears and decides all cases arising under the regulations of the Department of Environmental Quality, which was established in 1973 and reorganized in 1992. The department enforces measures to prevent pollution of Wyoming's surface water and groundwater, and it administers 21 air-monitoring sites to maintain air quality.

Wyoming typically spends the most money per capita on the environment and natural resources relative to all the states in the union. The state's principal environmental concerns are conservation of scarce water resources and preservation of air quality. Programs to dispose of hazardous waste and assure safe drinking water are administered by the federal Environmental Protection Agency (EPA); in 2002–05, the federal program to fund infrastructure for safe drinking water allocated 1% of its budget to Wyoming.

Wetlands cover about 1.25 million acres (505,857 hectares) of Wyoming and are administered and protected by the Wyoming Wetlands Act.

In 2003, 19.3 million lb of toxic chemicals were released in the state. Also in 2003, Wyoming had 42 hazardous waste sites listed in the US Environment Protection Agency (EPA) database, two of which, F.E. Warren Air Force Base and Mystery Bridge (US Highway 20 in Evansville), were on the National Priorities List as of 2006. In 2005, the EPA spent over $38,000 through the Superfund program for the cleanup of hazardous waste sites in the state. The same year, federal EPA grants awarded to the state included $8 million for the drinking water state revolving fund and $5.2 million for the water pollution control revolving fund.

6 POPULATION

Wyoming ranked 51st in population among the United States and the District of Columbia with an estimated total of 509,294 in 2005, an increase of 3.1% since 2000. Between 1990 and 2000, Wyoming's population grew from 453,588 to 493,782, an increase of 8.9%. The population was projected to reach 528,005 by 2015 and 529,031 by 2025.

In 2004 the median age was 38.4. Persons under 18 years old accounted for 23.1% of the population while 12.1% was age 65 or older.

Wyoming has the second-lowest population density in the country (5.2 persons per sq mi/2 persons per sq km in 2004); only Alaska is more sparsely populated. However, during the 1970s Wyoming was the third-fastest–growing state; its population grew by 41%, from 332,416 at the 1970 census to 469,557 according to the 1980 census, largely from in-migration. The growth rate reversed during the 1980s, shrinking the population to 453,588 in 1990 (-3.4%).

Leading cities, all with populations of less than 100,000, are Cheyenne, Casper, and Laramie. The Cheyenne metropolitan area had an estimated population of 85,296 in 2004; the Casper metropolitan area had an estimated population of 69,010.

7 ETHNIC GROUPS

There were some 11,133 American Indians residing in Wyoming in 2000, up from 9,000 at the 1990 census. In 2004, 2.4% of the state's total population was American Indian. The largest tribe is the Arapaho. Wind River (2000 population 23,250) is the state's only reservation; tribal lands covered 1,793,000 acres (726,000 hectares) in 1982.

The black population was 3,722 in 2000. In 2004, blacks made up 0.9% of the state's population. In 2000, the Asian population was 2,771; the largest group was the Chinese, who numbered 609. In 2004, 0.6% of the population was Asian and 0.1% Pacific Islander. That year, 6.7% of the population was of Hispanic or Latino origin. In 2004 as well, 1.2% of the population reported origin of two or more races. In 2002 about 95% of the population was white and mostly of European descent, the largest groups being German, English, and Irish.

8 LANGUAGES

Some place-names—Oshoto, Shoshoni, Cheyenne, Uinta—reflect early contacts with regional Indians.

Some terms common in Wyoming, like *comforter* (tied quilt) and *angleworm* (earthworm), evidence the Northern dialect of early settlers from New York State and New England, but generally Wyoming English is North Midland with some South Midland mixture, especially along the Nebraska border. Geography has changed the meaning of *hole, basin, meadow,* and *park* to signify mountain openings.

In 2000, over 433,000 Wyomingites—93.6% of the residents five years old or older (down slightly from 94.3% in 1990)—spoke only English at home.

The following table gives selected statistics from the 2000 Census for language spoken at home by persons five years old and over. The category "Other Native North American languages" includes Apache, Cherokee, Choctaw, Dakota, Keres, Pima, and Yupik.

LANGUAGE	NUMBER	PERCENT
Population 5 years and over	**462,809**	**100.0**
Speak only English	433,324	93.6
Speak a language other than English	29,485	6.4
Speak a language other than English	**29,485**	**6.4**
Spanish or Spanish Creole	18,606	4.0
German	2,382	0.5
Other Native North American languages	1,795	0.4
French (incl. Patois, Cajun)	1,618	0.3
Japanese	518	0.1
Chinese	512	0.1

9 RELIGIONS

The religiously active population in Wyoming is somewhat closely split between Protestants and Catholics. In 2004, the Roman Catholic Church had about 50,979 members. The next largest

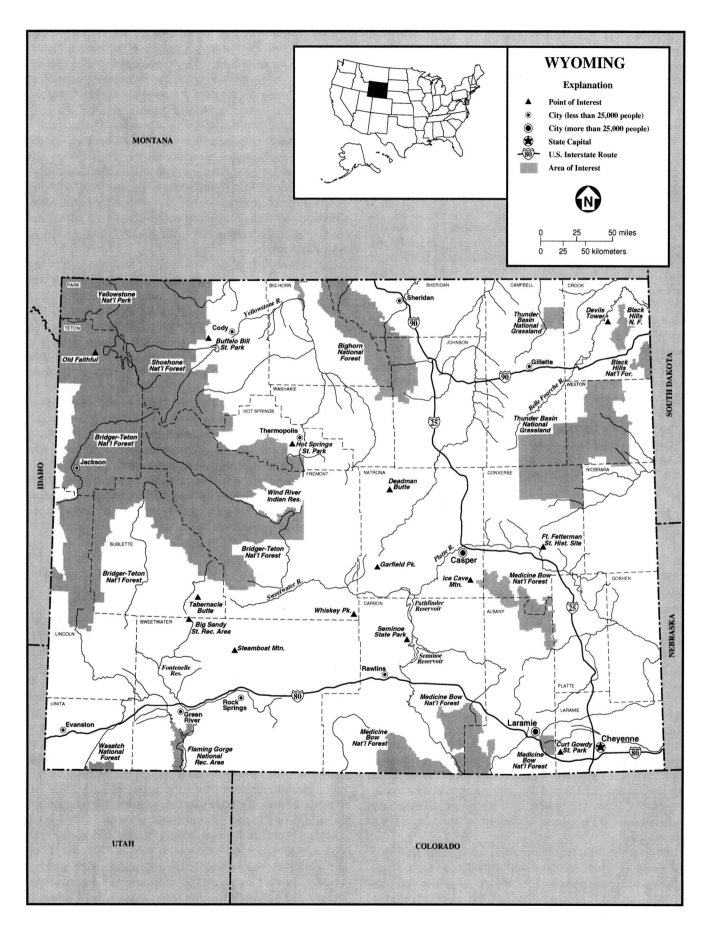

WYOMING

Explanation

▲ Point of Interest
⊙ City (less than 25,000 people)
◉ City (more than 25,000 people)
★ State Capital
(80) U.S. Interstate Route
▨ Area of Interest

N

0   25   50 miles
0   25   50 kilometers

MONTANA

IDAHO

UTAH

COLORADO

SOUTH DAKOTA

NEBRASKA

PARK

Yellowstone Nat'l Park

TETON

Old Faithful ▲

Shoshone Nat'l Forest

Cody ⊙
▲ Buffalo Bill St. Park

Yellowstone R.

BIG HORN

SHERIDAN

Sheridan ◉

CAMPBELL

CROOK

Thunder Basin National Grassland

Devils Tower ▲

Black Hills N. F.

Bighorn National Forest

JOHNSON

Gillette ◉

Black Hills Nat'l For.

Belle Fourche R.

WESTON

WASHAKIE

HOT SPRINGS

Thermopolis ⊙
▲ Hot Springs St. Park

FREMONT

Bridger-Teton Nat'l Forest

Jackson ⊙

Wind River Indian Res.

NATRONA

Deadman Butte ▲

CONVERSE

Thunder Basin National Grassland

NIOBRARA

SUBLETTE

Bridger-Teton Nat'l Forest

Bridger-Teton Nat'l Forest

Platte R.

Ft. Fetterman St. Hist. Site ▲

Garfield Pk. ▲

Casper ◉

Ice Cave Mtn. ▲

Medicine Bow Nat'l Forest

GOSHEN

Sweetwater R.

▲ Tabernacle Butte

Whiskey Pk. ▲

CARBON

Pathfinder Reservoir

ALBANY

SWEETWATER

▲ Big Sandy St. Rec. Area

Seminoe State Park ▲

Seminoe Reservoir

LINCOLN

▲ Steamboat Mtn.

Fontenelle Res.

Rawlins ⊙

PLATTE

Medicine Bow Nat'l Forest

LARAMIE

UINTA

Rock Springs ⊙

80

Green River ⊙

Evanston ⊙

Wasatch National Forest

Flaming Gorge National Rec. Area

Medicine Bow Nat'l Forest

Laramie ◉

Curt Gowdy St. Park ▲

Cheyenne ★

Medicine Bow Nat'l Forest

80

single denomination is the Church of Jesus Christ of Latter-day Saints (Mormons), with 56,665 members reported in 2006. Other leading denominations include the Southern Baptist Convention, with 17,101 members in 2000 (and 232 newly baptized members reported in 2002); the United Methodist Church. 11,431 members in 2000; the Lutheran Church—Missouri Synod, 11,113; and the Evangelical Lutheran Church in America, 10,038. Wyoming also had an estimated 430 Jews and 263 Muslims in 2000. That year, there were 263,057 people (about 53% of the population) who were not counted as members of any religious organization.

10 TRANSPORTATION

Wyoming as of 2003 was served by four railroads. Two of the largest were the Burlington Northern Santa Fe and the Union Pacific, both Class I lines. Out of a total of 1,882 mi (3,030 km) of railroad track these two companies accounted for nearly all of it at 1,846 mi (2,972 km). This was due to the double and triple-tracking, of their respective mainlines, primarily to haul coal from the Powder River Basin. In 2003, coal was the top commodity carried by rail that originated and terminated within the state. As of 2006, there was no Amtrak service in or through the state.

As of 2004, there were 27,594 mi (44,426 km) of public highways and roads in the state. In that same year, there were some 651,000 registered motor vehicles and 380,180 licensed drivers in the state.

In 2005, Wyoming had a total of 113 public and private-use aviation-related facilities. This included 90 airports and 23 heliports. Jackson Hole Airport in Jackson was the state's main airport. In 2004, the airport had 212,247 passenger enplanements.

11 HISTORY

The first human inhabitants of what is now Wyoming probably arrived about 11,500 BC. The forebears of these early Americans had most likely come by way of the Bering Strait and then worked their way south. Sites of mammoth kills south of Rawlins and near Powell suggest that the area was well populated. Artifacts from the period beginning in 500 BC include, high in the Big Horn Mountains of northern Wyoming, the Medicine Wheel monument, a circle of stones some 75 ft (23 m) in diameter with 28 "spokes" that were apparently used to mark the seasons.

The first Europeans to visit Wyoming were French Canadian traders. The Vérendrye brothers, Francois and Louis-Joseph, probably reached the Big Horn Mountains in 1743; nothing came of their travels, however. The first effective discovery of Wyoming was made by an American fur trader, John Colter, earlier a member of the Lewis and Clark expedition. In 1806–07, Colter traversed much of the northwestern part of the state, probably crossing what is now Yellowstone Park, and came back to report on the natural wonders of the area. After Colter, trappers and fur traders crisscrossed Wyoming. By 1840, the major rivers and mountains were named, and the general topography of the region was well documented.

Between 1840 and 1867, thousands of Americans crossed Wyoming on the Oregon Trail, bound for Oregon or California. Migration began as a trickle, but with the discovery of gold in California in 1848, the trickle became a flood. In 1849 alone it is estimated that more than 22,000 "forty-niners" passed through the state

via the Oregon Trail. Fort Laramie in the east and Fort Bridger in the west were the best-known supply points; between the two forts, immigrants encountered Independence Rock, Devil's Gate, Split Rock, and South Pass, all landmarks on the Oregon Trail. Although thousands of Americans crossed Wyoming during this period, very few stayed in this harsh region.

The event that brought population as well as territorial status to Wyoming was the coming of the Union Pacific Railroad. Railroad towns such as Cheyenne, Laramie, Rawlins, Rock Springs, and Evanston sprang up as the transcontinental railroad leapfrogged across the region in 1867 and 1868; in the latter year, Wyoming was organized as a territory. The first territorial legislature distinguished itself in 1869 by passing a women's suffrage act, the first state or territory to do so. Wyoming quickly acquired the nickname the Equality State.

After hostile Indians had been subdued by the late 1870s, Wyoming became a center for cattlemen and foreign investors who hoped to make a fortune from free grass and the high price of cattle. Thousands of Texas longhorn cattle were driven to the southeastern quarter of the territory. In time, blooded cattle, particularly Hereford, were introduced. As cattle "barons" dominated both the rangeland and state politics, the small rancher and cowboy found it difficult to go into the ranching business. However, overgrazing, low cattle prices, and the dry summer of 1886 and harsh winter of 1886/87 all proved disastrous to the speculators. The struggle between the large landowners and small ranchers culminated in the so-called Johnson County War of 1891–92, in which the large landowners were arrested by federal troops after attempting to take the law into their own hands.

Wyoming became a state in 1890, but growth remained slow. Attempts at farming proved unsuccessful in this high, arid region, and Wyoming to this day remains a sparsely settled ranching state. What growth has occurred has been primarily through the minerals industry, especially the development of coal, oil, and natural gas resources during the 1970s because of the national energy crisis. However, the world's oil glut in the early 1980s slowed the growth of the state's energy industries; in 1984, the growth of the state's nonfuel mineral industry slowed as well.

Wyoming's population, which had risen 41% during the minerals boom of the 1970s, declined, leaving the state ranking 50th in population in the 1990 census, having ceded 49th place to Alaska in the decade since 1980. In the 1990s, Wyoming's economy was spurred by a rise in oil prices and expanding coal production, as well as increased tourism. As of the 2000 census, the population stood at nearly 500,000, still ranking 50th in the nation.

In the summer of 1988, wild fires raged through Yellowstone National Park, damaging nearly one-third of the park's total area. Gray wolves, eradicated from the mountains of Wyoming and Idaho in the 1930s, were reintroduced to Yellowstone National Park and central Idaho in 1995 and 1996 as part of the US Fish and Wildlife Service's wolf reintroduction program. The program was initiated to fulfill a goal of the Endangered Species Act, passed in 1973. It was subjected to legal challenge in 1997, but the wolf reintroduction program was ruled legal in 2000. In 2003, the US Fish and Wildlife Service reclassified the gray wolves in the northern Rockies from an "endangered" to a "threatened" species, due to the growing wolf populations in those areas. In 2005, Governor Dave Freudenthal, elected in 2002, signed a petition requesting the Fish and Wildlife Service to remove the gray wolf from the list of threatened and endangered species. The final decision on whether to delist the species must be made by the Fish and Wildlife Service no later than July 2006.

Unlike most of the nation, Wyoming in 2003 had a $169 million budget surplus, largely due to an increase in mineral revenues. Rising health care costs and the need to pay for new state buildings and schools caused Democratic Governor Freudenthal to call for increases in property taxes.

12 STATE GOVERNMENT

Wyoming's state constitution was approved by the voters in November 1889 and accepted by Congress in 1890. By January 2005 it had been amended 94 times. Constitutional amendments require a two-thirds vote of the legislature and ratification by the voters at the next general election.

The legislature consists of a 30-member Senate and a 60-member House of Representatives. Senators are elected to staggered four-year terms. The entire House of Representatives is elected every two years for a two-year term. Legislators must be US citizens, citizens and residents of Wyoming, qualified voters, and residents of their districts for at least one year prior to election. The minimum age for senators is 25 and for representatives 21. Regular sessions begin in January or February and are limited to 40 legislative days in odd-numbered years and 20 legislative days in even-numbered years. The legislature may call special sessions by a petition of a majority of the members of each house. In 2004 the legislative salary was $125 per diem during regular sessions, unchanged from 1999.

Heading the executive branch are the following elected officials: the governor, secretary of state, auditor, treasurer, comptroller, commissioner of finance, and superintendent of public instruction. Each serves a four-year term. The governor is limited to serving two consecutive terms. His successor is the secretary of the Senate, as there is no lieutenant governor. A governor must be at least 30 years old, a US citizen, a state citizen, and at least a five-resident of the state. As of December 2004, the governor's salary was $130,000.

A bill passed by the legislature becomes law if signed by the governor, if left unsigned by the governor for three days while the legislature is in session (or 15 days after it has adjourned), or if passed over the governor's veto by two-thirds of the elected members of each house.

Voters must be US citizens, at least 18 years old, and bona fide residents of Wyoming. Convicted felons and those adjudicated as mentally incompetent may not vote.

13 POLITICAL PARTIES

The Republicans traditionally dominate Wyoming politics at the federal and state level, although the state elected a Democratic governor, Dave Freudenthal, in 2002. There were 246,000 registered voters in 2004. Both of Wyoming's senators, Craig Thomas (reelected in 2000) and Mike Enzi (elected in 1996 to succeed Alan Simpson and reelected in 2002), are Republicans, as is Wyoming's US Representative, Barbara Cubin, reelected in 2004.

As of mid-2005, there were 23 Republicans and 7 Democrats in the state Senate and 46 Republicans and 14 Democrats in the

Wyoming Presidential Vote by Major Political Parties, 1948–2004

YEAR	ELECTORAL VOTE	WYOMING WINNER	DEMOCRAT	REPUBLICAN
1948	3	*Truman (D)	52,354	47,947
1952	3	*Eisenhower (R)	47,934	81,049
1956	3	*Eisenhower (R)	49,554	74,573
1960	3	Nixon (R)	63,331	77,451
1964	3	*Johnson (D)	80,718	61,998
1968	3	*Nixon (R)	45,173	70,927
1972	3	*Nixon (R)	44,358	100,464
1976	3	Ford (R)	62,239	92,717
1980	3	*Reagan (R)	49,427	110,700
1984	3	*Reagan (R)	53,370	133,241
1988	3	*Bush (R)	67,113	106,867
1992**	3	Bush (R)	68,160	79,347
1996**	3	Dole (R)	77,934	105,388
2000	3	*Bush, G. W. (R)	60,481	147,947
2004	3	*Bush, G. W. (R)	70,776	167,629

*Won US presidential election.
**IND. candidate Ross Perot received 51,263 votes in 1992 and 25,928 votes in 1996.

state House. Republican George W. Bush received 69% of the vote in the 2000 presidential election, while Democratic candidate Al Gore won 28%. Bush garnered the same percentage (69%) in his 2004 bid for a second term, defeating Democrat John Kerry, who won just 29% of the vote. In 1998, 30% of registered voters were Democratic, 59% Republican, and 11% unaffiliated or members of other parties. The state had three electoral votes in the 2004 presidential election.

14 LOCAL GOVERNMENT

In 2005, Wyoming was subdivided into 23 counties, 98 municipal governments, 48 public school districts, and 546 special districts and authorities.

Counties, which can be geographically vast and include a relatively small population, are run by commissioners. Each county has a clerk, treasurer, assessor, sheriff, attorney, coroner, district court clerk, and from one to five county judges or justices of the peace. Municipalities may decide their own form of government, including mayor-council and council-manager.

In 2005, local government accounted for about 32,026 full-time (or equivalent) employment positions.

15 STATE SERVICES

To address the continuing threat of terrorism and to work with the federal Department of Homeland Security, homeland security in Wyoming operates under state statute; a homeland security director is designated as the state homeland security advisor.

The Board of Education has primary responsibility for educational services in Wyoming. Transportation services are provided by the Wyoming Department of Transportation; health and welfare matters fall under the jurisdiction of the Department of Health and the Department of Family Services. Among the many state agencies concerned with natural resources are the Department of Environmental Quality, Land Quality Advisory Board, Oil and Gas Conservation Commission, and Water Development

Commission. The Department of Employment is responsible for labor services.

16 JUDICIAL SYSTEM

Wyoming's judicial branch consists of a supreme court with a chief justice and four other justices, district courts with a total of 222 judges, and county judges and justices of the peace. Supreme court justices are appointed by the governor but must stand for retention at the next general election. Once elected, they serve eight-year terms.

As of 31 December 2004, a total of 1,980 prisoners were held in Wyoming's state and federal prisons, an increase from 1,872 of 5.8% from the previous year. As of year-end 2004, a total of 210 inmates were female, up from 175 or 20% from the year before. Among sentenced prisoners (one year or more), Wyoming had an incarceration rate of 389 per 100,000 population in 2004.

According to the Federal Bureau of Investigation, Wyoming in 2004, had a violent crime rate (murder/nonnegligent manslaughter; forcible rape; robbery; aggravated assault) of 229.6 reported incidents per 100,000 population, or a total of 1,163 reported incidents. Crimes against property (burglary; larceny/theft; and motor vehicle theft) in that same year totaled 16,889 reported incidents or 3,334.3 reported incidents per 100,000 people. Wyoming has a death penalty, of which lethal injection is the sole method of execution. However, if that method is declared unconstitutional, the use of lethal gas has been authorized. From 1976 through 5 May 2006, the state has carried out only one execution, in January 1992. As of 1 January 2006, Wyoming had only two inmates on death row.

In 2003, Wyoming spent $13,404,443 on homeland security, an average of $24 per state resident.

17 ARMED FORCES

In 2004, there were 5,125 active-duty military personnel and 524 civilian personnel stationed in Wyoming, nearly all of whom were at Wyoming's only US military installation—the Francis E. Warren Air Force Base at Cheyenne. The Air National Guard was stationed at Cheyenne Municipal Airport. Total defense contracts awarded in 2004 totaled more than $115 million, the lowest in the nation. Total defense payroll outlays for that same year were $302 million, second lowest only to Utah.

In 2003, there were 54,941 military veterans living in Wyoming. Of these, 6,344 were veterans of World War II; 5,477 of the Korean conflict; 18,625 of the Vietnam era; and 9,840 of the Gulf War. In 2004, the Veterans Administration expended more than $168 million in pensions, medical assistance, and other major veterans' benefits.

As of 31 October 2004, the Wyoming Highway Patrol employed 174 full-time sworn officers.

18 MIGRATION

Many people have passed through Wyoming, but relatively few have come to stay. Not until the 1970s, a time of rapid economic development, did the picture change. Between 1970 and 1983, Wyoming gained a net total of 45,500 residents through migration. In the 1980s, the state's total population grew only by 1.1%,

primarily offset by the net loss from migration of 52,000 persons. The urban population increased from 62.8% of the state's total in 1980 to 65% in 1990. Between 1990 and 1998, Wyoming had a net loss of less than 500 in domestic migration but a net gain of 2,000 in international migration. In 1998, the state admitted 159 foreign immigrants. Between 1990 and 1998, the state's overall population increased 6%. In the period 2000–05, net international migration was 2,264 and net internal migration was 1,771, for a net gain of 4,035 people.

19 INTERGOVERNMENTAL COOPERATION

Emblematic of Wyoming's concern for water resources is the fact that it belongs to seven compacts with neighboring states concerning the Bear, Belle Fourche, Colorado, Upper Colorado, Snake, Upper Niobrara, and Yellowstone rivers.

Wyoming has also joined the Interstate Oil and Gas Compact, the Western Interstate Energy Compact, the Western States Water Council, the Western Interstate Commission for Higher Education, and numerous other multistate bodies, including the Council of State Governments. Federal grants in fiscal year 2001 totaled over $1.2 billion. Mirroring a national trend, that figure declined significantly by 2005, to $675 million. Federal grants totaled an estimated $697 million in fiscal year 2006, and an estimated $713 million in fiscal year 2007.

20 ECONOMY

The economic life of Wyoming is largely sustained by agriculture, chiefly feed grains and livestock, and mining, including petroleum and gas production. Mining and petroleum production mushroomed during the 1970s, leading to a powerful upsurge in population. In the early 1980s, unemployment remained low, per capita income was high, and the inflation rate declined. The absence of personal and corporate income taxes helped foster a favorable business climate during the 1990s. The state economy's annual growth rate accelerated coming into the 21st century, from 1.1% in 1998 to 3.6% in 1999 to 12.3% in 2000. Not heavily involved in the information technology (IT) boom of the 1990s, Wyoming was relatively unaffected by its bust in 2001, registering annual growth of 6.8% for the year. The main growth sectors have been various service categories, with output from general services up 37.9% from 1997 to 2001; from trade, up 29.1%; from the government sector, up 24.3%; and from financial services, up 23.6%.

In 2004, Wyoming's gross state product (GSP) was $23.979 billion, of which mining accounted for $5.997 billion or 25% of GSP, while real estate accounted for $2.101 billion (8.7% of GSP) and construction at $1.272 billion (5.3% of GSP). In that same year, there were an estimated 56,740 small businesses in Wyoming. Of the 20,071 businesses that had employees, an estimated total of 19,388 or 96.6% were small companies. An estimated 2,519 new businesses were established in the state in 2004, up 4.1% from the year before. Business terminations that same year came to 2,737, down 6.3% from 2003. There were 65 business bankruptcies in 2004, up 47.7% from the previous year. In 2005, the state's personal bankruptcy (Chapter 7 and Chapter 13) filing rate was 484 filings per 100,000 people, ranking Wyoming as the 30th highest in the nation.

²¹INCOME

In 2005 Wyoming had a gross state product (GSP) of $27 billion which accounted for 0.2% of the nation's gross domestic product and placed the state at number 49 in highest GSP among the 50 states and the District of Columbia.

According to the Bureau of Economic Analysis, in 2004 Wyoming had a per capita personal income (PCPI) of $34,279. This ranked 15th in the United States and was 104% of the national average of $33,050. The 1994–2004 average annual growth rate of PCPI was 5.3%. Wyoming had a total personal income (TPI) of $17,341,215,000, which ranked 51st in the United States and reflected an increase of 7.0% from 2003. The 1994–2004 average annual growth rate of TPI was 5.8%. Earnings of persons employed in Wyoming increased from $11,534,759,000 in 2003 to $12,448,030,000 in 2004, an increase of 7.9%. The 2003–04 national change was 6.3%.

The US Census Bureau reports that the three-year average median household income for 2002 to 2004 in 2004 dollars was $43,641 compared to a national average of $44,473. During the same period an estimated 9.6% of the population was below the poverty line as compared to 12.4% nationwide.

²²LABOR

According to the Bureau of Labor Statistics (BLS), in April 2006 the seasonally adjusted civilian labor force in Wyoming 292,000, with approximately 9,400 workers unemployed, yielding an unemployment rate of 3.2%, compared to the national average of 4.7% for the same period. Preliminary data for the same period placed nonfarm employment at 271,900. Since the beginning of the BLS data series in 1976, the highest unemployment rate recorded in Wyoming was 10.1% in May 1983. The historical low was 1.9% in February 1979. Preliminary nonfarm employment data by occupation for April 2006 showed that approximately 7.9% of the labor force was employed in construction; 19.7% in trade, transportation, and public utilities; 6% in professional and business services; 12% in leisure and hospitality services; and 24.2% in government. Data for manufacturing, financial activities, and education and health services were unavailable.

The BLS reported that in 2005, a total of 18,000 of Wyoming's 228,000 employed wage and salary workers were formal members of a union. This represented 7.9% of those so employed, down slightly from 8% in 2004, and below the national average of 12%. Overall in 2005, a total of 22,000 workers (9.5%) in Wyoming were covered by a union or employee association contract, which includes those workers who reported no union affiliation. Wyoming is one of 22 states with a right-to-work law.

As of 1 March 2006, Wyoming had a state-mandated minimum wage rate of $5.15 per hour. In 2004, women in the state accounted for 46.1% of the employed civilian labor force.

²³AGRICULTURE

Agriculture—especially livestock and grain—is one of Wyoming's most important industries. In 2004, Wyoming had about 9,200 farms and ranches covering almost 34.4 million acres (13.9 million hectares). The state's acreage of 3,743 acres (1,514 hectares) per farm ranked second in the United States after Arizona. The

value of the lands and buildings of Wyoming's farms and ranches in 2004 was over $10.8 billion. Total farm marketings in 2005 amounted to $1.1 billion, ranking 38th among the 50 states. Of this, livestock and animal products accounted for $984 million; crops, $146 million.

Field crops in 2004 included barley, 6,900,000 bu; wheat, 3,750,000 bu; oats, 795,000 bu; sugar beets, 812,000 tons; dry beans, 541,000 cwt; and hay, 2,016,000 tons.

²⁴ANIMAL HUSBANDRY

For most of Wyoming's territorial and state history, cattle ranchers have dominated the economy, even though the livestock industry is not large by national standards. In 2005, Wyoming had an estimated 1.35 million cattle and calves, valued at $1.38 billion. During 2004, there were 114,000 hogs and pigs, valued at $13.7 million. Wyoming farms and ranches produced 28.8 million lb (13.1 million kg) of sheep and lambs in 2003, and an estimated 3.64 million lb (1.7 million kg) of shorn wool in 2004 (second after Texas). In 2003, Wyoming farmers sold 28,000 lb (12,700 kg) of chicken and produced 54 million lb (24.5 million kg) of milk.

²⁵FISHING

There is no important commercial fishing in Wyoming. Fishing is largely recreational, and fish hatcheries and fish-planting programs keep the streams well stocked. Wyoming's streams annually provide 1.3 million angler days and 3.4 million fish; lakes generate 1.6 million angler days and a harvest of 4.1 million fish. There are two national fish hatcheries in the state (Saratoga and Jackson) that stock native cutthroat trout into high mountain wilderness lakes to enhance the native stocks. In 2004, the state issued 247,583 sport fishing licenses.

²⁶FORESTRY

Wyoming has 10,995,000 acres (4,450,000 hectares) of forested land, equal to 17.8% of the state's land area. Of this, 5,739,000 acres (2,323,000 hectares) are usable as commercial timberland. As of 2003, the state's four national forests—Bighorn, Bridger-Teton, Medicine Bow, and Shoshone—covered a total of 9,238,000 acres (3,739,000 hectares). In 2004, lumber production totaled 165 million board feet. Ponderosa pine accounts for about 50% of the annual cut, and lodgepole pine most of the rest. The remainder consists of Douglas fir, larch, Engelmann spruce, and other species.

²⁷MINING

According to preliminary data from the US Geological Survey (USGS), the estimated value of nonfuel mineral production by Wyoming in 2003 was $1.01 billion, which was unchanged from estimated values for 2002. The USGS data ranked Wyoming as 13th among the 50 states by the total value of its nonfuel mineral production, accounting for over 2.5% of total US output.

According to preliminary data for 2003, soda ash was the state's top nonfuel mineral, followed by bentonite, Grade-A helium and portland cement, by value. Collectively, these four commodities accounted for almost 93% of all nonfuel mineral output, by value. By volume, Wyoming in 2003, was the nation's leading producer of soda ash and bentonite, and ranked second in the output of Grade-A helium. The state also ranked ninth in the production of gypsum.

Data for 2003 showed the production of bentonite as totaling 3.34 million metric tons, with a value of $145 million, construction sand and gravel output that year came to 7.5 million metric tons, with a value of $31.5 million. Crushed stone output in 2003 totaled 4 million metric tons and was valued at $19 million.

Major uses of Wyoming bentonite were as pet waste absorbent, in drilling mud, in the pelletizing of iron ore, in foundry sand, and as a waterproof sealant. Soda ash (sodium carbonate) is produced mostly from trona ore, of which Wyoming contains the largest known deposit of natural trona. Soda ash is used in the manufacturing of a number of products including glass, soap, detergents, and textiles, as well as in food products as sodium bicarbonate

Wyoming is also known to have deposits of gold and silver, diamonds, copper, and of metals belonging to the platinum group.

28 ENERGY AND POWER

As of 2003, Wyoming had 35 electrical power service providers, of which 13 were publicly owned and 15 were cooperatives. Of the remainder, five were investor owned, one was federally operated and one was the owner of an independent generator that sold directly to customers. As of that same year there were 290,971 retail customers. Of that total, 177,304 received their power from investor-owned service providers. Cooperatives accounted for 83,933 customers, while publicly owned providers had 29,730 customers. There were three federal customers and one independent generator or "facility" customer.

Total net summer generating capability by the state's electrical generating plants in 2003 stood at 6.562 million kW, with total production that same year at 43.626 billion kWh. Of the total amount generated, 96.9% came from electric utilities, with the remainder coming from independent producers and combined heat and power service providers. The largest portion of all electric power generated, 42.341 billion kWh (97.1%), came from coal-fired plants, with hydroelectric plants in second place at 593.555 million kWh (1.4%). Other renewable power sources, petroleum and natural gas fired plants accounted for the remaining output.

Wyoming is comparatively energy-rich, ranking first among the states in coal production and seventh in output of crude oil.

As of 2004, Wyoming had proven crude oil reserves of 628 million barrels, or 3% of all proven US reserves, while output that same year averaged 141,000 barrels per day. Including federal offshore domains, the state that year ranked sixth (fifth excluding federal offshore) in proven reserves and eighth (seventh excluding federal offshore) in production among the 31 producing states. In 2004 Wyoming had 9,468 producing oil wells and accounted for 3% of all US production. As of 2005, the state's five refineries had a combined crude oil distillation capacity of 152,000 barrels per day.

In 2004, Wyoming had 20,244 producing natural gas and gas condensate wells. In that same year, marketed gas production (all gas produced excluding gas used for repressuring, vented and flared, and nonhydrocarbon gases removed) totaled 1,592.203 billion cu ft (45.21 billion cu m). As of 31 December 2004, proven reserves of dry or consumer-grade natural gas totaled 22,632 billion cu ft (642.74 billion cu m).

Wyoming has the three largest producing coal mines in the United States and had total recoverable coal reserves estimated at 7.053 billion tons in 2004. In 1970, Wyoming's coal production accounted for only 1% of the US total. By 1998 the state's production had risen to 28% of national production. In 2004, Wyoming had 20 producing coal mines, all of which, except one, were surface operations. Coal production that year totaled 396,493,000 short tons, up from 376,270,000 short tons in 2003. Of the total produced in 2004, the state's lone underground mine accounted for 43,000 short tons. One short ton equals 2,000 lb (0.907 metric tons).

29 INDUSTRY

Although manufacturing has increased markedly in Wyoming over the last three decades, it remains insignificant by national standards.

According to the US Census Bureau's Annual Survey of Manufactures (ASM) for 2004, Wyoming's manufacturing sector was largely centered on only two product subsectors, chemicals and fabricated metal products. The shipment value of all products manufactured in the state that same year was $5.010 billion. Of that total, chemical manufacturing accounted for the largest share at $1.414 billion. It was followed by fabricated metal product manufacturing at $177.298 million.

In 2004, a total of 8,675 people in Wyoming were employed in the state's manufacturing sector, according to the ASM. Of that total, 6,472 were actual production workers. In terms of total employment, the chemical manufacturing industry accounted for the largest portion of all manufacturing employees with 1,531 (1,165 actual production workers). It was followed by fabricated metal product manufacturing, with 1,057 (780 actual production workers).

ASM data for 2004 showed that Wyoming's manufacturing sector paid $352.411 million in wages. Of that amount, the chemical manufacturing sector accounted for the largest share at $90.685 million and was followed by fabricated metal product manufacturing at $35.410 million.

30 COMMERCE

According to the 2002 Census of Wholesale Trade, Wyoming's wholesale trade sector had sales that year totaling $3.3 billion from 789 establishments. Wholesalers of durable goods accounted for 475 establishments, followed by nondurable goods wholesalers at 286 and electronic markets, agents, and brokers accounting for 28 establishments. Sales by durable goods wholesalers in 2002 totaled $1.3 billion, while wholesalers of nondurable goods saw sales of $1.6 billion. Electronic markets, agents, and brokers in the wholesale trade industry had sales of $283.01 million.

In the 2002 Census of Retail Trade, Wyoming was listed as having 2,861 retail establishments with sales of $5.7 billion. The leading types of retail businesses by number of establishments were: miscellaneous store retailers (410); gasoline stations (401); motor vehicle and motor vehicle parts dealers (371); building material/garden equipment and supplies dealers (289); and food and beverage stores (278). In terms of sales, motor vehicle and motor vehicle parts dealers accounted for the largest share of retail sales at $1.5 billion, followed by gasoline stations at $1.04 billion; general merchandise stores at $887.7 million; and food and beverage stores at $775.3 million. A total of 28,796 people were employed by the retail sector in Wyoming that year.

Wyoming's exports of products to other countries were valued at $669.07 million in 2005, ranking 50th among all states.

31 CONSUMER PROTECTION

The Attorney General's Consumer Protection Unit enforces the Wyoming Consumer Protection Act, which includes provisions regulating the promotional advertising of prizes and telephone solicitation, and creates a telemarketer "no-call" list. The unit also enforces statutes prohibiting price discrimination and other anticompetitive practices, as well as laws regarding pyramid schemes.

When dealing with consumer protection issues, the state's Attorney General's Office can initiate civil but not criminal proceedings. It can also: represent the state before state and federal regulatory agencies; administer consumer protection and education programs; and handle formal consumer complaints. However, the office has limited subpoena powers. In antitrust actions, the Attorney General's Office can act on behalf of those consumers who are incapable of acting on their own and initiate damage actions on behalf of the state in state courts. However, the office cannot initiate criminal proceedings or represent other governmental entities in recovering civil damages under state or federal law.

The office of the Consumer Protection Unit of the Office of the Attorney General is located in the state capitol, Cheyenne.

32 BANKING

As of June 2005, Wyoming had 44 insured banks, savings and loans, and saving banks, in addition to 33 federally chartered credit unions (CUs). Excluding the CUs, the Cheyenne market area accounted for the largest portion of the state's financial institutions and deposits in 2004, with 14 institutions and $1.066 billion in deposits, followed by the Casper market area with seven institutions and $1.048 billion in deposits. As of June 2005, CUs accounted for 16.9% of all assets held by all financial institutions in the state, or some $1.186 billion. Banks, savings and loans, and savings banks collectively accounted for the remaining 83.1% or $5.830 billion in assets held.

The median net interest margin) (the difference between the lower rates offered to savers and the higher rates charged on loans) for the state's insured institutions stood at 4.21% as of fourth quarter 2005, down from 4.34% for all of 2004and 4.225 for all of 2003. The median percentage of past-due/nonaccrual loans to total loans stood at 1.42% as of fourth quarter 2005, down from 1.73% for all of 2004 and 2% for all of 2003.

Regulation of Wyoming's state-chartered banks and other state-chartered financial institutions is the responsibility of the Department of Audit's Division of Banking.

33 INSURANCE

In 2004, there were 233,000 individual life insurance policies in force in Wyoming with a total value of $18.7 billion; total value for all categories of life insurance (individual, group, and credit) was

$28.4 billion. The average coverage amount is $80,500 per policy holder. Death benefits paid that year totaled $82.2 million.

As of 2003, there were two property and casualty and no life and health insurance companies domiciled in the state. In 2004, direct premiums for property and casualty insurance totaled $763 million. That year, there were 2,159 flood insurance policies in force in the state, with a total value of $306 million.

In 2004, 53% of state residents held employment-based health insurance policies, 7% held individual policies, and 23% were covered under Medicare and Medicaid; 15% of residents were uninsured. In 2003, employee contributions for employment-based health coverage averaged at 16% for single coverage and 20% for family coverage. The state offers a 12-month health benefits expansion program for small-firm employees in connection with the Consolidated Omnibus Budget Reconciliation Act (COBRA, 1986), a health insurance program for those who lose employment-based coverage due to termination or reduction of work hours.

In 2003, there were 444,587 auto insurance policies in effect for private passenger cars. Required minimum coverage includes bodily injury liability of up to $25,000 per individual and $50,000 for all persons injured in an accident, as well as property damage liability of $20,000. In 2003, the average expenditure per vehicle for insurance coverage was $617.46.

34 SECURITIES

Wyoming has no securities exchanges. In 2005, there were 110 personal financial advisers employed in the state and 170 securities, commodities, and financial services sales agents. In 2004, there were over 12 publicly traded companies within the state, with over five NASDAQ companies: Altair Intl., US Energy Corp., Crazy Woman Creek Bancorp, Double Eagle Petroleum Co., and Great Lakes Aviation Ltd.

35 PUBLIC FINANCE

Wyoming's biennial budget is prepared by the governor and submitted to the legislature at the beginning of each even-numbered calendar year. The fiscal year is 1 July through 30 June.

Fiscal year 2006 general funds were estimated at $1.25 billion for resources and $1.24 billion for expenditures. In fiscal year 2004, federal government grants to Wyoming were $1.6 billion.

In the fiscal year 2007 federal budget, Wyoming was slated to receive: $7.3 million in State Children's Health Insurance Program (SCHIP) funds to help the state provide health coverage to low-income, uninsured children who do not qualify for Medicaid. This funding is a 23% increase over fiscal year 2006; and $3.9 million for the HOME Investment Partnership Program to help Wyoming fund a wide range of activities that build, buy, or rehabilitate affordable housing for rent or homeownership, or provide direct rental assistance to low-income people. This funding is an 11% increase over fiscal year 2006.

36 TAXATION

In 2005, Wyoming collected $1,740 million in tax revenues or $3,418 per capita, which placed it third among the 50 states in per capita tax burden. The national average was $2,192 per capita.

Wyoming—State Government Finances

(Dollar amounts in thousands. Per capita amounts in dollars)

	AMOUNT	PER CAPITA
Total Revenue	5,151,978	10,181.77
General revenue	4,061,138	8,025.96
Intergovernmental revenue	1,976,603	3,906.33
Taxes	1,504,777	2,973.87
General sales	462,842	914.71
Selective sales	111,162	219.69
License taxes	101,712	201.01
Individual income tax	–	–
Corporate income tax	–	–
Other taxes	829,061	1,638.46
Current charges	122,014	241.13
Miscellaneous general revenue	457,744	904.63
Utility revenue	–	–
Liquor store revenue	56,361	111.39
Insurance trust revenue	1,034,479	2,044.42
Total expenditure	3,596,174	7,107.06
Intergovernmental expenditure	1,204,014	2,379.47
Direct expenditure	2,392,160	4,727.59
Current operation	1,588,024	3,138.39
Capital outlay	354,831	701.25
Insurance benefits and repayments	363,803	718.98
Assistance and subsidies	37,373	73.86
Interest on debt	48,129	95.12
Exhibit: Salaries and wages	486,718	961.89
Total expenditure	3,596,174	7,107.06
General expenditure	3,185,501	6,295.46
Intergovernmental expenditure	1,204,014	2,379.47
Direct expenditure	1,981,487	3,915.98
General expenditures, by function:		
Education	1,070,621	2,115.85
Public welfare	497,376	982.96
Hospitals	7,279	14.39
Health	168,603	333.21
Highways	415,425	821.00
Police protection	30,598	60.47
Correction	91,003	179.85
Natural resources	178,887	353.53
Parks and recreation	25,687	50.76
Government administration	122,063	241.23
Interest on general debt	48,129	95.12
Other and unallocable	529,830	1,047.09
Utility expenditure	–	–
Liquor store expenditure	46,870	92.63
Insurance trust expenditure	363,803	718.98
Debt at end of fiscal year	909,531	1,797.49
Cash and security holdings	11,569,706	22,865.03

Abbreviations and symbols: – zero or rounds to zero; (NA) not available; (X) not applicable.

SOURCE: *U.S. Census Bureau, Governments Division, 2004 Survey of State Government Finances,* January 2006.

Property taxes accounted for 10.4% of the total, sales taxes 30.0%, selective sales taxes 6.9%, and other taxes 52.7%.

As of 1 January 2006, Wyoming had no state income tax, a distinction it shared with Alaska, Washington, Nevada, Florida, Alaska, and South Dakota.

In 2004, state and local property taxes amounted to $683,963,000 or $1,352 per capita. The per capita amount ranks the state 10th highest nationally. Local governments collected $544,154,000 of the total and the state government $139,809,000.

Wyoming taxes retail sales at a rate of 4%. In addition to the state tax, local taxes on retail sales can reach as much as 2%, making for a potential total tax on retail sales of 6%. Food purchased for consumption off-premises is taxable, although an income tax credit is allowed to offset sales tax on food. The tax on cigarettes is 60 cents per pack, which ranks 31st among the 50 states and the District of Columbia. Wyoming taxes gasoline at 14 cents per gallon. This is in addition to the 18.4 cents per gallon federal tax on gasoline.

According to the Tax Foundation, for every federal tax dollar sent to Washington in 2004, Wyoming citizens received $1.11 in federal spending.

37 ECONOMIC POLICY

State policy in Wyoming has traditionally favored fiscal, social, and political conservatism. A pro-business and pro-family climate has generally prevailed. For example, Wyoming does not have a state personal income tax, a state business income tax, nor a business inventory tax. Not until 1969 was the minerals industry compelled to pay a severance tax on the wealth it was extracting from Wyoming soils. The state's leading industry is tourism, (the federal government owns over 50% of Wyoming's land), and Wyoming is first among US states in coal and iron production. The Wyoming Department of Commerce's Business Council encourages entrepreneurship, emphasizes community development, and supports retention and expansion of existing Wyoming businesses. Grant and loan programs also assist Wyoming communities and businesses. In 2006, the Wyoming Business Council maintained six regional offices around the state to provide personalized and localized technical assistance. These were part of a statewide network of partners, offering one-on-one business assistance.

38 HEALTH

The infant mortality rate in October 2005 was estimated at 5.8 per 1,000 live births. The birth rate in 2003 was 13.4 per 1,000 population. The abortion rate stood at 0.9 per 1,000 women in 2000. In 2003, about 86.4% of pregnant woman received prenatal care beginning in the first trimester. In 2004, approximately 83% of children received routine immunizations before the age of three.

The crude death rate in 2003 was 8.3 deaths per 1,000 population. As of 2002, the death rates for major causes of death (per 100,000 resident population) were: heart disease, 201.5; cancer, 172.2; cerebrovascular diseases, 48.7; chronic lower respiratory diseases, 65; and diabetes, 29.1. Wyoming had the highest suicide rate in the nation at 21.1 per 100,000 population. The mortality rate from HIV infection was not available that year. In 2004, the reported AIDS case rate was at about 3.6 per 100,000 population. In 2002, about 54.5% of the population was considered overweight or obese. As of 2004, about 21.6% of state residents were smokers.

In 2003, Wyoming had 23 community hospitals with about 1,800 beds. There were about 53,000 patient admissions that year and 900,000 outpatient visits. The average daily inpatient census was about 900 patients. The average cost per day for hospital care was $943. Also in 2003, there were about 39 certified nursing facilities in the state with 3,061 beds and an overall occupancy rate of about 80.9%. In 2004, it was estimated that about 68.1% of all state residents had received some type of dental care within the year. Wyoming had 191 physicians per 100,000 resident population in 2004 and 774 nurses per 100,000 in 2005. In 2004, there was a total of 266 dentists in the state.

About 15% of state residents were enrolled in Medicaid programs in 2003; 14% were enrolled in Medicare programs in 2004. Approximately 15% of the state population was uninsured in 2004. In 2003, state health care expenditures totaled $709,000.

39 SOCIAL WELFARE

In 2004, about 14,000 people received unemployment benefits, with the average weekly unemployment benefit at $238. In fiscal year 2005, the estimated average monthly participation in the food stamp program included about 25,482 persons (10,422 households); the average monthly benefit was about $88.22 per person. That year, the total of benefits paid through the state for the food stamp program was about $26.9 million.

Temporary Assistance for Needy Families (TANF), the system of federal welfare assistance that officially replaced Aid to Families with Dependent Children (AFDC) in 1997, was reauthorized through the Deficit Reduction Act of 2005. TANF is funded through federal block grants that are divided among the states based on an equation involving the number of recipients in each state. Wyoming's TANF program is called POWER (Personal Opportunities With Employment Responsibility). In 2004, the state program had 1,000 recipients; state and federal expenditures on this TANF program totaled $17 million in fiscal year 2003.

In December 2004, Social Security benefits were paid to 82,510 Wyoming residents. This number included 54,890 retired workers, 7,340 widows and widowers, 9,370 disabled workers, 4,720 spouses, and 6,190 children. Social Security beneficiaries represented 15.8% of the total state population and 94.5% of the state's population age 65 and older. Retired workers received an average monthly payment of $955; widows and widowers, $926; disabled workers, $896; and spouses, $491. Payments for children of retired workers averaged $516 per month; children of deceased workers, $637; and children of disabled workers, $270. Federal Supplemental Security Income payments in December 2004 went to 5,645 Wyoming residents, averaging $368 a month. An additional $56,000 of state-administered supplemental payments were distributed to 2,769 residents.

40 HOUSING

In 2004, there were an estimated 232,637 housing units in Wyoming, ranking the state as having the smallest housing stock in the country. About 202,496 units were occupied; 69.9% were owner-occupied. About 65.4% of all units were single-family, detached homes; 14.4% were mobile homes. It was estimated that 11,242 units lacked telephone service, 1,229 lacked complete plumbing facilities, and 1,198 lacked complete kitchen facilities. Utility gas was the most common energy source for heating. The average household had 2.43 members.

In 2004, 3,300 new privately owned housing units were authorized for construction. The median home value was $119,654. The median monthly cost for mortgage owners was $954. Renters paid a median of $534 per month. In 2006, the state received over $3.2 million in community development block grants from the US Department of Housing and Urban Development (HUD).

41 EDUCATION

In 2004, 91.9% of Wyoming residents age 25 and older were high school graduates, well above the national average of 84%. Approximately 22.5% had obtained a bachelor's degree or higher; the national average was 22.5%.

The total enrollment for fall 2002 in Wyoming's public schools stood at 88,000. Of these, 60,000 attended schools from kindergarten through grade eight, and 28,000 attended high school. Approximately 86% of the students were white, 1.4% were black, 8.2% were Hispanic, 1% were Asian/Pacific Islander, and 3.5% were American Indian/Alaskan Native. Total enrollment was estimated at 85,000 by fall 2003 and expected to be 89,000 by fall 2014. Expenditures for public education in 2003/04 were estimated at $947.5 million. In fall 2003 there were 2,079 students enrolled in 35 privates schools. The resulting report, *The Nation's Report Card*, stated that in 2005, eighth graders in Wyoming scored 282 out of 500 in mathematics compared with the national average of 278.

As of fall 2002, there were 32,605 students enrolled in college or graduate school; minority students comprised 7.8% of total postsecondary enrollment. In 2005 Wyoming had nine degree-granting institutions. Wyoming has seven community colleges. The state controls and funds the University of Wyoming in Laramie, as well as the seven community colleges. There are no private colleges or universities, although the National Outdoor Leadership School, based in Lander, offers courses in mountaineering and ecology.

42 ARTS

The Wyoming Arts Council helps fund local activities and organizations in the visual and performing arts, including painting, music, theater, and dance. In 2005, the Wyoming Arts Council and other Wyoming arts organizations received five grants totaling $655,200 from the National Endowment for the Arts (NEA). In 2005, the National Endowment for the Humanities contributed $503,322 for five state programs. Contributions to the arts also came from state and private sources.

The Grand Teton Music Festival (formerly the Jackson Hole Fine Arts Festival) has continued to present an annual program of symphonic and chamber music performed by some of the nation's top artists; in summer 2006, the festival celebrated its 45th season. The Cheyenne Civic Center serves as a venue for a variety of musical and theatrical groups, including the Cheyenne Symphony Orchestra. Cheyenne is also home to the Cheyenne Little Theater Players, a community theater group that marked a 75-year anniversary in 2005.

The University of Wyoming Art Museum houses a permanent collection that includes over 7,000 pieces. The diverse collection showcases European and American paintings, 19th century Japanese prints, and African and Native American artifacts, among other artwork.

43 LIBRARIES AND MUSEUMS

In 2001, Wyoming was served by 23 public library systems, with a total of 74 libraries, of which 51 were branches. In the same year, the state's library systems had a combined 2,415,000 volumes of books and serial publications, and a total circulation of 3,757,000. The system also had 78,000 audio and 65,000 video items, 8,000 electronic format items (CD-ROMs, magnetic tapes, and disks), and four bookmobiles. The University of Wyoming, in Laramie, had 1,227,000 volumes and 12,960 periodical subscriptions in 2000. In fiscal year 2001, operating income for the state's public library system totaled $15,740,000 and included $14,427,000 in local funding and $73,000 in federal funds. Operating expenditures that year totaled $14,852,000, of which 70.4% was spent on staff and 10.6% on the collection.

There are at least 53 museums and historic sites, including the Wyoming State Museum in Cheyenne; the Buffalo Bill Historical Center (Cody), which exhibits paintings by Frederic Remington; and the anthropological, geological, and art museums of the University of Wyoming at Laramie.

44 COMMUNICATIONS

In 2004, 94.6% of all Wyoming households had telephones. In addition, by June of that same year there were 277,658 mobile wireless telephone subscribers. In 2003, 65.4% of Wyoming households had a computer and 57.7% had Internet access. By June 2005, there were 55,884 high-speed lines in Wyoming, 49,585 residential and 6,299 for business.

In 2005, Wyoming had 28 major radio stations, 7 AM and 21 FM, plus 3 television stations. A total of 7,279 Internet domain names were registered in the state by 2000.

45 PRESS

There were nine daily newspapers and five Sunday newspapers in Wyoming in 2005. The major daily and its 2005 circulation was the *Casper Star–Tribune*, 30,790 (33,289 on Sunday).

46 ORGANIZATIONS

In 2006, there were over 825 nonprofit organizations registered within the state, of which about 590 were registered as charitable, educational, or religious organizations.

National organizations with headquarters within the state include the Dude Ranchers' Association, the National Park Academy of the Arts, and the Yellowstone Association. Local arts, history, and the environment are represented in part through the Arts Council (in Cheyenne) and the Wyoming Council for the Humanities. Outdoor sports and recreation organizations include the Wyoming Outfitters and Guides Association, Wyoming Ranch and Recreational Services, and the Wyoming Campgrounds Association.

47 TOURISM, TRAVEL, AND RECREATION

In 2004, the state hosted 8 million overnight visitors and 17.9 million day trip travelers. The tourism and travel industry, the state's second-leading industry, supports over 37,823 full-time and part-time jobs. In 2002–03, Wyoming tourism increased by 6.5%, the highest increase in travel and tourism of any US state.

There are two national parks in Wyoming—Yellowstone and Grand Teton—and 9 national forests. Devils Tower and Fossil Butte are national monuments, and Fort Laramie is a national historic site. Yellowstone National Park, covering 2,219,791 acres (898,349 hectares), mostly in the northwestern corner of the state, is the oldest (1 March 1872) and largest national park in the United States. The park features some 3,000 geysers and hot springs, including the celebrated Old Faithful. Just to the south of Yellowstone is Grand Teton National Park, 309,993 acres (125,454 hectares).Wyoming is home to major emigrant trails: Oregon, Mormon, California, and Pony Express. Devil's Tower National Monument, in the Black Hills National Forest, is a much-photographed landmark. The town of Cody was founded by Buffalo Bill Cody. The town of Kaycee was the home of the famous outlaws Butch Cassidy and the Sundance Kid.

Adjacent to Grand Teton is the National Elk Refuge, the feeding range of the continent's largest known herd of elk. Devils Tower, a rock formation in the northeast, looming 5,117 feet (1,560 meters) high, is the country's oldest national monument (24 September 1906).

48 SPORTS

There are no major professional sports teams in Wyoming, but there is a minor league baseball team in Casper. Participation sports in Wyoming are typically Western. Skills developed by ranch hands in herding cattle are featured at rodeos held throughout the state. Cheyenne Frontier Days is the largest of these rodeos. Skiing is also a major sport, with Jackson Hole being the largest, best-known resort.

In collegiate sports, the University of Wyoming competes in the Mountain West Conference. They won the Sun Bowl in 1956 and 1958, and they appeared in, but lost, the Holiday Bowl in 1987 and 1988.

49 FAMOUS WYOMINGITES

The most important federal officeholder from Wyoming was Willis Van Devanter (b.Indiana, 1859–1941), who served on the US Supreme Court from 1910 to 1937. Many of Wyoming's better-known individuals are associated with the frontier: John Colter (b.Virginia, 1775?–1813), a fur trader, was the first white man to explore northwestern Wyoming; and Jim Bridger (b.Virginia, 1804–81), perhaps the most famous fur trapper in the West, centered his activities in Wyoming. Late in life, William F. "Buffalo Bill" Cody (b.Iowa, 1846–1917) settled in the Big Horn Basin and established the town of Cody. A number of outlaws made their headquarters in Wyoming. The most famous were "Butch Cassidy" (George Leroy Parker, b.Utah, 1866–1908) and the "Sundance

Kid" (Harry Longabaugh, birthplace in dispute, 1863?–1908), who, as members of the Wild Bunch, could often be found there.

Two Wyoming women, Esther Morris (b.New York, 1814–1902) and Nellie Taylor Ross (b.Missouri, 1880–1979), are recognized as the first woman judge and the first woman governor, respectively, in the United States; Ross also was the first woman to serve as director of the US Mint. Few Wyoming politicians have received national recognition, but Francis E. Warren (b.Massachusetts, 1844–1929), the state's first governor, served 37 years in the US Senate and came to wield considerable influence and power.

Without question, Wyoming's most famous businessman was James Cash Penney (b.Missouri, 1875–1971). Penney established his first "Golden Rule" store in Kemmerer and eventually built a chain of department stores nationwide. The water-reclamation accomplishments of Elwood Mead (b.Indiana, 1858–1936) and the botanical work in the Rocky Mountains of Aven Nelson (b.Iowa, 1859–1952) were highly significant. Jackson Pollock (1912–56), born in Cody, was a leading painter in the abstract expressionist movement.

50 BIBLIOGRAPHY

Council of State Governments. *The Book of the States, 2006 Edition.* Lexington, Ky.: Council of State Governments, 2006.

Dubois, Muriel L. *Wyoming Facts and Symbols.* Mankato, Minn.: Hilltop Books, 2000.

Gottberg, John. *Hidden Wyoming.* Berkeley, Calif.: Ulysses Press, 1999.

Huser, Verne. *Wyoming's Snake River: A River Guide's Chronicle of People and Places, Plants and Animals.* Salt Lake City: University of Utah Press, 2001.

Lakes, Arthur. *Discovering Dinosaurs in the Old West: The Field Journals of Arthur Lakes.* Washington, D.C.: Smithsonian Institution Press, 2001.

Newby, Rick (ed.). *The Rocky Mountains.* Vol. 6 in *The Greenwood Encyclopedia of American Regional Cultures.* Westport, Conn.: Greenwood Press, 2004.

Parzybok, Tye W. *Weather Extremes in the West.* Missoula, Mont.: Mountain Press, 2005.

Pitcher, Don. *Wyoming Handbook: Including Yellowstone and Grand Teton National Parks.* 4th ed. Emeryville, Calif.: Moon, 2000.

Preston, Thomas. *Rocky Mountains: Montana, Wyoming, Colorado, New Mexico.* 2nd ed. Vol. 3 of *The Double Eagle Guide to 1,000 Great Western Recreation Destinations.* Billings, Mont.: Discovery Publications, 2003.

Rees, Amanda (ed.). *The Great Plains Region.* Vol. 1 in *The Greenwood Encyclopedia of American Regional Cultures.* Westport, Conn.: Greenwood Press, 2004.

US Department of Commerce, Economics and Statistics Administration, US Census Bureau. *Wyoming, 2000. Summary Social, Economic, and Housing Characteristics: 2000 Census of Population and Housing.* Washington, D.C.: US Government Printing Office, 2003.

DISTRICT OF COLUMBIA

District of Columbia

ORIGIN OF STATE NAME: From "Columbia," a name commonly applied to the United States in the late 18th century, ultimately derived from Christopher Columbus. **BECAME US CAPITAL:** 1 December 1800, when Congress first assembled in the city. **MOTTO:** *Justitia omnibus* (Justice for all). **FLAG:** The flag, based on George Washington's coat of arms, consists of three red stars above two horizontal red stripes on a white field. **OFFICIAL SEAL:** In the background, the Potomac River separates the District of Columbia from the Virginia shore, over which the sun is rising. In the foreground, Justice, holding a wreath and a tablet with the word "Constitution," stands beside a statue of George Washington. At the left of Justice is the Capitol; to her right, an eagle and various agricultural products. Below is the District motto and the date 1871; above are the words "District of Columbia." **BIRD:** Wood thrush. **FLOWER:** American beauty rose. **TREE:** Scarlet oak. **LEGAL HOLIDAYS:** New Year's Day, 1 January; Birthday of Martin Luther King Jr., 3rd Monday in January; Washington's Birthday, 3rd Monday in February; Memorial Day, last Monday in May; Independence Day, 4 July; Labor Day, 1st Monday in September; Columbus Day, 2nd Monday in October; Veterans' Day, 11 November; Thanksgiving Day, 4th Thursday in November; Christmas Day, 25 December. **TIME:** 7 AM EST = noon GMT.

¹LOCATION, SIZE, AND EXTENT

Located in the South Atlantic region of the United States, the District of Columbia has a total area of 69 sq mi (179 sq km), of which land takes up 63 sq mi (163 sq km) and inland water 6 sq mi (16 sq km). The District is bounded on the N, E, and S by Maryland and on the W by the Virginia shore of the Potomac River. The total boundary length is 37 mi (60 km).

For statistical purposes, the District of Columbia (coextensive since 1890 with the city of Washington, DC) is considered part of the Washington, DC, metropolitan area, which since 1985 has embraced Calvert, Charles, Frederick, Montgomery, and Prince George's counties in Maryland and Arlington, Fairfax, Loudoun, Prince William, and Stafford counties in Virginia, along with a number of other Virginia jurisdictions, most notably the city of Alexandria.

²TOPOGRAPHY

The District of Columbia, an enclave of western Maryland, lies wholly within the Atlantic Coastal Plain. The major topographical features are the Potomac River and its adjacent marshlands; the Anacostia River, edged by reclaimed flatlands to the south and east; Rock Creek, wending its way from the northwestern plateau to the Potomac; and the gentle hills of the north. The district's average elevation is about 150 ft (46 m). The highest point, 410 ft (125 m), is in the northwest, at Tenleytown; the low point is the Potomac, only 1 ft (30 cm) above sea level.

³CLIMATE

The climate of the nation's capital is characterized by chilly, damp winters and hot, humid summers. The normal daily average temperature is 58°F (14°C), ranging from 36°F (2°C) in January to 79°F (26°C) in July. The record low, -15°F (-26°C), was set on 11 February 1899; the all-time high, 106°F (41°C), on 20 July 1930. Precipi-

tation averaged 39.4 in (100 cm) yearly during 1971–2000; snowfall, 17 in (43 cm). The average annual relative humidity is 75% at 7 AM and 53% at 1 PM.

⁴FLORA AND FAUNA

Although most of its original flora has been obliterated by urbanization, the District has long been known for its beautiful parks, where about 1,800 varieties of flowering plants and 250 shrubs grow. Boulevards are shaded by stately sycamores, pin and red oaks, American lindens, and black walnut trees. Famous among the introduced species are the Japanese cherry trees around the Tidal Basin. Magnolia, dogwood, and gingko are also characteristic. The District's fauna is less exotic, with squirrels, cottontails, English sparrows, and starlings predominating. Two species (Hay's Spring amphipod and the puma) were listed as endangered and one (the bald eagle) as threatened by the US Fish and Wildlife Service as of April 2006.

⁵ENVIRONMENTAL PROTECTION

The Environmental Regulation Administration (ERA) administers district and federal laws, regulations and mayoral initiatives governing the environment and natural resources of the District of Columbia and the surrounding metropolitan area. The main duty is the protection of human health and the environment as they relate to pesticides, hazardous waste, underground storage tanks, water, air, soils, and fisheries programs. The ERA is responsible for administrating over 30 statutes and regulations.

In 1996, the District had about 250 acres of wetlands, all palustrine (marsh) or riverine, mostly along the tidal reaches of the Potomac and the Anacostia Rivers. The Potomac is an important tributary of the Chesapeake Bay Estuarine Complex, which was designated as a Ramsar Wetland of International Importance in 1987.

In 2003, the US Environment Protection Agency (EPA) database listed 29 hazardous waste sites in the District. Only one site, the Washington Naval Yard, was on the National Priorities List as of 2006. In 2004, the District received a federal EPA grant of $1.2 million for water pollution control projects.

6 POPULATION

In 2005, the District of Columbia ranked 50th in the nation with a larger population than the last-ranked state of Wyoming, at an estimated 550,521 residents, a decrease of 3.8% since 2000. Between 1990 and 2000, the District's population declined from 606,900 to 572,059, a decrease of 5.7%. The population is projected to decrease to 506,323 by 2015 and 455,108 by 2025.

In 2004, the median age was 35.8. Persons under 18 years old accounted for 19.8% of the population while 12.1% was age 65 or older.

In 1990, the District of Columbia outranked three states in population, with a census total of 606,900, a decline of almost 5% from 1980. As a city, the District ranked 27th in the United States in 2004. The population density in 2004 was 9,057.00 persons per sq mi.

Even as the capital's population has declined, the number of Washington, DC, metropolitan area residents has been increasing, from 3,040,000 in 1970 to 3,251,000 in 1980, to 3,924,000 in 1990, and to an estimated 5,139,549 in 2004. The District's population is 100% urban and extremely mobile.

7 ETHNIC GROUPS

Black Americans have long been the largest ethnic or racial group in the District of Columbia, accounting for 60% of the population in 2000 (when they numbered 343,312), among the highest percentages of any major US city. In 2004, that percentage had dropped to 57.7% of the population.

Between 1970 and 1980, the population of groups other than white and black almost quadrupled within the Washington metropolitan area, reaching 134,209 in 1980. Southeast Asians made up a significant proportion of the immigrants, as did Mexicans and Central and South Americans. The District's racial and ethnic minorities in 2000 included 44,953 Hispanics and Latinos (up from 33,000 in 1990) and 15,189 Asians (including 3,734 Chinese and 2,845 Asian Indians). There also were 1,713 American Indians living in the District. In 2004, 3% of the population was Asian, 0.3% was American Indian or Alaska native, 0.1% was Native Hawaiian or Pacific Islander, and 8.5% of the total population was or Hispanic or Latino origin. In 2004, 1.5% of the population reported origin of two or more races.

There were 73,561 foreign-born residents, accounting for 12.9% of the District's total population, in 2000. In addition, the many foreign-born residents attached to foreign embassies and missions contribute to Washington's ethnic diversity.

8 LANGUAGES

Dialectically, the Washington, DC, area is extremely heterogeneous. In 2000, 83.2% of all District of Columbia residents five years of age or older spoke only English at home, down from 87% in 1990.

The following table gives selected statistics from the 2000 Census for language spoken at home by persons five years old and over. The category "African languages" includes Amharic, Ibo, Twi, Yoruba, Bantu, Swahili, and Somali.

LANGUAGE	NUMBER	PERCENT
Population 5 years and over	**539,658**	**100.0**
Speak only English	449,241	83.2
Speak a language other than English	90,417	16.8
Speak a language other than English	**90,417**	**16.8**
Spanish or Spanish Creole	49,461	9.2
French (incl. Patois, Cajun)	9,085	1.7
African languages	5,181	1.0
Chinese	2,913	0.5
German	2,695	0.5
Arabic	2,097	0.4
Italian	1,723	0.3
Vietnamese	1,610	0.3
Tagalog	1,356	0.3
Russian	1,110	0.2
Portuguese or Portuguese Creole	1,013	0.2

9 RELIGIONS

As of 2000, the largest number of religious adherents in Washington, DC, were Roman Catholic, with about 160,048 adherents in 42 congregations. Mainline Protestants were next in numbers with the American Baptist Churches in the USA claiming 51,836 adherents in 62 congregations and the Episcopal Church claiming 19,698 adherents in 34 congregations. The Southern Baptist Convention had 38,852 adherents in about 49 congregations; the church reported 1,160 newly baptized members in the district in 2002. The Jewish population was estimated at 25,500 in 2000. About 26.8% of the population did not report affiliation with any religious organization.

The Washington National Cathedral was established by Congress through an 1893 charter with the Protestant Episcopal Cathedral Foundation. The charter was signed by President Benjamin Harrison. The building was completed in 1912.

The international headquarters of B'nai B'rith International is located in Washington, DC, as is the headquarters for Hillel, an organization of Jewish college students groups. The United States Conference of Catholic Bishops is also based in the District.

10 TRANSPORTATION

Union Station, located north of the Capitol, is the District's one rail terminal, from which Amtrak provides passenger service to the northeast corridor and southern points. As of 2006 Amtrak provided daily north south and east–west service from Union Station. In all, four railroads operated 45 rail mi (72 km) of track within the District. The Washington Metropolitan Area Transit Authority, or Metro, operates bus and subway transportation within the city and its Maryland and Virginia suburbs. About 40% of working District residents commute by public transportation. In 1994–95, the US Transit Authority awarded grants of $199 million for the Metro.

Within the District, as of 2004, were 1,500 mi (2,415 km) of public streets and roads. In that same year, some 228,000 motor vehicles were registered, and there were 349,122 driver's licenses in force. In 2005, a total of three major airports handled the District's commercial air traffic: Ronald Reagan Washington National Airport, just south of the city in Virginia; Dulles International Airport in Virginia; and Baltimore-Washington International Airport in Maryland. Enplanements for the three airports in 2004 totaled 7,661,532 for Reagan Washington National; 10,961,614 for

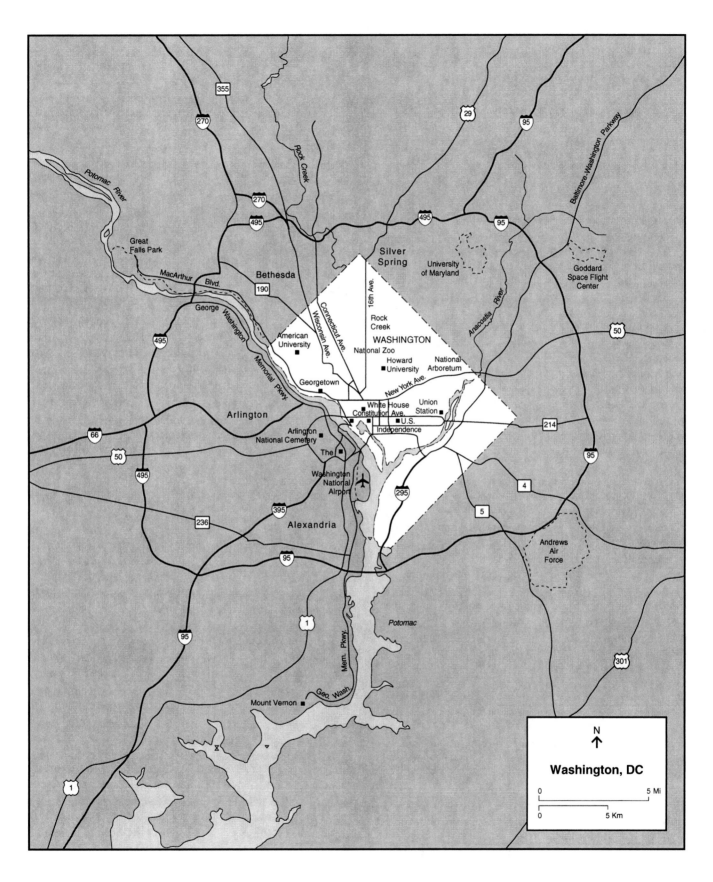

Washington, DC

N

Dulles; and 10,103,563 for Baltimore-Washington. The three airports were the 30th-, the 21st-, and the 23rd-busiest airports, respectively, in the United States that same year. The District also had 14 heliports in 2005.

Although Washington, DC, is not generally thought of as a traditional port, in 2004 the District did have 7 mi (11 km) of navigable inland waterways, and in 2003, it had waterborne shipments totaling 770,000 tons.

11 HISTORY

Algonkian-speakers were living in what is now the District of Columbia when Englishmen founded the Jamestown, Virginia, settlement in 1607. The first white person known to have set foot in the Washington area was the English fur trader Henry Fleete, who in 1622 was captured by the Indians and held there for several years. Originally part of Maryland Colony, the region had been carved up into plantations by the latter half of the 17th century.

After the US Constitution (1787) provided that a tract of land be reserved for the seat of the federal government, both Maryland and Virginia offered parcels for that purpose; on 16 July 1790, Congress authorized George Washington to choose a site not more than 10 mi (16 km) square along the Potomac River. President Washington made his selection in January 1791. He then appointed Andrew Ellicott to survey the area and employed Pierre Charles L'Enfant, a French military engineer who had served in the Continental Army, to draw up plans for the federal city. L'Enfant's masterful design called for a wide roadway (now called Pennsylvania Avenue) to connect the Capitol with the President's House (Executive Mansion, now commonly called the White House) a mile away, and for other widely separated public buildings with spacious vistas. However, L'Enfant was late in completing the engraved plan of his design, and he also had difficulty in working with the three commissioners who had been appointed to direct a territorial survey; for these and other reasons, L'Enfant was dismissed and Ellicott carried out the plans. Construction was delayed by lack of adequate financing. Only one wing of the Capitol was completed, and the President's House was still under construction when President John Adams and some 125 government officials moved into the District in 1800. Congress met there for the first time on 17 November, and the District officially became the nation's capital on 1 December. On 3 May 1802, the city of Washington was incorporated (the District also included other local entities), with an elected council and a mayor appointed by the president.

Construction proceeded slowly, while the city's population grew to about 24,000 by 1810. In August 1814, during the War of 1812, British forces invaded and burned the Capitol, the President's House, and other public buildings. These were rebuilt within five years, but for a long time, Washington remained a rude, rough city. In 1842, English author Charles Dickens described it as a "monument raised to a deceased project," consisting of "spacious avenues that begin in nothing and lead nowhere." At the request of its residents, the Virginia portion was retroceded in 1846, thus confining the federal district to the eastern shore of the Potomac. The Civil War brought a large influx of Union soldiers, workers, and escaped slaves, and the District's population rose sharply from 75,080 in 1860 to 131,700 by the end of the decade, spurring the development of modern Washington.

In 1871, Congress created a territorial form of government; this territorial government was abolished three years later because of alleged local extravagances, and in 1878, a new form of government was established, headed by three commissioners appointed by the president. During the same decade, Congress barred District residents from voting in national elections or even for their own local officials. In the 1890s, Rock Creek Park and Potomac Park were established, and during the early 1900s, city planners began to rebuild the monumental core of Washington in harmony with L'Enfant's original design. The New Deal period brought a rise in public employment, substantial growth of federal facilities, and the beginnings of large-scale public housing construction and slum clearance. After World War II, redevelopment efforts concentrated on demolishing slums in the city's southwest section. The White House was completely renovated in the late 1940s, and a huge building program coincided with the expansion of the federal bureaucracy during the 1960s.

Because it is the residence of the president, Washington, DC, has always been noted for its public events, in particular the Presidential Inauguration and Inaugural Ball. The District has also been the site of many historic demonstrations: the appearance in 1894 of Coxey's Army (some 300 unemployed workers); the demonstrations in 1932 of the Bonus Marchers (17,000 Army veterans demanding that the government cash their bonus certificates); the massive March on Washington by civil rights demonstrators in 1963; the march on the Pentagon in 1967 by antiwar activists and later Vietnam-era protests; and, in 1995, the Million Man March organized by the controversial Nation of Islam leader Louis Farrakhan.

The District's form of government has undergone significant changes. The 23rd Amendment to the US Constitution, ratified on 3 April 1961, permits residents to vote in presidential elections, and beginning in 1971, the District was allowed to send a nonvoting delegate to the US House of Representatives. Local self-rule began in 1975, when an elected mayor and council took office. The District both prospered and suffered in the 1980s and 1990s. In spite of an expanding economy, the city was wracked by poverty, drug-bred crime, and even gang warfare. In 1989, the federal government mandated $80 million for a program to combat drug abuse in the nation's capital. Crime in Washington has included corruption in high places. In the mid-1980s, the federal government launched an investigation into allegations of bribery, fraud, and racketeering in the award of millions of dollars in municipal and federal contracts. The investigation produced the conviction of 11 city officials. In 1990, the District's mayor of twelve years, Marion Barry, was videotaped smoking crack and was convicted of possessing cocaine. Barry was succeeded that year by Sharon Pratt Dixon, a black lawyer and former power company executive, but reelected in 1994. In 1998, he announced he would not run for reelection, completing four terms of office.

Since the 1970s, many of Washington's residents have supported statehood for the District of Columbia. A proposal for statehood won the majority of votes in a 1980 election, and the name "New Columbia" was approved by voters two years later. In 1992, the US House of Representatives passed a measure approving statehood for the capital, but the Senate refused to consider it.

Mayor Anthony A. Williams was reelected to a second term in November 2002. He pledged to target education, expand opportunities for all district residents, and to keep neighborhoods safe.

In 2004, the National World War II Memorial was completed and opened to the public. The Memorial lies between the Washington Monument and the Lincoln Memorial.

12 STATE GOVERNMENT

The District of Columbia is the seat of the federal government and is home to the principal organs of the legislative, executive, and judicial branches. Both the US Senate and House have subcommittees (of the Appropriations Committees) to oversee federal spending within the District. The District's residents have only limited representation in the House, where an elected delegate may participate in discussions and votes on bills within the District of Columbia subcommittees but may not vote on measures on the floor of the House. The District has no representation in the Senate. In 1978, Congress approved an amendment to the US Constitution granting the District two US senators and at least one representative; however, the amendment failed to become law when it was not ratified by the necessary 38 state legislatures by August 1985 (by that time only 16 states had approved the amendment).

In 1982, elected delegates to a District of Columbia statehood convention drafted a constitution for the proposed State of New Columbia. The petition for statehood was approved by voters within the District and sent to Congress. But in 1993 Congress voted on and rejected District statehood by 63 votes (277 against, 153 for, and 4 not voting). The bill, which polls have shown has wide public support within the District, can be reintroduced.

The Council of the District of Columbia, the unicameral legislative body for the district, is comprised of 13 representatives who serve four-year terms. Council members must be at least 18 years old, district residents and qualified voters. Prior to 1973, the mayor and council members were appointed by the US president; since 1973, they have been elected by the District's voters. The body was given full legislative powers in 1974. The council meets every year, beginning in January. In 2004, the legislative salary was $92,500 per year.

Voters must be US citizens, at least 18 years old, residents of Washington, DC for at least 30 days prior to election day, and not able to claim the right to vote elsewhere. Restrictions apply to convicted felons and those declared mentally incompetent by the court.

13 POLITICAL PARTIES

Washington, DC, is the headquarters of the Democratic and Republican parties, the nation's major political organizations. The District itself is overwhelmingly Democratic: in 1992 and again in 1996, Democratic presidential candidate Bill Clinton garnered an impressive 85% of the District's voters. Democrat Al Gore repeated this performance in 2000, capturing 85% of the vote to Republican candidate George W. Bush's 9% and Green Party candidate Ralph Nader's 5%. In fact, since 1964, when they were first permitted to vote for president, DC voters have unfailingly cast their ballots for the Democratic nominee. In 2002, there were 363,211 registered voters. As of 2003, the district had three electoral votes.

The first mayor, Walter Washington, was defeated for reelection in 1978 by Marion S. Barry Jr., who was reelected in 1982 and

District Presidential Vote by Major Parties, 1964–2004				
YEAR	ELECTORAL VOTE	DISTRICT WINNER	DEMOCRAT	REPUBLICAN
1964	3	*Johnson (D)	169,796	28,801
1968	3	Humphrey (D)	139,566	31,012
1972	3	McGovern (D)	127,627	35,226
1976	3	*Carter (D)	137,818	27,873
1980	3	Carter (D)	124,376	21,765
1984	3	Mondale (D)	180,408	29,009
1988	3	Dukakis (D)	159,407	27,590
1992	3	*Clinton (D)	192,619	20,698
1996	3	*Clinton (D)	158,220	17,339
2000	3	Gore (D)	171,923	18,073
2004	3	Kerry (D)	202,970	21,256

*Won US presidential election.

again in 1986. Sharon Pratt Dixon was elected mayor in 1990. In 1994, Marion S. Barry Jr., returning to political life after serving a six-month jail term for a 1990 drug conviction, defeated Republican Carol Schwartz in the mayoral contest. Schwartz previously lost to Barry in the mayoral election of 1986. Anthony Williams was elected mayor in 1998 and reelected in 2002.

Eleanor Holmes Norton serves as the District's delegate to the House of Representatives.

14 LOCAL GOVERNMENT

Local government in the District of Columbia operates under authority delegated by Congress. In 1973, for the first time in more than a century, Congress provided the District with a home-rule charter, allowing Washington, DC, residents to elect their own mayor and city council. Residents of the District approved the charter on 7 May 1974, and a new elected government took office on 1 January 1975.

The mayor has traditionally been the District's chief executive, and the council is the legislative branch; however, under constitutional authority, Congress can enact laws on any subject affecting the District, and all legislation enacted by the District is subject to congressional veto. In response to both a managerial and budgetary crisis, Congress passed the District of Columbia Financial Responsibility and Management Assistance Act of 1995. This law established a Control Board that has broad powers to review all actions of the DC government and must approve the financial plans and budget for the city before submission to Congress. Home rule was further eroded when in 1997 Congress took responsibility for most major agencies away from the mayor and gave them to the Control Board.

The council consists of 13 members: the council chairman and 4 members elected at large, and 8 elected by wards. The 12-member Board of Education consists of eight officials elected by ward and four elected at-large, including one at-large member elected by students. They serve for four years. As of 2005, there were two public school systems in the District. The charter also provides for 36 neighborhood advisory commissions, whose seats are filled through nonpartisan elections.

In 2005, local government accounted for about 45,951 full-time (or equivalent) employment positions.

15STATE SERVICES

To address the continuing threat of terrorism and to work with the federal Department of Homeland Security, homeland security in the District of Columbia operates under executive authority; the deputy mayor for public safety is designated as the state homeland security advisor for the District.

Public education in the District is the responsibility of a chief executive officer and board of trustees appointed by the Control Board and the University of the District of Columbia Board of Trustees. The elected Board of Education is left with very little authority. Transportation services are provided through the Department of Transportation and the Washington Metropolitan Area Transit Authority, while health and welfare services fall within the jurisdiction of the Department of Human Services. The Office of Consumer and Regulatory Affairs, Department of Corrections, District of Columbia National Guard, and Metropolitan Police Department provide public protection services, and the Department of Housing and Community Development is the main housing agency. Employment and job-training programs are offered through the Department of Employment Services.

16JUDICIAL SYSTEM

All judges in Washington, DC, are nominated by the president of the United States from a list of persons recommended by the District of Columbia Nomination Commission, and appointed upon the advice and consent of the Senate. The US Court of Appeals for the District of Columbia functions in a manner similar to that of a state supreme court; it also has original jurisdiction over federal crimes. The court consists of a chief judge and eight associate judges, all serving 15-year terms. The Superior Court of the District of Columbia, the trial court, consisted in 1999 of five divisions and 16 judges, also serving for 15 years. Washington, DC, is the site of the US Supreme Court and the US Department of Justice. The District of Columbia is the only US jurisdiction where the US Attorney's Office, an arm of the Justice Department, and not the local government, prosecutes criminal offenders for nonfederal crimes.

Prisoners sentenced to more than one year come under the jurisdiction of the Bureau of Prisons.

According to the Federal Bureau of Investigation, the District of Columbia in 2004 had a violent crime rate (murder/nonnegligent manslaughter; forcible rape; robbery; aggravated assault) of 1,371.2 reported incidents per 100,000 population, or a total of 7,590 reported incidents. Crimes against property (burglary; larceny/theft; and motor vehicle theft) in that same year totaled 26,896 reported incidents, or 4,859.1 reported incidents per 100,000 people. The District of Columbia has no death penalty. The last execution took place in 1957. District residents voted 2-1 against the death penalty in 1992. There is a provision for life without parole.

In 2003, Washington, DC, spent $1,891,475,962 on homeland security, an average of $2,364 per district resident.

17ARMED FORCES

In 2004, there were 24,328 active-duty military personnel stationed in the District of Columbia, with the vast majority, 10,109, at the Pentagon as the Washington Headquarters Services (WHS).

The WHS maintains and operates the Pentagon Reservation, the headquarters of the US Department of Defense, which covers 34 acres (14 hectares) of Arlington, Virginia, across the Potomac. In addition there were 21,549 civilian employees, of which 6,427 were at the Pentagon. An Air Force installation (Bolling Air Force Base) and the Army's Fort McNair are within the District. In 2005, the Base Realignment and Closure (BRAC) Commission recommended that Walter Reed Medical Center be realigned with the National Naval Medical Center to create a Walter Reed National Military Medical Center in Bethesda, Maryland. Firms in the District received $3.5 billion in federal defense contract awards in 2004, and defense payroll, including retired military pay, amounted to $1.9 billion.

There were 37,377 veterans of US military service in the District as of 2003, of whom 5,807 served in World War II; 4,384 in the Korean conflict; 10,474 during the Vietnam era; and 5,410 in the Gulf War. The federal government expenditures for veterans in Washington totaled $1.2 billion during 2004.

Because Washington is often the scene of political demonstrations and because high federal officials and the District's foreign embassy personnel pose special police-protection problems, the ratio of police personnel to residents is higher than in any state. In 2003, 3,963 police employees were employed in the District.

18MIGRATION

The principal migratory movements have been an influx of southern blacks after the Civil War and, more recently, the rapid growth of the Washington, DC, metropolitan area, coupled with shrinkage in the population of the District itself. Between 1950 and 1970, the District suffered a net loss from migration of as much as 260,000, much of it to Maryland and Virginia; there was, however, an estimated net inflow of 87,000 blacks in this period. Net emigration totaled between 150,000 and 190,000 during the 1970s, and roughly 23,000 more during 1981–83.

From 1985 to 1990, the District had a net loss from migration of over 30,000. Between 1990 and 1998, there was a net loss of 139,000 in domestic migration and a net gain of 28,000 in international migration. In 1998, 2,377 foreign immigrants arrived in Washington, DC. The District's overall population decreased 13.8% between 1990 and 1998. In the period 2000–05, net international migration was 20,618 and net internal migration was -53,550, for a net loss of 32,932 people.

19INTERGOVERNMENTAL COOPERATION

The District of Columbia, a member of the Council of State Governments and its allied organizations, also participates in such interstate regional bodies as the Washington Metropolitan Area Transit Authority Commission, and Potomac Valley Commission. Counties and incorporated cities in the Washington area are represented on the Metropolitan Washington Council of Governments, established in 1957. The District relies heavily on federal grants, which came to over $4 billion in fiscal year 2001. Following a national trend, by fiscal year 2005, that amount had dropped significantly, to $1.91 billion. In fiscal year 2006, federal grants amounted to an estimated $1.787 billion, and for fiscal year 2007 were estimated at $1.934 billion.

²⁰ECONOMY

During the 1990s, the number of jobs in the service sector grew by about 50%. Other sectors, however, declined in that decade. Not surprisingly, the public sector has a greater weight in DC's economy than is found in any of the 50 states, where the average contribution from the public sector in 2001 was 12% compared to 35.2% in DC. Also distinct from most of the states, the District's economy was not adversely affected by the national recession of 2001, as the strong annual growth rates at the end of the 20th century—6.2% in 1999 and 8.2% in 2000—continued into the 21st, averaging 7.5% for 2001. In 2002, the military build-up for the war in Iraq was one of the major growth points in an otherwise slowed national economy reeling from a precipitous drops in both domestic and foreign private investment. The recession and slowed economy also meant more work for government agencies.

In 2004, District's gross state product (GSP) totaled $76.685 billion, of which professional and technical services accounted for the largest portion, at $15.264 billion or nearly 20%, with real estate coming in a distant second at $6.068 billion or nearly 8%. In that same year, there were a total of 59,775 small businesses in DC. Of that total, 27,424 firms had employees, of which an estimated 25,600 or 93.4% were small businesses. An estimated 4,393 new businesses were established in DC in 2004, up 8.4% from the previous year. Business terminations that same year came to 3,440. Business bankruptcies totaled 41 in 2004, down 25.5% from 2003. In 2005, the personal bankruptcy (Chapter 7 and Chapter 13) filing rate was 395 filings per 100,000 people, ranking the District of Columbia 38th in the nation.

²¹INCOME

In 2005 District of Columbia had a gross state product (GSP) of $83 billion which accounted for 0.7% of the nation's gross domestic product and placed the state at number 35 in highest GSP among the 50 states and the District of Columbia.

According to the Bureau of Economic Analysis, in 2004 District of Columbia had a per capita personal income (PCPI) of $51,155. This ranked first in the United States and was 155% of the national average of $33,050. The 1994–2004 average annual growth rate of PCPI was 5.2%. District of Columbia had a total personal income (TPI) of $28,352,299,000, which ranked 45th in the United States and reflected an increase of 6.5% from 2003. The 1994–2004 average annual growth rate of TPI was 4.6%. Earnings of persons employed in District of Columbia increased from $57,332,497,000 in 2003 to $61,911,331,000 in 2004, an increase of 8.0%. The 2003–04 national change was 6.3%.

The US Census Bureau reports that the three-year average median household income for 2002–04 in 2004 dollars was $43,003, compared to a national average of $44,473. During the same period an estimated 16.8% of the population was below the poverty line, as compared to 12.4% nationwide.

²²LABOR

According to the Bureau of Labor Statistics (BLS), in April 2006, the seasonally adjusted civilian labor force in the District of Columbia numbered 288,500, with approximately 16,000 workers unemployed, yielding an unemployment rate of 5.5%, compared to the national average of 4.7% for the same period. Preliminary

data for the same period placed nonfarm employment at 690,500. Since the beginning of the BLS data series in 1976, the highest unemployment rate recorded in the District of Columbia was 11.4%, in March 1983. The historical low was 4.8% in December 1988. Preliminary nonfarm employment data by occupation for April 2006 showed that approximately 1.8% of the labor force was employed in construction; 21.8% in professional and business services; 8% in leisure and hospitality services; and 33.4% in government.

The US Department of Labor's Bureau of Labor Statistics reported that in 2005, a total of 29,000 of the District of Columbia's 259,000 employed wage and salary workers were formal members of a union. This represented 11.3% of those so employed, down from 12.7% in 2004, and below the national average of 12%. Overall in 2005, a total of 33,000 workers (12.8%) in the District were covered by a union or employee association contract, which included those workers who reported no union affiliation. The District of Columbia does not have a right-to-work law.

As of 1 March 2006, the District had a locally mandated minimum wage rate of $7.00 per hour. In 2004, women in the District accounted for 50.1% of the employed civilian labor force. The District of Columbia also serves as the headquarters of many labor organizations.

²³AGRICULTURE

There is no commercial farming in the District of Columbia.

²⁴ANIMAL HUSBANDRY

The District of Columbia has no livestock industry.

²⁵FISHING

There is no commercial fishing in the District of Columbia. Recreational fishing is accessible via a boat-launching facility on the Anacostia River. The Mammoth Spring National Fish Hatchery in Arkansas distributed 1,200 channel catfish within the district in 1995/96.

²⁶FORESTRY

There is no forestland or forest products industry in the District of Columbia.

²⁷MINING

There is no mining in the District of Columbia, although a few mining firms have offices there.

²⁸ENERGY AND POWER

As of 2003, the District of Columbia had five electrical power service providers, of which three were energy-only providers, one was a delivery-only provider and one was investor owned. As of that same year there were 225,500 retail customers. Of that total, 198,926 received their power from the sole investor-owned service provider. The energy-only provider had 26,574 customers. There was no data on the delivery-only power supplier.

Total net summer generating capability by the state's electrical generating plants in 2003 stood at 806,000 kW, with total production that same year at 74.144 million kWh. Of the total amount generated, 100% came from independent producers and combined heat and power service providers. Petroleum fired plants accounted for all the power produced.

The District of Columbia has no proven reserves or production of crude oil or natural gas. Nor is there any refining capacity. The states of Maryland and Virginia provide the District with its fossil fuel needs.

29INDUSTRY

Although the District of Columbia is best known as the nation's capital and a center of political administration, the District does have a small manufacturing sector. According to the US Census Bureau's Annual Survey of Manufactures (ASM) for 2004, the District's shipment value of all manufactured products totaled $271.285 million.

In 2004, a total of 1,876 people in the District earned their livelihood in the manufacturing sector, of which 1,155 were actual production workers. ASM data for 2004 showed that the District's manufacturing sector paid $70.970 million in wages.

Within the District is the Government Printing Office (established by Congress in 1860), which operates one of the largest printing plants in the United States. Also in the District is the Washington Post Co., publisher of the newspaper of that name and of *Newsweek* magazine; the company also owns television stations.

30COMMERCE

According to the 2002 Census of Wholesale Trade, the District of Columbia's wholesale trade sector had sales that year totaling $2.9 billion from 381 establishments. Wholesalers of durable goods accounted for 176 establishments, while the number of nondurable goods wholesalers stood at 186, with electronic markets, agents, and brokers accounting for 19 establishments. Sales data for durable goods wholesalers, nondurable goods wholesalers and those for electronic markets, agents, and brokers in the wholesale trade industry in 2002 was not available.

In the 2002 Census of Retail Trade, the District of Columbia was listed as having 1,877 retail establishments with sales of $3.06 billion. The leading types of retail businesses by number of establishments were: food and beverage stores (506); clothing and clothing accessories stores (355); miscellaneous store retailers (258); and health and personal care stores (185). In terms of sales, food and beverage stores accounted for the largest share of retail sales at $952.5 million, followed by health and personal care stores at $460.4 million; and clothing and clothing accessories stores at $416.2 million. A total of 18,513 people were employed by the retail sector in the District of Columbia that year.

Washington, DC, exported $825 million in merchandise in 2005.

31CONSUMER PROTECTION

The Department of Consumer and Regulatory Affairs has primary responsibility for consumer protection in the District. The Department regulates businesses; land and building use; occupational and professional standards; rental housing and condominiums; health and social service care facilities; and the natural environment.

When dealing with consumer protection issues, the District's Attorney General's Office can initiate civil but not criminal proceedings. It can also: represent the District before regulatory agencies; administer consumer protection and education programs; handle formal consumer complaints; and exercise broad subpoena powers. In antitrust actions, the Attorney General's Office can act on behalf of those consumers who are incapable of acting on their own; initiate damage actions on behalf of the District in court; initiate criminal proceedings; and represent other governmental entities in recovering civil damages under District or federal law.

32BANKING

Banking in the District of Columbia began with the chartering of the Bank of Alexandria in 1792 and the Bank of Columbia in 1793; both banks terminated in the early 19th century. The oldest surviving bank in the District is the National Bank of Washington, founded as the Bank of Washington in 1809.

As of June 2005, there were 7 banks/savings and loans/savings banks plus 65 credit unions (CUs) within the District of Columbia. As of that same date, CUs accounted for the vast majority of the assets held by financial institutions in the District, accounting for 85.4% of all assets held or $5.560 billion. Banks/savings and loans/savings banks accounted for the remaining 14.6% or $950 million in assets held. In addition, CUs had 470,150 members or 84.9% of the District's population. Financial institutions are regulated by the DC Department of Banking and Financial Institutions.

33INSURANCE

In 2004, District of Columbia policyholders held 363,000 individual life insurance policies worth over $26.6 billion; total value for all categories of life insurance (individual, group, and credit) was over $104.5 billion. The average coverage amount is $73,400 per policy holder. Death benefits paid that year totaled $148.5 million.

As of 2003, there were 10 property and casualty and 1 life and health insurance company incorporated or organized in the District of Columbia. In 2004, direct premiums for property and casualty insurance totaled over $1.4 billion. That year, there were 1,115 flood insurance policies in force in the District of Columbia, with a total value of over $118 million.

In 2004, 51% of residents held employment-based health insurance policies, 5% held individual policies, and 29% were covered under Medicare and Medicaid; 14% of residents were uninsured. In 2003, employee contributions for employment-based health coverage averaged at 19% for single coverage and 23% for family coverage. The District does not offer an expansion program in connection with the Consolidated Omnibus Budget Reconciliation Act (COBRA, 1986), a health insurance program for those who lose employment-based coverage due to termination or reduction of work hours.

In 2003, there were 210,515 auto insurance policies in effect for private passenger cars. Required minimum coverage includes bodily injury liability of up to $25,000 per individual and $50,000 for all persons injured in an accident, as well as property damage liability of $10,000. Uninsured motorist coverage is also required. In 2003, the average expenditure per vehicle for insurance coverage was $1,129.31, which ranked as the third-highest average in the nation (after New Jersey and New York).

34 SECURITIES

There are no securities exchanges in the District of Columbia. In 2005, there were 740 personal financial advisers employed in the District and 890 securities, commodities, and financial services sales agents. In 2004, there were over 34 publicly traded companies within the District, with 11 NASDAQ companies, 11 NYSE listings, and 2 AMEX listings. In 2006, the District had two Fortune 500 companies; Pepco Holdings (Potomac Electric Power Company) ranked first in the District and 283rd in the nation, with revenues of over $8 billion, followed by Danaher. Washington Post, Harman International Industries, and WGL Holdings made the Fortune 1,000 listing. All five companies are traded on the NYSE.

The headquarters of the US Securities and Exchange Commission is located in Washington, DC.

35 PUBLIC FINANCE

The budget for the District of Columbia is prepared in conjunction with the mayor's office and reviewed by the city council, but is subject to review and approval by the Congress. The fiscal year (FY) runs from 1 October through 30 September.

The local tax base is limited by a shortage of taxable real estate, much of the District being occupied by government buildings and federal reservations. Moreover, Congress has not allowed the District to tax the incomes of people who work in Washington but live in the suburbs, an objective the District government has urgently sought.

In fiscal year 2004, federal government grants to the District of Columbia were nearly $4.2 billion.

In the fiscal year 2007 federal budget, the District of Columbia was slated to receive: $214 million for the DC Court Services and Offender Supervision Agency, a $15 million increase over 2006; $35 million for the DC Resident Tuition Assistance program, an increase of $2 million over 2006. This program allows DC residents to attend public colleges nationwide at in-state tuition rates; $30 million to construct a new central library and renovate neighborhood branches for the District; $26 million to improve school facilities in the District; $20 million to expand the Navy Yard Metro station; $15 million for DC School Choice, a program that provides parents more options for obtaining a quality education for their children who are trapped in low-performing schools.

36 TAXATION

As of 1 January 2006, the District of Columbia had three individual income tax brackets ranging from 4.5% to 9.0%. The District of Columbia taxes corporations at a flat rate of 9.975%.

In 2004, the District collected $1,027,976,000 in property taxes, or $1,856 per capita. Only New Jersey, Connecticut, and New Hampshire have higher per capita property taxes.

The District of Columbia taxes retail sales at a rate of 5.75%. Food purchased for consumption off-premises is tax exempt. The tax on cigarettes is 100 cents per pack, which ranks 19th among the 50 states and the District of Columbia. The District of Columbia taxes gasoline at 22.5 cents per gallon. This is in addition to the 18.4 cents per gallon federal tax on gasoline.

According to the Tax Foundation, for every federal tax dollar sent to the federal government in 2004, DC citizens received $6.64

in federal spending, which ranks the District highest nationally by a wide margin.

37 ECONOMIC POLICY

The Business Resource Center offers information on doing business in the District. There is an Office of the Deputy Mayor for Planning and Economic Development. Community Development Corporations (CDCs) and other community-based organizations work to revitalize distressed neighborhoods throughout the District. The Department for Housing and Community Development (DHCD) facilitates the production and preservation of housing, community, and economic development opportunities. DHCD fosters partnerships with for-profit and nonprofit organizations to create and maintain stable neighborhoods; retain and expand the city's tax base; promote economic opportunities through community empowerment; and retain and create job and business opportunities for the benefit of DC residents. Business Improvement Districts (BIDs) are commercial areas of the District that collect a "self tax" from property owners to provide services and programs to the entire BID. These programs address cleanliness, maintenance, safety, promotion, economic development, among other issues. The Department of Small and Local Business Development (DSLBD) works with the Office of Contracting and Procurement (OCP) to match small, disadvantaged businesses with contracting opportunities with the DC government and elsewhere. DSLBD also fosters economic development of DC's small business community through technical assistance, business seminars, conferences, exhibits, and outreach forums, among other programs.

38 HEALTH

Health conditions in the nation's capital are no source of national pride. The infant mortality rate in October 2005 was estimated at 10.6 per 1,000 live births, the highest in the nation. The birth rate in 2003 was 13.5 per 1,000 population. In 2000, the District had the highest abortion rate in the country at 68.1 per 1,000 women (the national average was 21.3 per 1,000 that year); however, this figure represented a fairly substantial decrease from the 1992 rate of 133.1 per 1,000. In 2003, about 76.1% of pregnant woman received prenatal care beginning in the first trimester. In 2004, approximately 83% of children received routine immunizations before the age of three.

The crude death rate in 2003 was 9.8 deaths per 1,000 population. As of 2002, the death rates for major causes of death (per 100,000 resident population) were: heart disease, 291.8; cancer, 227.4; cerebrovascular diseases, 48.9; chronic lower respiratory diseases, 23.3; and diabetes, 33.5. The mortality rate from HIV infection in 2002 was the highest in the nation at 40.8 per 100,000 population. In 2004, the reported AIDS case rate was at about 179.2 per 100,000 population, the highest in the nation and well above the national average of 15 per 100,000. In 2002, the District had the lowest rate of suicides in the nation, at about 5.4 per 100,000, but also had the distinction of having the highest rate of homicides at 40.1 per 100,000; the national average rate of homicides that year was 6.1 per 100,000. In 2002, about 50.2% of the population was considered overweight or obese, one of the lowest rates in the nation. As of 2004, about 20.8% of state residents were smokers.

In 2003, the District had 10 community hospitals with about 3,400 beds. There were about 135,000 patient admissions that year and 1.6 million outpatient visits. The average daily inpatient census was about 2,500 patients. The average cost per day for hospital care was $1,824. Also in 2003, there were about 21 certified nursing facilities in the state with 3,114 beds and an overall occupancy rate of about 91.9%. In 2004, it was estimated that about 72,2% of all state residents had received some type of dental care within the year. The District had 752 physicians per 100,000 resident population in 2004 and 1,515 nurses per 100,000 in 2001; these represents the highest health care worker–population rates in the nation. In 2004, there was a total of 575 dentists in the District.

About 28% of District residents were enrolled in Medicaid programs in 2003, with this percentage, the District was tied with California and Tennessee as having the second-highest percentage of Medicaid recipients in the country (after Maine). Approximately 14% were uninsured in 2004.

³⁹SOCIAL WELFARE

In 2004, about 17,000 people received unemployment benefits, with the average weekly unemployment benefit at $257. In fiscal year 2005, the estimated average monthly participation in the food stamp program included about 88,799 persons (44,362 households); the average monthly benefit was about $96.94 per person. That year, the total of benefits paid through the state for the food stamp program was about $103.2 million.

Temporary Assistance for Needy Families (TANF), the system of federal welfare assistance that officially replaced Aid to Families with Dependent Children (AFDC) in 1997, was reauthorized through the Deficit Reduction Act of 2005. TANF is funded through federal block grants that are divided among the states based on an equation involving the number of recipients in each state. In 2004, the District program had 44,000 recipients; District and federal expenditures on this TANF program totaled $68 million in fiscal year 2003.

In December 2004, Social Security benefits were paid to 71,670 District of Columbia residents. This number included 46,910 retired workers, 6,770 widows and widowers, 9,270 disabled workers, 2,460 spouses, and 6,260 children. Social Security beneficiaries represented 13% of the District's total population and 77.3% of the District's population age 65 and older. Retired workers received an average monthly payment of $782; widows and widowers, $755; disabled workers, $824; and spouses, $415. Payments for children of retired workers averaged $431 per month; children of deceased workers, $488; and children of disabled workers, $268. Federal Supplemental Security Income payments in December 2004 went to 20,856 District of Columbia residents, averaging $430 a month.

⁴⁰HOUSING

In 2004, the District of Columbia had an estimated 276,600 housing units, of which 248,563 were occupied. Only 43.6% were owner occupied, ranking the District as having the least number of homeowners in the nation. About 38% of all units dated from 1939 or earlier. Only about 13% of all units were single-family, detached homes; the lowest percentage in the country. About 30% of all housing units were in buildings of 20 units or more; which is the highest percentage in the country for this category of housing.

It was estimated that about 9.625 units were without telephone service, 985 lacked complete plumbing facilities, and 961 lacked complete kitchen facilities. Most households relied on gas and electricity for heating. The average household had 2.08 members.

In 2004, 1,900 new privately owned housing units were authorized for construction. The median home value was $334,702, placing the District as third in the nation for highest home values. The median monthly cost for mortgage owners was $1,612 while renters paid a median of $799 per month. In 2006, the district was awarded over $19.2 million in community development block grants from the US Department of Housing and Urban Development (HUD).

⁴¹EDUCATION

The District of Columbia's first public schools were opened in 1805. Until 1954, public schools for whites and blacks were operated separately. Although legally integrated, the public school system remains virtually segregated. Most white and many black students attend private schools. In 2004, 86.4% of all residents 25 years of age or older were high school graduates. Some 45.7%, compared to the national average of 26%, obtained a bachelor's degree or higher.

The total enrollment for fall 2002 in the District of Columbia's public schools stood at 76,000. Of these, 59,000 attended schools from kindergarten through grade eight, and 17,000 attended high school. In 2001/02, approximately 86.6% of students enrolled in public elementary and secondary schools were minorities. Total enrollment was estimated at 75,000 in fall 2003 and was expected to be 74,000 by fall 2014, a decrease of 2.8% during the period 2002 to 2014. There were 16,376 students enrolled in 82 private schools in fall 2003. Expenditures for public education in 2003/04 were estimated at $1,077,584 or $12,801 per student, the third-highest among the 50 states. Since 1969, the National Assessment of Educational Progress (NAEP) has tested public school students nationwide. The resulting report, *The Nation's Report Card,* stated that in 2005 eighth graders in the District of Columbia scored 245 out of 500 in mathematics compared with the national average of 278.

As of fall 2002, there were 91,014 students enrolled in college or graduate school; minority students comprised 42.5% of total postsecondary enrollment. As of 2005, the District of Columbia had 16 degree-granting institutions, 14 private and 2 public. Some of the best-known private universities are American, Georgetown, George Washington, and Howard. The University of the District of Columbia, created in 1976 from the merger of three institutions, has an open admissions policy for District freshman undergraduate students. It has five academic colleges. The US Department of Agriculture Graduate School also operates within the District.

⁴²ARTS

The District of Columbia Commission on the Arts and Humanities was founded in 1968 and is a partner with the Mid-Atlantic Arts Foundation. In 2005, District arts organizations received 57 grants totaling $3,028,225 from the National Endowment for the Arts. The Humanities Council of Washington, DC, was established in 1980 and as of 2004, awarded approximately $125,000 annually to support local programming. In 2005, the National Endowment for the Humanities contributed $5,003,912 for 43 programs within the District.

The National Endowment for the Humanities contributed $400,000 to the Historical Society of Washington, DC, for community educational programs and exhibits, humanities fellowships of $149,565 to the American Councils for International Education in 2002, and $378,000 to the Folger Shakespeare Library in 2003.

The John F. Kennedy Center for the Performing Arts, officially opened on 8 September 1971, is the District's principal performing arts center. Its five main halls—the Opera House, Concert Hall, Eisenhower Theater, Terrace Theatre, and American Film Institute Theater—display gifts from at least 30 foreign governments, ranging from stage curtains and tapestries to sculptures and crystal chandeliers. Major theatrical productions are also presented at the Arena Stage-Kreeger Theater, National Theatre, Folger Theatre, and Ford's Theatre. Rep, Inc., is one of the few professional black theaters in the United States; the New Playwrights' Theatre of Washington is a nonprofit group presenting new plays by American dramatists.

The District's leading symphony is the National Symphony Orchestra, which performs from October through April at the Concert Hall of the Kennedy Center. On a smaller scale, the Phillips Collection, National Gallery of Art, and Library of Congress offer concerts and recitals. The Washington Opera performs at the Kennedy Center's Opera House.

During the summer months, the Carter Barron Amphitheater presents popular music and jazz. Concerts featuring the US Army, US Navy, and US Marine Corps bands, and the Air Force Symphony Orchestra are held throughout the District.

43 LIBRARIES AND MUSEUMS

Although Washington, DC, is best known as the site of the world's largest library, the Library of Congress, the District, or the city proper, had its own public library system, which for the fiscal year ending in September 2001, consisted of a central or main library and 26 branch libraries. In that same year the system had 2,472,000 volumes of books and serial publications, with a circulation of 1,191,000. The system also had 298,000 audio and 17,000 video items, and one bookmobile. Operating income for fiscal year 2001 totaled $27,223,000, of which $550,000 came from federal sources and $26,412,000 came from local sources. In that same year, operating expenditures totaled $27,223,000, of which 72.4% was spent on the staff and 9.6% on the collection.

The Library of Congress, as of 1998, had a collection of more than 80 million items, including 26 million books and pamphlets. The Library, which is also the cataloging and bibliographic center for libraries throughout the United States, has on permanent display a 1455 Gutenberg Bible, Thomas Jefferson's first draft of the Declaration of Independence, and Abraham Lincoln's first two drafts of the Gettysburg Address. Also in its permanent collection are the oldest known existing film (Thomas Edison's *The Sneeze,* lasting all of three seconds), maps believed to date from the Lewis and Clark expedition, original musical scores by Charles Ives, and huge libraries of Russian and Chinese texts. The Folger Shakespeare Library contains not only rare Renaissance manuscripts but also a full-size re-creation of an Elizabethan theater. The District's own public library system has a main library and 26 branch-es—including the Martin Luther King Memorial Library—with 2,863,296 volumes in 1998.

The District of Columbia was home to at least 93 museums in 2000. The Smithsonian Institution—endowed in 1826 by an Englishman, James Smithson, who had never visited the United States—operates a vast museum and research complex that includes the National Air and Space Museum, National Museum of Natural History, National Museum of History and Technology, many of the District's art museums, and the National Zoological Park. Among the art museums operated by the Smithsonian are the National Gallery of Art, housing one of the world's outstanding collections of Western art from the 13th century to the present; the Freer Gallery of Art, housing a renowned collection of Near and Far Eastern treasures, along with one of the largest collections of the works of James McNeill Whistler, whose Peacock Room is one of the museum's highlights; the National Collection of Fine Arts; the National Portrait Gallery; and the Hirshhorn Museum and Sculpture Garden. Among the capital's other distinguished art collections are the Phillips Collection, the oldest museum of modern art in the United States; the Museum of African Art, located in the Frederick Douglass Memorial Home; and the Corcoran Gallery of Art, devoted primarily to American paintings, sculpture, and drawings of the last 300 years. Washington is also the site of such historic house-museums as Octagon House, Decatur House, Dumbarton Oaks, and the Woodrow Wilson House. Many national associations maintain exhibitions relevant to their areas of interest. The US National Arboretum, US Botanic Garden, and National Aquarium are in the city. In 1999, lawmakers debated plans to build a memorial for Reverend Dr. Martin Luther King Jr. between the Jefferson and Lincoln memorials.

44 COMMUNICATIONS

Washington, DC, is the headquarters of the US Postal Service. As of 2004, about 91.9% of households had telephones. In addition, by June of that same year there were 555,958 mobile wireless telephone subscribers. In 2003, 64.3% of the District households had a computer and 56.8% had Internet access. By June 2005, there were 126,609 high-speed lines in the District, 94,320 residential and 32,289 for business.

In 2005, the District had 4 AM and 13 FM radio stations and 7 television stations. The District had 1,999,870 television households, 70% of which ordered cable in 1999. A total of 47,433 Internet domain names were registered in the District in 2000.

45 PRESS

Because the District of Columbia is the center of US government activity, hundreds of US and foreign newspapers maintain permanent news bureaus there. The District's major newspaper is the *Washington Post.* In 2005, the *Post,* a morning paper, had an average daily circulation of 707,690 and a Sunday circulation of 1,007,487. In 2004, the *Washington Post* had the sixth-largest daily circulation and the third-largest Sunday circulation in the country. The *Washington Times,* also published on weekday mornings, had a circulation of 100,603 (43,660 on Sunday).

Press clubs active within the District include the National Press Club, Gridiron Club, American Newspaper Women's Club, Washington Press Club, and White House Correspondents Association.

There are more than 30 major Washington-based periodicals. Among the best known are the *National Geographic, U.S. News & World Report, Smithsonian,* and *New Republic.* Important periodicals covering the workings of the federal government are the *Congressional Quarterly* and its companion, *CQ Weekly Report.*

46 ORGANIZATIONS

In 2006, there were over 4,000 nonprofit organizations registered within the District, of which about 2,849 were registered as charitable, educational, or religious organizations. Service and patriotic organizations with headquarters in the District include the Air Force Association, Daughters of the American Revolution, and the 4-H Program. Among the cultural, scientific, and educational groups are the American Film Institute, American Theatre Association, Federation of American Scientists, American Association for the Advancement of Science, National Academy of Sciences, National Geographic Society, Association of American Colleges, American Council on Education, National Education Association, American Association of University Professors, American Association of University Women, and US Student Association. District cultural and educational organizations include the Cultural Alliance of Greater Washington, the United States Capitol Historical Society, and the Historical Society of Washington, DC.

Among the environmental and animal protection organizations in the District are the Animal Welfare Institute and the Humane Society of the United States. Medical, health, and charitable organizations include the American Red Cross. Groups dealing with the elderly include the National Association of Retired Federal Employees and the American Association of Retired Persons. Among ethnic and religious bodies with headquarters in the District are the National Association of Arab Americans, B'nai B'rith International, and the US Conference of Catholic Bishops.

Trade, professional, and commercial organizations include the American Advertising Federation, American Federation of Police, Air Line Pilots Association, American Bankers Association, National Cable Television Association, Chamber of Commerce of the United States, American Chemical Society, and National Press Club.

Virtually every major public interest group maintains an office in Washington, DC. Notable examples are the Consumer Federation of America, National Consumers League, National Abortion Rights Action League, National League of Cities, Common Cause, US Conference of Mayors, National Organization for Women, and the American Federation of Labor and Congress of Industrial Organizations (AFL-CIO). Among the important world organizations with headquarters in the District are the Organization of American States, International Monetary Fund, and International Bank for Reconstruction and Development.

47 TOURISM, TRAVEL, AND RECREATION

As the nation's capital, the District of Columbia is one of the world's leading tourist centers. Tourism in Washington, DC, generates over $10 billion in direct spending each year and sustains some 260,000 full and part-time jobs. In 2004, there were over 17.7 million domestic visitors and over 1 million international visitors. In 2003, the District of Columbia employed 56, 200 people directly in the tourism industry.

The most popular sites are The National Air and Space Museum, the National Museum of Natural History, National Gallery of Art, Museum of American History, the National Zoo (featuring pandas), the US Holocaust Memorial Museum, Smithsonian Castle, the Vietnam Veterans Memorial, Lincoln Memorial, Library of Congress, White House, and US Capitol tours. Besides the many museums, there are federal buildings and landmarks, parks and gardens, cemeteries, and war memorials.

Across the Potomac, in Virginia, are Arlington National Cemetery, site of the Tomb of the Unknown Soldier and the grave of John F. Kennedy, and George Washington's home at Mt. Vernon.

48 SPORTS

There are six major professional sports teams in Washington, DC: the Redskins of the National Football League, the Nationals (formerly the Montreal Expos) of Major League Baseball, the Wizards (formerly the Bullets), of the National Basketball Association, the Mystics of the Women's National Basketball Association, the Capitals of the National Hockey League, and DC United of Major League Soccer. Hockey and basketball are played in downtown Washington at the MCI Arena, which was opened for the 1997–98 season. In 2005, the Nationals opened their first season in Washington, DC, at the Robert F. Kennedy Memorial Stadium. The Redskins began the 1997 season in the new Jack Kent Cooke Stadium in Landover, Maryland. The Redskins have reached football's Super Bowl five times, winning in 1983, 1988, and 1992. The Bullets won the National Basketball Association (NBA) championship in 1978.

In collegiate sports the Georgetown University Hoyas were a dominant force in basketball during the 1980s, reaching the National Collegiate Athletic Association (NCAA) championship game in 1982, 1984, and 1985, and winning the title in 1984.

49 FAMOUS WASHINGTONIANS

Although no US president has been born in the District of Columbia, all but George Washington (b.Virginia, 1732–99) lived there while serving as chief executive. Seven presidents died in Washington, DC, including three during their term of office: William Henry Harrison (b.Virginia, 1773–1841), Zachary Taylor (b.Virginia, 1784–1850), and Abraham Lincoln (b.Kentucky, 1809–65). In addition, John Quincy Adams (b.Massachusetts, 1767–1848), who served as a congressman for 17 years after he left the White House, died at his desk in the House of Representatives; and William Howard Taft (b.Ohio, 1857–1930) passed away while serving as US chief justice. Retired presidents Woodrow Wilson (b.Virginia, 1856–1924) and Dwight D. Eisenhower (b.Texas, 1890–1969) also died in the capital. Federal officials born in Washington, DC, include John Foster Dulles (1888–1959), secretary of state; J(ohn) Edgar Hoover (1895–1972), director of the Federal Bureau of Investigation (FBI); and Robert C. Weaver (1907–97), who as secretary of housing and urban development during the administration of President Lyndon B. Johnson was the first black American to hold cabinet rank. Walter E. Fauntroy (b.1933) was the District's first delegate to Congress in the 20th century, appointed when that office was reestablished in 1971.

Among the outstanding scientists and other professionals associated with the District were Cleveland Abbe (b.New York, 1838–1916), a meteorologist who helped develop the US Weather Service; inventor Alexander Graham Bell (b.Scotland, 1842–1922), president of the National Geographic Society (NGS) in his later years; Henry Gannett (b.Maryland, 1846–1914), chief geographer with the US Geological Survey, president of the NGS and a pioneer in American cartography; Charles D. Walcott (b.New York, 1850–1927), director of the Geological Survey and secretary of the Smithsonian Institution; Emile Berliner (b.Germany, 1851–1929), a pioneer in the development of the phonograph; Gilbert H. Grosvenor (b.Turkey, 1875–1966), editor in chief of *National Geographic* magazine; and Charles R. Drew (1904–50), developer of the blood bank concept. Leading business executives who have lived or worked in the District include William W. Corcoran (1798–1888), banker and philanthropist, and Katharine Graham (b.New York, 1917–2001), publisher of the *Washington Post* and chairman of its parent company; the two *Post* reporters who received much of the credit for uncovering the Watergate scandal are Carl Bernstein (b.1944), a native Washingtonian, and Robert "Bob" Woodward (b.Illinois, 1943). Mary Elizabeth "Tipper" Gore (b.1948), wife of Vice President Al Gore, was born in Washington, DC. Washingtonians who achieved military fame include Benjamin O. Davis (1877–1970), the first black to become an Army general, and his son, Benjamin O. Davis Jr. (1912–2002), who was the first black to become a general in the Air Force. John Shalikashvili (b.Poland, 1936) was the first foreign-born commander in chief of the Joint Chiefs of Staff.

The designer of the nation's capital was Pierre Charles L'Enfant (b.France, 1754–1825), whose grave is in Arlington National Cemetery; also involved in laying out the capital were surveyor Andrew Ellicott (b.Pennsylvania, 1754–1820) and mathematician-astronomer Benjamin Banneker (b.Maryland, 1731–1806), a black who was an early champion of equal rights. Among Washingto-nians to achieve distinction in the creative arts were John Philip Sousa (1854–1932), bandmaster and composer; Herblock (Herbert L. Block, b. Illinois, 1909), political cartoonist; and playwright Edward Albee (b.1928), winner of the Pulitzer Prize for drama in 1967 and 1975. Famous performers born in the District of Columbia include composer-pianist-bandleader Edward Kennedy "Duke" Ellington (1899–1974) and actress Helen Hayes (Helen Hayes Brown, 1900–92). Alice Roosevelt Longworth (b.New York, 1884–1980) dominated the Washington social scene for much of this century.

⁵⁰BIBLIOGRAPHY

Aikman, Lonnelle. *The Living White House.* 11th ed. Washington, D.C.: White House Historical Association, 2003.

Allen, Thomas B. *The Washington Monument: It Stands for All.* New York: Discovery Books, 2000.

Caroli, Betty Boyd. *Inside the White House: America's Most Famous Home.* Pleasantville, N.Y.: Reader's Digest Association, 1999.

Cary, Francine Curro (ed.). *Urban Odyssey: A Multicultural History of Washington, D.C.* Washington, D.C.: Smithsonian Institution, 1996.

Council of State Governments. *The Book of the States, 2006 Edition.* Lexington, Ky.: Council of State Governments, 2006.

Detzer, David. *Dissonance: The Turbulent Days between Fort Sumter and Bull Run.* Orlando: Harcourt, 2006.

Furgurson, Ernest B. *Freedom Rising: Washington in the Civil War.* New York: Alfred A. Knopf, 2004.

Luria, Sarah. *Capital Speculations: Writing and Building Washington, D.C.* Durham: University of New Hampshire Press, 2006.

Lüsted, Marcia Amidon. *The National Mall.* Detroit: Lucent Books, 2006.

Moore, John L. *Speaking of Washington: Facts, Firsts, and Folklore.* Washington, D.C.: Congressional Quarterly, 1993.

PUERTO RICO

Commonwealth of Puerto Rico

ORIGIN OF STATE NAME: Spanish for "rich port." **NICKNAME:** Island of Enchantment. **CAPITAL:** San Juan. **BECAME A COMMONWEALTH:** 25 July 1952. **SONG:** "La Borinquena." **MOTTO:** *Joannes est nomen ejus.* (John is his name.) **FLAG:** From the hoist extends a blue triangle, with one white star; five horizontal stripes—three red, two white—make up the balance. **OFFICIAL SEAL:** In the center of a green circular shield, a lamb holding a white banner reclines on the book of the Apocalypse. Above are a yoke, a cluster of arrows, and the letters "F" and "I," signifying King Ferdinand and Queen Isabella, rulers of Spain at the time of discovery; below is the commonwealth motto. Surrounding the shield, on a white border, are the towers of Castile and lions symbolizing Spain, crosses representing the conquest of Jerusalem, and Spanish banners. **BIRD:** Reinita. **FLOWER:** Maga. **TREE:** Ceiba. **LEGAL HOLIDAYS:** New Year's Day, 1 January; Three Kings Day (Epiphany), 6 January; Birthday of Eugenio Maria de Hostos, 2nd Monday in January; Birthday of Martin Luther King Jr., 3rd Monday in January; Presidents' Day, 3rd Monday in February; Abolition Day, 22 March; Good Friday, Friday before Easter, March or April; Birthday of José de Diego, 3rd Monday in April; Memorial Day, last Monday in May; Independence Day, 4 July; Birthday of Luis Muñoz Rivera, 3rd Monday in July; Constitution Day, 25 July; Birthday of José Celso Barbosa, 25 July; Labor Day, 1st Monday in September; Discovery of America (Columbus Day), 12 October; Veterans' Day, 11 November; Discovery of Puerto Rico Day, 19 November; Thanksgiving Day, 4th Thursday in November, Christmas Day, 25 December. **TIME:** 8 AM Atlantic Standard Time = noon GMT.

¹LOCATION, SIZE, AND EXTENT

Situated on the NE periphery of the Caribbean Sea, about 1,000 mi (1,600 km) SE of Miami, Puerto Rico is the easternmost and smallest island of the Greater Antilles group. Its total area is 3,515 sq mi (9,104 sq km), including 3,459 sq mi (8,959 sq km) of land and 56 sq mi (145 sq km) of inland water.

Shaped roughly like a rectangle, the main island measures 111 mi (179 km) E-W and 36 (58 km) N-S. Offshore and to the E are two major islands, Vieques and Culebra.

Puerto Rico is bounded by the Atlantic Ocean to the N, the Virgin Passage and Vieques Sound to the E, the Caribbean Sea to the S, and the Mona Passage to the W. Puerto Rico's total boundary length is 378 mi (608 km).

²TOPOGRAPHY

About 75% of Puerto Rico's land area consists of hills or mountains too steep for intensive commercial cultivation. The Cordillera Central range, separating the northern coast from the semiarid south, has the island's highest peak, Cerro de Punta (4,389 ft–1,338 m). Puerto Rico's best-known peak, El Yunque (3,496 ft–1,066 m), stands to the east, in the Luquillo Mountains (Sierra de Luquillo). The north coast consists of a level strip about 100 mi (160 km) long and 5 mi (8 km) wide. Principal valleys are located along the east coast, from Fajardo to Cape Mala Pascua, and around Caguas, in the east-central region. Off the eastern shore are two small islands: Vieques, with an area of 51 sq mi (132 sq km), and Culebra, covering 24 sq mi (62 sq km). Uninhabited Mona Island (19 sq mi–49 sq km), off the southwest coast, is a breeding ground for wildlife.

Puerto Rico has 50 waterways large enough to be classified as rivers, but none is navigable by large vessels. The longest river is the Rio de la Plata, extending 46 mi (74 km) from Cayey to Dorado, where it empties into the Atlantic. There are few natural lakes but numerous artificial ones, of which Dos Bocas, south of Arecibo, is one of the most beautiful. Phosphorescent Bay, whose luminescent organisms glow in the night, is a tourist attraction on the south coast.

Like many other Caribbean islands, Puerto Rico is the crest of an extinct submarine volcano. About 45 mi (72 km) north of the island lies the Puerto Rico Trench, at over 28,000 feet (8,500 meters) one of the world's deepest chasms.

³CLIMATE

Tradewinds from the northeast keep Puerto Rico's climate equable, although tropical. San Juan has a normal daily mean temperature of 80°F (27°C), ranging from 77°F (25°C) in January to 82°F (28°C) in July; the normal daily minimum is 73°F (23°C), the maximum 86°F (30°C). The lowest temperature ever recorded on the island is 39°F (4°C), at Aibonito, the highest 103°F (39°C), at San Lorenzo. The recorded temperature in San Juan has never been lower than 60°F (16°C) or higher than 97°F (37°C).

Rainfall varies by region. Ponce, on the south coast, averages only 32 in (81 cm) a year, while the highlands average 108 in (274 cm); the rain forest on El Yunque receives an annual average of 183 in (465 cm). San Juan's average annual rainfall is 54 in (137 cm), the rainiest months being May through November.

The word "hurricane" derives from *hurakán*, a term the Spanish learned from Puerto Rico's Taino Indians. Nine hurricanes have struck Puerto Rico in this century, the most recent being the devastating Hurricane Georges in 1998. On 7 October 1985, torrential rains created a mud slide that devastated the hillside barrio of Mameyes, killing hundreds of people; not only was this Puerto Rico's worst disaster of the century, but it was the single most destructive landslide in US history. On 15–16 September 2004, Hurricane Jeanne, the tenth named storm and the seventh hurricane of the 2004 hurricane season, entered southeast Puerto Rico near Maunabo and traveled west then north across Puerto Rico and exited over the northwest tip of the island near Aguadilla. Following the storm, Puerto Rico was declared a federal disaster area. As the storm approached, the entire power grid of Puerto Rico was shut down by the government, indirectly causing over $100 million in damage and resulting in 600,000 people left without running water. Seven deaths were attributed to Jeanne and there was also landslide damage.

⁴FLORA AND FAUNA

During the 19th century, forests covered about three-fourths of Puerto Rico. As of the 21st century however, only one-fourth of the island is forested. Flowering trees still abound, and the butterfly tree, African tulip, and flamboyán (royal poinciana) add bright reds and pinks to Puerto Rico's lush green landscape. Among hardwoods (now rare) are nutmeg, satinwood, Spanish elm, and Spanish cedar. Pre-Columbian peoples cultivated yucca, yams, peanuts, hot peppers, tobacco, and cotton. Pineapple, guava, tamarind, and cashews are indigenous, and such fruits as mamey, jobo guanábana, and quenepa are new to most visitors. Coconuts, coffee, sugarcane, plantains, mangoes, and most citrus fruits were introduced by the Spanish.

The only mammal found on the island by the conquistadores was a kind of barkless dog, now extinct. Virtually all present-day mammals have been introduced, including horses, cattle, cats, and dogs. The only troublesome mammal is the mongoose, brought in from India to control reptiles in the cane fields and now wild in remote rural areas. Mosquitoes and sand flies are common pests, but the only dangerous insect is the giant centipede, whose sting is painful but rarely fatal. Perhaps the island's best-known inhabitant is the golden coqui, a tiny tree frog whose call of "ko-kee, ko-kee" is heard all through the night; it is a threatened species. Marine life is extraordinarily abundant, including many tropical fish, crabs, and corals. Puerto Rico has some 200 bird species, many of which live in the rain forest. Thrushes, orioles, grosbeaks, and hummingbirds are common, and the reinita and pitirre are distinctive to the island. Several parrot species are rare, and the Puerto Rican parrot is endangered. Also on the endangered list are the yellow-shouldered blackbird and the Puerto Rican plain pigeon, Puerto Rican whippoorwill, Culebra giant anole, Puerto Rican boa, and Monita gecko. The Mona boa and Mona ground iguana are threatened. Also, on the endangered list is the hawksbill sea turtle, which nests in Puerto Rico. There are three national wildlife refuges, covering a total of 2,425 acres (981 hectares).

⁵ENVIRONMENTAL PROTECTION

US environmental laws and regulations are applicable in Puerto Rico. Land-use planning, overseen by the Puerto Rico Planning Board, is an especially difficult problem, since residential, industrial, and recreational developers are all competing for about 30% of the total land area on an island that is already more densely populated than any US state except New Jersey. Pollution from highland latrines and septic systems and from agricultural and industrial wastes is a potential hazard; the rum industry, for example, has traditionally dumped its wastes into the ocean. Moreover, the US requirement that sewage receive secondary treatment before being discharged into deep seas may be unrealistic in view of the commonwealth government's claim, in the late 1970s, which it could not afford to build secondary sewage treatment facilities when 45% of its population lacks primary sewage treatment systems. As of 2003, sewage discharges into the ocean remained a problem: in August 2000, the US Environmental Protection Agency (EPA) granted the Puerto Rico Aqueduct and Sewage Authority's Aguadilla treatment plant a 20-year waiver for discharging primary treated sewage into the ocean, threatening coral reefs. In 2003, the EPA database listed 16 hazardous waste sites in Puerto Rico. As of 2006, 10 sites were on the National Priorities List, including the Atlantic Fleet Weapons Training Area and the Upjohn facility; Pesticide Warehouse I in Arecibo was a proposed site.

In 2003, total on- and off-site release of toxic chemicals was 8.8 million pounds. In January 1994, 750,000 gallons of oil were spilled off the coast of Puerto Rico, resulting in a fine of over $75 million levied against the three companies responsible. Wetlands on the island have been devastated by development, but in recent years, efforts have been mounted to save and expand these resources. An example is the restoration of one of the most important waterfowl habitats on the island, the freshwater wetlands of Laguna Cartagena.

⁶POPULATION

Puerto Rico's population was estimated at 3,912,054 in 2005, an increase of about 0.4% from 2004 and up from 3,522,037 in 1990. From 1990 to 2000, the population increased by 8.1%. The population was projected to reach 4.4 million by 2010. The population density in 2004 was about 1,137.4 persons per sq mi (439.2 per sq km).

In 2004, about 26.8% of the population was under 18 years of age and 12.2% were 65 years or over. The median age was 33.8 years. In 2003, there were 93 Puerto Rican males for every 100 females.

The population was estimated to be 75.2% urban and 24.8% rural in 2000. San Juan is Puerto Rico's capital and largest city, with an estimated 2005 population of 428,591, followed by Bayamon, 222,195; Carolina, 187,472; Ponce, 182,387; and Caguas, 142,378. Approximately one-third of all residents live in the San Juan–Carolina–Bayamon metropolitan area.

⁷ETHNIC GROUPS

Three main ethnic strands reflect the heritage of Puerto Rico: the Taino Indians, most of whom fled or perished after the Spanish conquest; black Africans, imported as slaves under Spanish rule; and the Spanish themselves. With an admixture of Dutch, English, Corsicans, and other Europeans, Puerto Ricans today enjoy a distinct Hispanic-Afro-Antillean heritage. In 2006, about 80.5% of the population was white (primarily of Spanish origin), 8% were black, 0.4% was Amerindians, and 10.9% were of other or mixed race.

Residents of Puerto Rico have been considered as US citizens since 1917, when the island was ceded to the United States at the end of the Spanish-American War. However, Puerto Ricans do not pay federal income tax to the Untied States and they do not vote in US presidential elections. Despite this link to the United States, most Puerto Ricans describe themselves as "Puertorriqueños" rather than Americans.

Less than two-thirds of all ethnic Puerto Ricans live on the island. Virtually all the remainder resides on the US mainland; in 2000 there were 3,407,000 people who identified themselves as Puerto Rican in the 50 states. The state of New York had the largest US ethnic Puerto Rican population (some 1.1 million) and ethnic Puerto Ricans made up 5.5% of that state's total population. New Yorkers who were born in Puerto Rico or who are of Puerto Rican descent sometimes refer to themselves as "Nuyorican." Florida's total ethnic population in 2000 stood second to New York's, at approximately one-half million.

8LANGUAGES

Spanish and English are the official languages of Puerto Rico, but Spanish remains dominant among the residents. The issue of language has been an ongoing concern between residents and US authorities. A 1902 law established both languages for official use, but US officials pushed for many years to make English the dominant language in school and government use. In 1991, the Puerto Rican legislature issued a bill making Spanish the official language, but this decision was reversed in 1993, restoring both languages to official status.

Puerto Rican Spanish contains many Taino influences, which can be found in such place-names as Arecibo, Guayama, and Mayagüez, as well as *hamaca* (hammock) and *canoa* (canoe). Among many African borrowings are food terms like *quimbombó* (okra), *guince* (banana), and *mondongo* (a spicy stew). Some English words are incorporated into Spanish in what is commonly referred to as "Spanglish."

9RELIGIONS

Until 1850, Roman Catholicism was the only religion permitted in Puerto Rico. Most of the population is Christian, with Roman Catholics accounting for about 85% of the population in 2006. The Catholic Church maintains numerous hospitals and schools on the island. Most of the remaining Puerto Ricans belong to other Christian denominations, which have been allowed on the island since the 1850s. Pentecostal churches have attracted a significant following, particularly among the urban poor of the barrios.

A small number of residents (an estimated 0.71% or 27,799 adherents in 2001) are Spiritists, incorporating native and African beliefs into their faith practices. Santeria, a syncretic religion originating in Cuba and Brazil that incorporates African and native Caribbean beliefs (including voodoo) with Catholicism, is practiced by some residents. As of 2001, Puerto Rico had 3,446 Hindus, 2,818 Baha'is, 2,715 Jews, 1,135 Muslims, and 509 Buddhists.

In 2006, the United Evangelical Church of Puerto Rico (Iglesia Evangelical Unida de Puerto Rico—IEUPR) voted to end a 40-year partnership with the United Church of Christ (UCC) due to the denomination's liberal polices on lesbian, gay, bisexual, and transgender issues. The IEUPR, which was established in 1931 and became a conference of the UCC in 1961, planned to con-

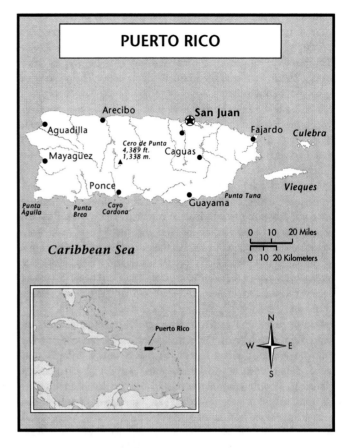

tinue to operate as an independent denomination, much as it had before affiliation with the UCC.

10TRANSPORTATION

Puerto Rico's inland transportation network consists primarily of roads and motor vehicles. A system of public buses operated by the Metropolitan Bus Authority (MBA) provides intercity passenger transport in the capital of San Juan and nearby cities. As of 2000, the bus service carried 135,000 daily passengers, up from 60,000 daily passengers in 1995, a 125% increase. The *públicos*, a privately owned jitney service of small buses and cars, offers transportation between fixed destinations in cities and towns.

As of 2004, Puerto Rico had 264 mi (424 km) of interstate highways and 15,673 mi (25,217 km) of local roads. In 2000, the territory had approximately two million registered automobiles.

The Tren Urbano (Urban Train), a heavy rail transit train, began operations in December 2004. Tren Urbano connects San Juan to the surrounding urban areas with 16 stations along a 10.7-mi (17-km), 30-minute route. The cost of the Tren Urbano project was $2.25 billion.

In 1996/97, the Puerto Rico Hotel and Tourism Association invested nearly $750 million to complete the strategic highway network system around the island, as well as other roads that connect small towns with the nearby cities. By 2000, the majority of the projects to improve the highway system had been completed, including improvements to Highways 2, 3, 22, 26, 30, and 52. The PR-10 Expressway crosses from the north to the central mountainous region. The PR-53 toll road provides a new route for the towns of the northeast. The Baldorioty de Castro Expressway allows rapid travel between the main airport and the capital. In 2000, a $200 million master plan for a new north-south expressway was being developed, which would involve the Martinez Nadal Expressway (Highway 20), improvements to Highway 1 to Caguas, an intersection in Caparra, and the Kennedy Expressway. The project was to be completed by 2008.

San Juan, the island's principal port and a leading containerized cargo-handling facility, handled 9.6 million tons of cargo in 2001. Ponce and Mayagüez handle considerable tons of cargo as well. Ferries link the main island with the islands of Vieques and Culebra.

As of 2006, the first of four phases was completed in the development of the "Port of the Americas," a world-class transshipment port and adjoining free industrial zone extending from Ponce to Guayanilla. Extensive tracts of land and the natural deep-water bay were an advantageous site for the port. The port was designed to handle all of Puerto Rico's foreign trade, and a good deal of the international container traffic crossing the Caribbean. It was expected that 12,000 jobs would be created with the establishment of the port.

Puerto Rico receives flights from 38 US mainland cities, and from the Virgin Islands, the British West Indies, Jamaica, the Dominican Republic, Great Britain, France, Spain, and the Netherlands. Luis Muñoz Marin International Airport in San Juan enplaned 10.4 million passengers in 2002. Puerto Rico shipped 495.8 million tons of air cargo in 2002. San Juan had 1.29 million passenger airline seats in January 2003. Other leading air terminals are located at Ponce, Mayagüez, and Aguadilla. There were 30 airports in Puerto Rico in 2004, 17 of which had paved runways. As of 2003, 52 airlines serviced Puerto Rico.

11 HISTORY

Archaeological finds indicate that at least three Indian cultures flourished on the island now known as Puerto Rico long before its discovery by Christopher Columbus on 19 November 1493. The first group, belonging to the Archaic Culture, is believed to have come from Florida. Having no knowledge of agriculture or pottery, it relied on the products of the sea; the remains of its members have been found mostly in caves. The second group, the Igneri, came from northern South America. Descended from Arawak stock, the Igneri brought agriculture and pottery to the island; their remains are found mostly in the coastal areas. The third culture, the Taino, also of Arawak origin, combined fishing with agriculture. A peaceful, sedentary tribe, the Taino were adept at stonework and lived in many parts of the island; Taino relics have been discovered not only along the coastal perimeter but also high in the mountains, where the Taino performed ritual games in ball parks that have been restored in recent times. To the Indians, the island was known as Boriquén.

Columbus, accompanied by a young nobleman named Juan Ponce de León, landed at the western end of the island—which he called San Juan Bautista (St. John the Baptist)—and claimed it for Spain. Not until colonization was well under way would the island acquire the name Puerto Rico (literally, "rich port"), with the name San Juan Bautista applied to the capital city. The first settlers arrived on 12 August 1508, under the able leadership of Ponce de León, who sought to transplant and adapt Spanish civilization to Puerto Rico's tropical habitat. The small contingent of Spaniards compelled the Taino, numbering perhaps 30,000, to mine for gold; the rigors of forced labor and the losses from rebellion reduced the Taino population to about 4,000 by 1514, by which time the mines were nearly depleted. With the introduction of slaves from Africa, sugarcane growing became the leading economic activity. Since neither mining nor sugarcane was able to provide sufficient revenue to support the struggling colony, the treasury of New Spain began a subsidy, known as the *situado*, which until the early 19th century defrayed the cost of the island's government and defense.

From the early 16th century onward, an intense power struggle for control of the Caribbean marked Puerto Rico as a strategic base of the first magnitude. After a French attack in 1528, construction of La Fortaleza (still in use today as the governor's palace) was begun in 1533, and work on El Morro fortress in San Juan commenced six years later. The new fortifications helped repel a British attack led by Sir Francis Drake in 1595; a second force, arriving in 1598 under George Clifford, Earl of Cumberland, succeeded in capturing San Juan, but the British were forced to withdraw by tropical heat and disease. In 1625, a Dutch attack under the command of Boudewijn Hendrikszoon was repulsed, although much of San Juan was sacked and burned by the attackers. By the 18th century, Puerto Rico had become a haven for pirates, and smuggling was the major economic activity. A Spanish envoy that came to the island in 1765 was appalled, and his report to the crown inaugurated a period of economic, administrative, and military reform. The creation of a native militia helped Puerto Rico withstand a fierce British assault on San Juan in 1797, by which time the island had more than 100,000 inhabitants.

Long after most of the Spanish colonies in the New World had obtained independence, Puerto Rico and Cuba remained under Spanish tutelage. Despite several insurrection attempts, most of them inspired by the liberator, Simón Bolivar, Spain's military might concentrated on these islands precluded any revolution.

Puerto Rico became a shelter for refugees from Santo Domingo, Haiti, and Venezuela who were faithful to Spain, fearful of disturbances in their own countries, or both. As in Cuba, the sugar industry developed in Puerto Rico during this period under policies that favored foreign settlers. As a result, a new landowner class emerged—the hacendados—who were instrumental in strengthening the institution of slavery on the island. By 1830, the population was 300,000. Sugar, tobacco, and coffee were the leading export crops, although subsistence farming still covered much of the interior. Sugar found a ready market in the US, and trade steadily developed, particularly with the northeast.

The 19th century also gave birth, however, to a new Puerto Rican civil and political consciousness. Puerto Rican participation in the short-lived constitutional experiments in Spain (1812–14 and 1820–23) fostered the rise of a spirit of liberalism, expressed most notably by Ramón Power y Giralt, at one time vice president of the Spanish Cortes (parliament). During these early decades, Spain's hold on the island was never seriously threatened. Although the Spanish constitution of 1812 declared that the people of Puerto Rico were no longer colonial subjects but were full-fledged citizens of Spain, the crown maintained an alert, centralized, absolutist government with all basic powers concentrated in the captain general.

Toward the middle of the 19th century, a criollo generation with strong liberal roots began a new era in Puerto Rican history. This group, which called for the abolition of slavery and the introduction of far-reaching economic and political reforms, at the same time developed and strengthened Puerto Rican literary tradition. The more radical reformers espoused the cause of separation from Spain and joined in a propaganda campaign in New York on behalf of Cuban independence. An aborted revolution, beginning in the town of Lares in September 1868 (and coinciding with an insurrection in Spain that deposed Queen Isabella II), though soon quelled, awakened among Puerto Ricans a dormant sense of national identity. "El Grito de Lares" (the Cry of Lares) helped inspire a strong anti-Spanish separatist current that was unable to challenge Spanish power effectively but produced such influential leaders as Ramón Emeterio Betances and Eugenio Maria de Hostos.

The major reform efforts after 1868 revolved around abolitionism and autonomia, or self-government. Slavery was abolished in 1873 by the First Spanish Republic, which also granted new political rights to the islanders. The restoration of the Spanish monarchy two years later, however, was a check to Puerto Rican aspirations. During the last quarter of the century, leaders such as Luis Muñoz Rivera sought unsuccessfully to secure vast new powers of self-government. By this time, Puerto Rico was an island with a distinct Antillean profile, strong Hispanic roots, and a mixed population that, borrowing from its Indian-Spanish-African background and an influx of Dutch, English, Corsicans, and other Europeans, had developed its own folkways and mores.

The imminence of war with the US over Cuba, coupled with autonomist agitation within Puerto Rico, led Spain in November 1897 to grant to the island a charter with broad powers of self-rule. Led by Luis Muñoz Rivera, Puerto Ricans began to establish new organs of self-government; but no sooner had an elected government begun to function in July 1898 than US forces, overcoming Spanish resistance, took over the island. A cease-fire was proclaimed on 13 August, and sovereignty was formally transferred to the US with the signing in December of the Treaty of Paris, ending the Spanish-American War. The US government swept aside the self-governing charter granted by Spain and established military rule from 1898 to 1900. Civilian government was restored in 1900 under a colonial law, the Foraker Act, which gave the federal government full control of the executive and legislative branches, leaving some local representation in the lower chamber, or House of Delegates. Under the Jones Act, signed into law by President Woodrow Wilson on 2 March 1917, Congress extended US citizenship to the islanders and granted them an elective senate, but still reserved vast powers over Puerto Rico to the federal bureaucracy.

The early period of US rule saw an effort to Americanize all insular institutions, even to the point of superseding the Spanish language as the vernacular. In the meantime, American corporate capital took over the sugar industry, developing a plantation economy so pervasive that, by 1920, 75% of the population relied on the cane crop for its livelihood. Glaring irregularities of wealth resulted, sharpening social and political divisions. This period also saw the development of three main trends in Puerto Rican political thinking. One group favored the incorporation of Puerto Rico into the US as a state; a second group, fearful of cultural assimilation, favored self-government; while a third group spoke for independence.

The Depression hit Puerto Rico especially hard. With a population approaching 2 million by the late 1930s and with few occupational opportunities outside the sugar industry, the island's economy deteriorated, and mass unemployment and near-starvation were the results. Controlling the Puerto Rican legislature from 1932 to 1940 was a coalition of the Socialist Party, led by Santiago Iglesias, a Spanish labor leader who became a protégé of the American Federation of Labor, and the Republican Party, which had traditionally espoused statehood and had been founded in Puerto Rico by José Celso Barbosa, a black physician who had studied in the US. The coalition was unable to produce any significant improvement, although under the New Deal a US government effort was made to supply emergency relief for the "stricken island."

Agitation for full political and economic reform or independence gained ground during this period. A violent challenge to US authority in Puerto Rico was posed by the small Nationalist Party, led by Harvard-educated Pedro Albizu Campos. A broader attack on the island's political and economic ills was led by Luis Muñoz Marin and the Popular Democratic Party (PDP), founded in 1938; within two years, the PDP won control of the senate. Under Muñoz Marin, a new era began in Puerto Rico. Great pressure was put on Washington for a change in the island's political status, while social and economic reform was carried to the fullest extent possible within the limitations of the Jones Act. Intensive efforts were made to centralize economic planning, attract new industries through local tax exemptions (Puerto Rico was already exempt from federal taxation), reduce inequality of income, and improve housing, schools, and health conditions. Meanwhile, a land distribution program helped the destitute peasants who were the backbone of the new party. All these measures—widely publicized as Operation Bootstrap—coupled with the general US economic expansion after World War II, so transformed Puerto Rico's economy that income from manufacturing surpassed that from agriculture by 1955 and was five times as great by 1970. Annual income per capita rose steadily from $296 in 1950 to $1,384 in 1970.

The PDP, the dominant force in Puerto Rican politics from 1940 to 1968, favored a new self-governing relationship with the US, distinct from statehood or independence. The party succeeded not only in bringing about significant social and economic change but also in obtaining from Congress in 1950 a law allowing Puerto Ricans to draft their own constitution with full local self-government. This new constitution, approved in a general referendum on 3 March 1952, led to the establishment on 25 July of the Commonwealth of Puerto Rico (Estado Libre Asociado de Puerto Rico), which, according to a resolution approved in 1953 by the United Nations Committee on Information from Non-Self-Governing Territories, was constituted as an autonomous political entity in voluntary association with the United States.

An island-wide plebiscite in 1967 showed that 60% of those voting favored continuation and improvement of the commonwealth relationship, 39% preferred statehood, and less than 1% supported independence; the turnout among eligible voters was 65%. The result of the plebiscite, held to support a movement for additional home-rule powers, met with indifference from the US executive branch and outright opposition from the pro-statehood minority in Puerto Rico. Consequently, efforts to obtain passage by Congress of a "Compact of Permanent Union between Puerto Rico and the United States," although approved at the subcommittee level by the House of Representatives, failed to produce any change in the commonwealth arrangement.

The result was renewed agitation for either statehood or independence, with growing internal political polarization. The island's Republican Party rearranged itself after the plebiscite as the New Progressive Party (NPP), and came to power in 1968 as a result of a split in PDP ranks that led to the creation of the splinter People's Party. The two major blocs have been evenly balanced since that time, with the PDP returning to power in 1972 but losing to the NPP in 1976 and again, by a very narrow margin, in 1980, before regaining the governorship in 1984. The independence movement, in turn, divided into two wings: the moderates favored social democracy, while the radicals pursued close ties with the Fidel Castro regime in Cuba. Capitalizing on the increased power of Third World countries in the United Nations, and with Soviet support, the radicals challenged US policies and demanded a full transfer of sovereign rights to the people of Puerto Rico. Their position won the support of the UN Special Committee on the Situation with Regard to the Implementation of the Declaration on the Granting of Independence to Colonial Countries and Peoples (more generally known as the Committee of 24), which on 15 August 1979 reaffirmed "the inalienable right of the people of Puerto Rico to self-determination and independence...." The US government replied that the people of Puerto Rico had already exercised their right of self- determination in the 1967 plebiscite, and noted that Congress in 1979 had restated its "commitment to respect and support the right of the people of Puerto Rico to determine their own political future through peaceful, open and democratic processes."

More advanced than most Caribbean countries in education, health, and social development, Puerto Rico suffered from growing political tensions in the early 1980s, with occasional terrorist attacks on US military installations and personnel. These tensions may have been exacerbated by the national recession of 1980–81, which had a particularly severe impact on Puerto Rico. The commonwealth's gross national product declined by 6% in 1982 and 1983, and federal budget cuts ended a jobs program and reduced access to food stamps. At the same time, the island's economy experienced a structural shift. Whereas 50% of jobs in Puerto Rico had been in agriculture in 1940, by 1989 that figure had dropped to 20%. Manufacturing jobs, in contrast, rose from 5 to 15% of total employment between 1940 and 1989. Although Puerto Rico's economy began to expand in the mid- 1980s, growing at an annual rate of 3.6%, the island continued to depend heavily on the federal government, which in 1989 employed 25% of Puerto Rican workers. The economy grew at an estimated rate of 2.2% in 2001. (Due to adverse conditions in the global economy, however, the GDP growth rate stood at 0.5% in 2002).

Puerto Rico's political status remains a source of controversy. Statehood would give Puerto Rico representation in the US Congress and would make the island eligible for billions of dollars more a year in food stamps, medical insurance, and income support payments, which are currently set at levels far below those of states. However, statehood would also incur the loss of tax benefits. Under current federal tax law for the commonwealth, individuals pay no federal income tax. More importantly, corporations pay no federal tax on profits, which has persuaded many companies, particularly manufacturers of pharmaceuticals, chemicals, and electronics, to build plants in Puerto Rico. In 1993 and 1998 plebiscites, a slight majority of Puerto Rican voters chose to maintain the island's status as an American commonwealth rather than opt for statehood or independence.

In 1989, Hurricane Hugo caused 12 deaths and $1 billion in damage in Puerto Rico. In 1994, the island suffered its worst drought in almost 30 years, and narrowly avoided serious damage to its beaches and wildlife when over half a million gallons (2.3 million liters) of heavy oil were spilled by a barge that ran aground on a coral reef. In October 1998, Hurricane Georges ravaged the island, causing damage estimated in the billions of dollars.

Pedro Rosselló was reelected governor in 1994; he announced in 1999 that he would not seek a third term in elections of fall 2000. In the 2000 election, Sila M. Calderón was elected the island's first woman governor.

In 1999 one Puerto Rican civilian had been killed and four others were seriously wounded in an accident during a US military training exercise on the island of Vieques. Widespread protests following the accident led US president Bill Clinton to temporarily suspend military training on the island, pending an investigation, and subsequent exercises used inert weapons only. The residents of Vieques, however, maintained that the military exercises were responsible for health and environmental problems. Governor Calderón, who opposed the US Navy maneuvers, pressured President George W. Bush, Clinton's successor, to halt the activity. On 1 May 2003, the US Navy withdrew from Vieques, and approximately 15,000 acres of land previously used by the military were turned over to the US Department of the Interior's Fish and Wildlife Service, to be dedicated to a wildlife refuge closed to the public.

That same month (May 2003), Calderón announced she would not run for reelection in 2004. The announcement set off a chain of events that brought the island commonwealth to the brink of financial insolvency in 2006.

During Governor Calderón's administration, Puerto Rico was faced with a growing crime rate, fueled by the drug trade, and a sick economy, made worse by the phasing out of tax breaks that had been given to US companies to set up operations on the island and Washington's general disinterest in the island. In addition, Puerto Rico had been losing population to the US mainland, further demoralizing those who chose to stay on the island. Shortly after Calderón announced her retirement, her predecessor, Pedro Rosselo, announced that he would run for the governorship in the 2004 election.

When Rosselo left office in 2001, unresolved charges of corruption leveled against him and members of his administration remained. In the 2004 election, Rosselo's opponent was Anibal Acevedo Vila, a member of Governor Calderón's pro-commonwealth party and the son of a former governor. During the campaign however, the interest centered upon the political theatrics between Rosselo (whose party favored statehood) and Calderón.

The election was bitter and hard fought and the results were very close: Acevedo Vila's margin of victory, only 3,880 votes out of around 2 million paper votes cast, led to a recount and a challenge by Rosselo in federal court. In the end, Acevedo Vila was pronounced the victor. However, this left the legislature and the office of the island's second-highest government official (the resident commissioner in Washington, DC, held by Luis Fortuno) under the control of the pro-statehood party. The result was political gridlock, mainly over a failure to agree on the budget.

The lack of a budget since 2004 caused a $740-million budget shortfall, and on 1 May 2006, the government ran out of money. Nearly 100,000 Puerto Rican government employees lost their jobs, some 43 government agencies shut down, and the island's 1,600 public schools were closed. The disruption to the Puerto Rican economy was severe and the island's bonds hovered at near junk status, seriously impacting the ability of the commonwealth to raise money for needed public works and other government needs.

Feeling the pressure, a meeting was arranged between the governor, the speaker of Puerto Rico's House, and the president of its Senate. Also invited to participate was a religious delegation that included the Roman Catholic archbishop of Puerto Rico. On 13 May 2006, a deal was approved that included a $741 million loan from the Government Development Bank of Puerto Rico and authorized the creation of an "urgent needs" fund, which would raise money through a new sales tax.

Although Puerto Rico banned capital punishment in 1929, in 2003, two men who were charged with first degree murder and extortion were being considered for execution under the 1994 Federal Death Penalty Act, which broadened the range of crimes punishable by death. Many Puerto Ricans claimed the imposition of the death penalty would infringe upon the commonwealth's right to self-government.

12 STATE GOVERNMENT

Since 1952, Puerto Rico has been a commonwealth of the US, governed under the Puerto Rican Federal Relations Act and under a constitution based on the US model. The Puerto Rican constitution specifically prohibits discrimination "on account of race, color, sex, birth, social origin or condition, or political ideas." The constitution has been amended a number of times, and in 2002, plans to hold a constitutional assembly to amend the constitution were proposed, providing for the elimination of the House of Representatives and the senate and the creation of a unicameral legislature. In 2005, the administration of President George W. Bush asked Congress to set a vote for the Puerto Ricans to decide on their status as a free nation.

The commonwealth legislature comprises a Senate (Senado) of 27 or more members, 2 from each of 8 senatorial districts, and 11 elected at large; and a House of Representatives (Cámara de Representantes) of 51 or more members, 1 from each of 40 districts and 11 at large. Each Senate district consists of five House districts. The Law of Minorities holds that if a single party wins two-thirds or more of the seats in either house, but does not win two-thirds of the vote in the gubernatorial election, the opposition parties are eligible for additional seats, in order to give the opposition (collectively) one-third of the seats in either house. The number of seats therefore, can be expanded (up to a limit of 9 in the senate and 17 in the house), if opposition parties receive at least 3% of the gubernatorial vote. In the 2000 election, one seat was added to the Senate according to this law, but no seats were added to the House of Representatives. Senators must be at least 30 years of age, representatives must be 25. Legislators must have been commonwealth residents for two years and district or municipal residents for one year. All legislators serve four-year terms.

The governor, who may serve an unlimited number of four-year terms, is the only elected executive. Candidates for the governorship must be US citizens for at least five years, must be at least 35 years of age, and must have resided in Puerto Rico for at least five years.

A bill becomes law if approved by both houses and either signed by the governor or left unsigned for 10 days while the legislature is in session. A two-thirds vote of the elected members of each house is sufficient to override a gubernatorial veto. The governor can employ the item veto or reduce amounts in appropriations bills. The governor also has the power to declare martial law in cases of rebellion, invasion, or immediate danger of rebellion or invasion. The constitution may be amended by a two-thirds vote of the legislature and ratification by popular majority vote.

Residents of Puerto Rico may not vote in US presidential elections. A Puerto Rican who settles in one of the 50 states automatically becomes eligible to vote for president; conversely, a state resident who migrates to Puerto Rico forfeits such eligibility. Puerto Rico has no vote in the US Senate or House of Representatives, but a nonvoting resident delegate, elected every four years, may speak on the floor of the House, introduce legislation, and vote in House committees.

Qualified voters must be US citizens, be at least 18 years of age, and have registered 50 days before a general election; absentee registration is not allowed.

13 POLITICAL PARTIES

Taking part in Puerto Rican elections during recent years were two major and three smaller political parties. The Popular Democratic (PPD), founded in 1938, favors the strengthening and development of commonwealth status. The New Progressive Party (PNP), created in 1968 as the successor to the Puerto Rican Republican Party, is pro-statehood. The National Republican Party of Puerto Rico is led by Luis Ferré. Two smaller parties, each favoring independence for the island, were the Puerto Rican Independence Party (PIP), founded in the mid-1940s and committed to democratic socialism, and the more radical Puerto Rican Socialist Party, which had close ties with Cuba until it became defunct. A breakaway group, the Renewal Party, led by the mayor of San Juan, Hernán Padilla, left the PNP and took part in the 1984 elections.

In 1980, Governor Carlos Romero Barceló of the PNP, who had pledged to actively seek Puerto Rico's admission to the Union if elected by a large margin, retained the governorship by a plurality of fewer than 3,500 votes, in the closest election in the island's history, while the PPD won control of the legislature and 52 out of 78 mayoralty contests. Former governor Rafael Hernández Colón defeated Romero Barceló's bid for reelection in 1984 by more than 54,000 votes. Colón was reelected in 1988 and was succeeded in 1992 by Pedro Rosselló, a New Progressive and a supporter of statehood, who was reelected in 1996. In 2000, Sila M. Calderón was elected Puerto Rico's first female governor, with 48.6% of the vote. The 2004 General Elections were the second-closest in Puerto Rican history. A recount confirmed the winner, Anibal Acevedo-Vila of the PPD; he was the first governor in Puerto Rican history not to have a resident commissioner of his same party, given that Luis Fortuno of the PNP won the post.

Puerto Rico Gubernatorial Vote by Political Parties, 1948–2004

YEAR	WINNER	POPULAR DEMOCRAT (PPD)	NEW PROGRESSIVE (PNP)	REPUBLICAN	PUERTO RICAN INDEPENDENCE (PIP)	SOCIALIST	LIBERAL REFORMIST
1948	Luis Muñoz Marin (PPD)	392,033	—	88,819	66,141	64,121	28,203
1952	Luis Muñoz Marin (PPD)	429,064	—	85,172	125,734	21,655	—
1956	Luis Muñoz Marin (PPD)	433,010	—	172,838	86,386	—	—
1960	Luis Muñoz Marin (PPD)	457,880	—	252,364	24,103	—	—
						CHRISTIAN ACTION	
1964	Roberto Sanchez Vitella (PPD)	487,280	—	284,627	22,201	26,867	—
						PEOPLE'S	
1968	Luis A Ferré (PNP)	367,903	390,623	4,057	24,713	87,844	—
							PR UNION
1972	Rafael Hernández Colón (PPD)	609,670	524,039	—	52,070	2,910	1,608
1976	Carlos Romero Barceló (PNP)	634,941	682,607	—	58,556	9,761	—
1980	Carlos Romero Barceló (PNP)	756,434	759,868	—	87,275	5,225	—
							RENEWAL
1984	Rafael Hernández Colón (PPD)	822,040	767,710	—	61,101	—	68,536
1988	Rafael Hernández Colón (PPD)	865,309	813,448	—	96,230	—	—
1992	Pedro Rosselló (PNP)	845,372	919,029	—	76,357	—	—
1996	Pedro Rosselló (PNP)	1,006,331	875,852	—	75,304	—	—
2000	Sila María Calderón (PPD)	978,860	919,194	—	104,705	—	—
2004	Aníbal Acevedo-Vilá (PPD)	963,303	959,737	—	54,551	—	—

* Residents of Puerto Rico are barred from voting in US presidential elections.

The question of Puerto Rico's status remained controversial as of 2006. Governor Rosselló called a plebiscite in November of 1993 to enable voters to choose between independence, commonwealth or statehood. A narrow majority of Puerto Rican voters decided to maintain the island's status as an American commonwealth. However, they conditioned their vote on a demand that the terms of the island's commonwealth status be modified. Such modifications would include eliminating the federal limits on food stamps and expanding Supplemental Security Income to encompass elderly and handicapped Puerto Ricans. Puerto Rican voters also requested that recent changes in Federal Tax Law 936, which had lowered by 60% the exemptions corporations could claim from taxes on profits, be removed and that the law be restored to its original form. Although Puerto Ricans have no vote in US presidential elections, the island does send voting delegates to the national conventions of the Democratic and Republican parties. In 1980, for the first time, those delegates were chosen by presidential preference primary.

Puerto Rico's political parties have generally committed themselves to peaceful change through democratic methods. One exception was the pro-independence Nationalist Party, whose followers were involved in an attempt to assassinate US president Harry S. Truman in 1950 and in an outbreak of shooting in the House of Representatives that wounded five congressman in 1954. A US-based terrorist group, the Armed Forces of Puerto Rican National Liberation (FALN), claimed credit during the late 1970s for bombings in New York and other major cities. FALN members briefly took over the Statue of Liberty in New York Harbor on 25 October 1977. Another group, the Macheteros, apparently based on the island, claimed responsibility for an attack on a US Navy bus in 1980 and for blowing up eight US Air Force planes at a Puerto Rico Air National Guard installation early in 1981.

14 LOCAL GOVERNMENT

The Commonwealth of Puerto Rico had 78 municipalities in 2006, each governed by a mayor and municipal assembly elected every four years. In fact, these governments resemble US county governments in that they perform services for both urban and rural areas. Many of the functions normally performed by municipal governments in the US—for instance, fire protection, education, water supply, and law enforcement—are performed by the commonwealth government directly.

15 STATE SERVICES

The executive branch of Puerto Rico's highly centralized government is organized into departments, agencies, and public corporations. The departments are as follows: agriculture, consumer affairs, correction and rehabilitation, economic development and commerce, education, family services, health, housing, justice, labor and human resources, natural resources and the environment, recreation and sports, state, transportation and public works, and treasury. Lodged within the Office of the Governor are the Office of Management and Budget, Planning Board, Commission on Women's Affairs, and Environmental Quality Board, as well as offices of economic opportunity, energy, youth affairs, cultural affairs, labor affairs, child development, and development of the disabled, and commissions for the protection and strengthening of the family and of agricultural planning and action.

Puerto Rico is more heavily socialized than any US state. Almost one-fourth of all those employed work for the commonwealth government, which operates hotels, marine transports, the telephone company, and all sugar mills, among other enterprises.

16 JUDICIAL SYSTEM

Puerto Rico's highest court, the Supreme Court, consists of a chief justice and six associate justices, appointed, like all other judges, by the governor with the consent of the senate and serving until compulsory retirement at age 70. The court may sit in separate panels for some purposes, but not in cases dealing with the constitutionality of commonwealth law, for which the entire body convenes. Decisions of the Supreme Court of Puerto Rico regarding US constitutional questions may be appealed to the US Supreme Court.

The Circuit Court of Appeals consists of 33 justices named by the governor with the consent of the senate. Decisions of the court may revise those of the trial courts of first instance. The Circuit Court of Appeals was created in 1994 as an intermediary tribunal between the courts of first instance and the Supreme Court. The tribunal sits in San Juan.

The nine superior courts are the main trial courts; superior court judges are appointed to 12-year terms. In 2003, superior courts were divided into 13 districts. These courts have original jurisdiction in civil cases not exceeding $10,000 and in minor criminal cases. District courts also hear preliminary motions in more serious criminal cases. Municipal judges, serving for five years, and justices of the peace, in rural areas, decide cases involving local ordinances.

San Juan is the seat of the US District Court for Puerto Rico, which has the same jurisdiction as federal district courts on the US mainland.

The death penalty is constitutionally forbidden; however, in 2003, the 1994 Federal Death Penalty Act was being invoked in a case involving two men accused of murder and extortion. This attempt met with increased activism against the death penalty, and reinforced the belief that the death penalty infringes on Puerto Rico's right to self-government. The last execution in Puerto Rico took place in 1927.

17 ARMED FORCES

In 2004, there were 611 active-duty military personnel stationed in Puerto Rico. Principal of the US military installations in Puerto Rico are the Naval Security Station at Sabana Seca and the Roosevelt Roads Naval Reservation, near Ceiba (a BRAC closing in 2004). Under BRAC Ft. Buchanan in Guaynabo became an army reserve base in 2005. Use of Vieques for training maneuvers, including shelling and bombing, forced many of that island's residents to move; the US Navy withdrew its forces in May 2003. Aerial and naval target practice on Culebra by the US Navy was halted by protests and legal action. Defense spending decreased dramatically in 2002: US defense agencies spent $133.8 million on procurement contracts greater than $25,000 during the first nine months of 2002.

As of 2004, some 131,448 veterans of US military service were living on the island, including 12,449 World War II veterans, 28,434 from the Korean Conflict, 34,195 Vietnam veterans and 17,345 from the Persian Gulf War. Total VA expenditures were $820, 565. Puerto Ricans suffered 731 combat deaths in Korea and 270 in Vietnam.

Reserve and National Guard personnel in Puerto Rico totaled 7,605 in 2004, with the army accounting for the vast majority (6,693).

18 MIGRATION

Although migration from Puerto Rico to the US mainland is not an entirely new phenomenon—several Puerto Rican merchants were living in New York City as early as 1830—there were no more than 70,000 islanders in the US in 1940. Mass migration, spurred by the booming postwar job market in the US, began in 1947. The out-migration was particularly large from 1951 through 1959, when the net outflow of migrants from the island averaged more than 47,000 a year. According to the 2003 American Community Profile an estimated 3,717,941 ethnic Puerto Ricans were living in the 50 states, or about 1.31% if the US population. At least 32 cities had Puerto Rican communities of 5,000 or more. Puerto Ricans are found in significant numbers not only in New York State but also in New Jersey, Illinois, Pennsylvania, California, and Florida. Connecticut, and Massachusetts. Indeed, 58% of ethnic Puerto Ricans living in the 50 states were concentrated in the Northeast in 2002.

During the 1970s, in part because of the economic decline of many US urban centers, the migration trend slowed; official estimates show that the net flow of migrants from the island totaled only 65,900. But with the Puerto Rican economy worsening in the early 1980s, the net migration from early 1980 to mid-1983 was about 90,000. From 1990 to 1992, there was a net loss from migration of about 40,000.

One striking aspect of the US-Puerto Rico migration pattern is its fluidity. As US citizens, Puerto Ricans can move freely between the island and the mainland. Even in 1953, when the heaviest net outflow was recorded—74,603—fully 230,307 persons emigrated from the US mainland to Puerto Rico, as 304,910 Puerto Ricans were migrating the other way. In 2000, 242,973 people living on the US mainland said that they had lived in Puerto Rico in 1995, while 112,788 people living in the commonwealth in 2000 said that they had lived on the mainland in 1995. This extreme mobility, though sensitive to the job market, would not be possible were it not for the increased income available to Puerto Ricans on both the island and the US mainland, and the fact that Puerto Ricans who come to the continental US generally preserve their ties of family and friendship with those in the commonwealth, thus finding it easy to return, whether for a short stay at Christmastime or for a new job on the island.

19 INTERGOVERNMENTAL COOPERATION

A member of the US Council of State Governments, Puerto Rico subscribes to the Compact for Education, the Interstate Compact for the Supervision of Parolees and Probationers, the Southern States Energy Board, and the Southern Growth Policies Compact. In its relations with the US government, the commonwealth is in most respects like a state, except in the key areas of taxation and representation. US laws are in effect, federal agencies regulate aviation and broadcasting, and Puerto Ricans participate in such federally funded programs as Social Security and food stamps. US grants to Puerto Rico totaled almost $5.3 billion in fiscal year 2004.

20 ECONOMY

The island's most important industrial products are pharmaceuticals, electronics, apparel, and food products. The sugar industry has gradually lost ground to dairy production and other livestock products in the agricultural sector. Tourism is the backbone of a large service industry, and the government sector has also grown. Tourist revenues and remittances from workers on the US mainland largely counterbalance Puerto Rico's chronic trade deficit. Federal funds to the government and directly to the people have been important to the Puerto Rican economy.

Puerto Rico's major problem is lack of jobs for an expanding population, a problem exacerbated when rising unemployment in the United States persuades Puerto Ricans to return to the island. From its former dependence on subsistence agriculture, Puerto Rico became a center for low-wage textile manufacturing, then a home for refining cheap crude oil from abroad—mainly Venezuela. The sharp rise of overseas oil prices that began in 1973 devastated this economic sector. Since then, high-technology industries, such as pharmaceutical and biotechnology industries, have become a major presence on the island.

Section 936 of the US internal revenue code, passed in 1976 and discontinued in 1996, established a substantial tax credit for US corporations doing business in Puerto Rico and possessions of the United States. Some corporations were also allowed to import their products into the United States duty-free. Section 936 was replaced with Section 30A, which allowed companies to claim 60% of wages and capital investment as non-taxable income. Pharmaceutical companies and high-tech industries based in Puerto Rico were to have an advantage over NAFTA member Mexico, whose low wages in low-skill labor-intensive jobs competed with Puerto Rican jobs. Due to the elimination of Section 936, however, many companies in Puerto Rico closed.

The downturn in the US economy that began in 2001 negatively impacted the Puerto Rican economy more severely than the mainland economy. The 11 September 2001 terrorist attacks on the United States also had an adverse effect on the Puerto Rican tourist industry. By 2003, the economy was beginning to show signs of stabilizing: unemployment stood at 11.9% in the first quarter of 2003, down from over 13% in 2002. However, some of the same factors affecting the US economy, such as the ongoing war with Iraq and rising oil prices, continue to impact the Puerto Rican economy as well. In May 2006, the unemployment rate was at 19.5%. Gross national product (GNP) in 2004 was at about $50.3 billion with an annual growth rate of 6.1%. GDP the same year was $78.8 billion with an annual growth rate of 5.4%. In 2004, the overall sales of goods and services totaled about $66.3 billion while the purchase of goods and services totaled $80.2 billion. Government net recurrent revenues were totaled at $11.2 billion.

21 INCOME

The minimum wage laws of the Untied States apply to Puerto Rico as well. In 2004, the mean hourly wage was $10.38, lower than the US national mean of $17.80. One of the highest mean hourly wages ($24.45) was paid to those in legal occupations, while those in the food service industry received one of the lowest mean hourly wages ($6.55). Per capita personal income in Puerto Rico was $12,031 in 2004. The average family income was about $37,990 per year. Government jobs accounted for 30% of payroll employment as of 2004. The next largest sector was trade, transportation, warehouse, and utilities, which accounted for 18% of payroll employment.

22 LABOR

Puerto Rico's civilian labor force as of May 2006 numbered 1,417,300. The unemployment rate in May 2006 averaged 19.5%.

In 2003, services accounted for 28% of employment; government, 21%; trade, 21%; manufacturing, 11%; construction and mining, 7%; transportation and other public utilities, 5%; finance, insurance, and real estate, 4%; and agriculture, 2%. In 2004, approximately 62,124 people were employed in construction, natural resources, and mining; 118,597, manufacturing; 182,037, trade, transportation, warehouse, and utilities; 22,067, information; 46,402, finance; 102,102, professional and business; 97,951, educational and health; 70,512, leisure and hospitality; 303,137, government; and 20,643, other services.

Less than 10% of the labor force belongs to trade unions. There are four main Puerto Rican unions represented on the island, the largest of which is the General Confederation of Puerto Rican Workers. Wages tend to adhere closely to the US statutory minimum, which applies to Puerto Rico.

23 AGRICULTURE

In 1940, agriculture employed 43% of the work force; by 2000, about 3% of the Puerto Rican labor force had agricultural jobs. Nowhere is this decline more evident than in the sugar industry. Production peaked at 1,300,000 tons in 1952, when 150,000 cane cutters were employed; by 1978, however, production was 300,000 tons, fewer than 20,000 cutters were in the fields, and the industry was heavily subsidized. By 2000, only 2,500 people were employed in the sugar industry, mostly in the fields, and Puerto Rico was importing most of its sugar from the US mainland and the Dominican Republic. The hilly terrain makes mechanization difficult, and manual cutting contributes to production costs that are much higher than those of Hawaii and Louisiana. In 2002, out of 17,659 farms sugarcane accounted for 21; vegetables and melons, 337; coffee, 7,167; fruits and coconuts, 4,544; and grains, 102. Despite incentives and subsidies, tobacco production has practically ceased, and coffee production—well adapted to the highlands—falls far short of domestic consumption, although about 10% of the best quality crops are exported to Asia, Europe, and the United States. Plantains are an important crop as well as ornamental plants. As of 2006, other important agricultural products included sugarcane, coffee, pineapples, and bananas, which are also grown on plots and on former sugarcane fields.

24 ANIMAL HUSBANDRY

In 2002 there were 281,371 cattle (down from 386,980 in 1998) and 87,490 hogs and pigs (down from 101,619 in 1998) on 4,000 cattle and 1,200 hog and pig farms and ranches. Sales of cattle and calves amounted to $36.5 million in 2002 (down from $53.4 million in 1998); hogs and pigs, $9.7 million (down from $11.4 million in 1998).

Dairy cattle numbered 153,097 in 2002 (down from 163,537 in 1998); poultry for meat numbered 7.7 million (down from 10.9 million in 1998); and chickens for egg production numbered 1.9 million in 2002 (up from 1.6 million in 1998). Puerto Rican dairy farms produced 373.3 million quarts of milk products valued at $194.2 million in 2002; egg production that year reached 17.6 million dozen. Sales of dairy products and poultry products in 2002 totaled $194.2 million and $78.7 million, respectively.

Meat and dairy production did not meet domestic demand in the early 2000s, so these products were being imported.

25 FISHING

Although sport fishing, especially for blue marlin, is an important tourist attraction, the waters surrounding Puerto Rico are too deep to lend themselves to commercial fishing. Tuna brought in from African and South American waters and processed on the western shore provided much of the canned tuna sold in eastern US markets until the late 1990s, when many tuna processing plants were closed in favor of lower-cost production elsewhere in the world. Approximately 4,497,000 lb of fish were produced in 2002, for a total value of $10.3 million.

Fifty aqua cultural farms were operating in 2002, up from 44 in 1998; aquaculture accounted for $2.9 million in sales that year. Products include prawns, saltwater shrimp, red tilapia fish, and ornamental species.

26 FORESTRY

Puerto Rico lost its self-sufficiency in timber production by the mid-19th century, as population expansion, increasing demand for food, and extraction of native and endemic woods for export led to massive deforestation. Puerto Rico must import nearly all of its wood and paper products. The public forest system covers 86,095 acres (34,842 hectares), of which 58,249 acres (23,573 hectares) are part of the Puerto Rico State Forest system and 27,846 acres (11,269 hectares) are part of the Caribbean National Forest.

27 MINING

The estimated value of nonfuel mineral commodities produced in Puerto Rico was $159 million in 2000; Puerto Rico, when compared to the 50 US states, ranked 42nd in nonfuel mineral production. Portland cement was the leading nonfuel mineral commodity. To protect proprietary data, statistics on specific nonfuel mineral products were not reported as of the early 2000s.

A multiyear study of the island's known and undiscovered mineral resources indicated that at least 11 different types of metallic mineral deposits, including copper, iron, gold, manganese, silver, molybdenum, zinc, lead, and other minerals, occur on the island in addition to the industrial minerals (cement, stone, clay, and sand and gravel) currently being produced.

Approximately 1,500 people were employed in mining, which was limited to quarry operations, in 2002.

28 ENERGY AND POWER

Puerto Rico is almost totally dependent on imported crude oil for its energy needs, particularly electricity generation. Oil accounted for 93% of total primary energy consumption in 2001. The island has not yet developed any fossil fuel resources of its own, and its one experimental nuclear reactor, built on the south coast at Rincon in 1964, was shut down after a few years. Solar- powered hot-water heaters have been installed in a few private homes and at La Fortaleza. Inefficiency in the public transport system has encouraged commonwealth residents to rely on private vehicles, thereby increasing the demands for imported petroleum. In 2003, Puerto Rico consumed an estimated 218,000 barrels per day of oil;

the vast majority of its imports came from American and Caribbean suppliers.

As of January 2004, the commonwealth's refining capacity was 114,400 barrels per day, from two operating refining facilities, the Caribbean Petroleum Refining facility on Bayamon, and the Shell Chemical's facility in Yabucoa. A third refinery at Guayama is used for storage. Puerto Rico also has petroleum storage at its Proterm facility.

Puerto Rico began importing liquefied natural gas in 2000 to feed its 540-MW EcoEléctrica gas-fired plant in Peñuelas. In 2003, an estimated 740 million cu m was consumed.

As of 2002, Puerto Rico consumed 176,370 short tons of coal each year, all of it imported. Since becoming operational in 2002, a new 454-MW coal-fired plant in Guayama increased the use of coal. The plant was recognized as one of the cleanest coal-fired plants in the world.

The commonwealth generated approximately 23.0 billion kilowatt hours of electricity in 2003, mostly from five oil-fired generators, but a fraction came from small hydroelectric dams. The Puerto Rico Electric Power Authority (PREPA) is Puerto Rico's only distributor of electric power.

The first non-incineration waste-to-energy power plant in the United States was being developed as of 2003 in Caguas. The proposed plant is to use a gasification process that will break down approximately 3,300 tons of waste per day into basic elements and electricity.

29 INDUSTRY

Value added by manufacture surpassed $8.6 billion in 1982, more than double the total for 1977. In 1949, about 55,200 Puerto Rican workers were employed in industrial jobs, 26% of them in sugar refining. By 1992, despite the loss of many jobs in the sugar industry, the number was 158,181 with a total payroll of $2.7 billion. The leading employment categories in 1992 were apparel and textiles, 30,700; chemicals and allied products, 25,400; food and kindred products, 21,000; electric and electronic equipment, 18,400; and instruments, 15,900. The growth areas were electric and electronic equipment, up 47% from 1977, and instruments and related products, up 60%.

According to the 1992 Census of Manufactures, the value of shipments amounted to $31 million, of which chemicals and allied products accounted for $13.3 billion; food and kindred products, $5.2 billion; and electronic and electric equipment, $2.8 billion.

There were more than 90 pharmaceutical plants representing 20 of the world's leading drug and health companies. The largest included Johnson & Johnson (Rio Piedras), Abbott Chemicals (Barceloneta), Bristol-Myers Squibb (Humacao), Warner-Lambert (Vega Baja), and Schering-Plough (Manati). In 1991, Baxter International (medical devices) was one of the commonwealth's largest non–locally based manufacturers, with 10 plants; Westinghouse Electric (electric components) had 15; Sara Lee (men's underwear), 6; and Motorola (radio equipment), 4.

In addition to the production of pharmaceuticals, electrical and electronic products, and textiles, other industries include: bottling, chemicals, clay and glass, distilling, leather, metal (including precision instruments), printing, publishing, and software manufacturing.

Industries tend to be labor intensive. The construction industry has been a growth area in recent years; in 1997, construction growth was estimated at around 15%. By 2003, however, the construction sector saw a downward trend. Manufacturing in 2003 accounted for 42.1% of GDP, more than double the percentage share of the US mainland. In 2002, employment in manufacturing declined by 8.5%, compared with a decline of 6.9% on the mainland. And, in 2005, there was an annual decline of 2.3% in manufacturing employment. However, in the face of the phase-out of federal tax incentives for U.S. firms the pharmaceutical industry continued to thrive. In 2005, the pharmaceutical industry employed over 30,000 people, approximately 26% of GDP, compared with less than 2% in the United States.

Puerto Rico has two foreign free-trade zones, in Mayagüez and San Juan. In January 1987, the Puerto Rico Industrial Incentives Act was passed to make more manufacturing and export service industries eligible for tax exemptions.

30 COMMERCE

Wholesale trade in Puerto Rico in 2002 involved about 2,313 establishments and major distributors, with sales of over $16.1 billion. Merchant wholesalers accounted for 94.3% of establishments and 97% of wholesale trade. Durable goods accounted for only 34.2% of sales. E-commerce accounted for about $71 million of the wholesale trade. There were approximately 39,316 employees engaged in wholesale trade in 2002.

Retail trade during 2002 involved 11,465 establishments; total retail trade amounted to over $20.4 billion. There were about 122,435 paid employees involved in retail trade. Motor vehicles and parts dealers accounted for the largest portion of retail trade sales at about $4.6 billion, followed by food and beverage stores at $3.5 billion. E-commerce accounted for about $115.7 million in retail trade sales.

Two large shopping centers, Plaza las Americas and Plaza Carolina, are in the San Juan area. The San Juan area alone had retail sales of nearly $3.3 billion in 1992, or over 28.1% of the total. Radio Shack announced at the end of 2002 that its best selling store in the world was the one at Plaza las Americas, with $6 million in revenue for fiscal year 2002.

Foreign trade is a significant factor in Puerto Rico's economy. Trade between the United States and Puerto Rico is unrestricted. In 2003, the islands' imports totaled about $33.7 billion and exports $55.2 billion. The primary import commodities were chemicals, machinery and equipment, clothing, food, fish, and petroleum products. Major exports included pharmaceuticals, medical equipment, electronics, apparel, canned tuna, rum, and beverage concentrates.

During 2001, the United States received $41.4 billion of Puerto Rico's exports and supplied about $15.6 billion of its imports. In 2003, the primary export partners were the United States (86.4%), the Netherlands (2.1%), and Belgium (2%). The primary import partners were the United States (48.9%), Ireland (20.7%), and Japan (3.9%). More than 100 of the US Fortune 500 multinational companies have industrial plants located in Puerto Rico.

31 CONSUMER PROTECTION

Consumer protection is the responsibility of Puerto Rico's cabinet-level Department of Consumer Affairs.

32 BANKING

Puerto Rico's first bank began operations in 1850. As of 2006, there were 19 commercial banks in Puerto Rico (most are local corporations, with the rest being US branches and foreign interests). The government owns and operates two banks, the Government Development Bank (GDB—founded in 1948) and the Economic Development Bank (EDB—created in 1985). The EDB fosters the development of local businesses engaged in agriculture, manufacturing, commerce, and other services, thus decreasing the need to import goods and services. The Economic Development Bank's loan portfolio was $128.7 million in 2003, and loan disbursements amounted to $82.7 million. The average of loan principal by sector in 2003 was: agriculture, 30%; services, 27%; business, 23%; manufacturing, 14%; and tourism, 6%. The Government Development Bank's liquidity increased 69.4% in fiscal year 2002, with $2.2 billion in reported capital.

Banco Popular de Puerto Rico continues to be the largest domestic bank in Puerto Rico, with more than 100 branches (2006). The second-largest bank, Banco Santander Puerto Rico, and Banco Bilbao-Vizcaya, are foreign banks.

Since 1992, a new type of institution has flourished in Puerto Rico, promoted by the government: the international banking entity. International banking entities are completely tax-exempt but can only receive deposits from non-residents. As the end of 2002, there were 34 international banking entities in Puerto Rico with total combined assets of $50 billion. Citibank controls 40% of these assets.

The credit union industry is also thriving in Puerto Rico. There were 144 credit unions throughout the island in 2002.

US corporations no longer operate tax-free in Puerto Rico. Amendments made to the US Internal Revenue Code tax laws require the payment of federal taxes on a portion of their income.

Banks in Puerto Rico are insured by the Federal Deposit Insurance Corporation (FDIC). Automatic teller machines are located all across the island.

33 INSURANCE

Due to Hurricane Hugo, the insurance industry suffered underwriting losses of $19.5 million in 1989. The largest life insurance company in 1990 was Seguro de Service de Salud de Puerto Rico, Inc., with written premiums exceeding $275 million. More than 200 Puerto Rican insurance companies collected revenues of $82.4 million (life insurance companies, $18.1 million; property and casualty, $64.3 million) in 1990/91, enforcing policies exceeding $1.5 billion. Hurricane Georges in 1998 caused $1 billion in insured property losses in Puerto Rico and the Virgin Islands.

In 2003, there were 21 property and casualty and 15 life and health insurance companies domiciled in Puerto Rico. In 2004, approximately 60,995 flood insurance policies were in force with an estimated value of over $4.2 billion.

34 SECURITIES

There are no securities exchanges in Puerto Rico. Bonds issued by the Government Development Bank, exempt from federal income taxes and from the income taxes of all US states and cities, are offered for sale on the world securities market. The Puerto Rico Stock Index (PRSI) is a market-value-weighted index composed of eight businesses with their main headquarters or main places of business in Puerto Rico. The companies included in the index are traded on national stock markets, such as the NYSE and AMEX, and in the over-the-counter market (NASDAQ). There are several hundred broker-dealer firms registered to do business in Puerto Rico. Approximately 100 organizations providing security investment advice are registered in Puerto Rico.

35 PUBLIC FINANCE

Puerto Rico's annual budget is prepared by the Bureau of Budget and Management and submitted by the governor to the legislature, which has unlimited power to amend it. The fiscal year extends from 1 July to 30 June.

In 1959/60, transfers from the US government amounted to $44 million, or less than 13% of all revenues. By 1972/73, receipts from the US government represented 23% of all revenues; by 1977/78, more than 29%. In 1995/96 intergovernmental transfers from the US government amounted to $2.9 billion, or 30.0% of the commonwealth government's receipts.

Puerto Rico's revenues were $6.7 billion, with expenditures of $9.6 billion during fiscal year 2000, the most recent year for which data was available.

Of expenditures, 3.3% were assigned to economic development and 26.2% to public housing and welfare; education accounted for 25.4% of the central government's expenditures.

36 TAXATION

The Puerto Rican Federal Relations Act stipulates that the commonwealth is exempt from US internal revenue laws. The US federal income tax is not levied on permanent residents of Puerto Rico, but federal Social Security and unemployment taxes are deducted from payrolls and the commonwealth government collects an income tax. Corporations in Puerto Rico are also taxed.

The commonwealth internal revenue tax system is a self-assessment system modeled on that of the United States. In 2004, the treasury reported total tax revenues of $7.24 billion. About $97.8 million was collected in property taxes. Income tax provided revenues of about $5.3 billion, with $2.7 billion from individual income tax and $1.8 billion from corporations and partnerships.

Section 936 of the Internal Revenue Code exempted certain corporations from paying taxes for periods ranging from 10 to 25 years, allowing subsidiaries of US corporations virtual exemption from US corporate income taxes. The exemption was passed in 1976 to encourage economic development on the island. At the time of repatriation of profits to the US stockholder, the Puerto Rican government imposed a "tollgate" of 5–10%. Section 936 was replaced with Section 30A in 1996, which reduced the amount of income companies could claim as non-taxable to 60% of wages and capital investment. In 2004, the tollgate tax revenues totaled about $31.6 million.

The government in 2001 also enacted a series of 27 laws to further economic development and foreign investment, primary among them Laws 145, 169, and 225. These provide incentives or tax credits that could in effect reduce corporate income tax to as low as 2%; a 10% income tax credit for companies that purchase locally produced goods for export, or to be used in local manufacturing for local consumption; and lower tax rates directed to businesses that establish hemispheric, global, or Latin American headquarters in Puerto Rico.

There is no general sales tax, but there is a 5% tax on jewelry. There are also taxes on room charges levied at 11% for hotels with casinos, 9% for those without casinos, and 7% for rooms at small inns. An excise tax applies for all inbound shipments and there are taxes on alcohol and motor vehicles as well. Merchandise arriving from the United States is subject to a tax of about 6.6%. In 2004, excise taxes brought in revenues of about $1.7 billion. US excises on off-shore shipments totaled over $328 million.

37 ECONOMIC POLICY

Inaugurated during the 1940s, Operation Bootstrap had succeeded by 1982 in attracting investments from more than 500 US corporations. The principal Puerto Rican agencies responsible for this transformation are the Administración de Fomento Económico, known as Fomento (Development), and its subsidiary, the Puerto Rico Industrial Development Co. (PRIDCO), which help select plant sites, build factories, hire and train workers, and arrange financing. Fomento reorganized certain industries, taking a direct role, for example, in promoting export sales of Puerto Rican rum. At first, Fomento brought in apparel and textile manufacturers,

who needed relatively unskilled workers. More recently, with the improvement in Puerto Rico's educational system, Fomento has emphasized such technologically advanced industries as pharmaceuticals and electronics. Industrialization has also required heavy investment in roads, power, water facilities, and communications systems.

PRIDCO reported that 253 new businesses were established in 2002 with 11,296 new jobs created with $1.1 billion in investment. Approximately 5,200 jobs were retained with a $170 million investment. In 2002, the government invested $2 billion in public works, with $2 billion budgeted for 2003. In 2001–03, $4.3 billion was offered for six economic development regions, including the Mayaguez-Ponce Expressway and the Santiago Channel.

The Puerto Rico Manufacturers' Association and the Puerto Rico Technoeconomic Corridor (PRTEC) also work to encourage and sustain industrial activities on the island. PRTEC is a nonprofit organization public and private entities working to facilitate economic development. This organization has been instrumental in implementing six major strategies for economic development, including an industrial cluster concept, which promotes networking and competition among similar industries.

The primary incentives to investment in Puerto Rico have been lower wage scales than in the continental US and the exemption of up to 90% of corporate profits from island corporate and property taxes for five years, with a descending rate of exemption that could last as long as 235 years in some regions. The commonwealth government created a 218-acre (88-hectare) free- trade zone in the San Juan area that allows companies to assemble imports duty-free in government-built warehouses for export from the island.

The government's plans for urban center rehabilitation in 2003 included $165.5 million for 80 revitalization projects in 18 municipalities. Economic development was being geared toward five sectors: pharmaceuticals, biotechnology, medical instruments, communication and information technology, and health services. The government has also launched "Puerto Rico 2025," a long-term economic and social development plan directed to ensuring the commonwealth's competitiveness in the global economy.

³⁸HEALTH

Health conditions in Puerto Rico have improved remarkably since 1940, when the average life expectancy was only 46 years. A resident of Puerto Rico born in 2006 is expected to live 78.4 years (74.46 years for males, 82.54 years for females). The infant mortality rate has declined from 113 per l,000 live births in 1940 to 9.38 in 1999 to an estimate of 9.14 in 2006. As of 2003, about 82.4% of all mothers received prenatal care within the first trimester of pregnancy.

In 2002, about 59.5% of the population was considered to be overweight or obese; the US national average was at 56%. As of 2004, about 12.6% of the adult population were smokers. The leading causes of death in 1940 were diseases brought on by malnutrition or infection: diarrhea, enteritis, tuberculosis, and pneumonia. In 2002, the most common causes of death, in order of prevalence, were heart disease (154.2 per 100,000 population); cancer (120.9 per 100,000); and diabetes mellitus (63.9 per 100,000). That year, the diabetes death rate was higher than that of any state in the United States. Cardiovascular diseases claimed a death rate of 40.8 per 100,000 and death by homicide was rated at 19 per 100,000 population (higher than any state, but lower than Washington, DC, which had a rate of 40 per 100,000).

At the end of 2004, there were an estimated 10,079 residents with AIDS. The same year, new AIDS cases were reported at an estimated rate of 23.4 per 100,000 population; a total of 2,049 new cases of HIV infection were reported as well. In 2003, the death rate for HIV was estimated at 13.6 per 100,000 population.

In 2002, Puerto Rico had 45 private hospitals and 13 public hospitals. There were 12,178 hospital beds available. In 2004, there were 254 physicians and 1,552 dentists per 100,000 people. In 2004, about 70% of the population had received dental care within the year. In 2005, there were 383 registered nurses per 100,000 population.

Annual national health expenditure as a percentage of GDP was 6.03% in 2002. The budget for health in 1999/00 was $993.3 million; of that amount, $570.3 came from federal contributions. As a result of health reform, the government now finances a medical insurance program contracted to the private sector. As of late 2000, all 78 municipalities had been incorporated into the health insurance plan, with 99% insured and 1.8 million participants in the plan.

³⁹SOCIAL WELFARE

Since the mid-1960s, residents of Puerto Rico have been eligible for most of the social welfare programs that apply throughout the 50 states. About one-fourth of the commonwealth's budget is appropriated for public housing and welfare. Federal grants, transfers, and expenditures in Puerto Rico amounted to nearly one-quarter of the GNP in 1990.

In 2004, Nutrition Assistance Grants, a program similar to the US Food Stamp Program, were offered through the US government to provide $1.3 billion in benefits to 1.01 million low-income residents. In FY 2005, there were 369,889 students participating in the national school lunch program.

Temporary Assistance for Needy Families (TANF), the system of US federal welfare assistance that officially replaced Aid to Families with Dependent Children (AFDC) in 1997, was reauthorized through the Deficit Reduction Act of 2005. TANF is funded through federal block grants that are divided among the states based on an equation involving the number of recipients in each state. In 2004, the program in Puerto Rico had 49,000 recipients.

Because unemployment is high and wages are low, Social Security benefits are below the US average. In 2004, 704,880 residents received social security benefits, including 327,620 retired workers, 81,610 widows and widowers, 134,540 disabled workers, 63,480 spouses, and 97,630 children. Retired workers received an average monthly payment of $635; widows and widowers, $555; disabled workers, $767; and spouses, $283. Payments for children of retired workers averaged $287 a month, children of deceased workers received $422 a month, and children of disabled workers received $205 per month. Monthly benefits for December 2004 totaled at about $404 million dollars. Approximately 96,000 workers received unemployment benefits in 2004, with the average weekly benefit at $107.

⁴⁰HOUSING

In 2000, there were a total of about 1,418,476 housing units, up from 1,184,382 units in 1990. About 1,261,325 units were occupied that year; 72.9% of occupied units were owner-occupied. About 68% of all units were single-family detached homes and just over 25% of all units were built between 1970 and 1979. About 58% of all households did not have modern heating systems; 31.1% had electric heating systems. Nearly 24% of all units had no telephone service, 5.2% lacked complete plumbing facilities, and 1.5% lacked complete kitchen facilities. The median home value was $75,100. The median monthly cost for a mortgage was $625 and the median monthly cost for rent was $297. The average household size was 2.98 persons.

In 2001, the Puerto Rico Housing Bank and Finance Agency was reorganized as the Puerto Rico Housing Finance Authority. One of the goals of the new agency was to build and renovate at least 50,000 units for low and moderate income families by 2005. Between 2001 and 2003, about $1.35 million was spent to renovate 139 public housing projects. Investment in elderly housing was $105 million for 994 units in 22 public housing projects. There were 15,985 housing units constructed during this period.

For those who have a gross annual income of up to $45,000 a year, the authority offers home loans of up to $90,000 with a 6.5% annual interest rate.

⁴¹EDUCATION

Puerto Rico has made enormous strides in public education. In 1900, only 14% of the island's school-age children were in school; the proportion had increased to 50% by 1940 and 85% by the late 1970s. The government encouraged school attendance among the poor in the 1940s and 1950s by providing inexpensive shoes, free lunches, school uniforms, and small scholarships. Education is compulsory for children between 6 and 16 years of age, and nearly two out of ten commonwealth budget dollars goes to education. About 94.1% of the population is literate (2002).

In 2004, there were 584,916 students attending public school. Instruction is carried out in Spanish, but English is taught at all levels. In 2004, there were 1,489 public schools and 545 private schools in Puerto Rico.

The main state-supported institution of higher learning is the University of Puerto Rico, with its main campus at Rico Piedras. The system also includes doctorate-level campuses at Mayagüez and San Juan (for medical sciences), and four-year colleges at Aguadilla, Arecibo, Bayamon, Carolina, Cayey, Humacao, Ponce, and Utuado. The 39 private institutions in 2002/03 included Interamerican University, with campuses at Hato Rey, San German, and other locations, and the Catholic University of Puerto Rico, at Ponce. In 2002/03, 191,552 students were enrolled at higher education institutions in Puerto Rico.

42 ARTS

The Tapia Theater in Old San Juan is the island's major showcase for local and visiting performers, including the Taller de Histriones group and zarzuela (comic opera) troupes from Spain. Claimed as one of the oldest theaters in the Western Hemisphere, Tapia Theater (Teatro Tapia) was built in 1832. The Institute of Puerto Rican Culture is headed by ASPIRA Association, Inc., a nonprofit organization focused on developing education and leadership in the communities. The Fine Arts Center (Centro de Bellas Artes) is the largest center of its kind in the Caribbean. The Fine Arts Center features entertainment ranging from ballet, opera, and symphonies to drama, jazz, and popular music.

Puerto Rico has its own symphony orchestra and conservatory of music. Both were formerly directed by Pablo Casals, and the annual Music Festival Casals, which he founded, still attracts world-renowned musicians to the island each year. In 2006, the festival celebrated its 50th anniversary with one full month of concerts, including the first performance by the Philadelphia Orchestra in Puerto Rico. The Opera de Camara tours several houses. Puerto Rico supports both a classical ballet company (the Ballets de San Juan) and the Areyto Folkloric Group, which performs traditional folk dances. Salsa, a popular style pioneered by Puerto Rican musicians like Tito Puente, influenced the development of pop music on the US mainland during the 1970s. In 2002, the Puerto Rican government devoted $25 million to a public arts project, developing 97 works of art in 18 municipalities as part of an urban revitalization program. Puerto Rico was awarded seven grants totaling $654,898 in 2005 from the National Endowment for the Humanities (NEH). That same year the National Endowment for the Arts (NEA) contributed five grants totaling $662,100. The NEA has also contributed to the arts education programs developed by the Institute of Puerto Rican Culture, and supported the Opera de Camara in Old San Juan, and the Ballet Concierto de Puerto Rico. The Puerto Rican Community Foundation, Inc., has received funding through the NEA's challenge grant program.

43 LIBRARIES AND MUSEUMS

In 1996–97, Puerto Rico's public libraries contained about 609,391 volumes and had a combined circulation of 479,133. The University of Puerto Rico Library at Rio Piedras held 1,804,010 books in 2003; the library of the Puerto Rico Conservatory of Music, in San Juan, has a collection of music written by Puerto Rican and Latin American composers. Also in San Juan are La Casa del Libro, a library-museum of typographic and graphic arts, and the Museo del Indio, a museum dedicated to the indigenous peoples of the Caribbean. There were some 50 museums in Puerto Rico in 2003, among them the Museo de Arte de Ponce (Luis A. Ferre Foundation), which has paintings, sculptures, and archaeological artifacts, as well as a library. The Marine Station Museum in Mayagüez exhibits Caribbean marine specimens and sponsors research and field trips.

44 COMMUNICATIONS

Puerto Rico is one of the most advanced and fastest growing telecommunications markets in the Caribbean region. The Puerto Rico Telephone Co. was founded in 1914 by two German sugar brokers, Sosthenes and Hernand Behn, best known today as the creators of International Telephone and Telegraph (ITT). In 1974, the Puerto Rican government bought the phone company from ITT. In 2004, there were an estimated 1.112 million telephone lines on the island. That same year there were an estimated 2.682 million cellular phone subscribers.

On 12 September 1996, Law 213 (known as Puerto Rico's Telecommunications Act of 1996) was enacted. The act created the Puerto Rico Telecommunications Regulatory Board with jurisdiction over all telecommunications companies providing services on the island. As of 2003, as a result of the 1996 law, 233 telecommunications companies had begun operations on the island. The Puerto Rico Telephone Co. has a 93% market share of the local telecommunications market and Centennial of Puerto Rico holds the remaining 7%. However, the Puerto Rico Telecommunications Regulatory Board, as of 2003, was attempting to promote competition within the telecommunications industry.

WKAQ, the island's first radio station, came on the air in 1923 and the first television station, WKAQ-TV, began broadcasting in 1954. As of 2006, there were 74 AM and 53 FM radio stations. In 2003, there were four commercial television channels/networks with six affiliates, one public broadcast television channel/network, three cable television service companies (with 360,579 subscribers), and four satellite television providers. The total number of television broadcast stations reached 32 in 2006.

There were 132 internet hosts in 2005, servicing approximately 1 million internet users.

45 PRESS

Puerto Rico has four major dailies: *El Nuevo Dia, El Vocero, Primera Hora,* and the *San Juan Star.* There are 22 weekly newspapers, including *El Estrella de Puerto Rico* and *Caribbean Business,* Puerto Rico's leading business publication. There are also eight monthly newspapers. The 2005 circulation for *El Nuevo Dia* (Puerto Rico's daily with the largest circulation), was 203,153 mornings and 245,500 Sundays. The English-language *San Juan Star* won a Pulitzer Prize in 1961.

46 ORGANIZATIONS

Important organizations on the island include the Puerto Rico Medical Association, Puerto Rico Manufacturers' Association, and Puerto Rico Bar Association. Also maintaining headquarters in Puerto Rico are the Association of Island Marine Laboratories of the Caribbean, Puerto Rico Rum Producers Association, Caribbean Hotel Association, and Caribbean Studies Association.

Some American professional organizations have chapters in Puerto Rico, including the American Physical Therapy Association and the American Library Association. Fondos Unidos is the local branch of Untied Way of America. Puerto Rico has chapters of Caritas and Amnesty International. There are also chapters of the YWCA/YMCA and the Young Democrats.

US-based agencies such as the National Puerto Rican Forum and the Puerto Rican Community Development Project assist Puerto Ricans living on the mainland. "Hometown clubs" consisting of "absent sons" *(hilos ausentes)* of various Puerto Rican towns are a typical feature of the barrios in New York and other cities in the continental United States.

47 TOURISM, TRAVEL, AND RECREATION

Only government and manufacturing exceed tourism in importance to the Puerto Rican economy. The industry has grown rapidly, from 65,000 tourists in 1950 to 1.1 million in 1970 to over 3 million in 2003. Tourism employs approximately 60,000 workers. Many hotels are located in San Juan, though the eastern part of the island also features hotels and resorts. Most tourists come for sunning, swimming, deep-sea fishing, and the fashionable shops, night clubs, and casinos of San Juan's Condado Strip. Attractions of old San Juan include two fortresses, El Morro and San Cristobal, San Jose Church (one of the oldest in the New World), and La Fortaleza, the governor's palace. The government has been encouraging tourists to journey outside of San Juan to such destinations such as the Arecibo Observatory (with its radio telescope used for research astronomy, ionospheric studies, and radar mapping), the rain forest of El Yunque, Phosphorescent Bay, colonial-style San German, and the bird sanctuary and mangrove forest on the shores of Torrecilla Lagoon. The 53-acre (21-hectare) San Juan harbor fortifications are a national historic site.

As of 2003, there were 3,238,300 total arrivals of non-resident tourists, including 2,454,300 from the United States. In that same year, 1,304,610 of the total non-resident tourists arrived at hotels and *paradores*. The occupancy rate of tourist hotels was 66.7% as of December 2005. During 2000/01, visitors spent $2.7 billion in Puerto Rico, a 14.2% increase over 1999/00. The 11 September 2001 terrorist attacks on the United States had a negative impact on the Puerto Rican tourist industry, as did the 2003 US-led war in Iraq. The World Travel and Tourism Council estimated that the war in Iraq cost Puerto Rico $262 million in lost tourism revenue and 3,800 jobs. Although industry growth decreased in 2001–03 in response to the slowdown in the US economy, Puerto Rico's tourism began to recover in 2004–05. There was an estimated tourist arrival total of almost five million for 2004.

48 SPORTS

Baseball is very popular in Puerto Rico. There is a six-team professional winter league, in which many ball players from American and National League teams participate. There were 50 games played in the league's six ballparks in 2002. Horse races are held every Sunday at El Nuevo Comandante, along with the annual Clasico del Caribe. Cockfighting, boxing, and basketball are also popular. Puerto Rico, which has its own Olympic Committee, sent a delegation to the 1980 Olympics in Moscow despite the US boycott. Other annual sporting events include the Copa Velasco Regatta, the Maraton de San Blas, the International Cycling Competition in Sabana Grande, the first leg of the Caribbean Ocean Racing Triangle, and the International Billfish Tournament in San Juan.

49 FAMOUS PUERTO RICANS

Elected to represent Puerto Rico before the Spanish Cortes in 1812, Ramón Power y Giralt (1775–1813), a liberal reformer, was the leading Puerto Rican political figure of the early 19th century. Power, appointed vice president of the Cortes, participated in drafting the new Spanish constitution of 1812. Ramón Emeterio Betances (1827–98) became well known not only for his efforts to alleviate a cholera epidemic in 1855, but also for his crusade to abolish slavery in Puerto Rico and as a leader of a separatist movement that culminated in 1868 in the "Grito de Lares." Eugenio Maria de Hostos (1839–1903), a writer, abolitionist, and educator, spent much of his adult life in Latin America, seeking to establish a free federation of the West Indies to replace colonial rule in the Caribbean. Luis Muñoz Rivera (1859–1916), a liberal journalist, led the movement that obtained the Autonomic Charter of 1897 for Puerto Rico, and he headed the cabinet that took office in 1898. With the island under United States rule, Muñoz Rivera served between 1911 and 1916 as Puerto Rico's resident commissioner to the US Congress. Other important Puerto Rican historical figures include Juan Alejo Arizmendi (1760?–1814), the first Puerto Rican–born bishop, appointed to the See of San Juan; José de Diego (1866–1918), a noted poet and gifted orator who, under the Foraker Act, became the first speaker of the island house of delegates and was a champion of independence for Puerto Rico.

The dominant political figure in 20th-century Puerto Rico was Luis Muñoz Marin (1898–1980), founder of the Popular Democratic Party in 1938 and president of the Puerto Rico senate from 1940–48. Muñoz, the first native-born elected governor of the island (1948–64), devised the commonwealth relationship that has governed the island since 1952. Another prominent 20th-century figure, Antonio R. Barceló (1869–1939), who led the Unionista Party after Muñoz Rivera's death, was the first president of the senate under the Jones Act, and was later the leader of the Liberal Party. In 1946, Jesús T. Pinero (1897–1952) became the first Puerto Rican appointed governor of the island by a US president; he had been elected as resident commissioner of Puerto Rico to the US Congress two years before. Pedro Albizu Campos (1891–1965), a Harvard Law School graduate, presided over the militant Nationalist Party and was, until his death, the leader of forces that advocated independence for Puerto Rico by revolution. In 1945, Gilberto Concepción de Gracia (1909–68), also a lawyer, helped found the more moderate Puerto Rican Independence Party. Herman Badillo (b.1929) was the first person of Puerto Rican birth to be a voting member of the US House of Representatives, as congressman from New York, and Maurice Ferré (b.1935), elected mayor of Miami in 1973, was the first native-born Puerto Rican to run a large US mainland city. Hernán Padilla (b.1938), mayor of San Juan, became the first Hispanic American elected to head the US Conference of Mayors (1984).

Women have participated actively in Puerto Rican politics. Ana Roqué de Duprey (1853–1933) led the Asociación Puertorriquena de Mujeres Sufragistas, organized in late 1926, while Milagros Benet de Mewton (1868–1945) presided over the Liga Social Sufragista, founded in 1917. Both groups actively lobbied for the extension of the right to vote to Puerto Rican women, not only in Puerto Rico but also in the United States and other countries. Felisa Rincón de Gautier (1897–1994), mayor of San Juan from 1946 to 1968, was named Woman of the Americas in 1954, the year she presided over the Inter-American Organization for Municipalities. Carmen Delgado Votaw (b.1935) was the first person of Puerto Rican birth to be elected president of the Inter-American Commission of Women, the oldest international organization in the field of women's rights. Sila María Calderón, elected in 2000, became the commonwealth's first female governor.

Manuel A. Alonso (1822–89) blazed the trail for a distinctly Puerto Rican literature with the 1849 publication of *El Gibaro*, the first major effort to depict the traditions and mores of the island's rural society. Following him in the development of a rich Puerto Rican literary tradition were, among many others, that most prolific of 19th century Puerto Rican writers, Alejandro Tapia y Rivera (1826–82), a writer adept in history, drama, poetry, and other forms of literary expression; essayist and critic Manuel Elzaburu (1852–92); novelist Manuel Zeno Gandia (1855–1930); and poets Lola Rodriguez de Tió (1843–1924) and José Gautier Benitez (1848–80). Tió's patriotic lyrics, popularly acclaimed, were adapted to become Puerto Rico's national anthem. Among 20th century Puerto Rican literary figures are poets Luis Lloréns Torres (1878–1944), Luis Palés Matos (1898–1959), and Julia de Burgos (1916–53); and essayists and critics Antonio S. Pedreira (1898–1939), Tomás Blanco (1900–75), José A. Balseiro (1900–62), Margot Arce de Vázquez (1904–90), Concha Meléndez (1904–83), Nilita Vientós Gastón (1908–89), and Maria T. Babin (1910–89). In the field of fiction, René Marqués (1919–79), Abelardo Diaz Alfaro (1919–99), José Luis González (b.1926), and Pedro Juan Soto (b.1928) are among the best known outside Puerto Rico.

In the world of entertainment, Academy Award winners José Ferrer (1912–92) and Rita Moreno (b.1931), and two-time Tony winner Chita Rivera (b.1933) are among the most famous. Notable in classical music are cellist-conductor Pablo Casals (b.Spain, 1876–1973), a longtime resident of Puerto Rico; pianist Jesús Maria Sanromá (1902–84); and opera star Justino Diaz (b.1940). Well-known popular musicians include Tito Puente (b.New York, 1923–2000) and José Feliciano (b.1945).

Roberto Clemente (1934–72), one of baseball's most admired performers and a member of the Hall of Fame, played on 12 National League All-Star teams and was named Most Valuable Player in 1966.

50 BIBLIOGRAPHY

Colonial Dilemma: Critical Perspectives on Contemporary Puerto Rico. Boston: South End Press, 1993.

Curet, L. Antonio. *Caribbean Paleodemography: Population, Culture, History, and Sociopolitical Processes in Ancient Puerto Rico.* Tuscaloosa: University of Alabama Press, 2005.

Fernandez, Ronald. *The Disenchanted Island: Puerto Rico and the United States in the Twentieth Century.* Westport, Conn.: Praeger, 1996.

———. *Puerto Rico Past and Present: An Encyclopedia.* Westport, Conn.: Greenwood Press, 1998.

Janer, Zilkia. *Puerto Rican Nation-building Literature: Impossible Romance.* Gainesville: University Press of Florida, 2005.

Maraniss, David. *Clemente: The Passion and Grace of Baseball's Last Hero.* New York: Simon & Schuster, 2006.

Morales Carrion, Arturo. *Puerto Rico: A Political and Cultural History.* New York: Norton, 1984.

Morris, Nancy. *Puerto Rico: Culture, Politics, and Identity.* Westport, Conn.: Praeger, 1995.

Picó, Fernando. *A General History of Puerto Rico: A Panorama of Its People.* Princeton, N.J.: Markus Wiener Publishers, 2006.

Villaronga, Gabriel. *Toward a Discourse of Consent: Mass Mobilization and Colonial Politics in Puerto Rico, 1932–48.* Westport, Conn.: Praeger, 2004.

UNITED STATES
CARIBBEAN DEPENDENCIES

NAVASSA

Navassa, a 5-sq-km (2-sq-mi) island between Jamaica and Haiti, was claimed by the United States under the Guano Act of 1856. The island, located at 18°24′ N and 75°1′ W, is uninhabited except for a lighthouse station under the administration of the coast guard.

VIRGIN ISLANDS OF THE UNITED STATES

The Virgin Islands of the United States lie about 64 km (40 mi) E of Puerto Rico and 1,600 km (1,000 mi) SSE of Miami, between 17°40′ and 18°25′ N and 64°34′ and 65°3′ N. The island group extends 82 km (51 mi) N–S and 80 km (50 mi) E–W with a total area of at least 353 sq km (136 sq mi). Only 3 of the more than 50 islands and cays are of significant size: St. Croix, 218 sq km (84 sq mi) in area; St. Thomas, 83 sq km (32 sq mi); and St. John, 52 sq km (20 sq mi). The territorial capital, Charlotte Amalie, on St. Thomas, has one of the finest harbors in the Caribbean.

St. Croix is relatively flat, with a terrain suitable for sugarcane cultivation. St. Thomas is mountainous and little cultivated, but it has many snug harbors. St. John, also mountainous, has fine beaches and lush vegetation; about two-thirds of St. John's area has been declared a national park. The subtropical climate, with temperatures ranging from 21–32°C (70–90 °F) and an average temperature of 25°C (77°F), is moderated by northeast trade winds. Rainfall, the main source of fresh water, varies widely, and severe droughts are frequent. The average yearly rainfall is 114 cm (45 in), mostly during the summer months.

The population of the US Virgin Islands was estimated at 123,498 in 2002, up from 96,569 at the time of the 1980 census. St. Croix has two principal towns: Christiansted and Frederiksted. Economic development has brought an influx of new residents, mainly from Puerto Rico, other Caribbean islands, and the US mainland. Most of the permanent inhabitants are descendants of slaves who were brought from Africa in the early days of Danish rule, and about 80% of the population is black. English is the official and most widely spoken language.

Some of the oldest religious congregations in the Western Hemisphere are located in the Virgin Islands. A Jewish synagogue there is the second-oldest in the New World, and the Lutheran Congregation of St. Thomas, founded in 1666, is one of the three oldest congregations in the United States. As of 1999, Baptists made up an estimated 42% of the population, Roman Catholics 34%, and Episcopalians 17%.

In 2000 there were 856 km (531.6 mi) of roads in the US Virgin Islands; the US Virgin Islands has the only US roads where driving is done on the left side of the road. Cargo-shipping services operate from Baltimore, Jacksonville, and Miami via Puerto Rico. In addition, weekly shipping service is available from Miami. Both St. Croix and St. Thomas have airports, with St. Croix's

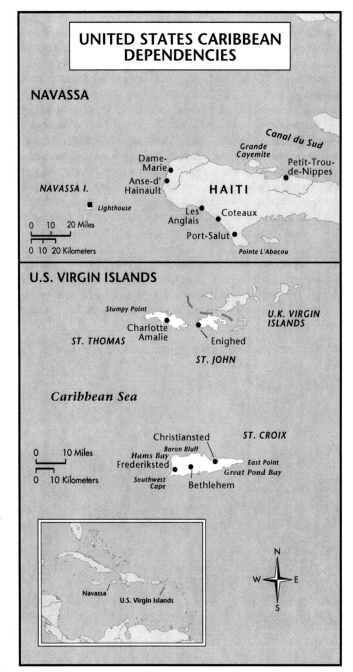

facility handling the larger number of jet flights from the continental United States and Europe.

Excavations at St. Croix in the 1970s uncovered evidence of a civilization perhaps as ancient as AD 100. Christopher Columbus, who reached the islands in 1493, named them for the martyred virgin St. Ursula. At this time, St. Croix was inhabited by Carib

Indians, who were eventually driven from the island by Spanish soldiers in 1555. During the 17th century, the archipelago was divided into two territorial units, one controlled by the British, the other (now the US Virgin Islands) controlled by Denmark. The separate history of the latter unit began with the settlement of St. Thomas by the Danish West India Company in 1672. St. John was claimed by the company in 1683 and St. Croix was purchased from France in 1733. The holdings of the company were taken over as a Danish crown colony in 1754. Sugarcane, cultivated by slave labor, was the backbone of the islands' prosperity in the 18th and early 19th centuries. After brutally suppressing several slave revolts. Denmark abolished slavery in the colony in 1848. A long period of economic decline followed, until Denmark sold the islands to the United States in 1917 for $25 million. Congress granted US citizenship to the Virgin Islanders in 1927. In 1931, administration of the islands was transferred from the Department of the Navy to the Department of the Interior, and the first civilian governor was appointed. In the late 1970s, the Virgin Islands government began to consider ways to expand self-rule. A UN delegation in 1977 found little interest in independence, however, and a locally drafted constitution was voted down by the electorate in 1979.

The chief executive of the Virgin Islands is the territorial governor, elected by direct popular vote (prior to 1970, territorial governors were appointed by the US president). Constitutionally, the US Congress has plenary authority to legislate for the territory. Enactment of the Revised Organic Act of the Virgin Islands on 22 July 1954 vested local legislative power—subject to veto by the governor—in a unicameral legislature. Since 1972, the islands have sent one nonvoting representative to the US House of Representatives. Courts are under the US federal judiciary; the two federal district court judges are appointed by the US president. Territorial court judges, who preside over misdemeanor and traffic cases, are appointed by the governor and confirmed by the legislature. The district court has appellate jurisdiction over the territorial court.

Tourism, which accounts for approximately 70% of both GDP and employment is the islands' principal economic activity. The number of tourists rose dramatically throughout the late 1960s and early 1970s, from 448,165 in 1964 to over 2 million per year in the 1990s, continuing into the early 2000s. Rum remains an important manufacture, with petroleum refining (on St. Croix) a major addition in the late 1960s. Economic development is promoted by the US-government-owned Virgin Islands Corp. In 2002 the gross domestic product per capita was $14,500. The unemployment rate was 6.2% in 2003. Exports for 1992 totaled $1.8 billion while imports totaled $2.2 billion. The island's primary export is refined petroleum products. Raw crude oil constitutes the Virgin Island's principal import. In 1990, median family income was $24,036.

The territorial Department of Health provides hospital and medical services, public health services, and veterinary medicine. Education is compulsory. The College of the Virgin Islands is the territory's first institution of higher learning. There were about 70,900 main line telephones in 2004, and 41,000 mobile cellular phones. The Virgin Islands had 22 radio stations (6 AM, 16 FM) and 5 broadcast television stations in 2004.

UNITED STATES PACIFIC DEPENDENCIES

AMERICAN SAMOA

American Samoa, an unincorporated and unorganized insular US territory in the South Pacific Ocean, comprises that portion of the Samoan archipelago lying E of longitude 171°w. (The rest of the Samoan islands comprise the independent state of Western Samoa.) While the Samoan group as a whole has an area of 3,121 sq km (1,205 sq mi), American Samoa consists of only seven small islands (between 14° and 15°s and 168° and 171°w) with a total area (land and water) of 197 sq km (76 sq mi). Five of the islands are volcanic, with rugged peaks rising sharply, and two are coral atolls.

The climate is hot and rainy; normal temperatures range from 24°c (75°F) in August to 32°c (90°F) during December–February; mean annual rainfall is 330 cm (130 in), the rainy season lasting from December through March. Hurricanes are common. The native flora includes flourishing tree ferns, coconut, hardwoods, and rubber trees. There are few wild animals.

As of mid-2005, the estimated population was 57,881, an increase over the 1986 population estimate of 37,500. However, the total population has remained relatively constant for many years because of the substantial number of Samoans who migrate to the United States. The inhabitants, who are concentrated on the island of Tutuila, are almost pure Polynesian. Most people are bilingual: English and Samoan are the official languages. Most Samoans are Christians.

The capital of the territory, Pago Pago, on Tutuila, has one of the finest natural harbors in the South Pacific and is a duty-free port. Passenger liners call there on South Pacific tours, and passenger and cargo ships arrive regularly from Japan, New Zealand, Australia, and the US west coast. There are regular air and sea services between American Samoa and Western Samoa, and scheduled flights between Pago Pago and Honolulu.

American Samoa was settled by Melanesian migrants in the 1st millennium BC. The Samoan islands were visited in 1768 by the French explorer Louis-Antoine de Bougainville, who named them the Îles des Navigateurs as a tribute to the skill of their native boatmen. In 1889, the United States, the United Kingdom, and Germany agreed to share control of the islands. The United Kingdom later withdrew its claim, and under the 1899 Treaty of Berlin, the United States was internationally acknowledged to have rights extending over all the islands of the Samoan group lying east of 171° w, while Germany was acknowledged to have similar rights to the islands west of that meridian. The islands of American Samoa were officially ceded to the United States by the various ruling chiefs in 1900 and 1904, and on 20 February 1929 the US Congress formally accepted sovereignty over the entire group. From 1900 to 1951, the territory was administered by the US Department of the Navy, and thereafter by the Department of the Interior. The basic law is the Constitution of 1966.

The executive branch of the government is headed by a governor who, along with the lieutenant governor, is elected by popular vote; before 1977, the two posts were appointed by the US government. Village, county, and district councils have full authority to regulate local affairs.

The legislature (Fono) is composed of the House of Representatives and the Senate. The 15 counties elect 18 *matais* (chiefs) to four-year terms in the senate, while the 20 house members are elected for two-year terms by popular vote within the counties. (There is one appointed member from Swains Island.) The secretary for Samoan affairs, who heads the Department of Local Government, is appointed by the governor. Under his administration are three district governors, the county chiefs, village mayors, and police officials. The judiciary, an independent branch of the government, functions through the high court and five district courts. Samoans living in the islands as of 17 April 1900 or born there since that date are nationals of the United States. The territory sends one delegate to the US House of Representatives.

The economy is primarily agricultural. Small plantations occupy about one-third of the land area; 90% of the land is communally owned. The principal crops are bananas, breadfruit, taro, papayas, pineapples, sweet potatoes, tapioca, coffee, cocoa, and yams. Hogs and poultry are the principal livestock raised; dairy cattle are few. The principal cash crop is copra. A third of the total labor force is employed by the federal and territorial government. The largest employers in the private sector, with more than 15% of the labor force, are two modern tuna canneries supplied with fish caught by Japanese, us, and Taiwanese fishing fleets. Canned tuna is the primary export. Most foreign trade is conducted with the United States.

Samoans are entitled to free medical treatment, including hospital care. Besides district dispensaries, the government maintains a central hospital, a tuberculosis unit, and a leprosarium. US-trained staff physicians work with Samoan medical practitioners and nurses. The LBJ Tropical Medical Center opened in 1986.

Education is a joint undertaking between the territorial government and the villages. School attendance is compulsory for all children from 6 through 18. The villages furnish the elementary-school buildings and living quarters for the teachers; the territorial government pays teachers' salaries and provides buildings and supplies for all but primary schools. Since 1964, educational television has served as a basic teaching tool in the school system. About 97% of the population is literate. In 1997, total enrollment in American Samoa's 29 public elementary and secondary schools was over 19,000. American Samoa Community College enrolled 1,178 in the fall of 2001.

Radiotelegraph circuits connect the territory with Hawaii, Fiji, and Western Samoa. Every village in American Samoa has telephone service.

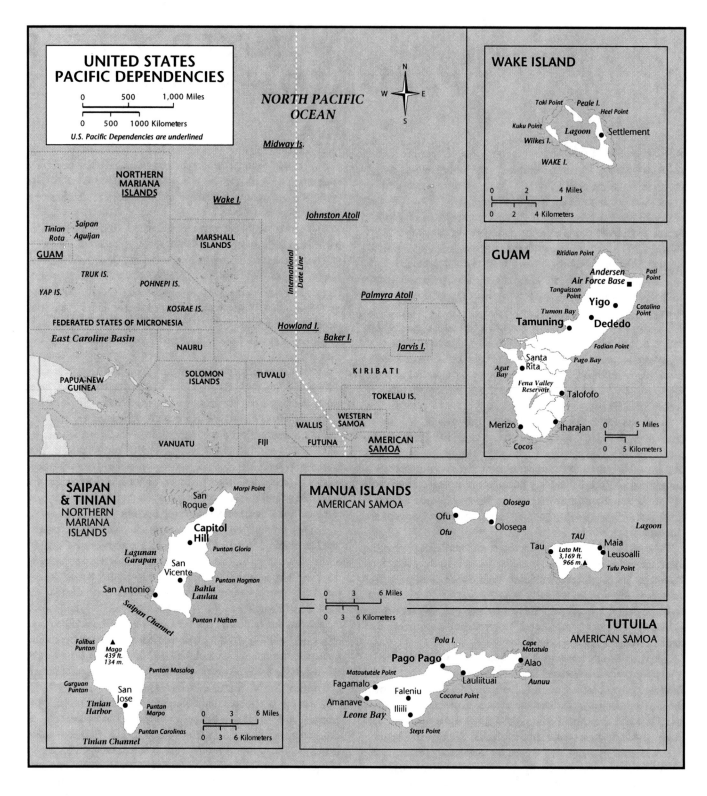

GUAM

The largest and most populous of the Mariana Islands in the Western Pacific, Guam (13° 28′ N and 144° 44′ E) has an area, including land and water, of 540 sq km (208 sq mi) and is about 48 km (30 mi) long and from 6–12 km (4–7 mi) wide. The island is of volcanic origin; in the south, the terrain is mountainous, while the northern part is a plateau with shallow fertile soil. The central part of the island (where the capital, Agana, is located) is undulating country.

Guam lies in the typhoon belt of the Western Pacific and is occasionally subject to widespread storm damage. In May 1976, a typhoon with winds of 306 km/hr (190 mph) struck Guam, causing an estimated $300 million in damage and leaving 80% of the island's buildings in ruins. Guam has a tropical climate with little seasonal variation. Average temperature is 26°C (79°F); rainfall is substantial, reaching an annual average of more than 200 cm (80 in). Endangered species include the giant Micronesian kingfisher and Marianas crow.

The mid-2005 population, excluding transient US military and civilian personnel and their families, was estimated at 168,564, an increase over the 1986 estimate of 117,500. The increase was attributed largely to the higher birthrate and low mortality rate. The present-day Chamorro, who comprise about 37% of the permanent resident population, descend from the intermingling of the few surviving original Chamorro with the Spanish, Filipino, and Mexican settlers, plus later arrivals from the United States, United Kingdom, Korea, China, and Japan. Filipinos (26%) are the largest ethnic minority. English and Chamorro are official languages. The predominant religion is Roman Catholicism.

The earliest known settlers on Guam were the original Chamorro, who migrated from the Malay Peninsula to the Pacific around 1500 BC. When Ferdinand Magellan landed on Guam in 1521, it is believed that as many as 100,000 Chamorro lived on the island; by 1741, their numbers had been reduced to 5,000—most of the population either had fled the island or been killed through disease or war with the Spanish. A Spanish fort was established in 1565, and from 1696 until 1898, Guam was under Spanish rule.

Under the Treaty of Paris that ended the Spanish-American War in 1898, the island was ceded to the United States and placed under the jurisdiction of the Department of the Navy. During World War II, Guam was occupied by Japanese forces; the United States recaptured the island in 1944 after 54 days of fighting. In 1950, the island's administration was transferred from the Navy to the US Department of the Interior. Under the 1950 Organic Act of Guam, passed by the US Congress, the island was established as an unincorporated territory of the United States; Guamanians were granted US citizenship, and internal self-government was introduced.

The governor and lieutenant governor have been elected directly since 1970. A 15-member unicameral legislature elected for two years by adult suffrage is empowered to legislate on all local matters, including taxation and appropriations. The US Congress reserves the right to annul any law passed by the Guam legislature, but must do so within a year of the date it receives the text of any such law.

Judicial authority is vested in the district court of Guam, and appeals may be taken to the regular US courts of appeal and ultimately to the US Supreme Court. An island superior court and other specialized courts have jurisdiction over certain cases arising under the laws of Guam. The judge of the district court is appointed by the US president; the judges of the other courts are appointed by the governor. Guam's laws were codified in 1953.

Guam is one of the most important US military bases in the Pacific, and the island's economy has been profoundly affected by the large sums of money spent by the US defense establishment. During the late 1960s and early 1970s, when the United States took the role of a major combatant in the Vietnam conflict, Guam served as a base for long-range US bombers on sorties over Indochina. In 2005, there were 3,384 active-duty US military personnel stationed on the island.

Prior to World War II, agriculture and animal husbandry were the primary activities. By 1947, most adults were wage earners employed by the US armed forces, although many continued to cultivate small plots to supplement their earnings. In 2002, agriculture accounted for 7% of GDP; a considerable amount of arable land is taken up by military installations. Fruits and vegetables are grown and pigs and poultry are raised for local consumption, but most food is imported. Current fish catches are insufficient to meet local demand.

Tourism became a major industry and sparked a boom in the construction industry in the mid-1980s. The number of visitors grew rapidly from 6,600 in 1967 to around one million per year in the mid-2000s, 90% of whom come from Japan. The stagnation in the Japanese economy since the early 1990s slowed the growth of Guam's tourism sector.

The Guam Rehabilitation Act of 1963 has funded the territory's capital improvement program. Further allocations in 1969 and 1977 provided over $120 million for additional capital improvements and development of the island's power installations. More than $200 million of federal funds were authorized for typhoon relief in 1977–78. Total expenditures by the government of Guam were $445 million in 2000; revenues were $340 million.

Guam's foreign trade usually shows large deficits. The bulk of Guam's trade is with the United States, Japan, Singapore, and South Korea.

US income tax laws are applicable in Guam; all internal revenue taxes derived by the United States from Guam are paid into the territory's treasury. US customs duties, however, are not levied. Guam is a duty-free port. In its trade with the US mainland, Guam is required to use US shipping.

Typical tropical diseases are practically unknown today in Guam. Tuberculosis, long the principal killer, was brought under control by the mid-1950s. The Guam Memorial Hospital has a capacity of 208 beds. Village dispensaries serve both as public health units and first-aid stations. In addition, there are a number of physicians in private practice. Specialists from the US Naval Hospital in Guam, assisting on a part-time basis, have made possible a complete program of curative medicine.

School attendance is compulsory from the age of 6 through 16. Twenty-five elementary schools, seven middle schools, four high schools and an alternative school serve over 30,000 students.

HOWLAND, BAKER, AND JARVIS ISLANDS

Howland Island (0° 48′ N and 176° 38′ W), Baker Island (0° 14′ N and 176° 28′ W), and Jarvis Island (0° 23′ S and 160° 1′ W) are three small coral islands, each about 2.6 sq km (1 sq mi) in area, belonging to the Line Islands group of the Central Pacific Ocean. All are administered directly from Washington as US unincorporated territories. Public entry is by special permit and generally restricted to scientists and educators. Howland was discovered in 1842 by US sailors, claimed by the United States in 1857, and formally proclaimed a US territory in 1935–36. It was worked for guano by US and British companies until about 1890.

Baker, 64 km (40 mi) s of Howland, and Jarvis, 1,770 km (1,100 mi) E of Howland, also were claimed by the United States in 1857, and their guano deposits were similarly worked by US and British enterprises. The United Kingdom annexed Jarvis in 1889. In 1935, the United States sent colonists from Hawaii to all three islands, which were placed under the US Department of the Interior in 1936 and are administered as part of the National Wildlife Refuge system. Baker was captured by the Japanese in 1942 and recaptured by the United States in 1944. The three islands lack fresh water and have no permanent inhabitants. They are visited annually by the US Coast Guard. A lighthouse on Howland Island is named in honor of the US aviatrix Amelia Earhart, who vanished en route to the island on a round-the-world flight in 1937.

JOHNSTON ATOLL

Johnston Atoll, located in the North Pacific 1,151 km (715 mi) SW of Honolulu, consists of two islands, Johnston (16° 44′ N and 169° 31′ W) and Sand (16° 45′ N and 169° 30′ W), with a total land and water area of about 2.6 sq km (1 sq mi). The islands are enclosed by a semicircular reef. It was discovered by English sailors in 1807 and claimed by the United States in 1858. For many years, it was worked for guano and was a bird reservation. Commissioned as a naval station in 1941, it remains an unincorporated US territory under the control of the US Department of the Air Force. In the 1950s and 1960s, it was used primarily for the testing of nuclear weapons. Until late in 2000, it was maintained as a storage and disposal site for chemical weapons. Munitions destruction is now complete, and cleanup and closure of the facility was completed by May 2005.

The population usually stood at 1,100 government personnel and contractors, but decreased significantly after the September 2001 departure of the US Army Chemical Activity Pacific (USACAP). As of May 2005, all US government personnel had left the island. The atoll is equipped with an excellent satellite and radio telecommunications system.

MIDWAY

The Midway Islands (28° 12′–17′ N and 177° 19′–26′ W) consist of an atoll and two small islets, Eastern Island (177° 20′ W) and Sand Island (177° 22′–24′ W), 2,100 km (1,300 mi) WNW of Honolulu. Total land and water area is 5 sq km (2 sq mi). As of 2005, 40 people made up the staff of the US Fish and Wildlife service on the atoll.

Discovered and claimed by the United States in 1859 and formally annexed in 1867, Midway became a submarine cable station early in the 20th century and an airlines station in 1935. Made a US naval base in 1941, Midway was attacked by the Japanese in December 1941 and January 1942. In one of the great battles of World War II, a Japanese naval attack on 3–6 June 1942 was repelled by US warplanes. Midway is a US unincorporated territory; there is a closed naval station, and the islands are important nesting places for seabirds. In 1993, administrative control of Midway was transferred from the US Department of the Navy to the US Department of the Interior's Fish and Wildlife Service.

NORTHERN MARIANAS

The Northern Marianas, a US commonwealth in the Western Pacific Ocean, is comprised of the Mariana Islands excluding Guam (a separate political entity). Located between 12° and 21°N and 144° and 146° E, it consists of 16 volcanic islands with a total land area of about 475 sq km (183.5 sq mi). Only six of the islands are inhabited, and most of the people live on the three largest islands—Rota, 85 sq km (33 sq mi); Saipan, 122 sq km (47 sq mi); and Tinian, 101 sq km (39 sq mi).

The climate is tropical, with relatively little seasonal change; temperatures average 21–29°C (70–85°F), and relative humidity is generally high. Rainfall averages 216 cm (85 in) per year. The southern islands, which include Rota, Saipan, and Tinian, are generally lower and covered with moderately heavy tropical vegetation. The northern islands are more rugged, reaching a high point of 959 m (3,146 ft) on Agrihan, and are generally barren due to erosion and insufficient rainfall. Pagan and Agrihan have active volcanoes, and typhoons are common from August to November. Insects are numerous and ocean birds and fauna are abundant. The Marianas mallard is a local endangered species.

The Northern Marianas had an estimated population of 80,362 in mid-2005. Three-fourths of the population is descended from the original Micronesian inhabitants, known as Chamorros. There are also many descendants of migrants from the Caroline Islands and smaller numbers of Filipino and Korean laborers and settlers from the US mainland. English, Chamorro, and Carolinian are official languages. However, only 10.8% of the population speaks English in the home. About 90% of the people are Roman Catholic.

It is believed that the Marianas were settled by migrants from the Philippines and Indonesia. Excavations on Saipan have yielded evidence of settlement around 1500 BC. The first European to reach the Marianas, in 1521, was Ferdinand Magellan. The islands were ruled by Spain until the Spanish defeat by the United States in the Spanish-American War (1898). Guam was then ceded to the United States and the rest of the Marianas were sold to Germany. When World War I broke out, Japan took over the Northern Marianas and other German-held islands in the Western Pacific. These islands (the Northern Marianas, Carolines, and Marshalls) were placed under Japanese administration as a League of Nations mandate on 17 December 1920. Upon its withdrawal from the League in 1935, Japan began to fortify the islands, and in World War II they served as important military bases. Several of the islands were the scene of heavy fighting during the war. In the battle for control of Saipan in June 1944, some 23,000 Japanese and 3,500 US troops lost their lives in one day's fighting. As each island was occupied by US troops, it became subject to US authority in accordance with the international law of belligerent occupation. The US planes that dropped atomic bombs on Hiroshima and Nagasaki, bringing an end to the war, took off from Tinian.

On 18 July 1947, the Northern Mariana, Caroline, and Marshall islands formally became a UN trust territory under US administration. This Trust Territory of the Pacific Islands was administered by the US Department of the Navy until 1 July 1951, when administration was transferred to the Department of the Interior. From 1953 to 1962, the Northern Marianas, with the exception of Rota, were administered by the Department of the Navy.

The people of the Northern Marianas voted to become a US commonwealth by a majority of 78.8% in a plebiscite held on 17 June 1975. A covenant approved by the US Congress in March 1976 provided for the separation of the Northern Marianas from the Caroline and Marshall island groups, and for the Marianas' transition to a commonwealth status similar to that of Puerto Rico. The islands became internally self-governing in January 1978. On 3 November 1986, US president Ronald Reagan proclaimed the Northern Marianas a self-governing commonwealth; its people became US citizens. The termination of the trusteeship was approved by the UN Trusteeship Council in May 1986 and received the required approval from the UN Security Council. On 3 November 1986, the Constitution of the Commonwealth of the Northern Marianas Islands came into force.

A governor and a lieutenant governor are popularly elected for four-year terms. The legislature consists of 9 senators elected for four-year terms and 18 representatives elected for two-year terms. A district court handles matters involving federal law and a commonwealth court has jurisdiction over local matters.

The traditional economic activities were subsistence agriculture, livestock raising, and fishing, but much agricultural land was destroyed or damaged during World War II and agriculture has never resumed its prewar importance. Garment production and tourism are the mainstays of the economy. Tourism employs about 50% of the work force. The construction industry is also expanding, and there is some small-scale industry, chiefly handicrafts and food processing.

The Northern Marianas is heavily dependent on federal funds. The United States also pays to lease property on Saipan, Tinian, and Farallon de Medinilla islands for defense purposes. The principal exports are garments, milk, and meat; imports include foods, petroleum, construction materials, and vehicles. US currency is the official medium of exchange.

Health care is primarily the responsibility of the commonwealth government and has improved substantially since 1978. Tuberculosis, once the major health problem, has been controlled. There is a hospital on Saipan and health centers on Tinian and Rota. The largest hospital in the commonwealth is a 76-bed, full service facility.

Education is free and compulsory for children between the ages of 8 and 14, and literacy is high. Northern Marianas College had an enrollment of 1,101 in 2006. There are 2 AM, 3 FM, and 1 television stations.

PALMYRA ATOLL

Palmyra, an atoll in the Central Pacific Ocean, containing some 50 islets with a total area of some 10 sq km (4 sq mi), is situated about 1,600 km (1,000 mi) ssw of Honolulu at 5° 52′ N and 162° 5′ W. It was discovered in 1802 by the USS *Palmyra* and formally annexed by the United States in 1912, and was under the jurisdiction of the city of Honolulu until 1959, when Hawaii became the 50th state of the United States. It is now the responsibility of the US Fish and Wildlife Service. The atoll is privately owned by the Nature Conservancy.

Kingman Reef, NW of Palmyra Atoll at 6° 25′ N and 162° 23′ N, was discovered by the United States in 1874, annexed by the United States in 1922, and became a naval reservation in 1934. Now abandoned, it is under the control of the US Department of the Navy. The reef only has an elevation of 1 m (3 ft) and is awash most of the time, making it hazardous for ships.

WAKE ISLAND

Wake Island, actually a coral atoll and three islets (Wake, Peale, and Wilkes) about 8 km (5 mi) long by 3.6 km (2.25 mi) wide, lies in the North Pacific 3,380 km (2,100 mi) w of Honolulu at 19° 17′ N and 166° 35′ E. The total land and water area is about 8 sq km (3 sq mi). Discovered by the British in 1796, Wake was long uninhabited.

In 1898, a US expeditionary force en route to Manila landed on the island. The United States formally claimed Wake in 1899. It was made a US naval reservation in 1934, and became a civil aviation station in 1935. Captured by the Japanese on 23 December 1941, Wake was subsequently the target of several US air raids. It was surrendered by the Japanese in September 1945 and has thereafter remained a US unincorporated territory under the jurisdiction, since 1972, of the Department of the Air Force.

As of 2001, only around 200 contractor personnel inhabited Wake Island. The island was no longer being used for missile launches by the US Army's Space and Strategic Defense Command. It is a stopover and fueling station for civilian and military aircraft flying between Honolulu, Guam, and Japan.

UNITED STATES

United States of America

CAPITAL: Washington, D.C. (District of Columbia). **FLAG:** The flag consists of 13 alternate stripes, 7 red and 6 white; these represent the 13 original colonies. Fifty 5-pointed white stars, representing the present number of states in the Union, are placed in 9 horizontal rows alternately of 6 and 5 against a blue field in the upper left corner of the flag. **OFFICIAL SEAL:** Obverse: An American eagle with outstretched wings bears a shield consisting of 13 alternating white and red stripes with a broad blue band across the top. The right talon clutches an olive branch, representing peace; in the left are 13 arrows, symbolizing military strength. The eagle's beak holds a banner with the motto "E pluribus unum" (From many, one); overhead is a constellation of 13 five-pointed stars in a glory. Reverse: Above a truncated pyramid is an all-seeing eye within a triangle; at the bottom of this triangle appear the roman numerals MDCCLXXVI (1776). The pyramid stands on a grassy ground, against a backdrop of mountains. The words "Annuit Coeptis" (He has favored our undertakings) and, on a banner, "Novus Ordo Seclorum" (A new order of the ages) surround the whole. **ANTHEM:** The Star-Spangled Banner. **MOTTO:** In God We Trust. **MONETARY UNIT:** The dollar ($) of 100 cents is a paper currency with a floating rate. There are coins of 1, 5, 10, 25, and 50 cents and 1 dollar, and notes of 1, 2, 5, 10, 20, 50, and 100 dollars. Although issuance of higher notes ceased in 1969, a limited number of notes of 500, 1,000, 5,000, and 10,000 dollars remain in circulation. A gold-colored 1 dollar coin featuring Sacagawea was introduced in 2000. **WEIGHTS AND MEASURES:** The imperial system is in common use; however, the use of metrics in industry is increasing, and the metric system is taught in public schools throughout the United States. Common avoirdupois units in use are the avoirdupois pound of 16 oz or 453.5924277 gm; the long ton of 2,240 lb or 35,840 oz; and the short ton, more commonly used, of 2,000 lb or 32,000 oz. (Unless otherwise indicated, all measures given in tons are in short tons.) Liquid measures: 1 gallon = 231 cu in = 4 quarts = 8 pints. Dry measures: 1 bushel = 4 pecks = 32 dry quarts = 64 dry pints. Linear measures: 1 ft = 12 in; 1 statute mi = 1,760 yd = 5,280 ft. Metric equivalent: 1 m = 39.37 in. **FEDERAL HOLIDAYS:** New Year's Day, 1 January; Birthday of Martin Luther King, Jr., 3rd Monday in January; Lincoln's Birthday, 12 February (only in the northern and western states); Washington's Birthday, 3rd Monday in February; Memorial or Decoration Day, last Monday in May; Independence Day, 4 July; Labor Day, 1st Monday in September; Columbus Day, 2nd Monday in October; Election Day, 1st Tuesday after the 1st Monday in November; Veterans or Armistice Day, 11 November; Thanksgiving Day, 4th Thursday in November; Christmas, 25 December. **TIME:** Eastern, 7 am = noon GMT; Central, 6 am = noon GMT; Mountain, 5 am = noon GMT; Pacific (includes the Alaska panhandle), 4 am = noon GMT; Yukon, 3 am = noon GMT; Alaska and Hawaii, 2 am = noon GMT; western Alaska, 1 am = noon GMT.

¹LOCATION, SIZE, AND EXTENT

Located in the Western Hemisphere on the continent of North America, the United States is the fourth-largest country in the world. Its total area, including Alaska and Hawaii, is 9,629,091 sq km (3,717,813 sq mi). The conterminous United States extends 4,662 km (2,897 mi) ENE—WSW and 4,583 km (2,848 mi) SSE–NNW. It is bordered on the N by Canada, on the E by the Atlantic Ocean, on the S by the Gulf of Mexico and Mexico, and on the W by the Pacific Ocean, with a total boundary length of 17,563 km (10,913 mi). Alaska, the 49th state, extends 3,639 km (2,261 mi) E–W and 2,185 km (1,358 mi) N–S. It is bounded on the N by the Arctic Ocean and Beaufort Sea, on the E by Canada, on the S by the Gulf of Alaska, Pacific Ocean and Bering Sea, and on the W by the Bering Sea, Bering Strait, Chukchi Sea, and Arctic Ocean, with a total land boundary of 12,034 km (7,593 mi) and a coastline of 19,924 km (12,380 mi). The 50th state, Hawaii, consists of islands in the Pacific Ocean extending 2,536 km (1,576 mi) N–S

and 2,293 km (1,425 mi) E–W, with a general coastline of 1,207 km (750 mi).

The nation's capital, Washington, D.C., is located on the mid-Atlantic coast.

²TOPOGRAPHY

Although the northern New England coast is rocky, along the rest of the eastern seaboard the Atlantic Coastal Plain rises gradually from the shoreline. Narrow in the north, the plain widens to about 320 km (200 mi) in the south and in Georgia merges with the Gulf Coastal Plain that borders the Gulf of Mexico and extends through Mexico as far as the Yucatán. West of the Atlantic Coastal Plain is the Piedmont Plateau, bounded by the Appalachian Mountains. The Appalachians, which extend from southwest Maine into central Alabama—with special names in some areas—are old mountains, largely eroded away, with rounded contours and forested, as a rule, to the top. Few of their summits rise much above 1,100 m

(3,500 ft), although the highest, Mt. Mitchell in North Carolina, reaches 2,037 m (6,684 ft).

Between the Appalachians and the Rocky Mountains, more than 1,600 km (1,000 mi) to the west, lies the vast interior plain of the United States. Running south through the center of this plain and draining almost two-thirds of the area of the continental United States is the Mississippi River. Waters starting from the source of the Missouri, the longest of its tributaries, travel almost 6,450 km (4,000 mi) to the Gulf of Mexico.

The eastern reaches of the great interior plain are bounded on the north by the Great Lakes, which are thought to contain about half the world's total supply of fresh water. Under US jurisdiction are 57,441 sq km (22,178 sq mi) of Lake Michigan, 54,696 sq km (21,118 sq mi) of Lake Superior, 23,245 sq km (8,975 sq mi) of Lake Huron, 12,955 sq km (5,002 sq mi) of Lake Erie, and 7,855 sq km (3,033 sq mi) of Lake Ontario. The five lakes are now accessible to oceangoing vessels from the Atlantic via the St. Lawrence Seaway. The basins of the Great Lakes were formed by the glacial ice cap that moved down over large parts of North America some 25,000 years ago. The glaciers also determined the direction of flow of the Missouri River and, it is believed, were responsible for carrying soil from what is now Canada down into the central agricultural basin of the United States.

The great interior plain consists of two major subregions: the fertile Central Plains, extending from the Appalachian highlands to a line drawn approximately 480 km (300 mi) west of the Mississippi, broken by the Ozark Plateau; and the more arid Great Plains, extending from that line to the foothills of the Rocky Mountains. Although they appear flat, the Great Plains rise gradually from about 460 m (1,500 ft) to more than 1,500 m (5,000 ft) at their western extremity.

The Continental Divide, the Atlantic-Pacific watershed, runs along the crest of the Rocky Mountains. The Rockies and the ranges to the west are parts of the great system of young, rugged mountains, shaped like a gigantic spinal column, that runs along western North, Central, and South America from Alaska to Tierra del Fuego, Chile. In the continental United States, the series of western ranges, most of them paralleling the Pacific coast, are the Sierra Nevada, the Coast Ranges, the Cascade Range, and the Tehachapi and San Bernardino mountains. Between the Rockies and the Sierra Nevada–Cascade mountain barrier to the west lies the Great Basin, a group of vast arid plateaus containing most of the desert areas of the United States, in the south eroded by deep canyons.

The coastal plains along the Pacific are narrow, and in many places the mountains plunge directly into the sea. The most extensive lowland near the west coast is the Great Valley of California, lying between the Sierra Nevada and the Coast Ranges. There are 71 peaks in these western ranges of the continental United States that rise to an altitude of 4,267 m (14,000 ft) or more, Mt. Whitney in California at 4,418 m (14,494 ft) being the highest. The greatest rivers of the Far West are the Colorado in the south, flowing into the Gulf of California, and the Columbia in the northwest, flowing to the Pacific. Each is more than 1,900 km (1,200 mi) long; both have been intensively developed to generate electric power, and both are important sources of irrigation.

Separated from the continental United States by Canadian territory, the state of Alaska occupies the extreme northwest portion of the North American continent. A series of precipitous mountain ranges separates the heavily indented Pacific coast on the south from Alaska's broad central basin, through which the Yukon River flows from Canada in the east to the Bering Sea in the west. The central basin is bounded on the north by the Brooks Range, which slopes down gradually to the Arctic Ocean. The Alaskan Peninsula and the Aleutian Islands, sweeping west far out to sea, consist of a chain of volcanoes, many still active.

The state of Hawaii consists of a group of Pacific islands formed by volcanoes rising sharply from the ocean floor. The highest of these volcanoes, Mauna Loa, at 4,168 m (13,675 ft), is located on the largest of the islands, Hawaii, and is still active.

The lowest point in the United States is Death Valley in California, 86 m (282 ft) below sea level. At 6,194 m (20,320 ft), Mt. McKinley in Alaska is the highest peak in North America. These topographic extremes suggest the geological instability of the Pacific Coast region, which is part of the "Ring of Fire," a seismically active band surrounding the Pacific Ocean. Major earthquakes destroyed San Francisco in 1906 and Anchorage, Alaska, in 1964, and the San Andreas Fault in California still causes frequent earth tremors. In 2004, there was a total of 3550 U.S. earthquakes documented by the United States Geological Survey National Earthquake Information Center. Washington State's Mt. St. Helens erupted in 1980, spewing volcanic ash over much of the Northwest.

3 CLIMATE

The eastern continental region is well watered, with annual rainfall generally in excess of 100 cm (40 in). It includes all of the Atlantic seaboard and southeastern states and extends west to cover Indiana, southern Illinois, most of Missouri, Arkansas, Louisiana, and easternmost Texas. The eastern seaboard is affected primarily by the masses of air moving from west to east across the continent rather than by air moving in from the Atlantic. Hence its climate is basically continental rather than maritime. The midwestern and Atlantic seaboard states experience hot summers and cold winters; spring and autumn are clearly defined periods of climatic transition. Only Florida, with the Gulf of Mexico lying to its west, experiences moderate differences between summer and winter temperatures. Mean annual temperatures vary considerably between north and south: Boston, 11°C (51°F); New York City, 13°C (55°F); Charlotte, N.C., 16°C (61°F); Miami, Fla., 24°C (76°F).

The Gulf and South Atlantic states are often hit by severe tropical storms originating in the Caribbean in late summer and early autumn. In the past few years, the number of hurricanes and their severity have measurably increased. From 1970–94, there were about three hurricanes per year. From 1995 to 2003, there were a total of 32 major hurricanes with sustained winds of 111 miles per hour or greater.

In 2005 there were a record-breaking 23 named Atlantic hurricanes, three of which caused severe damage to the Gulf Coast region. On 25 August 2005, Hurricane Katrina hit Florida as a category 1 hurricane. By 29 August, the storm developed into a category 4 hurricane that made landfall in southern Louisiana. Several levees protecting the low-lying city of New Orleans broke, flooding the entire region under waters that rose over the rooftops of homes. Over 1,000 were killed by the storm. Over 500,000 people were left homeless and without jobs.

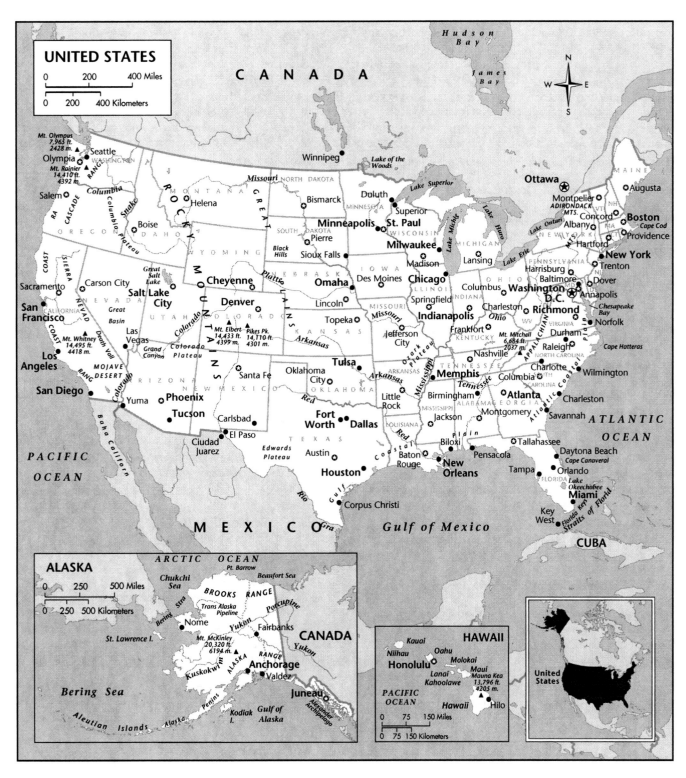

LOCATION: Conterminous US: 66°57′ to 124°44′ W; 24°33′ to 49°23′ N. Alaska: 130° W to 172°28′ E; 51° to 71°23′ N. Hawaii: 154°48′ to 178°22′ W 18°55′ to 28°25′ N. **BOUND-ARY LENGTHS:** Conterminous US: Canada, 6,416 kilometers (3,987 miles); Atlantic Ocean, 3,330 kilometers (2,069 miles); Gulf of Mexico coastline, 2,625 kilometers (1,631 miles); Mexico, 3,111 kilometers (1,933 miles); Pacific coastline, 2,081 kilometers (1,293 miles). Alaska: Arctic Ocean coastline, 1,706 kilometers (1,060 miles); Canada, 2,475 kilometers (1,538 miles); Pacific coastline, including the Bering Sea and Strait and Chukchi coastlines, 8,980 kilometers (5,580 miles). Hawaii: coastline, 1,207 kilometers (750 miles).

One month later, Hurricane Rita swept first into Florida and continued to make landfall between Sabine Pass, Texas, and Johnson's Bayou, Louisiana, on 24 September 2005 as a category 3 hurricane. Before reaching land, however, the storm had peaked as a category 5 hurricane that was placed on record as the strongest measured hurricane to ever have entered the Gulf of Mexico and the fourth most intense hurricane ever in the Atlantic Basin. Over 100 people were killed.

Hurricane Wilma followed on 24 October when it made landfall north of Everglades City in Florida as a category 3 hurricane. There were about 22 deaths in the United States from Wilma; however, the storm also hit Cuba, Haiti, Jamaica, and Mexico, reaching a death toll of at least 25 people from those countries combined.

The prairie lands lying to the west constitute a subhumid region. Precipitation usually exceeds evaporation by only a small amount; hence the region experiences drought more often than excessive rainfall. Dryness generally increases from east to west. The average midwinter temperature in the extreme north—Minnesota and North Dakota—is about –13°C (9°F) or less, while the average July temperature is 18°C (65 °F). In the Texas prairie region to the south, January temperatures average 10–13°C (50–55 °F) and July temperatures 27–29°C (80–85 °F). Rainfall along the western border of the prairie region is as low as 46 cm (18 in) per year in the north and 64 cm (25 in) in the south. Precipitation is greatest in the early summer—a matter of great importance to agriculture, particularly in the growing of grain crops. In dry years, the prevailing winds may carry the topsoil eastward (particularly from the southern region) for hundreds of miles in clouds that obscure the sun.

The Great Plains constitute a semiarid climatic region. Rainfall in the southern plains averages about 50 cm (20 in) per year and in the northern plains about 25 cm (10 in), but extreme year-to-year variations are common. The tropical air masses that move northward across the plains originate on the fairly high plateaus of Mexico and contain little water vapor. Periods as long as 120 days without rain have been experienced in this region. The rains that do occur are often violent, and a third of the total annual rainfall may be recorded in a single day at certain weather stations. The contrast between summer and winter temperatures is extreme throughout the Great Plains. Maximum summer temperatures of over 43°C (110°F) have been recorded in the northern as well as in the southern plains. From the Texas panhandle north, blizzards are common in the winter, and tornadoes at other seasons. The average minimum temperature for January in Duluth, Minn., is –19°C (–3 °F).

The higher reaches of the Rockies and the mountains paralleling the Pacific coast to the west are characterized by a typical alpine climate. Precipitation as a rule is heavier on the western slopes of the ranges. The great intermontane arid region of the West shows considerable climatic variation between its northern and southern portions. In New Mexico, Arizona, and southeastern California, the greatest precipitation occurs in July, August, and September, mean annual rainfall ranging from 8 cm (3 in) in Yuma, Ariz., to 76 cm (30 in) in the mountains of northern Arizona and New Mexico. Phoenix has a mean annual temperature of 22°C (71°F), rising to 33°C (92°F) in July and falling to 11°C (52°F) in January. North of the Utah-Arizona line, the summer months usually are very dry; maximum precipitation occurs in the winter and early spring. In the desert valleys west of Great Salt Lake, mean annual precipitation adds up to only 10 cm (4 in). Although the northern plateaus are generally arid, some of the mountainous areas of central Washington and Idaho receive at least 152 cm (60 in) of rain per year. Throughout the intermontane region, the uneven availability of water is the principal factor shaping the habitat.

The Pacific coast, separated by tall mountain barriers from the severe continental climate to the east, is a region of mild winters and moderately warm, dry summers. Its climate is basically maritime, the westerly winds from the Pacific Ocean moderating the extremes of both winter and summer temperatures. Los Angeles in the south has an average temperature of 13°C (56 °F) in January and 21°C (69°F) in July; Seattle in the north has an average temperature of 4°C (39 °F) in January and 18°C (65°F) in July. Precipitation in general increases along the coast from south to north, extremes ranging from an annual average of 4.52 cm (1.78 in) at Death Valley in California (the lowest in the United States) to more than 356 cm (140 in) in Washington's Olympic Mountains.

Climatic conditions vary considerably in the vastness of Alaska. In the fogbound Aleutians and in the coastal panhandle strip that extends southeastward along the Gulf of Alaska and includes the capital, Juneau, a relatively moderate maritime climate prevails. The interior is characterized by short, hot summers and long, bitterly cold winters, and in the region bordering the Arctic Ocean a polar climate prevails, the soil hundreds of feet below the surface remaining frozen the year round. Although snowy in winter, continental Alaska is relatively dry.

Hawaii has a remarkably mild and stable climate with only slight seasonal variations in temperature, as a result of northeast ocean winds. The mean January temperature in Honolulu is 23°C (73 °F); the mean July temperature 27°C (80 °F). Rainfall is moderate—about 71 cm (28 in) per year—but much greater in the mountains;

United States—Outlying Areas of the United States[1]

NAME	AREA SQ MI	SQ KM	CAPITAL	YEAR OF ACQUISITION	POPULATION 1980	POPULATION 1999
Puerto Rico	3,515	9,104	San Juan	1898	3,196,520	3,887,652
Virgin Islands of the United States	136	352	Charlotte Amalie	1917	96,569	119,827
Trust Territory of the Pacific Islands, of which:	713	1,847	Saipan	1947	132,929	87,865
Northern Marianas[2]	182	471	Saipan[3]	–	16,780	69,398
Republic of Palau[2]	191	495	Koror[3]	–	12,116	18,467
Other Pacific territories:						
American Samoa	77	199	Pago Pago	1899	32,297	63,786
Guam	209	541	Agaña	1898	105,979	151,716
Midway Islands	2	5	–	1867	468	n.a.
Wake Island	3	8	–	1899	302	n.a.

[1]Excludes minor and uninhabited islands.
[2]Although governed under separate constitutional arrangements by the mid–1980s, these territories formally remained part of the Trust Territory of the Pacific Islands pending action by the US Congress, the US president, and the UN Security Council.
[3]Centers of constitutional government. The entire Trust Territory of the Pacific Islands is administered from Saipan.

Mt. Waialeale on Kauai has a mean annual rainfall of 1,168 cm (460 in), highest in the world.

The lowest temperature recorded in the United States was -62°c (-79.8°F) at Prospect Creek Camp, Alaska, on 23 January 1971; the highest, 57°c (134° F) at Greenland Ranch, in Death Valley, Calif., on 10 July 1913. The record annual rainfall is 1,878 cm (739 in) recorded at Kukui, Maui in 1982; the previous record for a one-year period was 1,468 cm (578 in) recorded at Fuu Kukui, Maui, in 1950; in 1 hour, 30 cm (12 in), at Holt, Mo., on 22 June 1947, and on Kauai, Hawaii, on 24–25 January 1956.

[4] FLORA AND FAUNA

At least 7,000 species and subspecies of indigenous US flora have been categorized. The eastern forests contain a mixture of soft-woods and hardwoods that includes pine, oak, maple, spruce, beech, birch, hemlock, walnut, gum, and hickory. The central hardwood forest, which originally stretched unbroken from Cape Cod to Texas and northwest to Minnesota—still an important timber source—supports oak, hickory, ash, maple, and walnut. Pine, hickory, tupelo, pecan, gum, birch, and sycamore are found in the southern forest that stretches along the Gulf coast into the eastern half of Texas. The Pacific forest is the most spectacular of all because of its enormous redwoods and Douglas firs. In the southwest are saguaro (giant cactus), yucca, candlewood, and the Joshua tree.

The central grasslands lie in the interior of the continent, where the moisture is not sufficient to support the growth of large forests. The tall grassland or prairie (now almost entirely under cultivation) lies to the east of the 100th meridian. To the west of this line, where rainfall is frequently less than 50 cm (20 in) per year, is the short grassland. Mesquite grass covers parts of west Texas, southern New Mexico, and Arizona. Short grass may be found in the highlands of the latter two states, while tall grass covers large portions of the coastal regions of Texas and Louisiana and occurs in some parts of Mississippi, Alabama, and Florida. The Pacific grassland includes northern Idaho, the higher plateaus of eastern Washington and Oregon, and the mountain valleys of California.

The intermontane region of the Western Cordillera is for the most part covered with desert shrubs. Sagebrush predominates in the northern part of this area, creosote in the southern, with salt-brush near the Great Salt Lake and in Death Valley.

The lower slopes of the mountains running up to the coastline of Alaska are covered with coniferous forests as far north as the Seward Peninsula. The central part of the Yukon Basin is also a region of softwood forests. The rest of Alaska is heath or tundra. Hawaii has extensive forests of bamboo and ferns. Sugarcane and pineapple, although not native to the islands, now cover a large portion of the cultivated land.

Small trees and shrubs common to most of the United States include hackberry, hawthorn, serviceberry, blackberry, wild cherry, dogwood, and snowberry. Wildflowers bloom in all areas, from the seldom-seen blossoms of rare desert cacti to the hardiest alpine species. Wildflowers include forget-me-not, fringed and closed gentians, jack-in-the-pulpit, black-eyed Susan, columbine, and common dandelion, along with numerous varieties of aster, orchid, lady's slipper, and wild rose.

An estimated 428 species of mammals characterize the animal life of the continental United States. Among the larger game ani-

mals are the white-tailed deer, moose, pronghorn antelope, bighorn sheep, mountain goat, black bear, and grizzly bear. The Alaskan brown bear often reaches a weight of 1,200–1,400 lbs. Some 25 important furbearers are common, including the muskrat, red and gray foxes, mink, raccoon, beaver, opossum, striped skunk, woodchuck, common cottontail, snowshoe hare, and various squirrels. Human encroachment has transformed the mammalian habitat over the last two centuries. The American buffalo (bison), millions of which once roamed the plains, is now found only on select reserves. Other mammals, such as the elk and gray wolf, have been restricted to much smaller ranges.

Year-round and migratory birds abound. Loons, wild ducks, and wild geese are found in lake country; terns, gulls, sandpipers, herons, and other seabirds live along the coasts. Wrens, thrushes, owls, hummingbirds, sparrows, woodpeckers, swallows, chickadees, vireos, warblers, and finches appear in profusion, along with the robin, common crow, cardinal, Baltimore oriole, eastern and western meadowlarks, and various blackbirds. Wild turkey, ruffed grouse, and ring-necked pheasant (introduced from Europe) are popular game birds. There are at least 508 species of birds found throughout the country.

Lakes, rivers, and streams teem with trout, bass, perch, muskellunge, carp, catfish, and pike; sea bass, cod, snapper, and flounder are abundant along the coasts, along with such shellfish as lobster, shrimp, clams, oysters, and mussels. Garter, pine, and milk snakes are found in most regions. Four poisonous snakes survive, of which the rattlesnake is the most common. Alligators appear in southern waterways and the Gila monster makes its home in the Southwest.

Laws and lists designed to protect threatened and endangered flora and fauna have been adopted throughout the United States. Generally, each species listed as protected by the federal government is also protected by the states, but some states may list species not included on federal lists or on the lists of neighboring states. (Conversely, a species threatened throughout most of the United States may be abundant in one or two states.) As of November 2005, the US Fish and Wildlife Service listed 997 endangered US species (up from 751 listed in 1996), including 68 species of mammals, 77 birds, 74 fish, and 599 plants; and 275 threatened species (209 in 1996), including 11 species of mammals, 13 birds, 42 fish, and 146 plants. The agency listed another 520 endangered and 46 threatened foreign species by international agreement.

Threatened species, likely to become endangered if recent trends continue, include such plants as Lee pincushion cactus. Among the endangered floral species (in imminent danger of extinction in the wild) are the Virginia round-leaf birch, San Clemente Island broom, Texas wild-rice, Furbish lousewort, Truckee barberry, Sneed pincushion cactus, spineless hedgehog cactus, Knowlton cactus, persistent trillium, dwarf bear-poppy, and small whorled pogonia.

Endangered mammals included the red wolf, black-footed ferret, jaguar, key deer, northern swift fox, San Joaquin kit fox, jaguar, jaguarundi, Florida manatee, ocelot, Florida panther, Utah prairie dog, Sonoran pronghorn, and numerous whale species. Endangered species of rodents included the Delmarva Peninsula fox squirrel, beach mouse, salt-marsh harvest mouse, 7 species of bat (Virginia and Ozark big-eared Sanborn's and Mexican long-nosed,

Hawaiian hoary, Indiana, and gray), and the Morro Ba, Fresno, Stephens', and Tipton Kangaroo rats and rice rat.

Endangered species of birds included the California condor, bald eagle, three species of falcon (American peregrine, tundra peregrine, and northern aplomado), Eskimo curlew, two species of crane (whooping and Mississippi sandhill), three species of warbler (Kirtland's, Bachman's, and golden-cheeked), dusky seaside sparrow, light-footed clapper rail, least tern, San Clemente loggerhead shrike, bald eagle (endangered in most states, but only threatened in the Northwest and the Great Lakes region), Hawaii creeper, Everglade kite, California clapper rail, and red-cockaded woodpecker. Endangered amphibians included four species of salamander (Santa Cruz long-toed, Shenandoah, desert slender, and Texas blind), Houston and Wyoming toad, and six species of turtle (green sea, hawksbill, Kemp's ridley, Plymouth and Alabama redbellied, and leatherback). Endangered reptiles included the American crocodile, (blunt nosed leopard and island night), and San Francisco garter snake.

Aquatic species included the shortnose sturgeon, Gila trout, eight species of chub (humpback, Pahranagat, Yaqui, Mohave tui, Owens tui, bonytail, Virgin River, and Borax lake), Colorado River squawfish, five species of dace (Kendall Warm Springs, and Clover Valley, Independence Valley, Moapa and Ash Meadows speckled), Modoc sucker, cui-ui, Smoky and Scioto madtom, seven species of pupfish (Leon Springs, Gila Desert, Ash Meadows Amargosa, Warm Springs, Owens, Devil's Hole, and Comanche Springs), Pahrump killifish, four species of gambusia (San Marcos, Pecos, Amistad, Big Bend, and Clear Creek), six species of darter (fountain, watercress, Okaloosa, boulder, Maryland, and amber), totoaba, and 32 species of mussel and pearly mussel. Also classified as endangered were two species of earthworm (Washington giant and Oregon giant), the Socorro isopod, San Francisco forktail damselfly, Ohio emerald dragonfly, three species of beetle (Kretschmarr Cave, Tooth Cave, and giant carrion), Belkin's dune tabanid fly, and 10 species of butterfly (Schaus' swallowtail, lotis, mission, El Segundo, and Palos Verde blue, Mitchell's satyr, Uncompahgre fritillary, Lange's metalmark, San Bruno elfin, and Smith's blue).

Endangered plants in the United States include: aster, cactus, pea, mustard, mint, mallow, bellflower and pink family, snapdragon, and buckwheat. Several species on the federal list of endangered and threatened wildlife and plants are found only in Hawaii. Endangered bird species in Hawaii included the Hawaiian darkrumped petrel, Hawaiian gallinule, Hawaiian crow, three species of thrush (Kauai, Molokai, and puaiohi), Kauai 'o'o, Kauai nukupu'u, Kauai 'alialoa, 'akiapola'au, Maui'akepa, Molokai creeper, Oahu creeper, palila, and 'o'u.

Species formerly listed as threatened or endangered that have been removed from the list include (with delisting year and reason) American alligator (1987, recovered); coastal cutthroat trout (2000, taxonomic revision); Bahama swallowtail butterfly (1984, amendment); gray whale (1994, recovered); brown pelican (1984, recovered); Rydberg milk-vetch (1987, new information); Lloyd's hedgehog cactus (1999, taxonomic revision), and Columbian white-tailed Douglas County Deer (2003, recovered).

There are at least 250 species of plants and animals that have become extinct, including the Wyoming toad, the Central Valley

grasshopper, Labrador duck, Carolina parakeet, Hawaiian crow, chestnut moth, and the Franklin tree.

5 ENVIRONMENTAL PROTECTION

The Council on Environmental Quality, an advisory body contained within the Executive Office of the President, was established by the National Environmental Policy Act of 1969, which mandated an assessment of environmental impact for every federally funded project. The Environmental Protection Agency (EPA), created in 1970, is an independent body with primary regulatory responsibility in the fields of air and noise pollution, water and waste management, and control of toxic substances. Other federal agencies with environmental responsibilities are the Forest Service and Soil Conservation Service within the Department of Agriculture, the Fish and Wildlife Service and the National Park Service within the Department of the Interior, the Department of Energy, and the Nuclear Regulatory Commission. In addition to the 1969 legislation, landmark federal laws protecting the environment include the Clean Air Act Amendments of 1970 and 1990, controlling automobile and electric utility emissions; the Water Pollution Act of 1972, setting clean-water criteria for fishing and swimming; and the Endangered Species Act of 1973, protecting wildlife near extinction.

A measure enacted in December 1980 established a $1.6-billion "Superfund," financed largely by excise taxes on chemical companies, to clean up toxic waste dumps such as the one in the Love Canal district of Niagara Falls, N.Y. In 2005, there were 1,238 hazardous waste sites on the Superfund's national priority list.

The most influential environmental lobbies include the Sierra Club (founded in 1892; 700,000 members in 2003) and its legal arm, the Sierra Club Legal Defense Fund. Large conservation groups include the National Wildlife Federation (1936; over 4,000,000), the National Audubon Society (1905; 600,000), and the Nature Conservancy (1917; 1,000,000). Greenpeace USA (founded in 1979) has gained international attention by seeking to disrupt hunts for whales and seals.

Among the environmental movement's most notable successes have been the inauguration (and mandating in some states) of recycling programs; the banning in the United States of the insecticide dichlorodiphenyltrichloroethane (DDT); the successful fight against construction of a supersonic transport (SST); and the protection of more than 40 million hectares (100 million acres) of Alaska lands (after a fruitless fight to halt construction of the trans-Alaska pipeline); and the gradual elimination of chlorofluorocarbon (CFC) production by 2000. In March 2003, the US Senate narrowly voted to reject a Bush administration plan to begin oil exploration in the 19 million acre (7.7 million hectare) Arctic National Wildlife Refuge (ANWR). In 2003, about 25.9% of the total land area was protected. The United States has 12 natural UNESCO World Heritage Sites and 22 Ramsar wetland sites. Yellowstone National Park, founded in 1872, was the first national park established worldwide.

Outstanding problems include acid rain (precipitation contaminated by fossil fuel wastes); inadequate facilities for solid waste disposal; air pollution from industrial emissions (the United States leads the world in carbon dioxide emissions from the burning of fossil fuels); the contamination of homes by radon, a radio-

United States—State Areas, Entry Dates, and Populations

STATE	TOTAL AREA SQ MILE	TOTAL AREA SQ KM	RANK	CAPITAL	ENTRY ORDER	DATE OF ENTRY	POPULATION AT ENTRY†	POPULATION CENSUS 1990	POPULATION CENSUS 2000
Alabama	51,705	133,916	19	Montgomery	22	14 December 1819	127,901	4,040,587	4,447,100
Alaska	591,004	1,530,699	1	Juneau	49	3 January 1959	226,167	550,043	626,932
Arizona	114,000	295,260	6	Phoenix	48	14 February 1912	204,354	3,665,228	5,130,632
Arkansas	53,187	137,754	27	Little Rock	25	15 June 1836	57,574	2,350,725	2,673,400
California	158,706	411,048	3	Sacramento	31	9 September 1850	92,597	29,760,021	33,871,648
Colorado	104,091	269,595	8	Denver	38	1 August 1876	39,864	3,294,394	4,301,261
Connecticut*	5,018	12,997	48	Hartford	5	9 January 1788	237,946	3,287,116	3,405,565
Delaware*	2,044	5,294	49	Dover	1	7 December 1787	59,096	666,168	783,600
Florida	58,664	151,940	22	Tallahassee	27	3 March 1845	87,445	12,937,926	15,982,378
Georgia*	58,910	152,577	21	Atlanta	4	2 January 1788	82,548	6,478,316	8,186,453
Hawaii	6,471	16,760	47	Honolulu	50	21 August 1959	632,772	1,108,229	1,211,537
Idaho	83,564	216,431	13	Boise	43	3 July 1890	88,548	1,006,749	1,293,953
Illinois	56,345	145,933	24	Springfield	21	3 December 1818	55,211	11,430,602	12,419,293
Indiana	36,185	93,719	38	Indianapolis	19	11 December 1816	147,178	5,544,159	6,080,485
Iowa	56,275	145,752	25	Des Moines	29	28 December 1846	192,214	2,776,755	2,926,324
Kansas	82,277	213,097	14	Topeka	34	29 January 1861	107,206	2,477,574	2,688,418
Kentucky	40,409	104,659	37	Frankfort	15	1 June 1792	73,677	3,685,296	4,041,769
Louisiana	47,752	123,678	31	Baton Rouge	18	30 April 1812	76,556	4,219,973	4,468,976
Maine	33,265	86,156	39	Augusta	23	15 March 1820	298,335	1,227,928	1,274,923
Maryland*	10,460	27,091	42	Annapolis	7	28 April 1788	319,728	4,781,468	5,296,486
Massachusetts*	8,284	21,456	45	Boston	6	6 February 1788	378,787	6,016,425	6,349,097
Michigan	58,527	151,585	23	Lansing	26	26 January 1837	212,267	9,295,297	9,938,444
Minnesota	84,402	218,601	12	St. Paul	32	11 May 1858	172,023	4,375,099	4,919,497
Mississippi	47,689	123,514	32	Jackson	20	10 December 1817	75,448	2,573,216	2,844,658
Missouri	69,697	180,515	19	Jefferson City	24	10 August 1821	66,586	5,117,073	5,595,211
Montana	147,046	380,849	4	Helena	41	8 November 1889	142,924	799,065	902,195
Nebraska	77,355	200,349	15	Lincoln	37	1 March 1867	122,993	1,578,385	1,711,263
Nevada	110,561	286,353	7	Carson City	36	31 October 1864	42,491	1,201,833	1,998,257
New Hampshire*	9,279	24,033	44	Concord	9	21 June 1788	141,885	1,109,252	1,235,786
New Jersey*	7,787	20,168	46	Trenton	3	18 December 1787	184,139	7,730,188	8,414,350
New Mexico	121,593	314,926	5	Santa Fe	47	6 January 1912	327,301	1,515,069	1,819,046
New York*	49,108	127,190	30	Albany	11	26 July 1788	340,120	17,990,455	18,976,457
North Carolina*	52,669	136,413	28	Raleigh	12	21 November 1789	393,751	6,628,637	8,049,313
North Dakota	70,702	183,118	17	Bismarck	39	2 November 1889	190,983	638,800	642,200
Ohio	41,330	107,045	35	Columbus	17	1 March 1803††	43,365	10,847,115	11,353,140
Oklahoma	69,956	181,186	18	Oklahoma City	46	16 November 1907	657,155	3,145,585	3,450,654
Oregon	97,073	251,419	10	Salem	33	14 February 1859	52,465	2,842,321	3,421,399
Pennsylvania*	45,308	117,348	33	Harrisburg	2	12 December 1787	434,373	11,003,464	12,281,054
Rhode Island*	1,212	3,139	50	Providence	13	29 May 1790	68,825	1,003,464	1,048,319
South Carolina*	31,113	80,583	40	Columbia	8	23 May 1788	393,751	3,486,703	4,012,012
South Dakota	77,116	199,730	16	Pierre	40	2 November 1889	348,600	696,004	754,844
Tennessee	42,144	109,153	34	Nashville	16	1 June 1796	35,691	4,877,185	5,689,283
Texas	266,807	691,030	2	Austin	28	29 December 1845	212,592	16,986,510	20,851,820
Utah	84,899	219,888	11	Salt Lake City	45	4 January 1896	276,749	1,722,850	2,233,169
Vermont	9,614	24,900	43	Montpelier	14	4 March 1791	85,425	562,758	608,827
Virginia*	40,767	105,586	36	Richmond	10	25 June 1788	747,610	6,187,358	7,078,515
Washington	68,139	176,480	20	Olympia	42	11 November 1889	357,232	4,866,692	5,894,121
West Virginia	24,231	62,758	41	Charleston	35	20 June 1863	442,014	1,793,477	1,808,344
Wisconsin	56,153	145,436	26	Madison	30	29 May 1848	305,391	4,891,769	5,363,675
Wyoming	97,809	253,325	9	Cheyenne	44	10 July 1890	62,555	453,588	493,782

†Census closest to entry date.
††Date fixed in 1953 by congressional resolution.
*One of original 13 colonies.

active gas that is produced by the decay of underground deposits of radium and can cause cancer; runoffs of agricultural pesticides, pollutants deadly to fishing streams and very difficult to regulate; continued dumping of raw or partially treated sewage from major cities into US waterways; falling water tables in many western states; the decrease in arable land because of depletion, erosion, and urbanization; the need for reclamation of strip-mined lands and for regulation of present and future strip mining; and the expansion of the US nuclear industry in the absence of a fully sat-isfactory technique for the handling and permanent disposal of radioactive wastes.

6 POPULATION

The population of United States in 2005 was estimated by the United Nations (UN) at 296,483,000, which placed it at number 3 in population among the 193 nations of the world. In 2005, approximately 12% of the population was over 65 years of age, with another 21% of the population under 15 years of age. There were

97 males for every 100 females in the country. According to the UN, the annual population rate of change for 2005–2010 was expected to be 0.6%, a rate the government viewed as satisfactory. The projected population for the year 2025 was 349,419,000. The population density was 207 per sq km (80 per sq mi), with major population concentrations are along the northeast Atlantic coast and the southwest Pacific coast. The population is most dense between New York City and Washington, D.C.

At the time of the first federal census, in 1790, the population of the United States was 3,929,214. Between 1800 and 1850, the population almost quadrupled; between 1850 and 1900, it tripled; and between 1900 and 1950, it almost doubled. During the 1960s and 1970s, however, the growth rate slowed steadily, declining from 2.9% annually in 1960 to 2% in 1969 and to less than 1% from the 1980s through 2000. The population has aged: the median age of the population increased from 16.7 years in 1820 to 22.9 years in 1900 and to 34.3 years in 1995.

Suburbs have absorbed most of the shift in population distribution since 1950. The UN estimated that 79% of the population lived in urban areas in 2005, and that urban areas were growing at an annual rate of 1.33%. The capital city, Washington, D.C. (District of Columbia), had a population of 4,098,000 in that year. Other major metropolitan areas and their estimated populations include: New York, 18,498,000; Los Angeles, 12,146,000; Chicago, 8,711,000; Dallas, 4,612,000; Houston, 4,283,000; Philadelphia, 5,325,000; San Diego, 2,818,000; and Phoenix, 3,393,000. Major cities can be found throughout the United States.

7 ETHNIC GROUPS

The majority of the population of the United States is of European origin, with the largest groups having primary ancestry traceable to the United Kingdom, Germany, and Ireland; many Americans report multiple ancestries. According to 2004 American Community Survey estimates, about 75.6% of the total population are white, 12.1% are blacks and African Americans, and 4.2% are Asian. Native Americans (including Alaskan Natives) account for about 0.8% of the total population. About 1.8% of the population claim a mixed ancestry of two or more races. About 11.9% of all US citizens are foreign-born, with the largest numbers of people coming from Latin America (17,973,287) and Asia (9,254,705).

Some Native American societies survived the initial warfare with land-hungry white settlers and retained their tribal cultures. Their survival, however, has been on the fringes of North American society, especially as a result of the implementation of a national policy of resettling Native American tribes on reservations. In 2004, estimates place the number of Native Americans (including Alaska Natives) at 2,151,322. The number of those who claim mixed Native American and white racial backgrounds is estimated at 1,370,675; the 2004 estimate for mixed Native American and African American ancestry was 204,832. The largest single tribal grouping is the Cherokee, with about 331,491 people. The Navajo account for about 230,401 people, the Chippewa fro 92,041 people, and the Sioux for 67,666 people. Groups of Native Americans are found most numerously in the southwestern states of Oklahoma, Arizona, New Mexico, and California. The 1960s and 1970s saw successful court fights by Native Americans in Alaska, Maine, South Dakota, and other states to regain tribal lands or to receive cash settlements for lands taken from them in violation of treaties during the 1800s.

The black and African American population in 2004 was estimated at 34,772,381, with the majority still residing in the South, the region that absorbed most of the slaves brought from Africa in the 18th and 19th centuries. About 1,141,232 people claimed mixed black and white ethnicity. Two important regional migrations of blacks have taken place: (1) a "Great Migration" to the North, commencing in 1915, and (2) a small but then unprecedented westward movement beginning about 1940. Both migrations were fostered by wartime demands for labor and by postwar job opportunities in northern and western urban centers. More than three out of four black Americans live in metropolitan areas, notably in Washington, D.C., Atlanta, Chicago, Detroit, New Orleans, Newark, Baltimore, and New York City, which had the largest number of black residents. Large-scale federal programs to ensure equality for African Americans in voting rights, public education, employment, and housing were initiated after the historic 1954 Supreme Court ruling that barred racial segregation in public schools. By 1966, however, in the midst of growing and increasingly violent expressions of dissatisfaction by black residents of northern cities and southern rural areas, the federal Civil Rights Commission reported that integration programs were lagging. Throughout the 1960s, 1970s, and 1980s, the unemployment rate among nonwhites in the United States was at least double that for whites, and school integration proceeded slowly, especially outside the South.

Also included in the US population are a substantial number of persons whose lineage can be traced to Asian and Pacific nationalities, chiefly Chinese, Filipino, Japanese, Indian, Korean, and Vietnamese. The Chinese population is highly urbanized and concentrated particularly in cities of over 100,000 population, mostly on the West Coast and in New York City. According to 2004 estimates, there are over 2.8 million Chinese in the United States. Asian Indians are the next largest group of Asians with over 2.2 million people in 2004. About 2.1 million people are Filipino. The Japanese population has risen steadily from a level of 72,157 in 1910 to about 832,039 in 2004. Hawaii has been the most popular magnet of Japanese emigration. Most Japanese in California were farmers until the outbreak of World War II, when they were interned and deprived of their landholdings; after the war, most entered the professions and other urban occupations.

Hispanics or Latinos make up about 14% of the population according to 2004 estimates. It is important to note, however, that the designation of Hispanic or Latino applies to those who are of Latin American descent; these individuals may also belong to white, Asian, or black racial groups. Although Mexicans in the 21st century were still concentrated in the Southwest, they have settled throughout the United States; there are over 25 million Mexicans in the country. Spanish-speaking Puerto Ricans, who often represent an amalgam of racial strains, have largely settled in the New York metropolitan area, where they partake in considerable measure of the hardships and problems experienced by other immigrant groups in the process of settling in the United States; there are about 3.8 million Puerto Ricans in the country. Since 1959, many Cubans have settled in Florida and other eastern states. As of 2004, there are about 1.4 mullion Cubans in the Untied States.

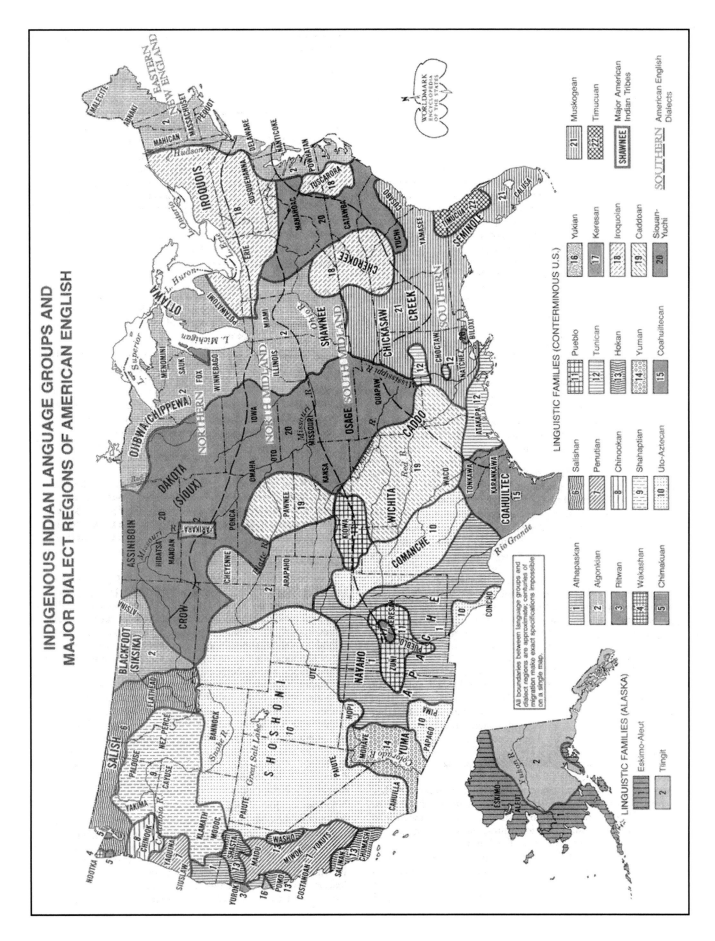

⁸LANGUAGES

The primary language of the United States is English, enriched by words borrowed from the languages of Indians and immigrants, predominantly European. Very early English borrowed from neighboring French speakers such words as *shivaree, butte, levee,* and *prairie;* from German, *sauerkraut, smearcase,* and *cranberry;* from Dutch, *stoop, spook,* and *cookie;* and from Spanish, *tornado, corral, ranch,* and *canyon.* From various West African languages, blacks have given English *jazz, voodoo,* and *okra.* According to 2004 estimates of primary languages spoken at home, about 81% of the population speak English only.

When European settlement began, Indians living north of Mexico spoke about 300 different languages now held to belong to 58 different language families. Only 2 such families have contributed noticeably to the American vocabulary: Algonkian in the Northeast and Aztec-Tanoan in the Southwest. From Algonkian languages, directly or sometimes through Canadian French, English has taken such words as *moose, skunk, caribou, opossum, woodchuck,* and *raccoon* for New World animals; *hickory, squash,* and *tamarack* for New World flora; and *succotash, hominy, mackinaw, moccasin, tomahawk, toboggan,* and *totem* for various cultural items. From Nahuatl, the language of the Aztecs, terms such as *tomato, mesquite, coyote, chili, tamale, chocolate,* and *ocelot* have entered English, largely by way of Spanish. A bare handful of words come from other Indian language groups, such as *tepee* from Dakota Siouan, *catalpa* from Creek, *sequoia* from Cherokee, *hogan* from Navaho, and *sockeye* from Salish, as well as *cayuse* from Chinook.

Professional dialect research, initiated in Germany in 1878 and in France in 1902, did not begin in the United States until 1931, in connection with the *Linguistic Atlas of New England* (1939–43). This kind of research, requiring trained field-workers to interview representative informants in their homes, subsequently was extended to the entire Atlantic Coast, the north-central states, the upper Midwest, the Pacific Coast, the Gulf states, and Oklahoma. The New England atlas, the *Linguistic Atlas of the Upper Midwest* (1973–76), and the first two fascicles of the *Linguistic Atlas of the Middle and South Atlantic States* (1980) have been published, along with three volumes based on Atlantic Coast field materials. Also published or nearing publication are atlases of the north-central states, the Gulf states, and Oklahoma. In other areas, individual dialect researchers have produced more specialized studies. The definitive work on dialect speech, the American Dialect Society's monumental *Dictionary of American Regional English,* began publication in 1985.

Dialect studies confirm that standard English is not uniform throughout the country. Major regional variations reflect patterns of colonial settlement, dialect features from England having dominated particular areas along the Atlantic Coast and then spread westward along the three main migration routes through the Appalachian system. Dialectologists recognize three main dialects—Northern, Midland, and Southern—each with subdivisions related to the effect of mountain ranges and rivers and railroads on population movement.

The Northern dialect is that of New England and its derivative settlements in New York; the northern parts of Ohio, Indiana, Illinois, and Iowa; and Michigan, Wisconsin, northeastern South Dakota, and North Dakota. A major subdivision is that of New England east of the Connecticut River, an area noted typically by the loss of /r/ after a vowel, and by the pronunciation of *can't, dance, half,* and *bath* with a vowel more like that in *father* than that in *fat.* Generally, however, Northern speech has a strong /r/ after a vowel, the same vowel in *can't* and *cat,* a conspicuous contrast between *cot* and *caught,* the /s/ sound in *greasy, creek* rhyming with *pick,* and *with* ending with the same consonant sound as at the end of *breath.*

Midland speech extends in a wide band across the United States: there are two main subdivisions, North Midland and South Midland. North Midland speech extends westward from New Jersey, Delaware, and Pennsylvania into Ohio, Illinois, southern Iowa, and northern Missouri. Its speakers generally end *with* with the consonant sound that begins the word *thin,* pronounce *cot* and *caught* alike, and say *cow* and *down* as /caow/ and /daown/. South Midland speech was carried by the Scotch–Irish from Pennsylvania down the Shenandoah Valley into the southern Appalachians, where it acquired many Southern speech features before it spread westward into Kentucky, Tennessee, southern Missouri, Arkansas, and northeast Texas. Its speakers are likely to say *plum peach* rather than *clingstone peach* and *snake doctor* rather than *dragonfly.*

Southern speech typically, though not always, lacks the consonant /r/ after a vowel, lengthens the first part of the diphthong in *write* so that to Northern ears it sounds almost like *rat,* and diphthongizes the vowels in *bed* and *hit* so that they sound like /beuhd/ and /hiuht/. *Horse* and *hoarse* do not sound alike, and *creek* rhymes with *meek. Corn bread* is *corn pone,* and *you-all* is standard for the plural.

In the western part of the United States, migration routes so crossed and intermingled that no neat dialect boundaries can be drawn, although there are a few rather clear population pockets.

Spanish is spoken by a sizable minority in the United States; according to 2004 estimates, about 11.4% of the population speak Spanish as the primary language of their household. The majority of Spanish speakers live in the Southwest, Florida, and eastern urban centers. Refugee immigration since the 1950s has greatly increased the number of foreign-language speakers from Latin America and Asia.

Educational problems raised by the presence of large blocs of non-English speakers led to the passage in 1976 of the Bilingual Educational Act, enabling children to study basic courses in their first language while they learn English. A related school problem is that of black English, a Southern dialect variant that is the vernacular of many black students now in northern schools.

⁹RELIGIONS

US religious traditions are predominantly Judeo-Christian and most Americans identify themselves as Protestants (of various denominations), Roman Catholics, or Jews. As of 2000, over 141 million Americans reported affiliation with a religious group. The single largest Christian denomination is the Roman Catholic Church, with membership in 2004 estimated at 66.4 million. Immigration from Ireland, Italy, Eastern Europe, French Canada, and the Caribbean accounts for the predominance of Roman Catholicism in the Northeast, Northwest, and some parts of the Great Lakes region, while Hispanic traditions and more recent immigration from Mexico and other Latin American countries account for the historical importance of Roman Catholicism in California and throughout most of the sunbelt. More than any other US religious body, the Roman Catholic Church maintains an extensive network of parochial schools.

Jewish immigrants settled first in the Northeast, where the largest Jewish population remains; at last estimates, about 6.1 million Jews live in the United States. According to data from 1995, there are about 3.7 million Muslims in the country. About 1.8 million people are Buddhist and 795,000 are Hindu. Approximately 874,000 people are proclaimed atheists.

Over 94 million persons in the United States report affiliation with a Protestant denomination. Baptists predominate below the Mason-Dixon line and west to Texas. By far the nation's largest Protestant group is the Southern Baptist Convention, which has about 16.2 million members; the American Baptist Churches in the USA claim some 1.4 million members. A concentration of Methodist groups extends westward in a band from Delaware to eastern Colorado; the largest of these groups, the United Methodist Church has about 8.2 million members. A related group, the African Methodist Episcopal Church, has about 2.5 million members. Lutheran denominations, reflecting in part the patterns of German and Scandinavian settlement, are most highly concentrated in the north-central states, especially Minnesota and the Dakotas. Two Lutheran synods, the Lutheran Church in America and the American Lutheran Church, merged in 1987 to form the Evangelical Lutheran Church in America, with more than 5 million adherents in 2004. In June 1983, the two major Presbyterian churches, the northern-based United Presbyterian Church in the USA and the southern-based Presbyterian Church in the United States, formally merged as the Presbyterian Church (USA), ending a division that began with the Civil War. This group claimed 3.4 adherents in 2004. Other prominent Protestant denominations and their estimated adherents (2004) include the Episcopal Church 2,334,000, and the United Church of Christ 1,331,000.

A number of Orthodox Christian denominations are represented in the United States, established by immigrants hoping to maintain their language and culture in a new world. The largest group of Orthodox belong to the Greek Orthodox Archdiocese of America, which has about 1.5 million members.

A number of religious groups, which now have a worldwide presence, originated in the United States. One such group, the Church of Jesus Christ of Latter-Day Saints (Mormons), was organized in New York in 1830 by Joseph Smith, Jr., who claimed to receive a revelation concerning an ancient American prophet named Mormon. The group migrated westward, in part to escape persecution, and has played a leading role in the political, economic, and religious life of Utah; Salt Lake City is the headquarters for the church. As of 2004, there are about 5.4 million members of the , the Church of Jesus Christ of Latter-Day Saints. The Jehovah's Witnesses were established by Charles Taze Russell in Pittsburgh, Pennsylvania, in 1872. They believe that Biblical prophecies are being fulfilled through world events and that the kingdom of God will be established on earth at the end of the great war described in the Bible. In 2004, there were about 1 million members in the Untied States.

The Church of Christ Scientist was established by Mary Baker Eddy (1821–1910) and her book *Science and Health with Key to the Scriptures*. A primary belief of the group is that physical injury and illness might be healed through the power of prayer and the correction of false beliefs. The Mother Church is located in Boston, Massachusetts. Christian Scientists have over 1,000 congregations in the nation. The Seventh-Day Adventists were also established in the Untied States by William Miller, a preacher who believed that the second coming of Christ would occur between 1843 and 1844. Though his prediction did not come true, many of his followers continued to embrace other practices such as worship on Saturday, vegetarianism, and a focus on preparation for the second coming. In 2004, the Seventh-Day Adventist Church had 919,000 members in the United States.

^{10}TRANSPORTATION

Railroads have lost not only the largest share of intercity freight traffic, their chief source of revenue, but passenger traffic as well. Despite an attempt to revive passenger transport through the development of a national network (Amtrak) in the 1970s, the rail sector has continued to experience heavy losses and declining revenues. In 1998 there were nine Class I rail companies in the United States, down from 13 in 1994, with a total of 178,222 employees and operating revenues of $32.2 billion. In 2003 there were 227,736 km (141,424 mi) of railway, all standard gauge. In 2000, Amtrak carried 84.1 million passengers.

The most conspicuous form of transportation is the automobile, and the extent and quality of the United States road-transport system are without parallel in the world. Over 226.06 million vehicles—a record number—were registered in 2003, including more than 130.8 million passenger cars and over 95.3. commercial vehicles. In 2000, there were some 4,346,068 motorcycles registered.

The United States has a vast network of public roads, whose total length as of 2003 was 6,393,603 km (3,976,821 mi), of which, 4,180,053 km (2,599,993 mi) were paved, including 74,406 km (46,281 mi) of expressways. The United States also has 41,009 km (25,483 mi) of navigable inland channels, exclusive of the Great Lakes. Of that total, 19,312 km (12,012 mi) are still in commercial use, as of 2004.

Major ocean ports or port areas are New York, the Delaware River areas (Philadelphia), the Chesapeake Bay area (Baltimore, Norfolk, Newport News), New Orleans, Houston, and the San Francisco Bay area. The inland port of Duluth on Lake Superior handles more freight than all but the top-ranking ocean ports. The importance of this port, along with those of Chicago and Detroit, was enhanced with the opening in 1959 of the St. Lawrence Seaway. Waterborne freight consists primarily of bulk commodities such as petroleum and its products, coal and coke, iron ore and steel, sand, gravel and stone, grains, and lumber. The US merchant marine industry has been decreasing gradually since the 1950s. In 2005, the United States had a merchant shipping fleet of 486 vessels of 1,000 GRT or more, with a combined GRT of 12,436,658.

In 2004, the United States had an estimated 14,857 airports. In 2005 a total of 5,120 had paved runways, and there were also 153 heliports. Principal airports include Hartsfield at Atlanta; Logan International at Boston; O'Hare International at Chicago; Dallas-Fort Worth at Dallas; Detroit Metropolitan; Honolulu International; Houston Intercontinental; Los Angeles International; John F. Kennedy, La Guardia, and Newark International at or near New York; Philadelphia International; Orlando International; Miami International; San Francisco International; L. Munoz Marin at San Juan, Seattle-Tacoma at Seattle, and Dulles International at Washington. Revenue passengers carried by the airlines in 1940 totaled 2.7 million. By 2003, the figure was estimated at 588.997 million for US domestic and international carriers, along with freight traffic estimated at 34,206 million freight ton-km.

11 HISTORY

The first Americans—distant ancestors of the Native Americans—probably crossed the Bering Strait from Asia at least 12,000 years ago. By the time Christopher Columbus came to the New World in 1492 there were probably no more than 2 million Native Americans living in the land that was to become the United States.

Following exploration of the American coasts by English, Portuguese, Spanish, Dutch, and French sea captains from the late 15th century onward, European settlements sprang up in the latter part of the 16th century. The Spanish established the first permanent settlement at St. Augustine in the future state of Florida in 1565, and another in New Mexico in 1599. During the early 17th century, the English founded Jamestown in Virginia Colony (1607) and Plymouth Colony in present-day Massachusetts (1620). The Dutch established settlements at Ft. Orange (now Albany, N.Y.) in 1624, New Amsterdam (now New York City) in 1626, and at Bergen (now part of Jersey City, N.J.) in 1660; they conquered New Sweden—the Swedish colony in Delaware and New Jersey—in 1655. Nine years later, however, the English seized this New Netherland Colony and subsequently monopolized settlement of the East Coast except for Florida, where Spanish rule prevailed until 1821. In the Southwest, California, Arizona, New Mexico, and Texas also were part of the Spanish empire until the 19th century. Meanwhile, in the Great Lakes area south of present-day Canada, France set up a few trading posts and settlements but never established effective control; New Orleans was one of the few areas of the United States where France pursued an active colonial policy.

From the founding of Jamestown to the outbreak of the American Revolution more than 150 years later, the British government administered its American colonies within the context of mercantilism: the colonies existed primarily for the economic benefit of the empire. Great Britain valued its American colonies especially for their tobacco, lumber, indigo, rice, furs, fish, grain, and naval stores, relying particularly in the southern colonies on black slave labor.

The colonies enjoyed a large measure of internal self-government until the end of the French and Indian War (1745–63), which resulted in the loss of French Canada to the British. To prevent further troubles with the Indians, the British government in 1763 prohibited the American colonists from settling beyond the Appalachian Mountains. Heavy debts forced London to decree that the colonists should assume the costs of their own defense, and the British government enacted a series of revenue measures to provide funds for that purpose. But soon, the colonists began to insist that they could be taxed only with their consent and the struggle grew to become one of local versus imperial authority.

Widening cultural and intellectual differences also served to divide the colonies and the mother country. Life on the edge of the civilized world had brought about changes in the colonists' attitudes and outlook, emphasizing their remoteness from English life. In view of the long tradition of virtual self-government in the colonies, strict enforcement of imperial regulations and British efforts to curtail the power of colonial legislatures presaged inevi-

table conflict between the colonies and the mother country. When citizens of Massachusetts, protesting the tax on tea, dumped a shipload of tea belonging to the East India Company into Boston harbor in 1773, the British felt compelled to act in defense of their authority as well as in defense of private property. Punitive measures—referred to as the Intolerable Acts by the colonists—struck at the foundations of self-government.

In response, the First Continental Congress, composed of delegates from 12 of the 13 colonies—Georgia was not represented—met in Philadelphia in September 1774, and proposed a general boycott of English goods, together with the organizing of a militia. British troops marched to Concord, Mass., on 19 April 1775 and destroyed the supplies that the colonists had assembled there. American "minutemen" assembled on the nearby Lexington green and fired "the shot heard round the world," although no one knows who actually fired the first shot that morning. The British soldiers withdrew and fought their way back to Boston.

Voices in favor of conciliation were raised in the Second Continental Congress that assembled in Philadelphia on 10 May 1775, this time including Georgia; but with news of the Restraining Act (30 March 1775), which denied the colonies the right to trade with countries outside the British Empire, all hopes for peace vanished. George Washington was appointed commander in chief of the new American army, and on 4 July 1776, the 13 American colonies adopted the Declaration of Independence, justifying the right of revolution by the theory of natural rights.

British and American forces met in their first organized encounter near Boston on 17 June 1775. Numerous battles up and down the coast followed. The British seized and held the principal cities but were unable to inflict a decisive defeat on Washington's troops. The entry of France into the war on the American side eventually tipped the balance. On 19 October 1781, the British commander, Cornwallis, cut off from reinforcements by the French fleet on one side and besieged by French and American forces on the other, surrendered his army at Yorktown, Va. American independence was acknowledged by the British in a treaty of peace signed in Paris on 3 September 1783.

The first constitution uniting the 13 original states—the Articles of Confederation—reflected all the suspicions that Americans entertained about a strong central government. Congress was denied power to raise taxes or regulate commerce, and many of the powers it was authorized to exercise required the approval of a minimum of nine states. Dissatisfaction with the Articles of Confederation was aggravated by the hardships of a postwar depression, and in 1787—the same year that Congress passed the Northwest Ordinance, providing for the organization of new territories and states on the frontier—a convention assembled in Philadelphia to revise the articles. The convention adopted an altogether new constitution, the present Constitution of the United States, which greatly increased the powers of the central government at the expense of the states. This document was ratified by the states with the understanding that it would be amended to include a bill of rights guaranteeing certain fundamental freedoms. These freedoms—including the rights of free speech, press, and assembly, freedom from unreasonable search and seizure, and the right to a speedy and public trial by an impartial jury—are assured by the first 10 amendments to the constitution, adopted on 5 December 1791; the constitution did however recognize slavery, and did not

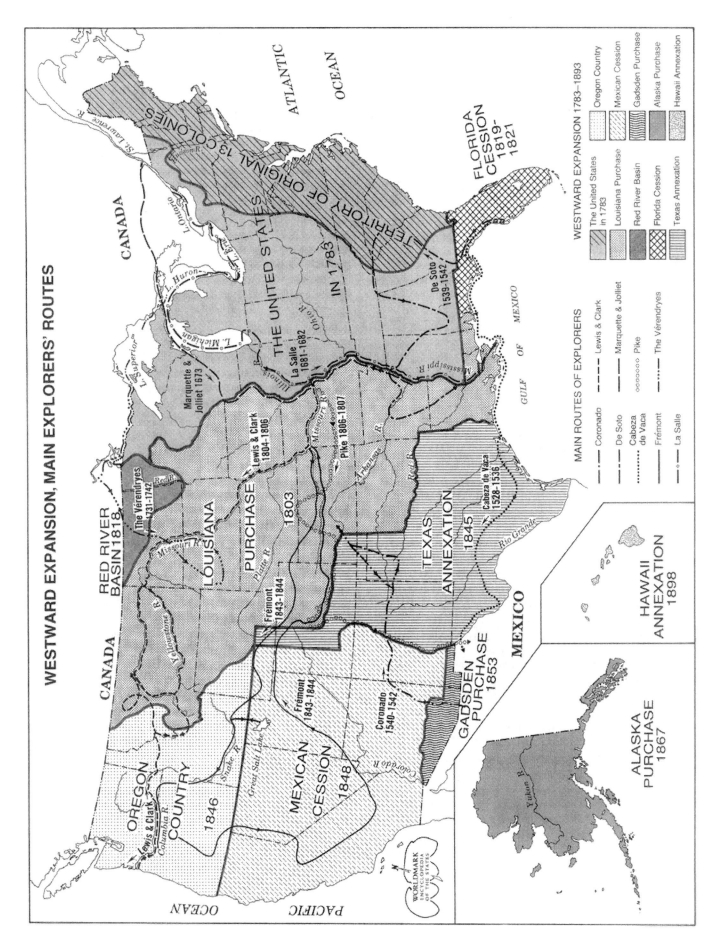

WESTWARD EXPANSION, MAIN EXPLORERS' ROUTES

TERRITORY OF ORIGINAL 13 COLONIES

THE UNITED STATES IN 1783

FLORIDA CESSION 1819-1821

CANADA

ATLANTIC OCEAN

Marquette & Jolliet 1673

La Salle 1681-1682

De Soto 1539-1542

Lewis & Clark 1804-1806

Pike 1806-1807

The Vérendryes 1731-1742

RED RIVER BASIN 1818

LOUISIANA PURCHASE 1803

Frémont 1843-1844

TEXAS ANNEXATION 1845

Cabeza de Vaca 1528-1536

GULF OF MEXICO

MEXICO

GADSDEN PURCHASE 1853

Frémont 1843-1844

Coronado 1540-1542

MEXICAN CESSION 1848

OREGON COUNTRY 1846

Lewis & Clark

PACIFIC OCEAN

WESTWARD EXPANSION 1783-1893

Oregon Country
Mexican Cession
Gadsden Purchase
Alaska Purchase
Hawaii Annexation

The United States in 1783
Louisiana Purchase
Red River Basin
Florida Cession
Texas Annexation

MAIN ROUTES OF EXPLORERS

Coronado
De Soto
Cabeza de Vaca
Frémont
La Salle

Lewis & Clark
Marquette & Jolliet
Pike
The Vérendryes

HAWAII ANNEXATION 1898

ALASKA PURCHASE 1867

WORLDMARK ENCYCLOPEDIA OF THE STATES

provide for universal suffrage. On 30 April 1789 George Washington was inaugurated as the first president of the United States.

During Washington's administration, the credit of the new nation was bolstered by acts providing for a revenue tariff and an excise tax; opposition to the excise on whiskey sparked the Whiskey Rebellion, suppressed on Washington's orders in 1794. Alexander Hamilton's proposals for funding the domestic and foreign debt and permitting the national government to assume the debts of the states were also implemented. Hamilton, the secretary of the treasury, also created the first national bank, and was the founder of the Federalist Party. Opposition to the bank as well as to the rest of the Hamiltonian program, which tended to favor northeastern commercial and business interests, led to the formation of an anti-Federalist party, the Democratic-Republicans, led by Thomas Jefferson.

The Federalist Party, to which Washington belonged, regarded the French Revolution as a threat to security and property; the Democratic-Republicans, while condemning the violence of the revolutionists, hailed the overthrow of the French monarchy as a blow to tyranny. The split of the nation's leadership into rival camps was the first manifestation of the two-party system, which has since been the dominant characteristic of the US political scene (Jefferson's party should not be confused with the modern Republican Party, formed in 1854.)

The 1800 election brought the defeat of Federalist President John Adams, Washington's successor, by Jefferson; a key factor in Adam's loss was the unpopularity of the Alien and Sedition Acts (1798), Federalist-sponsored measures that had abridged certain freedoms guaranteed in the Bill of Rights. In 1803, Jefferson achieved the purchase from France of the Louisiana Territory, including all the present territory of the United States west of the Mississippi drained by that river and its tributaries; exploration and mapping of the new territory, notably through the expeditions of Meriwether Lewis and William Clark, began almost immediately. Under Chief Justice John Marshall, the US Supreme Court, in the landmark case of *Marbury v. Madison*, established the principle of federal supremacy in conflicts with the states and enunciated the doctrine of judicial review.

During Jefferson's second term in office, the United States became involved in a protracted struggle between Britain and Napoleonic France. Seizures of US ships and the impressment of US seamen by the British navy led the administration to pass the Embargo Act of 1807, under which no US ships were to put out to sea. After the act was repealed in 1809, ship seizures and impressment of seamen by the British continued, and were the ostensible reasons for the declaration of war on Britain in 1812 during the administration of James Madison. An underlying cause of the War of 1812, however, was land-hungry Westerners' coveting of southern Canada as potential US territory.

The war was largely a standoff. A few surprising US naval victories countered British successes on land. The Treaty of Ghent (24 December 1814), which ended the war, made no mention of impressment and provided for no territorial changes. The occasion for further maritime conflict with Britain, however, disappeared with the defeat of Napoleon in 1815.

Now the nation became occupied primarily with domestic problems and westward expansion. Because the United States had been cut off from its normal sources of manufactured goods in Great Britain during the war, textiles and other industries developed and prospered in New England. To protect these infant industries, Congress adopted a high-tariff policy in 1816.

Three events of the late 1810s and the 1820s were of considerable importance for the future of the country. The federal government in 1817 began a policy of forcibly resettling the Indians, already decimated by war and disease, in what later became known as Indian Territory (now Oklahoma); those Indians not forced to move were restricted to reservations. The Missouri Compromise (1820) was an attempt to find a nationally acceptable solution to the volatile dispute over the extension of black slavery to new territories. It provided for admission of Missouri into the Union as a slave state but banned slavery in territories to the west that lay north of 36°30'. As a result of the establishment of independent Latin American republics and threats by France and Spain to reestablish colonial rule, President James Monroe in 1823 asserted that the Western Hemisphere was closed to further colonization by European powers. The Monroe Doctrine declared that any effort by such powers to recover territories whose independence the United States had recognized would be regarded as an unfriendly act.

From the 1820s to the outbreak of the Civil War, the growth of manufacturing continued, mainly in the North, and was accelerated by inventions and technological advances. Farming expanded with westward migration. The South discovered that its future lay in the cultivation of cotton. The cotton gin, invented by Eli Whitney in 1793, greatly simplified the problems of production; the growth of the textile industry in New England and Great Britain assured a firm market for cotton. Hence, during the first half of the 19th century, the South remained a fundamentally agrarian society based increasingly on a one-crop economy. Large numbers of field hands were required for cotton cultivation, and black slavery became solidly entrenched in the southern economy.

The construction of roads and canals paralleled the country's growth and economic expansion. The successful completion of the Erie Canal (1825), linking the Great Lakes with the Atlantic, ushered in a canal-building boom. Railroad building began in earnest in the 1830s, and by 1840, about 3,300 mi (5,300 km) of track had been laid. The development of the telegraph a few years later gave the nation the beginnings of a modern telecommunications network. As a result of the establishment of the factory system, a laboring class appeared in the North by the 1830s, bringing with it the earliest unionization efforts.

Western states admitted into the Union following the War of 1812 provided for free white male suffrage without property qualifications and helped spark a democratic revolution. As eastern states began to broaden the franchise, mass appeal became an important requisite for political candidates. The election to the presidency in 1928 of Andrew Jackson, a military hero and Indian fighter from Tennessee, was no doubt a result of this widening of the democratic process. By this time, the United States consisted of 24 states and had a population of nearly 13 million.

The relentless westward thrust of the United States population ultimately involved the United States in foreign conflict. In 1836, US settlers in Texas revolted against Mexican rule and established an independent republic. Texas was admitted to the Union as a state in 1845, and relations between Mexico and the United States steadily worsened. A dispute arose over the southern boundary of Texas, and a Mexican attack on a US patrol in May 1846 gave President James K. Polk a pretext to declare war. After a rapid advance, US forces captured Mexico City, and on 2 February 1848, Mexico formally gave up the unequal fight by signing the Treaty of Guadalupe Hidalgo, providing for the cession of California and the territory of New Mexico to the United States. With the Gadsden Purchase of 1853, the United States acquired from Mexico for $10 million large strips of land forming the balance of southern Arizona and New Mexico. A dispute with Britain over the Oregon Territory was settled in 1846 by a treaty that established the 49th parallel as the boundary with Canada. Thenceforth the United States was to be a Pacific as well as an Atlantic power.

Westward expansion exacerbated the issue of slavery in the territories. By 1840, abolition of slavery constituted a fundamental aspect of a movement for moral reform, which also encompassed women's rights, universal education, alleviation of working class hardships, and temperance. In 1849, a year after the discovery of gold had precipitated a rush of new settlers to California, that territory (whose constitution prohibited slavery) demanded admission to the Union. A compromise engineered in Congress by Senator Henry Clay in 1850 provided for California's admission as a free state in return for various concessions to the South. But enmities dividing North and South could not be silenced. The issue of slavery in the territories came to a head with the Kansas-Nebraska Act of 1854, which repealed the Missouri Compromise and left the question of slavery in those territories to be decided by the settlers themselves. The ensuing conflicts in Kansas between northern and southern settlers earned the territory the name "bleeding Kansas."

In 1860, the Democratic Party, split along northern and southern lines, offered two presidential candidates. The new Republican Party, organized in 1854 and opposed to the expansion of slavery, nominated Abraham Lincoln. Owing to the defection in Democratic ranks, Lincoln was able to carry the election in the electoral college, although he did not obtain a majority of the popular vote. To ardent supporters of slavery, Lincoln's election provided a reason for immediate secession. Between December 1860 and February 1861, the seven states of the Deep South—South Carolina, Mississippi, Florida, Alabama, Georgia, Louisiana, and Texas—withdrew from the Union and formed a separate government, known as the Confederate States of America, under the presidency of Jefferson Davis. The secessionists soon began to confiscate federal property in the South. On 12 April 1861, the Confederates opened fire on Ft. Sumter in the harbor of Charleston, S.C., and thus precipitated the US Civil War. Following the outbreak of hostilities, Arkansas, North Carolina, Virginia, and Tennessee joined the Confederacy.

For the next four years, war raged between the Confederate and Union forces, largely in southern territories. An estimated 360,000 men in the Union forces died of various causes, including 110,000 killed in battle. Confederate dead were estimated at 250,000, including 94,000 killed in battle. The North, with great superiority in manpower and resources, finally prevailed. A Confederate invasion of the North was repulsed at the battle of Gettysburg, Pennsylvania, in July 1863; a Union army took Atlanta in September 1864; and Confederate forces evacuated Richmond, the Confederate capital, in early April 1865. With much of the South in Union hands, Confederate Gen. Robert E. Lee surrendered to Gen. Ulysses S. Grant at Appomattox Courthouse in Virginia on 9 April.

The outcome of the war brought great changes in US life. Lincoln's Emancipation Proclamation of 1863 was the initial step in freeing some 4 million black slaves; their liberation was completed soon after the war's end by amendments to the Constitution. Lincoln's plan for the reconstruction of the rebellious states was compassionate, but only five days after Lee's surrender, Lincoln was assassinated by John Wilkes Booth as part of a conspiracy in which US Secretary of State William H. Seward was seriously wounded.

During the Reconstruction era (1865–77), the defeated South was governed by Union Army commanders, and the resultant bitterness of southerners toward northern Republican rule, which enfranchised blacks, persisted for years afterward. Vice President Andrew Johnson, who succeeded Lincoln as president, tried to carry out Lincoln's conciliatory policies but was opposed by radical Republican leaders in Congress who demanded harsher treatment of the South. On the pretext that he had failed to carry out an act of Congress, the House of Representatives voted to impeach Johnson in 1868, but the Senate failed by one vote to convict him and remove him from office. It was during Johnson's presidency that Secretary of State Seward negotiated the purchase of Alaska (which attained statehood in 1959) from Russia for $7.2 million.

The efforts of southern whites to regain political control of their states led to the formation of terrorist organizations like the Ku Klux Klan, which employed violence to prevent blacks from voting. By the end of the Reconstruction era, whites had reestablished their political domination over blacks in the southern states and had begun to enforce patterns of segregation in education and social organization that were to last for nearly a century.

In many southern states, the decades following the Civil War were ones of economic devastation, in which rural whites as well as blacks were reduced to sharecropper status. Outside the South, however, a great period of economic expansion began. Transcontinental railroads were constructed, corporate enterprise spurted ahead, and the remaining western frontier lands were rapidly occupied and settled. The age of big business tycoons dawned. As heavy manufacturing developed, Pittsburgh, Chicago, and New York emerged as the nation's great industrial centers. The Knights of Labor, founded in 1869, engaged in numerous strikes, and violent conflicts between strikers and strikebreakers were common. The American Federation of Labor, founded in 1886, established a nationwide system of craft unionism that remained dominant for many decades. During this period, too, the woman's rights movement organized actively to secure the vote (although woman's suffrage was not enacted nationally until 1920), and groups outraged by the depletion of forests and wildlife in the West pressed for the conservation of natural resources.

During the latter half of the 19th century, the acceleration of westward expansion made room for millions of immigrants from Europe. The country's population grew to more than 76 million by 1900. As homesteaders, prospectors, and other settlers tamed the frontier, the federal government forced Indians west of the Mississippi to cede vast tracts of land to the whites, precipitating a series of wars with various tribes. By 1890, only 250,000 Indians remained in the United States, virtually all of them residing on reservations.

The 1890s marked the closing of the United States frontier for settlement and the beginning of US overseas expansion. By 1892, Hawaiian sugar planters of US origin had become strong enough to bring about the downfall of the native queen and to establish a republic, which in 1898, at its own request, was annexed as a territory by the United States. The sympathies of the United States with the Cuban nationalists who were battling for independence from Spain were aroused by a lurid press and by expansionist elements. A series of events climaxed by the sinking of the USS *Maine* in Havana harbor finally forced a reluctant President William McKinley to declare war on Spain on 25 April 1898. US forces overwhelmed those of Spain in Cuba, and as a result of the Spanish-American War, the United States added to its territories the Philippines, Guam, and Puerto Rico. A newly independent Cuba was drawn into the United States orbit as a virtual protectorate through the 1950s. Many eminent citizens saw these new departures into imperialism as a betrayal of the time-honored US doctrine of government by the consent of the governed.

With the marked expansion of big business came increasing protests against the oppressive policies of large corporations and their dominant role in the public life of the nation. A demand emerged for strict control of monopolistic business practice through the enforcement of antitrust laws. Two US presidents, Theodore Roosevelt (1901–09), a Republican and Woodrow Wilson (1913–21), a Democrat, approved of the general movement for reform, which came to be called progressivism. Roosevelt developed a considerable reputation as a trustbuster, while Wilson's program, known as the New Freedom, called for reform of tariffs, business procedures, and banking. During Roosevelt's first term, the United States leased the Panama Canal Zone and started construction of a 42-mi (68-km) canal, completed in 1914.

US involvement in World War I marked the country's active emergence as one of the great powers of the world. When war broke out in 1914 between Germany, Austria-Hungary, and Turkey on one side and Britain, France, and Russia on the other, sentiment in the United States was strongly opposed to participation in the conflict, although a large segment of the American people sympathized with the British and the French. While both sides violated US maritime rights on the high seas, the Germans, enmeshed in a British blockade, resorted to unrestricted submarine warfare. On 6 April 1917, Congress declared war on Germany. Through a national draft of all able-bodied men between the ages of 18 and 45, some 4 million US soldiers were trained, of whom more than 2 million were sent overseas to France. By late 1917, when US troops began to take part in the fighting on the western front, the European armies were approaching exhaustion, and US intervention may well have been decisive in ensuring the eventual victory of the Allies. In a series of great battles in which US soldiers took an increasingly major part, the German forces were rolled back in the west, and in the autumn of 1918 were compelled to sue for peace. Fighting ended with the armistice of 11 November 1918. President Wilson played an active role in drawing up the 1919 Versailles peace treaty, which embodied his dream of establishing a League of Nations to preserve the peace, but the isolationist bloc in the Senate was able to prevent US ratification of the treaty.

In the 1920s, the United States had little enthusiasm left for crusades, either for democracy abroad or for reform at home; a rare

instance of idealism in action was the Kellogg-Briand Pact (1928), an antiwar accord negotiated on behalf of the United States by Secretary of State Frank B. Kellogg. In general, however, the philosophy of the Republican administrations from 1921 to 1933 was expressed in the aphorism "The business of America is business," and the 1920s saw a great business boom. The years 1923–24 also witnessed the unraveling of the Teapot Dome scandal: the revelation that President Warren G. Harding's secretary of the interior, Albert B. Fall, had secretly leased federal oil reserves in California and Wyoming to private oil companies in return for gifts and loans.

The great stock market crash of October 1929 ushered in the most serious and most prolonged economic depression the country had ever known. By 1933, an estimated 12 million men and women were out of work; personal savings were wiped out on a vast scale through a disastrous series of corporate bankruptcies and bank failures. Relief for the unemployed was left to private charities and local governments, which were incapable of handling the enormous task.

The inauguration of the successful Democratic presidential candidate, Franklin D. Roosevelt, in March 1933 ushered in a new era of US history, in which the federal government was to assume a much more prominent role in the nation's economic affairs. Proposing to give the country a "New Deal," Roosevelt accepted national responsibility for alleviating the hardships of unemployment; relief measures were instituted, work projects were established, the deficit spending was accepted in preference to ignoring public distress. The federal Social Security program was inaugurated, as were various measures designed to stimulate and develop the economy through federal intervention. Unions were strengthened through the National Labor Relations Act, which established the right of employees' organizations to bargain collectively with employers. Union membership increased rapidly, and the dominance of the American Federation of Labor was challenged by the newly formed Congress of Industrial Organizations, which organized workers along industrial lines.

The depression of the 1930s was worldwide, and certain nations attempted to counter economic stagnation by building large military establishments and embarking on foreign adventures. Following German, Italian, and Japanese aggression, World War II broke out in Europe during September 1939. In 1940, Roosevelt, disregarding a tradition dating back to Washington that no president should serve more than two terms, ran again for reelection. He easily defeated his Republican opponent, Wendell Willkie, who, along with Roosevelt, advocated increased rearmament and all possible aid to victims of aggression. The United States was brought actively into the war by the Japanese attack on the Pearl Harbor naval base in Hawaii on 7 December 1941. The forces of Germany, Italy, and Japan were now arrayed over a vast theater of war against those of the United States and the British Commonwealth; in Europe, Germany was locked in a bloody struggle with the Soviet Union. US forces waged war across the vast expanses of the Pacific, in Africa, in Asia, and in Europe. Italy surrendered in 1943; Germany was successfully invaded in 1944 and conquered in May 1945; and after the United States dropped the world's first atomic bombs on Hiroshima and Nagasaki, the Japanese capitulated in August. The Philippines became an independent republic soon after the war, but the United States retained most of its other Pacific possessions, with Hawaii becoming the 50th state in 1959.

Roosevelt, who had been elected to a fourth term in 1944, died in April 1945 and was succeeded by Harry S Truman, his vice president. Under the Truman administration, the United States became an active member of the new world organization, the United Nations. The Truman administration embarked on large-scale programs of military aid and economic support to check the expansion of communism. Aid to Greece and Turkey in 1948 and the Marshall Plan, a program designed to accelerate the economic recovery of Western Europe, were outstanding features of US postwar foreign policy. The North Atlantic Treaty (1949) established a defensive alliance among a number of West European nations and the United States. Truman's Point Four program gave technical and scientific aid to developing nations. When, following the North Korean attack on South Korea on 25 June 1950, the UN Security Council resolved that members of the UN should proceed to the aid of South Korea. US naval, air, and ground forces were immediately dispatched by President Truman. An undeclared war ensued, which eventually was brought to a halt by an armistice signed on 27 June 1953.

In 1952, Dwight D. Eisenhower, supreme commander of Allied forces in Europe during World War II, was elected president on the Republican ticket, thereby bringing to an end 20 years of Democratic presidential leadership. In foreign affairs, the Eisenhower administration continued the Truman policy of containing the USSR and threatened "massive retaliation" in the event of Soviet aggression, thus heightening the Cold War between the world's two great nuclear powers. Although Republican domestic policies were more conservative than those of the Democrats, the Eisenhower administration extended certain major social and economic programs of the Roosevelt and Truman administrations, notably Social Security and public housing. The early years of the Eisenhower administration were marked by agitation (arising in 1950) over charges of Communist and other allegedly subversive activities in the United States—a phenomenon known as McCarthyism, after Republican Senator Joseph R. McCarthy of Wisconsin, who aroused much controversy with unsubstantiated allegations that Communists had penetrated the US government, especially the Army and the Department of State. Even those who personally opposed McCarthy lent their support to the imposition of loyalty oaths and the blacklisting of persons with left-wing backgrounds.

A major event of the Eisenhower years was the US Supreme Court's decision in *Brown v. Board of Education of Topeka* (1954) outlawing segregation of whites and blacks in public schools. In the aftermath of this ruling, desegregation proceeded slowly and painfully. In the early 1960s, sit-ins, "freedom rides," and similar expressions of nonviolent resistance by blacks and their sympathizers led to a lessening of segregation practices in public facilities. Under Chief Justice Earl Warren, the high court in 1962 mandated the reapportionment of state and federal legislative districts according to a "one person, one vote" formula. It also broadly extended the rights of defendants in criminal trials to include the provision of a defense lawyer at public expense for an accused person unable to afford one, and established the duty of police to advise an accused person of his or her legal rights immediately upon arrest.

In the early 1960s, during the administration of Eisenhower's Democratic successor, John F. Kennedy, the Cold War heated up as Cuba, under the regime of Fidel Castro, aligned itself with the Soviet Union. Attempts by anti-Communist Cuban exiles to invade their homeland in the spring of 1961 failed despite US aid. In October 1962, President Kennedy successfully forced a showdown with the Soviet Union over Cuba in demanding the withdrawal of Soviet-supplied "offensive weapons"—missiles—from the nearby island. On 22 November 1963, President Kennedy was assassinated while riding in a motorcade through Dallas, Texas; hours later, Vice President Lyndon B. Johnson was inaugurated president. In the November 1964 elections, Johnson overwhelmingly defeated his Republican opponent, Barry M. Goldwater, and embarked on a vigorous program of social legislation unprecedented since Roosevelt's New Deal. His "Great Society" program sought to ensure black Americans' rights in voting and public housing, to give the underprivileged job training, and to provide persons 65 and over with hospitalization and other medical benefits (Medicare). Measures ensuring equal opportunity for minority groups may have contributed to the growth of the woman's rights movement in the late 1960s. This same period also saw the growth of a powerful environmental protection movement.

US military and economic aid to anti-Communist forces in Vietnam, which had its beginnings during the Truman administration (while Vietnam was still part of French Indochina) and was increased gradually by presidents Eisenhower and Kennedy, escalated in 1965. In that year, President Johnson sent US combat troops to South Vietnam and ordered US bombing raids on North Vietnam, after Congress (in the Gulf of Tonkin Resolution of 1964) had given him practically carte blanche authority to wage war in that region. By the end of 1968, American forces in Vietnam numbered 536,100 men, but US military might was unable to defeat the Vietnamese guerrillas, and the American people were badly split over continuing the undeclared (and, some thought, ill-advised or even immoral) war, with its high price in casualties and materiel. Reacting to widespread dissatisfaction with his Vietnam policies, Johnson withdrew in March 1968 from the upcoming presidential race, and in November, Republican Richard M. Nixon, who had been the vice president under Eisenhower, was elected president. Thus, the Johnson years—which had begun with the new hopes of a Great Society but had soured with a rising tide of racial violence in US cities and the assassinations of civil rights leader Martin Luther King, Jr., and US senator Robert F. Kennedy, among others—drew to a close.

President Nixon gradually withdrew US ground troops from Vietnam but expanded aerial bombardment throughout Indochina, and the increasingly unpopular and costly war continued for four more years before a cease-fire—negotiated by Nixon's national security adviser, Henry Kissinger—was finally signed on 27 January 1973 and the last US soldiers were withdrawn. The most protracted conflict in American history had resulted in 46,163 US combat deaths and 303,654 wounded soldiers, and had cost the US government $112 billion in military allocations. Two years later, the South Vietnamese army collapsed, and the North Vietnamese Communist regime united the country.

In 1972, during the last year of his first administration, Nixon initiated the normalization of relations—ruptured in 1949—with the People's Republic of China and signed a strategic arms limitation agreement with the Soviet Union as part of a Nixon-Kissinger policy of pursuing détente with both major Communist powers. (Earlier, in July 1969, American technology had achieved a national triumph by landing the first astronaut on the moon.) The Nixon administration sought to muster a "silent majority" in support of its Indochina policies and its conservative social outlook in domestic affairs. The most momentous domestic development, however, was the Watergate scandal, which began on 17 June 1972 with the arrest of five men associated with Nixon's reelection campaign, during a break-in at Democratic Party headquarters in the Watergate office building in Washington, D.C. Although Nixon was reelected in 1972, subsequent disclosures by the press and by a Senate investigating committee revealed a complex pattern of political "dirty tricks" and illegal domestic surveillance throughout his first term. The president's apparent attempts to obstruct justice by helping his aides cover up the scandal were confirmed by tape recordings (made by Nixon himself) of his private conversations, which the Supreme Court ordered him to release for use as evidence in criminal proceedings. The House voted to begin impeachment proceedings, and in late July 1974, its Judiciary Committee approved three articles of impeachment. On 9 August, Nixon became the first president to resign the office. The following year, Nixon's top aides and former attorney general, John N. Mitchell, were convicted of obstruction and were subsequently sentenced to prison.

Nixon's successor was Gerald R. Ford, who in October 1973 had been appointed to succeed Vice President Spiro T. Agnew when Agnew resigned following his plea of *nolo contendere* to charges that he had evaded paying income tax on moneys he had received from contractors while governor of Maryland. Less than a month after taking office, President Ford granted a full pardon to Nixon for any crimes he may have committed as president. In August 1974, Ford nominated Nelson A. Rockefeller as vice president (he was not confirmed until December), thus giving the country the first instance of a nonelected president and an appointed vice president serving simultaneously. Ford's pardon of Nixon, as well as continued inflation and unemployment, probably contributed to his narrow defeat by a Georgia Democrat, Jimmy Carter, in 1976.

President Carter's forthright championing of human rights—though consistent with the Helsinki accords, the "final act" of the Conference on Security and Cooperation in Europe, signed by the United States and 34 other nations in July 1974—contributed to strained relations with the USSR and with some US allies. During 1978–79, the president concluded and secured Senate passage of treaties ending US sovereignty over the Panama Canal Zone. His major accomplishment in foreign affairs, however, was his role in mediating a peace agreement between Israel and Egypt, signed at the camp David, Md., retreat in September 1978. Domestically, the Carter administration initiated a national energy program to reduce US dependence on foreign oil by cutting gasoline and oil consumption and by encouraging the development of alternative energy resources. But the continuing decline of the economy because of double-digit inflation and high unemployment caused his popularity to wane, and confusing shifts in economic policy (coupled with a lack of clear goals in foreign affairs) characterized his administration during 1979 and 1980; a prolonged quarrel with Iran over more than 50 US hostages seized in Tehrān on 4 November 1979 contributed to public doubts about his presidency. Ex-

actly a year after the hostages were taken, former California Governor Ronald Reagan defeated Carter in an election that saw the Republican Party score major gains throughout the United States. The hostages were released on 20 January 1981, the day of Reagan's inauguration.

Reagan, who survived a chest wound from an assassination attempt in Washington, D.C., in 1981, used his popularity to push through significant policy changes. He succeeded in enacting income tax cuts of 25%, reducing the maximum tax rate on unearned income from 70% to 50%, and accelerating depreciation allowances for businesses. At the same time, he more than doubled the military budget, in constant 1985 dollars, between 1980 and 1989. Vowing to reduce domestic spending, Reagan cut benefits for the working poor, reduced allocations for food stamps and Aid to Families With Dependent Children by 13%, and decreased grants for the education of disadvantaged children. He slashed the budget of the Environmental Protection Agency and instituted a flat rate reimbursement system for the treatment of Medicare patients with particular illnesses, replacing a more flexible arrangement in which hospitals had been reimbursed for "reasonable charges."

Reagan's appointment of Sandra Day O'Connor as the first woman justice of the Supreme Court was widely praised and won unanimous confirmation from the Senate. However, some of his other high-level choices were extremely controversial—none more so than that of his secretary of the interior, James G. Watt, who finally resigned on October 1983. To direct foreign affairs, Reagan named Alexander M. Haig, Jr., former NATO supreme commander for Europe, to the post of secretary of state; Haig, who clashed frequently with other administration officials, resigned in June 1982 and was replaced by George P. Shultz. In framing his foreign and defense policy, Reagan insisted on a military buildup as a precondition for arms-control talks with the USSR. His administration sent money and advisers to help the government of El Salvador in its war against leftist rebels, and US advisers were also sent to Honduras, reportedly to aid groups of Nicaraguans trying to overthrow the Sandinista government in their country. Troops were also dispatched to Lebanon in September 1982, as part of a multinational peacekeeping force in Beirut, and to Grenada in October 1983 to oust a leftist government there.

Reelected in 1984, President Reagan embarked on his second term with a legislative agenda that included reduction of federal budget deficits (which had mounted rapidly during his first term in office), further cuts in domestic spending, and reform of the federal tax code. In military affairs, Reagan persuaded Congress to fund on a modest scale his Strategic Defense Initiative, commonly known as Star Wars, a highly complex and extremely costly space-based antimissile system. In 1987, the downing of an aircraft carrying arms to Nicaragua led to the disclosure that a group of National Security Council members had secretly diverted $48 million that the federal government had received in payment from Iran for American arms to rebel forces in Nicaragua. The disclosure prompted the resignation of two of the leaders of the group, Vice Admiral John Poindexter and Lieutenant Colonel Oliver North, as well as investigations by House and Senate committees and a special prosecutor, Lawrence Walsh. The congressional investigations found no conclusive evidence that Reagan had authorized or known of the diversion. Yet they noted that because Reagan had approved of the sale of arms to Iran and had encouraged his staff to assist Nicaraguan rebels despite the prohibition of such assistance by Congress, "the President created or at least tolerated an environment where those who did know of the diversion believed with certainty that they were carrying out the President's policies."

Reagan was succeeded in 1988 by his vice president, George H.W. Bush. Benefiting from a prolonged economic expansion, Bush handily defeated Michael Dukakis, governor of Massachusetts and a liberal Democrat. On domestic issues, Bush sought to maintain policies introduced by the Reagan administration. His few legislative initiatives included the passage of legislation establishing strict regulations of air pollution, providing subsidies for child care, and protecting the rights of the disabled. Abroad, Bush showed more confidence and energy. While he responded cautiously to revolutions in Eastern Europe and the Soviet Union, he used his personal relationships with foreign leaders to bring about comprehensive peace talks between Israel and its Arab neighbors, to encourage a peaceful unification of Germany, and to negotiate broad and substantial arms cuts with the Russians. Bush reacted to Iraq's invasion of Kuwait in 1990 by sending 400,000 soldiers to form the basis of a multinational coalition, which he assembled and which destroyed Iraq's main force within seven months. This conflict became known as the Gulf War.

One of the biggest crises that the Bush administration encountered was the collapse of the savings and loan industry in the late eighties. Thrift institutions were required by law to pay low interest rates for deposits and long-term loans. The creation of money market funds for the small investor in the eighties which paid higher rates of return than savings accounts prompted depositors to withdraw their money from banks and invest it in the higher yielding mutual funds. To finance the withdrawals, banks began selling assets at a loss. The deregulation of the savings and loan industry, combined with the increase in federal deposit insurance from $40,000 to $100,000 per account, encouraged many desperate savings institutions to invest in high-risk real-estate ventures, for which no state supervision or regulation existed. When the majority of such ventures predictably failed, the federal government found itself compelled by law to rescue the thrifts. It is estimated that this will cost to taxpayers $345 billion, in settlements that will continue through 2029.

In his bid for reelection in 1992, Bush faced not only Democratic nominee Bill Clinton, Governor of Arkansas, but also third-party candidate Ross Perot, a Dallas billionaire who had made his fortune in the computer industry. In contrast to Bush's first run for the presidency, when the nation had enjoyed an unusually long period of economic expansion, the economy in 1992 was just beginning to recover from a recession. Although data released the following year indicated that a healthy rebound had already begun in 1992, the public perceived the economy during election year as weak. Clinton took advantage of this perception in his campaign, focusing on the financial concerns of what he called "the forgotten middle class." He also took a more centrist position on many issues than more traditional Democrats, promising fiscal responsibility and economic growth. Clinton defeated Bush, winning 43% of the vote to Bush's 38%. Perot garnered 18% of the vote.

At its outset, Clinton's presidency was plagued by numerous setbacks, most notably the failure of his controversial health care reform plan, drawn up under the leadership of first lady Hillary Rod-

ham Clinton. Major accomplishments included the passage, by a narrow margin, of a deficit-reduction bill calling for tax increases and spending cuts and Congressional approval of the North American Free Trade Agreement, which removed or reduced tariffs on most goods moving across the borders of the United States, Canada, and Mexico. Although supporters and critics agreed that the treaty would create or eliminate relatively few jobs—two hundred thousand—the accord prompted heated debate. Labor strenuously opposed the agreement, seeing it as accelerating the flight of factory jobs to countries with low labor costs such as Mexico, the third largest trading partner of the United States. Business, on the other hand, lobbied heavily for the treaty, arguing that it would create new markets for American goods and insisting that competition from Mexico would benefit the American economy.

By the fall of 1994, many American workers, still confronting stagnating wages, benefits, and living standards, had yet to feel the effects of the nation's recovery from the recession of 1990–91. The resulting disillusionment with the actions of the Clinton administration and the Democrat-controlled Congress, combined with the widespread climate of social conservatism resulting from a perceived erosion of traditional moral values led to an overwhelming upset by the Republican party in the 1994 midterm elections. The GOP gained control of both houses of Congress for the first time in over 40 years, also winning 11 gubernatorial races, for control of a total of 30 governorships nationwide. The Republican agenda—increased defense spending and cuts in taxes, social programs, and farm subsidies—had been popularized under the label "Contract with America," the title of a manifesto circulated during the campaign.

The ensuing confrontation between the nation's Democratic president and Republican-controlled Congress came to a head at the end of 1995, when Congress responded to presidential vetoes of appropriations and budget bills by refusing to pass stop gap spending measures, resulting in major shutdowns of the federal government in November and December. The following summer, however, the president and Congress joined forces to reform the welfare system through a bill replacing Aid to Families with Dependent Children with block grants through which welfare funding would largely become the province of the states.

The nation's economic recovery gained strength as the decade advanced, with healthy growth, falling unemployment, and moderate interest and inflation levels. Public confidence in the economy was reflected in a bull market on the stock exchange, which gained 60% between 1995 and 1997. Bolstered by a favorable economy at home and peace abroad, Clinton's faltering popularity rebounded and in 1996 he became the first Democratic president elected to a second term since Franklin D. Roosevelt in 1936, defeating the Republican candidate, former Senate majority leader Robert Dole, and Independent Ross Perot, whose electoral support was greatly reduced from its 1992 level. The Republicans retained control of both houses of Congress. In 1997, President Clinton signed into law a bipartisan budget plan designed to balance the federal budget by 2002 for the first time since 1969, through a combination of tax and spending cuts. In 1998–99, the federal government experienced two straight years of budget surpluses.

In 1998, special prosecutor Kenneth Starr submitted a report to Congress that resulted in the House of Representatives passing four articles of impeachment against President Clinton. In the subsequent trial in the Senate, the articles were defeated.

Regulation of the three large financial industries underwent significant change in late 1999. The Gramm-Leach-Bliley Act (also known as the Financial Modernization Act) was passed by Congress in November 1999. It cleared the way for banks, insurance companies, and securities companies to sell each other's services and to engage in merger and acquisition activity. Prior to the Act's passage, activities of the banking, insurance and securities industries were strictly limited by the Glass Steagall Act of 1933, which Gramm-Leach-Bliley repealed.

Health care issues received significant attention in 2000. On 23 November 1998, 46 states and the District of Columbia together reached a settlement with the large US tobacco companies over compensation for smoking-related health-care costs incurred by the states. Payments to the states, totaling $206 billion, were scheduled to be made over 25 years beginning in 1999. Most states passed Patients' Rights legislation, and all 50 states and the District of Columbia passed Children's Health Insurance Programs (CHIP) legislation to provide health care to children in low-income families.

The ongoing strong economy continued through the late 1990s and into 2000. Economic expansion set a record for longevity, and—except for higher gasoline prices during summer 2000, stemming from higher crude oil prices—inflation continued to be relatively low. By 2000, there was additional evidence that productivity growth had improved substantially since the mid-1990s, boosting living standards while helping to hold down increases in costs and prices despite very tight labor markets.

In 2000, Hispanics replaced African Americans as the largest minority group in the United States. (Hispanics numbered 35.3 million in 2000, or 12.5% of the population, compared with 34.7 million blacks, or 12.3% of the population.)

The 2000 presidential election was one of the closest in US history, pitting Democratic Vice President Al Gore against Republican Party candidate George W. Bush, son of former President George H. W. Bush. The vote count in Florida became the determining factor in the 7 November election, as each candidate needed to obtain the state's 25 electoral college votes in order to capture the 270 needed to win the presidency. When in the early hours of 8 November Bush appeared to have won the state's 25 votes, Gore called Bush to concede the election. He soon retracted the concession, however, after the extremely thin margin of victory triggered an automatic recount of the vote in Florida. The Democrats subsequently mounted a series of legal challenges to the vote count in Florida, which favored Bush. Eventually, the US Supreme Court, in *Bush v. Gore*, was summoned to rule on the election. On 12 December 2000, the Court, divided 5–4, reversed the Florida state supreme court decision that had ordered new recounts called for by Al Gore. George W. Bush was declared president. Gore had won the popular vote, however, capturing 48.4% of votes cast to Bush's 47.9%.

Once inaugurated, Bush called education his top priority, stating that "no child should be left behind" in America. He affirmed support for Medicare and Social Security, and called for pay and benefit increases for the military. He called upon charities and faith-based community groups to aid the disadvantaged. Bush announced a $1.6 trillion tax cut plan (subsequently reduced to

$1.35 trillion) in his first State of the Union Address as an economic stimulus package designed to respond to an economy that had begun to falter. He called for research and development of a missile-defense program, and warned of the threat of international terrorism.

The threat of international terrorism was made all too real on 11 September 2001, when 19 hijackers crashed 4 passenger aircraft into the North and South towers of the World Trade Center, the Pentagon, and a field in Stony Creek Township in Pennsylvania. The World Trade Center towers were destroyed. Approximately 3,000 people were confirmed or reported dead as a result of all four 11 September 2001 attacks. The terrorist organization al-Qaeda, led by Saudi-born Osama bin Laden, was believed to be responsible for the attacks, and a manhunt for bin Laden began.

On 7 October 2001, the United States and Britain launched air strikes against known terrorist training camps and military installations within Afghanistan, ruled by the Taliban regime that supported the al-Qaeda organization. The air strikes were supported by leaders of the European Union and Russia, as well as other nations. By December 2001, the Taliban were defeated, and Afghan leader Hamid Karzai was chosen to lead an interim administration for the country. Remnants of al-Qaeda still remained in Afghanistan and the surrounding region, and a year after the 2001 offensive more than 10,000 US soldiers remained in Afghanistan to suppress efforts by either the Taliban or al-Qaeda to regroup. As of 2005, Allied soldiers continued to come under periodic attack in Afghanistan.

As a response to the 11 September 2001 terrorist attacks, the US Congress that October approved the USA Patriot Act, proposed by the Bush administration. The act gave the government greater powers to detain suspected terrorists (or also immigrants), to counter money-laundering, and increase surveillance by domestic law enforcement and international intelligence agencies. Critics claimed the law did not provide for the system of checks and balances that safeguard civil liberties in the United States.

Beginning in late 2001, corporate America suffered a crisis of confidence. In December 2001, the energy giant Enron Corporation declared bankruptcy after massive false accounting practices came to light. Eclipsing the Enron scandal, telecommunications giant WorldCom in June 2002 disclosed that it had hid $3.8 billion in expenses over 15 months. The fraud led to WorldCom's bankruptcy, the largest in US history (the company had $107 billion in assets).

In his January 2002 State of the Union Address, President Bush announced that Iran, Iraq, and North Korea constituted an "axis of evil," sponsoring terrorism and threatening the United States and its allies with weapons of mass destruction. Throughout 2002, the United States pressed its case against Iraq, stating that the Iraqi regime had to disarm itself of weapons of mass destruction. In November 2002, the UN Security Council passed Resolution 1441, calling upon Iraq to disarm itself of any chemical, biological, or nuclear weapons it might possess and to allow for the immediate return of weapons inspectors (they had been expelled in 1998). UN and IAEA (International Atomic Energy Agency) weapons inspectors returned to the country, but the United States and the United Kingdom expressed dissatisfaction with their progress, and indicated military force might be necessary to remove the Iraqi regime, led by Saddam Hussein. France and Russia, permanent members of the UN Security Council, and Germany, a nonpermanent member, in particular, opposed the use of military force. The disagreement caused a diplomatic rift in the West that was slow to repair.

After diplomatic efforts at conflict resolution failed by March 2003, the United States, on 19 March, launched air strikes against targets in Baghdād and war began. On 9 April, Baghdād fell to US forces, and work began on restoring basic services to the Iraqi population, including providing safe drinking water, electricity, and sanitation. On 1 May, President Bush declared major combat operations had been completed. Iraqi dictator Saddam Hussein was captured by US forces on 13 December 2003 and placed in custody.

In May 2004, the Abu Ghraib scandal erupted. Photographs of US soldiers engaged in acts of abuse—including physical, sexual, and psychological—against Iraqi prisoners being held at the Abu Ghraib military prison outside Baghdād were made public. The fact that the prison had been a place of torture and execution under Saddam Hussein's rule made the abuse seem even more degrading. Seven US suspects were named for carrying out the abuse; most were given prison sentences on charges ranging from conspiracy to assault, but some thought higher-ranking officials, including Secretary of Defense Donald Rumsfeld, should resign as well.

US forces increasingly became the targets of attacks in Iraq as an insurgency against the US military presence began. By late 2005, nearly 1,900 US soldiers had been killed since major combat operations were declared over on 1 May 2003. Some 138,000 US troops remained in Iraq in late 2005, and that number was expected to increase as a referendum on a new Iraqi constitution in October 2005 and national elections in December 2005 were to be held.

The 2004 presidential election was held on 2 November. President George W. Bush and Vice President Dick Cheney defeated Democratic challengers John F. Kerry and John R. Edwards. Bush received approximately 3 million more popular votes than Kerry, and won the electoral vote 286 to 251 (One electoral vote went to John Edwards when an elector pledged to Kerry voted for "John Edwards" instead.) The vote in Ohio was the deciding factor, and upon conceding Ohio, Kerry conceded the election. The campaign was run on such issues as terrorism, the War in Iraq, the economy, and to a lesser extent issues of morality and values (Anti-gay marriage measures were on the ballots in 11 states, and all passed.)

In August 2005, Hurricane Katrina landed on the Gulf Coast of the United States, in what was one of the worst natural disasters in US history. The city of New Orleans, Louisiana, was evacuated, but some 150,000 people were unable to leave before the storm hit. A day after the storm appeared to have bypassed the city's center, levees were breached by the storm surge and water submerged the metropolis. Rescuers initially ignored the bodies of the dead in the search to find the living. Those unable to leave the city were sheltered in the Louisiana Superdome and New Orleans Convention Center; air conditioning, electricity, and running water failed, making for unsanitary and uncomfortable conditions. They were later transferred to other shelters, including the Houston Astrodome. Looting, shootings, and carjackings exacerbated already devastating conditions. The costs of the hurricane and flooding were exceedingly high in terms of both loss of life and economic damage: more than 1,000 people died and damages were estimated to reach $200 billion. Katrina had global economic consequences, as imports, exports, and oil supplies—including production, importation, and refining—were disrupted. The Federal Emergency Management Agency (FEMA) of the Department of Homeland Security, and President Bush were criticized in varying degrees for their lack of adequate response to the disaster. FEMA director Michael D. Brown resigned his position amid the furor. Race and class issues also came to the fore, as the majority of New Orleans residents unable to evacuate the city and affected by the catastrophe were poor and African American.

12 FEDERAL GOVERNMENT

The Constitution of the United States, signed in 1787, is the nation's governing document. In the first 10 amendments to the Constitution, ratified in 1791 and known as the Bill of Rights, the federal government is denied the power to infringe on rights generally regarded as fundamental to the civil liberties of the people. These amendments prohibit the establishment of a state religion and the abridgment of freedom of speech, press, and the right to assemble. They protect all persons against unreasonable searches and seizures, guarantee trial by jury, and prohibit excessive bail and cruel and unusual punishments. No person may be required to testify against himself, nor may he be deprived of life, liberty, or property without due process of law. The 13th Amendment (1865) banned slavery; the 15th (1870) protected the freed slaves' right to vote; and the 19th (1920) guaranteed the franchise to women. In all, there have been 27 amendments, the last of which, proposed in 1789 but ratified in 1992, denied the variation of the compensation of Senators and Representatives until an election intervened. The Equal Rights Amendment (ERA), approved by Congress in 1972, would have mandated equality between the sexes; only 35 of the required 38 states had ratified the ERA by the time the ratification deadline expired on 30 June 1982.

The United States has a federal form of government, with the distribution of powers between the federal government and the states constitutionally defined. The legislative powers of the federal government are vested in Congress, which consists of the House of Representatives and the Senate. There are 435 members of the House of Representatives. Each state is allotted a number of representatives in proportion to its population as determined by the decennial census. Representatives are elected for two-year terms in every even-numbered year. A representative must be at least 25 years old, must be a resident of the state represented, and must have been a citizen of the United States for at least seven years. The Senate consists of two senators from each state, elected for six-year terms. Senators must be at least 30 years old, must be residents of the states from which they are elected, and must have been citizens of the United States for at least nine years. One-third of the Senate is elected in every even-numbered year.

Congress legislates on matters of taxation, borrowing, regulation of international and interstate commerce, formulation of rules of naturalization, bankruptcy, coinage, weights and measures, post offices and post roads, courts inferior to the Supreme Court, provision for the armed forces, among many other matters. A broad interpretation of the "necessary and proper" clause of the Constitution has widened considerably the scope of congressional legislation based on the enumerated powers.

A bill that is passed by both houses of Congress in the same form is submitted to the president, who may sign it or veto it. If the president chooses to veto the bill, it is returned to the house in which it originated with the reasons for the veto. The bill may become law despite the president's veto if it is passed again by a two-thirds vote in both houses. A bill becomes law without the president's signature if retained for 10 days while Congress is in session. After Congress adjourns, if the president does not sign a bill within 10 days, an automatic veto ensues.

The president must be "a natural born citizen" at least 35 years old, and must have been a resident of the United States for 14 years. Under the 22nd Amendment to the Constitution, adopted in 1951, a president may not be elected more than twice. Each state is allotted a number of electors based on its combined total of US senators and representatives, and, technically, it is these electors who, constituted as the electoral college, cast their vote for president, with all of the state's electoral votes customarily going to the candidate who won the largest share of the popular vote of the state (the District of Columbia also has three electors, making a total of 538 votes). Thus, the candidate who wins the greatest share of the popular vote throughout the United States may, in rare cases, fail to win a majority of the electoral vote. If no candidate gains a majority in the electoral college, the choice passes to the House of Representatives.

The vice president, elected at the same time and on the same ballot as the president, serves as ex officio president of the Senate. The vice president assumes the power and duties of the presidency on the president's removal from office or as a result of the president's death, resignation, or inability to perform his duties. In the case of a vacancy in the vice presidency, the president nominates a successor, who must be approved by a majority in both houses of Congress. The Congress has the power to determine the line of presidential succession in case of the death or disability of both the president and vice president.

Under the Constitution, the president is enjoined to "take care that the laws be faithfully executed." In reality, the president has a considerable amount of leeway in determining to what extent a law is or is not enforced. Congress's only recourse is impeachment, to which it has resorted only three times, in proceedings against presidents Andrew Johnson, Richard Nixon, and Bill Clinton. Both the president and the vice president are removable from office after impeachment by the House and conviction at a Senate trial for "treason, bribery, or other high crimes and misdemeanors." The president has the power to grant reprieves and pardons for offenses against the United States except in cases of impeachment.

The president nominates and "by and with the advice and consent of the Senate" appoints ambassadors, public ministers, consuls, and all federal judges, including the justices of the Supreme Court. As commander in chief, the president is ultimately responsible for the disposition of the land, naval, and air forces, but the power to declare war belongs to Congress. The president conducts foreign relations and makes treaties with the advice and consent of the Senate. No treaty is binding unless it wins the approval of two-thirds of the Senate. The president's independence is also limited by the House of Representatives, where all money bills originate.

The president also appoints as his cabinet, subject to Senate confirmation, the secretaries who head the departments of the executive branch. As of 2005, the executive branch included the following cabinet departments: Agriculture (created in 1862), Commerce (1913), Defense (1947), Education (1980), Energy (1977), Health and Human Services (1980), Housing and Urban Development (1965), Interior (1849), Justice (1870), Labor (1913), State (1789), Transportation (1966), Treasury (1789), Veterans' Affairs (1989), and Homeland Security (2002). The Department of Defense—headquartered in the Pentagon, the world's largest office building—also administers the various branches of the military: Air Force, Army, Navy, defense agencies, and joint-service schools. The Department of Justice administers the Federal Bureau of Investigation, which originated in 1908; the Central Intelligence Agency (1947) is under the aegis of the Executive office. Among the several hundred quasi-independent agencies are the Federal Reserve System (1913), serving as the nation's central bank, and the major regulatory bodies, notably the Environmental Protection Agency (1970), Federal Communications Commission (1934), Federal Power Commission (1920), Federal Trade Commission (1914), and Interstate Commerce Commission (1887).

Regulations for voting are determined by the individual states for federal as well as for local offices, and requirements vary from state to state. In the past, various southern states used literacy tests, poll taxes, "grandfather" clauses, and other methods to disfranchise black voters, but Supreme Court decisions and congressional measures, including the Voting Rights Act of 1965, more than doubled the number of black registrants in Deep South states between 1964 and 1992. In 1960, only 29.1% of the black voting-age population was registered to vote; by the mid-1990s, that percentage had risen to over 65%.

As of the November 2004 presidential election, there were over 16 million registered African American voters (64.4% of those African Americans eligible to vote). The number of registered Hispanic voters increased from 2.5 million in 1972 to 9 million in 2004 (34.3% of eligible Hispanic voters). Sixty-four percent of eligible voters cast ballots in the 2004 presidential election, up from 60% in 2000. Voter registration was reported to be 72% nationwide. The next presidential election was to be held November 2008.

13 POLITICAL PARTIES

Two major parties, Democratic and Republican, have dominated national, state, and local politics since 1860. These parties are made up of clusters of small autonomous local groups primarily concerned with local politics and the election of local candidates to office. Within each party, such groups frequently differ drastically in policies and beliefs on many issues, but once every four years, they successfully bury their differences and rally around a candidate for the presidency. Minority parties have been formed at various periods in US political history, but most have generally allied with one of the two major parties, and none has achieved sustained national prominence. The most successful minority party in recent decades—that of Texas billionaire Ross Perot in 1992—was little more than a protest vote. Various extreme groups on the right and left, including a small US Communist Party, have had little political significance on a national scale; in 1980, the Libertarian Party became the first minor party since 1916 to appear on the ballot in all 50 states. The Green Party increased its showing in the 2000 election, with presidential candidate Ralph Nader winning 2.7% of the vote. Independent candidates have won state and local office, but no candidate has won the presidency without major party backing.

Traditionally, the Republican Party is more solicitous of business interests and gets greater support from business than does the Democratic Party. A majority of blue-collar workers, by contrast, have generally supported the Democratic Party, which favors more lenient labor laws, particularly as they affect labor unions; the Republican Party often (though not always) supports legislation that restricts the power of labor unions. Republicans favor the enhancement of the private sector of the economy, while Democrats generally urge the cause of greater government participation and regulatory authority, especially at the federal level.

Within both parties there are sharp differences on a great many issues; for example, northeastern Democrats in the past almost uniformly favored strong federal civil rights legislation, which was anathema to the Deep South; eastern Republicans in foreign policy are internationalist-minded, while midwesterners of the same party constituted from 1910 through 1940 the hard core of isolationist sentiment in the country. More recently, "conservative" headings have been adopted by members of both parties who emphasize decentralized government power, strengthened private enterprise, and a strong US military posture overseas, while the designation "liberal" has been applied to those favoring an increased federal government role in economic and social affairs, disengagement from foreign military commitments, and safeguards for civil liberties.

President Nixon's resignation and the accompanying scandal surrounding the Republican Party hierarchy had a telling, if predictable, effect on party morale, as indicated by Republican losses in the 1974 and 1976 elections. The latent consequences of the Vietnam and Watergate years appeared to take their toll on both parties, however, in growing apathy toward politics and mistrust of politicians among the electorate. Ronald Reagan's successful 1980 presidential bid cut into traditional Democratic strongholds throughout the United States, as Republicans won control of the US Senate and eroded state and local Democratic majorities. On the strength of an economic recovery, President Reagan won reelection in November 1984, carrying 49 of 50 states (with a combined total of 525 electoral votes) and 58.8% of the popular vote; the Republicans retained control of the Senate, but the Democrats held on to the House. Benefiting from a six-year expansion of the economy, Republican George H.W. Bush won 54% of the vote in 1988. As Reagan had, Bush successfully penetrated traditionally Democratic regions. He carried every state in the South as well as the industrial states of the North.

Bush's approval rating reached a high of 91% in March of 1991 in the wake of the Persian Gulf War. By July of 1992, however, that

US Popular Vote for President by National Political Parties, 1948–2004

YEAR	WINNER	VOTES CAST	VOTERS	DEMOCRAT	REPUBLICAN	PROHIBITION	SOC. LABOR	SOC. WORKERS	SOCIALIST	PROGRESSIVE	STATES' RIGHTS DEMOCRAT	CONSTITUTION	OTHER[1]
1948	Truman (D)	48,692,442	51	24,105,587	21,970,017	103,489	29,038	13,614	138,973	1,157,057	1,169,134	—	5,533
1952	Eisenhower (R)	61,551,118	62	27,314,649	33,936,137	73,413	30,250	10,312	20,065	140,416	—	17,200	8,676
1956	Eisenhower (R)	62,025,372	59	26,030,172	35,585,245	41,937	44,300	7,797	2,044	—	2,657	108,055	203,165
											NATL. STATES' RIGHTS		
1960	Kennedy (D)	68,828,960	63	34,221,344	34,106,761	44,087	47,522	40,166	—	—	209,314	—	159,856
												UNPLEDGED DEM	
1964	Johnson (D)	70,641,104	62	43,126,584	27,177,838	23,266	45,187	32,701	—	—	6,953	210,732	17,843
									COMMUNIST	PEACE AND FREEDOM	AMERICAN IND.		
1968	Nixon (R)	73,203,370	61	31,274,503	31,785,148	14,915	52,591	41,390	1,076	83,720[2]	9,901,151	—	48,876
										LIBERTARIAN		AMERICAN	
1972	Nixon (R)	77,727,590	55	29,171,791	47,170,179	12,818	53,811	94,4152	25,343	3,671	—	1,090,673	104,889
							US LABOR						
1976	Carter (D)	81,552,331	54	40,829,046	39,146,006	15,958	40,041	91,310	58,992	173,019	170,531	160,773	866,655[3]
						CITIZENS	RESPECT FOR LIFE						
1980	Reagan (R)	86,495,678	54	35,481,435	43,899,248	230,377	32,319	40,105	43,871	920,859	41,172	6,539	5,799,753[4]
							POPULIST				IND. ALLIANCE		
1984	Reagan (R)	92,652,793	53	37,577,137	54,455,074	72,200	66,336	24,706	36,386	228,314	46,852	13,161	132,627[5]
1988	Bush(R)	91,594,809	50	41,809,074	48,886,097	30,905	47,047	15,604	—	432,179	217,219	3,475	153,209
						US TAX PAYER							
1992	Clinton(D)	104,426,659	55	44,909,889	39,104,545	43,398	107,002	23,091	39,163	291,628	73,708	3,875	19,830,360[6]
						US TAX PAYER	GREEN			LIBERTARIAN	NATURAL LAW		
1996	Clinton (D)	96,277,223	49	47,402,357	39,198,755	184,658	684,902	8,476	4,765	485,798	113,668	1,847	8,196,762[7]
						REFORM							
2000	Bush,GW (R)	105,405,100	48	50,999,897	50,456,002	448,895	2,882,955	7,378	—	384,431	87,714	98,020	39,808
2004	Bush,GW (R)	122,295,345	57	59,028,444	62,040,610	465,650	119,859	10,791[8]	—	397,265	10,837	143,630	78,259

[1]Includes votes for state parties, independent candidates and unpledged electors.
[2]Total includes votes for several candidates in different states under the same party label.
[3]Includes 756,631 votes for Eugene McCarthy, an independent.
[4]Includes 5,719,437 votes for John Anderson, an independent.
[5]Includes 78,807 votes for Lyndon H. LaRouche, an independent.
[6]Includes 19,742,267 votes for Ross Perot, an independent.
[7]Includes 8,085,402 votes for Ross Perot, a Reform candidate.
[8]Includes 7,102 votes for James Harris and 3,689 for Róger Calero

rating had plummeted to 25%, in part because Bush appeared to be disengaged from domestic issues, particularly the 1991 recession. Bill Clinton, governor of Arkansas and twenty years younger than Bush, presented himself to the electorate as a "New Democrat." He took more moderate positions than traditional New Deal Democrats, including calling for a middle-class tax cut, welfare reform, national service, and such traditionally Republican goals as getting tough on crime. The presidential race took on an unpredictable dimension with the entrance of Independent Ross Perot, a Texas billionaire. Perot, who attacked the budget deficit and called for shared sacrifice, withdrew from the race in July and then re-entered it in October. Clinton won the election with 43% of the vote, Bush received 38%, and Perot captured 18%, more than any third-party presidential candidate since Theodore Roosevelt in 1912. As of 1992, Democrats enjoyed a large advantage over Republicans in voter registration, held both houses of congress, had a majority of state governorships, and controlled most state legislative bodies. In 1996 Bill Clinton became the first Democratic president since Franklin Roosevelt to be elected to a second term, with 49% of the popular vote to 41% for Republican Bob Dole, and 8% for Ross Perot, who once again ran as an Independent. Republicans retained control of the House and Senate.

Aided by a growing climate of conservatism on moral issues and popular discontent with the pace of economic recovery from the recent recession, the Republicans accomplished an historic upset in the 1994 midterm elections, gaining control of both houses of Congress for the first time since 1952. They gained 52 seats in the House, for a majority of 230–204, and 8 seats in the Senate, for a majority that came to 53–47 once Democrat Richard Shelby of Alabama changed parties shortly after the election. The Republicans also increased their power at the state level, winning 11 governorships, for a national total of 30. The number of state legislatures under Republican control increased from 8 to 19, with 18 controlled by the Democrats and 12 under split control. After the 1998 election, the Republican majority had eroded slightly in the House, with the 106th Congress including 223 Republicans, 210 Democrats, and 2 Independents; the Senate included 55 Republicans and 45 Democrats.

The major candidates in the 2000 presidential election were Republican George W. Bush, son of former president George H.W. Bush; his vice presidential running mate was Dick Cheney. The Democratic candidate was Vice President Al Gore, Jr. (Clinton administration 1992–2000). Gore chose Joseph Lieberman, senator from Connecticut, as his running mate. Lieberman, an Orthodox Jew, became the first Jew to run for national office. Following the contested presidential election of 2000, George W. Bush emerged as president following a ruling by the US Supreme Court. Gore won the popular vote, with 48.4%, to 47.9% for Bush, but Bush won the electoral college vote, 271–266, with one blank vote in the electoral college cast. Sectional and demographic differences were evident in the 2000 election, with the Northeast, parts of the Midwest, the Pacific states, and most urban areas voting Democratic, and the South, West, and rural communities voting Republican.

Following the November 2002 mid-term elections, Republicans held 229 of 435 seats in the House of Representatives, and there were 205 Democrats and 1 independent in the House. The Republicans held an extremely thin margin in the Senate, of 51 seats, to the Democrats' 48. There was one independent in the Senate, former Republican Jim Jeffords. Following the election, Nancy Pelosi became the Democratic Majority Leader in the House of Representatives, the first woman to head either party in Congress. As a result of the 2002 election, there were 60 women, 37 African Americans, and 22 Hispanics in the House of Representatives, and 14 women in the Senate. There were no African American or Hispanic senators following the 2002 election.

The 2004 presidential election was won by incumbent George W. Bush and his running mate Dick Cheney. They defeated Democrats John F. Kerry and John Edwards. Bush received 286 electoral votes, Kerry 251, and Edwards 1 when an elector wrote the name "John Edwards" in on the electoral ballot. Bush received a majority of the popular vote—50.73%, to Kerry's 48.27%—or 3 million more votes than Kerry. Voter turnout was the highest since 1968, at 64%. The composition of the 109th Congress after the 2004 election was as follows: 55 Republicans, 44 Democrats, and 1 Independent in the Senate, and 232 Republicans, 202 Democrats, and 1 Independent in the House of Representatives. The next elections for the Senate and House of Representatives were to be held November 2006.

The 1984 election marked a turning point for women in national politics. Geraldine A. Ferraro, a Democrat, became the first female vice presidential nominee of a major US political party; no woman has ever captured a major-party presidential nomination. In the 109th Congress (2005–06), 14 women served in the US Senate, and 68 women held seats in the US House of Representatives (including delegates).

The 1984 presidential candidacy of Jesse L. Jackson, election, the first African American ever to win a plurality in a statewide presidential preference primary, likewise marked the emergence of African Americans as a political force, especially within the Democratic Party. In 1992 an African American woman, Democrat Carol Moseley Braun of Illinois, won election to the Senate, becoming the first black senator; Moseley Braun lost her reelection bid in 1998. She was a candidate for president in 2004.

There were 42 African Americans in the House of Representatives and one in the Senate in the 109th Congress. Twenty-six Hispanics were serving in the House and two in the Senate, a record number. Eight members of Congress were of Asian/Hawaiian/or other Pacific Islander ethnicity, six in the House of Representatives and two in the Senate. There was one Native American in the House. (These numbers include delegates.)

14 LOCAL GOVERNMENT

Governmental units within each state comprise counties, municipalities, and such special districts as those for water, sanitation, highways, and parks. and recreation. There are more than 3,000 counties in the United States; more than 19,000 municipalities, including cities, villages, towns, and boroughs; nearly 15,000 school districts; and at least 31,000 special districts. Additional townships, authorities, commissions, and boards make up the rest of the nearly 85,000 local governmental units.

The 50 states are autonomous within their own spheres of government, and their autonomy is defined in broad terms by the 10th Amendment to the US Constitution, which reserves to the states such powers as are not granted to the federal government and not denied to the states. The states may not, among other restrictions, issue paper money, conduct foreign relations, impair the obligations of contracts, or establish a government that is not republican in form. Subsequent amendments to the Constitution and many Supreme Court decisions added to the restrictions placed on the states. The 13th Amendment prohibited the states from legalizing the ownership of one person by another (slavery); the 14th Amendment deprived the states of their power to determine qualifications for citizenship; the 15th Amendment prohibited the states from denying the right to vote because of race, color, or previous condition of servitude; and the 19th, from denying the vote to women.

Since the Civil War, the functions of the state have expanded. Local business—that is, business not involved in foreign or interstate commerce—is regulated by the state. The states create subordinate governmental bodies such as counties, cities, towns, villages, and boroughs, whose charters they either issue or, where home rule is permitted, approve. States regulate employment of children and women in industry, and enact safety laws to prevent industrial accidents. Unemployment insurance is a state function, as are education, public health, highway construction and safety, operation of a state highway patrol, and various kinds of personal relief. The state and local governments still are primarily responsible for providing public assistance, despite the large part the federal government plays in financing welfare.

Each state is headed by an elected governor. State legislatures are bicameral except Nebraska's, which has been unicameral since 1934. Generally, the upper house is called the senate, and the lower house the house of representatives or the assembly. Bills must be passed by both houses, and the governor has a suspensive veto, which usually may be overridden by a two-thirds vote.

The number, population, and geographic extent of the more than 3,000 counties in the United States—including the analogous units called boroughs in Alaska and parishes in Louisiana—show no uniformity from state to state. The county is the most conspicuous unit of rural local government and has a variety of powers, including location and repair of highways, county poor relief, determination of voting precincts and of polling places, and organization of school and road districts. City governments, usually headed by a mayor or city manager, have the power to levy taxes; to borrow; to pass, amend, and repeal local ordinances; and to grant franchises for public service corporations. Township government through an annual town meeting is an important New England tradition.

From the 1960s into the 21st century, a number of large cities began to suffer severe fiscal crises brought on by a combination of factors. Loss of tax revenues stemmed from the migration of middle-class residents to the suburbs and the flight of many small and large firms seeking to avoid the usually higher costs of doing business in urban areas. Low-income groups, many of them unskilled blacks and Hispanic migrants, came to constitute large segments of city populations, placing added burdens on locally funded welfare, medical, housing, and other services without providing the commensurate tax base for additional revenues.

15 STATE SERVICES

All state governments provide services in the fields of education, transportation, health and social welfare, public protection (including state police and prison personnel), housing, and labor. The 1970s saw an expansion of state services in four key areas:

energy, environment, consumer protection, and governmental ethics. Each state provides some form of consumer advocacy, either through a separate department or agency or through the office of the attorney general. State government in the 1970s and early 1980s also showed the effects of the so-called post-Watergate morality. Laws mandating financial disclosure by public officials, once rare, had become common by 1983. Also notable were "sunshine laws," opening legislative committee meetings and administrative hearings to the public, and the use of an ombudsman either with general jurisdiction or with special powers relating, for example, to the problems of businesses, prisoners, the elderly, or racial minorities. Other trends in state administration, reflected on the federal level, include the separation of education from other services and the consolidation of social welfare programs in departments of human resources.

The distribution of federal funds to state, local, and territorial governments was placed at more than $2.1 trillion in 2004. The largest outlays of aid were for retirement and disability funds, at $666.9 billion; Medicare, $259 billion; Medicaid, $172 billion; and supplemental security income, $36.9 billion.

California received more funds than any other state, $232.3 billion, followed by New York state at $143.9 billion; Texas at $141.8 billion; Florida, at $121.9 billion; Pennsylvania at $94.9 billion, and Virginia at $90.6 billion.

16 JUDICIAL SYSTEM

The Supreme Court, established by the US Constitution, is the nation's highest judicial body, consisting of the chief justice of the United States and eight associate justices. All justices are appointed by the president with the advice and consent of the Senate. Appointments are for life "during good behavior," otherwise terminating only by resignation or impeachment and conviction.

The original jurisdiction of the Supreme Court is relatively narrow; as an appellate court, it is open to appeal from decisions of federal district courts, circuit courts of appeals, and the highest courts in the states, although it may dismiss an appeal if it sees fit to do so. The Supreme Court, by means of a writ of certiorari, may call up a case from a district court for review. Regardless of how cases reach it, the Court enforces a kind of unity on the decisions of the lower courts. It also exercises the power of judicial review, determining the constitutionality of state laws, state constitutions, congressional statutes, and federal regulations, but only when these are specifically challenged.

The Constitution empowers Congress to establish all federal courts inferior to the Supreme Court. On the lowest level and handling the greatest proportion of federal cases are the district courts—including one each in Puerto Rico, Guam, the Virgin Islands, the Northern Mariana Islands, and the District of Columbia—where all offenses against the laws of the United States are tried. Civil actions that involve cases arising under treaties and laws of the United States and under the Constitution, where the amount in dispute is greater than $5,000, also fall within the jurisdiction of the district courts. District courts have no appellate jurisdiction; their decisions may be carried to the courts of appeals, organized into 13 circuits. These courts also hear appeals from decisions made by administrative commissions. For most cases, this is usually the last stage of appeal, except where the court rules that a statute of a state conflicts with the Constitution of the United

States, with federal law, or with a treaty. Special federal courts include the Court of Claims, Court of Customs and Patent Appeals, and Tax Court.

State courts operate independently of the federal judiciary. Most states adhere to a court system that begins on the lowest level with a justice of the peace and includes courts of general trial jurisdiction, appellate courts, and, at the apex of the system, a state supreme court. The court of trial jurisdiction, sometimes called the county or superior court, has both original and appellate jurisdiction; all criminal cases (except those of a petty kind) and some civil cases are tried in this court. The state's highest court, like the Supreme Court of the United States, interprets the constitution and the laws of the state.

The grand jury is a body of from 13 to 24 persons that brings indictments against individuals suspected of having violated the law. Initially, evidence is presented to it by either a justice of the peace or a prosecuting county or district attorney. The trial or petit jury of 12 persons is used in trials of common law, both criminal and civil, except where the right to a jury trial is waived by consent of all parties at law. It judges the facts of the case, while the court is concerned exclusively with questions of law. The US accepts the compulsory jurisdiction of the International Court of Justice with reservations.

¹⁷ARMED FORCES

The armed forces of the United States of America in 2005 numbered 1.473 million on active duty and 1.29 million in the Ready Reserve, a category of participation that allows regular training with pay and extended active duty periods for training. Membership in all U.S. armed forces is voluntary and has been since 1973 when conscription expired as the Vietnam war was winding down. The active duty force includes 196,100 women, who serve in all grades and all occupational specialties except direct ground combat units and some aviation billets.

In the 1990s, the armed forces reduced their personnel numbers and force structure because of the diminished threat of a nuclear war with the former Soviet Union or a major conflict in central Europe. Despite the interlude of the Gulf War, 1990–91, the force reductions continued throughout the decade, forcing some restructuring of the active duty forces, with emphasis on rapid deployment to deter or fight major regional conflicts much like the Gulf War, in Korea, elsewhere in the Middle East, or Latin America (e.g. Cuba). The conventional force debate centered on whether the United States could or should maintain forces to fight two regional conflicts simultaneously. In the spring of 1999, the United States took part in the NATO air campaign in response to the crisis in Kosovo, and the ensuing US participation in peacekeeping operations in the region brought with it the prospect of another long-term overseas deployment.

For the purposes of administration, personnel management, logistics, and training, the traditional four military services in the Department of Defense remain central to strategic planning. The US Army numbers 502,000 soldiers on active duty, and are deployed into 10 divisions (two armored, four mechanized infantry, two light infantry, one air assault and one airborne), as well as into various armored cavalry, aviation, artillery, signals, psychological operations, ranger, Special Forces, civil affairs and air defense units. Army missions involving special operations are given

to Special Forces groups, an airborne ranger regiment, an aviation group, and a psychological warfare group, with civil affairs and communications support units. The Army had 7,620 main battle tanks, 6,719 infantry fighting vehicles, 14,900 armored personnel carriers, 6,530 towed or self-propelled artillery pieces, some 268 fixed wing aircraft, and 4,431 armed and transport helicopters. The Army National Guard (355,900) emphasizes the preparation of combat units up to division size for major regional conflicts, while the Army Reserve (351,350) prepares individuals to fill active units or provide combat support or service support/technical/medical units upon mobilization. In addition, the National Guard retains a residual state role in suppressing civil disturbances and providing disaster relief.

The US Navy had 376,750 active personnel. The service has seen its role shift from nuclear strategic deterrence and control of sea routes to Europe and Asia, to the projection of naval power from the sea. Naval task forces normally combine three combat elements: air, surface, and subsurface. The Navy had up to 80 nuclear-powered submarines, that consisted of 16 strategic ballistic missile (SSBN) and 64 tactical/attack (SSGN and SSN) submarines. The latter ships can launch cruise missiles at land targets.

As of 2005, naval aviation was centered on 12 carriers (nine nuclear-powered) and 11 carrier aircraft wings, which included armed ASW helicopters and armed long-range ASW patrol aircraft, as well as a large fleet of communications and support aircraft. The Navy controled 983 combat capable fixed wing aircraft and 608 helicopters of all types. Naval aviation reserves provided additional wings for carrier deployment. The surface force included 27 cruisers (22 with advanced anti-air suites), 49 destroyers, 30 frigates, 38 amphibious ships, 26 mine warfare ships, and 21 patrol and coastal combatants. More ships are kept in ready reserve or were manned by surface line reserve units. The fleet support force also included specialized ships for global logistics that are not base-dependent.

The Marine Corps, a separate branch of the Navy, was organized into three active divisions and three aircraft wings of the Fleet Marine Force, which also included three Force Service Support groups and special operations and anti-terrorism units. The Marine Corps (173,350; 11,311 reservists) emphasized amphibious landings but trained for a wide-range of contingency employments. The Marines had 344 combat capable fixed wing aircraft, 304 helicopters of all types, 403 main battle tanks, 1,311 amphibious armored vehicles, and about 1,511 artillery pieces (926 towed).

As of 2005, the US Air Force had 379,500 active personnel, and was focused on becoming rapidly deployable rather than US-based. Almost all its aircraft are now dedicated to nonstrategic roles in support of forward deployed ground and naval forces. The Air Force stressed the missions of air superiority and interdiction with complementary operations in electronic warfare and reconnaissance, but it also included 29 transport squadrons. Air Force personnel manage the US radar and satellite early-warning and intelligence effort. The Air Force Reserve and Air National Guard (roughly 183,200 active reserves) provided a wide range of flying and support units, and its flying squadrons had demonstrated exceptional readiness and combat skills on contingency missions. Air Force reserves, for example, were the backbone of the air refueling and transport fleets.

The armed forces were deployed among a range of functional unified or specified commands for actual missions. Strategic forces were under the US Strategic Command, which was a combined service command that controled the U.S.' strategic nuclear deterrence forces, which as of 2005, was made up of 550 land-based ICBMs, 16 Navy fleet ballistic missile submarines (SSBNs), and 85 operational long-range bombers (B-52s and B-1As). Land-based ICBMs are under the Air Force Space Command, while the long-range bomber force was under the Air Force Air Combat Command. The Strategic Command was also responsible for strategic reconnaissance and intelligence collection, and the strategic early warning and air defense forces. In 2002 the Treaty of Moscow was signed between the United States and Russia to reduce deployed nuclear weapons by two-thirds by the year 2012. As of 2002, the United States had more than 10,000 operational nuclear warheads.

The conventional forces were deployed to a mix of geographic and organizational commands, including the Atlantic, European, Central, Southern, Northern and Pacific commands, as well as to specific organizational commands such as the Transportation Command, Special Operations Command and Air Mobility Command. Major operational units are deployed to Germany, Korea, and Japan as part of collective security alliances, in addition to forces stationed throughout other countries in the Middle East, Africa, Southeast Asia, Western and Eastern Europe, and Latin America. Approximately 19,000 US troops are stationed in Afghanistan with Operation Enduring Freedom.

Patterns of defense spending reflected the movement away from Cold War assumptions and confrontation with the former Soviet Union and the People's Republic of China. During the 1980s when defense spending hovered around $300 billion a year and increased roughly 30% over the decade, defense spending absorbed roughly 6% of the gross domestic spending, 25% of federal spending, and 16% of net public spending. In the early 1990s, when the defense budget slipped back to the $250–$260 billion level, the respective percentages were 4.5, 18, and 11, the lowest levels of support for defense since the Korean War (1950). In 1999, the defense budget was $276.7 million or 3.2% of GDP. In 2005, US defense budget outlays totaled $465 billion.

18 MIGRATION

Between 1840 and 1930, some 37 million immigrants, the overwhelming majority of them Europeans, arrived in the United States. Immigration reached its peak in the first decade of the 20th century, when nearly 9 million came. Following the end of World War I, the tradition of almost unlimited immigration was abandoned, and through the National Origins Act of 1924, a quota system was established as the basis of a carefully restricted policy of immigration. Under the McCarran Act of 1952, one-sixth of 1% of the number of inhabitants from each European nation residing in the continental United States as of 1920 could be admitted annually. In practice, this system favored nations of northern and western Europe, with the UK, Germany, and Ireland being the chief beneficiaries. The quota system was radically reformed in 1965, under a new law that established an annual ceiling of 170,000 for Eastern Hemisphere immigrants and 120,000 for entrants from the Western Hemisphere; in October 1978, these limits were replaced by a worldwide limit of 290,000, which was lowered to 270,000 by 1981. A major 1990 overhaul set a total annual ceiling of 700,000 (675,000 beginning in fiscal 1995), of which 480,000 would be family sponsored and 140,000 employment based. The 1996 Immigration Reform Law addressed concerns about illegal immigration and border enforcement. The 1996 Welfare Reform Law revised legal and illegal immigrants' access to different forms of public assistance, and raised the standards for US residents who sponsor immigrants. The 2000 H-1B Visa Legislation increased temporary immigration visas for high-tech workers. In 2004, President Bush proposed a fair and secure immigration reform with a new temporary worker program.

In 2002, 1,063,732 immigrants entered the United States, of whom 416,860 were subject to the numerical limits. Some 342,099 immigrants in 2002 were from Asia; 404,437 were from North America; 74,506 were from South America; 174,209 from Europe; 60,269 from Africa, and 5,557 from Oceania. A direct result of the immigration law revisions has been a sharp rise in the influx of Asians (primarily Chinese, Filipinos, Indians, Japanese, and Koreans), of whom 2,738,157 entered the country during 1981–90, as compared with 153,249 during the entire decade of the 1950s. Most immigrants in 2002 came from Mexico (219,380).

Since 1961, the federal government supported and financed the Cuban Refugee Program; in 1995, new accords were agreed to by the two countries. More than 500,000 Cubans were living in southern Florida by 1980, when another 125,000 Cuban refugees arrived; by 1990, 4% of Florida's population was of Cuban descent. Some 169,322 Cubans arrived from 1991–2000, and 27,520 arrived in 2002. Between 1975 and 1978, following the defeat of the US-backed Saigon (Vietnam) government, several hundred thousand Vietnamese refugees came to the United States. Under the Refugee Act of 1980, a ceiling for the number of admissible refugees is set annually; in fiscal 2002, the ceiling for refugees was 70,000. Since Puerto Ricans are American citizens, no special authorization is required for their admission to the continental United States. The population of refugees, resettled refugees, and asylum-seekers with pending claims was estimated at 5,250,954 in June 2003, a 34% increase over June 2002. During the same year, the newly-formed Bureau of Citizenship and Immigration Services (BCIS—formerly the Immigration and Naturalization Service or INS) received 66,577 applications for asylum, a decline of 36% from 2002. In 2004, the US hosted 684,564 persons of concern to UNHCR, 420,854 refugees, and 263,710 asylum-seekers. For that year, the US was the fifth largest asylum country. UNHCR reports the United States as the leading destination of refugees, accounting for 63% of all resettlement worldwide.

Large numbers of aliens—mainly from Latin America, especially Mexico—have illegally established residence in the United States after entering the country as tourists, students, or temporary visitors engaged in work or business. In November 1986, Congress passed a bill allowing illegal aliens who had lived and worked in the United States since 1982 the opportunity to become permanent residents. By the end of fiscal year 1992, 2,650,000 of a potential 2,760,000 eligible for permanent residence under this bill had attained that status. In 1996 the number of illegal alien residents was estimated at 5 million, of which 2 million were believed to be in California. As of 2002, an estimated 33.1 million immigrants (legal and illegal) lived in the United States. Of this total, the Census Bureau estimated in 2000 that 8–9 million of them were illegal alien residents. In 2004, there were 36 million foreign-born US residents, almost 30% were unauthorized, or some 10.3 million foreigners. Of these 57% are unauthorized Mexicans. Foreign-born persons are 11 % of the US population, and 14 % of US workers.

As of 2006, there are three major immigration-related agencies in the US: the Department of Homeland Security; the US Customs and Border Protection (CBP) agency which apprehends foreigners; and, Immigration and Customs Enforcement (ICE) which is responsible for enforcement of immigration laws within the US, together with identifying and removing unauthorized foreigners, and those ordered removed.

The major migratory trends within the United States have been a general westward movement during the 19th century; a long-term movement from farms and other rural settlements to metropolitan areas, which showed signs of reversing in some states during the 1970s; an exodus of southern blacks to the cities of the North and Midwest, especially after World War I; a shift of whites from central cities to surrounding suburbs since World War II; and, also during the post–World War II period, a massive shift from the North and East to the Sunbelt region of the South and Southwest.

In 2005, the net migration rate was estimated as 3.31 migrants per 1,000 population.

[19]INTERNATIONAL COOPERATION

The United States is a charter member of the United Nations, having joined on 24 October 1945. The United States participates in ECE, ECLAC, ESCAP, and all the nonregional specialized agencies. The United States is a permanent member of the UN Security Council. The United States participates in numerous intergovernmental organizations, including the Asian Development Bank, the African Development Bank, OECD, APEC, the Colombo Plan, the Euro-Atlantic Partnership Council, the European Bank for Reconstruction and Development, G-5, G-7. G-8, the Paris Club (G-10), OSCE, and the WTO. Hemispheric agencies include the Inter-American Development Bank and the OAS. The country is an observer in the Council of Europe and a dialogue partner with ASEAN.

In 1992, the United States, Canada, and Mexico signed the North American Free Trade Agreement (NAFTA), creating a free-trade zone among the three countries. It was ratified by all three governments in 1993 and took effect the following year.

NATO is the principal military alliance to which the United States belongs. The ANZUS alliance was a mutual defense pact between Australia, New Zealand, and the United States; in 1986, following New Zealand's decision to ban US nuclear-armed or nuclear-powered ships from its ports, the United States renounced its ANZUS treaty security commitments to New Zealand. The country is a signatory of the 1947 Rio Treaty, an inter-American security agreement. The Untied States has supported UN missions and operations in Kosovo (est. 1999), Liberia (est. 2003), Georgia (est. 1993), and Haiti (est. 2004). The Untied States belongs to the Nuclear Suppliers Group (London Group), the Zangger Committee, the Nuclear Energy Agency, and the Organization for the Prohibition of Chemical Weapons. It holds observe status in the European Organization for Nuclear Research (CERN).

In environmental cooperation, the United States is part of the Central American-US Joint Declaration (CONCAUSA), the Antarctic Treaty, Conventions on Air Pollution and Whaling, Ramsar, CITES, the London Convention, International Tropical Timber Agreements, the Montréal Protocol, MARPOL, the Nuclear Test Ban Treaty, and the UN Conventions on Climate Change and Desertification.

[20]ECONOMY

The US economy is the world's largest. In variety and quantity, the natural resources of the United States probably exceed those of any other nation, with the possible exception of the former Soviet Union. The United States is among the world's leading exporters of coal, wheat, corn, and soybeans. However, because of its vast economic growth, the United States depends increasingly on foreign sources for a long list of raw materials, including oil.

By the middle of the 20th century, the United States was a leading consumer of nearly every important industrial raw material. The industry of the United States produced about 40% of the world's total output of goods, despite the fact that the country's population comprised about 6% of the world total and its land area about 7% of the earth's surface.

In absolute terms the United States far exceeds every other nation in the size of its gross domestic product (GDP), which more than tripled between 1970 and 1983. In 1998 the nation's GDP in purchasing power parity terms (PPP) reached a record $8.5 trillion in current dollars, with per capita GDP reaching $31,500. Per capita GDP (PPP) stood at $40,100 in 2004, and the nation's GDP (PPP) was $11.75 trillion.

Inflation was not as significant a factor in the US economy in the 1990s and early 2000s as it was in the 1970s and 1980s. The US inflation rate tends to be lower than that of the majority of industrialized nations. For the period 1970–78, for example, consumer prices increased by an annual average of 6.7%, less than in every other Western country except Austria, Luxembourg, Switzerland, and West Germany, and well below the price increase in Japan. The double-digit inflation of 1979–81 came as a rude shock to most Americans, with economists and politicians variously blaming international oil price rises, federal monetary policies, and US government spending.

The United States entered the post–World War II era with the world's largest, and strongest, economy. Public confidence in both business and government was strong, the nation enjoyed the largest peacetime trade surplus in its history, and the gross national product grew to a record $482.7 billion by the end of the 1950s. In the sixties the country enjoyed the most sustained period of economic expansion it had known, accompanied by rising productivity and low unemployment. Real income rose 50% during the decade, and US investment in foreign countries reached $49 billion in 1965, up from $11.8 billion in 1950. Big business and big government were both powerful forces in the economy during this period, when large industrial corporations accounted for vast portions of the national income, and the federal government expanded its role in such areas as social welfare, scientific research, space technology, and development of the nation's highway system.

After two decades of prosperity, Americans experienced an economic downturn in the 1970s, a period known for the unprecedented combination of lagging economic growth and inflation that gave birth to the term *stagflation*. Foreign competitors in Japan and Europe challenged the global dominance of American manufacturers, and oil crises in 1973–74 and 1979 shook public confidence in the institutions of both government and business. The forced bailouts of Chrysler and Lockheed were symbolic of the difficult transition to a new economic era, marked by the growing importance of the service sector and the ascendancy of small businesses.

During Ronald Reagan's first presidential term, from 1980 to 1984, the nation endured two years of severe recession followed by two years of robust recovery. The inflation rate was brought down, and millions of new jobs were created. The economic boom of the early and mid-eighties, however, coincided with a number of alarming developments. Federal budget deficits, caused by dramatic increases in the military budget and by rising costs of entitlement programs such as Medicaid and Medicare, averaged more than $150 billion annually. By 1992, the total deficit reached $290 billion, or $1,150 for every American. In addition, corporate debt rose dramatically, and household borrowing grew twice as fast as personal income. The eighties also witnessed a crisis in the banking industry, caused by a combination of factors, including high inflation and interest rates, problem loans to developing countries, and speculative real estate ventures that caused thousands of banks to fail when the real estate boom of the early eighties collapsed.

The disparity between the affluent and the poor widened at the end of the 20th century. The share of the nation's income received by the richest 5% of American families rose from 18.6% in 1977 to 24.5% in 1990, while the share of the poorest 20% fell from 5.7% to 4.3%. Externally, the nation's trade position deteriorated, as a high level of foreign investment combined with an uncompetitive US dollar to create a ballooning trade deficit. In 1990, the American economy plunged into a recession. Factors contributing to the slump included rising oil prices following Iraq's invasion of Kuwait, a sharp increase in interest rates, and declining availability of credit. Output fell 1.6% and 1.7 million jobs were cut. Unemployment rose from 5.2% in 1989 to 7.5% in 1991, but had fallen to 4.5% by 1998.

The recovery that began in March 1991 inaugurated a sustained period of expansion that, as of mid-2000, was the third longest since World War II, characterized by moderation in the key areas of growth, inflation, unemployment, and interest rates. Real GDP growth, which fluctuated between 2% and 3.5% throughout the period, was 3.9% for 1998. After peaking at 7.5%, unemployment declined steadily throughout the early and mid-1990s, falling to 5.6% in 1995, 5.3% at the end of 1996, and in 1998, remaining below 5%. After 1993/94, inflation mostly remained under 3%. One exception to the generally moderate character of the economy was the stock market, which rose 60% between 1995 and 1997, buoyed by the combination of low unemployment and low inflation, as well as strong corporate earnings. Further cause for optimism was the bipartisan balanced-budget legislation enacted and signed into law in 1997. The plan, combining tax and spending cuts over a five-year period, was aimed at balancing the federal budget by 2002 for the first time since 1969. In early 2001, the government projected a budget surplus of $275 billion for the fiscal year ending that September. That surplus would soon be reversed.

At the beginning of the 21st century, significant economic concerns—aside from the inevitable worry over how long the boom could last without an eventual downturn—included the nation's sizable trade deficit, the increasing medical costs of an aging population, and the failure of the strong economy to improve conditions for the poor. Since 1975, gains in household income were experienced almost exclusively by the top 20% of households. However, in the late 1990s and early 2000s, productivity was continuing to grow, inflation was relatively low, and the labor market was tight.

Economic growth came to a standstill in the middle of 2001, largely due to the end of the long investment boom, especially in the information technology sector. The economy was in recession in the second half of 2001, and the service sector was affected as well as manufacturing. The 11 September 2001 terrorist attacks on the United States exacerbated the poor economic situation. Average real GDP growth rose by only 0.3% in 2001. The US economy, which had driven global economic growth during the 1990s, became the cause of a worldwide economic downturn, including in the rest of North America, Europe, Japan, and in the developing economies of Latin America and Southeast Asia strongly influenced by trends in the US economy.

The economy began to recover, slowly, in 2002, with GDP growth estimated at 2.45%. Analysts attributed the modest recovery to the ability of business decision-makers to respond to economic imbalances based on real-time information, on deregulation, and on innovation in financial and product markets. Nevertheless, domestic confidence in the economy remained low, and coupled with major corporate failures (including Enron and WorldCom) and additional stock market declines, growth remained sluggish and uneven. Economic growth slowed at the end of 2002 and into 2003, and the unemployment rate rose to 6.3% in July 2003. The CPI inflation rate fell to under 1.5% at the beginning of 2003, which raised concerns over the risk of deflation. As well, there was a substantial rise in military spending as a result of the war in Iraq which began in March 2003.

Following the start of the war in Iraq, consumer spending rebounded, as did stock prices; the housing market remained strong; inflation was low; the dollar depreciated on world markets; additional tax cuts were passed; there was an easing of oil prices; and productivity growth was strong. Nevertheless, in 2003, the federal budget deficit was projected to reach $455 billion, the largest shortfall on record.

The American economy grew at the rate of 4.3% in the third quarter of 2005, despite the ravages of Hurricane Katrina, which destroyed the port city of New Orleans and closed down a large portion of the energy industry. Unemployment hovered around 5% in 2005. Productivity had grown by 4.7%. But the nation's fast-growing economy had shaky underpinnings. Oil prices were at their highest level in real terms since the early 1980s, at $53.27/barrel. The inflation rate, which ran above 4% in late 2005, was at its highest level since 1991 (although core inflation, which excludes volatile energy and food prices, was still relatively modest). Wage growth was sluggish, and the jobs market was lagging the recovery. The current account deficit ballooned to record levels, and consumer spending was increasingly tied to prices in the overinflated housing market. The government ran a deficit of $412 billion in 2004, or 3.6% of GDP, but the deficit was forecast to narrow to $331 billion in 2006. Analysts project US deficits will average about 3.5% of GDP until about 2015.

21 INCOME

The US Central Intelligence Agency (CIA) reports that in 2005 the United States's gross domestic product (GDP) was estimated at $12.4 trillion. The CIA defines GDP as the value of all final goods and services produced within a nation in a given year and computed on the basis of purchasing power parity (PPP) rather than value as measured on the basis of the rate of exchange based on current dollars. The per capita GDP was estimated at $41,800. The annual growth rate of GDP was estimated at 3.5%. The average inflation rate in 2002 was 3.2%. It was estimated that agriculture accounted for 1% of GDP, industry 0.7%, and services 78.3%.

According to the World Bank, in 2003 remittances from citizens working abroad totaled $3.031 billion or about $10 per capita.

The World Bank reports that in 2003 household consumption in United States totaled $7.385 trillion or about $25,379 per capita based on a GDP of $10.9 trillion, measured in current dollars rather than PPP. Household consumption includes expenditures of individuals, households, and nongovernmental organizations on goods and services, excluding purchases of dwellings. It was estimated that for the period 1990 to 2003 household consumption grew at an average annual rate of 3.7%. In 2001 it was estimated that approximately 13% of household consumption was spent on food, 9% on fuel, 4% on health care, and 6% on education. It was estimated that in 2004 about 12% of the population had incomes below the poverty line.

22 LABOR

The US labor force, including those who were unemployed, totaled 149.3 million in 2005. Of that total in that same year, farming, fishing and forestry accounted fo 0.7% of the workforce, with manufacturing, extraction, transportation and crafts at 22.9%, managerial, professional and technical at 34.7%, sales and office at 25.4% and other services at 16.3%. Also that year, the unemployment rate was put at 5.1%. Earnings of workers vary considerably with type of work and section of country. In the first quarter of 2003, the national average wage was $15.27 per hour for nonagricultural workers, with an average workweek of 33.8 hours. Workers in manufacturing had a national average wage of $15.64, (including overtime), with the longest average workweek of all categories of workers at 40.4 hours in the first quarter of 2003.

In 2002, 13.2% of wage and salary workers were union members—16.1 million US citizens belonged to a union that year. In 1983, union membership was 20.1%. In 2002, there were 34 national labor unions with over 100,000 members, the largest being the National Educational Association with 2.7 million members as of 2003. The most important federation of organized workers in the United States is the American Federation of Labor–Congress of Industrial Organizations (AFL–CIO), whose affiliated unions had 13 million members as of 2003, down from 14.1 million members in 1992. The major independent industrial and labor unions and their estimated 2002 memberships are the International Brotherhood of Teamsters, 1,398,412, and the United Automobile Workers, some 710,000 (the majority of whom work for General Motors, Ford, and Daimler-Chrylser). Most of the other unaffiliated unions are confined to a single establishment or locality. US labor

unions exercise economic and political influence not only through the power of strikes and slowdowns but also through the human and financial resources they allocate to political campaigns (usually on behalf of Democratic candidates) and through the selective investment of multibillion-dollar pension funds.

The National Labor Relations Act of 1935 (the Wagner Act), the basic labor law of the United States, was considerably modified by the Labor-Management Relations Act of 1947 (the Taft-Hartley Act) and the Labor-Management Reporting and Disclosure Act of 1959 (the Landrum-Griffin Act). Closed-shop agreements, which require employers to hire only union members, are banned. The union shop agreement, however, is permitted, if it allows the hiring of nonunion members on the condition that they join the union within a given period of time.

As of 2003, 23 states had right-to-work laws, forbidding the imposition of union membership as a condition of employment. Under the Taft-Hartley Act, the president of the United States may postpone a strike for 90 days in the national interest. The act of 1959 requires all labor organizations to file constitutions, bylaws, and detailed financial reports with the Secretary of Labor, and stipulates methods of union elections. The National Labor Relations Board seeks to remedy or prevent unfair labor practices and supervises union elections, while the Equal Employment Opportunity Commission seeks to prevent discrimination in hiring, firing, and apprenticeship programs.

The number of work stoppages and of workers involved reached a peak in the late 1960s and early 1970s, declining steadily thereafter. In 2002, there were 19 major stoppages involving 46,000 workers resulting in 660,000 workdays idle, compared with 1995, when there were 31 major stoppages involving 191,500 workers resulting in 5,771,000 days idle; a major stoppage was defined as one involving 1,000 workers or more for a minimum of one day or shift.

23 AGRICULTURE

In 2004, the United States produced a substantial share of the world's agricultural commodities. Agricultural exports reached almost $63.9 billion in 2004. The United States had an agricultural trade surplus of $4 billion in 2004, 14th highest among the nations.

Between 1930 and 2004, the number of farms in the United States declined from 6,546,000 to an estimated 2,110,000. The total amount of farmland increased from 399 million hectares (986 million acres) in 1930 to 479 million hectares (1.18 billion acres) in 1959 but declined to 380 million hectares (938 million acres) in 2002. From 1930 to 2004, the size of the average farm tripled from 61 to 179 hectares (from 151 to 443 acres), a result of the consolidation effected by large-scale mechanized production. The farm population, which comprised 35% of the total US population in 1910, declined to 25% during the Great Depression of the 1930s, and dwindled to less than 2% by 2004.

A remarkable increase in the application of machinery to farms took place during and after World War II (1939–45). Tractors, trucks, milking machines, grain combines, corn pickers, and pickup bailers became virtual necessities in farming. In 1920 there was less than one tractor in use for every 400 hectares (1,000 acres) of cropland harvested; by 2003 there were five tractors per 400 hectares. Two other elements essential to US farm productivity are chemical fertilizers and irrigation. Fertilizers and lime represent more than 6% of farm operating expenses. Arable land under irrigation amounted to 12% of the total in 2003.

Substantial quantities of corn, the most valuable crop produced in the United States, are grown in almost every state; its yield and price are important factors in the economies of the regions where it is grown. Production of selected US crops in 2004 (in 1,000 metric tons), and their percent of world production were wheat, 58,737 (9.3%); corn, 299,917 (33.2%); rice, 10,469 (1.7%); soybeans, 85,013 (41.6%); cotton, 5,062 (20.5%); and tobacco, 398.8 (6.1%).

24 ANIMAL HUSBANDRY

The livestock population in 2005 included an estimated 95.8 million head of cattle, 60.6 million hogs, and 6.1 million sheep and lambs. That year, there were 1.9 billion chickens, and 88 million turkeys. Milk production totaled 80.1 million metric tons in that year, with Wisconsin, California, and New York together accounting for much of the total. Wisconsin, Minnesota, and California account for more than half of all US butter production, which totaled 608,900 metric tons in 2005; in that year, the United States was the world's largest producer of cheese, with almost 4.5 million metric tons (24% of the world's total). The United States produced an estimated 15% of the world's meat supply in 2005. In 2005, meat animals accounted for $4.97 billion in exports; dairy and eggs, $1.17 billion.

25 FISHING

The 2003 commercial catch was 5.48 million tons. Food fish make up 80% of the catch, and nonfood fish, processed for fertilizer and oil, 20%. Aquaculture accounts for about 10% of total production.

Alaska pollock, with landings of 1,524,904 tons, was the most important species in quantity among the commercial fishery landings in the United States in 2003. Other leading species by volume included Gulf menhaden, 522,195 tons; Atlantic menhaden, 203,263 tons; Pacific cod, 257,436 tons; North Pacific hake, 140,327 tons; and American cupped oyster, 183,940 tons. In 2003, exports of fish products totaled $3,398 million (fourth after China, Thailand, and Norway).

Aquacultural production consists mostly of catfish, oysters, trout, and crayfish. In 2004, there were 1,147 catfish and 601 trout farms in the United States, with sales of $425 million and $64 million, respectively.

Pollution is a problem of increasing concern to the US fishing industry; dumping of raw sewage, industrial wastes, spillage from oil tankers, and blowouts of offshore wells are the main threats to the fishing grounds. Overfishing is also a threat to the viability of the industry in some areas, especially Alaska.

26 FORESTRY

US forestland covers about 226 million hectares (558.4 million acres), or 25% of the land area. Major forest regions include the eastern, central hardwood, southern, Rocky Mountain, and Pacific coast areas. The National Forest Service lands account for approximately 19% of the nation's forestland. Extensive tracts of land (4 million acres or more) are under ownership of private lumber companies in Alabama, Arkansas, Florida, Georgia, Maine, Ore-

gon, and Washington. During 1990–2000, forested area increased by an annual average of 38,000 hectares (93,900 acres) per year.

Domestic production of roundwood during 2004 amounted to 458.3 million cu m (16.2 billion cu ft), or 1.7% of world production, of which softwoods accounted for roughly 60%. Other forest products in 2004 included 54.3 million metric tons of wood pulp, 83.6 million metric tons of paper and paperboard (excluding newsprint), and 44.2 million cu m (1.56 billion cu ft) of wood-based panels. Rising petroleum prices in the late 1970s sparked a revival in the use of wood as home heating fuel, especially in the Northeast. Fuelwood and charcoal production amounted to 43.6 million cu m (1.5 billion cu ft) in 2004.

Throughout the 19th century, the federal government distributed forestlands lavishly as a means of subsidizing railroads and education. By the turn of the century, the realization that the forests were not inexhaustible led to the growth of a vigorous conservation movement, which was given increased impetus during the 1930s and again in the late 1960s. Federal timberlands are no longer open for private acquisition, although the lands can be leased for timber cutting and for grazing. In recent decades, the states also have moved in the direction of retaining forestlands and adding to their holdings when possible.

27 MINING

Rich in a variety of mineral resources, the United States was a world leader in the production of many important mineral commodities, such as aluminum, cement, copper, pig iron, lead, molybdenum, phosphates, potash, salt, sulfur, uranium, and zinc. The leading mineral-producing states were Arizona (copper, sand and gravel, portland cement, molybdenum); California (portland cement, sand and gravel, gold, boron); Michigan (iron ore, portland cement, sand and gravel, magnesium compounds); Georgia (clays, crushed and broken stone, portland and masonry cement, sand and gravel); Florida (phosphate rock, crushed and broken stone, portland cement, sand and gravel); Utah (copper, gold, magnesium metal, sand and gravel); Texas (portland cement, crushed and broken stone, magnesium metal, sand and gravel); and Minnesota (iron ore, construction and industrial sand and gravel, crushed and broken stone). Oklahoma and New Mexico were important for petroleum and natural gas, and Kentucky, West Virginia, and Pennsylvania, for coal. Iron ore supported the nation's most basic nonagricultural industry, iron and steel manufacture; the major domestic sources were in the Lake Superior area, with Minnesota and Michigan leading all other states in iron ore yields.

28 ENERGY AND POWER

The United States (US) is the world's leading energy producer and consumer.

According to British Petroleum (BP), as of end 2003, the US had proven oil reserves of 29.4 billion barrels. Oil production that year averaged 7,400,000 barrels per day, with domestic demand averaging 20,033,000 barrels per day. As a result, the US in 2003 was a net oil importer. In 2003, imports of all oil products averaged 12,264.380 barrels per day, of which crude oil accounted for an average of 9,664,920 barrels per day. Refined oil production in 2003 averaged 17,793,990 barrels per day.

As of end 2003, the US had proven reserves of natural gas totaling 5.29 trillion cu m (186.9 trillion cu ft), according to BP. Gross

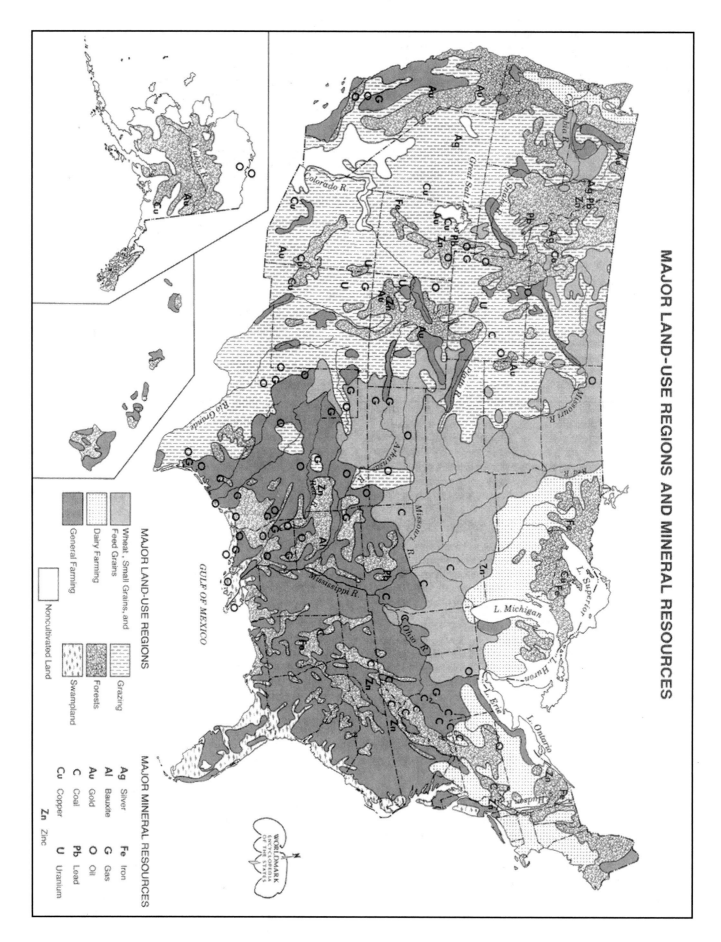

MAJOR LAND-USE REGIONS AND MINERAL RESOURCES

MAJOR LAND-USE REGIONS

Wheat, Small Grains, and
Feed Grains

Dairy Farming

General Farming

Grazing

Forests

Swampland

Noncultivated Land

MAJOR MINERAL RESOURCES

Ag Silver
Al Bauxite
Au Gold
C Coal
Cu Copper

Fe Iron
G Gas
O Oil
Pb Lead
U Uranium

Zn Zinc

GULF OF MEXICO

production that year, according to the Energy Information Administration (EIA), totaled 24,056.00 billion cu ft. Of that amount in 2003, 98 billion cu ft was vented or flared, and 3,548 billion cu ft was re-injected. Marketed production totaled 19,912 billion cu ft, with dry production at 19,036 billion cu ft. Demand in that same year for dry production totaled 22,375 billion cu ft. As with oil, the US was a net importer of natural gas. Imports of dry natural gas in 2003 totaled 3,996 billion cu ft, while dry exports totaled 692 billion cu ft, according to the EIA.

The US had recoverable coal reserves of 246,643 million metric tons at the end of 2004, according to BP. Of that amount, anthracite and bituminous coal reserves totaled 111,338 million metric tons, with sub-bituminous and lignite reserves totaling 135,305 million metric tons, according to BP. In 2003 according to the EIA, coal production by the US totaled 1,069,496,000 short tons, of which 987,613,000 short tons consisted of bituminous coal, with anthracite output totaling 1,289,000 short tons. Lignite or brown coal output that year totaled 80,595,000 short tons, according to the EIA.

In 2003, US electric power generation capacity by public and private generating plants totaled 932.832 million kW, of which 736.728 million kW of capacity belonged to conventional thermal fuel plants, followed by nuclear plant at 98.794 million kW. Hydroelectric capacity that year totaled 79.366 million kW, with geothermal/other capacity at 17.944 million kW. Electric power output in 2003 totaled 3,891.720 billion kWh, of which conventional thermal plants generated 2,758.650 billion kWh, followed by nuclear plants at 763.733 billion kWh, hydroelectric facilities at 275.806 billion kWh and geothermal/other facilities at 93.531 billion kWh.

During the 1980s, increasing attention was focused on the development of solar power, synthetic fuels, geothermal resources, and other energy technologies. Such energy conservation measures as mandatory automobile fuel-efficiency standards and tax incentives for home insulation were promoted by the federal government, which also decontrolled oil and gas prices in the expectation that a rise in domestic costs to world-market levels would provide a powerful economic incentive for consumers to conserve fuel. In 2001 the United States had 1,694 MW of installed wind power.

29INDUSTRY

Although the United States remains one of the world's preeminent industrial powers, manufacturing no longer plays as dominant a role in the economy as it once did.

Between 1979 and 1998, manufacturing employment fell from 20.9 million to 18.7 million, or from 21.8% to 14.8% of national employment. Throughout the 1960s, manufacturing accounted for about 29% of total national income; by 1987, the proportion was down to about 19%. In 2002, manufacturing was experiencing a decline due to the recession that began in March 2001. In 2004, industry accounted for 19.7% of GDP. That year, 22.7% of the labor force was engaged in manufacturing, extraction, transportation, and crafts.

Industrial activity within the United States has been expanding southward and westward for much of the 20th century, most rapidly since World War II. Louisiana, Oklahoma, and especially Texas are centers of industrial expansion based on petroleum

refining; aerospace and other high technology industries are the basis of the new wealth of Texas and California, the nation's leading manufacturing state. The industrial heartland of the United States is the east–north–central region, comprising Ohio, Indiana, Illinois, Michigan, and Wisconsin, with steelmaking and automobile manufacturing among the leading industries. The Middle Atlantic states (New Jersey, New York, and Pennsylvania) and the Northeast are also highly industrialized; but of the major industrial states in these two regions, Massachusetts has taken the lead in reorienting itself toward such high-technology industries as electronics and information processing.

Large corporations are dominant especially in sectors such as steel, automobiles, pharmaceuticals, aircraft, petroleum refining, computers, soaps and detergents, tires, and communications equipment. The growth of multinational activities of US corporations has been rapid in recent decades.

The history of US industry has been marked by the introduction of increasingly sophisticated technology in the manufacturing process. Advances in chemistry and electronics have revolutionized many industries through new products and methods: examples include the impact of plastics on petrochemicals, the use of lasers and electronic sensors as measuring and controlling devices, and the application of microprocessors to computing machines, home entertainment products, and a variety of other industries. Science has vastly expanded the number of metals available for industrial purposes, notably such light metals as aluminum, magnesium, and titanium. Integrated machines now perform a complex number of successive operations that formerly were done on the assembly line at separate stations. Those industries have prospered that have been best able to make use of the new technology, and the economies of some states have been largely based on it.

In the 1980s and 1990s, the United States was the world leader in computer manufacturing. At the beginning of the 21st century, however, the high-tech manufacturing industry registered a decline. Semiconductor manufacturing had been migrating out of the United States to East Asian countries, especially China, Taiwan, and Singapore, and research and development in that sector declined from 1999–2003. Certain long-established industries—especially clothing and steelmaking—have suffered from outmoded facilities that (coupled with high US labor costs) have forced the price of their products above the world market level. In 2005, the United States was the world's third-leading steel producer (after China and Japan). Employment in the steel-producing industry fell from 521,000 in 1974 to 187,500 in 2002. Automobile manufacturing was an ailing industry in the 1980s, but rebounded in the 1990s. The "Big Three" US automakers—General Motors, Ford, and Daimler-Chrysler—manufactured over 60% of the passenger cars sold in the United States in 1995. In 2005, however, General Motors announced it was cutting 30,000 North American manufacturing jobs, the deepest cuts since 1991, when GM eliminated 74,000 jobs over four years. Passenger car production, which had fallen from 7.1 million units in 1987 to 5.4 million in 1991, rose to 6.3 million by 1995 and to 8.3 million in 1999. In 2003, over 12 million motor vehicles were produced in the United States.

The United States had a total of 148 oil refineries as of January 2005, with a production capacity as of September 2004 of 17.1

million barrels per day. Crude oil and refined petroleum products are crucial imports, however.

30 COMMERCE

Total retail sales for 2004 were $3.5 trillion. Total e-commerce sales were estimated at $69.2 billion, an increase of 23.5% over 2003. The growth of great chains of retail stores, particularly in the form of the supermarket, was one of the most conspicuous developments in retail trade following the end of World War II. Nearly 100,000 single-unit grocery stores went out of business between 1948 and 1958; the independent grocer's share of the food market dropped from 50% to 30% of the total in the same period. With the great suburban expansion of the 1960s emerged the planned shopping center, usually designed by a single development organization and intended to provide different kinds of stores in order to meet all the shopping needs of the particular area. Between 1974 and 2000, the square footage occupied by shopping centers in the United States grew at a far greater rate than the nation's population.

Installment credit is a major support for consumer purchases in the United States. Most US families own and use credit cards, and their frequency of use has grown significantly in the 1990s and 2000s with aggressive marketing by credit card companies which have made cards available to households that didn't qualify in the past. The number of credit cards per household in 2004 was 8. The number of credit cards in circulation in 2004 was 641 million. The average household credit card debt in the United States in 2004 was approximately $8,650, and the total credit card debt in the United States in 2004 was some $800 billion. The use of debit cards was expected to exceed the use of credit cards in 2005.

The US advertising industry is the world's most highly developed. Particularly with the expansion of television audiences, spending for advertising has increased almost annually to successive record levels. Advertising expenditures in 2003 reached an estimated $249 billion, up from $66.58 billion in 1982 and $11.96 billion in 1960. Of the 2003 total, $87.8 billion was spent in radio, broadcast television, and cable television; $57.2 billion was spent on print media (newspapers and magazines); and internet advertising amounted to $5.6 billion.

In 2003 merchant wholesalers had combined total sales of $2.88 trillion.

31 CONSUMER PROTECTION

Consumer protection has become a major government enterprise during the 20th century. The Federal Trade commission (FTC), established in 1914, administers laws governing the granting and use of credit and the activities of credit bureaus; it also investigates unfair or deceptive trade practices, including price fixing and false advertising. The Securities and Exchange Commission, created in 1934, seeks to protect investors, while the Consumer Product Safety Commission, created in 1972, has the authority to establish product safety standards and to ban hazardous products. Overseeing the safety of air and highway transport is the National Transportation Safety Board, established in 1975. The Consumer Information Center Program of the General Services Administration (Pueblo, Colo.) and the Food Safety and Inspection Service and Food and Nutrition Service of the Department of Agriculture also serve consumer interests. Legislation that would have established

a Department of Consumer Affairs failed to win congressional approval several times during the 1970s, however.

Public interest groups have been exceptionally effective in promoting consumer issues. The Consumer Federation of America (CFA; founded in 1967), with 220 member organizations, is the largest US consumer advocacy body; its concerns include product pricing, credit, and the cost and quality of health care, education, and housing. The CFA also serves as a clearinghouse for consumer information. Consumers Union of the US, founded in 1936, publishes the widely read monthly Consumer Reports, which tests, grades, and comments on a variety of retail products. The National Consumers League, founded in 1899, was a pioneer in the consumer movement, focusing especially on labor laws and working conditions. Much of the growth of consumerism in the 1970s resulted from the public relations efforts of one man—Ralph Nader. Already a well-known consumer advocate concerned particularly with automobile safety, Nader founded Public Citizen in 1971 and an affiliated litigation group the following year. In 1994, Public Citizen claimed 100,000 supporters; its activities include research committees on tax reform, health care, work safety, and energy.

Other avenues open to consumers in most states include small claims courts, generally open to claims between $100 and $1,500 at modest legal cost. Complaints involving professional malpractice may also be brought to state licensing or regulatory boards. Supported by the business community, the US Better Business Bureau provides general consumer information and can help arbitrate some customer-company disputes.

The US government also publishes helpful consumer guides. A listing of the guides is available from the US government through its "Consumer Information Catalog." This catalog is free and lists about 142 of the best federal consumer publications. The federal publications range from planning a diet to financial planning. The publication, published quarterly by the Consumer Information Center of the US General Services Administration is available in most public libraries or online at www.pueblo.gsa.gov.

32 BANKING AND SECURITIES

The Federal Reserve Act of 1913 provided the United States with a central banking system. The Federal Reserve System dominates US banking, is a strong influence in the affairs of commercial banks, and exercises virtually unlimited control over the money supply. The Federal Reserve Bank system is an independent government organization, with important posts appointed by the President and approved by the Senate.

Each of the 12 federal reserve districts contains a federal reserve bank. A board of nine directors presides over each reserve bank. Six are elected by the member banks in the district: of this group, three may be bankers; the other three represent business, industry, or agriculture. The Board of Governors of the Federal Reserve System (usually known as the Federal Reserve Board) appoints the remaining three, who may not be officers, directors, stockholders, or employees of any bank and who are presumed therefore to represent the public.

The Federal Reserve Board regulates the money supply and the amount of credit available to the public by asserting its power to alter the rediscount rate, by buying and selling securities in the open market, by setting margin requirements for securities purchases, by altering reserve requirements of member banks in the

United States—2005 Exports, Imports, and Trade Balance by Country and Area

In millions of dollars. Details may not equal totals due to rounding. (X) Not applicable. (-) Represents zero or less than one-half of value shown.
January–December, Cumulative.

COUNTRY	TRADE BALANCE	RANK	EXPORTS F.A.S.	RANK	IMPORTS CUSTOMS	RANK
Total, BOP Basis	-782,740.2	(X)	894,630.8	(X)	1,677,371.0	(X)
Net Adjustments	-15,263.3	(X)	-11,346.8	(X)	3,916.5	(X)
Total, Census Basis	-767,476.9	(X)	905,977.6	(X)	1,673,454.5	(X)
Afghanistan	194.8	205	262.2	93	67.3	132
Albania	-18.7	102	18.5	179	37.2	146
Algeria	-9,279.0	20	1,167.4	60	10,446.4	27
Andorra	9.9	152	10.5	187	0.7	203
Angola	-7,555.3	24	929.0	66	8,484.4	33
Anguilla	28.4	168	32.2	160	3.8	180
Antigua and Barbuda	186.0	204	190.4	105	4.4	177
Argentina	-461.8	67	4,121.9	32	4,583.6	46
Armenia	19.3	160	65.5	142	46.2	143
Aruba	-2,360.8	36	558.9	76	2,919.7	54
Australia	8,486.0	229	15,828.2	14	7,342.2	35
Austria	-3,509.7	30	2,593.3	42	6,102.9	39
Azerbaijan	87.1	193	132.5	116	45.4	144
Bahamas	1,086.8	222	1,786.7	51	699.9	80
Bahrain	-80.8	92	350.8	88	431.6	89
Bangladesh	-2,373.3	35	319.8	90	2,693.0	56
Barbados	363.0	212	394.9	84	31.9	150
Belarus	-310.2	71	34.9	158	345.2	97
Belgium	5,667.7	226	18,690.6	12	13,022.9	24
Belize	119.3	199	217.6	101	98.3	124
Benin	71.8	187	72.3	138	0.5	205
Bermuda	403.2	216	490.5	82	87.3	128
Bhutan	2.4	135	3.1	208	0.6	204
Bolivia	-73.7	94	219.5	99	293.2	102
Bosnia-Herzegovina	-52.9	96	17.6	181	70.5	131
Botswana	-110.9	88	67.3	141	178.2	112
Brazil	-9,063.8	21	15,371.7	15	24,435.5	15
British Indian Ocean Territories	0.4	125	0.8	219	0.4	208
British Virgin Islands	91.3	194	124.9	117	33.6	148
Brunei	-513.1	64	49.6	150	562.7	82
Bulgaria	-186.3	81	267.9	92	454.3	85
Burkina	23.0	163	25.1	174	2.1	188
Burma (Myanmar)	5.4	142	5.5	201	0.1	220
Burundi	3.7	137	8.1	198	4.4	176
Cambodia	-1,697.3	45	69.7	139	1,767.0	64
Cameroon	-40.8	98	117.3	119	158.2	117
Canada	-78,485.6	3	211,898.7	1	290,384.3	1
Cape Verde	7.2	148	9.9	190	2.6	185
Cayman Islands	627.2	219	680.7	70	53.5	138
Central African Republic	9.1	151	14.8	183	5.7	171
Chad	-1,444.3	49	53.8	149	1,498.1	67
Chile	-1,441.7	50	5,222.6	29	6,664.3	37
China	-201,544.8	1	41,925.3	4	243,470.1	2
Christmas Island	1.6	132	2.0	214	0.4	210
Cocos (Keeling) Island	0.6	128	1.0	217	0.5	207
Colombia	-3,387.0	31	5,462.4	28	8,849.4	31
Comoros	-1.2	113	0.3	224	1.4	192
Congo (DROC)	-198.6	78	65.0	143	263.6	107
Congo (ROC)	-1,518.8	47	104.1	123	1,622.9	65
Cook Islands	-0.4	116	1.4	216	1.7	189
Costa Rica	183.3	203	3,598.6	36	3,415.3	50
Côte d'Ivoire	-1,073.7	55	124.2	118	1,198.0	72
Croatia	-205.7	77	158.6	109	364.3	94
Cuba	369.0	213	369.0	86	(-)	226
Cyprus	53.6	181	84.2	131	30.5	152
Czech Republic	-1,139.3	54	1,053.6	63	2,192.9	59
Denmark	-3,225.8	32	1,918.4	49	5,144.2	43
Djibouti	46.5	177	47.6	151	1.1	198
Dominica	58.2	183	61.5	146	3.3	183
Dominican Republic	115.0	198	4,718.7	30	4,603.7	45
East Timor	8.6	150	8.7	197	0.1	219
Ecuador	-3,794.9	29	1,963.8	47	5,758.7	41
Egypt	1,068.0	221	3,159.3	38	2,091.2	60
El Salvador	-134.5	86	1,854.3	50	1,988.8	62

United States—2005 Exports, Imports, and Trade Balance by Country and Area (cont.)

COUNTRY	TRADE BALANCE	RANK	EXPORTS F.A.S.	RANK	IMPORTS CUSTOMS	RANK
Equatorial Guinea	-1,279.7	51	281.5	91	1,561.1	66
Eritrea	29.8	172	31.1	163	1.3	196
Estonia	-366.0	70	145.4	113	511.4	84
Ethiopia	448.3	217	510.1	81	61.8	134
Falkland Islands	-0.2	117	9.0	195	9.3	164
Faroe Islands	-1.7	111	2.5	210	4.3	178
Federal Republic of Germany	-50,567.2	4	34,183.7	6	84,750.9	5
Federated States of Micronesia	23.8	164	25.3	173	1.6	191
Fiji	-141.3	85	28.2	169	169.5	114
Finland	-2,087.6	40	2,254.1	44	4,341.7	47
France	-11,431.7	16	22,410.4	9	33,842.1	10
French Guiana	26.9	167	27.0	172	0.1	217
French Polynesia	51.7	179	111.8	121	60.1	135
French Southern and Antarctic Lands	0.2	124	0.3	225	0.1	222
Gabon	-2,716.5	34	99.1	125	2,815.6	55
Gambia	30.2	173	30.6	165	0.4	209
Gaza Strip Administered by Israel	-1.2	112	0.2	226	1.4	193
Georgia	19.5	161	213.9	102	194.4	111
Ghana	179.0	202	337.4	89	158.4	116
Gibraltar	158.6	201	163.3	108	4.6	174
Greece	308.5	211	1,192.2	59	883.7	78
Greenland	-12.2	105	5.1	202	17.3	156
Grenada	76.6	188	82.4	133	5.9	169
Guadeloupe	52.4	180	54.5	148	2.1	187
Guatemala	-302.0	72	2,835.4	40	3,137.4	53
Guinea	18.9	159	93.6	129	74.7	130
Guinea-Bissau	2.0	133	2.1	213	0.1	218
Guyana	56.8	182	176.7	107	119.9	121
Haiti	262.4	209	709.6	69	447.2	87
Heard and McDonald Islands	0.1	122	0.2	227	(-)	225
Honduras	-495.4	66	3,253.8	37	3,749.2	49
Hong Kong	7,459.3	228	16,351.0	13	8,891.7	30
Hungary	-1,537.9	46	1,023.3	64	2,561.2	57
Iceland	243.0	208	512.0	80	269.0	105
India	-10,814.8	18	7,989.4	22	18,804.2	18
Indonesia	-8,960.4	22	3,053.9	39	12,014.3	26
Iran	-78.7	93	95.8	127	174.5	113
Iraq	-7,679.7	23	1,374.0	55	9,053.7	29
Ireland	-19,397.4	11	9,335.7	20	28,733.1	13
Israel	-7,093.1	25	9,737.3	19	16,830.5	19
Italy	-19,484.9	10	11,524.3	16	31,009.3	12
Jamaica	1,325.2	223	1,700.8	52	375.6	93
Japan	-82,519.2	2	55,484.5	3	138,003.7	4
Jordan	-622.7	59	644.2	71	1,266.8	69
Kazakhstan	-562.9	62	538.3	77	1,101.1	74
Kenya	284.5	210	632.5	72	348.0	96
Kiribati	1.3	130	2.4	211	1.1	197
Korea, North	5.8	145	5.8	199	(-)	227
Korea, South	-16,016.5	12	27,765.0	7	43,781.4	7
Kuwait	-2,359.9	37	1,974.9	46	4,334.8	48
Kyrgyzstan	26.5	166	31.1	162	4.6	175
Laos	5.6	144	9.8	191	4.2	179
Latvia	-184.6	82	177.5	106	362.2	95
Lebanon	379.3	214	465.7	83	86.4	129
Lesotho	-399.6	68	4.0	205	403.6	91
Liberia	-21.5	100	69.3	140	90.8	127
Libya	-1,506.5	48	83.8	132	1,590.3	(X)
Liechtenstein	-276.0	74	19.7	178	295.7	101
Lithuania	-243.9	75	390.0	85	633.9	81
Luxembourg	393.6	215	782.4	68	388.8	92
Macao	-1,147.4	53	101.6	124	1,249.0	70
Macedonia (Skopje)	-16.6	104	31.6	161	48.1	142
Madagascar	-295.4	73	28.2	168	323.6	99
Malawi	-87.5	90	28.0	170	115.5	122
Malaysia	-23,224.3	7	10,460.8	18	33,685.2	11
Maldives	3.8	138	9.3	193	5.5	172
Mali	28.8	170	32.4	159	3.6	182
Malta	-88.9	89	193.7	104	282.7	103
Marshall Islands	58.3	184	75.5	136	17.2	157

United States—2005 Exports, Imports, and Trade Balance by Country and Area (cont.)

COUNTRY	TRADE BALANCE	RANK	EXPORTS F.A.S.	RANK	IMPORTS CUSTOMS	RANK
Martinique	12.7	157	35.0	157	22.2	155
Mauritania	85.3	192	86.1	130	0.8	202
Mauritius	-191.0	79	30.9	164	221.9	109
Mayotte	(-)	120	(-)	230	(-)	228
Mexico	-49,743.8	5	120,364.8	2	170,108.6	3
Moldova	-10.2	106	40.1	154	50.2	140
Monaco	-20.7	101	16.8	182	37.5	145
Mongolia	-121.8	87	21.9	177	143.6	118
Montserrat	3.9	139	4.8	203	1.0	201
Morocco	79.2	190	525.0	79	445.8	88
Mozambique	50.9	178	62.8	144	11.9	160
Namibia	-17.3	103	112.2	120	129.6	120
Nauru	1.5	131	1.6	215	0.1	215
Nepal	-86.5	91	24.7	175	111.2	123
Netherlands	11,622.6	230	26,484.6	8	14,862.0	22
Netherlands Antilles	215.2	206	1,137.6	61	922.4	77
New Caledonia	11.2	154	38.4	155	27.2	153
New Zealand	-503.4	65	2,651.8	41	3,155.2	52
Nicaragua	-555.3	63	625.5	73	1,180.8	73
Niger	13.0	158	78.5	135	65.5	133
Nigeria	-22,618.2	8	1,621.2	53	24,239.4	16
Niue	0.5	127	0.6	220	0.1	216
Norfolk Island	0.2	123	0.4	223	0.2	214
Norway	-4,834.4	28	1,941.9	48	6,776.3	36
Oman	39.9	175	594.9	75	555.0	83
Pakistan	-2,001.6	41	1,251.6	57	3,253.2	51
Palau	11.7	155	12.2	185	0.5	206
Panama	1,835.0	224	2,162.0	45	327.1	98
Papua New Guinea	-3.1	107	55.3	147	58.5	136
Paraguay	844.2	220	895.8	67	51.6	139
Peru	-2,809.7	33	2,309.4	43	5,119.2	44
Philippines	-2,355.0	38	6,895.4	25	9,250.4	28
Pitcairn Island	-0.6	114	0.5	221	1.0	200
Poland	-680.8	58	1,267.7	56	1,948.6	63
Portugal	-1,196.8	52	1,131.9	62	2,328.7	58
Qatar	538.8	218	986.6	65	447.9	86
Republic of Yemen	-59.6	95	219.0	100	278.6	104
Reunion	-2.0	110	3.8	206	5.8	170
Romania	-598.7	60	608.9	74	1,207.6	71
Russia	-11,344.3	17	3,962.4	33	15,306.7	20
Rwanda	4.2	140	10.5	188	6.3	167
San Marino	3.3	136	4.7	204	1.4	194
São Tomé and Príncipe	9.9	153	10.2	189	0.2	213
Saudi Arabia	-20,379.8	9	6,812.8	26	27,192.6	14
Senegal	154.8	200	158.5	110	3.7	181
Serbia and Montenegro	77.9	189	132.5	115	54.6	137
Seychelles	12.0	156	17.9	180	5.9	168
Sierra Leone	28.5	169	37.8	156	9.3	163
Singapore	5,532.2	225	20,642.2	11	15,110.1	21
Slovakia	-810.9	57	149.8	112	960.7	76
Slovenia	-179.2	83	233.8	98	413.0	90
Solomon Islands	0.9	129	2.3	212	1.4	195
Somalia	8.5	149	8.8	196	0.3	211
South Africa	-1,978.7	42	3,906.9	34	5,885.6	40
Spain	-1,701.0	44	6,913.6	24	8,614.6	32
Sri Lanka	-1,885.3	43	197.6	103	2,082.9	61
St. Helena	-0.5	115	2.7	209	3.3	184
St. Kitts and Nevis	44.4	176	94.1	128	49.7	141
St. Lucia	103.0	197	135.4	114	32.4	149
St. Pierre and Miquelon	-0.1	118	1.0	218	1.1	199
St. Vincent and the Grenadines	29.8	171	45.4	153	15.7	158
Sudan	94.5	195	108.1	122	13.6	159
Suriname	80.4	191	245.7	95	165.3	115
Svalbard, Jan Mayen Island	5.6	143	5.7	200	(-)	223
Swaziland	-187.0	80	11.9	186	198.9	110
Sweden	-10,105.6	19	3,715.4	35	13,821.0	23
Switzerland	-2,280.0	39	10,719.8	17	12,999.9	25
Syria	-168.5	84	155.0	111	323.6	100
Taiwan	-12,756.6	13	22,069.2	10	34,825.8	8

United States—2005 Exports, Imports, and Trade Balance by Country and Area (cont.)

COUNTRY	TRADE BALANCE	RANK	EXPORTS F.A.S.	RANK	IMPORTS CUSTOMS	RANK
Tajikistan	-212.2	76	28.8	167	241.0	108
Tanzania	62.7	185	96.4	126	33.7	147
Thailand	-12,633.1	14	7,256.6	23	19,889.8	17
Togo	21.5	162	27.9	171	6.4	166
Tokelau	69.0	186	79.8	134	10.8	161
Tonga	4.3	141	9.7	192	5.4	173
Trinidad and Tobago	-6,474.1	26	1,416.7	54	7,890.9	34
Tunisia	-2.6	108	261.2	94	263.8	106
Turkey	-913.1	56	4,269.0	31	5,182.1	42
Turkmenistan	101.8	196	237.1	97	135.3	119
Turks and Caicos Islands	228.3	207	237.8	96	9.4	162
Tuvalu	(-)	119	(-)	228	0.1	221
Uganda	36.8	174	62.6	145	25.8	154
Ukraine	-565.1	61	533.0	78	1,098.0	75
United Arab Emirates	7,014.1	227	8,482.4	21	1,468.3	68
United Kingdom	-12,444.8	15	38,587.8	5	51,032.6	6
Uruguay	-375.6	69	356.7	87	732.3	79
Uzbekistan	-21.8	99	73.8	137	95.6	125
Vanuatu	6.6	147	9.1	194	2.5	186
Vatican City	23.9	165	24.2	176	0.3	212
Venezuela	-27,557.2	6	6,420.9	27	33,978.1	9
Vietnam	-5,438.0	27	1,193.2	58	6,631.2	38
Wallis and Futuna	0.4	126	0.4	222	(-)	224
West Bank Administered by Israel	2.1	134	3.7	207	1.6	190
Western Sahara	(-)	121	(-)	229	(-)	229
Western Samoa	6.6	146	14.5	184	7.9	165
Zambia	-2.6	109	29.1	166	31.7	151
Zimbabwe	-48.8	97	45.5	152	94.3	126
Unidentified	216.3	(X)	216.3	(X)	(-)	(X)
North America	-128,229.4	(X)	332,263.5	(X)	460,492.9	(X)
Western Europe	-125,453.7	(X)	200,260.3	(X)	325,714.0	(X)
Euro Area	-91,384.0	(X)	137,496.7	(X)	228,880.7	(X)
European Union (25)	-122,338.2	(X)	186,437.3	(X)	308,775.5	(X)
European Union (15)	-117,160.3	(X)	181,718.3	(X)	298,878.5	(X)
European Free Trade Association	-7,147.4	(X)	13,193.5	(X)	20,340.9	(X)
Eastern Europe	-18,539.6	(X)	10,994.0	(X)	29,533.6	(X)
Former Soviet Republics	-13,566.9	(X)	6,604.3	(X)	20,171.2	(X)
Organization for Economic Cooperation & Development (OECD) in Europe	-125,232.5	(X)	199,207.8	(X)	324,440.4	(X)
Pacific Rim Countries	-328,066.4	(X)	223,334.0	(X)	551,400.4	(X)
Asia–Near East	-30,550.8	(X)	31,893.6	(X)	62,444.3	(X)
Asia–(NICS)	-15,781.6	(X)	86,827.5	(X)	102,609.1	(X)
Asia–South	-16,966.6	(X)	10,045.2	(X)	27,011.8	(X)
Assoc. of South East Asia Nations (ASEAN)	-49,278.2	(X)	49,636.7	(X)	98,914.9	(X)
APEC	-488,815.3	(X)	575,440.1	(X)	1,064,255.4	(X)
South/Central America	-50,460.1	(X)	72,413.0	(X)	122,873.0	(X)
Twenty Latin American Republics	-96,587.6	(X)	182,836.4	(X)	279,424.0	(X)
Central American Common Market	-1,304.0	(X)	12,167.5	(X)	13,471.5	(X)
Latin American Free Trade Association	-97,865.1	(X)	162,709.5	(X)	260,574.6	(X)
North Atlantic Treaty Organization (NATO) Allies	-198,120.9	(X)	406,259.2	(X)	604,380.0	(X)
Organization of Petroleum Exporting Countries (OPEC)	-92,866.6	(X)	32,073.8	(X)	124,940.4	(X)
Unidentified	216.3	(X)	216.3	(X)	(-)	(X)

(1) Detailed data are presented on a Census basis. The information needed to convert to a BOP basis is not available.

(2) Countries included in Euro Area are also included in European Union. See Page 27 of the FT-900 release for a list of countries.

(3) Selected countries are included in more than one area grouping. Indonesia is included in both OPEC and Pacific Rim; Venezuela is included in both OPEC and Other South/Central America.

(4) The export totals reflect shipments of certain grains, oilseeds, and satellites that are not included in the country/area totals.

NOTE: For information on data sources, nonsampling errors and definitions, see the information section on page 27 of the FT-900 release, or at www.census.gov/ft900 or www.bea.gov/bea/di/home/trade.htm.

system, and by resorting to a specific number of selective controls at its disposal. The Federal Reserve Board's role in regulating the money supply is held by economists of the monetarist school to be the single most important factor in determining the nation's inflation rate.

Member banks increase their reserves or cash holdings by re-discounting commercial notes at the federal reserve bank at a rate of interest ultimately determined by the Board of Governors. A change in the discount rate, therefore, directly affects the capacity of the member banks to accommodate their customers with loans. Similarly, the purchase or sale of securities in the open market, as determined by the Federal Open Market Committee, is the most commonly used device whereby the amount of credit available to the public is expanded or contracted. The same effect is achieved in some measure by the power of the Board of Governors to raise or lower the reserves that member banks must keep against de-mand deposits. Credit tightening by federal authorities in early 1980 pushed the prime rate-the rate that commercial banks charge their most creditworthy customers-above 20% for the first time since the financial panics of 1837 and 1839, when rates reached 36%. As federal monetary policies eased, the prime rate dropped below 12% in late 1984; as of 2000 it was below 10%. In mid-2003 the federal funds rate was reduced to 1%, a 45-year low.

The financial sector is dominated by commercial banks, in-surance companies, and mutual funds. There was little change in the nature of the sector between the 1930s, when it was rescued through the creation of regulatory bodies and deposit insurance, and the 1980s, when the market was deregulated. In the 1980s, the capital markets underwent extensive reforms. The markets be-came increasingly internationalized, as deregulation allowed for-eign-owned banks to extend their operations. There was also ex-tensive restructuring of domestic financial markets-interest-rate ceilings were abolished and competition between different finan-cial institution intensified, facilitated by greater diversification.

Commercial and investment banking activities are separated in the United States by the Glass Steagall Act, which was passed in 1933 during the Great Depression. Fears that investment banking activities put deposits at risk led to a situation where commercial banks were unable to deal in non-bank financial instruments. This put them at severe commercial disadvantage, and the pressure for reform became so strong that the Federal Reserve Board has al-lowed the affiliates of commercial banks to enter a wide range of securities activities since 1986. Attempts to repeal the act were un-successful until November 1999, when the Gramm-Leach-Bliley Act (also known as the Financial Modernization Act) was passed by Congress. The Gramm-Leach-Bliley Act repealed Glass-Stea-gall and allows banks, insurance companies, and stock brokers and mutual fund companies to sell each other's products and ser-vices. These companies are also now free to merge or acquire one another.

The expansion and diversification in financial services was fa-cilitated by information technology. Financial deregulation led to the collapse of many commercial banks and savings and loan as-sociations in the second half of the 1980s. In the 1990s, change has continued in the form of a proliferation of bank mergers; with the passage in 1999 of Gramm-Leach-Bliley, further consolidation of the industry was predicted.

Prior to 1994 the banking system was highly fragmented; na-tional banks were not allowed to establish branches at will, as they were subject to the banking laws of each state. Within states, lo-cal banks faced similar restraints on their branching activities. In 1988, only 22 states permitted statewide banking of national banks, while 18 allowed limited banking and ten permitted no branches. Consequently in 1988 over 60% of US commercial banks had as-sets of less the $150 million, while only 3% had assets valued at $500 million or more.

Such regulation rendered US banks vulnerable to merger and acquisition. Acquisitions have generally taken place through

United States—Government Finances

(Dollar amounts in thousands. Per capita amounts in dollars.)

	AMOUNT	PER CAPITA
Total Revenue	1,589,856,242	5,424.22
General revenue	1,197,346,812	4,085.07
Intergovernmental revenue	394,497,492	1,345.93
Taxes	593,821,649	2,025.98
General sales	198,208,985	676.24
Selective sales	95,567,053	326.05
License taxes	39,626,991	135.20
Individual income tax	197,878,965	675.12
Corporate income tax	30,896,860	105.41
Other taxes	31,642,795	107.96
Current charges	114,842,943	391.82
Miscellaneous general revenue	94,184,728	321.34
Utility revenue	12,954,913	44.20
Liquor store revenue	4,865,703	16.60
Insurance trust revenue	374,688,814	1,278.35
Total expenditure	1,406,039,800	4,797.08
Intergovernmental expenditure	389,706,202	1,329.59
Direct expenditure	1,016,333,598	3,467.50
Current operation	691,570,727	2,359.48
Capital outlay	91,189,148	311.12
Insurance benefits and repayments	170,914,840	583.12
Assistance and subsidies	28,104,471	95.89
Interest on debt	34,554,412	117.89
Exhibit: Salaries and wages	185,827,096	634.00
Total expenditure	1,406,039,800	4,797.08
General expenditure	1,209,524,629	4,126.62
Intergovernmental expenditure	389,706,202	1,329.59
Direct expenditure	819,818,427	2,797.03
General expenditures, by function:		
Education	429,340,569	1,464.81
Public welfare	339,408,778	1,157.98
Hospitals	40,425,954	137.92
Health	49,559,091	169.08
Highways	86,428,773	294.88
Police protection	10,766,134	36.73
Correction	39,313,812	134.13
Natural resources	18,651,542	63.63
Parks and recreation	5,843,274	19.94
Government administration	44,682,549	152.45
Interest on general debt	32,883,864	112.19
Other and unallocable	112,220,289	382.87
Utility expenditure	21,676,258	73.95
Liquor store expenditure	3,924,073	13.39
Insurance trust expenditure	170,914,840	583.12
Debt at end of fiscal year	750,409,895	2,560.23
Cash and security holdings	2,928,805,805	9,992.41

Abbreviations and symbols: – zero or rounds to zero; (NA) not available; (X) not applicable.

SOURCE: U.S. Census Bureau, Governments Division, 2004 Survey of State Government Finances, January 2006.

bank holding companies, which then fall under the jurisdiction of the Federal Reserve System. This has allowed banks to extend their business into non-bank activities such as insurance, financial planning, and mortgages, as well as opening up geographical markets. The number of such holding companies is estimated at 6,500. These companies are believed to control over 90% of total bank assets.

The Riegle-Neal Interstate Banking and Branching Efficiency Act of 1994 removed most of the barriers to interstate bank acquisitions and interstate banking. The new act allowed banks to merge with banks in other states although they must operate them as separate banks. In addition, banks are allowed to establish branches in neighboring states. Restrictions on branching activity were lifted as of June 1997. The legislation allowed banks to lessen their exposure to regional economic downturns. It also ensured a continuing stream of bank mergers. Liberalization has encouraged a proliferation of in-store banking at supermarkets. International Banking Technologies, Inc., reported that the number of supermarket bank branches rose to 7,100 in 1998, up from 2,191 in 1994. In the mid-1990s, the number of supermarket branch banks grew at an annual rate of around 30%, but growth from 1997 to 1998 slowed to just over 10%.

Under the provisions of the Banking Act of 1935, all members of the Federal Reserve System (and other banks that wish to do so) participate in a plan of deposit insurance (up to $100,000 for each individual account as of 2003) administered by the Federal Deposit Insurance Corporation (FDIC).

Savings and loan associations are insured by the Federal Savings and Loan Insurance Corporation (FSLIC). Individual accounts were insured up to a limit of $100,000. Savings and loans failed at an alarming rate in the 1980s. In 1989 the government signed legislation that created the Resolution Trust Corporation. The RTC's job is to handle the savings and loans bailout, expected to cost taxpayers $345 billion through 2029. Approximately 30 million members participated in thousands of credit unions chartered by a federal agency; state-chartered credit unions had over 20 million members.

The International Monetary Fund reports that in 2001, currency and demand deposits—an aggregate commonly known as M1—were equal to $1,595.5 billion. In that same year, M2—an aggregate equal to M1 plus savings deposits, small time deposits, and money market mutual funds—was $6,961.2 billion. The money market rate, the rate at which financial institutions lend to one another in the short term, was 3.89%. The discount rate, the interest rate at which the central bank lends to financial institutions in the short term, was 1.25%.

33 INSURANCE

The number of life insurance companies has shrunk in recent years. Between 1985 and 1995 the number fell from 2,261 to 1,840. In 1998, there were 51 life insurance mergers and acquisitions. Competition between financial institutions has been healthy and premium income has risen steadily. The overwhelming majority of US families have some life insurance with a legal reserve company, the Veterans Administration, or fraternal, assessment, burial, or savings bank organization. The passage in 1999 of the Gramm-Leach-Bliley Act allowed insurance companies, banks, and securities firms to sell each other's products and services; re-

strictions were also lifted on cross-industry mergers and acquisitions. In 2003, the value of all direct insurance premiums written totaled $1,055.498 billion, of which nonlife premiums accounted for $574.579 billion. In that same year, State Farm Mutual Group was the top nonlife insurer, with direct written nonlife premiums of $47,226 million, while Metropolitan Life and Affiliated was the nation's leading life insurer, with direct written life insurance premiums of $27,649.1 million.

Hundreds of varieties of insurance may be purchased. Besides life, the more important coverages include accident, fire, hospital and medical expense, group accident and health, automobile liability, automobile damage, workers' compensation, ocean marine, and inland marine. Americans buy more life and health insurance than any other group except Canadians and Japanese. During the 1970s, many states enacted a "no fault" form of automobile insurance, under which damages may be awarded automatically, without recourse to a lawsuit.

34 SECURITIES

When the New York Stock Exchange (NYSE) opened in 1817, its trading volume was 100 shares a day. On 17 December 1999, 1.35 billion shares were traded, a record high for shares traded in a single day. Record-setting trading volume occurred for 1999 as a whole, with 203.9 billion shares traded (a 20% increase over 1998) for a total value of $8.9 trillion, up from $7.3 trillion in 1998. In 1996, 51 million individuals and 10,000 institutional investors owned stocks or shares in mutual funds traded on the NYSE. The two other major stock markets in the United States are the American Stock Exchange (AMEX) and the NASDAQ (National Association of Securities Dealers). The NASD (National Association of Securities Dealers) is regulated by the SEC (Securities and Exchange Commission). As of 2004, the New York Stock Exchange, the NASDAQ and the American Stock Exchange had a combined total of 5,231 companies listed. Total market capitalization that same year came to $16,323.726 billion.

35 PUBLIC FINANCE

Under the Budget and Accounting Act of 1921, the president is responsible for preparing the federal government budget. In fact, the budget is prepared by the Office of Management and Budget (established in 1970), based on requests from the heads of all federal departments and agencies and advice from the Board of Governors of the Federal Reserve System, the Council of Economic Advisers, and the Treasury Department. The president submits a budget message to Congress in January. Under the Congressional Budget Act of 1974, the Congress establishes, by concurrent resolution, targets for overall expenditures and broad functional categories, as well as targets for revenues, the budget deficit, and the public debt. The Congressional Budget Office monitors the actions of Congress on individual appropriations bills with reference to those targets. The president exercises fiscal control over executive agencies, which issue periodic reports subject to presidential perusal. Congress exercises control through the comptroller general, head of the General Accounting Office, who sees to it that all funds have been spent and accounted for according to legislative intent. The fiscal year runs from 1 October to 30 September. The public debt, subject to a statutory debt limit, has been raised by Congress 70 times since 1950. The debt rose from $43 billion in

1939/40 to more than $3.3 trillion in 1993 to more than $8.2 trillion in early 2006. In fiscal year 1991/92, the federal deficit reached $290 million, a record high. Pressured by Congressional Republicans, President Clinton introduced a taxing and spending plan to reduce the rate of growth of the federal deficit when he began his term in 1993. The Clinton Administration calculated the package of tax increases and spending would cut the deficit by $500 billion over a four-year period; in fiscal year 1997/98, the budget experienced an estimated surplus of $69 billion. However, the tax cuts and extensive military spending of President George W. Bush in the first term of the new millenium erased the surplus and pushed the economy toward a record $455 billion deficit projected for the 2003 fiscal year ($475 billion projected for 2004). The total public debt as of March 2006 exceeded $8 trillion.

The US Central Intelligence Agency (CIA) estimated that in 2005 the United States' central government took in revenues of approximately $2.1 trillion and had expenditures of $2.4 trillion. Revenues minus expenditures totaled approximately $-347 billion. Public debt in 2005 amounted to 64.7% of GDP. Total external debt was $8.837 trillion.

The International Monetary Fund (IMF) reported that in 2003, the most recent year for which it had data, central government revenues in billions of dollars were 1,902.4 and expenditures were 2,311.9. The value of revenues in millions of US dollars was $1,902 and expenditures $2,312. Government outlays by function were as follows: general public services, 12.2%; defense, 19.1%; public order and safety, 1.4%; economic affairs, 7.0%; housing and community amenities, 2.0%; health, 23.4%; recreation, culture, and religion, 0.2%; education, 2.6%; and social protection, 32.0%.

³⁶TAXATION

Measured as a proportion of the GDP, the total US tax burden is less than that in most industrialized countries. Federal, state, and local taxes are levied in a variety of forms. The greatest source of revenue for the federal government is the personal income tax, which is paid by citizens and resident aliens on their worldwide income. The main state-level taxes are sales and income taxes. The main local taxes are property and local income taxes.

Generally, corporations are expected to prepay, through four installments, 100% of estimated tax liability. US corporate taxes are famous for their complexity, and it is estimated that amount spent trying to comply with, minimize and/or avoid business taxes is equal to half the tax yield. As of 2004, the US had a top corporate federal tax rate of 35%, although the effective rate is actually 39.5%. Generally, corporations having taxable income in excess of $75,000 but not over $10 million are taxed at a 34% rate, with the first $75,000 taxed at graduated rates of 15% to 25%. However those whose income falls between $335,000 and $10 million are taxed at the full 34% which includes the initial $75,000. Corporations with income of over $15 million but not over $18,333,333 are subject to an additional 3% tax, while those corporations whose taxable income is over $18,333,333 are taxed at the 35% rate. The federal government also imposes an Alternative Minimum Tax (AMT). The purpose of the AMT is to prevent what is considered an overuse of tax deductions. As a result, the AMT is effectively a separate tax system with its own credit limitations and allowable deductions. Under the AMT, a 20% flat rate is applied to alternative minimum taxable income (AMTI), which the corporation

must pay if the calculated AMT is greater than the regular tax. Conversely, if the calculated regular tax is more than the calculated AMT, then the regular tax must be paid. State and local governments may also impose their own corporate income taxes. Generally, these taxes use the federal definitions of taxable income as the starting point when applying their income taxes. Capital gains from assets held as investments are taxed at the same rates as ordinary income. Dividends, interest and royalties paid to non-residents are subject to a withholding tax of 30%.

The United States has a progressive personal income tax structure that as of 2004, had a top rate of 35%. As with corporations, individuals can be subject to an AMT. With rates of 26% and 28%, the AMT, as it applies to individuals, is similar to the AMT charged to corporations in that the individual must pay whichever is highest, the regular tax or the AMT. Individuals may also be subject to inheritance and gift taxes, as well as state and local income taxes, all of which vary from state-to-state and locality-to-locality. Capital gains from assets held for under a year (short term) are taxed at higher rates than gains derived from assets held for more than a year (long term). Long term capital gains for individuals are taxed at a 15% rate, while those individuals who fall into lower-income tax brackets would be subject to a 5% rate. Certain capital gains derived from real estate are subject to a 25% tax rate.

The United States has not adopted a national value-added tax (VAT) system. The main indirect taxes are state sales taxes. There is an importation duty of 0.7% on imported goods. Excise taxes are levied on certain motor vehicles, personal air transportation, some motor fuels (excluding gasohol), alcoholic beverages, tobacco products, tires and tubes, telephone charges, and gifts and estates.

³⁷ECONOMIC POLICY

By the end of the 19th century, regulation rather than subsidy had become the characteristic form of government intervention in US economic life. The abuses of the railroads with respect to rates and services gave rise to the Interstate Commerce Commission in 1887, which was subsequently strengthened by numerous acts that now stringently regulate all aspects of US railroad operations.

The growth of large-scale corporate enterprises, capable of exercising monopolistic or near-monopolistic control of given segments of the economy, resulted in federal legislation designed to control trusts. The Sherman Antitrust Act of 1890, reinforced by the Clayton Act of 1914 and subsequent acts, established the federal government as regulator of large-scale business. This tradition of government intervention in the economy was reinforced during the Great Depression of the 1930s, when the Securities and Exchange Commission and the National Labor Relations Board were established. The expansion of regulatory programs accelerated during the 1960s and early 1970s with the creation of the federal Environmental Protection Agency, Equal Employment Opportunity Commission, Occupational Safety and Health Administration, and Consumer Product Safety Commission, among other bodies. Subsidy programs were not entirely abandoned, however. Federal price supports and production subsidies remained a major force in stabilizing US agriculture. Moreover, the federal government stepped in to arrange for guaranteed loans for two large private firms—Lockheed in 1971 and Chrysler in

1980—where thousands of jobs would have been lost in the event of bankruptcy.

During this period, a general consensus emerged that, at least in some areas, government regulation was contributing to inefficiency and higher prices. The Carter administration moved to deregulate the airline, trucking, and communications industries; subsequently, the Reagan administration relaxed government regulation of bank savings accounts and automobile manufacture as it decontrolled oil and gas prices. The Reagan administration also sought to slow the growth of social-welfare spending and attempted, with only partial success, to transfer control over certain federal social programs to the states and to reduce or eliminate some programs entirely. Ironically, it was a Democrat, Bill Clinton, who, in 1996, signed legislation that replaced Aid to Families with Dependent Children with a system of block grants that would enable the states to design and run their own welfare programs.

Some areas of federal involvement in social welfare, however, seem safely entrenched. Old age and survivors' insurance, unemployment insurance, and other aspects of the Social Security program have been accepted areas of governmental responsibility for decades. With the start of the 21st century, the government faced the challenge of keeping the Medicare program solvent as the postwar baby-boomer generation reached retirement age. Federal responsibility has also been extended to insurance of bank deposits, to mortgage insurance, and to regulation of stock transactions. The government fulfills a supervisory and regulatory role in labor-management relations. Labor and management customarily disagree on what the role should be, but neither side advocates total removal of government from this field.

Since the Reciprocal Trade Agreement Act of 1934, government regulation of foreign trade has tended toward decreased levels of protection, a trend maintained by the 1945 Trade Agreements Extension Act, the 1962 Trade Expansion Act, and the 1974 Trade Act. The goals of free trade have also been furthered since World War II by US participation in the International Monetary Fund (IMF), the World Bank, and the General Agreement on Tariffs and Trade (GATT). With the formation in 1995 of the World Trade Organization (WTO), most-favored-nation policies were expanded to trade in services and other areas.

In 1993, Congress approved the North American Free Trade Agreement, which extended the Free Trade Agreement between Canada and the United States to include Mexico. NAFTA, by eliminating tariffs and other trade barriers, created a free trade zone with a combined market size of $6.5 trillion and 370 million consumers. The effect on employment was uncertain—estimates varied from a loss of 150,000 jobs over the ensuing ten years to a net gain of 200,000. Labor intensive goods-producing industries, such as apparel and textiles, were expected to suffer, while it was predicted that capital goods industries would benefit. It was anticipated that US automakers would benefit in the short run by taking advantage of the low wages in Mexico and that US grain farmers and the US banking, financial, and telecommunications sectors would gain enormous new markets. As of 2005, the pros and cons of NAFTA were still being hotly debated. Spokespersons for organized labor claimed in 2000 that the agreement had resulted in a net loss of 420,000 jobs, while advocates of free trade insisted that 311,000 new jobs had been created to support record

US exports to Canada and Mexico, with only 116,000 workers displaced—a net gain of 195,000 jobs.

In 2003, President George W. Bush introduced, and Congress passed a tax cut of $350 billion designed to stimulate the economy, which was in a period of slow growth. This came on the heels of a $1.35 trillion tax cut passed in 2001 and a $96 billion stimulus package in 2002. Democrats cited the loss of 2.7 million private sector jobs during the first three years of the Bush administration as evidence that the president did not have control over the economy. In 1998, for the first time since 1969, the federal budget closed the fiscal year with a surplus. In 2000, the government was running a surplus of $236 billion, or a projected $5.6 trillion over 10 years. By mid-2003, the federal budget had fallen into deficit; the deficit stood at $455 billion, which was 4.2% of gross domestic product (GDP). The budget deficit stood at $412 billion in 2004, or 3.6% of GDP, and was forecast to decline to $331 billion in 2006.

US businesses are at or near the forefront of technological advances, but the onrush of technology has created a "two-tier" labor market, in which those at the bottom lack the education and professional and technical skills of those at the top, and, increasingly, fail to receive comparable pay raises, health insurance coverage, and other benefits. Since 1975, practically all the gains in household income have gone to the top 20% of households. Other long-term problems facing the US economy are inadequate investment in economic infrastructure, the rapidly rising medical and pension costs of an aging population, significant trade, current account, and budget deficits, and the stagnation of family income in the lower economic groups. Congress in 2003 passed an overhaul of the Medicare program, to provide prescription drug coverage for the elderly and disabled, which went into effect in January 2006.

38 HEALTH

The US health care system is among the most advanced in the world. Escalating health care costs resulted in several proposals for a national health care program in the 1970s, early 1980s, and early 1990s. Most reform measures relied either on market-oriented approaches designed to widen insurance coverage through tax subsidies on a federally controlled single-payer plan, or on mandatory employer payments for insurance coverage. The health care industry continues to struggle with continued rising costs, as well as the financial burden of providing care to over 40 million people who were uninsured. The percentage among the nation's poor was much higher.

In response to rising costs, the popularity of managed care grew rapidly in the latter half of the 1990s. By 2000, 59% of the population was insured by either an HMO (health maintenance organization) or PPO (preferred provider organization). In such organizations, medical treatment, laboratory tests, and other health services for each patient are subject to the approval of the insurer before they can be covered. From 1987 to 1996, enrollment in health maintenance organizations (HMOs) doubled. By the end of the decade, however, the quality of treatment under managed care organizations was coming under increased scrutiny.

Life expectancy for someone born in 2005 was 77.71 years. Infant mortality has fallen from 38.3 per 1,000 live births in 1945 to 6.50 per 1,000 live births in 2005. The birth rate in 2002 was 14.1

per 1,000 people. In 1999, 56.5% of US adults were overweight and 21.1% were obese. Although health indicators continued to improve overall 2004, pronounced disparities between different segments of the population remained.

The overall death rate is comparable to that of most nations—an estimated 8.7 per 1,000 people as of 2002. Leading causes of death were: heart disease, cancer, cerebrovascular diseases, chronic lower respiratory diseases, accidents, diabetes mellitus, pneumonia and influenza, Alzheimer's disease, suicide and homicide.

Cigarette smoking has been linked to heart and lung disease; about 20% of all deaths in the United States were attributed to cigarette smoking. Smoking has decreased overall since the late 1980s. The overall trend in smoking mortality suggests a decrease in smoking among males since the 1960s, but an increase in mortality for female smokers. On 23 November 1998, the Master Settlement Agreement was signed, the result of a lawsuit brought by 46 states and the District of Columbia against tobacco companies for damages related to smoking. Payments from the settlement, totaling $206 billion, began in 1999.

The rate of HIV infection (resulting in acquired immune deficiency syndrome—AIDS), first identified in 1981, has risen in the intervening years. There were a cumulative total of 750,000 AIDS cases in the 1980s and 1990s, with 450,000 deaths from the disease. In the latter 1990s, both incidence and mortality decreased with the introduction of new drug combinations to combat the disease. The number of AIDS cases declined by 30% between 1996 and 1998 and deaths were cut in half. In 2004, the number of people living with HIV/AIDS was estimated at 950,000, with the number of deaths from AIDS that year estimated at 14,000. AIDS continued to affect racial and ethnic minorities disproportionately. HIV prevalence was 0.60 per 100 adults in 1999.

Medical facilities in the United States included 5,810 hospitals in 2000, with 984,000 beds (down from 6,965 hospitals and 1,365,000 beds in 1980). As of 2004, there were an estimated 549 physicians, 773 nurses, 59 dentists and 69 pharmacists per 100,000 people. Of the total number of active classified physicians, the largest areas of activity were internal medicine, followed by general and family practice, then pediatrics.

Per capita health care expenditures rose from $247 in 1967 to about $3,380 in 1993. National health care spending reached $1 trillion in 1996 and is projected to rise to $1.9 trillion by 2006. Hospital costs, amounting to over $371 billion in 1997, represented 34% of national health care spending in that year. In the late 1990s, total health care expenditures stabilized at around 13% of GDP, with most expenditures being made by the private sector.

Medicare payments have lagged behind escalating hospital costs; payments in 2000 totaled $215.9 billion. Meanwhile, the elderly population in the United States is projected to increase to 18% of the total population by 2020, thus exacerbating the conundrum of health care finance.

³⁹SOCIAL WELFARE

Social welfare programs in the United States depend on both the federal government and the state governments for resources and administration. Old age, survivors', disability, and the Medicare (health) programs are administered by the federal government; unemployment insurance, dependent child care, and a variety of other public assistance programs are state administered, although the federal government contributes to all of them through grants to the states.

The Food and Nutrition Service of the US Department of Agriculture oversees several food assistance programs. Eligible Americans take part in the food stamp program, and eligible pupils participate in the school lunch program. The federal government also expends money for school breakfasts, nutrition programs for the elderly, and in commodity aid for the needy. The present Social Security program differs greatly from that created by the Social Security Act of 1935, which provided that retirement benefits be paid to retired workers aged 65 or older. Since 1939, Congress has attached a series of amendments to the program, including provisions for workers who retire at age 62, for widows, for dependent children under 18 years of age, and for children who are disabled prior to age 18. Disabled workers between 50 and 65 years of age are also entitled to monthly benefits. Other measures increased the number of years a person may work; among these reforms was a 1977 law banning mandatory retirement in private industry before age 70. The actuarial basis for the Social Security system has also changed. In 1935 there were about nine US wage earners for each American aged 65 or more; by the mid–1990s, however, the ratio was closer to three to one.

In 1940, the first year benefits were payable, $35 million was paid out. By 1983, Social Security benefits totaled $268.1 billion, paid to more than 40.6 million beneficiaries. The average monthly benefit for a retired worker with no dependents in 1960 was $74; in 1983, the average benefit was $629.30. Under legislation enacted in the early 1970s, increases in monthly benefits were pegged to the inflation rate, as expressed through the Consumer Price Index. Employers, employees, and the self-employed are legally required to make contributions to the Social Security fund. Currently, 6.2% of employee earnings (12.4% of self-employed earnings) went toward old-age, disability, and survivor benefits. Wage and salary earners pay Social Security taxes under the Federal Insurance Contributions Act (FICA). As the amount of benefits and the number of beneficiaries have increased, so has the maximum FICA payment. As of 2004 the maximum annual earnings for contribution and benefit purposes was $87,000.

Workers compensation laws vary according to states. Most laws were enacted before 1920; the program covering federal employees was instituted in 1908. Insurance is compulsory through public or private carriers. In most states the employer fund the total cost. There is a special federal program for miners with black lung disease (pneumoconiosis). The laws governing unemployment compensation originate in the states as well, and therefore benefits vary from state to state in duration and amount. Generally unemployment benefits amount to 50% of earnings, and federal law provides an additional 13 weeks of payments in states with high unemployment. Federal and state systems provide aid in the form of cash payments, social services, and job training to assist needy families.

Private philanthropy plays a major role in the support of relief and health services. The private sector plays an especially important role in pension management.

⁴⁰HOUSING

The housing resources of the United States far exceed those of any other country, with 122,671,734 housing units serving about

109,902,090 households, according to 2004American Community Survey estimates. About 67% of all occupied units were owner-occupied. About 10% of the total housing stock was vacant. The average household had 2.6 people. The median home value was estimated at $151,366. The median payment for rent and utilities of rental properties was $694 per month. California had the highest number of housing units at over 12 million (in 2000); the state also had the highest median housing value of owner-occupied units at $391,102 (2004 est.). Wyoming had the lowest number of housing stock with 223,854 (2000). The lowest median housing value of owner-occupied units was found in Arkansas at $79,006 (2004 est.).

The vast majority of housing units are single-unit structures; 61% are single-family detached homes. Over 9.5 million dwellings are found in buildings of 20 units or more. Over 8.7 million dwellings are mobile homes. About 14.9% of the total housing stock was built in 1939 or before. The decade of 1970–79 had the most homes built, with 21,462,868 units, 17.6% of the existing stock. During the period 1990–99, there were 19,007,934 units built, about 15% of the existing stick. Houses being built in the 1990s were significantly larger than those built in the 1970s. The average area of single-family housing built in 1993 was 180.88 sq m (1,947 sq ft), compared to 139.35 sq m (1,500 sq ft) in 1970. The median number of rooms per dwelling was estimated at 5.4 in 2004.

41 EDUCATION

Education is the responsibility of state and the local governments. However, federal funds are available to meet special needs at primary, secondary, or higher levels. Each state specifies the age and circumstances for compulsory attendance. The most common program of compulsory education requires attendance for ages 6 to 16; however, most school programs continue through twelve years of study, with students graduating at age 17 or 18. The high school diploma is only granted to students who complete this course of study, no certificates of completion are granted at previous intervals. Those who leave school before completion of grade 12 may choose to take a General Educational Development Test (GED) that is generally considered to be the equivalent to a state-approved diploma.

"Regular" schools, which educate a person toward a diploma or degree, include both public and private schools. Public schools are controlled and supported by the local authorities, as well as state or federal governmental agencies. Private schools are controlled and supported by religious or private organizations. Elementary schooling generally extends from grade one through grade five or six. Junior high or middle school programs may cover grades six through eight, depending on the structure of the particular school district. High schools generally cover grades 9 through 12. At the secondary level, many schools offer choices of general studies or college preparatory studies. Vocational and technical programs are also available. Some schools offer advanced placement programs through which students (after appropriate exams) may earn college credits while still in high school. The school year begins in September and ends in June.

In 2003, about 58% of children between the ages of three and five were enrolled in some type of preschool program. Primary school enrollment in 2003 was estimated at about 92% of age-eligible students. The student-to-teacher ratio for primary school was at about 14:1 in 2003; the ratio for secondary school was about 15:1. In 2003, private schools accounted for about 10.8% of primary school enrollment and 9.2% of secondary enrollment. As of 2003, about 87% percent of all 25- to 29-year-olds had received a high school diploma or equivalency certificate.

In 2003, about 1.1 million students were home schooled. In a home schooling program, students are taught at home by their parents or tutors using state-approved curriculum resources. Most of these students (about 82%) receive their entire education at home. Others may attend some classes at local schools or choose to attend public high school after completing preliminary grades through home schooling.

Colleges include junior or community colleges, offering two-year associate degrees; regular four-year colleges and universities; and graduate or professional schools. Both public and private institutions are plentiful. Eight of the most prestigious institutions in the country are collective known as the Ivy League. These schools are some of the oldest in the country and are known for high academic standards and an extremely selective admissions process. Though they are all now independent, nonsectarian organizations, most of them were founded or influenced by religious groups. They include: Yale University (1701, Puritans), University of Pennsylvania (1740, Quaker influence), Princeton University (1746, Presbyterian), Harvard University (1638, Puritan), Dartmouth College (1769, Puritan), Cornell University (1865), Colombia University (1754, Anglican), and Brown University (1764, Baptist).

The cost of college education varies considerably depending on the institution. There are county and state universities that receive government funding and offer reduced tuition for residents of the region. Students attending both public and private institutions may be eligible for federal aid in the form of grants or loans. Institutions generally offer their own scholarship and grant programs as well.

There are over 4,000 non-degree institutions of higher learning, including educational centers offering continuing education credits for professionals as well as general skill-based learning programs. Certificate programs are available in a number of professions and trades. Technical and vocational schools are also available for adults. In 2003, it was estimated that about 83% of the tertiary age population were enrolled in tertiary education programs. The adult literacy rate has been estimated at about 97%.

Beyond this, there are numerous public and private community organizations that offer educational programming in the form of workshops, lectures, seminars, and classes for adults interested in expanding their educational horizons.

As of 2003, public expenditure on education was estimated at 5.7% of GDP, or 17.1% of total government expenditures.

42 ARTS

The nation's arts centers are emblems of the importance of the performing arts in US life. New York City's Lincoln Center for the Performing Arts, whose first concert hall opened in 1962, is now the site of the Metropolitan Opera House, three halls for concerts and other musical performances, two theaters, the New York Public Library's Library and Museum of the Performing Arts, and the Juilliard School. The John F. Kennedy Center for the Performing

Arts in Washington, D.C., opened in 1971; it comprises two main theaters, two smaller theaters, an opera house, and a concert hall.

The New York Philharmonic, founded in 1842, is the nation's oldest professional musical ensemble. Other leading orchestras include those of Boston, Chicago, Cleveland, Los Angeles, Philadelphia, Pittsburgh, and Washington, D.C. (the National Symphony). Particularly renowned for artistic excellence are the Lyric Opera of Chicago, San Francisco Opera, Opera Company of Boston, Santa Fe Opera, New York City Opera, and the Metropolitan Opera.

The recording industry is an integral part of the music world. The US accounts for fully one-third of the global total of $33 billion in sales. Popular music (mostly rock), performed in halls and arenas in every major city and on college campuses throughout the US, dominates record sales. The Internet website Napster has challenged the recording industry's copyright rights by offering free downloads of popular music. The industry, threatened by the freedom that the Internet granted to those wishing to share music, succeeded in having Napster's operations suspended by an appeals judge in 2001.

Though still financially insecure, dance is winning an increasingly wide following. The American Ballet Theater, founded in 1940, is the nation's oldest dance company still active today; the New York City Ballet is equally acclaimed. Other important companies include those of Martha Graham, Merce Cunningham, Alvin Ailey, Paul Taylor, and Twyla Tharp, as well as the Feld Ballet, Joffrey Ballet, and Pilobolus.

Drama remains a principal performing art, not only in New York City's renowned theater district but also in regional, university, summer, and dinner theaters throughout the US. Television and the motion picture industry have made film the dominant modern medium.

The National Council on the Arts, established in 1964, advises the Chairman of the National Endowment for the Arts (NEA). Fourteen members of the Council, and six members of Congress serve in this function. As the largest single funder of the nonprofit arts sector in the United States, the NEA generated a total budget of $115.7 million in 2003. Grants are awarded to state, local, and regional organizations for projects in the following categories: creation and presentation, education and access, heritage and preservation, and planning and stabilization. Fellowship awards are made in the categories of Literature, American Jazz Masters, and National Heritage.

Since 1985, the NEA has assisted in the selection process for the National Medal of Arts, which is awarded by the president of the United States. Several winners are chosen each year, representing a variety of fields. Past medalists include: Dolly Parton (singer, 2005); Ray Bradbury (author, 2004); Ron Howard (director and actor, 2003);William "Smokey" Robinson (songwriter and musician, 2002); Al Hirschfeld (illustrator, 2002); Johnny Cash (singer, 2001); Yo-Yo Ma (cellist, 2001); Kirk Douglas (actor and producer, 2001); Mikhail Baryshnikov (dancer and director, 2000); Maya Angelou (poet and writer, 2000); Aretha Franklin (singer, 1999); Michael Graves (architect, 1999); Frank Gehry (architect, 1998); Edward Albee (playwright, 1997); Harry Callahan (photographer, 1996); Bob Hope (entertainer, 1995); Gene Kelly (dancer, 1994); Arthur Miller (playwright, 1993); and Frank Capra (film director, 1986), to name just a few. Organizations that have received medals

include the Alvin Ailey Dance Foundation (2001), National Public Radio (2000), the Julliard School (1999), Steppenwolf Theater Company (1998), the Sarah Lee Corporation (corporate arts patron, 1998), and the Boys Choir of Harlem (1994).

The National Endowment for the Humanities (NEH) was created as an independent federal agency in 1965. It is the largest funder of humanities programs in the country. Grants are distributed to state and local programs in the following categories: Challenge Grants, Education Programs, Preservation and Access, Public Programs, and Research Programs. Besides offering support to outside organizations, the NEH sponsors touring exhibitions and programs through chapters in most states. The NEH budget request for the year 2006 was $138.6 million.

The NEH sponsors the Jefferson Lecture in the Humanities award, which was established in 1972 as the highest honor the federal government bestows for distinguished intellectual and public achievement in the humanities. Recipients have included Tom Wolfe (2006); David McCullough (2003); Henry Louis Gates, Jr., (2002); Arthur Miller (2001); Toni Morrison (1996); Gwendolyn Brooks (1994); Saul Bellow (1977); and Robert Penn Warren (1974). The National Humanities Medals, established in 1997, are awarded to individuals or groups whose work has had an impact on the understanding and preservation of the humanities. Medalists include the Iowa Writers' Workshop (2002); Donald Kagan (2002); Art Linkletter (2002); Richard Peck (2001); Ernest J. Gaines (2000); Garrison Keillor (1999); Jim Lehrer (1999); Steven Spielberg (1999); Stephen Ambrose (1998); Don Henley (1997); and Maxine Hong Kingston (1997).

Since 1950, the National Book Foundation, based in New York, has sponsored the National Book Awards, which have become the nation's preeminent literary prizes. The 2005 prizes went to *Europe Central* by William Vollman (fiction), *Year of Magical Thinking* by Joan Didion (non-fiction), *New and Selected Poems* by W.S. Merwin (poetry), and *The Penderwicks* by Jeanne Birdsall (young people's literature). Notable past winners include: *United States: Essays 1952-1992* by Gore Vidal (1993); *Cold Mountain* by Charles Frazier (1997); *The White House* by Henry A. Kissinger (1980); *A Swiftly Tilting Planet* by Madeleine L'Engle (1980); *The Fall of America: Poems of these States, 1965-1971* by Allen Ginsberg (1974); *Death at an Early Age* by Jonathan Kozol (1968); *The Centaur* by John Updike (1964); *The Invisible Man* by Ralph Ellison (1953); *Collected Poems* by Marianne Moore (1952); and *The Collected Stories of William Faulkner* (1951).

43 LIBRARIES AND MUSEUMS

The American Library Association has reported that, as of 2004, there were an estimated 117,664 libraries in the country, including 9,211 public libraries (with over 16,500 buildings), 3,527 academic libraries, 93,861 school libraries, 9,526 special libraries, 314 armed forces libraries, and 1,225 government libraries.

The largest library in the country and the world is the Library of Congress, with holdings of over130 million items, including 29 million books and other printed materials, 2.7 million recordings, 12 million photographs, 4.8 million maps, and 58 million manuscripts. The Library of Congress serves as the national library and the site of the U.S. Copyright Office. The government maintains a system of Presidential Libraries and Museums which serve as archive and research centers that preserve documents and other materials of historical value related to the presidency. Starting with Herbert Hoover, the 31st president of the United States, there has been a library and museum established for each president. State governments maintain their own libraries as well.

The country's vast public library system is administered primarily by municipalities. The largest of these is the New York Public Library system with 89 branch locations and over 42.7 million items, including 14.9 million bound volumes. Other major public library systems include the Cleveland Public Library (over 9.7 million items), Los Angeles County Public Library (over 9.6 million items, 8.7 million books), the Chicago Public Library (6.5 million), the Boston Public Library system (6.1 million books, including 1.2 million rare books and manuscripts), and the Free Library of Philadelphia (6 million items).

Noted special collections are those of the Pierpont Morgan Library in New York; the Huntington Library in San Marino, Calif.; the Folger Shakespeare Library in Washington, D.C.; the Hoover Library at Stanford University; and the rare book divisions of Harvard, Yale, Indiana, Texas, and Virginia universities.

Among the leading university libraries are those of Harvard (with about 15 million volumes in 90 libraries), Yale, Illinois (Urbana-Champaign), Michigan (Ann Arbor), California (Berkeley), Columbia, Stanford, Cornell, California (Los Angeles), Chicago, Wisconsin (Madison), and Washington (Seattle).

There are over 5,000 nonprofit museums in the United States. The most numerous type is the historic building, followed in descending order by college and university museums, museums of science, public museums of history, and public museums of art. The Smithsonian Institute in Washington, D.C., sponsors 18 national museums and the National Zoo. Sixteen of the Smithsonian national museums are located in the Smithsonian complex of Washington, D.C.; these include the Natural History Museum, the American History Museum, the Air and Space Museum, American Art Museum, and the American Indian Museum. The American Indian Museum, Heye Center, and the Cooper-Hewitt, National Design Museum are Smithsonian-sponsored museums located in New York.

Other eminent US museums include the American Museum of Natural History, the Metropolitan Museum of Art, the Museum of Modern Art, the Guggenheim Museum, the Whitney Collection of American Art, the Frick Collection, and the Brooklyn Museum, all in New York City; the Boston Museum of Fine Arts; the Art Institute of Chicago and the Chicago Museum of Natural History; the Franklin Institute and Philadelphia Museum of Art, both in Philadelphia; and the M. H. de Young Memorial Museum in San Francisco. Also of prominence are the Cleveland Museum of Art, the St. Louis Museum of Art, and the Baltimore Museum of Art.

44 COMMUNICATIONS

All major electric communications systems are privately owned but regulated by the Federal Communications Commission. The United States uses wire and radio services for communications more extensively than any other country in the world. In 2003, there were an estimated 621 mainline telephones for every 1,000 people. The same year, there were approximately 543 mobile phones in use for every 1,000 people. The Post Office Department of the United States was replaced on 1 July 1971 by the US Postal Service, a financially autonomous federal agency. In addition to mail delivery, the Postal Service provides registered, certified, insured, express and COD mail service, issues money orders, and operates a postal savings system. Since the 1970s, numerous privately owned overnight mail and package delivery services have been established.

Radio serves a variety of purposes other than broadcasting. It is widely used by ships and aircraft for safety; it has become an important tool in the movement of buses, trucks, and taxicabs. Forest conservators, fire departments, and the police operate with radio as a necessary aid; it is used in logging operations, surveying, construction work, and dispatching of repair crews. In 2004, broadcasting stations on the air comprised over 12,000 radio stations (both AM and FM) and more than 1,500 television stations. Nearly 1,000 stations were affiliated with five major networks: NBC, ABC, CBS, FOX (all commercial), and PBS (Public Broadcasting System). As of 1997 the United States had some 9,000 cable television systems. In 2003, there were an estimated 2,109 radios and 938 television sets for every 1,000 people. About 255 of every 1,000 people were cable subscribers. Also in 2003, there were 658.9 personal computers for every 1,000 people and 551 of every 1,000 people had access to the Internet. There were 198,098 secure Internet servers in the country in 2004.

45 PRESS

In 2005 there were over 1,500 daily newspapers in the United States. It has been estimated that about 20 large newspaper chains account for almost 60% of the total daily circulation. The US daily newspapers with the largest circulations as of 2004 were: *USA Today* (national), 2,220,863; *Wall Street Journal* (national), 2,106,774; *New York Times*, 1,121,057; *Los Angeles Times* (CA), 902,3164; *New York Daily News*, 715,052; *Washington Post* (DC), 707,690; *New York Post*, 686,207; *Chicago Tribune* (IL), 600,988; *Houston Chronicle* (TX), 554,783; *Dallas Morning News* (TX), 519,014; *San Francisco Chronicle* (CA), 505,022; *Chicago Sun-Times* (IL), 481,980; *Long Island/New York Newsday*, 481,816; *Boston Globe* (MA), 451,471; *Arizona Republic*, 413,268; *Star-Ledger* (Newark, NJ), 400,042; *Journal-Constitution* (Atlanta, GA), 386,015; *Star Tribune* (Minneapolis, MN), 381,094; *Philadelphia Inquirer* (PA), 368,883; and *Cleveland Plain Dealer* (OH), 354,309. *The Christian Science Monitor* is published for daily national circulation by the Christian Science Church based in Massachusetts; circulation in 2004 was about 60,723. Investor's Business Daily, based in Los Angeles, California, also has a national circulation, reaching about 191,846 in 2004.

In 2004, the most popular consumer magazine in the country was AARP the Magazine, published bimonthly by the American Association of Retired Persons (AARP) with a circulation of over 22.6 million. The AARP Bulletin came in second with a circulation of about 22.1 million. The two general circulation magazines that appealed to the largest audiences were *Reader's Digest* (about 10 million) and *TV Guide* (about 9 million). *Time* and *Newsweek* were the leading news magazines, with 2004 weekly circulations of 4,034,272 and 3,135,476 respectively.

The US book-publishing industry consists of the major book companies (mainly in the New York metro area), nonprofit university presses distributed throughout the United States, and numerous small publishing firms. In 1994, 51,863 book titles were published in the United States.

The US Constitution provides for freedom of speech and of the press in its Bill of Rights, and the government supports these rights. Citizens enjoy a wide range of opinions in all media, where debate, editorial opinion, and government opposition viewpoints are represented in some form or another. Nearly all media are privately owned.

⁴⁶ORGANIZATIONS

A number of industrial and commercial organizations exercise considerable influence on economic policy. The National Association of Manufacturers and the US Chamber of Commerce, with numerous local branches, are the two central bodies of business and commerce. Various industries have their own associations, concerned with cooperative research and questions of policy alike.

Practically every profession in the United States is represented by one or more professional organizations. Among the most powerful of these are the American Medical Association, comprising regional, state, and local medical societies; the American Bar Association, also comprising state and local associations; the American Hospital Association; and the National Education Association. The most prestigious scientific and technical institution s are the National Academy of Sciences (founded 1863) and the National Academy of Engineering (1964).

Many private organizations are dedicated to programs of political and social action. Prominent in this realm are the National Association for the Advancement of Colored People (NAACP), the Urban League, the American Civil Liberties Union (ACLU), Common Cause, and the Anti-Defamation League. The League of Women Voters, which provides the public with nonpartisan information about candidates and election issues, began sponsoring televised debates between the major presidential candidates in 1976. The National Organization for Women, and the National Rifle Association have each mounted nationwide lobbying campaigns on issues affecting their members. There are thousands of political action committees (PACs) that disburse funds to candidates for the House and Senate and other elected offices.

The great privately endowed philanthropic foundations and trusts play an important part in encouraging the development of education, art, science, and social progress in the United States. Prominent foundations include the Carnegie Corporation and the Carnegie Endowment for International Peace, the Ford Foundation, the Guggenheim Foundation, the Mayo Association for the Advancement of Medical Research and Education, and the Rockefeller Foundation.

Private philanthropy was responsible for the establishment of many of the nation's most eminent libraries, concert halls, museums, and university and medical facilities; private bequests were also responsible for the establishment of the Pulitzer Prizes. Merit awards offered by industry and professional groups include the "Oscars" of the Academy of Motion Picture Arts and Sciences, the "Emmys" of the National Academy of Television Arts and Sciences, and the "Grammys" of the National Academy of Recording Arts and Sciences.

Funds for a variety of community health and welfare services are funneled through United Way campaigns, which raise funds annually. The American Red Cross has over 3,000 chapters, which pay for services and activities ranging from disaster relief to blood donor programs. The Salvation Army is also a prominent national organization supporting programs of social welfare and advancement. There are several national associations dedicated to research and education for specific fields of medicine and particular diseases and conditions, such as the American Cancer Society, the American Heart Association, and the March of Dimes.

There are numerous youth clubs and associations across the country. The Boy Scouts of America, the Girl Scouts of the USA, rural 4-H Clubs, and the Young Men's and the Young Women's Christian Associations are among the organizations devoted to recreation, sports, camping, and education. There are youth organizations for political parties, such as the Young Republicans and Young Democrats, and Junior ROTC (Reserve Officers' Training Corps) for the Army, Navy, Air Force, and Marines. Most national religious and service associations have youth chapters.

The largest religious organization in the United States is the National Council of the Churches of Christ in the USA, which embraces 32 Protestant and Orthodox denominations, whose adherents total more than 42 million. Many organizations, such as the American Philosophical Society, the American Association for the Advancement of Science, and the National Geographic Society, are dedicated to the enlargement of various branches of human knowledge. National, state, and local historical societies abound, and there are numerous educational, sports, and hobbyist groups.

The larger veterans' organizations are the American Legion, the Veterans of Foreign Wars of the United States, the Catholic War Veterans, and the Jewish War Veterans. Fraternal organizations, in addition to such international organizations as the Masons, include indigenous groups such as the Benevolent and Protective Order of Elks, the Loyal Order of Moose, and the Woodmen of the World. Many, such as the Ancient Order of Hibernians in America, commemorate the national origin of their members. One of the largest fraternal organizations is the Roman Catholic Knights of Columbus.

⁴⁷TOURISM, TRAVEL, AND RECREATION

Among the most striking scenic attractions in the United States are: the Grand Canyon in Arizona; Carlsbad Caverns in New Mexico; Yosemite National Park in California; Yellowstone National Park in Idaho, Montana, and Wyoming; Niagara Falls, partly in New York; and the Everglades in Florida. The United States has a total of 49 national parks. Popular coastal resorts include those of Florida, California, and Cape Cod in Massachusetts. Historical attractions include the Liberty Bell and Constitution Hall in Philadelphia; the Statue of Liberty in New York City; the White House, the Capitol, and the monuments to Washington, Jefferson, and Lincoln in the District of Columbia; the Williamsburg historical restoration in Virginia; various Revolutionary and Civil War battlefields and monuments in the East and South; the Alamo in San Antonio; and Mt. Rushmore in South Dakota. Among many other popular tourist attractions are the movie and television studios in Los Angeles; the cable cars in San Francisco; casino gambling in Las Vegas and in Atlantic City, N.J.; thoroughbred horse racing in Kentucky; the Grand Ole Opry in Nashville, Tenn.; the many jazz clubs of New Orleans; and such amusement parks as Disneyland (Anaheim, Calif.) and Walt Disney World (near Orlando, Fla.). For abundance and diversity of entertainment—theater, movies, music, dance, and sports—New York City has few rivals. In April

1993, Amtrak began the country's first regularly scheduled transcontinental passenger service, from Los Angeles to Miami.

Americans' recreational activities range from the major spectator sports—professional baseball, football, basketball, ice hockey, soccer; and horse racing; and collegiate football and basketball—to home gardening. Participant sports are a favorite form of recreation, including jogging, aerobics, tennis, and golf. Skiing is a popular recreation in New England and the western mountain ranges, while sailing, power boating, rafting, and canoeing are popular water sports.

Foreign visitors to the United States numbered 41,212,213 in 2003, down from 51 million in 2000. Of these visitors, 31% came from Canada and 25% from Mexico. Hotel rooms numbered 4,415,696 with an occupancy rate of 61%. With a few exceptions, such as Canadians entering from the Western Hemisphere, all visitors to the United States are required to have passports and visas.

The cost of traveling in the United States varies from city to city. According to 2005 US government estimates, daily expenses were approximately $187 in Chicago, $272 in New York, $230 in Washington, D.C., and $174 in Miami. Costs are lower in smaller cities and rural areas.

48 SPORTS

Baseball, long honored as the national pastime, is the nation's leading professional team sport, with two major leagues having 30 teams (one in Canada). In the 1998 season, two teams were added to Major League Baseball—the Arizona Diamondbacks, playing in the National League West, and the Tampa Bay Devil Rays, playing in the American League East. In 2005, the Montreal Expos became the Washington DC Nationals, following the team's move to Washington DC from Montreal. During the 2005 regular season, almost 75 million fans attended Major League Baseball games. In 1992, the Toronto Blue Jays became the first non-US team to win the World Series. In addition, there is an extensive network of minor league baseball teams, each of them related to a major league franchise. The National Basketball Association, created in 1946, included 30 teams in 2005. A labor dispute resulted in a lockout of the players for nearly half the 1999–2000 NBA season. The Women's National Basketball Association (WNBA), founded in 1997, included 14 teams as of 2005. During the WNBA's third season (1999), 1,959,733 fans attended regular season games, establishing an attendance record for women's professional sports. In 2005, WNBA attendance totaled 1,805,937. In 2005, the National Football League included 32 teams; Houston, Texas, was awarded a franchise in 2002 to establish the 32nd team. The National Hockey League (NHL) expanded to 30 teams in 2000, when teams in St. Paul, Minnesota (Minnesota Wild), and Columbus, Ohio (Columbus Blue Jackets), played their inaugural seasons. Prior expansion occurred in the 1998–99 season, with the Nashville Predators, and in 1999–2000, with the Atlanta Thrashers. In the 2003/2004 season, 20.3 million fans attended regular NHL season games. However, the entire NHL schedule for the 2004/2005 season was cancelled because of a labor dispute between the players and the team owners. Hockey players also held strikes in 1992 and 1994. Play resumed for the 2005/2006 season after both sides agreed to a new labor contract. The North American Soccer League (NASL), which appeared to be growing popular in the late 1970s, discontinued outdoor play in 1985. Indoor soccer continued, however,

with the Major Indoor Soccer League. In 1994, however, soccer's World Cup games were played in nine US cities, with the final match held in Los Angeles. As of 2005, Major League Soccer fielded 12 teams in two divisions. Radio and television contracts are integral to the popular and financial success of all professional team sports. In 1994, a strike by baseball players caused the World Series to be canceled for the first time since 1904.

Several other professional sports are popular nationwide. Thoroughbred racing is among the nation's most popular spectator sports, with an estimated 12 million fans visiting horse-racing tracks annually. Annual highlights of thoroughbred racing are the three jewels of the Triple Crown—the Kentucky Derby, the Preakness, and the Belmont Stakes—most recently won by Seattle Slew in 1977 and by Affirmed in 1978. In 2000, jockey Julie Krone became the first woman jockey to be inducted into the Horse Racing Hall of Fame. Harness racing is also popular; attracting millions of spectators annually and involving over $1.5 billion in wagering. In 1997, over 14.3 million fans watched greyhound racing. The prize money that Henry Ford won on a 1901 auto race helped him start his now-famous car company two years later; since then, automobile manufacturers have backed sports car, stock car, and motorcycle racing at tracks throughout the US. From John L. Sullivan to Muhammad Ali, the personality and power of the great boxing champions have drawn millions of spectators ringside. Glamour and top prizes also draw national followings for tennis and golf, two professional sports in which women are nationally prominent. Other professional sports include bowling and rodeo.

Football has been part of US college life since the game was born on 6 November 1869 with a New Jersey match between Rutgers and Princeton. The National Collegiate Athletic Association (NCAA) and National Association of Intercollegiate Athletics (NAIA) coordinate collegiate football and basketball. Colleges recruit top athletes with sports scholarships in order to win media attention, and to keep the loyalty of the alumni, thereby boosting fund-raising. Baseball, hockey, swimming, gymnastics, crew, lacrosse, track and field, and a variety of other sports also fill the intercollegiate competitive program

The Amateur Athletic Union (AAU), a national nonprofit organization founded in 1888, conducts the AAU/USA Junior Olympics, offering competition in 22 sports in order to help identify candidates for international Olympic competition. St. Louis hosted the 1904 summer Olympics; Los Angeles was home to the games in 1932 and 1984. The winter Olympic games were held in Squaw Valley, Calif., in 1960, and at Lake Placid, New York, in 1932 and 1980. Atlanta hosted the summer Olympic games in 1996. Salt Lake City, Utah, was the site of the 2002 winter Olympic games.

49 FAMOUS AMERICANS

Printer, publisher, inventor, scientist, statesman, and diplomat, Benjamin Franklin (1706–90) was America's outstanding figure of the colonial period. George Washington (1732–99), leader of the colonial army in the American Revolution, became first president of the United States and is known as the "father of his country." Chief author of the Declaration of Independence, founder of the US political party system, and third president was Thomas Jefferson (1743–1826). His leading political opponents were John Adams (1735–1826), second president, and Alexander Hamilton (b.West Indies, 1755–1804), first secretary of the treasury, who secured the new nation's credit. James Madison (1751–1836), a leading figure in drawing up the US Constitution, served as fourth president. John Quincy Adams (1767–1848), sixth president, was an outstanding diplomat and secretary of state.

Andrew Jackson (1767–1845), seventh president, was an ardent champion of the common people and opponent of vested interests. Outstanding senators during the Jackson era were John Caldwell Calhoun (1782–1850), spokesman of the southern planter aristocracy and leading exponent of the supremacy of states' rights over federal powers; Henry Clay (1777–1852), the great compromiser, who sought to reconcile the conflicting views of the North and the South; and Daniel Webster (1782–1852), statesman and orator, who championed the preservation of the Union against sectional interests and division. Abraham Lincoln (1809–65) led the United States through its most difficult period, the Civil War, in the course of which he issued the Emancipation Proclamation. Jefferson Davis (1808–89) served as the only president of the short-lived Confederacy. Stephen Grover Cleveland (1837–1908), a conservative reformer, was the strongest president in the latter part of the 19th century. Among the foremost presidents of the 20th century have been Nobel Peace Prize winner Theodore Roosevelt (1858–1919); Woodrow Wilson (1856–1924), who led the nation during World War I and helped establish the League of Nations; and Franklin Delano Roosevelt (1882–1945), elected to four terms spanning the Great Depression and World War II. The presidents during the 1961–2000 period have been John Fitzgerald Kennedy (1917–63), Lyndon Baines Johnson (1908–73), Richard Milhous Nixon (1913–94), Gerald Rudolph Ford (Leslie Lynch King, Jr., b.1913), Jimmy Carter (James Earl Carter, Jr., b.1924), Ronald Wilson Reagan (1911–2004), George Herbert Walker Bush (b.1924), and Bill Clinton (William Jefferson Blythe III, b.1946). George Walker Bush (b.1946) became the 43rd president and first president of the 21st century.

Of the outstanding US military leaders, four were produced by the Civil War: Union generals Ulysses Simpson Grant (1822–85), who later served as the eighteenth president, and William Tecumseh Sherman (1820–91); and Confederate generals Robert Edward Lee (1807–70) and Thomas Jonathan "Stonewall" Jackson (1824–63). George Catlett Marshall (1880–1959), army chief of staff during World War II, in his later capacity as secretary of state under President Harry S Truman (1884–1972), formulated the Marshall Plan, which did much to revitalize Western Europe. George Smith Patton, Jr. (1885–1945) was a leading general who commanded major units in North Africa, Sicily, and Europe in World War II. Douglas MacArthur (1880–1964) commanded the US forces in Asia during World War II, oversaw the postwar occupation and reorganization of Japan, and directed UN forces in the first year of the Korean conflict. Dwight D. Eisenhower (1890–1969) served as supreme Allied commander during World War II, later becoming the thirty-fourth president. William Childs Westmoreland (1914–2005) commanded US military operations in the Vietnam War from 1964 to 1968 and served as US Army Chief of Staff from 1968 to 1972. H. Norman Schwarzkopf (b.1934) commanded the successful allied invasion of Iraq in the Persian Gulf War. General Colin Luther Powell (b.1937), former Secretary of State (2001–2005) and highest ranking African American government official in the history of the US (a position assumed by Condoleezza Rice

in 2005), was a general in the army who also served as National Security Advisor (1987–1989) and Chairman of the Joint Chiefs of Staff (1989–1993).

John Marshall (1755–1835), chief justice of the United States from 1801 to 1835, established the power of the Supreme Court through the principle of judicial review. Other important chief justices were Edward Douglass White (1845–1921), former president William Howard Taft (1857–1930), and Earl Warren (1891–1974), whose tenure as chief justice from 1953 to 1969 saw important decisions on desegregation, reapportionment, and civil liberties. The justice who enjoyed the longest tenure on the court was William O. Douglas (1898–1980), who served from 1939 to 1975; other prominent associate justices were Oliver Wendell Holmes (1841–1935), Louis Dembitz Brandeis (1856–1941), and Hugo Lafayette Black (1886–1971).

Indian chiefs renowned for their resistance to white encroachment were Pontiac (1729?–69), Black Hawk (1767–1838), Tecumseh (1768–1813), Osceola (1804?–38), Cochise (1812?–74), Geronimo (1829?–1909), Sitting Bull (1831?–90), Chief Joseph (1840?–1904), and Crazy Horse (1849?–77). Other significant Indian chiefs were Hiawatha (fl. 1500), Squanto (d.1622), and Sequoya (1770?–1843). Historical figures who have become part of American folklore include pioneer Daniel Boone (1734–1820); silversmith, engraver, and patriot Paul Revere (1735–1818); frontiersman David "Davy" Crockett (1786–1836); scout and Indian agent Christopher "Kit" Carson (1809–68); James Butler "Wild Bill" Hickok (1837–76); William Frederick "Buffalo Bill" Cody (1846–1917); and the outlaws Jesse Woodson James (1847–82) and Billy the Kid (William H. Bonney, 1859–81).

Inventors and Scientists

Outstanding inventors were Robert Fulton (1765–1815), who developed the steamboat; Eli Whitney (1765–1825), inventor of the cotton gin and mass production techniques; Samuel Finley Breese Morse (1791–1872), who invented the telegraph; and Elias Howe (1819–67), who invented the sewing machine. Alexander Graham Bell (b.Scotland, 1847–1922) gave the world the telephone. Thomas Alva Edison (1847–1931) was responsible for hundreds of inventions, among them the long-burning incandescent electric lamp, the phonograph, automatic telegraph devices, a motion picture camera and projector, the microphone, and the mimeograph. Lee De Forest (1873–1961), the "father of the radio," developed the vacuum tube and many other inventions. Vladimir Kosma Zworykin (b.Russia, 1889–1982) was principally responsible for the invention of television. Two brothers, Wilbur Wright (1867–1912) and Orville Wright (1871–1948), designed, built, and flew the first successful motor-powered airplane. Amelia Earhart (1898–1937) and Charles Lindbergh (1902–74) were aviation pioneers. Pioneers in the space program include John Glenn (b.1921), the first US astronaut to orbit the earth, and Neil Armstrong (b.1930), the first man to set foot on the moon.

Benjamin Thompson, Count Rumford (1753–1814), developed devices for measuring light and heat, and the physicist Joseph Henry (1797–1878) did important work in magnetism and electricity. Outstanding botanists and naturalists were John Bartram (1699–1777); his son William Bartram (1739–1832); Louis Agassiz (b.Switzerland, 1807–73); Asa Gray (1810–88); Luther Burbank (1849–1926), developer of a vast number of new and improved

Presidents of the United States

	NAME	BORN	DIED	OTHER MAJOR OFFICES HELD	RESIDENCE AT ELECTION
1	George Washington	Westmoreland County, Va., 22 February 1732	Mt. Vernon, Va., 14 December 1799	Commander in Chief, Continental Army (1775–83)	Mt. Vernon, Va.
2	John Adams	Braintree (later Quincy), Mass., 30 October 1735	Quincy, Mass., 4 July 1826	Representative, Continental Congress (1774–77); US vice president (1797–97)	Quincy, Mass.
3	Thomas Jefferson	Goochland (now Albemarle) County, Va., 13 April 1743	Monticello, Va., 4 July 1826	Representative, Continental Congress (1775–76); governor of Virginia (1779–81); secretary of state (1790–93); US vice president (1797–1801)	Monticello, Va.
4	James Madison	Port Conway, Va., 16 March 1751	Montpelier, Va., 28 June 1836	Representative, Continental Congress (1780–83; 1786–88); US representative (1789–97); secretary of state (1801–9)	Montpelier, Va.
5	James Monroe	Westmoreland County, Va. 28 April 1758	New York, N.Y., 4 July 1831	US senator (1790–94); governor of Virginia (1799–1802); secretary of state (1811–17); secretary of war (1814–15)	Leesburg, Va.
6	John Quincy Adams	Braintree (later Quincy), Mass., 11 July 1767	Washington, D.C., 23 February 1848	US senator (1803–8); secretary of state (1817–25); US representative (1831–48)	Quincy, Mass.
7	Andrew Jackson	Waxhaw, Carolina frontier, 15 March 1767	The Hermitage, Tenn., 8 June 1845	US representative (1796–97); US senator (1797–98)	The Hermitage, Tenn.
8	Martin Van Buren	Kinderhook, N.Y., 5 December 1782	Kinderhook, N.Y., 24 July 1862	US senator (1821–28); governor of New York (1829); secretary of state (1829–31); US vice president (1833–37)	New York
9	William Henry Harrison	Charles City County, Va., 9 February 1773	Washington, D.C., 4 April 1841	Governor of Indiana Territory (1801–13); US representative (1816–19); US senator (1825–28)	North Bend, Ohio
10	John Tyler	Charles City County, Va., 29 March 1790	Richmond, Va., 18 January 1862	US representative (1816–21); governor of Virginia (1825–27); US senator (1827–36); US vice president (1841)	Richmond, Va.
11	James K. Polk	Mecklenburg County, N.C., 2 November 1795	Nashville, Tenn., 15 June 1849	US representative (1825–39); governor of Tennessee (1839–41)	Nashville, Tenn.
12	Zachary Taylor	Orange County, Va., 24 November 1784	Washington, D.C., 9 July 1850	—	Louisiana
13	Millard Fillmore	Cayuga County, N.Y., 7 January 1800	Buffalo, N.Y., 8 March 1874	US representative (1833–35; 1837–43); US vice president (1849–50)	Buffalo, N.Y.
14	Franklin Pierce	Hillsboro, N.H., 23 November 1804	Concord, N.H., 8 October 1869	US representative, (1833–37); US senator (1837–43)	Concord, N.H.
15	James Buchanan	Mercersburg, Pa., 23 April 1791	Lancaster, Pa., 1 June 1868	US representative (1821–31); US senator (1834–45); secretary of state (1845–49)	Lancaster, Pa.
16	Abraham Lincoln	Hodgenville, Ky., 12 February 1809	Washington, D.C., 15 April 1865	US representative (1847–49)	Springfield, Ill.
17	Andrew Johnson	Raleigh, N.C., 29 December 1808	Carter Station, Tenn., 31 July 1875	US representative (1843–53); governor of Tennessee (1853–57; 1862–65); US senator (1857–62); US vice president (1865)	Greeneville, Tenn.
18	Ulysses S. Grant	Point Pleasant, Ohio, 27 April 1822	Mount McGregor, N.Y., 23 July 1885	Commander, Union Army (1864–65); secretary of war (1867–68)	Galena, Ill.
19	Rutherford B. Hayes	Delaware, Ohio, 4 October 1822	Fremont, Ohio, 17 January 1893	US representative (1865–67); governor of Ohio (1868–72; 1876–77)	Fremont, Ohio
20	James A. Garfield	Orange, Ohio, 19 November 1831	Elberon, N.J., 19 September 1881	US representative (1863–80)	Mentor, Ohio
21	Chester A. Arthur	Fairfield, Vt., 5 October 1829	New York, N.Y., 18 November 1886	US vice president (1881)	New York, N.Y.
22	Grover Cleveland	Caldwell, N.J., 18 March 1837	Princeton, N.J., 24 June 1908	Governor of New York (1882–84)	Albany, N.Y.
23	Benjamin Harrison	North Bend, Ohio 20 August 1833	Indianapolis, Ind., 13 March 1901	US senator (1881–87)	Indianapolis, Ind.

PARTY	% OF POPULAR VOTE	% OF ELECTORAL VOTE[1,2]	TERMS IN OFFICE[5]	VICE PRESIDENTS	NOTABLE EVENTS	
Federalist	—	50.0	30 April 1789–4 March 1793	John Adams	Federal government organized; Bill of Rights enacted (1791); Whiskey Rebellion suppressed (1794); North Carolina, Rhode Island, Vermont, Kentucky, Tennessee enter Union.	1
Federalist	—	25.7	4 March 1797–4 March 1801	Thomas Jefferson	Alien and Sedition Acts passed (1798); Washington, D.C., becomes US capital (1800)	2
Dem.–Rep.	—	26.4[3] 92.0	4 March 1801–4 March 1805	Aaron Burr George Clinton	Louisiana Purchase (1803); Lewis and Clark Expedition (1803–6); Ohio enters Union.	3
Dem.–Rep.	—	69.7 58.9	4 March 1809–4 March 1818 4 March 1813–4 March 1817	George Clinton Elbridge Gerry	War of 1812 (1812–14); protective tariffs passed (1816); Louisiana, Indiana enter Union.	4
Dem.–Rep.	—	84.3	4 March 1817–4 March 1821 4 March 1821–4 March 1825	Daniel D. Tompkins Daniel D. Tompkins	Florida purchased from Spain (1819–21); Missouri Compromise (1820); Monroe Doctrine (1823); Mississippi, Illinois, Alabama, Maine, Missouri enter Union.	5
National Republican	30.9	38.0[4]	4 March 1825–4 March 1829	John C. Calhoun	Period of political antagonisms, producing little legislation; road and canal construction supported; Erie Canal opens (1825).	6
Democrat	56.0 54.2	68.2 76.6	4 March 1829–4 March 1833	John C. Calhoun Martin Van Buren	Introduction of spoils system; Texas Republic established (1836); Arkansas, Michigan enter Union.	7
Democrat	50.8	57.8	4 March 1837–4 March 1841	Richard M. Johnson	Financial panic (1837) and subsequent depression.	8
Whig	52.9	79.6	4 March 1841–4 April 1841	John Tyler	Died of pneumonia one month after taking office.	9
Whig	—	—	4 April 1841–4 March 1845	—	Monroe Doctrine extended to Hawaiian Islands (1842); Second Seminole War in Florida ends (1842).	10
Democrat	49.5	61.8	4 March 1845–4 March 1849	George M. Dallas	Boundary between US and Canada set at 49th parallel (1846); Mexican War (1846–48), ending with Treaty of Guadalupe Hidalgo (1848); California gold rush begins (1848); Florida, Texas, Iowa, Wisconsin enter Union.	11
Whig	47.3	56.2	4 March 1849–9 July 1850	Millard Fillmore	Died after 16 months in office.	12
Whig	—	—	9 July 1850–4 March 1853	—	Fugitive Slave Law (1850); California enters Union.	13
Democrat	50.8	85.8	4 March 1853–4 March 1857	William R. King	Gadsden Purchase (1853); Kansas–Nebraska Act (1854); trade opened with Japan (1854).	14
Democrat	45.3	58.8	4 March 1857–4 March 1861	John C. Breckinridge	John Brown's raid at Harpers Ferry, Va. (now W. Va.; 1859); South Carolina secedes (1860); Minnesota, Oregon, Kansas enter Union.	15
Republican	39.8 55.0	59.4 91.0	4 March 1861–4 March 1865 4 March 1865–15 April 1865	Hannibal Hamlin Andrew Johnson	Confederacy established, Civil War begins (1851); Emancipation Proclamation (1863); Confederacy defeated (1865); Lincoln assassinated (1865); West Virginia, Nevada attain statehood.	16
Republican	—	—	15 April 1865–4 March 1869	—	Reconstruction Acts (1867); Alaska purchased from Russia (1867); Johnson impeached but acquitted (1868); Nebraska enters Union.	17
Republican	52.7 55.6	72.8 78.1	4 March 1869–4 March 1873 4 March 1873–4 March 1877	Schuyler Colfax Henry Wilson	Numerous government scandals; financial panic (1873); Colorado enters Union.	18
Republican	48.0	50.1	4 March 1877–4 March 1881	William A. Wheeler	Federal troops withdrawn from South (1877); civil service reform begun.	19
Republican	48.3	58.0	4 March 1881–19 Sept. 1881	Chester A. Arthur	Shot after 4 months in office, dead 2½ months later.	20
Republican	—	—	19 Sept. 1881–4 March 1885	—	Chinese immigration banned despite presidential veto (1882); Civil Service Commission established by Pendleton Act (1883).	21
Democrat	48.5	54.6	4 March 1885–4 March 1889	Thomas A. Hendricks	Interstate Commerce Act (1887)	22
Republican	47.8	58.1	4 March 1889–4 March 1893	Levi P. Morton	Sherman Silver Purchase Act (1890); North Dakota, South Dakota, Montana, Washington, Idaho, Wyoming enter Union.	23

Presidents of the United States

	NAME	BORN	DIED	OTHER MAJOR OFFICES HELD	RESIDENCE AT ELECTION
24	Grover Cleveland	Caldwell, N.J., 18 March 1837	Princeton, N.J., 24 June 1908	Governor of New York (1882–84)	New York, N.Y.
25	William McKinley	Niles, Ohio, 29 January 1843	Buffalo, N.Y., 14 September 1901	US representative (1877–83; 1885–91); governor of Ohio (1892–96)	Canton, Ohio
26	Theodore Roosevelt	New York, N.Y., 27 October 1858	Oyster Bay, N.Y., 6 January 1919	Governor of New York (1899–1900); US vice president (1901)	Oyster Bay, N.Y.
27	William H. Taft	Cincinnati, Ohio, 15 September 1857	Washington, D.C., 8 March 1930	Governor of Philippines (1901–4); secretary of war (1904–8); chief justice of the US (1921–30)	Washington, D.C.
28	Woodrow Wilson	Staunton, Va., 28 December 1856	Washington, D.C., 3 February 1924	Governor of New Jersey (1911–13)	Trenton, N.J.
29	Warren G. Harding	Blooming Grove, Ohio, 2 November 1865	San Francisco, Calif., 2 August 1923	US senator (1915–21)	Marion, Ohio
30	Calvin Coolidge	Plymouth Notch, Vt., 4 July 1872	Northampton, Mass., 5 January 1933	Governor of Massachusetts (1919–20); US vice president (1921–23)	Boston, Mass.
31	Herbert Hoover	West Branch, Iowa, 10 August 1874	New York, N.Y., 20 October 1964	Secretary of commerce (1921–29)	Stanford, Calif.
32	Franklin D. Roosevelt	Hyde Park, N.Y., 30 January 1882	Warm Springs, Ga., 12 April 1945	Governor of New York (1929–1933)	Hyde Park, N.Y.
33	Harry S Truman	Lamar, Mo., 8 May 1884	Kansas City, Mo., 26 December 1972	US senator (1935–45); US vice president (1945)	Independence, Mo.
34	Dwight D. Eisenhower	Denison, Tex., 14 October 1890	Washington, D.C., 28 March 1969	Supreme allied commander in Europe (1943–44); Army chief of staff (1945–48)	New York
35	John F. Kennedy	Brookline, Mass., 29 May 1917	Dallas, Tex., 22 November 1963	US representative (1947–52); US senator (1953–60)	Massachusetts
36	Lyndon B. Johnson	Stonewall, Tex., 27 August 1908	Johnson City, Tex., 22 January 1973	US representative (1937–48); US senator (1949–60); US vice president (1961–63)	Johnson City, Tex.
37	Richard M. Nixon	Yorba Linda, Calif., 9 January 1913	New York, N.Y., 22 April 1994	US representative (1947–51); US senator (1951–53); US vice president (1953–61)	New York, N.Y.
38	Gerald R. Ford	Omaha, Neb., 14 July 1913	—	US representative (1949–73); US vice president (1973–74)	Grand Rapids, Mich.
39	James E. Carter	Plains, Ga., 1 October 1924	—	Governor of Georgia (1951–75)	Plains, Ga.
40	Ronald W. Reagan	Tampico, Ill., 6 February 1911	Bel-Air, Calif., 5 June 2004	Governor of California (1967–76)	Los Angeles, Calif.
41	George H. W. Bush	Milton, Mass., 12 June 1924	—	US representative (1967–71) Vice president (1980–88)	Houston, Texas
42	William J. Clinton	Hope, Arkansas, 19 August 1946	—	Attorney general of Arkansas (1977–79) Governor of Arkansas (1979–81; 1983–92)	Little Rock, Arkansas
43	George W. Bush	New Haven, Conn. 6 July 1946	—	Governor of Texas (1994–2000)	Midland, Texas

[1]Percentage of electors actually voting.

[2]In the elections of 1789, 1792, 1796, and 1800, each elector voted for two candidates for president. The candidate receiving the highest number of votes was elected president; the next highest, vice president. Percentages in table are of total vote cast. From 1804 onward, electors were required to designate which vote was for president and which for vice president, and an electoral majority was required.

PARTY	% OF POPULAR VOTE	% OF ELECTORAL VOTE[1,2]	TERMS IN OFFICE[5]	VICE PRESIDENTS	NOTABLE EVENTS	
Democrat	46.1	62.4	4 March 1893–4 March 1897	Adlai E. Stevenson	Financial panic (1893); Sherman Silver Purchase Act repealed (1893); Utah enters Union.	24
Republican	51.0	60.6	4 March 1897–4 March 1901	Garret A. Hobart Theodore Roosevelt	Spanish–American War (1898); Puerto Rico, Guam, Philippines ceded by Spain; independent Republic of Hawaii annexed; US troops sent to China to suppress Boxer Rebellion (1900); McKinley assassinated.	25
Republican	56.4	70.6	14 Sept. 1901–4 March 1905 4 March 1905–4 March 1909	Charles W. Fairbanks	Antitrust and conservation policies emphasized; Roosevelt awarded Nobel Peace Prize (1906) for mediating settlement of Russo–Japanese War; Panama Canal construction begun (1907); Oklahoma enters Union.	26
Republican	51.6	66.5	4 March 1909–4 March 1913	James S. Sherman	Federal income tax ratified (1913); New Mexico, Arizona enter Union.	27
Democrat	41.8 49.2	81.9 52.2	4 March 1913–4 March 1917 4 March 1917–4 March 1921	Thomas R. Marshall Thomas R. Marshall	Clayton Antitrust Act (1914); US Virgin Islands purchased from Denmark (1917); US enters World War I (1917); Treaty of Versailles signed (1919) but not ratified by US; constitutional amendments enforce prohibition (1919), enfranchise women (1920).	28
Republican	60.3	76.1	4 March 1921–2 Aug. 1923	Calvin Coolidge	Teapot Dome scandal (1923–24).	29
Republican	54.1	71.9	3 Aug. 1923–4 March 1925 4 March 1925–4 March 1929	Charles G. Dawes	Kellogg–Briand Pact (1928).	30
Republican	58.2	83.6	4 March 1929–4 March 1933	Charles Curtis	Stock market crash (1929) inaugurates Great Depression.	31
Democrat	57.4 60.8 54.7 53.4	88.9 98.5 84.6 81.4	4 March 1933–20 Jan. 1937 20 Jan. 1937–20 Jan. 1941 20 Jan. 1941–20 Jan. 1945 20 Jan. 1945–12 April 1945	John N. Garner John N. Garner Henry A. Wallace Harry S Truman	New Deal social reforms; prohibition repealed (1933); US enters World War II (1941).	32
Democrat	—	—	12 April 1945–20 Jan. 1949 20 Jan. 1949–20 Jan. 1953	Alben W. Barkley	United Nations founded (1945); US nuclear bombs dropped on Japan (1945); World War II ends (1945); Philippines granted independence (1946); Marshall Plan (1945); Korean conflict begins (1950); era of McCarthyism.	33
Republican	55.1 57.4	83.2 86.1	20 Jan. 1953–20 Jan. 1957 20 Jan. 1957–20 Jan. 1961	Richard M. Nixon Richard M. Nixon	Korean conflict ended (1953); Supreme Court orders school desegregation (1954); Alaska, Hawaii enter Union.	34
Democrat	49.7	56.4	20 Jan. 1961–22 Nov. 1963	Lyndon B. Johnson	Conflicts with Cuba (1961–62); aboveground nuclear test ban treaty (1963); Kennedy assassinated.	35
Democrat	61.1	90.3	22 Nov. 1963–20 Jan. 1965 20 Jan. 1965–20 Jan. 1969	Hubert H. Humphrey	Great Society programs; Voting Rights Act (1965); escalation of US military role in Indochina; race riots, political assassinations.	36
Republican	43.4 60.7	55.9 96.7	20 Jan. 1969–20 Jan. 1973	Spiro T. Agnew Spiro T. Agnew Gerald R. Ford	First lunar landing (1969); arms limitation treaty with Soviet Union (1972); US withdraws from Viet–Nam (1973); Agnew resigns in tax scandal (1973); Nixon resigns at height of Watergate scandal (1974).	37
Republican	—	—	9 Aug. 1974–20 Jan. 1977	Nelson A. Rockefeller	First combination of unelected president and vice president; Nixon pardoned (1974).	38
Democrat	50.1	55.2	20 Jan. 1977–20 Jan. 1981	Walter F. Mondale	Carter mediates Israel-Egypt peace accord (1978); Panama Canal treaties ratified (1979); tensions with Iran (1979–81).	39
Republican	50.8 58.8	90.9 97.6	20 Jan. 1981–20 Jan. 1985 20 Jan. 1985–20 Jan. 1989	George H. W. Bush George H. W. Bush	Defense buildup; social spending cuts; rising trade and budget deficits; tensions with Nicaragua.	40
Republican	54.0	79.2	20 Jan. 1989–20 Jan. 1993	J. Danforth Quayle	Multi-national force repelled Iraqi invaders from Kuwait; savings and loan crisis; 1991 recession.	41
Democrat	43.0 49.2	69.7 70.4	20 Jan. 1993–20 Jan. 1997 20 Jan. 1997–20 Jan. 2001	Albert Gore, Jr.	Passed North American Free Trade Agreement; enacted crime bill banning assault weapons; sent troops to Haiti to restore first democratically elected Haitian president to power after military coup.	42
Republican	47.87 50.73	50.37 53.1	20 Jan. 2001–20 Jan. 2005 20 Jan. 2005–	Richard B. Cheney Richard B. Cheney	Lowered taxes. Engaged in war in Afghanistan and Iraq after terrorist attacks on Washington and New York. Created the Department of Homeland Security. Substantially increased the federal deficit.	43

[3]Electoral vote tied between Jefferson and Aaron Burr; elections decided in House of Representatives.
[4]No candidate received a majority; election decided in House.
[5]In the event of a president's death or removal from office, his duties are assumed to devolve immediately upon his successor, even if he does not immediately take the oath of office.

varieties of fruits, vegetables, and flowers; and George Washington Carver (1864–1943), known especially for his work on industrial applications for peanuts. John James Audubon (1785–1851) won fame as an ornithologist and artist.

Distinguished physical scientists include Samuel Pierpont Langley (1834–1906), astronomer and aviation pioneer; Josiah Willard Gibbs (1839–1903), mathematical physicist, whose work laid the basis for physical chemistry; Henry Augustus Rowland (1848–1901), who did important research in magnetism and optics; and Albert Abraham Michelson (b.Germany, 1852–1931), who measured the speed of light and became the first of a long line of US Nobel Prize winners. The chemists Gilbert Newton Lewis (1875–1946) and Irving Langmuir (1881–1957) developed a theory of atomic structure.

The theory of relativity was conceived by Albert Einstein (b.Germany, 1879–1955), generally considered the greatest mind in the physical sciences since Newton. Percy Williams Bridgman (1882–1961) was the father of operationalism and studied the effect of high pressures on materials. Arthur Holly Compton (1892–1962) made discoveries in the field of X rays and cosmic rays. The physical chemist Harold Clayton Urey (1893–1981) discovered heavy hydrogen. Isidor Isaac Rabi (b.Austria, 1898–1988), nuclear physicist, did important work in magnetism, quantum mechanics, and radiation. Enrico Fermi (b.Italy, 1901–54) created the first nuclear chain reaction, in Chicago in 1942, and contributed to the development of the atomic and hydrogen bombs. Also prominent in the splitting of the atom were Leo Szilard (b.Hungary, 1898–1964), J. Robert Oppenheimer (1904–67), and Edward Teller (b.Hungary, 1908–2003). Ernest Orlando Lawrence (1901–58) developed the cyclotron. Carl David Anderson (1905–91) discovered the positron. Mathematician Norbert Wiener (1894–1964) developed the science of cybernetics.

Outstanding figures in the biological sciences include Theobald Smith (1859–1934), who developed immunization theory and practical immunization techniques for animals; the geneticist Thomas Hunt Morgan (1866–1945), who discovered the heredity functions of chromosomes; and neurosurgeon Harvey William Cushing (1869–1939). Selman Abraham Waksman (b.Russia, 1888–1973), a microbiologist specializing in antibiotics, was codiscoverer of streptomycin. Edwin Joseph Cohn (1892–1953) is noted for his work in the protein fractionalization of blood, particularly the isolation of serum albumin. Philip Showalter Hench (1896–1965) isolated and synthesized cortisone. Wendell Meredith Stanley (1904–71) was the first to isolate and crystallize a virus. Jonas Edward Salk (1914–95) developed an effective killed-virus poliomyelitis vaccine, and Albert Bruce Sabin (1906–93) contributed oral, attenuated live-virus polio vaccines.

Adolf Meyer (b.Switzerland, 1866–1950) developed the concepts of mental hygiene and dementia praecox and the theory of psychobiology; Harry Stack Sullivan (1892–1949) created the interpersonal theory of psychiatry. Social psychologist George Herbert Mead (1863–1931) and behaviorist Burrhus Frederic Skinner (1904–90) were influential in the 20th century. Psychiatrist Aaron Temkin Beck (b.1921) is regarded as the founder of cognitive therapy, and Albert Ellis (b.1913) developed rational-emotive therapy.

A pioneer in psychology who was also an influential philosopher was William James (1842–1910). Other leading US phi-

losophers are Charles Sanders Peirce (1839–1914); Josiah Royce (1855–1916); John Dewey (1859–1952), also famous for his theories of education; George Santayana (b.Spain, 1863–1952); Rudolf Carnap (b.Germany, 1891–1970); Willard Van Orman Quine (1908–2000), Richard Rorty (b.1931), Hilary Putnam (b.1926), John Rawls (1921–2002), Robert Nozick (1938–2002), and linguist and political philosopher Noam Chomsky (b.1928). Educators of note include Horace Mann (1796–1859), Henry Barnard (1811–1900), and Charles William Eliot (1834–1926). Noah Webster (1758–1843) was the outstanding US lexicographer, and Melvil Dewey (1851–1931) was a leader in the development of library science. Thorstein Bunde Veblen (1857–1929) wrote books that have strongly influenced economic and social thinking. Also important in the social sciences have been sociologists Talcott Parsons (1902–79) and William Graham Sumner (1840–1910) and anthropologist Margaret Mead (1901–78).

Social Reformers

Social reformers of note include Dorothea Lynde Dix (1802–87), who led movements for the reform of prisons and insane asylums; William Lloyd Garrison (1805–79) and Frederick Douglass (Frederick Augustus Washington Bailey, 1817–95), prominent abolitionists; Elizabeth Cady Stanton (1815–1902) and Susan Brownell Anthony (1820–1906), leaders in the women's suffrage movement; Clara Barton (1821–1912), founder of the American Red Cross; economist Henry George (1839–97), advocate of the single-tax theory; Eugene Victor Debs (1855–1926), labor leader and an outstanding organizer of the Socialist movement in the United States; Jane Addams (1860–1935), who pioneered in settlement house work; Robert Marion La Follette (1855–1925), a leader for progressive political reform in Wisconsin and in the US Senate; Margaret Higgins Sanger (1883–1966), pioneer in birth control; Norman Thomas (1884–1968), Socialist Party leader; and Martin Luther King, Jr. (1929–68), a central figure in the black civil rights movement and winner of the Nobel Peace Prize in 1964. Betty Friedan (1921–2006), Gloria Steinem (b.1934), and bell hooks (b. Gloria Jean Watkins, 1952) are contemporary feminists.

Religious leaders include Roger Williams (1603–83), an early advocate of religious tolerance in the United States; Jonathan Edwards (1703–58), New England preacher and theologian; Elizabeth Ann Seton (1774–1821), the first American canonized in the Roman Catholic Church; William Ellery Channing (1780–1842), a founder of American Unitarianism; Joseph Smith (1805–44), founder of the Church of Jesus Christ of Latter-day Saints (Mormon) and his chief associate, Brigham Young (1801–77); and Mary Baker Eddy (1821–1910), founder of the Christian Science Church. Paul Tillich (b.Germany, 1886–1965) and Reinhold Niebuhr (1892–1971) were outstanding Protestant theologians of international influence. Pat Robertson (b.1930), televangelist and leader of the Christian Coalition organization, and Jerry Falwell (b.1933), a fundamentalist Baptist pastor, televangelist, and founder of the Moral Majority movement and Liberty University, are contemporary leaders of the Christian religious right.

Famous US businessmen include Éleùthere Irénée du Pont de Nemours (b.France, 1771–1834), John Jacob Astor (Johann Jakob Ashdour, b.Germany, 1763–1848), Cornelius Vanderbilt (1794–1877), Andrew Carnegie (b.Scotland, 1835–1919), John Pierpont Morgan (1837–1913), John Davison Rockefeller (1839–1937),

Chief Justices of the United States, 1789-2006

	NAME	BORN	DIED	APPOINTED	SUPREME COURT TERM	MAJOR COURT DEVELOPMENTS
1	John Jay	New York City 12 December 1745	Bedford, N.Y., 17 May 1829	Washington	October 1789 June 1795	Organized court, established procedures.
2	John Rutledge	September 1739	Charleston, S.C., 18 July 1800	Washington		Presided for one term in 1795, but Senate refused to confirm his appointment.
3	Oliver Ellsworth	Windsor, Conn., 29 April 1745	Windsor, Conn. 26 Nov. 1807	Washington	March 1796 December 1800	
4	John Marshall	Fauquier County, Va., 24 September 1755	Philadelphia, Pa. 6 July 1835	Adams	February 1801 July 1835	Established principle of judicial review (Marbury v. Madison, 1803); formulated concept of implied powers (McCulloch v. Maryland, 1819).
5	Roger Brooke Taney	Calvert County, Md., 17 March 1777	Washington, D.C., 12 October 1864	Jackson	March 1836 October 1864	Held that slaves could not become citizens, ruled Missouri Compromise illegal (Dred Scott v. Sanford, 1857).
6	Salmon Portland Chase	Cornish, N.H., 13 January 1808	New York, N.Y. 7 May 1873	Lincoln	December 1864 May 1873	Ruled military trials of civilians illegal (Ex parte Milligan, 1866); Chase presided at A. Johnson's impeachment trial.
7	Morrison Remick Waite	Old Lynne, Conn., 29 November 1816	Washington, D.C., 23 March 1888	Grant	March 1874 March 1888	Held that businesses affecting the "public interest" are subject to state regulation (Munn v. Illinois, 1877).
8	Melville Weston Fuller	Augusta, Me., 11 February 1833	Sorvento, Me., 4 July 1910	Cleveland	October 1888 July 1910	Issued first opinions on cases under the Sherman Antitrust Act. (US v. E.C. Knight Co., 1895; Northern Securities Co. v. US, 1904); held the income tax unconstitutional (Pollock v. Farmers' Loan, 1895).
9	Edward Douglass White	Lafourche Parish, La., 3 November 1845	Washington, D.C., 19 May 1921	Taft	December 1910 May 1921	Further qualified the Sherman Antitrust Act (Standard Oil Co. v. US, 1911) by applying the "rule of reason."
10	William Howard Taft	Cincinnati, Ohio 15 September 1857	Washington, D.C., 8 March 1930	Harding	July 1921 February 1930	Held against congressional use of taxes for social reform (Bailey v. Drexel Furniture, 1922).
11	Charles Evans Hughes	Glens Falls, N.Y., 11 April 1862	Osterville, Mass., 27 August 1948	Hoover	February 1930 June 1941	Upheld constitutionality of National Labor Relations Act, Social Security Act, invalidated National Industrial Recovery Act (Schechter v. US, 1935); F. Roosevelt's attempt to pack Court opposed.
12	Harlan Fiske Stone	Chesterfield, N.H., 11 October 1872	Washington, D.C., 22 April 1946	F. Roosevelt	July 1941 April 1946	Upheld Court's power to invalidate state laws (Southern Pacific Co. v. Arizona, 1945).
13	Frederick Moore Vinson	Louisa, Ky., 22 January 1890	Washington, D.C., 8 September 1953	Truman	June 1946 September 1953	Overturned federal seizure of steel mills (Youngstown Sheet and Tube Co. v. Sawyer, 1952), Vinson dissenting.
14	Earl Warren	Los Angeles, Calif., 19 March 1891	Washington, D.C., 9 July 1974	Eisenhower	October 1953 June 1969	Mandated public school desegregation (Brown v. Topeka, Kans., Board of Education, 1954) and reapportionment of state legislatures (Baker v. Carr, 1962); upheld rights of suspects in police custody (Miranda v. Arizona, 1966).
15	Warren Earl Burger	St. Paul, Minn., 17 September 1907	Washington, D.C., 25 June 1995	Nixon	June 1969 August 1986	Legalized abortion (Roe v. Wade, 1973); rejected claim of executive privilege in a criminal case (US v. Nixon, 1974); first female justice (1981).
16	William Hubbs Rehnquist	Shorewood Village, Wis., 1 October 1924	Arlington, Va., 3 September 2005	Nixon	September 1986 September 2005	Applied constitutional prohibition against taking of property without compensation to invalidate government regulation of property. (Nollan v. California Coastal Commission, 1987). Strengthened states' rights although invalidated Florida election procedures (Bush v. Gore, 2000) on equal protection grounds. Limited enforcement of school desegregation. Narrowed the scope of affirmative action.
17	John Glover Roberts, Jr.	Buffalo, New York, 27 January 1955	—	Bush	September, 2005	

Andrew William Mellon (1855–1937), Henry Ford (1863–1947), and Thomas John Watson (1874–1956). William Henry "Bill" Gates III (b.1955), co-founder of the Microsoft Corp., was the richest person in the world as of 2006. Other corporate leaders in the 21st century include: Warren Edward Buffett (b.1930), Louis V. Gerstner, Jr., (b.1942), H. Wayne Huizenga (b.1937), Steve Jobs (b.1955), Sam Walton (1918–1992), John Francis "Jack" Welch Jr. (b.1935), and Sanford I. Weill (b.1933).

Literary Figures

The first US author to be widely read outside the United States was Washington Irving (1783–1859). James Fenimore Cooper (1789–1851) was the first popular US novelist. Three noted historians were William Hickling Prescott (1796–1859), John Lothrop Motley (1814–77), and Francis Parkman (1823–93). The writings of two men of Concord, Mass.—Ralph Waldo Emerson (1803–82) and Henry David Thoreau (1817–62)—influenced philosophers, political leaders, and ordinary men and women in many parts of the world. The novels and short stories of Nathaniel Hawthorne (1804–64) explore New England's Puritan heritage. Herman Melville (1819–91) wrote the powerful novel *Moby-Dick,* a symbolic work about a whale hunt that has become an American classic. Mark Twain (Samuel Langhorne Clemens, 1835–1910) is the best-known US humorist. Other leading novelists of the later 19th and early 20th centuries were William Dean Howells (1837–1920), Henry James (1843–1916), Edith Wharton (1862–1937), Stephen Crane (1871–1900), Theodore Dreiser (1871–1945), Willa Cather (1873–1947), and Sinclair Lewis (1885–1951), first US winner of the Nobel Prize for literature (1930). Later Nobel Prize–winning US novelists include Pearl Sydenstricker Buck (1892–1973), in 1938; William Faulkner (1897–1962), in 1949; Ernest Hemingway (1899–1961), in 1954; John Steinbeck (1902–68), in 1962; Saul Bellow (b.Canada, 1915–2005), in 1976; Isaac Bashevis Singer (b.Poland, 1904–91), in 1978; and Toni Morrison (b.1931), in 1993. Among other noteworthy writers are Zora Neale Hurston (1891–1960), Henry Miller (1891–1980), James Thurber (1894–1961), Francis Scott Key Fitzgerald (1896–1940), Vladimir Nabokov (b. Russia, 1899–1977), Thomas Wolfe (1900–1938), Richard Wright (1908–60), Eudora Welty (1909–2001), John Cheever (1912–82), Bernard Malamud (1914–1986), Carson McCullers (1917–1967), Norman Mailer (b.1923), James Baldwin (1924–87), Jack Kerouac (1922–1969), John Updike (b.1932), Philip Roth (b.1933), Paul Auster (b.1947), John Barth (b.1930), Donald Barthelme (1931–1989), T. Coraghessan Boyle (b.1948), Sandra Cisneros (b.1954), Joan Didion (b.1934), Stephen Dixon (b.1936), E.L. Doctorow (b.1931), Louise Erdrich (b.1954), William Gaddis (1922–1998), Carl Hiaasen (b.1953), Oscar Hijuelos (b.1951), John Irving (b.1942), Jamaica Kincaid (b. Elaine Cynthia Potter Richardson, 1949), Jhumpa Lahiri (b. Nilanjana Sudeshna, 1967), Jonathan Lethem (b.1964), Cormac McCarthy (b.1933), Larry McMurtry (b.1936), Bharati Mukherjee (b.1940), Joyce Carol Oates (b.1938), Marge Piercy (b.1936), E. Annie Proulx (b.1935), Thomas Pynchon (b.1937), J.D. Salinger (b.1919), Wallace Stegner (1909–93), Gore Vidal (b.1925), Kurt Vonnegut Jr. (b.1922), Alice Walker (b.1944), Tom Wolfe (b.1931), and Tobias Wolff (b.1945).

Noted US poets include Henry Wadsworth Longfellow (1807–82), Edgar Allan Poe (1809–49), Walt Whitman (1819–92), Emily Dickinson (1830–86), Edwin Arlington Robinson (1869–1935),

Robert Frost (1874–1963), Wallace Stevens (1879–1955), William Carlos Williams (1883–1963), Marianne Moore (1887–1972), Edward Estlin Cummings (1894–1962), Hart Crane (1899–1932), Langston Hughes (1902–67), and Rita Dove (b.1952). Ezra Pound (1885–1972) and Nobel laureate Thomas Stearns Eliot (1888–1965) lived and worked abroad for most of their careers. Wystan Hugh Auden (b.England, 1907–73), who became an American citizen in 1946, published poetry and criticism. Elizabeth Bishop (1911–79), Robert Lowell (1917–77), Allen Ginsberg (1926–97), and Sylvia Plath (1932–63) are among the best-known poets since World War II. Robert Penn Warren (1905–89) won the Pulitzer Prize for both fiction and poetry and became the first US poet laureate. Carl Sandburg (1878–1967) was a noted poet, historian, novelist, and folklorist. The foremost US dramatists are Eugene (Gladstone) O'Neill (1888–1953), who won the Nobel Prize for literature in 1936; Tennessee Williams (Thomas Lanier Williams, 1911–83); Arthur Miller (1915–2005); and Edward Albee (b.1928). Neil Simon (b.1927) is among the nation's most popular playwrights and screenwriters. August Wilson (1945–2005) won the Pulitzer Prize twice, for *Fences* (1985) and *The Piano Lesson* (1990), both of which depicted the African American experience.

Artists

Two renowned painters of the early period were John Singleton Copley (1738–1815) and Gilbert Stuart (1755–1828). Outstanding 19th-century painters were James Abbott McNeill Whistler (1834–1903), Winslow Homer (1836–1910), Thomas Eakins (1844–1916), Mary Cassatt (1845–1926), Albert Pinkham Ryder (1847–1917), John Singer Sargent (b.Italy, 1856–1925), and Frederic Remington (1861–1909). More recently, Edward Hopper (1882–1967), Georgia O'Keeffe (1887–1986), Thomas Hart Benton (1889–1975), Charles Burchfield (1893–1967), Norman Rockwell (1894–1978), Ben Shahn (1898–1969), Mark Rothko (b.Russia, 1903–70), Jackson Pollock (1912–56), Andrew Wyeth (b.1917), Robert Rauschenberg (b.1925), and Jasper Johns (b.1930) have achieved international recognition.

Sculptors of note include Augustus Saint-Gaudens (1848–1907), Gaston Lachaise (1882–1935), Jo Davidson (1883–1952), Daniel Chester French (1850–1931), Alexander Calder (1898–1976), Louise Nevelson (b.Russia, 1899–1988), and Isamu Noguchi (1904–88). Henry Hobson Richardson (1838–86), Louis Henry Sullivan (1856–1924), Frank Lloyd Wright (1869–1959), Louis I. Kahn (b.Estonia, 1901–74), and Eero Saarinen (1910–61) were outstanding architects. Contemporary architects of note include Richard Buckminster Fuller (1895–1983), Edward Durrell Stone (1902–78), Philip Cortelyou Johnson (1906–2005), Ieoh Ming Pei (b.China, 1917), and Frank Gehry (b.1929). The United States has produced many fine photographers, notably Mathew B. Brady (1823?–96), Alfred Stieglitz (1864–1946), Edward Steichen (1879–1973), Edward Weston (1886–1958), Ansel Adams (1902–84), and Margaret Bourke-White (1904–71).

Entertainment Figures

Outstanding figures in the motion picture industry are D. W. (David Lewelyn Wark) Griffith (1875–1948), Sir Charles Spencer "Charlie" Chaplin (b.England, 1889–1978), Walter Elias "Walt" Disney (1906–66), and George Orson Welles (1915–85). John Ford (1895–1973), Howard Winchester Hawks (1896–1977), Frank Capra (b.Italy, 1897–1991), Sir Alfred Hitchcock (b.England,

1899–1980), and John Huston (1906–87) were influential motion picture directors; Mel Brooks (Kaminsky, b.1926), George Lucas (b.1944), and Steven Spielberg (b.1947) have achieved remarkable popular success. Woody Allen (Allen Konigsberg, b.1935) has written, directed, and starred in comedies on stage and screen. World-famous American actors and actresses include the Barrymores, Ethel (1879–1959) and her brothers Lionel (1878–1954) and John (1882–1942); Humphrey Bogart (1899–1957); James Cagney (1899–1986); Spencer Tracy (1900–1967); Helen Hayes Brown (1900–93); Clark Gable (1901–60); Joan Crawford (Lucille Fay LeSueur, 1904–77); Cary Grant (Alexander Archibald Leach, b.England, 1904–86); Greta Garbo (Greta Louisa Gustafsson, b.Sweden, 1905–90); Henry Fonda (1905–82) and his daughter, Jane (b.1937); John Wayne (Marion Michael Morrison, 1907–79); Bette (Ruth Elizabeth) Davis (1908–89); Katharine Hepburn (1909–2003); Judy Garland (Frances Gumm, 1922–69); Marlon Brando (1924–2004); Marilyn Monroe (Norma Jean Mortenson, 1926–62); and Dustin Hoffman (b.1937). Among other great entertainers are W. C. Fields (William Claude Dukenfield, 1880–1946), Al Jolson (Asa Yoelson, b.Russia, 1886–1950), Jack Benny (Benjamin Kubelsky, 1894–1974), Fred Astaire (Fred Austerlitz, 1899–1987), Bob (Leslie Townes) Hope (b.England, 1903–2003), Bing (Harry Lillis) Crosby (1904–78), Frank (Francis Albert) Sinatra (1915–98), Elvis Aaron Presley (1935–77), and Barbra (Barbara Joan) Streisand (b.1942). The first great US "showman" was Phineas Taylor Barnum (1810–91).

Composers and Musicians

The foremost composers are Edward MacDowell (1861–1908), Charles Ives (1874–1954), Ernest Bloch (b.Switzerland, 1880–1959), Virgil Thomson (1896–89), Roger Sessions (1896–1985), Roy Harris (1898–1979), Aaron Copland (1900–90), Elliott Carter (b.1908), Samuel Barber (1910–81), John Cage (1912–92), and Leonard Bernstein (1918–90). George Rochberg (1918–2005), George Crumb (b.1929), Steve Reich (b.1936), and Philip Glass (b.1937) have won more recent followings. The songs of Stephen Collins Foster (1826–64) have achieved folk-song status. Leading composers of popular music are John Philip Sousa (1854–1932), George Michael Cohan (1878–1942), Jerome Kern (1885–1945), Irving Berlin (Israel Baline, b.Russia, 1888–1989), Cole Porter (1893–1964), George Gershwin (1898–1937), Richard Rodgers (1902–79), Woody Guthrie (1912–67), Stephen Joshua Sondheim (b.1930), Paul Simon (b.1941), and Bob Dylan (Robert Zimmerman, b.1941). Preeminent in the blues traditions are Leadbelly (Huddie Ledbetter, 1888–1949), Bessie Smith (1898?–1937), and Muddy Waters (McKinley Morganfield, 1915–83). Leading jazz figures include the composers Scott Joplin (1868–1917), James Hubert "Eubie" Blake (1883–1983), Edward Kennedy "Duke" Ellington (1899–1974), and William "Count" Basie (1904–84), and performers Louis Armstrong (1900–1971), Billie Holiday (Eleanora Fagan, 1915–59), John Birks "Dizzy" Gillespie (1917–93), Charlie "Bird" Parker (1920–55), John Coltrane (1926–67), and Miles Davis (1926–91).

Many foreign-born musicians have enjoyed personal and professional freedom in the United States; principal among them were pianists Artur Schnabel (b.Austria, 1882–1951), Arthur Rubinstein (b.Poland, 1887–1982), Rudolf Serkin (b.Bohemia, 1903–91), Vladimir Horowitz (b.Russia, 1904–89), and violinists Jascha Heif-

etz (b.Russia, 1901–87) and Isaac Stern (b.USSR, 1920). Among distinguished instrumentalists born in the United States are Benny Goodman (1909–86), a classical as well as jazz clarinetist, and concert pianist Van Cliburn (Harvey Lavan, Jr., b.1934). Singers Paul Robeson (1898–1976), Marian Anderson (1897–1993), Maria Callas (Maria Kalogeropoulos, 1923–77), Leontyne Price (b.1927), and Beverly Sills (Belle Silverman, b.1929) have achieved international acclaim. Isadora Duncan (1878–1927) was one of the first US dancers to win fame abroad. Martha Graham (1893–91) pioneered in modern dance. George Balanchine (b.Russia, 1904–83), Agnes De Mille (1905–93), Jerome Robbins (1918–98), Paul Taylor (b.1930), and Twyla Tharp (b.1941) are leading choreographers; Martha Graham (1893–1991) pioneered in modern dance.

Sports Figures

Among the many noteworthy sports stars are baseball's Tyrus Raymond "Ty" Cobb (1886–1961) and George Herman "Babe" Ruth (1895–1948); football's Samuel Adrian "Sammy" Baugh (b.1914), Jim Brown (b.1936), Francis A. "Fran" Tarkenton (b.1940), and Orenthal James Simpson (b.1947); and golf's Robert Tyre "Bobby" Jones (1902–71) and Mildred "Babe" Didrikson Zaharias (1914–56). William Tatum "Bill" Tilden (1893–1953), Billie Jean (Moffitt) King (b.1943), Chris Evert (b.1954), Martina Navratilova (b.Czechoslovakia, 1956), Andre Agassi (b.1970), Peter ("Pete") Sampras (b.1971), and sisters Venus (b.1980) and Serena (b.1981) Williams have starred in tennis; Joe Louis (Joseph Louis Barrow, 1914–81) and Muhammad Ali (Cassius Marcellus Clay, b.1942) in boxing; William Felton "Bill" Russell (b.1934) Wilton Norman "Wilt" Chamberlain (1936–99), and Michael Jordan (b.1963) in basketball; Mark Spitz (b.1950) and Michael Phelps (b.1985) in swimming; Eric Heiden (b.1958) in speed skating; and Jesse Owens (1913–80) in track and field.

50 BIBLIOGRAPHY

America's Century: Year by Year from 1900–2000. London: Dorling Kindersley, 2000.

Benjamin, Daniel (ed.). *America and the World in the Age of Terror: A New Landscape in International Relations.* Washington, D.C.: CSIS Press, 2005.

Chambers, S. Allen. *National Landmarks, America's Treasures: the National Park Foundation's Complete Guide to National Historic Landmarks.* New York: J. Wiley and Sons, 2000.

Davies, Philip John (ed.). *An American Quarter Century: US Politics from Vietnam to Clinton.* New York: Manchester University Press, 1995.

Donaldson, Gary. *America at War since 1945: Politics and Diplomacy in Korea, Vietnam, and the Gulf War.* Westport, Conn.: Praeger, 1996.

Hart, James David (ed.). *Oxford Companion to American Literature.* 6th ed. New York: Oxford University Press, 1995.

Health in the Americas, 2002 edition. Washington, D.C.: Pan American Health Organization, Pan American Sanitary Bureau, Regional Office of the World Health Organization, 2002.

Hummel, Jeffrey Rogers. *Emancipating Slaves, Enslaving Free Men: A History of the Civil War.* Chicago: Open Court, 1996.

Jenness, David. *Classic American Popular Song: The Second Half-Century, 1950–2000.* New York: Routledge, 2006.

Kaplan, Edward S. *American Trade Policy, 1923–1995*. Westport, Conn.: Praeger, 1996.

Kennedy, David M. *Freedom from Fear: The American People in Depression and War*. New York: Oxford University Press, 2001.

McElrath, Karen (ed.). *HIV and AIDS: A Global View*. Westport, Conn.: Greenwood Press, 2002.

McNickle, D'Arcy. *Native American Tribalism: Indian Survivals and Renewals*. New York: Oxford University Press, 1993.

Newell, Clayton R. *United States Army, a Historical Dictionary*. Lanham, Md.: Scarecrow Press, 2002.

Rein, Meiling, Nancy R. Jacobs, Maek S. Siegel (eds.). *Immigration and Illegal Aliens: Burden or Blessing?* Wylie, Tex.: Information Plus, 1999.

Robinson, Cedric J. *Black Movements in America*. New York: Routledge, 1997.

Sampanis, Maria. *Preserving Power through Coalitions: Comparing the Grand Strategy of Great Britain and the United States*. Westport, Conn.: Praeger, 2003.

Sinclair, Andrew. *A Concise History of the United States*. Rev. ed. Stroud: Sutton, 1999.

Summers, Randal W., and Allan M. Hoffman (ed.). *Domestic Violence: A Global View*. Westport, Conn.: Greenwood Press, 2002.

Tocqueville, Alexis de. *Democracy in America*. New York: Knopf, 1994.

US Bureau of the Census. *Historical Statistics of the United States, Colonial Times to 1970*. Washington, D.C.: US Government Printing Office, 1879-date.

Who's Who in America: A Biographical Dictionary of Notable Living Men and Women. Chicago: Marquis, 1899—.

ISBN-13: 978-1-4144-1122-4
ISBN-10: 1-4144-1122-7

90000

9 781414 411224

Alabama	Alaska	Arizona	Arkansas	California
Hawaii	Idaho	Illinois	Indiana	Iowa
Massachusetts	Michigan	Minnesota	Mississippi	Missouri
New Mexico	New York	North Carolina	North Dakota	Ohio
South Dakota	Tennessee	Texas	Utah	Vermont

Puerto Rico	District of Columbia	United States